Rogers

Alan

2007

Europe

Quality camping & caravanning sites

Alan Rogers

Compiled by: Alan Rogers Guides Ltd

Designed by: Paul Effenberg, Vine Design Ltd

Maps created by Customised Mapping (01769 540044)
contain background data provided by GisDATA Ltd
Maps are © Alan Rogers Guides and Gis DATA Ltd 2006

Published by: Alan Rogers Guides Ltd,
Spelmonden Old Oast, Goudhurst, Kent TN17 1HE
www.alanrogers.com Tel: 01580 214000

British Library Cataloguing-in-Publication Data:
A catalogue record for this book is available from the
British Library.

ISBN-13 978-0-9550486-5-4
ISBN-10 0-9550486-5-6

Printed in Great Britain by J H Haynes & Co Ltd

Contents

 4 Introduction

 6 How To Use This Guide

 10 Alan Rogers Awards

 12 Alan Rogers Travel Service

 15 Andorra

 17 Austria

 46 Belgium

 61 Croatia

 74 Czech Republic

 79 Denmark

 93 Finland

 99 France

 205 Germany

 249 Greece

 253 Hungary

 259 Italy

 341 Liechtenstein

 342 Luxembourg

 350 Netherlands

 381 Norway

 397 Portugal

 407 Slovakia

 411 Slovenia

 415 Spain

 473 Sweden

 490 Switzerland

 515 Open All Year

 517 Dogs

 518 Naturist Sites

 519 Travelling in Europe

 521 Insurance

 534 Maps

 546 Town and Village Index

 551 Index by Campsite Number

 556 Index by Country and Campsite Name

the Alan Rogers
approach

THIS YEAR WE CELEBRATE THE PUBLICATION OF THE FORTIETH EDITIONS OF THE ALAN ROGERS GUIDES. SINCE ALAN ROGERS PUBLISHED THE FIRST CAMPSITE GUIDE THAT BORE HIS NAME, THE RANGE HAS EXPANDED TO SIX TITLES COVERING 27 COUNTRIES. NO FEWER THAN 20 OF THE CAMPSITES SELECTED BY ALAN FOR THE FIRST GUIDE ARE STILL FEATURED IN OUR 2007 EDITIONS – LOOK OUT FOR THE 'CELEBRATING 40 YEARS' SYMBOL BESIDE OUR REPORTS.

THERE ARE MANY THOUSANDS OF CAMPSITES IN EUROPE OF VARYING QUALITY: THIS GUIDE CONTAINS IMPARTIALLY WRITTEN REPORTS ON 892 OF THE VERY FINEST, IN NO LESS THAN 22 COUNTRIES. EACH ONE IS INDIVIDUALLY INSPECTED AND SELECTED. THIS GUIDE DOES NOT INCLUDE SITES IN BRITAIN AND IRELAND, FOR WHICH WE PUBLISH A SEPARATE GUIDE, AND IT CONTAINS ONLY A LIMITED SELECTION OF SITES IN FRANCE, ITALY, SPAIN & PORTUGAL AND THE CENTRAL EUROPE COUNTRIES AS WE ALSO PUBLISH SEPARATE GUIDES FOR THESE DESTINATIONS. ALL THE USUAL MAPS AND INDEXES ARE ALSO INCLUDED, DESIGNED TO HELP YOU FIND THE CHOICE OF CAMPSITE THAT'S RIGHT FOR YOU. WE HOPE YOU ENJOY SOME HAPPY AND SAFE TRAVELS – AND SOME PLEASURABLE 'ARMCHAIR TOURING' IN THE MEANTIME!

A question of quality

The criteria we use when inspecting and selecting sites are numerous, but the most important by far is the question of good quality. People want different things from their choice of campsite so we try to include a range of campsite 'styles' to cater for a wide variety of preferences: from those seeking a small peaceful campsite in the heart of the countryside, to visitors looking for an 'all singing, all dancing' site in a popular seaside resort. Those with more specific interests, such as sporting facilities, cultural events or historical attractions, are also catered for.

The size of the site, whether it's part of a chain or privately owned, makes no difference in terms of it being required to meet our exacting standards in respect of its quality and it being 'fit for purpose'. In other words, irrespective of the size of the site, or the number of facilities it offers, we consider and evaluate the welcome, the pitches, the sanitary facilities, the cleanliness, the general maintenance and even the location.

" ...the campsites included in this book have been chosen entirely on merit, and no payment of any sort is made by them for their inclusion."

Alan Rogers, 1968

INSPECTED & SELECTED SINCE 1968

Independent and honest

Whilst the content and scope of the Alan Rogers guides have expanded considerably since the early editions, our selection of campsites still employs exactly the same philosophy and criteria as defined by Alan Rogers in 1968.

'telling it how it is'

Firstly, and most importantly, our selection is based entirely on our own rigorous and independent inspection and selection process. Campsites cannot buy their way into our guides – indeed the extensive Site Report which is written by us, not by the site owner, is provided free of charge so we are free to say what we think and to provide an honest, 'warts and all' description. This is written in plain English and without the use of confusing icons or symbols.

Expert opinions

We rely on our dedicated team of Site Assessors, all of whom are experienced campers, caravanners or motorcaravanners, to visit and recommend sites. Each year they travel some 100,000 miles around Europe inspecting new campsites for the guide and re-inspecting the existing ones. Our thanks are due to them for their enthusiastic efforts, their diligence and integrity.

We also appreciate the feedback we receive from many of our readers and we always make a point of following up complaints, suggestions or recommendations for possible new sites. Of course we get a few grumbles too – but it really is a few, and those we do receive usually relate to overcrowding or to poor maintenance during the peak school holiday period.

Please bear in mind that, although we are interested to hear about any complaints, we have no contractual relationship with the campsites featured in our guides and are therefore not in a position to intervene in any dispute between a reader and a campsite.

INSPECTED & SELECTED CAMPSITES

Highly respected by site owners and readers alike, there is no better guide when it comes to forming an independent view of a campsite's quality. When you need to be confident in your choice of campsite, you need the Alan Rogers Guide.

- ☑ Parks only included on merit
- ☑ Parks cannot pay to be included
- ☑ Independently inspected, rigorously assessed
- ☑ Impartial reviews
- ☑ **40** years of expertise

Country

The Site Reports – *Example of an entry*

Site Number Site name

Postal Address (including county)

Telephone number. Email address

A description of the site in which we try to give an idea of its general features – its size, its situation, its strengths and its weaknesses. This section should provide a picture of the site itself with reference to the facilities that are provided and if they impact on its appearance or character. We include details on pitch numbers, electricity (with amperage), hardstandings etc. in this section as pitch design, planning and terracing affects the site's overall appearance. Similarly we include reference to pitches used for caravan holiday homes, chalets, and the like. Importantly at the end of this column we indicate if there are any restrictions, e.g. no tents, no children, naturist sites.

Facilities	Directions
Lists more specific information on the site's facilities and amenities and, where available, the dates when these facilities are open (if not for the whole season). Off site: here we give distances to various local amenities, for example, local shops, the nearest beach, plus our featured activities (bicycle hire, fishing, horse riding, boat launching). Where we have space we list suggestions for activities and local tourist attractions.	Separated from the main text in order that they may be read and assimilated more easily by a navigator en-route. Bear in mind that road improvement schemes can result in road numbers being altered. GPS: references are provided as we obtain them for satellite navigation systems (in degrees and minutes).
Open: Site opening dates.	**Charges 2007**

Indexes

Our three indexes allow you to find sites by country, site number and name, by country and site name (alphabetically) or by the town or village where the site is situated. See also the handy Quick Reference sections at the back.

Campsite Maps

The maps of each country are designed to show the country in relation to others and will help you to identify the approximate position of each campsite. The colour of the campsite number indicates whether it is open all year or not. You will certainly need more detailed maps and we have found the Michelin atlas to be particularly useful.

Facilities

Toilet blocks

We assume that toilet blocks will be equipped with a reasonable number of British style WCs, washbasins with hot and cold water and hot showers with dividers or curtains, and will have all necessary shelves, hooks, plugs and mirrors. We also assume that there will be an identified chemical toilet disposal point, and that the campsite will provide water and waste water drainage points and bin areas. If not the case, we comment. We do mention certain features that some readers find important: washbasins in cubicles, facilities for babies, facilities for those with disabilities and motorcaravan service points. Readers with disabilities are advised to contact the site of their choice to ensure that facilities are appropriate to their needs.

Shop

Basic or fully supplied, and opening dates.

Bars, restaurants, takeaway facilities and entertainment

We try hard to supply opening and closing dates (if other than the campsite opening dates) and to identify if there are discos or other entertainment.

Children's play areas

Fenced and with safety surface (e.g. sand, bark or pea-gravel).

Swimming pools

If particularly special, we cover in detail in our main campsite description but reference is always included under our Facilities listings. Opening dates, charges and levels of supervision are provided where we have been notified.

Leisure facilities

For example, playing fields, bicycle hire, organised activities and entertainment.

Dogs

If dogs are not accepted or restrictions apply, we state it here. Check the quick reference list at the back of the guide.

Off site

This briefly covers leisure facilities, tourist attractions, restaurants etc nearby.

Charges

These are the latest provided to us by the sites. In those few cases where 2006 or 2007 prices are not given, we try to give a general guide.

Reservations

Necessary for high season (roughly mid-July to mid-August) in popular holiday areas (i.e. beach resorts). You can reserve via our own Alan Rogers Travel Service or through tour operators. Or be wholly independent and contact the campsite(s) of your choice direct, using the contact details shown in the site reports.

Telephone numbers

The numbers given assume you are actually IN the country concerned. If you are phoning from the UK remember that the first '0' is usually disregarded and replaced by the appropriate country code. For the latest details you should refer to an up-to-date telephone directory.

Opening dates

These are advised to us during the early autumn of the previous year – sites can, and sometimes do, alter these dates before the start of the following season, often for good reasons. If you intend to visit shortly after a published opening date, or shortly before the closing date, it is wise to check that it will actually be open at the time required. Similarly some sites operate a restricted service during the low season, only opening some of their facilities (e.g. swimming pools) during the main season; where we know about this, and have the relevant dates, we indicate it – again if you are at all doubtful it is wise to check.

Some site owners are very laid back when it comes to opening and closing dates. They may not be fully ready by their stated opening dates – grass and hedges may not all be cut or perhaps only limited sanitary facilities open. At the end of the season they also tend to close down some facilities and generally wind down prior to the closing date. Bear this in mind if you are travelling early or late in the season – it is worth phoning ahead.

The Camping Cheque low season touring system goes some way to addressing this in that participating campsites are encouraged to have all key facilities open and running by the opening date and to remain fully operational until the closing date.

Whether you're an 'old hand' in terms of camping and caravanning or are contemplating your first trip, a regular reader of our Guides or a new 'convert', we wish you well in your travels and hope we have been able to help in some way. We are, of course, also out and about ourselves, visiting sites, talking to owners and readers, and generally checking on standards and new developments.

We wish all our readers thoroughly enjoyable Camping and Caravanning in 2007 – favoured by good weather of course!

THE ALAN ROGERS TEAM

have you visited **www.alanrogers.com** yet?

INSPECTED CAMPSITES & SELECTED

Alan Rogers

Our website has fast become the first-stop for countless caravanners, motorhome owners and campers all wanting reliable, impartial and detailed information for their next trip.

It features a fully searchable database of the best campsites in the UK & Ireland, and the rest of Europe: over 2,000 campsites in 26 countries. All are Alan Rogers inspected and selected, allowing you to find the site that's perfect for you, with the reassurance of knowing we've been there first.

Countries

Finland

Norway

Sweden

Denmark

Netherlands

Belgium

Czech Republic

Luxembourg

Slovakia

Germany

Austria

France

Hungary

Switzerland

Liechtenstein

Slovenia

Croatia

Andorra

Portugal

Italy

Greece

Spain

In 2004 we introduced the first ever Alan Rogers Campsite Awards.

BEFORE MAKING OUR AWARDS, WE CAREFULLY CONSIDER MORE THAN 2000 CAMPSITES FEATURED IN OUR GUIDES, TAKING INTO ACCOUNT COMMENTS FROM OUR SITE ASSESSORS, OUR HEAD OFFICE TEAM AND, OF COURSE, OUR READERS.

OUR AWARD WINNERS COVER A MASSIVE GEOGRAPHICAL AREA FROM THE IBERIAN PENINSULA TO HUNGARY, AND THIS YEAR WE ARE MAKING AWARDS TO CAMPSITES IN 12 DIFFERENT COUNTRIES.

NEEDLESS TO SAY, IT'S AN EXTREMELY DIFFICULT TASK TO CHOOSE OUR EVENTUAL WINNERS, BUT WE BELIEVE THAT WE HAVE IDENTIFIED A NUMBER OF CAMPSITES WITH TRULY OUTSTANDING CHARACTERISTICS.

IN EACH CASE, WE HAVE SELECTED AN OUTRIGHT WINNER, ALONG WITH TWO HIGHLY COMMENDED RUNNERS-UP.

Listed below are full details of each of our award categories and our winners for 2006.

Alan Rogers Progress Award 2006

This award reflects the hard work and commitment undertaken by particular site owners to improve and upgrade their site.

WINNER

Camping International Marina, Spain

RUNNERS-UP

Camping La Grande Métairie, France

Newlands Caravan Park, England

Alan Rogers Welcome Award 2006

This award takes account of sites offering a particularly friendly welcome and maintaining a friendly ambience throughout reader's holidays.

WINNER

Mannix Point Caravan Park, Ireland

RUNNERS-UP

Castel Camping Sequoia Park, France

Balatontourist Napfeny, Hungary

Alan Rogers Active Holiday Award 2006

This award reflects sites in outstanding locations which are ideally suited for active holidays, notably walking or cycling, but which could extend to include such activities as winter sports or water sports

WINNER

Sportcamp Woferlgut, Austria

RUNNERS-UP

Klim Strand Camping, Denmark

Camping Bijela Uvala, Croatia

Alan Rogers Motorhome Award 2006

Motorhome sales are increasing and this award acknowledges sites which, in our opinion, have made outstanding efforts to welcome motorhome clients.

WINNER

Spessart-Camping Schönrain, Germany

RUNNERS-UP

Camping El Astral, Spain

Gaasper Camping, Netherlands

Alan Rogers 4 Seasons Award 2006

This award is made to outstanding sites with extended opening dates and which welcome clients to a uniformly high standard throughout the year.

WINNER

Komfort-Campingpark Burgstaller, Austria

RUNNERS-UP

Recreatiecentrum de Schatberg, Netherlands

Caravaning La Manga, Spain

Alan Rogers Seaside Award 2006

This award is made for sites which we feel are outstandingly suitable for a really excellent seaside holiday.

WINNER

Playa Montroig Camping Resort, Spain

RUNNERS-UP

Camping Baia Blu La Tortuga, Italy

Camping Bois Soleil, France

Alan Rogers Country Award 2006

This award contrasts with our former award and acknowledges sites which are attractively located in delightful, rural locations.

WINNER

Stowford Farm Meadows, England

RUNNERS-UP

Castel Camping La Paille Basse, France

Camping Romantische Strasse, Germany

Alan Rogers Rented Accommodation Award 2006

Given the increasing importance of rented accommodation on many campsites, and the inclusion in many Alan Rogers guides, of a rented accommodation section, we feel that it is important to acknowledge sites which have made a particular effort in creating a high quality 'rented accommodation' park.

WINNER

Camping Cambrils Park, Spain

RUNNERS-UP

Castel Camping Caravaning Esterel, France

Camping Kovacine, Croatia

Alan Rogers Unique Site Award 2006

This award acknowledges sites with unique, outstanding features – something which simply cannot be found elsewhere and which is an important attraction of the site.

WINNER

Camping Jésolo International, Italy

RUNNERS-UP

The Plassey Touring Park, Wales

Vakantiepark Duinrell, Netherlands

Alan Rogers Family Site Award 2006

Many sites claim to be child friendly but this award acknowledges the sites we feel to be the very best in this respect.

WINNER

Camping Capalonga, Italy

RUNNERS-UP

Beverley Park Holiday Centre, England

Domaine Le Pommier, France

Alan Rogers Readers' Award 2006

In 2005 we introduced a new award, which we believe to be the most important, our Readers' Award. We simply invited our readers (by means of an on-line poll at www.alanrogers.com) to nominate the site they enjoyed most. The outright winner for 2006 is:

WINNER

Camping Le Paradis, France

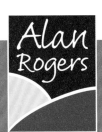

Alan Rogers.travel

The Alan Rogers Travel Service was set up to provide a low cost booking service for readers. We pride ourselves on being able to put together a bespoke holiday, taking advantage of our experience, knowledge and contacts. We can tailor-make a holiday to suit your requirements, giving you maximum choice and flexibility: exactly what we have been offering for some 7 years now.

2007 PRICE CRASH

For 2007 we offer more choice than ever before (around 500 campsites) and have thousands of holidays at significantly reduced prices - guaranteed.

unbeatable ferry deals

☑ CARAVANS GO FREE

☑ TRAILERS GO FREE

☑ MOTORHOMES PRICED AS CARS

ON CERTAIN ROUTES - CONDITIONS APPLY

At the Alan Rogers Travel Service we're always keen to find the best deals and keenest prices. There are always great savings on offer, and we're constantly negotiating new ferry rates and money-saving offers, so just call us on

0870 405 4055

and ask about the latest deals.

or visit
Alan Rogers.travel

Whether you book on-line or book by phone, you will be allocated an experienced Personal Travel Consultant to provide you with personal advice and manage every stage of your booking. Our Personal Travel Consultants have first-hand experience of many of our campsites and access to a wealth of information. They can 'paint a picture' of individual campsites, check availability, provide a competitive price and tailor your holiday arrangements to your specific needs.

- Discuss your holiday plans with a friendly person with first-hand experience

- Let us reassure you that your holiday arrangements really are taken care of

- Tell us about your special requests and allow us to pass these on

- Benefit from advice which will save you money – the latest ferry deals and more

- Remember, our offices are in Kent not overseas and we do NOT operate a queuing system!

THE AIMS OF THE TRAVEL SERVICE ARE SIMPLE

- To provide convenience - a one-stop shop to make life easier.
- To provide peace of mind - when you need it most.
- To provide a friendly, knowledgeable, efficient service – when this can be hard to find.
- To provide a low cost means of organising your holiday – when prices can be so complicated.

HOW IT WORKS

1 Choose your campsite(s) – we can book around 500 across Europe. Look for the yellow coloured campsite entries in this book. You'll find more info and images at www.alanrogers.travel.

   Please note: the list of campsites we can book for you varies from time to time.

2 Choose your dates – choose when you arrive, when you leave.

3 Choose your ferry crossing – we can book most routes with most operators at extremely competitive rates.

Then just call us for an instant quote

0870 405 4055
or visit

Alan Rogers.travel

LOOK FOR A CAMPSITE ENTRY LIKE THIS TO INDICATE WHICH CAMPSITES WE CAN BOOK FOR YOU.

THE LIST IS GROWING SO PLEASE CALL FOR UP TO THE MINUTE INFORMATION.

The tiny independent principality of Andorra is situated high in the Pyrenees between France and Spain. With a diverse landscape of mountains, valleys, forests, lakes and hot springs, it is probably best known for skiing and duty-free shopping.

CAPITAL: ANDORRA LA VELLA

Tourist Office

Embassy of the Principality of Andorra
63 Westover Road, London SW18 2RF
Tel/Fax: 020 8874 4806 (visits by appointment only)
Internet: www.turisme.ad

Shopping and skiing aside, Andorra has plenty to offer the visitor in terms of leisure activities. One of the most unspoilt areas of the country is the hamlet of Llorts. Set amidst fields of tobacco overlooked by mountains, it's a great place for hiking. The enormous spa complex in Caldea offers the perfect place to relax. Fed by natural thermal springs, it houses lots of pools, hot tubs and saunas. Village festivals are a popular event with many Andorran towns and hamlets celebrating their heritage with music, dancing, wine and feasts. Most fall in the high season.

Administratively Andorra is divided up into seven parishes: Canillo, Encamp, Ordino, La Massana, Andorra la Vella, Sant Julià de Lòria and Escaldes-Engordany. The Principality of Andorra can be accessed by road from France through Pas de la Casa and the Envalira Pass and from Spain via Sant Julià de Lòria. The nearest main cities are Barcelona (185 km) and Lleida (151 km) on the Spanish side and Toulouse (187 km) and Perpignan (169 km) on the French side.

Population

66,500

Climate

The climate is temperate, with cold winters with a lot of snow and warm summers. The country's mountain peaks often remain snowcapped until July.

Language

The official language is Catalan, with French and Spanish widely spoken.

Telephone

The country code is 00 376.

Money

Currency: The Euro
Banks: Mon-Fri 09.00-13.00 and 15.00-17.00, Sat 09.00-12.00.

Shops

Mon-Sat 09.00-20.00, Sun 09.00-19.00.

Public Holidays

New Year's Day; Epiphany; Constitution Day, Mar 14; Holy Thursday to Easter Monday; Labour Day; Ascension; Whit Sunday; Whit Monday; St John's Day Jun 24; Assumption Aug 15; National Day Sep 8; All Saints' Day Nov 1; St Charles' Day; Nov 4; Immaculate Conception; Dec 8; Christmas Dec 24-26; New Year's Eve.

Motoring

There are no motorways in Andorra. Main roads are prefixed 'N' and side roads 'V'. Certain mountain passes may prove difficult in winter and heavy snowfalls could cause road closures. Expect traffic queues in the summer, with a high volume of motorists coming to and from France.

AN7143 Camping Xixerella

Ctra de Pals, Xixerella, La Massana (Andorra)

Tel: 836 613. Email: c-xixerella@campingxixerella.com

Andorra is a country of narrow valleys and pine and birch forested mountains. Xixerella is attractively situated in just such a valley below towering mountains and beside a river. The site is made up of several sections of gently sloping grass, accessed by tarmac or gravel roads which lead to informal pitching. Electricity (3/6A) is available for most of the 150 places. Barbecues and picnic area with bridge access to walks in the woods. Pleasant bar and restaurant with pool-side terrace. The site can be very busy from mid-July to mid-August, but otherwise it is usually quite peaceful. Do not forget to explore Andorra for that duty-free shopping.

Facilities

The satisfactory main sanitary building is fully equipped, including British style WCs (no paper) and some children's toilets, some washbasins in cabins, showers with curtains. Laundry facilities. Further modern facilities in novel round building by the pool, including toilets, a laundry, baby bath and dishwashing sinks. Small shop, bar and restaurant (closed Oct). Swimming pool and paddling pool (mid-June - mid-Sept). Play area. Minigolf. Volleyball. Basketball. Table football. Electronic games. Disco in season. Torch useful. Off site: Volleyball and basketball pitch close by. Riding 3 km. Skiing possible at Arinsal (5 km) or Pal (6 km).

Open: All year.

Directions

Site is 8 km. from Andorra la Vella on the road to Pal (this road can only be accessed on the north side of town), via La Massana.

Charges 2006

Per person	€ 4,60
child	€ 4,30
pitch	€ 9,00 - € 9,20
electricity (3A)	€ 4,85

AN7145 Camping Valira

Avda Salou, s/n, Andorra la Vella (Andorra)

Tel: 722 384. Email: campvalira@andorra.ad

This small and unusual site is named after the river in the town of Andorra La Vella. It has a steep curving entrance which can become congested at peak times. You pass the pleasant restaurant and bar and the heated indoor pool as you enter the site. Maximum use has been made of space here and it is worth looking at the picture of the site in reception as it was in 1969. The 150 medium sized pitches are mostly level on terraces with some shading. One of the family will guide you to your place which can be an interesting experience if the site is busy. All pitches have access to electricity, but some may need long leads, and there are drinking water points around the site. As this is a town site there is some ambient noise but the site is ideal for duty-free shopping. Some pitches at the south end of the site have a free 'birds eye' view of any event in the sports stadium.

Facilities

The facilities are modern and spotless, with provision for disabled campers, plus separate room with toddlers' toilet and good baby room. Two washing machines and dryer. The two blocks can be heated in winter. Bar/restaurant with good menu at realistic prices. Well stocked small shop. Small heated indoor pool. Paddling pool. Play area. Barrier closed 11 pm - 7 am. Off site: Town shops 10 minutes walk.

Open: All year.

Directions

Site is on the south side of Andorra La Vella, on left travelling south behind sports stadium. It is well signed off the N145. Watch signs carefully – an error with a diversion round town will cost you dear at rush hour.

Charges 2006

Per person	€ 5,35
child (1-10 yrs)	€ 4,50
pitch	€ 10,70
electricity (3-10A)	€ 3,00 - € 5,35

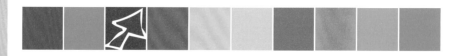

MAP 1

Austria is primarily known for two contrasting attractions: the capital Vienna with its fading Imperial glories, and the variety of its Alpine hinterland. It is an ideal place to visit year round, whether you want to admire the spectacular scenery and participate in winter sports or to visit historical sites and cultural attractions.

CAPITAL: VIENNA

Tourist Office

Austrian National Tourist Office (ANTO)
PO Box 2363, London W1A 2QB
Tel: 020 7629 0461
Fax: 020 7499 6038
Email: info@anto.co.uk
Internet: www.austria.info

Perhaps the best known area and the most easily accessible part of the country is the Tirol in the west. A charming region with picturesque valleys to explore, you'll be able to enjoy folk-lore entertainment year round. Situated in the centre is the Lake District and Salzburg. With its ancient castles, curative spas and salt mines to visit, Salzburg also has plenty of music, art and drama festivals to enjoy. Vienna, too, offers plenty of cultural pursuits with its museums, opera and famous choirs. The neighbouring provinces of Lower Austria, Burgenland and Styria, land of vineyards, mountains and farmland, are off the tourist routes, but provide good walking territory. Further south, in the Carinthia region, lakes and mountains dominate the landscape. The beautiful scenery and rural way of life offers a quieter retreat. There are a few large towns to explore, lots of pleasant villages and good, often uncrowded roads.

Population

8.1 million

Climate

Temperate, with moderately hot summers, cold winters and snow in the mountains.

Language

German

Telephone

The country code is 0043.

Money

Currency: The Euro
Banks: Mon, Tues, Wed & Fri 08.00-12.30 and 13.30-15.00. Thurs 08.00-12.30 and 13.30-17.30.

Shops

Mon-Fri 08.00-18.30, some close 12.00-14.00; Sat 08.00-17.00.

Public Holidays

New Year; Epiphany; Easter Mon; Labour Day; Ascension; Whit Mon; Corpus Christi; Assumption 15 Aug; National Day 26 Oct; All Saints 1 Nov; Immaculate Conception 8 Dec; Christmas 25, 26 Dec.

Motoring

Visitors using Austrian motorways and 'A' roads must display a Motorway Vignette on their vehicle as they enter Austria. Failure to have one will mean a heavy, on-the-spot fine. Vignettes are obtained at all major border crossings into Austria and at larger petrol stations. All vehicles above 3.5 tonnes maximum permitted laden weight are required to use a small device called the 'GO-Box' - see page 18.

AU0010 Alpencamping Nenzing

Garfrenga 1, A-6710 Nenzing (Vorarlberg)

Tel: 05525 62491. Email: office@alpencamping.at

Although best known for its ski-ing resorts, the forests and mountains of the Vorarlberg province make it equally suitable for a peaceful summer visit. Alpencamping Nenzing, is some 690 m. above sea level, set in a natural bowl surrounded by trees with some views across the pleasant countryside. You wind your way up from the main road or motorway, following a narrow road (you leave by a different route). Some of the 168 level, but small, tourist pitches are in a flat area with others on neat terraces beyond. All have electricity (12-16A) and 105 also have water, drainage, sewage, TV, gas and phone connections.

Facilities

The new sanitary facilities opened in 2005 are state of the art and contain 20 free private bathrooms with either shower or bath and washbasin and wc. The other 2 sanitary blocks remain and provide good facilities. Excellent new children's washroom. Baby room. Facilities for disabled visitors. Motorcaravan service point. Small shop. Bar. Restaurant with terrace. Heated swimming pool (20 x 8 m). Small play area with another larger one on the top terrace. Practice climbing wall and large football field. Sauna, solarium, massage and relax room. Internet access. Off site: Bicycle hire, riding, tennis and fishing near.

Open: All year excl. week after Easter-30 April.

Directions

From A14 Feldkirch - Bludenz motorway take exit for Nenzing on B190 and then follow small 'Camping' signs which have the site logo – a butterfly. GPS: N47:10.965 E09:40.929

Charges guide

Per unit incl. 2 persons	€ 15,00 - € 26,20
incl. 1 child	€ 18,60 - € 29,00
incl. 2 children	€ 22,20 - € 31,90
electricity	€ 0,65
full services	€ 1,50

No credit cards.

AU0015 Camping Grosswalsertal

Plazera 21, A-6741 Raggal (Vorarlberg)

Tel: 05553 209. Email: info@camping-austria.info

As we climbed up to this site we seemed to be above the clouds. We then descended into a beautiful green valley and saw the site on a flat plateau below. When we arrived, Siegmar Zech, the owner was busy siting a caravan, so we followed the sound of happy children and campers playing. Our immediate impressions were that this is a good site and one from which you could base an excellent holiday. From almost every pitch there are the most fantastic views down the valley. On open grass, there are 60 slightly sloping, un-numbered and unmarked pitches all with 10A electricity.

Facilities

The modern sanitary block has ample and clean toilets, hot showers and washbasins. Washing machine and dryer. Dishwashing facilities. Chemical toilet disposal point. Small shop with essential supplies. Swimming pool (1/6-15/9). Play area. Bicycle hire. Off site: Fishing 2 km. Golf 14 km. Riding 2 km.

Open: 15 May - 30 September.

Directions

From the A14 take exit for Nenzing and Gr. Walsertal and proceed to Ludesch. Turn right toward Raggal where you take the left fork, pass a Spa supermarket and 2 km. downhill to the site. GPS: N47:12.951 E9:51.222

Charges 2006

Per unit incl. 2 persons	€ 14,50 - € 17,00
incl. electricity	€ 16,00 - € 18,50
extra person	€ 4,00
child (0-13 yrs)	€ 2,00 - € 3,00

NOTE: From 1 January 2004, all vehicles above 3.5 tonnes maximum permitted laden weight using the Austrian network of motorways and expressways are required to attach a small device called the 'GO-Box' to their windscreen. The Go-Box uses the high frequency range to communicate with the around 400 fixed-installation toll points covering Austria, making it possible to effect an automatic toll deduction without slowing the flow of traffic. The on-board devices can be obtained for a one-off handling fee of Euro 5.00 at about 220 sales centres in Austria and in neighbouring countries or via the Internet. For further information visit the website at http://www.austria.info

AU0232 Terrassencamping Sonnenberg

Hinteroferst 12, A-6714 Nüziders bei Bludenz (Vorarlberg)

Tel: 05552 64035. Email: sonnencamp@aon.at

A friendly welcome awaits you at this well equipped site on the western end of Austria, at the junction of five alpine valleys. The views are captivating and ever-changing, ideal for keen photographers. The site is mostly terraced with pitches for longer stay units having gravel hardstandings at one side of the site, while shorter stay units have an area closer to the entrance. A large car park area reduces the traffic congestion on the site at peak times, and there are eight pitches designated for motorcaravans. There are 120 good sized pitches, all with electric hooks ups (13A), 24 are fully serviced. In the summer months these are all touring pitches. Traditional Tirolean musical evenings are a feature of this site, and on Sundays during the summer the men of the Dünser family, dressed in traditional costume, play the 'Alpenhorns'. The family also take parties of campers on guided walking tours, highly recommended, but do make sure that you are properly equipped, and reasonably fit. Good English is spoken.

Facilities

A superb new two storey building contains high quality facilities. On the lower floor you will find WCs, spacious hot showers, and washbasins (some in cubicles), and a baby room. The upper floor has a drying room, laundry, and a dishwashing room. The reception building has on its upper floor a TV and cinema room, and a sleeping loft for four campers (used in inclement weather). Secure storage room for campers' bicycles. Seven studio apartments. Shop. Playground. Table tennis. Motorcaravan service point. Chemical disposal point. Gas stocked. Baker calls daily in July/August. Only one dog per unit is allowed. Internet access. Off site: Village with shops and an ATM machine 500 m. Fishing 3 km. Riding and bicycle hire 4 km. Golf 8 km.

Open: 3 May - 3 October.

Directions

Nüziders is about 25 km. south east of Feldkirch. From A14 exit 57 (Bludenz-Nüziders) turn north on road 190 and turn left at roundabout into village. Follow camping signs through village to site. GPS: N47:10.191 E09:48.448

Charges 2006

Per person	€ 5,00 - € 5,70
child (2-14 yrs)	€ 3,50
pitch	€ 5,00 - € 10,00
electricity (4 kWh/day)	€ 2,60
extra kWh	€ 0,50

No credit cards.

AU0060 Ferienparadies Natterer See

Natterer See 1, A-6161 Natters (Tirol)

Tel: 0512 546732. Email: info@natterersee.com

Above Innsbruck, seven kilometres southwest of the town, this excellent site is in a quiet and isolated location around two small lakes. One of these is for bathing with a long 67 m. slide (free to campers, on payment to day visitors), while boats such as inflatables can be put on either lake. There are many fine mountain views and a wide variety of scenic excursions. For the more active, signed walks start from the site. There are 210 individual pitches (180 for tourists) of varying size. Some are quite small, either on flat ground by the lake or on higher, level terraces where views can be obscured by trees in the summer and some access roads are narrow. All pitches have electricity (6A), with 50 also having water and drainage. Many are reinforced by gravel (possibly tricky for tents). For winter camping the site offers ski and drying rooms and a free ski-bus service. A toboggan run and langlauf have been developed with ice skating, ice hockey and curling on the lake. Occasional services are held in the small chapel. The excellent restaurant with bar and large terrace overlooking the lake has a good menu. Three 'theme pavilions' overlooking the water provide special dinners (4-8 persons). Very good English is spoken. This family-run campsite must rate as one of the best in Austria and can therefore become very busy. Used by a tour operator (20 pitches).

Facilities

Two large sanitary blocks have under-floor heating, some washbasins in cabins, plus excellent facilities for babies, children and disabled people. Laundry facilities. Motorcaravan services. Fridge boxes for hire. Bar/restaurant (20/3-2/10). Pizzeria and takeaway. Good mini market (20/3-2/10). Playgrounds. Children's activity programme with Indian 'topi' tents. Child minding (day nursery) in high season. Sports field. Archery. Youth room with games, pool and billiards. TV room with Sky. Internet point and WIFI Internet. Open air cinema. Mountain bike hire. 'Aquapark' with water trampoline, bumper boats, slide and other attractions (1/5-30/9). Surf-bikes and wind-glider. Canoes and mini sailboats for rent. During main season (mid May-mid Oct) extensive daily entertainment programme. No dogs are accepted in high season (2/7-27/8). Off site: Tennis, minigolf nearby. Riding 6 km. Golf 12 km.

Open: All year excl. 1 November - 14 December.

Directions

From Inntal autobahn (A12) take Brenner autobahn (A13) as far as Innsbruck-sud/Natters exit (no. 3) without payment. Turn left by garage onto the B182 to Natters. Turn first right and immediately right again and follow signs to site 4 km. Note: Care is needed when negotiating site entrance and there is a separate entrance for large units or vehicles over 3 m. high – ask reception. GPS: N47:14.258 E11:20.557

Charges 2006

Per person	€ 5,70 - € 7,70
child (under 13 yrs)	€ 4,40 - € 5,30
pitch	€ 7,80 - € 10,00
with water and drainage	€ 9,30 - € 13,50
dog (excl. 2/7-27/8)	€ 3,00

Special weekly, winter, summer or Christmas packages. Camping Cheques accepted.

AU0040 Ferienanlage Tiroler Zugspitze

Obermoos 1, A-6632 Ehrwald (Tirol)

Tel: 05673 2309. Email: camping@zugspitze.at

Although Ehrwald is in Austria, it is from the entrance of Zugspitzcamping that the cable car runs to the summit of Germany's highest mountain. Standing at 1,200 feet above sea level at the foot of the mountain, the 200 pitches (120 for tourists), mainly of grass over stones, are on flat terraces with fine panoramic views in parts. All have electricity connections (16A). The modern reception building at the entrance also houses a fine restaurant with a terrace which is open to those using the cable car, as well as those staying on the site.

Facilities

Two good sanitary blocks (cleaning may be variable) provide some washbasins in cabins and 20 private bathrooms for rent. Separate children's sanitary unit. Baby room. Unit for disabled people. Washing machines, dryers and dishwashers. Drying rooms. Motorcaravan service point. Shop. Bar. Restaurant. Indoor pool with sauna, whirlpool and fitness centre with solarium and massage room. Outdoor pool and children's pool with slide. Internet access. Bicycle hire. Play area. Organised activities in season. Off site: Hotel, souvenir shop and cable car station 100 m. Sports in Ehrwald 5 km.

Open: All year.

Directions

Follow signs in Ehrwald to Tiroler Zugspitzbahn and then signs to camp. GPS: N47:25.595 E10:56.486

Charges 2006

Per person	€ 10,00 - € 12,00
child (4-15 yrs)	€ 7,50 - € 8,50
pitch	€ 6,00 - € 8,00
electricity per kWh.	€ 0,80
dog	€ 4,00

Special seasonal weekly offers. Mastercard accepted.

Your ★★★★★ Holiday Paradise in the Tirol Alps near Innsbruck...

full of life

Natterer See

8 convincing reasons for you to spend your holiday with us:

- the **unique scenic location** in the middle of unspoiled nature
- the **well-placed situation** - also perfect when en route to the South
- the **thrilling water experience** of our own swimming lake (average 22°C)
- the **guarantee for sports, amusement, fun and animation** - ideal for all the family
- the **weekly discounted prices for senior citizens** and bargain hunters and our special mountain-bike-packages
- the comfortable **appartments and guest rooms** for friends and relatives
- the central position in the **„Olympia" ski region** Innsbruck / Seefeld / Stubaital
- the **high praise of ADAC** for the facilities at our site

Facilities • **individual terraced pitches** with electricity and telephone hook-up, partly water and drainage, sat-TV and Internet connection • motorhome service station • top quality sanitation facilities • mini-market • Pizzeria „da Giorgio" • restaurant with lake terrace • **comfortable guest rooms** • **holiday appartments** • mini-club • pool room • youth room • sport & games areas • streetball • beach volleyball • indian camp • **swimming lake** with 66 m giant waterslide • water-trampoline • windgliders • surfbikes • canoes • bumper boats • children's swimming bay • archery • tabletennis • open-air chess • mountainbike and cycle hire • **top animation programme** from May to September • attractive walks

ski and drying room • ice skating • ice hockey • curling and tobogganing on-site • cross country skiing • „Olympia" ski region • ski bus

New plans for 2007
- ▶ new and wider access road
- ▶ new central building with
  - • reception • cafe bistro
  - • shop • sanitary facilities
- ▶ luxury pitches 110 to 130 m²
- ▶ new and bigger „Kids-Club"
- ▶ new, bigger rooms for the young

planned to be finished in spring 2007

We will be pleased to send you our detailed brochure.

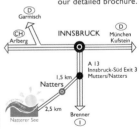

```
                 (D)
               Garmisch
(CH)                    INNSBRUCK    (D)
Arlberg                              München
                                     Kufstein
                              A 13
                         1,5 km  Innsbruck-Süd Exit 3
                                 Mutters/Natters
              Natters
                    2,5 km
  Natterer See          Brenner
                          (I)
```

Terrassencamping Natterer See
A-6161 Natters/Tirol/Austria

Tel. ++43(0)512/546732...
Fax ++43(0)512/54673216...

email: info@natterersee.com
http://www.natterersee.com

Servus in Österreich

TOP CAMPING AUSTRIA   **Tirol**

Ask for our free CD-ROM !

ADAC Super-Platz **2006**

AU0035 Camp Alpin Seefeld

Leutascherstrasse 810, A-6100 Seefeld (Tirol)

Tel: 05212 4848. Email: info@camp-alpin.at

Alpin Seefeld is a pleasant, modern campsite with very good facilities in an attractive setting some 1,200 metres high. With excellent views of the surrounding mountains and forests there are 140 large, individual pitches mainly on flat grass (a few hardstandings), all with gas, TV, electricity and waste water, with 10 water points around, but no shade. Some pitches at the back and edge of the site are terraced. This is a good base for summer or winter activity, whether you wish to take a gentle stroll or participate in something more demanding, including skiing direct from the site.

Facilities

Excellent heated sanitary facilities include nine private bathrooms for hire, some private cabins. Washing machines and dryer. Sauna, Turkish bath and solarium. Shop. Bar, snack bar and takeaway. Fishing. Play area. Bicycle hire. Off site: Sports centre with heated indoor and outdoor pools and restaurant are close. The popular Tirolean village of Seefeld 1 km. Golf 1.5 km.

Open: All year.

Directions

Seefeld is about 17 km. northwest of Innsbruck. The site is about 2 km. from Seefeld on the road signed to Leutasch. It is well signed as you approach the town.

Charges 2007

Per person	€ 5,00 - € 9,90
over 65 yrs	€ 4,00 - € 8,90
child (3-14 yrs)	€ 3,00 - € 7,90
pitch	€ 6,00 - € 12,90

AU0045 Campingplatz Ötztal

A-6444 Längenfeld (Tirol)

Tel: 052 53 53 48. Email: info@camping-oetztal.com

Camping Ötztal, a family run site, is situated some 400 metres from the pretty village of Längenfeld, at the edge of a forest. Next door are the local sports centre and swimming pool and a restaurant. In summer the campsite is ideal for walking and cycling, as well as mountaineering tours. In the winter you can enjoy cross-country skiing right from the doorstep and a free bus shuttle operates to the Ötztal Ski arena. The site provides 200 level grass pitches of which 170 are for tourers. All pitches have electricity and 100 have also gas, water, drainage and TV point.

Facilities

Excellent sanitary facilities include 4 bathrooms to rent for private use. Baby room. Facilities for disabled people. Sauna and solarium. Female hairdressing room. Dog shower. Washing machines and dryer. Ski room. Motorcaravan service point. Internet access. Bicycle hire. Off site: Längenfeld and Aqua Dome thermal spa facility.

Open: All year.

Directions

From the A12 take exit 123 and follow the 186 along the Ötztal Valley towards Sölden. Längenfeld is about 20 km. from the autobahn.

Charges 2006

Per person	€ 5,40 - € 5,90
child (4-13 yrs)	€ 4,00 - € 4,60
pitch incl. electricity	€ 8,40 - € 12,60

AU0065 Camping Seehof

Reintalersee, A-6233 Kramsach (Tirol)

Tel: 05337 63541. Email: info@camping-seehof.com

Camping Seehof, an excellent site in every respect, is situated in a marvellous, sunny and peaceful location on the eastern shores of the Reintalersee lake. Add to this that it is very much a family run site and you have almost perfection itself. It separates into two areas; a small area next to the lake, good for sunbathing, and a bigger one nearer the large excellent sanitary block. All the large pitches are served by good access roads and have electricity and TV point and many have waste water drainage. Water points are conveniently located around the site. Seehof provides an ideal starting point for walking, cycling or riding (with a riding stable nearby), and in the winter for cross-country skiing, ice-skating and curling. A free shuttle bus operates from the site during the skiing season.

Facilities

New and refurbished sanitary facilities are first class and include four bathrooms, which are free for campers' use, and a further six to rent for private use. Baby room. Facilities for disabled visitors. Medical room; including bed. Dog shower. Washing machine and dryer. Ski room. Motorcaravan service point. Small shop for basics. Good restaurant. Playground and children's playroom. Internet access. Bicycle hire. Fishing. Off site: Kramsach. Kristallwelten and the Swarovski Factory.

Open: All year.

Directions

From the A12 take exit 32 to Kramsach. At roundabout turn right and immediately turn left following signs for 'Zu den Seen' in village. After 3 km. turn right at camp sign.

Charges 2006

Per person	€ 4,50 - € 6,50
child (2-14 yrs)	€ 3,00 - € 4,50
pitch	€ 5,20 - € 9,20
electricity	€ 2,80
dog	€ 3,00

AU0055 Camping Arlberg

A-6574 Pettneu am Arlberg (Tirol)

Tel: 05448 22266-0. Email: info@camping-arlberg.at

This is a very unusual site, opened in December 2003, located alongside, and lower than, the S16 autobahn, just a few kilometres to the east of the 13 km. long Arlberg toll tunnel. Inevitably there is some traffic noise. The site is unusual because it offers 145 pitches (out of 185) which are provided with an excellent on-pitch wooden cabin housing a shower, WC, washbasin and sink. Electricity (which also provides the hot water) is metered and there are external points for electricity hook-ups and TV connection. The grass and hardcore pitches are of medium size. The other 40 pitches are near the new reception building and offer electricity with a prepayment meter only (€ 1 coins). There are no other sanitary facilities, so on these pitches you have to use your own.

Facilities

145 private bathrooms. Chemical disposal point. Motorcaravan service point. Off site: Pettnau, swimming pool and the Tyrol. Skiing; ski bus operates in the season.

Open: All year.

Directions

From S16 (B316) take exit to Pettneu. Just at the end of the slip road between a swimming complex and a new children's play area you will find the entrance to the site.

Charges 2007

Per unit incl. 2 adults and 2 children under 4 yrs	€ 18,00 - € 36,00
extra adult	€ 7,00 - € 8,00
child (4-14 yrs)	€ 3,50
Camping Cheques accepted.	

23

Austria

AU0070 Camping Hofer

Gerlosstrasse 33, A-6280 Zell-am-Ziller (Tirol)

Tel: 05282 2248. Email: info@campingdorf.at

Zell-am-Ziller is in the heart of the Zillertal valley at the junction of the B169 and B165 Gerlos Pass road and nestles round the unusual 18th century church noted for its paintings. Camping Hofer, owned by the same family for over 50 years, is on the edge of the village just five minutes walk from the centre on a quiet side road. The 100 pitches, all with electricity (6/10A, long leads may be needed) are grass on gravel. A few trees decorate the site and offer some shade.

Facilities

Good quality, heated sanitary provision is on the ground floor of the apartment building and has some washbasins in cabins. Baby room. Washing machines, dryers and irons. Gas supplies. Motorcaravan services. Restaurant with bar (closed 1/11-10/12 and 30/4-31/5). Shop opposite. Swimming pool (1/4-31/10). Bicycle hire. WiFi internet. Organised entertainment and activities in high season. Ski room. Youth room. Off site: Town and supermarket within walking distance.

Open: All year.

Directions

Site is well signed from the main B169 road at Zell-am-Ziller. Site is at southern end of town close to the junction of the B169 and B165.
GPS: N47:13.724 E11:53.157

Charges 2006

Per person	€ 4,50 - € 6,00
child (under 14 yrs)	€ 3,00 - € 4,00
pitch incl. electricity	€ 8,00 - € 9,00

No credit cards (debit cards accepted).
Camping Cheques accepted.

AU0085 Mountain Camp Pitztal

Niederhof 206, A-6474 Jerzens (Tirol)

Tel: 05414 87571. Email: mountain-camp@aon.at

Mountain Camp Pitztal was opened in 2002 by Tobias Eiter and his wife and is the only site in the Pitztal valley. It is an ideal base for walks in the Tiroler Mountains or for mountain bike tours on the numerous paths through the woods and on the Schotterpiste or Wildspitze, the highest mountain in Tirol. Being a new site, the pitches are rather in the open, but all 38 have 13A electricity, water, waste water and gas supplies. The pitches are laid out on level, rectangular fields on a grass and gravel base, with gravel access roads. There are beautiful views of the Tiroler mountains.

Facilities

One new, centrally located toilet block (heated) with toilets, washbasins (open style and in cabins) and free, controllable hot showers. Bathroom. Free washing machine. Dryer. Restaurant with bar and covered terrace. Fishing. Bicycle hire. Skate ramp. Swimming pond with small beach. Full activity programme for all ages in high season. Off site: Riding 2 km. Golf 25 km.

Open: All year.

Directions

From the A12, take exit 132 at Imst and continue south on minor road. Site is on the right, just before entering Jerzens. GPS: N47:08.552 E10:44.789

Charges 2007

Per unit with 2 persons	€ 18,00 - € 24,00
extra person	€ 4,00 - € 5,00
child (4-14 yrs)	€ 3,00 - € 3,50
electricity (per kw/h on meter)	€ 0,50

AU0090 Camping Zillertal-Hell

Gragering 212b, A-6263 Fügen (Tirol)

Tel: 05288 62203. Email: info@zillertal-camping.at

The village of Fügen lies about six kilometres from the A12 autobahn at the start of the Zillertal, so is well placed for exploring the valley and the area around Schwaz. Easy to reach, Camping Zillertal-Hell is an attractive small site with excellent facilities and 170 marked pitches (140 for tourists) on flat grass. All have electricity (10A), 80 also have water and drainage and there are some hardstandings for motorcaravans. The site could make a good overnight stop or for a longer stay but, being on a main road, there is a little daytime road noise.

Facilities

New modern heated sanitary block of top quality has some washbasins in cabins, a children's wash room, and private bathrooms for hire. Unit for disabled campers. Washing machine, dryer, iron and drying room. Drive over motorcaravan service point. Attractive bar with terrace and small restaurant. Shop for basic supplies. Pleasantly landscaped, heated swimming pool (1/5-15/10). Solarium, sauna and steam room. Games room with TV. Playground. Internet point. Organised entertainment. Bicycle hire. Dogs are not accepted. Off site: Fishing 500 m. Riding 2 km. Golf 15 km. Village 800 m.

Open: All year.

Directions

From the A12 Innsbruck - Worgl motorway take exit 39 and turn south on B169 towards Mayrhofen for 5 km. Turn into service road (on right) 1 km. north of Fugen (signed Gagering and site) and site entrance is on right. Note: this is a fast road, care is needed exiting site. GPS: N47:21.576 E11:51.128

Charges 2006

Per person	€ 4,20 - € 7,50
child (2-13 yrs)	€ 3,00 - € 5,00
pitch incl. electricity	€ 9,00 - € 13,50

Less for longer stays.

AU0080 Schloß-Camping

A-6111 Volders (Tirol)

Tel: 05224 52333. Email: campingvolders@utanet.at

The Inn valley is not only central to the Tirol, but is a very beautiful and popular part of Austria. Volders, some 15 km. from Innsbruck, is one of the little villages on the banks of the Inn river and is perhaps best known for the 17th century Baroque Servite Church and monastery. Conveniently situated here is the very pleasant Schloss-Camping, dominated by the castle, from which it gets its name, that towers at the back of the site with mountains beyond. The 160 numbered grass pitches are on level or slightly sloping ground. Electricity connections throughout (16A long leads may be necessary). The well laid out camping area is in two areas, divided by a fence and is closely mown, making this a most attractive site and the English speaking Baron who owns and runs it gives a most friendly welcome. This is an excellent base from which to explore the region and visit Innsbruck, Salzburg, the Royal Castles at Schwangau, the Bavarian Alps and northern Italy over the Brenner Pass for day trips. Caravans only accepted up to 7.5 m.

Facilities

The small, sanitary block of old design is near the entrance and has some washbasins in cabins. Washing machine and covered dishwashing area. Motorcaravan service point. Bar/restaurant. Snack bar with terrace. Shop for basics (all May - end Sept). Fenced and heated swimming pool (mid May-mid Sept). Minigolf. Playground. Car wash. Games and entertainment for children in high season. Off site: Supermarket 400 m. Bicycle hire 500 m. Golf and riding 7 km.

Open: 15 April - 15 October.

Directions

From A12 motorway, travelling east, leave at exit 68 for Hall, going westwards, take exit 61 for Wattens and follow the B171 and signs for Volders where site is signed. GPS: N47:17.231 E11:34352

Charges 2006

Per person	€ 5,10 - € 6,00
child (2-14 yrs)	€ 3,20 - € 3,70
pitch incl. car	€ 6,60 - € 7,80
electricity	€ 2,50

No credit cards. Reductions for stays of 3 nights or more in low season.

AU0100 Camping Seeblick Toni

Reintalersee, Moosen 46, A-6233 Kramsach (Tirol)

Tel: 05337 63544. Email: info@camping-seeblick.at

Austria has some of the finest sites in Europe and Seeblick Toni Brantlhof is one of the best. In a quiet, rural situation on the edge of the small Reintalersee lake, it is well worth considering for holidays in the Tirol with many excursions possibile. The surrounding mountains give scenic views and the campsite has a neat and tidy appearance. The 243 level pitches (215 for tourists) are in regular rows off hard access roads and are of good size with grass and hardstanding. All pitches have electricity (10A), 150 are fully serviced including cable TV and phone connections. The large, well appointed restaurant has a roof-top terrace where one can enjoy a meal, drink or snack and admire the lovely scenery. A path leads to the lake for swimming, boating and a sunbathing meadow. With a good solarium, sauna, whirlpool and fitness centre, this site provides for an excellent summer holiday and, with ski areas near, an excellent winter holiday also. This is a family run site with good English spoken and there is a friendly welcome.

Facilities

Two quite outstanding (heated in cool weather) sanitary blocks. One includes en-suite toilet/basin/shower rooms, the other also has individual bathrooms to let. Facilities for disabled visitors. New facilities for children. Baby room. Laundry facilities. Drying rooms. Freezer. Motorcaravan services. Restaurant. Bar. Snack kiosk. Mini-market. Fitness centre. Playground. New indoor play area. Topi club, kindergarten and organised activities for children in high season. Youth room. Fishing. Bicycle hire. Riding. Internet point (July/Aug. only). Off site: Kramsach 3km.

Open: All year.

Directions

Take exit 32 for Kramsach from A12 autobahn and turn right at roundabout, then immediately left following signs 'Zu den Seen' in village. After 3 km. turn right at camp sign. Note: there are two sites side by side at the lake – ignore the first and continue through to Seeblick Toni. GPS: N47:27.673 E11:54.396

Charges 2006

Per person	€ 5,50 - € 8,00
child (under 14 yrs)	€ 5,00 - € 6,00
pitch	€ 7,10 - € 12,50
electricity	€ 3,20

Camping Cheques accepted.

AU0102 Seen Camping Stadlerhof

Seebühel 14, A-6233 Kramsach (Tirol)

Tel: 05337 63371. Email: camping.stadlerhof@chello.at

This child-friendly family run site is in a beautiful location near the Krummsee. There are 130 sensibly sized pitches (99 for tourists) all with electric hook-ups (10A). Many are individual and divided by hedges and shrubs, and some mature trees offer shade in parts. 50 multi-serviced pitches are available. The site has a heated outdoor pool complex with cafe and Wellness Centre as well as its own small lake, a panorama walk and a dog walk. Reasonable English is spoken. A 'Quickstop' facility with grassy pitches and electric hook-up for overnighting is also offered. The Wellness Centre provides pampering and luxury for the adults with sauna, solarium, steam room, aromatherapy, massage rooms, skin therapy treatments, fitness centre, plus a relaxation area and an FKK naturist terrace. The children meanwhile, have an enticing array of play equipment including climbing frames, tubes, fort, bridge, conventional swings and slides, a skateboard ramp, table tennis and a games room with machines - plenty to keep them amused for an entire holiday.

Facilities

Spacious sanitary facilities include showers, some washbasins in cubicles, and 5 family bathrooms for rent. Laundry and dishwashing facilities. No dedicated facilities for disabled people. Small restaurant and bar. Basic provisions available. 'Wellness Centre', an outdoor heated stainless steel swimming pool (12.5m. x 6m and open in winter) with spa pool and children's pool, and a cafe. Comprehensive playground. TV room. Drying room, ski room. Off site: Kramsach is within walking distance. Reintalersee 3 km.

Open: All year.

Directions

Kramsach is approximately mid-way between Innsbruck and Kufstein. From A12 exit 32 turn right at roundabout and immediately left following signs for 'Zu den Seen' in village. Site is just outside village on left, after a right hand bend.
GPS: N47:27.395 E11:52.886

Charges 2006

Per person	€ 4,60 - € 5,80
child (under 14 yrs)	€ 2,95 - € 4,00
electricity per kWh	€ 0,65

No credit cards.

AU0110 Tirol Camp

Lindau 20, A-6391 Fieberbrunn (Tirol)

Tel: 05354 56666. Email: office@tirol-camp.at

This is one of many Tirol campsites that caters equally for summer and winter (here seemingly more for winter, when reservation is essential and prices 50% higher). Tirol Camp is in a quiet and attractive mountain situation and has 280 pitches all on wide flat terraces, set on a gentle slope (193 for touring units). Marked out mainly by the electricity boxes or low hedges, they are said to be 80-100 sq.m. and all have electricity (10A), gas, water/drainage, TV and telephone connections. A small, heated outdoor swimming pool with a paddling pool is open in summer. A new 'Wellness Centre' (free to campers) with indoor/outdoor pool complex, sauna, steam room, solarium and aromatherapy massage was opened in 2004. For winter stays, the site is very close to a ski lift centre and a 'langlauf' piste. Good English is spoken.

Facilities

The original refurbished toilet block in the main building is excellent with some washbasins in cabins and some private bathrooms on payment. A splendid, modern heated block at the top end of the site has spacious showers and all washbasins in cabins. Facilities for the disabled. Washing machines, dryers and drying room. Motorcaravan services. Self-service shop and snacks. Restaurant (closed Oct, Nov and May). Separate general room. Outdoor swimming pool (12 x 8 m; 1/6-30/9). Indoor pool and Wellness Centre (all year). Sauna. Tennis. Lake fishing. Riding. Bicycle hire. Outdoor chess. Playground and children's zoo. Entertainment and activity programmes (July/Aug). Internet point.

Open: All year.

Directions

Site is on the east side of Fieberbrunn, which is on the B164 St Johann-Saalfelden road. Turn south off the B164, 2 km. east of Fieberbrunn and follow camp signs up the hill to the site.
GPS: N47:28.095 E12:33.237

Charges 2006

Per person	€ 8,00 - € 10,00
child (4-14 yrs)	€ 4,00
pitch	€ 5,00 - € 14,00
electricity (per kWh on meter)	€ 0,70 - € 0,75

Winter charges higher.
Special weekly package deals with half-board offered in summer. Reductions for over 60s.
Camping Cheques accepted.

AU0170 Camping Innsbruck Kranebitten

Kranebitter Allee 214, A-6020 Innsbruck (Tirol)

Tel: 05122 84180. Email: campinnsbruck@hotmail.com

This basic site is in a pleasant situation just outside Innsbruck. The 120 pitches are numbered, but not marked out, on mostly sloping grass, with good shade cover. There are three separate terraces for caravans and motorcaravans and all pitches have electricity (6A, long leads are on loan for some). By the side of the site, with access to it, is a large open field with a good playground and plenty of space for ball games. Being so near the attractive town of Innsbruck, the site makes an excellent base from which to visit the ancient city and also to explore the many attractions nearby. The 'Innsbruck-Card', available from the site, gives various discounts for attractions in the city, plus free travel on public transport (park-and-ride from the site, even if you don't stay overnight). A private taxi also runs a shuttle service to and from the city for €5. Some road and aircraft noise may be heard. Good English is spoken.

Facilities

The large, toilet block shows signs of age, is heated, clean and acceptable, with some washbasins in cabins and renovated showers. Washing machines and dryers. Motorcaravan services. Bar/restaurant with terrace (open all year, but opening times may vary). Internet point. Shop for basic supplies. Playground with large play field adjoining. Games for children and barbecues in summer. Free mountain hiking and cycling tours in summer, free ski bus in winter. Bicycle hire. Off site: Swimming pool 2 km.

Open: All year.

Directions

From A12 Innsbruck - Arlberg motorway, take Innsbruck-Kranebitten exit 83 from where site is well signed, directly on B171 (Telfs-Innsbruck non-toll road). GPS: N47:15.821 E11:19.579

Charges 2006

Per person	€ 5,40
child (4-14 yrs)	€ 3,50
pitch incl. car	€ 6,80
electricity	€ 3,30

Less 10% for stays over 10 days.
Special offers for sporting groups.

Ideally located near the forest yet so close to a town!
Open year-round, great bus connection to the old part of the town of Innsbruck, "Inntal" bike way only 150m away, motor caravan services, restaurant, Internet access point Bus tickets, excursion and rambling tips as well as the All-inclusive Innsbruck Card are available at reception point. Receive many discounts with guest cards. Free guided mountain hikes from June to September. Free ski bus service in winter in the Olympic ski world surrounding Innsbruck.
www.campinginnsbruck.com, Tel. + Fax +43 512 28 41 80

Innsbruck-Kranebitten

AU0120 Erlebnis-Comfort-Camping Aufenfeld

Distelberg 1, A-6274 Aschau im Zillertal (Tirol)

Tel: 00435282 29160. Email: camping.fiegl@tirol.com

This site is attractively situated in a mountain region with fine views and good facilities. The main area of the site itself is flat with pitches of 100 sq.m. on grass between made-up access roads, with further pitches on terraces at the rear. There are around 350 pitches (240 for touring units with 6A electricity) including around 40 with individual sanitary cubicles. The site can become full mid-July until mid-August and at Christmas, but usually has space at other times. Ski lifts are nearby, one for beginners particularly close. A splendid indoor swimming pool has been added and there is a heated outdoor pool, paddling pool, and a tennis court for summer use. A 'Wellness centre' is planned. A lake and leisure area has been created alongside the site, together with a 'Western' village for children. There are around 60 privately owned or rental units and 50 seasonal units on site. Note: pylons and power lines cross the site over some pitches. Member of the Leading Campings Group.

Facilities

Four well kept, heated sanitary blocks of excellent quality and size, each with a few washbasins in cabins for each sex, baby rooms and nine units for disabled people. Four additional units provide 40 private cabins for luxury pitches and several family bathrooms for rent. Laundry and drying room. Ski room. Motorcaravan services. Shop. Restaurant. TV. Indoor pool, sauna and sun-beds. Outdoor pool (May - Sept). Football field. Playground. Multi-court. Tennis. Riding. Fishing. Trampolines. Bicycle hire. ATM. Western village. Mineral museum. Entertainment in high season includes line dancing, Western shows and archery. Off site: Walking and cycling in the Zillertall valley. Cross country skiing (winter).

Open: All year excl. 3 November - 8 December.

Directions

From A12 Inntal motorway, take exit for Zillertal (no. 39, 32 km. northeast of Innsbruck. Follow road no. 169 to village of Aschau from which site is well signed. GPS: N47:15.800 E11:53.960

Charges 2006

Per person	€ 5,00 - € 10,00
child (under 12 yrs)	€ 3,30 - € 6,50
pitch incl. electricity and TV hook-up	€ 7,00 - € 11,00
with private sanitary cabin	€ 15,00 - € 26,50

Winter prices are higher.

27

AU0130 Terrassen Camping Schloßberg Itter

Brixenialer Stobe 11, A-6305 Itter ba Hopfgarten (Tirol)
Tel: 05335 2181. Email: info@camping-itter.at

With some 200 pitches, this well kept site with good facilities is suitable both as a base for longer stays and also for overnight stops, as it lies right by a main road west of Kitzbühel. It is on a slight slope but most of the 200 numbered pitches are on level terraces. Some pitches are individual and divided by hedges and have electricity (8/10A) and cable TV connections, 150 have water and drainage. Space is usually available. Good English is spoken.

Facilities

The main sanitary facilities are heated and of very high standard. The newest section has a large room with private cubicles. Some of these have vanity style washbasins and others have baths. Two slightly larger units for families, with baby baths. Facilities for disabled visitors. Fridge. Washing machines and dryers. Motorcaravan services. Cooking facilities. Small shop, bar/restaurant (both closed Nov). Solar heated swimming pool (1/5-30/9). Sauna and solarium. Playground and playroom for wet weather.Naturist sun deck. WiFi internet. Ski and drying rooms. Off site: Tennis, fishing, riding, bicycle hire within 2 km. Golf 10 km.

Open: All year excl. 16-30 November.

Directions

Site is 2 km. northwest of Hopfgarten. From A12 exit 17 (Worgl-Ost) turn right on B178 towards St Johann for 5 km then take the B170 towards Hopfgarten for 2 km. Site is signed to left on a right hand bend opposite a Peugeot/Talbot garage.
GPS: N47:27.976 E12:08.376

Charges 2006

Per person	€ 5,80 - € 6,90
child (1-13 yrs)	€ 3,70 - € 3,90
pitch incl. electricity	€ 11,20 - € 12,70

Prices higher for winter. Less 50% on pitch fee in mid-seasons. No credit cards.

AU0140 Euro Camping Wilder Kaiser

Kranebittau 18, A-6345 Kössen (Tirol)
Tel: 05375 6444. Email: info@eurocamp-koessen.com

The village of Kössen lies to the south of the A8 Munich - Salzburg autobahn and east of the A93/A12 motorway near Kufstein. Wilder Kaiser is located at the foot of the Unterberg with views of the Kaisergebirge (the Emperor's mountains) and surrounded by forests. About 125 of the 190 pitches (grass over gravel) are available for tourists, plus an area for tents and a new area for motocaravans. Arranged on either side of paved roads, around 100 pitches have electricity (10A), water, drainage, TV and gas points. There is a little shade from specimen trees and all have views. English is spoken.

Facilities

The heated, central sanitary block is of good quality with spacious showers, some washbasins in cubicles. Baby room. Washing machines and dryers. Motorcaravan services. Shop. Large restaurant/bar (closed Nov). Snack bar (high season). Club room with TV and playstation. Heated swimming pool (May - Sept). Youth room. Sauna and solarium. Tennis. Large imaginative adventure playground. In high season, special staff run a Topi club and other activities for adults and children. Off site: Bicycle hire 1 km. Golf 2 km. Fishing and Riding 4 km. Beach and boat launching 6 km.

Open: All year excl. 2 November - 2 December.

Directions

From A8 autobahn (München - Salzburg), take Grabenstatt exit 109 and go south on B307/B176 to Kössen. Cross the river and at roundabout follow signs for 'Bergbahnen' and Euro Camp. After 600 m. follow signs to site. From A93 (Rosenheim - Kufstein) autobahn take Oberaudorf exit and go east on B172 to Walchsee and Kössen.
GPS: N47:39.222 E12:24.915

Charges 2006

Per person	€ 6,20 - € 7,20
pitch with electricity and TV	€ 7,00 - € 9,00
pitch with all services	€ 6,30 - € 8,30
electricity	€ 2,30 - € 4,30

AU0150 Camping Riffler

Bruggenfeldstraße 2, A-6500 Landeck (Tirol)
Tel: **05442 64898**. Email: **riffler@aon.at**

This small, pretty site is almost in the centre of the small town of Landeck and, being on the main through route from the Vorarlberg to the Tirol, would serve as a good overnight stop. Square in shape, it has just 40 pitches on either side of hard access roads on level grass, with the main road on one side and the fast flowing River Sanna on the other edge. Trees and flowers adorn the site giving good shade and all pitches have electricity (10A).

Facilities

The small toilet block has been rebuilt to a good standard. Washing machine and dryer. Basic motorcaravan services. Shop. Small general room with T.V. Table tennis. Fishing. Off site: Supermarket just outside the gate, other shops 100 m. Restaurants about 100 m. Bicycle hire and swimming pool 500 m. Reshen and Arlberg mountain passes within easy driving distance. Opportunities for watersports and hang-gliding. Schnapps distillery in Stanz.

Open: All year excl. May.

Directions

Site is at the western end of Landeck. Take exit for Landeck-West from the A12 and turn left towards Landeck. Site on the left (sharp left bend) just before entering town centre. GPS: N47:08.525 E10:33.665

Charges 2006

Per person	€ 6,80
pitch incl. electricity	€ 10,50 - € 11,70
car	€ 2,80

Winter prices slightly more. No credit cards.

AU0155 Aktiv-Camping Prutz

Beim Sauerbrunn, A-6522 Prutz (Tirol)
Tel: **05472 2648**. Email: **info@aktiv-camping.at**

Aktiv-Camping is a long site which lies beside, and is fenced off, from the River Inn. Most of the 131 individual level pitches are for touring and range in size from 70 to 90 sq.m. They all have 6A electrical connections and in the larger area fit together sideways and back to back, so at times, it can give the appearance of being quite crowded. There is a separate overnight area for motorcaravans. This is an attractive area with many activities in both summer and winter for all ages and you may well consider using this site not just as an overnight stop, but also for a longer stay.

Facilities

The sanitary facilities are of a high standard, with private cabins and good facilities for disabled visitors. Baby room. Washing machine. Dog shower. Small mini-market. Bar. Takeaway. Play room. Ski room. Skating rink. Internet point. Children's entertainment. Guided walks, skiing (free shuttle service). Wifi. Off site: Indoor pool at Feichten, Pilgrim's Church at Kaltenbrunn. Kaunertaler Glacier.

Open: All year.

Directions

Travelling west from Innsbruck on the E60/A12 for about 65 km. turn south onto the B180 signed Bregenz, Arlberg, Innsbruck and Fernpass for 11 km. to Prutz. Site is signed from the B180 over the bridge. GPS: N47:04.807 E10:39.564

Charges 2006

Per person	€ 6,70 - € 8,30
pitch incl. electricity	€ 7,00 - € 12,00

Camping Cheques accepted.

AU0185 Campingplatz Seewiese

Tristachersee 2, A-9900 Lienz (Tirol)
Tel: **04852 69767**. Email: **seewiese@hotmail.com**

High above the village of Tristach and 5 km. from Lienz, this is a perfect location for a good campsite. When we arrived the owner said, 'This is a green paradise at the gateway to the Dolomites' – it did not take us many minutes to agree totally with his assessment. The 110 pitches all have 6A electricity and the 11 pitches for motorcaravans near reception each have electricity, water and internet access. Caravans are sited on a gently sloping field which has level areas although pitches are unmarked and unnumbered.

Facilities

Toilet facilities are clean, heated and modern with free showers. Washing machine and dryer. Motorcaravan service point. Excellent restaurant/bar. Small play area. Internet access. Swimming in adjoining lake. Off site: Lienz 5 km.

Open: 5 May - 30 September.

Directions

In Lienz initially follow signs for Spittal and at traffic lights turn right towards Tristach. Go under the railway, over a small bridge then left, still towards Tristach. Go through Tristach and after about 1.5 km. turn right up to site (at the top of a 1:10 climb). GPS: N46:48.098 E12:48.172

Charges 2007

Per unit incl. 2 persons	€ 21,60
incl. electricity	€ 24,10

No credit cards.
Camping Cheques accepted.

AU0220 Øtztal Arena Camp Krismer

A-6441 Umhausen (Tirol)

Tel: 05255 5390. Email: info@oetztal-camping.at

This is a delightful site with lovely views, in the beautiful Øtz valley, on the edge of the village of Umhausen. Situated on a gentle slope in an open valley, it has an air of peace and tranquillity and makes an excellent base for mountain walking, particularly in spring and autumn, skiing in winter or a relaxing holiday. The 98 pitches, some on individual terraces, are all marked and numbered and have electricity (12/16A); charges relate to the area available, long leads may be necessary.

Facilities

With under-floor heating, open washbasins, hairdressing room and showers on payment, the toilet facilities are of good quality. One small toilet/wash block is for summer use. Sauna. Baby room. Laundry facilities. Motorcaravan services. Bar/restaurant (May-Sept, Dec-April). No shop, but bread can be ordered. TV room (satellite). Ski room. Fishing. Bicycle hire. Playground. Off site: Swimming pool and tennis 100 m. Village 200 m. Golf 20 m.

Open: All year.

Directions

Take Øtztal Valley exit 123 from Imst - Innsbruck A12 motorway, and Umhausen is 13 km. towards Solden on the B186; site is well signed to south of village. GPS: N47:08.122 E10:55.951

Charges 2006

Per person	€ 5,80
child (2-13 yrs)	€ 4,30
pitch	€ 2,40 - € 8,00
electricity (plus € 0.75 per kWh)	€ 0,75

AU0227 Comfort Camp Grän

Engetalstr. 13, A-6673 Grän (Tirol)

Tel: 05675 6570. Email: comfortcamp@aon.at

In a village location in the Tannheimer Tal, with panoramic mountain scenery, Comfort Camp Grän is a family run site with excellent heated sanitary facilities and a stylish modern indoor swimming pool complex. It makes a good base for exploring this border region of Austria and Germany. The site has 210 pitches of 80-100 sq.m. (170 for tourists) all with 16A electric hook-ups, water (only for summer use) and waste water on fairly level grass, over gravel terrain with some shallow terraces.

Facilities

The main sanitary unit is impressive with superb facilities, spacious, light and airy. There are controllable hot showers, washbasins in cubicles, a children's section in the ladies, a baby room and many family bathrooms for rent. First aid room. A second smaller unit is equally good. Indoor swimming pool, sauna and steam room. Solarium. Mini-market. Restaurant and bar. Playground. Indoor playroom. Internet. Teenagers' room. Off site: The Haldensee (lake) 3 km. Fishing 2 km. Riding 6 km. Beach 2 km. German Border 10 km. Walking trails and ski runs.

Open: 23 May - 2 November; 15 December - 18 April.

Directions

Grän is close to the German border, to the southwest of Füssen. From Germany on the autobahn A7, turn off at exit 137, and turn south on road 310 to Oberjoch, then take road 308 (road 199 in Austria) east to Grän. At eastern end of village turn north signed Pfronten, and site is 1.5 km. on left. GPS: N47:30.610 E10:33.050

Charges 2006

Per person	€ 7,50 - € 10,00
child (2-14 yrs)	€ 5,00 - € 8,00
pitch incl electricity	€ 8,15 - € 13,15

AU0225 Romantik Camping Schloß Fernsteinsee

Am Fernpaß Tirol, A-6465 Nassereith (Tirol)

Tel: 05265 5210. Email: hotel@fernsteinsee.at

This is a secluded and attractive site in a sheltered location in the protected area of the Fernstein Lakes and part of the Schloss Fernsteinsee estate. There are 125 pitches, all for tourists, in two separate areas and 80 have electricity hook-ups (4/13A), water and waste water. The pitches are on level grass in the area in front of the reception and services building on four shallow terraces divided by low rails or shrubs. A new area with flat, gravel pitches and all services has been developed at the bottom of the site. There is good shade here and gravel access roads. The second area, which is further from the services, is more open and with less formal pitching, served by a central tarmac road.

Facilities

Modern heated facilities with a generous supply of controllable hot showers, washbasins (open style and in cabins) and facilites for disabled visitors. Laundry room. Table tennis. Boules. Small playground. Games room. Sauna and solarium. Fishing and boating on the lake. Off site: The Hotel Schloss Fernsteinsee with bar and restaurant 500 m. Nassereith village, shops and indoor swimming pool 1.5 km. The Fern Pass and alpine road.

Open: 15 April - 26 October.

Directions

Nassereith is 15 km. north of Imst, just south of the Fern Pass. From Imst take road 189 north for 13 km., then left on road 179 and continue past Nassereith, taking tarmac entry road 500 m. before the bridge (well signed). GPS: N47:20.258 E10:49.092

Charges 2006

Per unit incl. 2 persons	€ 18,00 - € 24,00
extra person	€ 5,00
electricity (plus € 0.20 kWh)	€ 2,10

AU0250 AlpencampingMark

Bundesstraße 12, Maholmhof, A-6114 Weer bei Schwaz (Tirol)

Tel: **05224 68146**. Email: **alpcamp.mark@aon.at**

This pleasant Tirol site is run by a family who provides not only a neat, friendly site and a warm welcome, but also a variety of outdoor activities. Formerly a farm, they now breed horses, giving a free ride each day to youngsters and organise treks. Herr Mark junior (a certified alpine ski guide and ski instructor) runs courses for individuals or groups in climbing (there are practice climbing walls on site), rafting, mountain bike riding, trekking, hiking, etc. Guided alpine tours can be arranged and there are pleasant walks up the lower slopes of the mountains directly from the site. Set in the Inn valley, between mountain ranges, the site has 96 flat, grass pitches (71 for touring units) on either side of gravel roads, with electricity connections (6/10A).

Facilities

Good quality, modern, heated sanitary facilities are provided in the old farm buildings. Freezer. Washing machines and dryer. Motorcaravan services. Small, cheerful bar/restaurant and shop (1/6-1/9). Small heated pool (15/5-15/9). An attractive wooden chalet houses reception and the activities are administered from here. Activity programme with instruction. Bicycle hire. Riding (free for children). Glacier tours. Table tennis. Large play area with good equipment. A further barn is for use by children in wet weather. Off site: Imtal Valley, good for mountain biking.

Open: 1 April - 31 October.

Directions

Site is 200 m. east of the village of Weer on the Wattens - Schwaz road no. B171 which runs parallel to the A12, just 10 km east of Innsbruck. (If using A12 take exit 61 from west or 53 from east). GPS: N47:18.446 E11:38.875

Charges 2006

Per person	€ 4,30 - € 5,50
child (under 14 yrs)	€ 3,00 - € 3,50
pitch	€ 4,50 - € 6,00
electricity	€ 2,50
dog	€ 3,00

AU0160 Seecamp Zell am See

Thumersbacherstraße 34, A-5700 Zell-am-See (Salzburg)

Tel: **06542 72115**. Email: **zell@seecamp.at**

Zellersee, delightfully situated in the south of Salzburg province and near the start of the Grossglocknerstrasse, is ideally placed for enjoying the splendid southern Austria countryside. Seecamp is right by the water about 3 km. from the town of Zell and with fine views to the south end of the lake. One is immediately struck by the order and neat appearance of the site, with 176 good level, mainly grass-on-gravel pitches of average size, all with electricity (10/16A). About half have water, drainage and TV connections. Units can be close together in peak season. A large, modern building in the centre, houses the amenities. The lake is accessible for watersports, including both surfing and sailing schools. All in all, this is a splendid site for a relaxing or active holiday. Good English is spoken.

Facilities

Excellent, heated sanitary facilities include facilities for disabled visitors and a baby room. Washing machines, dryers and irons. Motorcaravan services (access difficult for larger units). Restaurant (closed for 2 weeks after Easter and Oct-Nov). Shop (June-Aug. and Dec-mid Jan). Beach volleyball. Play area. Playroom with play stations. Fishing. Bicycle hire. 'Topi' Club and summer entertainment for children. Activity programme for adults with rafting, canoeing, mountain biking, water ski-ing and hiking. Winter ski packages and free ski bus. Glacier ski-ing possible in summer. Off site: Free entry to nearby lake beach, swimming pools and ice skating.

Open: All year.

Directions

Approaching from the north on the B311 take the Thumersbach exit just before tunnel entrance (2 km. north of Zell-am-See town). After 500 m. turn left and site entrance is 750 m. on the right. Note: This road has a 3.5 ton weight restriction but it is the only access to site. GPS: N47:20.384 E12:48.536

Charges 2006

Per person	€ 7,70
child (5-15 yrs)	€ 4,30
pitch	€ 9,00 - € 11,20
tent pitch	€ 4,50
car	€ 2,50

Gas on meter. Less 20% in low season.
Special winter package prices.

AU0265 Park Grubhof

A-5092 St Martin bei Lofer (Salzburg)

Tel: 06588 8237. Email: camping@lofer.net

Park Grubhof is a well organised spacious site in a scenic riverside location, once the pleasure park of the adjacent Schloss (now a hotel). The 200 pitches all with electric hook-ups (10A, long leads may be required), have been carefully divided into separate areas for different types of camper – dog owners, couples, young people, families and groups. In 2005, 26 very large pitches, all with electricity, water and waste water, were added along the bank of the river Saarlach. There are wooded areas with plenty of shade, other more open areas, and some very attractive log cabins which have been rescued from the old logging camps. The main activities are based around the River Saalach, where you will find barbecue areas, canoeing and white water rafting, fishing and swimming (when the river level reduces). Good English is spoken. Parents of small children should be aware that the site is adjacent to a fast flowing river which is unfenced.

Facilities

Two sanitary units - one recently built unit by the riverside, and the original unit, completely rebuilt for 2006 nearer reception, give a good provision of all facilities including some washbasins in cubicles, laundry and dishwashing sinks. A suite for disabled campers is in the older unit. Motorcaravan service point. Shop, restaurant and bar. Playground. Games room. Watersports. Off site: Lofer 1 km. Gorges and caves 5-7 km. Salzburg 40 minutes drive. Many marked walking and cycling trails.

Open: 1 May - 30 September.

Directions

From A12 exit 17 (south of Kufstein) take road B178 east to St Johann in Tyrol, then continue on the B178 north west to Lofer, and finally south on B311. Just past Schloss Grubhof at the northern edge of St Martin, turn left (site signed) and follow lane to site. GPS: N47:34.474 E12:42.391

Charges 2006

Per person	€ 5,30 - € 5,90
child (under 15 yrs)	€ 3,30 - € 3,50
pitch incl. electricity	€ 4,30 - € 8,00

AU0212 Panoramacamping Stadtblick

Rauchenbichl, Rauchenbichler Straße 21, A-5020 Salzburg (Salzburg)

Tel: 06624 50652. Email: info@panorama-camping.at

With a panoramic view over the city of Salzburg this site is well named, and you can be sure of a warm welcome from the multi-lingual owner, Herr Wörndl. The site has 70 pitches all with electric hook-ups (4A) and water points, on grass over gravel terraces, plus 10 grassy tent pitches. They are reasonably sized for a city site location, and the view and the good value restaurant amply compensate for any shortcomings. This is an ideal site for a short stay to see all the sights of the city, with a bus stop within walking distance, and local tour buses pick up from the site. The site also sells the Salzburg Card.

Facilities

The single sanitary unit is in the older style, but is neat and well maintained. It provides some washbasins in cabins, controllable hot showers with limited changing space. No facilities for babies or the disabled. Laundry. Dishwashing sinks. Motorcaravan service point. Shop for basic supplies, gas and souvenirs. Restaurant (May-Sept). TV, lounge, and baby-foot. Small playground. Off site: Golf, bicycle hire and swimming pool within 3 km.

Open: 20 March - 5 November; 28 December - 6 January.

Directions

From A1 exit 288 (Salzburg Nord) turn south towards city. Approaching the first set of traffic lights you will need to be in right hand lane, turn right here on a minor road (site signed) and continue to top of hill, and follow site signs. GPS: N47:49.708 E13:03.145

Charges 2006

Per person	€ 6,50
child (2-15 yrs)	€ 3,00
pitch	€ 2,00 - € 7,00
pet	€ 1,50

AU0180 Sport Camp Woferlgut

Kroessenbach 40, A-5671 Bruck (Salzburg)

Tel: 06545 73030. Email: info@sportcamp.at

The village of Bruck lies at the junction of the B311 and the Grossglocknerstrasse in the Hohe Tauern National Park, with Salzburg to the north and Innsbruck to the northwest. Sport Camp Woferlgut, a family run site, is one of the best in Austria. Although surrounded by mountains, the site is quite flat with pleasant views. The 350 level, grass pitches are marked out by shrubs (300 for touring units) and each has electricity (16A), water, drainage, cable TV socket and gas point. The fitness centre has a fully equipped gym, whilst the other building contains a sauna and cold dip, Turkish bath, solarium (all free) massage on payment and a bar. In summer there is a free activity programme, evenings with live music, club for children, weekly barbecues and guided cycle and mountain tours. The site's own lake is used for swimming and fishing, surrounded by a landscaped sunbathing area. In winter a cross-country skiing trail and toboggan run lead from the site and a free bus service is provided to nearby skiing facilities. A high grass bank separates the site and the road. The management is pleased to advise on local attractions and tours, making this a splendid base for a family holiday. Good English is spoken. Used by tour operators (45 pitches).

Facilities

Three modern sanitary blocks– the newest in a class of its own - have excellent facilities, providing private cabins, under-floor heating and music. Washing machines and dryers. Facilities for disabled visitors. Family bathrooms for hire. Motorcaravan services. Cooking and dishwashing facilities. Well stocked shop, bar, restaurant and takeaway (20/12-20/4 and 28/4-1/11). Small, heated outdoor pool and children's pool (28/4-30/9). Fitness centre. Two playgrounds, indoor play room and children's cinema. General room. Tennis. Volleyball. Football area. Bicycle hire. Hobby room with billiards, table tennis and TV. Fishing. Watersports and lake swimming. Hiking and skiing (all year) nearby. Collection of small animals with pony rides for children. Off site: ATM 500 m. Skiing 2.5 km. Golf 3 km. Boat launching and sailing 3.5 km.

Open: All year.

Directions

Site is southwest of Bruck. From road B311, Bruck by-pass, take southern exit (Grossglockner) and site is signed from the junction of B311 and B107 roads (small signs).

Charges 2006

Per person	€ 4,90 - € 7,50
child (under 10 yrs)	€ 4,00 - € 5,50
pitch	€ 9,40 - € 12,00
luxury large pitch	€ 15,40 - € 18,00
electricity (plus meter)	€ 2,10

Special offers for low season, longer stays.
Camping Cheques accepted.

AU0262 Oberwötzlhof Camp

Erlfeld 37, A-5441 Abtenau (Salzburg)

Tel: **06243 2698**. Email: **oberwoetzlhof@sbg.at**

High up in the Lammertal Valley is this small farm site with amazing views of the surrounding mountains. Part of a working farm, it has a total of 70 pitches, of which 30 are for long stay units, leaving 40 places for tourers. All are serviced with electric hook-ups (10A), water and drainage. Amateur astronomers will appreciate the lack of site lighting, but campers may find a torch useful. The small fenced swimming pool (10 x 5 m.) is unheated, and has paved surrounds. The restaurant is only open during the winter, but breakfasts, drinks and ices are available during the summer season. Despite the slightly dated facilities, we think that the friendly atmosphere and stunning location amply compensate for any shortcomings.

Facilities

The current sanitary unit is a little dated and could be stretched if the site was full, but it does provide some washbasins in cubicles, laundry and dishwashing facilities, drying room, and solarium, however there are no special facilities for babies or disabled campers. A new unit is under construction but it could be some time before it is finished (the shell was complete at the time of our visit, but needed internal fitting and decorating). Restaurant open in winter only. Swimming pool. Internet terminal. Off site: Abtenau is 2.5 km. (about 25 minutes walk we were told). Skiing 2.5 km. Riding 8 km. Hallstättersee and salt mines 30 km.

Open: All year.

Directions

Abtenau lies to the south east of Salzburg. From the A10 exit 28 (Golling), take B162 east for 14 km. and site is signed to the left about 2.5 km before Abtenau. GPS: N47:35.171 E13:19.474

Charges 2006

Per person	€ 5,50
child (under 15 yrs)	€ 3,50
pitch	€ 5,00 - € 10,00
electricity	€ 0,60

No credit cards.

AU0350 Camp Mond See Land

Wiedlroither & Leidl KEG, Punz Au 21, A-5310 Mondsee (Upper Austria)

Tel: **06232 2600**. Email: **austria@campmondsee.at**

Mond See Land underwent a make-over in 2000 and now offers excellent facilities in a pleasant part of Austria, to the east of Salzburg, between the lakes of Mondsee and Irrsee. It is peacefully situated in a natural setting, with mountain views, yet less than 10 minutes drive from the autobahn. There are 60 good sized, level touring pitches (80 long stay), set amongst the trees at the lower level and on terraces, each with water, waste water and 16A electricity. There is a small fishing lake (unfenced) and a small children's playground. Good English is spoken.

Facilities

The sanitary facilities are in the reception and pool complex and offer first class facilities including some washbasins in cabins and a suite for disabled visitors. Laundry with washing machines and dryer. Kitchen with cooking facilities and dishwashing sinks. Motorcaravan service point. Shop and restaurant, both all season. Heated covered swimming pool (free) and sunbathing terrace. Playground. Riding. Off site: Mondsee is a popular large lake with many sporting opportunities. Golf 5 km.

Open: 1 April - 31 October.

Directions

From A1/E55 exit 265 (signed Straßwalchen) turn north onto B154. In approx 1.5 m. turn left at crossroads (by glassworks) and then 2 km to site (signed). Note: Signs can be difficult to spot. GPS: N47:52.008 E13:18.379

Charges 2006

Per person	€ 4,90 - € 5,50
child (6-15 yrs)	€ 3,50 - € 3,80
pitch	€ 6,50 - € 7,50
electricity	€ 2,50

AU0340 Camping am See

Winkl 77, A-4831 Obertraun (Upper Austria)

Tel: 06131 265. Email: camping.am.see@chello.at

It is unusual to locate a campsite so deep in the heart of spectacular mountain scenery, yet with such easy access. Directly on the shores of Halstattersee, near Obertraun and the Dachstein range of mountains, this 2.5 hectare, flat site, with 160 pitches is an excellent, peaceful holiday base which has been upgraded. Owners, cum professional artists, Carola and Lorenzo, both speak English and their talents are reflected around the central amenity building. The grass site is basically divided into two, with tents in a more shady area, whilst caravans and motorcaravans are more in the open. There are no specific pitches although the owners, within reason, control where you place your unit. At the time of our visit there were only 36 electricity hook-ups (10A).

Facilities

Completely refurbished, fully equipped and modern, the toilet block includes a small baby room. Washing machine. New, open barn style area for dishwashing and a similar area with purpose built barbecues, seating and tables. Bar and limited restaurant with hot meals and fine wines available to order. Basic daily provisions kept such as bread and milk. Small playground. Off site: Activities nearby.

Open: 1 May - 30 September.

Directions

Due south from Bad Ischl on road B145, take road B166 to Hallstatt. After single carriageway tunnel, site is 4 km. on left on entering village of Winkl. Note: Road is a little narrow in places so care is needed. GPS: N47:32.927 E13:40.661

Charges 2006

Per unit incl. 2 persons	€ 21,80 - € 25,30
child (5-14 yrs)	€ 3,37
electricity	€ 3,00
No credit cards.	

AU0345 Seecamping Gruber

Dorfstraße 63, A-4865 Nußdorf am Attersee (Upper Austria)

Tel: 07666 80450. Email: office@camping-grabei.at

The Attersee is the largest of a group of lakes just to the east of Salzburg in the very attractive Salzkammergut area. Seecamping Gruber is a small crowded site halfway up the western side of the lake. There are 150 individual pitches, with an increasing number of seasonal units taking the larger pitches. There are still some 60 pitches for tourers, all with 16A electrical connections, 16 with water and waste water as well and many with shade. Pitches tend to be small to medium size and the access roads are narrow making entrance and exit difficult and this is not helped by the seasonal pitches erecting fences, etc. to utilise every last inch of their pitches. Sadly only from the 25 metre swimming pool and the shallow children's play pool (both heated to 26 degrees and with sunbathing areas) are there views across the lake to the hills beyond.

Facilities

Modern sanitary facilities offer some private cabins, washing machine and dryer, good unit for the disabled and baby room. Restaurant and takeaway. Shop. Play area. Swimming and paddling pools. Sauna, solarium and gym. Fishing. Off site: Windsurfing, sailing, both with courses available. Mountain bikes, diving and balloon rides all available locally.

Open: 15 April - 15 October.

Directions

From the A1/E55/E60 between Salzburg and Linz, take exit 243 to Attersee and then south on the B151 to Nußdorf. Site is on the southern edge of the village.

Charges 2006

Per unit incl 2 persons and electricity	€ 21,30 - € 26,00

AU0240 Camping Appesbach

Au 99, A-5360 St Wolfgang (Upper Austria)

Tel: 06138 2206. Email: camping@appesbach.at

St Wolfgang, a pretty little village on the lake of the same name which was made famous by the operetta 'White Horse Inn', is ringed round by hills in a delightful situation. The location of Appesbach, on the banks of the lake with a good frontage, is one of its main assets. The site has 170 pitches, with 100 for tourists (including 20 tent pitches) with some in regular rows and the rest on open meadows that could become full in high season. The welcoming owners, Maria and Christian Peter both speak good English.

Facilities

The two toilet blocks have been combined into one, extended and refurbished to a good standard. Drive over Motorcaravan service point, with adjacent chemical disposal facility, sink and water. Good shop. Bar (1/5-31/8). Restaurant with TV (Easter-30/9). Snack bar with terrace (Easter-30/9). Small playground. Table tennis, billiards, darts. Off site: Village 1 km. Excursions possible.

Open: Easter - 31 October.

Directions

From B158 Salzburg-Bad Ischl road, turn towards St Wolfgang just east of Strobl and site is on the left 1 km. before St Wolfgang.

GPS: N47:43.947 E13:27.826

Charges 2006

Per person	€ 4,10 - € 6,10
child (3-15 yrs)	€ 2,55 - € 3,55
pitch incl. electricity	€ 7,80 - € 15,80

AU0290 Donaupark Camping Tulln

Hafenstraße, A-3430 Tulln (Lower Austria)

Tel: 02272 65200. Email: camptulln@oeamtc.at

The ancient town of Tulln (the 'city of roses') lies on the southern bank of the River Danube, about 20 miles northwest of Vienna. Donaupark, owned by the Austrian Motor Club, is imaginatively laid out village-style with unmarked grass pitches grouped around six circular gravel areas. Further pitches are to the side of the hard road which links the circles and these include some with grill facilities for tents; 100 of the 120 tourist pitches have electricity (3/6A) and cable TV sockets. Tall trees offer shade in parts. At the back of the site there are 120 long stay caravans. This is a quiet location.

Facilities

Three identical, modern, octagonal sanitary blocks can be heated. One is at reception (next to the touring area), the other two are at the far end of the site. Facilities for disabled visitors. Washing machines and dryers. Cooking rings. Gas supplies. Bar and restaurant with terrace which keeps open quite late (1/5-15/9). Shop (15/5-15/9). Bicycle and canoe hire. Excursion programme. Off site: Lake swimming in adjacent park. Fishing 500 m. Bus service into Vienna 9/7-24/8. Train to Vienna.

Open: Easter - 31 October.

Directions

From Vienna follow south bank of the Danube on B14; from the west, leave A1 autobahn at either St Christophen or Altenbach exits and go north on B19 to Tulln. Site is on the east side of Tulln.

Charges 2006

Per person	€ 6,50
child (5-14 yrs)	€ 3,00
pitch incl. electricity	€ 9,50 - € 13,00
Camping Cheques accepted.	

AU0280 Camping Stumpfer

A-3392 Schönbühel (Lower Austria)

Tel: 02752 8510. Email: office@stumpfer.com

This small, well appointed site with just 60 pitches is directly on the River Danube, near the small town of Schönbühel, and could make a convenient night stop being near the Salzburg - Vienna autobahn. The 50 unmarked pitches for touring units, all with electricity (16A), are on flat grass and the site is lit at night. There is shade in most parts and a landing stage for boat trips on the Danube. The main building also houses a Gasthof, with a bar/restaurant of the same name, that can be used by campers. This is very much a family run site.

Facilities

Part of the main building, the toilet block is of good quality with hot water on payment. Facilities for disabled visitors include ramps by the side of steps up to the block. Washing machine and dryer. Motorcaravan services. Small shop for basics. Playground. Fishing. Off site: Swimming pool, bicycle hire or riding within 5 km.

Open: 1 April - 31 October.

Directions

Leave Salzburg - Vienna autobahn at Melk exit. Drive towards Melk, but continue towards Melk Nord. Just before bridge turn right (Schönbühel, St Polten), at T-junction turn right again and continue down hill. Turn right just before BP station (Schönbühel) and site is 3 km. on left with narrow entrance.

GPS: N48:14.233 E15:22.250

Charges 2007

Per person	€ 5,60
child (6-15 yrs)	€ 2,60
pitch incl. electricity	€ 4,70 - € 8,20

AU0300 Camping Rodaun

Breitenfurter Straße 487, An der Au 2, A-1230 Wien-Südwest-Rodaun (Vienna)

Tel: **01 8884 154**

This good little site is within the Vienna city boundary and is a pleasant base for visiting this old, interesting and world famous city. Just 9 km. from the centre, there is an excellent public transport system for viewing the sights as car parking is almost impossible in the city. Situated in a southern suburb, it has space for about 40 units on flat grass pitches or on concrete bases and an additional area for about 20 tents. With little shade, the pitches are not numbered or marked, either in the centre or outside the circular tarmac road running round the camping area, with electricity provided.

Facilities

The toilet block has some washbasins in cabins and hot showers for which a token is needed, buy them at reception. Laundry service provided by Frau Deihs. Off site: Supermarket and restaurant within 250 m. Swimming pool 2 km.

Open: 1 April - 5 November.

Directions

Take Pressbaum exit from Westautobahn or Vosendorf exit from Sudautobahn and follow signs. It is worth writing for a brochure which gives a good sketch map showing how to find the site.

Charges guide

Per person	€ 5,50
pitch incl. car	€ 5,46 - € 6,10
electricty	€ 0,70

AU0302 Aktiv Camping Neue Donau

Am Kleehäufel, A-1220 Wien-Ost (Vienna)

Tel: **01 202 4010**. Email: **neuedonau@campingwien.at**

This is the sister site of Camping Wien-Sud and closer to Vienna. Near two busy motorways there is inevitably some background traffic noise. However it is perhaps easier to find and has similar facilities and standards. With 254 level touring pitches with electricity and a further 12 with water and drainage also, the site has a large and changing population. The site is close to the 'Donauinsel', a popular recreation area. The Neue Donau (New Danube), a 20 km. long artificial side arm of the Danube provides swimming, sports and play areas, while the Danube bicycle trail runs past the site.

Facilities

Modern toilet facilities are clean, and well maintained with free showers. Facilities for disabled visitors. Washing machines and dryers. Motorcaravan service point. Campers' kitchen with cooking, fridges, freezers and TV. Shop. Small restaurant. Play area. Volleyball. Internet access. Barbecue areas. Bicycle hire and free guided bicycle tours. Off site: Vienna city centre 5 km. Prater Park 1 km.

Open: Easter - 15 September.

Directions

Site is close to the A23 and A22. From A23 heading east turn off at first exit after crossing the Donau (signed Lobau). At first traffic lights, near Shell station, turn left and after 200 m. turn right into site. GPS: N48:12.555 E16:26.669

Charges 2007

Per person	€ 5,90 - € 6,90
child (4-15 yrs)	€ 3,50 - € 4,00
pitch	€ 5,50 - € 12,00

AU0304 Camping Wien-Sud

Breitenfursterstr. 269, A-1230 Wien-Atzgersdorf (Vienna)

Tel: **01 867 3649**. Email: **sued@campingwien.at**

This site, which is in a former Palace park and was closed for some years, reopened in 2003 with new facilities and new management. It is now probably the best site in the greater Vienna area, with good public transport links to the city centre and a friendly and welcoming atmosphere. With 154 touring pitches with electricity (16A) and 42 with water and drainage, the site provides a good base for city sightseeing. Right next door is a Merkur supermarket. With mature trees and some shade you will find this a peaceful and quiet site. Walking and cycling are popular.

Facilities

Excellent modern toilet facilities are clean and well maintained with free showers. Facilities for disabled visitors. Washing machine and dryer. Some cooking facilities. Motorcaravan service point. Small play area. Tickets for Schloss Schönbrunn and other attractions sold at reception. Off site: Vienna 6 km.

Open: 1 June - 31 August.

Directions

From the A2 turn onto the A21 towards Linz (if you're heading north the slip is just past IKEA). Turn off the A21 at first exit, Brunn am Gebirge, and head north. Site is well signed but keep going on this road to site on the right in Atzgersdorf. From the A23 (Süd-Ost Tangene) take the Altmannsdorf exit and follow the signs.

Charges 2007

Per person	€ 5,90 - € 6,90
child (4-15 yrs)	€ 3,50 - € 4,00
pitch	€ 5,10 - € 17,00

AU0306 Camping Wien West

Hüttelbergstrasse 80, A-1140 Wien (Vienna)

Tel: **01 914 2314**. Email: **west@campingwien.at**

Opera, classical music, museums, shopping and the Danube; whatever it is you want in Vienna you are spoilt for choice. Wien West is an all year round site with good transport links to the city centre. It is the parent site of Wien Sud and Neue Donau and is inevitably busier. The site is located on the edge of the Vienna Woods with direct access to walking and mountain bike trails. There are 202 level and numbered pitches, all with 13A electricity. Buses to the metro stop right outside the gates and you can be in centre in 35 minutes.

Facilities

Three modern toilet blocks provide ample and clean toilets, hot showers and washbasins. Washing machine and dryer. Kitchen and dishwashing facilities. Chemical toilet disposal point. Motorcaravan services. Small shop for essentials. Restaurant (1/4-1/10). WiFi (free) and internet point. Games room. Playground. Bicycle hire. Off site: Vienna centre 8 km, Schönbrunn palace. Bicycle and walking trails. Tennis.

Open: All year excl. Februrary.

Directions

From city centre follow signs to autobahn west and Linz. Site is well signed from the main roads. From the A1 drive over the Bergmillergasse (bridge). Stay on this road to Huttelbergstraße after the first traffic lights. GPS: N48:12.554 E16:26.668

Charges 2007

Per person	€ 5,90 - € 6,90
child (4-15 yrs)	€ 3,50 - € 4,00
pitch incl. electricity	€ 8,50 - € 13,50

AU0330 Camping Central

Martinhofstraße 3, A-8054 Graz (Steiermark)

Tel: **06763 785 102**. Email: **guenther_walter@utanet.at**

Although not as well known as Vienna, Salzburg and Innsbruck, Graz in the southern province of Styria, is Austria's second largest city. Camping Central's name is misleading as it is situated in the southwest of the town in the Strassgang district, some 6 km. from the centre. Always an acceptable site, it has now been given a face-lift including a new and refurbished sanitary provision. The 136 level tourist pitches are either in regular rows either side of tarmac roads under a cover of tall trees or on an open meadow where they are not marked out. All have electricity (6A).

Facilities

The new, well built toilet block is of good quality and the other two blocks have been refurbished. Each can be heated in cool weather. Facilities for disabled visitors. Washing machines and dryer. Swimming pool. Small restaurant at the pool. Tennis, playground and jogging track. Limited animation during high season. Off site: Two restaurants within 300 m. Shop 400 m.

Open: 1 April - 31 October.

Directions

From the west take the exit 'Graz-west', from Salzburg exit 'Graz-sud' follow signs to Central and Strassgang and turn right past traffic lights for site.

Charges 2006

Per unit incl. 2 persons and electricity	€ 24,00 - € 28,00
extra person	€ 7,00
No credit cards.	

AU0502 Camping Im Thermenland

Bairisch Kölldorf 240, A-8344 Bairisch Kölldorf (Steiermark)

Tel: **03159-3941**. Email: **gemeinde@bairisch-koelldorf.at**

Near both the Slovakian and Hungarian borders and set in the rolling countryside of southeast Austria, this is a real hidden gem. Not shown on many maps, but well worth the trip, if you want a good quiet site with modern amenities and excellent standards then come right here. There are 100 pitches of which 70 are for touring and all have electricity, water and drainage. The site is near numerous spas and thermal baths and close to Styrassic Park, a must for younger campers.

Facilities

Excellent toilet facilities are clean, well maintained and include free showers. Facilities for disabled visitors. Washing machine and dryer. Dog shower. Restaurant (all year). Unheated outdoor, but covered, swimming pool (May - Sept). Small play area. Off site: Styrassic Park 4 km. Fishing 100 m. Golf 3 km.

Open: All year.

Directions

Southeast of Graz. Leave A2 at exit 157 and head towards Feldbach on the 68. Continue on the 66 to Bad Gleichenberg, go straight over the first roundabout and left at second (supermarket). About 2.8 km. along this road, just past giant 'fire engine' turn left by a chapel and immediately turn right towards site - a further 600 m.

Charges 2006

Per person	€ 6,15
pitch	€ 3,99 - € 7,25
electricity per kwh	€ 0,50
Camping Cheques accepted.	

AU0505 Camping Leibnitz

Rudolf Hans Bartsch-Gasse 33, A-8430 Leibnitz (Steiermark)

Tel: 03452 82463. Email: leibnitz@camping-steiermark.at

Near the Slovakian border, close to the small town of Leibnitz, this site is set in the rolling wine-growing countryside of southeast Austria. A small site with only 52 pitches, it is set in a lovely park area and close to an excellent swimming pool complex which is available for campers' use (with access arrangements for disabled visitors). Minigolf, tennis, volleyball and a multitude of local cycle paths are nearby. All the pitches are of a good size, level and with 16A electricity connections, and some have shade. The town has shops and restaurants with weekly events held at the Jazz Club.

Facilities

Excellent toilet facilities are clean and well maintained. Showers cost € 0.50. Facilities for disabled visitors. Washing machine. Small restaurant but many more within walking distance. Small play area. Off site: Leibnitz 500 m. Leisure centre with two heated outdoor swimming pools 100 m.

Open: 1 May - 30 September.

Directions

From the A9 turn off at exit for Leibnitz, go straight over two roundabouts (through factory outlet centre), over traffic lights and after about 300 m. turn left (site signed). Go straight over roundabout and enter Leibnitz, turn right and site 500 m. on left.

Charges 2006

Per person	€ 4,50
pitch incl. car	€ 6,50
electricity	€ 1,80

AU0515 Katschtal Camping

Peterdorf 100, A-8842 Peterdorf (Steiermark)

Tel: 03584 22813. Email: katschtalcamping@yahoo.de

The small, quiet campsite with only 48 pitches is ideally located for exploring southwest Styria and the beautiful Mur valley, and the Niedere Tauern alps (highest point Greimberg 2472 m). Close to the towns of Oberwolz, which grew rich through its trade in salt and the smelting of silver, and Murau, with the Matthauskirche, the Schloss Murau and the Elisabethkirche, you have much to see and do. Not too far away is Turracher Hohe, the small ski resort that nestles at an altitude of 1700 m. high in the Nocky mountains, one of Austria's most scenic Alpine ranges between Styria and Carinthia.

Facilities

The modern sanitary block provides ample and clean facilities including toilets, hot showers and washbasins. Washing machine. Chemical toilet disposal point. Kitchen with dishwashing facilities.

Open: All year.

Directions

From the Murau - Scheifling 96 road, turn north towards Katsch just west of Frojach. Follow this road up the valley towards and through Peterdorf to the site on the right set back from the road but clearly signed. GPS: N47:10.848 E14:13.003

Charges guide

Per unit incl. 2 persons	€ 13,50
extra person	€ 3,50
electricity per kWh	€ 0,55

AU0520 Camping am Badesee

Hitzmonn Solorf 28, A-8822 Mühlen (Steiermark)

Tel: 03586 2418. Email: office@camping-am-badesee.at

Set in a beautiful open alpine valley alongside a lake in the southern part of the Steiermark region, this family run site will provide you with a warm welcome, and a relaxing holiday. The 60 good sized pitches are well spaced on open grassy terraces, and with only 10 long stay units, there should be around 50 available for tourists. All have electric hook-ups (6A). From reception you can order shopping – bread, milk and eggs and basic requirements. The small cafe/snack bar with a terrace overlooks the lake which is used for swimming, fishing, canoes and non-powered craft.

Facilities

A modern heated sanitary unit provides spacious hot showers, some washbasins in cubicles, with child size showers and basins. Hairdressing and shaving areas. Laundry room also has a baby bath and changing facility. No dedicated facilities for disabled persons. Communal barbecue. Playground. Pets corner. Lake for swimming, fishing and boating. Bicycle hire. Off site: Two restaurants and services in Mühlen (15 minutes walk). Riding 1 km. Neumarkt (6 km.) has more comprehensive shopping facilities. Golf 14 km.

Open: 1 May - 30 September.

Directions

Mühlen is southwest of Judenburg. From the west using the A10, take exit 104 (St Michael im Lungau) and head east on road 96 through Murau to Scheiffling. Turn right (south) on B317 to Neumarkt, and towards the end of village turn left on B92 to Mühlen. Site is 5.8 km on right hand side. GPS: N47:02.225 E14:29.243

Charges 2006

Per unit with 2 persons and electricity	€ 16,00 - € 17,90
extra person	€ 4,50

AU0415 Camping Rosental Roz

Gotschuchen 34, A-9173 St Margareten im Rosental (Carinthia)

Tel: **04226 81000**. Email: **camping.rosental@roz.at**

In the picturesque Drau valley, southeast of Flagenfurt, Rosental Roz has magnificent views along the valley and of the cliffs that form the northern boundary. The site is also close to the Slovakian and Italian borders. With 430 pitches (all for touring) and 4 mobile homes to rent around a small swimming lake, the site is good for short or long stays. All pitches have 6A electricity and 50 pitches have water and drainage. An active children's club provides lots to occupy the youngsters.

Facilities

Toilet facilities are clean and modern with free showers, 10 family washrooms and a large shower facility for young children. Washing machine and dryer. Restaurant/bar (1/5-30/9). Shop (1/6-15/9). Children's club (1/6-30/8). Playgrounds and large games area. Off site: Fishing 1 km. Riding 2 km. Many walks.

Open: Easter - 15 October.

Directions

Site is southeast of Klagenfurt. From the 91 road turn onto the 85 towards Feriach. Before getting to St Margareten in the centre of the small hamlet of Gotschuchen turn left towards site. It is about 1.5 km. but well signed (watch the overhanging gutters especially when passing another vehicle).

Charges guide

Per person	€ 7,10
pitch	€ 8,20 - € 10,10

AU0400 Camping Arneitz

Seeuferlandesstraße 53, A-9583 Faak am See (Carinthia)

Tel: **04254 2137**. Email: **camping@arneitz.at**

Directly on Faakersee, Camping Arneitz is one of the best sites in this area, central for the attractions of the region, watersports and walking. Family run, Arneitz led the way with good quality and comprehensive facilities. A newly built reception building reflects the quality of the site and apart from reception facilities, has a good collection of tourist literature and three desks with telephones for guests to use. The 400 level, marked pitches are mainly of gravel, off hard roads, with electricity available. Some have good shade from mature trees. Grass pitches are available for tents.

Facilities

Splendid family washroom, large, heated and airy, with family cubicles around the walls and in the centre, washbasins at child height in a circle with a working carousel in the middle. Extra, small toilet block nearer the lake. Hair washing room. Washing machines, spin dryer, irons. Motorcaravan services. Supermarket. Self-service restaurant, bar and terrace. Small cinema for children's films. Beauty salon. Large sauna/solarium. Minigolf. Playground. Football field. Fishing. Riding. Bicycle hire.

Open: 28 April - 30 September.

Directions

Site is southeast of Villach, southwest of Veldon. Follow signs for Faakersee and Egg rather than for Faak village. From A11 take exit 3 and head towards Egg, turn left at T-junction and go through Egg village. Just after leaving village, site is on right.

Charges 2006

Per person	€ 6,80 - € 7,50
child (under 10 yrs)	€ 6,40 - € 7,00
pitch incl. electricity	€ 10,00 - € 13,00

AU0410 Strandcamping Turnersee

A-9123 St Primus (Carinthia)

Tel: **04239 2350**. Email: **info@breznik.at**

The southern Austrian province of Kärnten (Carinthia) is a gentle rural area of mountains, valleys and lakes. Strandcamping lies between Villach and Graz, just south of the A2 Villach - Vienna motorway, giving the opportunity to visit Croatia and northern Italy. The neat, tidy site is situated in a valley with views of the mountains. The 300 marked and numbered pitches for touring units vary in size, on level grass terraces. Although there are many trees, not all parts have shade. All pitches have electricity (6A) and 50 also have water, drainage, TV and phone connections. There are 110 static caravans.

Facilities

Four modern sanitary blocks spread around the site, providing the usual facilities including special provision for young children and babies in the largest block. Facilities for disabled people. Central building housing shop, restaurant with terrace (10/5-14/9), takeaway (7/6-23/8) and play room for small children. Play areas for children and small zoo with goats and rabbits. 'Topi' club and organised activities for adults and children. Games room, bicycle hire, watersports. Internet access. Off site: Fishing and golf 1.5 km. Riding 3 km. Boat launching 5 km.

Open: 3 April - 3 October.

Directions

Leave A2 motorway at exit 296 signed Grafenstien. Go onto road 70 for a few kilometres and turn right for site via Tainach and St Kanzian. Site is on left before St Primus.

Charges guide

Per person	€ 4,50 - € 7,50
child (4-14 yrs)	€ 3,00 - € 5,10
pitch	€ 6,00 - € 12,50
dog	€ 1,50 - € 3,00
Camping Cheques accepted.	

AU0480 Komfort Campingpark Burgstaller

Seefeldstraße 16, A-9873 Döbriach (Carinthia)

Tel: 04246 7774. Email: service@qualitycamp.com

This is one of Austria's top sites in a beautiful location and with all the amenities you could want. You can always tell a true family run site by the attention to detail and this site oozes perfection. The latest sanitary block warrants an architectural award and of course it provides exceptional facilities for campers of all ages. The site entrance is directly opposite the park leading to the bathing lido, to which campers have free access. There is also a heated swimming pool. The 600 pitches (560 for tourists) are on flat, well drained grass, backing onto hedges and marked out, on either side of access roads. These vary in size (65-120 sq.m.), all with electricity, water, drainage, sewer, satellite TV and WiFi and there are special pitches for motorcaravans. Much activity is organised here, including games and competitions for children in summer with a winter programme of skiing, curling and skating. At Christmas, trees are gathered from the forest and there are special Easter and autumn events. This is an excellent family site for winter and summer camping with a very friendly atmosphere, particularly in the restaurant in the evenings. Good English spoken.

Facilities

Three exceptionally good quality toilet blocks have been creatively built and would not look amiss in Disneyland! There are washbasins in cabins, facilities for children and disabled visitors, dishwashers and under-floor heating for cool weather. Seven private sanitary rooms for rent (3 with jacuzzi baths). Motorcaravan services. Good restaurant with terrace (May-Oct). Shop (May-Sept). Bowling alley. Disco (July/Aug). TV room. Sauna and solarium. Two play areas (one for under 6s, the other for 6-12 yrs). Beach volleyball. Basketball. Bathing and boating in lake. Special entrance rate for lake attractions. Fishing. Bicycle hire. Mountain bike area. Riding. Comprehensive entertainment programmes. Covered stage and outdoor arena provide for church services (Protestant and Catholic, in German) and folk and modern music concerts. Off site: Mountain walks, climbing and farm visits all in local area.

Open: All year.

Directions

Site is well signed from around Döbriach.
GPS: N46:46.208 E13:38.875

Charges 2006

Per person	€ 5,00 - € 8,00
child (4-14 yrs)	€ 3,50 - € 6,00
pitch	€ 4,30 - € 11,50
electricity	€ 1,90

Discounts for retired people in low season.
No credit cards.

Check real time availability and at-the-gate prices...

www.alanrogers.com

AU0490 Camping Terrassen Maltatal

Malta 6, A-9854 Maltatal (Carinthia)

Tel: 04733 234. Email: info@maltacamp.at

With easy access to the Malta high alpine road, just 6 km. from the autobahn and 15 km. from Millstättersee, this site is good for an overnight stop and its pleasant situation and the good-sized pool on site encourage many to stay longer. The pool is over 300 sq.m. with a grassy lying out area and is open to all (free for campers). There are 220 grassy pitches on narrow terraces (70-100 sq.m.) and mostly in rows on either side of narrow access roads. Numbered and marked, some separated with low hedges, all have electricity (6/10A) and 90 have water and drainage connections, (the electric boxes are often inconveniently located on the next terrace). The 'Kärnten-card' is available from the site which gives free travel on public transport and free entry to various attractions. Local church bells ring at 06.00 every morning.

Facilities

Two toilet blocks, one with under-floor heating, have about half the washbasins in cabins and 10 family wash cabins. Facilities for babies and children. Washing machines, dryers and irons. Motorcaravan services. Only basic provisions kept. Restaurant (all season). Swimming pool (20/5-15/9). Sauna. Playground. Bicycle hire. Riding. Entertainment programme and many walks and excursions. Off site: Village 500 m. Fishing or golf 6 km. Malta High alpine road, Reisseck mountain railways and The Porsche Museum in Gmund are all nearby.

Open: Easter - 31 October.

Directions

Site is 6 km. up a mountain valley from an exit at the southern end of the A10 Salzburg - Carinthia autobahn. Take autobahn exit 129 for Gmund and Maltatal and proceed up Maltatal 6 km. to site. GPS: N46:56.990 E13:30.576

Charges guide

Per person	€ 4,80 - € 6,70
child (3-14 yrs)	€ 3,40 - € 4,20
pitch with electricity	€ 6,20 - € 9,00
incl. water and drainage	€ 8,80 - € 10,60

Electricity included. Less for longer stays.
Camping Cheques accepted.

The campsite at 800 m altitude between the «Hohe Tauern» and «Nockberge» national parks, with amazing panoramic views.

Terrassencamping Maltatal

A-9854 Malta 5-6, Kärnten • Tel. 0043-4733-234 • Fax 0043-4733-23416 • www.maltacamp.at • info@maltacamp.at

AU0450 Naturpark Schluga Seecamping

A-9620 Hermagor (Carinthia)

Tel: 04282 2051. Email: camping@schluga.com

This site is pleasantly situated on natural wooded hillside. It is about 300 m. from a small lake with clean water, where the site has a beach of coarse sand and a large grassy meadow. It also has a sunbathing area for naturists although this is not a naturist site. The 250 pitches for touring units are on individual, level terraces, many with light shade and all with electricity (10A); 124 pitches also have water, drainage and satellite TV and a further 47 pitches are occupied by a tour operator. Close by is Schluga Camping, under the same ownership, which is open all year. English is spoken.

Facilities

Four heated modern toilet blocks with some washbasins in cabins and family washrooms for rent. A suite for disabled people and baby facilities. Washing machines and dryer. Motorcaravan services. Shop. Restaurant/bar and takeaway (all 20/5-10/9). Playground. Film room. Kiosk and bar with terrace at beach. Surf school. Pedalo and canoe hire. Aqua jump and Ice-berg. Pony rides. Bicycle hire. Fishing. Weekly activity programme. Mountain walks and climbs. Internet point.

Open: 10 May - 20 September.

Directions

Site is on the B111 road (Villach - Hermagor) 6 km. east of Hermagor town. GPS: N46:37.908 E13:26.802

Charges 2007

Per person	€ 4,90 - € 7,80
child (5-14 yrs)	€ 3,45 - € 5,20
pitch	€ 6,80 - € 9,40

Camping Cheques accepted.

AU0440 Schluga Camping

Obervellach 15, A-9620 Hermagor-Presseggersee (Carinthia)

Tel: **04282 2051**. Email: **camping@schluga.com**

Schluga Camping is under the same ownership as Schluga Seecamping, some four kilometres to the west of that site in a flat valley with views of the surrounding mountains. The 223 tourist pitches are of varying size, 115 with water, drainage and satellite TV connections. Electricity connections are available throughout (10A). Mainly on grass covered gravel on either side of tarmac surfaced access roads, they are divided by shrubs and hedges. Entertainment in high season includes a disco and cinema. A weekly programme sheet details events at both Schluga sites and nearby. The site is open all year, to include the winter sports season, and has a well kept tidy appearance, although it may be busy in high seasons. English is spoken. New bar and terrace by the lake.

Facilities

Four sanitary blocks (a splendid new one, plus one modern and two good older ones) are well constructed and heated in cold weather. Most washbasins in cabins and good showers. Family washrooms for rent. Baby rooms and suite for disabled people. Washing machines and dryers. Drying rooms and ski rooms. Motorcaravan services. Well stocked shop (1/5-30/9). Bar/restaurant with terrace (closed Nov). Kiosk for snacks/ice creams. Heated swimming pool (12 x 7 m; 1/5-30/9). Playground. Youth games room. Bicycle hire. Sauna. Fitness centre. TV room. Internet point. Badminton. Kindergarten programme for small children. Off site: Tennis nearby.

Open: All year.

Directions

Site is on the B111 Villach - Hermagor road (which is better quality than it appears on most maps) just east of Hermagor town. GPS: N46:07.890 E13:20.749

Charges 2007

Per person	€ 4,90 - € 7,80
child (5-14 yrs)	€ 3,45 - € 5,20
pitch	€ 6,80 - € 9,40
dog	€ 1,90 - € 2,60

AU0445 Alpencamp

A-9640 Kötschach Mauthen (Carinthia)

Tel: **04715 429**. Email: **info@alpencamp.at**

Like most towns in Carinthia, Kötschach offers a wealth of sporting opportunities. Just 50 metres from the Gail river, Alpencamp offers a pleasant and quiet atmosphere with all the modern amenities you could want and is good for short or longer term stays. There are 85 pitches, all with electricity (16A) and wireless internet access, and including 9 'super' pitches close to the site's restaurant. Whilst bicycles and kayaks can be hired on site, these are just a taster for the range of sporting opportunities the area has to offer. These include rafting, canyoning and hydrospeeding in the summer to skiing, snowboarding and 'snow-cross' in winter.

Facilities

A modern sanitary block provides ample and clean toilets, hot showers and washbasins. Washing machine and dryer. Dishwashing facilities. Motorcaravan service point. Small shop with essential supplies. Restaurant. Apartments, bungalows and chalets to rent. Off site: Fishing 50 m. Golf 30 km. Riding 1 km. Ski lift 400 m. Aquarena 10 minutes walk.

Open: 15 December - 15 October.

Directions

Kötschach is at the junction of the 111 and the 110 roads. The site is well signed in the town and is on the left as you head towards Lesachtal. GPS: N46:40.185 E12:59.477

Charges 2007

Per person	€ 4,10 - € 6,40
child (under 14 yrs)	€ 2,50 - € 3,90
pitch incl. electricity	€ 6,40 - € 8,90

AU0425 Seecamping Berghof

Ossiachersee Süduferstraße 241, A-9523 Villach Landskron (Carinthia)

Tel: **04242 41133**. Email: **office@seecamping-berghof.at**

This surely must be the ultimate camping experience: a perfect location, excellent facilities, great pitches and a welcome to match. The Ertl family and their staff manage this 480 pitch site to perfection. Use of the natural topography means that you actually think you are in a small site wherever you camp. With lovely lake views from almost every spot, this is a great site to stop for a short or long stay. Constant improvements mean that slowly the number of pitches reduces as larger and more equipped places are provided. There are 150 pitches with water, electricity and drainage and many pitches have access to the internet.

Facilities

Five modern toilet blocks spread around the site, provide the usual facilities including special provision for young children and babies in two blocks. Facilities for disabled people. Large, central building housing well stocked supermarket and helpful reception. Restaurant with terrace. Takeaway. Games room. Play area. Daily club for 4-11 year olds all season. Bicycle hire. Watersports. Boat hire. Windsurfing school. Minigolf. Lake swimming. Skateboard park. Off site: Fishing. Villach 5 km.

Open: 1 April - 20 October.

Directions

From A10 take exit 178, which travelling south is just after the tunnel. Head towards Ossiacher See and after 1 km. turn right towards Ossiacher See Sud. At traffic lights turn left and site is 3.5 km. on the left just after entering hamlet of Heiligengestade. GPS: N46:39.272 E13:55.768

Charges 2007

Per person	€ 5,00 - € 8,00
child (10-15 yrs)	€ 3,80 - € 7,00
pitch	€ 7,50 - € 12,50

AU0405 Sommer und Winter Camping Ramsbacher

Gries 53, A-9863 Rennweg (Carinthia)

Tel: **04734 663**

Although this site is near the motorway, at this point the A10 (Salzburg - Villach motorway) is in a deep tunnel (toll payable) and from the site you would not know it is there. This is a beautiful small site set in a high alpine valley with great views in every direction. With only 72 touring pitches, all with electricity, this would make a great short or longer term stop for those seeking peace and quiet and the opportunity to explore the local area by either bike or on foot.

Facilities

Toilet facilities are clean, heated and modern with free showers but a communal changing area. Washing machine, dryer and drying area. Restaurant/bar. Small play area. Off site: Swimming pool, minigolf, tennis and play area 25 m.

Open: All year.

Directions

From the A10 take exit 113 which is just south of the Katschberg toll tunnel. Turn towards Rennweg, turn right a little later into the village and then right again towards Oberdorf where site is well signed. GPS: N47:01.56 E13:35.43

Charges guide

Per person	€ 5,20 - € 5,80
child (6-17 yrs)	€ 4,00 - € 5,80
pitch incl. electricity	€ 8,50 - € 9,00

AU0460 Terrassen Camping Ossiacher See

Ostriach 67, A-9570 Ossiach (Carinthia)

Tel: **04243 436**. Email: **martinz@camping.at**

This gently sloping site has been partly terraced to provide good, level pitches. The thick growth of reeds at the water's edge all around the lake means that access is limited to two small clearings within the site. One of these has a beach for bathing and a jetty, and boats may be launched from the other. The site is protected by rising hills and enjoys lovely views across the lake to the mountains beyond. Trees, flowers, hedges and bushes abound, adding atmosphere to this neat, tidy site. The 530 pitches (429 with electricity) are in rows on the level grass terraces, separated by hard roads and marked by hedges. There is shade in parts and electricity connections (4/6A) throughout. The site does become full in high season and although there is sufficient room on the pitches, it may give the initial impression of being overcrowded. A friendly, lively site, all ages and sports inclinations are catered for in a scenic location in a very beautiful part of Austria. A separate area (25 pitches only) is provided for campers with dogs. Used by tour operators (28 pitches). Good English is spoken.

Facilities

Although the facilities in the five sanitary blocks vary, they are all of good quality, heated in cool weather, and with some washbasins in cabins. The newest block has 10 family washrooms (charged), baby rooms and facilities for disabled campers. Washing machines, dryers and irons. Motorcaravan services. Restaurant (15/5-30/9). Well stocked supermarket. ATM. High season entertainment programme giving a wide range of sports and activities. Playgrounds, games rooms and disco dancing courtyard. Watersports including waterskiing and windsurfing schools and boats for hire. Water trampoline. Tennis, volleyball and badminton. Football field. Bicycle and moped hire. Fishing. Riding. Off site: Cycle path around lake. Hang-gliding possibilities in area.

Open: 1 May - 30 September.

Directions

Site is directly on the lake shore just south of Ossiach village. Leave the A10 autobahn at exit 178 for Ossiachersee, turn left onto road B94 towards Feldkirchen and shortly right to Ossiach Sud. The site is shortly before Ossiach.
GPS: N46:39.825 E13:58.495

Charges guide

Per person	€ 5,00 - € 7,50
child (3-12 yrs)	free - € 4,90
pitch acc. to season and location	€ 7,10 - € 11,20
small tent pitch	€ 4,30 - € 6,50

AU0475 Camping Brunner am See

Glanzerstraße 108, A-9873 Döbriach (Carinthia)

Tel: **04246 7189**. Email: **camping.brunner@aon.at**

This well appointed site at the eastern end of the Millstätter See, is the only site in the area with its own private beach directly accessible from the site. Consisting of fairly coarse sand, it is regularly cleaned and has a marked bathing area and separate boating area. There are 240 marked pitches (100 sq.m.), all for tourers and serviced with water, drainage and electric hook-ups (4A). They are arranged in rows on level grass, with tarmac access roads. The site is fairly open with only a little shade from a few trees. There are three playgrounds for children. The site owns land on the opposite side of the road, which includes forest walks, a dog walk, a parking area and one of the playgrounds.

Facilities

A new building behind reception houses the well appointed and generously supplied sanitary unit. Good facilities for disabled campers, especially handicapped children, plus a children's room with low level showers, basins, baby baths, changing deck etc. Family bathrooms (some for rent), some washbasins in cubicles, laundry and dishwashing rooms. Site owned supermarket adjacent. Communal barbecue. Internet terminal. Motorcaravan services. Fishing and watersports. Off site: Supermarket (1/5-30/10), Restaurant (Easter - 1/11). Bicycle hire 300 m. Tennis 500 m. Riding 1.5 km. Golf 10 km.

Open: All year.

Directions

Döbriach is at the eastern end of the Millstätter See, about 25 km. from Spittal. From A10 exit 139, follow road 98 (Döbriach), alongside northern side of lake for 13 km., then take right fork for 1.5 km. and turn right at roundabout. Site entrance is on right after 100 metres. GPS: N46:46.060 E13:38.913

Charges guide

Per person	€ 5,00 - € 7,50
child (4-14 yrs)	€ 3,50 - € 5,60
child (14-18 yrs)	€ 4,00 - € 6,90
pitch incl. electricity	€ 7,00 - € 11,20

Discounts for senior citizens (low season).

MAP 2

A small country divided into three regions, Flanders in the north, Wallonia in the south and Brussels the capital. Belgium is rich in scenic countryside, culture and history, notably the great forest of Ardennes, the historic cities of Bruges and Ghent and the western coastline with its sandy beaches.

CAPITAL: BRUSSELS

Tourist Office

Belgian Tourist Office Brussels & Wallonia,
217 Marsh Wall, London E14 9FJ
Tel: 0906 3020 245 Fax: 020 7531 0393
Email: info@belgiumtheplaceto.be
Internet: www.visitbelgium.com

Tourism Flanders-Brussels,
31 Pepper Street, London E14 9RW
Tel: 020 7867 0311 Fax: 020 7458 0045
Email: office@visitflanders.co.uk

Brussels is at the very heart of Europe and doubles as the capital of the European Union. A multi-cultural and multi-lingual city full of remarkable monuments, interesting museums and highly acclaimed restaurants. In the French speaking region of Wallonia lies the mountainous Ardennes, an area famous for its forests, lakes, streams and grottoes, making it a popular holiday destination, especially for those who like nature and walking. The safe, sandy beaches on the west coast run for forty miles. Here lies Ostend, a popular seaside resort with an eight kilometre long beach and a promenade coupled with a bustling harbour and shops. Bruges is Europe's best preserved medieval city and is certainly one of the most attractive, whether you want to relax on a boat trip along the canals, explore the narrow streets or visit one of the many churches and art museums.

Population
10.2 million

Climate
Temperate climate similar to Britain.

Language
There are three official languages. French is spoken in the south, Flemish in the north, and German is the predominant language in the eastern provinces.

Telephone
The country code is 00 32.

Money
Currency: The Euro
Banks: Mon-Fri 09.00-15.30.
Some banks open Sat 09.00-12.00.

Shops
Mon-Sat 09.00-17.30/18.00 hrs - later on Thurs/Fri; closed Sundays.

Public Holidays
New Year's Day; Easter Mon; Labour Day; Ascension; Whit Monday; Flemish Day 11 July; National Day 21 July; Assumption 15 Aug; French Day 27 Sept; All Saints 1, 2 Nov; Armistice Day 11 Nov; King's Birthday 15 Nov; Christmas 25, 26 Dec.

Motoring
For cars with a caravan or trailer, motorways are toll free except for the Liefenshoek Tunnel in Antwerp. Maximum permitted overall length of vehicle/trailer or caravan combination is 18 m. Blue Zone parking areas exist in Brussels, Ostend, Bruges, Liège, Antwerp and Gent. Parking discs can be obtained from police stations, garages, some shops.

BE0520 Camping de Blekker

Jachtwakersstraat 12, B-8670 Koksijde aan Zee (West Flanders)

Tel: 058 51 16 33. Email: camping.deblekker@belgacom.net

This family-owned site, adjacent to a 186-hectare nature reserve on the Belgium coast, is divided into two sections: Blekker and Blekkerdal. De Blekker has 178 pitches with 75 allocated for tourists, all with 10A electricity. The pitches are grassy with some dividing hedges and trees, and all have 10A electricity connections. Visitors should drive to the Blekker reception but will be given a choice of where to park. Local attractions include the Koksijde annual Flower Market and Floral Pageant, National Fishery Museum and horseback shrimp fishing in Oostduinkerke, and Plopsaland (a small theme park) or Clown City in De Panne.

Facilities

Each section has a single modern sanitary unit including washbasins in cubicles, dishwashing and laundry sinks, washing machine and dryer, facilities for babies and disabled persons (other than for washbasins, hot water is on payment throughout). Laundry. Small infirmary with bed. Bicycle hire. Internet access (in reception). Barbecues are not permitted in hot weather. Off site: Shop in nearest village 300 m. Restaurant and bars 0.4-3 km. Riding 1 km. Fishing and boat launching 1.5 km.

Open: 1 April - 15 November.

Directions

From A16 (E40) take junction 1A, then the N8 towards Koksijde. At roundabout take N396 towards Koksijde Dorp and then turn towards Koksijde-aan-zee. Follow small yellow camp signs. Site entrance road is on the right.

Charges 2007

Per unit incl. 4 persons   € 19,00 - € 27,00

Special rates for Ascension, Pentecost and Easter weekends. 10% discount on production of Alan Rogers Guide. Camping Cheques accepted.

BE0550 Kompas Camping Nieuwpoort

Brugsesteenweg 49, B-8620 Nieuwpoort (West Flanders)

Tel: 058 23 60 37. Email: nieuwpoort@kompascamping.be

Near Ostend, this large site with 952 pitches caters particularly for families. There are many on site amenities including a heated pool complex with two pools, a children's pool and a water slide, many sporting activities, and a children's farm. The numbered pitches, all with electricity, are in regular rows on flat grass. With 386 seasonal units and 79 caravan holiday homes, the site becomes full during Belgian holidays and in July/August. A network of footpaths links all areas of the site and gates to the rear lead to a reservoir reserved for sailing, windsurfing and canoeing (canoes for hire) during certain hours only. The site is well fenced, with a card operated barrier and a night guard.

Facilities

Seven functional, clean and well maintained toilet blocks include washbasins in cubicles. The blocks are accessible to disabled people. Dishwashing and laundry facilities. Motorcaravan services. Supermarket, bakery, restaurant and café/bar (weekends and Belgian holidays outside July/Aug). Takeaway. Swimming pools with waterslide and pool games (19/5-15/9). Tennis. Adventure playground. Minigolf. Sports and show hall. Off site: Fishing and bicycle hire within 500 m. Riding 3 km. Golf driving range 5 km. Nearest village is 2 km. Beach 4 km.

Open: 31 March - 12 November.

Directions

From E40 take exit 4 (Middelkerke - Diksmuide). Turn towards Diksmuide following signs to Nieuwport. Pass through Sint-Joris and IC-Camping is on right.

Charges guide

Per family (max 6 persons)
in Jul/Aug and B.Hs   € 29,50
at other times   € 19,00

Largest unit accepted 2.5 x 8 m.
Less 10% with camping carnet.
Camping Cheques accepted.

BE0530 Camping du Waux-Hall

Avenue Saint-Pierre 17, B-7000 Mons (Hainault)

Tel: 065 33 79 23. Email: ot1@ville.mons.be

Waux-Hall is a useful and convenient site for a longer look at historic Mons and the surrounding area. It is a well laid out municipal site, close to the town centre and E42 motorway. The 75 pitches, most with electricity (10A), are arranged on either side of an oval road, on grass and divided by beds of small shrubs; the landscape maintenance is excellent. The pitches are small and manoevering could be difficult for larger units. A large public park with refreshment bar, tennis, a children's playground and lake is adjacent, with direct access from the site when the gate is unlocked. Places to visit include the house of Van Gogh, the Fine Arts Museum, Decorative Arts Museum and the Collegiate church.

Facilities

A single, heated toilet block is of older style, basic but clean, with most washbasins in cubicles for ladies. Washing machine and dryer. Dishwashing and laundry sinks under cover. Soft drinks machine and ice cream. Bicycle hire. Tennis. Playground. Off site: Public park adjacent. Town centre shops and restaurants within easy walking distance. Fishing 300 m. Riding 2 km. Golf 4 km.

Open: All year.

Directions

From Mons inner ring road, follow signs for Charleroi, La Louviere, Binche, Beaumont. When turning off the ring-road, keep to right hand lane, turning for site is immediately first right. (signed Waux-Hall and camping).

Charges guide

Per unit incl. 1 person	€ 5,20 - € 6,10
extra person	€ 3,35
electricity after 2 nights (per kWh)	€ 0,15

No credit cards.

BE0555 Recreatiepark Klein Strand

Varsenareweg 29, B-8490 Jabbeke (West Flanders)

Tel: 050 811 440. Email: info@kleinstrand.be

In a convenient location, only 10 km. from Bruges, this site is in two distinct areas divided by an access road. The touring half of the campsite has 128 large pitches on flat grass and all with electricity (10A). This central block of touring pitches is surrounded by semi-permanent caravans on the outer edges and it is a surprisingly relaxing area. The static half is closer to the lake and this area has most of the amenities. These include the main reception building, two restaurants (French, Chinese), takeaways, bar, mini-market, and most of the sports facilities. Water-ski shows take place on the lake (every Sunday in July/August at 5pm), and there is a water-ski school (charged for). The lake also has a swimming area with waterslide (lifeguard), boat and kayak rental, and beach volleyball area. A comprehensive programme of activities and entertainment is provided in July/August. Indeed, this is a family holiday site with plenty of activities and, off season, a good base for sightseeing.

Facilities

A single modern, heated, toilet block in the touring area provides the usual facilities including good sized showers (charged) and vanity style open washbasins. Baby bath in the ladies section. Facilities for disabled campers. Laundry. Additional toilet facilities are opened for July/August. Motorcaravan service point. In high season a fun pool for small children and an adventure playground for older children. Barrier card deposit € 25. Off site: Golf 10 km. Riding 5 km.

Open: All year.

Directions

From Dunkirk take A10, then exit 6B signed Jabbeke. At roundabout take first exit signed for site. If missed, there is a second turn after a further 200 m. GPS: N51:11.071 E03:06.268

Charges 2006

Per unit incl. up to 6 persons and electricity	€ 15,00 - € 28,00

Check real time availability and at-the-gate prices...

www.alanrogers.com

BE0560 Camping De Lombarde

Elisabethlaan 4, B-8434 Lombardsijde Middelkerke (West Flanders)

Tel: 058 23 68 39. Email: info@delombarde.be

De Lombarde is a spacious, good value holiday site, between Lombardsijde and the coast. It has a pleasant atmosphere and modern buildings. The 360 pitches are set out in level, grassy bays surrounded by shrubs, all with electricity (16A, long leads may be needed). Vehicles are parked in separate car parks. There are many seasonal units and 22 holiday homes, leaving 180 tourist pitches. There is a range of activities (listed below) and an entertainment programme in season. This is a popular holiday area and the site becomes full at peak times. A pleasant stroll takes you into Lombardsijde or you can catch the tram to the town or beach.

Facilities

Three modern heated, clean sanitary units are of an acceptable standard, with some washbasins in cubicles. Facilities for disabled people. Motorcaravan services. Shop (1/4-31/8). Restaurant/bar and takeaway (July/Aug. plus weekends and holidays 21/3-11/11). Tennis. Boules. Fishing lake. Playground. Internet access. Torch useful. Off site: Beach 400 m. Bicycle hire 1 km.

Open: All year.

Directions

Coming from Westende, follow the tramlines. From traffic lights in Lombarsijde, turn left following tramlines into Zeelaan. Continue following tramlines until crossroads and tram stop, turn left into Elisabethlaan. Site is on right after 200 m.

Charges guide

Per unit incl. electricity	€ 14,00 - € 25,90
small tent incl. 2 persons	€ 2,80 - € 3,30

BE0565 Kompas Camping Westende

Bassevillestraat 141, B-8434 Westende (West Flanders)

Tel: 058 22 30 25. Email: westende@kompascamping.be

Part of the Kompas chain, Campng Westende is another large holiday site with 429 pitches. Of these 130 are taken by seasonal units and 5 chalets, leaving around 300 tourist pitches. These are generally individual, on grass and with 10A electricity hook-ups. There are 39 multi-service pitches with water, waste water drain and electricity. When we visited some pitches were looking rather well worn and untidy. The rigid pitching policy dictates that caravans have to be placed on a specific side of the pitch, which may mean that you have to manhandle your UK built van into a nose in situation. The main services are grouped around reception which can be a fair walk from the far end of the site.

Facilities

Four main toilet blocks are in modern style but suffer from heavy use and variable maintenance and cleaning. They provide the usual facilities, including those for children and disabled people at each block, plus some washbasins in cubicles. Block 4 facilities for disabled people. Although the shop, bar, restaurant and takeaway are open Easter - 14 November, outside July/August and certain public holidays, they only operate at weekends. Adventure playground.Off site: Fishing 20 m. Golf 100 m. Beach 800 m. Bicycle hire 200 m. Riding and sailing 5 km.

Open: Easter - 14 November.

Directions

Westende is about 15 km. southwest of Ostende. From A18 (E40) take exit 3 to Nieuwpoort, turn right at traffic lights in town centre, and follow signs to Westende. Once in Westende continue along the main street, passing two campsites on the right, turn left into Hoveniersstraat (site sign is very small). GPS: N51:09.487 E02:45.628

Charges 2006

Per unit incl. 4 persons	€ 19,50 - € 30,25
electricity	€ 2,20
Camping Cheques accepted.	

BE0580 Camping Memling

Veltemweg 109, B-8310 Brugge (West Flanders)

Tel: 325 03 55 84 5. Email: info@campingmemling.be

This traditional site is ideal for visiting Brugge. The 100 unmarked pitches (60 for touring units) are on slightly undulating grass, with gravel roads and trees and hedges providing some shade. Electricity (6A) is available to 40 pitches. There is a separate area for tents. Bars, restaurants, local shops and supermarkets are within walking distance. Brugge itself has a network of cycleways and for those on foot a bus runs into the centre from nearby. Visitors with large units should telephone in advance to ensure an adequate pitch.

Facilities

Heated toilet facilities are clean and tidy, including some washbasins in cubicles. Facilities for babies and disabled visitors. Laundry with washing machine and dryer. Freezer for campers' use. Club/TV room for 30 persons. Tiny playground. Bicycle hire. Internet access. Off site: Municipal swimming pool (open all year) and park nearby. Supermarket 250 m, hypermarket 250 m.

Open: All year.

Directions

From R30 Brugge ring road take exit 6 onto the N9 towards Maldegem. At Sint-Kruis turn right at traffic lights, where site signed (close to garage and supermarket, opposite MacDonalds).

Charges 2006

Per person	€ 5,00
child (under 15 yrs)	€ 4,00
pitch incl. electricity	€ 14,00 - € 20,00

49

BE0570 Camping Jeugdstadion

Bolwerkstraat 1, B-8900 Ieper (West Flanders)
Tel: **057 21 72 82**. Email: **info@jeugdstadion.be**

Camping Jeugdstadion is a small developing municipal close to the historic old town. At present there are only 21 caravan pitches, 12 on hardstandings and all with electricity (6A), plus a separate area for 15 tents. The barrier key also operates the lock for the toilet block. At the end of Leopold III Laan is the Menin Gate built in 1927, which bears the names of British and Commonwealth soldiers who lost their lives between 1914-1918. The last post is sounded beneath the gate at 8 pm. every evening in their honour. The Commonwealth War Graves Commission is a little further away in Elverdingestraat. The vehicle access is at the rear of the site, signed from Steverlyncklaan (second left off Picanolaan), but reception will give you a map and a barrier key. Alternatively go straight to the vehicle gate and walk through the site to book in (easier for large units).

Facilities

The modern, heated but fairly basic toilet block can struggle to cope in busy periods. It has cold water to washbasins and three sinks for dishwashing outside. Bicycle hire. Minigolf. Boules. Barrier key deposit € 24.79 or £20. Off site: The adjacent sports complex has courts for volleyball, petanque and squash, whilst indoor and outdoor swimming pools are only 500 m. away, and there is a very large playground. Minigolf. During school holidays these facilities are extensively used by local children and can therefore be fairly busy and lively.

Open: 16 March - 31 October.

Directions

Site is southeast of the city centre. From N336 (Lille) at roundabout by the Lille Gate, turn left on Picanolaan and first right on Leopold III laan. Jeugdstadion entrance is on the right. Use roadside parking spaces and book in at 'Kantine' (08.00-19.00 hrs) on left inside gates.

Charges 2006

Per person	€ 3,00
child (6-12 yrs)	€ 1,50
pitch incl. electricity	€ 4,50

BE0578 Camping Ter Duinen

Wenduinesteenweg 143, B-8421 De Haan (West Flanders)
Tel: **050 41 35 93**

Ter Duinen is a large, seaside holiday site with 120 touring pitches and over 700 privately owned static holiday caravans. Pitches are laid out in straight lines each side of tarmac roads and the site has three immaculate toilet blocks. Other than a bar, a playing field and a little shop, the site has little else to offer, but it is only a 400 metre walk to the sea and next door to the site is a large sports complex with a sub-tropical pool and several sporting facilities. Opportunities for riding and golf (18 hole course) are close by and it is possible to hire bicycles in the town. Best places to visit for a daytrip are Oostende with the Atlantic Wall from WWII, Knokke (with many summer festivals) and Brugge.

Facilities

Three modern toilet blocks have good fittings, washbasins in cubicles (cold water only) and showers (€ 1.20). Baby bath. Facilities for disabled visitors. Dishwashing sinks. Two launderettes with two washing machines and a dryer, irons and ironing boards. Motorcaravan service point. Shop (closed Wed). Snack bar. Off site: Sea with sandy beach 400 m. Bicycle hire 400 m. Riding 1 km. Golf 3 km. Boat launching 6 km. A bus for Brugge stops 200 m. from the site, a tram for the coast 400 m.

Open: 16 March - 15 October.

Directions

On E40 in either direction take exit for De Haan and Jabbeke. In De Haan drive through centre and turn right in front of the station (don't cross the tram-lines). Follow the Wenduinesteenweg to the site on the right.

Charges guide

Per uunit incl. 2 persons and electricity	€ 15,00 - € 20,00
extra person	€ 2,25
child (under 10 yrs)	€ 1,50

Camping Cheques accepted.

BE0735 Camping Petite Suisse

Al Bounire 27, B-6960 Dochamps (Luxembourg)

Tel: **084 444 030**. Email: **info@petitesuisse.be**

A member of the same group as Parc de la Clusure (BE0670), this quiet site is set in the picturesque countryside of the Belgium Ardennes, a region where rivers flow through valleys bordered by vast forests where horses are still usefully employed. Set on a southerly slope, the site is mostly open and offers wide views of the surrounding countryside. The 205 touring pitches, all with 10A electricity, are either on open sloping ground or in terraced rows with hedges between the rows and with trees providing some separation. Gravel site roads provide access. To the right of the entrance barrier a large wooden building houses reception, a bar and restaurant and some sanitary facilities. Close by is an attractive outdoor swimming pool with wide terraces surrounded by grass. Behind this is a large children's play area adjoining a small terrace. Although the site has many activities on offer the opportunity should not be missed to make excursions into the countryside with its hills and forests. The villages are filled with houses built from the local stone and small inviting bars and restaurants.

Facilities

All the facilities that one would expect of a large site are available. Showers are free, washbasins both open and in cabins. Baby changing room. Laundry room with washing machines and dryers. Shop. Restaurant, bar and takeaway meals. Swimming pool, paddling pool and water slide. Sports field. Tennis. Bicycle hire. Playground and club for children. Entertainment programme (1/6-1/9). Activity programme, including canoeing, climbing, abseiling and walking trips. Off site: La Roche en Ardennes 10 km. Baraque de Fraiture (ski resort) 10 km. Golf 20 km.

Open: All year.

Directions

From E25/A26 autoroute (Liège - Luxembourg) take exit 50 then the N89 southwest towards La Roche. After 8 km. turn right (north) on N841 to Dochamps where site is signed. GPS: N50:13.832 E05:37.87

Charges 2006

Per pitch incl. 2 persons	€ 17,50 - € 21,00
extra person (over 4 yrs)	€ 4,00 - € 4,50
electricity	€ 3,00

No credit cards.
Camping Cheques accepted.

BE0740 Camping l'Eau Rouge

Cheneux 25, B-4970 Stavelot (Liège)

Tel: **080 86 30 75**. Email: **info@eaurouge.nl**

A popular, lively and attractively situated site, L'Eau Rouge is in a sheltered valley close to Spa and the Grand Prix circuit. There are 180 grassy pitches of 110 sq.m. on sloping ground either side of a central road (speed bumps) – 60 are taken by permanent units and 120 for tourists. There are plenty of sporting activities in the area including skiing and luge in winter. The site is close to the motor race circuit at Spa Francorchamps and is within walking distance for the fit.

Facilities

There is a main block but a smaller unit serves the touring area. It includes good numbers of British WCs, mostly open washbasins, but rather fewer hot showers (free), which could be stretched at times. Additional facilities should be available in the near future. Shop. Baker calls daily at 8.30 am. in season. Takeaway (in summer). Bar. Football. Boules. Table tennis. Archery (free lessons in high season). Barbecues. Playground. Entertainment in season. Off site: Bicycle hire 6 km. Riding 10 km. Spa.

Open: All year.

Directions

The site is 1 km. to the east of Stavelot on the road to the race circuit. Leave E42 exit 11 Malmédy, at roundabout follow signs for Stavelot. At end of road 'T' junction turn right then first right. GPS: N50:24.722 E05:57.19

Charges guide

Per person	€ 2,25
child (4-12 yrs)	€ 2,00
pitch	€ 10,00
electricity (10A)	€ 2,00

BE0670 Camping Parc La Clusure

Chemin de la Clusure 30, B-6927 Bure-Tellin (Luxembourg)

Tel: 084 360 050. Email: info@parclaclusure.be

Set in a river valley in the lovely wooded uplands of the Ardennes, known as the L'Homme Valley touring area, La Clusure has 425 large marked, grassy pitches (350 for touring units). All have access to electricity (16A), cable TV and water taps and are mostly in avenues off a central, tarmac road. It is a busy site that could feel crowded during the high season. There is a very pleasant, well lit riverside walk (the river is shallow in summer and popular for children to play in), a heated swimming pool with pool-side bar/terrace. The site is used by a tour operator (number of pitches varies).

Facilities

Four sanitary units (one heated in winter) include some washbasins in cubicles facilities for babies and family bathrooms. Room for disabled persons. Dishwashing and laundry facilities may be stretched at times. Motorcaravan services. Well stocked shop, bar, restaurant, snack bar and takeaway (all 25/3-2/11). Bicycle hire. Tennis. Swimming pools (29/4-11/9). New playgrounds. Activity programme (July/Aug). Fishing (licence essential). Off site: Riding 7 km.

Open: All year.

Directions

Site is signed north at the rounabout off the N803 Rochefort - St Hubert road at Bure, 8 km. southeast of Rochefort with a narrow, steepish, winding descent to site. GPS: N50:05.788 E05:17.23

Charges 2007

Per pitch incl. 2 persons	€ 19,00 - € 26,00
extra person	€ 4,00 - € 5,00
electricity (16A)	€ 3,50

Camping Cheques accepted.

BE0590 Camping de Gavers

Onkerzelestraat 280, B-9500 Geraardsbergen (East Flanders)

Tel: 054 41 63 24. Email: gavers@oost-vlaanderen.be

Domein de Gavers is a modern, well organised holiday site in a peaceful location adjacent to a large sports complex, about 5 km. outside Geraardsbergen. A busy site in season, there is good security and a card operated barrier. Most of the 448 grassy, level pitches are taken by seasonal units but about 80 are left for tourists. Pitches are arranged on either side of surfaced access roads with some hedges and few trees to provide shade in parts, with electricity (5/10A) available to most. The site offers an extensive range of sporting activities and a full entertainment programme over a long season.

Facilities

Six modern, well equipped sanitary buildings provide hot showers on payment (€ 0.50). Modern rooms for disabled people and babies. Launderette. No motorcaravan service point. Shop (July/Aug). Restaurant and takeaway (all year). Cafeteria and bars (daily 1/4-30/9, otherwise weekends). Heated indoor pool. Outdoor pool (1/5-31/8). Excellent playground. Tennis. Boules. Minigolf. Fishing. Sailing. Boats for hire. Bicycle hire.

Open: All year.

Directions

From E429/A8 exit 26 (Edingen), take N255 and N495 to Geraardsbergen. Down a steep hill, then left at sign towards Onkerzele, through village and turn north to site. From E40/A10, exit at junction 17 on to N42, turn left on to N495 and as above.

Charges guide

Per unit incl. electricity	€ 10,00 - € 20,00

Discounts of 5-30% for longer stays.

BE0595 Kompas-Camping Oudenaarde

Kortrijkstraat 342, B-9700 Oudenaarde (East Flanders)

Tel: 055 31 54 73. Email: oudenaarde@kompascamping.be

This is an extensive holiday site with 381 pitches but there are only around 179 for tourists. The remainder are occupied by 190 seasonal units, rental or private chalets, and a few pitches for a tour operator. Pitches are generally on grass with 10A electric hook-ups and are of a reasonable size, some divided by hedges. A separate area for motorcaravans is close to the main entrance with a drive-over service point adjacent (tokens from reception). The shop here is unusual in that it is two 'automat' machines, always open for business but with an extremely limited variety of stock.

Facilities

Four toilet blocks all of a similar design provide all the usual services with some facilities for babies and disabled campers. In low season cleaning and maintenance appears to be of low priority. Recycling. Bar/restaurant and takeaway (1/4-14/11, full time in July/August, public holidays and at weekends, but are not during low season weekdays. Shop. Swimming pool. Indoor playroom and several playgrounds. Bicycle hire. Fishing. Children's entertainment in July/Aug. Off site: Oudenaarde 4 km.

Open: 1 April - 14 November.

Directions

Oudenaarde is about 25 km. south of Ghent. From main N60 (Ghent-Ronse) road, take exit to Avelgem on N453. (just north of River Schelde). Continue west for 2.5 km. and follow camp signs to your right (site signs are rather small). GPS: N50:50.459 E03:34.476

Charges 2006

Per unit incl. 4 persons	17,50 - € 26,25

Camping Cheques accepted.

BE0600 Camping Groeneveld

Groenevelddreef, Bachte-Maria-Leerne, B-9800 Deinze (East Flanders)

Tel: 093 80 10 14. Email: info@campinggroeneveld.be

Quiet and clean is how Rene Kuys describes his campsite. Groeneveld is a traditional site in a small village within easy reach of Gent. It has a friendly atmosphere and is also open over a long season. Although this site has 108 pitches, there are a fair number of seasonal units, leaving around 50 large tourist pitches with electricity (10A). Hedges and borders divide the grassy area, access roads are gravel and there is an area for tents. Family entertainment and activities organised in high season include themed, musical evenings, barbecues, petanque matches, etc. The city of Gent is just 15 km. north of the site and 5 km. to the south is the pleasant town of Deinze.

Facilities

Two clean sanitary units of differing age and design provide British style WCs, washbasins and free hot showers (new facilities are planned for 2007/8). Motorcaravan services. Freezer (free). Bar/café (July/Aug. and weekends). Small coarse fishing lake. Floodlit petanque court. Adventure style play area. TV room. Internet access (at reception). Off site: Shops and restaurants nearby. Golf 3 km. Swimming pool 5 km.

Open: 26 March - 12 November.

Directions

From A10 (E40) exit 13, turn south on N466. After 3 km. continue straight on at roundabout and site is on left on entering village (opposite a large factory). Note: yellow signs are very small.

Charges 2006

Per unit incl. 2 persons, electricity	€ 17,00 - € 20,00
2 persons and tent	€ 3,00 - € 3,50
dog	€ 2,00

No credit cards.

BE0610 Camping Blaarmeersen

Zuiderlaan 12, B-9000 Gent (East Flanders)

Tel: 09 266 81 60. Email: camping.blaarmeersen@gent.be

Blaarmeersen is a comfortable, well managed municipal site in the west of the city. It adjoins a sports complex and a fair-sized lake which provide facilities for a variety of watersports, tennis, squash, minigolf, football, athletics track, roller skating and a playground. The 205 individual, flat, grassy touring pitches are separated by tall hedges and mostly arranged in circular groups; with electricity to 178. There are 40 hardstandings for motorcaravans, plus a separate area for tents with barbecue facility. Some noise is possible as the the city ring road is close.

Facilities

Four sanitary units of a decent standard vary in size. Most of the 36 free hot showers are in one block. Showers and toilets for disabled people. Laundry. Motorcaravan services. Shop, café/bar (both daily March - Oct). Takeaway. Sports facilities. Playground. Fishing on site in winter, otherwise 500 m. Lake swimming. Off site: Bicycle hire 5 km. Riding and golf 10 km.

Open: 1 March - 15 October.

Directions

From E40 take exit 13 (Gent-West) and follow road for 5 km. Cross second bridge and look for Blaarmeersen sign, turning sharp right and following signs to leisure complex.
GPS: N51:02.833 E03:41.000

Charges guide

Per person	€ 3,25 - € 4,00
pitch incl. electricity	€ 6,25 - € 7,25

BE0630 Camping Grimbergen

Veldkantsraat 64, B-1850 Grimbergen (Brabant)

Tel: 0479 76 03 78. Email: camping.grimbergen@telenet.be

A popular little municipal site with a friendly atmosphere, Camping Grimbergen has 90 pitches on fairly level grass, of which around 50 have electricity (10A). The municipal sports facilities are adjacent and the site is well placed for visiting Brussels. The bus station is by the traffic lights at the junction of N202 and N211 and buses run into the city centre every 15 minutes. In Grimbergen itself visit Norbertine Abbey, St Servaas church, and the Sunday morning market. Also worth a visit are the nearby towns of Lier and Mechelen, and the botanical gardens at Meise. The site is not really suitable for large units, although four pitches for motorcaravans have been added.

Facilities

Immaculate new sanitary facilities are heated in colder months. Three dishwashing sinks under cover. Separate facilities for disabled people. Motorcaravan services. Adventure playground. Off site: Fishing 800 m.

Open: 1 April - 31 October.

Directions

From Brussels ring road take exit 7 (N202) to Grimbergen for about 2.5 km, turn right at traffic lights on N211 towards Vilvoorde (site is signed), then left at second lights (slightly oblique turn). Site entrance is on right in about 500 m.

Charges 2007

Per person	€ 4,50
pitch incl. electricity	€ 7,00

No credit cards.

BE0640 Camping Druivenland

Nijvelsebaan 80, B-3090 Overijse (Brabant)

Tel: **02 687.93.68**. Email: **camping.druivenland@pandora.be**

This small, peaceful site is within easy reach of Brussels and also close to 25,000 hectares of woodland where you can enjoy some of the best Belgian countryside by foot or by cycle. Neat and mature, the site is well looked after and family run. It has a large open touring field or further pitches available in the sheltered area of the static park. The pitches are slightly sloping but almost all have views over the countryside – in total there are 150 pitches, with 80 for touring units, all with electricity (10/16A) and some with internet access. This is a very pleasant relaxing site at which to stay and tour this part of Belgium. Brussells and Leuven are nearby and, perhaps of interesting note, there are over 60 eating places in the town of Overijse.

Facilities

Fully equipped toilet block with some washbasins in cabins and toilets for children. Well laid out provision for disabled visitors (shower room and toilet/washroom). Dishwashing sinks (€ 1). Laundry sinks, washing machine and dryer. Kept extremely clean at all times, it is of a very high standard. Limited shop with some fresh food. Table tennis. Boules. Basketball. Off site: Golf 3 km.

Open: 1 April - 30 September.

Directions

From E411 Brussels - Namur road take exit 3 to Overijse (not exit 2). After 1 km turn right signed Tombeek, Waver and Terlanen. Site is 1 km. on right (it is quite a long walk from the barrier to reception).

Charges guide

Per unit incl. 2 persons	€ 14,00 - € 16,00
extra person	€ 1,50
electricity	€ 2,00
dog	€ 1,50

BE0655 Camping De Lilse Bergen

Strandweg 6, Gierle, B-2275 Lille (Antwerp)

Tel: **014 55 79 01**. Email: **info@lilsebergen.be**

This attractive, quietly located holiday site has 503 shady pitches, of which 241 all with electricity (10A) are for touring units. Set on sandy soil among pine trees and rhododendrons and arranged around a large lake, the site has a Mediterranean feel. It is well fenced, with a night guard and comprehensive, well labelled, fire fighting equipment. Cars are parked away from units. The site is really child-friendly with each access road labelled with a different animal symbol to enable children to find their own unit easily. The lake has marked swimming and diving areas (adult), a sandy beach, an area for watersports, plus a separate children's pool complex (depth 60 cm.) with a most imaginative playground. There are lifeguards and the water meets 'Blue Flag' standards. A building by the lake houses changing rooms, extra toilets and showers and a baby room. There are picnic areas and lakeside or woodland walks. An entertainment programme is organised in high season.

Facilities

Four of the six main toilet blocks have been fully refitted to a good standard and can be heated. Some washbasins in cubicles and good hot showers (on payment). Well equipped baby rooms. Facilities for disabled campers. Laundry and dishwashing rooms. Barrier 'keys' can be charged up with credit units for operating showers, washing machine etc. First aid post. Recycling centre. Drive-over motorcaravan service point. Restaurant (all year, weekends only in winter), takeaway and well stocked shop (Easter - 31/9; weekends only outside July/Aug). Tennis. Table tennis. Minigolf. Boules. Multi-court. Volleyball. Climbing wall. Playground, trampolines and skateboard ramp. Pedaloes, windsurfers, lifejackets and bicycles for hire. Children's electric cars and pedal Kart tracks (charged for). Off site: Golf 1 km. Riding 1 km.

Open: All year.

Directions

From E34 Antwerp-Eindhoven take exit 22. On the roundabout take the exit for 'Lilse Bergen' and follow forest road to site entrance.
GPS: N51:17.345 E04:51.305

Charges 2007

Per unit incl. electricity (10A)	€ 18,00 - € 24,00
dog	€ 4,00

BE0700 Camping Spa d'Or

Stockay 17, B-4845 Sart-lez-Spa (Liège)

Tel: 087 474400. Email: info@campingspador.be

Camping Spa d'Or is set in a beautiful area of woodlands and picturesque villages, 4 km. from the town of Spa (the 'Pearl of the Ardennes'). The site is on the banks of a small river and is an ideal starting point for walks and bicycle trips through the forests. The Dutch owners have long-term plans to upgrade the site which had been rather neglected. The 230 touring pitches have an open aspect, most are slightly sloping and all have 10A electricity connections. With 300 pitches in total, 220 are for touring units and 40 places are reserved for tents. The remainder are used for site owned mobile homes and tents. Indoor accomodation is provided for groups of up to 50 persons. The bar and restaurant, brightly illuminated with coloured lights outside, offer a cosy environment for eating and drinking. This is an acceptable campsite within easy reach of many tourist attractions.

Facilities

Two sanitary blocks are old but clean. Most of the showers are very small with little or no room for changing. Three showers in the ladies section are equipped with a washbasin, otherwise these are open. Family room with shower, WC and baby bath. Room for visitors with disabilities. Laundry. Shop (1/4-24/10). Bar, restaurant and takeaway (1/4-24/10). Outdoor heated swimming pool (15/5-15/9). Play area with good equipment. TV in bar. Entertainment during July and August. Off site: Fishing 2 km. Golf and riding 5 km.

Open: All year.

Directions

From E42 take exit 9 and follow the signs to Spa d'Or. GPS: N50:30.455 E05:55.171

Charges guide

Per unit incl. 2 persons	€ 18,00
extra person (over 3 yrs)	€ 4,00
tent incl. 2 persons.	€ 12,50
electricity	€ 3,00
dog	€ 3,00

Camping Spa d'Or, Stockay 17, 4845 Sart-lez-Spa, België
Tel.: +32 (0)87 474 400 / Fax: +32 (0)87 475 277
E-mail: info@campingspador.be
www.campingspador.be

- gelegen bij Spa/Francorchamps
- modern en schoon sanitair
- verhuur stacaravans
- restaurant, bar en winkel
- animatie en buitensport

- nearby Spa/Francorchamps
- modern and clean sanitary
- mobile homes for rent
- restaurant, bar and shop
- animation and outdooractivities

BE0770 Camping le Vieux Moulin

Petite Strument 62, B-6980 La Roche-en-Ardenne (Luxembourg)

Tel: 084 411 380. Email: info@strument.com

Located in one of the most beautiful valleys in the heart of the Ardennes, Le Vieux Moulin has 183 pitches and, although there are 127 long stay units at the far end of the site, the 60 tourist pitches do have their own space. Some are separated by hedges, others for tents and smaller units are more open, all are on grass, and there are 50 electric hook-ups (6A). The 19th century water mill has been owned and operated by the owner's family for many years, but has now been converted into a small hotel and a fascinating mill museum (visits with an audio guide in English). La Roche is a pretty little town in an unspoiled area, a very scenic region of rolling tree-clad hills and small deep valleys, with rocks for climbing, castles to explore and rivers to fish.

Facilities

A newly constructed, centrally located toilet block is between the tourist and long stay areas. It can be heated in cool weather and provides washbasins in cubicles and controllable hot showers on payment. Dishwashing and laundry sinks with washing machine. No facilities for disabled persons. A further older unit is at the end of the mill building. Restaurant and bar with hotel (8 rooms). Mill museum. Off site: Town facilities 800 m.

Open: 1 April - 11 November.

Directions

From town centre take N89 south towards St Hubert, turning right towards Hives where site is signed. Site is 800 m. from the town centre. GPS: N50:10.417 E05:34.65

Charges 2006

Per person	€ 2,50
pitch	€ 8,00 - € 10,50
electricity	€ 2,50

55

BE0660 Camping Baalse Hei

Roodhuisstraat 10, B-2300 Turnhout (Antwerp)

Tel: 014 44 84 70. Email: info@baalsehei.be

The 'Campine' is an area covering three-quarters of the Province of Antwerp, noted for its nature reserves, pine forests, meadows and streams and is ideal for walking and cycling, while Turnhout itself is an interesting old town. Baalse Hei, a long-established, friendly site, is a recent Benelux campsite award winner. It has 454 pitches including a separate touring area of 61 large pitches (all with 16A electricity, TV connections and shared water point) on a large grass field, thoughtfully developed with young trees and bushes. Cars are parked away from the pitches. Large motorhomes can be accommodated (phone first to check availability). It is 100 m. from the edge of the field to the modern, heated, sanitary building. There is a small lake for swimming with a beach, a boating lake and a large fishing lake (on payment). Entertainment and activities are organised July/Aug. Walk in the woods and you will undoubtedly come across some of the many red squirrels or take the pleasant 1.5 km. riverside walk to the next village. Arrival after 4 pm. departure before 12 noon.

Facilities

The toilet block provides hot showers on payment (€ 0.50), some washbasins in cabins and facilities for disabled visitors. Dishwashing facilities (hot water € 0.12), Launderette. Motorcaravan services. Café/restaurant (daily 1/6-30/9, w/ends only other times, closed 16/11-25/1). Breakfast served in high season. Shop (all year). Club/TV room. Lake swimming. Fishing. Two tennis courts. Adventure play area. Bicycle hire. English is spoken. Off site: Riding 1.5 km. Golf 15 km.

Open: 16 January - 15 December

Directions

Site is northeast of Turnhout off the N119. Approaching from Antwerp on E34/A12 go onto Turnhout ring road to the end (not a complete ring) and turn right. There is a small site sign to right in 1.5 km. then a country lane.

Charges 2007

Per unit all inclusive	€ 15,00 - € 23,00
electricity	€ 1,00
2 cyclists and tent	€ 10,00 - € 13,00

No credit cards.

Baalse Hei offers a calm and quiet environment, boarding a nature reserve north of Turnhout. There are several lakes used for swimming, fishing and rowing. Football, volley- basket- and tennis facilities. A lot of cycling routes in the area. Caravans, Hikers' cabins and bicycle hire. Via E34/A12 Eindhoven-Antwerpen, exit n° 24. **Roodhuisstraat 10, 2300 Turnhout (Belgium) Tel. +32 (0)14 44 84 70 • Fax +32 (0)14 44 84 74 www.baalsehei.be • info@baalsehei.be**

Baalse Hei
't Groene Caravanpark

BE0675 Camping Spineuse

Rue de Malome 7, B-6840 Neufchâteau (Luxembourg)

Tel: 061 277 320. Email: info@camping-spineuse.be

This Dutch owned site lies about 2 km. from the town centre. It is on low lying, level grass bordered by a river, with trees and shrubs dotted around the 87 grassy pitches. The main gravel access road can be dusty in dry weather. Seasonal units take 25 pitches leaving 62 for tourists, all with electricity hook-ups (10/15A . There is also a separate area for tents. Reception is in the main building and keeps basic food items in July/August. A tiny bistro/bar offers a limited range of dishes, drinks and a takeaway service with a friendly, family atmosphere. Leisure activities include walking or cycling and there is a fishing lake. Parents of small children should be aware that there is unfenced water on site and a foot bridge over the river with no guard rails.

Facilities

Toilet facilities are in the central building and are looking dated with some cubicles rather small. Pre-set showers and open washbasins. However the building can be heated and was reasonably clean when seen. No facilities for disabled campers. Dishwashing and laundry sinks outside at the end of the building (not under cover). Washing machine and dryer. Extra facilities are available in a portacabin for July-August. Drive-over motorcaravan service point. Bistro/bar (1/4-31/10). Small inflatable children's pool (1/6-30/9). Tennis court. Table tennis. Boules. Small playground. Fishing. Bicycle hire. Off site: Riding 10 km. Golf 30 km.

Open: All year.

Directions

Located 2 km. southwest of Neufchâteau on the N15 towards Florenville. (There are 3 sites fairly close together, this is the last one on the left hand side). GPS: N49:49.899 E05:24.909

Charges guide

Per person	€ 3,10
child (0-6 yrs)	€ 2,00
pitch	€ 9,00
incl. electricity	€ 11,25

BE0680 Camping Sud

Voie de la Liberté 75, B-6717 Attert (Luxembourg)
Tel: 063 223715. Email: info@campingsudattert.com

This is a pleasant family run site which would make a good base for a short stay and is also well sited for use as an overnight halt. The 86 touring pitches are on level grass with 6A electricity hook-ups and are arranged around an oval loop access road. There are 11 drive-through pitches especially for one-nighters, plus four hardstandings for motorcaravans and a tent area. The far end of the site is close to the N4 and may suffer from some road noise. On-site facilities include a small restaurant/bar with takeaway facility and a shop for basics. An outdoor swimming pool (12 x 6 m) has a separate paddling pool and there is an open sports field at the far end of the site.

Facilities

A single building provides modern sanitary facilities including some washbasins in cubicles and baby areas. Showers are free in low season but are limited in July/August by use of a charge 'key' system. Extra showers can be purchased if required. No facilities for disabled campers. Small bar/restaurant and takeaway (1/4 - 25/10) TV in bar. Swimming pool (May-Sept). Small playground. Children's entertainment during July/August. Off site: Riding 5 km. Golf 8 km. Supermarket 5 km.

Open: 1 April - 25 October.

Directions

Attert is about 8 km. north of Arlon. From N4 take Attert exit, continue east for about 1 km. to Attert village, site entrance is immediately on your left as you join the main street.
GPS: N49:44.894 E05:47.219

Charges 2006

Per person	€ 4,00
pitch with electricity	€ 10,25
No credit cards.	

BE0705 Camping L'Hirondelle

Château 1, B-4210 Oteppe (Liège)
Tel: 085 711131. Email: info@lhirondelle.be

This site is set in 20 hectares of woodland in the grounds of a castle that dates back to the 14th century. From the entrance one gets a glimpse of the restaurant in one part of the castle. There are 800 pitches with 300 for tourers, all with 6A electricity. The pitches are arranged around a huge playground, basketball court and a building which houses a games room, a supermarket and a bar. In high season (5/7-21/8) the site offers a full animation programme with film nights, sports tournaments, discos and contests. This is a pleasant site which has a lot to offer for children and teenagers. The large open air pool (15 x 25 m.) will accommodate both youngsters and teenagers.

Facilities

The two toilet blocks for tourers provide some washbasins in cabins, children's toilets and basins and a unisex baby room. Washing machine and dryer. Good provision for disabled vsitors. Shop. Bar. Restaurant. Huge adventure type playground. Basketball. Boules. Playing field. Animation team (5/7-21/8). Open air swimming pool (15 x 25 m). Games room.

Open: 1 April - 31 October.

Directions

From Namen on the E42 take exit 10 towards Biewart then continue on the 80 to Burdinne. In Burdinne follow signs for Oteppe. The site is signposted just before entering Oteppe.
GPS: N50:34.055 E05:07.031

Charges guide

Per unit incl. 2 persons	€ 13,75 - € 21,00
extra person	€ 2,75 - € 4,00

BE0710 Camping Colline de Rabais

Rue de Bonlieu, B-6760 Virton (Luxembourg)
Tel: 063 57 11 95. Email: info@campingcollinederabais.be

Colline de Rabais is a large site with an unusual lay-out. This consists of a circular road with smaller roads leading to circular pads with wedge shaped pitches. In a hill top setting, the site is surrounded by forest. The forest is open to walkers and cyclists alike – you can go for ages without seeing another person. Various activities are organised throughout the season. There are around 250 pitches for touring units, all with 16A electricity (some long leads needed), plus 43 mobile homes and bungalows for rent and 22 tour operator tents. Site lighting is poor – a torch is recommended.

Facilities

Three toilet blocks including one which has been modernised with shower/washbasin cubicles and an en-suite room for disabled people. Not all blocks are open in low season. Laundry. Motorcaravan service point. Bar/restaurant and shop (opening times vary). Small outdoor swimming pool with Bicycle hire. Off site: Fishing 1 km. Riding 3 km.

Open: All year.

Directions

From E25/E411 take exit 29 towards Etalle and Virton. Follow signs for Vallée de Rabais. Turn right at sports complex. At crossroads turn right and uphill to site at end of road. GPS: N49:34.809 E05:32.864

Charges 2006

Per unit incl. 2 persons	€ 17,60 - € 22,00
extra person (over 3 yrs)	€ 4,00 - € 4,50
electricity	€ 3,00

BE0712 Camping Ile de Faigneul

Rue de la Cherizelle 54, B-6830 Poupehan-sur-Semois (Luxembourg)
Tel: **061 46 68 9**. Email: **iledefaigneul@belgacom.net**

Few campsites are in sole possession of an island, and when that island lies in a beautiful tree lined valley the site is likely to be something special. Camping Isle de Faigneul is! This quiet, peaceful site, surrounded by the River Semois, is near the small village of Poupehan in the picturesque Belgium Ardennes. All of the 130 level pitches, all with electricity, on this grass covered island are for tourists. A homely bar/restaurant with its terrace is entirely in keeping with this comfortable, natural site. The region has plenty to interest visitors.

Facilities

The well appointed sanitary block is new and maintained to the highest standard. Ultra modern, it has pre-set showers operated by key (deposit € 25) and some washbasins in cabins, others open. Facilities for disabled visitors, family shower room, baby changing area. Laundry room with sinks, washing machines and dryer plus iron and board. Dishwashing outside (free hot water). Shop. Bar and restaurant. Mountain bike and canoe rental. Fishing. Archery. Playground.

Open: 1 April - 30 September.

Directions

From Brussels southeast on motorway A4/E411 towards Luxembourg. At exit 25 Libramont/Bouillon take N89 southwest to Bouillon. In Bouillon follow signs for Poupehan. The twisting road ends up alongside the Semois just before Poupehan. Left over the stone bridge and immediately right (site signed). GPS: N49:48.963 E05:00.94

Charges guide

Per unit incl. 2 person	€ 19,70
incl. electricity	€ 22,05

BE0715 Camping De Chênefleur

Norulle 16, B-6730 Tintigny (Luxembourg)
Tel: **063 44 40 78**. Email: **info@chenefleur.be**

This is a comfortable site with 220 pitches (185 for tourers), set beside the Semois river, close to Luxembourg and France. All pitches have 6A electricity and are separated by young trees. On the whole the site is open but there is some shade. One of the guests we spoke to, a first time visitor, was very pleased with the spacious pitches and the peace and quiet on site. The site is still being developed, but Fred, the owner, is very enthusiastic and is working hard. It has a swimming pool (also used by the locals) and in high season entertainment is organised six days each week. The playground and beach volleyball court are brand new and it is possible to rent bicycles.

Facilities

A newly refurbished sanitary block and a temporary portacabin complex (a new block was due to be completed for 2006) provide showers (€ 0,80), a washing machine, a dryer and dishwashing under cover. Shop. Bar. Restaurant. Swimming pool (5 x 15 m). Two new play areas. Beach volleyball. Table tennis. Full animation programme in season. Bicycle hire. Off site: Riding 12 km. Luxembourg City 40 km.

Open: 1 April - 1 November.

Directions

From Luik follow E25 towards Luxembourg and continue on E411. Take exit 29 Habay-La-Neuve and continue to Etalle. From Etalle follow N83 to Florenville. Drive through Tintigny and follow camp signs. GPS: N49:41.098 E05:31.23

Charges guide

Per unit incl. 2 persons	€ 16,00 - € 20,00
electricity (6A)	€ 3,00
Camping Cheques accepted.	

BE0720 Camping Tonny

Tonny 35, B-6680 Amberloup (Luxembourg)
Tel: **061 68 82 85**. Email: **camping.tonny@belgacom.net**

With a friendly atmosphere, this family campsite is in pleasant valley by the River Ourthe. It is an attractive small site with 75 grassy touring pitches, with wooden chalet buildings giving a Tyrolean feel. The pitches (80-100 sq.m.) are separated by small shrubs and fir trees and electricity (4/6A) is available. Cars are parked away from the units and there is a separate meadow for tents. Surrounded by natural woodland, Camping Tonny is an ideal base for outdoor activites.

Facilities

Two fully equipped sanitary units (both heated in cool weather) include dishwashing and laundry sinks (all hot water is on payment). Baby changing area and laundry. Freezer for campers use. Small shop. Cafe/bar. TV lounge and library. Sports field. Boules. Games room. Playgrounds. Skittle alley. Bicycle hire. Fishing. Canoeing. Cross country skiing.

Open: 15 February - 15 November.

Directions

From N4 take exit for Libramont at km. 131 (N826), then to Amberloup (4 km.) where site is signed just outside of the south west town boundary. GPS: N50:01.594 E05:30.77

Charges 2006

Per person	€ 3,50
child (0-12 yrs)	€ 2,00
pitch with electricity (4A)	€ 9,60 - € 10,10
Off season discounts for over 55s and longer stays.	

BE0725 Camping Le Val de L'Aisne

Rue du TTA, 1, B-6997 Erezee (Luxembourg)

Tel: 086 47 00 67. Email: info@levaldelaisne.be

From a nearby hill Château de Blier overlooks Camping Le Val de L'Aisne, a large site attractively laid out around a 1.5 hectare lake in the Belgium Ardennes. The site has 450 grass pitches with 150 for touring units, on level ground and with 10A electricity. Tarmac roads circle the site providing easy access. Trees provide some shade although the site is fairly open allowing views of the surrounding hills and the château. To the left of the entrance a building houses reception and the bar/restaurant. Behind this is a large fenced playground. Activities play a large part on this site, ranging from quiet fishing in the lake to hectic quad bike tours in the surrounding hills. This is an attractive region with a lot to offer the visitor. There are many places to visit, marked walks though the forests or for the more adventurous, mountain bike tracks to ride or kayak descents down the region's rivers.

Facilities

Three toilet blocks provide showers (paid for by token) and mainly open washbasins. Facilities for disabled people. Baby changing room. Laundry rooms with washing machines and dryers. Motorcaravan service point. Bar/restaurant and snack bar with takeaway food. Bread can be ordered in reception. On the lake: fishing, swimming, kayaks and pedal boats (to hire). Quad bike hire and tours arranged. Kayaks and mountain bike hire. Play area and entertainment programme during summer and adventure games in the nearby wooded area. Off site: Riding, cycle and walking in the Ardennes woods.

Open: All year.

Directions

Leave the E411/A4 (Brussels - Luxembourg) motorway at exit 18 for Courière and Marche en Famenne, then southeast on the N4 to Marche. At Marche head northeast on N86 to Hotton, crossing the bridge over the river Ourthe. In Hotton follow signs for Soy and Erezée. Just to the west of Erezée at roundabout follow signs for La Roche. Site is 900 m. on the left.

Charges guide

Per pitch incl. 2 persons	€ 12,00 - € 18,00
extra person (over 3 yrs)	€ 3,00
electricity (3A)	€ 3,00

No credit cards.
Reductions for longer periods of stay.

Go for adventure... or to enjoy nature!

camping LE VAL DE L'AISNE

Summer and winter camping! Up to 30% discount in low season! Mobile homes and pre-erected tents for rent!

Camping Le Val de L'Aisne
Rue du T.T.A. 6997 Blier-Erezée
tel: 086/47 00 67 fax: 086/47 00 43
E-mail: info@levaldelaisne.be
Website: www.levaldelaisne.be

BE0730 Camping Moulin de Malempré

1 Malempre, B-6960 Manhay (Luxembourg)

Tel: 086 45 55 04. Email: camping.malempre@cybernet.be

This pleasant countryside site, very close to the E25, is well worth a visit and the Dutch owners will make you very welcome. The reception building houses the office and a small shop, above which is an attractive bar and restaurant with open fireplace. The 140 marked tourist pitches are separated by small shrubs and gravel roads on sloping terrain. All have electricity (10A), 40 have water and drainage as well and the site is well lit. The star of this site is the main sanitary unit, an ultra modern, two storey Scandinavian style building; this is complemented by a unisex unit. There is a little traffic noise from the nearby E25 (not too intrusive). English is spoken.

Facilities

Modern toilet facilities include some washbasins in cubicles and family bathrooms on payment. The unisex unit can be heated and has a family shower room. Unit for disabled people with automatic taps, hoists and rails. Baby room. Motorcaravan services. Shop for basic provisions only (15/5-31/8). Baker calls 08.30 - 09.15. Restaurant and bar (both 15/5-15/9 and weekends). Takeaway (15/5-15/9). Heated swimming pool and children's pools (one with mushroom fountain (15/5-15/9). TV. Playground and trampoline. Off site: Bicycle hire 3 km, Riding 6 km. Fishing 10 km.

Open: 1 April - 31 October.

Directions

From E25/A26 (Liege-Bastogne) exit 49. Turn onto N651 (south west) towards Manhay. After 220 m. turn sharp left (east) towards Lierneux. Follow signs for Malempré and site. GPS: N50:17.699 E05:43.39

Charges 2007

Per unit incl. 2 persons	€ 18,50 - € 22,00
extra person	€ 4,00
child (3-12 yrs)	€ 2,75
electricity	€ 2,85
dog	€ 2,85

Less 20% in low season.

BE0780 Family Camping Wilhelm Tell

Hoeverweg 87, B-3660 Opglabbeek (Limburg)

Tel: **089 85 44 44**. Email: **receptie@wilhelmtell.com**

Wilhelm Tell is a family run site that caters particularly well for children with its indoor and outdoor pools and lots of entertainment throughout the season. There is a total of 128 pitches with 70 available for touring units, some separated, others on open fields. There are 60 electricity connections (10A) and, for winter use, 20 hardstandings. The super bar/restaurant has access for wheelchair users. M. Lode Nulmans has a very special attitude towards his customers and tries to ensure they leave satisfied and want to return. For example, in his restaurant he says 'it serves until you are full'. The Limburg region is a relaxing area with much to do, including shopping or touring the historic towns with a very enjoyable choice of food and drink!

Facilities

Toilet facilities are adequate. Facilities around the pool supplement at busy times. Baby room in reception area. Two en-suite units for disabled visitors. Dishwashing and laundry facilities. Motorcaravan service point. Fridge hire. Bar/restaurant and snack bar (times vary acc. to season). Swimming pools (well supervised), the outdoor heated pool with slide and wave machine open 1/7-31/8, the indoor open all year. Play area. Table tennis.

Open: All year.

Directions

From E314 take exit 32 for Maaseik and follow 730 road towards As. From As follow signs to Opglabbeek. In Opglabbeek take first right at roundabout (Weg van Niel) then first left (Kasterstraat) to site. GPS: N51:01.711 E05:35.888

Charges 2006

Per person	€ 6,00
child	€ 3,00
pitch incl. electricity	€ 15,00

Less 30% in low season.
Camping Cheques accepted.

Wilhelm Tell RECREATIEOORD

Request your free brochure now from www.wilhelmtell.com!

Cycling, walking, family holidays - a real feast!!

Hoeverweg 87
B-3660 Opglabbeek-Limburg
Tel. 089 81 00 14 - Fax 089 81 00 10
receptie@wilhelmtell.com

To let: luxury holiday apartments and chalets!

camping **Zavelbos**

Kattebeekstraat 1
B-3680 Opoeteren
Tel. 089 75 81 46
Fax 089 75 81 48
receptie@zavelbos.com

5000 acres of land perfect for cycling and walking!

Request your free brochure now from www.zavelbos.com!

BE0732 Camping Floreal La Roche

Route de Holiffalize 18, B-6980 La Roche-en-Ardenne (Luxembourg)

Tel: **084 21 94 67**. Email: **camping.laroche@florealclub.be**

Maintained to very high standards, this site is set in a beautiful wooded valley bordering the Ourthe river. Open all the year round, the site is located on the outskirts of the attractive small town of La Roche en Ardenne in an area understandably popular with tourists. The site is large with 600 grass pitches, of which 280 are for touring units. The pitches are on level ground and all have electricity. Amenities on site include a well stocked shop, a bar and restaurant and takeaway food. In the woods and rivers close by, there are opportunities for walking, mountain biking, rafting and canoeing. The Ardennes as a region is rightly proud of its cuisine in which game, taken from the forests that cover the region is prominent; for those who really enjoy eating, a visit to a restaurant should be planned.

Facilities

Six modern, well maintained sanitary blocks provide washbasins (open and in cabins), free pre-set showers. Facilities for disabled visitors. Baby changing room. Laundry room with sinks, washing machines and dryers. Motorcaravan service point. Shop. Bar, restaurant, snack bar and takeaway. At Camping Floreal 1: outdoor heated swimming pool. Sports field. Tennis courts. Minigolf. Pétanque. Kayaks to rent. Off site: Indoor pool 800 m. Golf, riding and bicycle hire 1 km. Skiing 15 km.

Open: All year.

Directions

From E25/A26 autoroute take exit 50 and follow N89 southwest to La Roche. In La Roche follow signs for Houffalize (beside Ourthe river). Floral Club Camping 1 is 1.5 km. along this road. N.B. Go to Camping 1 not 2.

Charges 2006

Per person	€ 3,10
child (3-11 yrs)	€ 2,25
pitch incl. electricity (4A)	€ 10,40
dog (max. 1)	€ 2,75

MAP 13

Croatia

Croatia has thrown off old communist attitudes and blossomed into a lively and friendly place to visit. A country steeped in history, it boasts some of the finest Roman ruins in Europe and you'll find plenty of traditional coastal towns, clusters of tiny islands and mediaeval villages to explore.

CAPITAL: ZAGREB

Tourist Office

Croatian National Tourist Office
2 The Lanchesters
162-164 Fulham Palace Road
London W6 9ER
Tel: 0208 563 7979 Fax: 0208 563 2616
Email: info@cnto.freeserve.co.uk
Internet: www.croatia.hr

The heart-shaped peninsula of Istria, located in the north, is among the most developed tourist regions in Croatia. Here you can visit the preserved Roman amphitheatre in Pula, the beautiful town of Rovinj with its cobbled streets and wooded hills, and the resort of Umag, well-known for its recreational activities, most notably tennis. Islands are studded all around the coast, making it ideal for sailing and diving enthusiasts. Istria also has the highest concentration of campsites.

Further south, in the province of Dalmatia, Split is the largest city on the Adriatic coast and home to the impressive Diolectian's Palace. From here the islands of Brac, Hvar, Vis and Korcula, renowned for their lively fishing villages and pristine beaches, are easily accessible by ferry. The old walled city of Dubrovnik is 150 km south. At over 2 km. long and 25 m. high, with 16 towers, a walk along the city walls affords spectacular views.

Population
4.7 million

Climate
Predominantly warm and hot in summer with temperatures of up to 40°C.

Language
Croat

Telephone
The country code is 00 385.

Money
Currency: Kuna
Banks: Mon-Fri 08.00 - 19.00.

Shops
Mainly Mon-Sat 08.00-20.00, although some close on Monday.

Public Holidays
New Year's Day; Epiphany 6 Jan; Good Friday; Easter Monday; Labour Day 1 May; Parliament Day 30 May; Day of Anti-Fascist Victory 22 June; Statehood Day 25 June; Thanksgiving Day 5 Aug; Assumption 15 Aug; Independence Day 8 Oct; All Saints 1 Nov; Christmas 25, 26 Dec.

Motoring
Croatia is proceeding with a vast road improvement programme. There are still some roads which leave a lot to be desired but things have improved dramatically. Roads along the coast can become heavily congested in summer and queues are possible at border crossings. Tolls: some motorways, bridges and tunnels. Cars towing a caravan or trailer must carry two warning triangles. It is illegal to overtake military convoys.

CR6720 Naturist Centre Ulika

Cervar, HR-52440 Porec (Istria)

Tel: 052 436 325. Email: mail@plavalaguna.hr

One of the many naturist campsites in Croatia, Ulika is run by the same concern as Zelena Laguna (CR6722) and Bijela Uvala (CR6724) and offers similar facilities. The site is well located, occupying a small peninsula of some 15 hectares. This means that there is only a short walk to the sea from anywhere on the site. The ground is mostly gently sloping with a covering of rough grass and there are 388 pitches with electricity connections. One side of the site is shaded with mature trees but the other side is almost devoid of shade and could become very hot. There are many activities on site (see below) and an excellent swimming pool. The reception office opens 24 hours for help and information. Single men are not accepted. All in all, this is a pleasant, uncomplicated site which is well situated, well managed and peaceful.

Facilities

Six toilet blocks provide mostly British style WCs, washbasins (half with hot water) and showers (around a third with controllable hot water). Facilities for disabled visitors. Dishwashing and laundry sinks (half with hot water). Laundry. Motorcaravan service point. Supermarket (seven days per week). Restaurant, pizzeria and snacks. Bicycle hire. Swimming pool. Fishing. Tennis. Table tennis. Minigolf. Water sports - water skiing, windsurfing, etc. Volleyball. Boating - marina on site. Off site: Bicycle hire 3 km. Riding 15 km. Porec the nearest town is 6 km. (a must to visit) with a regular bus service running from site reception.

Open: 19 March - 7 October.

Directions

Site is about 3 km. off the main Novigrad - Porec road, signed in village of Cevar.
GPS: N45:15.424 E13:35.027

Charges guide

Per person	€ 3,70 - € 6,70
child (4-9 yrs)	free - € 4,60
pitch	€ 5,50 - € 12,80
electricity	€ 2,20 - € 3,00
dog	€ 3,00 - € 5,40

CR6722 Autokamp Zelena Laguna

HR-52440 Porec (Istria)

Tel: 052 410 101. Email: mail@plavalaguna.hr

A busy medium sized site (by Croatian standards), Zelena Laguna (green lagoon) is very popular with families and boat owners. Part of the Plava Laguna Leisure group that has three other campsites and seven hotels in the vicinity, it is long established and is improved and modernised each year as finances permit. Within the last 10 years, amongst other things, a new pool has been built. The 1,100 pitches (540 for touring units) are a mixture of level, moderately sloping and terraced ground and range in size from 40-120 sq.m. Slopes will be encountered on the site with a quite steep hill leading to the highest point allowing impressive views over the sea. Access to the pitches is by hard surfaced roads and shingle tracks which generally allow adequate space to manoeuvre. There are plenty of electrical hook-ups (10A; some German plugs in most). 42 super pitches are very popular and in other areas there is around one water point to every four pitches. Like all others in the area, Zelena Laguna can get very crowded in late June, July and August and as it can get very hot in high summer (40 degrees), the pitches nearest the sea and therefore the sea breezes, are recommended (book ahead). The sea runs along two sides of the site and has a mostly rocky beach with blue flag status into which paved sunbathing areas have been inserted. At one end of the beach is an impressive marina where visitors may park their yachts. About 25% of the beach area is reserved for naturists. There are open air showers on the beach and toilets are a short walk away. There are many attractions to amuse you here or ample opportunity to just chill out as it is quite peaceful.

Facilities

The sanitary blocks are good but being improved for 2005. About half the washbasins have hot water and there are free hot controllable showers in all blocks. Toilets are mostly British style and there are facilities for disabled campers. Supermarket and mini-market. Several restaurants and snack bars (from 1/5). Swimming pool. Sub-aqua diving (with instruction). Tennis (instruction available). Five-a-side football. Bicycle hire. Boat hire (motor and sailing). Boat launching. Beach volleyball. Riding. Aerobics. Animation programme for the family. Off site: Small market and parade of shops selling beach wares, souvenirs etc. immediately outside site. Regular bus service and also a small 'land train' into the centre of Porec. Nearest large supermarkets are in Porec (4 km). Fishing 5 km. (permit required). Riding 300 m.

Open: 19 March - 7 October.

Directions

Site is between the coast road and the sea with turning approx. 2 km. from Porec towards Vrsar. It is very well signed and is part of a large multiple hotel complex. GPS: N45:11.777 E13:35.333

Charges 2006

Per person	€ 3,80 - € 6,90
child (4-9 yrs)	€ -2,00 - € 4,80
pitch	€ 5,60 - € 13,10
electricity	€ 2,30 - € 3,10
dog	€ 3,10 - € 5,60

CR6724 Camping Bijela Uvala

Bijela Uvala, Zelena Laguna, HR-52440 Porec (Istria)

Tel: 052 410 551. Email: mail@plavalaguna.hr

Bijela Uvala is a large friendly campsite with an extensive range of facilities and direct sea access which makes the site very popular in high season. The topography of the site is undulating and the gravelled or grassy pitches are divided into zones which vary considerably. As the coastline winds along the site, the rocky and intermittently paved sea access is increased with boat launching facilities, beach volleyball and eateries dispersed along it. The 2000 pitches, 1476 for touring, are compact and due to the terrain some have excellent sea views and breezes, however as usual these are the most sought after so book early. They range from 60-120 sq.m. and all have electricity, 400 also have water connections. Some are formal with hedging, some are terraced and most have good shade from established trees or wooded areas. There is also very informal areas where pitches are not demarcated and generally on uneven ground. The smaller of the two pools is in a complex adjacent to the sea along with a large animation area where the active animation program can be seen and a family style restaurant. There are many sporting facilities and fair ground style amusements (at extra cost). The adjoining campsite Zelenga Laguna is owned by the same organisation and access to its beach (including naturist section) and facilities is via a gate between sites or along the beach. A large sports complex is also within walking distance. This site is very similar to Camping Zelegna Laguna with fewer permanent pitches.

Facilities

Eight sanitary blocks are clean and well equipped with mainly British style WCs. Free hot showers but no hot water for dishwashing or laundry. Washing machines. Facilities for disabled visitors. Motorcaravan service point. Gas. Fridge boxes. Two restaurants, three fast food cafés, two bars and a bakery. Large well equipped supermarket and a mini market. Two swimming pool complexes, one with a medium size pool and the other a larger lagoon style. Tennis. Playground. Amusements. TV room. Animation centre with active children's club. Minigolf. Boat launching and harbour. Off site: Zelenga Laguna campsite facilities. Naturist beach 25 m.

Open: 19 March - 7 October.

Directions

The site adjoins Zelena Laguna. From the main Porec to Vrsar coast road turn off towards coast and the town of Zelena Laguna approximately 4 km. south of Porec and follow campsite signs.
GPS: N45:11.515 E13:35.805

Charges 2006

Per person	€ 3,80 - € 6,90
child (4-9 yrs)	free - € 4,80
pitch	€ 5,60 - € 13,10
electricity	€ 2,30 - € 3,10
dog	€ 3,10 - € 5,60

CR6727 Camping Valkanela

Valkanela, HR-52450 Vrsar (Istria)

Tel: **052 445 216**. Email: **valkanela@maistra.hr**

Camping Valkanela is located in a beautiful green bay, right on the Adriatic Sea, between the villages of Vrsar and Funtana. It offers 1200 pitches, all with 6A electricity. Pitches near the beach are numbered, have shade from mature trees and are slightly sloping towards the sea. Those towards the back of the site are on open fields without much shade and are not marked or numbered. Most numbered pitches have water points close by, but the back pitches have to go to the toilet blocks for water. Unfortunately the number of pitches has increased dramatically over the years, many are occupied by seasonal campers and statics of every description, and parts of the site resemble a shanty town. Access roads are gravel. For those who like activity, Valkanela has four gravel tennis courts, beach volleyball and opportunities for diving, waterskiing and boat rental. There is a little marina for mooring small boats and a long rock and pebble private beach, with some grass lawns for sunbathing. It is a short stroll to the surrounding villages with their bars, restaurants and shops. There may be some noise nuisance from the disco outside the entrance and compared to most the site looks overcrowded and depressing.

Facilities

Fifteen toilet blocks of varying styles and ages provide toilets, open style washbasins and controllable hot showers. Child-size toilets, basins and showers. Bathroom (free). Facilities for disabled visitors. Laundry with sinks and washing machines. Dishwashing under cover. Two supermarkets. Souvenir shops and newspaper kiosk. Bars and restaurants with dance floor and stage. Patisserie. Tennis. Minigolf. Fishing. Bicycle hire. Games room. Marina with boat launching. Boat and pedalo hire. Disco outside entrance. Daily animation programme for children up to 12 yrs. Excursions organised. Off site: Riding 2 km.

Open: 7 April - 30 September.

Directions

Follow campsite signs from Vrsar.
GPS: N45:09.913 E13:36.434

Charges 2006

Per person	€ 4,40 - € 6,60
child (5-12 yrs)	free - € 4,80
pitch incl. electricity	€ 5,20 - € 12,90
dog	€ 3,10 - € 5,30

CR6728 Camping Orsera

HR-52450 Vrsar (Istria)

Tel: **052 441 330**. Email: **turist@riviera.hr**

Part of the Riviera group, this site is very close to the fishing port of Vrsar, and there is direct access from the site. The views of the many small islands from the site are stunning and it is very relaxing to sit on the beaches and enjoy the Croatian sunshine with a beer in your hand. The site is very proud of its beach's Blue Flag status and a safe rock pool has been created for children and a splash pool is at the base of a large flume in the beach area. This is a 30 hectare site with 833 pitches of which 593 are available to tourists. Marked and numbered, the pitches vary in size with 90 sq.m. being the average. The ground is undulating with sandy soil, grass and some terracing. There is ample shade from mature pines and oak trees, 16A electricity and 60 pitches with water and electricity. The site has no pool but a long beach area with attractive coves provide easy access for sea bathing from rock surfaces. The direct access to the old town of Vrsar is very popular.

Facilities

Three old and four new toilet blocks provide a mixture of British and Turkish style WCs, and washbasins and showers, not all with hot water. Some have facilities for disabled campers, private cabins and baby rooms. Beach bars. Laundry. Supermarket (1/5-15/9). Bar/restaurant (1/5-15/9). Sports centre. Cinema. Bicycle hire. Fishing. Off site: Golf 7 km. Riding 3 km. Excursions. Shops in Vrsar, although the nearest main shopping centre is Porec.

Open: 22 March - 15 October.

Directions

Site is on the main Porec (7 km.) - Vrsar (1 km.) road, well signed. GPS: N45:09.323 E13:36.639

Charges guide

Per person	€ 3,80 - € 6,65
child (5-10 yrs)	€ 2,75 - € 4,75
pitch incl. 10A electricity	€ 6,30 - € 17,55
dog	€ 3,30 - € 4,55

Highest prices are for pitches by the sea.

CR6725 Camping Porto Sole

Porto Sole, HR-52450 Vrsar (Istria)

Tel: **052 441 198**. Email: **petalon-portosole@maistra.hr**

Located near the pretty town of Vrsar and its charming marina, Porto Sole is a large campsite with 800 pitches. The pitches vary, some are in the open with semi shade and are fairly flat, others are under a heavy canopy of pines on undulating land. There is some terracing near the small number of water frontage pitches. The site could be described as almost a clover leaf shape with one area for rental accommodation and natural woods, another for sporting facilities and the other two for pitches. There is a large water frontage and two tiny bays provide delightful sheltered rocky swimming areas. In peak season the site is buzzing with activity and the hub of the site is the pools, disco and shopping arcade area where there is also a pub and both formal and informal eating areas. The food available is varied but simple with a tiny terrace restaurant by the water.

Facilities

Five older style toilet blocks with British and Turkish style WCs were clean and well maintained. The low numbers of showers (common to most Croatian sites) result in long queues. Facilities for disabled visitors. Washing machines, dishwashing and laundry (cold water). Large well stocked supermarket. Small shopping mall. Pub. Pizzeria. Formal and informal restaurants. Swimming pools. Play area (alongside beach). Boules. Tennis. Minigolf. Massage studio. Disco. Animation in season. Scuba diving courses. Boat launching. Off site: Marina 1 km. Vrsar 2 km.

Open: 1 April - 1 October.

Directions

Follow signs towards Vrsar and take turn towards Koversada, then follow campsite signs.
GPS: N45:08.527 E13:36.136

Charges 2006

Per person	€ 4,50 - € 6,40
child (5-12 yrs)	€ -2,00 - € 4,20
pitch	€ 6,40 - € 13,00
dog	€ 3,10 - € 5,30

Camping Cheques accepted.

CR6729 Naturist Camping Koversada

Koversada, HR-52450 Vrsar (Istria)

Tel: **052 441 378**. Email: **koversada-camp@maistra.hr**

According to history, the first naturist on Koversada was the famous adventurer Casanova. Today Koversada is an enclosed holiday park for naturists with bungalows, 1,700 pitches (700 for tourers, all with 6/8A electricity), a shopping centre and its own island. The main attraction of this site is the Koversada island, connected to the mainland by a small bridge. It is only suitable for tents, but has a restaurant and two toilet blocks. Between the island and the mainland is an enclosed, shallow section of water for swimming and, the other side of the bridge, an area for mooring small boats. The pitches are of average size on grass and gravel ground and slightly sloping. Pitches on the mainland are numbered and partly terraced under mature pine and olive trees. Pitching on the island is haphazard, but there is also shade from mature trees. The bottom row of pitches on the mainland have views over the island and the sea. The site is surrounded by a long beach, part sand, part paved.

Facilities

Seventeen toilet blocks provide British and Turkish style toilets, washbasins and controllable hot showers. Child-size toilets and basins. Family bathroom (free). Facilities for disabled visitors. Dishwashing under cover. Laundry service. Supermarket. Kiosks with newspapers and tobacco. Several bars and restaurants. Playing field. Tennis. Minigolf. Fishing. Boats, surf boards, canoes and kayaks for hire. Paragliding. 'Tweety club' for children. Live music. Sports tournaments. Off site: Riding 2 km.

Open: 15 April - 30 September.

Directions

Site is just south from Vrsar. From Vrsar, follow site signs. GPS: N45:08.573 E13:36.316

Charges 2006

Per person	€ 4,60 - € 6,40
child (5-11 yrs)	free - € 3,80
child (12-18 yrs)	€ 3,20 - € 4,50
pitch	€ 6,20 - € 15,00
dog	€ 3,10 - € 5,30

Naturist park Koversada *Vrsar*

New pitches by the sea, Mini Clubs!

Istria
Green Mediterranean.

A Mediterranean paradise in a superb natural setting; the gentle climate and clean seas have made this a favourite summer holiday destination for many generations of naturists.

tel: +385 (0)52 441 378 / fax: 441 761 / koversada-camp@maistra.hr

www.maistra.hr   *maistra*

CR6731 Naturist Camping Valalta

Cesta Valalta-Lim bb., HR-52210 Rovinj (Istria)

Tel: **052 804 800**. Email: **valalta@valalta.hr**

When we visited in August there were 6,000 naturist campers here but there was still a pleasant open atmosphere. The passage through reception is efficient and pleasant and this feeling is maintained around the well organised site. A friendly, family atmosphere is to be found here. All pitches are the same price with 16A electricity, although they vary in size and surroundings. The variations include shade, views, sand, grass, sea frontage, level ground or terracing. It is not possible to reserve a particular pitch and campers do move pitches at will. The impressive pool is in lagoon style with water features. Unusually for Croatia, the beach has soft sand (with some help from imported sand).

Facilities

Twenty high quality new or refurbished sanitary blocks of which four are smaller units of plastic 'pod' construction. Hot showers (coin operated). Facilities for disabled campers. Washing machines. Supermarket. Four restaurants. Pizzeria. Two bars. Large lagoon style pool complex. Doctor. Beauty saloon. Running track. Minigolf. Tennis. Football. Bocce. Sailing. Play area. Bicycle hire. Beach. Beach volleyball. Boat launching. Diving club. Windsurfing. Internet. Animation all season. Animals are not allowed. Off site: Gas close by. Riding 7 km.

Open: 24 April - 2 October.

Directions

Site is located on the coast 8 km. north of Rovinj. If approaching from the north turn inland (follow signs to Rovinj) to drive around the Limski Kanal. Then follow signs towards Valalta about 2 km. east of Rovinji. Site is at the end of the road and is well signed. GPS: N45:07.334 E13:37.848

Charges 2007

Per person	€ 5,00 - € 8,00
child (3-14 yrs)	free - € 4,00
pitch	€ 7,50 - € 13,50

CR6730 Camping Amarin

Monsena bb, HR-52210 Rovinj (Istria)

Tel: 052 802 000. Email: ac-amarin@maistra.hr

Situated 4 km. from the centre of the lovely old port town of Rovinj this site has much to offer. The complex is part of Maistra. It has 12.6 hectares of land and is adjacent to the Amarin bungalow complex, campers can take advantage of the facilities afforded by both areas. There are 670 pitches for touring units on various types of ground and between 80-120 sq.m. Most are separated by foliage, 10A electricity is available. A rocky beach backed by a grassy sunbathing area is very popular, but the site has its own superb, supervised round pool with corkscrew slide plus a splash pool for children. Boat owners have a mooring area and launching ramp, and a breakwater is popular with sunbathers. The port of Rovinj contains many delights, particularly if you are able to contend with the hundreds of steps which lead to the church above the town from where the views are well worth the climb.

Facilities

Thirteen toilet blocks have a mixture of British style and Turkish toilets. Half the washbasins have hot water. Some showers have hot water, the rest have cold and are outside. Some blocks have one private cabin on the female side and a unit for disabled visitors (shower, toilet and washbasin). Fridge boxes for hire. Washing machines. Security boxes. Drive over motorcaravan service point (key for hose from reception). Waste bins are emptied daily using an electric powered silent vehicle. Supermarket. Small market selling beach wares, and fresh fruit and vegetables. Two restaurants, taverna, pizzeria and terrace grill. Swimming pool. Flume and splash pool. Watersports. Bicycle hire. Fishing (subject to permit). Daily animation for children and adults. Barbecues are not accepted. Hairdresser. Massage. Off site: Hourly minibus service to Rovinj. Excursions from site including day trips to Venice. Riding nearby.

Open: 20 May - 23 September.

Directions

Follow signs towards Rovinj and if approaching from the north turn off about 2 km. before the town towards Amarin and Valalta. Then follow signs to Amarin and the campsite.
GPS: N45:06.556 E13:37.169

Charges 2006

Per person	€ 4,00 - € 6,60
child (5-12 yrs)	free - € 3,30
pitch incl. electricity	€ 6,00 - € 11,00
dog	€ 3,10 - € 5,30

For stays less than 3 nights in high season add 10%.

Camping Amarin *Rovinj*   Istria Green Mediterranean.   CROATIA

Family package includes Acquagun, Sport, Gratis for children, entertainment programmes!

The unique natural environment here is only one small piece of the larger picture for a summer holiday filled with magical experiences.

tel: +385 (0)52 802 000 / fax: 813 354 / ac-amarin@maistra.hr   www.maistra.hr   *maistra*

67

CR6732 Camping Polari

Polari bb, HR-52210 Rovinj (Istria)

Tel: **052 801 501**. Email: **crs@maistra.hr**

This 60 hectare site has facilities for both textile and naturist campers, the latter having a reserved area of 12 hectares called Punta Eva. Prime places are taken by permanent customers but there are some numbered pitches which are better. Swimming pools have been added and since our last visit we are informed that there have been many improvements.

Facilities

We have been informed by the site that new sanitary facilities have been added. Washing up and laundry sinks. Washing machines and dryers. Laundry service including ironing. Two shops, one large and one small, one restaurant and snack bar. Tennis. Volleyball, basketball, minigolf and table tennis. Some children's animation with all major European languages spoken. Off site: Riding 1 km. Five buses daily to and from Rovinj (3 km).

Open: 25 March - 30 September.

Directions

From any access road to Rovinj look for red signs to AC Polari (amongst other destinations). The site is about 3 km. south of Rovinj.
GPS: N45:03.815 E13:40.468

Charges 2006

Per person	€ 3,90 - € 6,90
child (5-11 yrs)	free - € 3,45
pitch incl. electricity	€ 5,50 - € 12,00

For stays less than 3 nights in high season add 20%. Camping Cheques accepted.

Camping Polari *Rovinj*   Istria   CROATIA

Motor Caravan parking, Mini Clubs!

A picturesque cove, ideal for all those who relish the pleasant shade of olive trees and the cleanest sea in the Mediterranean.

tel: +385 (0)52 801 501 / fax: 811 395 / e-mail: polari@maistra.hr   www.maistra.hr   *maistra*

CR6742 Camping Stoja

Stoja 37, HR-52100 Pula (Istria)

Tel: **052 387 144**. Email: **marketing@arenaturist.hr**

Camping Stoja in Pula, one of the famous little Istrian harbour towns, is on a little peninsula and therefore almost completely surrounded by the waters of the clear Adriatic. In the centre of the site is the old Fort Stoja, built in 1884 for coastal defence. Some of its buildings are now used as a toilet block or laundry and its courtyard is used by the animation team. The pitches here vary greatly in size (50-120 sq.m) and are marked by round, concrete, numbered blocks and separated by young trees. About half have shade from mature trees and all are slightly sloping on grass and gravel. Pitches close to the pebble and rock beach have beautiful views of the sea and Pula. This site is an ideal base for visiting Pula, considered to be the capital of Istrian tourism and full of history, tradition and natural beauty, including a spectacular Roman Coliseum.

Facilities

Five toilet blocks with British and Turkish style toilets, open plan washbasins with cold water only and controllable hot showers. Child-size basins. Facilities for disabled visitors. Laundry and ironing service. Fridge box hire. Dishwashing under cover. Dog shower. Chemical disposal. Motorcaravan service pioint. Supermarket. Bar/restaurant. Mini club and teen club. Bicycle hire. Waterskiing. Boat hire. Boat launching. Surfboard and pedalo hire. Island excursions. Off site: Pula (walking distance).

Open: 24 March - 1 November.

Directions

From Pula follow site signs.
GPS: N44:51.583 E13:48.870

Charges guide

Per person	€ 2,70 - € 6,00
child (2-12 yrs)	€ 1,50 - € 3,10
pitch	€ 2,20 - € 8,80
with electricity	€ 4,60 - € 14,20
dog	€ 1,90 - € 3,50

CR6733 Camping Vestar

HR-52210 Rovinj (Istria)

Tel: 052 800 250. Email: **crs@maistra.hr**

Camping Vestar, just 5 km. from the historic harbour town of Rovinj, is one of the rare sites in Croatia with a partly sandy beach. Right behind the beach is a large area, attractively landscaped with young trees and shrubs, with grass for sunbathing. The site has 750 large pitches, of which 600 are for tourers, all with 16A electricity (the rest being taken by seasonal units and 14 pitches for tour operators). It is largely wooded with good shade and from the bottom row of pitches there are views of the sea. Pitching is on two separate fields, one for free camping, the other with numbered pitches. The pitches at the beach are in a half circle around the shallow bay, making it safe for children to swim. Vestar has a small marina and a jetty for mooring small boats and excursions to the islands are arranged. There is a miniclub and live music with dancing at one of the two bar/restaurants in the evenings. The restaurants all have open air terraces, one covered with vines to protect you from the hot sun.

Facilities

Five modern and one refurbished toilet block with mainly Turkish style toilets and some British style, open washbasins and controllable hot showers. Child-size basins. Family bathroom. Facilities for disabled people. Laundry service. Fridge box hire. Motorcaravan services. Shop. Two bar/restaurants. Large pool. Playground. Tennis. Fishing. Boat and pedalo hire. Miniclub (5-11 yrs). Excursions. Off site: Riding 2 km. Rovinj 5 km.

Open: 1 May - 1 October.

Directions

Follow site signs from Rovinj.
GPS: N45:03.259 E13:41.141

Charges 2006

| Per person | € 3,90 - € 7,50 |
| child (5-11 yrs) | free - € 3,75 |

Camping Veštar *Rovinj*

GRATIS – children up to 7 years old, senior discount, luxurious sanitary facilities, pitches with drainage!

Istria Green Mediterranean.

This campsite has a special charm – a warm welcome is guaranteed, in a stunning beachside setting.

tel: +385 (0)52 829-150 / fax: 829 151 / e-mail: vestar@maistra.hr   www.maistra.hr   *maistra*

CR6745 Camping Bi-Village

Dragonja 115, HR-52212 Fazana (Istria)

Tel: 052 380 700. Email: **bivillage@inet.hr**

Camping Bi Village is large new holiday village, close to the historic town of Pula and opposite the Brioni National Park. The location is excellent and there are some superb sunsets. The site is landscaped with many flowers, shrubs and rock walls and offers 1,522 pitches, of which 922 pitches are for tourers, the remainder being taken by bungalows and chalets. The campsite is separated from the holiday bungalows by the main site road, that runs from the entrance to the beach. Pitching is off long, gravel lanes, slightly sloping towards the sea, with only the pitches at the bottom having shade from mature trees and good views over the Adriatic. Pitches are separated by young trees and shrubs, which have difficulty growing in the hot Croatian climate. Bi Village has a long pebble beach, but also offers two attractive, new swimming pools with a fun pool, a whirlpool, slides and flumes.

Facilities

Four modern toilet blocks with toilets, open plan washbasins and controllable hot showers. Baby room. Facilities for disabled visitors. Washing machine. Shopping centre. Several bars and restaurants. Two swimming pools. Playground on gravel. Tennis. Minigolf. Fishing. Jet skis, motorboats and pedaloes for hire. Sports tournaments and professional entertainment. Internet.

Open: All year.

Directions

Follow no. 2 road south from Rijeka to Pula. In Pula follow site signs. Site is close to Fazana.
GPS: N44:55.075 E13:48.643

Charges guide

Per person	€ 4,00 - € 7,50
child	€ 2,80 - € 4,00
pitch	€ 7,00 - € 16,00

Camping Cheques accepted.

69

CR6765 Camping Kovacine

Cres, HR-51557 Cres Island (Kvarner)

Tel: **051 573 150**. Email: **campkovacine@kovacine.com**

Camp Kovacine is located on a peninsula on the beautiful Dalmatian island Cres, just 2 km. from the town of Cres. Kovacine has 417 numbered, mostly level pitches, of which 382 are for tourers (300 with 10A electricity). On sloping ground, partially shaded by mature olive and pine trees. Pitching is on the large, open spaces between the trees. Some places have views of the Valun lagoon. Kovacine is partly an FKK (naturist) site, which is quite common in Croatia, and has a pleasant atmosphere. Here one can enjoy Croatian camping with local live music on a stage close to the pebble beach, where there is also a restaurant and bar. The site has its own private beach, part concrete, part pebbles, and a jetty for mooring boats and fishing. It is close to the historic town of Cres, the main town on the island, which offers a rich history in fishing, shipyards and authentic Dalmatian style houses. There are also several bars, restaurants and shops.

Facilities

Five modern, comfortable toilet blocks (two refurbished) offer British style toilets, open plan washbasins (some cabins for ladies) and hot showers. Bathroom for hire. Facilities for disabled people (although access is difficult). Laundry sinks and washing machine. Fridge box hire. Dishwashing under cover. Motorcaravan service point. Dog shower. Car wash. Supermarket. Bar, restaurant and pizzeria. Playground. Daily children's club. Evening shows with live music. Boat launching. Fishing. Diving centre. Motor boat hire. Off site: Historic town of Cres with bars, restaurants and shops 2 km.

Open: 15 April - 15 October.

Directions

From Rijeka take no. 2 road south towards Labin and take ferry to Cres at Brestova. Continue to Cres and follow site signs. GPS: N44:57.713 E14:23.790

Charges 2006

Per person	€ 4,60 - € 9,40
child (3-11 yrs)	€ 2,20 - € 3,40
pitch	€ 3,80 - € 8,00
dog	€ 1,00 - € 3,00

CR6768 Camping Slatina

Martinscica, HR-51556 Cres Island (Kvarner)

Tel: **051 574 127**. Email: **info@camp-slatina.com**

Camping Slatina lies about halfway along the island of Cres, beside the fishing port of Martinscica on a bay of the Adriatic Sea. It has 370 pitches for tourers, some with 10A electricity, off very steep, tarmac access roads, sloping down to the sea. The pitches are large and level on a gravel base and enjoy plenty of shade from mature laurel trees, although hardly any have views. Whilst there is plenty of privacy, the site does have an enclosed feeling. Some pitches in the lower areas have water, electricity and drainage. Like so many sites in Croatia, Slatina has a private diving centre, which will take you to the remote island of Lastovo. Lastovo is surrounded by reefs and little islands and the crystal clear waters of the Adriatic make it perfect for diving. Martinscica owes its name to the medieval church of the Holy Martin and has a Glagolite monastery, standing next to the 17th century castle, built by the Patrician Sforza. Both are well worth a visit.

Facilities

Two new and three refurbished toilet blocks provide toilets, open style washbasins and controllable hot showers. Facilities for disabled visitors. Laundry with sinks and washing machine. Fridge box hire. Dishwashing under cover. Dog shower. Car wash. Shop. Bar, restaurant, grill restaurant, pizzeria and fish restaurant. Playground. Minigolf. Fishing. Bicycle hire. Diving centre. Boat launching. Beach volleyball. Pedalo, canoe and boat hire. Excursions to the 'Blue Cave'. Off site: Martinscica with bars, restaurants and shops 2 km.

Open: Easter - 31 October.

Directions

From Rijeka take no. 2 road south towards Labin and take ferry to Cres at Brestova. From Cres go south towards Martinscica and follow site signs.

Charges 2006

Per person	€ 4,09 - € 6,65
child	€ 1,02 - € 3,07
pitch	€ 3,40 - € 7,00
dog	€ 1,02 - € 1,53

CR6736 Camping Valdaliso

Monsena bb,, HR-52210 Rovinj (Istria)

Tel: **052 815 025**. Email: **info@rovinjturist.hr**

Unusually Valdaliso Camping has its affiliated hotel in the centre of the site. The advantage for campers is that they can use the hotel and, as breakfast is served there but not in the restaurant, it may appeal to some. The fine Barabiga restaurant within the hotel offers superb Istrian and fish cuisine and the pool is also within the hotel. You are close to the beautiful old town of Rovinj and parts of this site enjoy views of the town. A water taxi makes exploring Rovinj very easy, compared with the impossible parking for private cars. A bus service is also provided but this involves much walking. The pitches are mostly flat with shade from pine trees and the site is divided into three sections all with 16A electricity. The choice of formal numbered pitches, informal camping or proximity to the sea impacts on the prices. The kilometre plus of beach has crystal clear water and a pebble beach. The animation programme is extremely professional and there is a lot to do at Valdaliso, which is aimed primarily at families. The variety of activities here and the bonus of the use of the hotel make this a great choice for campers

Facilities

Two large clean sanitary blocks have hot showers (coin operated), The northeastern block has facilities for disabled campers. Hotel facilities. Shop. Pizzeria. Restaurant. Table tennis. Volleyball. Basketball. Tennis. Fitness centre. Games room. Billiards. Children's games. Bicycle hire. Summer painting courses. Exchange. Water taxi. Bus service. Boat rental. Watersports. Boat launching. Fishing. Diving school. Internet. Animals are not accepted. Off site: Town 1 km. Excursions.

Open: 23 March - 15 October.

Directions

Follow signs to Rovinj on the main coast road then turn north 2 km. west of Rovinj and follow signs towards Monsena and campsite signs.
GPS: N45:06.256 E13:37.511

Charges 2006

Per person	€ 3,50 - € 6,00
child (7-12 yrs)	€ 2,00 - € 3,30
pitch	€ 5,50 - € 13,50

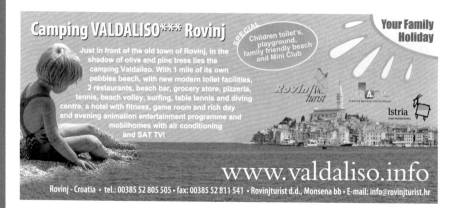

CR6761 Camp Zablace

E. Geistlicha 38, HR-51523 Baska (Kvarner)

Tel: **051 856 909**. Email: **ac-zablace@hotelibaska.hr**

Camping Zablace is at the southern end of the beautiful island of Krk, in the ancient ferry port of Baöka. Like most sites in Croatia it has direct access to a large, pebble beach and from the bottom row of pitches one has views over the Adriatic and the little island Koöljun with its Franciscan Monastery. The site has 500 pitches with 400 used for touring units. Zone 1 (nearest the beach) provides 200 individual pitches with electricity and water. The quietest zone, if further away (and across a public road that splits the site in two) has electricity and water taps. There is not much shade anywhere. There are not many amenities on the site, but it is an easy five minute walk along the promenade to the centre of Baöka where there are bars, restaurants and pizzerias.

Facilities

Four toilet blocks (three new, one old) with toilets, open plan basins and controllable hot showers (key access for the toilets nearest the beach; € 5 deposit). Facilities for disabled visitors. Motocaravan service point. Shop. Kiosks with fruit, cold drinks, tobacco, newspapers and beach wear. Fishing. Off site: Tennis and minigolf 200 m.

Open: Easter - 15 October.

Directions

On Krk follow 29 road south to Baöka. Follow site signs from Baöka (site is well signed).
GPS: N44:57.879 E14:44.858

Charges 2006

Per person	€ 4,00 - € 5,00
child (7-11 yrs)	€ 2,00 - € 2,50
pitch with electricity	€ 9,40 - € 10,50

CR6845 Camp Adriatic

Huljerat b.b., HR-22202 Primosten (Dalmatia)
Tel: **022 571223**. Email: **info@camp-adriatic.hr**

As we drove south down the Dalmatian coast road, we looked across a clear turquoise bay and saw a few tents, caravans and motorcaravans camped under some trees. A short distance later we were at the entrance of Camping Adriatic. With 500 pitches that slope down to the sea, the site is deceptive and enjoys a one kilometre beach frontage which is ideal for snorkelling and diving. Close to the delightful town of Primosten (with a taxi boat service in high season) the site boasts good modern amenities and a fantastic location. Tour operators use some pitches on the sea front and there are 20 wooden chalets to rent at the back of the site. Most pitches are level and have shade from pine trees. There are 212 numbered pitches and 288 unnumbered, all with 10/16A electricity.

Facilities

Four modern sanitary blocks provide clean toilets, hot showers and washbasins. Facilities for disabled visitors. Bathroom for children. Washing machine and dryer. Kitchen facilities. Small supermarket (15/5-30/9). Restaurant and bar (all season). Beach. Diving school. Sailing school and boat hire. Entertainment programme in July/Aug. Internet point. New sports centre and mini-club for children.

Open: 1 May - 15 October.

Directions

Take the new A1 motorway south and leave at the Sibenik exit. Follow the 33 road into Sibenik and then go south along the coast road (no. 8), signed Primosten. Site is 2.5 km. north of Primosten. GPS: N43:36.391 E15:55.257

Charges 2006

Per person	Kn 30,00 - 42,00
child (5-12 yrs)	Kn 20,00 - 25,00
pitch	Kn 30,00 - 58,00

Camping Cheques accepted.

CR6850 Camp Seget

Hrvatskih zrtava 121, HR-21218 Seget Donji (Dalmatia)
Tel: **021 880394**. Email: **kamp@kamp-seget.hr**

Seget is a pleasant, quiet site with only 120 pitches, just 2 km. from the interesting old harbour town of Trogir. It is an ideal base for exploring this part of the Dalmatian Coast, or for visiting Trogir and Split. The site is set up on both sides of a tarmac access lane that runs down to the Adriatic Sea. Pitches to the left are off three separate, gravel lanes. They are fairly level and from most there are views of the sea. Pitches to the right are slightly sloping and mostly used for tents. Of reasonable size (50-80 sq.m) the pitches are on grass and gravel (firm tent pegs may be needed), mostly in the shade of mature fig and palm trees. All have access to 16A electricity (long leads may be necessary). To the front of the site a paved promenade gives access to the pebble beach. Via the promenade it is an easy five minute stroll to the first restaurants (we can recommend Frankie's), where you can enjoy good quality, good value meals.

Facilities

One good and one 'portacabin' style toilet block with British style toilets, open style washbasins and controllable, hot showers (free). Campers' kitchen. Fridge box hire. Shop. Beach. Fishing. Boat rental. Barbecues permitted only on communal area. Off site: Golf, riding and bicycle hire 1 km. Boat launching 500 m.

Open: 15 April - 15 October.

Directions

Follow no. 8 coastal road south towards Split and in Trogir follow site signs. Site is signed on the right. It is a sharp right and a descending bend off the main road. GPS: N43:31.116 E16:13.450

Charges 2006

Per person	€ 2,65 - € 3,30
child (5-12 yrs)	€ 1,90 - € 2,30
pitch incl. car	€ 5,00 - € 8,10
electricity	€ 2,00

73

MAP 7

The Czech Republic is a land full of fascinating castles, romantic lakes and valleys, picturesque medieval squares and famous spas. It is divided into two main regions, Bohemia to the west and Moravia in the east.

CAPITAL: PRAGUE

Tourist Office

Czech Tourist Authority
95 Great Portland Street, London W1N 5RA
Tel. 020 7291 9925 Fax. 020 7436 8300
Email: ctainfo@czechcentre.org.uk
Internet: www.visitczech.cz

Although small, the Czech Republic is crammed with attractive places to explore. Indeed, since the new country first appeared on the map in 1993, Prague has become one the most popular cities to visit in Europe. Steeped in history with museums, architectural sights, art galleries, and theatres, it is an enchanting place. The beautiful region of Bohemia, known for its Giant Mountains, is popular for skiing, hiking and other sports. The town of Karlovy Vary, world famous for its regenerative waters, is Bohemia's oldest Spa town, with 12 hot springs containing elements that are said to treat digestive and metabolic ailments. It also has many picturesque streets to meander through and peaceful riverside walks. Moravia is quieter, the most favoured area Brno and from here it is easy to explore historical towns such as Olomouc and Kromeriz. North of Brno is the Moravian Karst, with around 400 caves created by the underground Punkya River. Some caves are open to the public, with boat trips along the river and out of the caves.

Population

10.3 million

Climate

Temperate, continental climate with four distinct seasons. Warm in summer with cold, snowy winters.

Language

The official language is Czech.

Telephone

The country code is 00420.

Money

Currency: The Koruna
Banks: Mon-Fri 0830-1630.

Shops

Mon-Fri 08.00-18.00, some close at lunchtime. Sat 09.00 until midday.

Public Holidays

New Year; Easter Mon; May Day; Prague Uprising 5 May; National Day 8 May; Saints Day 5 July; Festival (John Huss) Day 6 July; Independence Day 28 Oct; Democracy Day 17 Nov; Christmas 24-26 Dec.

Motoring

There is a good and well signposted road network throughout the Republic and, although stretches of cobbles still exist, surfaces are generally good. An annual road tax is levied on all vehicles using Czech motorways and express roads, and a disc can be purchased at border crossings, post offices and filling stations. Do not drink any alcohol before driving. Dipped headlights are compulsory throughout winter months. Always give way to trams and buses.

CZ4850 Camp Sokol Troja

Trojská 171A, CZ-17100 Praha (Prague)

Tel: **233 542 908**

This site is very close to the Vltava river although you cannot see it. It was subject to heavy flooding in 2002 and some of the facilities were washed away. The is clearly a continuing risk of flooding so care is needed when visiting this site. Nevertheless, it is only a 15 or 20 minute journey to the centre of the city by bus (stop in front of the site) or tram no. 17 (300 m. walk). Unlike many of the municipal sites near Prague, this site has few facilities and little entertainment. There are 75 touring pitches (10 with 16A electricity). The pitches are small (80-90 sq.m) and can become muddy with rain. The access road is narrow and manoeuvring space is limited so the site may be less suitable for large caravans and motorhomes. The site restaurant serves real Czech meals at very reasonable prices (many locals eat here) - you don't have to go to town for good value meals.

Facilities	Directions
The single, refurbished toilet block is a good provision with toilets, washbasins with hot and cold water and pre-set showers in cabins without curtain or door. Cleaning can be variable. Facilities for disabled people. Dishwashing and laundry sinks (free hot water). Campers' kitchen with hob. Good restaurant. Off site: Fishing 1 km.	From Dresden or Teplice, follow signs to the centre and turn right before the first bridge over the Moldau into the Kozlovka Pátkova, in the Troja district. Site is well signed from here. GPS: N50:07.010 E14:25.500

Open: All year.

Charges 2006

Per person	CZK 105 - 120
child (under 18 yrs)	CZK 70 - 80
caravan	CZK 120 - 190
motorcaravan	CZK 170 - 200
electricity	CZK 100

CZ4840 Camping Oase Praha

Zlatniky - Liben, CZ-25241 Dolni Brezany (Prague)

Tel: **241 932 044**. Email: **post@campoase.cz**

Camping Oase Praha is an exceptional site, only five kilometres from Prague and with easy access. You can take the bus (from outside the site) or drive to the underground stop (10 minutes). The site has 100 pitches, all around 100 sq.m, with 6A electricity and 60 with water and drainage, on level, well kept fields. The site is very well kept and has just everything one may expect, including a new toilet block, a well maintained pool and separate paddling pool, a restaurant and a bar. The main attraction here is, of course, the Czech capital. However, this site will provide a relaxing environment to return to and another advantage is that Mr Hess, the helpful owner, speaks English.

Facilities	Directions
An outstanding, new toilet block includes washbasins (open style and in cabins) with hot and cold water, spacious, controllable showers and child size toilets. Facilities for disabled visitors. Laundry with washing machines and dryer. Campers kitchen with hob, fridge and freezer. Motorcaravan services. Restaurant and bar. Simple shop. Swimming pool (9 x 15 m) and paddling pool with slide (both 1/6-31/8). New adventure style playgrounds. Trampolines. Minigolf. Internet point. TV and video. Board games. Bicycle hire. Closed circuit security cameras. Barbecues are permitted. Off site: Fishing 2 km. Riding 3 km. Golf 10 km. Boat launching 15 km.	Go southeast from Prague on the D1 towards Brno and take exit 11 to Jesenice via road 101. At Jesenice turn right then immediately left, following camping signs to the site in Zlatn'ky where you turn left at the roundabout. Site is 700 m.

Charges 2007

Per person	CZK 120
child (under 12 yrs)	CZK 90
pitch incl. electricity	CZK 220 - 650
tent and car	CZK 150

Less 20% discount 15/4-31/5 and 1/9-30/9.
Less 3% discount for payment in cash.
Camping Cheques accepted.

Open: 20 April - 20 September.

CZ4780 Autocamping Konopiste

CZ-25601 Benesov u Prahy (Stredocesky)

Tel: **317 729 083**. Email: **reserve@cckonopiste.cz**

Benesov's chief claim to fame is the Konopiste Palace, the last home of Archduke Franz Ferdinand whose assassination in Sarajevo sparked off the First World War in 1914. Konopiste, now under new ownership, is part of a motel complex with excellent facilities situated in a very quiet, tranquil location south of Prague. On a hillside, rows of terraces separated by hedges provide 65 grassy pitches of average size, 50 with electricity. However, 34 are occupied all year by a tour operator's tents. One of the best Czech campsites, Konopiste has much to offer those who stay there. A fitness centre and heated pool are shared with motel guests. The whole complex has a well tended air.

Facilities

The good quality sanitary block is central to the caravan pitches. Washing machine and irons. Kitchen. Site's own bar/buffet (high season) with simple meals and basic food items. Motel bar and two restaurants (all year). Swimming pool (1/6-31/8). Tennis. Minigolf. Bicycle hire. Badminton. Fitness centre. Playground. Club room with TV. Chateau and park. Off site: Shop 200 m. Fishing 1.5 km. Riding 5 km. Prague 48 km. (public transport available).

Open: 1 May - 30 September.

Directions

Site is signed near the village of Benesov on the main Prague - Ceske Budejovic road no. 3/E55.

Charges 2006

Per person	CZK 90 - 120
child (6-15 yrs)	CZK 50 - 90
pitch incl. electricity	CZK 150 - 390
dog	CZK 50

CZ4820 Caravan Camp Valek

Chrustenice 155, CZ-26712 Lodenice (Stredocesky)

Tel: **311 672 147**. Email: **info@campvalek.cz**

Only 2.5 km. from the E50 motorway, this well maintained, family owned site creates a peaceful, friendly base enjoyed by families. Surrounded by delightful countryside, it is possible to visit Prague even though it is about 28 km. from the city centre. It is best to use public transport. The medium sized, gently sloping grass site is divided in two by a row of well established trees (some shade) and the toilet block. Most pitches are relatively flat, in the open and not specifically marked. However this does not appear to cause overcrowding and generally there is plenty of space. Some places have pleasant views of the sunbathing area in front of the pool with a pine-forested hillock as a backdrop.

Facilities

The single clean toilet block has limited numbers of toilets and showers, but during our visit in high season coped well. Small shop. Good waiter service restaurant with terrace. Natural swimming pool (20 x 60 m). Extensive games room with arcade machines and internet. Live musical nights on Saturday. Tennis. Off site: Prague 28 km. Plzen 69 km.

Open: 1 May - 30 September.

Directions

From E50 (D5) motorway take exit 10 for Lodenice. Follow camping signs and or Chrustenice. Site is 300 m. on right on leaving Chrustenice. GPS: N50:00.687 E14:09.033

Charges 2006

Per unit with 2 persons	CZK 75 - 155
extra person	CZK 110
electricity	CZK 90

Less 10% in May and Sept.

CZ4690 Camping Slunce

CZ-47107 Zandov (Severocesky)

Tel: **487 861116**

Away from larger towns, near the border with the former East Germany, this is pleasant rural country with a wealth of Gothic and Renaissance castles. Zandov has nothing of particular interest but Camping Slunce is a popular campsite with local Czech people. There is room for about 50 touring units with 35 electrical connections (12A) on the level, circular camping area which has a hard road running round. Outside this circle are wooden bungalows and tall trees. The general building at the entrance houses all the facilities including reception.

Facilities

The satisfactory toilet block is good by Czech standards. Kitchen with electric rings, full gas cooker and fridges. Restaurant (all year) but under separate management has live music during high season. Kiosk for basics (May - Sept). Tennis. Swimming pool. Mountain bike hire. Playground. Barbecues are not permitted. Dogs are not accepted. Off site: Fishing 1 km. Riding 2 km.

Open: 15 May - 28 August.

Directions

Zandov is 20 km. from Decin and 12 km. from Ceske Lipa on the 262 road. Signed in the centre of Zandov village. GPS: N50:40.281 E14:24.179

Charges guide

Per person	CZK 52 - 64
piitch	CZK 104 - 128
electricity per kWh	CZK 6

CZ4590 Holiday Park Lisci Farma

Dolni Branna 350, CZ-54362 Vrchlabi (Vychodocesky)

Tel: **499 421 473**. Email: **info@liscifarma.cz**

This is truly an excellent site that could be in Western Europe considering its amenities, pitches and welcome. However, Eurocamp Lisci Farma is a fully Czech site and has a pleasant Czech atmosphere. The helpful young manager welcomes many Dutch visitors throughout the year, but in the winter months, when local skiing is available, snow chains are essential. The 242 pitches are fairly flat, although the terrain is slightly sloping and some pitches are terraced. There is shade. The site is well equipped for the whole family to enjoy with its adventurous playground with trampolines for children, archery, beach volleyball, Russian bowling and outdoor bowling court for older youngsters. A beautiful sandy, lakeside beach is 800 m. from the entrance. The more active amongst you can go paragliding or rock climbing, with experienced people to guide you. This site is very suitable for relaxing or exploring the culture of the area. Excursions to Prague are organised and, if all the sporting possibilities are not enough, the children can take part in the activities of the entertainment team, while you are walking or cycling or enjoying live music at the Fox Saloon. The site reports the addition of completely new electrical connections, restaurant, games room and mini-market.

Facilities

Two good sanitary blocks, one new in 2005 near the entrance and another modern block next to the hotel, both include toilets, washbasins and spacious, controllable showers (on payment). Child size toilets and baby room. Toilet for disabled visitors. Launderette. Shop (15/6-15/9). Bar/snack bar. Games room. Swimming pool (6 x 12 m). Adventure style playground on grass. Trampolines. Tennis courts. Minigolf. Archery. Russian bowling. Paragliding. Rock climbing. Bicycle hire. Excursions to Prague. Shuttle bus for skiing. Off site: Fishing and beach 800 m. Riding 2 km. Golf 5 km.

Open: 1 December - 31 March and 1 May - 31 October.

Directions

Follow road no. 14 from Liberec to Vrchlabi. At the roundabout turn in the direction of Prague and site is about 1 mile on the right.
GPS: N50:36.516 E15:36.056

Charges 2007

Per person	CZK 105
child (4-14 yrs)	CZK 80
pitch incl. electricity	CZK 410 - 570
dog	CZK 90

Various discounts available in low seasons.
Camping Cheques accepted.

Holiday Park Lišči Farma
www.liscifarma.cz

Camping**** - Wintercamping**** - Hotel*** - Cottages - Restaurant - Swimmingpool
Tennis Court - Minigolf - Big Children's Playground - Adrenalin Sports - Music Nights
Ski school - Ski bus - Bustrips

Dolní Branná 350 - 543 62 - Vrchlabí - tel./fax.: 00420/ 499/ 421 656 E-mail: info@liscifarma.cz

CZ4860 Autocamping Orlice

PO Box 26, CZ-51741 Kostelec n Orlice (Vychodocesky)

Tel: **494 323 970**. Email: **orlice@wo.cz**

Kostelec does have an ancient castle and a large Ferodo factory, although not a lot else to commend it, but is a good centre from which to explore the interesting town of Hradec Kralove, East Bohemia, the Orlicke Hory and other high districts near the Polish border. Autocamping Orlice, situated on the edge of town near the swimming pool, has a river running by and is in a quiet location and a pleasant appearance. Surrounded by tall trees, the grass pitches are of generous size although not marked or numbered. There is room for 80 units, half having electricity and with shade in parts.

Facilities

The central sanitary block includes hot water in washbasins, sinks and good showers. Limited food supplies are available in a bar/lounge during July/Aug. Café/bar (15/5-30/9). Off site: Town swimming pool near (15/6-31/8). Tennis 100 m. Fishing 0.5 km. Riding 5 km.

Open: 15 May - 30 September.

Directions

Site is signed from the centre of town.
GPS: N50:06.949 E16:13.010

Charges 2006

Per person	CZK 46 - 50
child (6-14 yrs)	CZK 22 - 26
pitch incl. electricity	CZK 129 - 170

77

CZ4710 Camping Chvalsiny

Chvalsiny 321, CZ-38208 Chvalsiny (Jihocesky)

Tel: 380 739123. Email: info@campingchvalsiny.nl

Camping Chvalsiny is Dutch owned and has been developed from an old farm. It has been developed into real camping fields which are terraced and level. A newly built toilet block houses excellent facilities and everything looks well maintained. The 200 pitches are of average size but look larger because of the open nature of the terrain which also means there is little shade. Chvalsiny is a real family site and children are kept occupied with painting, crafts and stories. Older youngsters take part in soccer, volleyball and rafting competitions. The location in the middle of the Blanky Les nature reserve, part of the vast Sumava forest, provides excellent opportunities for walking, cycling and fishing but it also has a rich culture and heritage. You can visit charming villages of which Cesky Krumlov with its impressive castle and scenic centre is the most important.

Facilities

Modern, clean and well kept toilet facilities include washbasins in cabins and controllable showers (coin operated). Laundry. Dishwashing under cover. Kiosk (1/6-15/9) with bread and daily necessities. Snack bar (1/6-15/9). Play attic. Lake swimming. Climbing equipment and swings. Crafts, games, table tennis and soccer. Torches useful. Off site: Village restaurants close. Riding 10 km.

Open: 1 May - 15 September.

Directions

Take exit 114 at Passau in Germany (near the Austrian border) towards Freyung in the Czech Republic. Continue on this road to Philipsreut and take no. 4 road towards Vimperk. Turn right on no. 39 road to Horni Plana and Cesky Krumlov. Turn left 4 km. before Cesky Krumlov on no. 166 to Chvalsiny and follow camp signs through the village. GPS: N48:51.35 E14:12.51

Charges 2006

Per person	CZK 90
child (under 12 yrs)	CZK 50
pitch incl. electricity	CZK 300
No credit cards.	

CZ4650 Autocamping Luxor

Plzenska, CZ-35301 Velká Hledsebe (Zapadocesky)

Tel: 354 623 504. Email: autocamping.luxor@seznam.cz

An orderly site, near the German border, Luxor is adequate as a stopover for a couple of days. Now under new management, it is in a quiet location by a small lake on the edge of the village of Velká Hled'sebe, four kilometres from Marianbad. The 100 pitches (60 for touring units) are in the open on one side of the entrance road (cars stand on a tarmac park opposite the caravans) or in a clearing under tall trees away from the road. All pitches have access to electricity (10A) but connection in the clearings section may require long leads. Forty bungalows occupy one side of the site. There is little to do here but it is a good location for visiting the spa town of Marianbad.

Facilities

Toilet buildings are old and should be refurbished, but the provision is more than adequate. Cleaning could be better. No chemical disposal point. Restaurant with self-service terrace (1/5-30/9). Rest room with TV, kitchen and dining area. Small playground. Fishing. Bicycle hire. Off site: Very good motel restaurant and shops 500 m. in village. Riding 5 km. Golf 8 km.

Open: 1 May - 31 September.

Directions

Site is directly by the Stribo - Cheb road no. 21, 500 m. south of Velká Hledsebe. GPS: N49:57.145 E12:40.100

Charges 2006

Per unit incl. 2 persons and electricity	CZK 301 - 343
extra person	CZK 53
child (under 10 yrs)	free
No credit cards.	

MAP 6

Denmark offers a diverse landscape all within a relatively short distance. The countryside is green and varied with flat plains, rolling hills, fertile farmland, many lakes and fjords, wild moors and long beaches, interrupted by pretty villages and towns.

Denmark

CAPITAL: COPENHAGEN

Tourist Office

The Danish Tourist Board
55 Sloane Street, London SW1X 9SY
Tel: 020 7259 5959.
Fax: 020 7259 5955
Email: dtb.london@dt.dk
Internet: www.visitdenmark.com

Denmark is the easiest of the Scandinavian countries to visit, both in terms of cost and distance. There are many small islands but the main land masses that make up the country are the islands of Zeeland and Funen and the peninsula of Jutland, which extends northwards from the German border. Zeeland is the most visited region, its main draw being the capital, Copenhagen. This vibrant city has a beautiful old centre, an array of museums and art galleries plus a boisterous night life. Funen is the smaller of the two main islands and known as the Garden of Denmark, with its neat green fields and fruit and vegetable plots. Sandy beaches and quaint villages can be found here. Jutland has the most varied landscape ranging from heather-clad moors, dense forests to plunging gorges. It's also home to one of the most popular attractions in Denmark, Legoland, and the oldest town in Scandinavia, Ribe.

Population
5.3 million

Climate
Generally mild although changeable throughout the year.

Language
Danish, but English is widely spoken.

Telephone
The dialling code for Denmark is 00 45.

Money
Currency: Danish Krone
Banks: Mon-Wed & Fri 09.30-16.00, Thurs to 18.00. Closed Sat. In the provinces opening hours vary.

Shops
Hours may vary in the main cities. Regular openings are Mon-Thu 09.00-17.30, Fri 09.00- 19.00/20.00, and Sat 09.00-13.00/14.00.

Public Holidays
New Year's Day; Three Kings Day 6 Jan; April Fools Day 1 April; Maundy Thursday; Good Friday; Easter Monday; Queen's Birthday 16 April; Flag Day 18 April; Ascension; Whit Mon; Constitution Day 5 Jun; Valdemars 15 June; Mortens Day 11 Nov; Christmas 24- 26 Dec; New Year's Eve

Motoring
Driving is much easier than at home as roads are much quieter. Driving is on the right. Do not drink and drive. Dipped headlights are compulsory at all times. Strong measures are taken against unauthorised parking on beaches, with on the spot fines.

DK2000 Nordsø Camping

Tingodden 3, Årgab, DK-6960 Hvide Sande (Ringkøbing)
Tel: 96 59 17 22. Email: info@nordsoe-camping.dk

Located beside the North Sea, behind the sand dunes and next to a fjord, Nordsø not only has beach access but also provides a splendid indoor pool complex. There are 300 regularly laid out, level pitches, quite close together, most of which have 16A electricity with 80 fully serviced and 43 cabins. The site has a wide range of activities for children with a restaurant for evening use and a pizzeria for day time. The site is situated on the West Coast Path, a 40 km. long cycle path. The site is very popular with German visitors.

Facilities
Two fully equipped toilet blocks one heated. Family bathrooms (charged). Facilities for the disabled visitors. Laundry. Restaurant, bar, pizzeria and takeaway. Supermarket. Kitchen. Outdoor pool and indoor pool complex (DKK. 10-20). Sauna, solarium and spa bath. Tennis, table tennis, minigolf. TV and games room. Play areas. Fishing.
Open: 11 April - 14 September.

Directions
From E20 take exit 73, Korskroen. Take main road 11 to Varde then 181 towards Nymindegab and Hvide Sande. Site is 6 km. south of Hvide Sande.

Charges guide
Per person	€ 8,78
pitch incl. electricity (10A)	free - € 10,54
water and drainage	€ 1,35 - € 2,03
Camping Cheques accepted.	

kawan-villages.com tel: 00 333 59 59 03 59   *kawan*

DK2015 Ådalens Camping

Gudenåvej 20, DK-6710 Esbjerg V-Sædding (Ribe)
Tel: 75 15 88 22. Email: info@adal.dk

Owned and run by Britta and Peter Andersen, this superb site is in the northeast of Esbjerg and is a great starting point from which to tour the city with its harbour, museums and sea water aquarium. It is also convenient for those arriving on the ferry from Harwich (16 hours). From the attractive, tree lined drive, gravel lanes lead to large fields with well-mown grass and good services. Ådalens has 193 pitches for touring visitors and 30 seasonal places. The pitches are split into groups of 5 or 10 by mature trees that provide some shade. There are 16 concrete hardstandings for large caravans or motorcaravans, 4 of which are fully serviced.

Facilities
Two modern toilet blocks with free hot showers. Special children's section in bright colours and family shower rooms. Excellent facilities for disabled visitors. Baby room. Laundry. Campers' kitchen. Motorcaravan services. Basics from reception (order bread). Outdoor pool (15 x 10 m.) with slide, flume and paddling pool. Playground. Animal farm. Minigolf. Internet access. Off site: Fishing, golf and bicycle hire 5 km. City centre 5 km.
Open: All year.

Directions
From Esbjerg, take the 447 road northeast and continue along the coast. Turn right at sign for site and follow the signs. GPS: N55:30.778 E08:23.349

Charges 2007
Per person	DKK 69
child (1-11 yrs)	DKK 41
Camping Cheques accepted.	

DK2020 Møgeltonder Camping

Sonderstregsvej 2, Møgeltonder, DK-6270 Tonder (Sønderjylland)
Tel: 74 73 84 60. Email: moegeltoender.camping@post.tele.dk

This site is only five minutes walk from one of Denmark's oldest villages and ten minutes drive from Tønder with its well preserved old buildings and magnificent pedestrian shopping street. The old town of Ribe is just 43 km. It is also convenient for the ferry ports. A quiet family site, Møgeltønder has 285 large, level, numbered pitches on grass, most with electricity (10A), divided up by new plantings of shrubs and small hedges. Only 35 pitches are occupied by long stay units, the remainder solely for tourists, and there are 15 cabins.

Facilities
Two superb, modern, heated sanitary units include showers (on payment), washbasins with divider/curtain or in private cubicles. Bathrooms for families and disabled visitors. Baby room. Kitchens with hobs. Dishwashing sinks. Laundry. Motorcaravan services. Shop (bread to order). Swimming and paddling pools. Playground. TV. Games rooms. Internet access. Off site: Golf or bicycle hire 10 km.
Open: All year.

Directions
Turn left off no. 419 Tønder - Højer road, 4 km. from Tønder. Drive through Møgeltønder village and past the church where site is signed. The main street is cobbled so drive slowly.

Charges 2006
Per person	DKK 56
child (0-12 yrs)	DKK 29
electricity	DKK 22

DK2010 Hvidbjerg Strand Camping

Hvidbjerg Strandvej 27, DK-6857 Blavand (Ribe)

Tel: 75 27 90 40. Email: info@hvidbjerg.dk

A family owned, 'TopCamp' holiday site, Hvidbjerg Strand is on the west coast near Blåvands Huk, 43 km. from Esbjerg. It is a high quality, seaside site with a wide range of amenities and facilities. Most of the 570 pitches have electricity (6/10A) and the 130 'comfort' pitches also have water, drain and satellite TV. Many are individual and divided by hedges, in rows on flat sandy grass, with areas also divided by small trees and hedges. On-site leisure facilities include an impressive, tropical style indoor pool complex with stalactite caves and 70 m. water chute, 'the black hole' with sounds and lights plus water slides, spa baths, Turkish bath and a sauna. The latest indoor suite of supervised play rooms is designed for all ages with Lego, computers, video games, TV, etc. The most recent sanitary facilities are also impressive, thatched in the traditional style and one with a central, glass covered atrium. A Blue Flag beach and windsurfing school are adjacent to the site and the town offers a full activity programme during the main season. Member of Leading Campings Group.

Facilities

Four superb toilet units, two just renovated to very high standards, include washbasins (many in cubicles), roomy showers, spa baths, suites for disabled visitors, family bathrooms, kitchens and laundry facilities. The most recent units include a children's bathrooms decorated with dinosaur or Disney characters, racing car baby baths, low height WCs, basins and showers, plus many high quality family bathrooms, suites for disabled visitors and two kitchens with hobs, microwave ovens and cosy dining areas. Some family bathrooms for rent. Motorcaravan services. Supermarket. Café/restaurant. TV rooms. Pool complex, solarium and sauna. Play areas. Supervised play rooms (09.00-16.00 daily). Barbecue areas. Minigolf, football, squash and badminton. Riding. Fishing. Dog showers. ATM machine. Off site: Legoland 70 km.

Open: 31 March - 22 October.

Directions

From Varde take roads 181/431 to Blåvand. Site is signed left on entering the town (mind speed bump on town boundary).

Charges guide

Per person	€ 9,93
child (0-11 yrs)	€ 7,31
pitch	€ 12,69
electricity (6/10A)	€ 3,72
dog	€ 3,75

DK2140 Jesperhus Feriecenter & Camping

Legindvej 30, DK-7900 Nykobing Mors (Viborg)

Tel: 96 70 14 00. Email: jesperhus@jesperhus.dk

Jesperhus is an extensive, well organised and busy site with many leisure activities, adjacent to Blomsterpark. It is a 'TopCamp' site with 662 numbered pitches, mostly in rows with some terracing, divided by shrubs and trees and with shade in parts. Many pitches are taken by seasonal, tour operator or rental units, so advance booking is advised for peak periods. Electricity (6A) is available on all pitches and water points are in all areas. The indoor and outdoor pool complex (daily charge) has three pools, diving boards, water slides with the 'Black Hole', spa pools, saunas and a solarium. With all the activities at this site an entire holiday could be spent here regardless of weather, but Jesperhus is also an excellent centre for touring a lovely area of Denmark. Although it may appear to be just part of Jutland, Mors is an island in its own right surrounded by the lovely Limfjord. It is joined to the mainland by a fine 2,000 m. bridge at the end of which are signs to Blomsterpark (Northern Europe's largest flower park which also houses a Bird Zoo, Butterfly World, Terrarium and Aquarium) and the campsite – both under the same ownership.

Facilities

Four first rate sanitary units are cleaned three times daily. Facilities include washbasins in cubicles or with divider/curtain, family and whirlpool bathrooms (on payment), suites for babies and disabled people. Free sauna. Superb kitchens with full cookers and hoods, microwaves, dishwashing sinks and a fully equipped laundry. Supermarket (1/4-1/11) with gas. Restaurant. Bar. Café, takeaway. Pool complex with solarium. Activities include a 10 lane bowling centre, 'space laser' game, attractive minigolf, volleyball, tennis, go-carts and other outdoor sports. An indoor hall includes badminton, table tennis, and children's 'play-world'. Playgrounds. Pets corner. Golf. Fishing pond. Practice golf (3 holes). Off site: Riding 2 km. Bicycle hire 6 km. Beach 2 km.

Open: All year.

Directions

From south or north, take road no. 26 to Salling Sund bridge, site is signed Jesperhus, just north of the bridge. GPS: N56:45.049 E08:48.948

Charges guide

Per person	DKK 68
child (1-11 yrs)	DKK 49
pitch	free - DKK 50
electricity	DKK 30
dog	DKK 10

DK2022 Vikær Diernæs Strand Camping

Dundelum 29, Diernæs, DK-6100 Harderslev (Sønderjylland)

Tel: **74 57 54 64**. Email: **info@vikaercamp.dk**

The warm and humorous welcome at Vikær Diernæs will start your holiday off in the right way. This family site in Southern Jutland lies in beautiful surroundings, right on the Diernæs Bugt beaches – ideal for both active campers and relaxation seekers. The attractively laid out site has 330 grass pitches (210 for touring units), all with 10/16A electricity and separated by low, partly new planted hedges. Access is off long, gravel access lanes. The upper part of the site provides newly developed fully serviced pitches with electricity, water, sewage, TV aerial point and internet. From these, and from the front pitches on the lower fields, there are marvellous views over the Diernæs Bugt. For the active there are several routes for walking and cycling and, of course, sea fishing trips are possible. In the area are a newly developed swamp nature reserve, Schackenborg Castle and the battlefields of Dybbøl Banke. The site is next to a 'Blue Flag' beach providing safe swimming.

Facilities

Three modern toilet blocks with British style toilets, washbasins in cabins and controllable hot showers. Family shower rooms. Baby room with bath and changing mat. En-suite facilities for disabled visitors. Laundry with sink, 2 washing machines and dryer. Campers' kitchen. Dishwashing. Motorcaravan services. Shop (Thursday – Sunday). Playground. Football field. Minigolf. Fishing. Archery. Watersports and boat launching. Petanque. Play house for children. Daily activities for children in high season. TV room. Billiards. Torch useful. English is spoken. Off site: Golf 30 minutes. Riding 2 km.

Open: 1 April - 18 September.

Directions

From German/Danish border follow E45 north. Take exit 69 and follow to Hoptrup. From Hoptrup follow to Diernæs and Diernæs Strand.

Charges 2006

Per person	DKK 67
child (under 12 yrs)	DKK 45
pitch	DKK 15 - 45
electricity	DKK 28
dog	DKK 10

DK2030 Sandersvig Camping & Tropeland

Espagervej 15-17, DK-6100 Haderslev (Sønderjylland)

Tel: **74 56 62 25**. Email: **sandersvig@dk-camp.dk**

An attractively laid out, family run site, Sandersvig offers the very best of modern facilities in a peaceful and beautiful countryside location, 300 metres from the beach. The 470 very large grassy pitches (270 for tourers) are divided by hedges, shrubs and small trees into small enclosures, many housing only four units, most with electricity (10A). The site is well lit, very quiet at night and there are water taps close to most pitches. The playground boasts Denmark's largest bouncing cushion! Opposite the site, on the road to the beach, the site owners have planted new woodland. Sandersvig makes a very comfortable base for excursions. Visit nearby historic Kolding with its castle, museums and shops, the beautiful old town of Christiansfeld or the restored windmill at Sillerup. The drive to the island of Fyn takes less than an hour, with miles of country lanes around the site for cycling and walking.

Facilities

Four heated sanitary blocks offer some washbasins in cubicles and roomy showers (on payment). Suites for disabled visitors, six family bathrooms and baby rooms. Excellent kitchens with ovens, electric hobs, dishwashing sinks. Very good laundry. Fish cleaning area. Motorcaravan services. Well stocked supermarket and fast food service, with dining room adjacent (Easter-15/9). Takeaway (15/6-15/8). Indoor heated swimming pool with sauna, whirlpool and slide (DKK 12,50). Solarium. Playground. New football field. Games room with pool table, 'air hockey' and arcade machines. TV lounge. Two hard tennis courts. Boat launching. Off site: Riding 4 km. Bicycle hire 6 km. Fishing 7 km. Golf 16 km.

Open: 7 April - 17 September.

Directions

Leave E45 at exit 66 and turn towards Christianfeld. Turn right at roundabout onto 170 and follow signs for Fjelstrup and Knud village, turning right 1 km. east of the village from where site is signed.

Charges 2006

Per person	DKK 62
child (0-11 yrs)	DKK 34
pitch	DKK 15 - 40
electricity (10A)	DKK 25
dog	free

DK2036 Gammelmark Strand Camping

Gammelmark 16, DK-6310 Broager (Sønderjylland)
Tel: **74 44 17 42**. Email: **info@gammelmark.dk**

This site combines Danish hospitality with historical interest. In 1864 war was waged between the Danes and the Germans over the Flensburger Förde and this site organises excursions to the war museum in Dybbøl Banke where you can learn all about this devastating period in Danish history. Especially interesting for children, in summer a guide will take them out for a day to show them how tough it was to drag the canons uphill. The Siegers, a Danish/Dutch couple, have owned this site since 2001. There are 240 level, grass pitches (180 for tourers), all with 13A electricity. English is spoken.

Facilities

Modern, heated facilities with British style toilets, washbasins (open and in cabins) and controllable hot showers (DKK 2). Child-size toilets and basins. Baby room. En-suite facilities for disabled visitors. Laundry facilities. Motorcaravan services. Shop. Playground. Football. Fishing. Riding. Sailing. Beach. Activity programme (high season). Animal farm. TV room. Torch useful. Off site: Bar, restaurant 2 km. Bicycle hire 6 km. Golf 10 km.

Open: 1 April - 30 September.

Directions

From Flensburg take no. 7 road north and at exit 75 turn east towards Sønderborg. Take exit Dynt and follow site signs.

Charges 2006

Per person	DKK 62
child (1-11 yrs)	DKK 31
pitch	DKK 15 - 31
electricity	DKK 32

DK2040 TopCamp Riis

Osterhovedvej 43, DK-7323 Give (Vejle)
Tel: **75 73 14 33**. Email: **info@topcampriis.dk**

TopCamp Riis is a good quality touring site ideal for visiting Legoland (18 km) and Givskov Zoo (3 km). It is a friendly, family run 'TopCamp' site with 280 large touring pitches on sheltered, gently sloping, well tended lawns surrounded by trees and shrubs. Electricity (6A) is available to 220 pitches, and there are 51 site owned cabins. The outdoor heated pool and water-slide complex and the adjacent small bar that serves beer, ice cream, soft drinks and snacks are only open in main season. This is a top class site suitable for long or short stays in this very attractive part of Denmark.

Facilities

Two excellent sanitary units include washbasins with divider/curtain and controllable showers (on payment). Suites for babies and disabled visitors, family bathrooms (one with whirlpool bath, on payment) and solarium. Two kitchens with hobs, ovens, and sinks (on payment). Laundry. Motorcaravan services. Shop. Pool complex. Cafe/bar. Minigolf. Train ride for children. Animal farm. Bicycle hire. Off site: Fishing and golf 4 km. Beach 23 km.

Open: 31 March - 30 September.

Directions

Turn onto Osterhovedvej southeast of Give town centre (near Shell Garage) at sign to Riis and site. After 4 km. turn left into drive which runs through the forest to the site. Alternatively, turn off the 442 Brande - Jelling road at Riis village north of Givskud.

Charges 2006

Per person	DKK 69
child (0-11 yrs)	DKK 46
pitch incl. electricity	DKK 77 - 107

DK2044 Hampen Sø Camping

Hovedgaden 31, DK-7362 Hampen (Vejle)
Tel: **75 77 52 55**. Email: **info@hampen-soe-camping.dk**

If you are heading up towards Denmark to cross to Norway or Sweden, then this site in a natural setting close to lakes and moors could be a useful stop-over. There are 230 pitches in total, with 80 seasonal units plus 34 cabins, but there will always be space for touring units. The pitches are arranged in large grassy bays taking around 15 units, and there are 10A electric hook-ups (some long leads may be needed). The nearby Hampen See lake is a pleasant walk through the forest and is said to be one of the cleanest lakes for swimming in Denmark.

Facilities

Two toilet blocks, one at the upper end, the other near the entrance, one basic, the other with newer facilities including family shower rooms, children's room and laundry. En-suite facilities for disabled people. Laundry. Good supermarket and restaurant open all year (weekends in winter). Takeaway. Kitchen. Games and TV rooms. Small outdoor pool (15/6-1/9). Covered minigolf. Playground. Race track for mini cars. Wifi internet access. Off site: Riding 500 m. Fishing 3 km. Golf 18 km.

Open: All year.

Directions

Site lies on road no.176, approx. 500 m. southwest of its junction with road no.13 between Vejle and Viborg (around 50 km. south of Viborg). Look for Spar mini-market and camping signs.
GPS: N56:00.855 E09:21.856

Charges 2006

Per person	€ 8,96
child (0-11 yrs)	€ 4,82
electricity	€ 3,86
Camping Cheques accepted.	

DK2046 Trelde Næs Supercamp

Trelde Næsvej 297, Trelde, DK-7000 Fredericia (Vejle)

Tel: 75 95 71 83. Email: info@supercamp.dk

Trelde Næs Supercamp is one of the larger Danish sites with 500 level and numbered pitches. The 400 touring pitches all have 10A electricity and there are 37 fully serviced pitches with electricity, water, wastewater and internet. Seasonal units take up the remaining 100 pitches. Pitching is off tarmac access roads on well-kept, grassy fields with some shade from bushes at the rear. The toilet buildings are older in style but the fittings are good. At the front of the site is a heated, open air, fun pool with large slide, bubble bath, water curtain and play island. This is connected to a room with a sauna, Turkish baths and massage chairs, with play stations for children. Trelde Næs is right next to the beach, but also close to the nature reserve of Trelde Næs which has been part of the Royal estates since the 14th century. City and culture lovers are well off too, for the historic town of Fredericia is close. Here we recommend you take the tour of the Walls, built by King Christian IV, and visit Den Historiske Miniby, a miniature model park of Fredericia.

Facilities

Four traditional but refurbished toilet blocks have British style toilets, washbasins in cabins and controllable hot showers (card operated). Child size toilets and basins. Family shower room. Baby room. Laundry with sinks, washing machines and dryer. Fun pool (10 x 20 m.) with island, large slide, Turkish bath, solarium and sauna. Shop. Takeaway. Several playgrounds. Football field. Minigolf. Fishing. Watersports. Full entertainment programme in high season for children. TV room. English is spoken. Off site: Golf 6 km. Bicycle hire 6 km.

Open: All year.

Directions

From Fredericia follow road no. 28 north and take Trelde exit. Follow signs for Trelde and Trelde Næs.

Charges 2006

Per person	DKK 66
child (0-11 yrs)	DKK 42
pitch	DKK 50
with services	DKK 30 - 70
electricity	DKK 25

Camping Cheques accepted.

DK2048 Fårup Sø Camping

Fårupvej 58, DK-7300 Jelling (Vejle)

Tel: 75 87 13 44. Email: faarup-soe@dk-camp.dk

This site was originally set up on the old farm woodlands of Jelling Skov where local farmers each had their own plot. Owned since January 2004 by the Dutch/Danish Albring family, this is a rural location on the Fårup Lake. This family site is ideal for those who want to enjoy a relaxed holiday on the lakeside beaches or walking or cycling through the surrounding countryside. Some of Denmark's best-known attractions such as Legoland and the Lion Park are nearby. Fårup Sø Camping has 240 pitches, mostly on terraces (from top to bottom the site has a height difference of 53 metres). The terraces provide beautiful views of the countryside and the Fårup lake. There are 180 pitches for touring units, most with 10A electricity, and some tent pitches without electricity. Next to the top toilet block is an open-air barbecue area with a terrace and good views. A neighbour rents out water bikes and takes high season excursions onto the lake with a real Viking Ship which campers can join. The last weekend of May the site celebrates the Jelling Musical Festival when it is advisable to book in advance.

Facilities

One modern and one older toilet block have British style toilets, open style washbasins and controllable hot showers (card operated). Family shower rooms. Baby room. Facilities for disabled visitors. Laundry. Campers' kitchen. Motorcaravan services. Shop (bread to order). Outdoor swimming pool (15 x 5 m.) Playground. Football field. Minigolf. Basketball. Volleyball. Games room. Pony riding. Lake with fishing, watersports and Viking ship. Animation for children (high season). Off site: Golf and riding 2 km. Boat launching 10 km. Legoland 20 km. Lion Park 8 km.

Open: 13 April - 3 September.

Directions

From Vejle take the 28 road towards Billund. In Skibet turn right towards Fårup Sø/Jennum/Jelling and follow the signs to Fårup Sô. GPS: N55:44.159 E09:25.063

Charges 2006

Per person	DKK 61
child	DKK 34
pitch	DKK 25
electricity	DKK 27

DK2080 Holmens Camping

Klostervej 148, DK-8680 Ry (Århus)

Tel: 86 89 17 62. Email: info@holmens-camping.dk

Holmens Camping lies between Silkeborg and Skanderborg in a very beautiful part of Denmark. The site is close to the waters of the Gudensø and Rye Møllesø lakes which are used for boating and canoeing. Walking and cycling are also popular activities. Both Skanderborg and Silkeborg are worth a visit and in Ry you can attend the Skt. Hans party which takes place at midsummer. Holmens has 225 grass touring pitches, partly terraced and divided by young trees and shrubs. The site itself is surrounded by mature trees. Almost all the pitches have 6A electricity and vary in size between 70-100 sq.m. A small tent field is close to the lake, mainly used by those who travel by canoe. The lake is suitable for swimming but the site also has an attractive pool complex consisting of two circular pools linked by a bridge and a paddling pool with water canon. There are opportunities for activities including boat hire on the lake and for fishing (the site has its own fishing pond).

Facilities

One traditional and one modern toilet block have British style toilets, washbasins (open and in cabins) and controllable hot showers (on payment). En-suite facilities with toilet, basin, shower. Baby room. Excellent facilities for disabled visitors. Laundry. Campers' kitchen. Shop for basics. Open-air pool with jet stream and paddling pool with water canon. Pool bar. Extensive games room. Playground. Football. Tennis. Minigolf. Fishing. Bicycle hire. Boat rental. Off site: Golf 14 km. Riding and beach 2 km.

Open: 8 April - 24 September.

Directions

Going north on E45, take exit 52 at Skanderborg turning west on 445 road towards Ry. In Ry follow the camp signs. GPS: N56:04.568 E09:45.601

Charges 2007

Per person	DKK 62 - 73
child (3-11 yrs)	DKK 35 - 40
pitch	DKK 20

Klostervej 148 · DK-8680 Ry · Tlf. +45 86 89 17 62 · Fax +45 86 89 17 12 · www.holmens-camping.dk

DK2050 Terrassen Camping

Himmelbjergvej 9 A, Laven, DK-8600 Silkeborg (Århus)

Tel: 86 84 13 01. Email: info@terrassen.dk

Terrassen Camping is a family run site that is arranged on terraces, overlooking Lake Julso and the surrounding countryside. There are 260 pitches with good views, most with electricity (6/10A) and three new hardstanding pitches for motorcaravans. A small area for tents (without electricity) is at the top of the site where torches may be required. There are also 29 seasonal units, and some site owned cabins. The solar heated swimming pool (8 x 16 m, open June - end August) has a paved terrace and is well fenced. This is a comfortable base from which to explore this area of Denmark.

Facilities

The main modern sanitary unit is heated and includes many washbasins in cubicles, controllable showers (on payment), family bathrooms, children's bathroom, baby room, and facilities for disabled visitors. Kitchen with hobs, ovens and sinks. Motorcaravan services. Well stocked shop. Swimming pool (15/5-31/8). Games/TV rooms. Adventure playground, trampolines, bouncing cushion, toddlers play room and pets corner. Basketball, volleyball and boules. Canoe hire. Off site: Fishing 200 m. Golf, bicycle hire and boat launching 5 km.

Open: 18 March - 18 September.

Directions

From the harbour in the centre of Silkeborg follow signs and minor road towards Sejs (5 km.) and Ry (20 km). Site lies on the northern side of the road at village of Laven (13 km.). Note: Height restriction of 3 m. on railway bridge over this road.

Charges guide

Per person	DKK 65
child (1-11 yrs)	DKK 41
pitch	DKK 20 - 45
electricity	DKK 26

85

DK2070 Fornæs Camping

Stensmarkvej 36, DK-8500 Grenå (Århus)

Tel: **86 33 23 30**. Email: **fornaes@1031.inord.dk**

In the grounds of a former farm, Fornæs Camping is about 5 km from Grenå. From reception a wide, gravel access road descends through a large grassy field to the sea. Pitches to the left are mostly level, to the right slightly sloping with some terracing and views of the Kattegat. The rows of pitches are divided into separate areas by colourful bushes and each row is marked by a concrete tub containing a young tree and colourful flowers. Fornæs has 320 pitches of which 240 are for tourers, the others being used for seasonal visitors. All touring pitches have 10A electricity. At the foot of the site is a pebble beach with a large grass area behind it for play and sunbathing.

Facilities	Directions
Two modern toilet blocks have British style toilets, washbasins in cabins and controllable hot showers (DKK 2). Child-size toilets. Family shower rooms. Baby room. Facilities for disabled people. Laundry. Campers' kitchen. Motorcaravan service point. Shop. Café/grill with bar and takeaway. Swimming pool (80 sq.m) with paddling pool. Sauna and solarium. Play area. Minigolf. Fishing. Watersports. Off site: Golf and riding 5 km.	From Århus follow the 15 road towards Grenå and then the 16 road towards town centre. Turn north and follow signs for Fornæs and the site. GPS: N56:27.361 E10:56.464

Open: Easter - 28 September.

Charges guide

Per person	DKK 60 - 68
child (1-12 yrs)	DKK 32 - 36
electricity (10A)	DKK 25

Credit cards 5% surcharge.

DK2100 Blushoj Camping

Elsegårdevej 55, DK-8400 Ebeltoft (Århus)

Tel: **86 34 12 38**

This is a traditional type of site where the owners are making a conscious effort to keep mainly to touring units – there are only six seasonal units and four rental cabins. The site has 200 pitches on levelled grassy terraces surrounded by mature hedging and shrubs. Some have glorious views of the Kattegat and others overlook peaceful rural countryside. Most pitches have electricity (10A), but long leads may be required. There is a heated and fenced swimming pool (14 x 7 m) with a water-slide and the beach below the site provides opportunities for swimming, windsurfing and sea fishing.

Facilities	Directions
One toilet unit includes washbasins with dividers and showers with divider and seat (on payment). The other unit has a kitchen with electric hobs, dishwashing sinks, dining/TV room, laundry and baby facilities. A heated extension provides six very smart family bathrooms, and additional WCs and washbasins. Motorcaravan service point. Well stocked shop. Swimming pool (20/5-20/8). Minigolf. Play area. Games room. Beach. Fishing. Off site: Riding, bicycle hire, boat launching and golf 5 km.	From road 21 northwest of Ebeltoft turn off at junction where several sites are signed. Follow signs through the outskirts of Ebeltoft turning southeast to Elsegårde village. Turn left for Blushøj and follow camp signs. GPS: N56:10.066 E10:43.843

Open: 15 April - 15 September.

Charges 2006

Per person	DKK 72
child	DKK 38

No credit cards.

DK2130 Hobro Camping Gattenborg

Skivevej 35, DK-9500 Hobro (Nordjylland)

Tel: **98 52 32 88**. Email: **hobro@dk-camp.dk**

This neat and very well tended municipal site is imaginatively landscaped and has 130 pitches on terraces arranged around a bowl shaped central activity area. Most pitches (100 for touring units) have electricity (10A) and there are many trees and shrubs. Footpaths connect the various terraces and activity areas. There are 30 seasonal units and 10 cabins. The reception building with a small shop and tourist information, has a covered picnic terrace behind, and houses a large TV lounge.

Facilities	Directions
The main heated sanitary building includes washbasins in cubicles and hot showers (on payment). Two family bathrooms. Facilities for disabled people. Baby room. Kitchen with hobs. Small laundry. A further tiny unit has two unisex WCs and basins (cold water only). Motorcaravan services. Shop (order bread before 9 pm). Swimming pool (high season). Play areas. Minigolf. Off site: Town 500 m. Fishing 7 km. Beach 1 km.	From E45 exit 35, take road 579 towards Hobro Centrum. Site is well signed to the right, just after railway bridge. GPS: N56:38.083 E09:46.953

Open: 1 April - 1 October.

Charges 2007

Per person	DKK 60 - 70
child (2-11 yrs)	DKK 30 - 36
electricity	DKK 25

DK2150 Solyst Camping

Logstorvej 2, DK-9240 Nibe (Nordjylland)

Tel: 98 35 10 62. Email: soelyst@dk-camp.dk

You will always be near the water in Denmark, either open sea or, as here, alongside the more sheltered waters of a fjord – Limfjord. Sølyst is a family run site providing 200 numbered pitches, most with electricity (6A), on gently sloping grass arranged in fairly narrow rows separated by hedges (150 for touring units). There are facilities for watersports and swimming in the fjord, the site also has a small heated swimming pool (8 x 16 m), waterslide and splash pool with a children's pool all with paved sunbathing area, and paddle boats can be rented. A little train provides rides for children. Good paths have been provided for superb, easy walks in either direction, and indeed right into the nearby town of Nibe. This is a delightful example of an old Danish town with picturesque cottages and handsome 15th century church. Its harbour, once prosperous from local herring boats, is now more concerned with pleasure craft.

Facilities

A central sanitary unit includes washbasins in cubicles, four family bathrooms, a baby room and facilities for disabled visitors. Very good kitchen with hobs, microwave, oven, dishwashing sinks and small dining area. Fully equipped laundry. A second unit provides extra facilities. Hot water (except in washbasins) is charged for. Motorcaravan services. Mini-market. Snack bar and takeaway (open main season). Swimming pool. Solarium. Play area. Minigolf. Boules. TV room. Games room with amusement machines. Fishing. Bicycle hire. Boat launching. Beach. Off site: Riding 1 km. Town of Nibe 1 km. Golf 4 km.

Open: All year.

Directions

Site is clearly signed from the no. 187 road west of Nibe town, with a wide entrance.
GPS: N56:58.332 E09:37.475

Charges guide

Per person	DKK 55 - 63
child (under 12 yrs)	DKK 29 - 33
pitch	DKK 25

DK2165 Skiveren Camping

Niels Skiverenrej 5-7, DK-9982 Skiveren/Aalbæk (Nordjylland)

Tel: 98 93 22 00. Email: info@skiveren.dk

This friendly seaside site, a member of the Danish 'TopCamp' organisation, is set up in 'maritime style' with the pitches separated by low wooden poles connected by a sailor's rope. Skiveren Camping has 670 pitches (595 for tourers), almost all with 6/10A electricity. Around the site are different varieties of low spruces and firs which give the site a pleasing appearance and atmosphere. The level pitches are of a good size (up to 120 sq.m), some having a picnic table and all are separated from the main tarmac access road by the low wooden fences. Toilet facilities look immaculate and the main block has a new attractive, light-blue children's section in maritime style again, with a lighthouse and a boat. The site has its own fitness centre with an outdoor pool, sauna, steam bath and solarium. However, this whole area is also great for a seaside holiday on the Ålbæk Bugt beaches. Other possibilities are walking and cycling on the surrounding moors or a visit to the interesting old harbour town of Skagen.

Facilities

Three immaculate toilet blocks with the usual facilities, free family showers and private facilities with shower, toilet and basin for rent. Facilities for disabled visitors. Laundry. Campers' kitchen. Dishwashing (free hot water). Motorcaravan services. Supermarket. Strand Café for meals, drinks and takeaway meals. Outdoor pool (15 x 8 m) with whirlpool and sauna. Playground with play area for toddlers. Football field. Tennis. Games room with wide-screen TV and air hockey. Bicycle hire. Children's club daily (from 16.00). Live music and dancing. Off site: Fishing 14 km. Golf 7 km. Riding 10 km.

Open: Easter - 30 September.

Directions

From the no. 40 road going north from Ålbæk, turn left at sign for 'Skiveren'. Follow this road all the way to the end. GPS: N57:36.997 E10:16.803

Charges 2007

Per person	DKK 55 - 73
child (1-11 yrs)	DKK 36 - 51
pitch	DKK 25 - 65
with water and drainage	DKK 45 - 95
electricity (6/10A)	DKK 27 - 37
Credit cards 4% surcharge.	

DK2170 Klim Strand Camping

Havvejen 167, Klim Strand, DK-9690 Fjerritslev (Nordjylland)

Tel: 98 22 53 40. Email: ksc@klim-strand.dk

A large family holiday site right beside the sea, Klim Strand is a paradise for children. It is a privately owned 'TopCamp' site with a full complement of quality facilities, including its own fire engine and trained staff. The site has 560 numbered touring pitches, all with electricity (10A), laid out in rows, many divided by trees and hedges and shade in parts. Some 220 of these are fully serviced with electricity, water, drain and 18 channel TV hook-up. On site activities include an outdoor water-slide complex, a newly renovated indoor pool complex, tennis courts, pony riding (all free), numerous play areas, an adventure playground with aerial cable ride, roller skating area and ramp. Recent additions include a kayak school and a large bouncy castle for toddlers. Live music and dancing are organised twice a week in high season. Suggested excursions include trips to offshore islands, visits to local potteries, a brewery museum and bird watching on the Bygholm Vejle. Member of Leading Campings Group.

Facilities

Two large, central toilet blocks, recently renovated to high standards, are heated. Spacious showers and some washbasins in cubicles. Separate children's room. Baby rooms. Bathrooms for families (some charged) and disabled visitors. Sauna, solariums, whirlpool bath, hairdressing rooms, fitness room. Dog bathroom. Two smaller units are by reception and beach. Laundry. Well equipped kitchens and barbecue areas with sinks, microwaves, gas hobs, and two TV lounges. Motorcaravan services. Supermarket. Pizzeria. Restaurant and bar. Internet cafe. TV rental. Pool complex. Play areas. Crèche. Bicycle hire. Cabins to rent. Off site: Golf 10 km. Boat launching 25 km.

Open: 1 April - 20 October.

Directions

Turn off Thisted-Fjerritslev no. 11 road to Klim from where site is signed. GPS: N57:08.000 E09:10.14

Charges 2006

Per person	€ 10,35
child (1-11 yrs)	€ 7,60
pitch	free - € 10,35
electricity	€ 3,45
dog	€ 4,15

DK2180 Nordstrand Camping

Apholmenvej 40, DK-9900 Frederikshaven (Nordjylland)

Tel: 98 42 93 50. Email: info@nordstrand-camping.dk

An excellent site, Nordstrand is 2 km. from Frederikshaven and the ferries to Sweden and Norway. It is another 'TopCamp' site and provides all the comforts one could possibly need with all the attractions of the nearby beach, town and port. The 430 large pitches are attractively arranged in small enclosures of 9-13 units surrounded by hedges and trees. Many hedges are of flowering shrubs and this makes for a very pleasant atmosphere. 250 pitches have electricity (10A) and drainage, a further 20 have water and there are 16 on hardstandings. There are 64 seasonal units, plus 23 site owned cabins. The roads are all paved and the site is well lit and fenced with the barrier locked at night. The reception complex also houses a café (high season), with a telephone pizza service available at other times. The beach is a level, paved 200 m. walk. On the roof of the indoor pool a small terrace gives views of the beach and the Ålbæk Bugt. There is much to see in this area of Denmark and this site would make a very comfortable holiday base.

Facilities

Centrally located, modern, large toilet blocks provide spacious showers (on payment) and washbasins in cubicles, together with some family bathrooms, rooms for disabled people and babies. Laundry with free ironing. All are spotlessly clean. Good kitchens at each block provide mini-ovens, microwaves, hobs (free) and dishwashing sinks with free hot water. Motorcaravan services. Supermarket (all season). Café (15/6-15/8). Pizza service. Indoor swimming pool. Sauna. Solarium. 'Short' golf course, minigolf, tennis, table tennis, billiards and chess. Bicycle hire. Play areas. Internet access (free). Off site: Frederikshavn with shops, etc.

Open: 1 April - 20 October.

Directions

Turn off the main no. 40 road 2 km. north of Frederikshavn at roundabout just north of railway bridge. Site is signed. GPS: N57:27.853 E10:31.653

Charges 2006

Per person	DKK 56 - 67
child (0-11 yrs)	DKK 39 - 49
pitch	DKK 30 - 40
electricity	DKK 29

DK2200 Bojden Strandcamping

Bojden Landevej 12, Bojden, DK-5600 Fåborg (Fyn)

Tel: **62 60 12 84**. Email: **bojden@dk-camp.dk**

Bøjden is located in one of the most beautiful corners of southwest Fyn (Funen in English) known as the 'Garden of Denmark'. Now run by the original owner's son and his wife, this is a well equipped site separated from the beach only by a hedge. Arranged in rows on mainly level grassy terraces and divided into groups by hedges and some trees, many pitches have sea views as the site slopes gently down from the road. The 314 pitches (200 for touring units) all have electricity (10A) and include 32 new fully serviced pitches (water, drainage and TV aerial point). Four special motorcaravan pitches also have water and waste points.

Facilities

The superb quality, heated toilet block includes washbasins in cubicles, controllable showers, family bathrooms (some with whirlpools and double showers), a baby room and facilities for disabled people. Kitchen with hobs, oven and sinks, plus laundry facilities. Motorcaravan services. Supermarket. Takeaway. Swimming pool (20/5-20/8). Solarium. Fenced toddler play area and separate adventure playground. Bicycle and boat hire. Fishing. Riding. Off site: Beach. Restaurant 100 m. Golf 12 km.

Open: 1 April - 15 September.

Directions

From Faaborg follow road no. 8 to Bøjden and site is on right 500 m. before ferry terminal (from Fynshav).

Charges guide

Per person	DKK 59
child (under 12 yrs)	DKK 35
pitch (18/6-15/8)	DKK 30 - 60
electricity	DKK 26

Credit cards accepted with 5% surcharge.
Camping Cheques accepted.

DK2205 Løgismosestrand Camping

Løgismoseskov 7, DK-5683 Hårby (Fyn)

Tel: **64 77 12 50**. Email: **info@logismose.dk**

A countryside site with its own beach and pool, Løgismosestrand is surrounded by picturesque villages and the new owners are a friendly young couple. The former owner, Per Blaabjerg, has now taken over Bøjden Camping from his father. The 220 pitches here are arranged in rows and groups divided by hedges and small trees which provide a little shade. All the 140 pitches for touring units have 6-10A electricity points.

Facilities

Heated toilet units, kept very clean, include washbasins in cubicles, roomy showers (on payment), baby room, bathrooms for families and disabled people. Good laundry. Kitchen with gas hobs, microwave (charged for). Motorcaravan services. Well stocked shop. Café with pizzeria. Takeaway (high season). Swimming pool (1/6-1/9). Minigolf. Bicycle and boat hire. Pony riding. Adventure playground. Off site: Riding 2 km. Golf 12 km.

Open: 27 March - 18 September.

Directions

Southwest of Hårby via Sarup and Nellemose to Løgismoseskov, site is well signed. Lanes are narrow, large units should take care.

Charges guide

Per person	DKK 59
child (under 12 yrs)	DKK 35
pitch incl. electricity	DKK 36 - 66

Credit cards accepted with 5% surcharge.

DK2210 Bøsøre Strand Feriepark

Bøsørevej 16, DK-5874 Hesselager (Fyn)

Tel: **62 25 11 45**. Email: **info@bosore.dk**

A themed holiday site on the eastern coast of Fyn, the tales of Hans Christian Andersen are evident in the design of the heated indoor pool complex and the main outdoor children's playground at this site. The former has two pools on different levels, two hot tubs and a sauna and features characters from the stories, the latter has a fairytale castle with moat as its centrepiece. There are 300 pitches in total, and with only 25 seasonal units there should always be room for tourists out of main season. All have 6A electric hook-ups, there are 124 multi-serviced pitches and 20 hardstandings.

Facilities

Sanitary facilities are housed in one main central block and a smaller unit close to reception. They provide all usual facilities plus some family bathrooms, special children's section, baby rooms, facilities for disabled people. Motorcaravan service point. Shop, bar/restaurant, pizzeria, take-away all open all season. Kitchen (water charged). Solarium. Indoor pool complex. Playground with moat. Animal farm. Internet access. Bicycle hire. Entertainment in main season. Off site: Golf 20 km.

Open: Easter - 22 October.

Directions

The site lies on the coast about midway between Nyborg and Svendborg. From road no. 163 just north of Hesselager, take turning towards coast signed Bøsøre Strand. GPS: N55:11.572 E10:48.318

Charges guide

Per person	DKK 63
pitch	free - DKK 55
electricity	DKK 28

Camping Cheques accepted.

DK2220 Helnæs Camping

Strandbakken 21, Helnæs, DK-5631 Ebberup (Fyn)

Tel: **64 77 13 39**. Email: info@helnaes-camping.dk

Helnæs Camping is on the remote Helnæs peninsula to the southeast of Fyn (Funen in English), connected to the mainland by a small road. The site is adjacent to a nature reserve making it ideal for walkers, cyclists and bird spotters, or for those who enjoy sea fishing. Helnæs Camping has 160 pitches, some terraced, on grassy fields sloping down towards to the sea. From almost all the pitches there are beautiful views of Helnæs Bugt and the site is only 300 m. from the beach. Low rock walls and newly planted trees and low shrubs separate pitches. All have 6A electricity.

Facilities

Two toilet blocks, one partly refurbished, one new, with British style toilets, basins in cabins and controllable showers (Dkr. 2). Baby room (heated). Laundry with 2 washing machines, 2 dryers and spin dryer. Dishwashing. Campers' kitchen. Shop. Takeaway. New adventure type playground. Football field. Minigolf. Bicycle hire. Canoe hire. Watersports. In high season small circus for children. TV lounge. Covered barbecue area. English is spoken. Off site: Sea fishing.

Open: 1 April - 17 October.

Directions

From Nørre Åby follow 313 road south to Ebberup. In Ebberup turn south to Helnæs and follow the signs Helnæs Strand.

Charges guide

Per person	DKK 56
child	DKK 28
electricity	DKK 22

No credit cards.

DK2235 Sakskobing Gron Camping

Saxes Allé 15, DK-4990 Sakskobing (Lolland)

Tel: **54 70 47 57**

This small, traditional style site provides a useful stop-over on the route from Germany to Sweden within easy reach of the Puttgarden - Rødby ferry. There are 125 level grassy pitches, most with electricity (10A) and, although there are a fair number of seasonal units, one can usually find space. The pool at the nearby sports centre is said to be the most modern in Europe. The site has a well stocked shop, which is open long hours. The town centre is semi-pedestrianised, and has a good range of shops and a supermarket. The town is noted for its unusual 'smiling' water tower.

Facilities

Two sanitary units provide basic, older style facilities, including push-button hot showers on payment (DKK. 2 token), some curtained washbasin cubicles and a baby room, plus cooking, dishwashing and laundry facilities. Motorcaravan services. Shop. New play area. Off site: Town 500 m.

Open: 1 April - 27 October.

Directions

From E47, exit 46, turn towards town on road no. 9. Turn right at crossroads towards town centre (site is signed), cross railway and then turn right again, and site entrance is 250 m. on left.

Charges guide

Per unit incl. 2 persons	€ 19,00

DK2257 Vesterlyng Camping

Ravnholtvej 1, DK-4591 Føllenslev (Sjælland)

Tel: **59 20 00 66**. Email: info@vesterlyng-camping.dk

Vesterlyng is a pleasant, quiet site, close to Føllenslev on Sjælland. The ground slopes towards the sea and there are good views from some pitches It is an open site but some mature trees provide shade. Vesterlyng has 181 mostly level touring pitches, 150 with 6/13A electricity. A further 100 pitches are used by mostly elderly, seasonal units. The pitches are on long, grassy meadows each taking 16-20 units, off tarmac access roads. Facilities on this site are basic, but clean. The local beaches are ideal for swimming and a relaxing beach holiday.

Facilities

Two traditional style toilet blocks include washbasins (open style and in cabins) and controllable hot showers. Family shower rooms (Dkr. 5). Basic facilities for disabled people. Laundry with sink, washing machine and dryer. Dishwashing (free hot water). Small shop. Bar (daily). Playing field. Minigolf. Fishing. Riding trips organised. Bicycle hire. Water sports. Internet. Massages. Beach volleyball. Boules. Circus workshop. Animal farm. Live musical nights. Weekly theme meal organised. Off site: Fishing 1 km. Golf 30 km. Boat launching 1 km.

Open: 22 March - 30 September.

Directions

From Kalundborg follow 23 road east and exit on 155 road towards Svinninge. From Snertinge, continue north on 255 road and follow site signs. GPS: N55:44.504 E11:18.540

Charges guide

Per person	DKK 60
child (4-12 yrs)	DKK 8
pitch	DKK 15 - 25
electricity	DKK 24

No credit cards.

DK2250 Hillerød Camping

Blytækkervej 18, DK-3400 Hillerød (Sjælland)
Tel: **48 26 48 54**. Email: **info@hillerodcamping.dk**

The northern-most corner of Sjælland is packed with interest, based not only on fascinating parts of Denmark's history but also its attractive scenery. Centrally situated, Hillerød is a hub of main roads from all directions, with this neat campsite clearly signed. It has a park-like setting in a residential area with five acres of well kept grass and some attractive trees. There are 92 pitches, of which 50 have electricity (10-13A) and these are marked. The site amenities are all centrally located in modern, well maintained buildings which are kept very clean. The centre of Hillerød, like so many Danish towns, has been pedestrianised making shopping or outdoor refreshment a pleasure. Visit Frederiksborg Slot, a fine Renaissance Castle and home of the Museum of Danish national history. Hillerød, however is a fine base for visiting Copenhagen and only 25 km. from the ferries at Helsingør and the crossing to Sweden.

Facilities

The bright, airy toilet block is older in style and includes washbasins with partitions and curtain. Facilities for babies can be used by disabled people. Campers' kitchen adjoins the club room and includes free new electric hot plates and coffee making machine. Dishwashing sinks. Laundry room (free iron). Motorcaravan services. Small shop with basic supplies. Good comfortable club room with TV and children's corner. New large sand play area. Free bicycles, some with buggy for small children. Off site: Tennis courts and indoor swimming pool 1 km. Riding 2 km. Golf 3 km. Electric train service every 10 minutes (20 minutes walk) to Copenhagen. The site sells the Copenhagen card.

Open: Easter - 30 September.

Directions

Follow road no. 6 bypassing road to south until sign for Hillerød S. Turn towards town at sign for 'Centrum' on Roskildvej road no. 233 and site is signed to the right. GPS: N55:55.436 E12:17.722

Charges 2007

Per person	DKK 60 - 67
child (2-11 yrs)	DKK 30 - 35
electricity	DKK 25 - 30
dog	free

DK2255 Topcamp Feddet

Feddet 12, DK-4640 Fakse (Sjælland)
Tel: **56 72 52 06**. Email: **info@feddetcamping.dk**

This interesting spacious site with ecological principles is located on the Baltic coast. It has a fine, white, sandy beach (Blue Flag) which runs the full length of one side, with the Præstø fjord on the opposite side of the peninsula. There are 862 pitches, generally on sandy grass, with mature pine trees giving adequate shade. All have 10/13A electricity and 20 are fully serviced (water, electricity, drainage and sewage). There are 676 pitches for touring units. Two, recently constructed sanitary buildings have been specially designed to have natural ventilation, with ventilators controlled by sensors for heat, humidity and smell. The shaped blades on the roof increase ventilation on windy days. All this saves power and provides a comfortable climate inside. Heating is by a wood chip furnace (backed up by an oil seed rape furnace), is CO_2 neutral and replaces 40,000 litres of heating oil annually. The buildings are clad with larch panels from sustainable local trees, and are insulated with flax mats. Rainwater is used for toilet flushing, but showers and basins are supplied from the normal mains, and urinals are water free.

Facilities

Both sanitary buildings are impressive, equipped to very high standard and include family bathrooms (with twin showers), complete small children and baby suites. Facilities for disabled people. Laundry. Kitchens with ovens, hobs and rental fridges, dining room and a TV lounge. Each block has a chemical disposal facility complete with hand basin, soap, and paper towel. Excellent drive-over motorcaravan service point. Well stocked licensed shop. Licensed bistro and takeaway (1/5-20/10 but weekends only outside peak season). Minigolf, games room and table tennis. Indoor toddlers' playroom and several playgrounds for all ages, trampolines and bouncing cushion. Event camp for children. Pet zoo. Bungee jump. Internet access. Gym, massage, reflexology and sun beds. Watersports. Fishing. Off site: Activities with guides or instructors, including Land Rover safaris, abseiling, Icelandic pony riding, educational courses, ocean kayaking, and seal watching in Fakse Bay. Indoor pool complex nearby. Amusement park.

Open: All year.

Directions

From south on E47/55 take exit 38 towards Præstø. Turn north on 209 road towards Fakse and from Vindbyholt follow site signs. From the north on E47/55 take exit 37 east towards Fakse. Just before Fakse turn south on 209 road and from Vindbyholt, site signs.

Charges 2007

Per person	DKK 67
child (0-11 yrs)	DKK 46
pitch	free - DKK 95
electricity	DKK 30
dog	DKK 15

DK2260 DCU Nærum Camping

Ravnbakken, DK-2850 Nærum (Sjælland)

Tel: **45 80 19 57**. Email: **info@dcu.dk**

Obviously everyone arriving in Sjælland will want to visit 'wonderful, wonderful Copenhagen', but like all capital cities, it draws crowds during the holiday season and traffic to match. This friendly, sheltered site is near enough to be convenient but distant enough to afford peace and quiet (apart from the noise of nearby traffic) and a chance of relaxing after sightseeing. Nærum, one of the Danish Camping Union sites, is only 15 km. from the city centre and very near a suburban railway that takes you there. The long narrow site covers a large area alongside the ancient royal hunting forests, adjacent to the small railway line and the main road. Power lines do cross the site but there is lots of grassy open space. The 275 touring pitches are in two areas – in wooded glades taking about six units each (mostly used by tents) or on more open meadows where electrical connections (6/10A) are available. Nærum is a useful site to know for Copenhagen, but is also very near the interesting friendly shopping complex of Rødøvre and the amusement park at Bakken. Note: Should you wish to drive into the city, there is a useful car park on the quayside. It is within easy walking distance of the centre and is located where the Kalvebød Brygge meets the Langebrø bridge (suitable for motorcaravans and caravans).

Facilities

Two modern toilet blocks, one in the meadow area has been refurbished and includes partitioned washbasins. Good block at reception can be heated and also provides a laundry, dishwashing and a campers' kitchen. Good facilities for babies and disabled people. Four family bathrooms (free). Motorcaravan service point. Reception and shop for basics (closed 12.00-14.00 and 22.00-07.00). Café/restaurant near. Club room and TV. Barbecue. Play field and adventure playground. Off site: Full range of sporting facilities within easy reach of the site and café/restaurant within a few hundred metres. Train service to Copenhagen (400 m. on foot, change at Jaegersborg).

Open: 19 March - 25 September.

Directions

From E55/E47, take Nærum exit (no. 14), 15 km. north of Copenhagen. Turn right at first set of traffic lights (site signed), right on road 19 at second lights, cross bridge and turn left, following signs to site. GPS: N55:48.498 E12:31.865

Charges guide

Per person	DKK 62
child (0-11 yrs)	DKK 31
pitch	DKK 20
electricity	DKK 25

DK2265 Camping Charlottenlund Fort

Strandvejen 144B, DK-2920 Charlottenlund (Sjælland)

Tel: **39 62 36 88**. Email: **info@campingcopenhagen.dk**

On the northern outskirts of Copenhagen, this unique site is within the walls of an old fort which still retains its main armament of twelve 29 cm. howitzers (disabled, of course). The fort was constructed during 1886-1887 and was an integral link in the Copenhagen fortifications until 1932. The site is only six kilometres from the centre of Copenhagen, with a regular bus service (every 20 minutes) from just outside the site. Alternatively you could use the excellent cycle network to visit the city. There are 63 pitches, mostly on grass, all with 10A electric hook-ups. The obvious limitation on the space available means that pitches are relatively close together, but many are quite deep. The site is very popular and is usually full every night, so we suggest that you either make a reservation or arrive well before mid-day.

Facilities

Sanitary facilities located in the old armoury are rather basic, but clean, well maintained and heated. Showers on payment, but kitchen facilities include gas hobs and a dining area free of charge. Laundry. Motorcaravan service point. Small kiosk in front of site. Bicycle hire. Beach. Off site: Small restaurant (separate management) is adjacent, with good sea views to Sweden and the spectacular ʾresund Bridge. Riding 1.5 km. Golf 2 km.

Open: 15 May - 14 September.

Directions

Leave E47/E55 at junction 17, and turn southeast on Jægersborgvej. After a short distance turn left (east) on Jægersborg Allé, following signs for Charlottenlund (5 km) and follow all the way to the end. Finally turn right (south) on to Strandvejen, and site entrance is on left after 500 m. GPS: N55:44.688 E12:35.123

Charges 2006

Per person	DKK 80
child (3-12 yrs)	DKK 35
electricity	DKK 5

MAP 11

Situated in the far north, Finland is a long and mainly flat county, dominated by huge dense forests and glorious lakes. The unspoilt wilderness of this country makes it a perfect place for relaxing in natural, peaceful surroundings.

Finland

CAPITAL: HELSINKI

Tourist Office

Finnish Tourist Board
PO Box 33213
London W6 8KX
Tel: 020 8600 5680
Fax: 020 8600 5681
Email: finlandinfo.lon@mek.fi
Internet: www.visitfinland.com

There is a considerable difference in the landscape between north and south, with the gently rolling, rural landscape of the south giving way to the hills and vast forests of the north and treeless fells and peat-lands of Lapland, where reindeer and moose run free. Forests of spruce, pine and birch cover three quarters of the country's surface and are inhabited by hares, elks and occasional wolves and bears.

The other outstanding feature of Finland is its thousands of post-glacial lakes and islands. The main Lake District is centred on the beautiful Lake Saimaa in the south east, where you can swim, sail and fish. In the south, the capital Helsinki retains a small town feel, with open air cafes, green parks, waterways and a busy market square surrounded by 19th century architecture and museums. The flat western coastal regions include Turku and the Åland islands, ideal for sailing and fishing.

Population
5.2 million

Climate
Temperate climate, but with considerable variations. Summer is warm, winter is very cold.

Language
Finnish

Telephone
The country code is 00 358.

Money
Currency: The Euro
Banks: Mon-Fri 09.15 - 16.15
(regional variations may occur).

Shops
Mon-Fri 09.00-17.00/18.00.
Sat 09.00-14.00/15.00, department stores usually remain open to 18.00. Supermarkets usually open to 20.00 Mon-Fri.

Public Holidays
New Year; Epiphany; Saints Day 16 Mar; Language Day 9 April; Good Friday; Easter Mon; May Day 30 Apr/1 May; All Saints Day 1 Nov; Independence Day 6 Dec; Christmas 25, 26 Dec.

Motoring
Main roads are excellent and relatively uncrowded outside city limits. Traffic drives on the right. Horn blowing is frowned upon. There are many road signs warning motorists of the danger of elk dashing out on the road. If you are unfortunate enough to hit one, it must be reported to police. Do not drink and drive, penalties are severe if any alcohol is detected.

FI2850 Rastila Camping

Karavaanikatu 4, FIN-00980 Helsinki (Uusimaa)

Tel: **09 321 6551**. Email: **rastilacamping@hel.fi**

No trip to Finland would be complete without a few days stay in Helsinki, the capital since 1812. This all year round site has exceptional transport links with the metro; only five minutes walk from the campsite gates. It provides 265 pitches, 165 with electrical hook-ups, plus an additional small field for tent campers. Shrubs have been planted between the tarmac and grass pitches. All visitors will want to spend time in the Capital and a 24 hour bus, tram and metro pass costs a little over € 6 and can be bought at the metro station. Once on the metro you are in the city centre within 20 minutes on this regular fast train service. Essential visits will include Senate Square, in the heart of the city, and Suomenlinna, a marine fortress built on six islands in the 1700s. This garrison town is one of the most popular sights in Finland and is the world's largest maritime fortress. Helsinki, on the other hand, is one of Europe's smallest capitals and walking around the centre and port is popular as well as visiting the market square alongside the ferry port. The city also has a wide variety of art galleries and museums, many of which are free with the Helsinki card.

Facilities

Four sanitary blocks (one heated) provide toilets and showers. Kitchens with cooking rings and sinks. Facilities for disabled visitors and babies. Laundry room. Saunas. Motorcaravan service point. Fully licenced restaurant. Playground. Games and TV room. Bicycles, kajaks and rowing boats for hire. Off site: Small beach adjacent. Golf 5 km. Tallinn the capital of Estonia is only 90 minutes away from Helsinki by fast jetliner ferry.

Open: All year.

Directions

Well signed from 170 or Ring I. From the 170, turn at Itakeskus shopping complex towards Vuosaari. After crossing bridge go up slip road to Rastila. At top of road turn left. Site is directly ahead. GPS: N60:12.395 E25:07.279

Charges 2006

Per pitch incl. 2 persons	€ 16,00 - € 24,00
electricity	€ 4,50

Discounts for weekly or monthly bookings.

FI2820 Tampere Camping Härmälä

Leirintäkatu 8, FIN-33900 Tampere (Häme)

Tel: **03 265 1355**. Email: **harmala@lomaliitto.fi**

Härmelä is a lively campsite near Lake Pyhäjärvi. It is situated only four kilometres from Tampere city centre. You can chose from a large, unspecified number of unmarked pitches (about 180). The site has 111 cabins of various sizes and facilities. Amenities include a beach, saunas, playgrounds for children, a small shop and a pizzeria. The site seems a little run down but is acceptable for a couple of nights. Tampere is beautifully situated beside Lake Näsijärvi. A stroll along the harbour with its yachts and through the parks is a pleasant experience. Another must is the Sänkänniemi Adventure Park with its 168 m. high tower and revolving restaurant, children's zoo, aquarium and amusements such as roller coasters and rapid rides.

Facilities

There are four sanitary blocks, one block is new, three are rather basic. Washbasins and showers have free hot water. Facilities for disabled visitors. Laundry room. Campers' kitchen with cooking rings, microwave. Chemical disposal and motorhome service point. Small shop. Pizzeria. Off site: Golf and riding 5 km.

Open: 17 May - 27 August.

Directions

Turn off the E12 and follow signs. GPS: N61:28.318 E23:44.367

Charges 2006

Per person	€ 4,00
child (0-14 yrs)	€ 2,00
pitch	€ 10,00 - € 11,50
electricity	€ 4,00

FI2830 Camping Lakari

Lakarintie 405, FIN-34800 Virrat (Häme)

Tel: 034 758639. Email: virtain.matkailu@phpoint.fi

The peace and tranquillity of the beautiful natural surroundings are the main attractions at this vast (18 hectares) campsite which is located on a narrow piece of land between two lakes. This site is a must if you want to get away from it all. There is a variety of cabins to rent, some with their own beach and jetty! Marked pitches for tents and caravans are beside the beach or in little meadows in the forest. You pick your own place. Site amenities include a café and a beach sauna. This is a spectacular landscape with deep gorges and steep lakeside cliffs. There is a nature trail from the site to the lakes of Toriseva or pleasant excursions to the Esteri Zoo and the village shop in Keskinen. The Helvetinjärvi National Park is nearby. Facilities at the site are rather basic but very clean and well kept. This is a glorious place for a nature loving tourist looking to relax.

Facilities

Two toilet blocks, basic but clean and well kept include toilets, washbasins and showers. Free hot water. Chemical disposal and motorcaravan service point. Covered camper's kitchen with fridge, cooking rings and oven. Washing machine. Small shop and cafeteria. TV. Fishing. Bicycle hire. Off site: Golf 1 km. Riding 5 km.

Open: 1 May - 30 September.

Directions

Site is 7 km south of Virrat on road 66. Follow signs. GPS: N62:12.589 E23:50.266

Charges 2006

Per person	€ 2,00
child	€ 1,00
pitch	€ 12,00
electricity	€ 2,00

FI2922 Camping Taipale

Leiritie, FIN-78250 Varkaus (Kuopio)

Tel: 017 552 6644. Email: tuija.jalkanen@campingtaipale.inet.fi

Camping Taipale is situated right in the middle of an area of a thousand lakes, along the banks of Lake Haukivesi, which stretches to Savonlinna. Being at latitude of 62 degrees, daylight at Camping Taipale lasts for almost twenty four hours during the months of June and July. This site has 52 pitches, (all with electricity) in two lightly wooded areas, with a further grassy area for 90 tents and 16 log cabins to rent. To the south of the site there is a fine sandy beach and a small island with its own fishing dock for campers use. Savonlinna is the hub of the Lake Saimaa waterways traffic. The town is famous for its medieval castle Ovalinlinna, which is transformed each year for the world famous opera festival. To the north of the site is Kuopio, where Lake Kallavesi encircles the town centre. From the Puijo tower you can admire one of the most spectacular panoramas of Finnish lakes and forest while having lunch in the tower's revolving restaurant.

Facilities

Two sanitary blocks with good clean toilets and showers. The central block also provides a laundry with washing machines, driers, ironing facilities and good kitchen facilities. Two lakeside saunas (charged). Motorcaravan service point. Shop. Bar. Restaurant. Takeaway. Bicycle hire. Pedal boats. Beach volleyball. Minigolf. Trampoline. Off site: Old canal and museum within 1 km. The steamship 'Paul Wahl' has cruises on the lake. Varkaus 3 km. (home to the museum of mechanical music). Cruises from Kuopio.

Open: 26 May - 20 August.

Directions

Leave main road 5 at Varkaus and proceed through town. Site is about 7 km. from the route 5 junction. Turn at the traffic lights towards Taipale, then bear left. Site is on right about 1 km. further along.

Charges 2006

Per person	€ 3,00
child (2-15 yrs)	€ 1,00
pitch	€ 10,00

FI2960 Koljonvirta Camping

Ylemmäisentie 6, FIN-74120 Iisalmi (Kuopio)

Tel: 017 825252. Email: info@campingkoljonvirta.fi

Korljonvirta Camping is a large but quiet site located about five kilometres from the centre of Iisalmi. There are 200 marked grass pitches, 120 with electricity (16A). The site adjoins a lake and has a small beach and facilities for boating and fishing. Iisalmi town itself is on the northern edge of the Finnish Lake District and provides a good variety of shops, including some factory outlets, and an interesting variety of events during June, July and August. These vary from the world famous Wife-Carrying World Championships to the Lapinlahti Cattle Calling Competition and the International Midnight Marathon.

Facilities

The sanitary blocks provide showers, toilets and a sauna in one block. Launderette. Shop. Snack bar. Fully licenced restaurant. Motorcaravan service point. Lake and small beach with facilities for boating and fishing. The site exhibits large wooden sculptures of animals. Off site: Riding 100 m. Golf 5 km.

Open: May - September.

Directions

From road 5 turn onto the 88 (towards Oulu) just north of Iisalmi. Go straight over the roundabout and the site is about 1 km on the left. Follow signs. GPS: N63:35.649 E27:09.646

Charges 2006

Per person	€ 4,00
child	€ 1,00
pitch incl. electricity	€ 12,50

FI2970 Nallikari Camping

PL 55, FIN-90015 Oulun Kaupunki (Oulu)

Tel: 08 5586 1350. Email: nallikari.camping@ouka.fi

This is probably one of the best sites in Scandinavia, set in a recreational wooded area alongside a sandy beach on the banks of the Baltic Sea, with the added bonus of the adjacent Eden Spa complex. Nallikari provides 200 pitches with electricity (some also have water and drainage), plus an additional 79 cottages to rent, 28 of which are suitable for winter occupation. Oulu is a modern town about 100 miles south of the Arctic Circle that enjoys long, sunny and dry summer days. The Baltic however is frozen for many weeks in winter and then the sun barely rises for 2 months.

Facilities

The modern shower/WC blocks also provide male and female saunas, kitchen and launderette facilities. Facilities for disabled visitors. Motorcaravan service point. Playground. New reception with café/restaurant, souvenir and grocery shop. TV room. WiFi. Bicycle hire. Off site: The adjacent Eden centre provides excellent modern spa facilities where you can enjoy a day under the glass-roofed pool with its jacuzzis, saunas, Turkish Baths and an Irish Bath. Fishing 5 km. Golf 15 km.

Open: All year.

Directions

Leave Route 4/E75 at junction with route 20 and head west down Kiertotie. Site well signed, Nallikari Eden, but continue on, just after traffic lights, cross a bridge and take the second on the right. Just before the Eden Complex turn right towards Lerike and new reception. GPS: N65:01.784 E25:25.076

Charges 2006

Per pitch incl. 2 persons	€ 13,00 - € 24,00
extra person	€ 4,00
child (under 15 yrs)	€ 1,00
electricity	€ 3,50 - € 5,00

FI2975 Manamansalo Camping

Teeriniemientie 156, FIN-88340 Manamansalo (Oulu)

Tel: 08 874 138. Email: manamansalo@kainuunmatkailu.fi

Manamansalo is a top class, 'Wild North' tourist centre on the island of Manamansalo in Lake Oulojärvi. You come by ferry or via a bridge from the mainland. This site is a real find if you are looking for peace and quiet and is also very good for families. It has 200 pitches, 140 with electricity, very attractively laid out in the forest with natural dividers of pine trees. The site stretches along the lake and has a long, narrow sandy beach. Nature lovers will appreciate the network of trails in the pine forest. Choose between walking and cycling or even skiing in spring.

Facilities

Three toilet blocks have toilets, washbasins and showers in cubicles with free hot water. Washing machines and dryers. Kitchen with sinks, cooking rings and ovens. Chemical disposal and motorcaravan service point. Fully licensed restaurant and small shop (from May). Playground. Canoes, pedaloes and rowing boats for hire. Fishing. WiFi.

Open: 1 March - 30 September.

Directions

Coming from the south on road 5/E63 turn at Mainau on road 28. At Vuottolahti turn on road 879 and follow signs to Manamansalo and site. From road 22 turn at Liminpuro or Melaillahti and follow signs. GPS: N64:23.365 E27:01.565

Charges 2006

Per person	€ 4,00
child (0-15 yrs)	€ 1,00
pitch incl. electricity	€ 15,50 - € 17,50

FI2980 Ounaskoski Camping

Jäämerentie 1, FIN-96200 Rovaniemi (Lapland)

Tel: **016 345 304**

Ounaskoski Camping is situated almost exactly on the Arctic Circle, 66 degrees north and just 8 km. south of the Santa Claus Post office and village, on the banks of the Kemijoki River. The site has 113 marked touring pitches, (68 with electricity), plus a further a small area for tents. Rovaniemi attracts many visitors each year, especially in the weeks leading up to Christmas, who fly direct to the local airport and pay Santa Claus a visit. The town has much to offer with a good selection of shops and some restaurants. Reindeer meat is well worth trying! Not to be missed is the Artikum Museum where you will learn much of how people in the North live with nature and on her terms. Slightly further afield you can visit Vaattunkiköngäs and enjoy one of the many walks, which are suitable for everyone, from the one kilometre walk to the most challenging 9 kilometre path. Alternatively sit back and enjoy the summer sun on the riverbank.

Facilities	Directions
There are two sanitary buildings each providing toilets, showers, laundry and kitchen. One also houses a sauna. Facilities for disabled visitors. Motorcaravan service point. Café. Small shop. Playground. TV room. Fishing. Bicycle hire. Organised coach trips. Off site: Ranua Zoo. The Kemijoki, Finland's largest river, offers numerous opportunities for sightseeing by boat. Santa Claus village and Santa Park.	Ounaskoski Camping is on the banks of the Kemijoki River in the middle of Rovaniemi. From the 4/E75 go via the centre across the river and turn right. Site is between the Jatkankynttilasilta Bridge and the Rautatiesilta Bridge. GPS: N66:29.847 E25:44.594

Open: 1 June - 15 September.

Charges 2006

Per person	€ 4,50
child (under 15 yrs)	€ 2,50
pitch	€ 13,00
electricity (16A)	€ 3,80

FI2985 Camping Sodankylä Nilimella

Kelukoskentie 4, FIN-99600 Sodankylä (Lapland)

Tel: **016 612181.** Email: antti.rintala@naturex-ventures.fi

Camping Sodankylä Nilimella is a small, quiet site situated alongside the Kitinen River, just one kilometre from the centre of Sodankylä. The site is split into two areas by a small, relatively quiet, public road. The good sized pitches (80 in total) are clearly marked with hedges and 40 have 16A electricity. The reception area also serves drinks and snacks. Sodankylä town itself, at the junction of routes 4 and 5, is home to a small Sami community and is an important trading post, so you will find a variety of shops including supermarkets. The town is also home to the Geophysical Observatory, which constantly surveys the earth's magnetic field and measures earthquakes using seismic recordings. The Sodankylä Light Infantry Brigade, (the Finnish version of the SAS) which specialises in survival in cold climates is also based near here. This whole area is ideal for walking and bird watching; there are plenty of well marked paths to choose from. You can try the 4 km Luosto Game trail or the 15 km Kaares Fell hiking trail, which will take you right into the wilderness. There are many easier walks in the Urho Kekkonen National Park, which is close by, some 10 km north of Vuotso.

Facilities	Directions
Two good sanitary blocks with toilets, hot showers and saunas. Facilities for disabled visitors. Campers' kitchen. Motorcaravan service point. Playground. River swimming, canoeing and waterskiing. Off site: Shops and supermarkets in Sodankylä town.	Turn off Route 4 onto Route 5. The site is on the left just after you cross the river, it is well signed and easy to find. GPS: N67:25.053 E26:36.482

Open: 1 June - 31 August.

Charges 2006

Per unit incl. 2 persons and electricity	€ 15,50

FI2990 Camping Tenorinne

FIN-99950 Karigasniemi (Lapland)

Tel: 016 676113. Email: camping@tenorinne.com

This is probably the most northerly campsite in Finland and makes an excellent stop over on route to North Cape. This is a small site with space for 48 units, on three levels with a small access road sloping down to the river. Electricity points (16A) are available throughout the site but the pitches are unmarked. This area is still largely unpopulated, scattered with only small Sami communities and herds of reindeer. Karigasniemi is a slightly larger town as it is a border post with Norway and is close to both the Kevo Nature reserve and the Lemmenjoki National Park. Finland has 19 nature reserves covering an area of 1,520 square kilometres, Kevo takes up almost half of that area. The campsite is on the banks of the Tenojoki River and is an excellent base for walking and bird watching. A little further north you will find Nuvvus-Ailigas, the holy fell of the ancient sami, which rises to a height of 400m above the level of the Teno river. Karigasniemi is at the junction of the 970 with route 92 and is a good base to absorb all that Finnish Lapland has top offer.

Facilities	Directions
Sanitary block includes showers, toilets and sauna. Launderette. Kitchen. Reception with TV.	If travelling south on the 970, site is on right as you enter town. If travelling west on the 92, turn right immediately before Norwegian customs point. Site shortly on left past petrol station. Entrance quite steep. GPS: N69:24.020 E25:50.670
Open: 1 June - 20 September.	

Charges 2006

Per person	€ 3,00
pitch	€ 12,00
electricity	€ 3,00

FI2995 Ukonjarvi Camping

Ukonjärventi 141, FIN-99801 Ivalo (Lapland)

Tel: 016 667501. Email: nuttu@ukolo.fi

Ukonjärvi Camping lies on the banks of Lake Inari, situated in a forested area alongside a nature reserve. It is a quiet, peaceful site, ideal for rest and relaxation, with 30 touring pitches which have electricity and are surrounded by pine and beech trees. Cottages are available to rent. A bar and restaurant are located at reception; a range of local dishes are produced including reindeer casserole. There is also a barbecue hut, located in the centre of the site, if you prefer to cook your own food. A climb up to the nearby view point offers spectacular views over the lake – you can even see over to Russia. The lake also provides plenty of opportunities for boating and fishing.

Facilities	Directions
Sanitary block includes toilets and showers. Laundry and campers' kitchen. Lakeside sauna (extra cost). Bar and restaurant. Barbecue hut with logs. Small beach. Fishing and boating on lake. TV room. WiFi. Off site: Local attractions include the Tankavaaran kansainvalinen Kulamuseo, a gold mining experience where you can try gold panning – keeping what you find! The Northern Lapland Centre and the Sami Museum, displaying cultural and natural history exhibitions.	Ukonjärvi Camping is 11 km. north of Ivalo on Route 4. Look for signs to Lake Inari viewpoint; site is about 1 km. down the narrow road (signed). GPS: N68:44.212 E27:28.612

Charges 2006

Per person	€ 3,00
child	€ 2,00
pitch with electricity	€ 17,00

Open: May - September.

Check real time availability and at-the-gate prices...

www.**alanrogers**.com

From the hot sunny climate of the Mediterranean to the more northerly and cooler regions of Normandy and Brittany, with the Chateaux of the Loire and the lush valleys of the Dordogne, France offers holidaymakers a huge choice of destinations to suit all tastes.

France

CAPITAL: PARIS

Tourist Office

The French Government Tourist Office (FGTO)
178 Piccadilly
London W1V 0AL
Tel: 0906 8244 123
Fax: 0207 493 6594
Email: info.uk@franceguide.com
Internet: www.franceguide.com

France boasts every type of landscape imaginable ranging from the wooded valleys of the Dordogne to the volcanic uplands of the Massif Central, the rocky coast of Brittany to the lavender covered hills of Provence and snow-capped peaks of the Alps. Each region is different and this is reflected in the local customs, cuisine, architecture and dialect. Many rural villages hold festivals to celebrate the local saints and you can also find museums devoted to the rural arts and crafts of the regions.

France has a rich architectural heritage with a huge variety of Gothic cathedrals, châteaux, Roman remains, fortresses and Romanesque churches to visit. Given the varied landscape and climate there is also great scope for outdoor pursuits with plenty of hiking and cycling opportunities across the country, and rock-climbing and skiing in the mountains. And of course a trip to France wouldn't be complete without sampling the local food and wine.

Population
60.2 million

Climate
France has a temperate climate but this varies considerably from region to region.

Language
French

Telephone
The country code is 00 33.

Money
Currency: The Euro
Banks: Mon-Fri 09.00-1200 and 14.00-16.00.

Shops
Mon-Sat 0900-1830. Some are closed between 1200-1430. Food shops are open 0700-1830/1930. Some food shops (particularly bakers) are open Sunday mornings. Many shops close Mondays.

Public Holidays
New Year; Easter Mon; Labour Day; VE Day 8 May; Ascension; Whit Mon; Bastille Day 14 July; Assumption 15 Aug; All Saints 1 Nov; Armistice Day 11 Nov; Christmas Day.

Motoring
France has a comprehensive road system from motorways (Autoroutes), Routes Nationales (N roads), Routes Départementales (D roads) down to purely local C class roads. Tolls are payable on the autoroute network which is extensive but expensive, and also on certain bridges.

FR22210 Camping Bellevue

Route de Pléneuf Val-André, F-22430 Erquy (Côtes d'Armor)

Tel: 02 96 72 33 04. Email: campingbellevue@yahoo.fr

Situated a mile from the beaches between Erquy and Pléneuf Val-André, Camping Bellevue offers a quiet country retreat with easy access to the cliffs of Cap Fréhel, Sables d'Or and St Cast. There are 140 pitches of which 120 are available for touring units, most with electricity (6/10A) and 15 with water and drainage. The site also has 20 mobile homes, chalets and bungalows to rent. A 'Sites et Paysages' member. Children are well catered for at this campsite – there are heated swimming and paddling pools, three play areas and minigolf, petanque and volleyball. Indoor entertainment for all includes theme evenings, Breton dancing and visits to a local cider house. There are numerous walks in the area and a vast range of aquatic sports at nearby Erquy.

Facilities

Two modern, unisex toilet blocks are of a high standard. Some washbasins in cubicles. Facilities for disabled visitors. Dishwashing and laundry facilities. Shop and bar (15/6-10/9). Restaurant and takeaway (12/6-31/8). Swimming and paddling pools (10/5-10/9). Play areas. Pool table. TV room. Table football, video games and library. Minigolf. Petanque. Volleyball. Entertainment and organised activities in high season. Off site: Beach and fishing 2 km. Golf 3 km. Bicycle hire and boat launching 5 km. Riding 6 km.

Open: 31 March - 30 September.

Directions

From St Brieuc road take D786 towards Erquy. Site is adjacent to the D786 at St Pabu and is well signed.

Charges 2006

extra person	€ 3,80 - € 4,80
child (2-13 yrs)	free - € 4,20
Per unit incl. 2 persons	€ 14,20 - € 18,00
electricity	€ 3,20 - € 4,50
dog	€ 1,20 - € 1,60

FR29030 Camping du Letty

F-29950 Bénodet (Finistère)

Tel: 02 98 57 04 69. Email: reception@campingduletty.com

The Guyader family have ensured that this excellent and attractive site has plenty to offer for all the family. The site on the outskirts of the popular resort of Bénodet spreads over 22 acres with 493 pitches, all for touring units. Groups of four to eight pitches are set in cul-de-sacs, each group divided by mature hedging and trees. Most pitches have electricity, water and drainage. The site has direct access to a small sandy beach with a floating pontoon (safe bathing depends on the tides).

Facilities

Six well placed toilet blocks are of good quality and include mixed style WCs, washbasins in large cabins and controllable hot showers (charged). Baby rooms. Separate facility for disabled visitors. Launderette. Hairdressing room. Motorcaravan services. Mini-market. Extensive snack bar and takeaway (22/6-30/8). Bar with games room and night club. Fitness centre (no charge). Saunas, jacuzzi and solarium (all on payment). Two tennis and two squash courts (charged). Play area.

Open: 15 June - 6 September.

Directions

From N165 take D70 Concarneau exit. At first roundabout take D44 to Fouesnant. Turn right at T-junction. After 2 km. turn left to Fouesnant (still D44). Continue through La Forêt Fouesnant and Fouesnant, picking up signs for Bénodet. Shortly before Bénodet at roundabout turn left (signed Le Letty). GPS: N47:52.02 W04:05.27

Charges 2007

Per person	€ 5,40
pitch	€ 9,00 - € 11,00

FR29050 Castel Camping L'Orangerie de Lanniron

Château de Lanniron, F-29336 Quimper (Finistère)
Tel: **02 98 90 62 02**. Email: **camping@lanniron.com**

L'Orangerie is a beautiful and peaceful, family site set in 10 acres of a XVIIth century, 42 acre country estate on the banks of the Odet river, formerly the home of the Bishops of Quimper. The site has 200 grassy pitches (146 for touring units) of three types varying in size and services. They are on flat ground laid out in rows alongside access roads with shrubs and bushes providing pleasant pitches. All have electricity and 88 have all three services. With lovely walks within the grounds, the restaurant and the gardens are both open to the public and in spring the rhododendrons and azaleas are magnificent. The site is just to the south of Quimper and about 15 km. from the sea and beaches at Bénodet. The family owner's five year programme to restore the park, the original canal, fountains, ornamental 'Bassin de Neptune', the boathouse, the gardens and avenues is very well advanced. The original outbuildings have been attractively converted around a walled courtyard. Used by tour operators (30 pitches). All facilities are available when the site is open.

Facilities

Excellent heated block in the courtyard and second modern block serving the top areas of the site. Facilities for disabled people and babies. Washing machines and dryers. Motorcaravan services. Shop (15/5-9/9). Gas supplies. Bar, snacks and takeaway. New restaurant (open daily). New pool complex. New golf driving range and 9 hole course (with academy). Small play area. Tennis. Minigolf. Table tennis. Fishing. Archery. Bicycle hire. General reading, games and billiards rooms. TV/video room. Karaoke. Outdoor activities. Large room for indoor activities. Off site: Two hypermarkets 1 km. Historic town of Quimper under 3 km. Activities in the area include golf, cycling, walking, fishing, canoeing, surfing and sailing. Beach 15 km.

Open: 15 May - 15 September.

Directions

From Quimper follow 'Quimper Sud' signs, then 'Toutes Directions' and general camping signs, finally signs for Lanniron.

Charges 2006

Per person	€ 4,20 - € 6,50
child (2-10 yrs)	€ 2,70 - € 4,20
pitch (100 sq.m.)	€ 10,20 - € 15,80
with electricity (10A)	€ 13,20 - € 20,00
special pitch (120/150 sq.m.) with water and electricity	€ 16,80 - € 25,20
Less 15% outside July/Aug.	

Camping Cheques accepted.

FR29010 Castel Camping le Ty Nadan

Route d'Arzano, F-29310 Locunolé (Finistère)

Tel: **02 98 71 75 47**. Email: **infos@camping-ty-nadan.fr**

Ty Nadan is a well organised site set amongst wooded countryside along the bank of the River Elle. The 183 pitches for touring units are grassy, many with shade and 99 are fully serviced. The pool complex with slides and paddling pool is very popular as is the large indoor pool complex and an indoor games area with a climbing wall. There is also an adventure play park and a 'Minikids' park for 5-8 year olds, not to mention tennis courts, table tennis, pool tables, archery and trampolines. This is a wonderful site for families with children. Several tour operators use the site. An exciting and varied programme of activities is offered throughout the season – canoe and sea kayaking expeditions, rock climbing, mountain biking, aqua-gym, paintball, riding or walking – all supervised by qualified staff. A full programme of entertainment for all ages is provided in high season including concerts, Breton evenings with pig roasts, dancing, etc. (be warned, you will be actively encouraged to join in!)

Facilities

Two older, split-level toilet blocks are of fair quality and include washbasins in cabins and baby rooms. A newer block provides easier access for disabled people. Washing machines and dryers. Restaurant, takeaway, bar and well stocked shop. Crêperie (July/Aug). Heated outdoor pool (17 x 8 m.) and new indoor pool. Small river beach (unfenced). Indoor badminton and rock climbing facility. Activity and entertainment programmes (high season). Bicycle hire. Boat hire. Fishing. Off site: Beaches 20 minutes by car. Golf 12 km.

Open: 1 April - 7 September.

Directions

Make for Arzano which is northeast of Quimperlé on the Pontivy road and turn off D22 just west of village at camp sign. Site is about 3 km.

Charges 2006

Per person	€ 4,30 - € 8,40
child (under 7 yrs)	€ 1,70 - € 5,20
pitch	€ 8,70 - € 21,00
electricity (10A)	€ 2,60 - € 6,30
dog	€ 1,70 - € 5,20

Less 15-20% outside July/Aug.
Camping Cheques accepted.

kawan-villages.com **tel: 00 333 59 59 03 59**

kawan VILLAGES CAMPINGS

FR29190 Camping les Prés Verts

B.P. 612, Kernous-Plage, F-29186 Concarneau Cedex (Finistère)

Tel: **02 98 97 09 74**. Email: **info@presverts.com**

What sets this family site apart from the many others in this region are its more unusual features – its stylish pool complex with Romanesque style columns and statue, and its plants and flower tubs. The 150 pitches are mostly arranged on long, open, grassy areas either side of main access roads. Specimen trees, shrubs or hedges divide the site into smaller areas. There are a few individual pitches and an area towards the rear of the site where the pitches have sea views. A 'Sites et Paysages' member. Concarneau is just 2.5 km. and there are many marked coastal walks to enjoy in the area, plus watersports or boat and fishing trips available nearby.

Facilities

Two toilet blocks provide unisex WCs, but separate washing facilities for ladies and men. Pre-set hot showers and washbasins in cabins for ladies, both closed 9 pm - 8 am. Some child-size toilets. Laundry facilities. Pizza service twice weekly. Heated swimming pool (1/7-31/8) and paddling pool. Playground (0-5 yrs only). Minigolf (charged). Off site: Path to sandy/rocky beach (300 m.) and coastal path. Riding 1 km. Supermarket 2 km. Bicycle hire 3 km. Golf 5 km.

Open: 1 April - 22 September.

Directions

Turn off C7 road, 2.5 km. north of Concarneau, where site is signed. Take third left after Hotel de l'Océan. GPS: N47:53. W03:56

Charges 2007

Per unit incl. 2 persons	€ 16,00 - € 22,00
extra person	€ 4,70 - € 6,50
child (2-7 yrs)	€ 3,10 - € 4,30
electricity (2-6A)	€ 3,20 - € 6,00

FR29080 Camping le Panoramic

Route de la Plage-Penker, F-29560 Telgruc-sur-Mer (Finistère)

Tel: **02 98 27 78 41**. Email: **info@camping-panoramic.com**

This medium sized traditional site is situated on quite a steep, ten acre hillside with fine views. It is personally run by M. Jacq and his family who all speak good English. The 200 pitches are arranged on flat, shady terraces, in small groups with hedges and flowering shrubs and 20 pitches have services for motorcaravans. Divided into two parts, the main upper site is where most of the facilities are located, with the swimming pool, its terrace and a playground located with the lower pitches across the road. A 'Sites et Paysages' member. Some up-and-down walking is therefore necessary, but this is a small price to pay for such pleasant and comfortable surroundings. This area provides lovely coastal footpaths.

Facilities

The main site has two well kept toilet blocks with another very good block opened for main season across the road. All three include British and Turkish style WCs, washbasins in cubicles, facilities for disabled people, baby baths, plus laundry facilities. Motorcaravan services. Small shop (1/7-31/8). Bar/restaurant with takeaway (1/7-31/8). Barbecue area. Heated pool, paddling pool and jacuzzi (1/6-15/9). Playground. Games and TV rooms. Tennis. Volleyball. Bicycle hire. Off site: Beach and fishing 700 m. Riding 6 km. Golf 14 km. Sailing school nearby.

Open: 1 June - 15 September.

Directions

Site is just south of Telgruc-sur-Mer. On D887 pass through Ste Marie du Ménez Horn. Turn left on D208 signed Telgruc-sur-Mer. Continue straight on through town and site is on right within 1 km. GPS: N48:13.428 W04:22.382

Charges 2006

Per person	€ 5,00
child (under 7 yrs)	€ 3,00
pitch	€ 12,00
electricity (6-10A)	€ 3,10 - € 4,50
water and drainage connection	€ 2,50

Less 20% outside July/Aug.

FR35040 Camping le P'tit Bois

Saint Malo, F-35430 Saint Jouan des Guerets (Ille-et-Vilaine)

Tel: **02 99 21 14 30**. Email: **camping.ptitbois@wanadoo.fr**

On the outskirts of Saint Malo, this neat, family oriented site is very popular with British visitors, being ideal for one night stops or for longer stays in this interesting area. Le P'tit Bois provides 274 large level pitches with 114 for touring units. In two main areas, either side of the entrance lane, these are divided into groups by mature hedges and trees, separated by shrubs and flowers and with access from tarmac roads. Nearly all have electrical hook-ups and over half have water taps. There are site-owned mobile homes and chalets so the facilities are open over a long season.

Facilities

Two fully equipped toilet blocks, include washbasins in cabins. Baby baths. Laundry facilities. Simple facilities for disabled people. Motorcaravan service point. Small shop (from 1/5). Bar with entertainment in July-Aug. Snack bar with takeaway. TV room. Games rooms. Heated swimming pool, paddling pool and two water slides (from 1/5). Heated indoor pool (from 8/4). Playground. Multi-sports court. Tennis court, minigolf. Charcoal barbecues not permitted. Off site: Beach, fishing 1.5 km. Buses 2 km. Bicycle hire or riding 5 km. Golf 15 km.

Open: 7 April - 8 September.

Directions

St Jouan is west off the St Malo - Rennes road (N137) just outside St Malo. Site is signed from the N137 (exit St Jouan on the D4). GPS: N48:36.579 W01:59.27

Charges 2007

Per person	€ 5,00 - € 8,00
child (under 7 yrs)	€ 3,00 - € 6,00
pitch and car	€ 8,00 - € 19,00
electricity (6A)	€ 4,00

FR29180 Camping les Embruns

Rue du Philosophe Alain, Le Pouldu, F-29360 Clohars-Carnoét (Finistère)

Tel: **02 98 39 91 07**. Email: **camping-les-embruns@wanadoo.fr**

This site is unusual in that it is located in the heart of a village, yet is only 250 metres from a sandy cove. The entrance with its card operated barrier and wonderful floral displays, is the first indication that this is a well tended and well organised site, and the owners have won numerous regional and national awards for its superb presentation. The 180 pitches (100 occupied by mobile homes) are separated by trees, shrubs and bushes, and most have electricity, water and drainage. There is a covered, heated swimming pool, a circular paddling pool and a water play pool. It is only a short walk to the village centre with all its attractions and services. It is also close to beautiful countryside and the Carnoët Forest which are good for walking and cycling.

Facilities

Two modern sanitary blocks, recently completely renewed, include mainly British style toilets, some washbasins in cubicles, baby baths and good facilities for disabled visitors. Family bathrooms. Laundry facilities. Motorcaravan service point. Mini-market and restaurant by site entrance. Bar and terrace (1/7-31/8). Takeaway (20/6-5/9). Covered, heated swimming and paddling pools. Large games hall. Play area. Football field, volleyball and minigolf. Communal barbecue area. Daily activities for children and adults organised in July/Aug. Off site: Nearby sea and river fishing and watersports. Bicycle hire 50 m. Beach 250 m. Riding 2 km.

Open: 7 April - 15 September.

Directions

From N165 take either 'Kervidanou, Quimperlé Ouest' exit or 'Kergostiou, Quimperlé Centre, Clohars Carnoét' exit and follow D16 to Clohars Carnoét. Then take D24 for Le Pouldu and follow site signs in village. GPS: N47:46 W03:32

Charges 2007

Per unit incl. 2 persons	€ 10,50 - € 15,40
fully serviced pitch	€ 15,90 - € 28,20
extra person	€ 3,90 - € 5,30
child (under 7 yrs)	€ 2,60 - € 3,20
electricity on ordinary pitch	€ 3,90

Less in low seasons.
Use of motorcaravan services € 4.

250 m from one of Brittany's sandy beaches Mr & Mrs Leguennou welcome you in their particularly well maintained campsite where you are assured of a good holiday.
• First class facilities and amenities in a green and floral environment • Mobile homes to let • Motorcaravan service point • Covered heated swimming pool right from the opening •

LE POULDU - F-29360 CLOHARS-CARNOET
TEL: 0033 298 39 91 07 - FAX: 0033 298 39 97 87
www.camping-les-embruns.com
E-mail: camping-les-embruns@wanadoo.fr

FR44100 Sunêlia le Patisseau

29 rue du Patisseau, F-44210 Pornic (Loire-Atlantique)

Tel: **02 40 82 10 39**. Email: **contact@lepatisseau.com**

Le Patisseau is situated in the countryside just a short drive from the fishing village of Pornic. It is a relaxed site with a large number of mobile homes and chalets, and popular with young families and teenagers. The 115 touring pitches all with electrical connections (6A), are divided between the attractive 'forest' area with plenty of shade from mature trees and the more open 'prairie' area some are on a slight slope and access to others might be tricky for larger units. A railway runs along the bottom half of the site with trains several times a day, (but none overnight) and the noise is minimal.

Facilities

The modern heated toilet block is very spacious and well fitted; most washbasins are open style, but the controllable showers are all in large cubicles which have washbasins (very popular). Facilities for disabled visitors and babies, laundry rooms and dishwashing facilities. Shop (15/5-8/9). Bar, restaurant and takeaway (1/7-31/9). Indoor heated pool with sauna, jacuzzi and spa. Small heated outdoor pools and water slides (15/5-3/9). Play area. Multisport court. Bicycle hire. Off site: Fishing and beach 2.5 km. Riding, golf and sailing all 5 km.

Open: 8 April - 6 November.

Directions

Pornic is 19 km. south of the St Nazaire bridge. Access to site is at junction of D751 Nantes - Pornic road with the D213 St Nazaire - Noirmoutier 'Route Bleue'. From north take exit for D751 Nantes. From south follow D751 Clion-sur-Mer. At roundabout north of D213 take exit for Le Patisseau. Follow signs. Avoid Pornic centre. GPS: N47:07.183 W02:04.397

Charges 2006

Per unit incl. 2 persons	€ 20,00 - € 30,50
incl. electricity (6A)	€ 24,00 - € 34,50
extra person	€ 5,50 - € 7,50

FR35000 Camping le Vieux Chêne

Baguer-Pican, F-35120 Dol-de-Bretagne (Ille-et-Vilaine)

Tel: **02 99 48 09 55**. Email: **vieux.chene@wanadoo.fr**

This attractive, family owned site is situated between Saint Malo and Mont Saint Michel. Developed in the grounds of a country farmhouse dating from 1638, its young and enthusiastic owner has created a really pleasant, traditional atmosphere. In spacious, rural surroundings it offers 199 good sized pitches on gently sloping grass, most with 10A electricity, water tap and light. They are separated by bushes and flowers, with mature trees for shade. A very attractive tenting area (without electricity) is in the orchard. Used by a Dutch tour operator (10 pitches). There are three lakes in the grounds and centrally located leisure facilities include a restaurant with a terrace overlooking an attractive pool complex. Some entertainment is provided in high season, which is free for children.

Facilities

Three very good, unisex toilet blocks, which can be heated, include washbasins in cabins, a baby room and facilities for disabled people. Small laundry. Motorcaravan services. Shop, takeaway and restaurant (15/5-15/9). Heated swimming pool, paddling pool, slides (15/5-15/9; lifeguard July/Aug). TV room (satellite) and games room. Tennis court. Minigolf. Giant chess. Play area. Riding in July/Aug. Fishing. Off site: Supermarket in Dol 3 km. Golf 12 km. Beach 20 km.

Open: 31 March - 22 September.

Directions

Site is by the D576 Dol-de-Bretagne - Pontorson road, just east of Baguer-Pican. It can be reached from the new N176 taking exit for Dol-Est and Baguer-Pican. GPS: N48:32.972 W01:41.03

Charges 2007

Per person	€ 4,50 - € 5,75
child (under 13 yrs)	free - € 3,90
pitch with electricity	€ 10,00 - € 21,50

FR44150 Camping la Tabardière

F-44770 La Plaine-sur-Mer (Loire-Atlantique)

Tel: **02 40 21 58 83**. Email: **info@camping-la-tabardiere.com**

Owned and managed by the Barre family, this campsite lies next to the family farm. Pleasant, peaceful and immaculate, it will suit those who want to enjoy the local coast and towns but return to an 'oasis' for relaxation. It still, however, provides activities and fun for those with energy remaining. The pitches are mostly terraced either side of a narrow valley. Care needs to be taken in manoeuvring caravans into position – although the effort is well worth it. Most pitches have access to electricity and water taps are conveniently situated. The site is probably not suitable for wheelchair users. A 'Sites et Paysages' member.

Facilities

Two good, clean toilet blocks are well equipped and include laundry facilities. Motorcaravan service point. Bar. Shop. Snacks and takeaway. Good sized swimming pool, paddling pool and slides (supervised). Playground. Minigolf. Table tennis. Volleyball and basketball. Half size tennis courts. Boules. Overnight area for motorcaravans (€ 9 per night). Off site: Beach 3 km. Sea fishing, golf, riding all 5 km.

Open: 1 April - 30 September.

Directions

Site is well signed, situated inland off the D13 Pornic - La Plaine sur Mer road.

Charges 2006

Per unit incl. 2 persons	€ 12,50 - € 21,00
extra person	€ 3,30 - € 5,50
child (2-10 yrs)	€ 2,50 - € 3,50
dog	€ 2,70
electricity (3/8A)	€ 2,80 - € 4,20

FR44090 Camping Château du Deffay

B.P. 18 Le Deffay, Ste Reine de Bretagne, F-44160 Pontchâteau (Loire-Atlantique)

Tel: 02 40 88 00 57. Email: campingdudeffay@wanadoo.fr

A family managed site, Château du Deffay is a refreshing departure from the usual formula in that it is not over organised or supervised and has no tour operator units. The 142 good sized, fairly level pitches have pleasant views and are either on open grass, on shallow terraces divided by hedges, or informally arranged in a central, slightly sloping wooded area. Most have electricity. The facilities are located within the old courtyard area of the smaller château (that dates from before 1400). With the temptation of free pedaloes and the fairly deep, unfenced lake, parents should ensure that children are supervised. The landscape is natural right down to the molehills, and the site blends well with the rural environment of the estate, lake and farmland which surround it. For these reasons it is enjoyed by many. The larger château (built 1880) and another lake stand away from this area providing pleasant walking. The reception has been built separately to contain the camping area. Alpine type chalets overlook the lake and fit in well with the environment. The site is close to the Brière Regional Park, the Guérande Peninsula, and La Baule with its magnificent beach is 20 km.

Facilities

The main toilet block is well equipped including washbasins in cabins, provision for disabled people and a baby bathroom. Laundry facilities. Maintenance can be variable and hot water can take time to reach temperature in low season. Shop, bar, small restaurant with takeaway and solar heated swimming pool and paddling pool (all 15/5-15/9). Play area. TV. Animation in season including children's miniclub. Torches useful. Off site: Golf and riding 5 km.

Open: 1 May - 30 September.

Directions

Site is signed from D33 Pontchâteau - Herbignac road near Ste Reine. Also signed from the D773 and N165.

Charges 2006

Per person	€ 3,00 - € 4,90
child (2-12 yrs)	€ 2,00 - € 3,30
pitch	€ 7,20 - € 11,00
with electricity (6A)	€ 10,40 - € 14,90
with 3 services	€ 12,20 - € 16,80

Camping Cheques accepted.

FR44180 Camping de la Boutinardière

Rue de la Plage de la Boutinardière, F-44210 Pornic (Loire-Atlantique)

Tel: 02 40 82 05 68. Email: info@laboutinardiere.com

This is truly a holiday site to suit all the family whatever their age, just 200 m. from the beach. It has 250 individual good sized pitches, 100-120 sq.m. in size, many bordered by three metre high, well maintained hedges for shade and privacy. All pitches have electricity available. It is a family owned site and English is spoken by the helpful, obliging reception staff. Beside reception is the excellent site shop and across the road is a complex of indoor and outdoor pools, paddling pool and a twin toboggan water slide. On site there are sports and entertainment areas. Facing the water complex, the bar, restaurant and terraces are new and serve excellent food, be it a snack or in the restaurant or perhaps a takeaway. This site is difficult to better in the South Brittany, Loire-Atlantique area. This campsite has it all – two kilometres from the beautiful harbour town of Pornic and 200 metres from the sea, together with the very best of amenities and facilities.

Facilities

Toilet facilities are in three good blocks, one large and centrally situated and two supporting blocks. The quality, maintenance and cleanliness are amongst the best. Washbasins are in cabins, dishwashing is under cover. Laundry facilities. Shop (15/6-15/9). New complex of bar, restaurant, terraces (1/4-30/9). Three heated swimming pools, one indoor (1/4-15/9), a paddling pool and water slides (15/5-22/9). Games room. Sports area. Playground. Off site: Sandy cove 200 m. Restaurants, cafés, golf, riding, fishing, sailing and windsurfing, all within 5 km.

Open: 1 April - 30 September.

Directions

From north or south on D213, take Nantes D751 exit. At roundabout (with McDonalds) take D13 signed Bemarie-en-Retz. After 4 km. site is signed to right. Note: do NOT exit from D213 at Pornic Ouest or Centre.

Charges 2006

Per unit incl. 2 persons	€ 14,00 - € 32,00
extra person	€ 3,00 - € 6,00
child (2-10 yrs)	€ 2,00 - € 4,50
electricity (6-10A)	€ 3,50 - € 5,00

FR44210 Camping L'Océan

44490 Le Croisic (Loire-Atlantique)

Tel: 02 40 23 07 69. Email: info@camping-ocean.com

Camping de l'Océan is located on the Le Croisic peninsula, an area which enjoys a microclimate, thanks to the gulf stream. The site is within walking distance of the Atlantic Ocean and the white sandy beaches of the Côte d'Amor. L'Océan has been recommended by our French agent and we hope to undertake a full inspection in 2007. There are many facilities here including a large swimming pool complex with water slides, an indoor pool and paddling pool.

Facilities

Laundry and ironing facilities. Restaurant. Takeaway food. Bar. Supermarket. Motorcaravan service point. Swimming pool complex comprising an indoor pool, outdoor pool and paddling pool. Volleyball. Football. Basketball. Tennis. Off site: Archery. Sailing. Scuba diving. Cycling. Fishing.

Open: April - September.

Directions

From Nantes take the N165 and then the N171 to Guérande. At the roundabout before Guérande follow signs to Le Croisic using the D774. Just before the centre of Le Croisic, the site is signed.

Charges 2007

Per unit incl 2 persons and electricity	€ 16,50 - € 36.50
extra person	€ 3,00 - € 7,00
child (under 7 years)	€ 2,00 - € 5,50

This is just a sample of the campsites we have inspected and selected in France. For more campsites and further information, please see the Alan Rogers France guide.

*3 campsites with water park
in the lovely region of south Brittany...*

3 covered swimming pools with heated water and air.

Aquaticamp

* water park
Domaine de Léveno

* water park la Boutinardière

Domaine de Léveno
Camping - Locatière
★★★★

only 5 km from la Baule !
www.camping-leveno.com
route de Sandun
44350 GUÉRANDE - FRANCE
Tel. : 00 33 (0)2 40 24 79 30
Fax : 00 33 (0)2 40 62 01 23

la Baule

le Croisic

La Boutinardière
Camping Village
★★★

Camping
Qualité

Airotel

only 200 m from the beach !
www.camping-boutinardiere.com
rue de la plage de la Boutinardière
44210 PORNIC - FRANCE
Tel. : 00 33 (0)2 40 82 05 68
Fax : 00 33 (0)2 40 82 49 01

Guérande

* water park de l'Océan

l'Océan
Camping Village ★★★

Camping
Qualité

only 150 m from the beach !
www.camping-ocean.com
15, route Maison Rouge - B.P. 15
44490 LE CROISIC - FRANCE
Tel. : 00 33 (0)2 40 23 07 69
Fax : 00 33 (0)2 40 15 70 63

Pornic

Réalisation Koro Marketing © 2006 - www.koromarketing.com.fr

FR44190 Camping le Fief

57, chemin du Fief, F-44250 St Brévin-les-Pins (Loire-Atlantique)

Tel: **02 40 27 23 86**. Email: **camping@lefief.com**

If you are a family with young children or lively teenagers, this could be the campsite for you. Le Fief is a well established site only 800 metres from sandy beaches on the southern Brittany coast. It has a magnificent 'aqua park' with outdoor and covered swimming pools, paddling pools, slides, river rapids, fountains, jets and more. The site has 220 pitches for touring units (out of 413). Whilst these all have electricity (5A), they vary in size and many are worn and may be untidy. There are also 143 mobile homes and chalets to rent and 55 privately owned units. This is a lively site in high season with a variety of entertainment and organised activity for all ages. This ranges from a miniclub for 5-12 year olds, to 'Tonic Days' with aquagym, jogging and sports competitions, and to evening events which include karaoke, themed dinners and cabaret. There are plenty of sporting facilities for active youngsters.

Facilities

One excellent new toilet block and three others of a lower standard. Laundry facilities. Shop (15/5-15/9). Bar, restaurant and takeaway (15/4-15/9) with terrace overlooking the pool complex. Outdoor pools, etc. (15/5-15/9). Covered pool (all season). Play area. Tennis. Archery. Games room. Internet access. Organised entertainment and activities (July/Aug). Off site: Beach, bicycle hire 800 m. Bus stop 1 km. Riding 1 km. Golf 15 km.

Open: 1 April - 15 October.

Directions

From the St Nazaire bridge take the fourth exit from the D213 signed St Brévin - L'Océan. Continue over first roundabout and bear right at the second to join Chemin du Fief. The site is on the right, well signed.

Charges 2006

Per pitch incl. 2 persons	€ 14,00 - € 35,00
extra person	€ 4,00 - € 8,50
child (0-7 yrs)	€ 2,00 - € 4,25
electricity	€ 4,00 - € 5,00

FR44220 Parc de Léveno

Route de Sandun, F-44350 Guérande (Loire-Atlantique)

Tel: **02 40 24 79 30, or 02 40 24 79**. Email: **domaine.leveno@wanadoo.fr**

There have been many changes to this extensive site over the past three years and considerable investment has been made to provide some excellent new facilities. The number of mobile homes and chalets has increased considerably, leaving just 47 touring pitches. However, these are mainly grouped at the far end of the site. Pitches are divided by hedges and trees which offer a good deal of shade and all have electricity (10A). Access is tricky to some and the site is not recommended for larger units. Twin axle caravans and American motorhomes are not accepted. The site is close to the historic town of Guérande, its salt marshes, some good beaches and the Natural Reserve of La Brière.

Facilities

Main refurbished toilet block offers pre-set showers, washbasins in cubicles and facilities for disabled visitors. Laundry facilities. Small shop selling basics and takeaway snacks. Bar with TV and games (all July/Aug). Indoor pool. Heated outdoor pool complex with water slides and a flume, paddling pool (15/5-15/9). Aquatic Centre. Fitness room. Play area. Multisport court. Programme of activities and events (high season). Off site: Hypermarket 1 km. Fishing 2 km. Beach, golf and riding all 5 km.

Open: Easter - 30 September.

Directions

Site is less than 3 km. from the centre of Guérande. From D774 and from D99/N171 take D99E Guérande by-pass. Turn east following signs for Villejames and Leclerc Hypermarket and continue on D247 to site on right. GPS: N47:19.987 W02:23.478

Charges 2006

Per unit incl. 2 persons,	
electricity and water	€ 15,00 - € 25,00
extra person	€ 3,00 - € 5,00
child (under 7 yrs)	€ 1,80 - € 3,00

See advertisement on page 109

FR56280 Airotel les Sept Saints

B.P. 14, F-56410 Erdeven (Morbihan)

Tel: **02 97 55 52 65**. Email: **info@septsaints.com**

One is attracted to this campsite on arrival, with a well-tended shrubbery and reception to the left of the entrance and a landscaped pool complex on the right. The 200 pitches are divided equally between mobile homes and touring pitches, arranged in three separate groups: 60 normal touring pitches with electricity (10A), mobile homes, and an area under the trees across the play area for tents. Touring pitches are separated by manicured hedges and are level grass. The heated swimming pool complex, with its slides, jacuzzi and padding pool, and overlooked by the bar terrace, provides a focal point. In July and August there are separate children's clubs for younger children and teenagers and a variety of entertainment in the evenings. The site offers a complete holiday within itself as well as access to the Brittany coast.

Facilities

Two modern toilet blocks include en-suite facilities for disabled visitors and attractive baby rooms. Two laundry rooms. Bar, takeaway and shop (10/6-9/9). Heated swimming pool with slides, Jacuzzi,and paddling pool with mushroom and baby slide (15/5-15/9). Excellent play areas. Multisports pitch. Boules. Grass area for ball games. Bicycle hire. Games room. TV room. Gas supplies. Internet. Off site: Fishing 1.5 km. Riding 3 km. Golf 3 km. Beach and sailing 3 km.

Open: 15 May - 15 September.

Directions

From N165 at Auray take exit for D768 to Carnac and Quiberon. At roundabout entering Plouharnel turn west on D781, following signs to Erdeven and L'Orient. Continue through Erdeven, turn left where site is signed after 1.5 km. and site is 150 m. on the right. GPS: N47:39.317 W03:10.307

Charges 2006

Per person	€ 4,00 - € 6,00
child (under 7 yrs)	€ 3,00 - € 5,00
pitch incl. electricity	€ 15,00 - € 22,00

FR56020 Camping de la Plage

Plage de Kervilaine, F-56470 La Trinité-sur-Mer (Morbihan)

Tel: **02 97 55 73 28**. Email: **camping@camping-plage.com**

The Carnac/La Trinité area of Brittany is popular with British holiday makers. Camping de la Plage is one of two sites, close to each other and owned by members of the same family, with direct access to the safe sandy beach of Kervillen Plage. There are 198 grass pitches of which 112 are for touring (64 are used by tour operators). All are hedged and have electricity (6/10A), water and drainage. The site has a pronounced slope and some pitches reflect this. With narrow roads and sharp bends, it is not suitable for large units. The shop, restaurant and bar, 200 m. along the coast opposite Camping de la Baie, are used by local residents and provide excellent value. The restaurant and takeaway have extensive menus. A lively entertainment programme for all ages in high season makes this an attractive site for family holidays.

Facilities

Toilet blocks have washbasins in cubicles and facilities for disabled people and small children. Laundry facilities. Small swimming pool with water slides. Play areas including ball pool. Tennis, basketball, table tennis. TV. Entertainment programme in high season for all ages. Bicycle hire. Beach. Guided tours. Internet access. Communal barbecue areas (gas or electric only on pitches). Off site: Fishing 50 m. Shop with bakery. Bar, restaurant, crêperie, takeaway (all 200 m). Sailing 1.5 km. Riding 3.5 km. Golf 5 km.

Open: 12 May - 16 September.

Directions

From N165 at Auray take D28 (La Trinité-sur-Mer). On through town following signs to Carnac-Plage on D186. Site signed off this road to the south. Take care to take road signed to Kervillen Plage where it forks. At sea front turn right. Site is 300 m. on right. GPS: N47:34.538 W03:01.734

Charges 2006

Per unit incl. 2 persons	€ 16,90 - € 32,30
extra person	€ 5,00
child (2-18 yrs)	€ 3,00 - € 4,00
electricity (6/10A)	€ 2,20 - € 3,20

FR56110 Camping le Moustoir

Route du Moustoir, F-56340 Carnac (Morbihan)

Tel: **02 97 52 16 18**. Email: **info@lemoustoir.com**

Camping le Moustoir is a friendly, family run site situated about three kilometres inland from the many beaches of the area and close to the famous 'alignments' of standing stones. Pitches are grassy and separated by shrubs and hedges, with several shaded by tall pine trees. There is a popular pool area with slides, a separate swimming pool and a paddling pool with 'mushroom' fountain. The bar and terrace become the social centre of the site in the evenings. A high season entertainment programme includes a daily 'Kid's club' attracting children of several nationalities. Several small tour operators use the site.

Facilities

The substantial, traditional style toilet block is well maintained (outside peak season some sections may be closed). Motorcaravan service facilities. Shop. Bar and takeaway (from 20/5). Heated swimming pool (21 x 8 m.), water slides, and paddling pool (from 20/5). Adventure playground. Tennis. Boules. Volleyball, football and basketball. Table tennis and pool. 'Kids Club'. Barrier deposit € 20. Off site: Watersports at Carnac Plage. Fishing, bicycle hire, riding 2 km. Beach 3 km. Golf 10 km.

Open: 6 June - 22 September.

Directions

From N165, take exit to D768 (Carnac and Quiberon). At second crossroads after 5 km. turn left (D119) towards Carnac. After 3 km. turn left (oblique turning) after a hotel. Site is 500 m. on left. GPS: N47:36 W03:03

Charges 2006

Per person (over 2 yrs)	€ 4,40
pitch incl. car	€ 5,00 - € 16,00
electricity	€ 3,20
animal	€ 1,50
Camping Cheques accepted.	

kawan-villages.com tel: **00 333 59 59 03 59**

FR14070 Camping de la Vallée

88 rue de la Vallée, F-14510 Houlgate (Calvados)

Tel: **02 31 24 40 69**. Email: **camping.lavallee@wanadoo.fr**

Camping de la Vallée is an attractive site with good, well maintained facilities, situated on one of the rolling hillsides overlooking the seaside resort of Houlgate. The original farmhouse building has been converted to house a good bar and comfortable TV lounge and billiards room overlooking the pool. The site has 373 pitches with around 100 for touring units. Large, open and separated by hedges, all the pitches have 4 or 6A electricity. Part of the site is sloping, the rest level, with gravel or tarmac roads. Shade is provided by a variety of well kept trees and shrubs. The town and its beach are only 900 metres walk. This is a popular site which is busy in high season with entertainment provided. It is used by tour operators (104 pitches), there are 150 mobile homes on site and around 40 seasonal units. The site has its own chalets to rent in two different areas of the site. English is spoken in season.

Facilities

Three good toilet blocks include washbasins in cabins, mainly British style toilets, facilities for disabled people and baby bathrooms. Laundry facilities (no washing lines allowed). Motorcaravan services. Shop (from 1/5). Bar. Snack bar with takeaway in season (from 15/5). Heated swimming pool (15/5-20/9; no shorts). Games room. Playground. Bicycle hire. Volleyball, football, tennis, petanque. Entertainment in Jul/Aug. Internet access. Off site: Riding 500 m. Beach, town 1 km. Golf 2 km.

Open: 1 April - 30 September.

Directions

From A13 take exit for Cabourg following signs for Dives/Houlgate. Go straight on at two roundabouts, then four sets of traffic lights. Turn left along sea front. After 1 km. at lights turn right, after about 1 km. go over mini-roundabout - look for flag poles on right. GPS: N49:17.644 W00:04.097

Charges 2006

Per unit incl. 2 persons and electricity	€ 21,00 - € 30,00
extra person	€ 5,00 - € 6,00
child (under 7 yrs)	€ 3,00 - € 4,00

Credit card minimum € 50.
Camping Cheques accepted.

www.campinglavallee.com
Tél. : +33 (0)2 31 24 40 69
88, rue de la Vallée
14510 HOULGATE

La Vallée ★★★★

Authentic Normandy...
900 m away from the beaches

FR50050 Camping le Cormoran

Ravenoville-Plage, F-50480 Sainte Mère Eglise (Manche)

Tel: **02 33 41 33 94**. Email: **lecormoran@wanadoo.fr**

Set in a flat, open landscape and separated from the beach by the coast road, Le Cormoran is ideal for a holiday or short break quite near Cherbourg (33 km.) and the Landing Beaches close by. It does get full in peak season. Mobile homes, many privately owned, take 136 places and include 40 for rent. The remaining 80 pitches for touring units are sheltered from the wind by neat hedges and have 6A electricity available. A 'Sites et Paysages' member.

Facilities

Four toilet blocks of varying styles and ages. Washbasins in cabins. Dishwashing sinks. Laundry facilities. A sanitary block serves 15 extra large pitches (150 sq.m.) at the back of the site. Small shop, bar with snacks and takeaway. Swimming pool (heated 1/5-15/9, unsupervised). Play areas. Tennis. Boules. Entertainment, TV and games room. Bicycle and shrimp net hire. Communal barbecue. Off site: Beach 50 m. Utah Beach, golf 5 km.

Open: 1 April - 24 September.

Directions

From N13 take Ste Mère Eglise exit and in centre of town take road to Ravenoville (6 km), then Ravenoville-Plage (3 km). Just before beach turn right and site is 500 m. GPS: N49:27.960 W01:14.104

Charges 2006

Per unit incl. 1 or 2 persons	€ 16,20 - € 25,00
extra person	€ 4,60 - € 7,00
electricity (6A)	€ 3,80

Camping Cheques accepted.

FR50080 Camping Haliotis

Chemin des Soupirs, F-50170 Pontorson (Manche)

Tel: 02 33 68 11 59. Email: info@camping-haliotis-mont-saint-michel.com

The Duchesne family have achieved a remarkable transformation of this former municipal site. Situated on the edge of the little town of Pontorson and next to the river Couesnon, Camping Haliotis is within walking, cycling and canoeing distance of Mont Saint Michel. The site has 154 pitches, including 110 for touring units. Most pitches have electricity and several really large ones also have water and drainage. The large, comfortable reception area has been developed to incorporate a bar and restaurant. A 'Sites et Paysages' member.

Facilities

Very clean, renovated and well-equipped toilet block. Laundry facilities. Bar and restaurant. No shop or takeaway on site, facilities available in nearby town. Swimming pool (cleaned daily) with jacuzzi, separate paddling pool. Sauna and solarium. Good fenced play area. Large games room. Tennis court. Bicycle hire. Fishing in the River Couesnon. Japanese garden and animal park. Off site: Local services in Pontorson within walking distance. Riding 5 km. Golf 18 km. Beach 30 km.

Open: 1 April - 5 November.

Directions

Site is 300 m. from the town centre, west of D976, alongside the river, and is well signed from the town. GPS: N48:33.424 W01:30.67

Charges 2007

Per person	€ 4,50 - € 6,00
child (under 7 yrs)	€ 2,00 - € 3,50
pitch	€ 5,00 - € 7,00
electricity	€ 2,50 - € 3,00

No credit cards.
Camping Cheques accepted.

kawan-villages.com tel: 00 333 59 59 03 59 ———— *kawan*

FR27070 Camping l'Ile de Trois Rois

FR27700 Les Andelys (Eure)

Tel: 02 32 54 23 79. Email: campingtroisrois@aol.com

One hour from Paris and 30 minutes from Rouen, L'Ile des Trois Rois has an attractive setting on the banks of the Seine and has a private fishing lake within the grounds of Château-Gaillard. The site has 300 spacious, shady pitches all with electricity. There are also mobile homes for rent. Recommended by our French agent and we plan to undertake a full inspection in 2007.

Facilities

Swimming pool. Fishing in the Seine or in the private lake. Volleyball. Games room. Animation, evening entertainment in peak season. Off site: Day trips to Paris and Rouen. Cycling and walking trails. Golf, riding.

Open: March - November.

Directions

From the A13 motorway, take exit 17 and join the D316 to Les Andelys. In Les Andelys follow signs to Evreux, and the campsite is located before passing the bridge over the Seine.

Charges 2007

Per unit (incl 2 persons and electricity	€ 15,00
extra person	€ 10,00
child (under 3 years)	free

L'Ile des Trois Rois

swimming pool opens during summer of 2007

The park Ile des Trois Rois is situated in the most beautiful bend of the Seine nearby Castle Gaillard in Normandy and is a haven of peace. Paris is situated of less than than an hour and Rouen is half an hour driving from the camp site.

Facilities: two heated swimming pools, ping pong, camper service, bar and restaurant (high season) and play area

1, Rue Gilles Nicole - F-27700 Les Andelys - France
Tel. 0033 (0) 2 32 54 23 79 - Fax 0033 (0) 2 32 51 14 54 - Email campingtroisrois@aol.com

Check real time availability and at-the-gate prices...

www.alanrogers.com

FR60010 Camping Campix

B.P. 37, F-60340 St Leu-d'Esserent (Oise)

Tel: **03 44 56 08 48**. Email: **campixfr@aol.com**

This informal site has been unusually developed in a former sandstone quarry on the outskirts of the small town. The quarry walls provide a sheltered, peaceful environment and trees soften the slopes. The 160 pitches are in small groups on the different levels with stone and gravel access roads (some fairly steep and possibly muddy in poor weather). Electricity (6A) is available to about 140 pitches. There are secluded corners mostly for smaller units and tents and space for children to explore (parents must supervise – some areas, although fenced, could be dangerous). Torches are advised.

Facilities

A large building houses reception and two clean, heated sanitary units - one for tourers, the other usually reserved for groups. Two suites for disabled people double as baby rooms. Laundry facilities. At quieter times only one unit open but facilities may be congested at peak times. Motorcaravan service facilities. Daily bread and milk. Pizza and other Italian food delivery in the evenings. Off site: Fishing 1 or 5 km. Riding, golf 5 km.

Open: 7 March - 30 November.

Directions

St Leu-d'Esserent is 11 km. west of Senlis, 5 km. northwest of Chantilly. From north on A1 autoroute take Senlis exit, from Paris the Chantilly exit. Site north of town off D12 towards Cramoisy, and signed in village. GPS: N49:13.509 E02:25.638

Charges 2007

Per person	€ 3,00 - € 5,50
child (under 9 yrs)	€ 2,00 - € 3,00
pitch	€ 3,50 - € 5,50
electricity	€ 2,50 - € 3,50

FR62030 Camping Château du Gandspette

F-62910 Eperlecques (Pas-de-Calais)

Tel: **03 21 93 43 93**. Email: **contact@chateau-gandspette.com**

This spacious family-run site, in the grounds of a 19th century château, conveniently situated for the Channel ports and tunnel, provides overnight accommodation together with a range of facilities for longer stays. There are 100 touring pitches, all with electric hook-ups, inter-mingled with 50 French-owned mobile homes and caravans, and a further 18 for hire. Pitches are delineated by trees and hedging and mature trees form the perimeter of the site. A 'Sites et Paysages' member.

Facilities

Two sanitary blocks with a mixture of open and cubicled washbasins. Good facilities for disabled people and babies. Dishwashing sinks. Laundry facilities. Motorcaravan service point. Bar, grill restaurant and takeaway (all 15/5-15/9). Swimming pools (15/5-30/9). Playground and field. Tennis, petanque and a children's room. Entertainment in season. Off site: Supermarket 1 km. Fishing 3 km. Riding, golf 5 km. Bicycle hire 9 km. Beach 30 km.

Open: 1 April - 30 September.

Directions

From Calais follow N43 (St Omer) for 25 km. Southeast of Nordausques take D221 (east). Follow camp signs for 5-6 km. From St Omer follow N43 to roundabout at junction with D600. Turn right on D600 (Dunkirk). After 5 km. turn left on D221. Site is 1.5 km. on right. GPS: N50:49.137 E02:10.740

Charges 2006

Per unit incl. 2 persons	€ 16,00 - € 22,00
extra person (over 6 yrs)	€ 5,00 - € 6,00
electricity (6A)	€ 4,00

Camping Cheques accepted.

tel: **00 333 59 59 03 59** *kawan-villages.com*

FR80040 Camping le Royon

1271 route de Quend, F-80120 Fort-Mahon-Plage (Somme)

Tel: **03 22 23 40 30**. Email: **info@campingleroyon.com**

This busy site, some two kilometres from the sea, has 300 pitches of which 100 are used for touring units. The marked and numbered pitches (of either 95 or 120 sq.m.) are divided by hedges. Electricity (6A) and water points are available to all. The site is well lit, fenced and guarded at night (€ 30 deposit for barrier card). Entertainment is organised in July/Aug when it will be very full. Nearby there are opportunities for windsurfing, sailing, sand yachting, canoeing, climbing and shooting.

Facilities

Slightly dated toilet blocks provide unisex facilities with British WCs and washbasins in cubicles. Units for disabled people. Baby baths. Dishwashing and laundry sinks. Shop. Mobile takeaway calls evenings in July/Aug. Clubroom and bar. Heated, covered pool (16 x 8 m). Open air children's pool and sun terrace. Playground. Multi-court. Bicycle hire. Off site: Fishing, riding, golf within 1 km. Baie de l'Authie - an area noted for migrating birds.

Open: 10 March - 1 November.

Directions

From A16 exit 24, take D32 around Rue (road becomes D940 for a while)then continues as D32 (Fort-Mahon-Plage). Site is on right after 19 km. GPS: N50:19.98 E01:34.811

Charges 2006

Per pitch 95 sq.m. incl. caravan, car, water tap, electricity (6A) and 3 persons	€ 17,00 - € 27,00
extra person (over 1 yr)	€ 7,00

115

FR80060 Camping le Val de Trie

Bouillancourt-sous-Miannay, F-80870 Moyenneville (Somme)

Tel: **03 22 31 48 88**. Email: **raphael@camping-levaldetrie.fr**

Le Val de Trie is a natural countryside site in woodland, near a small village. The 100 numbered, grassy pitches are of a good size, divided by hedges and shrubs with mature trees providing good shade in most areas, and all have electricity (6A) and water. Access roads are gravel (site is possibly not suitable for the largest motorcaravans). It can be very quiet in April, June, September and October. If there is no-one on site, just choose a pitch or call at farm to book in. There are a few Dutch tour operator tents (5). This is maturing into a well managed site with modern facilities and a friendly, relaxed atmosphere. There are good walks around the area and a notice board keeps campers up to date with local market, shopping and activity news. English is spoken.

Facilities	Directions
Two clean sanitary buildings include washbasins in cubicles, units for disabled people, babies and children. Laundry and dishwashing facilities. Motorcaravan services. Shop (from 1/4), bread to order and butcher visits in season. Bar with TV (1/4-31/10), snack-bar with takeaway (29/4-10/9). Children's club (high season). Small heated pool (29/4-10/9), paddling pool and jacuzzi. Table tennis, boules and volleyball. Fishing. Play areas and animal enclosure. Off site: Riding 2 km. Golf 10 km. Beach 12 km.	From exit 2 on A28 near Abbeville take D925 to Miannay and turn left on D86 to Bouillancourt-sous-Miannay: site is signed in village. GPS: N50:05.038 E01:42.779

Open: 1 April - 1 November.

Charges 2007

Per unit incl. 2 persons	€ 14,60 - € 19,60
with electricity	€ 16,70 - € 23,60
extra person	€ 3,10 - € 4,90
child (under 7 yrs)	€ 1,90 - € 2,90
dog	€ 0,80 - € 1,30

Camping Cheques accepted.

Camping le Val de Trie ***

Situated at only 1 hour from Calais (A16)
Ideal spot for first or last night or longer stay
12 km from the coast

Cottages to rent.

Seven days stay, six days to pay
(outside July /August).

Quiet and relaxing
Swimming pools
Fishing pond

Moyenneville   Tel: 00 33 (0)3 22 31 48 88   www.camping-levaldetrie.fr
raphael@camping-levaldetrie.fr

HOLIDAY CHEQUE

Camping Cheque

FR80070 Camping la Ferme des Aulnes

1 rue du Marais, Fresne-sur-Authie, F-80120 Nampont-St Martin (Somme)

Tel: 03 22 29 22 69. Email: contact@fermedesaulnes.com

This peaceful site, with 120 pitches, has been developed on the meadows of a small, 17th century farm on the edge of Fresne and is lovingly cared for by its hard-working enthusiastic owner and his hard-working team. Restored outbuildings house reception and the facilities, around a central courtyard that boasts a fine heated swimming pool. A new development outside, facing the main gate, has 20 large level grass pitches for touring. There is also an area for tents. In the centre, a warden lives above a new facility building. The remaining 22 touring pitches are in the main complex, hedged and fairly level. From here you can visit Crécy, Agincourt, St Valéry and Montreuil (where Victor Hugo wrote 'Les Misérables'). The nearby Bay of the Somme has wonderful sandy beaches and many watersports.

Facilities

Both sanitary areas are heated and include washbasins in cubicles with a large cubicle for disabled people. Dishwashing and laundry sinks. Shop. Piano bar and restaurant. Motorcaravan service point. TV room. Swimming pool (16 x 9 m. heated and with cover for cooler weather). Fitness room. Aquagym and Balneo therapy. Playground. Beach volleyball, table tennis, boules and archery. Rooms with play stations and videos. Off site: River fishing 100 m. Golf 3 km. Riding 8 km.

Open: 1 April - early November.

Directions

From Calais, take A16 to exit 25 and turn for Arras for 2 km. and then towards Abbeville on N1. At Nampont St Martin turn west on D485 and site will be found in 2 km. GPS: N50:20.157 E01:42.740

Charges 2006

Per person	€ 7,00
child (under 7 yrs)	€ 4,00
pitch	€ 7,00
electricity (6/10A)	€ 6,00 - € 12,00

Camping Cheques accepted.

FR80090 Camping Caravaning le Val d'Authie

20 route de Vercourt, F-80120 Villers-sur-Authie (Somme)

Tel: **03 22 29 92 47**. Email: **camping@valdauthie.fr**

In a village location, this well organised site is fairly close to several beaches, but also has its own excellent pool complex, small restaurant and bar. The owner has carefully controlled the size of the site, leaving space for a leisure area with an indoor pool complex. There are 170 pitches in total, but with many holiday homes and chalets, there are only 60 for touring units. These are on grass, some are divided by small hedges, with 3 or 6A electric hook-ups, and 15 have full services. A 'Sites et Paysages' member.

Facilities

Good toilet facilities include some shower and washbasin units, washbasins in cubicles, and limited facilities for disabled people and babies. Facilities may be under pressure in high season and cleaning variable. Shop (not October). Bar/restaurant (8/4-15/10; hours vary). Swimming and paddling pools (8/4-15/10, with lifeguards in July/Aug). Playground, club room with TV. Weekend entertainment in season (discos may be noisy until midnight, once weekly). Multi-court. Beach volleyball.

Open: 31 March - 15 October.

Directions

Villers-sur-Authie is about 25 km. NNW of Abbéville. From A16 junction 24 take N1 to Vron, then left on D175 to Villers-sur-Authie. Or use D85 from Rue, or D485 from Nampont St Martin. Site is at southern end of village at road junction.
GPS: N50:18.815 E01:41.729

Charges 2007

Per person	€ 6,00
pitch incl. electricity (4-10A)	€ 9,50 - € 13,00

Camping Cheques accepted.

kawan-villages.com tel: **00 333 59 59 03 59** — *kawan*

FR77020 Camping le Chêne Gris

24, place de la Gare de Faremoutiers, F-77515 Pommeuse (Seine-et-Marne)

Tel: **01 64 04 21 80**. Email: **info@lechenegris.com**

This site is currently being developed by a new Dutch/Italian company and when we visited in July 2006, work was very much behind schedule. A new building which houses reception on the ground floor and an airy restaurant/bar plus a takeaway is of high quality. Of the 190 pitches, 134 are for touring many of which are on rough aggregate stone, the rest (higher up the hill on which the site is built) being occupied by mobile homes and tents of a Dutch tour operator. Terraces look out onto the heated leisure pool complex and an adventure-type play area for over-fives, whilst the play area for under-fives is at the side of the bar with picture windows overlooking it. The site is next to a railway station with trains to Paris (45 minutes). Disneyland is 20 km.

Facilities

One basic toilet block with push-button showers, washbasins in cubicles and a dishwashing and laundry area. At busy times these facilities may be under pressure. Facilities for disabled visitors (although grab-rail only for WC and shower seemed to be set too high). Children's area with toilets and baby bath but showers at adult height! Bar, restaurant and takeaway. Pool complex (all season). Off site: Shops, bars and restaurants within walking distance. Fishing and riding 2 km.

Open: 28 April - 31 October.

Directions

Pommeuse is 55 km. east of Paris. From A4 at exit 16 take N34 towards Coulommiers. In 10 km. turn south for 2 km. on D25 to Pommeuse; site on right after level-crossing. Also signed from south on D402 Guignes - Coulommiers road, taking D25 to Faremoutiers. GPS: N48:48.514 E02:59.530

Charges 2006

Per unit incl. 2 persons and electricity	€ 29,00 - € 35,00
extra person	€ 2,00 - € 3,50
child (3-11 yrs)	€ 2,00 - € 3,00

FR77030 Camping International de Jablines

Base de Loisirs, F-77450 Jablines (Seine-et-Marne)

Tel: 01 60 26 09 37. Email: welcome@camping-jablines.com

Jablines is a modern site which, with the accompanying leisure facilities of the adjacent 'Espace Loisirs', provides an interesting, if a little impersonal alternative to other sites in the region. Man-made lakes provide marvellous water activities. The 'Great Lake' as it is called, is said to have the largest beach on the Ile-de-France! The site itself provides 150 pitches, of which 132 are for touring units. Most are of a good size with gravel hardstanding and grass and marked by fencing panels and shrubs. All have 10A electrical connections, 60 with water and waste connections also.

Facilities	Directions
Two toilet blocks, heated in cool weather, include push-button showers, some washbasins in cubicles. Dishwashing and laundry facilities. Motorcaravan service (charged). Shop. Play area. Bar/restaurant adjacent at leisure centre/lake complex with watersports including 'water cable ski', riding activities, tennis and minigolf. Whilst staying on the campsite, admission to the leisure complex is free. Internet point. Ticket sales for Disneyland and Asterix. Off site: Golf 24 km.	From A4 Paris - Rouen turn north on A104. Take exit 8 on D404 Meaux and Base de Loisirs. From A1 going south, follow signs for Marne-la-Vallée using A104. Take exit 6A Clay-Souilly on the N3 (Meaux). After 6 km. turn south on D404 and follow signs. GPS: N48:54.817 E02:44.051

Open: 31 March - 28 October.

Charges 2007

Per pitch incl. 2 persons	€ 20,00 - € 25,00
extra person	€ 5,00 - € 6,00

Camping Cheques accepted.

FR77070 Camping la Belle Etoile

Quai Joffre, La Rochette, F-77000 Melun (Seine-et-Marne)

Tel: 01 64 39 48 12. Email: info@campinglabelleetoile.com

Alongside the River Seine, this site has an overall mature and neat appearance, although the approach road has several industrial plants. However, you'll discover that La Belle Etoile enjoys a pleasant position with pitches to the fore of the site within view of the barges which continually pass up and down. The 170 touring pitches, with electricity (6/10A), are on grass and laid out between the many shrubs and trees. A friendly, family run site with pleasant, helpful English speaking owners.

Facilities	Directions
The toilet blocks are not new but they are kept very clean and the water is very hot. Laundry room. Baby bath. Facilities for disabled visitors (shower, washbasin and WC). Motorcaravan service point. Small bar, snacks and shop (28/6-30/8). Takeaway (1/5-15/9). Swimming pool (1/5-15/9). Play area. Fishing. Bicycle hire. Tickets for Disney and Vaux le Vicomte are sold by the site. Off site: Fontainebleau and Paris. Golf 15 km.	Travelling north on N6 Fontainebleau - Melun road, on entering La Rochette, pass petrol station on left. Turn immediately right into Ave de la Seine. At end of road turn left at river, site on left in 500 m. GPS: N48:31.501 E02:40.164

Open: 1 April - 22 October.

Charges 2006

Per person	€ 4,90 - € 5,40
pitch	€ 5,00 - € 5,40

Camping Cheques accepted.

tel: 00 333 59 59 03 59 *kawan-villages.com*

FR88040 Camping Club Lac de Bouzey

19 rue du Lac, F-88390 Sanchey (Vosges)

Tel: 03 29 82 49 41. Email: camping.lac.de.bouzey@wanadoo.fr

Camping-Club Lac de Bouzey is eight kilometres west of Épinal, overlooking the lake, at the beginning of the Vosges Massif. The 125 individual 100 sqm. back-to-back grass pitches are arranged on either side of tarmac roads with electricity; 100 are fully serviced. They are on a gentle slope, divided by trees and hedging and some overlook the 130 haectare lake with its sandy beaches. Units can be close when site is busy. A site, with lots going on for all ages. A 'Sites et Paysages' member.

Facilities	Directions
Sanitary block includes a baby room and one for disabled people (there is up and down hill walking). In winter a small, heated section in main building with toilet, washbasin and shower is used. Laundry. Motorcaravan service point. Shop. Bar and restaurant. Heated pool (1/5-30/9). Fishing, riding and bicycle hire. Internet access. Cinema shows and discos. Off site: Golf 8 km.	Site is 8 km. west of Épinal on D460 and is signed from some parts of Épinal. Follow signs for Lac de Bouzey and Sanchey. GPS: N48:10.015 E06:21.594

Open: All year.

Charges 2007

Per unit incl. 2 persons	€ 15,00 - € 25,00
child (4-10 yrs)	free - € 6,00
electricity (6-10A)	€ 5,00 - € 6,00

Camping Cheques accepted.

tel: 00 333 59 59 03 59 *kawan-villages.com*

Check real time availability and at-the-gate prices...

FR88130 Camping Vanne de Pierre

5, rue du camping, F-88100 Saint Dié-des-Vosges (Vosges)

Tel: 03 29 56 23 56. Email: **vannedepierre@wanadoo.fr**

La Vanne de Pierre is a neat and attractive site with 118 pitches, many of which are individual with trimmed hedges giving plenty of privacy. There are 9 chalets and mobile homes (for rent) and a few seasonal units, leaving around 105 tourist pitches, all multi-serviced with water, drainage and electricity (6/10A). The reception building has been refitted and provides a small shop and a bar that includes a restaurant and takeaway (all year, opening hours vary). A 'Sites et Paysages' member.

Facilities

Main unit is heated with good facilities including washbasins in cubicles. Three family rooms each with WC, basin, and shower and two similar units fully equipped for disabled campers. Dishwashing and laundry rooms. A second, older unit (opened July/Aug). Shop. Bar/restaurant and takeaway. Swimming pool (1/4-30/9, weather permitting). Internet terminal. Bicycle hire. Off site: Golf, tennis, archery, riding all 1 km. Fishing. Supermarkets (some have 2.5 m. height barriers).

Open: All year.

Directions

St Dié is south east of Nancy. Site is east of town on north bank of river Meurthe and south of D82 to Nayemont les Fosses. Site well signed. GPS: N48:17.160 E06:58.199

Charges 2007

Per unit incl. 2 persons	€ 15,00 - € 22,00
extra person	€ 4,00 - € 6,00
electricity	€ 4,00 - € 5,00

Camping Cheques accepted.

kawan-villages.com **tel: 00 333 59 59 03 59**

kawan VILLAGES CAMPINGS

FR52030 Camping Lac de la Liez

Peigney, F-52200 Langres (Haute-Marne)

Tel: 03 25 90 27 79. Email: **campingliez@free.fr**

Managed by the enthusiastic Baude family, this newly renovated lakeside site is near the city of Langres. Only 10 minutes from the A5, Camping Lac de la Liez provides an ideal spot for an overnight stop en-route to the south of France. There is also a lot on offer for a longer stay. The site provides 131 fully serviced pitches, some with panoramic views of the 200 hectare lake with its sandy beach and small harbour where boats and pedaloes may be hired. Lake access is down steps and across quite a fast road (in total 150 m). With its old ramparts and ancient city centre, Langres was elected one of the 50 most historic cities in France.

Facilities

Two toilet blocks have all facilities in cabins (only one is open in low season). Facilities for disabled people and babies. Laundry facilities. Motorcaravan services. Shop, bar and restaurant (with takeaway food). Indoor pool complex with spa and sauna. Heated outdoor pool (1/6-30/9). Games room. Playground. Extensive games area and tennis court (free in low season). Off site: Lake with beach. Boat and bicycle hire and cycle tracks around lake. Fishing 100 m. Riding 5 km. Golf 40 km.

Open: 1 April - 1 November

Directions

From Langres take the N19 towards Vesoul. After approximately 3 km. turn right, straight after the large river bridge, then follow site signs. GPS: N47:52.44 E05:22.628

Charges 2006

Per person	€ 4,50 - € 6,00
child (2-12 yrs)	€ 3,00 - € 4,50
pitch	€ 15,00 - € 20,00
electricity	€ 3,00 - € 4,50

Camping Cheques accepted.

kawan-villages.com **tel: 00 333 59 59 03 59**

kawan VILLAGES CAMPINGS

Camping du Lac de la Liez ★★★★

In the heart of the Champagne and Ardenne regions, Camping du Lac de la Liez is a top quality 4 star site, ideal for the whole family

Open 01ˢᵗ April - 01ˢᵗ November.

Peigney, F-52200 Langres • tel 0033 (0)325 90 27 79 • fax 0033 (0)325 90 66 79
e-mail campingliez@free.fr • http://campingliez.free.fr

Check real time availability and at-the-gate prices...

www.**alanrogers**.com

FR17220 Camping la Brande

Route des Huitres, F-17480 Le Château-d'Oléron (Charente-Maritime)

Tel: **05 46 47 62 37**. Email: **info@camping-labrande.com**

A quality site, run and maintained to the highest standard, La Brande offers an ideal holiday environment on the delightful Ile d'Oléron, famed for its oysters. La Brande is situated on the oyster route and close to a sandy beach. Pitches here are generous and mostly separated by hedges and trees, the greater number for touring outfits. All are on level grassy terrain and have electricity hook-ups, some are fully serviced. The many activities during the high season, plus the natural surroundings, make this an ideal choice for families. A feature of this site is the heated swimming pool which can be covered under a sliding roof in cool weather and is open all season. The Barcat family ensures that their visitors not only enjoy quality facilities, but Gerard Barcat offers guided bicycle tours and canoe trips. This way you discover the nature, oyster farming, vineyards and history of Oléron, which is joined to the mainland by a 3 km. bridge.

Facilities

Three heated, clean sanitary blocks have spacious, well equipped showers and washbasins (mainly in cabins). Baby facilities. Excellent facilities for people with disabilities (separate large shower, washbasin and WC). Laundry room. Motorcaravan service point. Shop. Restaurant/takeaway and bar (July/Aug). Grass play area. Football field, tennis, minigolf, fishing and archery. Bicycle hire. Canoe hire. Internet access. Off site: Beach 300 m.

Open: 15 March - 15 November.

Directions

After crossing bridge to L'Ile d'Oléron turn right towards Le Château d'Oléron. Continue through village and follow sign for Route des Huitres. Site is on left after 3 km. GPS: N45:90.353 W01:21.53

Charges 2007

Per unit incl. 2 persons and electricity	€ 19,20 - € 39,00
extra person	€ 5,00 - € 8,00

Camping Cheques accepted.

Alain Barcat and his team welcomes you at La Brande - an open air hotel, camping and caravan site. Situated 1,5 miles outside of Château d'Oléron on la route des huîtres nearby the seaside, you will discover the peace of the country and the pleasures of the sea...

Route des Huitres • 17480 Le Château d'Oléron
Tél. +33 (0)5 46 47 62 37
Fax +33 (0)5 46 47 71 70
info@camping-labrande.com
www.camping-labrande.com

FR17030 Camping le Bois Roland

82 Route Royan - Saujon, F-17600 Medis (Charente-Maritime)

Tel: **05 46 05 47 58**. Email: **bois.roland@wanadoo.fr**

This campsite is in an urban area on a busy N-road but, nevertheless, has some unique features. Over the past 30 years, M. Dupont, the owner, has planted a very large number of tree varieties to mark and separate the pitches and they provide some shade. The site has 88 pitches for touring units, mainly between 80-90 sq.m. All have electricity (some may need long leads) and access to water close at hand. The family run a bar and provide simple takeaway food in July and August and there is a welcoming swimming pool.

Facilities

Two modernised toilet blocks contain a mixture of Turkish and British style toilets (no seats and no paper). Modern showers. Baby changing room. Special facilities for disabled campers. Dishwashing under cover. Laundry room with washing machines. Play area for young children. Off site: Buses pass the gate. Riding 1 km. Fishing 4 km. Bicycle hire 5 km. Golf 10 km. Supermarket with ATM 2 km. Beach 5 km.

Open: 23 April - 30 September.

Directions

Site is clearly signed on the west side of the N150, 600 m. north of the village of Medis (the N150 runs between Saujon and Royan).

Charges 2006

Per unit incl. 2 persons	€ 14,00 - € 17,00
extra person	€ 4,50
child (0-5 yrs)	€ 3,50
electricit (5A)	€ 4,00
dog (max. 1)	€ 2,50

FR17010 Camping Bois Soleil

2 avenue de Suzac, F-17110 St Georges-de-Didonne (Charente-Maritime)

Tel: 05 46 05 05 94. Email: camping.bois.soleil@wanadoo.fr

Close to the sea, Bois Soleil is a fairly large site in three parts, with 165 serviced pitches for touring units and a few for tents. All touring pitches are hedged, and have electricity, with water and a drain between two. The main part, 'Les Pins', is attractive with trees and shrubs providing shade. Opposite is 'La Mer' with direct access to the beach, some areas with less shade and an area for tents. The third part, 'La Forêt', is for static holiday homes. It is best to book your preferred area and can be full mid-June - late August. There are a few pitches with lockable gates. The areas are well tended with the named pitches (not numbered) cleared and raked between visitors and with an all-in charge including electricity and water. This lively site offers something for everyone, whether they like a beach-side spot or a traditional pitch, plenty of activities or the quiet life. The sandy beach here is a wide public one, sheltered from the Atlantic breakers although the sea goes out some way at low tide.

Facilities

Each area has one large sanitary block, and smaller blocks with toilets only. Heated block near reception. Cleaned twice daily, they include washbasins in cubicles, facilities for disabled people and babies. Launderette. Nursery. Supermarket, bakery (July/Aug). Beach shop. Restaurant and bar. Takeaway. Pool (heated 15/6-15-9). Steam room. Tennis. Bicycle hire. Play area. TV room and library. Internet terminal. Charcoal barbecues not permitted. Pets not accepted 24/6-2/9). Off site: Fishing, riding 500 m. Golf 20 km.

Open: 1 April - 4 November.

Directions

From Royan centre take coast road (D25) along the sea-front of St Georges-de-Didonne towards Meschers. Site is signed at roundabout at end of the main beach. GPS: N45:35.13 W00:59.128

Charges 2006

Per unit incl. 2 persons, 6A electricity	€ 19,00 - € 33,00
3 persons	€ 22,00 - € 33,00
tent incl. 2 persons	€ 14,00 - € 29,00
extra person	€ 3,50 - € 6,50
child (3-7 yrs)	€ 1,50 - € 4,50

Less 20% outside July/Aug.
Camping Cheques accepted.

FR17140 Castel Camping Séquoia Parc

La Josephtrie, F-17320 St Just-Luzac (Charente-Maritime)

Tel: 05 46 85 55 55. Email: sequoia.parc@wanadoo.fr

This is definitely a site not to be missed. Approached by an avenue of flowers, shrubs and trees, Séquoia Parc is a Castel site set in the grounds of La Josephtrie, a striking château with beautifully restored outbuildings and courtyard area with a bar and restaurant. Most pitches are 140 sq.m. with 6A electricity connections and separated by mature shrubs providing plenty of privacy. The site has 300 mobile homes and chalets, with 125 used by tour operators. This is a popular site with a children's club and entertainment throughout the season and reservation is necessary in high season. Member of Leading Campings Group. The site itself is designed to a high specification with reception in a large, light and airy room retaining its original beams and leading to the courtyard area where you find the bar and restaurant. The pool complex with water slides, large paddling pool and sunbathing area is impressive.

Facilities

Three spotlessly clean luxurious toilet blocks, include units with washbasin and shower and facilities for disabled visitors and children. Dishwashing sinks. New large laundry. Motorcaravan service point. Gas supplies. Large new supermarket. Restaurant/bar and takeaway. Impressive swimming pool complex with water slides and large paddling pool. Tennis, volleyball, football field. Games and TV rooms. Bicycle hire. Pony trekking. Organised entertainment all season. Off site: Sailing, fishing, golf 25 km. Flying trips.

Open: 13 May - 10 September, with all services.

Directions

Site is 5 km. southeast of Marennes. From Rochefort take D733 south for 12 km. Turn west on D123 to Ile d'Oléron. Continue for 12 km. Turn southeast on D728 (Saintes). Site signed, in 1 km. on left. GPS: N45:48.699 W01:03.637

Charges 2006

Per unit incl. 2 persons and electricity	€ 15,00 - € 37,00
extra person	€ 6,00 - € 8,00
child (3-12 yrs)	€ 3,00 - € 5,00

Bois Soleil

Camping ★★★★
Charente-Maritime

...rounded by pine trees and a sandy beach on the Atlantic ...ast, with one direct access to the beach, Bois Soleil ...poses to you many attractions like tennis, tabletennis, ...ldren playgrounds and entertainment. ...ps, take-away and snack-bar with big TV screen.

Camping Qualité

Spring and Summer 2007

2, avenue de Suzac - 17110 ST GEORGES DE DIDONNE
Tel: 0033 546 05 05 94 - Fax: 0033 546 06 27 43
...w.bois-soleil.com / e-mail: camping.bois.soleil@wanadoo.fr

FR17230 Camping de L'Océan

La Passe, La Couarde-sur-Mer, F-17670 Ile de Ré (Charente-Maritime)

Tel: **05 46 29 87 70**. Email: **campingdelocean@wanadoo.fr**

L'Océan lies close to the centre of the Ile de Ré, just 50 m. from a sandy beach. There are 338 pitches here with 161 for touring units, the remainder occupied by mobile homes and chalets. The camping area is well shaded and pitches are of a reasonable size, all with electricity (10A). A pleasant bar/restaurant overlooks the large heated swimming pool which is surrounded by an attractive sunbathing terrace. Bicycle hire is popular here as the island offers over 100 km. of cycle routes.

Facilities

The new toilet blocks are modern and well maintained with facilities for disabled visitors. Motorcaravan services. Shop. Bar/restaurant and takeaway (all season). Swimming pool. Riding. Bicycle hire. Tennis court. Fishing pond adjacent. Basketball. Play area. Minigolf (free). Helicopter rides, subaqua diving and pony riding (high season). Entertainment in high season. No charcoal barbecues. Internet access. Off site: Beach 50 m. La Couarde 2.5 km. Golf 5 km.

Open: 25 March - 24 September.

Directions

After toll bridge, join D735 which runs along the north side of the island until you pass La Couarde. The site is 2.5 km. beyond village (in direction of Ars-en-Re). GPS: N46:12.260 W01:28.06

Charges 2006

Per unit incl. 1-3 persons	€ 14,65 - € 37,08
extra person	€ 4,25 - € 9,37
electricity	€ 5,05
dog	€ 1,77 - € 4,42

Camping Cheques accepted.

kawan-villages.com tel: **00 333 59 59 03 59**

FR17280 Camping la Grainetière

Route de Saint-Martin, F-17630 La Flotte-en-Ré (Charente-Maritime)

Tel: **05 46 09 68 86**. Email: **la-grainetiere@free.fr**

A truly friendly welcome awaits you from the owners, Isabelle and Eric, at La Grainetière. It is a peaceful campsite set in almost three hectares of pine trees which provide some shade for the 65 touring pitches of various shapes and sizes. There are also 50 well spaced chalets for rent. Some pitches are suitable for units up to 7 metres (book in advance). There are no hedges for privacy and the pitches are sandy with some grass. Ample new water points and electricity (10A) hook-ups (Euro plugs) serve the camping area. The site is well lit.

Facilities

The unisex sanitary block is first class, with washbasins in cubicles, showers, British style WCs, facilities for children and people with disabilities. Shop (1/4-30/9). Takeaway (July/Aug). Swimming pool (heated 1/4-30/9). Bicycle hire. Fridge hire. TV room. Charcoal barbecues are not permitted. Off site: Beach and sailing 2 km. Fishing and boat launching 2 km. Riding 3 km. Golf 10 km. Bar and restaurant 2 km.

Open: 1 April - 30 September.

Directions

Follow camping signs from La Flotte, 1 km. from the village. GPS: N46:11.253 W01:20.696

Charges 2006

Per unit incl. 2 persons	€ 14,00 - € 22,00
extra person	€ 3,00 - € 6,00
child (0-7 yrs)	€ 2,00 - € 3,00
electricity (10A)	€ 3,50

La Grainetiere

Between St. Martin harbor and la Flotte. All kinds of shops at proximity. Isabelle and Eric welcome you in a wooded park. Friendly family atmosphere.

Route de Saint Martin - 17630 La Flotte - France - Tel: 0033 (0)5 46 09 68 86 - Fax: 0033 (0)5 46 09 53 13
lagrainetiere@free.fr - www.la-grainetiere.com

FR85150 Camping la Yole

Chemin des Bosses, Orouet, F-85160 St Jean-de-Monts (Vendée)

Tel: **02 51 58 67 17**. Email: **contact@la-yole.com**

La Yole is an attractive and well run site, 2 kilometres from a sandy beach. It offers 278 pitches, the majority of which are occupied by tour operators and mobile homes to rent. There are 100 touring pitches, most with shade and separated by bushes and trees. A newer area at the rear of the site is more open. All the pitches are of at least 100 sq.m. and have electricity (10A), water and drainage. The pool complex includes an outdoor pool, a paddling pool, slide and an indoor heated pool with jacuzzi. Entertainment is organised in high season.

Facilities

Two toilet blocks include washbasins in cabins and facilities for disabled people and babies. A third block has a baby room. Laundry facilities. Shop. Bar, restaurant and takeaway (18/5-10/9). Outdoor pool and paddling pool. Indoor heated pool with jacuzzi. Play area. Ball games. Club room. Tennis. Table tennis, pool and video games. Entertainment in high season. Gas barbecues only. Off site: Beach, bus service, bicycle hire 2 km. Riding 3 km. Fishing, golf and watersports 6 km.

Open: 2 April - 28 September.

Directions

Signed off the D38, 6 km. south of St Jean de Monts in the village of Orouet.
GPS: N46:45.383 W02:00.466

Charges 2007

Per unit incl. 2 persons	
and electricity	€ 16,00 - € 29,00
extra person	€ 3,70 - € 6,00
child (2-9 yrs)	€ 2,15 - € 4,50
baby (0-2 yrs)	free - € 3,30
dog	€ 4,00 - € 5,00

Camping Cheques accepted.

Wake up to the sound of birdsong in a wooded park of 17 acres with four star comfort. Space, security, informal atmosphere: la yole, tucked away between fields and pine trees, only 2 km from the beach.

– Chemin des Bosses - Orouet - F 85160 Saint Jean de Monts –
– Tel: 0033 251 58 67 17 - Fax: 0033 251 59 05 35 –
– contact@la-yole.com / www.la-yole.com –

FR85480 Camping Caravaning le Chaponnet

Rue du Chaponnet N16, F-85470 Brem sur Mer (Vendée)

Tel: **02 51 90 55 56**. Email: **campingchaponnet@wanadoo.fr**

This well established family run site is within five minutes walk of Brem village and 1.5 km. from a sandy beach. The 80 touring pitches are level with varying amounts of grass, some with shade from mature trees. Pitches are separated by tall hedges and serviced by tarmac or gravel roads and have frequent water and electricity points (long leads may be required). Tour operators have mobile homes and tents on 70 pitches and there are 55 privately owned mobile homes and chalets. The swimming pool complex also has a jacuzzi, slides and a children's pool, together with a sauna and fitness centre. It is overlooked by the spacious bar and snack bar. Entertainment is provided for all ages and three or four musical evenings a week provide family fun rather than teenage activities.

Facilities

The six sanitary blocks are well maintained with washbasins in cubicles, some showers and basins have controllable water temperature. Facilities for babies and disabled people. Laundry facilities. Bar (15/5-6/9), snack bar and takeaway (1/6-30/9). No shop but bread and croissants available. Indoor (heated) and outdoor pools. Play area with space for ball games. Table tennis, tennis and bicycle hire. Indoor games room. Off site: Shops and restaurants. Beach 1.5 km. Fishing 5 km. Golf 12 km. Riding 10 km.

Open: 1 May - 15 September.

Directions

Brem is on the D38 St Gilles - Les Sables d'Olonne road. Site is clearly signed, just off the one-way system in centre of village.

Charges 2006

Per unit incl. 3 persons	€ 17,70 - € 27,20
with electricity	€ 21,60 - € 30,90
extra person	€ 3,90 - € 5,00
child (under 5 yrs)	€ 2,40 - € 3,40
dog	€ 2,00

FR85220 Camping Acapulco

Avenue des Epines, F-85160 St Jean-de-Monts (Vendée)

Tel: **02 51 59 20 64**. Email: **info@sunmarina.com**

Ideal for family beach holidays, this friendly site is situated mid-way between St Jean-de-Monts and St Hilaire-de-Riez, and is 600 m. from the beach. It is one of four sites on the Vendée coast owned by the Sunmarina group. Most of the pitches here are taken by mobile homes, leaving about 20 for touring. All are about 100 sq.m. on grass and divided by hedges which give some shade. The central part of the site has an excellent pool complex complete with five slides, a children's pool and a terrace for sunbathing. Adjacent to this is a spacious bar, restaurant and a safe play area.

Facilities

Two sanitary blocks are clean and include washbasins in cabins and showers. Facilities for disabled visitors. Laundry facilities. Motorcaravan service point. Shop with basic supplies. Bar, restaurant and takeaway. Large heated pool complex with five water slides and paddling pool. Play area. Entertainment in high season. Off site: Shopping centre 400 m. Sancy beach 600 m.

Open: 15 May - 15 September.

Directions

Follow the coastal road of St Jean de Monts south towards St Hilaire-de-Riez. Just past signs of Commune St Hilaire, turn left at first roundabout. Site is 400 m. on right (signed).

Charges 2006

Per unit incl. 3 persons and electricity	€ 30,00
extra person	€ 9,00
child (under 5 yrs)	€ 5,00

FR85210 Camping les Ecureuils

Route des Goffineaux, F-85520 Jard-sur-Mer (Vendée)
Tel: **02 51 33 42 74**. Email: **camping-ecureuils@wanadoo.fr**

Les Ecureuils is a wooded site in a quieter part of the southern Vendée. It is undoubtedly one of the prettiest sites on this stretch of coast, with an elegant reception area, attractive vegetation and large pitches separated by low hedges with plenty of shade. Of the 261 pitches, some 128 are for touring units, each with water and drainage, as well as easy access to 10A electricity. This site is very popular with tour operators (103 pitches). Jard is rated among the most pleasant and least hectic of Vendée towns. The harbour is home to some fishing boats and rather more pleasure craft, and has a public slipway for those bringing their own boats.

Facilities

Two toilet blocks, well equipped and kept very clean, include baby baths, and laundry rooms. Small shop (bread baked on site). New snack-bar. Takeaway service (pre-order 1/6-15/9). Snacks and ice-creams available from the friendly bar. Good sized L-shaped swimming pool and separate paddling pool (30/5-15/9). Indoor pool and fitness centre (all season). Two play areas for different age groups. Modern play area. Minigolf, table tennis and a pool table. Club for children (5-10 yrs) daily in July/Aug. Bicycle hire. Only gas barbecues are allowed. Dogs are not accepted. Internet access. Off site: Beach, fishing 400 m. Marina and town.

Open: 1 April - 30 September.

Directions

Jard-sur-Mer is on D21 between Talmont St Hilaire and Longeville sur Mer. Site is signed from main road – caravanners follow signs to avoid tight bends and narrow roads. GPS: N46:24.683 W01:35.382

Charges 2006

Per person	€ 5,00 - € 6,50
child (0-4 yrs)	€ 1,50 - € 2,00
child (5-9 yrs)	€ 4,00 - € 4,50
pitch with water and drainage	€ 13,00 - € 15,50

Less 10% outside 30/6-1/9.

FR85330 Camping Naturiste Cap Natur'

151 avenue de la Faye, F-85270 St Hilaire-de-Riez (Vendée)
Tel: 02 51 60 11 66. Email: info@cap-natur.com

Situated on the northern outskirts of St Hilaire-de-Riez, this family campsite for naturists is in an area of undulating sand dunes and pine trees. The 140 touring pitches nestle among the dunes and trees and offer a wide choice to suit most tastes, including the possibility of electrical connections (10A), although in some cases long leads are needed. Despite the undulating terrain, some pitches are quite level and thus suitable for motorcaravans. The whole of the indoor complex is a designated non-smoking area. A number of apartments, tents and mobile homes are on site.

Facilities

Basic, but clean sanitary facilities, two indoor (heated) and one outdoor (roofed) block. Open plan hot showers, British style WCs, washbasins, baby baths and children's toilets. Shop (with takeaway pizzas) and restaurant, bar, with TV, indoor table games. Indoor and outdoor pools. Fitness classes (high season). Massage room. Play area. Volleyball. Torches useful. Bicycle hire. Not suitable for American motorhomes. Off site: Beach 2 km. Fishing 5 km. Naturist beach 6 km. Golf, riding 10 km.

Open: 1 April - 1 November.

Directions

From Le Pissot roundabout go south on D38, for St Hilaire. At roundabout (first exit), next roundabout turn right ('Les Plages'). At third Y-shaped junction turn right ('Parée Prèneau'). Site is 2 km. on left.

Charges 2006

Per unit incl. 2 persons	€ 14,80 - € 28,10
extra person	€ 2,60 - € 6,80
child (under 13 yrs)	€ 1,60 - € 5,10
electricity (10A)	€ 4,20

Camping Cheques accepted.

FR37060 Camping L'Arada Parc

Rue de la Baratière, F-37360 Sonzay (Indre-et-Loire)
Tel: 02 47 24 72 69. Email: laradaparc@free.fr

A good, well maintained site in a quiet location, Camping L'Arada Parc is a popular base from which to visit the numerous châteaux in this beautiful part of France. The 79 grass pitches all have electricity and 22 have water and drainage. The clearly marked pitches, some slightly sloping, are separated by trees and shrubs some of which are now providing a degree of shade. An attractive, heated pool is on a pleasant terrace beside the restaurant. Entertainment, themed evenings and activities for children are organised in July/August. A new site with modern facilities and developing well. A 'Sites et Paysages' member.

Facilities

Two modern toilet blocks provide unisex toilets, showers and washbasins in cubicles. Baby room. Facilities for disabled visitors (wheelchair users may find the gravel access difficult). Dishwashing and laundry facilities. Shop, bar, restaurant and takeaway (24/3-31/10). Swimming pool (no Bermuda style shorts; 1/5-13/9). Play area, games area. Boules, volleyball, badminton and table tennis. TV room. Bicycle hire. Internet access. Off site: Tennis 200 m. Riding 7 km. Fishing 9 km. Golf 12 km.

Open: 24 March - 1 November.

Directions

Sonzay is northwest of Tours. From the new A28 north of Tours take the exit to Neuillé-Pont-Pierre which is on the N139 Le Mans - Tours road. Then take D766 towards Château la Vallière and turn southwest to Sonzay. Follow campsite signs. GPS: N47:31.687 E00:27.18

Charges 2006

Per unit incl. 2 persons	€ 13,50 - € 17,50
extra person	€ 3,50 - € 4,50
child (2-10 yrs)	€ 2,75 - € 3,50
electricity (10A)	€ 3,50

Camping Cheques accepted.

FR37050 Camping Caravanning la Citadelle

Avenue Aristide Briand, F-37600 Loches en Touraine (Indre-et-Loire)
Tel: 02 47 59 05 91. Email: camping@lacitadelle.com

A pleasant, well maintained site, La Citadelle is within walking distance of Loches, noted for its perfect architecture and its glorious history, at the same time offering a rural atmosphere in the site itself. Most of the 128 level, good-sized touring pitches (all with 10A electricity and 42 fully serviced) offer some shade from trees, although sun lovers can opt for a more open spot. The most recent addition is an on-site outdoor swimming pool with paddling pool (solar heated). A 'Sites et Paysages' member. Loches, its château and dungeons, is 500 m.

Facilities

Three sanitary blocks provide British and Turkish style WCs, washbasins (mostly in cabins) and showers. Dishwashing and laundry facilities. Motorcaravan service area. Two excellent baby units and provision for disabled people. Play equipment. Boules, volleyball and games room. Small bar and snack bar offering a variety of food and drink in a lively environment (15/6-13/9). Internet access and TV. Off site: Riding 3 km. Supermarket 3 km. Market on Wednesday and Saturday mornings. Golf 7 km.

Open: 19 March - 19 October.

Directions

From any direction take town bypass (RN143) and leave via roundabout at southern end (supermarket). Site signed towards town centre on right in 800 m. Do not enter centre. GPS: N47:07.382 E01:00.134

Charges 2006

Per pitch incl. 2 adults with electricity, water	€ 15,20 - € 20,00
and drainage	€ 17,90 - € 25,50
extra person	€ 3,90 - € 4,80

Camping Cheques accepted.

FR37130 Domaine Résidential Le Parc des Allais

FR37220 Trogues (Indre-et-Loir)
Tel: 05 38 50 70 90. Email: contact@parc-des-allais.com

This campsite has been recommended by our French agent and we plan to undertake a full inspection in 2007. Parc des Allais was previously known as Chlorophylle Parc and it is well located in the heart of the Loire Valley, convenient for exploring the surrounding countryside and the region's world class chateaux. The site is situated within a 16 acre park and borders an attractive lake. Pitches here are large and grassy and the site also offers a range of mobile homes and chalets for rent.

Facilities

Modern toilet blocks include a laundry room and facilities for disabled visitors. Restaurant. Bar. Supermarket. Indoor heated swimming pool. Outdoor pool with water slide. Fitness facilities. Tennis. Mountain bike track. Lake and river fishing. Play areas. Games room. Bicycle and mountain bike rental. Small boat rental. Multisport court. Trampoline. Cycle excursions. pétanque. Theme evenings. Entertainment for children.

Open: February - November.

Directions

Take exit 25 from the A10 motorway (Ste Maure de Touraine). Then follow directions to Pouzay and the site is well signed.

Charges 2007

Per unit incl 2 persons and electricity	€ 21,95 - € 26,35
extra person	€ 3,95 - € 4,75
child (under 7 yrs)	€ 2,45 - € 3,20

FR37030 Camping le Moulin Fort

F-37150 Francueil-Chenonceaux (Indre-et-Loire)

Tel: **02 47 23 86 22**. Email: **lemoulinfort@wanadoo.fr**

Camping Le Moulin Fort is a tranquil, riverside site that has been redeveloped by British owners, John and Sarah Scarratt. The 137 pitches are enhanced by trees and shrubs offering some shade and 110 pitches have electricity (6A). The swimming pool (unheated) is accessed by a timber walkway over the mill race from the snack bar terrace adjacent to the restored mill building. Although not intrusive there is some noise from the railway across the river and a few trains run at night. The site is more suitable for couples and families with young children, although the river is unfenced. All over the campsite, visitors will find little information boards about local nature (birds, fish, trees and shrubs), about the history of the mill and fascinating facts about recycling. The owners are keen to encourage recycling on the site. The picturesque Château of Chenonceaux is little more than 1 km. along the Cher riverbank and many of the Loire châteaux are within easy reach, particularly Amboise and its famous Leonardo de Vinci museum.

Facilities

Two toilet blocks with all the usual amenities of a good standard, including washbasins in cubicles and baby baths. Shop (1/4-30/9). Bar, restaurant and takeaway (all 1/4-30/9). Swimming pool (15/5-30/9). Petanque. Minigolf. Games room and TV. Library. Regular family entertainment including wine tasting, quiz evenings, activities for children and light-hearted games and tournaments. Motorcaravan service point. Fishing. Bicycle and canoe hire. Petanque. Live music events. Off site: Riding 12 km. Golf 20 km.

Open: 1 April - 30 September.

Directions

Site signed from N76 Tours - Vierzon road. From D40 (Tours - Chenonceaux), go through village and after 2 km. right on D80 to cross river at Chisseaux. Site on left just after bridge.
GPS: N47:19.637 E01:05.358

Charges 2007

Per unit incl. 2 persons	€ 9,00 - € 20,00
extra person	€ 3,00 - € 5,00
child (4-12 yrs)	€ 2,00 - € 4,00
electricity (6A)	€ 4,00

FR37090 Camping du Château de la Rolandière

F-37220 Trogues (Indre-et-Loire)

Tel: **02 47 58 53 71**. Email: **contact@larolandiere.com**

This is a charming site set in the grounds of a château. The owners, Sabine Toulemonde and her husband, offer a very warm welcome. There are 30 medium sized, flat pitches, some gently sloping front to rear, separated by hedges. All but four have 10A electricity and water taps nearby and parkland trees give shade. The château and adjoining buildings contain rooms to let. The site has a pleasant swimming pool (14 x 6 m.) with a sunny terrace and paddling pool, minigolf through the parkland and a play area. Situated between Ille Bouchard and St Maure-de-Touraine, the site is convenient for an overnight break or for longer stays to explore the area.

Facilities

The toilet block is older in style but has been refurbished to provide adequte facilities with shower, washbasin, dishwashing and laundry areas around central British style WCs. Provision for disabled visitors. Bar with terrace and snacks/takeaway. Small shop for basics (July/Aug). Swimming pool (15/5-30/9). Minigolf (no children under 12 yrs). Play area. Fitness room. Bicycle hire 25 km. Off site: Fishing 1 km. to River Vienne. Restaurant 5 km. St Maure 8 km.

Open: 15 April - 30 September.

Directions

Site is 5 km. west from exit 25 on A10 at St Maure-de-Touraine on D760 towards Chinon. Entrance is signed and marked by a model of the château. GPS: N47:06.460 E00:30.631

Charges 2006

Per person	€ 5,00 - € 6,00
child (under 7 yrs)	€ 2,50 - € 3,00
pitch	€ 7,00 - € 8,50
electricity	€ 3,50

No credit cards.

FR45010 Camping les Bois du Bardelet

Route de Bourges, Poilly, F-45500 Gien (Loiret)

Tel: 02 38 67 47 39. Email: contact@bardelet.com

This attractive, lively family site, in a rural setting, is well situated for exploring the less well known eastern part of the Loire Valley. Two lakes (one for boating, one for fishing) and a pool complex have been attractively landscaped in 12 hectares of former farmland, blending old and new with natural wooded areas and more open field areas with rural views. Bois du Bardelet provides 260 pitches with around 130 for touring units. All are larger than 100 sq.m. and have electrical connections, with some fully serviced. The communal areas are based on attractively converted former farm buildings with a wide range of leisure facilities. A family club card can be purchased to make use of the many activities on a daily basis (some high season only). Various activities and excursions are organised, the most popular being to Paris on Wednesdays, which can be pre-booked.

Facilities

Two sanitary blocks (only one open outside 15/6-31/8) include washbasins in cabins. Facilities for disabled visitors and babies. Washing machines. Shop (1/4-17/9). Bar. Snack bar, takeaway, restaurant (all 1/4-17/9) and pizzeria (8/7-21/8). Outside pool (1/5-31/8). Indoor children's pool. Indoor pool, heated (with purchased club card). Aqua gym, fitness and jacuzzi room. Games area. Archery. Canoeing and fishing. Tennis, minigolf, boules. Bicycle hire. Playground. Internet access. Off site: Supermarket 5 km. Riding 7 km. Golf 25 km. Walking and cycling.

Open: 1 April - 30 September.

Directions

From Gien take D940 (Bourges). After 5 km. turn right and right again to cross road and follow site signs. From Argent sur Sauldre take D940 (Gien). Site signed to right after 15 km. Entrance is 200 m. past what looks like the first opening to site. GPS: N47:38.497 E02:36.891

Charges 2006

Per unit incl. 2 persons
incl. electricity   € 18,00 - € 30,00
Less 15-25% in low seasons (20-40% for over 60s).
Camping Cheques accepted.

kawan-villages.com tel: 00 333 59 59 03 59

Les Bois du Bardelet ★★★★

Loire Valley
Poilly - 45500 GIEN
Tel. 00 33/238 67 47 39 - Fax. 00 33/238 38 27 16
Internet: www.bardelet.com
E-mail: contact@bardelet.com

2 lakes, 3 swimming pools, relaxing area with indoor pool, jacuzzi, fitness room. Children aquatic play area with paddling indoor pool.

Other activities : fishing, canoe, tennis, crazy golf, ping pong.

Weekly and weekend-renting. Chalets and mobile-homes.

FR41030 Yelloh! Village le Parc des Alicourts

Domaine des Alicourts, F-41300 Pierrefitte-sur-Sauldre (Loir-et-Cher)

Tel: 02 54 88 63 34. Email: parcdesalicourts@wanadoo.fr

A secluded holiday village set in the heart of the forest and with many sporting facilities, Parc des Alicourts is midway between Orléans and Bourges, to the east of the A71. There are 490 pitches, 150 for touring and the remainder occupied by mobile homes and chalets. All pitches have electricity connections (6A) and good provision for water, and most are 150 sq.m. (min. 100 sq.m). Locations vary from wooded to more open areas, thus giving a choice of amount of shade. All facilities are open all season and the leisure amenities are exceptional. Member of Leading Campings Group.

Facilities

Three modern sanitary blocks include some washbasins in cabins and baby bathrooms. Laundry facilities. Facilities for disabled visitors (shallow step to reach them). Motorcaravan services. Shop. Restaurant. Takeaway in bar with terrace. Water complex. 7 hectare lake (fishing, bathing, canoes, pedaloes). 9-hole golf course. Play area. Football, volleyball, tennis, minigolf, table tennis, boules. Roller skating/skateboarding (bring own equipment). Bicycle hire. Internet access. Walk and cycle path.

Open: Mid May - 7 September.

Directions

From A71, take Lamotte Beuvron exit (no 3) or from N20 Orléans to Vierzon turn left on to D923 towards Aubigny. After 14 km. turn right at camping sign on to D24E. Site signed in about 4 km. GPS: N47:32.639 E02:11.516

Charges 2006

Per unit incl. 2 persons
and electricity   € 15,00 - € 38,00
extra person   € 6,00 - € 9,00
child (1-17 yrs)   free - € 7,00

Check real time availability and at-the-gate prices...

www.**alanrogers**.com

FR41070 Camping Caravaning la Grande Tortue

3 route de Pontlevoy, F-41120 Candé-sur-Beuvron (Loir-et-Cher)

Tel: **02 54 44 15 20**. Email: **grandetortue@wanadoo.fr**

This is a pleasant, shady site that has been developed in the surroundings of an old forest. It provides 169 touring pitches the majority of which are more than 100 sq.m. 150 have 10A electricity and the remainder are fully serviced. The family owners continue to develop the site with a new multisports court already created. During July and August, they organise a programme of trips including wine/cheese tastings, canoeing and horse riding excursions. Used by tour operators. This site is well placed for visiting the châteaux of the Loire or the cities of Orléans and Tours. A 'Sites et Paysages' member.

Facilities

Three sanitary blocks offer British style WCs, washbasins in cabins and push-button showers. Laundry facilities. Shop selling provisions. Terraced bar and restaurant with reasonably priced food and drink (15/4-15/9). Swimming pool and two shallower pools for children (1/5-30/9). Trampolines, a ball crawl with slide and climbing wall, bouncy inflatable, table tennis. New multisport court. Off site: Walking and cycling. Bicycle hire 1 km. Fishing 500 m. Golf 10 km. Riding 12 km.

Open: 9 April - 30 September.

Directions

Site is just outside Candé-sur-Beuvron on D751, between Amboise and Blois. From Amboise, turn right just before Candé, then left into campsite. GPS: N47:29.389 E01:15.515

Charges 2007

Per unit incl. 2 persons	€ 15,00 - € 26,00
incl. electricity	€ 19,50 - € 30,00
extra person	€ 5,00 - € 7,50
child (3-9 yrs)	€ 3,50 - € 5,50

Camping Cheques accepted.

TRAVEL SERVICE SITE
TO BOOK CALL **0870 405 4055**
Advice & low ferry-inclusive prices

Check real time availability and at-the-gate prices...

www.**alanrogers**.com

FR49040 Camping de l'Etang

Route de St Mathurin, F-49320 Brissac (Maine-et-Loire)

Tel: **02 41 91 70 61**. Email: info@campingetang.com

At Camping de l'Etang many of the 150 level touring pitches have pleasant views across the countryside. Separated and numbered, some have a little shade and all have electricity with water and drainage nearby. 21 are fully serviced. A small bridge crosses the river Aubance which runs through the site (well fenced) and there are two lakes where fisherman can enjoy free fishing. The site has its own vineyard and the wine produced can be purchased on the campsite. Tour operators use 16 pitches. A 'Sites et Paysages' member. Originally the farm of the Château de Brissac (yet only 24 km. from the lovely town of Angers), this is an attractive campsite retaining much of its rural charm. The adjacent Parc de Loisirs is a paradise for young children with many activities including boating, pony rides, miniature train, water slide, bouncy castle and swings (free entry for campers).

Facilities

Three well maintained toilet blocks provide all the usual facilities. Laundry facilities. Baby room. Disabled visitors are well catered for. Motorcaravan service point. The farmhouse houses reception, small shop and takeaway snacks when bar is closed. A bar/restaurant serves crêpes, salads, etc (evenings June-August). Swimming pool (heated and covered) and paddling pool. Fishing. Play area. Bicycle hire. Variety of evening entertainment in high season. Off site: Golf and riding 10 km. Sailing 25 km.

Open: 15 May - 15 September.

Directions

Brissac-Quincé is 17 km. southeast of Angers on D748 towards Poitiers. Do not enter the town but turn north on D55 (site signed) in direction of St Mathurin. GPS: N47:21.560 W00:26.065

Charges 2006

Per unit incl. 2 persons	€ 15,00 - € 26,00
extra person	€ 4,50 - € 6,50
child (0-10 yrs)	€ 3,00 - € 3,50
electricity	€ 3,00
dog	€ 2,50

On the route of the châteaux of the Loire, 2 campsites welcome you

The same spirit of hospitality

CAMPING DE CHANTEPIE ★★★★
S-Hilaire-S'-Florent - 49400 SAUMUR
Tél. +33 (0)2 41 67 95 34 - Fax +33 (0)2 41 67 95 85
e-mail : info@campingchantepie.com
www.campingchantepie.com

Association de
Chantepie et de l'Etang
N° 2002/DRTEFP/280

CAMPING DE L'ETANG ★★★★
Route de S'-Mathurin
49320 BRISSAC
Tél. +33 (0)2 41 91 70 61 - Fax +33 (0)2 41 91 72 65
e-mail : info@campingetang.com
www.campingetang.com

FR49080 Camping Ile d'Offard

Rue de Verden, Ile d'Offard, F-49400 Saumur (Maine-et-Loire)

Tel: **02 41 40 30 00**. Email: iledoffard@cutloisirs.fr

This site is situated on an island between the banks of the Loire. The 224 touring pitches are at present on grass at the far end or hardstanding nearer the entrance. Some 34 pitches are occupied by tour operators and caravan holiday homes and these can be intrusive in some areas. Pitches have access to electricity hook-ups (10A). A new heated outdoor swimming pool has been completed together with paddling and spa pools. Within walking distance of the centre of Saumur, this site is useful as an overnight stop en-route south or as a short-term base from which to visit the numerous châteaux in the region. Fishing is possible in the Loire (permits are available from Saumur).

Facilities

Three sanitary blocks, one heated in winter, include provision for disabled visitors. Toilet facilities are unisex. Block one has a well equipped laundry. The other blocks are only open in high season. Motorcaravan service point € 4.50 - € 7.50 (free to campers). Restaurant and bar (early May - late Sept) with takeaway. Internet access. Volleyball. Play area. Some activities with a children's club, wine tastings, etc. in high season. Off site: Thursday market 500 m. Saturday market 2 km. Riding 5 km.

Open: 1 March - 31 October.

Directions

From north and A85 exit 3, take N147 south (Saumur). After 2.5 km. turn left (N147 bears right). Follow old road towards river and town. Cross bridge onto island, then first left. Site ahead. GPS: N47:15.457 W00:03.660

Charges 2007

Per unit incl. 2 persons	€ 15,50 - € 24,00
extra person	€ 4,00 - € 5,00
electricity	€ 3,50
Camping Cheques accepted.	

kawan-villages.com **tel: 00 333 59 59 03 59**

kawan
VILLAGES CAMPING

Check real time availability and at-the-gate prices...

www.**alanrogers**.com

FR49090 Camping l'Isle Verte

Avenue de la Loire, F-49730 Montsoreau (Maine-et-Loire)

Tel: 02 41 51 76 60. Email: isleverte@cutloisirs.fr

This friendly, natural site, with pitches overlooking the Loire, is just 100 m. from the centre of Montsoreau, an ideal starting point to visit the western Loire area. Most of the 90 shaded, level and good-sized tourist pitches are separated by low hedges but grass tends to be rather sparse during dry spells. All have electricity (16A). Excellent English is spoken in the reception and bar. Fishermen are particularly well catered for here, there being an area to store equipment and live bait (permits are available in Saumur). There are many attractions within walking distance of the campsite.

Facilities	Directions
A single building provides separate male and female toilets. Washbasins, some in cabins, and showers are unisex. Separate facilities for disabled campers. Baby room. Laundry facilities. Motorcaravan services. Bar and snack bar (1/5-30/9). Swimming pool (15/5-30/9). Play area. Bicycle hire (June - August or by special request). Fishing. Off site: Golf 6 km. Riding 15 km.	Take D947 from Saumur to Montsoreau and site is clearly signed on left along the road into town. GPS: N47:13.092 E00:03.159

Open: 1 April - 30 September.

Charges 2007

Per unit incl. 1 or 2 persons	€ 12,90 - € 17,50
extra person	€ 3,00 - € 3,50
electricity	€ 3,00

Camping Cheques accepted.

tel: 00 333 59 59 03 59 *kawan-villages.com*

FR79020 Camping de Courte Vallée

F-79600 Airvault (Deux-Sèvres)

Tel: 05 49 64 70 65. Email: camping@caravanningfrance.com

A warm welcome is given to all visitors with a glass of wine and a friendly chat from the British owners. This very attractive site, within walking distance of Airvault, has 65 pitches on level grass amongst trees and shrubs, all with electricity (8A). The owners have spent lots of time and work improving what was already a well laid out site, and have recently added several hardstanding pitches and four 'super' pitches. This is an ideal location for a short stay or as a base for touring the Poitou-Charentes region and the Loire valley including the châteaux of Saumur and Oiron.

Facilities	Directions
A modern unisex block has spacious cubicles for showers and washbasins, and shower and WC cubicles for disabled visitors, all kept to a very high standard of cleanliness. Dishwashing area under cover. Washing machine and dryers. Reception sells 'frites', snacks, beers, wine and ice cream. Internet access. Swimming pool. Boules. Play area. Caravan storage. Wine tasting events and barbecues. Coffee bar. Off site: Airvault (birthplace of Voltaire) 10-15 minute walk. Fishing 300 m. Riding 8 km.	From D938 (Parthenay-Thouars) take D725 Airvault. On approaching village turn left over bridge. At T-junction turn sharp left, second exit at roundabout, left at junction to site on left. Note: caravans are not allowed in village. GPS: N46:49.937 W00:08.909

Open: All year.

Charges 2006

Per person	€ 6,00 - € 7,00
pitch	€ 9,00 - € 11,00
electricity (8A)	€ 11,00 - € 13,00

No credit cards.

FR86090 Camping Flower du Lac de Saint Cyr

F-86130 Saint Cyr (Vienne)

Tel: 05 49 62 57 22. Email: contact@parcdesaintcyr.com

This well organised, five hectare campsite is part of a 300 hectare leisure park, based around a large lake with sailing and associated sports, and an area for swimming (supervised July/Aug). The campsite has around 185 tourist pitches, 10 mobile homes and 3 'yurts' (canvas and wooden tents) for rent. The marked and generally separated pitches are all fully serviced with electricity (10A), water and drainage. In high season there is a kids club and an entertainment programme and also a sailing school and various watersports (charged). Campers can also use the golf courses.

Facilities	Directions
The main toilet block is modern and supplemented for peak season by a second unit, although they do attract some use by day-trippers to the leisure facilities. Washbasins in cubicles. Laundry facilities. Facilities for babies and disabled persons. Shop, restaurant and takeaway (April - Sept). Playground on beach. Bicycle hire. Fitness suite. Fishing. Off site: Riding 200 m. Golf 800 m.	Saint Cyr is about midway between Châtellerault and Poitiers. Site signed to east of N10 at Beaumont along D82 towards Bonneuil-Matours, and is part of the Parc de Loisirs de Saint Cyr.

Open: 1 April - 30 September.

Charges 2006

Per person	€ 2,50 - € 5,00
child (1-7 yrs)	€ 1,50 - € 2,00
pitch incl. electricity	€ 6,00 - € 12,00

FR86040 Camping le Futuriste

F-86130 Saint Georges-les-Baillargeaux (Vienne)

Tel: 05 49 52 47 52. Email: camping-le-futuriste@wanadoo.fr

Le Futuriste is a neat, modern site, open all year and close to Futuroscope. With a busy atmosphere, there are early departures and late arrivals. The reception office is open 08.00-22.00 hrs. There are 118 individual, flat, grassy pitches divided by young trees and shrubs which are beginning to provide some shelter for this elevated and otherwise rather open site (possibly windy). 82 pitches have electricity (6A) and a further 30 have electricity, water, waste water and sewage connections. All are accessed via neat, level and firmly rolled gravel roads. On raised ground with panoramic views over the strikingly modern buildings and night-time bright lights that comprise the popular attraction of Futuroscope, this site is ideal for a short stay to visit the park which is only 1.5 km. away (tickets can be bought at the site) but it is equally good for longer stays to see the region. Details of attractions are available from the enthusiastic young couple who run the site. Note: it is best to see the first evening show at Futuroscope otherwise you will find yourself locked out of the site – the gates are closed at 23.30 hrs.

Facilities

Excellent, clean sanitary facilities in two insulated blocks (can be heated). Those in the newest block are unisex. and include some washbasins in cabins and facilities for disabled people. Dishwashing and laundry facilities. Shop (bread to order), bar/restaurant (all 1/5-30/9) . Snack bar and takeaway (1/7-31/8). Two heated outdoor pools, one with slide and paddling pool (1/5-30/9). Games room. TV. Volleyball, boules and table tennis. Lake fishing. Youth groups not accepted. Off site: Bicycle hire 500 m. Hypermarket 600 m. Golf 5 km. Riding 10 km.

Open: All year.

Directions

From either A10 autoroute or N10, take Futuroscope exit. Site is east of both roads, off D20 (St Georges-Les-Baillargeaux). Follow signs to St Georges. Site on hill; turn by water tower and site is on left. GPS: N46:39.928 E00:23.668

Charges 2007

Per pitch incl. 1-3 persons	€ 14,20 - € 19,50
extra person	€ 1,90 - € 2,60
electricity	€ 2,60 - € 3,50
animal	€ 1,80

Camping Cheques accepted.

kawan-villages.com tel: 00 333 59 59 03 59

kawan
VILLAGES CAMPING

Open all year. Panoramic view over the Futuroscope situated at 2 kms.
Heated swimming pool, pond, snack, bar, restaurant. Chalets for hire.

86130 St-Georges les Baillargeaux
Tel: 0033 549 52 47 52
Fax: 0033 549 37 23 33
www.camping-le-futuriste.fr

kawan
VILLAGES CAMPINGS

83 quality campsites in 7 countries

Decidedly Kuality
Decidedly Komfort
Decidedly Konvivial

decidedly Kamping!

kawan-villages.com
free brochure
00333 59 59 03 59

Low Season
Super Savers

Camping Cheque

HOLIDAY CHEQUE

From £24.75 per night in deluxe chalets and mobile homes

£10.30 per night for 2 persons per standard pitch

FR71070 Castel Camping Château de l'Epervière

F-71240 Gigny-sur-Saône (Saône-et-Loire)

Tel: **03 85 94 16 90**. Email: **domaine-de-leperviere@wanadoo.fr**

Peacefully situated on the edge of the little village of Gigny-sur-Saône, yet within easy distance of the A6 autoroute, this site nestles in a woodland area near the Saône river. There are 135 pitches, 75 for touring, nearly all with 10A electricity. The site is in two distinct areas. The original part, close to the château and fishing lake, has semi-hedged pitches on part-level ground with shade from mature trees, The centre of the second area has a more open aspect, with large hedged pitches and mature trees offering shade around the periphery. A partly fenced road across the lake connects the two areas of the site (care is needed with children). The managers, Gert-Jan and Francois, and their team enthusiastically organise a range of activities for visitors that includes wine tastings in the cellars of the château and a Kids' Club in July/Aug. You may need earplugs in the mornings because of the ducks.

Facilities

Two well equipped toilet blocks include washbasins in cabins, dishwashing and laundry areas. Washing machine and dryer. Basic shop (1/5-30/9). Château restaurant with a French menu (1/4-30/9). Second restaurant with basic menu and takeaway. Converted barn houses attractive bar, large TV and games room. Unheated swimming pool (1/5-30/9) partly enclosed by old stone walls. Smaller indoor heated pool, Jacuzzi, sauna, paddling pool. Play area. Outdoor paddling pool. Bicycle hire. Off site: Riding 15 km. Golf 20 km.

Open: 1 April - 30 September.

Directions

From N6 between Châlon-sur-Saône and Tournus, turn east on D18 (just north of Sennecey-le-Grand) and follow site signs for 6.5 km. From A6, exit Châlon-Sud from the north, or Tournus from the south.

Charges 2006

Per person	€ 5,40 - € 6,90
child (under 7 yrs)	€ 3,30 - € 4,80
pitch	€ 7,90 - € 10,20
dog	€ 2,20 - € 2,90
electricity	€ 2,20 - € 2,90

Camping Cheques accepted.

 *kawan-villages.com* **tel: 00 333 59 59 03 59**

FR71140 Camping du Pont de Bourgogne

Rue Julien Leneveu, Saint Marcel, F-71380 Chalon sur Saône (Saône-et-Loire)

Tel: **03 85 48 26 86**. Email: **campingchalon71@wanadoo.fr**

This is a well presented site, useful for an overnight stop or for a few days if exploring the local area and you want a simple site without the frills. It does get crowded in the third week of July during the Chalon street theatre festival. There are 93 fairly small pitches with 6/10A electricity, 10 with a gravel surface. The new owners of the site plan to replace or improve the facilities in the near future, but when we visited there was a bar/restaurant with an outdoor terrace and serving a good selection of simple, inexpensive meals. Although alongside the Saône river, the site is well fenced. The staff are friendly and helpful.

Facilities

Three toilet blocks, two centrally located amongst the pitches and traditional in style and fittings, the third new and modern, alongside the reception building (including facilities for disabled visitors). Dishwashing facilities but no laundry. Modern bar/restaurant. No shop but essentials kept in the bar (bread to order). Simple play area. Bicycle hire arranged. Off site: Municipal swimming pool 300 m. Golf 1 km. Riding 10 km.

Open: 1 April - 30 September.

Directions

From A6 exit 26 (Chalon-Sud) bear right to roundabout and take N80 (Dole) straight on to roundabout at St Marcel. Turn left (fourth exit) and fork right into Les Chavannes. At central traffic lights turn right and under modern river bridge to site entrance.

Charges 2006

Per person	€ 3,10 - € 3,80
child (under 7 yrs)	€ 1,90 - € 2,50
pitch	€ 3,90 - € 4,70
electricity	€ 2,90 - € 3,50

Domaine du Château de l'Epervière

Castel Camping ★★★★

Bourgogne du Sud

FRANCE

CAMPING DU Pont de BOURGOGNE

Chalon sur Saône - Bourgogne du Sud

FR71050 Camping Moulin de Collonge

F-71390 Saint Boil (Saône-et-Loire)

Tel: 03 85 44 00 32. Email: millofcollonge@wanadoo.fr

This well run, family site offers an 'away from it all' situation surrounded by sloping vineyards and golden wheat fields. It has an instant appeal for those seeking a quiet, relaxing environment. There are 57 level pitches, most with electrical hook-ups although long cables may be required. Flower arrangements are in abundance and, like the shrubs and grounds, are constantly being attended. Beyond the stream that borders the site are a swimming pool, patio and a pizzeria (also open to the public all year). A new lake, 1.8 m. deep, has been created for leisure activities.

Facilities

Well kept toilet facilities housed in a converted barn. Laundry and dishwashing sinks. Washing machine and dryer. Freezer for campers' use. Bread each morning. Basic shop (1/6-3/9). Pizzeria, snack bar (1/7-31/8). Swimming pool covered - walls can be opened in good weather. Playgrounds. Bicycle hire. Table tennis. Fishing. Pony trekking. Off site: Riding 4 km. 'Voie Vert', 117 km. track for cycling or walking near the site.

Open: 15 March - 30 September.

Directions

From Chalon-sur-Saône travel 9 km. west on the N80. Turn south on D981 through Buxy (6 km). Continue south for 7 km. to Saint Boil and site is signed at south end of the village.

Charges 2006

Per person	€ 4,50 - € 5,50
child (under 7 yrs)	€ 2,29 - € 3,50
pitch incl. electricity	€ 8,50 - € 11,50

Camping Cheques accepted.

FR25080 Camping les Fuvettes

F-25160 Malbuisson (Doubs)

Tel: 03 81 69 31 50. Email: lesfuvettes@wanadoo.fr

High in the Jura and close to the Swiss border, Les Fuvettes is a well-established family site with a fine, lakeside setting on Lac Saint Point. The lake is large – over 1000 hectares and a wide range of watersports are possible from the site, including sailing, windsurfing and pedaloes. Most equipment can be hired on site. Pitches here are grassy and of a reasonable size, separated by hedges and small trees. The new swimming pool is impressive with water slides and a separate children's pool. The site's bar/snack bar is housed in an attractive, steep roofed building and offers panoramic views across the lake. Walking and mountain biking are popular pursuits and many trails are available in the surrounding countryside. The Château de Joux is a popular excursion and the nearby Mont d'Or offers fine views towards the Alps. In high season, the site runs an entertainment and excursion programme, including a children's club. Mobile homes and chalets for rent.

Facilities

Three toilet blocks include facilities for babies and disabled people. Shop. Bar and snack bar. Swimming pool with waterslides and jacuzzi. Paddling pool. Play area. Minigolf. Archery. Beach volleyball. Bicycle hire. Sports pitch. Fishing (permit needed). Boat and pedalo hire. Games room. TV room. Children's club in peak season. Entertainment and excursion programme (July and August). Off site: Sailing school. Tennis. Cycling and walking trails. Restaurants, cafes and shops in nearby Malbuisson (walking distance).

Open: 1 April - 30 September.

Directions

From Besançon, head south on the N57 and join the D437 beyond Pontarlier signed Lac St Point and Mouthe. This road runs along the easten shores of the lake and passes through Malbuisson. Site is at the end of the village on the right.

Charges 2006

Per unit incl. 2 persons	€ 14,00 - € 21,00
extra person	€ 3,00 - € 4,90
child (under 7 yrs)	€ 1,50 - € 2,70
electricity (6A)	€ 3,90

FR39040 Camping la Pergola

1, rue des Vernois, F-39130 Marigny (Jura)

Tel: 03 84 25 70 03. Email: contact@lapergola.com

Close to the Swiss border and overlooking the sparkling waters of Lac de Chalain, La Pergola is a neat, tidy, terraced site set amongst the rolling hills of the Jura. It is very well appointed, with 350 pitches, 127 for touring, mainly on gravel and separated by small bushes, all with electricity, water and drainage. Arranged on numerous terraces, connected by steep steps, some have shade and the higher ones have good views over the lake. A fence protects the site from the public footpath that separates the site from the lakeside but there are frequent access gates.

Facilities

Latest sanitary block serving the lower pitches is well appointed. Slightly older blocks serve the other terraces. Facilities for disabled visitors on lower terraces. Shop (1/6-18/9). Bar. Restaurant. Pizzeria/takeaway. Pool complex (two heated). Play areas and children's club. Windsurfing, pedaloes, canoes and small boats for hire. Organised programme in high season. Disco twice weekly. Internet access. Off site: Hang-gliding 2 km. Riding 3 km.

Open: 15 May - 18 September.

Directions

Site is 2.5 km. north of Doucier on D27 next to Lake Chalain. It is signposted from Marigny. GPS: N46:40.621 E05:46.851

Charges 2006

Per unit incl. 2 persons	€ 20,00 - € 36,00
extra person	€ 4,40 - € 6,50
child (2-7 yrs)	free - € 5,50

Camping Cheques accepted.

tel: 00 333 59 59 03 59 *kawan-villages.com*

FR39080 Camping du Domaine de l'Epinette

15, rue de l'Epinette, F-39130 Chatillon (Jura)

Tel: 03 84 25 71 44. Email: info@domaine-epinette.com

This site is set in charming wooded countryside on land sloping down to the river Ain, which is shallow and slow moving. There are 150 grassy pitches, 126 are available for touring units, some slightly sloping. These are arranged on terraces and separated by hedges and young bushes and trees, about half being shaded. Nearly all have electricity hook-ups, although some long leads are needed. There is an attractive swimming pool, paddling pool and surrounds.

Facilities

Two modern toilet blocks. Unit for disabled visitors. Baby bath. Dishwashing and laundry sinks. Washing machine and dryer. Small shop for basics. Snack bar and takeaway (evenings). New reception, bar, TV room and shop. Playground. Table tennis under marquee. Boules. Direct access to river for swimming and canoeing. Activity club for children (high season). Off site: Riding 6 km. Golf 25 km. Shops, etc. in Doucier 6 km.

Open: Mid-June - mid-September.

Directions

From Lons-le-Saunier take D471 eastwards towards Champagnole. After about 8 km. fork right onto D39 towards Doucier. After 11 km. at Chatillon turn right on D151 south towards Blye. Site is 2 km.

Charges 2006

Per unit incl. 2 persons and electricity	€ 16,00 - € 26,50
extra person	€ 2,00 - € 4,00

Camping Cheques accepted.

tel: 00 333 59 59 03 59 *kawan-villages.com*

FR74060 Camping la Colombière

Saint Julien-en-Genevois, F-74160 Neydens (Haute-Savoie)

Tel: 04 50 35 13 14. Email: la.colombiere@wanadoo.fr

La Colombière, a family owned site, is on the edge of the small residential village of Neydens, a few minutes from the A40 autoroute and only a short drive from Geneva. It is an attractive site with only 104 pitches (82 for touring), all reasonably level and separated by fruit trees, flowering shrubs and hedges. Neydens makes a good base for visiting Geneva and the region around the lake.

Facilities

Good sanitary blocks (one heated) include facilities for disabled people. Motorcaravan services. Good bar/ restaurant (all season) and terrace overlooking the pool (15/5-15/9). Heated, indoor spa pool. Internet (WiFi). Organised visits and activities (all season). Bicycle hire. Playground. Off site: Fishing 2 km. Riding 3 km. Golf 6 km. St Julien-en-Genevois (5 km). Switzerland 3 km.

Open: 1 April - 15 October.

Directions

Take exit 13 from A40 autoroute south of Geneva, and then N201 towards Annecy. After 2 km. turn left into village of Neydens and follow campsite signs to site in just over 1 km. GPS: N46:07.213 E06:06.323

Charges 2007

Per unit incl. 2 persons	€ 16,00 - € 25,50
child (2-7 yrs)	€ 3,50 - € 4,50
electricity (5/6A)	€ 4,70

Camping Cheques accepted.

tel: 00 333 59 59 03 59 *kawan-villages.com*

FR74070 Camping Caravaning L'Escale

Famille Baur, F-74450 Le Grand-Bornand (Haute-Savoie)
Tel: 04 50 02 20 69. Email: contact@campinglescale.com

The 149 fairly sunny pitches (142 for touring with electricity) are of average size (some now 100 sq.m.), clearly marked with a part grass, part gravel surface and separated by trees and shrubs, 86 being fully serviced. Rock pegs are essential. The village (200 m.) has all the facilities of a major resort with ongoing activity for summer or winter holidays. In summer a variety of well signed footpaths and cycle tracks provide forest or mountain excursions of all degrees of difficulty.

Facilities

Good heated toilet blocks have all the necessary facilities. Drying room for skis and boots. Superb complex with interconnected indoor (all season) and outdoor pools and paddling pools (10/6-31/8). Bar/restaurant (all season). Play area. Tennis. WiFi. Off site: Village (5 minutes walk), shops, bars, restaurants, paragliding, hang-gliding. Activities organised. Ice skating, ice hockey in winter. Bicycle hire 200 m. Riding and golf 3 km.

Open: 15 December - 22 April, 20 May - 24 September.

Directions

From Annecy follow D16 and D909 roads towards La Clusaz. At St Jean-de-Sixt, turn left at roundabout on D4 signed Grand Bornand. Just before village turn right signed Vallée de Bouchet and camping. Site in 1 km. GPS: N45:56.261 E06:25.416

Charges 2006

Per unit incl. 2 persons	€ 17,50 - € 22,00
electricity (2-10A)	€ 3,80 - € 8,40

Camping Cheques accepted.

FR38080 Camping Caravaning Au Joyeux Réveil

Le Château, F-38880 Autrans (Isère)
Tel: 04 76 95 33 44. Email: camping-au-joyeux-reveil@wanadoo.fr

The small town of Autrans is set on a plateau, 1,050 m. high, in the Vercors region. The well organised site is run by a very friendly family (English is spoken). It is on the outskirts of the town, set below a ski jump and short lift. There are 111 pitches with 80 for touring, electricity 2-10A. They are mainly on grass, in a sunny location with fantastic views over the surrounding wooded mountains with small trees giving little shade. There is a new swimming pool area.

Facilities

The new toilet block is very well appointed, with under-floor heating and all the expected facilities. Another new building houses a bar with terrace, snack bar/takeaway (July and August). New pool area with two pools, toboggan for children and separate paddling pool. Small play area. TV room. Internet point. Off site: Autrans with a few shops 500 m. Villard de Lans, 16 km. Short ski lift near site and a shuttle bus runs (in winter) to the longer runs (5 km). Fishing, bicycle hire, riding 300 m.

Open: 1 December - 31 March, 1 May - 30 September.

Directions

From A48, northwest of Grenoble at exit 13 (going south) or 3A (going north). Take N532 to Sassenage, turn west on D531 to Lans en Vercors. Turn right on D106 (Autrans). Entering Autrans turn right at roundabout and very shortly right again. Site on left. GPS: N45:10.515 E05:32.87

Charges 2006

Per unit incl. 1 or 2 persons	€ 16,50 - € 26,00
electricity (2-6A)	€ 2,00 - € 6,00

Camping Cheques accepted.

kawan-villages.com **tel: 00 333 59 59 03 59**   *kawan*
VILLAGES CAMPINGS

FR38010 Le Coin Tranquille

F-38490 Les Abrets (Isère)
Tel: 04 76 32 13 48. Email: contact@coin-tranquille.com

Les Abrets is well placed for visits to the Savoie regions and the Alps. Le Coin Tranquille is an attractive and well maintained site of 192 grass pitches (178 for tourers), all with electricity. They are separated by hedges of hydrangea, flowering shrubs and trees to make a lovely environment enhanced by the marvellous views across to the mountains. This is a popular, family run site with friendly staff that makes a wonderful base for exploring the area. A 'Sites et Paysages' member.

Facilities

Three well appointed sanitary blocks are well kept, heated in low season. Facilities for children and disabled people. Busy shop. Excellent restaurant. Swimming pool and paddling pool (15/5-30/9; no Bermuda style shorts) with sunbathing areas. Play area. TV/video room, games room and quiet reading room. Weekly entertainment for children and adults (July/Aug) including live music (not discos). Bicycle hire. Off site: Riding 6 km. Fishing 8 km. Golf 25 km. Les Abrets with shops and supermarket 2 km.

Open: 1 April - 31 October.

Directions

Site is east of Les Abrets. From roundabout in town take N6 towards Chambery, turning left in just under 2 km. (signed Restaurant and Camping). Follow signs along country lane for just over 1 km. and entrance is on right. GPS: N45:32.482 E05:36.489

Charges 2007

Per pitch incl. 2 persons and electricity	€ 16,30 - € 30,00
extra person	€ 4,00 - € 6,50

Camping Cheques accepted.

kawan-villages.com **tel: 00 333 59 59 03 59**   *kawar*
VILLAGES CAMPINGS

FR73030 Camping les Lanchettes

F-73210 Peisey-Nancroix (Savoie)

Tel: 04 79 07 93 07. Email: lanchettes@free.fr

A natural, terraced site, it has 90 good size, reasonably level and well drained, grassy/stony pitches, with 80 used for touring units, 70 having electricity (3-10A). Because it is very cold in winter and quite cold on some spring and autumn evenings (warm bedding necessary) there are no outside taps. For those who love walking and biking, the wonderful scenery, flora and fauna, this is the site for you. In winter it is ideal for the serious skier being close to the famous resort of Les Arcs (via free bus service and cable car). Underpowered units not advised.

Facilities

Well appointed heated toilet block. Motorcaravan services. Restaurant, takeaway (July/Aug. and winter). Playground. Club/TV room. Large tent/marquee used in bad weather. In winter a small bus (free) runs to all the hotels, bars, ski tows. Off site: Walks in National Park. Riding next to site. Peisey-Nancroix, restaurants, bars and shops 3 km. Les Arcs winter sports centre 6 km. Outdoor swimming pool and bicycle hire 6 km. Golf and indoor pool 8 km.

Open: 15 December - 15 October.

Directions

From Albertville take N90 towards Bourg-St-Maurice, through Aime. In 9 km. turn right on D87, signed Peisey-Nancroix. Follow a winding hilly road (with hairpin bends) for 10 km. Pass through Peisey-Nancroix; site on right about 1 km. beyond Nancroix. GPS: N45:31.882 E06:46.536

Charges 2006

Per unit incl. 2 persons	€ 11,60 - € 13,10
extra person	€ 4,00 - € 4,40
electricity (3-10A)	€ 3,00 - € 7,30

Camping Cheques accepted.

FR40140 Camping Caravaning Lou P'tit Poun

110 avenue du Quartier Neuf, F-40390 Saint Martin de Seignanx (Landes)

Tel: 05 59 56 55 79. Email: contact@louptitpoun.com

The manicured grounds surrounding Lou P'tit Poun give it a well kept appearance, a theme carried out throughout this very pleasing site. It is only after arriving at the car park that you feel confident it is not a private estate. Beyond this point an abundance of shrubs and trees are revealed. Behind a central sloping flower bed lies the open plan reception area. The avenues around the site are wide and the 168 pitches (99 for touring) are spacious. All have electricity (6/10A), many also have water and drainage and some are separated by low hedges. A 'Sites et Paysages' member. The jovial owners not only make their guests welcome, but extend their enthusiasm to organising weekly entertainment for young and old during high season.

Facilities

Two unisex sanitary blocks, maintained to a high standard and kept clean, include washbasins in cabins, a baby bath and provision for disabled people. Dishwashing sinks and laundry facilities with washing machine and dryer. Motorcaravan service point. Small shop (1/7-31/8). Café (1/7-31/8). Swimming pool (1/6-15/9). Play area. Games room, TV. Half court tennis. Table tennis. Off site: Bayonne 6 km. Fishing or riding 7 km. Golf 10 km. Sandy beaches of Basque coast ten minute drive.

Open: 1 June - 15 September.

Directions

Leave A63 at exit 6 and join N117 in the direction of Pau. Site is signed at Leclerc supermarket. Continue on N117 for 3.5 km. and site is clearly signed on right. GPS: N43:31.451 W01:24.730

Charges 2006

Per pitch incl. 1 or 2 persons	€ 10,40 - € 23,50
with 6A electricity	€ 13,50 - € 27,00
with water and drainage	€ 20,50 - € 31,50
extra person	€ 5,10 - € 6,50
child (under 7 yrs)	€ 2,10 - € 4,30

Check real time availability and at-the-gate prices...

www.alanrogers.com

FR33110 Airotel Camping de la Côte d'Argent

F-33990 Hourtin-Plage (Gironde)

Tel: **05 56 09 10 25**. Email: **info@camping-cote-dargent.com**

Côte d'Argent is a large, well equipped site for leisurely family holidays. It makes an ideal base for walkers and cyclists, with over 100 km. of cycle lanes. Hourtin-Plage is a pleasant invigorating resort on the Atlantic coast and a popular location for watersports enthusiasts, The site's top attraction is its pool complex with wooden bridges connecting the pools and islands, with sunbathing and play areas plus indoor heated pool. There are 550 touring pitches, not clearly defined, under trees with some on soft sand. Entertainment takes place at the bar near the entrance (until 12.30). Spread over 20 hectares of undulating sand-based terrain and in the midst of a pine forest. There are 48 hardstandings for motorcaravans outside the site, providing a cheap stop-over, but with no access to site facilities. The site is well organised and ideal for children.

Facilities

Very clean sanitary blocks include provision for disabled visitors. Washing machines. Motorcaravan service points. Large supermarket, restaurant, takeaway, pizzeria bar. Four outdoor pools with slides and flumes. Indoor pool. Massage. Astronomy once a week. Tennis. Pool tables. Play areas. Mini-club, organised entertainment in season. Fishing. Riding. Bicycle hire. Internet. ATM. Charcoal barbecues are not permitted. Off site: Path to the beach 300 m. Golf 30 km.

Open: 12 May - 16 September.

Directions

Turn off D101 Hourtin-Soulac road 3 km. north of Hourtin. Then join D101E signed Hourtin-Plage. Site is 300 m. from the beach.
GPS: N45:13.381 W01:09.868

Charges 2006

Per unit incl. 2 persons	€ 25,00 - € 39,00
tent incl. 2 persons	€ 19,00 - € 29,00
extra person	€ 3,00 - € 6,00
child (2-10 yrs)	€ 2,00 - € 5,00
electricity (6A)	€ 5,00

Camping Cheques accepted.

FR33080 Domaine de la Barbanne

Route de Montagne, F-33330 Saint Emilion (Gironde)

Tel: **05 57 24 75 80**. Email: **barbanne@wanadoo.fr**

La Barbanne is a pleasant, friendly, family-owned site in the heart of the Bordeaux wine region, only 2.5 km. from the famous town of St Emilion. With 174 pitches, most for touring, the owners have created a carefully maintained, well equipped site. The large, level and grassy pitches have dividing hedges and electricity (long leads necessary). Twelve pitches for motorcaravans have tarmac surrounded by grass. The owners run a free minibus service daily to St Emilion and also organise excursions in July and August. The original parts of the site bordering the lake have mature trees providing good shade, whilst in the newer area the trees have yet to provide full shade and it can be hot in summer. A 'Sites et Paysages' member.

Facilities

Two modern, fully equipped toilet blocks include facilities for campers with disabilities. Motorcaravan services. Well stocked shop. Bar, terrace, takeaway, restaurant (1/6-20/9). Two swimming pools, one heated with water slide (15/4-22/9). Enclosed play area with seats for parents, children's club (from 1/7). Evening entertainment (from 1/7). Tennis, boules, volleyball, table tennis, minigolf. The lake provides superb free fishing, pedaloes, canoes and lakeside walks. Bicycle hire. Off site: St Emilion and shops 2.5 km. Riding 8 km.

Open: 1 April - 22 September.

Directions

Site is 2.5 km. north of St Emilion. Caravans and motorhomes are forbidden through the village of St Emilion and they must approach the site from Libourne on D243 or from Castillon leave D936 and take D130/D243. GPS: N44:54.997 W00:08.513

Charges 2006

Per unit incl. 1 or 2 persons	€ 15,50 - € 23,90
extra person	€ 5,00 - € 7,50
child (under 7 yrs)	€ 3,50 - € 6,30
animal	free - € 2,50

Camping Cheques accepted.

Airotel Camping Caravaning
Côte d'Argent

★★★

Club Airotel

POOL COMPLEX OF 3500 M² WITH WATERSLIDES, JACUZZI AND COVERED HEATED SWIMMING POOL

Special low season offers (not in July and August)
14 = 11 and 7 = 6
campsite or accommodations

wifi - hotel - shops - restaurant - bar - provisions - animation (sports) - tennis - horse riding - archery - mini club - games room - sailing (4 km) - surfing (300 m)

Hourtin Plage - Aquitaine - Atlantique Sud

La Côte d'Argent is a beautiful sloping park of 20 ha in the heart of a pine tree forest. At 300 m of a long winding sandy beach at the Atlantic Ocean.
A site in the lee of dunes and the forest, this holiday village enjoys an ideal climate for enjoying relaxing nature holidays.

Sun, Life and fun

Airotel Camping Caravaning de la Côte d'Argent
33990 Hourtin Plage
Tél : 00033 (0)5.56.09.10.25
Fax : 0033 (0)5.56.09.24.96
www.camping-cote-dargent.com - www.cca33.com -
www.campingcoteouest.com

FR33130 Yelloh! Village les Grands Pins

Plage Nord, F-33680 Lacanau-Océan (Gironde)

Tel: **05 56 03 20 77**. Email: **reception@lesgrandspins.com**

This Atlantic coast holiday site with direct access to a fine sandy beach, is on undulating terrain amongst tall pine trees. A large site, with 600 pitches, 470 of varying sizes for touring units. One half of the site is a traffic free zone (except for arrival or departure day, caravans are placed on the pitch, with separate areas outside for parking). There are a good number of tent pitches, those in the centre of the site having some of the best views. This site is popular and has an excellent range of facilities available for the whole season. Especially useful for tenters are safety deposit and fridge boxes which are available for rent. The large sandy beach is a 350 metre stroll from the gate at the back of the site.

Facilities

Four well equipped toilet blocks, one heated, including baby room and facilities for disabled people. Launderette. Motorcaravan services. Supermarket. Bar, restaurant, snack bar, takeaway. Heated swimming pool (lifeguard in July/Aug) with sunbathing surround. Jacuzzi. Free fitness activities. Games room. Fitness suite. Tennis. Two playgrounds. Adventure playground. Bicycle hire. Organised activities. Entrance barrier with keypad access. Only gas barbecues are permitted. Off site: Fishing, golf, riding and bicycle hire 5 km.

Open: 15 April - 23 September.

Directions

From Bordeaux take N125/D6 west to Lacanau Ocean. At second roundabout, take second exit: Plage Nord, follow signs to 'campings'. Les Grand Pins signed to right at the far end of road. GPS: N45:00.664 W01:11.602

Charges 2006

Per unit incl. 2 persons and electricity	€ 16,00 - € 38,00
extra person	€ 5,00 - € 9,00
child (2-12 yrs)	free - € 6,00

Directly on the beach and in the heart of an extensive pine forest, this village is an ideal choice for family holidays, where you can relax and unwind in the open air. Discover Lacanau, the well-known surfing spot, play golf, ride a bike on one of the nice cycle tracks or chose a canoe trip between the lakes. For a full-day excursion, visit a Chateau in the world famous Médoc wine growing area, take a boat trip on the Bassin d'Arcachon or do some shopping in the majestic town of Bordeaux.

Yelloh ! Village ★★★★ Les Grands Pins

Camping and Mobile-homes 350m from the beach

Yelloh ! Village **LES GRANDS PINS**   F 33680 Lacanau Océan
Tél. + 33 (0)5 56 03 20 77   Fax. + 33 (0)5 57 70 03 89
www.lesgrandspins.com   www.yellohvillage-les-grands-pins.com
E-mail : info@yellohvillage-les-grands-pins.com

yelloh! VILLAGE

FR33220 Sunêlia le Petit Nice

Route de Biscarosse, F-33115 Pyla-sur-Mer (Gironde)

Tel: **05 56 22 74 03**. Email: **info@petitnice.com**

Le Petit Nice is a traditional seaside site, just south of the great Dune de Pyla (Europe's largest sand dune, and a genuinely remarkable sight). It is a friendly, if relatively unsophisticated, site with direct (steep) access to an excellent sandy beach. The 225 pitches are for the most part terraced, descending towards the sea. Many are quite small, with larger pitches generally occupied by mobile homes. For this reason it is likely to appeal more to campers and those with smaller motorcaravans and caravans. Most pitches are shaded by pine trees but those closest to the sea are unshaded. Unusually, the site also has a private hang-gliding and paragliding take-off strip (very popular activities here).

Facilities

Two refurbished toilet blocks include washbasins in cubicles, baby rooms and facilities for disabled people. New, very smart bar/restaurant. Well stocked shop. Games room. Attractive swimming pool with small slide, children's pool and jacuzzi. Good fenced play area. Tennis, table tennis and boules court.

Open: 7 April - 30 September.

Directions

The site is on the D218 (Arcachon - Biscarosse) south of the Dune de Pyla and is the fifth site you pass after the Dune. GPS: N44:34.339 W01:13.255

Charges 2006

Per pitch incl. 2 persons	€ 14,00 - € 28,00
with electricity (6A)	€ 17,00 - € 32,00
extra person	€ 4,00 - € 7,00
child (2-12 yrs)	€ 2,00 - € 6,00

Camping Cheques accepted.

FR40100 Camping du Domaine de la Rive

Route de Bordeaux, F-40600 Biscarosse (Landes)
Tel: **05 58 78 12 33**. Email: **info@camping-de-la-rive.fr**

Surrounded by pine woods, La Rive has a superb beach-side location on Lac de Sanguinet. It provides mostly level, numbered and clearly defined pitches of 100 sq.m. all with electricity connections (6A). The swimming pool complex is wonderful with pools linked by water channels and bridges. There is also a jacuzzi, paddling pool and two large swimming pools all surrounded by sunbathing areas and decorated with palm trees. An indoor pool is heated and open all season. There may be some aircraft noise from a nearby army base. This is a friendly site with a good mix of nationalities. The latest addition is a super children's aqua park with various games. The beach is excellent, shelving gently to provide safe bathing for all ages. There are windsurfers and small craft can be launched from the site's slipway.

Facilities

Five good clean toilet blocks have washbasins in cabins and mainly British style toilets. Facilities for disabled visitors. Baby baths. Motorcaravan service point. Shop. Propane gas. Restaurant. Bar serving snacks and takeaway. Games room. Pool complex (supervised July/Aug). Play area. Tennis. Bicycle hire. Hand-ball, basketball. Table tennis, boules, archery and football. Fishing. Water skiing. Watersports equipment hire. Tournaments (June-Aug). Skateboard park. Trampolines. Mini-club for children. No charcoal barbecues on pitches. Off site: Golf 8 km.

Open: 1 April - 30 September.

Directions

Take D652 from Sanguinet to Biscarosse and site is signed on the right in about 6 km. Turn right and follow new tarmac road for 2 km.
GPS: N44:27.607 W01:07.808

Charges 2006

Per pitch incl. 2 persons and electricity	€ 20,00 - € 38,00
with water and drainage	€ 23,00 - € 41,00
extra person	€ 3,40 - € 7,00
child (3-10 yrs)	€ 2,30 - € 5,50

Camping Cheques accepted.

FR40060 Camping Club International Eurosol

Route de la Plage, F-40560 Vielle-Saint Girons (Landes)
Tel: **05 58 47 90 14**. Email: **contact@camping-eurosol.com**

The site is on undulating ground amongst mature pine trees giving good shade and the pitches on the slopes are mainly only suitable for tents. The 405 pitches for touring units are numbered (although with nothing to separate them, there is little privacy) and 209 have electricity with 120 fully serviced (86 with mobile homes). A family site with entertainers who speak many languages, many games and tournaments are organised and a beach volleyball competition is held each evening in front of the bar.

Facilities

Four main toilet blocks and two smaller blocks, facilities for babies and disabled people. Motorcaravan services. Fridge rental. Well stocked shop and bar (12/5-15/9). Restaurant, takeaway (1/7-31/8). Stage for live shows (mainly performed by the versatile staff) in July/Aug. and finishing by midnight. Outdoor swimming pool (12/5-15/9). Tennis. Multi-sport court for basketball, handball and football. Bicycle hire. Charcoal barbecues are not permitted. Off site: Riding school opposite. Fishing 700 m.

Open: 12 May - 15 September.

Directions

Turn off D652 at St Girons on D42 towards St Girons-Plage. Site is on left before coming to beach (4.5 km). GPS: N43:57.100 W01:21.087

Charges 2006

Per unit incl.1 or 2 persons	€ 12,00 - € 25,50
with electricity	€ 15,00 - € 30,00
with water and drainage	€ 15,00 - € 33,00
extra person (over 4 yrs)	€ 3,00 - € 4,00
dog	€ 2,50

This is just a sample of the campsites we have inspected and selected in France. For more campsites and further information, please see the Alan Rogers France guide.

Domaine de La Rive

a Paradise for Children

ww.larive.fr

Pool complex and a covered heated swimming pool

Route de Bordeaux
40600 Biscarosse
Tél : 00 33 5 58 78 12 33
Fax : 00 33 5 58 78 12 92
info@camping-de-la-rive.fr

La Clef Verte

Chalets
and mobile homes
for rent.
At the banks
of a lake,
in the heart
of the landaise
forest

★ ★ ★ ★

Saint Martin

Airotel Camping
Caravaning

Avenue de l'Océan
40660 Moliets-Plage

Tél : (33) 05.58.48.52.30
Fax : (33) 05.58.48.50.73
www.camping-saint-martin.fr
contact @camping-saint-martin.fr

FR40190 Le Saint Martin Airotel Camping

Avenue de l'Océan, F-40660 Moliets-Plage (Landes)
Tel: **05 58 48 52 30**. Email: **contact@camping-saint-martin.fr**

A family site aimed mainly at couples and young families, Airotel St Martin is a welcome change to most of the sites in this area in that it has only a small number of mobile homes (85) compared to the number of touring pitches (575). First impressions are of a neat, tidy, well cared for site and the direct access to the beach is an added bonus. The pitches are mainly typically French in style with low hedges separating them plus some shade. Electric hook ups are 10-15A and a number of pitches also have water and drainage. Entertainment in high season is low key (with the emphasis on quiet nights) – daytime competitions and a 'miniclub' and the occasional evening entertainment, well away from the pitches and with no discos or karaoke. With pleasant chalets and mobile homes to rent, and an 18 hole golf course 700 m. away (special rates negotiated), this would be an ideal destination for a golfing weekend or longer stay.

Facilities

Seven toilet blocks of a high standard and very well maintained, have washbasins in cabins, large showers, baby rooms and facilities for disabled visitors. Motorcaravan service point. Washing machines and dryers. Fridge rental. Supermarket. Bars, restaurants and takeaways. Indoor pool, jacuzzi and sauna (charged July/Aug). Outdoor pool area with jacuzzi and paddling pool (15/6-15/9). Multi sports pitch. Play area. Internet access. Electric barbecues only. Off site: Excellent area for cycling, bicycle hire 500 m. Golf and tennis 700 m. Riding 8 km. .

Open: Easter - 31 October.

Directions

From the N10 take D142 to Lèon, then D652 to Moliets-et-Mar. Follow signs to Moliets-Plage, site is well signed. GPS: N43:51.145 W01:23.239

Charges 2006

Per unit incl. 1 or 2 adults,

and 1 child	€ 17,50 - € 31,50
with electricity	€ 21,00 - € 35,50
with services	€ 24,00 - € 39,00
extra person	€ 3,20 - € 5,50
dog	€ 3,00

Prices are for reserved pitches.

FR40200 Yelloh! Village le Sylvamar

Avenue de l'Océan, F-40530 Labenne Océan (Landes)

Tel: **05 59 45 75 16**. Email: **camping@sylvamar.fr**

Less than a kilometre from a long sandy beach, this campsite has a good mix of tidy, well maintained chalets, mobile homes and touring pitches. The 556 pitches (212 for touring) are level, numbered and mostly separated by low hedges. Most have electricity (10A), many also have water and drainage and there is welcoming shade. The swimming pool complex is superbly set in a sunny location. The pools are of various sizes (one heated, one not) with a large one for paddling. With four toboggans and a fast flowing channel for sailing down in the inflatable rubber rings provided, this is a haven for children. All are surrounded by ample sunbathing terraces and overlooked by the bar/restaurant.

Facilities

Four modern toilet blocks (one recently refurbished) have washbasins in cabins, and facilities for babies and disabled visitors. Washing machines. Shop. Bar/restaurant and takeaway. Play area. TV room. Mini-club (July/Aug). Fitness centre. Tennis. Bicycle hire. Extensive entertainment programme. No charcoal barbecues. Internet access. Off site: Beach 900 m. Fishing, riding 1 km. Golf 7 km.

Open: 14 April - 25 September.

Directions

Labenne is on the N10. In Labenne, head west on D126 signed Labenne Océan and site is on right in 4 km. GPS: N43:35.742 W01:27.383

Charges 2006

Per unit incl. 2 persons and electricity	€ 15,00 - € 36,00
extra person (over 7 yrs)	€ 3,00 - € 7,00
child (3-7 yrs)	free - € 5,00

Le Sylvamar

Avenue de l'Océan F-40530 - Labenne Océan - France
T [33] 05 59 45 75 16 - F [33] 05 59 45 75 16 - sylvamar@wanadoo.fr

Nestled in a 37-acre (15 hectares) pine forest, this village is paradise for nature lovers, beachgoers and marine activities. Located on the southern coast of France's Landes region, Sylvamar is right next to Basque country and Spain, between Biarritz and Hossegor. It's up to you to choose wether you'd like an active or relaxing vacation, with plenty of clean, fresh air to make the best of it.

A DREAM COME TRUE · THE AQUATIC AREA IS AT YOUR DISPOSAL:
Blue lagoon, quiet green, luxurious vegetation, natural surroundings. For aquatic fun, there are 2 heated pools, a play river and triple waterslide. For relaxation, use deck chairs to soak up sun, stroll about on bridges and whatever you feel like. It's all designed around games, having fun and taking it easy. Smiling children and parents and all in complete safety, with on-duty lifeguards

FR40240 Camping Mayotte Vacances

368 chemin des Roseaux, F-40600 Biscarrosse (Landes)

Tel: **05 58 78 00 00**. Email: **mayotte@yellohvillage.com**

This appealing site is set amongst pine trees on the edge of Lac de Biscarrosse. Drive down a tree and flower lined avenue and proceed toward the lake to shady, good sized pitches which blend well with the many tidy mobile homes that share the area. Divided by hedges, all the pitches have electricity (10A) and water taps. There may be some aircraft noise at times from a nearby army base. The pool complex is impressive, with various pools, slides, chutes, jacuzzi and sauna, all surrounded by paved sunbathing areas. The excellent lakeside beach provides safe bathing for all ages with plenty of watersports available. A comfortable restaurant and bar overlook the pool. A new, fully equipped gym is available free of charge. Children of all ages are catered for with organised clubs, play and sports areas and a games room. This well managed, clean and friendly site with helpful multilingual staff in reception should appeal to all and the facilities are open all season.

Facilities

Four good quality, clean toilet blocks (one open early season). Good facilities for visitors with disabilities. Unusual baby/toddler bathroom. Motorcaravan services. Laundry. Supermarket. Boutique. Rental shop (July/Aug). Restaurant. Swimming pools (one heated; supervised July/Aug. and weekends). Play area. Further children's area (extra cost) with trampolines, inflatables and a small train. Bicycle hire. Fishing. Watersports. Organised activities and entertainment (July/Aug). Charcoal barbecues not permitted. ATM. Internet access. Off site: Golf 4 km. Riding 100 m. Beach 10 km. Town 2 km.

Open: 30 April - 24 September.

Directions

From the north on D652 turn right on D333 (chemin de Goubern). Pass through Goubern and Mayotte Village. Take next right (signed to site) into chemin des Roseaux. GPS: N44:26.097 W01:09.303

Charges 2006

Per unit incl. 2 persons	€ 18,00 - € 29,00
extra person	€ 3,50 - € 5,00
child (3-7 yrs)	free - € 2,50
dog	€ 3,00 - € 5,00

151

FR40250 Camping les Grands Pins

1039 avenue de Losa, F-40460 Sanguinet (Landes)

Tel: **05 58 78 61 74**. Email: **info@campinglesgrandspins.com**

Approached by a road alongside the lake, this site is set amongst tall pine trees. The gravel pitches are of average size, mostly level and shaded. Hedges divide those available for tourers and these are set amongst the many mobile homes. Large units may find manoeuvring difficult. There may be some aircraft noise at times from a nearby army base. A central pool complex includes a covered heated indoor pool, an outdoor pool, water slide and flume. In early and late season this is a very quiet site with very few facilities open. However, there are plenty of walks, cycle rides and the lake to enjoy. The poolside bar, restaurant and shops are only open in July/August. In July and August the site becomes busy, offering watersports, minigolf, a children's club, boat trips and organised activities. All four sanitary blocks are open for July and August. Fishing is also available.

Facilities

Four toilet blocks include washbasins in cabins, showers and British style toilets (not all open in low seasons). Baby bath and provision for disabled visitors. Laundry facilities. Motorcaravan service point. Shop, bar, restaurant and takeaway (1/7-31/8). Indoor pool (all seson). Outdoor pool complex (1/7-31/8). Play area. Games room. Tennis. Bicycle hire (July/Aug). Pets are not accepted in July/Aug. Barbecues are not allowed. Off site: Beach 30 m. Fishing 2 km. Golf and riding 15 km. Boat launching 1 km.

Open: 1 April - 31 October.

Directions

Enter Sanguinet from the north on the D46. At one way system turn right. Do not continue on one way system but go straight ahead toward lake (signed) on Rue de Lac. Site is 2 km. on left.
GPS: N44:29.038 W01:05.383

Charges 2006

Per unit incl. 2 persons	
and electricity	€ 13,00 - € 33,50
extra person	€ 2,50 - € 4,00
child (3-10 yrs)	€ 2,00 - € 3,00

FR64150 Airotel Residence des Pins

Avenue de Biarritz, F-64210 Bidart (Pyrénées-Atlantiques)

Tel: **05 59 23 00 29**. Email: **lespins@free.fr**

This is a very pleasant, reasonably priced site which will appeal greatly to couples and young families. Set on a fairly gentle hillside, the top level has reception and the bar. Slightly lower are the paddling and swimming pools in a sunny location with sun-beds. Next comes the well stocked shop, tennis courts and the rest of the pitches. Some pitches are behind reception and others, lower down, some slightly sloping, are under trees and separated by hydrangea hedges. Some have electricity (long leads required). There is a varied entertainment programme in July and Aug. The site is not suitable for American motorhomes. It is used by tour operators and there are mobile homes around the outer edges of the site. Buses pass the gate. There is a little day-time road noise but not intrusive.

Facilities

The two toilet blocks have some washbasins and showers together. Washing machines, dryers, ironing boards and facilities for disabled people. Motorcaravan services. Shop and bar open all season, restaurant and takeaway (20/6-15/9). Pool open all season. Games room. Table tennis. Tennis (charged in July/Aug). Play area (3-8 yrs). Bicycle hire. Off site: Lake 600 m. with fishing (no licence required). Golf 1 km. Riding 1 km. Beach with lifeguard 600 m.

Open: 14 May - 30 September.

Directions

Heading south on the A63 towards Spain, take exit J4 onto the N10 towards Bidart. At the roundabout straight after Intermarche turn right towards Biarritz. The site is on the right after 1 km.
GPS: N43:27.185 W01:34.425

Charges 2006

Per unit with 2 persons	
Per unit with 2 persons	€ 13,50 - € 20,80
extra person (over 2 yrs)	€ 3,20 - € 5,70
electricity	€ 3,20 - € 5,00

Camping Cheques accepted.

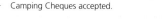

Check real time availability and at-the-gate prices...
www.**alanrogers**.com

FR40180 Camping le Vieux Port

Plage sud, F-40660 Messanges (Landes)

Tel: **01 72 03 91 60**. Email: contact@levieuxport.com

A well established destination appealing particularly to families with teenage children, this lively site has 1,406 pitches of mixed size, most with electricity (6/8A) and some fully serviced. The camping area is well shaded by pines and pitches are generally of a good size, attractively grouped around the toilet blocks. There are many tour operators here and well over a third of the site is taken up with mobile homes and another 400 pitches are used for tents. The heated pool complex is exceptional boasting five outdoor pools and three large water slides. There is also a heated indoor pool. The area to the north of Bayonne is heavily forested and a number of very large campsites are attractively located close to the superb Atlantic beaches. Le Vieux Port is probably the largest and certainly one of the most impressive of these. At the back of the site a path leads across the dunes to a good beach (500 m). A little train also trundles to the beach on a fairly regular basis in high season (small charge). All in all, this is a lively site with a great deal to offer an active family.

Facilities

Nine well appointed toilet blocks with facilities for disabled people. Motorcaravan services. Good supermarket and various smaller shops in high season. Several restaurants, takeaway and three bars (all open all season). Large pool complex (no Bermuda shorts) including new covered pool and Polynesian themed bar. Tennis, football, multi-sport pitch, minigolf. Bicycle hire. Riding centre. Organised activities in high season including frequent discos and karaoke evenings. Only communal barbecues are allowed. Off site: Fishing 1 km. Golf 8 km.

Open: 1 April - 30 September.

Directions

Leave RN10 at Magescq exit heading for Soustons. Pass through Soustons following signs for Vieux-Boucau. Bypass this town and site is clearly signed to the left at second roundabout.
GPS: N43:47.863 W01:23.959

Charges 2006

Per unit incl. 2 persons	€ 12,00 - € 35,00
extra person	€ 3,50 - € 6,00
child (under 10 yrs)	€ 2,50 - € 4,00
electricity (6/8A)	€ 4,00 - € 6,50
animal	€ 2,00 - € 3,50

Camping Cheques accepted.

FR64110 Sunêlia Col d'Ibardin

F-64122 Urrugne (Pyrénées-Atlantiques)

Tel: 05 59 54 31 21. Email: info@col-ibardin.com

This family owned site at the foot of the Basque Pyrénées is highly recommended and deserves praise. It is well run with emphasis on personal attention, the friendly family and their staff ensuring that all are made welcome and is attractively set in the middle of an oak wood. Behind the forecourt, with its brightly coloured shrubs and modern reception area, various roadways lead to the 191 pitches. These are individual, spacious and enjoy the benefit of the shade (if preferred a more open aspect can be found). There are electricity hook-ups (4/10A) and adequate water points. From this site you can enjoy the mountain scenery, be on the beach in 7-10 km. or cross the border into Spain in approximately 14 km.

Facilities

Two toilet blocks, one rebuilt to a high specification, are kept very clean. WC for disabled people. Dishwashing and laundry facilities. Motorcaravan service point. Shop for basics and bread orders (15/6-15/9). Catering, takeaway service and bar (15/6-15/9). Heated swimming pool. New paddling pool. Playground and club (adult supervision). Tennis courts, boules, table tennis, video games. Bicycle hire. New multi-purpose sports area. Not suitable for American motorhomes. Off site: Supermarket and shopping centre 5 km. Fishing and golf 7 km. Riding 20 km.

Open: 1 April - 30 September.

Directions

Leave A63 autoroute at St Jean-de-Luz sud, exit no. 2 and join RN10 in direction of Urrugne. Turn left at roundabout (Col d'Ibardin) on D4. Site on right after 5 km. Do not turn off to the Col itself, carry on towards Ascain. GPS: N43:20.035 W01:41.077

Charges 2007

Per unit incl. 2 persons and electricity	€ 16,50 - € 34,00
extra person	€ 3,00 - € 6,00
child (2-7 yrs)	€ 2,00 - € 3,00

Basque Country

Located between Biarritz (25 kms) and San Sebastian (25 kms), our campsite will pleased the chidren as much as their parents

Swimming Pool / Tennis / Playground / Bar/ Snack / Take Away / Launderette / Kid's Club / Mobil homes to rent...

Tél. : (00 33) 559 54 31 21 • Fax : (00 33) 559 54 62 28 • 64122 Urrugne
www.col-ibardin.com • info@col-ibardin.com

Check real time availability and at-the-gate prices...

www.alanrogers.com

FR12010 Camping le Val de Cantobre
F-12230 Nant-d'Aveyron (Aveyron)
Tel: 05 65 58 43 00. Email: info@valdecantobre.com

This very pleasant terraced site has been imaginatively and tastefully developed by the Dupond family over the past 30 years. Most of the 200 touring pitches (all with electricity and water) are peaceful, generous in size and blessed with views of the valley. A unique activity programme at Val de Cantobre is supervised by qualified instructors in July and August, some arranged by the owners and some at a fair distance from the site. The terrace design provides some peace and privacy, especially on the upper levels and a warm welcome awaits. Rock pegs are advised. The pool surrounds are bedecked by flowers and crowned by a large urn which dispenses water into the paddling pool. The magnificent carved features in the bar create a delightful ambience, complemented by a recently built terrace. Passive recreationists appreciate the scenery, especially Cantobre, a medieval village that clings to a cliff in view of the site. Nature lovers will be delighted to see black vultures wheeling in the Tarn gorge alongside more humble rural residents. Butterflies in profusion, orchids, huge edible snails, glow worms, families of beavers and the natterjack toad all live here.

Facilities
Fully equipped toilet block is beautifully appointed. Fridge hire. Small shop with wide variety of provisions; including many regional specialities. Attractive bar, restaurant, pizzeria, takeaway (some fairly steep up and down walking from furthest pitches to some facilities). Three swimming pools. Minigolf. Table tennis. Play area. River rafting, white water canoeing, rock climbing, paragliding. All weather sports pitch. Torch useful. There are some fairly steep climbs between the levels on the site. Off site: Fishing 4 km. Riding 15 km. Bicycle hire 25 km.

Open: 5 May - 9 September, with all facilities.

Directions
Site is 4 km. north of Nant, on D991 road to Millau. From Millau direction take D991 signed Gorge du Dourbie. Site is on left, just past turn to Cantobre.

Charges 2006
Per unit incl. 2 persons and 4A electricity	€ 19,00 - € 31,50
extra person (4 yrs and over)	€ 4,00 - € 7,00
dog	free - € 3,00

Camping Cheques accepted.

Pitches with stunning views... Facilities full of character... An area with fabulous scenery

LES CASTELS ★★★★

Castel-Camping Val de Cantobre ★★★★
www.valdecantobre.com

Camping Cheque

FR12020 Camping Caravaning les Rivages

Avenue de l'Aigoual, route de Nant, F-12100 Millau (Aveyron)

Tel: 05 65 61 01 07. Email: campinglesrivages@wanadoo.fr

Les Rivages is a large, well established site on the outskirts of the town. It is well situated, being close to the high limestone Causses and the dramatic gorges of the Tarn and Dourbie. Smaller pitches, used for small units, abut a pleasant riverside space suitable for sunbathing, fishing or picnics. Most of the 314 pitches are large, and well shaded. A newer part of the site has less shade but larger pitches. All pitches have electricity (6A), and 100 have water and drainage. The site offers a very wide range of sporting activities close to 30 in all (see facilities). Don't miss the night markets, but don't eat before you get there – there are thousands of things to taste, many of them grilled or spit roasted. Millau is a bustling and pleasant town with easy access via a footpath from the site. The gates are shut 11 pm.- 8 am, with night-watchman.

Facilities

Four well kept modern toilet blocks have all necessary facilities. Special block for children. Small shop (1/6-15/9). Terrace, restaurant and bar overlooking swimming pool, children's pool (from 10/5). Play area. Entertainment, largely for children, child-minding, mini-club. Impressive sports centre with tennis (indoor and outdoor), squash and badminton. Table tennis. Boules. River activities, walking, bird watching, fishing. Off site: Rafting and canoeing arranged. Bicycle hire 1 km. Riding 10 km. Hypermarket in Millau.

Open: 1 May - 30 September.

Directions

From Millau, cross the Tarn bridge and take D991 road east towards Nant. Site is about 400 m. from the roundabout on the right, on the banks of the Dourbie river.

Charges 2007

Per pitch incl. 2 persons and electricity	€ 18,00 - € 26,00
with water and drainage	€ 20,00 - € 28,00
extra person (over 3 yrs)	€ 3,00 - € 4,50
pet	free - € 3,00

Airotel
Les Rivages ★★★★
camping • caravaning • mobil-home • tentes

GORGES DU TARN • MILLAU • AVEYRON
Avenue de l'Aigoual - 12100 MILLAU - France
Tél. 00 33 (0)5 65 61 01 07 • Fax 00 33 (0)5 65 59 03 56

www.campinglesrivages.com
e-mail : campinglesrivages@wanadoo.fr

FR12150 Camping Marmotel

F-12130 Saint Geniez-d'Olt (Aveyron)

Tel: **05 65 70 46 51**. Email: **info@marmotel.com**

The road into Marmotel passes various industrial buildings and is a little off-putting – persevere, as they are soon left behind. The campsite itself is a mixture of old and new. The old part provides many pitches with lots of shade and separated by hedges. The new area is sunny until the trees grow. These pitches each have a private sanitary unit, with shower, WC, washbasin and dishwashing. New and very well designed, they are reasonably priced for such luxury. All the pitches have electricity (10A). A lovely restaurant has a wide terrace with views of the hills and overlooking the heated swimming and paddling pools. These have fountains, a toboggan and sun beds either on grass or the tiled surrounds. The Lot river runs alongside where you can fish or canoe. A 'Sites et Paysages' member.

Facilities

Good sanitary facilities include baby baths and facilities for disabled visitors. Washing machines. Bar/restaurant, takeaway (all season). Swimming pools. Small play area. Multi-sports area (tennis, volleyball, basketball). Entertainment July/Aug. including disco below bar, cinema, karaoke, dances, mini club for 4-12 yr olds. Bicycle hire. Fishing. Canoeing. Off site: Large supermarket 500 m. Riding 10 km. Bicycle tours and canoe trips on the Lot and rafting on the Tarn are organised.

Open: 10 May - 10 September.

Directions

Heading south on autoroute 75 (free) take exit 41 and follow signs for St Geniez d'Olt. Site is at western end of village. Site is signed onto D19 to Prades d'Aubrac, then 500 m. on left.

Charges 2006

Per unit incl. 1 or 2 persons, 10A electricity	€ 17,30 - € 30,00
extra person	€ 2,05 - € 5,80
child under 4 yrs	€ 1,00 - € 3,00
animal	free - € 1,60

Less 30% outside July/Aug.
Camping Cheques accepted.

kawan-villages.com **tel: 00 333 59 59 03 59**

FR12080 Camping Club les Genêts

Lac de Pareloup, F-12410 Salles-Curan (Aveyron)

Tel: **05 65 46 35 34**. Email: **contact@camping-les-genets.fr**

The 162 pitches include 102 grassy, mostly individual pitches for touring units. These are in two areas, one on each side of the entrance lane, and are divided by hedges, shrubs and trees. Most have electricity (6A) and many also have water and waste water drain. The site slopes gently down to the beach and lake with facilities for all watersports including waterskiing. A full animation and activities programme is organised in high season, and there is much to see and do in this very attractive corner of Aveyron. The site is not suitable for American style motorhomes.

Facilities

Two sanitary units with suite for disabled people. Refurbishment of the older unit is planned. Baby room. Laundry. Well stocked shop. Bar, restaurant, snacks (main season). Swimming pool, spa pool (from 1/6; unsupervised). Playground. Minigolf, volleyball, boules. Bicycle hire. Red Indian style tee-pees. Pedaloes, windsurfers, kayaks. Fishing licences available.

Open: 31 May - 11 September.

Directions

From Salles-Curan take D577 for about 4 km. and turn right into a narrow lane immediately after a sharp right hand bend. Site is signed at junction.

Charges 2006

Per unit incl. 1 or 2 persons and 6A electricity	€ 11,00 - € 29,00
lakeside pitch	€ 11,00 - € 36,00
extra person	€ 4,00 - € 7,00

FR12160 Camping Caravaning les Peupliers

Route des Gorges du Tarn, F-12640 Rivière-sur-Tarn (Aveyron)

Tel: 05 65 59 85 17. Email: lespeupliers12640@wanadoo.fr

Les Peupliers is a friendly, family site on the banks of the Tarn river. Most of the good-sized pitches have shade, all have electricity, water and a waste water point and are divided by low hedges. It is possible to swim in the river and there is a landing place for canoes. The site has its own canoes (to rent). In a lovely, sunny situation on the site is a swimming pool with a paddling pool, sun beds and a new slide, all protected by a beautifully clipped hedge and with a super view to the surrounding hills and the Château du Peyrelade perched above the village. Some English is spoken. A treat for us at dusk was to watch beavers playing and swimming on the far river bank. We were told this happens nearly every day. The site is near the village of Rivière-sur-Tarn and the mouth of the Gorges du Tarn. It is 10 km. from the town of Millau, now famous for its spectacular bridge designed by Norman Foster that carries the A75 over the Tarn valley.

Facilities

Large, light and airy toilet facilities, baby facilities with baths, showers and WCs, facilities for disabled visitors. Washing machines. Shop (1/6-30/9). Snack bar, takeaway (1/5-30/9). Bar, TV. Internet. Swimming pool (from 1/5). Games, competitions July/Aug. Fishing. Volleyball. Football. Badminton. Play area. Weekly dances July/Aug. Canoe hire. Off site: Village with shops and restaurant 300 m. Riding 0.5 km. Bicycle hire 2 km. Golf 25 km. Rock climbing, canyoning, cycling and walking.

Open: 1 April - 30 September.

Directions

Heading south from Clermont Ferrand to Millau on the A75 autoroute take exit 44-1 signed Aguessac/Gorges du Tarn. In Aguessac turn left and follow signs to Riviere sur Tarn (5 km.) and site is clearly indicated down a short road to the right. GPS: N44:11.061 E03:07.402

Charges 2006

Per unit incl. 2 persons	€ 16,00 - € 24,00
extra person	€ 5,00 - € 7,00
child (under 7 yrs)	€ 2,00 - € 4,00
electricity (6A)	€ 4,00

Camping Cheques accepted.

awan ——————————— tel: 00 333 59 59 03 59 *kawan-villages.com*

Camping Caravaning - Mobil-home rental
Canoë-Kayak
Open from april to september

12640 RIVIERE SUR TARN
Tél. : +33 (0)5 65 59 85 17
Fax : +33 (0)5 65 61 09 03
www.campinglespeupliers.fr

Gorges du Tarn   AVEYRON
PAYS D'EMOTIONS

FR12120 Camping du Rouergue

Avenue de Fondiès, F-12200 Villefranche-de-Rouergue (Aveyron)

Tel: 05 65 45 16 24. Email: **campingrouergue@wanadoo.fr**

A spacious and well appointed site in the Vallée de L'Aveyron, Camping du Rouergue is adjacent to the municipal sports facilities. Run by the Rouergue Tourisme Service, the managers are friendly and welcoming. The site has 98 grassy individual pitches of varying sizes, served by tarmac roads, and all serviced with electricity (16A), water and drain. Some pitches are shady. There are reduced rates for campers at the municipal swimming pool and shops and restaurants are within walking distance along the riverside foot and cycle path.

Facilities

The modern spacious sanitary unit includes washbasins in cubicles. Facilities for babies and disabled persons. Dishwashing and laundry sinks. Washing machine. With two identical sections to the block, only one is open during low season. Motorcaravan service point outside campsite entrance. Small bar (June-Oct). TV room. Well equipped playground. Bicycle hire. Off site: Fishing 1 km. Riding 5 km.

Open: 15 April - 15 October.

Directions

Villefranche de Rouergue is about midway between Cahors and Rodez. Site is 1 km. southwest of town on D47 towards Monteils, follow signs from D911 to campsite and 'Stade'.

Charges 2007

Per pitch incl. 2 persons	€ 11,00 - € 14,00
extra person (over 10 yrs)	€ 2,50
child (4-10 yrs)	€ 1,50
electricity	€ 3,00

FR16060 Camping Marco de Bignac

Lieudit 'Les Sablons', F-16170 Bignac (Charente)

Tel: 05 45 21 78 41. Email: **camping.marcodebignac@wanadoo.fr**

The small village of Bignac is set in peaceful countryside not too far from the N10 road, north of Angoulême. This mature site is arranged alongside an attractive lake on a level, grassy meadow. The 85 large touring pitches are marked by a trees so there is shade, most have electricity (3/6A). There is a hedged swimming pool and plenty of grassy space for ball games. This site is popular with British visitors and is a peaceful, relaxing location for couples or young families.

Facilities

Two traditional style, functional toilet blocks have functional facilities. Washing machine. Bar, snack bar (1/6-31/8). Small shop, baker calls (high season). Swimming pool (15/6-31/8, unsupervised). Football, badminton, tennis, table tennis, pedaloes, minigolf, boules, fishing, all free. Library. Play area. Pets' corner. Organised activities in high season. A torch may be useful. Off site: Local markets. Riding 5 km. Golf 25 km.

Open: 15 May - 15 September.

Directions

From N10 south of Poitiers, 14 km. north of Angoulême, take D11 west to Vars and Basse. Turn right onto D117 to Bignac. Site is signed at several junctions and in village (Camping Bignac). GPS: N45:47.850 E00:03.831

Charges 2007

Per pitch incl. 2 persons	€ 15,00 - € 21,00
extra person	€ 3,00 - € 5,00
electricity (3/6A)	€ 2,00 - € 3,00

FR24040 Castel Camping le Moulin du Roch

Route des Eyzies - Le Roch, D47, F-24200 Sarlat-la-Canéda (Dordogne)

Tel: 05 53 59 20 27. Email: **moulin.du.roch@wanadoo.fr**

The site has 199 pitches, of which 104 are for touring units. Pitches are mostly flat (some slope slightly) and grassy and all have electricity (6A). Pitches on the upper levels have plenty of shade, whilst those on the lower level near the amenities and the fishing lake are more open. Entertainment and activities are organised from June to September, with something for everyone from craft workshops and sports tournaments to canoeing and caving for the more adventurous. An excellent multi-lingual children's club runs in July and August. Walking and mountain biking from the site.

Facilities

Modern, well maintained, clean toilet blocks. Washing machines, dryers. Good shop (all season). Bar, terrace (1/6-31/8). Takeaway (2/5-16/9). Superb restaurant (13/5-9/9). Attractive swimming pool, paddling pool, sun terrace (all season). Fishing lake, tennis, table tennis, boules, volleyball, playground, discos twice weekly in high season. Pets are not accepted. Off site: Sarlat 10 km. Bicycle hire and riding 10 km. Golf 15 km.

Open: 28 April - 15 September.

Directions

Site is 10 km. west of Sarlat la Canéda, on south side of D47 Sarlat - Les Eyzies road. GPS: N44:54.516 E01:06.883

Charges 2007

Per pitch incl. 2 persons	€ 15,00 - € 27,00
with electricity	€ 19,00 - € 31,00
with full services	€ 23,00 - € 35,00
extra person	€ 4,00 - € 7,80
Camping Cheques accepted.	

FR24010 Camping Château le Verdoyer

Champs Romain, F-24470 Saint Pardoux (Dordogne)

Tel: 05 53 56 94 64. Email: chateau@verdoyer.fr

The 26 hectare estate has three lakes, two for fishing and one with a sandy beach and safe swimming area. There are 135 good sized touring pitches, level, terraced and hedged. With a choice of wooded area or open field, all have electricity (5/10A) and most share a water supply between four pitches. There is a swimming pool complex and in high season activities are organised for children (5-13 yrs) but there is no disco. This site is well adapted for those with disabilities, with two fully adapted chalets, wheelchair access to all facilities and even a lift into the pool. Le Verdoyer has been developed in the park of a restored château and is owned by a Dutch family. We particularly like this site for its beautiful buildings and lovely surroundings. It is situated in the lesser known area of the Dordogne sometimes referred to as the Périgord Vert, with its green forests and small lakes. The courtyard area between reception and the bar is home to evening activities, and provides a pleasant place to enjoy drinks and relax. The château itself has rooms to let and its excellent lakeside restaurant is also open to the public.

Facilities

Well appointed toilet blocks include facilities for disabled people and baby baths. Serviced launderette. Motorcaravan services. Fridge rental. Shop with gas. Bar, snacks, takeaway and restaurant, both open all season. Bistro (July/Aug). Two pools the smaller covered in low season, slide, paddling pool. Play areas. Tennis. Volleyball, basketball, badminton, table tennis, minigolf. Bicycle hire. Small library. Off site: Riding 15 km.

Open: 16 April - 15 October.

Directions

Site is 2 km. from Limoges (N21) - Chalus (D6bis-D85) - Nontron road, 20 km. south of Chalus and is well signed from main road. Site on D96 about 4 km. north of village of Champs Romain.

Charges 2006

Per unit incl. 2 persons and electricity	€ 18,00 - € 29,00
full services	free - € 4,50
extra person	€ 5,00 - € 6,00
child (under 2-8 yrs)	free - € 4,00

Camping Cheques accepted.

FR24090 Camping Soleil Plage

Caudon par Montfort, Vitrac, F-24200 Sarlat-la-Canéda (Dordogne)
Tel: 05 53 28 33 33. Email: info@soleilplage.fr

This site is in one of the most attractive sections of the Dordogne valley, with a riverside location. The site has 199 pitches, in three sections, around 104 are for touring units. The smallest section surrounds the main reception and other facilities. There are 59 mobile homes. 20 chalets and 17 bungalow tents. The site offers river bathing from a sizeable pebble or sand bank. All pitches are bounded by hedges and are of adequate size. Most pitches have some shade and have electricity and many have water and a drain. Various activities are organised during high season including walks and sports tournaments, and daily canoe hire is available from the site. Once a week in July and August there is a 'soirée' (charged for) usually involving a barbecue or paella, with band and lots of free wine – worth catching! The site is busy and reservation is advisable. Used by UK tour operators (42 pitches). English is spoken. The site is quite expensive in high season and you also pay more for a riverside pitch, but if you like a holiday with lots going on, you will like this one.

Facilities

Toilet facilities are in three modern unisex blocks (only two open). You will need to hire a plug (€5) for the baby bath. Washing machines and dryer (charged for). Motorcaravan service point. Pleasant bar with TV. Restaurant. Well stocked shop. Very impressive main pool, paddling pool, spa pool and two water slides. Tennis. Minigolf. Playground. Fishing. Canoe and kayak hire. Bicycle hire. Small library. Off site: Golf 1 km. Riding 5 km.

Open: 1 April - 30 September.

Directions

Site is 8 km. south of Sarlat. From A20 take exit 55 (Souillac) towards Sarlat. Follow the D703 to Carsac and on to Montfort. At Montfort castle turn left for 2 km. down to the river.

Charges 2007

Per person	€ 4,50 - € 7,00
child (2-9 yrs)	€ 2,50 - € 4,50
pitch with electricity	€ 9,00 - € 15,50
with full services	€ 12,00 - € 23,00

FR24060 Camping le Paradis

Saint Léon-sur-Vézère, F-24290 Montignac (Dordogne)
Tel: 05 53 50 72 64. Email: le-paradis@perigord.com

Le Paradis is a well maintained riverside site, halfway between Les Eyzies and Montignac. Well situated for exploring places of interest in the Dordogne region, the site is very well kept and laid out with mature shrubs and bushes of different types. It has 200 individual pitches of good size on flat grass, divided by trees and shrubs (146 for touring units). All have electricity, water and drainage, and there are some special pitches for motorcaravans. At the far end of the site, steps down to the Vézère river give access for canoe launching and swimming. The site welcomes a good quota of Dutch and British visitors, many through a tour operator. English is spoken.

Facilities

High quality, well equipped, heated toilet blocks (unisex), baby baths and toilets,. Well stocked shop (with gas). Good restaurant, takeaway. Good pool complex heated in low season, paddling pool. Tennis, football, BMX track, volleyball, table tennis and pool activities. Multisport court. Canoe hire. Fishing. Bicycle hire. Quad bike and horse riding excursions. Playground. Off site: Riding 2 km. Various trips organised to surrounding area.

Open: 1 April - 25 October.

Directions

Site is 12 km. north of Les Eyzies and 3 km. south of St Léon-sur-Vézère, on the east side of the D706.

Charges 2006

Per unit incl. 2 persons	€ 17,50 - € 25,50
extra person	€ 5,00 - € 7,00
child (3-12 yrs)	€ 4,00 - € 6,00
electricity (10A)	€ 3,00

Low season reductions.
Camping Cheques accepted.

FR24130 Camping les Grottes de Roffy

Sainte Nathalène, F-24200 Sarlat-la-Canéda (Dordogne)
Tel: 05 53 59 15 61. Email: roffy@perigord.com

A pleasantly laid out site, about 5 km. east of Sarlat, Les Grottes de Roffy has 162 clearly marked pitches, some very large. Set on very well kept grass terraces, they have easy access and good views across an attractive valley. Some have plentiful shade, although others are more open, and all have electricity (6A). The reception, bar, restaurant and shop are located within converted farm buildings surrounding a semi-courtyard. The campsite shop is well stocked with a variety of goods and a tempting charcuterie section (prepared on site) with plenty of ideas for the barbecue. Various entertainments and excursions are organised during high season. Conveniently located for Sarlat and all other Dordogne attractions, this is a good site for families. Used by tour operators (64 pitches).

Facilities

Two toilet blocks with modern facilities are more than adequate. Well stocked shop. Bar and restaurant with imaginative and sensibly priced menu. Takeaway (all amenities from 6/5). Good swimming pool complex comprising two deep pools (one heated), a fountain, children's pool and heated jacuzzi. Tennis and badminton courts. Games room. Play area. Off site: Fishing 2 km. Bicycle hire 7 km. Riding 10 km. Golf 15 km.

Open: 28 April - 15 September.

Directions

Take D47 east from Sarlat to Ste Nathalène. Just before Ste Nathalène the site is signed on the right hand side of the road. Turn here, and the site is about 800m along the lane.

Charges 2006

Per person	€ 5,45 - € 6,80
child (2-7 yrs)	€ 4,00 - € 4,80
pitch	€ 7,05 - € 8,70
with electricity	€ 9,60 - € 12,00
with full services	€ 11,00 - € 13,50

les Grottes de **Roffy** camping caravaning

★ ★ ★ ★

Sainte-Nathalèle • 24200 Sarlat • France
E-mail roffy@perigord.com Tél. +33 (0)5 53 59 15 61 • Fax +33 (0)5 53 31 09 11

FR24100 Camping le Moulinal

F-24540 Biron (Dordogne)
Tel: 05 53 40 84 60. Email: lemoulinal@perigord.com

A rural, lakeside site in woodland, Le Moulinal offers activities for everyone of all ages. Of the 280 grassy pitches, only around 62 are available for touring units and these are spread amongst the site's own mobile homes, chalets and a small number of British tour operator tents. All pitches are flat, grassy and have electricity (6A), but vary considerably in size from 75 sq.m. to 100 sq.m. The five-acre lake has a sandy beach and is suitable for boating (canoe hire available), swimming and fishing. Ambitious, well organised animation is run throughout the season including children's club.

Facilities

Toilet facilities, built to harmonise with the surroundings, include facilities for disabled people and babies. Washing machines, dryers. Motorcaravan services. Excellent restaurant. Bar. Snack bar/takeaway. Large, heated swimming pool with Jacuzzi and children's pool. Rustic play area. Multisport court. Boules. Tennis. Archery. Mountain bike hire. Off site: Riding and climbing 5 km. Monpazier, Villeréal and Monflanquin 15 km.

Open: 1 April - 16 September.

Directions

From D104 Villeréal - Monpazier road take the D53/D150 south. Just before Lacapelle Biron turn right on D255 towards Dévillac, (site signed), site is 1.5 km. on the left. GPS: N44:35.988 E00:52.249

Charges guide

Per pitch incl. 2 persons and electricity	€ 17,00 - € 42,00
extra person	€ 4,00 - € 9,00

Camping Cheques accepted.

FR24170 Camping le Port de Limeuil

F-24480 Allés-sur-Dordogne (Dordogne)

Tel: **05 53 63 29 76**. Email: **didierbonvallet@aol.com**

At the confluence of Dordogne and Vézère rivers, opposite the picturesque village of Limieul, this delightful family site exudes a peaceful and relaxed ambience. There are 90 marked, grassy, flat pitches, some spacious and all with electricity (5A). The buildings are in traditional Périgourdine style and surrounded by flowers and shrubs. A sports area on a large open grassy space between the river bank and the main camping area adds to the feeling of space and provides an additional recreation and picnic area (there are additional unmarked pitches for tents and camper vans along the bank).

Facilities

Two clean, modern toilet blocks provide excellent facilities. Bar/restaurant with snacks and takeaway (all 20/5-5/9). Small shop. Swimming pool with jacuzzi, paddling pool and children's slide (1/5- 30 /9). Badminton, football, boules and volleyball. Mountain bike hire. Canoe hire - launched from the site's own pebble beach. Off site: The pretty medieval village of Limeuil 200 m. Riding 1 km. Golf 10 km.

Open: 1 May - 30 September.

Directions

Site is 7 km. south of Le Bugue. From D51/D31E Le Buisson to Le Bugue road turn west towards Limeuil. Just before bridge into Limeuil, turn left (site signed), across another bridge. Site shortly on the right. GPS: N44:52.878 E00:53.444

Charges 2007

Per pitch incl. 2 persons	€ 14,00 - € 24,90
extra person	€ 4,50 - € 5,50
child (under 10 yrs)	€ 2,50 - € 3,50
electricity (5A)	€ 2,50 - € 3,50

FR24330 Camping de l'Etang Bleu

F-24340 Vieux-Mareuil (Dordogne)

Tel: **05 53 60 92 70**. Email: **marc@letangbleu.com**

There are 169 pitches, 151 for touring, with the remainder taken up by site owned mobile homes for rent. The pitches are a good size, flat and grassy, with mature hedging and trees providing privacy and plenty of shade. All pitches have water and 90 have electricity (10/16A). At the bottom of the site is a fishing lake stocked with carp (permit required) and various woodland walks start from the campsite grounds. The bright and cheerful 'bistro bar' provides good value food and drinks, and becomes a focal point for evening socialising on site.

Facilities

Modern well maintained toilet block provides facilities for babies and disabled people. Laundry. Small playground, paddling pool. Swimming pool, sun terrace. Bar with terrace (all season), restaurant (1/6-30/9), poolside bar. Takeaway (1/6-30/9). Small shop. Table tennis, boules, volleyball, badminton. Canoe and bicycle hire. Entertainments, sporting activities, excursions in high season. Off site: Restaurant adjacent. Mareuil (7 km).

Open: Easter/1 April -18 October.

Directions

Site is between Angoulême and Périgueux. Leave D939 in Vieux Mareuil, take D93, and follow narrow road. Just after leaving village site signed on right, just past Auberge de L'Etang Bleu. Turn right, follow signs to site.

Charges 2006

Per person	€ 3,75 - € 5,50
pitch and car	€ 5,75 - € 7,25
with electricity	€ 7,75 - € 11,50

FR46040 Camping Moulin de Laborde

F-46700 Montcabrier (Lot)

Tel: **05 65 24 62 06**. Email: **moulindelaborde@wanadoo.fr**

Based around a converted 17th century watermill, Moulin de Laborde has been created by the Van Bommel family to provide a tranquil and uncommercialised campsite for the whole family to enjoy. Bordered by woods, hills and a small river, there are 90 flat and grassy pitches, all of at least 100 sq.m. with electricity (6A). A variety of pretty shrubs and trees divide the pitches and provide a moderate amount of shade. A gate at the back of the site leads walkers onto a 'Grand Randonée' footpath which passes through the village of Montcabrier, 1 km. away.

Facilities

Well designed, clean toilet block, unit for disabled people. Washing machine, dryer. Basic shop (all season). Small bar, restaurant, takeaway. Swimming and paddling pools. Play area. Small lake, free rafts and rowing boats. Fishing. Volleyball. Badminton. Covered recreation area. Mountain bike hire. Rock climbing. Archery. No dogs. Off site: Riding 5 km. Golf 8 km. Tennis nearby and canoeing on the Lot. The Château of Bonaguil 6 km. Fumel 12 km.

Open: 28 April - 8 September.

Directions

Site is on the north side of the D673 Fumel - Gourdon road about 1 km. northeast of the turn to village of Montcabrier.

Charges 2007

Per person	€ 6,00
child (under 7 yrs)	€ 3,30
pitch incl. electricity (6A)	€ 11,00

Less 20% outside July/August. No credit cards.

FR46010 Castel Camping Domaine de la Paille Basse

F-46200 Souillac-sur-Dordogne (Lot)

Tel: 05 65 37 85 48. Email: paille.basse@wanadoo.fr

Set in a rural location some 8 km. from Souillac, this family owned site is easily accessible from the N20 and well placed to take advantage of excursions into the Dordogne. It is part of a large domain of 80 hectares, all available to campers for walks and recreation. The site is quite high up and there are excellent views over the surrounding countryside. The 262 pitches are in two main areas - one is level in cleared woodland with good shade, and the other on grass without shade. Numbered and marked, the pitches are a minimum 100 sq.m. and often considerably more. All have electricity (3/6A) with about 80 fully serviced. The site is well placed to take advantage of excursions into the Dordogne. A wide range of activities and entertainment are organised in high season. The site can get very busy in high season and is popular with three tour operators. If you like a livelier type of site, you will enjoy La Paille Basse.

Facilities

Three main toilet blocks all have modern equipment and are kept very clean. Laundry. Small shop. Restaurant, bar, terrace, takeaway. Crêperie. main swimming pool, a smaller one, paddling pool (unheated), water slides. Sun terrace. Sound-proofed disco (three times weekly in season). TV (with satellite). Cinema below the pool area. Tennis (charged), football, volleyball, table tennis. Play area. Library. Massage. Off site: Golf 4 km.

Open: 15 May - 15 September.

Directions

From Souillac take D15 and then D62 roads leading northwest towards Salignac-Eyvignes and after 6 km. turn right at camp sign and follow steep and narrow approach road for 2 km.

Charges 2007

Per person	€ 5,40 - € 7,00
child (under 7 yrs)	€ 3,80 - € 5,00
pitch	€ 7,80 - € 10,80
incl. water and drainage	€ 9,80 - € 13,00

Camping Cheques accepted.

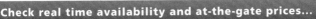

FR46190 Camping Domaine de la Faurie

F-46240 Séniergues (Lot)

Tel: 05 65 21 14 36. Email: contact@camping-lafaurie.com

A stunning array of tended shrubs and thoughtful flower plantings is spread throughout this very pretty site which is located on a hilltop with wide open views of the surrounding hills and valleys. Although hidden away, it is an excellent base for exploring the Lot and Dordogne regions. The site is separated into two distinct areas, an open, lightly shaded front section and a much more densely shaded area with tall pine trees all around the pitches. The pitches are large and most are at least 100 sq.m. The owners will tell you that they consider the three hectacre site their personal garden.

Facilities

The single sanitary block is clean and well maintained. Facilities for disabled visitors. Washing machine. Motorcaravan service point. Excellent gift shop selling regional wines, pâtés, specialist tinned meats, and local produce (bread available). Bar, restaurant and takeaway. Swimming pool and paddling pool. TV and games rooms. Bicycle hire. Play area. Small library. Weekly soirées in high season. Off site: Fishing 3 km. Golf 8 km. Riding 15 km.

Open: 7 April - 30 September.

Directions

From A20 exit 56, take D2 towards Montfaucon. Site is 5 km further on.

Charges 2006

Per person	€ 4,00 - € 4,80
child (2-10 yrs)	€ 3,00 - € 3,20
pitch	€ 5,50 - € 6,00
electricity (6A)	€ 3,20

kawan-villages.com **tel: 00 333 59 59 03 59**

kawan
VILLAGES CAMPINGS

FR47150 Domaine de Guillalmes

F-47500 Fumel (Lot-et-Garonne)

Tel: 05 53 71 01 99. Email: info@guillalmes.com

Pitches at Domaine de Guillalmes are exclusively for mobile homes and chalets, although in the near future the site may also provide for touring units.

Domaine de Guillalmes

Nestled on the banks of the River Lot, Domaine de Guillalmes is ideally situated for touring the beautiful Lot et Garonne region of South West France.

Domaine de Guillales - Condat - 47500 Fumel - France
info@guillalmes.com - www.guillalmes.com

This is just a sample of the campsites we have inspected and selected in France. For more campsites and further information, please see the Alan Rogers France guide.

FR47010 Camping Caravaning Moulin du Périé

F-47500 Sauveterre-la-Lemance (Lot-et-Garonne)

Tel: 05 53 40 67 26. Email: moulinduperie@wanadoo.fr

Set in a quiet area and surrounded by woodlands this peaceful little site is well away from much of the tourist bustle. It has 125 reasonably sized, grassy pitches, all with 6A electricity, divided by mixed trees and bushes with most having good shade. All are extremely well kept, as indeed is the entire site. The attractive front courtyard is complemented by an equally pleasant terrace at the rear. Two small, clean swimming pools overlook a shallow, spring water lake, ideal for inflatable boats and paddling and bordering the lake, a large grass field is popular for games. The picturesque old mill buildings, adorned with flowers and creepers, now house the bar and restaurant where the food is to be recommended, as is the owner's extensive knowledge of wine that he is pleased to share with visitors. A quiet, friendly site with regular visitors – reservation is advised for July/Aug. Bergerac Airport is an hour away so would suit those choosing a mobile home or bungalow tent and wanting to travel light. A 'Sites et Paysages' member.

Facilities

Two clean, modern and well maintained toilet blocks include facilities for disabled visitors. Motorcaravan services. Fridge, barbecue, chemical toilet hire (book in advance). Basic shop. Bar/reception, restaurant, takeaway. Two small swimming pools (no Bermuda-style shorts). Boules, table tennis, outdoor chess. Playground. Trampoline. Small, indoor play area. Bicycle hire. Organised activities in high season; including canoeing, riding, wine tasting visits, sight seeing trips, barbecues, gastronomic meals. Winter caravan storage. Off site: Fishing 1 km. Small supermarket in village and larger stores in Fumel.

Open: 12 May - 21 September.

Directions

From D710, Fumel - Périgueux, turn southeast into Sauveterre-le-Lemance. Turn left (northeast) at far end on C201 signed campsite, Château Sauveterre and Loubejec. Site is 3 km. on right.

Charges 2006

Per unit incl. 2 persons	€ 12,70 - € 21,20
with electricity	€ 16,50 - € 25,00
extra person	€ 4,10 - € 6,30
child (under 7 yrs)	€ 1,75 - € 3,35
animal	€ 2,10 - € 7,30

Camping Cheques accepted.

(167)

FR23010 Castel Camping le Château de Poinsouze

Route de la Châtre, B.P.12, F-23600 Boussac-Bourg (Creuse)

Tel: **05 55 65 02 21**. Email: **info.camping-de.poinsouze@wanadoo.fr**

Le Château de Poinsouze is a well established site with pitches arranged on the open, gently sloping, grassy park to one side of the Château's main drive – a beautiful plane tree avenue. It is a well designed, high quality site. The 150 touring pitches, some with lake frontage, all have electricity (6-25A), water, drain and 66 have sewage connections. The site has a friendly family atmosphere, there are organised activities in main season including dances, children's games and crafts, family triathlons and there are marked walks around the park and woods. All facilities are open all season. This is a top class site with a formula which should ensure a stress-free, enjoyable family holiday. Boussac (2.5 km) has a market every Thursday morning. The massive 12/15th century fortress, Château de Boussac, is open daily all year. The Château (not open to the public) lies across the lake from the site. Exceptionally well restored outbuildings on the opposite side of the drive house a new restaurant serving superb cuisine, other facilities and the pool area.

Facilities

High quality, sanitary unit, washing machines, dryer, ironing, suites for disabled people. Motorcaravan services. Well stocked shop. Takeaway. Bar, internet, two satellite TVs, library. Restaurant with new mini-bar for low season. Heated swimming pool, slide, children's pool. Fenced playground. Table tennis, petanque, pool table, table football. Bicycle hire. Free fishing in the lake, boats and lifejackets can be hired. Football, volleyball, basketball, badminton and other games. No dogs (7/7-21/8).

Open: 12 May - 15 September.

Directions

Site entrance is 2.5 km. north of Boussac on D917 (towards La Châtre). GPS: N46:22.356 E02:12.157

Charges 2006

Per pitch incl. 2 persons	€ 13,00 - € 22,00
with 6A electricity, water, drain	€ 18,00 - € 27,00
10A electricity, water, drain, and sewage connection	€ 24,00 - € 29,00
extra person	€ 3,00 - € 5,50

Camping Cheques accepted.

FR63070 Camping le Pré Bas

Lac Chambon, F-63790 Murol (Puy-de-Dôme)

Tel: **04 73 88 63 04**. Email: **prebas@campingauvergne.com**

Le Pré Bas is especially suitable for families and those seeking the watersports opportunities that the lake provides. Level, grassy pitches are divided up by mature hedging and trees and, with 63 mobile homes for rent, around 120 pitches are available for tourists, all with electricity (6A). A gate leads to the lakeside, where in high season there is windsurfing, pedaloes, canoes and fishing, and 50 m. away is a beach with supervised bathing and a snack bar. The site has a new pool complex with heated swimming pools (one covered), a large slide and a paddling pool. The site is in the heart of the Parc des Volcans d'Auvergne, beside the beautiful Lac Chambon with its clear, clean water, The cable car ride up to the Puy de Sancy, the highest peak in the area, provides superb views offering an excellent opportunity for trekking and mountain bike rides. Superb scenery abounds; wooded mountains rising to over 6,000 feet, flower filled valleys and deep blue lakes.

Facilities

Refurbished toilet building with facilities for disabled guests plus four smaller units. Washing machines, dryers, ironing, baby room. Motorcaravan services. Snack bar (10/6-10/9 and some weekends in low season). Three pools of different depths (20/5-10/9, lifeguard in July/Aug). Watersports, fishing in lake. Games room, table tennis, table football, pool, TV, library. Adventure style playground, football, basketball. Organised activities. Off site: Lakeside bars, restaurants, shops. Murol 4 km. St Nectaire famous for cheese. Puy de Dome, hang gliding, Vulcania Exhibition.

Open: 1 May - 30 September.

Directions

Leave A75 autoroute at exit 6 and take D978 signed St Nectaire and Murol, then D996. Site is located on left, 3 km. west of Murol towards Mont Dore, at the far end of Lac Chambon.
GPS: N45:34.513 E02:54.854

Charges 2006

Per pitch incl. 2 persons	€ 9,10 - € 14,70
extra person	€ 3,90 - € 5,20
child (5-10 yrs)	€ 2,50 - € 5,20
electricity (6A)	€ 4,10 - € 4,40

FR43030 Camping du Vaubarlet

Vaubarlet, F-43600 Sainte-Sigolène (Haute-Loire)

Tel: **04 71 66 64 95**. Email: **camping@vaubarlet.com**

This peacefully located, spacious riverside family site has 131 marked, level, grassy, open pitches, with those around the perimeter having shade, all having electricity (6A). With 102 pitches for tourists, the remainder are occupied by site owned tents or mobile homes. Those who really like to get away from it all can use a small 'wild camping' area on the opposite side of the river with its own very basic facilities. This area is reached either by footbridge or a separate road access. The main site is separated from the river (unfenced) by a large field used for sports activities.

Facilities

Good, clean toilet blocks, baby room, washing machine, dryer. Two family bathrooms are also suitable for disabled people. Small shop, bread. Takeaway, bar (all season). Attractive swimming pool, children's pool. Bicycle hire. Boules, volleyball and games area. Playground. Activities in season. Fishing. Birdwatching. Off site: Ste Sigolène 6 km. Riding 15 km. Walks and cycle tracks from site.

Open: 1 May - 30 September.

Directions

Site is 6 km. southwest of Ste Sigolène on the D43 signed Grazac. Keep left by river bridge, site signed. Site shortly on right. GPS: N45:12.936 E04:12.766

Charges 2006

Per unit incl. 2 persons	€ 17,00
extra person	€ 3,00
electricity	€ 3,00
Camping Cheques accepted.	

FR48020 Camping de Capelan

F-48150 Meyrueis (Lozère)

Tel: **04 66 45 60 50**. Email: **camping.le.capelan@wanadoo.fr**

The Lozère is one of France's least populated départements but offers some truly spectacular, rugged scenery, wonderful flora and fauna and old towns and villages. Meyrueis is accessible from the campsite via a riverside walk. Le Capelan is a friendly family site with English and Dutch spoken. It has 120 grassy pitches strung out alongside the river, most with some shade and all with electrical connections (6/10A). The site has direct river access and trout fishing is popular.

Facilities

Well maintained toilet blocks, facilities for disabled visitors. Three bathrooms for rent. Small shop (from 1/6). Bar (from 1/6), satellite TV, internet, pool table. Takeaway (from 1/7). Swimming, paddling pools, sunbathing terrace (from 1/6), access via 60 steps. Multi-sports terrain. Play area. Leisure activities including supervised rock climbing. Fishing. Communal barbecue area, only gas and electric barbecues. Off site: Town centre 1 km. Bicycle hire 1 km. Riding 3 km. Canoeing. Cévennes national park. Caves.

Open: 29 April - 16 September.

Directions

From Clermont Ferrand on the A75 take exit 44-1 Aguessac-le Rozier towards Meyrueis. The site is 1 km. west of Meyruels on the D996, the road to La Jonte. It is well signed from the centre of the town. GPS: N44:11.150 E03:25.193

Charges 2007

Per unit incl. 2 persons and electricity	€ 13,00 - € 19,00
extra person	€ 3,00 - € 4,10

Camping Cheques accepted.

kawan-villages.com tel: **00 333 59 59 03 59** *kawan*

FR07070 Camping les Ranchisses

Route de Rocher, F-07110 Largentière (Ardèche)

Tel: **04 75 88 31 97**. Email: **reception@lesranchisses.fr**

The site has been developed from an original 'camping á la ferme' into a very well equipped modern campsite. There are 165 good-sized, level, grassy pitches, 88 for tourists with electricity (10A) include 42 fully serviced pitches. They are in two distinct areas, the original site which is well shaded and the lower part with less shade. The site runs parallel to the road and there may be background traffic noise in some areas. A small lake provides opportunities for bathing, fishing or canoeing.

Facilities

Comprehensive toilet buildings include facilities for babies and disabled persons. Laundry. Motorcaravan services. Small shop, takeaway, bar, terrace (all season), new restaurant. Two large pools (both heated), paddling pool. Adventure playground. Amusements for children in high season. Minigolf. Canoeing. Tennis. Skate park. Off site: Canoe, kayaking arranged (mid -June - end Aug). Medieval village, Largentière 1.5 km.

Open: 7 April - 16 September.

Directions

Largentière is southwest of Aubenas best approached using D104. After 16 km, just beyond Uzer turn northwest on D5. After 5 km. at far end of Largentière, fork left downhill signed Valgorge. Site on left in about 1.8 km.

Charges 2007

Per unit incl. 2 persons	€ 24,00 - € 37,00
extra person (over 1 yr)	€ 4,50 - € 7,50

Camping Cheques accepted.

kawan-villages.com tel: **00 333 59 59 03 59** *kawan*

FR07110 Domaine le Pommier

Route Nationale 102, F-07170 Villeneuve-de-Berg (Ardèche)

Tel: **04 75 94 82 81**. Email: **info@campinglepommier.com**

Domaine Le Pommier is an extremely spacious Dutch owned site of 10 hectares in 32 hectares of wooded grounds. The site is steeply terraced (a tractor is available for assistance) and has wonderful views over the Ardèche mountains and beyond. There are 400 pitches with 275 for tourists. They are grassy/stony, of good size and well spaced. Separated by young trees and hedges, some have little or no shade. All have electricity and water is close by. The site is not recommended for large units.

Facilities

Four excellent toilet blocks, one with under-floor heating, provide all the necessary facilities. Comprehensive shop. Bar/restaurant. Swimming pool complex, paddling pools, etc. Everything opens from the end of April. Minigolf. Archery, water polo and tug of war. Bridge and water colour classes. Sound proof disco. Extensive programme of events on and off site. Off site: Villeneuve de Berg 1.5 km. River Ardèche 12 km.

Open: 1 May - 30 September.

Directions

Site is west of Montélimar on the N102. The entrance is adjacent to the roundabout at the eastern end of the Villeneuve-de-Berg bypass. GPS: N44:34.350 E04:30.669

Charges 2006

Per unit incl. 2 persons	€ 14,00 - € 29,50
extra person over 4 yrs	€ 4,00 - € 6,50
electricity	€ 4,00

Max. 6 persons per pitch.

FR01080 Camping Etang du Moulin
F-01240 Saint Paul de Varax (Ain)

Tel: **04 74 42 53 30**. Email: **moulin@campingendombes.fr**

This extremely spacious and well run campsite, which is owned by several villages, lies within a larger leisure complex which will be very busy at weekends. The major attraction here is one of the largest swimming pools in Europe – 5,500 sq.m. It is irregularly shaped, has shallow areas all around, two large toboggans and eight lifeguards always on duty – ideal for all the family and free for campers. The 165 very large, level grassy pitches include 156 for touring, with 4 hardstandings for motorcaravans. All have 6A electricity and are separated by hedges, with shade provided by a variety of trees. The reception, bar, restaurant and entertainment centre is at the entrance well away from the pitches. There is an extensive entertainment programme in high season. There is also a 13 hectare, well stocked fishing lake and large spaces set aside for sporting activities. This site would be Ideal for those active families seeking a campsite based holiday. No animals are accepted.

Facilities
Two very clean and well maintained toilet blocks, functional rather than luxurious, have all the necessary facilities including those for disabled visitors. Motorcaravan service point. All facilities open all season. Bar, TV room, restaurant and takeaway. Large swimming pool with toboggans and pebble sunbathing beach near to entrance. Marquee for entertainment. Bicycle hire. Large area for games. Off site: In adjacent leisure complex – fishing, tennis, minigolf. Bourg-en-Bresse (20 km) has a wide range of shops, bars/restaurants/banks/market.

Open: 24 May - 3 September.

Directions
Site is about 20 km. southwest of Bourg-en-Bresse. Leave the N83 at St Paul de Varax and turn southeast on the D17. In 3 km. turn right down the bumpy lane, signed Base de Loisirs. Site is 1 km. GPS: N46:05.206 E5:09.122

Charges 2006

Per person	€ 3,70
child (3-12 yrs)	€ 2,20
pitch incl. 6A electricity	€ 7,50
vehicle	€ 2,20

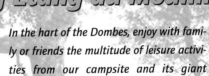

Camping Etang du Moulin

In the hart of the Dombes, enjoy with family or friends the multitude of leisure activities from our campsite and its giant Aquatic Park. An exceptional setting! Ideal for people looking for resting holidays but also those who are fond of sports!

01240 St.Paul-de-Varax
Tél.: [33] [0] 4 74 42 53 30
Fax: [33] [0] 4 74 42 51 57
www.campingendombes.fr

FR07140 Camping les Lavandes

Le Village, F-07170 Darbres (Ardèche)

Tel: **04 75 94 20 65**. Email: **sarl.leslavandes@online.fr**

Situated to the northeast of Aubenas, in a quieter part of this region, Les Lavandes is surrounded by magnificent countryside, vineyards and orchards. The enthusiastic French owners, who speak good English, run a site that appeals to all nationalities. The 70 pitches (58 for touring) are arranged on low terraces separated by a variety of trees and shrubs that give welcome shade in summer. Visit at the end of May to see the campsite trees laden with luscious cherries.

Facilities

Comprehensive and well maintained facilties, baby room, excellent facilities for disabled people. Washing machine. Small shop (1/7-31/8). Bar, terrace (1/6-31/8). Restaurant (1/7-31/8). Takeaway (14/4-31/8). Swimming pool, paddling pool, sunbathing areas, all with super views. Play areas. Table games, billiard room, open air chess. No electric barbecues. Off site: Fishing 1 km. Bicycle hire 3 km. Tennis 5 km. Canoeing, walking and cycling.

Open: 15 April - 30 September.

Directions

Site best approached from south. From Montélimar take N102 towards Aubenas. After Villeneuve, in Lavilledieu, turn right at traffic lights on D224 to Darbres (10 km). In Darbres turn sharp left by post office (care needed) and follow site signs.

Charges 2006

Per unit incl. 2 persons	€ 11,50 - € 16,50
extra person	€ 2,80 - € 3,50
electricity	€ 3,50

FR07150 Camping Domaine de Gil

Route de Vals-les-Bains, Ucel, F-07200 Aubenas (Ardèche)

Tel: **04 75 94 63 63**. Email: **info@domaine-de-gil.com**

This very attractive and well organised, smaller site in a less busy part of the Ardèche should appeal to couples and families with younger children. The 80, good sized, level pitches, 43 for touring, are surrounded by a variety of trees offering plenty of shade. All have 5-10A electricity with European type connectors. There is a swimming pool, paddling pool and sunbathing area, with the bar, restaurant and play areas adjacent. A sports area and shady picnic area are alongside the river Ardèche. You will receive a warm welcome from the enthusiastic new Dutch owners.

Facilities

Modern well appointed toilet block, washing machine and iron. Motorcaravan services. Basic shop. Bar/restaurant, takeaway (from June). Heated swimming pool, paddling pool. Two play areas. Volleyball, boules, minigolf, football, tennnis. Canoeing, boating, fishing. Organised activities in high season. Only gas and electric barbecues. Off site: Shops at Vals-les-Bain 1.5 km. Interesting old town of Aubenas 3 km. Organised canoe trips, canyoning on river Ardèche. Bicycle hire, riding 4 km.

Open: 14 April - 16 September.

Directions

Site north of Aubenas. From southeast (N102), after tunnel, turn right, roundabout (signed Privas), cross river into Pont d'Ucel. Bear right and at roundabout, last exit (signed Ucel). Shortly turn left (signed Ucel D18), then right (Ucel D578B). Site is 2 km. GPS: N44:38.558 E04:22.775

Charges 2006

Per unit incl. 2 persons	€ 14,00 - € 27,50
extra person	€ 3,50 - € 5,50
electricity	€ 3,80

FR07180 Ardèche Camping

Boulevard de Paste, F-07000 Privas (Ardèche)

Tel: **04 75 64 05 80**. Email: **jcray@wanadoo.fr**

This spacious, family run site is on the southern outskirts of Privas and would be a good base for exploring the lesser known parts of the Ardèche. Bus and coach trips are available to explore these areas. The site has 166 large, grass, reasonably level pitches, of which 153 are for tourers. A wide variety of trees provide reasonable shade and electricity (6/10A) should now be available on most pitches. Recent additions include new heated swimming and paddling pools.

Facilities

Two toilet blocks, only one open in low season. Facilities for disabled people. Motorcaravan service point. Bar and restaurant (1/5-30/9). Volleyball. Boule. Table tennis. Play area. Mini-club. Entertainment (high season). Only gas barbecues are permitted. Tents (4) for rent. Off site: Swimming pool and tennis courts adjacent. Supermarket 100 m. Bicycle hire 2 km. Riding 5 km.

Open: 1 April - 30 September.

Directions

At traffic lights in the centre of town take D2, signed Montélimar. Descend the winding road for about 1 km. then at roundabout (near Intermarché) turn right and then shortly left, signed Espace Ouvéze. Entrance is straight on. GPS: N44:43.569 E04:35.898

Charges 2006

Per unit incl. 2 persons	€ 14,00 - € 18,00
extra person	€ 3,50 - € 5,00
electricity (6A)	€ 3,50
Camping Cheques accepted.	

FR07120 Camping Nature Parc L'Ardéchois

Route touristique des Gorges, F-07150 Vallon-Pont-d'Arc (Ardèche)

Tel: 04 75 88 06 63. Email: ardecamp@bigfoot.com

This very high quality, family run site is within walking distance of Vallon-Pont-d'Arc. It borders the River Ardèche and canoe trips are run, professionally, direct from the site. This campsite is ideal for families with younger children seeking an active holiday. The facilities are comprehensive and of an extremely high standard, particularly the central toilet block. Of the 244 pitches, there are 197 for tourers, separated by trees and individual shrubs. All have electrical connections (6/10A) and 125 have full services. Forming a focal point is the bar and restaurant (good menus), with a terrace and stage overlooking the attractive heated pool. There is also a large paddling pool and sunbathing terrace. For children, there is a well thought out play area plus plenty of other space for youngsters to play, both on the site and along the river. Activities are organised throughout the season; these are family based – no discos. Patrols at night ensure a good night's sleep. Access to the site is easy and suitable for large outfits. Member of Leading Campings Group.

Facilities

Two well equipped toilet blocks, one superb with 'everything' working automatically, the other to be upgraded for 2007. Facilities are of the highest standard, very clean and include good facilities for babies, those with disabilities, washing up and laundry facilities. Four private bathrooms to hire. Washing machines. Shop. Swimming pool and paddling pool (no Bermuda shorts). Play area. Internet access. Organised activities, canoe trips. Off site: Vallon-Pont-d'Arc 800 m.

Open: Easter - 30 September.

Directions

From Vallon-Pont-d'Arc (western end of the Ardèche Gorge) at a roundabout go east on the D290. Site entrance is shortly on the right.
GPS: N44:23.873 E04:23.929

Charges 2007

Per pitch incl. 2 persons and electricity	€ 28,30 - € 47,50
extra person	€ 5,50 - € 8,50
child (2-13 yrs)	€ 4,00 - € 6,70

FR26040 Camping le Couspeau

F-26460 Le Poët Célard (Drôme)

Tel: 04 75 53 30 14. Email: info@couspeau.com

The site has 127 pitches with 87 for touring. Access to the 62 touring pitches on the older section of the site (6A electricity) is reasonably easy, although levelling blocks may be handy. Mature trees provide some shade. The 30 fully serviced pitches on the lower section are large, separated by small hedges with little shade. Access is via a steep road but tractor assistance is available. Rock pegs are advised. The site has a good restaurant/bar and terrace with panoramic views. In July and August there is weekly live music and a themed meal. As one approaches this site a magnificent landscape of mountains and valleys unfolds and the overall impression is one of beauty and tranquillity. Those seeking to relax should appreciate the delightful scenery and setting of this site. The most direct approach is via a steep road, and with several hairpin bends to negotiate, care is required. For many people the views are reward enough, for others there is an alternative, easier route via Bourdeaux.

Facilities

Three sanitary blocks. Washing machines, dryer. Facilities for disabled campers (but site is not ideal with steep roads and steps. Shop (15/4-14/9). Bar (20/6-14/9). Restaurant and takeaway (25/6-25/8). Pool (1/6-30/8) and small, heated, covered, toddler's pool (14/4-14/9). Play area, organised activities. Tennis, table tennis, volleyball. Bike hire. Rafting, canoe trips (on River Drôme), riding, paragliding. Off site: Riding, fishing 5 km. Ideal area for the serious cyclist, mountain biker and hiker. Medieval towns and villages, markets and châteaux. Crest, Poët-Laval. Vercors mountains.

Open: 15 April - 14 September.

Directions

From A7, exit 16, take D104 to Crest. At traffic lights, turn right, D538 towards Bourdeaux. Before Bourdeaux turn right over bridge, D328B, signed Le Poët Célard. Climb for 1.5 km. to T-junction, turn right. D328. Before Le Poët Célard turn left, D328A to site. GPS: N44:35.744 E05:06.680

Charges 2006

Per unit incl. 2 persons	€ 18,00 - € 26,00
extra person	€ 4,00 - € 6,00
child (under 7 yrs)	free - € 4,00
electricity (6A)	€ 3,00

Camping Cheques accepted.

English not spoken ... who cares ?

Just kidding... you like our accent!

At the gates of Alps and Provence, a great spot for your holiday !

Mobile homes and chalets, swimming pools, kids club, hiking and biking, quiet evenings...

www.couspeau.com
+33 475 533 014

FR26130 Camping L'Hirondelle

Bois de Saint Ferreol, F-26410 Menglon (Drôme)

Tel: 04 75 21 82 08. Email: contact@campinghirondelle.com

This natural, spacious and peaceful site is run by a very friendly family and you are assured a good welcome. It lies in a beautiful valley, south of the Vercors mountains and the Vercors National Park, beside the River Bez. In natural openings in woodland, the 100 large to very large pitches all have electricity and are stony and slightly bumpy (rock pegs advised). There are 64 for touring units. The large pitches are separated by trees and the river bank on one side. A 'Sites et Paysages' member.

Facilities

Two large toilet blocks offer all the necessary facilities. Very good bar/restaurant and takeaway. Small range of supplies from the bar. Swimming pool, plus new excellent pool complex with small slide, paddling pool, jacuzzi and Lazy river (1/5 -17/9). Playground. Club/TV room. Internet access. Fishing. Boules. Archery. Organised events. Advice on activities and bookings made. Occasional evening events. Off site: Riding and bicycle hire 3 km.

Open: 28 April - 17 September.

Directions

From Die follow D93 southwards and after 5 km, at Pont de Quart, turn left on D539 signed Châtillon. After approx. 4 km. turn right on D140, signed Menglon. Site entrance is on the right just after crossing a small river. GPS: N44:40.885 E05:26.846

Charges 2006

Per pitch incl. 2 persons	€ 16,20 - € 24,30
electricity (3-6A)	€ 3,15 - € 4,20

Camping Cheques accepted.

kawan-villages.com   tel: 00 333 59 59 03 59

kawan
VILLAGES CAMPINGS

FR26210 Camping Les Bois du Chatelas

Route de Dieulefit, F-26460 Bourdeaux (Drôme)

Tel: 04 75 00 60 80. Email: contact@chatelas.com

Located at the heart of the the the Drôme Provencale, Les Bois du Chatelas is a smart, family run site which has undergone many recent improvements. The site is just 1 km. from the delightful village of Bourdeaux which offers a good range of shops, cafés, etc. There are 120 pitches here of which 44 are occupied by mobile homes. Although situated on a hillside, the pitches are level and of a good size. They all offer electricity, water and drainage. Les Bois du Chatelas is a particularly good choice for those seeking an active holiday. Member of Sites et Paysages de France. The long distance GR9 footpath passes through the site and there are very many walking and cycle routes close at hand. A popular aquagym is organised in the large outdoor pool in peak season. In the high season, a lively entertainment programme is organized as well as a number of cycling and walking excursions.

Facilities

Two heated toilet blocks (on upper and lower levels) with facilities for babies and disabled people (note: the site is hilly and may be unsuitable). Shop. Bar. Restaurant/pizzeria. Indoor swimming pool. Outdoor pool with water slide, waterfall and jacuzzi. Sports pitch. Archery. Play area. Bicycle hire. Entertainment and excursion programme (July/Aug). Mobile homes for rent. Off site: Rafting and canoe trips. Riding 5 km. Fishing 1 km. Very extensive walking and cycle (mountain bike) opportunities. Vercors mountain range. Many stunning mediaeval villages.

Open: 15 April - 1 October.

Directions

From the north, leave A7 at exit 16 and join the eastbound D104 to Crest. Upon reaching Crest take D538 south to Bourdeaux and continue towards Dieulefit. Site is on the left 1 km. beyond Bourdeaux and is well signed.

Charges 2006

Per unit incl. 2 persons	€ 13,00 - € 23,00
extra person	€ 4,00 - € 4,50
child (1-7 yrs)	€ 2,50 - € 2,60
electricity (10A)	€ 4,20 - € 4,50

FR04020 Castel Camping le Camp du Verdon

Domaine du Verdon, F-04120 Castellane (Alpes-de Haute-Provence)

Tel: **04 92 83 61 29**. Email: **contact@camp-du-verdon.com**

Close to the 'Route des Alpes' and the Gorges du Verdon. Two heated swimming pools and numerous on-site activities during high season help to keep non-canoeists here. Du Verdon is a large level site, part meadow, part wooded, with 500 partly shaded, rather stony pitches (390 for tourists). Numbered and separated by bushes, they vary in size, have 6A electricity, and 120 also have water and waste water. They are mostly separate from the mobile homes (63) and pitches used by tour operators (110). Some overlook the unfenced river Verdon, so watch the children. This is a very popular holiday area, the gorge, canoeing and rafting being the main attractions, ideal for active families. One can walk to Castellane without using the main road. Dances and discos in July and August suit all age groups – the latest finishing time is around 11 pm. (after that time patrols make sure that the site is quiet). The site is popular and very busy in July and August.

Facilities

Refurbished toilet blocks include facilities for disabled visitors. Washing machines. Motorcaravan services. Restaurant, terrace, log fire for cooler evenings. New supermarket. Pizzeria/crêperie. Takeaway. Heated swimming pools, paddling pool with 'mushroom' fountain (all open all season). Organised entertainments (July and August). Playgrounds. Minigolf, table tennis, archery, basketball, volleyball. Organised walks. Bicycle hire. Riding. Small fishing lake. ATM. Room for games and TV. Internet access. Off site: Castellane and the Verdon Gorge 1 km. Riding 2 km. Boat launching 4.5 km. Golf 20 km. Water sports.

Open: 15 May - 15 September.

Directions

From Castellane take D952 westwards towards Gorges du Verdon and Moustiers. Site is 1 km. on left.

Charges 2006

Per unit with 2 or 3 persons incl. 6A electricity	€ 17,00 - € 30,00
	€ 21,00 - € 34,00
extra person (over 3 yrs)	€ 7,00 - € 11,00
dog	€ 2,50

Camping Cheques accepted.

FR04100 Camping International

Route Napoleon, F-04120 Castellane (Alpes-de Haute-Provence)

Tel: **04 92 83 66 67**. Email: **info@camping-international.fr**

Camping International has very friendly, English speaking owners and is a reasonably priced, less commercialised site situated in some of the most dramatic scenery in France with good views. The 274 pitches, 130 good sized ones for touring, are clearly marked, separated by trees and small hedges, and all have electricity and water. The bar/restaurant overlooks the swimming pool with its sunbathing area set in a sunny location, and all have fantastic views. In high season English speaking young people entertain children (3-8 years) and teenagers. Access is good for larger units. On some evenings the teenagers are taken to the woods for campfire 'sing-alongs' which can go on till the early hours without disturbing the rest of the site. There are guided walks into the surrounding hills in the nearby Gorges du Verdon – a very popular excursion, particularly in high season. The weather in the hills here is very pleasant without the excessive heat of the coast.

Facilities

Small toilet blocks are of an older design. One newer block has modern facilities, including those for disabled visitors. Washing machines and dryer. Motorcaravan services. Fridge hire. Shop. Restaurant/takeaway (May-Sept). Swimming pool (1/5-30/9). Club/TV room. Children's animation, occasional evening entertainment (July/Aug). Play area. Boules. Internet access. Off site: Riding 800 m. Castellane (1.5 km.), with river, canyon and rapids, ideal for canoeing, rafting and canyoning etc. Walking, biking. Boat launching 5 km.

Open: 31 March - 1 October.

Directions

Site is 1 km. north of Castellane on the N85 'Route Napoleon'. GPS: N43:50.50 E06:30.42

Charges 2006

Per unit incl. 2 persons	€ 14,00 - € 21,00
extra person	€ 3,00 - € 5,00
electricity (6A)	€ 3,00 - € 5,00
dog	€ 2,00 - € 3,00

Camping Cheques accepted.

kawan-villages.com **tel: 00 333 59 59 03 59**

Camping International
Route Napoléon
04120 Castellane
Tél : +33 492 836 667
Fax : +33 492 837 767
mail : info@campinginternational.fr
www.campinginternational.fr

Castel Camping Caravaning
Domaine du Verdon
04120 Castellane
Tél : +33 492 836 129
Fax : +33 492 836 937
E-mail : contact@camp-du-verdon.com
www.camp-du-verdon.com

Provence
Castellane
Canyon du Verdon

FR04010 Sunêlia Hippocampe

Route de Napoléon, F-04290 Volonne (Alpes-de Haute-Provence)

Tel: **04 92 33 50 00**. Email: camping@l-hippocampe.com

Hippocampe is a friendly family run, 'all action' lakeside site, with families in mind, situated in a beautiful area of France. The perfumes of thyme, lavender and wild herbs are everywhere and the higher hills of Haute Provence are not too far away. There are 447 level, numbered pitches (243 for touring units), medium to very large (130 sq.m.) in size. All have electricity (10A) and 220 have water and drainage, most are separated by bushes and cherry trees. Some of the best pitches border the lake. The restaurant, bar, takeaway and shop have all been completely renewed. Games, aerobics, competitions, entertainment and shows, plus a daily club for younger family members are organised in July/August. A soundproof underground disco is set well away from the pitches and is very popular with teenage customers. Staff tour the site at night ensuring a good night's sleep. The site is, however, much quieter in low season and, with its good discounts, is the time for those who do not want or need entertaining. The Gorges du Verdon is a sight not to be missed and rafting, paragliding or canoe trips can be booked from the site's own tourist information office. Being on the lower slopes of the hills of Haute-Provence, the surrounding area is good for both walking and mountain biking. All in all, this is a very good site for an active or restful holiday and is suitable for outfits of all sizes. Used by tour operators (20 pitches). English is spoken.

Facilities

Toilet blocks vary from old to modern, all with good clean facilities that include washbasins in cabins. Washing machines. Motorcaravan service point. Bread available (from 28/4). Shop, bar, restaurant, pizzeria (all 1/5-15/9). Large, pool complex (heated in early and late seasons). Tennis. Fishing. Canoeing. Boules. Several sports facilities (some with free instruction). Charcoal barbecues are not permitted. Off site: Village of Volonne 600 m. Bicycle hire 2 km. Riding 6 km. Various sporting opportunities.

Open: 4 April - 30 September.

Directions

Approaching from the north turn off N85 across river bridge to Volonne, then right to site. From the south right on D4, 1 km. before Château Arnoux. GPS: N44:06.366 E06:00.933

Charges 2007

Per unit with 2 persons	
simple pitch:	€ 13,00 - € 27,00
with electricity	€ 16,00 - € 32,00
with water/drainage 100 sq.m.	€ 16,00 - € 34,00
with water/drainage 140 sq.m.	€ 20,00 - € 39,00
extra person (over 4 yrs)	€ 3,00 - € 6,50

Special low season offers.
Camping Cheques accepted.

Check real time availability and at-the-gate prices...
www.**alanrogers**.com

FR04030 Camping Moulin de Ventre

Niozelles, F-04300 Forcalquier (Alpes-de Haute-Provence)

Tel: 04 92 78 63 31. Email: moulindeventre@aol.com

This is a friendly, family run site in the heart of Haute-Provence, near Forcalquier, a bustling small French market town. Attractively located beside a small lake and 28 acres of wooded, hilly land, which is available for walking. Herbs of Provence can be found growing wild and flowers, birds and butterflies abound – a nature lovers delight. The 124 level, grassy pitches for tourists are separated by a variety of trees and small shrubs, 114 of them having electricity (6A; long leads may be necessary). Some pitches are particularly attractive, bordering a small stream. English is spoken. A 'Sites et Paysages' member. The site is well situated to visit Mont Ventoux, the Luberon National Park, the Gorges du Verdon and a wide range of ancient hill villages with their markets and museums etc.

Facilities

Refurbished toilet block. Facilities for disabled people. Baby bath. Washing, drying machines. Fridge hire. Bread. Bar/restaurant, takeaway (all season), themed evenings (high season). Pizzeria. Swimming pools (15/5-15/9). New playground. Fishing, boules. Some activities organised in high season. No discos. Only electric or gas barbecues. Internet access. Off site: Shops, local market, doctor, tennis 2 km. Supermarket, chemist, riding, bicycle hire 5 km. Golf 20 km. Walking, cycling.

Open: 1 April - 30 September.

Directions

From A51 motorway take exit 19 (Brillanne). Turn right on N96 then turn left on N100 westwards (signed Forcalquier) for about 3 km. Site is signed on left, just after a bridge 3 km. southeast of Niozelles. GPS: N43:56.1 E05:52.52

Charges 2006

Per unit incl. 2 persons	€ 13,00 - € 20,00
incl. electricity	€ 16,00 - € 25,00
extra person (over 4 yrs)	€ 3,50 - € 5,50
child (2-4 yrs)	€ 2,00 - € 3,00

No credit cards.
Camping Cheques accepted.

FR84020 Domaine Naturiste de Bélézy

F-84410 Bédoin (Vaucluse)

Tel: 04 90 65 60 18. Email: info@belezy.com

At the foot of Mt Ventoux, surrounded by beautiful scenery, Bélézy is an excellent naturist site with many amenities and activities and the ambience is relaxed and comfortable. The 238 marked pitches are set amongst many varieties of trees and shrubs. Electricity points (12A) are plentiful but long leads are necessary. So far as naturism is concerned, the emphasis is on personal choice, the only stipulation being the requirement for complete nudity in the pools and pool area. An area of natural parkland with an orchard, fishpond and woodland has a good range of sports facilities.

Facilities

Sanitary blocks differ – newer ones are excellent, with showers and washbasins in cubicles, others have hot showers in the open air, screened by stone dividers. One block has a superb children's section. Shop (26/3-30/9). Excellent restaurant and takeaway. Two swimming pools. Sauna. Tennis. Adventure play area. Archery. Guided walks. Hydrotherapy centre (1/4-30/9). Barbecues are prohibited. Pets are not accepted. Off site: Bédoin 1 km.

Open: 20 March - 6 October.

Directions

From A7 autoroute or RN7 at Orange, take D950 southeast to Carpentras, then northeast via D974 to Bédoin. Site is signed in Bédoin (1.5 km. northeast of the village). GPS: N44:08.011 E05:11.247

Charges 2007

Per unit incl. 2 persons	€ 14,50 - € 35,00
extra person	€ 5,50 - € 10,00
pitch	€ 4,60 - € 5,30

Camping Cheques accepted.

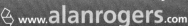

FR32010 Le Camp de Florence

Route Astaffort, F-32480 La Romieu (Gers)

Tel: **05 62 28 15 58**. Email: **info@lecampdeflorence.com**

Camp de Florence is an attractive site on the edge of an historic village in pleasantly undulating Gers countryside. The 183 large, part terraced pitches (95 for tourers) all have electricity, 10 with hardstanding and 25 fully serviced. They are arranged around a large field (full of sunflowers when we visited) with rural views, giving a feeling of spaciousness. The 13th century village of La Romieu is on the Santiago de Compostela pilgrim route. The Pyrénées are a two hour drive, the Atlantic coast a similar distance. It is run by the Mynsbergen family who are Dutch (although Susan is English) and they have sympathetically converted the old farmhouse buildings to provide facilities for the site. The collegiate church, visible from the site, is well worth a visit (the views are magnificent from the top of the tower), as is the local arboretum, the biggest collection of trees in the Midi-Pyrénées.

Facilities

Two toilet blocks. Washing machine, dryer. Motorcaravan services. Air-conditioned restaurant (open to the public) 1/5-30/9, barbecue. Takeaway. Bread. Swimming pool area with water slide. Jacuzzi, protected children's pool (open to public in afternoons). Adventure playground, games and pets areas. Games room, tennis, table tennis, volleyball, petanque. Bicycle hire. Video shows, discos, picnics, musical evenings. Excursions. Internet and WiFi. Off site: Shop 500 m. in village. Fishing 5 km. Riding 10 km. Walking tours, excursions and wine tasting arranged.

Open: 1 April - 8 October.

Directions

Site signed from D931 Agen - Condom road. Small units turn left at Ligardes (signed), follow D36 for 1 km, turn right turn La Romieu (signed). Otherwise continue until outskirts of Condom and take D41 left to La Romieu, through village to site. GPS: N43:58.975 E00:30.091

Charges 2007

Per unit incl. 2 persons and electricity	€ 16,00 - € 30,90
extra person	€ 3,50 - € 6,90
child (4-9 yrs)	€ 2,60 - € 4,80

Camping Cheques accepted.

kawan-villages.com tel: **00 333 59 59 03 59** *kawan*
VILLAGES CAMPINGS

Le Camp de Florence - 32480 La Romieu

Sun * Comfort * Nature * Water

The Gers - A region waiting to be discovered, an unspoilt landscape of rolling hills, sunflowers and historic fortified villages and castles. Peace, tranquillity, the home of Armagnac, Fois Gras and Magret de Canard. A four star camping / caravanning site with bungalows, mobil-homes and Trigano tents for hire.

Tel: 0033 562 28 15 58 - Fax: 0033 562 28 20 04
E-mail: info@campdeflorence.com - www.campdeflorence.com

FR09020 Camping L'Arize

Lieu-dit Bourtol, F-09240 La Bastide-de-Sérou (Ariège)

Tel: **05 61 65 81 51**. Email: **camparize@aol.com**

The site sits in a delightful, tranquil valley among the foothills of the Pyrénées and is just east of the interesting village of La Bastide-de-Sérou beside the River Arize (good trout fishing). The river is fenced for the safety of children on the site, but may be accessed just outside the gate. The 70 large pitches are neatly laid out on level grass within the spacious site. All have electricity and are separated into bays by hedges and young trees. An extension to the site gives 24 fully serviced pitches.

Facilities

Toilet block includes facilities for babies and disabled people. Laundry room, dryer. Motorcaravan services. Small swimming pool, sunbathing area. Entertainment, high season, weekly barbecues and welcome drinks on Sundays. Fishing, riding and bicycle hire on site. Off site: Golf 5 km. The nearest restaurant is at the national stud for the famous Merens horses just 200 m. away and will deliver takeaway meals to your pitch.

Open: 10 March - 6 November.

Directions

Site is southeast of the village La Bastide-de-Sérou. Take the D15 towards Nescus and site is on right after about 1 km. GPS: N43:00.109 E01:26.723

Charges 2006

Per pitch incl. 2 persons and electricity	€ 16,40 - € 23,70
extra person	€ 4,00 - € 5,20
child (0-7 yrs)	€ 3,00 - € 3,60

FR09060 Camping le Pré Lombard

F-09400 Tarascon-sur-Ariège (Ariège)
Tel: 05 61 05 61 94. Email: **leprelombard@wanadoo.fr**

This busy, good value site is located beside the attractive river Ariège near the town. There are 180 level, grassy, pitches with shade provided by a variety of trees (electricity 10A). At the rear of the site are 69 site-owned chalets and mobile homes. A gate in the fence provides access to the river bank for fishing. Open for a long season, it is an excellent choice for early or late breaks, or as a stop-over en-route to the winter sun destinations in Spain. This region of Ariège is in the foothills of the Pyrénées, 85 km. from Andorra. Didier Mioni, the manager here follows the town motto S'y passos, y demoros – 'if you wish to come here, you will stay here' in his aim to ensure your satisfaction.

Facilities

Five toilet blocks of varying age, facilities for disabled people. Laundry. Motorcaravan services. Bar and takeaway. Shop. Restaurant (15/5-15/9). Swimming pool (15/5-15/9). Playgrounds. Fishing. Internet. Entertainment (high season), nightclub, children's club, sports. Activity programmes for small groups. Off site: Supermarket 300 m. Town 600 m. Riding 5 km. Golf 30 km. Skiing 20 km.

Open: 29 January - 11 November.

Directions

Site is 600 m. south of town, adjacent to the river. From north, turn off main N20 into the town, site well signed. GPS: N42:50.391 E01:36.720

Charges 2007

Per unit incl. 2 persons and 6A electricity	€ 15,00 - € 30,00
extra person (over 2 yrs)	€ 5,00 - € 9,00

Camping Cheques accepted.

awan ——————————————— **tel: 00 333 59 59 03 59** *kawan-villages.com*

FR31000 Camping le Moulin

F-31220 Martres-Tolosane (Haute-Garonne)
Tel: 05 61 98 86 40. Email: **info@campinglemoulin.com**

Set in a 12 hectare estate of woods and fields, Camping Le Moulin is a family run campsite in the foothills of the Pyrénées, close to the interesting medieval village of Martres-Tolosane and situated on the site of an old mill on the bank of the River Garonne. There are 94 pitches (60 available for tourers) all of which have electrical connections. Most pitches are level and grassy, of a good size and with shade from mature trees. A number of very large (150-200 sq.m.) 'super' pitches are also available and there are 34 chalets/mobile homes for rent.

Facilities

Large modern sanitary block with showers and washbasins in cubicles. Facilities for disabled visitors. Baby bath. Laundry facilities. Outdoor bar with WiFi. Snackbar and takeaway (July/Aug). Heated swimming pool (July/Aug). BMX. Playground. Entertainment programme (high season). Off site: Martres-Tolosane 1.5 km.

Open: Easter - 30 September.

Directions

From the A64 motorway (Toulouse-Tarbes) take exit 21 (Boussens) or exit 22 (Martres-Tolosane) and follow signs to Martres-Tolosane. Site is well signed.

Charges 2006

Per person	€ 4,20 - € 6,00
child (2-7 ys)	€ 2,10 - € 3,00
pitch incl. electricity (6/10A)	€ 7,70 - € 16,50

FR65060 Castel Camping Pyrénées Natura

Route du Lac, F-65400 Estaing (Haute-Pyrénées)
Tel: 05 62 97 45 44. Email: **info@camping-pyrenees-natura.com**

Pyrénées Natura, at an altitude of 1,000 metres, on the edge of the National Park is the perfect site for lovers of nature. The 60 pitches (46 for tourists), all with electricity, are in a large, level, open and sunny field. Around 75 varieties of trees and shrubs have been planted – but they do not spoil the fantastic views. The reception and bar are in a traditional style stone building with an open staircase. The small shop in the old water mill is left unmanned and open all day and you pay at reception.

Facilities

First class toilet blocks include facilities for disabled visitors and babies. Washing machine and airers (no lines allowed). Motorcaravan services. Small shop, takeaway (15/5-15/9). Small bar (15/5-15/9). Lounge, library, TV. Sauna, solarium (free between 12.00-17.00). Music room. Play area for the very young. Small 'beach' beside river. Internet. Off site: Village restaurants.

Open: 1 May - 20 September.

Directions

From Lourdes take N21 towards Argelès-Gazost. Exit 2, N2021/D21, into Argelès. Approaching town turn on D918 (Aucun). After 8 km, turn left, D13 to Bun, right on D103 to site (5.5 km). Narrow road, few passing places. GPS: N42:56.451 W00:10.631

Charges 2007

Per unit incl. 2 persons and electricity (3A)	€ 24,00
extra person	€ 5,00

FR65080 Camping du Lavedan

Lau-Balagnas, F-65400 Argelès-Gazost (Haute-Pyrénées)

Tel: **05 62 97 18 84**. Email: **contact@lavedan.com**

Camping du Lavedan is an old established and very French site set in the Argelès-Gazost valley south of the Lourdes. It is beside the main road so there is some daytime road noise. The 105 touring pitches are set very close together on grass with some shade and all have electricity (2-10A). The area is fine for walking, biking, rafting and of course, in winter, skiing. There is a swimming pool which can be covered in inclement weather and events are organised in high season.

Facilities

Acceptable toilet block. Baby room. Facilities for disabled visitors. Washing machines and dryer in separate block heated in winter. Restaurant with takeaway and terrace (1/5-15/9). Bar, TV (all year). No shop, bread delivery (1/5-15/9). Swimming pool (with cover), paddling pool. Excellent play area. Internet (July/Aug). Boules, table tennis. Off site: Fishing or bicycle hire 1 km. Supermarket or rafting 2 km. Riding 5 km. Golf 15 km.

Open: All year.

Directions

Lau-Balagnas, 15 km. south of Lourdes. From Lourdes take the N21 south, exit 3 (Argelès-Gazost). Take N2021, D921 or D21 towards Luz St Sauveur for 2 km. to Lau Balagnas. Site is on right, southern edge of town. GPS: N42:59.293 W00:05.340

Charges 2006

Per unit incl. 2 persons	€ 15,00 - € 19,00
electricity (2A)	€ 2,00 - € 6,00

Camping Cheques accepted.

kawan-villages.com **tel: 00 333 59 59 03 59** ━━━━━━━━ kawar

FR65090 Camping Soleil du Pibeste

16 avenue du Lavedan, F-65400 Agos Vidalos (Haute-Pyrénées)

Tel: **05 62 97 53 23**. Email: **info@campingpibeste.com**

Soleil du Pibeste is a quiet, rural site with well tended grass and flower beds. It has 67 pitches for touring, all having electricity (3-15A) with some shade. The Dusserm family welcomes all arrivals with a drink and they are determined to ensure that you have a good stay. There is no shop but the supermarket is only 5 km. and ordered bread is delivered to your door daily. The swimming pool is on a terrace above the pitches, with sun beds, a paddling pool and waterfall and has the most magnificent view of the mountains.

Facilities

Two heated toilet blocks. Baby room. Facilities for disabled visitors (key). Cleaning can be variable. Washing machine, dryer. Motorcaravan services. Bar, snacks, piano, internet. Room for playing cards or reading. Swimming, paddling pools. Small play area. Boules. Bicycle hire. Tai Chi and other relaxation classes. Off site: Fishing 800 m. Golf 10 km. Rafting 2 km. Skiing 2 km.

Open: 1 May - 30 September.

Directions

Agos Vidalos is on the N21, 5 km. south of Lourdes. Leave express-way at second exit, signed Agos Vidalos and continue to site, a short distance on the right. GPS: N43:02.134 W00:04.256

Charges 2006

Per unit incl. 2 persons and 3A electricity	€ 15,00 - € 22,00
extra person	€ 3,00 - € 5,00

FR30000 Camping Domaine de Gaujac

Boisset-et-Gaujac, F-30140 Anduze (Gard)

Tel: **04 66 61 80 65**. Email: **gravieres@club-internet.fr**

The 293 level, well shaded pitches include 175 for touring with electricity (4-10A) with 22 serviced. Access to some areas can be difficult for larger units due to narrow winding access roads, trees and hedges. Larger units should ask for lower numbered pitches (1-148) where access is a little easier. In high season this region is dry and hot, thus grass quickly wears off many pitches leaving just a sandy base. There are 12 special hardstanding pitches for motorcaravans near the entrance.

Facilities

Heated toilet blocks include facilities for disabled visitors. Washing machines, dryer. Motorcaravan services. Good shop (2/6-27/8). Newsagent. Takeaway/crêperie (15/4-15/9). Bar, restaurant (15/4-15/9). New heated swimming, paddling pool (lifeguard 5/7-15/8) and jacuzzi. Playground, sports field. Tennis. Minigolf. Only gas and electric barbecues. Off site: Fishing 70 m. Bicycle hire 5 km. Riding, golf 8 km. River beach 70 km.

Open: 1 April - 30 September.

Directions

From Alès take N110 towards Montpellier. At St Christol-les-Alès fork right on D910 towards Anduze and in Bagard turn left on D246 to Boisset et Gaujac (5 km). GPS: N44:02.148 E04:01.455

Charges 2006

Per unit incl. 2 persons	€ 14,00 - € 22,00
extra person	€ 4,00 - € 4,70
electricity (4-10A)	€ 3,00 - € 3,50

Camping Cheques accepted.

kawan-villages.com **tel: 00 333 59 59 03 59** ━━━━━━━━ kawar

FR30080 Camping le Mas de Reilhe

F-30260 Crespian (Gard)

Tel: **04 66 77 82 12**. Email: **info@camping-mas-de-reilhe.fr**

This is a comfortable family site nestling in a valley with 95 pitches (76 for tourers), most have electricity (6/10A) and some of the upper ones may require long leads. The large lower pitches are separated by tall poplar trees and hedges, close to the main facilities and may experience some road noise. The large terraced pitches on the hillside are scattered under mature pine trees, some with good views, more suited to tents and trailer tents but with their own modern sanitary facilities. The heated pool is in a sunny position and overlooked by the attractive bar/restaurant. There are no shops in the village, the nearest being at the medieval city of Sommières 10 km. away (and well worth a visit). A 'Sites et Paysages' member.

Facilities

Good toilet facilities with washbasins in cabins and pre-set showers. Dishwashing and laundry sinks. Washing machine. Reception with limited shop (bread to order). Bar (6/4-23/9), takeaway and restaurant (1/6-15/9). Small play area. Heated swimming pool (all season). Internet access. Off site: Tennis 0.5 km. Fishing 3 km. Riding 5 km. Bicycle hire 10 km. Beach 30 km. Nîmes 25 km.

Open: 6 April - 23 September.

Directions

From the A9 take exit 'Nimes ouest' signed Alès, then onto the D999 towards Le Vigan. The site is on the N110 just north of the junction with the D999.

Charges 2006

Per unit incl. 2 persons	€ 13,00 - € 19,00
extra person	€ 3,40 - € 5,20
electricity (6/10A)	€ 3,30 - € 4,00

Camping Cheques accepted.

awan ————————————— tel: **00 333 59 59 03 59** *kawan-villages.com*

FR11060 Yelloh! Village Domaine d'Arnauteille

F-11250 Montclar (Aude)

Tel: **04 68 26 84 53**. Email: **Arnauteille@mnet.fr**

Enjoying some beautiful and varied views, this site is ideal exploring the little known Aude Département and for visiting the walled city of Carcassonne. However, access could be difficult for large, twin axle vans. The site is set in farmland on hilly ground with the original pitches on gently sloping, lightly wooded land and newer ones of good size with water, drainage and electricity (5/10A), semi-terraced and partly hedged. The facilities are quite spread out with the swimming pool complex, in the style of a Roman amphitheatre, set in a hollow basin surrounded by fine views. The reception building is vast; originally a farm building, with a newer top floor being converted to apartments. This is a developing site so be aware of on-going building work. Some very steep up and down walking between the pitches and facilities is unavoidable. A 'Sites et Paysages' member.

Facilities

Toilet blocks, one with a Roman theme. Laundry, facilities for disabled people and a baby bath. Motorcaravan services. Small shop (15/5-30/9). Restaurant in converted stable block, takeaway (15/5-30/9). Four pools including children's pool. Games court. Boules. Play area. Table tennis, volleyball. Riding (1/7-31/8). Day trips. Library, internet, games room, TV. Off site: Fishing 3 km. Bicycle hire 8 km. Golf 10 km. Rafting and canoeing near, plus many walks with marked paths.

Open: 7 April - 25 September.

Directions

D118 from Carcassonne, pass Rouffiac d'Aude. Before the end of dual carriageway, turn right to Montclar up narrow road (passing places) for 2.5 km. Site signed very sharp left up hill before village. GPS: N43:07.636 E02:15.571

Charges 2007

Per pitch incl. 2 persons	€ 14,00 - € 29,00
with 6A electricity	€ 18,00 - € 33,00
with electricity, water and drain	€ 21,00 - € 37,00

Camping Cheques accepted.

Domaine d'Arnauteille ★★★★
11250 Montclar (close to Carcassonne)
Tel: 0033 468 26 84 53 - Fax: 0033 468 26 91 10
Arnauteille@mnet.fr - www.arnauteille.com

New waterpark with 4 pools in a Greek-Roman style.

FR30100 Camping Naturiste de la Sablière

Domaine de la Sablière, St Privat de Champclos, F-30430 Barjac (Gard)

Tel: **04 66 24 51 16**. Email: **contact@villagesabliere.com**

Spectacularly situated in the Cèze Gorges, this naturist site with a surprising 497 pitches, 240 for touring, tucked away within its wild terrain offers a wide variety of facilities, all within a really peaceful, wooded and dramatic setting. The pitches themselves are mainly on flat stony terraces, attractively situated among a variety of trees and shrubs (some with a low overhang). Many are of a good size and have electricity (6/10A), very long leads may be needed. Nudity is obligatory only around the pool complex. You must expect fairly steep walking between the pitches and facilities.

Facilities

Six good unisex sanitary blocks have excellent free hot showers in typical open plan, naturist style, washbasins (cold water), baby baths and facilities for people with disabilities. Laundry. Good supermarket. Bar (1/4-22/9). Restaurant and takeaway (1/4-22/9). Small café/crêperie. Swimming pool complex. Activity programme. Barbecues are not permitted. Off site: Bicycle hire 8 km.

Open: 1 April - 1 October.

Directions

From Barjac take D901 east for 3 km. Turn right at site sign just before St Privat-de-Champclos and follow site signs along winding country lane to site entrance in 4 km. GPS: N44:16.021 E04:21.125

Charges 2006

Per pitch incl. 2 persons	€ 13,00 - € 32,55
extra person	€ 3,00 - € 6,50

Camping Cheques accepted.

FR11080 Camping la Nautique

La Nautique, F-11100 Narbonne (Aude)

Tel: **04 68 90 48 19**. Email: info@campinglanautique.com

This extremely spacious site is situated on the Etang de Bages, where flat water combined with strong winds make it one of the best windsurfing areas in France and it is owned and run by a very welcoming Dutch family. La Nautique has 390 huge, level pitches, there are also six or seven overnight pitches with electricity in a separate area. The flowering shrubs and trees give a pleasant feel. Each pitch is separated by hedges making some quite private and providing shade. All have electricity (10A) and water. Each pitch has an individual toilet cabin. Entertainments are organised for adults and children in July/Aug, plus a sports club for supervised surfing, sailing, rafting, walking and canoeing (some activities are charged for). The unspoilt surrounding countryside is excellent for walking or cycling and locally there is horse riding and fishing. English is spoken in reception by the very welcoming Schutjes family. This site caters for families with children including teenagers. The site is fenced off from the water for the protection of children and windsurfers can have a key for the gate (with deposit) that leads to launching points on the lake.

Facilities

Each cabin has a toilet, shower, washbasin. Pitches for disabled people. Laundry. Shop. Bar/restaurant, terrace, TV. Takeaway. All 1/5-15/9. Snack bar 1/7-31/8. Swimming pools, paddling pool, slide. Play areas, miniclub. Tennis, minigolf, boules. Teenagers' disco (high season). Recreation area. Internet. Only electric barbecues. Torch useful. Off site: Large sandy beaches at Gruissan (10 km.) and Narbonne Plage (15 km.). Narbonne is only 4 km. Canoeing, sailing and windsurfing on the Etang.

Open: 15 February - 15 November.

Directions

From A9 take exit 38 (Narbonne Sud). Go round roundabout to last exit and follow signs for La Nautique and site, then further site signs to site on right in 3 km.

Charges 2006

Per person	€ 4,20 - € 6,00
child (1-7 yrs)	€ 2,20 - € 4,50
pitch incl. electricity, water and sanitary unit	€ 8,50 - € 20,00
dog or cat	€ 1,50 - € 3,50

Private Sanitary facilities on every pitch.
Open from 15/02 till 15/11
www.campinglanautique.com
(+33) 04 68 90 48 19

FR11070 Camping les Mimosas

Chaussée de Mandirac, F-11100 Narbonne (Aude)
Tel: 04 68 49 03 72. Email: info@lesmimosas.com

Six kilometres inland from the beaches of Narbonne and Gruissan, this site benefits from a less hectic situation than others by the sea. The site is lively with plenty to amuse and entertain the younger generation whilst offering facilities for the whole family. A free club card is available in July/August to use the children's club, gym, sauna, tennis, minigolf, billiards etc. There are 250 pitches, 150 for touring, many in a circular layout of very good size, most with electricity (6A). There are a few 'grand confort', with reasonable shade, mostly from 2 m. high hedges. There are also a number of mobile homes and chalets to rent. This could be a very useful site offering many possibilities to meet a variety of needs, on-site entertainment (including an evening on Cathar history), and easy access to popular beaches. Nearby Gruissan is a fascinating village with its wooden houses on stilts, beaches, ruined castle, port and salt beds. Narbonne has Roman remains and inland Cathar castles are to be found perched on rugged hill tops.

Facilities

Refurbished high standard sanitary buildings. Washing machines. Shop and 'Auberge' restaurant (open all season). Takeaway. Bar. Small lounge, amusements (July and Aug). Landscaped heated pool with slides and islands (open 1 May), plus the original pool and children's pool (high season). Play area. Minigolf. Mountain bike hire. Tennis. Volleyball. Sauna, gym. Children's activities, sports, entertainment (high season). Bicycle hire. Multisports ground. Off site: Riding. Windsurfing/sailing school 300 m. Gruissan's beach 10 minutes. Lagoon, boating fishing via footpath (200 m).
Open: 24 March - 31 October.

Directions

From A9 exit 38 (Narbonne Sud) take last exit on roundabout, back over the autoroute (site signed from here). Follow signs La Nautique and then Mandirac and site (6 km. from autoroute). Also signed from Narbonne centre.

Charges 2007

Per pitch incl. 1 or 2 persons	€ 13,50 - € 21,00
pitch with electricity	€ 17,00 - € 27,00
with electricity, water and waste water	€ 21,20 - € 31,00
extra person	€ 4,00 - € 5,90

Camping Cheques accepted.

tel: 00 333 59 59 03 59 kawan-villages.com

FR34070 Yelloh! Village le Sérignan Plage

Le Sérignan Plage, F-34410 Sérignan (Hérault)

Tel: **04 67 32 35 33**. Email: **info@leserignanplage.com**

A large, friendly, family-orientated site with direct access to superb sandy beaches, including a naturist beach. Those looking for 'manicured' sites may be less impressed, as its situation on 'the littoral' close to the beach makes it difficult to keep things neat and tidy. It has 450 mainly good sized, level touring pitches, including some (with little shade) actually alongside the beach, coupled with perhaps the most comprehensive range of amenities we've come across. Perhaps the most remarkable aspect is the cluster of attractive buildings which form the 'heart' of this site with courtyards housing many of the amenities. The hugely enthusiastic owners, Jean-Guy and Katy, continually surprise us with new ideas and developments. New for 2004 was a superb 1,800 sq.m. 'Spa Water Fitness centre' with more new pools, a fitness centre and jacuzzi. The amenities are just too extensive to describe in detail, but they include a pool complex, with slides surrounded by large grassy sunbathing areas with sun loungers and another indoor pool. Sérignan Plage exudes a strongly individualistic style which we find very attractive.

Facilities

Several modern blocks of individual design, with good facilities, including showers with washbasin and WC. Facilities for disabled people. Washing machines. Maintenance variable. Supermarket, bakery, newsagent, ATM. Poissonnerie, boucherie (7/6-8/9). Launderette. Hairdresser. Bars, restaurant, takeaway (all 7/4-10/9). Children's activities, evening entertainment. Heated indoor and outdoor pool with lifeguards in the main season (April - Sept). Sporting activities organised. Bicycle hire. Off site: Riding 2 km. Golf 10 km. Bicycle hire. Sailing and windsurfing school on beach (lifeguard in high season).

Open: 6 April - 24 September.

Directions

From A9 exit 35 (Béziers Est) follow signs for Sérignan, D64 (9 km). Before Sérignan, turn left, Sérignan Plage (4 km). At small sign (blue) turn right. At T-junction turn left over small road bridge and after left hand bend. Site is 100 m.

Charges 2007

Per unit incl. 1 or 2 persons and 6 A electricity	€ 17,00 - € 43,00
extra person	€ 4,00 - € 8,00
pet	€ 3,00

Low season offers.
Camping Cheques accepted.

FR34130 Camping le Neptune

Route du Grau, F-34300 Agde (Hérault)

Tel: **04 67 94 23 94**. Email: **info@campingleneptune.com**

Camping Neptune is a rare find in this area. This small, family run site with only 165 pitches makes a delightful change. The pitches are mostly separated by flowering bushes, with some shade, most with 6A electricity. The Fray family are welcoming and, even though in a busy area, this site is an oasis of calm, suited to couples and young families. Alongside the D32 there may be a little daytime road noise. The swimming pool is in a sunny position overlooked by the bar. The only entertainment is in high season and is a twice weekly miniclub for children.

Facilities

Two toilet blocks provide roomy pre-set showers, washbasins in cabins, three cold showers for hot weather. Laundry and dishwashing sinks. Two washing machines, dryer. Small shop, bar (both 15/5-30/9). Heated swimming pool heated, bracelets required. Table tennis, field for sports. Boat mooring facility on the River Hérault across the road. Only one dog allowed. No barbecues. Off site: Beach 1.5 km. Golf and riding 1.5 km.

Open: 1 April - 30 September.

Directions

From A9 exit 34, N312, Agde, join N112. Cross river bridge, exit Grau d'Agde, top of exit road over road bridge turn left (roundabout), left at next roundabout, straight over next roundabout, towards river. Left at next roundabout signed Grau d'Agde, D32, parallel to river. Site on left. GPS: N43:17.882 E03:27.377

Charges 2006

Per unit incl. 2 persons	€ 16,00 - € 25,90
extra person	€ 4,50 - € 5,30

Camping Cheques accepted.

kawan-villages.com **tel: 00 333 59 59 03 59**

kawa VILLAGES CAMPING

Le Sérignan Plage

The magic of
the Mediterranean

Imagine – hot sunshine, blue sea, vineyards, olive and eucalyptus trees, alongside a sandy beach – what a setting for a campsite – not just any campsite either ! With three pool areas, one with four toboggans surrounded by sun bathing areas, an indoor pool for baby swimmers plus a magnificent landscaped, Romanesque spa-complex with half Olympic size pool and a superb range of hydro-massage baths to let you unwind and re-charge after the stresses of work. And that's not all – two attractive restaurants, including the atmospheric "Villa" in its romantic Roman setting beside the spa, three bars, a mini-club and entertainment for all ages, all add up to a fantastic opportunity to enjoy a genuinely unique holiday experience.

Le Sérignan-Plage - F-34410 SERIGNAN
Tel: 00 33 467 32 35 33 - Fax: 00 33 467 32 26 36
info@leserignanplage.com - www.leserignanplage.com

FR34190 Camping Caravaning les Champs Blancs

Route de Rochelongue, F-34300 Agde (Hérault)

Tel: **04 67 94 23 42**. Email: **champs.blancs@wanadoo.fr**

Les Champs Blancs is set in high trees, 2 km. from Agde and 2 km. from the sea in a shady environment. The 169 level, sandy, touring pitches are bordered with bushes and plenty of trees, all with 10A electricity and 60 have private sanitary cabins. The pool area has been augmented by a super irregular pool, with toboggans, cascade, Jacuzzi, bridges and palms but retaining the original pool and paddling pool. Games, shows and competitions are arranged in July and August. The area nearest the road is bordered by trees to deaden possible road noise.

Facilities

Refurbished toilet blocks, unit for disabled visitors, 60 en-suite private cabins containing WC, shower and washbasin with outside sink. Washing machines, dryers. Motor caravan services. Well stocked shop in high season, only bread low season. Bar (from 1/6). Restaurant (20/6-15/9). Swimming complex (from 8/4 depending on weather – bracelet required € 5). Good play area. Off site: Riding 1 km. Golf 1.5 km. Beach 2 km.

Open: 8 April - 30 September.

Directions

From A9 exit 34, follow N312 for Adge, joins the N112 Béziers - Sète road. Cross river, take first turning (Rochelongue), turn right, next left, then next left (Adge). Site on left before another bridge back over N112. GPS: N43:17.821 E03:28.528

Charges 2006

Per pitch incl. 2 persons	€ 18,00 - € 45,00
extra person	€ 5,00 - € 10,00

Camping Cheques accepted.

kawan-villages.com tel: **00 333 59 59 03 59** ━━━━━━ *kawan*

FR66020 Camping Caravaning Ma Prairie

Route de St Nazaire, F-66140 Canet-en-Roussillon (Pyrénées-Orientales)

Tel: **04 68 73 26 17**. Email: **ma.prairie@wanadoo.fr**

Ma Prairie is an excellent site and its place in this guide goes back over 30 years. Then it was simply a field surrounded by vineyards. The trees planted then have now matured, more have been planted, along with colourful shrubs providing a comfortable, park-like setting with some 260 pitches, all with electricity and 35 with water and drainage. It is a peaceful haven some 3 km. back from the sea but within walking distance of Canet village itself. The Gil family still provide a warm welcome.

Facilities

Fully equipped toilet blocks, baby bath. Laundry facilities. No shop but bread can be ordered. Snack bar and takeaway. Bar and restaurant. Swimming pool. Play area. Tennis. Bicycle hire. Dancing three times weekly, busy daily activity programme in season. Caravan storage. Off site: Supermarket 400 m. Riding 600 m. Golf 6 km. Canet Village within walking distance.

Open: 5 May - 25 September.

Directions

Leave autoroute A9 at Perpignan North towards Barcarès. Site access is from the D11 Perpignan road (exit 5), close to junction with D617 in Canet-Village. Go under bridge, right at roundabout the left to site.

Charges 2007

Per unit incl. 2 persons	€ 17,00 - € 30,00
electricity (10A)	€ 4,00 - € 5,00

Camping Cheques accepted.

kawan-villages.com tel: **00 333 59 59 03 59** ━━━━━━ *kawan*

FR66050 Camping le Haras

Domaine Saint Galdric, F-66690 Palau del Vidre (Pyrénées-Orientales)

Tel: **04 68 22 14 50**. Email: **haras8@wanadoo.fr**

A distinctly 'French' style site, Le Haras is midway between the coast (about 8 km.) and the Pyrénées, in quiet countryside away from the bustle of the coastal resorts. Le Haras has 75 pitches with electricity, 18 fully serviced, arranged informally in bays of four, in the grounds of an old hunting lodge. A mixture of trees, shrubs and flowers provides colour and shade. Some access roads are narrow. Rail noise is possible, although this is screened by large trees.

Facilities

Fully equipped toilet blocks, Renovation of smaller block near the pool planned. Covered dishwashing and laundry sinks. Washing machines. Fridge hire. Bar. Restaurant, open to the public (all year). Takeaway. Swimming pool (1/5-15/9). Play area. No charcoal barbecues. Internet access. Off site: Beaches 10 minutes drive. Fishing 500 m. Riding 2 km. Bicycle hire 6 km. Golf 7 km.

Open: 20 March - 20 October.

Directions

From A9, exit 43 (Le Boulou) follow D618 towards Argelès for 13 km. Bypass St André, turn left, Palau-del-Vidre (D11). Bear right through village, on D11 towards Elne. Site at end of village, before bridge.

Charges 2007

Per pitch incl. two persons	€ 14,00 - € 24,50
electricity (5A)	€ 4,00

Camping Cheques accepted.

kawan-villages.com tel: **00 333 59 59 03 59** ━━━━━━ *kawa*

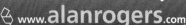

FR06120 Camping Green Park

159, Vallon des Vaux, F-06800 Cagnes-sur-Mer (Alpes-Maritimes)

Tel: 04 93 07 09 96. Email: info@greenpark.fr

Green Park has many facilities of a high standard and the family owners are justifiably proud. Situated just over 4 km. from the beaches at Cagnes-sur-Mer, Green Park is at the centre of the Côte d'Azur. The newer part of the site keeps all the family occupied with activities for children, teenagers and adults, while on the other side of the road is a quieter, traditional site, with limited facilities. There are 78 touring pitches mainly on grass, with electricity and 24 are fully serviced. The site has two swimming pools, one on each side of the quiet road. Green Park is situated in an area which benefits from a 'micro climate', hot during the day but pleasantly cooler at night. There are 67 mobile homes and chalets.

Facilities

All the toilets are modern and mostly British, with facilities for children and disabled visitors (the disabled facilities are superb). Showers and washbasins are modern and kept very clean. Dishwashing and laundry sinks and three washing machines. Bar, restaurant and takeaway (28/4-24/9). Two swimming pools (all season, one heated 5/5-24/9). Internet point. Games room. Electronic barrier (€5 card deposit) and a gate keeper on duty all night. Off site: Beach 4 km. Golf and riding 9 km.

Open: 31 March - 15 October.

Directions

From Aix, A8, exit 47 onto N7 towards Nice. Straight on at traffic lights, by racecourse, for 2 km. Turn left towards Val Fleuri, Av. du Val Fleuri. Over roundabouts to Chemin Vallon des Vaux, site on right 2 km. Avoid the town centre. GPS: N43:41.355 E07:09.409

Charges 2006

Per unit incl. 2 persons	€ 13,00 - € 33,20
extra person	€ 4,50 - € 5,70
child (7-17 yrs)	€ 3,00 - € 4,20
electricity	€ 4,10 - € 5,20

FR66070 Yelloh! Village le Brasilia

B.P. 204, F-66141 Canet-en-Roussillon (Pyrénées-Orientales)

Tel: **04 68 80 23 82**. Email: **camping-le-brasilia@wanadoo.fr**

An impressive family site beside the beach and well managed, Le Brasilia is pretty, neat and well kept with an amazingly wide range of facilities. There are 826 neatly hedged pitches all with electricity varying in size from 100 to 150 sq.m. Some of the longer pitches are suitable for two families together. With a range of shade from pines and flowering shrubs, less on pitches near the beach, there are neat access roads (sometimes narrow for large units). Over 100 of the pitches have mobile homes or chalets to rent. A 'Yelloh Village' member. Member of Leading Campings Group. The sandy beach here is busy, with a beach club (you can hire windsurfing boards) and a naturist section is on the beach to the west of the site. There is also a large California type pool, with sunbathing areas bounded by an attractive mosaic wall and bar. The village area of the site provides bars, a busy restaurant, entertainment (including a night club) and a range of shops. In fact you do not need to stir from the site which is almost a resort in itself also providing a cash dispenser, exchange facilities, telephone, post office, gas supplies and even weather forecasts. It does have a nice, lively atmosphere but is orderly and well run – very good for a site with beach access.

Facilities

Ten modern sanitary blocks are very well equipped and maintained, with British style WCs (some Turkish) and washbasins in cabins. Good facilities for children and for disabled people. Laundry room. Hairdresser. Bars and restaurant. Swimming pool with lifeguards (heated). Play areas. Sports field. Tennis. Sporting activities. Library, games and video room. Internet café. Daily entertainment programme. Bicycle hire. Fishing. Torches useful. Off site: Riding 5 km. Golf 12 km.

Open: 29 April - 30 September.

Directions

From A9 exit 41 (Perpignan Centre/Rivesalts) follow signs for Le Barcarès/Canet on D83 for 10 km, then for Canet (D81). At first Canet roundabout, turn fully back on yourself (direction Sainte-Marie) and watch for Brasilia sign almost immediately on right.

Charges 2006

Per unit incl. 2 persons and electricity (6A)	€ 16,00 - € 42,00
extra person	€ 4,60 - € 6,50
child (1-4 yrs)	free - € 4,00

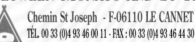

FR06080 Camping Caravaning les Cigales

505 avenue de la Mer, F-06210 Mandelieu-la-Napoule (Alpes-Maritimes)

Tel: **04 93 49 23 53**. Email: **campingcigales@wanadoo.fr**

It is hard to imagine that such a quiet, peaceful site could be in the middle of such a busy town and so near Cannes. The entrance (easily missed) has large electronic gates that ensure that the site is very secure. There are only 115 pitches (40 mobile homes) so this is quite a small, personal site. There are three pitch sizes, from small ones for tents to pitches for larger units and all have electricity (6A), some fully serviced. All are level with much needed shade in summer, although the sun will get through in winter when it is needed. The site is alongside the Canal de Siagne and for a fee, small boats can be launched at La Napoule, then moored outside the campsite's side gate. Les Cigales is open all year so it is useful for the Monte Carlo Rally, the Cannes Film Festival and the Mimosa Festival, all held out of the main season. English is spoken.

Facilities

Well appointed, clean, heated toilet blocks. Facilities for babies and disabled visitors. Washing machine. Motorcaravan services. Restaurant and takeaway (April - Oct). Heated swimming pool and large sunbathing area (April - Oct). Small play area. Table tennis. Two games machines. Canal fishing. Off site: Beach 800 m. The town is an easy walk. Two golf courses within 1 km. Railway station 1 km. for trains to Cannes, Nice, Antibes, Monte Carlo. Hypermarket 2 km. Bus stop 10 minutes.

Open: All year.

Directions

From A8, exit 40, bear right. Remain in right hand lane, continue right signed Plages-Ports, Creche-Campings. Casino supermarket on right. Continue under motorway to T-junction. Turn left, site is 60 m. on left opposite Chinese restaurant.

Charges 2006

Per person	€ 5,50
child (under 5 yrs)	€ 2,75
tent	€ 11,50 - € 18,50
caravan or motorcaravan	€ 14,00 - € 28,50

Les Cigales ★★★★

Camping
Caravaning
Accommodation
Swimming pool
Lagoon for kids
Solarium
Private pontoon

Open all year
800m from the beaches
and golf

LES CIGALES
505 avenue de la Mer
06210 MANDELIEU LA NAPOULE
Tél. : + 33 493 49 23 53
Fax. : + 33 493 49 30 45
www.lescigales.com
Mail : campingcigales@wanadoo.fr

FR06140 Ranch Camping

Chemin Saint Joseph, F-06110 Le Cannet (Alpes-Maritimes)

Tel: **04 93 46 00 11**. Email: **dstallis@free.fr**

Ranch Camping is a well run 'French flavoured' site. The ambience here is calm and there is relatively little by way of entertainment or leisure amenities. The site is very well located for the beaches of Cannes just 2 km. away; a regular bus service runs past the site entrance. Despite its urban setting the site enjoys a tranquil position on a wooded hillside. There are 108 touring pitches which are generally level and well shaded, all with 6A electrical connections. The swimming pool is quite small and can be covered in low season. Other leisure facilities are nearby.

Facilities

Principal toilet block has been recently refurbished, whereas the second block is of 'portacabin' style. Both very clean and well maintained. Facilities for disabled people. Washing machines and dryers. Small shop. Swimming pool (covered in low season). Play area. Games room. Mobile homes, rooms to rent. Off site: Beach 2 km. Bus stop at site entrance (regular service to Cannes and beaches). Tennis 200 m. Fishing. bicycle hire 2 km. Golf 4 km.

Open: 1 April - 30 October.

Directions

From A8 exit 42 follow signs to Le Cannet, then L'Aubarède to the right (D809). Follow this road until signs for La Bocca and site is signed from here. GPS: N43:33.883 E06:58.661

Charges 2006

Per unit incl. 1 person	€ 10,00 - € 16,00
extra person	€ 6,00
child (5-10 yrs)	€ 3,00
electricity (6A)	€ 3,00

191

FR83020 Castel Camping Caravaning Esterel

Avenue des Golf, F-83530 St Raphaël – Agay (Var)

Tel: **04 94 82 03 28**. Email: **contact@esterel-caravaning.fr**

Esterel is a quality caravan site east of St Raphaël, set among the hills at the back of Agay. The site is 3.5 km. from the sandy beach at Agay where parking is perhaps a little easier than at most places on this coast. It has 230 pitches for tourists, for caravans but not tents, all have electricity and tap, 18 special ones have individual en-suite washroom adjoining. Pitches are on shallow terraces, attractively landscaped with good shade and a variety of flowers, giving a feeling of spaciousness. Some 'maxi-pitches' from 110 to 160 sq.m. are available with 10A electricity. Developed by the Laroche family for over 30 years, the site has an attractive, quiet situation with good views of the Esterel mountains. A member of 'Les Castels' group. Wild boar come to the perimeter fence each evening to be fed by visitors. This is a very good site, well run and organised in a deservedly popular area. A pleasant courtyard area contains the shop and bar, with a terrace overlooking the attractively landscaped (floodlit at night) pool complex.

Facilities

Excellent refurbished, heated toilet blocks. Individual toilet units on18 pitches. Facilities for disabled people. Laundry room. Motorcaravan services. Shop. Gift shop. Takeaway. Bar/restaurant. Five circular swimming pools (two heated), one for adults, one for children, three arranged as a waterfall (1/4-30/9). Disco. Archery. Minigolf. Tennis. Pony rides. Petanque. Squash. Playground. Nursery. Bicycle hire. Organised events in season. No barbecues. Off site: Golf nearby. Trekking by foot, bicycle or by pony in L'Esterel forest park. Fishing, beach 3 km.

Open: 1 April - 6 October.

Directions

From A8, exit Fréjus, follow signs for Valescure, then for Agay, site on left. The road from Agay is the easiest to follow but it is possible to approach from St Raphaël via Valescure.
GPS: N43:27.253 E06:49.945

Charges 2007

Per unit incl. 2 persons,	
standard pitch	€ 23,00 - € 38,00
'maxi' pitch	€ 28,00 - € 47,00
deluxe pitch	€ 32,00 - € 51,00
extra person	€ 8,50
child (1-7 yrs)	€ 6,50

FR83010 Camping Caravaning les Pins Parasols

Route de Bagnols, F-83600 Fréjus (Var)

Tel: **04 94 40 88 43**. Email: **lespinsparasols@wanadoo.fr**

Not everyone likes very big sites and Les Pins Parasols with its 189 pitches is of a comfortable size which is quite easy to walk around. It is family owned and run. Although on very slightly undulating ground, virtually all the pitches (all have electricity) are levelled or terraced and separated by hedges or bushes with pine trees for shade. There are 48 pitches equipped with their own fully enclosed, sanitary unit, with WC, washbasin, hot shower and dishwashing sink. These pitches naturally cost more but may well be of interest to those seeking extra comfort. The nearest beach is the once very long Fréjus-Plage (5.5 km.) now reduced a little by the new marina, and adjoins St Raphaël.

Facilities

Average quality toilet blocks (one heated) providing facilities for disabled people. Small shop with reasonable stocks, restaurant, takeaway (both 15/4-30/9). General room, TV. Swimming pool, attractive rock backdrop, separate long slide with landing pool, small paddling pool (heated). Half-court tennis. Off site: Bicycle hire or riding 2 km. Fishing 6 km. Golf 10 km. Bus from the gate into Fréjus 5 km. Beach 6 km.

Open: 31 March - 29 September.

Directions

From A8 take exit 38 for Fréjus Est. Turn right immediately on leaving pay booths on a small road which leads across to D4, then right again and under 1 km. to site.

Charges 2006

Per unit incl. 2 persons	
and electricity	€ 17,40 - € 25,50
pitch with sanitary unit	€ 22,00 - € 31,80
extra person	€ 4,40 - € 6,00
child (under 7 yrs)	€ 2,90 - € 3,65

FR83030 Camping Caravaning Leï Suves

Quartier du Blavet, F-83520 Roquebrune-sur-Argens (Var)

Tel: 04 94 45 43 95. Email: camping.lei.suves@wanadoo.fr

This quiet, pretty site is a few kilometres inland from the coast, two kilometres north of the N7. Close to the unusual Roquebrune rock, it is within easy reach of St Tropez, Ste Maxime, St Raphaël and Cannes. The site entrance is appealing – wide and spacious, with a large bank of well tended flowers. Mainly on a gently sloping hillside, the 310 pitches are terraced with shade provided by the many cork trees which give the site its name. All pitches have electricity and access to water. A pleasant pool area is beside the bar/restaurant and entertainment area. It is possible to walk in the surrounding woods as long as there is no fire alert. A good number of the pitches are used for mobile homes.

Facilities

Modern, well kept toilet blocks include washing machines, facilities for disabled visitors. Shop. Good sized swimming pool, paddling pool. Bar, terrace, snack bar, takeaway (all 1/4-30/9). Outdoor stage near the bar for evening entertainment, high season. Excellent play area. Table tennis, tennis, sports area. Internet terminal. Only gas barbecues. Off site: Bus stop at site entrance. Riding 1 km. Fishing 3 km. Bicycle hire 5 km. Golf 7 km. Beach at St Aygulf 15 km.

Open: 31 March - 14 October.

Directions

Leave autoroute at Le Muy and take N7 towards St Raphaël. Turn left at roundabout onto D7 heading north signed La Boverie (site also signed). Site on right in 2 km. GPS: N43:28.677 E06:38.324

Charges 2007

Per unit incl. 2 persons	€ 19,00 - € 32,50
incl. 3 persons	€ 21,00 - € 34,50
extra person	€ 4,50 - € 7,30
electricity	€ 4,50

Camping Cheques accepted.

FR83170 Camping Domaine de la Bergerie

Vallée du Fournel, route du Col du Bougnon, F-83520 Roquebrune-sur-Argens (Var)

Tel: **04 98 11 45 45**. Email: **info@domainelabergerie.com**

This excellent site near the Côte d'Azur will take you away from all the bustle of the Mediterranean to total relaxation amongst the cork, oak, pine and mimosa. The 60 hectare site is quite spread out with semi-landscaped areas for mobile homes and, grassy avenues of 200 separated pitches for touring caravans and tents. All pitches average over 80 sq.m. and have electricity, with those in one area also having water and drainage. The restaurant/bar, a converted farm building, is surrounded by shady patios, whilst inside it oozes character with high beams and archways leading to intimate corners. Activities are organised daily and, in the evening, shows, cabarets, discos, cinema, karaoke and dancing at the amphitheatre prove popular (possibly until midnight). A superb new pool complex supplements the original pool adding more outdoor pools with slides and a river feature, an indoor pool and a fitness centre with jacuzzi, sauna, massage and gym.

Facilities

Four toilet blocks (two refurbished) are kept clean and include washbasins in cubicles, facilities for disabled people and babies. Supermarket. Bar/restaurant. Takeaway. Pool complex (1/4-30/9) with indoor pool and fitness centre (body building, sauna, gym, etc). Tennis courts. Archery. Roller skating. Minigolf. Mini-farm for children. Fishing. Only gas barbecues are permitted. Off site: Riding or golf 4 km. Bicycle hire 7 km. Beach, St Aygulf or Ste Maxime 7 km. Water skiing and rock climbing nearby.

Open: 27 April - 30 September.
Mobile homes 15 February - 15 November.

Directions

Leave A8 at Le Muy exit on N7 towards Fréjus. Proceed for 9 km. then right onto D7 signed St Aygulf. Continue for 8 km. and then right at roundabout on D8; site is on the right. GPS: N43:24.547 E06:40.481

Charges 2006

Per unit incl. 2 persons and electricity (5A)	€ 17,00 - € 39,00
3 persons and electricity, water and drainage	€ 22,50 - € 41,00
extra person	€ 4,00 - € 7,30
child (under 7 yrs)	€ 3,00 - € 5,70
electricity (10A)	€ 1,80 - € 2,80

Check real time availability and at-the-gate prices...
www.alanrogers.com

FR83060 Camping Caravaning de la Baume

Route de Bagnols, F-83618 Fréjus (Var)

Tel: **04 94 19 88 88**. Email: **reception@labaume-lapalmeraie.com**

La Baume is large, busy site about 5.5 km. from the long sandy beach of Fréjus-Plage, with its fine and varied selection of swimming pools many people do not bother to make the trip. The pools with their palm trees are remarkable for their size and variety (water slides, etc.) – the very large 'feature' pool a highlight. The site has nearly 250 adequate size, fully serviced pitches, with some separators and most have shade. Although tents are accepted, the site concentrates mainly on caravanning. It becomes full in season but one section, with unmarked pitches, is not reserved. Adjoining La Baume is its sister site La Palmeraie, containing self-catering accommodation, its own landscaped pool and providing some entertainment to supplement that at La Baume. There are 500 large pitches with mains sewerage for mobile homes. La Baume's convenient location has its 'downside' as there is some traffic noise from the nearby autoroute – somewhat obtrusive at first but we soon failed to notice it. A popular site with tour operators. An indoor pool and an aquatic play area were added in 2006.

Facilities

Seven refurbished toilet blocks. Supermarket, several shops. Bar, terrace overlooking pools, TV. Restaurant, takeaway. Five swimming pools (heated all season, two covered, plus steam room and jacuzzi). Fitness centre. Tennis. Archery (July/Aug). Organised events, daytime and evening entertainment, some English. Amphitheatre. Discos daily in season. Children's club (all season). Off site: Bus to Fréjus passes gate. Riding 2 km. Fishing 3 km. Golf 5 km. Beach 5 km.

Open: 1 April - 30 September, with full services

Directions

From west, A8, exit 37 Fréjus, take N7 southwest, Fréjus, 4 km, turn left on D4. Site 3 km. From east, A8, exit 38 Fréjus, turn right immediately on small road marked Musée, shortly turn right D4. Site is 3 km. GPS: N43:27.992 E06:43.396

Charges 2007

Per unit incl. 2 persons, 6A electricity, water and drainage	€ 18,00 - € 39,00
extra person	€ 4,00 - € 10,00
child (under 7 yrs)	free - € 6,00
dog	€ 4,00 - € 5,00
car	€ 4,00 - € 5,00

Min. stay for motorhomes 3 nights. Large units should book.

FR83230 Domaine du Colombier

Route de Bagnols en Forêt, 1052 rue des Combattants d'AFN, F-83600 Fréjus (Var)

Tel: **04 94 51 56 01**. Email: **info@domaine-du-colombier.com**

Domaine du Colombier is a busy site alongside a main road, some pitches will have some road noise. The majority are down a hillside and pine trees help to deaden the noise. The 408 variable size, level, terraced pitches (268 for touring) with 40 fully serviced, all have electricity. The sunny pool area and snack bar are a long way from many pitches, at the bottom of the site. New planting of attractive trees and shrubs has taken place with gazebos being provided on many pitches to provide shade.

Facilities

Well maintained, fully equipped toilet blocks (two heated), baby rooms, units for people in wheelchairs. Laundry. Well stocked shop. Bar/restaurant, takeaway. Snack bar (from 1/6). Underground disco. Large heated swimming pool, paddling pool. Internet. Two excellent play areas. Games room, miniclub room. Half court tennis. Boules. No barbecues, communal provided. Off site: Bus passes gate.

Open: 8 March - 1 October.

Directions

From A8 exit 38, follow D4 for Fréjus. Site is on left, well signed. GPS: N43:26.750 E06:43.636

Charges guide

Per unit incl. 2 or 3 persons	€ 19,00 - € 43,00
extra person	€ 6,00 - € 7,50
child (under 10 yrs)	€ 4,00 - € 5,50

Camping Cheques accepted.

kawan-villages.com **tel: 00 333 59 59 03 59** *kawa*

La Baume ★★★★
Camping - Caravaning

La Palmeraie ★★
Résidence de Tourisme

Fréjus Côte d'Azur

…eated sanitary blocks, marked-out …ches, 6 swimming pools, 2 covered …ated swimming pool, 6 water-slides. …kilometers from the sandy beaches of …éjus and Saint Raphaël.

On going entertainment
Cabaret, Show, Disco,
Children's club during the season

Le Sud Grandeur Nature

Heated swimming pool

1 covered heated swimming-pool

Provençal chalet,
Mobil-homes 4/6 persons
and Appartementen 6 of 10 persons
for hire

Special rates in low season

Rue des Combattants d'Afrique du Nord   83618 FREJUS Cedex
Tel : + 33 494 19 88 88   -   Fax: + 33 494 19 83 50
www.labaume-lapalmeraie.com   E-mail : reception@labaume-lapalmeraie.com

FR83200 Camping Caravaning les Pêcheurs

F-83520 Roquebrune-sur-Argens (Var)

Tel: 04 94 45 71 25. Email: **info@camping-les-pecheurs.com**

Les Pêcheurs will appeal to families who appreciate natural surroundings together with many activities, cultural and sporting. Interspersed with mobile homes, the 150 good size, touring pitches (electricity 6/10A) are separated by trees or flowering bushes The Provencal style buildings are delightful, especially the bar, restaurant and games room, with its terrace down to the river and the site's own canoe station (locked gate). Across the road is a lake used exclusively for water skiing with a sandy beach, a restaurant and minigolf. This popular Riviera site has some new spa facilities including steam pool, a sauna and a Turkish bath. Developed over three generations by the Simoncini family, this peaceful, friendly site is set in more than four hectares of mature and well shaded countryside at the foot of the Roquebrune Rock. Activities include climbing the 'Rock' with a guide. We became more and more intrigued with stories about the Rock and the Holy Hole, the Three Crosses and the Hermit all call for further exploration which reception staff are happy to arrange, likewise trips to Monte Carlo, Ventimigua (Italy) and the Gorges du Verdon, etc. The medieval village of Roquebrune is within walking distance.

Facilities

Modern, refurbished, well designed toilet blocks, baby baths, facilities for disabled visitors. Washing machines. Shop. Bar, restaurant, games room (all open all season). Heated outdoor swimming pool (all season), separate paddling pool (lifeguard in high season), ice cream bar. Spa facilities. Playing field. Fishing. Canoeing, water skiing. Activities for children and adults (high season), visits to local wine caves. Rafting and diving schools. Only gas or electric barbecues. Off site: Bicycle hire 1 km. Riding 4 km. Golf 5 km. (reduced fees).

Open: 31 March - 30 September.

Directions

From A8 take Le Muy exit, follow N7 towards Fréjus for 13 km. bypassing Le Muy. After crossing A8, turn right at roundabout towards Roquebrune sur Argens. Site is on left after 1 km. just before bridge over river.

Charges 2007

Per unit incl. 2 persons	€ 17,00 - € 32,50
incl. 3 persons	€ 19,00 - € 34,50
electricity (6/10A)	€ 4,20 - € 5,20
dog (max. 1)	€ 3,00
Camping Cheques accepted.	

kawan-villages.com tel: **00 333 59 59 03 59**

kawan

UN JARDIN EN PROVENCE

10 km away from the beaches of Fréjus St Raphaël, calm and shady. Wellness : spa, spa aqua trainer, sauna, Restaurant, canoeing, Mini tennis Mini golf, Family atmosphere, Rental of mobile homes, Cycle tracks to the beach, Wifi.

Camping ★★★★ Caravaning Les Pêcheurs
83520 Roquebrune sur Argens
Tél : 00 33 (0)4 94 45 71 25   Fax : 00 33 (0)4 94 81 65 13
www.camping-les-pecheurs.com

FR83220 Camping Caravaning Cros de Mouton

P.O. 116, F-83240 Cavalaire-sur-Mer (Var)

Tel: **04 94 64 10 87**. Email: **campingcrosdemouton@wanadoo.fr**

Cros de Mouton is a reasonably priced campsite in a popular area. High on a steep hillside, about 2 km. from Cavalaire and its popular beaches, the site is a calm oasis away from the coast. There are stunning views of the bay but, due to the nature of the terrain, some of the site roads are very steep – the higher pitches with the best views are especially so. There are 199 large, terraced pitches (electricity 10A) under cork trees with 73 suitable only for tents with parking close by, and 80 for touring caravans. English is spoken by the welcoming and helpful owners. The restaurant terrace and the pools share the wonderful view of Cavalaire and the bay. Olivier and Andre are happy to take your caravan up with their 4x4 Jeep if you are worried.

Facilities

Clean, well maintained toilet blocks have all the usual facilities including those for disabled customers (although site is perhaps a little steep in places for wheelchairs). Washing machine. Shop. Bar/restaurant, reasonably priced meals, takeaways. Swimming and paddling pools with lots of sun beds on the terrace and small bar for snacks and cold drinks. Small play area. Games room. Off site: Beach 1.5 km. Bicycle hire 1.5 km. Riding 3 km. Golf 15 km.

Open: 15 March - 31 October.

Directions

Take the D559 to Cavalaire-sur-Mer (not Cavalière 4 km. away). Site is about 1.5 km. north of the town, very well signed from the centre.

Charges 2006

Per person	€ 6,00 - € 7,30
child (under 7 yrs)	€ 4,10
pitch	€ 6,00 - € 7,30
electricity (10A)	€ 4,10
dog	free - € 2,00

Camping Cheques accepted.

awan
tel: **00 333 59 59 03 59** *kawan-villages.com*

FR83070 Caravaning L'Etoile d'Argens

F-83370 Saint Aygulf (Var)

Tel: **04 94 81 01 41**. Email: **info@etoiledargens.com**

First impressions of L'Etoile d'Argens are of space, cleanliness and calm. This is a site run with families in mind and many of the activities are free, making for a good value holiday. There are 493 level, fully serviced, grass pitches (265 for touring units – 10A electricity), separated by hedges, with five sizes, ranging from 50 sq.m. (for small tents) to 250 sq.m. mainly with good shade. The pool and bar area is attractively landscaped with olive and palm trees on beautifully kept grass. Two heated pools (one for adults, one for children) – both very much with families in mind. Reception staff are very friendly and English is spoken. The exceptionally large pitches could easily take two caravans and cars or one family could have a very spacious plot with a garden like atmosphere. The river runs alongside the site with a free boat service to the beach (15/6-15/9). This is a good family site for the summer but also good in low season for a quiet stay in a superb location with excellent pitches. Tour operators take 85 pitches and there are 175 mobile homes but for a large site it is unusually calm and peaceful even in July.

Facilities

Over 20, well kept, small toilet blocks. Supermarket and gas supplies. Bar, restaurant, pizzeria, takeaway. Two adult pools (heated 1/4-20/6), paddling pool, Jacuzzi, solarium. Floodlit tennis with coaching. Minigolf (both free in low season). Aerobics. Archery (July/Aug). Football and swimming lessons. Boules. Good play area. Children's entertainment (July/Aug). Activity programme with games, dances and escorted walking trips to the surrounding hills within 3 km. Off site: Golf and riding 2 km. Beach 3.5 km.

Open: 1 April - 30 September, with all services.

Directions

From A8 exit 36, take N7, Le Muy, Fréjus. After 8 km. at roundabout take D7 signed Roquebrune, St Aygulf. In 9.5 km. (after roundabout) turn left signed Fréjus. Site signed. Ignore width and height limit signs as site is before limit (500 m). GPS: N43:24.947 E06:42.326

Charges 2006

Per tent pitch (100 sq.m.) with electricity and 2 persons	€ 20,00 - € 45,00
'comfort' pitch (130 sq.m.) incl. 3 persons with water and drainage	€ 32,00 - € 56,00
'luxury' pitch incl. 4 persons 180 sq.m	€ 38,00 - € 64,00
extra person	€ 5,00 - € 8,00
child (under 7 yrs)	€ 4,00 - € 6,00

FR83240 Camping Caravaning Moulin des Iscles

Quartier La Valette, F-83520 Roquebrune-sur-Argens (Var)

Tel: **04 94 45 70 74**. Email: **moulin.iscles@wanadoo.fr**

Moulin des Iscles is a small, pretty site beside the river Argens with access to the river in places for fishing, canoeing and swimming with some sought after pitches overlooking the river. The 90 grassy, level pitches have water and electricity (6A) and a mixture of trees provides natural shade. There is a security barrier which is closed at night. This is a quiet site with little entertainment, but a nice restaurant. Handicapped visitors are made very welcome. It is a real campsite not a 'camping village'.

Facilities

Fully equipped toilet block, plus small block near entrance, ramped access for disabled visitors. Some Turkish style toilets. Washbasins have cold water. Baby bath and changing facilities. Washing machine. Restaurant, home cooked dish-of-the-day. Well stocked shop. Library - some English books. TV, pool table, table tennis. Play area, minigolf, boules all outside the barrier. Internet terminal. Canoeing possible. Off site: Riding and golf 4 km. Bicycle hire 1 km. (cycle way to St Aygulf). Beach 9 km.

Open: 1 April - 30 September.

Directions

From A8, exit Le Muy, follow N7 towards Fréjus for 13 km. Cross over A8 and turn right at roundabout through Roquebrune sur Argens towards St Aygulf for 1 km. Site signed on left. Follow private unmade road for 500 m. GPS: N43:26.708 E06:39.470

Charges 2006

Per unit incl. 2 or 3 persons	€ 19,50
extra person	€ 3,20
electricity	€ 2,70
Camping Cheques accepted.	

2007

L'Etoile d'Argens

✳ ✳ ✳ ✳ *Camping-Caravaning*

ESE COMMUNICATION - DRAGUIGNAN - 04 94 67 06 00

www.etoiledargens.com
E-mail : info@etoiledargens.com
83370 St Aygulf - Tél. +33 4 94 81 01 41

FR83410 Camping Club le Ruou

Les Esparrus RD 560, F-83690 Villecroze-Les Grottes (Var)

Tel: **04 94 70 67 70**. Email: **camping.lervou@wanadoo.fr**

This is a family oriented site in the Provencal countryside, very much geared for family holidays with children. Some 45 minutes by car from the coast at Fréjus, the site has a large and well kept pool area and a mobile stage for entertainment. Smaller than some other sites of this type, there are 110 good sized pitches (52 for touring units). On mainly terraced, rather stony, ground with good shade, all have 6/10A electricity. Some of the pitches for caravans are along a steep path but there is a 4x4 available to assist. The attractive pool complex with three slides is surrounded by a sunbathing area and some shade. Although Le Ruou has all the facilities, activities and entertainment expected of a holiday site, the atmosphere is very relaxed and much less frenzied than some similar sites. Outdoor activities, such as canoeing or rafting are personally arranged for you by the campsite owner.

Facilities

One new super de-luxe toilet block includes washbasins in cabins. Facilities for babies and disabled visitors. Laundry facilities. Snacks and takeaway (15/6-31/8). The main building houses a bar and entertainment room with TV. Area for shows, cabarets, etc. with mobile stage. Two swimming pools. Riding. Tennis. Boules. Miniclub for children and evening entertainment in season. Off site: Beach 30 km. Riding and bicycle hire 5 km. Fishing 10 km. Golf 17 km.

Open: 1 April - 30 October.

Directions

Directions: Villecroze-les-Grottes is northwest of Fréjus. From the A8 (Toulon - Mandelieu-la-Napoule) take exit 13 onto the N7 towards Le Muy. At Les Arcs turn left on D955 (Draguignan), then onto D557 to Villecroze. Site is on the left side of this road. GPS: N43:33.207 E06:17.879

Charges 2006

Per unit incl. 2 persons	€ 13,00 - € 21,00
extra person	€ 3,00 - € 5,00
child (2-9 yrs)	€ 2,00 - € 4,00
electricity (6/10A)	€ 2,00 - € 3,00

The biggest waterslide of the region – heated swimming pool – Wifi – Fitness

Le Ruou

Camping Club Le Ruou ★★★
83690 Villecroze les Grottes
Tél : 00 33 4 94 70 67 70
Fax : 00 33 4 94 70 64 65
E-mail : camping.leruou@wanadoo.fr

In the of the Provence between the sea and the Verdon river

www.leruou.com

Bar, take away, pool complex, sport area, large play ground. Childrensclub. Daily organised activities.
Mobile homes for rent

Camping Qualite

FR83250 Camping Douce Quiétude

3435 boulevard Jacques Baudino, F-83700 St Raphaël (Var)

Tel: **04 94 44 30 00**. Email: **sunelia@douce-quietude.com**

Douce Quiétude is five kilometres from the beaches at Saint Raphaël and Agay but is quietly situated at the foot of the Estérel massif. There are 400 pitches, only 70 of these are for touring set in pleasant pine woodland or shaded, green areas. The pitches are of a comfortable size, separated by bushes and trees with electricity (6A), water, drainage and telephone/TV points provided. This mature site offers a wide range of services and facilities complete with a pool complex. It can be busy in the main season yet is relaxed and spacious.

Facilities

Fully equipped modern toilet blocks, facilities for babies and disabled visitors. Launderette. Bar, restaurant, takeaway, pizzeria (3/4-3/9). Shop. Three swimming pools (two heated), water slide, Jacuzzi. Play area. Children's club, activities for teenagers (all July/Aug). Sports area. Games room. Tennis. Minigolf. Archery. Fitness centre, sauna. Evening entertainment (July/Aug). Mountain bike hire. Only gas barbecues. Off site: Bus route 1 km. Golf and riding 2 km. Windsurf hire and sea fishing 5 km.

Open: 3 April - 2 October.

Directions

From A8 exit 38 (Fréjus/St Raphaël) take D100, signed Valescure then Agay. Follow site signs (round the back of Fréjus/St Raphaël). Access via N98 coast road turning north at Agay on D100. Pass Esterel Camping. Site signed. GPS: N43:26.836 E06:48.360

Charges 2006

Per unit incl. 2 persons and electricity	€ 25,00 - € 46,00
extra person	€ 5,00 - € 9,00
Camping Cheques accepted.	

kawan-villages.com tel: **00 333 59 59 03 59**

kawan
VILLAGES CAMPINGS

Check real time availability and at-the-gate prices...

www.alanrogers.com

FR20040 Riva Bella Nature Resort & Spa

B.P. 21, F-20270 Alèria (Haute-Corse)

Tel: 04 95 38 81 10. Email: riva-bella@wanadoo.fr

This is a relaxed, informal, spacious naturist site alongside an extremely long and beautiful beach. Riva Bella is naturist camping at its very best, with great amenities. It offers a large number and variety of pitches, situated in a huge area of varied and beautiful countryside and seaside. It is difficult to believe that it could become overcrowded. The site is divided into several areas – pitches and bungalows, alongside the sandy beach, in a wooded glade with ample shade, or beside the lake, a feature of this site. Although electricity is available in most parts, a long cable may be needed.

Facilities

Refurbished, high standard toilet facilities, typical of naturist sites, facilities for disabled people and babies. Large shop (25/4-15/10). Fridge hire. Restaurant (all season) with reasonable prices. Snack bar. Watersports, sailing school, fishing, sub-aqua. Therapy centre. Sauna. Volleyball, aerobics, table tennis, giant draughts, archery. Fishing. Mountain bike hire. Half-court tennis. Walk with llamas. No barbecues. Interesting evening entertainment programme. Off site: Riding 5 km.

Open: 8 April - 1 November.

Directions

Site is 8 km. north of Aleria on N198 (Bastia) road. Watch for signs and unmade road to it and follow for 4 km. GPS: N42:09.598 E09:32.64

Charges guide

Per unit incl. 2 persons	€ 17,00 - € 31,00
extra person	€ 4,00 - € 8,50
child (3-8 yrs)	€ 2,00 - € 5,00
electricity	€ 3,80
dog	€ 3,00 - € 3,00

Camping Cheques accepted.

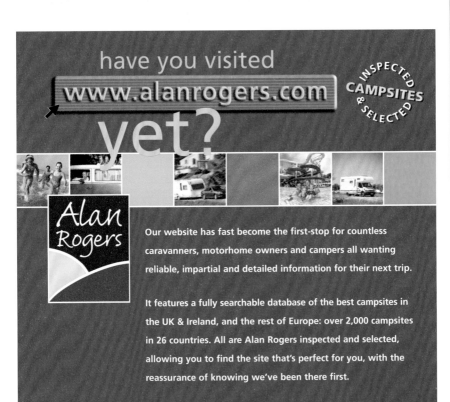

The Leading Campsites
in Europe

LeadingCampings – the pleasure of leisure.

We create that high level touring camping that you deserve for the most precious weeks of the year. 32 LeadingCampings throughout Europe guarantee first class vacations: in tent, caravan, motorcaravan or a wide range of rental accommodation. Enjoy also first class wellness spas, restaurants, sports and entertainment facilities. In this camping guide all entries of LeadingCampings are highlighted as 'member of the LeadingCampings'. Visit us on internet, order your personal LeadingCard and profit from all its benefits. You are welcome!

www.leadingcampings.com

LeadingCampings

MAP 6

With its wealth of scenic and cultural interests, Germany is a land of contrasts. From the flat lands of the north to the mountains in the south, with forests in the east and west, regional characteristics are a strong feature of German life and present a rich variety of folklore and customs.

CAPITAL: BERLIN

Tourist Office

German National Tourist Office
PO Box 2695. London W1A 3TN
Tel: 020 7317 0908
Fax: 020 7495 6129
Email: gntolon@d-z-t.com
Internet: www.germany-tourism.co.uk

Each region in Germany differs greatly to the next. Home of lederhosen, beer and sausages is Bavaria in the south, full of charming forest villages, beautiful lakes, and towering mountains dotted with castles. In the southwest, Baden Württemberg is famous for its ancient Black Forest, with dense woodlands, medieval towns and scenic lakes, this region is a walker's paradise. Further west is the stunningly beautiful, Rhine Valley full of romantic castles, wine villages, woodland walks and river trails. Eastern Germany is studded with lakes and rivers, undulating lowlands that give way to mountains. The north has its lively ports such as Bremen and Hamburg and picturesque coastal towns, where watersports are a popular pastime in the North Sea. The capital city of Berlin, situated in the northeast of the county, is an increasingly popular tourist destination, with its blend of old and modern architecture and huge variety of entertainment on offer.

Population
83.2 million

Climate
Temperate climate. In general winters are a little colder and summers a little warmer than in the UK.

Language
German

Telephone
The country code is 00 49.

Money
Currency: The Euro
Banks: Mon-Fri 08.30-12.30 and 14.00-16.00. Late opening on Thurs until 18.00.

Shops
Mon-Fri 08.30/09.00 to 18.00/18.30.

Public Holidays
New Year's Day; Good Fri; Easter Mon; Labour Day; Ascension; Whit Mon; Unification Day 3 Oct; Christmas, 25, 26 Dec. In some areas: Epiphany 6 Jan; Corpus Christi 22 Jun; Assumption 15 Aug; Reformation 31 Oct; All Saints 1 Nov (plus other regional days).

Motoring
An excellent network of (toll-free) motorways (autobahns) exists in the 'West' and the traffic moves fast. Remember in the 'East' a lot of road building is going on amongst other works so allow plenty of time when travelling and be prepared for poor road surfaces.

fDE3005 Camping Schnelsen Nord

Wunderbrunnen 2, D-22457 Hamburg (Hamburg)

Tel: **040 5594225**. Email: **service@campingplatz-hamburg.de**

Situated some 15 km. from the centre of Hamburg on the northern edge of the town, Schnelsen Nord is a suitable base either for visiting this famous German city, or as a night stop before catching the Harwich ferry or travelling to Denmark. A large number of trees and shrubs offer shade and privacy. There is some traffic noise because the autobahn runs alongside (despite efforts to screen it out) and also some aircraft noise. However, the proximity of the A7 (E45) does make it easy to find. The 145 pitches for short-term touring are of about 100 sq.m, on grass with access from gravel roads. All have 6A electricity, are numbered and marked out with small trees and hedges.

Facilities

A deposit is required for the key to the single sanitary block, a modern building with good quality facilities and heated in cool weather. Good facilities for disabled visitors, with special pitches close to the block. Washing machines and dryers. Motorcaravan service point (for site guests only). Shop (basics only). Playground. Off site: Swimming pool, tennis, golf and fishing nearby.

Open: 1 April - 31 October.

Directions

From A7 autobahn take Schnelsen Nord exit. Stay in outside lane as you will soon need to turn back left; follow signs for Ikea store and site signs. GPS: N53:38.998 E09:55.736

Charges 2007

Per person	€ 6,00
child (3-13 yrs)	€ 3,50
pitch	€ 7,20 - € 7,40

DE3021 Camping am Stadtwaldsee

Hochschulring 1, D-28359 Bremen (Bremen)

Tel: **0421 8410748**. Email: **contact@camping-stadtwaldsee.de**

This well designed and purpose built campsite overlooking a lake was opened in October 2005 and is ideally placed for those travelling to northern Europe and for people wishing to visit Bremen and places within the region. There is a bus stop outside the site. Of the 220 level pitches 168 are for touring units, standing on grass with openwork reinforcements at the entrances. All have electricity (16A), water and drainage. The pitches are positioned around the grass roofed sanitary block and are laid out in areas separated by young trees and hedges.

Facilities

Modern sanitary block with free hot showers, facilities for disabled people, five private bathrooms for rental. Laundry with washing machines and dryers. Kitchen. Children's play room. Lakeside café/restaurant. Small supermarket. Health centre with fitness courses. Play area. Lake swimming, FKK beach three minutes walk away. Windsurfing, fishing and scuba diving possible on lake. Off site: Riding 8 km. Golf 10 km.

Open: All year.

Directions

From A27 autobahn northeast of Bremen take exit 19 for 'Universitat' and follow signs for University and camping. Site is on the left 1 km. after leaving the university area. GPS: N53:06.890 E08:49.948

Charges 2006

Per person	€ 7,00
child (3-14 yrs)	€ 4,00
pitch	€ 5,50 - € 10,00
electricity (per KwH)	€ 0,50

DE3010 Kur und Feriencamping Röders Park

Ebsmoor 8, D-29614 Soltau (Lower Saxony)

Tel: **05191 2141**. Email: **info@roeders-park.de**

Although near Soltau centre (1.5 km), Ebsmoor is a peaceful location, ideal for visits to the famous Luneburg Heath or as a stop on the route to Denmark. Röders' Park is also close to the Soltau spa pool. The site has 100 pitches (90 touring), all with 6A electricity and 85 with water and drainage. Some 40 pitches have satellite TV connections. Most have hardstanding and there is reasonable privacy between pitches. The site is run by the third generation of the Röders family who make their visitors most welcome and speak excellent English.

Facilities

Two modern, very clean sanitary blocks (one with under-floor heating) contain all necessary facilities with a laundry room and an excellent, separate unit (including shower) for wheelchair users. Private bathrooms for rent. Motorcaravan services. Gas supplies. Shop. Restaurant and takeaway (all Easter - Oct). Play area. Bicycle hire. Internet (free), WiFi (on payment). Off site: Thermal swimming pool 1 km. Fishing and riding 1.5 km.

Open: All year.

Directions

From Soltau take B3 road north and turning to site is on left after 1.5 km. (opposite DCC camping sign) at yellow town boundary sign. GPS: N53:00.133 E09:50.317

Charges 2006

Per person	€ 5,50
child (4-14 yrs)	€ 4,00
pitch	€ 11,50

DE3025 Alfsee Ferien-und Erholungspark

Am Campingpark 10, D-49597 Rieste (Lower Saxony)

Tel: **05464 92120**. Email: **info@alfsee.com**

Improvements to this already well-equipped site continue. There are now over 800 pitches (many long stay but with 400 for tourers) on flat grass, 85 with 16A electricity, with some shade for those in the original area. A new camping area provides 290 large, serviced pitches. Alfsee offers a really good base for enjoying the many watersports activities available here on the two lakes. This site has plenty to offer for the active family and children of all ages. The smaller lake has a 780 m. water-ski 'tug' ski lift style (on payment) and there is also a separate swimming area here with a sandy beach (and beach volleyball). A little further along is a 600 m. go-kart track and a smaller track for youngsters. The Alfsee itself is a very large stretch of water with a sailing school, windsurfing, motor boats, row boats, canoes and pedaloes as well as fishing and a café/restaurant open daily. Member of Leading Campings Group.

Facilities

Three older, but still very good sanitary blocks serve the original area with two new first class, heated buildings with family bathrooms (to rent), baby rooms and laundry facilities. Washing machines and dryers. Cooking facilities. Motorcaravan services. Gas supplies. Shop, restaurants and takeaway. Pub and internet point. Watersports. Football practice field. New playground and entertainment for children. Grass tennis courts. Minigolf. Go-kart track. Fishing. Bicycle hire. Riding. Off site: Golf 8 km.

Open: All year.

Directions

From A1 autobahn north of Osnabrück take exit 67 for Neuenkirchen and follow signs for Rieste, Alfsee and site. GPS: N52:29.158 E07:59.529

Charges 2007

Per person	€ 3,20 - € 6,20
child or student	€ 2,90 - € 4,20
pitch	€ 8,10 - € 12,50
electricity (once only plus meter)	€ 1,00
dog	€ 2,50 - € 3,50

DE3055 Camping Prahljust

Lange Brüche 4, D-38678 Clausthal-Zellerfeld (Lower Saxony)

Tel: **05323 1300**. Email: **camping@prahljust.de**

In a woodland setting, 600 metres high and well away from main roads Camping Prahljust is a quiet site providing plenty of fresh air in an attractive location. The site slopes gently down to a lake which is used for swimming, boating, windsurfing and fishing or in winter ice skating. Of the 800 plus pitches 500 are reserved for tourists. These are arranged in larger open, grass areas separated by hedges with plenty of tree cover and all have electrical connections. The Oberharz is a winter sports region and January and February are the busiest months, with cross-country skiing from the site. During the rest of the year this attractive region has much to offer, rambling, mountain-biking and rock climbing are all popular and the list of interesting places to visit is almost unending.

Facilities

Modern, heated toilet blocks are well maintained and hold all the usual facilities. Showers are free. Facilities for disabled people. Baby room. Washing machines, dryers, drying room and kitchen. Motorcaravan service point and chemical disposal facilities. Shop, restaurant and bar (closed November). Indoor, heated pool (12 x 9 m; no shallow end). Sauna and solarium. Bicycle hire.

Open: All year.

Directions

Leave Clausthal-Zellerfeld on the B242 towards Braunlage. After 1 km. site is signed. Turn south and site is a further 1.5 km. GPS: N51:47.066 E10:20.985

Charges 2007

Per person	€ 4,70
pitch	€ 4,80
electricity per kWh	€ 0,55
Winter charges higher.	

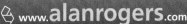

DE3065 Camping am Bärenbache

Bärenbachweg 10, Hohegeiss, D-38700 Braunlage (Lower Saxony)

Tel: 05583 1306. Email: info@campingplatz-hohegeiss.de

Pleasantly situated and over 600 metres high in the Harz, Campingplatz Bärenbache is a quiet, attractive, well run family site having direct access to the forests that surround it. This terraced site on a south facing slope reaps the maximum benefit from the sun throughout the year and offers views of the surrounding hills in an area known for its fresh air. At the lower end of the site is a large, heated, outdoor swimming pool complex adjoined by a bar/restaurant. Of the 140 pitches 90 are reserved for tourists all having 10A electrical connections. The level pitches are separated by hedges and are of various sizes, some suitable for one, others for several units. The Harz is a region steeped in geological, mythical, industrial and cultural history and the reception has a good selection of tourist information. In addition, the site owners are only too happy to give tourist advice. Roses, rambling, narrow gauge railways, witches, mines, mineral collections and medieval towns such as Goslar, all have their place in this fascinating region.

Facilities

As can be expected in a site that also has a winter season, all facilities are housed internally in the modern, well maintained and heated toilet block. Showers are free. Baby room. Laundry room with washing machines, dryers and iron, drying room. Small kitchen with cooking rings. Bar/restaurant (all year) beside the pool. Large outdoor heated pool with two separate pools for children. Playground. Off site: Shopping in the village centre is only a few minutes walk from the campsite.

Open: All year.

Directions

The village of Hohegeiß is 10 km. southeast of Braunlage on the B4 road. Leaving Hohegeiß in the direction of Zorge. site is signed.

Charges 2006

Per person	€ 4,10 - € 4,80
child (2-15 yrs)	€ 2,50 - € 2,90
pitch	€ 4,90
electricity per kWh	€ 0,50

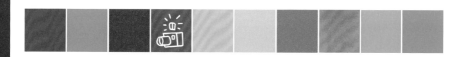

DE3070 Süd-See Camp

Lindhorstforst 66, D-29649 Wietzendorf (Lower Saxony)

Tel: 05196 98016. Email: forst28@suedseecamp.de

Südsee-Camp in the Lüneburger Heide is a large well organised holiday centre where children are especially well catered for. There are 1,000 touring pitches of varying types and sizes, all with electricity and most with fresh water, drainage and TV connection. The seven modern sanitary blocks are well maintained and contain all necessary facilities, including some areas specially built for children. Although centred around a large sandy shored lake, complete with ship wreck, the main swimming attraction is the South See Tropical swimming pool. This large, well designed glass roofed complex, has pools of different sizes with slides whirlpools and a pirate ship as well as a sauna, steam bath, sun benches and roof terrace. Adjoining is an outdoor pool. There is a full range of entertainment facilities and programmes for children of all ages. The campsite organises excursions to many interesting locations within the region. Next to the site is a stable with riding school. The reception has a wide range of tourist information brochures and, in addition, Südsee has its own brochures that include walking, cycling and car tours. In the reception good English is spoken and the staff are only too happy to help and advise. Member of Leading Campings Group.

Facilities

Seven, modern well maintained sanitary blocks with all the expected facilities, including facilities for disabled people and private bathrooms to rent. Hot showers need a token. Special areas for children (kinderland), facilities for babies. Laundry rooms. Kitchens. Choice of bars, restaurants and snack bars. Tropical swimming pool complex (charged). Disco. Fitness room. Bicycle and pedal car hire. Children's games room. Internet room.

Open: All year.

Directions

From A7 autobahn take exit 45 towards Bergen and Celle on the B3 (campsite is signed). After 6 km. turn left (site again signed).

Charges guide

Per unit incl. 2 persons	€ 18,00 - € 29,00
child (2-18 yrs)	€ 2,00 - € 2,50
electricity (10A)	€ 2,50

DE3080 Campingplatz am Hardausee

D-29556 Suderburg/Hosseringen (Lower Saxony)

Tel: 05826 7676. Email: info@camping-hardausee.de

The Hardausee site is evolving from a 'seasonals only' site into a site for touring units. When we visited, there were 80 touring pitches and 270 seasonal units, but as soon as a seasonal guest leaves, the pitch will be reallocated for touring. Hardausee is on sloping ground although the grassy, marked pitches are mostly level. Some pitches are numbered and most are 100 sq.m or larger. The newer pitches hardly have any shade, but mature trees surround the older field. There are now 28 serviced pitches with 16A electricity, water and drainage.

Facilities

Three toilet blocks, one heated and two refurbished, provide British style toilets, washbasins in cabins and free, controllable hot showers. Laundry with sinks, washing machines and dryer. Motorcaravan services. Shop (for basics). Bar, restaurant and takeaway (April - Oct, closed Mondays). Large adventure playground. Biking tours and excursions in the woods. Fishing. Lakeside beach. Off site: Riding 1 km. Bicycle hire 300 m.

Open: All year.

Directions

From Uelzen, follow 4/191 road south towards Braunschweig. Take exit for Suderburg and follow signs for Hösseringen. Site is signed on the right 2 km. before town. GPS: N52:52.475 E10:28.475

Charges 2007

Per person	€ 5,00
child (under 14 yrs)	€ 2,50
pitch incl. electricity	€ 7,00 - € 8,00

No credit cards.

DE3030 Regenbogen Camp Tecklenburg

Grafenstrasse 31, D-49545 Tecklenburg-Leeden (North Rhine-Westphalia)

Tel: 05405 1007. Email: tecklenburg@regenbogen-camp.de

This is a well designed and attractive countryside site with lots of trees and hedges where modern buildings have been built in keeping with the traditional, half timbered style of the region. The site has an excellent indoor and outdoor swimming pool complex. There are 500 grass touring pitches arranged on large, open areas divided by tall hedges. Trees provide good shade and all pitches have electrical connections. Access from the A30 autobahn is convenient, although this is offset by the fact that some noise from the autobahn is evident in the touring pitch area.

Facilities

Four modern, heated toilet blocks have free showers and provision for disabled visitors. Washing machines and dryer. Cooking facilities. Motorcaravan service point. Shop, bar and restaurant (Easter- end October and Christmas). Pool complex with indoor and outdoor pools and paddling pool. Play area. Minigolf.

Open: All year.

Directions

Leave A30/E30 autobahn at exit 13 towards Tecklenburg. Between the autobahn exit and Tecklenburg, at a roundabout, the site is signed.

Charges guide

Per person	€ 6,80
child (4-13 yrs)	€ 3,40
pitch incl. electricity	€ 12,50

DE3180 Camping Sonnenwiese

Borlefzen 1, D-32602 Vlotho (North Rhine-Westphalia)

Tel: 05733 8217. Email: info@sonnenwiese.com

Sonnenwiese is a first class, family run campsite where care has been taken to make everyone feel at home – there is even an insect hotel! The site is tastefully landscaped with lots of flowers, an ornamental pond crossed by a wooden bridge and large grass areas extending to the river. Situated between wooded hills to the north and bordering the river Weser to the south, this 500 pitch site offers 60 touring pitches, all with electricity and most also having water and drainage. In addition, there are special pitches with their own shower, toilet and washbasin unit. The site is particularly orientated towards families with children, having spacious play areas and in summer and at holiday weekends, entertainment programmes.

Facilities

The toilet block is modern and maintained to the highest standard. Showers are token operated. Baby room. Laundry room with washing machines, dryer and ironing board. Dishwashing sinks and cooking facilities. Supermarket. Panorama restaurant with good choice of dishes. Snack bar. Sauna, solarium and fitness room. Room used for children's entertainment. Large adventure play area. Lake for swimming. Fishing. Bicycle hire.

Open: All year.

Directions

Leave A2 autobahn at exit 31 or 33 just north of the bridge crossing The Weser in Vlotho is the signed turning for the campsite. After 3 km. on the right are the entrances to two campsites. Sonnenwiese is on the left at the end of the entrance road.

Charges 2007

Per person	€ 4,60
child (5-14 yrs)	€ 3,40
pitch incl. electricity (plus meter)	€ 8,50 - € 10,10

No credit cards.

DE3182 Ferienpark Teutoburger Wald

Fischteiche 4, D-32683 Barntrup (North Rhine-Westphalia)

Tel: 05263 2221. Email: info@ferienparkteutoburgerwald.de

Now under Dutch ownership, Ferienpark Teutoburger Wald is a long-established site which is rapidly undergoing redevelopment into a top-class site. The new toilet block has an ingenious system for water disposal, roomy showers and an attractive children's section. The site has 90 touring pitches, all 100-150 sq.m, and with 16A electricity. There are 8 with water, waste water and cable TV (Dutch and German channels). Although the site is on steep ground, most pitches are on level, grassy areas, with some shade from mature trees.

Facilities

Excellent, new heated toilet block with roomy showers (key), British style toilets and open washbasins. Attractive children's section. Family shower rooms (extra payment). Baby room. Washing machine, dryer, iron and board. Bread to order. Games room with internet. Animation team (high season). Children's disco. No twin axle caravans. Off site: Tennis, outdoor pool (free for campers) just outside gate. Barntrup town. Mountain bike trails.

Open: 20 March - 30 September.

Directions

From Hanover, take the A2 road west towards Osnabrück and at exit 35 continue on B83 road towards Hameln. In Hameln take the B1 road south towards Barntrup and follow signs. GPS: N51:59.209 E09:06.508

Charges 2006

Per pitch incl. 2 persons and electricity	€ 17,00 -	€ 31,00
extra person		€ 4,50

DE3185 Campingplatz Münster

Laerer Werseufer 7, (Wolbecker Strasse), D-48157 Münster (North Rhine-Westphalia)

Tel: 0251 311982. Email: campingplatz-muenster@t-online.de

This is a first class site on the outskirts of Münster. Of a total of 570 pitches, 120 are touring units, each with electricity, water, drainage and TV socket. The pitches are level, most with partial hardstanding and others are separated into groups by mature hedges and a number of trees provide shade. The university city of Münster with its many historical buildings and over five hundred bars and restaurants, many offering local traditional dishes, is only 5 km. from the site.

Facilities

The two toilet blocks are well designed, modern and maintained to the highest standards. Controllable showers are token operated. Two units for disabled guests. Baby room. Cooking facilities. Laundry room. Sauna and solarium. Hairdressing salon. Motorcaravan service point. Shop. Bar/restaurant. Minigolf. Play area. Tennis court. Play room. Bicycle hire. Off site: Public open air swimming pool, canoe paddling and fishing. Bus stop.

Open: All year.

Directions

Site is 5 km. southeast of Münster city centre. Leave A1 autobahn at exit 78 (Münster Süd) and take B51 towards Münster. After 2 km. stay on the B51 in the direction of Bielefeld/Warendorf. After 5 km. turn south (right) towards Wolbeck. WDR. Follow camping site signs. GPS: N51:56.784 E07:41.467

Charges 2006

Per unit incl. 3 persons and electricity (1 night)	€ 23,00
extra person	€ 4,00

DE3202 Erholungszentrum Grav-Insel

Gravinsel 1, D-46487 Wesel (North Rhine-Westphalia)

Tel: 0281 972830. Email: info@grav-insel.com

Grav-Insel claims to be the biggest family camping site in Germany, providing entertainment and activities to match, with over 2,000 permanent units as well as those for touring. It is a well maintained site, attractively situated on an island in the Rhine and is a good base for swimming (with a sandy beach by a quiet inlet), fishing and boating (with boat park). A long section for the touring units runs beside the water to the left of the entrance. The 500 pitches here are flat, grassy, mostly without shade and of about 100 sq.m. There are electricity boxes with multiple outlets (10/16A).

Facilities

Excellent, new sanitary facilities, augmented by older, very basic portacabin units in the touring area, have toilets with washbasins, some very large showers with triple sprays, baby room, launderette. Solarium. Supermarket. Restaurant (all year). Fishing. Swimming. Large play area on sand plus wet weather indoor area. Animation in high season. Boat park. Sailing. Off site: Bus service 500 m.

Open: All year.

Directions

Site is 5 km. WNW of the town of Wesel. From the A3 (Arnhem - Düsseldorf) take exit 6 and B58 towards Wesel, then right towards Rees. Turn left at sign for Flüren, through Flüren and left to site after 1.5 km. GPS: N51:40.237 E06:33.36

Charges guide

Per person	€ 3,00
child (under 12 yrs)	€ 1,50
pitch	€ 7,50
electricity	€ 3,00

DE3205 Campingplatz der Stadt Köln
Weidenweg 35, D-51105 Köln-Poll (North Rhine-Westphalia)

Tel: **0221 831966**. Email: **die-eckardts@netcologne.de**

This wooded park is pleasantly situated along the river bank, with wide grass areas (the manager takes great pains to keep it well) on either side of narrow tarmac access roads with low metal barriers separating it from the public park and riverside walks. Of 140 unmarked, level or slightly undulating touring pitches, 50 have 10A electricity and there is shade for some from various mature trees. Tents have their own large area. Because of its position close to the Autobahn bridge over the Rhine, there is road and river noise, but when we stayed the location and friendly atmosphere generated by the Eckhardt family, who have managed the site for 15 years, more than made up for it. The ancient city of Cologne offers much for the visitor, with many museums (including the popular Museum of Chocolate), art galleries, opera and open-air concerts, as well as the famous Cathedral. The 'Phantasialand' theme park is close at Brühl and Rhine cruises are another attraction.

Facilities
The small toilet block has fairly basic facilities, but is heated with free hot water (06.00-12.00, 17.00-23.00 hrs) in the washing troughs and by token in the showers. There is a large open-fronted room where you may cook, eat, and wash clothes and dishes (free hot water). Washing machine and dryer. Small shop opens in the mornings for bread and offers basic supplies (mid May-Sept). Microwave evening snacks (March-Oct). Fishing. Bicycle hire. Drinks machine. Off site: Bar/café by entrance. Trams and buses to city centre 1 km. across the bridge. Golf 5 km. Riding 15 km.

Open: Easter - 17 October.

Directions
Leave autobahn A4 at exit 13 for Köln-Poll (just to west off intersection of A3 and A4). Turn left at first traffic lights and follow site signs through a sometimes fairly narrow one-way system to the riverside, back towards the motorway bridge. GPS: N50:54.163 E06:59.44

Charges 2007

Per person	€ 5,50
child (4-12 yrs)	€ 2,50
pitch incl. car	€ 5,50 - € 6,50
electricity	€ 1,50

DE3210 Feriencamp Biggesee – Vier Jarheszeiten
Am Sonderner Kopf 3, D-57462 Olpe-Sondern (North Rhine-Westphalia)

Tel: **02761 944111**. Email: **info@biggesee-sondern.com**

Biggesee-Sondern is a high quality leisure complex and campsite, in an attractive setting on the shores of a large lake in the Südsauerland National Park, offering many leisure opportunities, as well as excellent camping facilities. It is therefore deservedly popular, and reservation is almost always advisable. Well managed, the same company also operates two other sites on the shores of the lake, where space may be available, which is useful as it is also popular for a short stay, being quite near the A45 and A4 roads. There are 300 flat or sloping numbered pitches of 100 sq.m, of which about 250 are available for tourists, either in rows or in circles, on terraces, with 6A electricity and water points grouped throughout. The leisure activities available are numerous. Watersports include diving, sailing and windsurfing, with lessons available. You may launch your own small boat, and also swim from the shore in a roped off area.

Facilities
Excellent sanitary facilities are in two areas, heated when necessary (bring your own paper). Many washbasins in cabins and special showers for children. Facilities for babies, laundry and people with disabilities. Motorcaravan services. Cooking facilities. Roller-skating. Playroom and playground for smaller children. Skiing. Watersports. Fishing. Bicycle hire. Solarium and sauna. Entertainment. Off site: Train service 1 km. Tennis near. Riding 8 km. Golf 12 km. Restaurant and snacks 300 m. (Easter-31/10).

Open: All year.

Directions
From A45 (Siegen-Hagen) autobahn, take exit 18 to Olpe (N), and turn towards Attendorn. After 6 km. turn right signed 'Erholungs anlage', then in another 100 m. turn right and follow campsite signs. GPS: N51:04.438 E07:51.39

Charges 2006

Per person	€ 3,90 - € 4,50
child (3-15 yrs)	€ 2,40 - € 2,50
pitch incl. electricity	€ 12,00 - € 14,00

No credit cards.

211

DE3002 Camping Park Schlei-Karschau

Karschau 56, D-24407 Rabenkirchen-Faulück (Schleswig-Holstein)

Tel: **04642 920820**. Email: **info@campingpark-schlei.de**

Schlei-Karschau is a pleasant, quiet site on the only Baltic Sea fjord in Germany. All you will hear is the wind from the sea and the calls of the birds. This site is ideal if you enjoy fishing or sailing, or you could visit one of the beaches on this coast, just 10 km. further on. The site has 160 open pitches, 100 for touring units, all with at least 6A electricity. Schlei-Karschau is not yet fully developed, but already completed are a fully equipped toilet block and a new playground. There is no shop as yet, but bread can be ordered from a kiosk and a restaurant with a bar and takeaway are open. Students provide an entertainment programme for children in high season with painting and crafts for toddlers and sporting events for older youngsters. There is no evening entertainment for adults but, after a hard day fighting with large fish or sails at sea you may prefer to relax in the restaurant or bar. Relaxing in front of your caravan or tent is another possibility – you are likely to see many rabbits passing by.

Facilities

The single, new sanitary block includes controllable hot showers in cabins with washbasin, child size toilets and washbasins and facilities for disabled visitors. Launderette with washing machines and dryers. Campers' kitchen with fridge. Motorcaravan services. Restaurant and bar (daily in high season). New playground. Sports field. Children's activity programme six days a week in high season. River fishing (permits from reception). Bicycle hire. Motor boat hire. Off site: Golf 4 km. Riding 6 km. Beach 10 km.

Open: All year.

Directions

Follow the A7 from Hamburg north to Flensburg and take exit Schleswig - Schuby. Take the B201 road towards Kappeln. Drive through Süderbrarup and turn right after 5 km. to Faulück. Follow signs to site. GPS: N54:37.176 E09:53.049

Charges 2006

Per person	€ 4,00 - € 5,00
child (1-14 yrs)	€ 2,00 - € 3,00
pitch	€ 8,00 - € 10,00
electricity and water	€ 2,50

Camping Cheques accepted.

DE3008 Klüthseecamp Seeblick

Klüthseehof 2, D-23795 Klein Rönnau (Schleswig-Holstein)

Tel: **04551 82368**. Email: **info@kluethseecamp.de**

Klüthseecamp Seeblick is a modern, family run site situated on a small hill between two lakes. For those travelling on the A1 to Denmark it is a convenient overnight site, but additionally it is a useful base to explore the region. The large, open grass, touring part of the site is divided into smaller areas by some low hedges and young trees. There are 120 pitches on fairly level ground, all with electricity (10/16A) and 70 with water and drain. The site has two other parts, one accommodating permanent campers, the other for those who prefer camping in natural surroundings. An attractive main building houses reception, a shop, a snack bar and most other facilities. The site has its own stables and plenty of open space for children to play. A half-covered, heated swimming pool overlooks a playground and playing field. Beside the lake is the site's restaurant with a beer garden serving local specialities and, of course, German wine and beer. Fishing and boating on the lake are popular.

Facilities

Two cheerful, modern, heated sanitary blocks have washbasins (open or in cabins), six bathrooms to rent and free controllable showers. Facilities for disabled visitors. Attractive baby room. Gas supplies. Laundry room. Sauna (Finish and Bio) steam bath, massage. TV room with projector. Children's play room. Bicycle hire. Minigolf. Off site: Golf 6 km. Beach 25 km.

Open: All year.

Directions

Leave A1 at exit 27 and travel north towards Kiel on the A 21 to exit 13 (Bad Segeberg Sud). Follow B432 (Hamburger Strasse) into Bad Segeberg and at T-junction turn left (north) and continue on B432. 300 m. Pass through Klein Rönnau turn right into Stripsdorferweg. GPS: N53:57.661 E10:20.289

Charges 2006

Per person	€ 4,90
child (under 14 yrs)	€ 2,50
pitch incl. electricity	€ 6,00 - € 9,40

DE3003 Camping Wulfener Hals

D-23769 Wulfen auf Fehmarn (Schleswig-Holstein)

Tel: 04371 86280. Email: camping@wulfenerhals.de

If you are travelling to Denmark or on to Sweden, taking the E47/A1 then B207 from Hamburg, and the ferry from Puttgarden to Rødbyhavn, this is a top class all year round site, either to rest overnight or as a base for a longer stay. Attractively situated by the sea, it is a large, mature site (34 hectares) and is well maintained. It has over 800 individual pitches of up to 160 sq.m. (half for touring) in glades and some separated by bushes, with shade in the older parts, less in the newer areas nearer the sea. There are many hardstandings and 552 pitches have electricity, water and drainage. A separate area has been recently developed for motorcaravans. It provides 60 extra large pitches, all with electricity, water and drainage, and some with TV aerial points, together with a new toilet block. There is much to do for old and young alike at Wolfener Hals, with a new heated outdoor pool and paddling pool (unsupervised), although the sea is naturally popular as well. The site also has many sporting facilities including its own golf courses and schools for watersports. Member of Leading Campings Group.

Facilities

Five heated sanitary buildings have first class facilities including showers on payment (€ 0.50) and both open washbasins and private cabins. Family bathrooms for rent. Facilities for disabled people. Dishwashing. Laundry. New motorcaravan services. Shop, bar and restaurants (one waiter, one self-service and takeaway (all year). Swimming pool (May-Oct). Sauna. Solarium. Jacuzzi. Sailing and windsurfing school. Diving school. Boat slipway. Golf courses (18 hole, par 72 and 9 hole, par 27). Roller skating. Riding. Fishing. Archery. Football area. Table tennis. Good play equipment for younger children. Bicycle hire. Catamaran hire. Only small dogs are accepted. Off site: Naturist beach 500 m. Village mini-market 2 km.

Open: All year.

Directions

From Hamburg take A1/E47 north to Puttgarden, cross the bridge onto the island of Fehmarn and turn right twice to Avendorf and follow the signs for Wulfen and the site. GPS: N54:24.386 E11:10.575

Charges 2007

Per unit incl. 2 persons	€ 11,60 - € 36,00
child (3-14 yrs)	€ 2,10 - € 5,30
electricity (6/10A)	€ 2,10 - € 2,90
water and drainage	€ 1,50
dog	€ 1,00 - € 7,50

Plus surcharges for larger pitches.
Many discounts available and special family prices.

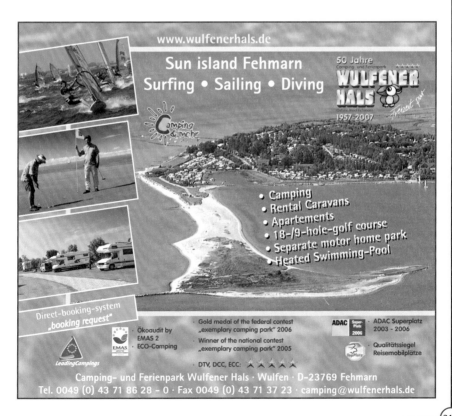

DE3827 Camping Sanssouci-Gaisberg

An der Pirschheide, Templiner See 41, D-14471 Potsdam (Brandenburg)

Tel: 0331 951 0988. Email: info@recra.de

Sanssouci is an excellent base for visiting Potsdam and Berlin, about 2 km. from Sanssouci Park on the banks of the Templiner See in a quiet woodland setting. Looking very attractive, reflecting the effort which has been put into its development, with modern reception, shop, takeaway, restaurant and bar. There are 240 pitches in total with some 90 odd being seasonal pitches but all the 150 touring pitches now have 6/10A electricity, many also with their own water and waste water connections. Tall trees mark out the tourist pitches, and access is good for larger units. There is a separate area for tents by the lake. Reception staff are helpful with English spoken and a comprehensive English language information pack has been prepared by the owners for local attractions. Free transport in the mornings and evenings is operated by the site to the nearby station. Tickets for public transport, boat trips and fishing can be bought at reception.

Facilities

Top class sanitary facilities are in two excellent, modern, heated blocks containing hot showers, washbasins in cabins and facilities for babies. Laundry. Very good facility for wheelchair users. A separate smaller toilet building also. Bathrooms to rent, kitchen, hairdresser and solarium. Gas supplies. Motorcaravan services. Restaurant/bar. Shop. Boats and pedaloes for hire. Fishing. Swimming in the lake. Play area. Bicycle hire. Internet café and WIFI Internet. Off site: The pool, sauna, solarium and skittle alley at the nearby Hotel Semiramis may (100 m.) be used by campers at a discount. Riding 3 km. Golf 10 km.

Open: 1 April - 4 November.

Directions

From A10 take Potsdam exit 22, follow B1 to within 4 km. of city centre then sign to right for camp just before the railway bridge. Or A10 exit 17 on the B2 into town and follow signs for Brandenburg/Werder. Site is southwest of Sanssouci Park on the banks of the Templiner See off Zeppelinstrasse 1.2 km. along a woodland drive. GPS: N52:21.514 E13:00.38

Charges 2007

Per person	€ 9,30
child (2-15 yrs)	€ 1,30
pitch incl. electricity	€ 8,90

Special low season offers. No credit cards.

DE3812 Seecamping Flessenow

Am Schweriner See 1A, D-19067 Flessenow (Mecklenburg-West Pomerania)

Tel: 03866 81491. Email: info@seecamping.de

Seecamping Flessenow is owned and run by an enthusiastic young, Dutch couple. It is right on the banks of the Schwerinner See and makes an ideal base for a beach holiday or for an active holiday on the water. There are 250 pitches of which 170 are for touring units, arranged on two rectangular fields to one side of a hardcore access lane (which can become muddy with heavy rain) and on one newer field to the rear of the site. Some pitches have views over the lake and these have some shade from mature trees. All the pitches are marked and numbered on level grass and separated by low wooden fences, all with 10A electricity and 45 with electricity, water and drainage. Centrally located on the site is a kiosk with covered terrace which also provides a takeaway service. The numerous watersport opportunities include a windsurfing school, sailing and some boats for high. In high season open air film nights are organised.

Facilities

Three toilet blocks (one older style) with British style toilets, open washbasins and controllable hot showers (token from reception). Baby room with shower. Dishwashing under cover. Washing machine and dryer. Motorcaravan services. Kiosk and takeaway (April - Oct; bread to order). Playground. TV room. Lake with beach. Fishing. Watersports. Riding. Bicycle hire. Boat launching. Sailing. Off site: Golf 20 km.

Open: April - October.

Directions

From Schwerin, take the A241 road north along the east side of the lake. At Schwerin Nord turn west towards Rampe and then north on a minor road towards Flessenow. Site is signed from there. GPS: N53:45.110 E11:19.780

Charges guide

Per unit incl. 2 persons	€ 14,00 - € 21,00
extra person	€ 3,50
child (4-13 yrs)	€ 2,00
electricity	€ 2,00

DE3820 Camping Park Havelberge am Woblitzsee

D-17237 Groß Quassow (Mecklenburg-West Pomerania)

Tel: 03981 24790. Email: info@haveltourist.de

The Müritz National Park is a very large area of lakes and marshes, popular for birdwatching as well as watersports, and Havelberge is a large, well-equipped site to use as a base for enjoying the area. It is quite steep in places here with many terraces, most with shade, less in newer areas, with views over the lake. There are 310 pitches in total with 140 good sized, numbered touring pitches most with 10A electrical connections and 60 pitches on a newly developed area to the rear of the site with water and drainage. Pitches on the new field are level and separated by low hedges and bushes but have no shade. Over 170 seasonal pitches with a number of attractive chalets and an equal number of mobile homes in a separate areas. In the high season this is a busy park with lots going on to entertain families of all ages, whilst in the low seasons this is a peaceful base for exploring an unspoilt area of nature. Member of Leading Campings Group.

Facilities

Four sanitary buildings (one new and of a very high standard) provide very good facilities, with private cabins, showers on payment and large children's section. Dishwashing, fully equipped kitchen and laundry. Motorcaravan service point. Small shop and modern restaurant (May - Sept). The lake provides fishing, swimming from a small beach and non-powered boats can be launched - canoes, rowing boats, windsurfers and bikes can be hired. Play areas and animation in high season. Volleyball. Internet access. Off site: Riding 3.5 km.

Open: All year.

Directions

From A19 Rostock - Berlin road take exit 18 and follow B198 to Wesenberg and go left to Klein Quassow and follow site signs.

Charges 2007

Per person	€ 3,80 - € 6,10
child (2-14 yrs)	€ 1,60 - € 4,10
caravan and car	€ 5,20 - € 12,00
tent	€ 3,50 - € 6,70
motorcaravan	€ 4,20 - € 7,20

Camping-und Ferienpark
Havelberge ★★★★★
am Woblitzsee
Mecklenburg lake district

Holiday at the countryside of a 1000 seas

Restaurant Havelberge with Sea-terrace

Holiday homes, rental caravans and mobil homes beautyfully situated

Canoe centre with school, hire and watertours

Gold medal of the federal contest „exemplary camping park in germany" 2006

Camping- und Ferienpark Havelberge • 17237 Groß Quassow
Tel. 0049 (0) 39 81 24 79 - 0 • Fax 0049 (0) 39 81 24 79 - 99
Haveltourist   www.haveltourist.de • info@haveltourist.de

ADAC Auszeich-nung 2006   LeadingCampings   EMAS

215

DE3833 Camping und Freizeitpark LuxOase

Arnsdorfer Straße 1, Kleinröhrsdorf, D-01900 Dresden (Saxony)

Tel: 035952 56666. Email: info@luxoase.de

This is a pleasantly situated new park about half an hour from the centre of Dresden, in a very peaceful location with good facilities. It is owned and run by a progressive young family. On open grassland with views across the lake (access to which is through a gate in the site fence) to the woods and low hills beyond, this is a sun-trap with little shade at present. There are 138 large touring pitches (plus 50 seasonal in a separate area), marked by bushes or posts on generally flat or slightly sloping grass. All have 10/16A electricity and 100 have water and waste water facilities. At the entrance is an area of hardstanding (with electricity) for late arrivals. The main entrance building houses the amenities and in front of the building is some very modern play equipment on bark. You may swim, fish or use inflatables in the lake. Entertainment is organised for children in high season. There are many interesting places to visit apart from Dresden and Meissen, with the fascinating National Park Sächsische Schweiz (Saxon Switzerland) on the border with the Czech Republic offering some spectacular scenery. Boat trips on the Danube can be taken from the tourist centres of Königstein and Bad Schandau and Saxony is also famous for its many old castles, for which an English language guide is available. Bus trips organised to Prague. Member of Leading Campings Group.

Facilities

A well equipped sanitary building provides modern, heated facilities with private cabins, a family room, baby changing room, units for disabled visitors and two units for hire. Jacuzzi. Rooms for cooking, laundry and dishwashing. Gas supplies. Motorcaravan services. Shop (am. All year, pm. In high season). Bar and restaurant with good value meals (Apr - Oct evenings and w/end lunchtimes). Bicycle hire. Lake swimming. Sports field with basketball and volleyball. Fishing. Play area enlarged and with much new equipment. Sauna. Train, bus and theatre tickets from reception. Internet point. Minigolf. Fitness room. Regular guided bus-trips to Dresden, Prague etc. Off site: Riding next door (lessons available). Public transport to Dresden 1 km. Golf 7.5 km. Nearby Dinosaur park, zoo and indoor karting etc.

Open: All year (phone in winter).

Directions

From A4 (Dresden - Görlitz) take exit 85 towards Radeberg, soon following signs to site via Leppersdorf and Kleinröhrsdorf.
GPS: N51:07.221 E13:58.78

Charges 2007

Per person	€ 5,00 - € 6,00
child (2-15 yrs)	€ 2,50 - € 4,00
motorcaravan or caravan/car	€ 7,50 - € 8,00
tent	€ 7,00 - € 7,50
electricity	€ 2,00

Various special offers in low season.

DE3836 Waldcamping Erzgebirgsblick

An der Dittersdorfer Höhe, D-09439 Amtsberg (Saxony)

Tel: 0371 7750833. Email: info@waldcamping-erzgebirge.de

The Scheibner family first thought of opening a campsite when touring through Canada in 1998, so it is not surprising to find reminders of their trip appearing in the site's buildings with pictures and Canadian names. They found their spot on land once belonging to the Stasi, the East German secret police, and turned it into a well kept and welcoming campsite. It has 90 touring pitches. either under mature pine trees in the woods or on open ground, partly separated by low bushes and shrubs, in front of reception and the sanitary block.

Facilities

Excellent sanitary facilities with British style toilets, free, controllable hot showers and washbasins (1 cabin each for men and women). Washbasin and toilet for children. Baby room. Bathroom for rent. Washing machines, dryers, iron and board. Fully equipped kitchen, including fridge and dishwashing machine. Small shop in reception (bread to order). Lounge with dining table, darts, satellite TV and library. Playground. Bicycle hire. Small outdoor paddling pool. Off site: Fishing 5 km. Golf 5 km. Riding 2 km.

Open: All year.

Directions

From Chemnitz, take the B174 southeast towards Gronau. Site is well signed in Amtsberg, off the B174. Take care on the steep roads and the bumpy access road (which is only 100 m).
GPS: N50:45.960 E13:00.869

Charges 2006

Per person	€ 5,00
child (2-13 yrs)	€ 3,50
pitch incl. electricity	€ 8,00

DE3847 Campingplatz Auensee

Gustav-Esche Strasse 5, D-04159 Leipzig (Saxony)
Tel: 0341 4651 600. Email: info@camping-auensee.de

It is unusual to find a good site in a city, but this large, neat and tidy site is one. It is far enough away from roads and the airport to be reasonably peaceful during the day and very quiet overnight and has 168 pitches, all for short-term tourers. It is set in a mainly open area with tall trees and very attractive flower arrangements around, with some chalets and 'trekker' huts for rent in the adjoining woodland, home to shoe-stealing foxes. The individual, numbered, flat grassy pitches are large (at least 100 sq.m.), all with 16A electrical connections and five on hardstanding, arranged in several sections with a separate area for young people with tents.

Facilities

Five sanitary buildings (all in one area and mind your head if you are over 6 feet tall) have differing mixtures of equipment and offer many washbasins in cabins and showers on payment (token). Well equipped rooms for babies and disabled visitors (key from reception). Kitchen and laundry rooms. Bar/restaurant and snack bar (all year). Several play areas. Bicycle hire. Motorcaravan service point. Fishing. Off site: Public transport to the city centre goes every 10 minutes from just outside the site.

Open: All year.

Directions

Site is signed 3 km. from Leipzig centre on the B6 to Halle. From the A9 Berlin - Nurnberg take exit 16 at Schkeuditz onto the B6 towards Leipzig. Turn right to Auensee just after the Church 3 km before the centre of the town. If you pass the railway station you are too far. Turn back and turn left at the Church. GPS: N51:22.185 E12:18.84

Charges 2006

Per person	€ 4,50
pitch incl. car	€ 5,50 - € 8,50

DE3855 Camping Oberhof

Am Stausee 09, Oberhof, D-99330 Frankenhain (Thuringia)
Tel: 036205 76518. Email: info@oberhofcamping.de

Beside a lake, at an altitude of 700 metres and quietly hidden in the middle of the Thüringer forest, Camping Oberhof has seen many changes since the departure of its former owners, the East German secret police. There are 200 touring pitches, all have 16A electricity and 100 with water and drainage. Access is now via a tarmac road replacing the former steeply descending forest track. From this fairly open site there are views of the surrounding forests and of the lake which is bordered by wide grass areas ideal for a picnic or for just lazing around and enjoying the view.

Facilities

New heated sanitary block with all usual facilities including free hot water, plus 15 bathrooms to rent. Facilities for disabled people. Baby changing room. Laundry room. Motorcaravan services. Modern reception building with shop and restaurant serving traditional dishes. Shop. TV room. Children's club room. Play area. On the lake: fishing (license required), swimming and boating. Off site: Bus service 1.5 km. Riding 5 km.

Open: All year.

Directions

From A4 autobahn between Eisenach and Dresden take exit 42 (Gotha). Travel south on the B247 to Ohrdruf then the B88 to Crawinkel then Frankenhain. In Frankenhain follow Lütsche Stausee and Campingpark signs. GPS: N50:44.020 E10:45.40

Charges 2006

Per person	€ 5,50
pitch incl. electricity	€ 8,00

Camping Cheques accepted.

DE3850 Camping Strandbad Aga

Reichenbacherstrasse 14, D-07554 Gera-Aga (Thuringia)
Tel: 036695 20209. Email: info@campingplatz-strandbad-aga.de

Strandbad Aga is a useful night stop near the A4/A9 and within reach of Dresden, Leipzig and Meissen. It is situated in open countryside on the edge of a small lake, with 350 individual, fenced pitches, mostly fairly level, without shade. The 200 touring pitches all have 16A electricity – for stays of more than a couple of days, over-nighters being placed on an open area. The lake is used for swimming, boating and fishing (very popular with day visitors at weekends and with a separate naturist area). The friendly, enthusiastic owner is improving the facilities each year.

Facilities

The sanitary building is at one side, with some washbasins in cabins and hot showers on payment. Washing machines and dryers. Motorcaravan services. Modern restaurant/bar open long hours. High season kiosk for drinks, ice creams, etc. Playground. Swimming and watersports in the lake. Entertainment in high season. No English spoken. Off site: Football 200 m. Shop in village (200 m). Riding, Go-and Tennis 1 km.

Open: All year.

Directions

From A4/E40 Chemnitz - Erfurt autobahn take Gera exit (no. 58) then the B2 towards Zeitz, following Bad Köstritz signs at first then site signs. GPS: N50:57.232 E12:05.21

Charges 2007

Per person	€ 4,00
child (3-13 yrs)	€ 2,00
pitch incl. electricity plus meter	€ 7,50 - € 9,00

No credit cards.

DE3605 Camping Rangau

Campingstraße 44, D-91056 Erlangen-Dechsendorf (Bavaria (N))

Tel: 09135 8866. Email: infos@camping-rangau.de

Run by the same family for many years now, this site makes a convenient stopover, quickly and easily reached from the A3 Würzburg - Nürnberg and A73 Bamberg - Nürnberg autobahns and is pleasant enough to stay a bit longer. It has 110 pitches which are mainly for tourists on flat ground, under trees, numbered and partly marked but only about 60-80 sq.m. so it can look cramped when busy. There are also 60 permanent units. There is usually space and, in peak season, overnight visitors can often be put on the adjacent football pitch. There is access to a lake for sailing or fishing on permit.

Facilities

A satisfactory sanitary block, heated when cold, has well spaced washbasins (some cabins for ladies) and showers. Good facilities for disabled visitors.Laundry facilities. Motorcaravan services. Gas supplies. Restaurant. Order bread from reception. Playground. Club/TV room Off site: Swimming 200 m. Erlangen centre 5 km.

Open: 1 April - 30 September.

Directions

Take exit for Erlangen-West from A3 autobahn, turn towards Erlangen. After 1 km. at Dechsendorf turn left by camp signs and follow to site.

Charges guide

Per person	€ 4,50
child (6-12 yrs)	€ 2,50
pitch incl. electricity (6A)	€ 6,30

DE3610 Knaus Campingpark Nürnberg

Hans Kalb Strasse 56, D-90471 Nürnberg (Bavaria (N))

Tel: 0911 9812717. Email: knaus.camp.nbg@freenet.de

This is an ideal site for visiting the fascinating and historically important city of Nuremberg. Since acquiring this pleasantly situated site, the Knaus group have made various improvements, and it now ranks as one of the best city sites anywhere. There are 150 shaded pitches, 118 with 10A electrical connections and with water taps in groups. On mainly flat grass among tall trees, some pitches are marked out with 'ranch' style boards, others still attractively 'wild', some others with hardstanding. Space allows for them to be quite big and many have the advantage of being drive through.

Facilities

A brand new heated sanitary building offers first class facilities including free showers. Washing machines and dryers. Cooking facilities. Unit for disabled visitors. Gas supplies. Motorcaravan services. Shop. Bar/bistro area with terrace and light meals served. Play area in woodland. Tennis court. Table tennis. Bicycle hire. Large screen TV. Off site: Swimming pool (free entry for campers) and football stadium 200 m. Boat launching 2 km. City centre 4 km. (a 20 minute walk following signs takes you to the underground station).

Open: All year.

Directions

From autobahns, take Nürnberg-Fischbach exit from A9 München-Bayreuth east of Nürnberg. Proceed 3 km. on dual carriageway towards city then left at first traffic lights. From city follow 'Stadion-Messe' signs. Site is signed. The entrance road to the site is not too obvious. It is opposite a large office block and the sign 'Knaus Campingpark Zufahrt' is quite close to the ground. GPS: N49:25.389 E11:07.28

Charges guide

Per person	€ 6,00
pitch incl. electricity	€ 12,00
No credit cards.	

DE3625 Knaus Camping Park Frickenhausen

Ochsenfurter Straße 49, D-97252 Frickenhausen (Bavaria (N))

Tel: 09331 3171. Email: frickenhausen@knauscamp.de

This is a pleasant riverside site with good facilities just south of Würzburg, situated towards the northern end of the 'Romantische Strasse' and not far from the A3 Frankfurt to Nürnberg. There are 115 fair sized, numbered touring pitches on generally flat grass, arranged in sections leading from tarred access roads with flowers around. Most have 6-16A electricity connections. About 80 long stay places are mostly separate nearer the river.

Facilities

Modernised, heated, sanitary facilities have washbasins (some private cabins), and dishwashing sinks. Soap and paper towels are provided for the toilets. Washing machine and dryer. Gas supplies. Restaurant, café/wine bar and shop (1/12-31/10, weekends only in low season). Bread to order. Small, free swimming pool (1/5-31/10). Play area on river island. Open air theatre. Bicycle hire. Fishing. Boat marina. Cooking facilities Off site: Public swimming pool 300 m. Riding 1 km. Golf 15 km.

Open: All year excl. November.

Directions

Take exit 71 (Ochsenfurt) from the A3 autobahn at Würzburg and continue on the B13 towards Ochsenfurt and Ansbach. Do not cross the Main into town but follow Frickenhausen and site signs. GPS: N49:40.176 E010:09.48

Charges guide

Per person	€ 6,00
child (3-14 yrs)	€ 3,00
pitch	€ 8,00
No credit cards.	

DE3632 Azur Camping Altmühltal

Am Festplatz 3, D-85110 Kipfenberg (Bavaria (N))

Tel: 08465 905167. Email: kipfenberg@azur-camping.de

In the beautiful Altmühltal river valley, this Azur site is in pretty woodland, with lots of shade for much of it. On flat grassland with direct access to the river, one looks from the entrance across to the old Schloss on the hill. Outside the main entrance is a large, flat, grass/gravel field for 60 overnight tourers (with electricity). The main site has 277 pitches, of which 178 are for touring, plus two small areas for tents and one large one (at the end in an open area). Ranging in size up to 90 sq.m. they are generally in small groups marked by trees or bushes.

Facilities

The main sanitary facilities are good, with free hot water (no private cabins), Baby room. Unit for disabled visitors. Launderette. Kitchen. These facilities are mostly duplicated 'portacabin' style at the other end of the site (toilets only in low season). Motorcaravan services. Shop. Beer garden serving snacks in July/Aug. Play area. Fishing. Off site: Bus service 50 m. Supermarket 100 m. Restaurants 300 m.

Open: All year.

Directions

From the A9/E45 Munich - Nuremberg, take exit 59 Denkendorf or 58 Eichstätt and follow the signs to Kipfenberg. GPS: N48:56.904 E11:23.36

Charges 2006

Per person	€ 5,50 - € 7,50
child (2-12 yrs)	€ 4,00 - € 6,00
pitch incl. electricity	€ 8,50 - € 11,50

Camping Cheques accepted.

DE3710 Azur Ferienpark Bayerischer Wald

Waldesruhweg 34, D-94227 Zwiesel (Bavaria (N))

Tel: 09922 802 595. Email: zwiesel@azur-camping.de

Bayerischerwald is a large site on the edge of town with views to the hills and a stream running through it. Pleasantly situated nearly 2,000 feet up (it can be cool at night) on a slight slope, there are around 500 pitches, just under 400 of which are individual numbered ones for tourers, but there is not much shade. There are various areas, with motorcaravans taken on a flat open, grassy section, whilst for caravans there are some flat and many sloping or undulating pitches, all with electricity (some 10A Euro, most 16A German) and water points along the central roadway.

Facilities

The two tiled sanitary blocks (one part modernised) have some private cabins. Facilities for disabled visitors. Baby room. Bread orders at reception. Pleasant restaurant/bar (not open November). Launderette. Badminton/Basketball area. Off site: Large pool complex next door comprising a deep Olympic pool, a separate pool for children and non-swimmers and a 'natural' pool, open say June-Sept. For other dates or rainy days there is an indoor pool.

Open: All year.

Directions

Site is on north side of Zwiesel. From autobahn A3 Regensburg-Passau, take Deggendorf exit and then B11 to Zwiesel. Take Zwiesel Nord exit and follow Azur signs. GPS: N49:01.530 E13:13.24

Charges 2006

Per person	€ 5,00 - € 7,00
child (2-12 yrs)	€ 3,50 - € 5,50
pitch with electricity	€ 8,00 - € 11,00

Camping Cheques accepted.

DE3739 Camping Katzenkopf

Am See, D-97334 Sommerach am Main (Bavaria (N))

Tel: 09381 9215

This is an excellent family run site, on the banks of the Main to the east of Wurzburg. For peace and quiet this site is likely to be at the top of the list. There are 250 pitches with some 150 for touring units. All pitches have electricity (16A) and 13 provide electricity, water, and drainage. English is spoken at reception which also houses a shop and good tourist information. Wurzburg is an important commercial and cultural centre that was substantially destroyed by bombing and has risen again from the ashes. The town is the home of the excellent Franconian wine. The village of Sommerach, a few minutes walk, is surrounded by vineyards which produce a special local vintage.

Facilities

Excellent, modern toilet blocks include private cabins, free showers and facilities for disabled people and children. Laundry. Motorcaravan service point. Shop, restaurant, bar and takeaway (all open all season). Fishing. Boat launching. Sailing courses. Dogs accepted in part of the site only. Off site: Sailing. Shops and vineyards.

Open: 31 March - 28 October.

Directions

From the A3 take Kitzingen exit and turn towards Schwarzach. After 4 km. turn right towards Sommerach. Just before the village turn left and site is well signed. GPS: N49:49.551 E10:12.334

Charges 2007

Per person	€ 6,00 - € 6,50
child (2-14 yrs)	€ 4,00 - € 4,50
pitch incl. electricity	€ 8,00 - € 9,00

No credit cards.

DE3735 Spessart-Camping Schönrain

Schönrainstraße 4 - 18, D-97737 Gemünden-Hofstetten (Bavaria (N))

Tel: 09351 8645. Email: info@spessart-camping.de

Situated a short distance from the town of Gemünden, with views of forested hills beside the Main river, this is a very friendly, family run site, with excellent facilities. There are 200 pitches, half of which are for touring. They vary in size from 70-150 sq.m. and most have 10A electricity, 20 also with water. Another area has been developed for tents. The site has an outdoor pool open from Whitsun to end Sept (weather permitting). A pleasant small restaurant and bar and a shop are on site with the local full-bodied Franconian wine and schnapps for sale. Frau Endres welcomes British guests and speaks a little English. There are opportunities for walking and riding in the adjacent woods, excursions are organised in the main season and it is possible to hire a bicycle, ride to Würzburg and catch the pleasure boat back, or take a combined bus and cycle ride. Fishing and boating are both very popular in the locality.

Facilities

A superb new sanitary building has card operated entry – the card is pre-paid and operates the showers, washing machines and dryers, coffee machine, dishwashing, gas cooker, baby bathroom, jacuzzi etc. Two private bathrooms (complete with wine and balcony!) for rent. Motorcaravan services. General room with sections for very young children, a pool table and arcade games and a TV. Upstairs is a library and internet café, fitness room and solarium. Bar/restaurant (closed Tuesdays). Shop. Swimming pool. Playground. Outdoor chess. Bicycle hire. Excursions organised. New 'Beauty and Wellness' programme. Off site: Bus service 200 m. Menus for local restaurants held in reception with booking service and transport provided. Fishing 400 m.

Open: 1 April - 30 September.

Directions

From Frankfurt - Würzburg autobahn, take Weibersbrunn-Lohr exit and then B26 to Gemünden. Turn over Main river bridge to Hofstetten. From Kassel - Wurzburg autobahn, leave at Hammelburg and take B27 to Gemünden, and as above.

Charges 2007

Per person	€ 6,10
child (under 14 yrs)	€ 3,80
pitch	€ 4,50 - € 10,30

Less 10% for stays over 14 days in mid and low seasons.

DE3750 Camping Schloss Issigau

Schloss Issigau, D-95188 Issigau (Bavaria (N))
Tel: 09293 7173. Email: info@schloss-issigau.de

This is an attractive, small family run site with very good facilities and of a type not often found in Germany with less than 50 pitches, all for tourers. Situated in northeast Bavaria, on the edge of a pretty village from where there are views of the surrounding fields and woods. Entering a large grass courtyard there are several sections, part terraced and with some old trees giving a little shade in places. As you go through the site it opens up to a largish, sloping tent area beside the small ponds, beyond which is the new young children's play area. There are 45 pitches – around half are individual ranging up to 120 sq.m.– all with 16A electricity, plus three also with water and waste water. There is a delightful café/bar and restaurant in the interesting old 'Schloss' (circa 1398 – a large fortified house is how we might describe it) with a museum of old armour, etc.

Facilities

Satisfactory heated sanitary facilities are in an old building with some modern fittings and some washbasins in cabins. Laundry facilities. Baby room. Café/bar and restaurant (open daily from 12.00 to 22.00). Games room. Hotel. Off site: Bus service and small supermarket 300 m. Riding 1.5 km. Fishing 6 km. Golf 10 km.

Open: 15 March - 31 October; 18 December - 9 January.

Directions

The small village of Issigau is on the road between Holle and Berg. From A9 (Berlin - Nuremberg) take exit 31 Berg/Bad Steben. Turn left and follow signs for Berg and then straight on (Holle). In Issigau site is signed. Follow 'Camping Schloß Issigau' sign, narrow in places. GPS: N50:22.451 E11:43.273

Charges 2007

Per person	€ 4,50
child (4-14 yrs)	€ 2,50
pitch	€ 5,00 - € 6,00

No credit cards.

DE3630 Camping Donau-Lech

Campingweg 1, D-86698 Eggelstetten (Bavaria (S))
Tel: 09090 4046. Email: info@donau-lech-camping.de

The Haas family have developed this friendly site just off the attractive 'Romantische Strasse' well and run it very much as a family site, providing a useful information sheet in English for their guests. The lake provides swimming and wildlife for children and adults to enjoy. Alongside it are 50 marked touring pitches with 16A electrical connections, on flat grass arranged in rows either side of a tarred access road. With an average of 120 sq.m. per unit, it is a comfortable site with an open feeling and developing shade. There are three separate pleasant, flat, grass areas near the entrance for people with tents (including youngsters, cyclists or motorcyclists) with unmarked pitches. Long stay pitches are located beyond the tourers. Suitable not only as a night stop on the way south, the site is also not far from Augsburg and Munich. From the local railway station (3 km.) a family railcard costs about € 24 for both main line services and Munich city transport system.

Facilities

All amenities are housed in the main building at the entrance with reception. Sanitary facilities are downstairs with free showers, warm water washbasins, (no cabins), dishwashing and laundry room, all of a good standard. Sauna. Washing machine and dryer. Motorcaravan services. Large bar area with terrace. Small shop for basics, bread to order (1/4-31/10). General room. Youth room. Table tennis. Play area. Health studio with massage, manicure and pedicure. Lake for swimming on site (own risk). Off site: Larger lake used for sailboarding 400 m. Golf course and driving range 1 km. Fishing 3 km. Restaurants and other amenities a short drive.

Open: All year excl. November.

Directions

Turn off main B2 road about 5 km. south of Donauwörth (site signed) at signs for Asbach-Bäumenheim Nord towards Eggelstetten, then follow camp signs for over 1 km. to site. GPS: N48:40.554 E10:50.45

Charges guide

Per person	€ 4,50
child (2-15 yrs)	€ 2,50
pitch	€ 5,00 - € 6,00
electricity (plus meter)	€ 2,00
dog	€ 2,00

DE3635 Camping München Obermenzing

Lochhausenerstraße 59, D-81247 München (Bavaria (S))

Tel: 089 8112235. Email: campingplatz-obermenzing@t-online.de

On the northwest edge of Munich, this site makes a good stopover for those wishing to see the city or pass the night. The flat terrain is mostly covered by mature trees, giving shade to most pitches. Caravan owners are well off here as they have a special section of 130 individual drive-through pitches, mainly separated from each other by high hedges and opening off the hard site roads with easy access. These have 10A electricity connections and about 30 have water and waste water connections also. About 200 tents and motorcaravans are taken on quite large, level grass areas, with an overflow section so space is usually available. There is a shop and rest room with TV and a drinks machine (including beer). There is some road noise, but we spent another reasonably undisturbed night here, helped by the new earth bank, and it is a very convenient site.

Facilities

The central sanitary block is large, having been extended, and together with a new 'portacabin' style unit, the provision should now be adequate. Cleaning is satisfactory and there is heating in the low season. Hot showers require tokens, as do some washbasins. Cooking facilities on payment. Washing machine and dryers. Gas supplies. Motorcaravan services. Shop (from May). Bar (from July). TV room. Charcoal barbecues not permitted. Off site: Baker and café nearby. Riding or golf 5 km. Bicycle hire 8 km. Public transport services to the city from very close by. By car the journey might take 20-30 minutes depending on the density of traffic.

Open: 15 March - 31 October.

Directions

Site is in the northwest of the city. From Stuttgart, Nuremberg, Deggendorf or Salzburg, leave A99 at 'Kreiss-West' for München - Lochhausen and turn left into Lochhausener Strasse. The site is a further 1.5 km. GPS: N48:10.489 E11:26.78

Charges 2006

Per person	€ 4,50
child (2-14 yrs)	€ 2,00
caravan and car	€ 9,00
motorcaravan	€ 6,00

No credit cards.

DE3640 Camping Municipal München-Thalkirchen

Zentralländstraße 49, D-81379 München (Bavaria (S))

Tel: 089 7231707. Email: munichtouristoffice@compuserve.com

This well cared for municipal site is pleasantly and quietly situated on the southern side of Munich in parkland formed by the River Isar conservation area, 4 km. from the city centre (there are subway and bus links) and tall trees offer shade in parts. The large city of Munich has much to offer and the Thalkirchen site becomes quite crowded during the season. There are 550 touring pitches, all with 10A electricity and shared water and waste water. The pitches are of various sizes (some quite small), marked by metal or wooden posts and rails. Like many city sites, groups are put in one area. and American motorhomes are accepted. The site is very busy (and noisy) during the Beer Festival (mid Sept - early Oct), but is well maintained and kept clean.

Facilities

There are five refurbished toilet blocks, two of which can be heated, with seatless toilets, washbasins with shelf, mirror and cold water. Hot water for showers and sinks is on payment. Facilities for disabled people. Shop (7 am - 8.30 pm). Snack bar with covered terrace (7 am - 10 pm), Drinks machine incl. Beer. General room with TV pool and games. Good small playground. Tourist information, souvenirs and other services. Treatment room. Washing machines and dryers. Maximum stay 14 days. Bikes for hire. Dormitory accommodation for groups (schools, scouts and guides etc.) Office hours 7 am - 11 pm. Off site: Restaurant 200 m. Pleasant walks may be taken in the adjacent park and the world famous Munich zoo is just 15 minutes walk along the river from the site.

Open: 15 March - end October.

Directions

From autobahns follow 'Mittel' ring road to SSE of the city centre where site is signed; also follow signs for Thalkirchen or the Zoo and site is close. Well signed now from all over the City.
GPS: N48:05.471 E11:32.69

Charges guide

Per person	€ 4,40 - € 8,10
child (2-14 yrs)	€ 1,30
caravan and car	€ 10,00
motorcaravan (acc. to size)	€ 5,50 - € 7,00
electricity	€ 1,80

Credit cards only accepted for souvenirs.

DE3650 Camping Gitzenweiler Hof

Gitzenweiler 88, D-88131 Lindau-Oberreitnau (Bavaria (S))

Tel: 08382 94940. Email: info@gitzenweiler-hof.de

Gitzenweiler Hof has been developed into a really well-equipped, first-class site for a family holiday. In a country setting it has about 380 permanent caravans as well as about 450 places for touring units (it is advisable to book for July/Aug). In the tourist section many pitches are without markings with siting left to campers, the others in rows between access roads. There are 450 electricity connections (6/16A) and 56 pitches for caravans and motorcaravans with water, drainage and TV connections. A large open-air swimming pool has attractive surrounds with seats (free for campers). Lindau is an interesting town, especially by the harbour, and possible excursions include the whole of the Bodensee (Lake Constance), the German Alpine Road, the Austrian Vorarlberg and Switzerland. This is a pleasant, friendly, well-run site with a separate area just outside for overnight stops. Member of Leading Campings Group.

Facilities

The toilet blocks have been beautifully renovated and include some washbasins in cabins, a children's bathroom and baby bath. Washing machines, dryers and dishwasher. Motorcaravan services. Shop (limited hours in low season). Two restaurants with takeaway. Large swimming pool in summer (33 x 25 m). Two playgrounds and play room with entertainment in summer. Organised activities all year. Hens, rabbits, ducks and ponies for children. Ground for football, etc. Free fishing in lake. Minigolf. Cinema. Club room with arcade games, library and internet points. Doctor comes if needed; hospital near. American motorhomes accepted up to 10 tons.

Open: All year.

Directions

Site is signed from the B12 about 4 km. north of Lindau. Also from A96 exit 3 (Weißensberg), and from in and around Lindau.
GPS: N47:35.120 E09:42.385

Charges guide

Per person	€ 6,50
child (3-9 yrs)	€ 2,00
child (10-15 yrs)	€ 4,50
pitch	€ 8,00
serviced pitch (in summer)	€ 14,00

Discounts for stays over 14 days and in low season. Overnight hardstanding with electricity outside camp barrier € 12.

Welcome on your holiday

Camping in comfort!

Caravan pitches+ (105 m²) on solid ground, with water, drainage, electricity, partly TV. Motorhome pitches+ on solid ground, with water, drainage, electricity, TV. Standard pitches for caravans, motorhomes and tents. Pitches for overnighters outside the gate, only for one night.

Come in!

Modern sanitary facilities, also for disabled guests, 'washland' for children, family bathrooms for rent, dog shower, swimming pool, leisure activities, canoes, Nordic walking, Inline skating, balloon trips and much nature awaits you.
Golf, scuba diving school, horse riding, ski school close by.

Family friendly!

Activity programmes for adults and children during the school holidays, 1500 m² natural play area with fireplace, football ground, playground, beach volleyball, street-basketball, cinema, table tennis, boules, chess, pet area, pony riding, Internet-Point, recreation room.

Twins up to 15 years old stay free of charge.

Senior Citizens 55+

The idyllic 'Gitz' offers pedestrian areas, Kneipp-treatements, bio-displays and more...

Campingpark
Gitzenweiler Hof
Lindau – Bodensee
★ ★ ★ ★ ★
D-88131 Lindau (Bodensee)
Gitzenweiler
Telefon +49 (0) 83 82 / 94 94-0
Telefax +49 (0) 83 82 / 94 94-15
info@gitzenweiler-hof.de
www.gitzenweiler-hof.de

DE3642 Lech Camping

Seeweg 6, D-86444 Mühlhausen bei Augsburg (Bavaria (S))

Tel: **08207/2200**. Email: **info@lech-camping.de**

Situated just north of Ausgburg, this beautifully run site is a pleasure to stay on. Gabi Ryssel, the owner, spends her long days working very hard to cater to every wish of her guests – from the moment you arrive and are given the key to one of the cleanest toilet blocks we have seen and plenty of tourist information, you are in very capable hands. The 40 level, grass and gravel pitches are roomy and have shade from pine trees. Electricity connections are available (10/16A). This is an immaculate site with a separate area for disabled people to park near the special facilities provided. The site has a very comprehensive camping shop (only a few basic foodstuffs as there is a supermarket over the road) and an excellent restaurant overlooking a small lake. A paddling pool (part of the lake cordoned off) is provided for children with a safe little sandy area (toys also thoughtfully supplied) along with sun beds to enjoy the view over the lake. Although this is a rural site, there is easy access by bus (a stop just over the road) to Ausburg, a beautiful German town, which has a brilliant beer festival in April (definitely a must!)

Facilities

The new toilet block (cleaned many times daily) provides British style WCs and good showers with seating area and non slip flooring. Baby room. Separate family bathroom for rent. Five star facilities for disabled visitors. Motorcaravan service point. Small shop. Restaurant. Small playground (partially fenced). Bicycle hire. WiFi. Off site: Bus service to city. Legoland 25 minute drive. Fishing 4 km. Golf 10 km. Riding 15 km.

Open: Easter - 15 September.

Directions

Site is northeast of Augsburg at the border of Muhlhausen. Leave E52 /A8 Munich - Stuttgart motorway at exit 73 and follow signs to Neuburg and Pöttmes. After 3 km. (past airport on right) on U49 at Muhlhausen sign. Lech Camping is on right.

Charges guide

Per person	€ 5,20
child (2-15 yrs)	€ 2,50
pitch incl. electricity	€ 9,60

DE3670 Camping Hopfensee

Fischerbichl 17, D-87629 Füssen im Allgäu (Bavaria (S))

Tel: **08362 917710**. Email: **info@camping-hopfensee.com**

Hopfensee is a high class site with excellent facilities, catering for discerning visitors, by a lake. It is well placed to explore the very attractive Bavarian Alpine region which, along with the architecture and historical interest of the Royal Castles at Hohenschwangau and the Baroque church at Wies, makes it a very popular holiday area. The 378 tourist pitches for caravans and motorhomes, most with shade, each have 16A electricity, water, drain and cable TV connections. They are marked, numbered and of a good size. Member of Leading Campings Group. At the centre of the site is a large building with an open village-like square in the middle, adorned with cascading flowers. It houses the exceptional sanitary facilities and, on the upper floors, a swimming pool, treatment and physiotherapy suites, a full spa centre, fitness centre, cinema and children's play room. There is direct access to the lake for sailing, canoeing etc. and a place for parking boats. Charges are high, but include the pool, super sports building, cinema, etc. Tents are not accepted.

Facilities

The exceptionally good, heated sanitary facilities provide British style WCs, free hot water in washbasins (some in cabins), large showers and sinks, laundry and washing-up rooms, as well as baby and children's wash rooms. Motorcaravan services. Restaurant. Bar. Takeaway. Shop. Indoor pool and spa centre. Sauna, solarium and steam bath. Playground. Large games room. Bicycle hire. Tennis. Fishing. Ski school in winter. Small golf academy and green fee discounts for two local courses. No tents taken. Off site: Riding and boat launching 1 km.

Open: 16 December - 5 November.

Directions

Site is 4 km. north of Füssen. Turn off B16 to Hopfen and site is on the left through a car park. If approaching from the west on B310, turn towards Füssen at T-junction with the B16 and immediately turn right again for the road to Hopfen. GPS: N47:36.167 E10:41.030

Charges 2006

Per person	€ 8,30 - € 9,50
child (2-12 yrs)	€ 5,00 - € 5,90
12-18 yrs	€ 6,40 - € 8,50
pitch with cable TV, electricity	€ 12,30 - € 13,65

No credit cards.

DE3672 Camping Elbsee

Am Elbsee 3, D-87648 Aitrang (Bavaria (S))

Tel: 08343 248. Email: camping@elbsee.de

This attractive site, with its associated hotel and restaurant about 400 m. away, lies on land sloping down to the lake. This is not an area well known to tourists, although the towns of Marktoberdorf (14 km), Kaufbeuren (16 km) and Kempten (21 km) merit a visit. With this in mind, the owners have set about providing good facilities and a developing program of activities. All the 120 touring pitches have access to electricity (16A) and 78 also have their own water supply and waste water outlet. Some of the pitches restricted to tents slope slightly. In high season there are organised outings, musical performances on site or at the hotel, painting courses and children's activities. Next to the site is a supervised lake bathing area, operated by the municipality, with a kiosk selling drinks and snacks, a playground and an indoor play area. Entrance to this is at a reduced price for campers.

Facilities

Two clean, well appointed heated sanitary blocks include free showers, washbasins all in cabins, a children's bathroom and family bathrooms to rent. Facilities for disabled visitors. Dog shower. Motorcaravan service point. Shop (bread can be ordered for following day). New playground, indoor play area and activity rooms. TV, games and meeting rooms. Sports field. Fishing. Bicycle hire. Riding. Boat launching. Activity programme (20/7-31/8). Off site: At hotel, very good restaurant, takeaway and bar. Shop and ATM point 2 km. Golf 12 km.

Open: 15 December - 5 November.

Directions

From centre of Marktoberdorf, take minor road northwest to Ruderatshofen and from there take minor road west towards Aitrang. Just south of Aitrang, site is signed to south of the road. The road to the site (2 km.) is winding and narrow, but two caravans can just about pass.
GPS: N47:48.166 E10:33.206

Charges guide

Per person	€ 5,00
child (4-14 yrs)	€ 3,00
pitch incl. car	€ 10,00 - € 14,00
electricity per kWh	€ 0,60

Camping Cheques accepted.

DE3680 Alpen-Caravanpark Tennsee

D-82494 Krün / Obb (Bavaria (S))

Tel: 08825 170. Email: info@camping-tennsee.de

Tennsee is an excellent site in truly beautiful surroundings high up (1,000 m.) in the Karwendel Alps with super mountain views, and close to many famous places of which Innsbruck (44 km) and Oberammergau (26 km) are two. Mountain walks are plentiful, with several lifts close by. It is an attractive site with good facilities including 120 serviced pitches with connections for electricity (up to 16A and two connections), gas, TV, radio, telephone, water and waste water. The other 80 pitches all have electricity and some of these are available for overnight guests at a reduced rate.

Facilities

The first class toilet block has under-floor heating, washbasins in cabins and private units with WC, shower, basin and bidet for rent. Unit for disabled people. Heated room for ski equipment. Washing machines. Gas. Motorcaravan services. Cooking facilities. Restaurants with takeaway. Bar. Shop. Solarium. Bicycle hire. Playground. WiFi. Activities. Excursions. Bus to ski slopes in winter. Off site: Fishing 400 m. Riding or golf 3 km.

Open: All year excl. 4 November - 15 December.

Directions

Site is just off main Garmisch-Partenkirchen to Innsbruck road no. 2 between Klais and Krün, 15 km. from Garmisch watch for small sign 'Tennsee, Barmersee' and turn right there for site.

Charges 2006

Per person	€ 7,00 - € 7,50
1-3 children (3-15 yrs)	€ 3,50 - € 5,00
pitch	€ 8,00 - € 12,00

Senior citizens special rates (not winter).

DE3688 Panorama Camping Harras

Harrasser Strasse 135, D-83209 Prien am Chiemsee (Bavaria (S))
Tel: 08051 904613. Email: info@camping-harras.de

Panorama Harras is a popular, friendly site on a small, wooded peninsula by the Chiemsee, with good views to the mountains across the lake. With some near the lake, the pitches vary in size (60-100 sq.m.) and most have electricity (6A). There are 80 numbered pitches marked by trees, but with no hedges, the site can look and feel crowded at busy times. A separate, all numbered section of gravel hardstanding is provided for motorhomes and an area for tents on grass and gravel. Sailing and windsurfing are very popular here and you can swim from the shingle beach. It is also a useful base for exploring this attractive area, with boat trips to the 'Herrenchiemsee' island with its castle, cycle trips and mountains to walk in.

Facilities

Toilet facilities include family shower rooms with washbasin and toilet (no paper). Push-button showers need a token. Baby room. Launderette. Good unit for disabled people. Well stocked shop. Restaurant with bar and takeaway (all open for the whole season). Bicycle hire. Off site: Bus services 1 km. in town. Boat trips on the lake. Golf and riding 5 km. Automobile museum 20 km.

Open: 6 April - 10 October.

Directions

The Chiemsee is north of the A8 (E52, E60) between Munich and Salzburg. Take exit 106 (Bernau) then north towards Prien. After 3 km, at the roundabout, turn east towards Harras (and Kreiskrankenhaus) following site signs. GPS: N47:50.450 E12:22.29

Charges 2007

Per person	€ 6,90
child (under 14 yrs)	€ 4,80
pitch	€ 3,50 - € 7,10

Surcharge 15% for stays of less than 4 nights.
Camping Cheques accepted.

★ ★ ★ ★
An idyllic holiday by the lake

New: luxury sanitary facilities

Panorama-Camping Harras • 83209 Prien / Chiemsee • 0049-8051/9046-0 • Fax -16
Internet: http://www.camping-harras.de • E-Mail: info@camping-harras.de

DE3685 Camping Allweglehen

D-83471 Berchtesgaden (Bavaria (S))
Tel: 08652 2396. Email: campingplatz.allweglehen@t-online.de

Berchtesgaden is a National Park with magnificent scenery, in an area of mountains, lakes, valleys, castles and churches. Hitler built his 'Eagles Nest' on top of the Kehlstein, which is visible from the site and open to the public (bus service, no cars). However, the trip there is mainly interesting for the views, as the Eagles Nest has now been turned into a commercial restaurant. From an historical point of view, the Visitor Centre below is more interesting. This all year site occupies a hillside position, with spectacular mountain views. The site access road is steep (14%), particularly at the entrance, but the proprietor will use his tractor to tow caravans . There are 180 pitches (160 for touring), arranged on gravel terraces, separated by hedges or fir trees and all with good views and electrical connections.

Facilities

Two adjacent older style toilet blocks near the restaurant can be heated. A further tiny unit serves the lowest terrace. Bathroom. Baby room. Cleaning and maintenance can be variable. Washing machines, dryers and iron. Motorcaravan services. Gas supplies. Restaurant. Kiosk for essentials (all year). Play area. Small heated pool (small charge, 15/5-15/10). Solarium. Minigolf. Table tennis. Fishing. Excursions. Internet access. Off site: Winter sports near. Walks. Riding 2 km. Bicycle hire 3 km. Golf 5 km.

Open: All year.

Directions

Easiest access is via the Austrian autobahn A10 (vignette necessary), Salzburg Sud exit and follow the B305 towards Berchtesgaden. Alternatively take the B305 from Ruhpolding (with 4 m. height limit) or the B20 from Bad Reichenhall. Site is 4 km. northeast of Berchtesgaden. GPS: N47:38.833 E13:02.387

Charges 2006

Per person	€ 5,40
pitch	€ 7,50 - € 8,50
electricity (per kWh)	€ 0,50

DE3686 Strandcamping

Am See 1, D-83329 Waging am See (Bavaria (S))

Tel: 08681 552. Email: info@strandcamp.de

This is an exceptionally big site on the banks of a large lake fed by clear alpine streams. There are some 700 pitches for touring units out of a total of over 1,200. All the grass, level touring pitches have electricity (16A) with 86 also providing water and drainage. As you would expect with a site of this kind, there is a considerable range of sports facilities and an extensive games and entertainment programme in high season. A small sandy beach offers facilities for swimming in the lake (lifeguards are in attendance in the high season) and an adjoining windsurfing school is available. The site has an large restaurant and beer garden on the banks of the lake. Member of Leading Campings Group.

Facilities

Good sanitary facilities include private cabins and free showers. Facilities for disabled people and children in the four modern blocks. 11 private bathrooms for rent. Laundry and dishwashing facilities. Motorcaravan service point. Shop and internet access at reception. Restaurant and bar. Lake beach. Windsurfing. Tennis courts. Minigolf. Fishing. Bicycle hire. Dogs are not accepted during July/Aug. Off site: Golf 1 km.

Open: 1 April - 31 October.

Directions

From A8 take exit 112 and head towards Traunstein. Turn right on road no. 304 then left towards Waging. Just before bridge turn right and then right towards site.

Charges 2006

Per person	€ 5,30 - € 6,70
child (3-9 yrs)	€ 2,50 - € 4,90
pitch	€ 5,90 - € 8,60
incl. services	€ 6,90 - € 10,90

DE3695 Dreiflüsse Camping

Am Sonnenhang 8, Donautat, D-94113 Irring bei Passau (Bavaria (S))

Tel: 08546 633. Email: dreifluessecamping@t-online.de

Although the site overlooks the Danube, it is in fact some 9 km. from the confluence of the Danube, Inn and Ilz. Dreiflüsse Camping occupies a hillside position, well above highwater level, to the west of Passau with pitches, flat or with a little slope on several rows of terraces. The 180 places for touring units are not all numbered or marked, although 16A electricity boxes determine where units pitch. Trees and low banks separate the terraces which are of gravel with a thin covering of grass. The energetic and jolly owner, Herr Pitscheneder, is most popular and gives the site a very friendly air.

Facilities

The sanitary facilities are acceptable, if a little old, with two private cabins for women, one for men. Laundry. New motorcaravan services. Gas supplies. Pleasant, modern Gasthof restaurant with terrace at site entrance, where the reception, shop and sanitary buildings are also located. Shop. Small heated indoor pool (May - 15 Sept on payment). Play area. Bicycle hire. Off site: Bus service for Passau (4 daily). Riding 3 km. Golf 10 km.

Open: 1 April - 31 October.

Directions

From A3, take exit 115 (Passau-Nord) from where site is signed. Follow signs from Passau on road to west of city and north bank of Danube towards Windorf and Irring. GPS: N48:36.377 E13:20.75

Charges 2007

Per person	€ 4,50
pitch	€ 5,00 - € 9,50
electricity (plus kWh charge)	€ 2,50
No credit cards.	

DE3697 Kur und Feriencamping Dreiquellenbad

Singham 40, D-94086 Bad Griesbach (Bavaria (S))

Tel: 085 32 96 13 50

This site is to the southwest of Passau which dates back to Roman times and lies on a peninsula between the rivers Danube and Inn, close to the Austrian border. Dreiquellenbad is an exceptional site in a quite rural area, with over 200 pitches, some 190 of which are used for touring units. All pitches have electricity and water and 50 are fully serviced with electricity, water, drainage, TV and telephone points. English is spoken at reception which also houses a shop. A luxury leisure complex includes a sauna, Turkish bath and jacuzzi. An adjoining building provides various beauty and complementary health treatments. Member of Leading Campings Group.

Facilities

Excellent sanitary facilities include private cabins and free showers, facilities for disabled visitors, special child facilities and a dog shower. Two private bathrooms for rent. Laundry and dishwashing facilities. Motorcaravan services. Shop. Internet point. Off site: Golf 2 km. Spa facilities of Bad Griesbach within walking distance.

Open: All year.

Directions

Site is 15 km. from the A3. Take exit 118 and follow signs for Pocking. After 2 km. turn right on B388. Site is in the hamlet of Singham - turn right into Karpfhan then left towards site.

Charges guide

Per person	€ 4,90
pitch	€ 8,30 - € 9,30
electricity (plus meter)	€ 1,00

227

DE3720 Internationaler Campingplatz Naabtal

Sistelhausen 2, D-93188 Pielenhofen (Bavaria (S))
Tel: 09409 373. Email: camping.pielenhofen@t-online.de

International Camping Naabtal is an attractive riverside site in a beautiful tree-covered valley and makes an excellent base for exploring the ancient city of Regensburg on the Danube and other areas of this interesting part of Germany. It is also a good overnight site for those wishing to visit or pass through Austria or the Czech Republic. The best 130 of the 340 pitches are reserved for tourists and they are mainly located on the banks of the river on flat or gently sloping ground under willow and other trees. This is good walking and mountain biking country with many marked trails. Small boats can be launched on the placid river (where you may also swim at your own risk) and there are two good size tennis courts. Reception will advise on local excursions, walks, cycle routes and sports.

Facilities

Two original, heated toilet blocks are part of larger buildings and there is a newer block for the tent area. Some washbasins are in cabins, showers are on payment. First class unit for disabled people. Washing machines, dryers and irons. Gas supplies. Motorcaravan services. Sauna and solarium. Bar/restaurant (1/4-31/10 plus Xmas/New Year). Small shop (Easter - end Sept). Skittle alley and tarmac curling rink. Playground. Bicycle hire. Fishing (permit required). Small boats on river. Off site: Shop and bus service in the village 1.5 km. Golf 15 km.

Open: All year.

Directions

Take exit 97 Nittendorf from A3 Nürnberg - Regensburg, and follow road to Pielenhofen where you must pass under the arch (Camping Naabtal is signed from exit). Cross river and turn right to site. Site is 11 km. from autobahn.
GPS: N49:03.547 E11:57.61

Charges 2007

Per person	€ 5,25
child	€ 3,25
pitch	€ 6,10
electricity (plus meter)	€ 0,50

No credit cards.

DE3420 Freizeitcenter Oberrhein

D-79244 Rheinmunster (Baden-Württemberg)
Tel: 07227 2500. Email: info@freizeitcenter-oberrhein.de

This large, well equipped holiday site provides much to do and is also a good base for visiting the Black Forest. To the left of reception are a touring area and a section of hardstanding for motorcaravans. The 285 touring pitches – out of 700 overall – all have electricity connections (mostly 16A, 3 pin, a few with 2 pin), and include 180 with water and drainage, but little shade. Two of the site's lakes are used for swimming (with roped-off areas for toddlers) and non-powered boating (the water was very clean when we visited), the third small one is for fishing. This site is well worth considering for a holiday, especially for families with young and early teenage children. Occasional live music is organised until late.

Facilities

Seven top quality, heated toilet buildings have free hot water and very smart fittings. Some have special rooms for children, babies and families. Excellent dog shower! Family wash cabins to rent. Motorcaravan services. Gas supplies. Shop (1/4-31/10). Lakeside restaurant; snack bar (both 1/4-31/10). Modern play areas on sand. Small zoo. Tennis. Table tennis. Bicycle hire. Minigolf. Windsurf school. Swimming and boating lakes. Fishing (charged). Off site: Supermarket 3 km. Riding 4 km. Golf 5 km.

Open: All year.

Directions

Leave autobahn A5/E35-52 at exit 51 and travel west in direction of Iffezheim. Turn south onto B36 passing through Hügelsheim to Stollhoffen where at the roundabout site is signed.
GPS: N48:46.346 E08:02.49

Charges 2006

Per person	€ 5,00 - € 8,00
child (6-16 yrs)	€ 3,00 - € 6,00
child (under 6 yrs)	€ 2,50 - € 4,50
pitch incl. car	€ 5,00 - € 8,00
electricity	€ 2,00

DE3415 Camping Adam

Campingstraße 1, D-77815 Bühl (Baden-Württemberg)

Tel: 07223 23194. Email: webmaster@campingplatz-adam.de

This very convenient lakeside site is by the A5 Karlsruhe - Basle autobahn near Baden-Baden, easily accessed from exit 52 Bühl (also from the French autoroute A35 just northeast of Strasbourg). It is also a useful base for the Black Forest. Most of the touring pitches (180 from 490 total) have electricity connections (10A), many with waste water outlets too. Tents are positioned along the outer area of the lake. At very busy times, units staying overnight only may be placed close together on a lakeside area of hardstanding. The site has a well tended look and good English is spoken. The lake is divided into separate areas for bathing or boating and windsurfing, with a long slide – the public are admitted to this on payment and it attracts many people on fine weekends. The shop and restaurant/bar remain open virtually all year (not Monday or Tuesday in low season), so this is a useful site to use out of season.

Facilities

Two heated sanitary buildings have mostly private cabins in the new block, hot showers on payment, facilities for babies and disabled people. Washing machine and dryer. Gas supplies. Motorcaravan services. Shop (1/4-31/10). Restaurant (1/3-30/10). Takeaway (1/5-31/8). Tennis. Playground. Bicycle hire. Fishing. Off site: Riding or golf 5 km.

Open: All year.

Directions

Take A5/E35-52, exit 52 (Bühl), turn towards Lichtenau, go through Oberbruch and left to site. From French autoroute A35 take exits 52 or 56 onto D2 and D4 respectively then turn onto A5 as above. GPS: N48:43.590 E08:05.100

Charges 2006

Per person	€ 4,80 - € 7,00
child (3-16 yrs)	€ 2,50 - € 4,00
pitch with services	€ 4,80 - € 8,50
electricity	€ 2,20

DE3406 Camping Kleinenzhof

D-75323 Bad Wildbad (Baden-Württemberg)

Tel: 07081 3435. Email: info@kleinenzhof.de

In the northern Black Forest, a very good area for walking and cross-country skiing, this site runs along the sloping bank of a stream big enough to play in but small enough not to be dangerous. There are excellent facilities, which the owner is still working on improving. The land is terraced and accommodates around 200 seasonal pitches, and 100 touring pitches. All have 16A electricity and all but five have water and drainage. At the far end of the site is a hotel with a heated indoor pool and an outdoor pool which are free to campers. A full programme of activities is arranged, including walks, other outings, visits to the site's own distillery, films and communal barbecues at weekends, and a children's club every afternoon from May to September.

Facilities

Four sanitary blocks, all heated, are clean with many washbasins in cabins and showers. Facilities for disabled visitors. Children's bathroom. 12 free family bathrooms (many for rent €3.70). Laundry facilities. Motorcaravan service point. Gas. Shop. Bar and restaurant (at hotel). Indoor pool. Outdoor pool (May-Sept) and paddling pool. Playground. TV and games room. Internet. Bicycle hire. Off site: Fishing 3 km. Riding 8 km. Golf 25 km.

Open: All year.

Directions

From Pforzheim take B294 south through Birkenfeld and Neuenbürg to Calmbach (about 20 km.) From here do not go to Bad Wildbad. Continue on B294 to Kleinenzhof (about 3 km). GPS: N48:44.284 E08:34.626

Charges 2006

Per person	€ 5,90 - € 6,10
pitch	€ 7,70 - € 7,90
electricity (per kWh)	€ 0,55

229

DE3432 Schwarzwald Camp Wolfach

Schiltacher Straße 80, D-77709 Wolfach-Halbmeil (Baden-Württemberg)

Tel: 07834 859309. Email: info@schwarzwald-camp.com

This site is set in a quiet position on the side of an attractive valley in the Black Forest. If you would like to dine or wake up to beautiful views across an alpine valley and watch herds of wild deer graze in the meadows opposite, then this is the site for you. Terraced but with little shade as yet, the site has fairly level pitches, many with electricity, water and drainage, and an area which is used for tents. In front of the main building is an area of hardstanding for overnight visitors (also with electricity).

Facilities

First class sanitary facilities include private cabins, large free showers including one multi-head, laundry, dishwashing, family bathrooms for hire and a kitchen, in the main building close to the entrance. It also houses reception with a small shop and the restaurant open daily all year. Off site: Wolfach 2 km. Outdoor swimming pool 5 km. Golf 20 km.

Open: All year.

Directions

From A5 Karlsruhe - Freiburg, take exit 55 Offenburg on B33/E531 to Haslach, then on 33/294 through Hausach and soon after left on 294 to Wolfach. Go through tunnel, stay on 294 for about 3 km. to Halbmeil. Site on left at end of village. GPS: N48:17.467 E08:16.69

Charges 2006

Per person	€ 6,00
pitch	€ 3,50 - € 6,00
electricity (plus 0.5 kWh)	€ 1,00

DE3437 Camping Hochschwarzwald

Oberhäuserstraße 6, D-79674 Todtnau-Muggenbrunn (Baden-Württemberg)

Tel: 07671 1288. Email: camping.hochschwarzwald@web.de

Hochschwarzwald is a small, peaceful, quality site in an attractive wooded valley high up in the Black Forest. This is an extremely popular area, with many summer visitors enjoying walking and cycling, but it is also ideal for winter stays, with skiing from the site. There are woods to walk in and you can paddle in a flat area of a stream. There is also an attractive barbecue area with seating. Of 85 marked pitches (some with shade), 50 are for tourers (all with 10A electrical connections) on level terraces of grass and gravel. There is an area at the entrance for overnight stays in high season.

Facilities

Two modern, heated sanitary buildings have good facilities with a few private cabins, a family room and a unit for disabled people. Washing machine, dryer and spin dryer, plus dishwashing, inside or out. Small shop for essentials. Restaurant/bar (closed Mondays). Off site: Bus to Freiburg 50 m. Bicycle hire 5 km. Fishing 6 km. Riding 12 km. Golf 12 km. Walking and skiing directly from the site. Heated indoor pool. Ski school in Muggenbrunn. Todtnau waterfalls 3 km. Freiburg and Titisee both 25 km.

Open: All year.

Directions

Site is about 1 km. beyond Muggenbrunn on the road from Todtnau towards Freiburg. GPS: N47:51.934 E07:54.97

Charges 2007

Per person	€ 4,80
child (2-12 yrs.)	€ 2,80
pitch	€ 5,90
electricity per kWh	€ 0,50
Camping Cheques accepted.	

DE3454 Kur- und Feriencamping Badenweiler

Weilertalstrasse 73, D-79410 Badenweiler (Baden-Württemberg)

Tel: 07632 1550. Email: info@camping-badenweiler.de

Badenweiler is an attractive spa centre on the edge of the southern Black Forest, and is the site of the largest Roman baths north of the Alps. It is easily accessed from the A5 or B3, but far enough from them to be peaceful. This well kept, family run campsite with pleasant views is on a hillside close to Badenweiler and the cure facilities. There are four terraces with 100 large, individual grass pitches, 96 for touring and all with electricity (16A), water and waste water connections.

Facilities

Top quality sanitary facilities, one with toilets, the other with free, controllable hot showers with full glass dividers and washbasins (cabins and vanity style). Family washrooms, facilities for babies and disabled visitors. Washing machines and dryers. Motorcaravan services. Gas supplies. Shop. Play area. Play room. Games room. Internet point and wi-fi access throughout site. Off site: Municipal outdoor, heated swimming pool, free entry for campers at 200 m. Restaurants 200 m. Shop 300 m. Golf 12 km.

Open: All year excl. 15 December - 15 January.

Directions

From the A5 about midway between Freiburg and Basel take exit 65 onto the B378 to Müllheim, then onto the L131 signed to Badenweiler-Ost from where the site is well signed. GPS: N47:48.592 E07:41.786

Charges 2007

Per person	€ 7,80
child (10-15 yrs)	€ 4,90
child (0-9 yrs)	€ 3,50
pitch	€ 8,50
No credit cards.	

DE3440 Camping Kirchzarten

Dietenbacher Straße 17, D-79199 Kirchzarten (Baden-Württemberg)

Tel: 07661 9040910

There are pleasant views of the Black Forest from this municipal site which is within easy reach by car of Titisee, Feldberg and Todtnau, and 8 km. from the large town of Freiburg in Breisgau. It is divided into 500 numbered pitches with electricity, 370 of which are for tourists (some used by tour operators). Most pitches, which are side by side on level ground, are of quite reasonable size and marked out at the corners, though there is nothing to separate them and there are some hardstanding motorcaravan pitches. From about late June to mid-August it does become full. The fine swimming pool complex adjoining the site is free to campers and is a main attraction, with pools for diving, fun, swimming and children, surrounded by spacious grassy sunbathing areas and a children's play area on sand. It is only a short stroll from the site to the village centre, which has supermarkets, restaurants, etc.

Facilities

The new sanitary building is a splendid addition and includes a large, central children's section, private cabins (some for hire), and a laundry room. Cooking stoves, washing machines, dryers, irons, sewing machines (all on payment by meter) are available among the other buildings. Restaurant/bar. Shop (May - Sept). Swimming pool complex (15/5-15/9). Large playground. Minigolf. Dogs are not accepted in July and August. New multi-purpose building housing TV room, children's play room and youth room. Off site: Tennis (covered court, can be booked from site). Adventure playground, fitness track, tennis and minigolf near. Riding 2 km. Golf 4 km.

Open: All year.

Directions

From Freiburg take B31 road signed Donaueschingen to Kirchzarten where site is signed (it is south of the village). GPS: N47:57.625 E07:57.050

Charges 2007

Per person	€ 9,20
child (4-16 yrs)	€ 4,70
pitch	€ 7,40
Every 15th day free.	

DE3442 Terrassen Campingplatz Herbolzheim

Im Laue, D-79336 Herbolzheim (Baden-Württemberg)

Tel: 07643 1460. Email: s.hugoschmidt@t-online.de

This well equipped campsite is in a quiet location on a wooded slope to the north of Freiburg. There are 70 touring pitches, all with electricity (16A) and grass surfaces, on terraces linked by hard access roads with a little shade for some. A separate meadow for tents is at the top of the site (with three cabin toilets) and some pitches are used by a tour operator. This is good walking country and with only occasional entertainment, this is a very pleasant place in which to relax between daily activities.

Facilities

The main toilet facilities are modern, with new facilities for babies and disabled visitors. Laundry and dishwashing facilities. Motorcaravan services. Bar/restaurant (Easter - Sept daily). Play area. Dogs are not accepted 15/7-15/8. Off site: Large open-air heated municipal swimming pool complex adjacent (1/5-15/9). Restaurants and shops in the village 3 km. Riding, bicycle hire 5 km. Local market on Friday mornings.

Open: Easter - 3 October.

Directions

From A5 Frankfurt - Basel autobahn take exit 57, 58 or 59 and follow signs to Herbolzheim. Site signed south side of town near swimming pool. Go through pool car park and about 350 yd. past the pool entrance. GPS: N48:12.966 E07:47.314

Charges 2006

Per person	€ 5,00
child (0-15 yrs)	€ 3,00
pitch incl. electricity	€ 8,00 - € 11,00

DE3455 Gugel's Dreiländer Camping

Oberer Wald 3, D-79395 Neuenburg (am Rhein) (Baden-Württemberg)

Tel: **07631 7719**. Email: **info@camping-gugel.de**

Set in natural heath and woodland, Gugel's is an attractive site with 220 touring pitches either in small clearings in the trees, in open areas or on a hardstanding section used for single night stays. All have electricity (16A), and some also have water, waste water and satellite TV connections. Opposite is a meadow where late arrivals and early departures may spend the night. There may be some road noise near the entrance. The site may become very busy in high season and at Bank Holidays but you should always find room. There is a good atmosphere and can be recommended for both short and long stays. There is a social room with satellite TV where guests are welcomed with a glass of wine and a slide presentation of the attractions of the area. The Rhine is within walking distance. Neuenburg is ideally placed not only for enjoying and exploring the south of the Black Forest, but also for night stops when travelling from Frankfurt to Basel on the A5 autobahn. The site is winner of a prestigious environmental award. The permanent caravans set away from the tourist area, with their well-tended gardens, enhance rather than detract from the natural beauty.

Facilities

Three good quality heated sanitary blocks include some washbasins in cabins. Baby room. Facilities for disabled visitors. Laundry facilities. Motorcaravan services. Shop. Excellent restaurant. Takeaway (weekends and daily in high season). Indoor pool. Boules. Tennis. Fishing. Minigolf. Table tennis. Chess. Barbecue. Bicycle hire. Community room with TV. Activity programme organised (high season). Play areas. Off site: Riding 1.5 km. Golf 5 km. Neuenburg, Breisach, Freiburg, Basel and the Black Forest.

Open: All year.

Directions

From autobahn A5 take Neuenburg exit, turn left, then almost immediately turn left at traffic lights, left at next junction and follow signs for 2 km. to site (called 'Neuenburg' on most signs). GPS: N47:47.816 E07:33.00

Charges 2006

Per person	€ 6,25
child (2-15 yrs)	€ 2,90
caravan or tent	€ 5,70
small tent	€ 3,80
car	€ 4,20

Discount every 10th night, persons free.
No credit cards.

DE3427 Ferienparadies Schwarzwälder Hof

Tretenhofstr. 76, D-77960 Seelbach (Baden-Württemberg)

Tel: **078 23 960 950**. Email: **camping-rezeption@seelbach.org**

This site lies in a wooded valley, just south of the pleasant village of Seelbach in the Black Forest. The old buildings have been replaced by very attractive ones built in the old traditional style, but containing very modern facilities. There are 160 well drained touring pitches, either grass or hardstanding, all with electricity (10A), water supply and waste water outlet. There is also space for groups in tents. Just at the entrance is the family hotel with a restaurant. Besides a comprehensive general menu, there are also menus for children and older people with smaller appetites. A short walk from the site is a well-equipped municipal swimming pool and surrounding grass area. In July/August a good range of activities is organised for all ages, including a children's club. Fishing is possible in the stream which runs along the bottom of the site. The surrounding countryside is good for walking and cycling, and Europa Park is 30 km.

Facilities

Three sanitary blocks, all heated, clean and well maintained, include many washbasins in cabins and free showers. Facilities for wheelchair users. Family rooms (free). Baby changing room, superb children's bathroom, child size toilets and washbasins. Dishwashing and laundry facilities. Motorcaravan services. Gas supplies. Small shop. Restaurant, snacks and takeaway. TV and club room. Playground. Sauna (free after two night stay). Off site: Swimming 150 m. Bicycle hire 1 km. ATM in Seelbach 1 km. Riding 2 km. Golf 5 km.

Open: All year.

Directions

From A5/E35 autobahn, leave at exit 56 (Lahr). Follow road east through Lahr, until turn south to Seelbach. Go through Seelbach and the site is about 1 km. south. GPS: N48:17.983 E07:56.653

Charges 2006

Per person	€ 8,70
child (3-15 yrs)	€ 5,70
pitch with services	€ 8,40 - € 9,90
electricity (plus 0.50 kWh)	€ 2,00
dog	€ 3,00

Your sunny holiday and health paradise between the Black Forest and the Rhine

The first class holiday campsite with friendly atmosphere for your holiday.

NEW: swimming pool 160 m², sauna, solarium, fitness room, massages, beauty parlour, steam room, private sanitary facilities

luxury pitches with water and drainage,
satellite TV connection
beautiful play area
room for youngsters, table tennis
recreation room, TV room
beach volleyball • football pitch
two tennis courts
18-hole minigolf
barbecue area
bicycle hire
cycle tours with guide
boule court
canoeing on the Rhine
fishing in the Rhine
children's motorbikes
open air chess
baby room
facilities for disabled people
washing machines and dryers
animation programmes
excursions
gas for sale, self-service shop
beautiful restaurant
golf course 2,5 km
Spas at Bad Krozingen,
Badenweiler and Bad Bellingen
**all year: 10th night, persons go free
other discounts in low season
and for longer stays.**

DE3428 Terrassen Camping Oase

Mühlenweg 34, D-77955 Ettenheim (Baden-Württemberg)

Tel: **07822 445918**. Email: **info@campingpark-oase.de**

This pleasant well run site lies on wooded land on the western edge of the Black Forest, a very good region for walking and cycling. The level area near the entrance holds the main facilities and 200 touring pitches, all with 6A electricity. Pitches for tents are on grass and there is grass or hardstanding for caravans and motorcaravans. On sloping land further away are 85 terraced seasonal pitches. Just outside the entrance is the family hotel/restaurant, which also has a playground, all open to campers. Europa Park is 7 km. away, and the city of Freiburg is 40 km. to the south. The site is only 5 km. from the A5/E35 autobahn, which makes it an ideal overnight stop on the way to Basel and Switzerland.

Facilities

Two sanitary blocks are heated, clean and well maintained. Many washbasins are in cabins. Showers are coin-operated. Facilities for wheelchair users. Baby changing room, children's bathroom. Motorcaravan services. Gas supplies. Shop. Restaurant and takeaway (at hotel). TV and club room. Off site: Leisure area (snack bar, playground, three small football pitches, table tennis, volleyball, badminton, minigolf, boules). Tennis, riding and bicycle hire within 1 km. Fishing 3 km. Golf 5 km.

Open: Week before Easter - 4 October.

Directions

From A5/E35 autobahn, exit 57A (Ettenheim), follow L103 road southeast to Ettenheim (about 2.5 km). From here site is signed, and is a further 1 km. along the same road. GPS: N48:14.862 E07:49.652

Charges 2006

Per person	€ 6,50
child (1-15 yrs)	€ 3,50
pitch	€ 6,00 - € 9,00
electricity	€ 2,00
dog	€ 1,50 - € 3,00

DE3439 Hirzberg Camping Freiburg

Kartäuserstrasse 99, D-79104 Freiburg (Baden-Württemberg)

Tel: **0761 3 50 54**. Email: **hirzberg@freiburg-camping.de**

Hirzberg Camping is a quiet city site backing onto meadows and wooded hills, yet within easy reach of Freiburg's old town quarter. To the right of the entrance is reception, a shop, the sanitary facilities and a children's room with a play area outside. Just opposite is a large convenient overnight parking area. The main part of the site is reached by a short climb passing a small reading room and flower decked sitting area. The upper part has 76 pitches, 60 for tourists almost all with 10A electricity connections. Hardcore roads lead to open grass pitches, many under mature trees. To the left of reception and conveniently reached through a gap in the hedge is a comfortable beer garden with tables spread out under tall trees. This belongs to a restaurant specialising in serving traditional meals. The site is ideally placed for visiting the city and there is easy access to the main road for visiting other regions. Reception holds plenty of tourist information material and the site owners, Herr and Frau Ziegler, both speak very good English and are most helpful with tourist advice.

Facilities

Modern heated, well maintained sanitary block provides free hot water, roomy adjustable showers and some washbasins in cabins. Laundry room with washing machines and dryer. Kitchen with cooking rings on payment. Play room and play area for children. Small shop with essential supplies. Bicycle hire. WIFI internet over whole site. Off site: Bus service at entrance, tram 300 m. Golf 6 km. Riding 8 km.

Open: All year.

Directions

Site is in the eastern part of the city of Freiberg. To reach it without having to drive through the city, from the B31 take exit Freiberg Kappel (F. Kappel) which is well to the east of the city and follow camping signs. GPS: N47:59.514 E07:52.41

Charges 2007

Per person	€ 6,00
child (0-12 yrs)	€ 1,00 - € 2,50
pitch incl. electricity	€ 5,00 - € 6,50

No credit cards.

DE3450 Feriencamping Münstertal

Dietzelbachstr. 6, D-79244 Münstertal (Baden-Württemberg)

Tel: 07636 7080. Email: info@camping-muenstertal.de

Münstertal is an impressive site pleasantly situated in a valley on the western edge of the Black Forest. It has been one of the top graded sites in Germany for 20 years, and first time visitors will soon realise why when they see the standard of the facilities here. There are 300 individual pitches in two areas, either side of the entrance road on flat gravel, their size varying from 70-100 sq.m. All have electricity (16A) and 200 have waste water drains, many also with water, TV and radio connections. The large indoor swimming pool with sauna and solarium, and the outdoor pool, are both heated and free and there is a large, grass sunbathing area. The health and fitness centre provides a range of treatments, massages, etc. Children are very well catered for here with a play area and play equipment, tennis courts, minigolf, a games room with table tennis, table football and pool table and fishing. Riding is popular and the site has its own stables. The latest addition is an ice rink for skating and ice hockey in winter. There are 250 km. of walks, with some guided ones organised, and winter sports with cross-country skiing directly from the site (courses in winter – for children or adults and ski hire). The site becomes full in season and reservations, especially in July, are necessary. Member of Leading Campings Group.

Facilities

Three toilet blocks are of truly first class quality, with washbasins, all in cabins, showers with full glass dividers, baby bath, a unit for disabled visitors and individual bathrooms, some for hire, others for general use. Dishwashers in two blocks. Laundry with washing machines, spin and tumble dryers. Drying room. Motorcaravan services. Well stocked shop (all year). Restaurant, particularly good and well patronised (closed Nov.). Heated swimming pools, indoor all year 07.30-21.00, outdoor (with children's area) May-Oct. New health and fitness centre. Sauna and solarium. Games room. Bicycle hire. Tennis courses in summer Off site: Village amenities and train station near. Golf 15 km. Freiburg and Basel easy driving distances.

Open: All year.

Directions

Münstertal is south of Freiburg. From A5 autobahn take exit 64, turn southeast via Bad Krozingen and Staufen and continue 5 km. to the start of Münstertal, where camp is signed from the main road on the left. GPS: N47:51.584 E07:45.825

Charges 2006

Per person	€ 6,60 - € 7,65
child (2-10 yrs)	€ 4,40 - € 4,90
pitch incl. services	€ 10,50 - € 13,40
dog	€ 3,00

Maestro cards accepted.

Holidays under the starry sky

feriencamping
Münstertal

The Leading Camping & Caravaning Parks of Europe

Feriencamping Münstertal
Familie Wilfried Ortlieb
Dietzelbachstr. 6 • D-79244 Münstertal

Phone 07636-7080 • Fax 07636-7448
www.camping-muenstertal.de

This campsite is one of the best in Europe. Best ADAC rating since 1983. Pitches with electricity-, water-, telephone- and TV-connection. Tennis courts (lessons), heated covered and outdoor swimming pools, sauna, solarium, midget golf, trout fishing, winter sports in the vicinity and lots of footpaths in the surroundings.

DE3436 Campingplatz Bankenhof

Bruderhalde 31, D-79822 Titisee (Baden-Württemberg)

Tel: 07652 1351. Email: info@bankenhof.de

This peacefully located, fairly informal woodland site, with a friendly atmosphere, is situated just beyond the western end of Lake Titisee. The 190 pitches are on sparse grass and gravel, with some shade from a variety of trees, and 30 are occupied by seasonal units. The site is generally level, although there is a separate grassy area for tents which does have a slight slope. All pitches have electric hook-ups (16A), with gravel roads, and water taps for each area. Although there is some site lighting a torch might be useful for the darker areas under the trees. There is enough space for American RVs and other large units (welcomed, but booking is advised). Unusual features of the site are the glass walled technical area in the sanitary facilities, where the inquisitive can check the temperature of the water before taking their morning shower, and the totally separate sanitary unit with bright cheerful child-sized facilities for the under 10s. A popular bar and restaurant is open all year round (except November). Children also have an excellent fenced adventure playground. The lake and beach are only 300 m. via a direct path. This is an excellent site for exploring this part of the Black Forest and the Titisee area.

Facilities

Two sets of quality sanitary facilities plus three family bath/shower rooms for rent. Well equipped and heated, they include controllable hot showers and some washbasins in cubicles. A separate building houses facilities for disabled campers, and a unit for children (under 10 yrs). Kitchen facilities provide an electric hob and a dishwasher (on payment). Laundry. Motorcaravan service point. Shop. New restaurant (excl. Nov). Fitness room. TV and cinema room. Adventure play area. Youth Room. Bicycle, go-kart and buggy hire. Off site: Free bus service 300 m. Fishing 0.5 km. Golf, riding and boat launching within 3 km.

Open: All year.

Directions

From Freiburg take road B31 east to Titisee. Pass through the town centre and continue for 2.5 km. following camping signs. The entrance to Bankenhof is on the left. GPS: N47:53.159 E08:07.842

Charges guide

Per person	€ 4,70
child (3-16 yrs)	€ 2,60
pitch	€ 6,90
electricity per kWh	€ 0,45
dog	€ 1,80

DE3452 Terrassen Camping Alte Sägemühle

Badstrasse 57, D-79295 Sulzburg (Baden-Württemberg)

Tel: 07634 551181

Situated beside a peaceful road leading only to a natural swimming pool (formerly the mill pond) and a small hotel, the site lies just beyond the picturesque old town of Sulzburg with its narrow streets. This attractive location is perfect for those seeking peace and quiet. Set in a tree-covered valley with a stream running through the centre, the site has been kept as natural as possible. It is divided into terraced areas, each surrounded by high hedges and trees. Electrical connections (16A) are available on 42 of the 45 large touring pitches, although long leads may be needed. The main building by the entrance houses reception, a small shop (which stocks a good selection of local wines) and the sanitary facilities. Run by the Geuss family (Frau Geuss speaks reasonable English) the site has won an award from the state for having been kept natural, for example, no tarmac roads, no minigolf, no playgrounds, etc. There are opportunities for walking straight from the site into the forest, and many walks and cycle rides are shown on maps available at reception. The tiny 500 year old Jewish Cemetery reached through the site has an interesting history.

Facilities

In the main building, facilities are of good quality with two private cabins, separate toilets, washing machine and dryer. Motorcaravan service point. Small shop for basics (all year). Natural, unheated swimming pool adjacent (June-Aug) with discount to campers. Torch may be useful. Off site: Public transport, restaurants and other shops in Sulzburg 1.5 km. Riding 2 km. Bicycle hire 6 km. Fishing 8 km.

Open: All year.

Directions

Site is easily reached (25 minutes) from autobahn A5/E35. Take exit 64 for Bad Krozingen just south of Freiburg onto the B3 south to Heitersheim, then on and up through Sulzburg, or if coming from the south, exit 65 through Müllheim, Heitersheim and Sulzburg. GPS: N47:50.129 E07:43.402

Charges guide

Per person	€ 5,50
child (1-15 yrs)	€ 3,00
pitch incl. electricity (plus meter)	€ 4,50 - € 7,00

DE3445 Camping Belchenblick

Münstertäler Straße 43, D-79219 Staufen (Baden-Württemberg)

Tel: 07633 7045. Email: camping.belchenblick@t-online.de

This site stands at the gateway, so to speak, to the Black Forest. Not very high up itself, it is just at the start of the long road climb which leads to the top of Belchen, one of the highest summits of the forest. It is well situated for excursions by car to the best areas of the forest, for example the Feldberg-Titisee-Höllental circuit, and many excellent walks are possible nearby. Staufen is a pleasant little place with character. The site has 200 pitches (170 for touring units), all with electrical connections (10-16A), and 100 with TV and water. On site is a small heated indoor swimming pool and adjacent is a municipal sports complex, including an open-air pool. Reservation is necessary from early June to late August at this popular site, which is not a cheap one. However, charges do include free hot water and the indoor pool. A little tractor will site your caravan if required.

Facilities

Three sanitary blocks are heated and have free hot water, individual washbasins (6 in private cabins), plus 21 family cabins with WC, basin and shower (some on payment per night for exclusive use). Washing machine. Gas supplies. Motorcaravan services. Shop (1/3-31/10). Bar (all year). Snacks and takeaway (1/3-31/10). Indoor and outdoor pools. Sauna and solarium. Tennis. Playground with barbecue section. Football fields. Bicycle hire. Off site: Restaurant near. Fishing 500 m. Riding 2 km.

Open: All year.

Directions

Take autobahn exit for Bad Krozingen, south of Freiburg, and continue to Staufen. Site is southeast of the town and signed, across an unmanned local railway crossing near the entrance.
GPS: N47:52.307 E07:44.20

Charges 2007

Per person	€ 6,00 - € 7,50
child (2-12 yrs)	€ 4,00
pitch	€ 8,00
dog	€ 2,50
electricity (per kWh)	€ 0,60

DE3465 Camping Wirthshof

Steibensteg 12, D-88677 Markdorf (Baden-Württemberg)

Tel: 07544 9627-0. Email: info@wirthshof.de

Lying 7 km. back from the Bodensee, 12 km. from Friedrichshafen, this friendly site with good facilities could well be of interest to Britons with young children. The 324 individual touring pitches have electrical connections (10A) and are of about 80 sq.m. on well tended flat grass, adjoining access roads. There are 100 larger pitches with water, waste water and electricity. No dogs are accepted in July/Aug. and there is a special section for campers with dogs at other times. Many activities are organised for children and adults over a long season. On site is a pleasant heated outdoor pool (10/5-10/9) with a grassy lying-out area; it is free to campers but is also open to outsiders on payment so can be busy in season.

Facilities

The three heated toilet blocks provide washbasins in cubicles, a unit for disabled people and a children's bathroom. Cosmetic studio. Gas supplies. Motorcaravan services. Shop. Restaurant/bar with takeaway. Swimming pool (25 x 12.5 m; open 10/5-10/9). Sports field. Adventure playgrounds. Bicycle hire. Activity programme. Off site: Tennis near. Riding 8 km. Golf and fishing 10 km.

Open: 15 March - 30 October.

Directions

Site is on eastern edge of Markdorf, turn south off B33 Ravensburg road. The site is signed (but not named) from Markdorf.
GPS: N47:42.869 E09:24.558

Charges 2006

Per person	€ 5,50 - € 6,50
child (1-14 yrs)	€ 3,00 - € 4,00
pitch incl. electricity	€ 10,00 - € 11,00
No credit cards.	

237

DE3490 Hegau Bodensee Camping

An der Sonnenhalde 1, D-78250 Tengen (Baden-Württemberg)

Tel: **07736 92470**. Email: **info@hegau-camping.de**

Located in the sunny southwest corner of Germany, this site, new in 2003, must be one of the best we have seen. It is ultra modern in design and exceptionally high standards are maintained. Located in meadowland in a quiet rural valley close to the Swiss border, it provides excellent opportunities for walking, cycling and sightseeing. All 150 touring pitches (out of a total of 200) have electricity (16A), water and drainage, although water points are shared. The pitches are grassy and level and of a good size. At the bottom of the site is an excellent heated swimming pool which also houses a sauna and Turkish bath. With the Swiss border only minutes away, it is well placed for visits to Schaffhausen and even as far afield as Zurich. It is also an excellent spot to rest from touring the southern Black Forest which is a drive of less than an hour to the west.

Facilities

New heated sanitary facilities include private cabins, showers, facilities for disabled visitors and for children. Laundry and dishwashing facilities. Three family shower rooms for rent (2 also have a bath). Motorcaravan service point. Restaurant, small shop and bar opposite reception. Swimming pool, sauna and Turkish bath (charged). Off site: Golf 20 km. Skiing for children possible in the adjoining meadows. Supermarket less than 1 km.

Open: All year.

Directions

From A81 take exit 42 on to B314. At roundabout in Tengen follow international camping signs. Turn right at supermarket on edge of village. From Kommingen follow camp signs turning left towards site at supermarket on edge of village.

Charges 2006

Per unit incl. 2 persons and electricity	€ 17,50 - € 30,00
extra person	€ 5,00
child (6-14 yrs)	€ 3,00
Camping Cheques accepted.	

DE3467 Isnycamping

Lohbauerstr. 59-69, D-88316 Isny (Baden-Württemberg)

Tel: **07562 2389**. Email: **info@isny-camping.de**

Isny is a delightful spot for families and for others looking for a peaceful stay in a very well-managed environment. The site has been developed to a high standard and lies just south of the village in a wood by a lake. In an open area there are 45 individual 100 sq.m. hardstanding pitches with a circular access road. A further area is on a terrace just above. A café with light snacks during the week and meals at the weekends is open long hours in high season. It has a terrace that overlooks the lake, which is used for swimming (unsupervised). The site also offers a large family play area and fly fishing for trout in September/October.

Facilities

The main sanitary unit is first class and has automatic toilet seat cleaning. There are cabins as well as vanity style washbasins, large controllable showers, with full curtain, token operated. Further facilities near the reception house showers, WCs, washbasins, and a good unit for disabled visitors. Laundry. Basic motorcaravan services. Café/bar. Reception keeps a few basic supplies. Bicycles to borrow. Off site: Tennis club. Recreation and play areas. Barbecue area. Restaurant and supermarket 1.5 km.

Open: All year excl. November and December.

Directions

From the B12 between Lindau and Kempten, turn south at sign in Isny at traffic lights and follow signs up into the woods. GPS: N47:40.697 E10:01.821

Charges 2006

Per person	€ 6,40
child per year of age	€ 0,40
pitch	€ 9,00
electricity per kWh	€ 0,50
Special rates for senior citizens (low season).	

DE3602 Camping Romantische Straße

D-97993 Creglingen-Münster (Baden-Württemberg)

Tel: 07933 20289. Email: camping.hausotter@web.de

The small village of Münster is on a scenic road just 3 km. from Creglingen and the 100 km. long Tauber valley cycle route, and about 16 km. from the beautiful and popular tourist town of Rothenburg on the Tauber which can become very busy during the summer. This site would, therefore, be appreciated for its peaceful situation in a wooded valley just outside Münster, with 100 grass touring pitches (out of 140), many level, others with a small degree of slope. They are not hedged or fenced, to keep the natural appearance of the woodland. All the pitches have electricity (16A), some shade, and are either side of a stream (fenced off from a weir at the top of the site).

Facilities

The main sanitary facilities are of good quality, with free hot water for washbasins (two for each male/female in private cabins) and showers. A further small unit is not of the same quality. Launderette. Motorcaravan services. Small shop. Bar/restaurant (1/4-12/11, closed Mondays). Heated indoor pool (caps required). Sauna. Play area. Bicycle hire. Rooms to let. Off site: Bus 200 m. Lakes for swimming 100 m. and fishing 1 km. Riding 3 km.

Open: 15 March - 15 November.

Directions

From the Romantische Strasse between Rothenburg and Bad Mergentheim, exit at Creglingen to Münster (3 km) and site is just beyond this village. GPS: N49:26.357 E10:02.52

Charges 2006

Per person	€ 4,70 - € 5,80
child (3-14 yrs)	€ 3,60 - € 3,90
pitch incl. electricity	€ 8,00 - € 9,00

No credit cards. Camping Cheques accepted.

awan — tel: 00 333 59 59 03 59 kawan-villages.com

DE3627 Azur Camping Ellwangen

Rotenbacher Strasse, D-73479 Ellwangen (Baden-Württemberg)

Tel: 07961 7921. Email: ellwangen@azur-camping.de

In a quiet position on the edge of town, with the river Jagst along one side, this modern six hectare site, from which you can see the large hilltop castle, has a park-like appearance with mature trees giving some shade. The 95 large, flat, grassy pitches (8 hardstandings) are unmarked off tarmac access roads. Electricity is available for all the pitches from central boxes (16A). All the facilities are in one area in modern units, with reception, the small shop for basics and a bar/restaurant.

Facilities

Heated sanitary facilities provide some private cabins. Dishwashing facilities, both inside and out, a small laundry, and room for babies and disabled visitors. Laundry facilities. Gas supplies. Motorcaravan service point. Shop. Restaurant/bar. Play equipment on sand. Fishing is very popular. Off site: Cycle paths. Heated indoor municipal wave-pool 200 m. Numerous other local attractions.

Open: All year; 18 November - 28 February by reservation.

Directions

From A7 Ulm - Würzburg autobahn take exit 113 and go into Ellwangen from where site is signed on road to Rotenbach village. It is next to the Hallenbad, with a fairly tight left turn into the entrance road. GPS: N48:57.495 E10:07.24

Charges 2006

Per person	€ 5,50 - € 7,50
pitch incl. electricity	€ 8,50 - € 11,50

No credit cards.

DE3411 Campingplatz Heidehof

Heidehofstr 50, D-89150 Laichingen (Baden-Württemberg)

Tel: 07333 6408. Email: heidehof.camping@t-online.de

This site is at an altitude of 725 m. in the pleasant countryside of the Swabian Alb. Although there is an emphasis on permanent caravans, there are about 110 pitches for tourists. For overnight stays, these are in an area outside the barrier, and for longer stays pitches are inside the site. All have electricity connections (16A), and the overnight section also has an area for tents. A hotel/restaurant (open all year), although not actually in the campsite, is attached to it and immediately accessible.

Facilities

Five good quality toilet blocks, all heated and well maintained. 25 bathrooms to rent plus 3 for disabled visitors. Some washbasins are in cabins. Facilities for disabled visitors. Baby rooms. Laundry. Motorcaravan service point. Gas supplies. Shop with bakery. Bar and restaurant (at hotel). Swimming pool. Playgrounds. Children's club (weekends July/Aug). Bicycle hire. Off site: Riding 1 km. Fishing 6 km. Golf 10 km.

Open: All year.

Directions

Site is 6 km. from exit 61.A5/E52 Stuttgart-Ulm autobahn. Follow signs for Blaubeuren. Heidehof is about 2 km. south of the village of Machtolsheim. GPS: N48:28.659 E09:44.693

Charges 2006

Per person	€ 5,50
child (under 15 yrs)	€ 2,50
pitch	€ 4,50 - € 6,50
electricity (plus 0.5 per kWh)	€ 2,00

239

DE3280 Camping und Ferienpark Teichmann

An der B252, D-34516 Vöhl-Herzhausen (Hesse)

Tel: 05635 245. Email: camping-teichmann@t-online.de

Situated by a six hectare lake (the Edersee) with tree-covered hills all around, this well cared for site blends in attractively with its surroundings. Windsurfing, rowing boats, pedaloes (no motor-boats), swimming and fishing are possible, all in different areas, and the site is also suitable for a winter sports holiday (with ski runs near). There are many local walks and the opportunity exists for taking a pleasure boat trip and riding home by bicycle. The 460 pitches (half for touring units) are mainly on flat grass, all with electricity (6-16A) and with some hardstandings. There is a separate area for tents with its own toilet block. The many amenities include a mini-market and café. A good site for families with children of all ages, there are many activities (listed below) and a pitch can usually be found even for a one night stay. A very large open air model railway is a special attraction.

Facilities

Three good quality sanitary blocks can be heated and have some private cabins, with baby rooms in two with facilities for wheelchair users. Café and shop (both summer only). Restaurant by entrance open all day (closed Feb). Watersports. Boat and bicycle hire. Lake swimming. Football. Fishing. Minigolf. Tennis. Playground. Large working model railway. Sauna and solarium. High season disco. Off site: Riding 0.5 km. Golf 25 km. Cable car (you can take bikes), Aquapark.

Open: All year.

Directions

From A44 Oberhausen - Kassel autobahn, take exit for Korbach. Site is between Korbach and Frankenberg on the B252 road, 1 km. to the south of Herzhausen, about 45 km. from the A44. GPS: N51:10.530 E08:53.44

Charges 2007

Per person	€ 3,50 - € 6,40
pitch	€ 8,00 - € 14,60
child (3-15 yrs)	€ 2,50 - € 3,80
electricity (10A)	€ 2,40

Camping-und Ferienpark ★★★★ TEICHMANN

34516 Vöhl-Herzhausen . Tel. 05635-245 . Fax 05635-8145
Internet: www.camping-teichmann.de . E-Mail: camping-teichmann@t-online.de

am Nationalpark Kellerwald-Edersee

The camping with ♥

ADAC 2004

Federal winner in competition for best compsites, surrounded by the glorious countryside of the Edersee

Our family-friendly campsite, in the heart of Germany offers unforgettable holiday enjoyment.

DE3265 Lahn Camping

Schleusenweg 16, D-65549 Limburg an der Lahn (Hesse)

Tel: 06431 22610. Email: lahncamping@limburg-net.de

Pleasantly situated on the bank of the river Lahn (with direct access to it) between the autobahn and the town – both the autobahn viaduct and the cathedral are visible – this is a useful overnight stop for travellers along the Köln-Frankfurt stretch of the A3. The site is on level grass with 200 touring pitches (out of 250 altogether and 140 have 6A electricity – may need long cable)) on either side of gravel tracks at right angles from the main tarmac road. There are some trees but it is mainly open. It is very popular and can become crowded at peak times, so arrive early. There is road and rail noise.

Facilities

The main sanitary block near reception is old and facilities are poor (showers need a token). A better, heated block at the other end of the site is a welcome addition. Motorcaravan services. Bar/restaurant offers drinks, simple meals and takeaway. Small shop.

Open: 18 April - 26 October.

Directions

Leave A3 autobahn at Limburg-Nord exit and follow road towards town and then signs for 'Camping-Swimming'. GPS: N50:23.357 E08:04.40

Charges guide

Per pitch incl. electricity	€ 15,20

No credit cards.

DE3225 Naturpark Camping Suleika
D-65391 Lorch am Rhine (Hesse)
Tel: 06726 9464

On a steep hillside in the Rhine-Taunus Nature Park and approached by a narrow and steep system of lanes through the vineyards, this site is steeply arranged on small terraces up the side of the wooded hill with a stream flowing through – the water supply is direct from springs. The surroundings are most attractive, with views over the vineyards to the river below. Of the 100 pitches, 50 are available for tourists. These are mostly on the lower terraces, in groups of up to four units. All have electricity and there are water points. Cars are parked away from the pitches near the entrance. There is a special area for younger campers. The site is popular for caravan rallies. A central block contains a very pleasant restaurant and small shop for basics (bread to order), with sanitary facilities alongside. With steep walks from most pitches to the facilities, this is probably not a site for visitors with disabilities; however, it is an attractive situation and reception staff are very friendly. This particular area is famous as it was briefly a 'Free State' (1919-23) and you will be able to taste and buy the site owner's wine and other items as souvenirs. The Riesling Walk footpath passes above the site. There are many local attractions (as well as the Lorelei) shown on a large map, and the helpful owner speaks good English.

Facilities
The excellent toilet block is heated in cool weather and provides some washbasins in cabins for each sex and a nicely furnished baby washroom, with WC, shower and bath. Laundry service. Motorcaravan services. Gas supplies. Restaurant (closed Mon. and Thurs.). Small shop (bread to order). Playground. Some entertainment in season. Off site: Bicycle hire. Fishing 300 m. Riding 4 km. The Riesling Walk footpath passes above the site.

Open: 15 March - 31 October.

Directions
Direct entrance from B42 (cars only), between Rudesheim and Lorch, with height limit of 2.25 m. under bridge. Higher vehicles: site signed on south side of Lorch. Site reached via a one-way system of lanes – follow signs. GPS: N50:01.047 E07:51.206

Charges 2006
Per person	€ 5,00
child	€ 2,00
pitch incl. electricity (plus meter)	€ 6,00 - € 8,00

No credit cards.

DE3275 Camping Seepark
D-36275 Kirchheim (Hesse)
Tel: 06628 1525. Email: info@campseepark.de

Kirchheim is just five kilometres from the A7 (50 km. south of Kassel) and also close to the Frankfurt to Dresden autobahns A5-A4 in eastern Hesse, which has the largest forested area in Germany. Pleasantly situated on the side of a valley, this is a large terraced park and is probably unique in offering a service for diabetics, with special food available and dialysis arranged in Bad Hersfeld hospital. There are 170 touring pitches (5 for people with disabilities) generally in their own areas (out of 370 altogether), varying in size from about 80 to 110 sq.m many marked with young trees in the corners. All have 16A electrical connections, just under half with water and drainage. They are mostly numbered in cul-de-sacs with access from tarmac roads leading up to an open area for larger vehicles and a tent field at the top. Thousands of bushes and trees have been planted over the years (but providing little shade for the pitches) and flowers are prominent around the service buildings. Opposite the entrance is a mainly sloping overnight area (including electricity and shower).

Facilities
The original sanitary facilities are in the complex at the entrance with further very good facilities at the modern restaurant building higher up the site (high season and holidays). They have under-floor heating and private cabins. The tent area is currently served by a portable unit. Launderette. Motorcaravan service point. Shop. Restaurant (breakfast available) open all year. Small free heated open air raised swimming pool (June-Aug; 1 m. deep; parents must supervise children which also applies to the lake swimming area at the left side of the site). Tennis. Table-tennis. Football. Volleyball. Minigolf. Diabetic service. Play areas. Tennis. Fishing. Volleyball. Football field. Water-skiing. Barbecue area. Off site: Bus service 500 m. Close by on the lake there is water-skiing, boat hire, trampolining, adventure pool, roller skating rink, indoor tennis and fishing. Golf 4 km.

Open: All year.

Directions
From A7 Kassel - Fulda/Wurzburg take exit 87 for Kirchheim and follow signs to Seepark for 4.5 km. The park is on a minor road between the small villages of Rimboldshausen and Kemmerode, just west of the lake. GPS: N50:48.872 E09:31.07

Charges guide
Per unit incl. up to 6 persons	€ 19,80
electricity	€ 2,50
water	€ 1,50

DE3220 Camping Burg Lahneck

Ortsteil Oberlahnstein, D-56112 Lahnstein (Rhineland Palatinate)

Tel: 02621 2765

The location of this site is splendid, high up overlooking the Rhine valley and the town of Lahnstein – many of the pitches have their own super views. It consists partly of terraces and partly of open grassy areas, has a cared for look and all is very neat and clean. One can usually find a space here, though from early July to mid-August it can become full. There are 100 individual touring pitches marked but not separated and mostly level, all with electricity (16A). Campers are sited by the management. Reception staff at the site are friendly and charges reasonable. Adjacent is a good outdoor swimming pool with extensive grassy areas, and the mediaeval castle Burg Lahneck (the home of the camp proprietor, which may be visited) with its smart restaurant. A ' Kurzentrum', under 2 km. from the site, has a thermal pool from warm springs (reduced admission to campers) with sauna and solarium. Very popular with British visitors, this site is in the best part of the Rhine valley, and close to Koblenz and the Mosel.

Facilities	Directions
The single central, heated toilet block is of a good standard, and well maintained and cleaned. There are some cabins for both sexes. Showers are on payment. Washing machine and dryer. Motorcaravan services. Gas supplies. Small shop. Small playground. Off site: Cafe/restaurant adjoining site. Town swimming pool (reduced charges for campers, 15/5-31/8). Riding 500 m. Fishing 3 km. Bicycle hire 2 km.	From B42 road bypassing the town, take Oberlahnstein exit and follow signs 'Kurcentrum' and Burg Lahneck. GPS: N50:18.338 E07:36.791

Open: Easter/1 April - 31 October.

Charges 2006

Per person	€ 5,50
children (3-14 yrs)	€ 3,00
pitch	€ 5,50 - € 8,50
electricity (plus meter)	€ 0,50

No credit cards.

DE3222 Camping Gülser Moselbogen

Am Gülser Moselbogen 20, Güls, D-56072 Koblenz (Rhineland Palatinate)

Tel: 0261 44474. Email: moselbogen@paffhausen.com

This site is set well above the river and has a pleasant outlook to the forested valley slopes. A large proportion of the 16 acre site is taken up by privately owned bungalows, but the touring section of 110 large individual pitches, is self contained and accessed by gravel paths leading off the main tiled roads. The flat pitches have little shade as yet, but all have connections for TV and 16A electricity and there are water points in each section. A new area of gravel hardstanding has been developed and RVs are accepted. The provision of first class sanitary facilities here, combined with the location being very convenient for sightseeing along the rivers Mosel and Rhein and the easy access to Koblenz, the A48 and A61, make this an attractive proposition for a short or longer-term stay.

Facilities	Directions
Entry to the excellent, heated sanitary building is by a coded card that also operates the hot water to the showers (free to the washbasins, many of which are in cabins). Unit for disabled visitors. Baby room. Dishwashing and cooking rings (charged). Laundry. Gas supplies. Motorcaravan services. Shop. Café and bistro. Play area. Bicycle hire. Off site: Fishing 200 m. Special area for swimming in the Mosel 200 m. Restaurant 500 m. Güls village 1.5 km. Riding 3 km.	Site is 1.5 km. west of village of Güls but easiest access is from the A61. Take exit 38 (Koblenz-Metternich). After 2 km. turn right at roundabout (Winningen). Keep on main road to Winningen until the B416 where you turn left towards Koblenz. Site on right in 3.5 km. GPS: N50:19.954 E07:33.185

Open: All year.

Charges 2006

Per person	€ 5,00
child (3-14 yrs)	€ 2,50
pitch	€ 5,00 - € 8,00
electricity (plus 1.00 connection)	€ 1,50
dog	€ 2,00

DE3215 Camping Goldene Meile

Simrockweg 9 - 13, D-53424 Remagen (Rhineland Palatinate)

Tel: 02642 22222. Email: info@camping-goldene-meile.de

This site is on the banks of the Rhine between Bonn and Koblenz. Although there is an emphasis on permanent caravans, there are about 300 pitches for tourists (out of 500), most with 6A electricity and 100 with water and drainage. They are either in the central, more mature area or in a newer area where the numbered pitches of 80-100 sq. m. are arranged around an attractively landscaped, small fishing lake. Just 5 are by the busy river and there is likely to be some noise from the trains that run beside it. Access to the river bank is through a locked gate. Adjacent to the site is a large complex of open-air public swimming pools (campers pay the normal entrance fee). They claim always to find space for odd nights, except perhaps at B.Hs. This site is in a popular area and, although busy at weekends and in high season, appears to be well run.

Facilities

The main toilet block is heated and clean, with some washbasins in cabins, showers and facilities for wheelchair users. Shower and wash rooms locked 10 pm. A smaller block serves the newer pitches (no showers). Laundry and cooking facilities. Motorcaravan services. Gas. Shop, bar, restaurant and takeaway (all 1/4-30/10 and some weekends). Play areas. Entertainment for children (July/Aug). Bicycle hire. Main gate locked at 10 pm. (also 1-3 pm). Off site: Pool complex adjacent (May-Sept).

Open: All year.

Directions

Remagen is 23 km. south of Bonn on N9 road towards Koblenz. Site is on road close to the Rhine from Remagen to Kripp, signed from N9 south of Remagen. From A61 autobahn take Sinzig exit. GPS: N50:34.549 E07:15.085

Charges 2006

Per person	€ 5,50
child (6-16 yrs)	€ 4,50
pitch incl. electricity	€ 9,75 - € 11,25

Eurocards accepted.

Campingplatz »Goldene Meile«
D-53424 Remagen
Tel. (0 26 42) 2 22 22
http://www.camping-goldene-meile.de
e-mail: info@camping-goldene-meile.de

On one of the most beautiful and modern camp sites in the romantic Rhine valley between Bonn (20 km) and Koblenz (40 km) you will find ideal conditions.

For a holiday: water sports on the Rhine and in the heated leissure time pool (86 m chute), sports and keep-fit (indoor and outdoor tennis courts, playing field, volleyball court, football ground), hiking in the Eifel and the Westerwald, boat trips on the Rhine and the Mosel, numerous wine festivals.

For a short stop: convenient location only 7 km from the A 61 motorway (Sinzig-Remagen exit), 2 km to the B 9. Shop, restaurant with terrace, first-class rating from ADAC for many years.

DE3212 Landal Wirfttal

Wirftstraße, D-54589 Stadtkyll (Rhineland Palatinate)

Tel: 06597 92920. Email: info@landal.de

Peacefully set in a small valley in the heath and forest of the hills of the northern Eifel near the Belgian border, Wirfttal has 250 numbered pitches of which 150 are for tourers. They mostly back onto fences, hedges etc. on fairly flat ground of different levels (steel pegs are required for tents and awnings). The pitches (many on gravel) are 80 sq.m or more, and all have electricity (8A) and TV aerial points with water points around. 5 individual pitches have their own water and waste water points. Also part of the site, but separate from the camping, is a large holiday bungalow complex.

Facilities

One main toilet block, and two small units, all heated. All ladies' washbasins and one for men in main block are in cabins. New shop. Restaurant and snacks. Swimming pool complex (discount for campers). Indoor pool (free) and sauna and solarium (on payment). Tennis. Riding. Fishing. Bicycle hire. Sports centre adjacent with squash hall. Play equipment. Adventure playground. Winter sports. Bicycle and sledge hire. Animation in season.

Open: All year.

Directions

Site is 1.5 km. south of Stadtkyll on road towards Schüller. Follow signs in Stadtkyll for Haus am der See). GPS: N50:20.326 E06:32.252

Charges 2006

Per unit incl. 2 persons and electricity	€ 13,00 - € 28,00
extra person	€ 3,00

DE3233 Campingplatz Holländischer Hof

D-56820 Senheim (Rhineland Palatinate)

Tel: 02673 4660. Email: holl.hof@t-online.de

This campsite lies along a bend of the river Moselle, surrounded on three sides by hills, and on the other by the river. An arm of the river intrudes here and a harbour for small boats has been made. A road bridge passes over the very last pitches at one end of the site, but this did not seem to generate any noise nuisance. There are some seasonal pitches, but the site caters mostly for tourists. All 150 pitches have electricity points (6/10A). Dogs are not allowed on the site, but there are a dozen pitches outside the barrier for those who have dogs with them. Many wine producing villages and towns are within easy reach, the largest and best known being Cochem (16 km. downstream). Boat trips are also a feature of the area. As well as the many events taking place in the villages, the site organises a good programme of daily activities.

Facilities	Directions
Main sanitary block – washbasins (some in cubicles), showers (by token), unit for disabled visitors. Laundry facilities. Other toilet facilities in a 'portacabin' unit. Motorcaravan service point. Shop. Gas. Restaurant, snack bar, pizzeria and takeaway (with children's menu) and terrace. Playground. TV room. Sports field. Fishing in river. Off site: Tennis 300 m. Bicycle hire 2 km. ATM point 2 km. Golf 4 km.	From Cochem (on the west bank) take B49 upstream (south). At Nehren, cross bridge towards Senheim. From the bridge the site is below on the left. If coming from upstream, take the B49 north from Alf. GPS: N50:04.931 E07:12.521

Open: Easter - 1 November.

Charges 2007

Per person	€ 4,10
child (3-10 yrs)	€ 3,00
pitch	€ 7,15
electricity per kWh	€ 0,55

No credit cards.

DE3237 Camping In der Enz

In der Enz 25, D-54673 Neuerburg (Rhineland Palatinate)

Tel: 06564 2660

This site is just outside the town, next to the municipal swimming pool complex, and the enthusiastic owners give a very warm welcome which makes this a very pleasant place to stay. The site is bisected by the unfenced River Enz which is little more than a stream at this point. The section nearest the road is occupied by 50 long stay units. The other half, on the other side of the river with its own access road and footbridge, is solely for tourists. This has 50 very large, open grass pitches, all with electricity (16A), of which 32 are multi-service with water and drainage. Reception keeps basic supplies, but there is a supermarket only 1.5 km. towards the town via a traffic free path/cycleway which runs along the route of the old railway line for 5 km, passing the site. At the end of June each year, on a Sunday, 38 km. of road between Arzfeld, through Neuerburg and Sinspelt to Irrel is closed to motorised traffic. Known as the 'Süd Eifel Tour', only pedestrians, cyclists, wheelchair users, roller-bladers etc. are allowed to enjoy this traffic free situation (avoid arrival or departure on this day).

Facilities	Directions
New sanitary block of very high quality with the usual facilities and provision for disabled visitors. Baby changing room. Kitchen and laundry. Family sauna room (extra charge). Play area. Bicycle hire. Internet point. The site is not suitable for American RVs. Off site: Swimming pool complex (May-Sept) and all year restaurant and bar (both adjacent). Fishing, riding and tennis within walking distance. Golf 13 km.	From A60 (E29) take exit 6 and head south to Bitburg, then take road 50 west to Sinspelt. Turn north for 6 km. to Neuerburg, through town and site is 1.5 km. north of the town. GPS: N50:01.668 E06:16.613

Open: All year excl. February and November.

Charges 2006

Per person	€ 2,50
child (3-15 yrs)	€ 2,00
pitch incl. car	€ 7,00
electricity per kWh	€ 0,50

DE3242 Country Camping Schinderhannes

D-56291 Hausbay-Pfalzfeld (Rhineland Palatinate)

Tel: 06746 80280. Email: info@countrycamping.de

About 30 km south of Koblenz, west of the Rhine and south of the Mosel, this site is set in a 'bowl' of land which catches the sun all day. With trees and parkland all around, it is a peaceful and picturesque setting. There are 150 permanent caravans in a separate area from 90 short stay touring pitches on hardstanding. For longer stays, an area around the lake has a further 160 numbered pitches. These are of over 80 sq.m. on grass, some with hardstanding and all with 8A electricity. You can position yourself for shade or sun. The lake is used for swimming, inflatable boats and fishing. English is spoken by the helpful reception staff. Country Camping could be a useful transit stop en-route to the Black Forest, Bavaria, Austria and Switzerland, as well as a family holiday. High in the Hunsruck (a large area with forests, ideal for walking and cycling), Schinderhannes himself was a legendary 'Robin Hood' character, whose activities were curtailed in Mainz, at the end of a rope.

Facilities

The sanitary buildings, which can be heated, are of a high standard with one section, in the reception/shop building, for the overnight pitches and the remainder close to the longer stay places. Facilities for disabled people. Laundry. Bar. Restaurant with takeaway. TV area. Skittle alley. Shop (all amenities 1/3-31/10 and Xmas). Tennis (on payment). Fishing. Play area. Rallies welcome. Torches useful. Barrier closed 22.00-07.00 hrs.

Open: All year.

Directions

From A61 Koblenz - Ludwigshafen road, take exit 43 Pfalzfeld (30 km. south of Koblenz) and on to Hausbay where site is signed.
GPS: N50:06.358 E07:34.093

Charges 2006

Per person	€ 6,00
child (under 14)	€ 3,00
pitch incl. electricity	€ 8,00

Camping Cheques accepted.

Country Camping Schinderhannes
HOLIDAY - RALLY & FAMILYCAMP
Between Rhine and Mosel
Free Brochure
GPS: N 50.1060 E 07.5679
see no. 3242

DE3232 Family Camping

Wiesenweg 25, D-56820 Mesenich bei Cochem (Rhineland Palatinate)

Tel: **02673 4556**. Email: **info@familycamping.de**

Situated beside the River Mosel with views of forest and vineyard, this attractive family run site is on a stretch of the river that is well away from the railway. The 94 touring pitches are among the vines, mainly level, with electric hook-ups (6/10A), separated by bushes and some with shade. 25 pitches have their own water tap and there are 35 tents for rent. The site roads are relatively narrow and are not suitable for larger units especially American RVs or twin axle caravans. On arrival you must stop in the lay-by on the approach road while booking in at reception. A very popular site in July and August with many activities organised for youngsters, the site has a small outdoor pool and a children's pool. There is direct access to the riverside path and good walks and cycling opportunities all around the site. Good English is spoken.

Facilities

Well equipped, heated toilet facilities provide good sized showers (on payment), washbasins mainly in cubicles or curtained. Good baby room. Laundry with washing machines and dryer. Shop, bar and restaurant (1/5-8/9). Takeaway (1/5-15/9). Swimming pools (1/6-15/9, weather dependant). Play area. Disco evenings and wine tours in July/Aug. River fishing (with permit). Dogs are not accepted in July/Aug. Off site: Bicycle hire 300 m. Golf 7 km. Riding 10 km. Wine museum. Cochem with its castle and leisure centre 15 km.

Open: 8 April - 8 October.

Directions

Mesenich is about 15 km. southwest of Cochem, on opposite side of the River Mosel. From B49 at Senheim, cross river and follow signs (Mesenich). Site in village on left. Or cross river at Cochem and follow L98 riverside road south to Mesenich. GPS: N50:06.093 E07:11.628

Charges 2007

Per unit incl. 2 persons	€ 10,00 - € 14,00
extra person	€ 4,00

No credit cards.

DE3245 Landal Sonnenberg

D-54340 Leiwen (Rhineland Palatinate)

Tel: **06507 93690**. Email: **info@landal.de**

With attractive views over the Mosel as you climb the approach road, 4 km. from the wine village of Leiwen and the river, this pleasant site is on top of a hill. It has a splendid free leisure centre incorporating an indoor activity pool with child's paddling pool, whirlpool, cascade and slides. Also in this building are tenpin bowling, a sauna, solarium and fitness room, tennis and badminton, plus a snack bar. Combining a bungalow complex (separate) with camping, the site has 150 large, individual and numbered grass/gravel pitches on terraces with electricity (6A) and TV connections. Excursions and entertainment are organised in season, with ranger guided walks, wine-tasting, daily cruises from Leiwen to Bernkastel and coach trips to the Rhine (both May-Oct). There is a good restaurant and shop, and the site is efficiently managed with a friendly and helpful English speaking reception staff.

Facilities

The single toilet block has under-floor heating, washbasins in cabins (all for women, a couple for men). It is stretched in busy times. Separate suite for disabled visitors. Large laundry. Motorcaravan services. Shop. Restaurant, bistro, bar and snacks. Indoor multi-purpose leisure centre with activity pool, climbing wall, 10 pin bowling, tennis and badminton. Volleyball. Football pitch. Minigolf. Playground. Bicycle hire (high season). Disco, entertainment and excursions at various busy times. Deer park. Off site: Fishing 5 km. Riding or golf 12 km.

Open: 23 March - 3 November.

Directions

From Trier-Koblenz A48/A1 take new exit 128 for Bekond, Föhren, Hetzerath and Leiwen. Follow signs for Leiwen and in town follow signs for Ferienpark, Sonnenberg or Freibad on very winding road up hill 4 km. to site. GPS: N49:48.227 E06:53.554

Charges 2006

Per unit incl. 2 persons and electricity	€ 22,00 - € 33,00
extra person	€ 3,00
dog	€ 3,00

DE3258 Camping Sägmühle

D-67705 Trippstadt (Rhineland Palatinate)

Tel: 06306 92190. Email: info@saegmuehle.de

Camping Sägmühle has been in the same family for over 50 years, during which time it has undergone several major developments which have turned it into a first class site. It is peacefully situated beside a lake, in a wooded valley in the heart of the Palatinate Nature Park, and there are many kilometres of walks to enjoy, as well as castles to explore. A first class restaurant offers you fine local wines, and there is plenty for younger children to enjoy with fishing, swimming and boating in the lake (pedaloes for hire), a fort, minigolf and tennis. The 200 touring pitches (half the total) are at least 80 sq.m. or more on flat grass, each with electricity (4A or more) and TV connections, with plenty of water points around. There are three separate areas of pitches, one of which is close to the lake, and it is a pleasant change to find a site that keeps the lakeside pitches for tourers.

Facilities

Each area has its own sanitary facilities, those beside the lake and the back being first class, while those at the side have been renovated. Private cabins, baby bathroom, facilities for disabled people, launderette. Motorcaravan services. Restaurant serving local specialties and takeaway food (lunchtime and evening). Bread available from the accessory shop in high season. Solarium. Two tennis courts. Play areas. Mountain bike hire. Boules, giant chess. Minigolf. Fishing in lake. Entertainment daily in high season. Off site: Shops and bus service 10 minutes walk in Trippstadt. Riding 4 km. Golf 25 km.

Open: 14 December - 31 October.

Directions

At Kaiserslautern on A6, take exit 15 (Kaiserslautern West) onto B270 towards Pirmasens. Turn left after 8 km. towards Karlstal and follow site signs. From the A65 between Karlsruhe and Neustadt take exit 15 or 17 towards Annweiler on the B10. After Annweiler right on B48 to Rinnthal and on towards Kaiserslautern. After 20 km. left to Trippstadt and the next left to Trippstadt. Follow site signs into the valley. GPS: N49:21.096 E07:46.862

Charges 2007

Per person	€ 6,20 - € 7,20
child (under 14 yrs)	€ 2,60 - € 3,20

Camping Cheques accepted.

DE3250 Landal Warsberg

In den Urlaub 1, D-54439 Saarburg (Rhineland Palatinate)

Tel: 06581 91460. Email: info@landal.de

On top of a steep hill in an attractive location, this site and the long winding approach road both offer pleasant views over the town and surrounding area. A large, well organised site, there are 500 numbered touring pitches of quite reasonable size on flat or slightly sloping ground, separated in small groups by trees and shrubs, with electrical connections (6A) available in most places. There are some tour operator pitches and a separate area of holiday bungalows to rent.

Facilities

Three toilet blocks of good quality provide washbasins (many in private cabins) and a unit for disabled visitors. Large launderette by reception. Motorcaravan services. Gas supplies. Shop. Restaurant and takeaway, games rooms adjacent. Swimming pool. Minigolf. Bicycle hire. Football. Playground. Entertainment in season. Reception opens 09.00 - 17.00. 530 metre long 'Rodelbahn' toboggan (small fee). Off site: Riding and fishing 5 km.

Open: 31 March - 30 October.

Directions

From Trier on road 51 site is well signed in the northwest outskirts of Saarburg off the Trierstrasse (signs also for 'Ferienzentrum') and from all round town. Follow signs up hill for 3 km. GPS: N49:37.195 E06:32.609

Charges 2006

Per unit incl. 2 persons	€ 19,00 - € 27,00
with electricity (6A)	€ 21,00 - € 29,00
extra person	€ 3,00

DE3255 Azur Camping am Königsberg

Am Schwimmbad 1, D-67752 Wolfstein (Rhineland Palatinate)

Tel: 06304 4143. Email: benspruijt@gmx.de

Situated in an area between the Rhine and Mosel rivers in a nature area at the foot of the Königsberg, this is a small attractive, well maintained site with plenty of facilities. Of the 100 pitches, 70 are reserved for tourists and most have electricity, fresh and waste water connections. The level, grass, mainly open pitches are easily reached by tarmac site roads. A large separate meadow is for tents and has a communal grill and covered eating area. Trees and hedges provide some shade and division of the site. A large attractive swimming pool complex next to the site is free to campers.

Facilities

Modern comfortable, heated sanitary block with all usual facilities including showers, free hot water and private cabins. Facilities for disabled people. Laundry room. Shop. Bar/restaurant (all year). Takeaway. Play area and games room for children with entertainment daily in summer. Minigolf. Bicycle hire. Fishing. Off site: Large swimming pool complex next to site, free to campers. Shops and other facilities in the village 300 m. Riding 2 km.

Open: All year.

Directions

From A6 Ludwigshafen - Saarbrücken autobahn take exit 15 for Kaiserslauten West and head north towards Lauterecken. In Erfenbach left on B270 towards Lauterecken and Idar-Oberstein. Stay on the B270. Site is signed 300 m. south of the village of Wolfstein.

Charges 2006

Per person	€ 5,50 - € 7,50
child (2-12 yrs)	€ 4,00 - € 6,00
pitch incl. electricity	€ 8,50 - € 11,50

DE3256 Azur Camping Hunsrück

Parkstr., D-54421 Reinsfeld (Rhineland Palatinate)

Tel: 06503 95123. Email: reinsfeld@azur-camping.de

This quiet countryside site, spread over 20 hectares, is situated close to the French and Luxembourg borders. With 980 pitches (600 for touring units), the site is constructed with 29 circular grassed areas, each surrounded by trees, and containing no more than 25 pitches. This creates the impression that you are staying on a smaller site, although you do have the facilities of a larger large site. A spacious central meadow opposite a lake is used for caravans and tents and is separated from a playing field by a tree lined stream. This is a quiet and relatively unknown comer of Germany.

Facilities

Six heated sanitary buildings with free hot showers, washbasins in cabins and family bathrooms to rent. Baby rooms. Facilities for disabled people. Laundry facilities. Motorcaravan service point. Gas supplies. Supermarket. Comfortable restaurant/bar with takeaway. Swimming pool. Tennis. Large play area and children's entertainment in summer. Sunday concerts.

Open: All year.

Directions

Site is 20 km. southeast of Trier. Leave A1 at exit 132 (Reinsfeld) and follow sign for Reinsfeld. Continue through village and site is signed to the left just before leaving village. GPS: N49:41.328 E006:52.00

Charges 2006

Per person	€ 5,50 - € 7,50
child (2-12 yrs)	€ 4,00 - € 6,00
pitch incl. electricity	€ 8,50 - € 11,50

DE3260 Knaus Camping Park Bad Dürkheim

In den Almen 3, D-67098 Bad Dürkheim (Rhineland Palatinate)

Tel: 06322 61356. Email: badduerkheim@knauscamp.de

This large site is comfortable and has some 550 pitches (about half occupied by permanent caravans) but, being the best site at this well known wine town, it is very busy in main season. However, with some emergency areas they can usually find space for everyone. The site is long with individual pitches of fair size arranged on each side of the central road, which is decorated with arches of growing vines. Growing trees provide sme shade and electrical connections are available throughout (16A). There is some noise from light aircraft, especially at weekends.

Facilities

Three large sanitary blocks are spaced out along the central avenue. They are of a high standard (private cabins, automatic taps, etc) and are heated in cool weather. Laundry facilities. Gas supplies. Motorcaravan services. Cooking facilities. Shop. Restaurant. Sports programme. Tennis. Sports field. Playground. Garden chess. Sauna and solarium. Bathing and non-powered boat launching in lake. Activity programme (guided tours, biking, canoeing and climbing). Dogs are not accepted.

Open: All year excl. November

Directions

Bad Dürkheim is on the no. 37 road west of Ludwigshafen. Site is on the eastern outskirts, signed from the Ludwigshafen road at traffic lights. GPS: N49:28.428 E08:11.502

Charges 2006

Per person	€ 6,00
child (4-14 yrs)	€ 3,00
pitch	€ 8,00
electricity (plus meter)	€ 2,00
No credit cards.	

MAP 14

The country's coastline offers huge variety – sheltered bays and coves, golden stretches of sand with dunes, pebbly beaches, coastal caves with steep rocks and volcanic black sand and coastal wetlands.

CAPITAL: ATHENS

Tourist Office

Greek National Tourism Organisation
4 Conduit Street, London, W1S 2DJ
Tel: 020 7495 9300 (Enquiries & Information)
Fax: 020 7287 1369
Email: info@gnto.co.uk
Internet: http://www.gnto.co.uk/

Stretching from the Balkans in the north to the south Aegean, Greece shares borders with Albania, Macedonia, Bulgaria and Turkey.

It is above all a mountainous country – the Pindus range forms the backbone of mainland Greece, extending through central Greece into the Peloponnese and Crete. The majority of islands throughout the Aegean are in fact the mountain peaks of the now submerged landmass of Aegeis, which was once the link between mainland Greece and Asia Minor. Mount Olympus in the north of the country, known from Greek mythology as the abode of the gods, is the highest mountain (2,917 m).

Six thousand islands are scattered in the Aegean and Ionian Seas, a unique phenomenon on the continent of Europe; of these islands, only 227 are inhabited.

Population

10.9 million

Climate

Greece has a Mediterranean climate with plenty of sunshine, mild temperatures and a limited amount of rainfall.

Language

Greek, but most of the people connected to tourism and the younger generations currently practise English and sometimes German, Italian or French.

Telephone

The country code for Greece is 00 30.

Currency

Euro

Time

GMT + 2 (GMT + 3 from last Sunday in March to last Sunday in October).

Public Holidays

New Year's Day 1 Jan; Epiphany 6 Jan; Shrove Monday Orth. Easter; Independence Day 25 Mar; Easter: Good Friday, Easter Sunday and Easter Monday (Orthodox); Labour Day 1 May; Whit Sunday and Monday (Orthodox); Assumption Day 15 Aug; Ochi Day (National Fest) 28 Oct; Christmas 25/26 Dec.

Motoring

Speed limits are 100-120 km/h on highways unless otherwise posted; 50 km/h in residential areas unless otherwise marked. An international driver's licence is required. Road signs are written in Greek and repeated phonetically in English. Road tolls exist on two highways in Greece, one leading to Northern Greece and the other to the Peloponnese.

GR8120 Camping Poseidon Beach

Platamon-Pieria, GR-60065 Neos Panteleimonas (Central Macedonia)

Tel: **23520 41654**. Email: **info@poseidonbeach.com**

This site is located in a rural area at the foot of Mount Olympus, just off the motorway which follows the coast from Thessalonica to Athens. The area is known for its golden beaches and, as its name suggests, this campsite enjoys direct access. The 250 pitches are on level ground shaded by mature trees and a variety of shrubs and all have 16A electricity. There is a good restaurant, which is open for most of the season. The site is also close to the tenth century castle of Platamon, which is the principal attraction of the area. There may be some noise from the nearby railway and motorway.

Facilities	Directions
Two modern and one refurbished sanitary blocks with mainly British style WCs (one Turkish toilet per block), open washbasins and controllable showers. Chemical disposal. Laundry sinks, washing machines and dryers. Covered dishwashing area. Shop, bar and restaurant (all May - Sept). Fishing.	From E75 Thessaloniki - Athens motorway (toll road) turn left signed Neos Panteleimonas. Cross over railway bridge and turn left onto coastal road. In 500 m. turn right at campsite sign next to Camping Heraklia. Site is on right in 300 m. GPS: N40:00.778 E22:35.430

Open: 1 March - 31 October.

Charges guide

Per person	€ 4,40 - € 5,00
pitch incl. electricity	€ 9,30 - € 11,10

GR8145 Camping Areti

GR-63081 Neos Marmaras (Central Macedonia)

Tel: **23750 71430**. Email: **info@camping-areti.gr**

If you imagine Greek campsites as being set immediately behind a small sandy beach in a quiet cove with pitches amongst the pine and olive trees which stretch along way back to the small coast road; then you have found your ideal site. Camping Areti is conveniently located just off the beaten track on the peninsula of Sithonia. It has 130 pitches, all for tourers (no static caravans are allowed). The olive groves at the rear provide hidden parking spaces for caravans and boats that can be brought to the site when the owner is present.

Facilities	Directions
Three excellent toilet blocks include showers, WCs and washbasins. Kitchen with sinks, electric hobs and fridges. Laundry with washing machines. Facilities for emptying chemical toilet. Small shop and restaurant. Sandy beach. Bungalows to rent. Fishing, sailing and swimming. Off site: Riding nearby. Sithonia, Mount Athos and the nearby Spalathronissia islands.	Although the postal address is Neos Marmaras the site is 12 km. south. So stay on the main coast road, go past casino at Porto Carras and 5 km. further on turn right (site signed). Then right again to the coast where turn left then 1.5 km. Turn right into site access road. GPS: N40:01.451 E23:48.957

Open: 1 May - 15 October.

Charges 2006

Per person	€ 8,10 - € 9,00
pitch incl. electricity	€ 13,00 - € 14,00

GR8235 Camping Kalami Beach

Plataria, GR-46100 Igoumenitsa (Epirus)

Tel: **26650 71211**

A warm welcome awaits you on your arrival at Camping Kalami Beach. This family run site is ideally situated 8 kilometres from the ferry port of Igoumenitsa, where it is possible to take cruises to several islands and to Italy. The site is very well cared for with an attractive floral display around the reception building. There are 75 pitches of varying sizes with 10A electricity. Although the site is quite steep in places, the pitches themselves are level and well drained and those at the front of the site above the beach have panoramic views across the sea and to the mountains of Corfu.

Facilities	Directions
One sanitary block with British style WCs, washbasins and showers. Second block has showers and washbasins in cabins. Chemical disposal point. Laundry room with sinks and washing machines and dryer (token operated). Dishwashing area inside. Shop. Bar and restaurant, takeaway. Beach at site.	From Igoumenitsa head south on the E55 towards Preveza. In 8 km. site is on right, well signed. Entrance is 300 m. down a steep narrow lane. GPS: N39:28.427 E20:14.449

Open: 1 March - 31 October.

Charges 2006

Per person	€ 5,00
child (4-10 yrs)	€ 2,50
pitch incl. electricity	€ 10,00 - € 13,00

Discounts available for low season and stays over ten nights in high season. No credit cards.

GR8285 Camping Hellas International

GR-38500 Kato Gatzea (Thessaly)

Tel: 24230 22267. Email: camping-hellas@argo.net.gr

There is a warm welcome from the English speaking brother and sister team who own and run Camping Hellas. The campsite has been in the family since the sixties, when tourists first asked if they could camp overnight and use the facilities of the taverna. It is in a beautiful setting in a 500 year old olive grove, right next to the beach and the calm blue waters of the Pagasitikos gulf. Everything is kept spotlessly clean and the owners have many plans for further improvements. There are around 100 pitches all with 16A electricity. Pitch sizes vary and some parts are more level than others, but shade is plentiful thanks to the olive trees.

Facilities

One modern and one old sanitary block, both very clean with British style toilets and open washbasins. Very good facilities for disabled visitors. Laundry room. Shop has essentials from 15 April, fully stocked from May. Bar. TV room. Restaurant (from April). Boat launching. Dogs are not allowed on the beach. Off site: Fishing 5 km. Sailing 5 km. Riding 18 km. Bicycle hire 18 km.

Open: 15 March - 31 October.

Directions

From the north follow the E75 towards Lamia. Turn left at sign for Volos onto E92. Follow coastal road south towards Argalasti for 18 km. Site is off coastal road on right at Kato Gatzea. GPS: N39:18.650 E23:06.546

Charges guide

Per person	€ 5,00 - € 6,00
pitch incl. electricity	€ 9,90 - € 11,90

GR8330 Ionion Beach

Glifa, GR-27050 Vartholomino Ilias (Western Greece)

Tel: 26230 96395. Email: ioniongr@otenet.gr

This is a well kept site in a beautiful location by the Ionian Sea, created from former farmland by the Fligos family. Much has changed since they welcomed their first guests in 1982, when they still left plenty of space for growing potatoes. Now it is a modern site with a large pool and a paddling pool and two blocks of apartments to rent. Separated by a variety of trees and oleander bushes, there are 235 pitches with 16A electricity and of between 80 and 100 sq.m. Those at the front of the site have a view over the sea and the island of Zakynthos.

Facilities

Two modern sanitary blocks with British style WCs and showers with washbasins in cabins. Motorcaravan service point. Laundry room with sinks and washing machine. Shop, bar, restaurant (15/4-15/11). Internet access in bar. Swimming pool and paddling pool (15/4-15/11). Caution is advised as there are no depth markings in the pool. Play area. Off site: Ferries to Zakynthos from Kilini, ancient city of Olympia, Frankish fortress of Chlemoutsi.

Open: All year.

Directions

From Patra head south on E55 towards Pyrgos. At sign for Vartholomio, turn right at sign for Glyfa and Ionion Beach. In 15 km. campsite sign is on right. Coming from the north of Greece, there is a toll for the Korinthian gulf bridge. GPS: N37:50.197 E21:08.028

Charges 2006

Per person	€ 5,00 - € 6,00
pitch incl. electricity	€ 8,10 - € 12,60

GR8525 Chrissa Camping

Chrisso, GR-33054 Delphi (Central Greece)

Tel: 22650 82050. Email: info@chrissacamping.gr

This well kept site is located close to Delphi which was once sacred to the god Apollo and is now the setting for some of the most important monuments of ancient Greek civilisation. The site's situation on a hill ensures stunning views across a vast olive grove to the Gulf of Corinth beyond. There are 60 pitches with electricity connections (16A). They are mainly arranged on terraces as the site is quite steep, which means that everyone can enjoy the views. The swimming pool has an adjacent bar and plenty of space around it for sunbathing or relaxing in the shade. Traditional Greek dishes prepared with local produce are served in the campsite restaurant accompanied by local wines.

Facilities

Modern toilet block with British style WCs, open washbasins and controllable showers. Plastic seats available in showers. Chemical disposal point. Laundry room with sinks, washing machine and dryer. Dishwashing room. Shop (1/4-30/10). Bar, restaurant and takeaway (weekends only in winter). Outdoor pool and paddling pool. Barbecues are not allowed. Internet point. Off site: Beach 10 km. skiing 18 km. Delphi.

Open: All year.

Directions

From Patra head west on E65 (48) towards Itea. Continue towards Delphi and 6 km. from Delphi there is a sign on the right for Chrisso. Site is directly opposite, clearly signed and entrance is 300 m. down a narrow lane. GPS: N38:28.346 E22:27.549

Charges 2007

Per person	€ 5,00 - € 6,00
pitch incl. electricity	€ 11,00 - € 11,50

Camping Cheques accepted.

251

GR8565 Camping Kokkino Limanaki

GR-19009 Rafina (Attica)

Tel: **22940 31604**. Email: **travelnet@otenet.gr**

This site is an ideal base for visiting the famous ancient sites of Athens as it lies just 20 minutes away from the Acropolis. It is also well placed for exploring the many islands of the Aegean with the port of Rafina five minutes away. The port of Piraeus is also within easy reach. The site is 100 m. above sea level, but also has access to the beach below. There are 100 pitches on partly sloping ground some with views over the Aegean sea and nearby islands. There is some aircraft noise.

Facilities	Directions
Single toilet block with open style washbasins and unisex showers. Dishwashing sinks, washing machine and ironing board. Fridges for hire. Chemical disposal. Bar and restaurant. Takeaway (July and August). Off site: Fishing 1 km. Boat launching 4.5 km. Beach 200 m.	Travelling south on E75 towards Athens turn right signed Varibobi. At traffic lights turn left and follow signs to Nea Makri. Enter town and follow signs to Rafina; 1.6 km. after Nea Makri turn left and follow signs to campsite. GPS: N38:01.899 E24:00.095
Open: 1 May - 30 September.	**Charges guide**

Per person	€ 5,60 - € 6,10
pitch incl. electricity	€ 12,60 - € 13,50

GR8640 Camping Kastraki

Assini, GR-21100 Nafplio (Peloponnese)

Tel: **27520 59386**. Email: **sgkamania@kastrakicamping.gr**

Ancient Assini, where Camping Kastraki is located, inspired the Nobel Prize winning poet, George Seferis to write one of his most beautiful poems. This alone attracts the more romantic traveller to head for this wonderful coast. Run personally by the owner, George Karmaniolas, this site offers 200 good pitches amongst eucalyptus and pine trees that border a narrow shingle beach.

Facilities	Directions
Refurbished toilet block includes showers, WCs and washbasins. Facilities for disabled visitors. Sinks for dishwashing. Gas hobs for cooking. Chemical toilet emptying point and motorcaravan service point. Washing machines. Small shop, bar and restaurant during high season. Flats to rent nearby. Slipway for small boats. Off site: Nafplio and Ancient Assini.	From Nafplio head towards Tolo and go through the modern town of Assini. Shortly before Tolo site is well signed on the left. From Drepano head towards Tolo and turn left at T-junction to site on the left. GPS: N37:31.680 E22:52.572
Open: 1 April - 20 October.	**Charges 2006**

Per person	€ 7,20 - € 8,00
pitch incl. electricity	€ 13,70 - € 16,10

GR8700 Camping Erodios

Koroni, Gialova, GR-24001 Pylos (Peloponnese)

Tel: **27230 28240**. Email: **erodioss@otenet.gr**

This brand new site sets a standard not seen anywhere else in Greece! Great thought has been given to what is needed and then provided it to the highest possible standard in an environmentally friendly way. The 90 pitches have high reed screens to provide shade which is most welcome given the high temperatures even in the low season. There is direct access to a sandy beach and the glorious turquoise sea in a sheltered bay north of the busy town of Pylos.

Facilities	Directions
Three excellent toilet blocks include showers, WCs and washbasins. Facilities for disabled visitors. Two kitchens include sinks, electric hobs and fridges. Laundry. Motorcaravan service points. Very good shop. Bar/café with Internet. Excellent restaurant. Bicycle, car and motorbike rental. Play area for under 5s. Off site: Pylos.	From Pylos head north on the main road and fork left towards Gialova. In the village turn left, signed to site and Golden Beach. Site is on the left in 700 m.
	Charges 2006
Open: 20 March - 31 October.	

Per person	€ 4,50 - € 5,50
pitch incl. electricity	€ 10,00 - € 13,50

This is just a sample of the campsites we have inspected and selected in Central Europe. For more campsites and further information, please see the Alan Rogers Central Europe guide.

MAP 7

Centrally located in Europe, Hungary comprises mountain ranges, hilly regions and flat plains, with the River Danube running through its length. The country also has over one thousand lakes, an abundance of thermal baths, Europe's largest cave system and several notable wine regions.

Hungary

CAPITAL: BUDAPEST

Tourist Office

Hungarian National Tourist Office
46 Eaton Place, London SW1X 8AL
Tel: 020 7823 1032
Fax: 020 7823 1459
Email: htlondon@btinternet.com
Internet: www.hungarytourism.hu

An increasingly popular destination, Budapest is divided into two parts by the Danube, the hilly side of Buda on the western bank and the flat plain of Pest on the eastern bank. A cruise along the river will enable you to appreciate this picturesque city with its grand buildings, romantic bridges, museums and art galleries. It also has plenty of spas to tempt you. North of the city, the Danube Bend is one of the grandest stretches of the river, along the banks of which you'll find historic towns and ruins. Further afield in the north-eastern hills, the caves at Aggtelek are another firm favourite.

One of the largest in Europe, Lake Balaton covers an area of nearly 600 square miles and is great for swimming, sailing, windsurfing and waterskiing. It has two distinct shores; the bustling south with its string of hotels, restaurants and beaches, and the north offering a quieter pace with beautiful scenery and sights.

Population

10.2 million

Climate

There are four fairly distinct seasons – hot in summer, mild spring and autumn, very cold winter with snow.

Language

The official language is Magyar, but German is widely spoken.

Telephone

The country code is 00 36.

Money

Currency: Hungarian forints
Banks: Mon-Fri 09.00-14.00,
Sat 09.00-12.00.

Shops

Mon-Fri 10.00-18.00, Sat 10.00-14.00.
Food shops open Mon-Fri 07.00-19.00,
Sat 07.00-14.00.

Public Holidays

New Year; Revolution Day 15 March; Easter Mon; Labour Day; Whitsun; Constitution Day 20 Aug; Republic Day 23 Oct; All Saints Day 1 Nov; Christmas 25, 26 Dec.

Motoring

Dipped headlights are compulsory at all times but main beams should not be used in towns. Motorway stickers must be purchased for the M1 to Budapest; the M7 from Budapest to Lake Balaton and also on the M3 eastward. Aso the full length of the M5 (Budapest - Kiskunfelegyhaza). Give way to trams and buses at junctions. Carrying spare fuel in a can is not permitted.

HU5070 Balatontourist Camping & Motel Kristof

H-8220 Balatonalmádi (Veszprem County)

Tel: **88 584 201**. Email: **ckristof@balatontourist.hu**

This is a delightfully small site with just 33 marked pitches and many tall trees. Square in shape, the generously sized pitches are on either side of hard roads, on level grass. There is some shade and all pitches have electricity points (6A). It is situated between the main road and railway line and the lake. Although there is no direct access to the lake, a public lakeside area adjoins the site, and site fees include the entry price. Balatonalmádi is at the northern end of the lake and well placed for excursions around the lake or to Budapest. Kristof is very suitable for anyone seeking a small, friendly site without the bustle of the larger camps.

Facilities	Directions
The excellent, fully equipped toilet facility is part of the reception building. Laundry room, kitchen and sitting room with TV. Motorcaravan service point. Café (12/5-19/9). Playground and organized entertainment every day except Sunday. Tennis. Off site: Fishing and beach 50 m. Bicycle hire and boat launching 500 m. Village shops and supermarket 500 m. Riding 5 km.	Site is on road no. 71 at Balatonalmádi, between the railway line and the lake and is signed. GPS: N47:01.507 E18:00.613

Open: 12 May - 24 September.

Charges 2006

Per person	HUF 600 - 1000
child (2-14 yrs)	HUF 450 - 850
pitch	HUF 1750 - 3550

HU5080 Balatontourist Diana Camping

H-8241 Aszófô (Veszprem County)

Tel: **87 445 013**. Email: **dianacamping@freemail.hu**

Once a very large site of about twelve hectares, Diana was developed many years ago as a retreat for the 'party faithful'. Now just 8 hectares are used by Mr and Mrs Keller-Toth, who have leased it from the Balatontourist organisation and run it as a quiet, friendly site. There is a great feeling of space and naturally, much woodland around in which you may wander. There are 27 hedged pitches of 120 sq.m. (where two 60 sq.m. ones have been joined) on grass. Many have shade from trees including about 65 smaller individual ones.

Facilities	Directions
Toilet facilities have been largely refurbished. Very smart, new sections now provide large showers with private dressing for men and women and washbasins with hot water. Splendid, new children's washroom (key from reception). Washing machines, dryers and ironing (key from reception). Motorcaravan service point. Large kitchen with 3 cookers. Well stocked shop. Restaurant (all season). Play area. Tennis. Club room with video nights. Off site: Lake fishing 3 km. Riding or bicycle 5 km.	From road 71 on the north side of the lake, turn towards Azsófô just west of Balatonfüred, through the village and follow the signs for about 1 km. along access road (bumpy in places). GPS: N46:56.368 E17:49.542

Open: 7 May - 17 September.

Charges 2006

Per pitch incl. electricity	HUF 1000 - 1950
person	HUF 800 - 1090

Special rates for disabled persons and low season long stays.

HU5380 Balatontourist Camping Venus

H-8252 Balatonszepezd (Veszprem County)

Tel: **87 568 061**. Email: **venus@balatontourist.hu**

For those who want to be directly beside Lake Balaton and would like a reasonably quiet location, Camping Venus site would be a good choice and it is also possibly the best site in Hungary. Apart from the rather noisy train that regularly passes the site, this is a quiet setting with views of the lake from almost all the pitches. From the front row of pitches you could almost dangle your feet from your caravan in the warm water of the lake. Varying in size from 70 to 100 sq.m, there are 150 flat pitches, all with at least 4/10A electricity and almost all with shade.

Facilities	Directions
Two good sanitary blocks provide toilets, washbasins (open style and in cabins) with hot and cold water, pre-set showers, facilities for disabled people and child size toilets and basins. Launderette. Motorcaravan services. Shop for basics. Bar. Restaurant. Snack bar. Playground. Daily activity programme. Canoe, pedalo, rowing boats and bicycle hire. Dogs are not accepted. Off site: Riding 3 km.	On the 71 road between Balatonfüred and Keszthely site is in Balatonszepezd on the lake side of the road.

Open: 18 May - 9 September, with all services

Charges 2007

Per person	HUF 670 - 1130
child (2-14 yrs)	HUF 510 - 820
pitch incl. electricity	HUF 1280 - 3470

HU5090 Balatontourist Camping Füred

H-8230 Balatonfüred (Veszprem County)

Tel: 87 343 823. Email: cfured@balatontourist.hu

This is a large international holiday village rather than just a campsite, pleasantly decorated with flowers and shrubs, with a very wide range of facilities and sporting activities. All that one could want for a family holiday can be found on this site. Directly on the lake with 800 m. of access for boats and bathing, it has a large, grassy lying out area, a small beach area for children with various watersports organised. There is also a swimming pool on site with lifeguards. Mature trees cover about two-thirds of the site giving shade, with the remaining area being in the open. The 944 individual pitches (60-120 sq.m), all with electricity (4-10A), are on either side of hard access roads on which pitch numbers are painted. Many bungalows are also on the site. Along the main road that runs through the site, are shops and kiosks, with the main bar/restaurant and terrace overlooking the lake. Other bars and restaurants are around the site. A water ski drag lift is most spectacular with its four towers erected in the lake to pull skiers around the circuit. Coach trips and pleasure cruises are organised. The site is part of the Balatontourist organisation and, while public access is allowed for the amenities, security is good. Some tour operators – Danish and German.

Facilities

Six fully equipped toilet blocks around the site include hot water for dishwashing and laundry. Private cabins for rent. Laundry service. Gas supplies. Numerous bars, restaurants, cafés, food bars and supermarket (all 15/4-15/10). Stalls and kiosks with wide range of goods, souvenirs, photo processing. Hairdresser. Excellent swimming pool with separate children's pool (20/6-25/9). Sauna. Fishing. Water ski lift. Windsurf school. Sailing. Pedaloes. Play area on sand. Bicycle hire. Tennis. Minigolf. Video games. Internet point. Dogs are not accepted. Off site: Riding 5 km. Close by a street of fast food bars, about 10 in all, offering a variety of Hungarian and international dishes with attractive outdoor terraces under trees.

Open: 15 April - 15 October.

Directions

Site is just south of Balatonfüred, on Balatonfüred - Tihany road and is well signed. Gates closed 1-3 pm. except Sat/Sun. GPS: N46:56.735 E17:52.626

Charges 2006

Per person	HUF 700 - 1500
child (2-14 yrs)	HUF 500 - 1100
pitch incl. electricity (120 sq.m)	HUF 3000 - 5500
100 sq.m.	HUF 2800 - 5000
70 sq m	HUF 2350 - 3800

Camping Cheques accepted.

HU5150 Fortuna Camping

Dózsa György út 164, H-2045 Törökbálint (Pest County)

Tel: 23 335 364. Email: fortunacamping@axelero.hu

This good site lies at the foot of a hill with views of the vineyards, but Budapest is only 25 minutes away by bus. The owner, Csaba Szücs, will provide visitors with a map and instructions on how to see the town in the best way. The site is surrounded by mature trees and Mr Szücs will proudly name all 150 varieties of bushes and shrubs which edge some of the pitches. The site has a small restaurant with very reasonable prices but it is only open from 18.00-21.00. An open air swimming pool with flume will help you to cool off in summer with an indoor pool for cooler weather. Concrete and gravel access roads lead to terraces where there are 170 individual pitches most bordered with hedges, all with electricity (up to 16A, long leads needed), and 14 with water, on slightly sloping ground. A special field area provides for group bookings, and has separate facilities. Mr Szücs and his family will endeavour to make your stay a comfortable one. His daughter organises tours to Budapest or the surrounding countryside, and will also explain the mysteries of public transport in Budapest. English is spoken.

Facilities

One fully equipped sanitary blocks and two smaller blocks. Good facilities for disabled people. Six cookers in sheltered area. Washing machine and dryer. Gas supplies. Motorcaravan services. Restaurant and bar (all year). Snack bar. Essentials from reception, order bread previous day). Outdoor swimming pool with slide (15/5-15/9). Indoor pool. Small play area. Excursions organised. Off site: Close to bus terminal for city centre 1 km. Riding 3 km. Fishing 4 km.

Open: All year.

Directions

From M1 Gyor - Budapest, exit for Törökbálint following signs for town and then site. Also accessible from M7 Budapest - Balaton road. GPS: N47:25.922 E18:54.066

Charges 2006

Per person	€ 6,00
child (4-14 yrs)	€ 4,00
pitch	€ 5,00
electricity	€ 2,00

No credit cards.

HU5180 Jumbo Camping

Budakalászi út 23-25, H-2096 Üröm (Pest County)

Tel: **26 351 251**

Jumbo Camping is a modern, thoughtfully developed site in the northern outskirts of Budapest. The concrete and gravel access roads lead shortly to 55 terraced pitches of varying size, a little on the small size for large units, and some slightly sloping. Hardstanding for cars and caravan wheels, as well as large hardstandings for motorhomes. There is a steep incline to some pitches and use of the site's 4x4 may be required. All pitches have 6A electricity (may require long leads) and there are 8 caravan pitches with water and waste water. They are mostly divided by small hedges and the whole area is fenced. Situated on a hillside 15 km from Budapest centre, with attractive views of the Buda hills and with public transport to the city near, this is a pleasant and comfortable small site (despite the name) where you will receive a warm welcome. It is possible to park outside the short, fairly steep entrance which has a chain across. Reception, where you are given a comprehensive English language information sheet, doubles as a café/bar area.

Facilities

Sanitary facilities are excellent, with large showers (communal changing). Terrace with chairs and tables. Washing machine, iron and cooking facilities on payment. Motorcaravan services. Café where bread (orders taken), milk and butter available. Small, attractive swimming pool (10/6-10/9). Playground with covered area for wet weather. Barbecue area. English spoken and information sheet provided in English. Off site: Shop and restaurant 500 m. The 'Old Swabian Wine-Cellar' said to serve extremely good food. Bus to city 500 m. every 30 minutes. Fishing 8 km.

Open: 1 April - 31 October.

Directions

Site signed on roads to Budapest - nos. 11 from Szentendre and 10 from Komarom. If approaching from Budapest use 11 (note: site sign appears very quickly after sharp right bend; signs and entry are clearer if using road 10). Can also approach via Gyor on M1/E60 and Lake Balaton on M7/E71. Turn into site is quite acute and uphill. GPS: N47:36.093 E19:01.200

Charges 2006

Per person	€ 3,80 - € 4,50
child (3-14 yrs)	€ 1,90 - € 2,80
pitch acc to size and season	€ 1,90 - € 6,40
electricity	€ 2,30

No credit cards (cash only).

HU5120 Gasthof Camping Pihenö

I-es föút, H-9011 Györszentivan-Kertváros (Gyor-Moson-Sopron County)

Tel: **96 523 008**. Email: **piheno@piheno_hu**

This privately owned site makes an excellent night stop when travelling to and from Hungary as it lies beside the main no. 1 road, near the end of the motorway to the east of Györ. It is set amidst pine trees with pitches which are not numbered, but marked out by small shrubs, in a small clearing or between the trees. With space for about 40 touring units, all with electrical connections (6A), and eight simple, one roomed bungalows and four en-suite rooms. On one side of the site, fronting the road, is the reception, bar and pleasant restaurant with terrace (menu in English). The food is of excellent quality and very well priced (typical main course and coffee £3.50). The management offer a very reasonably priced package (if desired) which includes pitch and meals. A very friendly German speaking owner runs the site and restaurant with his wife and daughters who speak a little English.

Facilities

A single, small, basic toilet block has just two showers for each sex (10 ft for one minute) and curtained, communal dressing space. Baby room. Room for washing clothes and dishes with small cooking facility. Washing machine. Bar. Restaurant with good menu and reasonable prices. Solar heated swimming pool and children's pool (10 x 5 m, open June -Sept). Order bread at reception the previous evening. Off site: Gyor with shops and swimming pool.

Open: 1 April - 30 October.

Directions

Coming from Austria, continue through Györ following signs for Budapest. Continue on road no. 1 past start of motorway for 3 km. and site is on left. From Budapest, turn right onto road no. 10 at end of motorway, then as above. GPS: N47:43.528 E17:42.883

Charges 2006

Per person	€ 4,20
pitch	€ 3,20
electricity	€ 1,50

Less 10% for stays over 4 days, 20% after 8.

This is just a sample of the campsites we have inspected and selected in Central Europe. For more campsites and further information, please see the Alan Rogers Central Europe guide.

Check real time availability and at-the-gate prices...

www.**alanrogers**.com

HU5025 Zalatour Thermal Camping

Gyogyfurdo 6, H-8749 Zalakaros (Zala County)

Tel: 93 34 01 05. Email: thermal@zalatour.hu

The Zalatour Thermál Camping in Zalakaros has 280 attractively laid out, level pitches, all with electricity and varying in size from 30-100 sq.m. (the larger pitches need to be reserved). There are 250 for touring units on grass and gravel (firm tent pegs may be needed) and 10 hardstandings for larger units and motorcaravans. Mature trees provide useful shade and access roads are gravel. Zalatour attracts many elderly people who spend their day at the thermal spa down the road – the waters are good for rheumatism and other joint problems.

Facilities

Modern and comfortable toilet facilities with British style toilets, open washbasins and controllable, hot showers (free). Facilities for disabled visitors. Full-service laundry including ironing. Campers' kitchen. Motorcaravan service point and car wash. Shop. Bar/restaurant. Massage, acupuncture and pedicure. Sauna. Hairdresser. Bicycle hire. Off site: Beach 3 km. Golf 500 m. Riding 2 km.

Open: 1 April - 30 September.

Directions

On E71 travelling northeast from Nagykanisza, take exit for Zalakaros. Follow good site signs. GPS: N46:33.136 E17:07.556

Charges 2006

Per person	HUF 2200
child (2-14 yrs)	HUF 500
pitch incl. electricity	HUF 1200 - 1650

HU5210 Diófaház Accommodations

Ady Endre út 12, H-3348 Szilvásvárad (Heves County)

Tel: 36 355 595. Email: info@diofahaz.hu

Diófaház is an ideal base in northeast Hungary for exploring this wooded part of the country, to visit the stud farm of the famous Lipizzaner horses (one of only five in the world) or to visit the town of Eger, world famous for its culture and red wine. The site is in private grounds on the edge of the village and provides a maximum of six pitches, all with electricity, which makes it quiet and peaceful. Gyöngyi Pap, the owner provides a warm welcome and if you're lucky you may arrive for weekly barbecue or the home made Hungarian goulash soup. Nearby are the famous Szalajka waterfalls. In winter this is a skiing resort and there is a local spa. English is spoken.

Facilities

The single, freshly painted toilet block includes washbasins in cabins with hot and cold water, controllable hot showers and sinks with free hot water. Fresh rolls to order every day but no shop. Internet access. Discounts at four restaurants in the village if you show your campers card. Off site: Riding 200 m. Bicycle hire 500 m. Fishing 6 km.

Open: All year.

Directions

Take the no. 25 road from Eger north to Szilvásvárad. Site is signed when entering the village. GPS: N48:05.890 E20:23.04

Charges 2007

Per unit incl. 2 persons	€ 8,75 - € 10,50
extra person	€ 3,15
electricity per kWh	€ 0,18

HU5300 Kek-Duna Camping

Hösök Tere 23, H-7020 Dunafoldvar (Tolna County)

Tel: 75 541 107. Email: postmaster@camping_gyogyfurdo.axelero.net

Dunafoldvár is a most attractive town of 10,000 people and you are in the heart of it in just two or three minutes by foot from this site, easily reached via the wide towpath on the west bank of the Danube. For a town site, Kék-Duna is remarkably peaceful. This is a pleasant small site on the banks of the Danube, fenced all round and locked at night, with flat concrete access roads to 50 pitches. All have electricity (16A), the first half being open, the remainder well shaded.

Facilities

Modern, tiled sanitary building with nicely decorated ladies' section offers curtained showers with communal changing. The rest of the facilities are of above average standard. Dishwashing outside with cold water. Washing machine. Shop and café (from mid June), town shops close. Bicycle hire. Excursion information. German speaking receptionist Off site: Tennis 50 m. Thermal swimming pool 200 m (under the same ownership). Riding 5 km.

Open: All year.

Directions

From the roundabout south of Dunafoldvar turn towards the town centre. At the traffic lights turn right and go down as far as the Danube then turn left, under the green bridge and follow the towpath about 300 m. to the site.

Charges guide

Per person	HUF 500
pensioner, student or child	HUF 250
caravan, car and electricity	HUF 1200
motorcaravan and electricity	HUF 1100
tent and car	HUF 550

MAP 8

Whether you want to explore historic cities, stroll around mediaeval hill towns, relax on sandy beaches or simply indulge in opera, good food and wine, Italy has it all. Roman ruins, Renaissance art and beautiful churches abound. For the more active, the Italian Alps are a haven for winter sports enthusiasts and also offer good hiking trails.

Italy

CAPITAL: ROME

Tourist Office

Italian State Tourist Board
1 Princes Street
London W1B 2AY
Tel: 020 7408 1254
Fax: 020 7399 3567
Email: italy@italiantouristboard.co.uk
Internet: www.enit.it

Italy only became a unified state in 1861, hence the regional nature of the country today. With 20 distinct regions, each one has retained its own individualism which is evident in the cuisine and local dialects.

In the north, the vibrant city of Milan is great for shopping and home to the famous opera house, La Scala, as well as Leonardo's Last Supper fresco. It is also a good starting-off point for the Alps; the Italian Lake District, incorporating Lake Garda, Lake Como and Lake Maggiore; the canals of Venice and the lovely town of Verona. Central Italy probably represents the most commonly perceived image of the country and Tuscany, with its classic rolling countryside and the historical towns of Florence, Siena, San Gimignano and Pisa, is one of the most visited areas. Further south is the historic capital of Rome and the city of Naples. Close to some of Italy's ancient sites such as Pompeii, Naples is within easy distance of Sorrento and the Amalfi coast.

Population

57.8 million

Climate

The south enjoys extremely hot summers and mild, dry winters, whilst the mountainous regions of the north are cooler with heavy snowfalls in winter.

Language

Italian. There are several dialect forms and some German is spoken near the Austrian border.

Telephone

The country code is 0039.

Money

Currency: The Euro. Banks: Mon-Fri 08.30-13.00 and 15.00-16.00.

Shops

Mon-Sat 08.30/09.00-13.00 and 15.30/16.00- 19.30/20.00, with some variations in larger cities.

Public Holidays

New Year; Easter Mon; Liberation Day 25 Apr; Labour Day; Republic Day 2 June; Assumption 15 Aug; All Saints 1 Nov; Unity Day 4 Nov; Immaculate Conception 8 Dec; Christmas 25, 26 Dec; plus some special local feast days.

Motoring

Tolls are payable on the autostrada network. If travelling distances, save time by purchasing a 'Viacard' from pay booths or service areas. An overhanging load, ie. bicycle rack, must be indicated by a large red/white hatched warning square. Failure to do so will result in a fine.

IT6246 Camping Village Isolino

Via per Feriolo 25, I-28924 Verbania Fondotoce (Piedmont)

Tel: 0323 496 080. Email: info@isolino.com

Lake Maggiore is one of the most attractive Italian lakes and Isolino Camping Village is one of the largest sites in the region. Most of the 600 closely knit tourist pitches have shade from a variety of trees. Some are of a good size, many in long, angled rows open only at one end which can mean extended walks to the facilities. All have electrical connections (6A) and a few pitches have lake views. There is a small sandy beach and a wide range of watersports can be enjoyed on the lake (no jet-skis are allowed). The very large, lagoon style swimming pool with its island sun-deck area has stunning views across the lake to the fir-clad mountains beyond is breathtaking and worth finding. The social life of the campsite is centred around the large bar which has a stage sometimes used for musical entertainment. When we visited, the evening programme for children was being held on the tennis court opposite the entrance and reception. It was a little chaotic and parental supervision was essential on occasion. The extensive poolside terrace is outside the bar, takeaway and casual eating area. In the restaurant on the floor above some tables share the magnificent views across the lake. The site is well situated for visiting the many attractions of the region which include the famous gardens on the islands in the lake and at the Villa Taranto, Verbania. The Swiss mountains and resort of Locarno are quite near. The site is owned by the friendly Manoni family who also own Camping Continental Lido at nearby Lake Mergozzo and good English is spoken.

Facilities

Six well-built toilet blocks have hot water for showers and washbasins but cold for dishwashing and laundry. Baby room. Laundry facilities. Fridge box hire. Motorcaravan services. Supermarket (6/4-24/8). Resaurant and takeaway (6/4-24/9). Most attractive swimming pool (29/4-24/9) with large sunbathing area. Football. Tennis. Fishing. Watersports. Bicycle hire and guided mountain bike tours. Long beach. Organised activities and weekly disco in July/Aug. Internet access. Bus to town (booking required). Off site: Golf 200 m. Riding 12 km.

Open: 26 March - 24 September.

Directions

Leave A26 motorway at exit for Stresa/Baveno, turn left towards Fondotoce and follow signs to site on right.

Charges 2006

Per unit incl. 2 persons	
and electricity	€ 17,90 - € 31,60
extra person	€ 4,20 - € 7,00
child 3-5 yrs	free - € 5,70
child 6-11 yrs	€ 3,10 - € 5,70
dog	€ 3,10 - € 7,00

Credit cards accepted with 1.4% commission.

The lightly leaning sandy beach is ideal for children - the campsite lies in a very quiet position with wonderful view • Bar • Pool bar • Restaurant • Supermarket • Free hot showers • Baby-room • Children's playground • Basketball and volleyball facilities • Windsurfing school • Table tennis • We rent bicycles, pedalò, canoes, boats and surfboards • Bungalows, mobile homes and apartments for rent • Animation • Internet Point • Internet Wireless.

ISOLINO camping village

Special Offer
FROM 5 NIGHTS From 30.03. to 17.05. and from 08.09. to 24.09.07
FROM 7 NIGHTS From 17.05. to 30.06. and from 25.08. to 08.09.07

Lago Maggiore

Dogs only on request and reservation from the 30.06 to the 25.08.07

Pool of 1000 sq. m. open from 28.04. to 23.09.07 - animation from 28.04. to 08.09.07

CHILDREN GRATIS
0-2 all the season long.
3-5 years till 07.07.
and from 18.08.07

Via Per Feriolo, 25 • I-28924 Fondotoce di Verbania • Tel. 0039/0323496080 • Fax 0039/0323496414
info@isolino.com • www.isolino.it

IT6249 Camping Continental Lido

Via 42 Martiri, 156, I-28924 Fondotoce di Verbania (Piedmont)
Tel: 0323 496300. Email: info@campingcontinental.com

Continental Lido is a charming site situated on the shore of the small Lake Mergozzo, about a kilometre from the better known Lake Maggiore. The 315 small to normal sized tourist pitches are back-to-back in regular rows on grass. All have electricity (6A) and there is shade from a variety of trees in some parts. There is a feeling of spaciousness here and the 185 mobile homes are not obtrusive. There is no swimming pool but a small sandy beach slopes gently into the lake where swimming and watersports can also be enjoyed (no powered craft may be used). Fir-clad mountains and a pretty village directly opposite the beach provide a pleasing, scenic background. An unusual feature here is the 9-hole golf course and when we visited, people were happy and having lots of fun. Under the same ownership as Isolino Camping Village, this site is managed by son Giano Paolo who speaks good English.

Facilities

Five high standard toilet blocks have free hot water, facilities for disabled visitors and washing machines and dryers. Mini-fridges. Well stocked shop and bar/restaurant with terrace and takeaway (all open all season). TV. Tennis courts. Volleyball, basketball. Nine-hole golf course. Playground. Fishing. Windsurfing, pedaloes, canoes, kayaks. Games room. Bicycle hire. Entertainment and activities (mid-June to mid-September). Bus on request to Verbania. Off site: Site is within easy range of botanical gardens and the Swiss Ticano canton.

Open: 30 March - 24 September.

Directions

Site is on the SS34 road between Fondotoce and Gravellona.

Charges 2006

Per unit incl. 2 persons	€ 16,85 - € 24,95
extra person	€ 4,10 - € 6,35
child (3-11 yrs)	free - € 4,55

Camping Cheques accepted.

IT6242 Camping Orta

Via Domodossola 28, I-28016 Orta San Giulio (Piedmont)

Tel: 03229 0267. Email: **info@campingorta.it**

Lake Orta is a charming, less visited small lake just west of Lake Maggiore in an area with understated charm. The flat grassy pitches are on either side of the main road. A pedestrian underpass joins both sides of the site and there appears to be little road noise. There are 140 pitches, the best 70 dedicated to tourers, all with 4A electricity. They are of a good size with established shady trees. Amenities include a large games and entertainment room and a traditional Italian bar and restaurant serving good value family meals. Some English is spoken by the Guarnori family, who take pride in maintaining their uncomplicated site to a high standard. Book ahead to enjoy the superb lakeside pitches or if you enjoy a more dramatic vista try the top terraces.

Facilities

Three modern sanitary blocks are clean and well maintained providing a mix of British and Turkish style toilets, coin operated showers and an excellent unit for disabled visitors. Laundry facilities. Motorcaravan services. Excellent mini-market. Bar and restaurant with basic menu serving good value Italian family meals. Playground. Large games/TV room. WiFi internet access in reception/bar area. Fishing. Bicycle hire. Boat launching. Off site: Riding, golf and sailing all within 10 km.

Open: All year.

Directions

Site is on the SR229 between Borgomanero and Omega, 600 m. north of the turn to Orta San Giulio, GPS: N45:48.137 E08:25.216

Charges 2006

Per person	€ 4,80 - € 6,00
child (0-11 yrs)	€ 4,50
pitch	€ 8,00 - € 14,00
electricity	€ 2,00
dog	€ 2,50 - € 4,00

Camping Cheques accepted.

CAMPING ORTA
Loc. Bagnera
I-28016 Orta S.Giulio (NO)
Tel. and Fax 0039/032290267
E-mail: info@campingorta.it
Http: www.campingorta.it

On the shores of Orta Lake - 1,5 km from the village - the campsite enjoys a beautiful view on the quite neighborhood and on the lake. The right place for families with young children. Terraces up to the shores. Ideal starting point for visit to the interesting places of the lake and the surroundings, like villas, museums, cloisters and churches. Hot shower, electrical connection, supermarket, bar, restaurant, play area for children, pier, lighting on pitches. Services and toilettes for disabled people.
Open all year with great discounts from 01.01 to 30.06 and from 30.08 to 31.12.

IT6412 Villaggio Camping Valdeiva

Localita Ronco, I-19013 Deiva Marina (Ligúria)

Tel: 0187 824174. Email: **camping@valdeiva.it**

A mature site, 3 km. from the sea between the famous Cinque Terre and Portofino, Valdeiva is open all year. It is situated in a valley amongst dense pines so views are restricted. On flat ground and separated, most of the 125 pitches are used for permanent Italian units. There are 40 pitches for tents and touring units but in high season tourers can expect to be put onto a sloping 'overflow' area by the road with no shade. The touring pitches are in a square at the bottom of the site, some with shade, all with electricity (3A). Cars may be required to park in a separate area depending on the pitch and season. A small busy bar/restaurant offers food at realistic prices. There was late night noise from residents when we stayed in high season. The site does have a small swimming pool, which is very welcome if you do not wish to take the free bus to the beach. The beach is pleasant and the surrounding village has several bars and restaurants. There are very pleasant walks and treks in the unspoilt woods of Liguria nearby or the most interesting tourist option is a visit to Cinque Terre, five villages, some of which can only be reached by rail, boat or by cliff footpath. Their history is one of fishing but now they also specialise in wines. Unusually some of the vineyards can only be reached by boat. We see this as a transit site rather than for extended stays.

Facilities

The toilet block nearest the touring pitches provides cramped facilities. A new block is in the centre of the site. WCs are mainly Turkish, but there are some of British style. Washing machines. Shop (15/6-15/9). Bar/restaurant and takeaway with reasonable menu and pizzas cooked in a traditional oven (15/6-15/9). Small swimming pool. Play area. Free bus to the beach. Torches required. Bicycle hire. Internet access. WiFi. Off site: Beach, fishing and boat launching 3 km.

Open: All year.

Directions

Leave A12 at Deiva Marina exit and follow signs to Deiva Marina. Site signs are clear at the first junction and site is on left 3 km. down this road. GPS: N44:13.482 E09:33.101

Charges 2006

Per person (over 6 yrs)	€ 6,00
pitch	€ 10,00 - € 20,00
small tent	€ 6,00 - € 12,00

IT6414 Camping Arenella

Localita Arenella, I-19013 Deiva Marina (Ligúria)

Tel: 01 87 82 52 59. Email: info@campingarenella.it

Situated at the back of the town of Deiva Marina, Camping Arenella is accessed from the A12 autostrada via a twisting 5 km. of road. The site is on a hillside amongst pines and there are some good views. There are around 70 pitches for permanent units with a further 50 pitches for tourists with electricity connections available (3A). Cars must be parked in a separate area. The rustic restaurant is accessed by a long flight of steep steps and offers a varied menu along with a chioce of pizzas and spaghetti to take away. The approach to it is not suitable for infirm or disabled campers. The most interesting tourist option is a visit to Cinque Terre, five villages which can only be reached by rail, boat or cliff footpath. Their history is one of fishing but they now also specialise in wines. There are very pleasant walks and treks in the Ligurian woods nearby.

Facilities

Two centrally situated, and quite dated sanitary blocks have predominantly Turkish style WCs. Free hot water in showers and washbasins. Laundry. Restaurant with keen prices plus small snack bar and shop (May-Sept). Satellite TV. Communal freezer. Free bus service to the beach. Off site: Beach, fishing, boat launching and watersports 1.8 km. Riding 5 km. Villages of Cinque Terre.

Open: All year excl November.

Directions

Leave A12 autostrada at Deiva Marina exit and follow signs to Deiva Marina. Site is well signed and can be found before the village to the right. GPS: N44:14 E09:32.09

Charges guide

Per person	€ 7,00 - € 8,50
child (2-5 yrs)	€ 3,40 - € 4,00
pitch	€ 6,00 - € 8,50
electricity	€ 2,00
car	€ 2,00

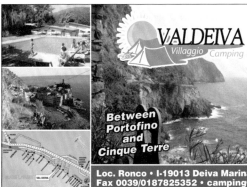

IT6401 Camping Villaggio dei Fiori

Via Tiro a Volo 3, I-18038 San Remo (Ligúria)
Tel: **0184 660635**. Email: **info@villaggiodeifiori.it**

Open all year round, this open and spacious site has high standards and is ideal for exploring the Italian Riviera or for just relaxing by the enjoyable, filtered sea water pools. Unusually all the pitch areas at the site are totally paved and there are some extremely large pitches for large units (ask reception to open another gate for entry). All pitches have electricity (3/6A), 50 also have water and drainage, and there is an outside sink and cold water for every four. There is ample shade from mature trees and shrubs, which are constantly watered and cared for in summer. The 'Gold' pitches and some wonderful tent pitches have pleasant views over the sea. There is a path to a secluded and pleasant beach with sparkling waters, overlooked by a large patio area. The rocky site surrounds are excellent for snorkelling and fishing with ladder access to the water. The friendly management speak excellent English and will supply detailed tourist plans. Activities and entertainment are organised in high season for adults and children. Excursions are offered (extra cost) along the Italian Riviera dei Fiori and the French Côte d'Azur, including night excursions to Nice and Monte Carlo.Buses run from outside the site to Monte Carlo, Nice, Cannes, Eze and many other places of interest. This is a very good site for visiting all the attractions in the local area.

Facilities

Three clean and modern toilet blocks have British and Turkish style WCs and hot water throughout. Baby rooms. Facilities for disabled campers. Laundry facilities. Motorcaravan services. Bar sells essential supplies. Large restaurant. Pizzeria and takeaway (all year). Sea water swimming pools (small extra charge in high season) and sophisticated whirlpool spa (June-Sept). Tennis. Play area. Fishing. Satellite TV. Internet access. Bicycle hire. Dogs are not accepted. Off site: Shop 150 m. Riding and golf 2 km.

Open: All year.

Directions

From SS1 (Ventimiglia - Imperia), site is on right just before San Remo. There is a sharp right turn if approaching from the west. From autostrada A10 take San Remo Ouest exit. Site is well signed. GPS: N43:48.07 E07:44.92

Charges 2007

Per unit incl. 4 persons	€ 27,00 - € 56,00
electricity (3/6A)	€ 2,00 - € 4,00

Some charges due on arrival. Discounts for stays in excess of 7 days. Discount for readers 10% in low season. Camping Cheques accepted.

IT6403 Camping Baciccia

Via Torino 19, I-17023 Ceriale (Ligúria)
Tel: **0182 990 743**. Email: **info@campingbaciccia.it**

This friendly, family run site is a popular holiday destination. Baciccia was the nickname of the present owner's grandfather who grew fruit trees and tomatoes on the site. Tall eucalyptus trees shade the 120 tightly packed pitches which encircle the central facilities block. The pitches are on flat ground and all have electricity. There is always a family member by the gate to greet you, and Vincenzina and Giovanni, along with their adult children Laura and Mauro, work tirelessly to ensure that you enjoy your stay. The restaurant is informal and, as no frozen food is served, the menu is necessarily simple but is traditional Italian food cooked to perfection. The restaurant overlooks a large swimming pool and there are organised water polo and pool games, as well as a half size tennis court and boule. The private beach is a short walk (or free shuttle service) and the town has the usual seaside attractions but it is also worth visiting the tiny traditional villages close by. This site may suit campers looking for a family atmosphere and none of the brashness of large seaside sites. If you have forgotten anything by way of camping equipment just ask and the family will lend it to you. Free shuttle service to Ceriale's beaches.

Facilities

Two clean and modern sanitary blocks near reception have British and Turkish style WCs and hot water throughout. Laundry. Motorcaravan services. Restaurant/bar. Shop. Pizzeria and takeaway. Two swimming pools (20/3-31/10) and private beach. Tennis. Table tennis. Bowls. Play area. Bicycle hire.Wood-burning stove and barbecue. Internet point. Fishing. Diving. Animation for children and adults in high season. Excursions. Off site: Department store 150 m. Aqua Park 500 m. Riding and golf 5 km. Parachuting school 10 km. Ancient town (2000 years old) of Albenga 3 km.

Open: All year.

Directions

From the A10 between Imperia and Savona, take Albenga exit. Follow signs Ceriale/Savona and Aquapark Caravelle (which is 500 m. from site) and then site signs. Site is just south of Savona.

Charges 2006

Per unit incl. up to 3 persons	€ 24,00 - € 46,00
extra person (over 2 yrs)	€ 5,00 - € 9,00
half pitch, no car	€ 15,00 - € 31,00
dog	€ 2,00 - € 4,00

Discounts for stays in excess of 7 days. Discount for readers 10% in low season. Camping Cheques accepted.

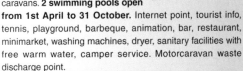

IT6419 Camping River

Loc. Armezzone, I-19031 Ameglia (Ligúria)

Tel: **0187 665629**. Email: **info@campingriver.com**

This campsite on the Ligurian coast has been recommended by our Italian agent and we plan to undertake a full inspection in 2007. Camping River has 250 individual pitches which vary in size from 60-90 sq.m. On site amenities include a supermarket, a restaurant and a bar. The site borders a river and site users can moor their boats alongside the 120 m. long quay. During high season many activities and excursions are organized. More unusual options include archery, sailing, scuba diving and even athletics. From the site a shuttle service conveys campers to the nearby beach.

Facilities	Directions
Modern toilet blocks include laundry and ironing facilities. Restaurant. Takeaway. Bar. Supermarket. Motorcaravan service point. Swimming pool with spa bath and cascades, children's pool. Fitness room. Volleyball. Football. Basketball. Riding. Off site: Tennis 200 m. Archery. Sailing. Scuba diving.	From the A12 Genoa-Livorno motorway, take the Sarzana exit. Follow the main road to Ameglia Bocca di Magra. Site is well signed from this point.

Open: April - October.

Charges 2006

Per person	€ 4,50 - € 8,80
child (2-10 yrs)	€ 2,30 - € 6,70
pitch	€ 9,50 - € 17,70

See advertisement on previous page.

IT6261 Camping Del Sole

Via per Rovato, 26, I-25049 Iseo (Lombardy)

Tel: **030 980288**. Email: **info@campingdelsole.it**

Camping Del Sole lies on the southern edge of Lake Iseo, just outside the pretty lakeside town of Iseo. The site has 360 pitches, some taken up with chalets and mobile homes, and many with fine views of the surrounding mountains and lake. The pitches are generally flat and of a reasonable size, most with electrical connections. The site has a wide range of excellent leisure amenities, notably a large swimming pool and smaller children's pool. There is a pleasant bar and restaurant with a pizzeria near the pool and entertainment area and a second bar that serves snacks by the lake. The site is near the delightful waterfront area of the town where you can enjoy classic Italian architecture, stroll around the shops or enjoy a meal in one of the many restaurants. There is a boat launching facility at the lakeside. A lively entertainment programme and excursions around the lake are organised, notably to Lake Iseo's three islands where you can sit at a street café or enjoy a walk while enjoying the magnificent scenery. Excursions are also organised to the wine cellars of Franciacorta.

Facilities	Directions
Sanitary facilities are modern and well maintained, including special facilities for disabled visitors. Washing machines and dryers. Bar, restaurant, pizzeria and snack bar. Supermarket. Motorcaravan service point. Bicycle and pedal boat hire. Tennis. Volleyball. Entertainment in high season. Off site: Golf 5 km. Riding 6 km.	From the A4 Milan - Venice autostrada take Rovato exit. Head towards Lago d'Iseo for 12 km. and the site is well signed. If you miss site signs follow signs to Rovato from Iseo town centre (1 km).

Open: 1 April - 30 September.

Charges 2006

Per person	€ 4,50 - € 8,10
child	free - € 6,60
pitch incl. electricity	€ 8,50 - € 16,80
tent pitch	€ 6,50 - € 12,00

Reductions in low season.
Camping Cheques accepted.

IT6260 Camping Europa Silvella

Via Silvella 10, I-25010 San Felice del Benaco (Lake Garda)

Tel: **0365 651095**. Email: **info@europasilvella.com**

This large, modern, lakeside site was formed from the merger of two different sites with the result that the 323 pitches (about 295 for tourists) are spread among a number of different sections of varying type. The chief difference between them is that the marked pitches alongside the lake are in smaller groups and closer together so that one has less space. However, in the larger, very slightly sloping or terraced grassy meadows further back, one can have 80 sq.m. or more instead of 50. There is reasonable shade in many parts and all pitches have electricity; 192 have water and drainage. Some areas also contain bungalows, mobile homes and log cabins. The site has frontage to the lake in two places (with some other property in between), with a beach, jetty and moorings. The private beach is very pleasant, with all manner of watersports available. There is a windsurfing school in season, along with an organised animation programme with live entertainment. A large modern swimming pool complex has a jacuzzi and a paddling pool.

Facilities

Toilet blocks include washbasins in cabins, facilities for disabled visitors and a superb children's room with small showers. Laundry. Supermarket. Bazaar. Restaurant/bar. Swimming pools (hats required). Fitness centre. Tennis courts. Volleyball courts and five-a-side soccer pitch. Table tennis. Playground. Bowling alley. Surf boards, canoes and bicycles for hire. Animation and entertainment (every night in season). Disco. Tournaments, swimming, windsurfing and tennis lessons. First aid room.

Open: 23 April - 27 September.

Directions

From Desenzano at southerly end of Lake Garda follow S572 north towards Salo. Following signs for San Felice turn off towards lake. Then follow yellow tourist signs bearing campsite name.
GPS: N45:34.471 E10:32.095

Charges 2006

Per person	€ 4,00 - € 8,00
child (0-5 yrs)	€ 3,50 - € 7,00
pitch incl. electricity	€ 11,00 - € 19,50
pitch with services	€ 12,50 - € 21,00

SUMMER 2007: new

> New swimming pool for adults with water games, lagoon and Jacuzzi.
> New swimming pool for children.
> New Tennis court.

> Modern mobile homes with air-conditioning and TV-sat; Chalets and Bungalows. New apartments with all comforts.
> 345 places for caravans and tents. 200 with electricity, water and drain. Some places are directly by the lake.
> An animation team organizes daily sport competitions, games, shows and miniclub.
> Swimming pool with lagoon and Jacuzzi, football field, volleyball field, bowling green and table tennis.
> Bar, restaurant, pizzeria, minimarket.
> Beach of more than 300m long with boat ramp. Boot mooring also available (booking required).
> We organize private excursions for our guests.

Via Silvella, 10 - 25010 S. Felice del Benaco, Brescia (Italy) Tel. +39.0365.651095 - Fax +39.0365.654395
info@europasilvella.it - www.europasilvella.it - SKYPE: europasilvella.eliana - europasilvella.jenny

267

IT6252 Camping San Francesco

Strada Vicinale, I-25015 Rivoltella (Lake Garda)

Tel: **0309 110245**. Email: **moreinfo@campingsanfrancesco.com**

San Francesco is a large, very well organised site situated to the west of the Simione peninsula on the southeast shores of Lake Garda. The pitches are generally on flat gravel and sand and enjoy shade from mature trees. There are three choices of pitch of different sizes with either 3A or 6A electricity, 35 are fully serviced. They are marked by stones but there is no division between them. A wooded beach area of about 400 metres on the lake is used for watersports and there is a jetty for boating. There are delightful lake views from the restarant and terrace. There is also a new shopping mall with games area, bazaar and takeaway. The sports centre, pools and entertainment area are all located across a busy road away from the pitches and safely accessed by a tunnel. This is a good quality site which is great for families.

Facilities

Sanitary facilities are in two large, modern, centrally located buildings, very clean when seen. Excellent facilities for disabled campers. Shop. Restaurant. Bar. Pizzeria. Takeaway. Across the road: swimming pools (15/4-20/9) and jacuzzi, sports centre, football stadium and tennis. Playground. Entertainmentt and activities. Bicycle hire. Internet access. Off site: Riding 5 km. Golf 10 km.

Open: 1 April - 30 September.

Directions

From autostrada A4, between Brescia and Verona, exit towards Simione and follow signs to Simione and site. GPS: N45:27.921 E10:35.681

Charges 2006

Per person	€ 5,50 - € 9,00
pitch incl. electricity	€ 11,50 - € 29,00

Camping Cheques accepted.

camping ★★★★ SanFrancesco

The camping site is located at the begin-ning of Sirmione peninsula. Restaurant, pizzeria, supermarket, clothes shop, winebar and take-away. The campingsite is situated on a shaded surface of 104.000 sm. right by the lake, with a 300m long beach. In the sport area you can enjoy the swimming pool with a childrens' pool and water games. In addition there is the possibility to practise more than 10 sports. To reach us follow exit Sirmione on the highway Milan-Venice. The camping site is an ideal starting point to reach Gardaland and Caneva. New mobile homes equipped with heating and air-conditioning

GPS: LOG 10° 32' 59,3" - LAD 45° 27' 56,2"

Strada Vic. S. Francesco • I-25015 Desenzano del Garda (BS) • Tel. 0039/0309110245
Fax 0039/0309119464 • moreinfo@campingsanfrancesco.com • www.campingsanfrancesco.com

IT6254 Camping Lido

Via Peschiera 2, I-37017 Pacengo (Lake Garda)

Tel: **045 759 0030 / 759 0611**. Email: **info@campinglido.it**

Camping Lido is one of the largest and amongst the best of the 120 campsites around Lake Garda and is situated at the southeast corner of the lake. There is quite a slope from the entrance down to the lake so many of the 683 grass touring pitches are on terraces which give lovely views across the lake. They are of varying size, separated by hedges, all have electrical connections and 57 are fully serviced. This is a most attractive site with tall, neatly trimmed trees standing like sentinels on either side of the broad avenue which runs from the entrance right down to the lake. A wide variety of trees provide shade on some pitches and flowers add colour to the overall appearance. Near the top of the site is a large, well designed pool with a paddling pool and slides into splash pools. The site has its own beach with a landing stage that marks off a large area for swimming on one side and on the other an area where boats can be moored. One could happily spend all the holiday here without leaving the site but with so many attractions nearby this would be a pity.

Facilities

Seven modern toilet blocks (three heated) include provision for disabled visitors and three family rooms. Washing machines and dryer. Restaurant, bars, pizzeria, takeaway and well stocked supermarket. Swimming pool, paddling pool and slides. Fitness centre. Playground. Tennis. Bicycle hire. Watersports. Fishing. Volleyball. High season activities. Dogs are not accepted in high season (3/7-15/8). Off site: Bus service 200 m. Gardaland.

Open: 1 April - 18 October.

Directions

Leave A4 Milan - Venice motorway at exit for Peschiera. Head north on east side of lake on SS249. Site entrance on left after Gardaland Theme Park.

Charges guide

Per person	€ 4,10 - € 6,10
child (3-5 yrs)	free - € 3,80
pitch incl. services	€ 8,00 - € 15,50

IT6256 Camping del Garda

Via Marzan 6, I-37019 Peschiera del Garda (Lake Garda)

Tel: 045 755 0540. Email: campingdelgarda@gardalake.it

Camping del Garda is directly on the lake with access through gates which provide security at night.
This is one of the largest campsites around Lake Garda and is more of a self contained holiday village
with many pitches used by tour operators, although they are generally separate from the touring
pitches. The mature trees provide shade for the 659 grass pitches of which 337 are for tourers.
Arranged in numbered rows, all have 4A electrical connections and hedges have been cleverly
trimmed for maximum attractiveness. Hard roads give access. This is a well kept site with colour
added by attractive flower beds. There is a very active animation programme throughout the season
for all ages and two good pools with lifeguards. A huge range of sports activities including
watersports is available and boat enthusiasts have launching close by. The picturesque little town of
Peschiera is 1 km. over the multiple bridges and the busy waterfront has pretty bars and restaurants.

Facilities

Eleven good quality toilet blocks have the usual facilities
with free hot water in sinks, washbasins and showers.
Facilities for disabled visitors in two blocks. Washing
machines and dryers. Bars, restaurant and takeaway.
Supermarket. Swimming pools. Tennis courts and school.
Minigolf. Watersports including windsurf school. Fishing.
Playground.Organised activities in high season. Dogs or
motorcycles are not accepted. Off site: Gardaland, Zoo
Safari, Verona, etc. Fishing 0.5 km. Golf and riding 2 km.

Open: 1 April - 30 September.

Directions

Leave the A4 (Milan - Venice) at Peschiera exit and
travel through the town in the direction of Garda.
After the second town bridge on Via Parcocatullo
look for Via Marzan off the complex four road
intersection. Campsite signs are small and difficult
to see (campsite is on Via Marzan).

Charges guide

Per person	€ 4,00 - € 8,50
child (under 5 yrs)	free - € 5,00
pitch incl. electricity (4A)	€ 9,50 - € 17,50

IT6253 Camping Piani di Clodia

Localita Bagatta, I-37017 Lazise (Lake Garda)

Tel: 045 7590456. Email: info@pianidiclodia.it

Piani di Clodia is one of the best large sites on Lake Garda and it has a positive impression of space and cleanliness. It is located on a slope between Lazise and Peschiera in the southeast corner of the lake, with lovely views across the water to Sirmione's peninsula and the opposite shore. The rectangular site slopes down to the water's edge and has over 950 pitches, all with electricity (6A), 250 with electricity, water and drainage, terraced where necessary and back to back from hard access roads. There is some shade from mature and young trees. The pool complex is truly wonderful with three pools,. a pleasant sunbathing area and a bar. The whole area is fenced and supervised. At the centre of the site is a quality rooftop restaurant, huge lower self service restaurant plus pizzeria and table service for drinks. A large choice of wine includes the delicious Lagana wines of the southern lake area. From most of this area you will be able to enjoy the free entertainment on the large stage. The enthusiastic animation team provide an ambitious variety of entertainment. There is a fence between the site and the lake with access points to a private beach and opportunities for a variety of watersports. You are greeted at the gate by English speaking attendants who are keen to please, as are reception staff. The site is very close to Gardaland, one of the biggest theme parks in Europe and the huge Caneva aqua park. Member of Leading Campings Group.

Facilities

Seven modern, immaculate sanitary blocks, well spaced around the site. British and Turkish style WCs. All have facilities for disabled visitors and one has a baby room. Washing machines, dryers and laundry service. Motorcaravan services. Shopping complex with supermarket, general shops for clothes, etc. Two bars. Self-service restaurant with takeaway and pizzeria and gelaterie. Swimming pools. Tennis. Table tennis. Gymnastics. Bicycle hire. Large playground. Outdoor theatre with animation programme. Off site: Riding near. Golf 12 km. Caneva aqua park, Gardaland theme park close by.

Open: 20 March - 5 October.

Directions

Site is south of Lazise on road SS249 before Peschiera. GPS: N45:28.963 E10:43.759

Charges 2006

Per person	€ 4,70 - € 9,20
child (1-9 yrs)	€ 3,00 - € 6,00
pitch with electricity	€ 9,50 - € 23,00
pitch with electricity and water	€ 10,50 - € 24,50

IT6358 Camping Park Delle Rose

Localitá Vanon, I-37017 Lazise (Lake Garda)

Tel: 045 6471181. Email: info@campingparkdellerose.it

An orderly, well designed site with a feeling of spaciousness, Delle Rose is on the east side of Lake Garda, three kilometres from the attractive waterside village of Peschiera. The 396 pitches are of average size, most with grass and shade and laid out in 30 short, terraced avenues. The ratio of recreational area to pitches is unusually high, particularly for sites at Lake Garda. Unusually, reception is located one third of the way into the site. On approach one sees the attractive restaurant, gardens and comprehensive sporting facilities including the pool complex with its stylish terraced bar and animation area close by.

Facilities

Five very clean, modern sanitary blocks provide hot water throughout. Britiish style toilets, some in cabins with washbasins. Private bathrooms for hire. Good baby rooms. Facilities (3) for disabled visitors. Washing machines. Motorcaravan service point. Fridge hire. Bar/restaurant, takeaway and pool bar serving snacks (all season), Shops (all season). Swimming pool (mid April-Sept). Tennis. Archery. Minigolf. Play area and miniclub for children. Fishing (with permit). Beach at site. Watersports, Kayak. Windsurfing. Daily medical services. Animation programme in high season. Excursions. Dogs are not accepted. Motorbikes are not accepted. Torches useful. Off site: Peschiera 2 km with ATM and usual town amenities. Riding 8 km. Golf 6 km. Gardaland close by.

Open: 1 April - 30 September.

Directions

From A4 Milan - Venice autostrada take exit for Perschiera, west of Verona. Travel north towards Lazise. The campsite is on the southeastern lakeside about 2.5 km north of Peschiera and well signed. GPS: N45:29 E10:43.91

Charges 2006

Per person	€ 4,50 - € 8,00
child (1-7 yrs)	free - € 4,60
pitch	€ 9,00 - € 16,50

PIANI DI CLODIA
★ ★ ★ ★

Feel the emotion!

ADAC Super-Platz 2006

The Leading Camping
& Caravaning Parks of Europe

www.pianidiclodia.it

Località Bagatta - 37017 Lazise (Verona) Italy
T. +39 045 7590456 - F. +39 045 7590939
info@pianidiclodia.it

 GS 490 - Via Peschiera (Lazise)

IT6255 Camping La Quercia

I-37017 Lazise sul Garda (Lake Garda)

Tel: **045 6470577**. Email: **laquercia@laquercia.it**

A spacious, popular site on a slight slope leading down to Lake Garda, La Quercia is decorated by palm trees and elegantly trimmed hedges. Accommodating up to 1,000 units, pitches are in regular double rows between access roads, all with electricity (6A). Most are shaded by mature trees, although those furthest from the lake are more open to the sun. Siting is not always easy but staff do help in high season. Much of the activity centres around the newly renovated pool with its fantastic slides and the terrace bar, restaurant and pizzeria which overlook the entertainment stage. The evening entertainment is very professional with the young team working hard to involve everyone – smaller children and some parents love it! La Quercia has a fine sandy beach on the lake, with diving jetties and a roped-off section for launching boats or windsurfing (high season).Another self-service restaurant serving traditional Italian food is located closer to the beach. The site is a short distance from the exquisite lakeside towns of Lazise and Peschiera, which have a wide choice of restaurants, and is a short drive from Verona, one of Italy's finest cultural centres where the open air Opera in the Roman Amphitheatre is a unique experience. La Quercia has always been a popular site and even though its prices are a little higher, it does offer a great deal for your money, including a wide choice of organised, mostly free, activities and amenities. Many of the courses require enrolment on a Sunday. The families we spoke to during our visit commented on how much they enjoyed La Quercia.

Facilities

Six toilet blocks are perfectly sufficient and are of a very high standard. Laundry. Supermarket. General shop. Bar, restaurant, self-service restaurant and pizzeria. Swimming pools (small charge). Tennis. Riding stables. Football. Aerobics and yoga. Scuba club. Playground with water play. Organised events (sports competitions, games, etc.) and free courses (e.g. swimming, surfboarding). Canoeing. Roller-blading. Archery, climbing, judo, multi-gym. Minigolf. Evening entertainment or dancing. Baby sitting service. Internet. ATM. Free weekly excursion. Medical service. Off site: Supermarkets en-route to Verona. Gardaland and the enormous Caneva Aqua Park nearby.

Open: 10 days before Easter - 30 September.

Directions

Site is on south side of Lazise. From north on Trento - Verona A22 autostrada take Affi exit then follow signs for Lazise and site. From south take Peschiera exit and site is 7 km. towards Garda and Lazise. GPS: N45:29.606 E10:43.969

Charges 2006

Per person	€ 5,20 - € 10,50
child (4-7 yrs)	€ 3,00 - € 7,00
pitch	€ 10,25 - € 23,40
dog	€ 3,50 - € 6,90

Low season discount for pensioners.

IT6275 Fornella Camping

Via Fornella 1, I-25010 San Felice del Benaco (Lake Garda)

Tel: **0365 62294**. Email: **fornella@fornella.it**

Fornella Camping is one of the few campsites on Lake Garda still surrounded by farmed olive trees and with a true country atmosphere. Parts of the site have lake views, others a back drop of mountains and attractive countryside. The 268 pitches are on flat grass, terraced where necessary and most have good shade, all with 6A electricity; 40 have water and waste as well. The owners speak excellent English and have family connections with the UK. This site has top class facilities for boat owners, having recently purchased the adjoining marina.

Facilities

Three very clean, modern toilet blocks, well dispersed around the site, have mainly British type WCs and hot water in washbasins (some in cabins), showers and sinks. Facilities for disabled people. Washing machines, dryer and irons. Motorcaravan services. Bar/restaurant. Pizzeria and takeaway at certain times. Shop. Supervised swimming pool and paddling pool (15/5-15/9). Tennis. Table tennis. Volleyball. Two playgrounds and animation for children in season. Beach. Fishing. Small marina, boat launching and repairs. Off site: Bicycle hire 4 km. Golf 8 km. Riding 10 km.

Open: 29 April - 24 August.

Directions

From main SS572 Desenzano-Salo road on the west side of the lake, head for San Felice and follow signs. GPS: N45:35.098 E10:33.949

Charges guide

Per person	€ 4,60 - € 8,80
child (3-7 yrs)	€ 3,60 - € 6,80
pitch incl. electricity (6A)	€ 9,30 - € 16,50
boat	€ 4,50 - € 11,50
dog	free - € 5,90

Various low season discounts.

Sought-after relaxation in the nature

Enjoy a unique relax in the Camping La Quercia, in a clean and safe environment with an exceptional comfort. In the spirit of the true camping, we make people happy since 49 years.

If you wish a place where everything smiles on you, discover our hospitality in the midst of Nature.

Shadow for everybody, in a place of extraordinary beauty.

A very clean beach where one can play in all safety.

A lot of services for a vacation of true relax.

Try AquaFun, an exciting amusement.

Shady parking places – Warmed toilet services for both grownups and children – Warm water 24 hours out of 24 – Restaurant – Pizzeria – Cocktail Bar – Funny Bar on the beach – Swimming-pools and 'Maxicaravan'-slides with sight on the lake – Professional animateurs – Animation for both children and boys – Warmed underwater massage bath – Full-comfort bungalows for 4 and 5 people – The widest beach in the lake – Theatre – Supermarket – Butcher's shop – Pastry-shop and bakery – Typical products of the lake – Fresh fruits and vegetables all days – Tobacconist's shop – International news-stall – Rent-a-car service – Fax service Tennis – Canoes – Archery – Surfing – Judo – Football – Fitness hall – Fencing – Spinning – Horse-riding.

Reserve at once your relax vacation!
Call now!

++39.045.6470577

CAMPING ★★★★
LA QUERCIA
...more than a camping!

LAZISE SUL GARDA
VERONA - **ITALY**

Anniversario
1958-2008

nformation
www.laquercia.it
laquercia@laquercia.it

New! *The only camp-site with V.S.C.*
Vehicle Safety Check *for cars and camper vans.*
*Free **check-up** for: Brakes, Suspension, Tyres, Lights, Windscreen wipers, Exhaust fumes.*
Immediate release of a safety certificate. www.laquercia.it/csa

IT6263 Camping Bella Italia

Via Bella Italia 2, I-37019 Peschiera del Garda (Lake Garda)

Tel: **045 640 0688**. Email: **bellaitalia@camping-bellaitalia.it**

Peschiera is a picturesque village on the southern shore of Lake Garda and Camping Bella Italia is an attractive, large, well organised site in the grounds of a former farm, just one kilometre west from the centre of the village. Although about one third of the total area is taken by the site's own accommodation (apartments and bungalows) and tour operators, there are some 700 tourist pitches, most towards the lakeside and reasonably level on grass under trees. All have electricity (3A) and are separated by shrubs and numbered on the campsite plan but not on the ground. There are fine views across the lake from many parts. The pitches are grouped in regular rows on either side of hard access roads (which are named after European cities) and the wide central road which leads to the shops, pleasant restaurants and terrace. The site slopes gently down to the lake with access to the water for swimming and boating and to the lakeside public path which includes a series of fitness stations. A feature of the site is the group of pools of varying shape and size with an entertainment area at the road end of the site. A range of supervised activities is organised. Regulations are in place to ensure a peaceful site particularly during the afternoon siesta and during the hours of darkness. English is spoken by the friendly management.

Facilities

Six modern toilet blocks have British style toilets, free hot water in washbasins (some in cabins), showers and facilities for disabled visitors. Washing machines. Motorcaravan services. Shops. Bars. Waiter service restaurant and terrace with splendid views across to the opposite shore and another restaurant in the old farm building. Swimming pools. Tennis. Football. Volleyball. Basketball. Playgrounds (small). Games room. Watersports. Bicycle hire. Organised activities. Dogs are not accepted. Off site: Fishing 1 km. Gardaland, Italy's most popular theme park is about 2 km. east of Peschiera.

Open: 24 March - 7 October.

Directions

From A4 take exit for Peschiera del Garda and follow SS11 towards Brescia. Site is at the large roundabout at the entrance to Peschiera. GPS: N45:26.499 E10:40.752

Charges 2007

Per person	€ 6,00 - € 11,50
child (3-5 yrs)	free - € 5,00
pitch	€ 12,00 - € 21,00

Four charging seasons. No credit/debit cards. Camping Cheques accepted.

IT6277 Camping Fontanelle

Via del Magone 13, I-25080 Moniga del Garda (Lake Garda)

Tel: **0365 502079**. Email: **info@campingfontanelle.it**

Camping Fontanelle is a sister site to Fornella (no. IT6275), situated near the historic village of Moniga and enjoying excellent views across the lake. The site sits on the southwest slopes of Lake Garda and has 188 pitches on flat and terraced ground. All are marked and have electrical connections. There are some very pleasant lakeside pitches (extra cost). Some for tents and tourers are very secluded but distant from the site facilities, although small blocks with toilets are close by.

Facilities

The two main toilet blocks are modern and clean, with hot water throughout. Facilities for disabled campers. Washing machines and dryers. Motorcaravan services. Large mini-market. Restaurant/bar. Takeaway. Shop. Swimming pools (from 15/5, supervised). Tennis. Animation and live entertainment in season. Off site: Bicycle hire 1 km. Golf 5 km. Riding 20 km.

Open: 28 April - 23 September.

Directions

From A4 or E70 Milano - Verona road travel north on the west side of the lake to Moniga - site is well signed. GPS: N45:31.515 E10:32.603

Charges 2006

Per person	€ 4,60 - € 7,50
child (3-7 yrs)	free - € 6,20
pitch incl. electricity	€ 9,30 - € 15,00

IT6357 Campings Cisano & San Vito

Via Peschiera 48, I-37010 Cisano di Bardolino (Lake Garda)

Tel: 045 622 9098. Email: cisano@camping-cisano.it

This is a combination of two sites and some of the 700 pitches have superb locations along the kilometre of shaded lakeside contained in Cisano. Some are on sloping ground and most are shaded but the San Vito pitches have no lake views. Both sites have a family orientation and considerable effort has been taken in the landscaping to provide maximum comfort even for the largest units. San Vito is the smaller and more peaceful location with no lakeside pitches and shares many of the facilities of Cisano which is a short walk across the road. Each site has its own reception. A reader reports that a 2 m. fence separating the pitches from the beach and lake has been constructed at Cisano, with several gates, but only two that open at the moment, at the extreme ends of the beach. The support facilities are constantly upgraded, although visitors with disabilities should select their pitch carefully to ensure an area appropriate to all their needs (there are some slopes in Cisano). On the San Vito site there is a pleasant family style restaurant (some road noise) which also sells takeaway food. San Vito is accessed through a tunnel under the road. The friendly efficient staff speak English at both sites.

Facilities

Plentiful, good quality sanitary facilities are provided in both sites (9 blocks at Cisano and 2 at San Vito) including facilities for disabled visitors. Fridge hire. Shop, bar, restaurant (open all season). Swimming pool. Play area. Fishing and sailing. Windsurfing and canoeing. Boat launching. Internet access. Dogs are not accepted. Off site: Indoor pool, bicycle hire and tennis 2 km.

Open: 1 April - 1 October.

Directions

Leave A4 autoroute at Pescheria exit and head north towards Garda on lakeside road. Pass Lazise and site is signed (small sign) on left halfway to Bardolina. Site is 12 km. beyond the Gardaland theme park.

Charges guide

Per person	€ 3,50 - € 9,00
pitch	€ 8,00 - € 16,50

Camping Cheques accepted.

IT6283 Camping La Rocca

Via Cavalle 22, I-25080 Manerba del Garda (Lake Garda)

Tel: 0365 551 738. Email: info@laroccacamp.it

Set high on a peninsula, there are delightful views from this very friendly, family-orientated campsite. With 180 attractive touring pitches enjoying shade from the tree canopy which also protects the campers from the summer heat, this is a 'real' campsite (20 pitches have lake views). Located in the idyllic Gulf of Manerba on Lake Garda, near the La Rocca natural park, it has the choice of two pretty, pebble lakeside beaches which can be accessed from the site, and a very nice pool complex. The site has a friendly family feel with all modern amenities without losing its distinctive Italian ambience. Nothing is too much trouble for the management. The director Livio is charming and very engaging with his pleasant, halting English.

Facilities

Two sanitary blocks with smart new units for disabled campers and baby changing areas which are kept in pristine condition at all times. Washing machines. Restaurant for basic meals with a pleasant terrace. Small shop. Swimming pools. Tennis. Play area. Fishing (permit). Music. Miniclub (high season). Off site: Bars and restaurants close. Theme parks. Fishing. Sailing. Golf 2 km.

Open: 31 March - 30 September.

Directions

From A4 autostrada take Desenzano exit and follow S572 towards Salo. Take minor road to Manerba from where site is signed. It is on road Cavalle 200 m. after 'Porto Torchio' (public towage).

Charges 2006

Per person	€ 3,80 - € 7,00
child (3-11 yrs)	€ 3,00 - € 5,50
pitch with electricity	€ 8,80 - € 17,00

IT6280 Camping Villaggio Weekend

Via Vallone della Selva 2, I-25010 San Felice del Benaco (Lake Garda)
Tel: 0365 43712. Email: info@weekend.it

Created among the olive groves and terraced vineyards of the Chateau Villa Louisa, which overlooks it, this modern well equipped site enjoys some superb views over the small bay which forms this part of Lake Garda. On reaching the site you will pass through a most impressive pair of gates. There are 230 pitches, all with electricity, of which about 30% are taken by tour operators and statics. The touring pitches are in several different areas, and many enjoy superb views. Some pitches for larger units are set in the upper terraces on steep slopes and manoeuvring can be challenging. Low olive branches may cause problems for long or high units. Although the site is 400 metres from the lake via a steep footpath, for many campers the views resulting from its situation on higher ground will be ample compensation for its not being an actual lakeside site. Being set in quiet countryside, it provides an unusually tranquil environment, although even here it can become very busy in the high season. The site has a supervised pool (25 x 12 m) and a paddling pool which make up for its not actually having frontage onto the lake. The large, attractive restaurant has a thoughtfully laid out terrace and lawn with attractive marble statues from where there are more wonderful views.

Facilities

Three sanitary blocks, one below the restaurant/shop, are modern and well maintained. Mainly British style WCs, a few washbasins in cabins and facilities for disabled people in one. Baby room. Laundry. Bar/restaurant (waiter service). Takeaway. Shop. Supervised swimming pool and paddling pool. Barbecues. Entertainment programme all season. Wide-screen TV. All facilities are open throughout the season. Two playgrounds. First aid room. English spoken. Internet points. Off site: Fishing 2 km. Golf 6 km. Riding 8 km. Windsurfing, water skiing and tennis near.

Open: 21 April - 22 September.

Directions

Approach from Saló (easier when towing) and follow site signs. From Milano - Venezia autostrada take Desenzano exit towards Saló and Localita Cisano - S. Felice. Watch for narrow right fork after Cunettone roundabout. Pass petrol station on left, then turn right towards San Felice for 1 km.

Charges 2007

Per person	€ 5,50 - € 9,00
child (3-10 yrs)	€ 3,50 - € 6,00
pitch incl. electricity	€ 14,50 - € 19,00

Camping Cheques accepted.

IT6286 Camping Baia Verde

I-25080 Manerba del Garda (Lake Garda)

Tel: **3463 366184**. Email: **info@campingbaiaverde.com**

Baia Verde is a new campsite to be opened in 2007 and which we will inspect during the coming season. It is located in the south western corner of Lake Garda, close to the popular resort of Manerba del Garda. Although still under construction, the site will have a swimming pool and a range of leisure facilites and will also offer mobile homes for rent. Pitches will be grassy and of a reasonable size and all will be equipped with electrical connections. However, given that the site is new, there will be little natural shade on most pitches. The site will obviously benefit from brand new amenities and some pitches will have private wash blocks. The lake is just two minutes walk away and other popular attractions such as the Gardaland theme park and Caneva water park are close at hand.

Facilities	Directions
(planned) Swimming pool, children's pool, sports pitch, children's playground, entertainment and activity programme in high season. Off site: Manerba del Garda 1 km. Lake Garda 400 m. Cycle and walking trails. Riding. Golf.	From Desenzano, head north on the S572 on the west side of the lake towards Salo and take the road to Manerba from where the site will be well signed (via dell' Edera).

Open: 26 May - 15 September.

Charges 2006

Per person	€ 5,00 - € 7,50
child (3-11 yrs)	€ 4,50 - € 5,00
pitch incl. electricity	€ 9,00 - € 14,00

IT6284 Camping Belvedere

Via Cavalle, 5, I-25080 Manerba del Garda (Lake Garda)

Tel: **03 65 55 11 75**. Email: **info@camping-belvedere.it**

Situated along a promontory reaching into Lake Garda, this campsite has been landscaped with terracing to give many of the 84 touring pitches a good vantage point to enjoy the wonderful views. There is access to the long pebbly beach for a relaxing swim and a dedicated area for boat launching. The delightful restaurant and bar with pretty flowers is under shady trees at the water's edge. The site has lots of grassy areas and alternated with attractive olive trees are others to give a cool canopy. This is a good site from which to explore all the exciting sights the area has to offer. Italian villages with lots of atmosphere are close by as are the huge theme parks the area is known for. The landscaping and atmosphere are delightfully Mediterranean with charming Italian vistas. There are no facilities for disabled campers and really young children would require supervision as the terracing is unguarded in places and there are steep slopes which may hinder the infirm.

Facilities

Five decent sanitary blocks are very much to the sites credit, but there are no facilities for disabled visitors. Shop selling basics. Restaurant, bar and takeaway. Play area. Full size tennis court. Music in bar. TV. Torches useful. Off site: Golf and bicycle hire 2 km. Riding 4 km. Fishing. Watersports. Theme parks. Bars and restaurant (limited menu).

Open: 1 April - 8 October.

Directions

From Desezano head north on road 572 towards Salo and take minor road to Manerba from where Belvedere is signed. The campsite is on road Cavadella along with two other campsites (San Biago and La Rocca).

Charges 2006

Per person	€ 3,75 - € 6,50
child	€ 3,00 - € 5,20
pitch with electricity	€ 7,80 - € 13,00
dog	€ 2,00 - € 3,50

On the shores of Lake Garda, in the suggestive gulf of Manerba, Camping Belvedere is the ideal place for a great relaxing holiday on the lakeside. Its unique position offers you shady terraced pitches with a fantastic view, 200 mt. Beach with private pear and buoys for boat anchorage in the calm and safe water of the gulf. A restaurant with a wide terrace on the beach, children-playground, swimming pools, boat-access, bar and mini-market are at disposal of the guests.

CAMPING BELVEDERE
Via Cavalle, 5 - 25080 MANERBA DEL GARDA (BS) ITALY
Tel. +39 0365 551175 - Fax +39 0365 552350
E-mail: info@camping-belvedere.it
www.camping-belvedere.it

IT6270 Villaggio Turistico La Gardiola

Via Gardiola, 36, I-25010 San Felice del Benaco (Lake Garda)

Tel: 0365 559240. Email: info@baiaholiday.com

This small site is a hidden gem amongst the jewels of Lake Garda. With only 50 pitches (25 for tourers) it is located at the end of a no-through road with direct lake access. The campsite is small and terraced, all the well maintained pitches having great views. The touring pitches are nearest the lake with electricity, water and drainage. The bar, café and reception area is modern but small and simple, in keeping with the private feel to the campsite. The café terrace overlooks the lake. The shared amenities are of a high standard and discretely built underground minimising the intrusion on the beautiful views. This is a lovely campsite for those campers keen to capture their own secluded piece of Lake Garda. On our visit we met Alan Rogers' readers Ena and Tom from Sunderland who were delighted with the intimacy of the site.

Facilities

The toilet block is just below ground level with a lift system for disabled visitors. The facilities are quite small but are adequate, although some gentlemen may prefer to use the cabin due to the lack of privacy around the urinals. Hot water is free throughout. Laundry. Small kiosk with terrace for coffee and snacks. Small playground. Table tennis. Fishing. Off site: Restaurants, shops, pizzerias nearby.

Open: 30 March - 21 October.

Directions

Near San Felice on SS572 Salo - San Felice road, site is well signed (La Gardiola) at San Felice. Access is via a long, narrow lane. GPS: N45:34.512 E10:33.092

Charges 2007

Per unit incl. 2 persons	€ 16,20 - € 36,20
extra person	€ 3,40 - € 8,20
child (3-9 yrs) and seniors (over 60)	€ 3,10 - € 7,10
dog	€ 1,50 - € 6,50

IT6000 Camping Mare Pineta

Sistiana 60 D, Duino - Aurisina, I-34019 Trieste (Friuli - Venézia Giúlia)

Tel: 040 299264. Email: info@baiaholiday.com

This site is 18 kilometres west of Trieste, and is on raised ground near the sea with views over the Sistiana Bay, Miramare Castle and the Gulf of Trieste. The development of this site continues with modern reception buildings and improved sanitary facilities. The majority of the 500 individual pitches are occupied by mobile homes, chalets, tour operator tents and seasonal units but there are said to be about 100 available for touring units. They are on gravel hardstanding (awnings possible) in light woodland, all with 3A electricity and with water nearby. Good English is spoken. The site is used by a tour operator.

Facilities

Six toilet blocks of varying quality, some recently modernised, provide some washbasins in cabins (the hot water supply does not always cope with demand) and WCs of both British and Turkish style. Facilities for disabled people. Laundry. Motorcaravan service point. Shop (all season). Bars. Pizzeria with terrace. Disco. Swimming pool (1/6-15/9). Playground. Tennis. Bicycle hire. Fishing. Organised entertainment in season. Dogs or other animals are accepted but ring first. Off site: Riding 2 km. Golf 10 km. Beach 1 km.

Open: 30 March - 21 October.

Directions

From the west take Sistiana exit from A4 autostrada, turn right on S14 towards Sistiana and then Duino. Site is 1 km. on the left past Sistiana. From the east approach on the S14. GPS: N45:46.292 E13:37.451

Charges 2007

Per unit incl. 2 persons	€ 15,40 - € 40,00
extra person	€ 3,40 - € 8,10
child (3-12 yrs) or senior (over 60)	€ 3,10 - € 6,60
dog	€ 2,50 - € 7,00

www.baiaholiday.com

BOOKING ON-LINE
CAMPING - VILLAGE - BLU RESORT

WELCOME TO OUR WORLD

❶ Camping-Village ★★★★
BAIA BLU LA TORTUGA
SARDEGNA
ADAC Auszeichnung 2006

❷ Camping-Village ★★★
LA GARDIOLA
LAGO DI GARDA

❸ Camping-Village ★★★★
CAVALLINO
VENEZIA
ADAC Auszeichnung 2006

❹ Camping-Village ★★★★
MARE PINETA BAIA SISTIANA
TRIESTE

❺ Camping-Village ★★★
POLJANA
MALI LOŠINJ - CROAZIA
ADAC Auszeichnung 2006

Booking Centre Baia Holiday
Tel: +39 041 5301210
Tel: +39 0365 554296
Fax: +39 041 5304012
E-mail: info@baiaholiday.com

Booking Centre in Germany
Tel: +49 089 54881677
Fax: +49 089 54881675
E-mail: info@baiaholiday.de

IT6359 Camping Serenella

Localitá Mezzariva, I-37011 Bardolino (Lake Garda)

Tel: **0457 211333**.. Email: **serenella@camping-serenella.it**

Situated alongside Lake Garda, Serenella has 300 average size pitches, some with good lake views. Movement around the site may prove difficult for large units (look for the wider roads). The pitches are shaded and have 3A electricity. A long promenade with brilliant views of the mountains and lake runs the length of the campsite. It is dotted with grassy relaxation areas and beach bars where snacks are served and the atmosphere is charming. The pleasant pool complex is near an older style 'taverna' where delicious, sensibly priced food is served. There is some road noise at some of the amenities and the pool. There is an animation programme from May to September, a small market and a variety of tiny bungalows throughout the site. Serenella is popular with Italians and international guests.

Facilities

Five clean, well equipped sanitary blocks, include three that are more modern with laundry facilities. British style toilets, free hot water. Facilities for disabled visitors. Washing machines and dryer. Freezer. Bar/restaurant, takeaway and shop (all season). Watersports. Animation programme in high season. Play area. Bicycle hire. Boat launching. Minigolf. Tennis. Satellite TV. Internet and WiFi. Dogs are not accepted. Off site: Beach with fishing and watersports. Golf 3 km. Riding 3.5 km. Town 3 km.

Open: Easter or 1 April - 22 October.

Directions

From E70 Milan - Venice autostrada take Pescheria exit and follow signs to Bardolino. Site is on lakeside between Bardolino and Garda, about 4 km. south of Garda. GPS: N45:33 E10:43.000

Charges 2006

Per person	€ 4,00 - € 8,50
child (4-10 yrs)	free - € 4,00
pitch	€ 9,00 - € 16,00

IT6008 Camping Sabbiadoro

Via Sabbiadoro 8, I-33054 Lignano Sabbiadoro (Friuli - Venézia Giúlia)

Tel: **0431 714 55**. Email: **campsab@lignano.it**

Sabbiadoro is a large, good quality site with a huge entrance and efficient reception. It has over 1,250 pitches and is ideal for families who like all their amenities to be close by. This does mean that the site is busy and noisy with people having fun. Quite tightly packed, the pitches vary in size, are shaded by attractive trees and have electricity. You may wish to cover your car and unit to prevent sap covering it over time. The facilities are all in excellent condition and well thought out, especially the pool complex, and everything here is very modern, safe and clean. A second site close by is opened for younger customers in high season – they use the main site facilities. The local resort town is just 200 metres away and this too buzzes with activity in high season. The fine beach is 250 metres and is safe for children.

Facilities

Well equipped sanitary facilities include superb facilities for disabled visitors. Washing machines and dryers. Motorcaravan service point. Huge supermarket (all season). Bazaar. Good restaurant and snack bar (31/5-29/9). Heated outdoor pool complex with separate fun pool area, slides (all season). Table tennis. Disco. TV room. Internet. Play areas. Tennis. Fitness centre. Entertainment in the main season. Off site: Riding, sailing and golf 2 km.

Open: 31 March - 30 September.

Directions

Leave A4 at Latisana exit, west of Trieste and head to Latisano. From Latisano follow road to Lignano, then Sabbiadoro. Site is well signed as you approach the town.

Charges 2006

Per person	€ 4,50 - € 8,60
child (3-12 yrs)	€ 3,00 - € 4,80
pitch	€ 7,80 - € 14,80

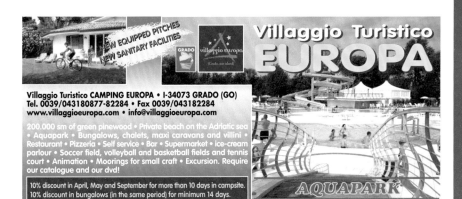

IT6005 Villaggio Turistico Camping Europa

Via Monfalcone 12, I-34073 Grado (Friuli - Venézia Giúlia)

Tel: 0431 80877. Email: info@villaggioeuropa.com

This large flat site beside the sea can take almost 500 units. All the pitches are marked, nearly all with good shade, and there are electrical connections in all areas. The terrain is undulating and sandy in the areas nearer the sea, where cars have to be left in parking places and not by your pitch. The site reports the building of a large new 'Aquatic Park' covering 1500 sq.m. with two slides (100 m. and 60 m. long and many other features. There is direct access to the beach but the water is shallow up to 200 m. from the beach, with growing seaweed. However, a narrow wooden jetty is provided which one can walk along to deeper water. This is a good honest site which, after recent improvements, is probably the best in the area.

Facilities

Six identical toilet blocks should make up a good supply, with free hot water in all facilities, half British style WCs and facilities for disabled people. Washing machines. Motorcaravan services. Large supermarket, small general shop (all season). Large bar and restaurant with takeaway (all season). Swimming pools (May - Sept). Tennis. Fishing. Bicycle hire. Playground. Dancing at times in season; some organised activities in high season. Off site: Golf 0.5 km. Riding 4 km.

Open: 28 April - 22 September.

Directions

Site is 4 km. east of Grado on road to Monfalcone. If road 35L is taken to Grado from west, continue through town to Grado Pineta.
GPS: N45:41.816 E13:27.302

Charges 2006

Per person	€ 5,50 - € 9,50
child (3-11 yrs)	free - € 6,50
pitch incl. electricity	€ 8,00 - € 18,50
dog	€ 2,50 - € 6,00

Less 10% for longer stays out of season.

283

IT6207 Camping Residence Sägemühle

Dornweg 12, I-39026 Prad am Stilfserjoch (Trentino - Alto Adige)

Tel: 0473 616078. Email: info@campingsaegemuehle.com

This small site in the countryside is beside a little village and has attractive views of the surrounding mountains where skiing is popular in the winter. The grass pitches are neat and level, some have shade and most have water, electricity drainage and pretty views. For a tiny campsite there is a lot on offer here. The indoor pool area is welcoming to cool oneself in the summer and relax in warm water after skiing in winter. The facilities are cleverly placed under the pool and include a tiny gymnasium, sauna and a TV/games room. The steps may prove difficult for those with mobility problems, although the facilities for disabled visitors are on ground level. Animation is provided in July and August and shared with a sister site. We visited in high summer season but the area is a renowned winter sports area. The friendly owners speak some English and Dutch. A sister site, Camping Kiefernhain, has 180 pitches with amenities provided at a nearby sports centre in the village. A public swimming pool is adjacent to the site.

Facilities

The main modern toilet block is under the pool complex. All WCs are British style and the showers are of high quality. Facilities for disabled visitors. Children's facilities and baby baths. Washing machines. Restaurant and bar. Indoor swimming pool. Spa and sauna. Animation programme in season. Mini-club. Play area. Internet. Torches useful. Off site: Town facilities. Natural spring for paddling close by. Bicycle hire 300 m. Riding 800 m. Golf 30 km.

Open: All year excl. 7 November. - 19 December.

Directions

Site is west of Bolzano. From A38/S40 west of Bolzano, take exit for Pso dello Stelvio/Stilfserjoch (also marked S38) and village of Prad am Stilfserioch. Site is well signed from here.

Charges 2006

Per person	€ 6,70 - € 7,70
child (11-15 yrs)	€ 5,80 - € 7,00
child (2-10)	€ 4,80 - € 5,50
pitch	€ 10,50 - € 12,00
electricity	€ 2,50

IT6204 Camping Seiser Alm

Sant Konstantin 16, I-39050 Völs am Schlern (Trentino - Alto Adige)

Tel: **0471 706459**. Email: **info@camping-seiseralm.com**

What an amazing experience awaits you at Seiser Alm! Elisabeth and Erhard Mahlknecht have created a superb site in the magnificent Sudtirol region of the Dolomite mountains. Catering for families and delightfully peaceful, towering peaks provide a magnificent backdrop when you dine in the charming restaurant on the upper terrace. The 150 touring pitches are of a very high standard with 16A electricity supply, 120 with gas, water, drainage and satellite connections. Guests were delighted with the site when we visited, many coming to walk or cycle, some just to enjoy the surroundings. There are countless things to see and do here. Local buses and cable cars provide an excellent service for summer visitors and skiers alike In keeping with the natural setting, the majority of the luxury facilities are set into the hillside. Elisabeth's designs incorporating Grimm fairy tales are tastefully developed in the superb children's bathrooms that are in a magic forest setting complete with blue sky, giant mushroom and elves! A brilliant family adventure park with an enclosure of tame rabbits is at the lower part of the site where goats also roam. If you wish for quiet, quality camping in a crystal clean environment, then visit this immaculate site.

Facilities

One luxury underground block is in the centre of the site. 16 private units are available. Excellent facilities for disabled visitors. Fairy tale facilities for children. Infra red sensors, under-floor heating and gently curved floors to prevent slippery surfaces. Washing machines and large drying room. Sauna. Supermarket. Quality restaurant and bar with terrace. Animation programme. Mini-club. Children's adventure park and play room. Torches useful. Off site: Riding alongside site. Golf 18 hole course (discounts) 1 km. Fishing 1 km. Bicycle hire 2 km. Lake swimming 2 km. ATM 3 km. Walks. Skiing in winter.

Open: All year excl. 5 November - 20 December.

Directions

Site is east of Bolzano. From A22-E45 take Bolzano Nord exit, then road for Prato Isarco/Blumau. Then follow road for Fie/Vols. Take care as the split in the road is sudden and if you miss the left fork as you enter a tunnel (Altopiano dello Sciliar/Schlerngebiet) you will pay a heavy price in extra kilometers. Enjoy the climb to Vols am Schlern and site is well signed.

Charges 2006

Per person	€ 6,10 - € 7,20
child (2-16 yrs)	€ 3,30 - € 5,80
pitch incl. electricity	€ 8,20 - € 11,52

Camping Cheques accepted.

IT6199 Camping Corones

I-39030 Rasun (Trentino - Alto Adige)

Tel: **0474 496490**. Email: **info@corones.com**

This campsite has been recommended by our Italian agent and we plan to undertake an inspection in 2007. It is a tranquil site, beautifully located in the Dolomites alongside a stream in a valley with fine views over wooded hillsides. Pitches are of a good size and all have electrical connections.

Facilities

Modern toilet blocks include private cabins for hire. Facilities for disabled visitors. Restaurant. Bar. Takeaway. Supermarket. Sauna, Jacuzzi and steam room. Outdoor swimming pool and paddling pool. Bicycle hire. Play area. Internet facilities. Television room. Chalets for rent. Off site: Tennis 800 m. Riding 5 km. Golf (9 holes) 11 km. Canoeing/kayaking 15 km.

Open: 2 December - 15 April and 20 May - 28 October.

Directions

Using the southbound Munich - Bolzano motorway, take Brixen/Pustertal exit. Head towards Toblach and Cortina. After the junction at Olang-Vaklaora continue towards Rasen and then towards Antholz/Anterselva. The site is well signed.

Charges 2006

Per unit incl 2 persons and electricity	€ 19,00 - € 26,20
extra person	€ 4,50 - € 7,00

285

IT6208 Camping Gamp

I-39043 Chiusa (Trentino - Alto Adige)
Tel: 0472 847425. Email: info@camping-gamp.com

This campsite has been recommended by our Italian agent and we will undertake a full inspection in 2007. The site is situated in the picturesque Isarco valley in the mountainous German speaking Sudtirol region of northern Italy. This is an excellent region for walking and mountain biking with magnificent views on all sides. On site amenities are modern and include a children's play area with mini zoo, an attractive swimming pool with a terrace offering fine panoramic views of the surrounding mountains. Open all year, the site is well located for winter sports holidays.

Facilities

Modern toilet block with family bathrooms, baby room, and special children's facilities. Motorcaravan service point. Restaurant. Coffee bar. mini-market. Fishing. Music and dancing. Mountain bike rental. Ski and sledge rental. Playground with small zoo.

Open: All year.

Directions

Camping Gamp is only 800 m. away from the A22 motorway (Brenner - Verona) exit for Klausen and Grödental. Site is well signed from here.

Charges 2006

Per person	€ 6,10 - € 6,60
child (10-14 yrs)	€ 4,70 - € 4,90
child ((3-9 yrs)	€ 3,10 - € 3,90
pitch	€ 8,30 - € 8,60
electricity	€ 0,60 - € 1,80

IT6226 Camping Punta Lago

Via Lungo Lago, 42, I-38050 Calceranica al Lago (Trentino - Alto Adige)
Tel: 0461 723229. Email: info@campingpuntalago.com

There is something quite delightful about the smaller Italian lakes. Lago di Caldonazzo is in a beautiful setting about two kilometres from the historic village of Calceranica which has summer time markets. This well designed campsite has 140 level, shaded and grassy pitches. Of a good size, all have electricity (3/6A) and 50 are serviced with water and drainage. Access roads are paved and the sanitary facilities are of the highest quality. A small road separates the site from the grassy banks of the lake where all kinds of non-motorised water sports can be enjoyed. There are excellent restaurants within 50 metres of the gate. The site itself has a large terraced snack bar with wonderful views of the lake and the most amazing ice cream (gelato, yogurt) and fruit concoctions. The campsite first opened 45 years ago and brothers Gino and Mauro continue the friendly family tradition of ensuring you enjoy your holiday.

Facilities

One central sanitary block has superb facilities with hot water throughout. Well designed bathroom and washbasin area. Excellent facilities for disabled campers and babies. Washing machines and dryer. Private units for rent, some with massage baths. Bar/snack bar and shop (all season). Fishing (with permit). Freezer. Modern comprehensive play area. Internet access. Cinema. TV. Five-a-side pitch. Volleyball. Off site: Town 1 km. and ATM. Watersports. Bicycle hire 1 km. Riding 3 km. Golf 20 km.

Open: 1 May - 15 September.

Directions

From A22 Bolzano - Trento autostrada take the SS47 towards Padova and then turn for Lago di Caldonazzo. Approaching town from the west beside the railway, continue along Via Donegani, turn left into Via al Lago and right at the lakeside into Via Lungolago. Site is on the right 200 m. before a sharp right turn. GPS: N46:00 E11:15.27

Charges 2006

Per person	€ 5,50 - € 8,00
child	€ 4,90 - € 7,00
pitch incl. electricity	€ 8,40 - € 14,00
dog	free - € 3,00

Check real time availability and at-the-gate prices...
www.alanrogers.com

IT6210 Camping Steiner

Kennedy Straße 32, I-39055 Laives (Bolzano) (Trentino - Alto Adige)
Tel: 0471 950105. Email: info@campingsteiner.com

Camping Steiner is very central for touring with the whole of the Dolomite region within easy reach, as well as Bolzano, Merano and other attractive places. It has its share of overnight trade but, with much on site activity, one could spend an enjoyable holiday here, especially now the S12 by which it stands has a motorway alternative. It is a fairly small site with part taken up by bungalows. The individual touring pitches, mostly with good shade and hardstanding, are in rows on either side of access roads. There are electricity connections. This friendly, family run site has a long tradition of providing a happy camping experience in the more traditional style – the owner remembers Alan Rogers who stayed here on many occasions. There is a family style restaurant and indoor and outdoor pools to provide exercise and relaxation.

Facilities

The two sanitary blocks, one new, can be heated in cool weather. Excellent small restaurant and takeaway service, with good choice. Cellar bar with taped music, dancing at times. Shop. Two free swimming pools – one open air, 20 x 10 m. (May-Sept. and heated in spring), and a 12 x 6 m. enclosed, heated pool (open all season, except July/Aug). Playground and paddling pool. Table tennis. Off site: 18 hole golf course 30 minutes away.

Open: 28 March - 7 November.

Directions

Site is by the S12 in northern part of Leifers, 8 km. south of Bolzano. If approaching from north, take Bolzano-Süd autostrada exit and follow Trento signs for 7 km; from south take Ora exit, then 14 km. towards Bolzano. GPS: N46:25.820 E11:20.635

Charges 2006

Per person	€ 5,00 - € 6,50
child (0-9 yrs)	€ 3,00 - € 4,50
pitch incl. car and 6A electricity	€ 11,00 - € 13,00
dog	€ 5,00

Less in low season. Less 5-10% after 2 weeks stay.

IT6232 Camping Al Sole

Via Maffei, 127, I-38060 Molina di Ledro (Trentino - Alto Adige)

Tel: **0464 508496**. Email: **info@campingalsole.it**

Lake Ledro is only 9 km. from Lake Garda, its sparkling waters and breathtaking scenery offering a low key alternative for those who enjoy a natural setting. The drive from Lake Garda is a real pleasure and prepares you for the treat ahead. This site has been owned by the same friendly family for over 40 years and their experience shows in the layout of the site with its mature trees and the array of facilities provided. Situated on the lake with its own sandy beach, pool and play area, the facilities were rebuilt in 2006 and now include an outstanding 'wellness' centre. The 'Chiva Som' centre provides a whirlpool, solarium, beauty therapies, aromatic showers and massage room. The sauna has panoramic views over the lake and mountains and there is a heated outdoor spa pool where one can relax under the stars at night. New fully serviced pitches were also added in 2006. This is a very pleasant, peaceful site for extended stays or sightseeing. It came as no surprise to hear that many people choose to return year after year. The local community welcomes tourists and offers hiking programmes beginning with Monday evening information nights so that you can choose the most appropriate guided walks.

Facilities

Superb new facilities block (2006) with free hot water throughout. Well appointed facilities include 5 private bathrooms with shower, toilet, basin and safe. Excellent facilities for disabled people. Baby room. Laundry facilities. Freezer. Motorcaravan services. Small supermarket. Pleasant restaurant and pizzeria. Bar serving snacks and takeaway. 'Chiva Som' wellness centre. Swimming pool. Play area. Bicycle hire. Boating, windsurfing, fishing and canoeing. Live music twice weekly in July/Aug. Children's club. Off site: Riding 2 km. Golf 20 km.

Open: Easter - 8 October.

Directions

From autostrada A22 exit for Lake Garda North to Riba del Garda. In Riva follow sign for Ledro valley. Site is well signed as you approach Lago di Ledra. GPS: N45:52.683 E10:46.064

Charges 2006

Per person	€ 5,50 - € 8,00
child (2-11yrs)	€ 4,00 - € 5,00
pitch incl. electricity	€ 7,00 - € 14,00

Camping Cheques accepted.

Family Camping Al Sole

Valle di Ledro - Trentino • 0039.0464.508496
www.campingalsole.it • info@campingalsole.it

IT6200 Camping Olympia

Camping 1, I-39034 Toblach (Trentino - Alto Adige)

Tel: **0474 972147**. Email: **info@camping-olympia.com**

In the Dolomite mountains, Camping Olympia, always good, maintains its high standards with the upgrading of the camping area and the refurbishment of the already excellent sanitary accommodation. Tall trees at each end of the site have been left, but most of those in the centre have been removed and the pitches relaid in a regular pattern. They include 16 fully serviced ones with electricity, water, waste, gas and TV and telephone points.

Facilities

Excellent sanitary provision, on two floor levels, is housed in the main building. Two small blocks at each end of the site provide further WCs and showers. Shop. Attractive restaurant (all day, all year). Snack bar (not April/May or Oct/Nov). Tennis. Swimming pool (when weather permits). Sauna, solarium, steam bath and whirl pools. Minigolf. Fishing. Bicycle hire. Play area. Animation programme.

Open: All year.

Directions

Site is between Villabassa and Toblach/Dobbiaco. From A22 (Innsbruck-Bolzano) take exit for Bressanone/Brixen and go east on SS49 for about 60 km. From Cortina take SS48 and SS51 north then west on SS49. GPS: N46:44.086 E12:11.638

Charges 2006

Per person	€ 8,00 - € 9,50
pitch	€ 7,00 - € 11,50

IT6229 Camping Lévico

Localitá Pleina, 5, I-38056 Lévico Terme (Trentino - Alto Adige)

Tel: 0461 706491. Email: mail@campinglevico.com

Sister site to Camping Jolly, Camping Levico is in a natural setting on the small, very pretty Italian lake also called Levico which is surrounded by towering mountains. The sites are owned by brothers – Andrea, who manages Levico, and Gino who is based at Jolly. Both campsites are charming, with Levico having some pitches along the lake edge and a quiet atmosphere. There is a shaded terrace for enjoying pizza and drinks in the evening. Pitches are of a good size, most grassed, well shaded and with 6A electricity. Staff are welcoming and fluent in many languages including English and Dutch. There is a small supermarket and it is a short distance to the local village. The beautiful grassy shores of the lake are ideal for sunbathing and the crystal clear water is ideal for enjoying (non-motorised) water activities. This is a site where the natural beauty of an Italian lake can be enjoyed without being overwhelmed by commercial tourism. All the amenities at Camping Jolly can be enjoyed by traversing a very pretty walkway along a stream where we saw many trout.

Facilities

Four modern sanitary blocks provide hot water for showers, washbasins and washing. Mostly British style toilets. Single locked unit for disabled visitors. Washing machines and dryer. Ironing. Freezer. Motorcaravan service point. Bar/restaurant, takeaway and good shop (all season). Play area. Miniclub and animation (high season). Fishing. Satellite TV and cartoon cinema. Internet acess. Five-a-side soccer pitch. Kayak hire. Tennis. Billiards. Medical services. Torches useful. Off site: Town 2 km. with all the usual facilities and ATM. Bicycle hire 1.5 km and bicycle track. Boat launching 500 m. Riding 3 km. Golf 7 km.

Open: 1 April - 5 October.

Directions

From A22 Verona - Bolzano road take turn for Trento on S47 to Levico Terme where campsite is very well signed. GPS: N46:00.700 E11:17.000

Charges 2006

Per person	€ 5,00 - € 9,50
child (3-11 years)	€ 4,00 - € 6,00
pitch incl. electricity (6A)	€ 7,50 - € 18,00

IT6233 Camping Al Lago

Via Alzer, 7/9, I-38060 Pieve di Ledro (Trentino - Alto Adige)

Tel: **0464 591250**. Email: **mb.penner@libero.it**

Camping Al Lago is a small, unassuming site on the banks of the serene Lake Ledro, with towering hills of rock and forest on two sides. The 105 pitches (with electricity) are fairly tightly placed and the site has very limited facilities. It is very peaceful here and the friendly owner Mario will give help and guidance on what to do in the area including leading bicycle and walking tours. The site is very popular with Dutch holidaymakers. Only snacks are served in the bar behind reception but there is a choice of restaurants just 200 m. from the gate. There is also a good supermarket nearby selling fresh foods and prepared meals. A hire service for bicycles and kayaks is offered and the site has two sections where there is direct access to the lake. A cool swim can be most welcome after a day of exploration in the hills. If you like very simple camping without the luxuries and amenities of the bigger sites and a sound night's sleep this may be for you.

Facilities

A single toilet block provides a very limited number of showers and toilets that are mixed British and Turkish style. Facilities are extremely busy at peak periods. Provision for disabled campers. Washing machines and spin dryers. Bar with terrace. Snacks. Bicycle hire. Kayaking. Lakeside areas. Organised walking and cycling. Off site: Riding 2 km. Sailing 200 m. Town 500 m.

Open: 25 April - 10 October.

Directions

Site is on the north side of Lake Ledro. From the A22 near Rovereto take S240 to Riva del Garda, then S240 to Pieve di Lago. Site is well signed approaching the village.

Charges 2006

Per person	€ 5,00 - € 7,50
child (2-12 yrs)	€ 3,50 - € 5,00
pitch incl. electricity	€ 6,00 - €10,00

IT6205 Camping International Dolomiti

Via Campo di Sotto, I-32043 Cortina d'Ampezzo (Veneto)

Tel: **0436 2485**. Email: **campeggiodolomiti@tin.it**

Cortina is a large provincial town with many interesting shops and restaurants. A bus from outside the gate of the campsite will take you the three kilometres to the town centre. The strength of this site is its beautiful mountain scenery and quiet location in a grassy meadow beside a fast flowing river (no fences). The site is dedicated to tourers with 390 good sized pitches, most with electricity and about half with shade. The site does not take reservations so arrive early in the day in the first three weeks of August to improve your chance of obtaining a pitch. There is a heated swimming pool on site, but otherwise it is a simple and uncomplicated site which makes a good centre for touring the Dolomites or for more active pursuits such as mountain walking.

Facilities

The main toilet block is large and should be adequate. Some British style WCs but mainly Turkish. Washbasins have hot water sprinkler taps. A heated block provides facilities for disabled visitors. Washing machines and ironing boards. Gas supplies. Coffee bar and small shop (long hours). Heated swimming pool (5/7-25/8). Basic playground (hard base). Dogs are not accepted. Off site: Restaurant 600 m. Fishing 1 km. Golf 2 km. Bicycle hire and riding 3 km.

Open: 1 June - 20 September.

Directions

Site is 2 km. west off the S51 (Dobbiaco - Veneto) at southern outskirts of Cortina. The S48 travels west of Cortina to the A22 between Bolzano and Trieste, but this road can be difficult to locate from Cortina (follow signs to Falzarego). The S48 has incredible views but is very slow between Cortina and Canazei. GPS: N46:30.974 E12:08.160

Charges 2007

Per person	€ 4,50 - € 7,50
pitch incl. electricity	€ 7,00 - € 9,00

IT6003 Centro Vacanze Pra' Delle Torri

P.O. Box 176, I-30021 Caorle (Veneto)

Tel: 0421 299063. Email: torri@vacanze-natura.it

Pra' delle Torri is another Italian Adriatic site which has just about everything! Pitches for camping, hotel, accommodation to rent, one of the largest and best equipped pool complexes in the country and a golf course where lessons for beginners are also available. Many of the 1,300 grass pitches (with electricity) have shade and they are arranged in zones – when you book in at reception you are taken by electric golf buggy to select your pitch. There are two good restaurants, bars and a range of shops arranged around an attractive square. Recent additions incude a crèche and a supervised play area for young children. The pool complex is the crowning glory with indoor (Olympic size) and outdoor pools with slides and many other features. Other super amenities include a large grass area for ball games, a good playground, a babies' car track, and a whole range of sports, fitness and entertainment programmes, along with a medical centre, skincare and other therapies. The site has its own sandy beach and Porto Santa Margherita and Caorle are nearby. One could quite happily spend a whole holiday here without leaving the site but the attractions of Venice, Verona, etc. might well tempt one to explore the area.

Facilities

Sixteen excellent, high quality toilet blocks with the usual facilities including very attractive 'Junior Stations' and units for disabled visitors. Motorcaravan service point. Large supermarket and wide range of shops, restaurants, bars and takeaways. Indoor and outdoor pools. Tennis. Minigolf. Fishing. Watersports. Archery. Diving. Fitness programmes and keep fit track. Crèche and supervised play area. Bowls. Mountain bike track. Wide range of organised sports and entertainment. Off site: Riding 3 km.

Open: 31 March - 29 September.

Directions

From A4 Venice - Trieste motorway leave at exit for Sto Stino di Livenze and follow signs to Caorle then Sta Margherita and signs to site.

Charges guide

Per person	€ 3,55 - € 8,20
child (1-5 yrs)	free - € 6,00
senior (over 60 yrs)	€ 2,75 - € 7,00
pitch incl. electricity	€ 6,80 - € 21,00
tent pitch	€ 4,75 - € 14,80

Min. stay 2 nights.

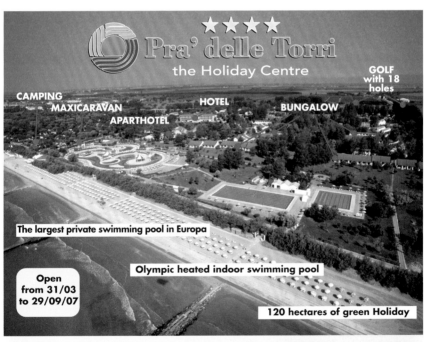

★★★★
Pra' delle Torri
the Holiday Centre

GOLF with 18 holes

CAMPING
MAXICARAVAN
APARTHOTEL
HOTEL
BUNGALOW

The largest private swimming pool in Europa

Olympic heated indoor swimming pool

Open from 31/03 to 29/09/07

120 hectares of green Holiday

  Tel. 0039/0421299063 - Fax 0039/0421299035
I-30021 Caorle (VENEZIA)
torri@vacanze-natura.it - www.pradelletorri.it

IT6010 Camping Capalonga

Via della Laguna 16, I-30020 Bibione-Pineda (Veneto)

Tel: **0431 438351**. Email: **capalonga@bibionemare.com**

A quality site right beside the sea, Capalonga is a large site with 1,350 pitches of variable size (70-90 sq.m). Nearly all marked out, all have electrical connections, some have water and drainage, and there is good shade almost everywhere. The site is pleasantly laid out – roads run in arcs which avoids the square box effect. Some pitches where trees define the pitch area may be tricky for large units. The very wide, sandy beach, which is cleaned by the site, shelves extremely gently so is very safe for children and it never becomes too crowded. A concrete path leads out towards the sea to avoid too much sand-walking and the water is much cleaner here than at most places along this coast. A large lagoon runs along the other side of the site where boating (motor or sail) can be practised and a landing stage and moorings are provided. There is also a swimming pool on site. Capalonga is an excellent site, with comprehensive facilities.

Facilities

Seven toilet blocks are well and frequently cleaned. Two newer blocks built side by side have facilities for disabled people and very fine children's rooms. British and some Turkish style toilets, some washbasins in private cabins. Launderette. Motorcaravan services. Large supermarket. General shop. Self-service restaurant and separate bar. Swimming pool (25 x 12-5 m; 19/5-15/9). Boating. Fishing. Playground. Free animation programme. First-aid room. Dogs are not accepted.

Open: 28 April - 30 September.

Directions

Bibione is about 80 km. east of Venice, well signed from afar on approach roads. 1 km. before Bibione turn right towards Bibione Pineda and follow camp signs. GPS: N45:37.830 E12:59.615

Charges 2006

Per person	€ 5,70 - € 10,00
child (1-4 yrs)	free - € 4,50
child (5-10 yrs)	free - € 7,00
pitch with electricity	€ 10,50 - € 20,00
pitch with water and drainage	€ 11,50 - € 21,00

IT6013 Camping Lido

Via Dei Ginepri, 115, I-30020 Bibione-Pineda (Veneto)

Tel: **0431 438480**. Email: **lido@bibionemare.com**

Camping Village Lido is a quiet green site with direct access to the sea front in the centre of the town of Bibione Pineda. The 420, mostly shaded, touring pitches are in three sizes, 380 with electricity, water and waste water facilities. All have convenient access to the long white sandy beach with its slowly shelving water ideal for swimming. There are 233 high quality mobile homes available for campers who choose to fly to the site (car hire is available in a package deal). This is a simple site with good sporting and children's facilities, and an uncomplicated bar and restaurant. An adjacent area is shared by the animation team and a very good supermarket. There are pleasant swimming pools for adults and children, although the site's main strength is the excellent beach and its central location convenient to Bibione Pineda's shopping area. Like other sites owned by the Sartori family, who have many years experience in the camping holiday industry, this is a well organised site with high standards of cleanliness and good sanitary facilities.

Facilities

Six sanitary blocks conveniently located, two new and all clean and well appointed. Car wash and motorcaravan service point. Bar, restaurant, supermarket and bazaar. Electronic games. First aid post. Archery. Canoeing. Children's play park. Table tennis. Football. Tennis and windsurfing schools. Boat mooring. Off site: Bibione Pineda. Marina. Excursions to Venice.

Open: 13 May - 17 September.

Directions

Bibione is about 80 km. east of Venice, well signed from afar on approach roads. 1 km. before Bibione turn right towards Bibione Pineda and follow camp signs. GPS: N45:37.963 E13:00.060

Charges 2006

Per person	€ 4,50 - € 8,00
child (1-4 yrs)	free - € 3,60
child (5-10 yrs)	free - € 5,50
pitch	€ 8,00 - € 16,00

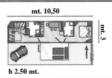

IT6015 Camping Residence Il Tridente

Via Baseleghe 12, I-30020 Bibione-Pineda (Veneto)
Tel: **0431 439600**. Email: **tridente@bibionemare.com**

This is an unusual site in that only half the area is used for camping. Formerly a holiday centre for deprived children, it occupies a strip of woodland 200 m. wide and 400 m. long stretching from the main road to the sea. It is divided into two parts by the Residence, an apartment block of first class rooms which are for rent. The 250 tourist pitches are located amongst tall pines in the area between the entrance and the Residence. Pitch size varies according to the positions of the trees, but they are of sufficient size and have electricity connections. The ground slopes gently from the main building to the beach of fine sand and this is used as the recreation area with two swimming pools – one 25 x 12.5 m. and a smaller children's pool – tennis courts, table tennis and sitting and play places. With thick woodland on both sides, Il Tridente is a quiet, restful site with excellent facilities.

Facilities

Three sanitary blocks, two in the main camping area and one near the sea, are of excellent quality. Mixed British and Turkish style WCs in cabins with washbasins and facilities for disabled people. Washing machines and dryers. Motorcaravan services. The Residence includes an excellent restaurant, bar and supermarket. Swimming pools. Playground. Tennis. Animation programme in high season. Dogs are not accepted.

Open: 12 April - 17 September.

Directions

From A4 Venice - Trieste autostrada, take Latisana exit and follow signs to Bibione and then Bibione Pineda and camp signs.
GPS: N45:38.084 E13:01.040

Charges 2006

Per person	€ 5,70 - € 9,00
child (1-4 yrs)	free - € 4,20
child (5-10 yrs)	free - € 6,50
pitch incl. electricity	€ 10,50 - € 18,00

See advertisement on page 293

IT6036 Camping Ca'Pasquali

Via A. Poerio, 33, I-30010 Cavallino-Treporti (Veneto)
Tel: **041 96 61 10**. Email: **info@capasquali.it**

On the attractive natural woodland coast of Cavallino with its wide sandy beach, Ca'Pasquali is a holiday resort with easy access to magnificent Venice. This is an ideal place for a holiday interspersed with excursions to Verona, Padova, the glassmakers of Murano, the local water park, pretty villages and many other cultural attractions. This is a large site affiliated with nos. IT6028 and IT6014. The detail is important here; there are superb pools, a fitness area, an arena for entertainment and a beachside restaurant. The generously sized pitches are shaded and flat, serviced with drainage and some have spectacular sea views. The fine sandy beach was alive with families playing games, flying kites and enjoying themselves as we watched from the restaurant as the sun set. A family site with many extras, Ca'Pasquali has been thoughtfully designed to a high standard – it is ideal for families as a resort holiday or to combine with sightseeing.

Facilities

Three spotless modern units have excellent facilities with mainly British style toilets, superb facilities for disabled campers and babies. Washing machines and dryers. Motorcaravan services. Restaurant. Snack bar. Supermarket. Very pleasant pool complex with slides, fun pool and fountains. Aerobics. Fitness centre. Pool bar. Play areas. Bicycle hire. Small boat launching. Animation. Amphitheatre. Mini-club. Excursion service. Caravan storage. Dogs and other animals are not accepted. Off site: Golf and riding 5 km. Sailing. Fishing. Theme parks.

Open: 30 April - 18 September.

Directions

Leave autostrada A4 at Sant Dona Noventa exit and head for Sant Dona di Piave, Losolo and on to peninsula of Cavallino. Site is well signed shortly after town of Cavallino.

Charges 2006

Per person	€ 4,20 - € 8,50
child (1-5 yrs)	free - € 6,00
senior (over 60 yrs)	€ 2,70 - € 8,50
pitch	€ 7,20 - € 22,50

See advertisement on page 297

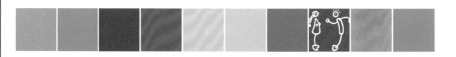

IT6022 Camping Village Portofelice

Viale Dei Fiori 15, I-30020 Eraclea Mare (Veneto)

Tel: **0421 66411**. Email: **info@portofelice.it**

Portofelice is a typical Italian coastal site with a sandy beach and plenty of well organised activity. It is unusual in being separated from the sea by a protected pine wood with a gravel path between the two. It is of medium size for this part of Italy with 546 tourist pitches and 230 occupied by static caravans, bungalows and tour operators' accommodation. The pitches are arranged in rectangular blocks or zones in regular rows, separated by hedges from hard access roads and with either natural or artificial shade. Cars are parked in numbered places under shade at the side of the zones. All pitches have electricity and 224 also have water, drainage and TV sockets. The social life of the site is centred around the pool complex where the shops, pizzeria, bar, café and restaurant are also located. A wide range of entertainment and activities are organised for adults and children. If you can drag yourself away from the holiday village, you can explore the region by car with Venice, the Dolomites and the Italian Lakes within range.

Facilities

Two modern sanitary blocks have the usual facilities with slightly more Turkish style toilets than British. Children's block (0-12 yrs). Facilities for disabled people. Shops. Pizzeria. Restaurant with most tables on a covered terrace with waiter service. Swimming pools with an area specifically equipped for disabled guests, whirlpool massage and sunbathing. Playgrounds. Tennis. Sandy beach. Bicycle hire. Organised activity and entertainment programmes. Off site: Riding 200 m. Golf 6 km.

Open: 5 May - 16 September.

Directions

From A4 Venice - Trieste motorway take exit for 'S. Dona/Noventa' and go south through S. Dona di Piave and Eraclea to Eraclea Mare where site is signed. GPS: N45:33.214 E12:46.051

Charges 2007

Per person	€ 3,40 - € 9,40
senior (over 60 yrs)	€ 2,40 - € 6,80
child (1-5 yrs)	free - € 6,80
pitch depending on type	€ 7,40 - € 20,70

IT6040 Camping Village Garden Paradiso

Via Baracca 55, I-30013 Cavallino-Treporti (Veneto)

Tel: **041 968075**. Email: **garden@vacanze-natura.it**

There are many sites in this area and there is much competition in providing a range of facilities. Garden Paradiso is a good seaside site which also provides three excellent, centrally situated pools, a fitness centre, minigolf, an excursion train and other activities for children. Compared with other sites here, this one is of medium size with 739 pitches. Most have electricity (from 6A), water and drainage points and all are marked and numbered with hard access roads, under a good cover of trees. Used by tour operators (35 pitches).

Facilities

Four brick, tiled toilet blocks are fully equipped with a mix of British and Turkish style toilets. Facilities for babies. Dishwashing and laundry sinks. Washing machines and dryers. Motorcaravan services. Shopping complex. Restaurant (22/4-28/9). Snack bar and takeaway. Swimming pools. Fitness centre. Tennis. Table tennis. Minigolf. Play area. Organised entertainment and excursions (high season). Bicycle hire. Dogs are not accepted. Off site: Riding 2 km. Fishing 2.5 km.

Open: 28 March - 30 September.

Directions

Leave Venice-Trieste autostrada either by taking airport or Quarto d'Altino exits; follow signs to Jesolo and Punta Sabbioni. Take first road left after Cavallino and site is a little way on the right.

Charges 2006

Per person	€ 4,32 - € 8,55
junior (3-6 yrs) or senior (over 60 yrs)	€ 2,72 - € 6,60
pitch with full services	€ 9,90 - € 21,70

IT6014 Villaggio Turistico Internazionale

Via Colonie 2, I-30020 Bibione (Veneto)

Tel: **0431 442611**. Email: **info@vti.it**

This is a large, professionally run tourist village which offers all a holidaymaker could want. The Granzotto family have owned the site since the sixties and the results of their continuous improvements are impressive. There are 300 clean pitches, many fully serviced, shaded by mature trees and mostly on flat ground. The site's large sandy beach is excellent (umbrellas and loungers for a small charge), as are all the facilities within the campsite where English speaking, uniformed assistants will help when you arrive. The tourist village is split by a main road with the main restaurant, cinema and children's club on the very smart 'chalet' side. The most professional hairdressing salon sets the luxury tone of the site. A comprehensive entertainment programme is on offer daily and the large pool provides a great flume and slides and a separate fun and spa pool. The local area is a major tourist resort but for more relaxation try the famous thermal baths at Bibione!

Facilities

Four modern toilet blocks house excellent facilities with mainly British style toilets. Excellent provision for children and disabled campers. Washing machines and dryers. Motorcaravan service point. Supermarket. Bazaar. Good restaurant with bright yellow plastic chairs. Snack bar. Pool complex. Fitness centre. Disco. TV. Cinema and theatre. Internet. Play areas. Football. Tennis. Billiards. Electronic games. Doctor's surgery. Off site: Bicycle hire 1 km. Riding 3 km. Golf 6 km. Fishing.

Open: 12 April - 24 September.

Directions

Leave A4 east of Venice at Latisana exit on Latisana road. Then take road 354 towards Lingano, after 12 km. turn right to Bavassano and then left to Bibione. Site is well signed on entering town. GPS: N45:38.6 E13:2.14

Charges 2006

Per person	€ 5,00 - € 9,50
senior	€ 3,50 - € 9,00
child (1-5 yrs)	free - € 7,00
pitch incl. electricity	€ 9,00 - € 17,00
with electricity and water	€ 12,00 - € 22,50

Camping Cheques accepted.

IT6028 Camping Vela Blu

Via Radaelli, 10, I-30013 Cavallino-Treporti (Veneto)

Tel: **041 968068**. Email: **info@velablu.it**

Thoughtfully landscaped within a natural wooded coastal environment, the tall pines here give shade while attractive flowers and paved roads enhance the setting while giving easy access to the pitches. The 230 pitches vary in size and shape, but all have electricity and many have drainage. A sister site to nos. IT6036 and IT6014, Vela Blu is a relatively new, small, family style site and a pleasant alternative to the other massive sites on Cavallino. The clean, fine sand beach runs the length of one side of the site with large stone breakwaters for fun and fishing. It is fenced making it safer for children and access is via a gate. There are outdoor showers and footbaths. The hub of the site is the charming restaurant and brilliant play area on soft sand, both adjoining a barbecue terrace and entertainment area. A well stocked shop is also in this area. For those who enjoy a small quiet site, Vela Blu fits the bill. Venice is easy to access as is the local water park (there is no pool here as yet). The entrance can become congested in busy periods due to limited waiting space.

Facilities

Two excellent modern toilet blocks include baby rooms and good facilities for disabled visitors. An attendant is on hand to maintain high standards. Laundry facilities. Motorcaravan service point. Medical room. Shop. Bar. Restaurant and takeaway. Games room. TV room. Table tennis. Volleyball. Windsurfing. Fishing. Bicycle hire. Entertainment for children and adults by a professional animation team. Off site: Bars, restaurants and shops. Ferry to Venice. Theme parks.

Open: 8 April - 18 September.

Directions

Leave A4 Venice - Trieste motorway at exit for 'Aeroporto' and follow signs for Jesolo and Punta Sabbioni. Site is signed after village of Cavallino.

Charges 2006

Per person	€ 3,90 - € 7,30
child (1-4 yrs)	free - € 6,50
seniors (over 60)	€ 3,00 - € 6,50
pitch	€ 8,20 - € 15,70
dog	€ 4,40

Camping Cheques accepted.

IT6020 Camping Union Lido Vacanze

Via Fausta 258, I-30013 Cavallino-Treporti (Veneto)
Tel: 041 2575111. Email: info@unionlido.com

This well known site is very large, but extremely well organised and it has been said to set the standard that others follow. It lies right beside the sea with direct access to a long, broad sandy beach which shelves very gradually and provides very safe bathing. The beach is well cleaned by the site. The site itself is regularly laid out with parallel access roads under a covering of poplars, pine and other trees typical of this area providing good shade. These mark out numbered pitches of adequate size (2,600 for touring units), all with electricity and 1,684 also with water and drainage. There are separate areas for caravans, tents and motorcaravans, plus one mixed part. At the entrance is a large off-road overnight parking area with electricity, toilets and showers for those arriving after 9 pm. An aqua-park covering 5,000 sq.m. includes a swimming pool, lagoon pool for children, heated whirlpool and a slow flowing 160 m. 'river'. A further heated pool for hotel and apartment guests is open to others on payment. A selection of sports is offered in the annexe across the road and fitness programmes are available in season. The golf 'academy' (with professional) has a driving range, pitching green, putting green and practise bunker, and a diving centre has a school and the possibility of open water dives. There are regular entertainment and activity programmes for adults and children. Union Lido is above all an orderly and clean site, which is achieved by regulations that suit those who like quiet, comfortable camping and by good management. Member of Leading Campings Group.

Facilities

Fifteen well kept, fully equipped toilet blocks which open and close progressively during the season. Eleven blocks have facilities for disabled people. Launderette. Motorcaravan service points. Gas supplies. Comprehensive shopping area set around a pleasant piazza (all open till late). Seven restaurants each with a different style. Nine pleasant and lively bars. Aqua-park (from 15/5). Tennis. Riding. Minigolf. Skating rink. Bicycle hire. Archery. Two fitness tracks in 4 ha. natural park with play area and supervised play for children. Golf academy. Diving centre and school. Windsurfing school in season. Boat excursions. Recreational events for adults and children, day and evening. Church service in English in July/Aug. Hairdressers. Medical centre. Dogs are not accepted. Off site: Boat launching 3.5 km.

Open: 1 May - 30 September, with all services.

Directions

From Venice - Trieste autostrada leave at exit for airport or Quarto d'Altino and follow signs first for Jesolo and then Punta Sabbioni, and camp will be seen just after Cavallino on the left.

Charges 2006

Per person	€ 6,20 - € 9,30
child (under 3 yrs)	€ 3,60 - € 6,40
child (3-12 yrs)	€ 5,10 - € 8,00
pitch with electricity	€ 11,40 - € 21,00
pitch with water and drainage	€ 14,30 - € 24,00

Three different seasons: (i) high season 29/6-31/8; (ii) mid-season 18/5-29/6 and 31/8-14/9, and (iii) off-season, outside these dates.

IT6021 Italy Camping Village

Via Fausta 272, I-30013 Cavallino-Treporti (Veneto)
Tel: 041 968 090. Email: info@campingitaly.it

Italy Camping Village, under the same ownership as the better known Union Lido which it adjoins, is suggested for those who prefer a smaller site where less activities are available (although those at Union Lido may be used). The 180 touring pitches are on either side of sand tracts off hard access roads under a cover of trees. All have electricity connections and some have water as well. Being on the small size (60-70 sq.m), they may be difficult for large units, particularly in high season when cars may have to be parked elsewhere. There is direct access to a gently sloping sandy beach and a good, heated, swimming pool which has a whirlpool at one end. There are over 30 campsites to choose from on the Littorale del Cavallino between Lido di Jesolo and Punta Sabbioni. Strict regulations regarding undue noise here make this a peaceful site and with lower charges than some in the area, this would be a good choice for families with young children where it is possible to book in advance.

Facilities

Two good quality, fully equipped sanitary blocks include facilities for disabled visitors. Washing machines. Shop. Restaurant. Bar beside beach. Heated swimming pool (17 x 7 m). Small playground, mini-club and children's disco. Weekly dance for adults. Barbecues are only permitted in a designated area. Dogs are not accepted. Off site: Sports centre 500 m. Golf or riding 500 m.

Open: 21 April - 22 September.

Directions

From Venice - Trieste A4 autostrada leave at exit for airport or Quarto d'Altino and follow signs for Jesolo and Punta Sabbioni. Site on left after Cavallino.

Charges 2007

Per person	€ 4,70 - € 7,65
child (1-6 yrs)	free - € 5,90
pitch with electricity	€ 8,00 - € 18,50
pitch with electricity and water	€ 8,50 - € 19,90

Three charging seasons.

PARK & RESORT
CAMPING • HOTEL

★ ★ ★

nion Lido Vacanze is situated on the green
avallino Riviera, between the splendid
netian lagoon and the Adriatic Sea.

pen from 1st May to 30th September.

Venice and it's magnificent islands can
be reached across water in approximately
30 minutes.

Spacious and well looked after pitches.

The modern washrooms are constantly
kept clean, complete with facilities for
the disabled, and baby rooms for the
smaller guests.

UNGALOWS, MOBILE HOMES,
AXI CARAVANS COMPLETE
ITH EVERY COMFORT.

oms, villas and apartments at the high quality
rk Hotel, **the only 4 star hotel in the area**,
h it's own heated swimming pool, Jacuzzi
d children's mini pool.

he Gourmet Club Union Lido boasts
3 restaurants and 9 bars on site

2 supermarkets and over 20 shops of various types

Exclusive beach **1km in length of fine sand**
and games for children

2 Aqua Parks with pools for a total of 11.000 m2;
Entrance to the parks is included in the price
of your holiday

The Marino Club health Spa with sea view,
salt water oasis with exclusive treatments

Entertainment for both **children and adults**.
Diving school, surf school, golf academy,
horse-riding, archery, rollerblade link.
Excursions and trips to unforgettable destinations.

sit our website **www.unionlido.com**
more information on our packages and super offers,
eck out the last minute offers too...
or unrepeatable opportunities!!

OUD MEMBER OF

  LeadingCampings

 SINCERT
UNITER
CERTIFIED QUALITY MANAGEMENT SYSTEM
ISO 9001

SINCERT
UNITER
CERTIFIED ENVIRONMENTAL MANAGEMENT SYSTEM
ISO 14001

MANIFESTO
Turistico Ambientale
V E N E T O

Turistico di
Cavallino Treporti

0013 CAVALLINO - VENEZIA - ITALIA
mping Park & Resort
. Camping +39 041 25 75 111
. Park Hotel +39 041 96 80 43
efax +39 041 5 37 03 55
o@unionlido.com - booking@unionlido.com

IT6032 Camping Village Cavallino

Via delle Batterie 164, I-30013 Cavallino-Treporti (Veneto)

Tel: **041 966133**. Email: **info@campingcavallino.com**

This large, well ordered site is run by a friendly, experienced family who have other sites in this guide. It lies beside the sea with direct access to a superb beach of fine sand, which is very safe and enjoys the cover of several lifeguards. The site is thoughtfully laid out with large numbers of unusually large pitches shaded by olives and pines. All pitches have electricity and there is a 10% tour operator presence. If you wish to visit Venice a bus service runs to the ferry at Punta Sabbioni, some 20 minutes distance. You then catch an interconnecting ferry which, after a charming journey of 40 minutes, drops you directly at Saint Marco Square after negotiating its way around the gondolas. A late return will mean a 2 km. walk at the end of a different bus service, but the night views of Venice from the sea are wonderful. Be sure to pay independently at the ferry rather than using the supposedly cheap 'all-in' tickets which in fact are more expensive.

Facilities

Clean and modern toilet blocks are well spaced and provide a mixture of Turkish and British style WCs with facilities for disabled campers. Launderette. Motorcaravan services. Large shop. Restaurant with large terrace. Takeaway. Pizzeria. (all open all season). Swimming pools (May-Sept). Table tennis. Minigolf. Play area. Bicycle hire. Fishing. Ambitious animation programme aimed mostly at younger guests. Dogs are not admitted.

Open: 30 March - 21 October.

Directions

From Venice - Trieste autostrada leave at exit for airport or Quarto and Altino. Follow signs, first for Jesolo, then Punta Sabbioni. Site signs are just after Cavallino on the left. GPS: N45:27.379 E12:30.055

Charges 2007

Per unit incl. 2 persons,	€ 15,40 - € 37,80
extra person	€ 3,40 - € 9,00
child (3-12 yrs) or senior	€ 3,10 - € 8,00
Min. stay in high season I week.	

IT6046 Camping Miramare

I-30010 Punta Sabbioni (Veneto)

Tel: **041 966150**. Email: **info@camping-miramare.it**

This campsite has been recommended by our Italian agent and we plan to undertake an inspection in 2007. Camping Miramare is well located, close to Cavallino, on a popular stretch of coastline. Although there are many sites in this area, this site has unusually long opening dates. It is ideally located for exploring Venice and its islands, as well as the Lido di Venezia. The site's restaurant is renowned for its excellent regional meals. Unusually, the site runs a free cycle loan scheme as well as a free shuttle to the nearest beach.

Facilities

Two toilet blocks (one heated in low season) with a baby room and facilities for disabled people. Motorcaravan service point. Bar, restaurant and takeaway. Supermarket. Play area. Internet point. TV room. Free bicycle hire. Dogs are not accepted. Free shuttle bus from Punta Sabbioni square (departure point for trips to Venice and the islands) and to the nearest beach on the Adriatic Coast.

Open: Easter - early November.

Directions

Leave the A4 autostrada at exit for Venezia Mestre and follow signs to Noventa/San Dona' di Piave, Eraclea, Jesolo Lido, Cavallino and finally Punta Sabbioni. Site is well signed.

Charges 2006

Per unit incl. 2 persons	€ 19,90 - € 20,50
extra person	€ 4,50 - € 6,80

Check real time availability and at-the-gate prices...

 www.**alanrogers**.com

IT6041 Camping Village Europa

Via Fausta, 332, I-30013 Cavallino-Treporti (Veneto)

Tel: **041 968069**. Email: **info@campingeuropa.com**

There are many popular campsites along this stretch of coast and our Italian agent has recommended this site to us. In common with many sites in the area, it benefits from direct access to a fine sandy beach. There are 600 touring pitches, all of which have electrical connections, some with satellite TV connections. Unusually, some are reserved for visitors with dogs. Some smaller pitches are also available for those with tents. This is a large site with an impressive array of restaurant, shopping and leisure amenities. Venice is easily accessible by bus and then ferry from Punta Sabbioni.

Facilities

Bar, restaurant and pizzeria. Shopping centre. Tennis. Football pitch. Games room. Playground. Children's club. Entertainment programme. Direct access to the beach. Mobile homes and chalets for rent. Off site: Excursions to Venice. Riding. Golf. Walking and cycling trails.

Open: 24 March - 30 September.

Directions

From A4 autostrada (approaching from Milan) take Mestre exit and follow signs initially for Venice airport and then Jesolo. From Jesolo, follow signs to Cavallino from where site is well signed.

Charges 2006

Per person	€ 4,30 - € 7,60
child (2-5 yrs)	€ 2,90 - € 6,60
adult over 60 yrs	€ 3,30 - € 7,50
pitch	€ 7,90 - € 19,80

Emerge Yourself in a Dream Vacation

www.campingeuropa.com

Several residential units which permit guests to keep animals are available

EUROPA CAMPING VILLAGE
Via Fausta, 332 • 30013 Cavallino
Venezia • Italy
Tel.: +39 041 968069 / 968261
Fax: + 39 041 5370150
info@campingeuropa.com

Europa Camping Village

IT6045 Camping Marina di Venezia

Via Montello 6, I-30010 Punta Sabbioni (Veneto)

Tel: **041 530 2511**. Email: **camping@marinadivenezia.it**

This is a very large site (2,300 pitches) with much the same atmosphere as many other large sites along this appealing stretch of coastline. Marina di Venezia, however, has the advantage of being within walking distance of the ferry to Venice. It will appeal particularly to those who enjoy an extensive range of entertainment and activities, and a lively atmosphere. Individual pitches are marked out on sandy ground, most separated by trees or hedges and all with electricity and water. The site's excellent sandy beach is one of the widest along this stretch of coast and has a pleasant beach bar. The main pool is Olympic sized and there is also a very large children's pool adjacent. This is a well run site with committed management and staff.

Facilities

Ten modern toilet blocks are maintained to a high standard with a reasonable proportion of British-style toilets. Good provision for disabled visitors. Washing machines. Range of shops. Several bars, restaurants and takeaways. Swimming pools (no slides). Play areas. Tennis. Windsurf and catamaran hire. Wide range of organised entertainment. WiFi internet access in all bars and cafés.

Open: 23 April - 30 September.

Directions

From A4 motorway, take Jesolo exit. After Jesolo continue towards Punta Sabbioni. Site is clearly signed to the left towards the end of this road, close to the Venice ferries.

Charges guide

Per person	€ 3,95 - € 7,80
child (0-5 yrs) or senior (over 60)	€ 3,35 - € 6,35
pitch with electricity and water	€ 9,95 - € 19,00

IT6037 Camping Jésolo International

Viale A. Da Giussano, I-30017 Lido di Jésolo (Veneto)

Tel: **0421 971826**. Email: **info@jesolointernational.it**

At this brilliant family resort style site with a focus on sporting activities, you can plan the cost of your holiday with confidence. The amazing array of on-site activities is free and there are large discounts for some off site attractions. Jesolo International is located on a beautiful promontory with 700 metres of uncrowded white sandy beach and slowly shelving waters for safe swimming. As the site is narrow, all the pitches are close to the sea. There is a choice of three types of pitch, all flat, well shaded and with 10-20A electricity, water and drainage. Most also have a satellite TV connection supplying 26 free channels. The superb pool complex, where an excellent animation programme is presented each night, is centrally located and very spacious. The pool is open one night a week for a supervised pool party. The dynamic director Sergio Comino works long hours to maintain and improve this high quality family orientated site, to combine a unique holiday experience for guests, with real value for money. As the site is community owned, profits are returned to the guests in the form of facilities, sporting opportunities and entertainment. Cleanliness and security are high priorities. Electronic tags are given to guests to gain entrance and exit to the beach gates and this, combined with video surveillance of these key locations, allows guests to feel secure. Children's passes exclude them from accessing the beach alone or the hydro massage whirlpools reserved for adults. A ferry service to Venice leaves from the marina adjoining the campsite and takes just 40 minutes to reach St Mark's Square in the heart of the city.

Facilities

Sanitary facilities include 72 modern, continually cleaned bathroom units (shower, toilet and basin), private bathrooms (extra cost) and baby rooms. Washing machines and dryers. Fridge boxes. Motorcaravan service point. Supermarket. Family style restaurant. Beach bar with snacks. Pool bar serving light lunches. Sports centre. Children's club and inflatable fun park. Indoor gym. Tennis courts and lessons (equipment provided). Golf (lessons, equipment and playing fees all free). Sailing with tuition and canoe courses. scuba dive lesson (followed by 50% discount on courses and excursions). Language courses. Large grassy play area with adventure style equipment. Free medical service (with doctor). Free internet. Dogs are not accepted. Off site: Golf 2 km. (free lesson and use of 18 hole course with equipment). Aqualandia 1.5 km. (30% discount). Ferry to Venice and Murano 200 m. Jesolo promenade with shops, restaurants and bars 500 m.

Open: 1 May - 30 September.

Directions

From A4 Venice - Trieste autostrada take Dona di Piave exit and follow signs to Jesolo then Punta Sabbioni. Turn off to Lido di Jesolo just before the Cavallino bridge where the site is well signed. GPS: N45:29.061 E12:35.319

Charges 2006

Per person (over 5 yrs)	€ 5,00 - € 10,00
child (1-5 yrs)	free - € 2,00
pitch incl. electricity	€ 9,00 - € 18,50
'super' pitch incl. services	€ 12,00 - € 23,50
'mega' pitch (170 sq.m)	€ 19,00 - € 42,00

IT6050 Camping Della Serenissima

Via Padana 334/a, I-30030 Oriago (Veneto)

Tel: **041 921850**. Email: **camping.serenissima@shineline.it**

This is a delightful little site of some 140 pitches (all with 16A electricity) where one could stay for a number of days whilst visiting Venice (12 km), Padova (24), Lake Garda (135) or the Dolomites. There is a good service by bus to Venice and the site is situated on the Riviera del Brenta, a section of a river with some very large old villas. A long, narrow and flat site, numbered pitches are on each side of a central road. There is good shade in most parts with many trees, plants and grass. The management is very friendly and good English is spoken. The site is used mainly by Dutch and British visitors, with some Germans, and is calm and quiet.

Facilities

Sanitary facilities are of a good standard with all facilities in private cabins. Facilities for disabled visitors. Motorcaravan services. Gas supplies. Shop (all season). Bar. Restaurant and takeaway (1/6-31/10). Play area. Fishing. Bicycle hire. Reduced price bus ticket to Venice if staying for 3 days. No organised entertainment but local markets, etc. all well publicised. Off site: Golf or riding 3 km.

Open: Easter - 10 November.

Directions

From the east take road S11 at roundabout SSW of Mestre towards Padova and site is 2 km. on right. From west, leave autostrada A4 at Dolo exit, follow signs to Dolo, continue on main road through this small village and turn left at T-junction (traffic lights). Continue towards Venice on S11 for site about 6 km on left. GPS: N45:45.234 E12:18.333

Charges 2006

Per person	€ 6,00 - € 7,50
child (3-10 yrs)	€ 4,00 - € 5,50
caravan and car	€ 12,00
tent and car	€ 11,00
motorcaravan	€ 12,00

for the ferries to Venice, the pitches are an average of just 60 metres from the beach. Unrivalled value for money because of the incredible number of services included in the price: banana boat, sun umbrellas and loungers on the beach and by the swimming-pool, unlimited access to Aqualandia (Italy's top water park, only 2 km away), green fees at Jesolo's 18-holes golf course (3 km away), deep-sea diving, pedal boats, canoes, catamarans, heated jacuzzis, tennis, Internet, car wash, pirates' galleon, go-kart races on the "Pista Azzurra" track (4 km away), top fitness centre, animation.
Reductions at the most exclusive Wellness Club in Jesolo.
Unique surveillance system. No booking fees.
NEW: Free access to "Adventure Minigolf"

NEW: Luxury mobile-homes with unmatched equipment and service.

IT6053 Camping Fusina

Via Moranzani, 79, I-30030 Fusina (Veneto)

Tel: **041 547 0055**. Email: **info@camping-fusina.com**

There are some sites that take one by surprise – this is one. This is old fashioned camping, but what fun, and we met English speaking people who have been coming here for 30 years. Choose from 500 well shaded, flat and grassy informal pitches or a position with views over the lagoon to the towers in Saint Mark's Square. With water on three sides there are welcoming cool breezes and fortunately many trees hide the industrial area close by. Those who don't wish to be disturbed by the lively bar can choose from the many super informal waterside pitches on the far end of the site. The site owns a large ferry car park and a 700-boat marina which accepts and launches all manner of craft. A deep water channel carries huge ships close by and the water views are never boring. Fusina offers a very easy and comfortable, 20 minute ferry connection to the cultural heart of Venice, Accademia. Several site buildings, including some of the showers and toilets, were designed by the famous modern architect Scarpa. These are heritage listed and are visited by design students, although this listing makes development and improvement difficult. Many of the staff are mature Australian/New Zealand people and English is used everywhere.

Facilities

Modern, well equipped facilities include units for disabled visitors, along with some existing older units. Many washing machines and dryers. Motorcaravan service point. Shop (15/3-31/10). Charming restaurant (no credit cards). Pizzeria. Very lively bar entertainment. Playground. Boat hire. Marina with cranes, moorings, and maintenance facilities. Air-conditioned London Cyber bus (really!) and another 'Info bus' for information and ticket sales. ATM. Torches useful. Off site: Excellent public transport and ferry connections to Venice.

Open: All year.

Directions

From SSII Padua - Venice road follow site signs on road east of Mira, turning right as signed. Site is in Fusina at end of peninsula and is well signed (also as 'Fusina parking'). GPS: N45:25.150 E12:15.416

Charges 2006

Per person	€ 8,00 - € 9,00
child (5-12yrs)	€ 4,50
caravan	€ 9,00
motorcaravan	€ 14,00
tent	€ 8,50 - € 9,00

This is just a sample of the campsites we have inspected and selected in Italy. For more campsites and further information, please see the Alan Rogers Italy guide.

IT6055 Villaggio Turistico Isamar

Isolaverde, Via Isamar, 9, I-30010 Santa Anna di Chioggia (Veneto)

Tel: 041 5535 811. Email: info@villaggioisamar.com

Many improvements have been made here over the years and these continue at this busy, well managed site. The largest camping area, which may be cramped at times, is under pines and grouped around the swimming pool, the large modern sanitary block, shops, etc. near reception. A smaller area is under artificial shade near the beach with an Olympic size, salt water swimming pool, paddling pool and four new pools, a covered entertainment section, pizzeria, bar/restaurant and a small toilet block. Between these sections are well constructed holiday bungalows. A third camping area has been developed mainly for the site's own accommodation. The pitches, on either side of hard access roads, vary in size and all have electrical connections. Although directly by the sea, with its own sandy beach, it is a fair way from the entrance to the sea. The site has a much higher proportion of Italian holidaymakers than many other sites. It is also popular with the Germans and Dutch and may become crowded in high season.

Facilities

The main toilet blocks are fully equipped and of good quality with British style WCs (small block has only Turkish style). Laundry. Motorcaravan services. Gas supplies. Fridge hire. Hairdresser. Supermarket and general shopping centre. Large bar/pizzeria and self-service restaurant. Swimming pools. Tennis. Playground. Disco. Games room. Riding. Bicycle hire. Extensive entertainment and fitness programme offered for adults and supervised play for children over 4 yrs old. Dogs are not accepted. Off site: Fishing 500 m.

Open: 13 May - 16 September.

Directions

Turn off main 309 road towards sea just south of Adige river about 10 km. south of Chioggia, and proceed 5 km. to site.

Charges 2006

Per person	€ 3,50 - € 9,50
child (2-5 yrs)	€ 2,50 - € 8,00
pitch with full facilities	€ 6,90 - € 22,00

Less 10% for stays in low season for over 2 weeks.

IT6033 Villaggio Turistico Malibu Beach

Viale Oriente 78, I-30017 Lido di Jesolo (Veneto)

Tel: **0421 362212**. Email: **info@campingmalibubeach.com**

Our Italian agent has recommended this family site which has direct access to a private beach and we intend to undertake an inspection in 2007. Malibu Beach has 270 pitches, shaded by pines, and includes some 'super' pitches with electricity and water. A central complex incorporates the site amenities include a large pool. Excursions to Venice are plentiful from Jesolo.

Facilities

Bar, restaurant and pizzeria. Shop. Fitness centre. Swimming pool. Playground. Entertainment programme. Direct access to the beach. Mobile homes and chalets for rent. Off site: Lido de Jesolo, excursions to Venice. Riding. Golf.

Open: 15 May - 13 September.

Directions

From A4 autostrada take Mestre exit and follow signs for Venice airport and then Jesolo. From Jesolo, follow signs to Jesolo Pineta and site is well signed.

Charges 2007

Per person	€ 3,40 - € 7,75
pitch with electricity	€ 8,30 - € 21,20

No credit cards. Minimum stay 2 nights.

IT6034 Camping Waikiki

Viale Oriente 144, I-30017 Lido di Jesolo (Veneto)

Tel: **0421 980186**. Email: **info@campingwakiki.com**

Waikiki has been recommended to us by our Italian agent and is located very close to IT6033 Malibu Beach. This site also benefits from direct access to a broad sandy beach. Pitches here are shaded by pines and mostly have electricity. On-site amenities include an attractive pool and a restaurant. A regular bus service runs from the site to Jesolo and its shops, bars and restaurants.

Facilities

Bar, restaurant/pizzeria and shop. Games room. Fitness centre. Swimming and paddling pools. Playground. Entertainment programme. Mobile homes and chalets for rent. Off site: Lido de Jesolo, excursions to Venice. Riding.

Open: 12 May - 11 September.

Directions

From A4 autostrada take Mestre exit and follow signs for Venice airport and then Jesolo. From Jesolo, follow signs to Jesolo Pineta and site is well signed.

Charges 2007

Per person	€ 2,80 - € 6,80
pitch with electricity	€ 6,90 - € 18,40

No credit cards. Minimum stay 2 nights.

IT6054 Camping Oasi

Via A. Barbarigo 147, I-30019 Sottomarina (Veneto)

Tel: **041 5541 145**. Email: **info@campingoasi.com**

Camping Oasi is a traditional, old style Italian family site where many Italian families return all summer, so it would be a good place to practice your Italian language skills. There is an excellent marina just outside the campsite gates for launching boats. Pitches, most with electricity, water and waste water, vary in size up to 80 sq.m. and are flat with a choice of shade or sun. The site has a good swimming pool with a small flume and a good sports area.A small restaurant, bar, TV room, pizzeria, takeaway, shop and terrace are on the site. Another small beach bar is at the fine grey sandy beach which is a long walk through the campsite and sports areas.

Facilities

Two older sanitary blocks each have one British style toilet. The numbers are low so facilities could get very busy. Good swimming pool and flume. Small play area. Sports area, beach volleyball, basketball, table tennis, boules, bicycle hire, watersports, fishing, tennis and football.

Open: 30 March - 30 September.

Directions

Site is off the S309 near Chioggia. Follow signs to Sottomaria then site. Signs can be unclear, but the turn is at a set of lights. Site is 3 km. down this narrow road. GPS: N45:10.15 E12:18.446

Charges 2006

Per person	€ 4,60 - € 7,20
pitch	€ 7,70 - € 16,30

Camping Cheques accepted.

IT6047 Camping Scarpiland

I-30010 Treporti (Veneto)

Tel: **041 966150**. Email: **info@scarpiland.com**

This campsite has been recommended by our Italian agent and we plan to undertake an inspection in 2007. Scarpiland faces the Adriatic and is adjacent to a fine sandy beach. This is a large site with shady pitches, varying in size from 70-90sq.m. A lively site in peak season, many activities are on offer, including many based on the beach, such as windsurfing lessons, banana boat hire and boat trips. The site's entertainment team organise many games and tournaments, including children's activities.

Facilities

Two recently refurbished, modern toilet blocks include facilities for babies and also for disabled visitors. Restaurant/pizzeria. Ice cream parlour. Newsagent. Supermarket. Butcher. Souvenir shop. Greengrocer and local produce. Bicycle hire. Sports field.

Open: 24 April - 22 September.

Directions

From Milan, take A4 to Venice and continue towards Trieste (Venezia-Trieste) as far as the A27 intersection, then follow signs to the airport. At end of bypass, follow signs to San Donà and Jesolo. At Jesolo, to Lido del Cavallino and Punta Sabbioni.

Charges 2006

Per unit incl 2 persons	€ 14,90 - € 30,30
extra person	€ 3,90 - € 7,40

IT6056 Camping Miramare

I-30019 Chioggia (Veneto)

Tel: 041 490610. Email: campmir@tin.it

This campsite has been recommended by our Italian agent and we plan to undertake an inspection in 2007. Camping Miramare has an attractive situation alongside a white sandy beach. The site lies close to Chioggia, an important resort to the south of Venice. On-site facilities include a restaurant, bar (with takeaway food) and a large swimming pool. This is a lively site in peak season with a children's club and many activities on offer. During high season many activities are organised. For those wishing to explore the region, there are many opportunities. An excursion to Venice naturally holds a strong appeal, but other stunning cities are also close at hand, notably Padova, Vicenza, Treviso and, a little further afield, Verona.

Facilities

Modern clean toilet blocks. Launderette. Bar. Restaurant. Takeaway. Mini-market. Swimming pool with water games. Play area. Entertainment, activities and children's activities in high season. Mobile homes to rent.
Off site: Excursions to Venice and other cities. Golf, tennis, bicycle hire.

Open: 5 April - 20 September.

Directions

From the eastbound A4 (Milan - Venice) autostrada, leave at the Padova Zona Industriale exit and join the Ravenna-Chioggia road (SS309). The site is well signed from Chioggia

Charges 2006

Per unit incl. 2 persons	€ 17,50 - € 31,00
extra person	€ 4,50 - € 7,40
child (under 6 yrs)	€ 2,25 - € 3,80

IIT6080 Camping Mare Pineta

Via delle Acacie, 67, I-44024 Lido Estensi (Emília-Romagna)

Tel: 0533 330110. Email: info@campingmarepineta.com

Camping Mare Pineta is a large site located within a pinewood at the heart of the Adriatic Riviera. The site enjoys direct access to a gently shelving sandy beach and has been recommended by our Italian agent. We plan to conduct a full inspection in 2007. The site has 1,050 shady pitches, all with electrical connections (3A). This is a lively site in high season with a varied entertainment programme, including activities on the beach such as volleyball. The site boasts a large number of amenities including a well equipped shopping complex and a large restaurant/pizzeria. Mare Pineta is well located for visiting the region; the Po Delta and fascinating cities such as Ravenna, Ferrara and Venice are all within reach.

Facilities

Bar. Restaurant/pizzeria. Shopping centre. Swimming pool (free in low season, small charge for use in high season) and children's pool. Sauna and solarium. Tennis. Archery. Gym. Football pitch. Hairdresser and beautician. Games room. Playground. Entertainment and activity programme, beach activities. Bungalows and mobile homes for rent. Direct access to the sea. Off site: Fishing trips. Argenta golf club. Mirabilandia theme park. Riding centre.

Open: 13 April - 18 September.

Directions

From the A13 autostrada (Padova - Bologna) take Ferrara South exit and join the SS309 express road signed Romea and Ravenna. Continue on this road until it meets the S309 and head south on this road. Lido degli Estensi and site is signed to the left.

Charges 2006

Per person	€ 3,80 - € 8.20
child (2-8 yrs)	€ 3,10 - € 6,30
pitch incl. electricity (3A)	€ 9,00 - € 15,60

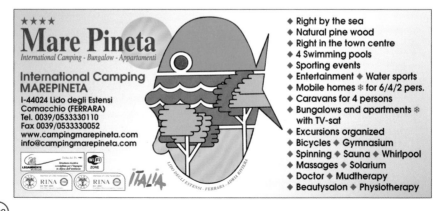

IT6090 Camping Arizona

Via Tabiano 42/A, I-43030 Tabiano di Salsomaggiore Terme (Emilia-Romagna)
Tel: **0524 565 648**. Email: **info@camping-arizona.it**

Tabbiano and Salsomaggiore Terme are thermal springs dating back to the Roman era and the beneficial waters have given rise to attractive inland resort towns. The focus on water is developed within this family-run site – the complex of four large pools, long water slides, jacuzzi and more set in open landscaped grounds with good views, is most impressive. Camping Arizona is 500 metres from Tabbiano and access is easy for even the largest of units. The 350 level pitches are large and well defined, most having shade from mature trees. All the pitches have access to electricity and water points are within 30 m. On-site traffic is kept to a minimum during the high season – with the exception of loading and unloading, vehicles must be parked in the large adjacent car park and golf trolleys are provided for use during your stay. Sporting facilities are extensive with tennis, volleyball and basketball courts and a five-a-side football pitch on synthetic grass. Younger children will be entertained by the large, supervised play centre with bouncy cushion, ball pool and other indoor and outdoor games. This site has everything required for an extended stay as well as for touring.

Facilities

Sanitary facilities in four blocks are clean and well maintained with British and Turkish style WCs, open style washbasins and free warm showers. Facilities for disabled visitors. Washing machines and dryers. Well stocked shop. Restaurant/bar. Swimming pools, slides and jacuzzi (22/5-14/9, also open to the public but free for campers). Tennis. Bowling. Table tennis. Play centre. Bicycle hire. Off site: Fidenza shopping village with designer outlets 8 km. Fishing 4 km. Golf 6 km.

Open: 1 April - 15 October.

Directions

From autostrada A1 take exit for Fidenza and follow signs for Tabiano. The site is on left 500 m. after Tabiano town centre. GPS: N44:48.379 E10:00.578

Charges 2006

Per person	€ 5,50 - € 7,75
child (2-9 yrs)	€ 4,00 - € 6,00
pitch	€ 6,00 - € 12,50
dog	€ 2,00

IT6620 Camping Riccione

Via Marsala, I-47838 Riccione (Emilia-Romagna)
Tel: **0541 690160**. Email: **info@campingriccione.it**

Situated on the Adriatic coast, 400 metres from the beach, in high season Camping Riccioni is a bustling, vibrant campsite with an Italian flavour and a carnival atmosphere. The pitches are of varying sizes, almost all have good shade and 75 are provided with water and drainage. Luigi Gobbi, who owns the site, takes pride in welcoming his guests and provides a very high standard of services proven by his high return custom figures. The noise from road and rail here is compensated by the fine beaches nearby and when we visited all campers appeared to be having great fun. The 30 metre pool and children's lagoon with waterfall have a lifeguard and the poolside bar serves light meals. Unusually the pools have extended hours and are very popular in the early evening, followed by a poolside animation programme which is varied and entertaining. The children's playground has a vast array of equipment and parents will find the supermarket extremely good value with a wide variety of fresh and prepared foods to choose from.

Facilities

Five refurbished toilet blocks are bright, clean and cheerful. WCs are mixed British and Turkish style. Facilities for disabled visitors. Great children's facilities and baby rooms. Washing machines. Two bars with TV. Restaurant and pizzeria with large terrace. Pool complex. Play areas. Games room. Animation programme in season. ATM. Animals not accepted in high season. Barbecues not permitted. Torches useful. Off site: Beach 400 m. Bicycle hire 1 km. Fishing 3 km. Riding 4 km. Golf 5 km.

Open: Easter - 15 September.

Directions

Site is in the village of Riccioni, south of Rimini. From A14 take road to Riccioni and then S16 southeast to Riccioni. Site is well signed in the village. GPS: 43.59 12.40

Charges 2006

Per person	€ 3,70 - € 7,70
child (2-12 yrs)	€ 3,00 - € 6,10
pitch incl. electricity	€ 11,30 - € 30,00

IT6075 Camping Florenz

Viale Alpi Centrali, 199, I-44020 Lido degli Scacchi (Emilia-Romagna)
Tel: **0533 380193**. Email: **info@campingflorenz.com**

Popular with Italian families for over 30 years Camping Florenz has many loyal campers who remain all season. The area which is most sought after by tourers is over the sand dunes along the seafront where there are good sized, shaded and level pitches with views. The gently shelving beach has fine grey sand, chairs and umbrellas. Away from the beach there is heavy shade cover from pine trees. The pitches are mostly a mixture of sand and grass, of a good size and level, all with electricity (3A).

Facilities

Six mixed mostly old sanitary blocks with half British, half Turkish style toilets and pre-set showers. Some unisex showers at beach. Good facilities for disabled people. Motorcaravan service point. Good supermarket. Restaurant and bar with TV. Large outdoor pool. Activities and children's club in season. Good play area. Excellent beach for swimming and boat launching. Beach bar. Bicycle hire. Off site: Small town with restaurants 1 km.

Open: Easter - 20 September.

Directions

Site is at Lido di Scacchi just off the S309 running between Chioggia and Ravenna. Both Lido di Scacchi and site are well signed from the S309. GPS: N44:42.084 E12:14.324

Charges 2006

Per person	€ 4,00 - € 8,30
pitch	€ 9,50 - € 20,00
boat	€ 4,00 - € 6,50
Camping Cheques accepted.	

IT6617 Camping Perticara

Via Serra Masini 10/d, Perticara, I-61017 Novafeltria (Marche)

Tel: 0541 927602. Email: info@campingperticara.com

High in the Marche hills, not far from San Marino, Ravenna and Rimini, is Camping Perticara, a brand new, purpose built camping site with glorious views across a valley to the mountains and the nearby traditional village of Perticara. Its 75 pitches have water and drainage and are very large, all arranged on terraces to take advantage of the fabulous scenery. Good-sized trees have been planted to provide shade in the future. The shop, bar and restaurant area is attractively presented, with a terrace overlooking the swimming pool which shares the incredible vistas. Dutch owners, Bert and Nel, have thoughtfully designed the campsite, which has everything a traditional camper could desire. This is a quiet country location with family activities, a place to relax and unwind. Or you may care to go further afield and enjoy the Roman mosaics at Ravenna, local castles, historic villages like Sant Leo, the beach at Rimini, or the fabulous mountain top country of San Marino, all less than an hour away. The facilities here are of the highest standard, although the steep slopes make this a difficult site for the infirm.

Facilities

Two immaculate modern units provide really excellent facilities with all the extras. Facilities are all in large luxury cabins with shower, toilet and basin. Units for disabled campers are of the same standard. Washing machine and dryers. Gas. Small shop. Restaurant (limited menu but good value). Snack bar. Swimming and paddling pools. Small play areas. Animation (mini-club) in high season. Torches useful. Off site: Bicycle hire 500 m. Fishing 10 km.

Open: 24 April - 1 October.

Directions

Leave E14 near Rimini and take SS258 for Novafeltria. Follow sign to Perticara (with direction signs). Travel uphill (northwest) for 7 km. Leave unit on the lower level and go to reception on the upper level on foot.

Charges 2006

Per person	€ 5,50 - € 8,00
child (4-12 yrs)	€ 3,50 - € 6,00
pitch	€ 11,00 - € 15,00

CampingPerticara.com

75 Pitches, 2 Apartments, 4 Mobil Homes
Tel. 0039 0541 927602

SPECIAL OFFER 2007
IN LOW SEASON
8 days = 7 days
14 days = 11 days

Camping Perticara is a beautiful campsite, situated in the Italian hills between the sea and the mountains of the Marche Region. Here you can still find peace, space, culture and nature in abundance.

IT6507 Camping Panorama

Strand Panorama, I-61010 Fiorenzuola di Focara (Marche)

Tel: 0721 20 81 45. Email: info@campingpanorama.it

Camping Panorama is a peaceful site located on a scenic coastal drive within a small national park (Parco del San Bartolo) and quite close to the delightful town of Pesaro. The site lies 100 metres above the sea and a pleasant path leads to the beach below. There are 140 pitches ranging in size from 45-100 sq.m. Most have electrical connections and all are well shaded. Leisure amenities include an attractive swimming pool (with smaller children's pool) and a sports court. This is a largely undeveloped area and has many opportunities for walking and mountain biking.

Facilities

Centrally located toilet block. Swimming pool and children's pool. Bar, pizzeria. TV room. Play area. Tourist information. Sports court. Off site: Riding. Golf. Nearest village is Fiorenzuola di Focara (2 km), a pretty village perched over the sea with bars, shops and restaurants. Pesaro 8 km. San Marino 42 km. Urbino 50 km. Mountain biking and walking.

Open: 21 April - 30 September.

Directions

From A14 (Bologna – Taranto) take Cattolica exit and join SS16 southbound towards Gabbice Mare. Here join the coast road (Strad Panoramico) towards Casteldimezzo. Site is beyond this town and Fiorenzuola di Focara and before reaching Pesaro. GPS: N43:56.501 E12:50.751

Charges 2006

Per person	€ 5,50 - € 8,50
child (under 6 yrs)	€ 3,50 - € 5,50
pitch incl. electricity	€ 11,50 - € 15,50

IT6606 Camping Europa

Viale dei Tigli - casella postale 115, I-55048 Torre del Lago Puccini (Tuscany)

Tel: **0584 350707**. Email: **info@europacamp.it**

Europa is a large, flat, rectangular site with roads on all four sides of the site. There are 400 pitches in 17 rows, several with well established permanent pitches, three with bungalows to rent. The site's facilities including a bar, shop and air conditioned reataurant, are in rows 5 and 6. The touring pitches in rows 12-17 are flat, very sandy and close together (55-70 sq.m). Some have shade from small trees or artificial cover and electricity (6A) is available. The site has been owned by the Morescalchi family since 1967 and they are very keen that you have an enjoyable stay. The pool and its separate paddling pool are pleasant (charged) and a jacuzzi is built into one end. A bicycle is a must for the beach 1 km. away, otherwise it is a brisk 20 minute walk through towering trees on a forest trail. However, once there the sand is soft and the beach shelves gently into the water. In high season a horse drawn wagon will take you there and back at a cost of €1.20. Europa is conveniently situated for visiting many of the interesting places around such as Lucca, Pisa, Florence and the wealth of Puccini related historical items.

Facilities

Two sanitary blocks provide hot and cold showers (€0.40 token from reception). Toilets are mixed Turkish and British style. Facilities for disabled visitors. Laundry facilities. Cleaning goes on non-stop here. Motorcaravan service point outside gate. Bar/restaurant (air conditioned). Small shop. Good swimming pool (caps required). Large play area. Entertainment. Mini-club. Bicycle hire. Satellite TV. Internet access. Dogs are not accepted 9/6-27/8. Torches useful. Off site: Beach 1 km. Fishing. Golf 17 km. Riding 2 km.

Open: 31 March - 13 October.

Directions

From A11-12 to Pisa Nord take Viareggio exit. Turn south on Via Aurelia towards Pisa and then towards the sea for Marina di Torre Lago Puccini. Follow clear signs for site. GPS: N43:49 E10:16.43

Charges 2006

Per person	€ 4,00 - € 8,50
child (2-10 yrs)	€ 2,50 - € 4,50
pitch	€ 6,00 - € 12,00
car	€ 4,00 - € 8,00

IT6608 Camping Torre Pendente

Viale delle Cascine 86, I-56122 Pisa (Tuscany)

Tel: **050 561704**. Email: **torrepen@campingtoscana.it**

Torre Pendente is a most friendly site, well run by the Signorini family who speak good English and make everyone feel welcome. It is amazingly close to the famous leaning tower of Pisa and obviously its position means it is busy throughout the main season. It is a medium sized site, on level, grassy ground with some shade from trees and lots of artificial shade. There are 220 touring pitches, 160 with electricity. All site facilities are near the entrance including a most pleasant swimming pool complex with pool bar and a large terrace. Here you can relax after hot days in the city and enjoy drinks and snacks or find more formal fare in the restaurant with a la carte menu. This is a very busy site in high season with many nationalities discovering the delights of Pisa. It is ideal for exploring the fascinating leaning tower and other attractions.

Facilities

Three new toilet blocks are clean and smart with British style toilets with good facilities for disabled campers. Private cabins for hire. Hot water at sinks. Washing machines. Motorcaravan services. New supermarket. New restaurant, bar and takeaway. Swimming pool with pool bar, paddling pool and spa. Playground. Boules. Animation in high season. Internet access. Accommodation. Off site: Bicycle hire. Riding 3 km. Fishing 10 km. Golf 15 km.

Open: 1st week before Easter - 15 October.

Directions

From A12, exit at Pisa Nord and follow for 5 km. to Pisa. Do not take first sign to town centre. Site is well signed at a later left turn (Viale delle Cascine).

Charges 2006

Per person	€ 8,00
child (3-10 yrs)	€ 4,50
pitch	€ 10,00 - € 11,50
dog	€ 1,60

See advertisement opposite

IT6611 Camping Il Poggetto

Via Il Poggetto 143, I-50010 Troghi - Firenze (Tuscany)

Tel: **055 8307323**. Email: **info@campingilpoggetto.com**

This superb site has a lot to offer. It benefits from a wonderful panorama of the Colli Fiorentini hills with acres of the Zecchi family vineyards to the east adding to its appeal and is just 15 km. from Florence. The charming and hard-working owners Marcello and Daniella have a wine producing background and you can purchase their fine wines at the site's shop. Their aim is to provide an enjoyable and peaceful atmosphere for families. All 106 pitches are of a good size and have electricity and larger units are welcome. On arrival you are escorted to view available pitches then assisted in taking up that place. The restaurant offers excellent Tuscan fare including pizzas, pastas and delicate 'cucina casalinga' (home cooking). The locals also come here to eat. An attractive flower-bedecked terrace overlooks the two pools. Enjoy the typically Tuscan views and revel in the choice of Chianti from the region. A regular bus service runs directly from the site to the city. English is spoken at this delightful family site.

Facilities

Two spotless sanitary blocks with a mix of British and Turkish style WCs are a pleasure to use. Three private sanitary units for hire. Five very well equipped units for disabled campers. Baby room. Laundry facilities. Motorcaravan services. Gas supplies. Shop. Bar. Restaurant. Takeaway. Swimming pools and jacuzzi (15/5-30/9). Bicycle and scooter hire. Playground and animation for children all season. Excursions and organised trekking. Internet point. Off site: Tennis 100 m. Fishing 2 km. Golf 12 km.

Open: 19 March - 14 October.

Directions

Site is south east of Florence. Police have banned caravans/motorcaravan from Troghi so now you must leave A1 at 'Incisa' and take the Troghi road turn left at first bridge. The site is well signed.
GPS: N43:42.05 E11:24.19

Charges 2006

Per person	€ 7,50
child (0-12 yrs)	€ 5,20
pitch	€ 13,00

IT6600 Camping Barco Reale

Via Nardini 11-13, I-51030 San Baronto di Lamporecchio (Tuscany)

Tel: 0573 88332. Email: info@barcoreale.com

Just forty minutes from Florence and an hour from Pisa, this site is beautifully situated high in the Tuscan hills close to the birthplace of Leonardo da Vinci, and the fascinating town of Pistoia. Part of an old walled estate, there are impressive views of the surrounding countryside. It is a quiet site of 15 hectares with 250 pitches with good shade from mature pines and oaks. Some pitches are huge with great views and others are very private. Most are for tourers, but some have difficult access (site provides tractor assistance). All have electricity and 50 have water and drainage. Member of Leading Campings Group. The site has an attractive bar, a smart restaurant with terraces (try the brilliant traditional dishes) and a leased shop (prices are a little high). The pools have really stunning views to the west (on a clear day you may see the island of Capraia). Pleasant walks are available in the grounds of the estate. This is a most attractive and popular site, which will appeal to those who prefer a quiet site but with plenty to do for all age groups. In high season an information kiosk supplies tourist information, makes bookings and help in general. Used by tour operators.

Facilities

Three modern sanitary blocks are well positioned and kept very clean. Good facilities for disabled people (dedicated pitches close by). Baby room. Laundry facilities. Motorcaravan services. Restaurant. Bar. Disco. Shop. Supervised swimming pool (caps required; 1/5-30/9). Ice cream shop (1/6-31/8). Playgrounds. Bowls. Bicycle hire. Internet point. Entertainment. Tuscan cooking lessons. Excursions. Charcoal fires are not permitted. Off site: Village and shops 1 km. Fishing 8 km. Golf 15 km.

Open: 1 April - 30 September.

Directions

From Pistoia take Vinci - Empoli - Lamporecchio signs to San Baronto. From Empoli signs to Vinci and San Baronto. Final approach involves a sharp bend and a steep slope. GPS: N43:50.514 E10:54.678

Charges 2006

Per person	€ 6,60 - € 9,10
child (0-2 yrs)	free - € 4,50
child (3-12 yrs)	€ 3,30 - € 5,50
pitch	€ 5,10 - € 8,30

Credit cards accepted for amounts over € 155. Discounts for longer stays.

IT6627 Camping Boschetto di Piemma

I-53037 San Gimignano (Tuscany)

Tel: 0577 940352. Email: camping@selvadelletorri.com

The mediaeval Manhattan of San Gimignano is one of Tuscany's most popular sites. This new site lies just 2 km. from the town and has been recommended by our Italian agent. We plan to undertake a full inspection here in 2007. There are 100 pitches here, all with electrical connections (10A). The site is in a wood surrounded by olive groves and vineyards and has been developed with much care for the environment, using rain water for irrigation, for example. A shuttle bus connects the site with San Gimignano (alternatively, it makes a pleasant walk).

Facilities

Restaurant/pizzeria and bar. Mini-market (specialising in local produce). Swimming pool (small charge). Tennis (lessons available). Sports pitch. Playground. Entertainment and activity programme in high season. Apartments for rent. Off site: San Gimignano 2 km. Cycle and walking trails, riding, golf.

Open: 2 May - 2 November.

Directions

Take the Poggibonsi Nord exit from the Florence – Siena superstrada. Then follow signs to San Gimignano. At first roundabout follow signs to Volterra and then take first road to the left, signed Santa Lucia. Site is located close to the sports area.

Charges 2006

Per person	€ 6,00 - € 7,80
pitch incl. electricity	€ 6,00 - € 10,90

IT6612 Camping Norcenni Girasole Club

Via Norcenni 7, I-50063 Figline Valdarno (Tuscany)

Tel: **055 915141**. Email: **girasole@ecvacanze.it**

The Norcenni Girasole Club is a brilliant, busy and well run resort style site in a picturesque, secluded situation with great views of Tuscan landscapes 19 km. south of Florence. Owned by the dynamic Cardini-Vannucchi family, care has been taken in its development and the buildings and infrastructure are most attractive and in sympathy with the surrounds. There are 470 roomy pitches for touring units, all with electricity (4A) and water, most shaded by well tended trees. The ground is hard and stony. Although on a fairly steep hillside, pitches are on level terraces accessed from good, hard roads. Tour operators occupy another 150 pitches and there are a few (20) permanent pitches. Absolutely everything is to hand and guests will only need to leave the site if they wish to explore the local attractions or go on one of the many organised tours. There is an amazing choice of superb pools both in the lower area where there are new pools in the already fantastic complex (one for aerobics, a wading pool, a covered pool), and then at the top of the site where a lagoon with amazing acres of pools allows children to ride the exciting water flume free, play in the waterfall and feature pool or revert to other themed pools with slides. A modern health complex provides saunas, jacuzzi, a fitness centre and massages (extra cost). An extensive animation programme is published each week with music, lots of activities for children, courses in the Italian language, Tuscan cooking and wine tasting. All information and most of the animation is in English. Three attractive restaurants with terraces serve wonderful food, the Vecchio specialising in typical Tuscan fare (try 'Bistecca alla Florentina' with one of the Chianti classico wines for a real treat; bookings advised). We also liked Lo Strettoio with its comprehensive menu and family atmosphere and the S. Andrea restaurant at the very top of the site which has fabulous views and offers more cosmopolitan food.

Facilities

Sanitary facilities are very good with British and Turkish style WCs. Five family bathrooms for rent (book). Facilities for disabled visitors. Laundry. Supermarket. Bar and restaurants. Pizzeria. Gelateria. Tennis. Riding. Wonderful swimming pools, one covered and heated (hats required). Fitness centre (charged). Soundproof disco. Internet café. ATM. Extensive animation programme. Excursions.

Open: 30 March - 2 November.

Directions

From Florence take Rome AI/E35 autostrada and take Incisa exit. Turn south on route 69 towards Arezzo. In Figline turn right for Greve and watch for Girasole signs - site is 4 km. up a twisting, climbing road.

Charges 2007

Per person	€ 7,00 - € 11,00
child (2-12 yrs)	€ 4,30 - € 6,50
pitch	€ 9,80 - € 15,20

IT6629 Camping Tripesce

Via Cavalleggeri 88, I-57018 Vada (Tuscany)
Tel: 0586 788167. Email: info@campingtripesce.com

Neat and tidy, this family owned and run site has the great advantage of direct beach access through three gates (CCTV). The beach is of fine sand with a very gentle shelving – super for children, watersports and with a lifeguard in season. This great beach makes up for the lack of a pool on the site and the fairly small size of the 230 pitches. All have 4A electricity and 60 are serviced with water and drainage with some shade provided by young trees and artificial shade. The site is contained within a rectangle and bungalows for rent are discreetly placed near reception. A pleasant bar with a terrace is alongside the small restaurant (limited but very reasonable menu), and just across the road is a well stocked shop. The play area is modern and pleasant but the slides end on gravel or concrete so children will need supervision. There is a small range of activities and a mini-club. Everything is kept spotlessly clean. The site has many German guests as demonstrated in the German language notices around the site. If you are a beach enthusiast this could be for you, especially the beach side pitches. This is a relaxing site without the razzamataz of the larger sites along the coast.

Facilities

Three clean, fresh toilet blocks provide hot and cold showers (water is solar heated and free). British and Turkish style toilets. Facility for disabled visitors. Washing machines. Motorcaravan services. Bar/restaurant and takeaway. Shop (all season). Excellent beach. Aquarobics and aerobics (high season). Play area (supervision required). Mini-club (high season). Internet and WiFi. Fishing. Dogs not accepted May - Sept. Off site: Bus service 300 m. Seaside town 1 km. Riding 5 km.

Open: Week before Easter - 20 October.

Directions

From S1 autostrada (free) between Livorno and Grosetto head south and take Vada exit. Site is well signed along with lots of others as you approach the town. GPS: N43:20 E10:27.49

Charges 2006

Per person	€ 4,00 - € 7,00
child (0-7 yrs)	€ 2,50 - € 4,00
pitch incl. car and electricity	€ 11,00 - € 17,00

No credit cards.

IT6631 Camping Mareblu

Localitá Mazzanta, I-57023 Cecina Mare (Tuscany)
Tel: 0586 629191. Email: info@campingmareblu.com

Mareblu is a well equipped family site with an impressive range of amenities, including a large swimming pool with an attractive terraced surround, and shopping complex incorporating a greengrocer, hairdressing salon, newsagent and internet centre. There is also a sandy beach, 300 metres away, accessed through a pine wood. The pitches at Mareblu are well shaded and are all equipped with electrical connections (6A). Parking for all cars is in a dedicated area at the front of the site which ensures a pleasant traffic-free ambience within the site. The site is close to Cecina Mare, a popular resort with easy access to some of Tuscany's great cities, and the island of Elba.

Facilities

Five modern toilet blocks include facilities for disabled visitors. Shopping centre. Bar, restaurant and self-service cafeteria, pizzeria and takeaway. Swimming and paddling pools. Play area. Games field. Boules. Bicycle hire. Animation. Miniclub. Internet access. Direct access to beach. Off site: Tennis. Riding. Watersports and diving. Excursions.

Open: 20 March - 16 October.

Directions

Site is south of Livorno. From north, take A12 to Rosignano and then join the E80 to Vada, then to La Mazzanta. From here site is well signed.

Charges 2006

Per person	€ 4,10 - € 7,70
child (0-10 yrs)	€ 3,10 - € 6,20
pitch incl. electricity	€ 5,20 - € 13,40
car	€ 1,50 - € 3,60

IT6638 Park Albatros Camping Village

Viale della Principessa, I-57027 San Vincenzo (Tuscany)
Tel: 0565 701018. Email: parkalbatros@ecvacanze.it

Camping Albatros is another venture for the Cardini/Vanucchi families and is situated on the historic Costa Degli Etruschi where natural parks abound. A group of conical buildings form the hub of the original, somewhat dated, infrastructure of Albatross. This theme of circles is continued through the peaceful new development in the form of round buildings and the placing of mobile homes in curves. The 300 new touring pitches are in a separate area on flat ground. Of 110 sq.m. all have water, drainage, 10A electricity and some shade from newly planted trees. The restaurant, bar and shopping complex are under natural pines at the hub. They provide a quality range of goods and services. There is also a vast new, air-conditioned supermarket and a new (2007) lagoon pool, bar and entertainment area. The new, architect designed, circular, bamboo covered toilet block on the touring side is amazing with brilliant children's rooms. Albatros aims to provide a wide range of services and your visits to the local beach some 800 m. away will be assisted by site transport. There is much to see and explore in the area and a wide range of excursions can be organized.

Facilities

Two toilet blocks are on site. The new circular block is superb! All WCs are British style and the showers are really good, as are facilities for disabled visitors and children. Washing machines. Central area includes bar, restaurant and pizzeria with large terrace. Animation programme in season. Miniclub (4-12 yrs). Play areas. Lagoon pool complex. Bicycle hire. No barbecues allowed. Internet. Torches very useful. Off site: Beach 800 m. Riding 1 km. Vast choice of excursions and walks. Public transport at gate in high season.

Open: Easter - 15 October.

Directions

Site is northwest of Grossetto and south of Livorno on the coast. From the SS1 take San Vincenzo exit. Site is well signed as you approach the village.

Charges 2006

Per person	€ 5,50 - € 10,50
child (2-12 yrs)	€ 4,00 - € 8,00
pitch	€ 8,00 - € 16,00
dog	€ 1,50

IT6645 Parco Delle Piscine

Via del Bagno Santo 29, I-53047 Sarteano (Tuscany)
Tel: 0578 26971. Email: info@parcodellepiscine.it

On the spur of Monte Cetona, Sarteano is a spa, and this large, smart site utilises that spa in its very open environs. The site is well run with an excellent infrastructure and there is a friendly welcome from the English speaking staff. The 509 individual, flat pitches, are all of a good size and fully marked with high neat hedges giving real privacy. The novel feature here is the three unique swimming pools fed by the natural thermo-mineral springs. These springs have been known since antiquity as 'del Bagno Santo' which flows at a constant temperature of about 24 degrees. Two of these pools (the largest is superb with water cascade and hydro-massage, and the other large shallow pool is just for children) are set in a huge park-like ground with many picnic tables. They are free to all those staying on the site. A third excellent pool is on the campsite itself and is opened in the main season. A very big building alongside the spa-pool houses a select restaurant on the first floor and a pizzeria on the second floor, the terrace gives fine views over the local area. Delle Piscine is really good as a sightseeing base or as an overnight stop from the Florence - Rome motorway (it is 6 km. from the exit). Access to the attractive town is directly outside the site gate and it is worth exploring, especially the massive fortress with its drawbridge (straight out of a toy box!).

Facilities
Two heated toilet blocks are of high quality with mainly British style WCs and numerous sinks for laundry and dishwashing (with hot water). Motorcaravan services. Restaurant/pizzeria with bar. Coffee bar. Swimming pools (one all season). Satellite TV room and mini-cinema with 100 seats and very large screen. Tennis. Exchange facilities. Free guided cultural tours. Internet. Gas supplies. Dogs are not accepted. Off site: Bicycle hire 100 m. Riding 3 km.
Open: 1 April - 30 September.

Directions
From autostrada A1 take Chiusi/Chianciano exit, from where Sarteano is well signed (6 km). In Sarteano follow camping signs to site (entrance sign reads Piscine di Sarteano).
GPS: N42:59.249 E11:51.898

Charges 2006
Per person	€ 10,00 - € 13,00
child (3-10 yrs)	€ 6,00 - € 8,00
pitch	€ 10,00 - € 13,00

IT6661 Toscana Village

Via Fornoli, 9, I-56020 Montopoli (Tuscany)
Tel: 0571 449032. Email: info@toscanavillage.com

Five years ago a forest stood here and was part of the attractive medieval Tuscan village of Montopoli. Toscana Village has been thoughtfully carved out of the mature pines and it is ideal for a sightseeing holiday in this central area. The 150 level pitches (some large) are on shaded terraces and are carefully maintained. Some pitches have full drainage facilities and water, most have electricity (3A). The amenities are centrally located at the top of the hill in a pleasant modern building. English is spoken by the helpful reception staff. The restaurant has a terrace where there are views of the forest. The unusually shaped pool is in a separate area of the site and will be a welcome break after touring the sights. This is a quality site tucked away from the bustle of the cities.

Facilities

One modern central block has excellent facilities including British style toilets, hot water at all the stylish sinks, private cabins and two large en-suite cubicles which may be suitable for disabled campers. Washing machines and dryer. Motorcaravan services. Shop. Gas. Restaurant with terrace (limited menu, evenings only). Takeaway. Bread to order. Swimming pool. Play area. Bicycle hire. Organised activities. Off site: Village 1 km. Fishing 6 km. Golf 7 km.

Open: All year.

Directions

From A12 (Genova-Florence) take Pisa Centro exit. Take F1,P1,L1 and then Montopoli exit. Follow signs to Montopoli. Look for cemetery on right. Opposite is Via Masoria leading to Via Fornoli and site.

Charges 2006

Per person	€ 4,70 - € 6,80
child (2-10 yrs)	free - € 5,00
pitch incl. electricity	€ 10,70 - € 14,20

Camping Cheques accepted.

IT6660 Camping Maremma Sans Souci

I-58043 Castiglione della Pescaia (Tuscany)
Tel: 0564 933765. Email: info@maremmasanssouci.it

This delightful seaside site is owned and run by the Perduca family and sits in natural woodland on the coast between Livorno and Rome. The minimum amount of undergrowth has been cleared to provide 400 individually marked and hedged, flat pitches for camping enthusiasts. This offers considerable privacy in individual settings. Some pitches are small and cars may not remain with tents or caravans but must go to a shaded and secure car park near the entrance. There is a wide road for motorcaravans but other roads are mostly narrow and bordered by trees (this is a protected area, and they cannot fell the trees). Only 3 km. from Castiglione della Pescaia, a lively holiday town with an old walled village and castle at the centre, the site is on a small cliff overlooking a marina. An excellent sandy beach is less than 100 m. from one end of the site (400 m. from the other) and is used only by campers. This is a most friendly site right by the sea which should appeal to many people who like a relaxed style of camping with a real personal touch.

Facilities

Five small, very clean, mature toilet blocks are well situated around the site. hree blocks have private cabins. Facilities for disabled campers. Motorcaravan services. Laundry. Shop. Excellent restaurant. Bar with snacks. Sailing school. Torches required in some areas. Dogs not accepted 16/6-31/8. Off site: Excursions organised.

Open: 1 April - 31 October.

Directions

Site is 2.5 km. northwest of Castiglione on road to Follonica. GPS: N42:46.406 E10:50.635

Charges 2006

Per person	€ 7,00 - € 10,00
child (2-6 yrs)	€ 5,00 - € 7,00
pitch and car	€ 8,00 - € 15,00

IT6667 Camping La Finoria

Via Monticello, 66, I-58023 Gavorrano (Tuscany)

Tel: 0566 844381. Email: info@campeggiolafinoria.it

An unusual site, primarily for tents, La Finoria is set high in the mountains with incredible views. It is a rugged site with a focus on nature. Italian schoolchildren attend education programmes here. The three motorcaravan pitches are at the top of the site for those who enjoy a challenge, with a dozen caravan pitches on lower terraces accessed by a steep gravel track. Under huge chestnut trees there is a very pretty terraced area for tents. These have a private natural feel which some might say is what camping is all about. Electricity (3A) is available to all pitches, although long leads may be needed. If you visit in November you can help collect the olives and make olive oil or in October gather chestnuts for purée, wild berries in May and make jam. The views of Elba and the Gulf of Follonica from the terace by day and night are stunning. After an exhausting day communing with nature, or exploring the area, there is a large pool for a refreshing swim before enjoying the night views.

Facilities

Two blocks provide British and Turkish style toilets, hot showers and cold water at washbasins and sinks. Facilities for disabled campers. Washing machines. Quaint, small shop (closed Jan/Feb). Good restaurant and bar (closed Jan/Feb). Swimming pool (May - Sept). Tennis. Lessons on the environment. Excursions. Torches essential. Off site: Riding 2 km. Tennis 3 km. Village 3 km. Bicycle hire 6 km. Golf 8 km. Private beach 12 km.

Open: All year.

Directions

From SS1 (Follonica – Grosseto) take Gavorrano exit, then Finoria road. This is a steady, steep climb for some 10 minutes. Start to descend and at junction (the only one), look left downhill for a large white sign to site. GPS: N42:55.35 E10:54.74

Charges 2006

Per person	€ 2,50 - € 8,50
child (1-6 yrs)	€ 2,00 - € 4,50
pitch	€ 4,00 - € 10,00

IT6673 PuntAla Camping Resort

I-58040 Punta Ala (Tuscany)

Tel: 0564 922294. Email: info@campingpuntala.it

This very large site was established some 35 years ago. Some of the original infrastructure remains and some has been renovated. The pitches vary tremendously in size and position relative to the amenities. With the size of the site some serious distances have to be covered from some areas to the amenities, most of which are near the entrance. There are 300 pitches for touring units on sand on a mainly flat site. All have 25A electricity (67 have water and waste water as well) and shade from very mature pines. Much hedging gives privacy and is quite extensive in parts. Bungalows and mobile homes are prevalent in the northern areas. More expensive, larger pitches are on offer to the north near the amenities and main beach access. We recommend avoiding a section adjacent to a huge treatment plan (alongside the fence)! A bicycle would be handy!

Facilities

The nine blocks are a confusing mixture of facilities with some unisex facilities and many private cabins to hire. Two blocks have been rebuilt and these are popular. The older blocks resemble old army blocks, and have mostly Turkish toilets. Unit for disabled campers. Motorcaravan services. Bars, restaurants and takeaway. Mini-market. Animation. Play areas. WiFi. Bicycle hire. Tennis. Beach with good sailing club. ATM. Animals are not accepted. Torches essential. Off site: Golf 14 km. Town 6 km.

Open: 1 April - 30 October.

Directions

From E80/S1 take Follonica Nord exit onto S322 (for Punta Ala). Look for Pian d'alma marked on maps – Total petrol station on the right, go 450 m. past it to small white restaurant. Site is now signed to the right. Watch for speed bumps. After 2 km. cross bridge and park on the left. Avoid town of Punta Ala – site is not on that road. GPS: N42:50 E10:46.78

Charges 2006

Per person	€ 5,50 - € 16,50
pitch	€ 5,30 - € 24,00

IT6675 Camping Cieloverde

Via della Trappola, 180, I-58046 Marina di Grosseto (Tuscany)
Tel: 0564 321611. Email: info@cieloverde.it

Cieloverde Camping Village lies at the heart of the Tuscan Maremma, between Marina di Grosseto and Principina, bordering the Maremma Nature Park. The huge site lies deep in a long-established pinewood, looking out onto the Costa d'Argento where a sandy beach slopes gently down to the sea. The 1,000 touring pitches (all around 100 sq.m.) are in circular zones around sanitary blocks and all have 3A electricity and offer telephone hook-ups. Parking is in designated areas away from the camping area. A wide range of entertainment is organized here, including shows, dance events, open-air cinema and games. The site also offers a 2.8 kilometre-long 'Percorso Verde', or 'Green Route', with 16 exercise areas. There is also a new adventure park, Tarzaland, where it's possible to explore the treetops thanks to a network of aerial walkways, ropes and swings. Surrounding the site is a large natural park where fallow deer, red deer, moufflon sheep and other animals roam in freedom. The site restaurant, takeaway and bars are centrally located and here you will find typical Maremma recipes, grills and other freshly caught fish dishes.

Facilities

Modern toilet blocks. Shops, restaurant and takeaway. Pizzeria. Bars. Hairdresser. Play area. Table tennis. Games room. Archery. Cinema. Chapel. Volleyball. Football. 'Tarzaland' adventure park. Transport to the beach. Pets allowed in low season only. Off site: Watersports. Fishing (with licence). Marina di Grossetto. Riding 5 km. Golf 30 km.

Open: 15 May - 19 September.

Directions

Site is west of Grosseto on the coast. Take care here as Grosseto has only one way of crossing the railway for anything other than cars. Follow Grosseto signs from S1 (the Aurelia) and cross town following road to Castiglione della Pescada until signs for Marina di Grosseto. We stress this is the only way across town.

Charges 2006

Per person	€ 5,00 - € 12,00
pitch	€ 6,90 - € 16,00

Camping Cheques accepted.

Check real time availability and at-the-gate prices...
www.alanrogers.com

IT6649 Camping Punta Navaccia

I-06069 Tuoro sul Trasimeno (Umbria)

Tel: 075 826357. Email: **navaccia@camping.it**

Situated on the north side of Lake Trasimeno and run by friendly and welcoming owners, this is a large site with over 70,000 sq.m. and 400 touring pitches (200 with 4A electricity) and all with shade. The campsite has a long (stony) beach with facilities for mooring and launching your boat. There are 60 mobile homes with air conditioning for rent. The site is ideally located for exploring Umbria and its famous cities, such as Assisi and Perugia. Tuscany and its cities of Siena and Florence are also within easy reach and it is even possible to visit Rome for a day trip.

Facilities

Sanitary block with British style WCs, showers and some private cabins. Washing machine and dryer. Motorcaravan service point. Heated swimming and paddling pools. Shop, restaurant and takeaway (April - November). Play area. Tennis. Table tennis. Large covered amphitheatre. Disco. Cinema screen. Miniclub. Animation is organised in high season (in Italian, English, German and Dutch). Boat launching. Off site: Sandy beach 200 m. Windsurfing, sailing and canoeing 200 m.

Open: 15 March - 31 October.

Directions

Going south on the A1 (Florence/Firenze - Rome), take exit for Val di Chiana to Perugia near Bettolle. After 15 km. take Tuoro sul Trasimeno exit. Site is well signed.

Charges 2006

Per unit incl. 2 persons	€ 17,00 - € 26,50
extra person	€ 5,50 - € 8,00
child (2-9 yrs)	€ 4,00 - € 6,00

IT6677 Camping Baia dei Gabbiani

I-58020 Scarlino (Tuscany)

Tel: 0566 866158. Email: **info@baiadeigabbiani.com**

Baia dei Gabbiani is a large seaside site located at Puntino di Scarlino, 4 km. from the seaside resort of Follonica. This site has been recommended by our Italian agent and we plan to undertake a full inspection in 2007. Pitches are on level ground and most have electrical connections. The site has direct access to the beach and a lively activity programme is organised in peak season.

Facilities

Restaurant and bar. Shop. Newsagent. Playground. Entertainment and activity programme in high season. Direct beach access. Chalets for rent. Off site: Puntone 400 m. Follonica 4 km. Siena, Florence and Pisa are all within 2 hours drive.

Open: 6 May - 16 September.

Directions

From Livorno take the southbound Via Aurelia (S1). Leave at Follonica Nord exit. Head initially towards Follonica and then towards Grosseto. Site is signed to the right (Castiglione della Pescaia and Punta Ala).

Charges 2006

Per person	€ 6,50 - € 10,90
pitch incl. electricity	€ 9,30 - € 14,70

IT6678 Camping Riva dei Butteri

Via del Buttero 2, I-58020 Scarlino (Tuscany)

Tel: 0566 54 006. Email: **info@rivadeibutteri.it**

This is a sister site of Camping Baia dei Gabbiani (IT6677) and is also located close to Follonica. The site is just 100 m. from the beach and 15 minutes from the town centre. This site has been recommended by our Italian agent and we plan to undertake a full inspection in 2007. Pitches are located beneath trees and most have electrical connections. The site has recently undergone a renovation programme and contains a good range of leisure amenities including a restaurant, bar and supermarket. A varied activity and entertainment programme is organised in peak season, including children's activities.

Facilities

Restaurant and bar. Shop and newsagent. Playground. Mountain bikes to hire. Entertainment and activity programme in high season. Children's mini-club. Chalets for rent. Off site: Nearest beach 100 m. Follonica 3 km. Siena, Florence and Pisa are all within 2 hours drive.

Open: 6 May - 16 September.

Directions

From Livorno take the southbound Via Aurelia (S1). Leave at Follonica Nord exit. Head initially towards Follonica and then towards Grosseto. Site is signed to the right (Castiglione della Pescaia and Punta Ala).

Charges 2006

Per person	€ 6,50 - € 10,90
child (3-7 yrs)	€ 4,90 - € 7,10
pitch incl. electricity	€ 9,30 - € 14,70

IT6643 Camping Village Europa

Localitá San Donato, 8, I-06065 Passignano sul Trasimeno (Umbria)

Tel: 075 827405. Email: info@camping-europa.it

The shores of Lake Trasimeno are dotted with a large number of campsites but we feel that Camping Village Europa has something different to offer. This is a high quality friendly site which, with just 100 pitches, is relatively small but which still manages to offer a wide range of amenities. The pitches are separated into four groups by clusters of mature trees, although shade on the pitches is quite limited. All the pitches offer 6A electrical connections. A regular bus service links the site with the nearby town of Passignano and its railway station. On-site amenities include a swimming pool, bar, restaurant, pizzeria and well-stocked shop. The site has its own private beach on Lake Trasimeno with a wide range of watersports available and beach parties in peak season.

Facilities

Three toilet blocks are maintained to a high standard with facilities for disabled users. Washing machines and dryers. Shop. Bar, restaurant, pizzeria and takeaway. Swimming pool. Play area. Children's club. Evening entertainment. Sports pitch. Direct access to lake and beach.
Off site: Passignano 2 km. Perugia 30 km. Assisi 45 km. Riding, tennis, watersports.

Open: Easter - 10 October.

Directions

From Passignano take the road towards Perugia. Turn off this road after 1 km. and the site is clearly signed. GPS: N43:10.933 E12:09.900

Charges 2007

Per person	€ 5,50 - € 7,00
child (3-10 yrs)	€ 4,70 - € 6,00
caravan	€ 6,00 - € 7,00
motorcaravan	€ 6,50 - € 7,50
tent	€ 5,30 - € 6,30

IT6651 Camping Polvese

I-06060 S Arcangelo sul Trasimeno (Umbria)

Tel: 0758 48078. Email: cpolvese@interfree.it

Beside the lake, Polvese takes its name from the island which can be seen clearly from the site. The 80 tourist pitches are in two areas, generally separated from the very permanent pitches rented by Italian and German guests. On flat ground, the older pitches are reasonably sized and shaded, with some by the lake. The new area has young trees and relies on artificial shading. Children have a separate shallow pool in which to play and the adult pool is clean and pleasant. The restaurant with its lake views and a pleasant terrace. It is run as a separate business. The very small bar doubles as a shop selling basics for campers. There is a mini-club in high season plus a little entertainment for adults in the evening, and a slightly tired outdoor cinema. Tours are organised along with tastings of the fare produced in Umbria. We see this as a site for short visits rather than extended stays.

Facilities

Single, basic sanitary block with tired exterior and dated interior but is relatively clean with free hot showers. British and Turkish style toilets and cold water at all the sinks. Facilities for disabled campers. Washing machine. Motorcaravan service point. Restaurant (not owned by site). Basic bar - doubles as shop. TV. Outdoor cinema (basic). Swimming pool. Bicycle hire. Mini-club. Barbecue area. Torches required. Off site: Riding 2 km. Golf (8 hole) 5 km.

Open: 1 April - 1 October.

Directions

Site is on south side of Lake Trasimino. From Florence - Rome autostrada take Magione exit and lakeside road south to S. Arcangelo. Site is well signed.

Charges 2006

Per person	€ 5,00 - € 6,00
child (3-10 yrs)	€ 3,50 - € 4,50
pitch	€ 4,00 - € 4,50
animal	€ 1,50 - € 2,00

Camping Cheques accepted.

kawan-villages.com **tel: 00 333 59 59 03 59** ━━━━━ *kawaⁿ*

IT6652 Camping Villaggio Italgest

Via Martiri di Cefalonia, I-06060 Sant Arcangelo Magione (Umbria)

Tel: 075 848 238. Email: camping@italgest.com

Directly on the shore on the south side of Lake Trasimeno, which is almost midway between the Mediterranean and the Adriatic, Sant Arcangelo is ideally placed for exploring Umbria and Tuscany. The area around the lake is fairly flat but has views of the distant hills and can become very hot during summer. Villaggio Italgest is a pleasant site with 248 tourist pitches on level grass and, except for the area next to the lake, under a cover of tall trees. All pitches have electricity. Cars are parked away from the pitches. The site offers a wide variety of activities, tours are organised and there is entertainment in high season. The bar/disco remains open until 2 am. There is a good sized pool and the site has a marina for boats. Whether you wish to use this site as a base for exploration, as a place to relax, you will find this a most pleasant place to stay. English is spoken.

Facilities

The one large and two smaller sanitary block have mainly British style WCs and free hot water in the washbasins and showers. Facilities for disabled people. Motorcaravan services. Washing machines and dryers. Kitchen. Bar, restaurant, pizzeria and takeaway (all season). Mini-market. Swimming pool. Tennis. Play area. TV (satellite) and games rooms. Disco. Films. Watersports, motor boat hire and lake swimming. Fishing. Mountain bike and scooter hire. Internet point. Activities, entertainment and excursions. Off site: Golf, riding and sailing close.

Open: 1 April - 30 September.

Directions

Site is on the southern shore of Lake Trasimeno. Take Magione exit from the Perugia spur of the Florence - Rome autostrada, proceed southwest round the lake to SAN Arcangelo where site is signed.

Charges 2006

Per person	€ 5,70 - € 8,00
child (3-9 yrs)	€ 4,00 - € 5,70
pitch	€ 6,00 - € 9,50
car	€ 1,80 - € 2,50

Camping Cheques accepted.

CAMPING & VILLAGE ☆☆☆☆
VILLAGGIO ITALGEST
Via Martiri di Cefalonia
I-06060 Sant'Arcangelo
MAGIONE (PERUGIA)
Tel. 0039/075848238
Fax 0039/075848085
camping@italgest.com
www.italgest.com

GPS:
Latit. 43°05'18''
Longit. 12°09'23''

NEW 2007: MOBILE HOMES WITH AIR-COND
PETS ADMITTED

Right on the lake, on the border between Umbria and Tuscany, the campsite is located within the Lake Trasimeno Natural Park. Comfort and fun make it ideal for family's holidays. The campsite, rated 4 stars, the maximum regional rating, has been recently rebuilt: sanitary facilities and bathrooms has been modernized following the highest European standards. With its geographical location, the campsite is an excellent starting point to art cities such as Rome, Florence, Siena, Perugia, Assisi and Orvieto, as well as to natural areas and places in Umbria and Tuscany renowned for their foods and wines. During July and August activities and entertainment are offered in English, with kids' club service.

IT6653 Camping Listro

Via Lungolago, I-06061 Castiglione del Lago (Umbria)

Tel: 075 951193. Email: listro@listro.it

This is a simple, pleasant, flat site with the best beach on Lake Trasimeno. Listro provides 110 pitches all with electricity with 70% of the pitches enjoying the shade of mature trees. Younger campers are in a separate area of the site ensuring no noise disturbance, and some motorcaravan pitches are right on the lakeside giving stunning views. Facilities are fairly limited with a small shop, bar and snack bar, and there is no organised entertainment. English is spoken and British guests are particularly welcome. If you enjoy the simple life and peace and quiet in camping terms then this site is for you. The campsite's beach is private and the lake has very gradually sloping beaches making it very safe for children to play and swim. Camping Listro is a few hundred yards north of the historic town of Castiglione and the attractive town can be seen rising up the hillside from the site.

Facilities

Two screened sanitary facilities are very clean with British and Turkish style WCs. Facilities for disabled visitors. Washing machine. Motorcaravan services. Bar. Shop. Snack bar. Play area. Table tennis. Private beach. Off site: The town is 800 m. and many bars and restaurants are near, as are sporting facilities including a good swimming pool and tennis courts (discounts using the campsite card).

Open: 1 April - 30 September.

Directions

From A1/E35 Florence-Rome autostrada take Val di Chiana exit and join the Perugia (75 bis) superstrada. After 24 km. take Castiglione exit and follow town signs. Site is clearly signed just before the town. GPS: N43:08.0 E12:02.39

Charges 2006

Per person (over 3 yrs)	€ 3,80 - € 4,50
pitch incl. car	€ 5,10 - € 6,30

Less 10% for stays over 8 days in low season.

IT6811 I Pini Camping

Via delle Sassete 1/A, Fiano Romano, I-00065 Roma (Lazio)

Tel: **0765 453349**. Email: **ipini@camping.it**

The many years Roberto and his Australian born wife Judy have spent in the camping industry are reflected in this site built only a few years ago. The 115 pitches are set on shaded grassy terraces with views of the nearby hills, access is easy for all units via tarmac roads, and everything is here, including a well stocked and reasonable supermarket. The beautifully designed restaurant with its high ceilings and wooden beams are typical of the thought that has gone into making I Pini a place where you can relax between exciting visits discovering the wonders of Rome or other nearby attractions. What could be more wonderful after several days or nights in Rome (travelling to and from I Pini by air conditioned bus) exploring all the amazing sights before returning to the cool breezes of this hillside site. Simone, Roberto's daughter is responsible for the restaurant and we recommend sampling the excellent menu on the large terrace with views and entertainment in high season. This is a family business with son Robbie sharing in the task of making your stay enjoyable. Thought has gone into the location of the bungalow village which is separate from the camping. This very friendly and well ordered site is great for families.

Facilities

The single excellent sanitary block is spotless and hot water is free in showers, washbasins and sinks. Two well equipped units for disabled visitors. Washing machines and dryers. Motorcaravan services. Bar. Restaurant. Snack bar and pizza oven. Pleasant market. Swimming pool (with lifeguard). Tennis. Play area. Entertainment (1/6-30/8). Internet access. Torches required in some areas. Air conditioned buses to Rome daily. Off site: Fishing 3 km. Golf and riding 20 km.

Open: 15 March - 1 November.

Directions

From Rome ring road (GRA) take A1 exit to Fiano Romano. As you enter the town turn right along via Belvedere opposite an IP petrol station and follow camping signs – there is only the one site.

Charges 2006

Per person	€ 8,50 - € 10,00
child (3-12 yrs)	€ 5,50 - € 6,60
pitch incl. car	€ 4,50 - € 9,80
Electricity included.	

IT6778 Fabulous Camping Village

Via Cristoforo Colombo, km. 18, I-00125 Roma (Lazio)

Tel: **06 5259354**. Email: **fabulous@ecvacanze.it**

Fabulous Camping Village is another new venture in the Cardini/Vannucchi family group of campsites. Purchased some three years ago, developments are under way to create a superb campsite on top of a hill, midway between Rome and the sea. The pitches are of varying size, all with 6/10A electricity. They are mainly under tall pines and access is by tarmac and hardcore roads. Whilst renovation is in progress some areas will be dusty. The pools, tennis courts and activity amenities are to one side of the site where there are lovely views toward Rome. The very large bar and entertainment area and the restaurant are stylish and new (2006). There is a large, well stocked supermarket attached to this building. Unusually there is an archaeological dig exposing a Roman villa within the site. We are sure that in a relatively short space of time this site will live up to its name and be really fabulous. Families will enjoy the facilities here and the closeness to sea and the delights of Rome.

Facilities

Three blocks, two in traditional style in the permanent area and one new for the tourers. This block is excellent. Facilities for disabled visitors. Baby rooms. Washing machines. Motorcaravan service area. Excellent new supermarket. New restaurant/pizzeria and bar. Three swimming pools, one for paddling, with lifeguards. Play area. Tennis. Mini-club (5 yrs plus) and teenage activities. Animation programme for all ages. Bicycle hire. Internet. Torches useful. Off site: Riding and golf 2 km. Public transport 2 km. Ostia and the coast 10 km.

Open: All year.

Directions

Site is southwest of Rome. It is on the GRA (Rome's M25 equivalent ring road). Take exit 27 or 26 depending on your approach of direction. Site is signed as 'camping' on a small yellow marker. Follow larger camping signs once off the GRA. GPS: N41:46.690 E12:23.807

Charges 2006

Per person	€ 7,00 - € 8,50
child (2-12 yrs)	€ 4,00 - € 5,50
pitch	€ 8,00 - € 11,00
dog	free - € 2,50

Italy

IT6780 Camping Village Roma

Via Aurelia 831, I-00165 Roma (Lazio)

Tel: **06 6623018**. Email: **campingroma@ecvacanze.it**

Perched high on a hilltop on the edge of Rome this is another of the Cardini/Vanucchi family ventures, who have other quality city sites in Italy IT6042, IT6614 and IT6612. Camping Village Roma has been brilliantly re-developed over the past three years into possibly the best city campsite in Europe. The diverse range of facilities are designed in particular to meet the needs of young travellers and the aim here is to provide a friendly helpful service all year round. There are 150 pitches of varying sizes on level terraces. Campervans are mostly in a separate area where 80 pitches are fully serviced. There is some shade and most have attractive views. There are new swimming pools and a jacuzzi on a terrace with beach volley ball on soft sand, a barbeque plus relaxation areas. The modern bar (nightclub) has a huge TV screen and a terrace to relax and enjoy the cool evening breezes and the views. We visited on a Saturday when there was a superb cheap buffet prepared in the large well appointed Italian themed restaurant. A vibrant site where all can have fun and get good value for money.

Facilities

Two superb toilet blocks with British style WCs and showers. Good facilities for disabled visitors and children. Baby baths. Washing machines. Motorhome service point. New supermarket. Large restaurant/late night bar with DJ plus pizzeria with terrace and poolside bar. Huge TV screen. Evening entertainment/disco and regular themed parties. Play area. Swimming pool and jacuzzi. Beach volleyball. Internet. Travel information. Off site: Public transport at gate. Golf 500 m.

Open: All year.

Directions

Site is west of Rome. From A1 autoroute take Roma North exit towards the airport Fuimcino. Take the GRA and exit 1 'Aurelia' towards San Pietro-Citta del Vaticano-Centro. At the 831 km. marker the site is well signed. GPS: N41:53.261 E12:24.252

Charges 2006

Per person	€ 8,50 - € 9,70
child (3-10 yrs)	€ 5,80 - € 7,00
pitch incl. car	€ 7,00 - € 12,60
dog	€ 1,50 - € 4,00

See advertisement on page 327

IT6810 Camping Seven Hills

Via Cassia 1216, I-00189 Roma (Lazio)

Tel: **06 30310826**. Email: **info@sevenhills.it**

Close to Rome, this site provides a quieter, garden setting in some areas, but has a very lively, busy atmosphere in others. It is situated in a delightful valley, flanked by two of the seven hills of Rome and is just off the autostrada ring road to the north of the city (4 km. from the city centre). The site runs a bus shuttle service every 30 minutes to the local station and one return bus to Rome each day (09.00, returning at 18.00). The 80 pitches for touring units (3A electricity to some) are not marked, but the management supervise in busy periods. Arranged in two sections, the top half, near the entrance, restaurant and shop consists of small, flat, grass terraces with two to four pitches on each, with smaller terraces for tents. Access to some pitches may be tricky. The flat section at the lower part of the site is reserved mainly for ready erected tents used by international tour operators who bring guests by coach. These tend to be younger people and the site, along with its often busy pool, has a distinctly youthful feel. Consequently there may be a little extra noise, so choose your pitch carefully. The site is a profusion of colour with flowering trees and shrubs and a good covering of trees provides shade. An unusual feature of the site is that numerous deer roam unhindered and peacocks strut around the terraces. English is spoken and many notices are in English. All cash transactions on the site are made with a card from reception. This is an extremely busy and bustling site with up to 15 touring buses with their occupants on the site during high season, in addition to a very busy camping routine.

Facilities

Three soundly constructed sanitary blocks are well situated around the site, with open plan washbasins, and hot water in the average sized showers. Facilities for disabled campers. Well stocked shop. Bar/restaurant and terrace. Money exchange. Swimming pool at the bottom of the site with bar/snack bar and a room where the younger element tends to congregate (separate pool charge). Disco. Excursions. Bungalows to rent. Off site: Golf 4 km.

Open: 15 March - 1 November.

Directions

From autostrada ring-road exit 3 take Via Cassia (signed SS2 Viterbo, NOT Via Cassia Bis) and look for site signs. Turn right after 1 km. and follow small road for 1 km. to site.

Charges 2006

Per person (over 4 yrs)	€ 8,50 - € 9,50
tent	€ 5,00 - € 6,00
caravan and car	€ 10,50 - € 12,00
car	€ 4,00 - € 4,50
motorcaravan	€ 9,00 - € 10,50
No credit cards.	

IT6809 Camping Tiber

Via Tiberina km 1,400, I-00188 Roma (Lazio)
Tel: **06 3361 0733**. Email: **info@campingtiber.com**

An excellent city site with sound facilities and a dynamic approach to hosting visitors during their stay, Camping Tiber is also remarkably peaceful. It is ideally located for visiting Rome with an easy train service (20 minutes to Rome) a free shuttle bus every 30 minutes and trams for later at night. The 350 tourist pitches (with electricity) are mostly shaded under very tall trees and many have very pleasant views over the river Tiber. This mighty river winds around two sides of the site boundary (safely fenced) providing a cooling effect for campers. There is a new section with some shade, and bungalows to rent are in a separate area. A small but pleasant outdoor pool with a bar awaits after a busy day in the city. The excellent main bar, beer garden and restaurant all have terraces and, along with the takeaway, give good value. The site is extremely well run and especially good for campers with disabilities. Visiting the delights of Rome is easy from here.

Facilities

Fully equipped, very smart sanitary facilities include hot water everywhere, private cabins, a baby room and very good facilities for disabled campers. Laundry facilities. Motorcaravan servicesShop. Bar, restaurant, pizzeria and takeaway. Swimming pool (hat required) and bar (15/5-30/9). Play area. Fishing. Internet access. Free shuttle bus to underground station. Torches useful. Off site: Local bars, restaurants and shops. Golf or riding 20 km.

Open: 15 March - 31 October.

Directions

From Florence, exit at Rome Nord Fiano on A1 and turn south onto Via Tibernia and site is signed. From other directions on Rome ring road (GRA) take exit 6 northbound on S3 Via Flaminia following signs to Tibernia.

Charges 2006

Per person	€ 9,20 - € 10,50
child (3-12 yrs)	€ 6,40 - € 7,60
pitch incl. car	€ 9,30 - € 13,40

Check real time availability and at-the-gate prices...
www.**alanrogers**.com

IT6814 Flaminio Village Camping Bungalow Park

Via Flaminia Nuova 821, I-00189 Roma (Lazio)
Tel: 06 333 2604 / 333 1429. Email: info@villageflaminio.com

We were impressed with Camping Flaminio - it is ideally situated for visiting the 'Eternal City'. An attractive, quite large campsite with some shade, it is clean and crisp with a youthful flavour. On ground that slopes in parts, it is 400 metres from the main road, which results in its being protected from traffic noise. There is reasonable space allocated to touring units and the majority of these pitches in the lower areas are of average size. All have 6A electricity and are approached by 'environmentally approved' brick access roads. There are also some 120 well-equipped bungalows, quite attractively arranged in a village-style setting. There is a regular bus/underground service into the centre of Rome from outside the site entrance, which operates until late evening. It is a site for those with culture in mind and the nearest antiquities, etc. are only 500 metres away. A smart pool complex (hats required) at the furthest point of this long, slim site has a bar and terrace.

Facilities

Some sanitary facilities are currently housed in old blocks, but the new block has high quality facilities, including provision for disabled visitors and a very good baby room. Bar/pizzeria and restaurant. Shop. Swimming pool, pool bar and solarium (15/6-5/9). Bicycle hire. Internet access. Bus service. Torches useful. Pick-up service to and from Ciampino airport. Off site: Shops, service station, bank and access to cycle route alongside river into the City. Buses and trains outside the gate.

Open: All year.

Directions

From the ring road north of the city take Via Flaminia exit 6 south towards the city centre. After 3 km. follow Flaminia signs and bear left where roads split in order to avoid tunnel. Warning: site entrance comes up suddenly on the right as the central barrier ends 150 m. after passing tunnel entrance. GPS: N41:57 E12:28.94

Charges 2006

Per person	€ 9,50 - € 10,70
child (under 12 yrs)	€ 6,50 - € 7,60
pitch	€ 10,40 - € 13,40

IT6812 Roma Flash Sporting

Via Settevene Palo km 19,800, I-00062 Bracciano (Lazio)
Tel: 0699 805458. Email: info@romaflash.it

This excellent family site is situated on the beautiful Lake Bracciano, the source of Rome's drinking water. Roma Flash Sporting is a friendly campsite which seems to improve each time we visit. Mature trees provide cover for the 200 pitches, some which have good lake views. The dynamic owners Elide and Eduardo speak excellent English and happily go out of their way to ensure guests enjoy their holiday. The simple restaurant has a large terrace and small indoor area both overlooking the lake where you can enjoy a basic menu and excellent pizza; a small shop shares this area.

Facilities

One new large toilet block is very well appointed and the second block should now have been replaced. Free hot water throughout and fully adjustable showers. Facilities for disabled visitors. Laundry facilities. Gas supplies. Bar/pizzeria. Small shop. Swimming pool (caps compulsory). Play area. Watersports. Games room. Animation for children in high season. Excursions.

Open: 1 April - 30 September.

Directions

From E35/E45 north of Rome, take Settebagni exit. Follow GRA orbital road west to Cassia exit. Follow sign for Lago Bracciano to town of Bracciano. Site is signed from town. GPS: N42:07.896 E12:10.423

Charges 2006

Per person	€ 5,00 - € 7,00
pitch	€ 6,00 - € 8,00
Camping Cheques accepted.	

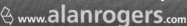

IT6819 Camping Villaggio Settebello

Via Flacca, km. 3,6, I-04020 Salto di Fondi (Lazio)

Tel: 0771 599132. Email: settebello@settebellocamping.com

The SS213 hugs this beautiful coast line for many miles, running between small towns and villages and alongside the pine forests that are directly behind the beach. Camping Settebello, an attractive and well managed site, is in a rural area but unfortunately the site straddles this busy road and inevitably there is traffic noise. The touring pitches are all on the beach side of the site in a wooded area. The ground rises before the beach and this is where many of the bungalows for rent have been built. With a total of 600 pitches about 260 are available for tourers. The remainder are used for seasonal caravans (225), mobile homes for rent (16) and bungalows (101). Given the site's popularity, it naturally provides many sporting and social activities. Being midway between Rome and Naples, it is a good point to break a journey when travelling, or perhaps for a longer stay in the low season. Most of the sporting activities are on the other side of the road but these can be accessed by a pedestrian subway. No dogs or cats allowed.

Facilities

Five toilet blocks include showers, WCs (Turkish and British style) and washbasins. Facilities for disabled visitors. Motorcaravan service point. Small shop. Bar and restaurant (1/6-10/9). New swimming pool and children's pool (1/6-30/8). Skating. Tennis. Minigolf. Entertainment and children's club. Disco. Amphitheatre and cinema. Pets are not accepted. Bungalows and mobile homes to rent. Off site: Narrow public beach. Bicycle hire 2 km. Fondi 10 km. Riding 20 km. Watersports.

Open: 1 April - 30 September.

Directions

The Via Flacca is a comparatively short stretch of the SS213 between Sperlonga and Terracina. The site straddles this road at km. 3.6 which is close to Terracina. Turn towards the beach to find reception. GPS: N41:17.689 E13:19.190

Charges 2006

Per unit incl. 2 persons	€ 23,00 - € 50,00
extra person	€ 7,00 - € 13,00
child (3-12 yrs)	€ 6,00 - € 12,00

Camping Cheques accepted.

CAMPING VILLAGE

SETTEBELLO

www.settebellocamping.com

To the south of Rome, directly on the sea, 500 pitches, 100 modern bungalows, 14 mobile homes with private toilet and kitchenette for 2 to 6 people. Bed linen, electricity, gas, fridge, sun shade parasol, deck chair and deck chair in the internal solarium.
Swimming pool, restaurant, pizzeria, market, bar, pub, shopping, newspaper kiosk, skate park, disco, sport fittings, internal car park.

**Via Flacca - Km 3,600 - I-04020 Salto di Fondi (LATINA) - Tel. 0039/0771599132 - Fax 0039/077157635
settebello@settebellocamping.com**

IT6813 Camping Porticciolo

Via Porticciolo, I-00062 Bracciano (Lazio)

Tel: 06 99803060. Email: info@porticciolo.it

This small family run site, useful for visiting Rome, has its own private beach on the southwest side of Lake Bracciano. A pleasant feature is that the site is overlooked by the impressive castle in the village of Bracciano. There are 170 pitches (160 for tourers) split into two sections, some with lake views and 120 having electricity. Pitches are large and shaded by very green trees that are continuously watered in summer by a neat overhead watering system. The bar has two large terraces, shared by the trattoria which opens for lunch and the pizzeria in the evenings.

Facilities

Three somewhat rustic, but clean, sanitary units with children's toilet and nursery. Hot showers (by token). Laundry facilities. Motorcaravan services. Gas supplies. Shop (basics). Bar. Trattoria/pizzeria (15/5-5/9). Tennis. Play area. Bicycle hire. Fishing. Internet point and free WiFi. Excursions 'Rome By Night' and nearby nature parks. Off site: Riding 2 km. Bus service from outside the gate runs to central Rome. Air conditioned train service from Bracciano (1.5 km) into the city.

Open: 1 April - 30 September.

Directions

From Rome ring road (GRA) northwest side take Cassia exit to Bracciano S493 (not 'Cassia bis' which is further northeast). Two kilometres before Bracciano village, just after going under a bridge follow site signs and turn along the lake away from Anguillara. Site is 1 km. and has a steep entrance. GPS: N42:06.335 E12:11.167

Charges 2007

Per person	€ 4,20 - € 6,00
pitch incl. electricity	€ 9,6 - € 13,75

IT6800 Camping Europe Garden

Via Belvedere 11, I-64028 Silvi (Abruzzo)

Tel: 085 930137. Email: info@europegarden.it

This site is 13 kilometres northwest of Pescara and, lying just back from the coast (2 km.) up a very steep hill, it has pleasant views over the sea. The 204 pitches, all with electricity, are mainly on good terraces – access may be difficult on some pitches. However, if installation of caravans is a problem a tractor is available to help. When we visited the site was dry but we suspect life might become difficult on some pitches after heavy rain. Cars stand by units on over half of the pitches or in nearby parking spaces for the remainder, and most pitches are shaded. There is a good swimming pool at the bottom of the site, with a small bar and an entertainment programme in season on a small stage and associated area within the pool boundary. The restaurant has large olive trees penetrating the floor and ceilings of the eating area and good views but the terrace views are fabulous. Electronic money is used throughout the site (credit is bought on the site's swipe cards). This site has very steep slopes and is not suitable for disabled or infirm campers.

Facilities

Two good toilet blocks are well cleaned and provide mixed British and Turkish style WCs. Washing machines. Restaurant. Bar. Swimming pool (300 sq.m; caps compulsory), small paddling pool and jacuzzi. Tennis. Playground. Entertainment programme. Free weekly excursions (15/6-8/9). Free bus service (18/5-7/9) to beach. Dogs are not accepted.

Open: 27 April - 20 September.

Directions

Turn inland off S16 coast road at km. 433 for Silvi Alta and follow camp signs. From autostrada A14 take Pineto exit from north or Pescara Nord exit from the south.

Charges 2006

Per person	€ 4,20 - € 8,00
child (0-3 yrs)	€ 3,80 - € 6,00
pitch	€ 9,80 - € 15,00
2-man tent	€ 5,40 - € 10,30
electricity	€ 2,50

No credit cards. Discounts for longer stays outside high season.

IT6804 Camping Village Eurcamping

Lungomare Trieste, I-64026 Roseto degli Abruzzi (Abruzzo)

Tel: 0858 993179. Email: eurcamping@camping.it

Our Italian agent has recommended this site and we hope to include a full report in a future edition of the guide. Eurcamping is situated directly beside the sea, in a quiet, green area, far from the railway and noisy roads. The sea here is ideal for windsurfing, sailing and sea fishing and the site has a private, sandy beach. A yacht club is behind the site and there is a small harbour nearby. The small town of Roseto degli Abruzzi is easy to reach by car, bus or bicycle, or on foot along the seashore. The site offers about 350 flat pitches, well shaded by various types of tall trees. All have good access with electricity hook ups (3/6A). There are good facilities and a team to provide entertainment and activities.

Facilities

Three sanitary blocks with free hot showers. Facilities for disabled people. Motorcaravan services. Laundry. Bar. Restaurant. Takeaway. Pizzeria. Shop. Swimming pools (hats must be worn) with solarium terrace. Play area and sports ground. Tennis. Bowling green. Internet point. Bicycle hire. Entertainment in high season. Clubs for children and teenagers. Pets are allowed only on assigned pitches. Off site: Beach. Canoe and pedalo hire.

Open: April - October.

Directions

From north or south on A14 motorway, take exit for Roseto degli Abruzzi. Turn on SS150 to Roseto degli Abruzzi. From Rome and L'Aquila on A24 motorway take exit for Villa Vomano-Teramo, onto SS150 (Roseto degli Abruzzi).

Charges 2006

Per person	€ 4,00 - € 9,00
child (3-7 yrs)	€ 3,00 - € 6,00
pitch	€ 8,00 - € 16,00

IT6838 Camping Nettuno

Via A. Vespucci, 39, Marina del Cantone, I-80061 Massa Lubrense (Campania)

Tel: **081 8081051**. Email: **info@villaggionettuno.it**

Situated in a protected area called the 'Punta Campanella', away from the busiest tourist areas of the Amalfi Coast, this tiny campsite of only 42 pitches (4A) is a delight. Owned and run by the friendly Mauro family, who speak excellent English, it is nestled in the bay of Marina del Cantone between Positano and Capri. Pitches are informally arranged some with fabulous sea views and almost all with shade. Across a minor road up a flight of steps are about 50 mobile homes, a bar, excellent restaurant, small, well stocked shop and terrace where there is animation in the high season. The single small sanitary block is centrally located and newly refurbished with quality finishes. The site has two pathways to the nearby beach that, unusually for the area, involves little walking, steps or steep inclines. With their own diving centre, this is a popular site for all divers. Excursions are arranged to the Isle of Capri and Amalfi Coast on alternate days, there are also diving or snorkelling trips and excursions into the natural park area only accessible by boat. There is an interesting 500 years old stone tower on the site that has been converted into four apartments. The small village of Marina del Cantone is just 100 metres walk away and is renowned for its beautiful quality cuisine - often boats moor outside the marina especially to dine here.

Facilities

One clean and newly refurbished sanitary block with excellent facilities for disabled people (and access via a ramp to the beach). Washing machine. Motorcaravan service point. Gas supplies. Small shop. Delightful restaurant with sea views. Bar (lively at night). Dive centre. Excursions. TV in bar area. Small play area. Free tennis arranged at court next door. Off site: Beach (pebbles) 5 m. from bottom of site. Excellent restaurants 100 m. Amalfi Coast, Capri, nature parks, walking etc.

Open: 1 March - 2 November.

Directions

From A3 motorway (Naples - Salerno), take Castellamare di Stabia exit onto S145. Pass Castellamare, follow signs to Meta di Sorrento through Vico Equense bypass tunnel and turn off towards Positano near Meta. After 5 km. turn to S. Agata (6.5 km.) then signs to Nerano and finally Marina del Cantone. Site is well signed. GPS: N40:34.996 E14:21.197

Charges 2006

Per person	€ 6,50 - € 9,00
child (3-10 yrs)	€ 4,00 - € 5,00
pitch	€ 9,50 - € 13,00

Camping Cheques accepted.

IT6820 Baia Domizia Villaggio Camping

I-81030 Baia Domizia (Campania)

Tel: 0823 930164. Email: info@baiadomizia.it

This large, beautifully maintained seaside site is about 70 kilometres northwest of Naples, and is within a pinewood, cleverly left in a natural state. Although it does not feel like it, there are 1000 touring pitches in clearings, either of grass and sand or on hardstanding, all with electricity. Finding a pitch may take time as there are so many good ones to choose from, but staff will help in season. Most pitches are well shaded, but there are some in the sun for cooler periods. The central complex is superb with well designed buildings providing for all needs (the site is some distance from the town). Restaurants, bars and a 'gelaterie' enjoy live entertainment and attractive water lily ponds surround the area. The entire site is attractive, with shrubs, flowers and huge green areas. Near the entrance are two excellent pools, which are a pleasant alternative to the sea on windier days. The supervised beach is 1.5 km. of soft sand and a great attraction. A large grassy field overlooking the sea is ideal for picnics and sunbathing. A wide range of sports and other amenities is provided. The site is very well organised with particular regulations (e.g. no dogs or loud noise), so the general atmosphere is relaxing and peaceful. Although the site is big, there is never very far to walk to the beach, and although it may be some 300 m. to the central shops and restaurant from the site boundaries, there is always a nearby toilet block. It is the ideal place to recover from the rigours of touring or to relax and allow the professionals to organise tours for you to Rome, Pompeii, Sorrento etc. Charges are undeniably high, but this site is well above average and most suitable for families with children. Member of Leading Campings Group.

Facilities

Seven new toilet blocks have hot water in washbasins (many cabins) and showers. Good access and facilities for disabled people. Washing machines, spin dryers. Motorcaravan services. Gas supplies. Supermarket and general shop. Large bar and restaurants with pizzeria and takeaway. Ice cream parlour. Playground. Tennis. Bicycle hire. Windsurfing hire and school. Disco. Excursions. Torches required in some areas. Dogs are not accepted. Off site: Fishing and riding 3 km.

Open: 28 April - 16 September.

Directions

The turn to Baia Domizia leads off the Formia - Naples road 23 km. from Formia. From Rome - Naples autostrada, take Cassino exit to Formia. Site is to the north of Baia Domizia and well signed. GPS: N41:12.432 E13:47.481

Charges 2006

Per person	€ 4,80 - € 10,40
child (1-3 yrs)	free - € 8,50
pitch incl. electricity	€ 10,90 - € 21,40

IT6889 Villaggio Camping Costa Verde

Capo Vaticano di Ricadi, I-89865 San Nicolo di Ricadi (Calabria)

Tel: 0963 663090. Email: tropea@costaverde.org

The coast near Capo Vaticano is listed as one of the best 100 in the world and one of the top three in Italy. From our pitch the sandy beach was just five metres below, down a flight of steps, and we had an unobstructed view of the turquoise sea, the beach and beyond – what more can you ask for? Camping Costa Verde nestles in a small bay, almost hidden from the surrounding area. With its 80 shaded pitches, it offers all year round camping in a beautiful location. The nearby small town of Tropea is one of the most picturesque on the Tyrrhenian coast.

Facilities

The toilet block includes showers, WCs and washbasins. Washing machine. Small shop (1/5-30/10). Bar/coffee shop and restaurant (1/5-30/10). Good sandy beach. Excursions arranged. Children's club in high season. Disco. Apartments to rent. Dogs are not accepted in July/Aug. Barbecues not permitted. Off site: Tropea and Capo Vaticano.

Open: All year.

Directions

From A3 (Naples - Reggio) take Rosarno exit and go through the town. Follow signs for Nicotera then Tropea. Before Tropea look for signs for Ricadi and at a fairly large junction, amongst others, for Costa Verde (if you reach the railway viaduct you have gone too far). Turn left here, then right for the site. The last 400 m. is down a narrow, steep and winding road. GPS: N38:38.344 E15:50.056

Charges 2006

Per person	€ 5,50 - € 11,00
pitch incl. car	€ 8,80 - € 16,50

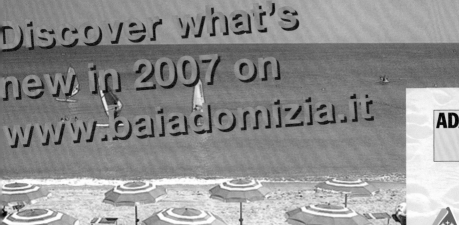

IT6865 Camping Riva di Ugento

Litoranea Gallipoli, Santa Maria di Leuca, I-73059 Ugento (Puglia)
Tel: **0833 933600**. Email: **info@rivadiugento.it**

There are some campsites where you can be comfortable, have all the amenities at hand and still feel you are connecting with nature. Under the pine and eucalyptus trees of the Bay of Taranto foreshore is Camping Riva di Ugento. Its 900 pitches are nestled in and around the sand dunes and the foreshore area. They have space and trees around them and the sizes differ as the environment dictates the shape of most. The sea is only a short walk from most pitches and some are at the water's edge. The site buildings resemble huge wooden umbrellas and are in sympathy with the environment. There are swimming and paddling pools, although these are expensive to use in high season. A free cinema also shows special events via satellite TV near the main bar and restaurant area. The area is sandy but well shaded, and the sea breezes, scented with pine give the site a cool fresh feel. This site has an isolated, natural feel that defies its size. Cycling along the kilometre of beach, we enjoyed the tranquillity of the amazing pitches - shaded, private and inviting. We were sorry to leave the site which was by far the best we found in the area.

Facilities

Twenty toilet blocks all with WCs, showers and washbasins. Bar. Restaurant and takeaway. Swimming and paddling pools. Tennis. Basketball. Volleyball. Watersports incl. windsurfing school. Cinema. TV in bar. Entertainment for children. Bicycle hire. Off site: Fishing. Riding 0.5 km. Boat launching 4 km. Golf 40 km.

Open: 15 May - 30 September.

Directions

From Bari take the Brindisi road to Lecce, then SS101 to Gallipoli, followed by the SR274 towards S. Maria di Leuca, and exit at Ugento. Site well signed and turn right at traffic lights on SS19. Bumpy approach road. GPS: N39:52.485 E18:08.467

Charges 2006

Per pitch incl. 2 persons	€ 18,00 - € 37,00
extra person (over 2 yrs)	€ 5,00 - € 9,00
Camping Cheques accepted.	

Check real time availability and at-the-gate prices...
www.**alanrogers**.com

IT6930 Camping Villaggio Marinello

Via del Sol, 17, I-98060 Oliveri (Sicily)
Tel: **0941 313000**. Email: **marinello@camping.it**

Camping Marinello is located alongside the sea with direct access to a lovely uncrowded beach with an informal marina at one end and a spit of sand and natural pool areas at the other. The 250 sandy pitches here are shaded by tall trees. We enjoyed a delicious traditional meal in the excellent terraced restaurant with its lovely sea views. Tours are arranged to major sightseeing destinations such as Mount Etna, Taormina and the nearby Aeolian Islands. The Greco family have been here for over 30 years and work hard to ensure that their guests enjoy a pleasant stay. The nearby resort area town has lots of attractions for the tourist and the site is easily accessible from the ferry at Messina.

Facilities

Two sanitary blocks with free hot showers, one has been refurbished and heated. Washing machines. Bazaar, market and supermarket. Bar with sea views. Restaurant and terraced eating area also with views. Electronic games. Piano bar in high season. Off site: Seaside resort style town of Oliveri.

Open: All year.

Directions

From A20 motorway take Falcone exit and follow signs to Oliveri. At the town turn north towards the beach (site sign), then turn west along the beach and continue 1 km. to site. GPS: N38:07.937 E15:03.263

Charges guide

Per person (over 3 yrs)	€ 4,50 - € 7,50
pitch with electricity	€ 12,00 - € 16,50

IT6923 Camping Jonio

Via Villini a Mare, 2, Ognina, I-95126 Catania (Sicily)
Tel: **095 491139**. Email: **camping@jonioeventi.it**

This is a small, uncomplicated and tranquil city site with the advantage of being on top of the cliff at the waters edge. The level pitches are on gravel with shade from some tall trees and artificial bamboo screens. There are some clean high quality sanitary facilities (also some private facilities for hire), although these may be overcrowded in peak season. There is no pool but the views of the water compensate and there are delightful rock pools in the sea just a few steps from the campsite. A new attractive restaurant offers food in the summer high season. Camping Jonio is ideal for a short stay to unwind whilst basking on the rocky platforms and diving into the clear waters, or to take advantage of the many excursions to the local historical sites. Excellent winter rates are available for long stay visitors. Five languages including English are spoken and access to the site is good.

Facilities

Sanitary facilities are in one small block for men and another for women. Modern and clean, but low numbers of showers and hot water at timed periods will mean showers will frequently be under stress. Laundry. Motorcaravan services. Shop. Bar and restaurant. Basic old style playground (supervision recommended). Animation (high season). Diving school. Access to small gravel beach. Excursions. Dogs are not accepted in July/August. Off site: Large town of Catania, many historical sites and Mount Etna.

Open: All year.

Directions

From A18 motorway take Catania exit and follow signs to the SS114 coast road in the direction of Ognina. Site is off the SS114 (signed) on the northeast outskirts of town. GPS: N37:31.939 E15:07.204

Charges 2006

Per person	€ 6,00 - € 8,00
pitch	€ 6,00 - € 11,00
car	€ 3,50 - € 5,50
electricity	€ 2,50
Camping Cheques accepted.	

337

IT6919 Camping Scarabeo

I-97017 San Croce Camerina (Sicily)

Tel: **0932 918096**. Email: **info@scarabeocamping.it**

Scarabeo Camping is located in Punta Braccetto, a little fishing port in Sicily's southeastern corner. This small site has been recommended by our Italian agent and we hope to undertake a full inspection here in 2007. The site has just 48 pitches, all with electrical connections (3A). All pitches are well shaded, some naturally and others with an artificial cane roof. Scarabeo lies adjacent to a sandy beach and the little village is close by. The site layout resembles a Sicilian farm courtyard and is divided into four principal areas. It has recently undergone an improvement programme.

Facilities	Directions
Direct access to beach, children's playground, entertainment programme in high season. Mobile homes for rent. Off site: Supermarket 4 km, Restaurant/café 500 m. Cycle and walking trails.	Site is 20 km. southwest of Ragusa. From Catania, take S194 towards Ragusa and, at Comiso, follow signs to S. Croce Camerina, then Punta Braccetto, from where site is well signed.
Open: All year.	

Charges 2006

Per person	€ 4,00 - € 8,00
child (under 6 yrs)	€ 2,00 - € 5,00
pitch	€ 4,00 - € 10,50

IT6925 Camping Il Peloritano

Contrada Tarantonio S.S. 113 dir., Rodia, I-98161 Messina (Sicily)

Tel: **090 348496**. Email: **il_peloritano@yahoo.it**

Set in a 100 year old olive grove which provides shade for the 50 informally arranged pitches, Camping Il Peloritano is a quiet uncomplicated site with clean facilities. It is a 200 metre walk to the sandy beach and approximately two kilometres to the nearest village. The friendly owners, Patrizia Mowdello and Carlo Oteri, provide assistance to arrange excursions to the Aeolian Islands, Taormina and Mount Etna and will do their best to make your stay a pleasant one.

Facilities	Directions
Hot showers (by token). Washing machine. Motorcaravan service point. Small shop. Meals can be ordered in from local restaurants. Excursions arranged. Sub aqua school and diving with guide. Bowls. Off site: Sandy beach 200 m. Small seaside village 2 km.	From Messina on the A20 motorway take Villafranca exit then follow 'Messina dir' and 'Tarantonio' for 2 km. From Palermo on the A20, take exit for Rometta and follow 'Messina - Tarantonio' for approx. 5 km. GPS: N38:15.559 E15:28.069
Open: 21 March - 31 October.	

Charges 2006

Per person	€ 5,00 - € 7,00
child (3-7 yrs)	€ 3,00
pitch	€ 4,80 - € 7,00
car	€ 2,00 - € 2,40
electricity	€ 2,40

IT6935 Camping Rais Gerbi

Contrada Rais Gerbi, S.S. 113, km 172.9, I-90010 Finale di Pollina (Sicily)

Tel: **0921 426 570**. Email: **camping@raisgerbi.it**

Rais Gerbi provides good quality camping with excellent facilities on the beautiful Tyrrhenian coast not far from Cefalu. This attractive terraced campsite is shaded by well established trees and the good size pitches vary from informal areas under the trees near the sea to gravel terraces and hardstandings. Most have stunning views, many with their own sinks and with some artificial shade to supplement the trees. From the mobile homes to the unusual white igloos, everything here is being established to a high quality. The large pool with its entertainment area and the restaurant, like so much of the site, overlook the beautiful rocky coastline and aquamarine sea. Vincenzo Cerrito who speaks excellent English has been developing the site for many years and is continually upgrading and improving the resort style facilities. An infrequently used rail line in a deep cutting, then a tunnel, divides part of the site. The cutting is well fenced and lined with trees and has minimal impact and one is unaware of the tunnel under the site. Budget airlines fly into a nearby airport and it is possible to rent tents or accommodation at the site. Packages are available to tour the island and use other campsites near major attractions in Sicily (reception staff will advise). This is a central location from which to explore many of the island's attractions, although it may prove difficult to leave the glorious coastline. Try to visit in spring and autumn when the weather is usually perfect and the site is less busy.

Facilities

Excellent new sanitary blocks with British style toilets, free hot showers in generous cubicles. Small shop. Casual summer terrace and indoor (winter) restaurant. Animation area and pool near the sea. Tennis court and football field. High quality accommodation and tents for rent. Rocky beach at site. Off site: Small village of Finale 500 m. Larger historic town of Cefalu 12 km.

Open: All year.

Directions

Site is on the SS113 running along the east - north coast of the island, between km. 172 and 173, just west of the village of Finale (the turn into site is at end of the bridge on the outskirts of the village). It is 12 km. east of Cefalu and 11 km. north of Pollina. GPS: N38:1.397 E14:09.238

Charges 2006

Per person	€ 4,50 - € 7,50
pitch	€ 6,00 - € 10,00
car	€ 3,00 - € 3,50
electricity	€ 3,00

339

IT6996 Camping Mariposa

Via Lido 22, I-07041 Alghero (Sardinia)
Tel: 079 950 360. Email: info@lamariposa.it

Mariposa is situated right by the sea with its own beach and the range of sports available here probably makes it best suited for active young visitors. Kite surfing, diving, windsurfing, sailing, surfing and paragliding courses are all available here on payment, whilst evening entertainment is provided free. Pitch size ranges from 50 to 90 sq.m. so they are also better suited for tents, although they do all have 6A electrical connections and caravans and motorcaravans are welcome. Cars must be parked away from the pitches. Alghero (1.5 km.) still has a strong Catalan flavour from its 400 year occupation by the Spanish. There are many small coves and the Neptune caves are well worth a visit.

Facilities

The sanitary facilities are fairly basic, partly open plan, with cold washbasins and troughs, dishwashing and laundry sinks and an equal amount of warm (token needed) and cold showers. Washing machines and dryer. Motorcaravan service point. Shop, self service restaurant and bar (all open all season). Bicycle hire. Dogs are not accepted in August.

Open: 1 April - 31 October.

Directions

Alghero is on the northwest coast, about 35 km. southwest of Sassari. Mariposa is at the north of the town.

Charges 2006

Per person	€ 7,50 - € 10,50
child (3-12 yrs)	€ 4,00 - € 8,50
tent or caravan	€ 3,50 - € 14,00
car	free - € 4,00
motorcaravan	€ 3,50 - € 14,00

IT6955 Camping Baia Blu La Tortuga

Pineta di Vignola Mare, I-07020 Aglientu (Sardinia)
Tel: 079 602200. Email: info@baiablu.com

In the northeast of Sardinia near the Costa Smeralda and well situated for the Corsica ferry, Baia Blu is a large, professionally run campsite. The beach with its golden sand, brilliant blue sea and pretty rocky outcrops is warm and inviting. The site's 550 touring pitches are of fine sand and shaded by tall pines with banks of colourful oleanders and wide boulevards providing good access for units. Four toilet blocks provide an exceptionally good ratio of facilities to pitches including some combined private shower/washbasin cabins for rent. This is a busy bustling site with lots to do and attractive restaurants. It is under the same ownership as Marepineta (no. IT6000) and is very popular with Italian families who enjoy the wide range of amenities here. It is used by tour operators.

Facilities

Four blocks with free hot showers and mixed British and Turkish toilets. Facilities for disabled people. Washing machines and dryers. Motorcaravan services. Supermarket. Gas. Bazaar. Bar. Restaurant, pizzeria, snack bar and takeaway (May-Sept). Playground. Tennis. Games and TV rooms. Windsurfing and diving schools. Entertainment and sports activities (high season). Excursions. Barbecue area (not permitted on pitches). Torches useful. Internet point. Massage centre. Off site: Disco 50 m. Riding 5 km.

Open: 30 March - 21 October.

Directions

Site is on the north coast between towns of Costa Paradiso and S. Teresa di Gallura (18 km.) at Pineta di Vignola Mare and is well signed. GPS: N41:07.463 E09:04.055

Charges 2007

Per unit incl. 2 persons and electricity	€ 15,40 - € 43,00
extra person	€ 3,40 - € 10,70
junior (3-12 yrs) or senior (over 60 yrs)	€ 3,10 - € 9,20

See advertisement on page 281

The independent principality of Liechtenstein is the fourth smallest country in the world. Nestled between Switzerland and Austria, it has a total area of 157.sq.km. (61 sq.miles).

If you like clean mountain air and peaceful surroundings, then a visit to Liechtenstein would be worthwhile. The little town of Vaduz (the Capital) is where you will find most points of interest, including the world famous art collection (Kunstmuseum), which holds paintings by Rembrandt and other world famous artists. Above the town of Vaduz is the restored twelfth century castle, now owned by the prince of Liechtenstein (not open to the public). Take a walk up to the top of the hill, you can view Vaduz and the mountains stretched out below. Situated on a terrace above Vaduz is Triesenberg village, blessed with panoramic views over the Rhine Valley, a pretty village with vineyards and ancient chapels. Malbun is Liechtenstein's premier mountain resort, popular in both winter and summer, for either skiing or walking.

FL7580 Camping Mittagspitze

Sägastrasse 29, FL 9495 Triesen (Liechtenstein)

Tel: **3923677**. Email: **info@campingtriesen.li**

Camping Mittagspitze is attractively and quietly situated for visiting the Principality. Probably the best site in the region, it is on a hillside and has all the scenic views that one could wish. Extensive broad, level terraces on the steep slope provide unmarked pitches (a reader tells us that spacing causes problems in high season) and electricity connections are available. There is little shade. Of the 240 spaces, 120 are used by seasonal caravans. Liechtenstein's capital, Vaduz, is 7 km, Austria is 20 km. and Switzerland 3 km.

Facilities

Two good quality sanitary blocks (the one near reception is new) provide all the usual facilities. Washing machine, dryer and ironing. Room where one can sit or eat with cooking facilities. Shop (1/6-31/8). Restaurant (all year). Small swimming pool (15/6-15/8), not heated but very popular in summer. Playground. Fishing. New TV room. Off site: Tennis and indoor pool nearby. Riding and bicycle hire 5 km.

Open: All year.

Directions

From A3 take Trübbach exit and follow road towards Balziers. Then head towards Vaduz and site is 2 km. south of Triesen on the right.

Charges 2006

Per person	€ 8,50
child (under 14 yrs)	€ 4,00
caravan or large tent and car	€ 12,00 - € 14,00
motorcaravan	€ 10,00
electricity	€ 5,00

341

MAP 2

The Grand Duchy of Luxembourg is a sovereign state, lying between Belgium, France and Germa Divided into two areas: the spectacular Ardennes region in the north and the rolling farmlands and woodland in the south, bordered the east by the wine growing area of the Moselle Valley.

CAPITAL: LUXEMBOURG CITY

Tourist Office

Luxembourg National Tourist Office
122 Regent Street, London W1B 5SA
Tel: 020 7434 2800
Fax: 020 7734 1205
Email: tourism@luxembourg.co.uk
Internet: www.luxembourg.co.uk

From wherever you are in Luxembourg you are always within easy reach of the capital, Luxembourg-Ville, home to about one fifth of the population. The city was built upon a rocky outcrop, and has superb views of the Alzette and Petrusse Valleys. Those who love the great outdoors must make a visit to the Ardennes, with its hiking trails, footpaths and cycle routes that take you through beautiful winding valleys and across deep rivers, a very popular region for visitors. If wine tasting takes your fancy, then head for the Moselle Valley, particularly if you like sweet, fruity wines. From late spring to early autumn wine tasting tours take place in cellars and caves. The Mullerthal region, known as the 'Little Switzerland', lies on the banks of the river Sûre. The earth is mostly made up of soft sandstone, so through the ages many fascinating gorges, caves and formations have emerged.

Population

435,700

Climate

A temperate climate prevails, the summer often extending from May to late October.

Language

Letzeburgesch is the national language, with French and German also being official languages.

Telephone

The country code is 00 352.

Money

Currency: The Euro
Banks: Mon-Fri 08.30/09.00-12.00 and 13.30-16.30.

Shops

Mon 14.00-18.30. Tues to Sat 08.30-12.00 and 14.00-18.30 (grocers and butchers at 15.00 on Sat).

Public Holidays

New Year; Carnival Day mid-Feb; Easter Mon; May Day; Ascension; Whit Mon; National Day 23 June; Assumption 15 Aug; Kermesse 1 Sept; All Saints; All Souls; Christmas 25, 26 Dec.

Motoring

Many holidaymakers travel through Luxembourg to take advantage of the lower fuel prices, thus creating traffic congestion at petrol stations, especially in summer. A Blue Zone area exists in Luxembourg City and various parts of the country (discs from tourist offices) but meters are also used.

LU7610 Camping Birkelt

1 rue de la Piscine, L-7601 Larochette

Tel: 879 040. Email: vilux@pt.lu

This is very much a family site, the price representing the range of facilities provided. It is well organised and well laid out, set in an elevated position in attractive undulating good walking countryside. A tarmac road runs around the site with 400 large grass pitches, some slightly sloping, many with a fair amount of shade, on either side of gravel access roads in straight rows or circles. All pitches have a 6A electric point. An all weather swimming pool complex is just outside the site entrance (free for campers). Entertainment for children is organised in high season. The site is very popular with tour operators (140 pitches).

Facilities

Three modern sanitary buildings well situated around the site include mostly open washbasins (6 cabins in one block). Dishwashers (on payment), baby baths, facilities for wheelchair users. Washing machines and dryers. Motorcaravan service point. Shop. Coffee bar. Restaurant with terrace. All weather swimming pool. Outdoor pool for toddlers. Massage. Playgrounds. Table tennis. Roller blade skating. Minigolf. Tennis. Football ground. Riding. Balloon flights. Internet points. Bicycle hire. Off site: Golf and bicycle hire 5 km. Fishing and kayaking 10 km.

Open: 1 March - 31 October.

Directions

From N7 From N7 Diekirch - Luxembourg city, turn onto N8 at Berschblach (just past Mersch) towards Larochette. Site is signed on the right about 1.5 km. from Larochette. Approach road is fairly steep and narrow. GPS: N49:47.105 E06:12.62

Charges 2006

Per unit incl. 2 persons and electricity	€ 18,50 - € 31,50
extra person	€ 3,75

Less 25% in low season.
Camping Cheques accepted.

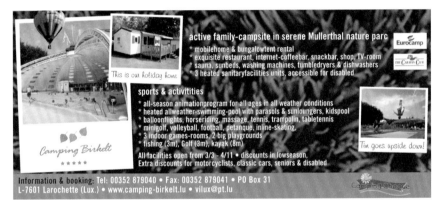
LU7620 Europacamping Nommerlayen

L-7465 Nommern

Tel: 878 078. Email: nommerlayen@vo.lu

This is a top quality site, in central Luxembourg, with fees to match, but it has everything! A large, central building housing most of the services and amenities opens onto a terrace around an excellent swimming pool complex with two main pools (one heated 1/5-15/9) and an imaginative watery playground. The 396 individual pitches (70-120 sq.m.) are on grassy terraces, all have access to electricity (2/16A) and water taps. Interestingly enough the superb new sanitary block is called 'Badtemple' (its architecture suggesting this title as the entrance with colonnades supporting a canopy is reminiscent of a Greek temple). Member of Leading Campings Group.

Facilities

A large, high quality, modern sanitary unit provides some washbasins in cubicles, facilities for disabled people, and family and baby washrooms. The new block includes all the usual features, with special rooms for children and disabled visitors, plus a sauna. Twelve private bathrooms for hire, including whirlpool bath. Laundry. Motorcaravan service point. Supermarket. Restaurant. Snack bar. Bar (all 23/3-1/11). Heated swimming pools (1/5-15/9). Solarium. Fitness programmes. Bowling. Table tennis. Snooker. Billiards. Volleyball. Football. Playground. Large screen TV. Entertainment in season. Bicycle hire. Bottle bank Off site: Riding 1 km. Fishing and golf 5 km.

Open: 1 February - 1 December.

Directions

Take the 118 between Mersch and Larochette. 3 km. north of Larochette the village of Nommer and the campsite are signposted on the 346 road. GPS: N49:47.097 E06:09.92

Charges 2006

Per unit incl. 2 persons and 2A electricity	€ 18,00 - € 36,00
extra adult	€ 4,40
child (under 18 yrs)	€ 3,85
dog	€ 2,75
electricity (16A) plus	€ 3,50

No credit cards.

LU7640 Camping Auf Kengert

L-7633 Larochette / Medernach

Tel: 837186. Email: info@kengert.lu

A friendly welcome awaits you at this peacefully situated, family run site, 2 km. from Larochette, which is 24 km. northeast of Luxembourg city, providing 180 individual pitches, all with electricity (4/16A). Some in a very shaded woodland setting, on a slight slope with fairly narrow access roads. There are also six hardened pitches for motorcaravans on a flat area of grass, complete with motorcaravan service facilities (space really only suitable for four motorhomes). Further pitches are in an adjacent and more open meadow area. There are also six site owned chalets and caravans. This site is popular in season, so early arrival is advisable, or you can reserve.

Facilities

The well maintained sanitary block in two parts includes a modern, heated unit with some washbasins in cubicles, and excellent, fully equipped cubicles for disabled visitors. The showers, facilities for babies, additional WCs and washbasins, plus laundry room are located below the central building which houses the shop, bar and restaurant. Motorcaravan services. Gas supplies. New indoor and outdoor play areas. Solar heated swimming pool (Easter - 30 Sept). Paddling pool. Open area for ball games. Off site: Bicycle hire. Golf, fishing and riding 8 km.

Open: 1 March - 8 November.

Directions

From Larochette take the CR118/N8 (towards Mersch) and just outside town turn right on the CR119 towards Schrondweiler, site is 2 km. on right. GPS: N49:47.995 E06:11.89

Charges 2007

Per person	€ 11,00 - € 14,00
child (4-18 yrs)	€ 5,00 - € 7,00
electricity	€ 2,00
dog	€ 1,25

20% reduction for students, walkers and cyclists. No credit cards.

LU7650 Camping de la Sûre

23 route de la Sûre, L-9390 Reisdorf

Tel: 836 246. Email: ren2@pt.lu

Camping de la Sûre is on the banks of the river that separates Luxembourg and Germany. It is a pleasant site close to Reisdorf with 180 numbered pitches (120 with 10A electricity). These are not separated but are marked with trees that provide some shade. There are caravan holiday homes in a fenced area towards the back of the site, leaving the prime pitches for touring units. Ongoing redevelopment is almost complete with new roads and a new toilet block should now be ready.

Facilities

Modern, clean sanitary facilities recently refitted and extended, including some washbasins in cubicles. New block planned. Laundry. Small shop. Café/bar. Takeaway. Playground. Minigolf. Sports field. Canoeing. Fishing. Off site: Town centre within easy walking distance. Cycle ways abound. Bicycle hire 200 m. Golf 8 km.

Open: 1 April - 30 October.

Directions

From the river bridge in Reisdorf, take the road to Echternach, de la Sûre is the second campsite on the left. GPS: N49:52.202 E06:16.05

Charges guide

Per person	€ 5,00
pitch	€ 5,50
electricity	€ 2,50

25% reduction in low season. No credit cards.

LU7660 Camping Kockelscheuer

22 route de Bettembourg, L-1899 Kockelscheuer
Tel: **471 815**. Email: **caravani@pt.lu**

Camping Kockelscheuer is 4 km. from the centre of Luxembourg city and quietly situated (although there can be some aircraft noise at times). On a slight slope, there are 161 individual pitches of good size, either on flat ground at the bottom or on wide flat terraces with easy access, all with electricity (16A). There is also a special area for tents. For children there is a large area with modern play equipment on safety tiles and next door to the site is a sports centre. Charges are reasonable. There is a friendly welcome, although little English is spoken.

Facilities

Two fully equipped, identical sanitary buildings, both very clean at time of visit. Washing machines. Motorcaravan services. Shop. (order bread the previous day). Snack bar. Restaurant in adjacent sports centre also with minigolf, tennis, squash, etc. No entry or exit for vehicles (reception closed) from 12.00-14.00 hrs. Off site: Bus 200 m. every 15 minutes to Luxembourg. Swimming pool 5 km.

Open: Easter - 31 October.

Directions

Site is SSW of Luxembourg city on the N13 to Bettembourg. Note: road is also known locally as the 186. From the south, exit A4 at junction signed Kockelscheuer onto N4. In 2 km. turn right (signed Kockelscheuer and campsite) and continue to follow the signs. GPS: N49:34.308 E06:06.54

Charges 2007

Per person	€ 3,75
child (3-14 yrs)	€ 2,00
pitch	€ 4,50
electricity (1 or 2 days)	€ 2,20

No credit cards.

LU7670 Camping des Ardennes

10, op der Héi, L-9809 Hosingen
Tel: **921 911**

A good value, small municipal site, Camping Ardennes is located on the edge of this attractive small town with an easy level walk to all amenities and parks and some floral arrangements to admire during the summer season. The 48 touring pitches are level, open and grassy. All have electricity (10A) and are arranged on either side of surfaced roads, with a few trees providing a little shade in places. This site is useful as a stopover if travelling along the N7.

Facilities

The single well appointed, modern, clean sanitary block can be heated in winter and includes separate men's and women's facilities. Facilities for dishwashing and laundry, with a washing machine, dryer and clothes lines. Café/bar (opening variable). Barbecue. Playground. Volleyball. Boule. Skis and winter sports equipment for hire. English spoken. Rooms for rent (B&B).

Open: All year.

Directions

Hosingen is on the N7 21 km. north of Diekirch. The site and sports complex are signed in the village. 20 m. after leaving the main road turn right. Site is 100 m. on the left. GPS: N50:00.463 E06:05.41

Charges guide

Per person	€ 4,50
child (3-12 yrs)	€ 2,25
pitch	€ 4,50
electricity	€ 2,25

LU7770 Camping Val d'Or

Llm Gaettchen 2, L-9747 Enscherange
Tel: 920 691. Email: **valdor@pt.lu**

Camping Val d'Or is one of those small family-run countryside sites where you easily find yourself staying longer that planned. Set on lush meadowland under a scattering of trees, the site is divided into two by the tree lined Clerve river as it winds its way slowly through the site. Two footbridges go some way to joining the site together and there are two entrances for vehicles. Children have three playgrounds, two conventional and the third, beside the river, a water playground with pump, various waterways, waterwheel and a small pool. The site's Dutch owners speak good English and Fred van Donk is active in the Luxemburg tourist industry. He is well able to give advice about this interesting, attractive and to most people unknown region of Europe which is within easy reach of the channel ports and Holland. There are 76 level grass touring pitches, all with electricity (4A). and with some tree shade. There are open views of the surrounding countryside with its wooded hills. The friendly bar is a popular meeting point. The site participates in the 'Wanderhütten' scheme providing wooded huts for rent to hikers. A local railway passes the site but it is not obtrusive and there are no night passenger services.

Facilities

Next to the reception is a heated sanitary block where some facilities are found, others including some showers are located, under cover, outside. Showers are token operated, washbasins open style. Dishwashing sinks. Laundry room with washing machine and dryer. Gas supplies. Bar. Swimming or paddling in river. Three play areas. Bicycle hire. Off site: Fishing and golf 10 km.

Open: All year.

Directions

Leave A26/E25 (Liège - Luxembourg) at exit 54 to Bastogne. From Bastogne take N84/N15 towards Diekirk for 15 km. At crossroads turn left (northeast) towards Wiltz (Clervaux). Pass though Wiltz. On entering Weldingen 500 m. after VW garage on the right; turn right on Wilderwiltz road. In Wilderwiltz follow signs for small village of Enscherange where site is signed. GPS: N50:00.012 E05:59.45

Charges 2006

Per person	€ 5,00
child (0-15 yrs)	€ 2,00
pitch incl. electricity (4A)	€ 9,00

No credit cards.

LU7780 Camping Woltzdal

Maison 12, L-9974 Maulusmühle
Tel: 998 938. Email: **info@woltzdal-camping.lu**

Set by a stream in a valley, Camping Wolzdal is one of the many delightful sites in the Ardennes, a region of wooded hills and river valleys that crosses the borders of Belgium, France and Luxembourg. This slightly sloping site has 85 touring pitches, set on grass amongst fir trees; all with 4A electricity. They are fairly open and have views of the surrounding wooded hills. A railway track passes the site on the far side of the stream, but there are only trains during the day and they are not disturbing. This is truly a family-run site where during the evenings in the small, friendly bar/restaurant, one brother cooks, the other serves the guests while their father runs the bar. In the surrounding hills there are kilometres of marked paths and mountain bike tracks for those wishing to enjoy the natural environment. For city life, a family ticket from the railway station close to the site is an economic and convenient way of visiting Luxembourg City with its museums, exhibitions and many other attractions. In the end this is a site of woods, water and wildlife.

Facilities

The heated sanitary block contains the usual facilities; showers are coin operated, washbasins open. Baby room. Laundry room. Reception and small shop are in the large house at the entrance where there is also a bar and a restaurant/snack bar. Children's library/activity room. Play area. Mountain bike hire. Entertainment programme for children in high season. Small hikers' chalets to rent. Off site: Fishing and golf 6 km. Riding 20 km.

Open: 8 April - 28 October.

Directions

Site is 6 km. north of Clervaux on the CR335 road. Leave Clervaux in the direction of Troisvierge and site is signed in the 12 house village of Maulusmühle. GPS: N50:05.477 E06:01.67

Charges 2006

Per person	€ 5,80
child (4-12 yrs)	€ 2,90
pitch	€ 5,20
electricity (4A)	€ 1,70

No credit cards.

LU7680 Camping Kohnenhof

Maison 1, L-9838 Obereisenbach
Tel: **929 464**. Email: **kohnenho@pt.lu**

Nestling in a valley with the River Our running through it, Camping Kohnenhof offers a very agreeable location for a relaxing family holiday. From the minute you stop at the reception you are assured of a warm and friendly welcome. Numerous paths cross through the wooded hillside so this could be a haven for walkers. A little wooden ferry crosses the small river across the border to Germany. The river is shallow and safe for children to play in (parental supervision essential). A large sports field and play area with a selection of equipment caters for younger campers. During the high season, an entertainment programme is organised for parents and children. The owner organises special golf weeks with games on different courses (contact the site for details). The restaurant is part of an old farmhouse and, with its open fire to keep it warm, offers a wonderful ambience to enjoy a meal.

Facilities	Directions
Heated sanitary block with showers and washbasins in cabins. Motorcaravan service point. Laundry. Bar, restaurant, takeaway. Games and TV room. Baker calls daily. Sports field with play equipment. Boules court. Bicycle hire. Golf weeks. Discounts on four local 18 hole golf courses. WiFi. Off site: Bus to Clervaux and Vianden stops (4 times daily) outside site entrance. Riding 5 km. Castle at Vianden 14 km. Monastery at Clervaux 14 km. Golf 15 km. **Open:** 25 March - 30 October.	Take N7 north from Diekirch. At Hosingen, turn right onto the narrow and winding CR324 signed Eisenbach. Follow campsite signs from Eisenbach or Obereisenbach. GPS: N50:00.961 E06:08.16

Charges 2006	
Per person	€ 5,50
child (under 12 yrs)	€ 3,00
pitch	€ 11,00
electricity	€ 2,80
dog	€ 2,80

Less 25% outside school holidays.
Camping Cheques accepted.

LU7850 Camping Fuussekaul

4 Fuussekaul, L-9156 Heiderscheid
Tel: **26 88 881**. Email: **info@fuussekaul.lu**

Children who visit Fuusse Kaul (the name means fox hole) won't want to leave as there is so much for them to do. Apart from a fun pool, exciting play areas, and an entertainment programme, children and parents can bake their own pizzas in the open-air oven. Of the 289 pitches, 196 of varying sizes are for touring units, all with a 10A electricity connection. The touring area (separate from the chalets and seasonal pitches) is well endowed with modern facilities, although there is no provision for visitors with disabilities. An entertainment programme continues throughout the main holiday season and includes mini shows and theatre productions, and sports. On the opposite side of the road (pedestrian access via a passage under the road) is a service and parking area for six motorcaravans. Each pitch has a hook-up, fresh water tap and waste water disposal point. There is also a drive-over service point for those not wishing to stay the night.

Facilities

Four excellent sanitary blocks provide showers (by token), washbasins (in cabins and communal) and children and baby rooms with small toilets, washbasins and showers. Laundry. Suite with sauna and sun beds etc. Beauty salon. Well-stocked shop, bar, restaurant and takeaway. Swimming pools, playgrounds, cross country skiing when snow permits. Bicycle hire. Children's club. Bowling. Off site: Bus stops outside site entrance. Riding 500 m. Fishing 3 km. Ettelbruckk 7 km.

Open: All year.

Directions

Take N15 from Diekirch to Heiderscheid. Site is on left at top of hill just before reaching the village. Motorhome service area is signed on the right. GPS: N49:52.650 E05:59.57

Charges 2006

Per unit incl. 2 persons	€ 11,50 - € 23,00
extra person	€ 2,50
electricity	€ 2,00
dog	€ 2,00

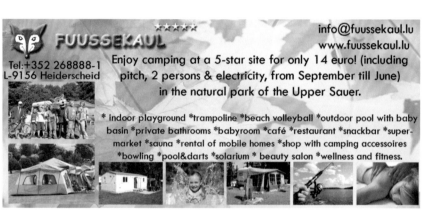

LU7700 Camping Gaalgebierg

Boite Postale 20, L-4001 Esch-sur-Alzette
Tel: **541 069**. Email: **gaalcamp@pt.lu**

Occupying an elevated position on the edge of town, near the French border, this pleasant good quality site is run by the local camping and caravan club. Although surrounded by hills and with a good variety of trees, not all pitches have shade. There are 150 pitches (100 for tourists) 100 sq.m., most on grass, marked out by trees, some on a slight slope. There is a gravel area set aside for one night stays, plus four all-weather pitches for motorcaravans although these are used mostly in the winter. All pitches have 16A electricity and TV points. The site operates its own minibus for visits to Luxembourg city and other excursions (free to campers) and also provides the Luxembourg card.

Facilities

The modern, well equipped toilet blocks can be heated and include some washbasins in cubicles, hot showers on payment and excellent facilities for disabled people and babies. Laundry. These facilities have a key-card entry system. Motorcaravan service point. Gas available. Shop for basics. Small bar and takeaway on demand. TV room. Excellent playground. Boules. Entertainment and activities programme in high season. Off site: Restaurant within walking distance. Swimming pool and tennis nearby.

Open: All year.

Directions

Site is well signed from centre of Esch, but a sharp look out is needed as there are two acute right hand bends on the approach to the site. GPS: N49:29.095 E05:59.194

Charges guide

Per person	€ 3,75
child (3-12 yrs)	€ 1,75
pitch incl. electricity (16A)	€ 7,60
No credit cards.	

LU7870 Camping de la Sûre

Route de Gilsdorf, L-9234 Diekirch

Tel: 80 94 25. Email: **tourisme@diekirch.lu**

The municipal Camping de la Sûre is within walking distance of the centre of Diekirch, a town that is brimming with things to see and do. Located on the banks of the Sûre, this site offers 196 flat grass pitches, most with a 16A electricity connection. One large building close to the entrance houses the reception and sanitary facilities, all of which were in pristine condition at the time of our visit. A path for walking and cycling runs alongside the campsite; maps are available in the Syndicat d'Initiative in the town centre. Diekirch, with a donkey as its mascot, is a happy town and well worth a visit.

Facilities

New reception building with bar and attached heated modern facilities including showers and communal washbasins. Baby room and suite for visitors with disabilities. Laundry. Play area. Children's entertainment during July and August. Off site: Diekirch has all leisure facilities within walking distance of the site. Large park adjacent. Walk/cycle path along site boundary.

Open: 1 April - 1 October.

Directions

Follow signs (only official camping signs, not site name) from centre of Diekirch.
GPS: N49:52.002 E06:09.85

Charges 2006

Per person	€ 5,00
child (3-14 yrs)	€ 2,25
pitch incl. electricity	€ 7,00

LU7880 Camping Trois Frontières

Maison 1, L-9972 Lieler

Tel: 998 608. Email: **camp.3front@cmdnet.lu**

On a clear day, it is possible to see Belgium, Germany and Luxembourg from the campsite swimming pool, hence its name: Les Trois Frontières. Martin and Esther Van Aalst own and manage the site themselves and all visitors receive a personal welcome and immediately become part of a large happy family. Most of the facilities are close to the entrance, leaving the camping area quiet, except for the children's play area. The restaurant/takeaway provides good quality food at reasonable prices, served either inside or on the pleasant terrace with flower borders and overlooking the pool.

Facilities

Unisex facilities include excellent showers, washbasins in cabins, British-style WCs, suite for visitors with disabilities, plus baby bath and changing station. More WCs in second building (down some steps). Laundry. Swimming pool now covered and heated (open 1/4-31/10). Play area. Boules. Games room. Bicycle hire. Off site: Shops 2.3 km. Golf and riding 12 km. Clervaux 12 km.

Open: All year.

Directions

Take N7 northward from Diekirch. 3 km. south of Weiswampach turn right onto CR338 to Lieler (campsite is signed here). Site is on right as you enter the village. GPS: N50:07.404 E06:06.31

Charges 2006

Per pitch incl. 2 persons	€ 15,30 - € 19,90
extra person	€ 6,20 - € 6,70
electricity (4A)	€ 2,50

LU7890 Camping Haute Sûre

34 rue J. de Busleyden, L-9639 Boulaide

Tel: 993 061. Email: **info@campinghautesure.com**

Located in a small village in a fairly remote area of the Grand Duchy, this site is very peaceful with some outstanding views over the Sûre valley. There are 87 pitches, 12 used by a Dutch tour operator tents, and two chalets for rent. The 73 large pitches for tourists are on well kept grass, generally with a slight slope, all have electricity hook-ups (6A) with a water tap serving four pitches. The reception complex contains a very well stocked shop and at the far end of the building is a bar and restaurant, with a takeaway service. The emphasis at Haute Sûre is very much geared towards families, especially those with younger children.

Facilities

A modern building with under floor heating and a central foyer provides good facilities including spacious showers (a water saving feature means that the pre-set showers are timed, giving 5 minutes use, then 5 minutes down time before being available for re-use). Children's washbasins. Separate unisex baby room. Excellent suite for disabled campers. Laundry. Shop, restaurant, bar and takeaway (all 15/4-15/9). Swimming pool (15/4-15/9). Adventure playground. Children's entertainment. Off site: Fishing 3 km. Golf 30 km. Riding in village.

Open: 15 April - 15 September.

Directions

Boulaide is about 15 km. northeast of Martelange on the Belgium/Luxembourg border. From Bastogne take N4 south for 22 km. to Martelange. From Martelange take N23 east and after about 4 km. turn north on minor road CR309, through Bigonville to Boulaide. Site is towards the northern end of village. GPS: N49:53.362 E05:48.899

Charges 2006

Per unit incl. 2 persons	€ 25,00
incl. 3 persons	€ 27,50

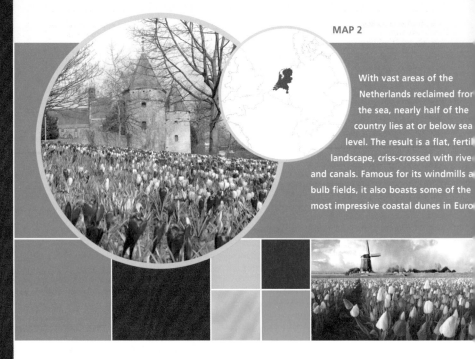

MAP 2

With vast areas of the Netherlands reclaimed fro[m] the sea, nearly half of the country lies at or below sea level. The result is a flat, fertil[e] landscape, criss-crossed with rive[rs] and canals. Famous for its windmills a[nd] bulb fields, it also boasts some of the most impressive coastal dunes in Euro[pe]

CAPITAL: AMSTERDAM

Tourist Office

Netherlands Board of Tourism
15-19 Kingsway, 7th Floor, Imperial House
London WC2B 6UN Tel: 020 7539 7950
Fax: 020 7539 7953
Email: information@nbt.org.uk
Internet: www.holland.com/uk

There is more to the Netherlands than Amsterdam and the bulb fields. Granted, both are top attractions and no visitor should miss the city of Amsterdam with its delight of bridges, canals, museums and listed buildings or miss seeing the spring-time riot of colour that adorns the fields and gardens of South Holland. This is a country with a variety of holiday venues ranging from lively seaside resorts to picturesque villages, idyllic old fishing ports and areas where nature rules. The Vecht valley is an area of natural beauty which centres around the town of Ommen. Giethoorn is justly dubbed the 'Venice of the North'. The Alblasserwaard polder offers time to discover the famed windmills of Kinderdijk, cheese farms and a stork village. The islands of Zeeland are joined by amazing feats of engineering, particularly the Oosterschelde storm surge barrier. Island hopping introduces lovely old towns such as Middelburg, the provincial capital Zierikzee with its old harbour or the quaint old town of Veere.

Population

15.9 million

Climate

Temperature with mild winters and warm summers.

Language

Dutch. English is very widely spoken, so is German and to some extent French. In Friesland a Germanic language, Frisian is spoken.

Telephone

The country code is 00 31.

Money

Currency: The Euro
Banks: Mon-Fri 09.00-16.00/1700.

Shops

Mon-Fri 09.00/09.30-17.30/18.00.
Sat to 16.00/17.00. Later closing hours in larger cities.

Public Holidays

New Year; April Fools Day 1 April; Good Fri; Easter Mon; Queen's Birthday 30 April; Labour Day; Remembrance Day 4 May; Liberation Day 5 May; Ascension; Whit Mon; SinterKlaas 5 Dec; Kingdom Day 15 Dec; Christmas 25, 26 Dec.

Motoring

There is a comprehensive motorway system but, due to the high density of population, all main roads can become very busy, particularly in the morning and evening rush hours. There are many bridges which can cause congestion. There are no toll roads but there are a few toll bridges and tunnels notably the Zeeland Bridge, Europe's longest across the Oosterschelde.

NL5500 Vakantiepark Pannenschuur

Zeedijk 19, NL-4504 PP Nieuwvliet (Zeeland)
Tel: 0117 37 23 00. Email: info@pannenschuur.nl

This is one of several coastal sites on the narrow strip of the Netherlands between the Belgian frontier near Knokke and the Breskens ferry. Quickly reached from the ports of Ostend, Zeebrugge and Vlissingen, it is useful for overnight stops or for a few days to enjoy the seaside. A short walk across the quiet coast road and steps over the dike bring you to the open, sandy beach. Quite a large site, most of the 595 pitches are taken by permanent or seasonal holiday caravans but there are also 165 pitches for tourists mostly in their own areas. Mostly in bays of six or eight units surrounded by hedges, all have electricity (6A) and 100 also have water, drainage and cable connections. Cars are not parked by units but in separate parking areas. A star attraction is the recently updated complex that provides a super indoor heated pool with baby and children's sections, jacuzzi, sauna, Turkish bath and solarium. It also includes a full restaurant and bar, a shop and the reception, plus for children, a special restaurant (Pedro's Piratenship) and an entertainment room. Overall, this is a very good site.

Facilities

Five toilet blocks including two new, heated buildings, provide first class facilities including children's washrooms, baby rooms and some private cabins. Hot water is free (using a key - deposit € 11). Launderette. Motorcaravan services. Supermarket. Restaurant, snack bar and takeaway. Swimming pool, sauna and solarium. All these amenities are closed 14/1-31/1. Large games room. Internet access. Playground and play field. Bicycle hire. Organised activities in season. Off site: Fishing 500 m. Riding 2 km. Golf 5 km.

Open: All year (all amenities closed 14/1-31/1).

Directions

At Nieuwvliet, on the Breskens - Sluis minor road, 8 km. southwest of Breskens, turn towards the sea at sign for Nieuwvliet-Bad and follow signs to site GPS: N51:23.013 E03:26.431

Charges 2006

Per unit (max. 5 persons)	
incl. electricity	€ 20,00 - € 39,00
extra person	€ 4,00

Rates available for weekly stays.

NL6925 Camping Weltevreden

Melsesweg, NL-4374 NG Zouteland (Zeeland)

Tel: **0118 561 321**. Email: **info@campingweltevreden.nl**

Camping Weltevreden is on Zeeland's 'Riviera', the area of the Dutch coast with the highest recorded annual hours of sunshine. It is a family site with a pleasant ambiance, located just behind the high, grassy dunes between Zoutelande and Westkapelle. This attractively landscaped site is only 100 m. from the sandy North Sea beaches. There are 144 pitches (50 for tourers) on well kept, grassy lawns, connected by narrow tarmac roads. Separated by a variety of low bushes and shrubs, all the touring pitches have 6A electricity, water and drainage.

Facilities

One central, modern toilet block with British style toilets, washbasins (open and in cabins), free hot showers, baby room and special children's section. Laundry with washing machines, dryer, spin dryer, iron and board. Well stocked shop. Boules. Small play area. Dogs are not accepted. English is spoken. Off site: Fishing 100 m. Riding 3 km. Golf 6 km. Bicycle hire 1 km. Beach 100 m.

Open: April - October.

Directions

From Zoutelande, follow the coastal road towards Westkapelle. Site is on the left just outside Zoutelande. GPS: N51:30.545 E03:25.046

Charges guide

Per unit incl. 2 persons	€ 12,50
incl. electricity	€ 19,00 - € 29,00
extra person	€ 5,00
child (0-5 yrs)	€ 2,75

NL6930 Camping Schoneveld

Schoneveld 1, NL-4511 HR Breskens (Zeeland)

Tel: **0117 38 32 20**. Email: **schoneveld@zeelandnet.nl**

This site is well situated within walking distance of Breskens and it has direct access to sand dunes. It has around 200 touring pitches and has many static vans, but these are kept apart. The touring pitches are behind reception, laid out in fields which are entered from long avenues that run through the site. There are also twelve car parking bays. One ultra modern and very clean toilet block serves this area of the site. The complex at the site entrance houses reception, a restaurant and a recreation room. Also near the entrance are the indoor pool, tennis courts and a football field.

Facilities

One large sanitary block provides showers, wash cubicles, child size toilets and washbasins, baby room, en-suite unit for disabled visitors. Motorcaravan service point. Restaurant. 'Fun Food Plaza' and takeaway (5/4-31/10). Bowling. Indoor pool. Tennis. Play area. Organised entertainment in July/Aug. Bicycle hire. WiFi internet access. Off site: Fishing 200 m. Golf or riding 10 km.

Open: All year.

Directions

From Breskens port follow N58 south for about 1 km. and turn right at camping sign. Site is 500 m. GPS: N51:24.064 E03:32.085

Charges 2006

Per unit incl. 2 persons	€ 31,00
incl. 3 persons	€ 35,50
incl. 5 persons	€ 39,50
tent pitch incl. 1 or 2 persons	€ 16,00

Weekly tariff and various discounts available. Camping Cheques accepted.

NL5510 Camping Groede

Zeeweg 1, NL-4503 PA Groede (Zeeland)

Tel: **0117 37 13 84**. Email: **info@campinggroede.nl**

Camping Groede is a friendly, fair-sized site by the same stretch of sandy beach as no. NL5500. Family run, it aims to cater for the individual needs of visitors and to provide a good all-round holiday. Campers are sited as far as possible according to taste – in family areas, in larger groups or on more private pitches for those who prefer peace and quiet. In total, there are 500 pitches for tourists (plus 380 seasonal units), all with electrical connections (4-10A) and 300 with water and drainage connections. A field has been added with 63 fully serviced large pitches.

Facilities

Toilet facilities are excellent with a high standard of cleanliness, including some wash cabins, baby baths, family room and a dedicated unit for disabled persons. Motorcaravan services. Gas supplies. Shop, restaurant and snack bar (all weekends only in low seasons). Recreation room. Internet access. Sports area. Several play areas (bark base). Football, volleyball, basketball, boules, table tennis. Plenty of activities for children in peak season. Bicycle hire. Fishing. Off site: Riding 1 km. Golf 11 km

Open: 24 March - 31 December.

Directions

From Breskens take the coast road for 5 km. to site. Alternatively, the site is signed from Groede village on the more inland Breskens - Sluis road. GPS: N51:23.749 E03:29.263

Charges guide

Per pitch incl. 2 persons	€ 17,00 - € 24,00
with 4A electricity	€ 19,00 - € 26,00
with water and drainage	€ 23,00 - € 30,00
extra person	€ 2,50

No credit cards.

NL5570 Camping de Molenhoek

Molenweg 69a, NL-4493 NC Kamperland (Zeeland)
Tel: **0113 37 12 02**. Email: **molenhoek@zeelandnet.nl**

This family-run site makes a pleasant contrast to the livelier coastal sites in this popular holiday area. It is rurally situated 3 km. from the Veerse Meer which is very popular for all sorts of watersports. Catering both for 300 permanent or seasonal holiday caravans and for 100 touring units, it is neat, tidy and relatively spacious. The marked touring pitches are divided into small groups with surrounding hedges and trees giving privacy and some shade, and electrical connections are available. A large outdoor swimming pool is Molenhoek's latest attraction. Entertainment is organised in season (dance evenings, bingo, etc.) as well as a disco for youngsters. Although the site is quietly situated, there are many excursion possibilities in the area including the towns of Middelburg, Veere and Goes and the Delta Expo exhibition.

Facilities

Sanitary facilities in one fully refurbished and one newer block, include some washbasins in cabins, dishwashing and laundry sinks. Toilet and shower facilities for disabled visitors and provision for babies. Motorcaravan services. Small shop. Simple bar/restaurant with terrace and TV room. Restaurant/bar. Swimming pool (15/5-15/9). Playground. Bicycle hire. Off site: Tennis and watersports close. Riding 1 km. Fishing 2.5 km.

Open: 1 April - 28 October.

Directions

Site is west of the village of Kamperland on the 'island' of Noord Beveland. From the N256 Goes to Zierikzee road, exit west onto the N255 Kamperland road. Site is signed south of this road. GPS: N51:34.704 E03:41.785

Charges 2006

Per unit incl. 2 or 3 persons and electricity	€ 20,10 - € 34,50
extra person	€ 3,75 - € 4,50

No credit cards.

★★★★ **Familiecamping de Molenhoek**

✓ **4-stars familiecampsite – 9,5 hectare large**
✓ **Annual-, seasonal- and touring piches**
✓ **Well maintained toilet blocks**
✓ Facilities for disabled – baby room
✓ Heated open air swimming pool
✓ Paddling pool for children
✓ Bar, restaurant and takeaway
✓ Caravans for rent
✓ First class animation in high season
✓ Dogs have a warm welcome!

info or direct booking 0113 371202 – e-mail: molenhoek@zeelandnet.nl – www.demolenhoek.com

NL5580 Camping de Veerhoeve

Veerweg 48, NL-4471 NC Wolphaartsdijk (Zeeland)
Tel: **0113 58 11 55**. Email: **deveerhoeve@zeelandnet.nl**

This is a family-run site near the shores of the Veerse Meer which is ideal for family holidays. It is situated in a popular area for watersports and is well suited for sailing, windsurfing or fishing enthusiasts, with boat launching 1 km. away. As with most sites in this area there are many mature static and seasonal pitches. However, part of the friendly, relaxed site is reserved for touring units with 60 marked pitches on grassy ground, all with electrical connections. A member of the Holland Tulip Parcs group.

Facilities

Sanitary facilities in three blocks have been well modernised with full tiling. Hot showers are on payment. Laundry facilities including ironing. Motorcaravan services. Supermarket (all season). Restaurant and snack bar (July/Aug. otherwise at weekends). TV room. Tennis. Playground and play field. Games room. Bicycle hire. Fishing. Accommodation for groups. Max. 1 dog per pitch. Off site: Riding 2 km. Golf 7 km.

Open: 3 April - 30 October.

Directions

From N256 Goes-Zierikzee road take Wolphaartsdijk exit. Follow through village and signs to site. GPS: N51:32.807 E03:48.807

Charges 2006

Per pitch incl. up to 4 persons	€ 20,50 - € 24,00
with services	€ 22,00 - € 26,50
extra person	€ 4,00

Camping Cheques accepted.

NL6920 Camping Veerse Meer

Veerweg 71, NL-4471 NB Wolphaartsdijk (Zeeland)
Tel: **0113 581423**. Email: **info@campingveersemeer.nl**

This well cared for family-run site is situated beside the Veerse Meer on the island of Noord Beveland in Zeeland. Not only is its location idyllic for watersports enthusiasts, it is also an excellent and picturesque setting for cyclists and walkers. Emphasis at this site is on a neat and tidy appearance, quality facilities and a friendly reception. The site spreads over both sides of the road. The area to the right provides 15 pitches with individual sanitary facilities (some seasonal), fully serviced hardstanding pitches for motorcaravans and a tent field at the far end. The original part of the site is where you will find reception, a bar and the main toilet block (recently renovated to provide water heated by solar panels). There are 40 generous touring pitches in this area, many fully serviced and separated by hedging. Further seasonal and static places are kept apart. A feature of this campsite is a narrow canal crossed by a bridge.

Facilities

The single updated toilet block has showers (token operated), open style wash areas, two wash cabins, child size WC and a baby bath. Dishwashing sinks. Laundry. Motorcaravan service point. Bar. Play area. Organised events for all age groups in high season. Bicycle hire. Fishing.

Open: 1 April - 31 October.

Directions

From N256 Goes-Zierikzee road take Wolphaartsdijk exit. Follow through village and signs to site.
GPS: N51:32.662 E03:48.769

Charges 2006

Per unit incl. 1 or 2 persons	€ 14,00 - € 18,00
incl. private sanitary facility	€ 23,00 - € 28,50
extra person	€ 2,50 - € 5,00

NL6915 Camping Linda

Oostelijke kanaalweg 4, NL-4424 NC Wemeldinge (Zeeland)
Tel: **0113 621259**. Email: **info@campinglinda.nl**

Camping Linda has been recommended by our Dutch agent. We plan to conduct a full inspection in 2007. The site lies within the Oosterschelde National Park and offers direct access to a small beach. Pitches are of a good size and are grassy. Most have electrical connections. Cycling and walking are very popular (including a windmill tour!) and the site organises a bicycle hire service. In the high season an entertainment and excursion programme is organised.

Facilities

Shop, snack bar. Motorcaravan service point. Play area. Games room. Bicycle hire. Sports field. Direct access to beach. Mobile homes and chalets for rent. Off site: Town of Kapelle 3 km. with indoor and outdoor swimming pools as well as a shopping centre. Various cycle and walking trails.

Open: 1 April - 1 October.

Directions

From the south, take A58 towards Vlissingen. Leave at exit 35 and head towards Kapelle on the N666, joining the N289. Pass Kapelle and continue towards Wemeldinge. Site is well signed.

Charges guide

Per unit with 2 persons	€ 16,50
extra person	€ 5,00
child (3-13 yrs)	€ 3,50
electricity	€ 3,00

NL5560 Camping de Wijde Blick

Lagezoom 23, NL-4325 CP Renesse (Zeeland)
Tel: 0111 46 88 88. Email: wijdeblick@ardoer.com

The Van Oost family run this neat campsite in a pleasant and personal way. It is located on the outskirts of the village of Renesse in a quiet rural spot. Much redevelopment took place in 2005 and De Wijde Blick now has a repositioned entrance. There are now 316 pitches of which 210 are for touring units which include 16 fully serviced pitches with private sanitary facilities and 10 attractively arranged motorcaravan pitches with hardstanding. All the touring pitches have 6/10A electricity and are 90-120 sq.m. in area. There are special 'bike & hike' pitches for those touring without a car. Those with cars must park away from the pitch areas. Children are welcomed by the campsite mascot, Billy Blick and will thoroughly enjoy the large new playground, the indoor activity room or an evening at the theatre wagon. The new toilet block is solar heated, with a special children's section and an interesting schedule of how the technology works. This is a real holiday area and there are restaurants and shops in the village (and a market on Wednesdays). The beach is 2 km. from the site.

Facilities

Three modern toilet blocks are first class, heated and with clean facilities including washbasins in cabins, controllable showers, facilities for disabled people. Bath (on payment). Laundry (with cartoons for children). Motorcaravan services. Shop. Restaurant/bar (16/3-31/10). Swimming pool (1/5-15/9). WiFi internet access. Good playground on sand. Bicycle hire. Activities for children. Dogs are not accepted. Off site: Tennis and minigolf. Riding and fishing 1.5 km. Golf 10 km. Beach 2 km.

Open: All year.

Directions

Renesse is on the island of Schouwen (connected to the mainland by a bridge and three dams). On the N57 from Middelburg take the Renesse exit. After 2 km follow road 106 to the left and then site signs. Site is on the east side of the village.
GPS: N51:43.106 E03:46.028

Charges 2007

Per unit incl. 2 persons	€ 12,50 - € 30,50
extra person	€ 3,50

CAMPING DE WIJDE BLICK - Lagezoom 23 - 4325 CP Renesse
T. +31 (0)111 468 888 - F +31 (0)111 468889 - E wijdeblick@ardoer.com - www.ardoer.com/wijdeblick

NL6950 Camping International Renesse

Scharendijkseweg 8, NL-4325 LD Renesse (Zeeland)
Tel: 0111 461391. Email: info@camping-international.net

Situated 300 metres from the beach at Renesse in Zeeland, this is a friendly, family run site. Its owners have set high standards, which is demonstrated by the immaculate and tastefully decorated sanitary facilities. There are 200 pitches, with 100 for touring units. These are a generous size and laid out in bays and avenues surrounded by hedging. Around a courtyard area beyond reception is a bar which is attractively decorated with novel figures and the owner's personal memorabilia. Outside bench seating and umbrellas turns this corner of the camping into a popular meeting place. Being close to one of Zeeland's excellent beaches makes this site an ideal choice for families.

Facilities

Two luxury sanitary blocks provide showers, washbasins (some in cabins) and a baby room. Dishwashing sinks (hot water on payment). Laundry room with washing machine, dryer and ironing board. Motorcaravan service point. Supermarket. Bar. Games room. Play area. Bicycle hire. Entertainment in high season for children and adults.

Open: 1 March - 31 October.

Directions

From Zierikzee follow N59 to Renesse for 15 km. and turn right at roundabout (before town) onto local road signed R101. Continue for 1 km. and turn left, then first right to site on right.

Charges 2006

Per unit incl. 2 persons	€ 21,00
extra person	€ 4,50
child (2-9 yrs)	€ 4,00
electricity	€ 2,50

NL5630 Camping Koningshof

Elsgeesterweg 8, NL-2231 NW Rijnsburg (Zuid-Holland)

Tel: 0714 02 60 51. Email: info@koningshofholland.nl

This popular site is run in a personal and friendly way. The 200 pitches for touring units are laid out in groups of four or twelve, divided by hedges and trees and all with 10A electrical connections. Cars are mostly parked in areas around the perimeter and 100 static caravans, confined to one section of the site, are entirely unobtrusive. Reception, a pleasant good quality restaurant, bar and a snack bar are grouped around a courtyard style entrance which is decorated with seasonal flowers. The site has a small outdoor, heated pool (13.5 x 7 m), with a separate paddling pool and imaginative children's play equipment. Recent additions are a recreation hall, an indoor swimming pool and a unique children's play pool with water streams, locks and play materials. The site has a number of regular British visitors from club connections who receive a friendly welcome, with English spoken. Used by tour operators (25 pitches). A very useful local information booklet (in English) is provided for visitors. A member of the Holland Tulip Parcs group.

Facilities

Three good toilet blocks, two with under-floor heating, include washbasins in cabins and provision for disabled visitors. Laundry room with washing machines and dryers. Motorcaravan services. Gas supplies. Shop (1/4-15/10). Bar (1/4-1/11). Restaurant (1/4-10/9). Snacks and takeaway (1/4-1/11). Small outdoor pool (unsupervised; 15/5-15/9). Indoor pool complex (15/3-15/11). Solarium. Adventure playground and sports area. Tennis courts. Fishing pond (free). Bicycle hire. Entertainment in high season. Room for shows. One dog per pitch accepted in a limited area of the site. Off site: Riding or golf 5 km. Sandy beach 5 km. Den Haag 15 km. Amsterdam 30 km.

Open: All year.

Directions

From N44/A44 Den Haag - Amsterdam motorway, take exit 7 for Oegstgeest and Rijnsburg. Turn towards Rijnsburg and follow camp signs

Charges 2006

Per pitch incl. 2 persons	€ 20,00 - € 26,50
extra person (over 3 yrs)	€ 3,50
dog (see text)	€ 2,50
electricity (10A)	€ 3,50

Senior citizen discounts, group rates and special packages.
Camping Cheques accepted.

kawan-villages.com **tel: 00 333 59 59 03 59** ——— kawar

NL5600 Recreatiecentrum Delftse Hout

Korftlaan 5, NL-2616 LJ Delft (Zuid-Holland)
Tel: 0152 13 00 40. Email: info@delftsehout.nl

Pleasantly situated in Delft's park and forest area on the eastern edge of the city, this well run, modern site is part of the Koningshof group. It has 200 tourist pitches quite formally arranged in groups of 4 to 6 and surrounded by attractive young trees and hedges. All have sufficient space and electrical connections (10A). Modern buildings near the entrance house the site amenities. A good sized first floor restaurant serves snacks or full meals and has an outdoor terrace overlooking the swimming pool and pitches. Walking and cycling tours are organised and there is a recreation programme in high season. A special package deal can be arranged including tickets to local Royal attractions and a visit to the Royal Delftware factory.

Facilities

Modern, heated toilet facilities include a spacious family room. Laundry. Motorcaravan services. Shop for basic food and camping items (1/4-1/11). Restaurant and bar (1/4-1/10). Small outdoor swimming pool (15/5-15/9). Adventure playground. Recreation room. Bicycle hire. Gas supplies Off site: Fishing 1 km. Riding or golf 5 km. Regular bus service to Delft centre.

Open: All year.

Directions

Site is 1 km. east of Delft. From A13 motorway take Delft - Pijnacker (exit 9), turn towards Pijnacker and then right at first traffic lights, following camping signs through suburbs and park to site.

Charges 2006

Per unit incl. 2 persons	€ 20,00 - € 24,50
supplement for services	€ 7,00
extra person (3 yrs and older)	€ 2,00
electricity (10A)	€ 3,50

Camping Cheques accepted.

tel: 00 333 59 59 03 59 *kawan-villages.com*

NL5640 Vakantiecentrum Kijkduinpark

Machiel Vrijenhoeklaan 450, NL-2555 NW Den Haag (Zuid-Holland)
Tel: 0704 48 21 00. Email: info@kijkduinpark.nl

This is now an ultra-modern, all year round centre and family park, with many huts, villas and bungalows for rent and a large indoor swimming pool complex. The wooded touring area is immediately to the left of the entrance, with 450 pitches in shady glades of bark covered sand. There are simple pitches for tents, some pitches with electricity only and many with electricity 10A, water, waste water and cable TV connections. In a paved central area stands a supermarket, snack bar and restaurant. The main attraction here is the Meeresstrand, 500 m. from the site entrance.

Facilities

There are five modern sanitary blocks (key entry). Launderette. Snack bar. Shop. Restaurant. Supermarket (all year). Indoor pool. Bicycle hire. Special golfing breaks. Entertainment and activities organised in summer Off site: Fishing 500 m. Riding 5 km,

Open: All year.

Directions

Site is southwest of Den Haag on the coast and Kijkduin is signed as an area from around Den Haag.

Charges 2006

Per unit incl. 2 persons and electricity	€ 18,00 - € 40,00
extra person	€ 1,21

NL6970 Camping 't Weergors

Zuiddijk 2, NL-3221 LJ Hellevoetsluis (Zuid-Holland)
Tel: 0181 312430. Email: weergors@publishnet.nl

A rustic style site built around old farm buildings, t'Weergors has a comfortable mature feel. At the front of the site is a well presented farmhouse which houses reception and includes the main site services. Around the courtyard area is one of the two sanitary blocks which is unsophisticated, but clean and functional. There are plans to replace this with a new reception and shop and build a new toilet block elsewhere. There are currently 100 touring pitches (plus seasonal and static places), with another field at the back of the site under development to provide a further 70 or 80 touring places.

Facilities

Two sanitary blocks have showers (by token), washbasins, some in cabins, child size WCs and a baby bath. Laundry area. Motorcaravan service point. Small shop (Easter - 1/9). Restaurant and bar (all year). Snack bar (Easter - 1/9). Tennis. Recreation room/TV. Internet access. Play area. Paddling pool. Organised entertainment in high season. Fishing. Bicycle hire.

Open: Easter - 31 October.

Directions

From Rotterdam join A15 west to Rozenburg exit 12 and join N57 south for 11 km. Turn left on N497 (Hellevoetsluis) and follow signs for 4.5 km. Turn right to site (1.5 km). GPS: N51:49.766 E04:06.971

Charges 2006

Per person	€ 3,50
pitch incl. electricity (6A)	€ 9.70

Camping Cheques accepted.

NL6960 Recreatiepark De Klepperstee

Vrijheidsweg 1, NL-3253 ZG Ouddorp (Zuid-Holland)

Tel: 0187 681511. Email: info@klepperstee.com

De Klepperstee is a good quality, family site. It offers excellent recreation areas that are spread over the centre of the site giving it an attractive open parkland appearance which is enhanced by many shrubs, trees and grass areas. The variety of play equipment ensures hours of non-stop fun for children and there is a special evening 'house' for older children with a television, etc. The site itself is peacefully located in tranquil countryside amid renowned nature reserves and just outside the village of Ouddorp in Zuid Holland. The 338 spacious touring pitches are in named avenues, mostly separated by hedging and spread around the perimeter, together with the seasonal and static caravans. De Klepperstee would be ideal for a beach holiday.

Facilities

One main sanitary block and a number of WC/shower units around the touring area provide hot showers (on payment), washbasins, some in cabins (hot water only), baby bath and shower, child size toilets and a unit for people with disabilities. Laundry. Motorcaravan service point. Supermarket. Restaurant, bar and takeaway. Small paddling pool. Play areas. TV, pool and electronic games. Entertainment with special team in high season. Bicycle hire. No animals are accepted and no single sex groups.

Open: Easter - 31 October.

Directions

From Rotterdam follow A15 west to Rozenburg exit 12 and join N57 south for 22 km. Take exit for Ouddorp and follow signs for 'Stranden'. Site is on the left after about 3 km.
GPS: N51:48.961 E03:53.983

Charges 2006

Per unit incl. up to 4 persons	€ 27,50
incl. 6A electricity	€ 30,00
incl. 10A electricity	€ 32,50
extra person	€ 2,75

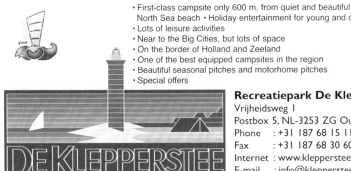

• First-class campsite only 600 m. from quiet and beautiful North Sea beach • Holiday entertainment for young and old
• Lots of leisure activities
• Near to the Big Cities, but lots of space
• On the border of Holland and Zeeland
• One of the best equipped campsites in the region
• Beautiful seasonal pitches and motorhome pitches
• Special offers

Recreatiepark De Klepperstee
Vrijheidsweg 1
Postbox 5, NL-3253 ZG Ouddorp
Phone : +31 187 68 15 11
Fax : +31 187 68 30 60
Internet : www.klepperstee.com
E-mail : info@klepperstee.com

NL5680 Camping Noordduinen

Campingweg 1, NL-2221 EW Katwijk (Zuid-Holland)

Tel: 0714 02 52 95. Email: info@noordduinen.nl

This is a large, well managed site surrounded by dunes and sheltered partly by trees and shrubbery, which also separate the various camping areas. The 200 touring pitches are marked and numbered but not divided. All have electricity (10A) and 45 are fully serviced with electricity, water, drainage and TV connection. There are also seasonal pitches and mobile homes for rent. The latter are placed mostly away from the touring areas and are unobtrusive. You are escorted to an allocated pitch and sited in a formal layout and cars are parked away from the pitches. Entertainment is organised in high season for various age groups. Bicycles can be hired nearby and worth a visit is Space Expo.

Facilities

The three sanitary blocks are modern and clean, with washbasins in cabins, a baby room and provision for people with disabilities. Hot water for showers and dishwashing is on payment. Laundry. Motorcaravan services. Supermarket with fresh bread daily. Restaurant/bar which doubles as a function room and a takeaway service. Games room. Play area. Only gas barbecues are permitted. No dogs are accepted.
Off site: Beach and Katwijk within walking distance.

Open: 31 March - 28 October.

Directions

Leave A44 at exit 8 (Leiden - Katwijk) to join N206 to Katwijk. Take Katwijk Noord exit and follow signs to site.

Charges guide

Per pitch	€ 22,00 - € 31,00
serviced pitch	€ 27,00 - € 34,00
electricity (10A)	€ 3,50

NL5620 Vakantiepark Duinrell

Duinrell 1, NL-2242 JP Wassenaar (Zuid-Holland)

Tel: 0705 15 52 57. Email: info@duinrell.nl

A very large site, Duinrell's name means 'well in the dunes' and the water theme is continued in the adjoining amusement park and in the extensive indoor pool complex. Entry to the popular pleasure park is free for campers – indeed the camping areas surround and open out from the park. The 'Tiki' tropical pool complex has many attractions which include slides ranging from quite exciting to terrifying (according to your age!), whirlpools, saunas and many other features. There are also free outdoor pools and the centre has its own bar and café. Entry to the Tiki complex is at a reduced rate for campers. Duinrell is open all year and a ski school (langlauf and Alpine) with 12 artificial runs, is a winter attraction. The campsite itself is very large with 1,150 tourist places on several flat grassy areas and it can become very busy in high season. As part of a continuing improvement programme, 950 marked pitches have electricity, water and drainage connections and some have cable TV. Amenities shared with the park include restaurants, a pizzeria and pancake house, supermarket and a theatre. There are now 425 smartly furnished bungalows to rent.

Facilities

Six toilet blocks, including two very good new ones, serve the tourist areas and can be heated in cool weather. Laundry facilities. Amusement park and Tiki tropical pool complex as detailed above. Restaurant, cafés, pizzeria and takeaways (weekends only in winter). Supermarket. Entertainment and theatre with shows in high season. 'Rope Challenge' trail and 'Forrest Frisbee' trail. Bicycle hire. Bowling. Artificial ski slopes and ski school (winter). All activities have extra charges.

Open: All year.

Directions

Site is signed from N44/A44 Den Haag-Amsterdam road, but from the south the turning is about 5 km. after passing sign for start of Wassenaar town – then follow camp signs.

Charges 2007

Per person (over 3 yrs)	€ 4,95 - € 9,50
pitch	€ 8,50

Special package offers.
Overnight stays between 17.00-10.00 hrs (when amusement park closed) less 25%.

NL5670 Gaasper Camping Amsterdam

Loosdrechtdreef 7, NL-1108 AZ Amsterdam (Noord-Holland)

Tel: 20 6967326

Amsterdam is probably the most popular destination for visits in the Netherlands, and Gaasper Camping is on the southeast side, a short walk from a Metro station with a direct 20 minute service to the centre. In high season the site becomes very crowded and it is necessary to arrive during the day to find space (in July/Aug. check-ins start at 11.00 hrs). The site is well kept and neatly laid out on flat grass with attractive trees and shrubs. There are 350 touring pitches in two main areas – one more open and grassy, mainly kept for tents, the other more formal with numbered pitches mainly divided by shallow ditches or good hedges. Areas of hardstanding are available and all caravan pitches have electrical connections (10A). There are 20 tent pitches with 10A connections. Some 60 seasonal and permanent units have their own area. Although this is a typical, busy city site, it is better than many and there is a friendly welcome, with good English spoken. The site is on the edge of a large park with nature areas and a lake (with sailing facilities and swimming beaches), so there are also opportunities for relaxation.

Facilities

Three modern, clean toilet blocks (one unisex) for the tourist sections are an adequate provision. Some washbasins in private cabins. Hot water for showers and some washing-up sinks on payment. Facilities for babies. Washing machine and dryer. Motorcaravan services. Gas supplies. Supermarket (1/4-15/10). Café/bar plus takeaway (1/4-15/10). Shopping centre and restaurant nearby. Play area on grass Off site: Riding 200 m. Fishing 1 km. Golf 4 km.

Open: 15 March - 1 November.

Directions

Take exit No.1 for Gaasperplas - Weesp (S113) from the section of A9 motorway which is on the east side of the A2. Note: do not take the Gaasperdam exit (S112) which comes first if approaching from the west. GPS: N52:18.776 E04:59.489

Charges 2006

Per person	€ 4,75
child (0-11 yrs)	€ 2,25
pitch incl. car	€ 8,50 - € 10,50
electricity (10A)	€ 3,50

No credit cards.

NL5660 Camping Het Amsterdamse Bos

Kleine Noorddijk 1, NL-1187 NZ Amstelveen (Noord-Holland)
Tel: 0206 41 68 68. Email: info@campingamsterdamsebos.com

Het Amsterdamse Bos is a very large park to the southwest of Amsterdam, one corner of which has been specifically laid out as the city's municipal site and is now under new ownership. Close to Schiphol Airport (we noticed little noise), it is about 12 km. from central Amsterdam. A high season bus service runs from the site during the day to the city (a local service at other times is 300 m). The site is well laid out alongside a canal, with unmarked pitches on separate flat lawns mostly backing onto pleasant hedges and trees, with several areas of hardstanding. It takes 400 tourist units, with 100 electrical connections (10A). An additional area is available for tents and groups.

Facilities

Two older style sanitary blocks rather let the site down, appearing somewhat small and well used. A third block is newer. Hot water is free to the washbasins but hot showers are on payment. Laundry facilities. Motorcaravan services. Gas supplies. Small shop. Cafe/bar and snack bar. Off site: Fishing, boating, pancake restaurant in the park. Riding and bicycle hire 5 km.

Open: All year.

Directions

Amsterdamse Bos and site are west of Amstelveen. From the A9 motorway take exit 6 and follow the N231 to site (2nd traffic light).
GPS: N52:17.614 E04:49.378

Charges 2006

Per person	€ 5,00
child (4-12 yrs)	€ 2,50
pitch incl. electricity	€ 10,00 - € 11,00

NL5700 Molengroet Recreatieverblijven

Molengroet 1, NL-1723 PX Noord-Scharwoude (Noord-Holland)
Tel: 0226 39 34 44. Email: info@molengroet.nl

Molengroet is a modern, pleasant site, close to a lake for watersports and 40 kilometres from Amsterdam. It is a useful stop on the way to the Afsluitdijk across the top of the Ijsselmeer or as an enjoyable stop for watersport enthusiasts. The 260 touring pitches are grouped according to services provided, ranging from simple pitches with no services, to those with electricity (4/10A), TV, water and waste water. There are 10 pitches with private sanitary facilities. The bar and restaurant are open all season and there is a snack bar in high season – order snacks from the restaurant. The nearby lake with surf school is an attractive proposition, particularly for those with teenagers. A site bus can take you to the local pool, the beach and Alkmaar with its famous cheese market. Friendly multi-lingual staff provide local information. A member of the Holland Tulip Parcs group.

Facilities

The best sanitary facilities, in a modern, heated building, are near the serviced pitches. Supplemented by two other blocks, all necessary facilities are provided. Motorcaravan services. Gas supplies. Shop (1/4-1/9), bread and milk from reception at other times. Restaurant/bar (1/4-1/9). Bouncy castle. Fishing. Bicycle hire. Surfboards and small boats for hire. Entertainment is organised in high season and at weekends in a large tent. Off site: Watersports close. Tennis, squash, sauna, and swimming nearby. Riding or golf 5 km.

Open: 1 April - 31 October.

Directions

From Haarlem on A9 to Alkmaar take N245 towards Schagen. Site is southwest of Noord Sharwoude on the N245, signed to west on road to Geestermerambacht GPS: N52:41.673 E04:46.262

Charges 2006

Per unit incl. 2 persons	€ 18,00 - € 25,00

Reductions in low season and for longer stays. Camping Cheques accepted.

NL5720 Camping Jachthaven Uitdam

Zeedijk 2, NL-1154 PP Uitdam (Noord-Holland)

Tel: 0204 03 14 33. Email: info@campinguitdam.nl

Situated beside the Markermeer which is used extensively for watersports, this large site has its own private yachting marina (300 yachts and boats). It has 200 seasonal and permanent pitches, many used by watersports enthusiasts, but also offers 260 marked tourist pitches (120 with 6A electricity) on open, grassy ground overlooking the water and 14 mobile homes to rent. There is a special area for campers with bicycles. Very much dominated by the marina, this site will appeal to watersports enthusiasts, with opportunities for sailing, windsurfing and swimming, or for fishing, but it is also on a pretty stretch of coast, 15 kilometres northeast of Amsterdam and is close to the ancient, small towns of Marken, Volendam and Monnickendam, which are well worth a visit.

Facilities

Two good toilet blocks and one rather basic toilet block with toilets only. Good facilities include hot showers on payment, toilets, washbasins and a baby room. Dishwashing. Motorcaravan services. Gas supplies. Shop (1/4-1/10). Bar/restaurant (weekends and high season). TV room. Tennis. Playground and paddling pool. Bicycle hire. Fishing. Yacht marina (with fuel) and slipway. Watersports facilities. Entertainment in high season.

Open: 1 March - 1 November.

Directions

From A10, take N247 towards Volendam then Monnickendam exit south in direction of Marken, then Uitdam. Site is just outside Uitdam. GPS: N52:25.668 E05:04.408

Charges 2007

Per unit incl. 2 persons	€ 22,50
extra person (over 3 yrs)	€ 3,00

Less 20% outside 1/5-7/9.

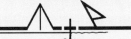

NL6870 Kennemer Duincamping de Lakens

Zeeweg 60, NL-2051 EC Bloemendaal aan Zee (Noord-Holland)

Tel: 075 6472393. Email: delakens@kennemerduincampings.nl

De Lakens is part of the Kennemer Duincampings group and is beautifully located in the dunes at Bloemendaal aan Zee. De Lakens has 940 reasonably large, flat pitches with a hardstanding of shells. There are 410 for tourers (235 with 10A electricity) and the sunny pitches are separated by low hedging. This site is a true oasis of peace in a part of the Netherlands usually bustling with activity. From this site it is possible to walk straight through the dunes to the North Sea. Although there is no pool, a lake on the site can be used for swimming or, of course, there is the sea. A separate area is provided for groups and youngsters to maintain the quiet atmosphere. It is not far to Amsterdam or Alkmaar and its cheese market. We feel you could have an enjoyable holiday here.

Facilities

The six toilet blocks for tourers (two brand new) include controllable showers, washbasins (open style and in cabins), facilities for disabled people and a baby room. Launderette. Two motorcaravan service points. Bar and restaurant. Snack bar. Supermarket. Adventure playgrounds. Bicycle hire. Entertainment in high season for all ages. Boat slipway. Fishing. Dogs are not accepted. Off site: Beach and riding 1 km. Golf 10 km.

Open: 1 April - 1 November.

Directions

From Amsterdam go west to Haarlem and follow the N200 from Haarlem towards Bloemendaal aan Zee. Site is on the N200, on the right hand side. GPS: N52:24.338 E04:35.191

Charges guide

Per pitch incl. 4 persons	€ 20,45 - € 31,85
incl. electricty	€ 22,20 - € 33,20
extra person	€ 4,00

Camping Cheques accepted.

NL5735 Camping Tempelhof

Westerweg 2, NL-1759 JD Callantsoog (Noord-Holland)

Tel: 0224 58 15 22. Email: info@tempelhof.nl

This first class site on the Dutch coast has 500 pitches with 250 for touring units, the remainder used by seasonal campers and a number of static units (mostly privately owned). All touring pitches have electricity (10/16A), water, drain and TV aerial point. The grass pitches are arranged in long rows which are separated by hedges and shrubs, with access from hardcore roads. There is hardly any shade. Tempelhof is close to the North Sea beaches (1 km), but the site has a heated indoor pool with a paddling pool, water slide and new gym. This also provides facilities for football, handball and tennis and has a climbing wall. In high season a full entertainment programme is arranged for children with water games, activities and music. With all these activities, you may not want to leave the site other than to go to the beach. However, the site is close to the ferry port of Den Helder where you can catch a ferry to the largest Dutch Island – Texel. Tempelhof is also close to the cheese market in Alkmaar and only 60 km. or so from Amsterdam. Member of Leading Campings Group.

Facilities

Two toilet blocks have modern facilities including washbasins (open style and in cabins) and controllable hot showers (card operated). Child size toilets, basins and showers. Baby room with bath and changing mat. Private bathroom with shower, toilet and basin (charged). Facilities for disabled visitors. Laundry with sinks, washing machines, dryers, spin dryer, iron and ironing board. Motorcaravan services. Shop, restaurant and takeaway (1/4-1/11) and bar (all year). Swimming pool with paddling pool (€ 3 p/d). Gym Trim court. Play area. Animal farm. Extensive animation programme in high season. Wifi internet access. Fishing. Bicycle hire. Off site: Beach 1 km. Golf 6 km. Riding 4 km. Boat launching 1 km.

Open: All year.

Directions

From Alkmaar take N9 road north towards Den Helder. Turn left towards Callantsoog on the N503 road and follow site signs.

Charges 2006

Per unit incl. 2 persons, electricity and services	€ 17,00 - € 31,00
extra person	€ 3,00
dog	€ 2,50

Electricity charge, plus per kwh charge (€ 0.20).

NL6830 Recreatiecentrum Mijnden

Bloklaan 22A, NL-1231 AZ Loosdrecht (Noord-Holland)

Tel: 0294 23 31 65. Email: info@mijnden.nl

Recreatiecentrum Mijnden is located amidst typical Dutch countryside alongside the River Drecht and close to cities such as Amsterdam, Utrecht and Hilversum. The site has 120 level pitches for tourers, some on hardstanding, all with 4/10A electricity and 20 with water and drainage. There are also 80 seasonal pitches and 250 mobile homes. The pitches are on grassy fields and almost all provide lovely views over the lake. The site has recently undergone major changes, including the addition of an extra camping field overlooking the water providing 36 extra pitches (20 for tourers), some with their own landing stage for boats. Mijnden is in a central position in the Vechtstreek, one of the most beautiful parts of the Netherlands, and you can explore this area by car, bike or on foot. There are some famous country estates and several charming castles to visit. The site itself has much to offer with evening entertainment including live music, and activities including swimming, sailing, water skiing or boating. The site has its own boat slipway so you could bring your own boat and navigate the Loosdrechtse Plassen. The waterfront is not fenced or gated.

Facilities

Three modern, heated sanitary blocks with showers on payment, washbasins, toilets and facilities for disabled visitors. Launderette with washing machines. Motorcaravan service point. Gas. Supermarket (1/4-15/9). Bar-café-restaurant 'Het Drechthuis' and snack bar (1/4-1/10). Room for teenagers. Zoo. Play area. Sports field. Boat slipway. Sailing and fishing competitions. Entertainment programme. Fishing. Bicycle hire. Caravan storage. Off site: Golf 10 km. Riding 5 km. Amsterdam and Utrecht 20 km. Loosdrechtse Plassen 100 m.

Open: 27 March - 3 October.

Directions

Take A2 from Utrecht to Amsterdam. Exit for Hilversum and after bridge turn right. Drive through village of Loenen and turn left to site. GPS: N52:12.156 E05:01.808

Charges guide

Per unit incl. 2 persons and electricity	€ 14,00 - € 19,50
extra person	€ 4,00
small tent pitch incl. 2 persons	€ 11,50 - € 13,50

NL6820 Camping Westerkogge

Kerkebuurt 202, NL-1647 MH Berkhout (Noord-Holland)

Tel: 0229 55 12 08. Email: info@camping-westerkogge.nl

Camping Westerkogge is near the A7 motorway and Hoorn, and close to the Ijsselmeer. The 300 pitches (100 for touring units) are on grassy fields, surrounded by high trees and bushes that provide shade; 80 pitches have 6A electricity and 28 of these also have water and drainage. From this site you can cycle through the lovely West Friesland countryside, sail on the Ijsselmeer or visit the attractive old town of Hoorn. It is also a good base for visiting Amsterdam or the harbour of Den Helder. This is a site for the whole family.

Facilities

Three toilet blocks include washbasins (open style and in cabins), child size washbasins and unisex showers. Facilities for disabled visitors. Laundry. Motorcaravan services. Shop (in reception). Café with bar and snacks. Covered pool (10 x 5 m) with separate paddling pool (also open to the public). Playground. Sports court. Tennis court. Bicycle hire. Go-kart and canoe hire. Boat trips through the polder. Off site: Riding 10 km. Golf 15 km.

Open: 1 April - 30 October.

Directions

Follow the A7 from Amsterdam north towards Hoorn and take exit Berkhout - Hoorn. Follow signs for Berkhout and site. GPS: N52:58.341 E04:59.392

Charges guide

Per unit incl. 2 persons,	
4A electricity	€ 18,80 - € 21,00
extra person	€ 2,10 - € 2,40
child (3-4 yrs)	€ 1,85
dog	€ 2,10 - € 2,40

NL6840 Camping Vogelenzang

2e Doodweg 17, NL-2114 AP Vogelenzang (Noord-Holland)

Tel: 023 584 7019. Email: camping@vogelenzang.nl

Camping Vogelenzang is a friendly campsite with 600 pitches, located 15 km. from the North Sea beaches. The cities of Haarlem and Amsterdam with their old streets are within reach. There are 300 pitches here for touring caravans and tents, about half with electricity connections. There is a separate area for tents. Arranged on flat grass, all the pitches are numbered and mature trees and hedges provide shade, but also give the site a somewhat enclosed feel. A family campsite, there is something for everyone.

Facilities

Four modern and one older toilet block provide toilets, open washbasins with cold water, washbasins in cabins with hot and cold water, controllable showers (on payment), a family shower room and baby room. Motorcaravan service point. Shop (1/4-15/9). Bar and snack bar (1/4-15/9). Open air swimming pool (10 x 5 m) with separate paddling pool. Play area. Sports field. Extensive high season recreation programme. Dogs are not accepted. Off site: Beach 15 km.

Open: 1 April - 15 September.

Directions

From Haarlem on the N206 traveling south take exit for Vogelenzang and follow campsite signs through Vogelenzang and Hillegom. The entrance road is to the right on a bend just after leaving Hillegom. GPS: N52:19.204 E04:33.975

Charges 2006

Per unit incl. up to 6 persons	€ 14,60
tent pitch (4 persons)	€ 10,30
extra person	€ 4,30
electricity (4A)	€ 10,30

NL5710 Camping It Soal

Suderséleane 27, NL-8711 GX Workum (Friesland)

Tel: 0515 541443. Email: info@itsoal.nl

This is an attractive, child-friendly site with 800 metres of beach, situated directly beside the Ijsselmeer with a canal on one side. It is ideal for those who enjoy water sports as there are many activities on the lake, including windsurfing, sailing, swimming, fishing, or you can launch your own boat. There are 650 pitches here, of which 400 are good sized, individual, flat and grassy for tourers, with 4/6A electrical connections. In separate areas, the other pitches are taken by seasonal guests and about 50 static units.

Facilities

Modern sanitary facilities include toilets, washbasins (open and in private cabins) and free, controllable showers. Facilities for disabled visitors. Baby room. Laundry. Shop, restaurant and takeaway (1/4-1/10). Several small play areas. Tennis courts. Video games room. Skate track. Bicycle hire. Fishing. Beach. Surfboards and sailing boats for hire. Entertainment programme. Off site: Golf 15 km. Riding 10 km.

Open: 1 April - 31 October

Directions

From Groningen on the A7 (via Drachten, Joure and Sneek), exit just before Bolsward onto the N359 towards Workum, then exit Workum and follow signs.

Charges 2006

Per unit incl. 1 or 2 adults	
with electricity	€ 18,00 - € 26,50
extra person	€ 2,50
dog	€ 4,00

NL6040 Recreatiecentrum Bergumermeer

Solcamastraat 30, NL-9262 ND Sumar (Friesland)
Tel: 0511 46 13 85. Email: info@bergumermeer.nl

Recreatiecentrum Bergumermeer's location beside the Bergum lake, makes it ideal for lovers of watersports, with sailing, surfing, water skiing and canoeing available, as well as swimming from two sandy beaches. There is also a large, heated indoor swimming pool, fun paddling pool and a solarium. The site provides 300 good sized, flat touring pitches for both caravans and tents, some having attractive views over the Prinses Margrietkanaal and the surrounding countryside, others with views over the lake. All pitches are fully serviced with 10A electricity, water and drainage, and there are 10 large hardstandings. In high season there are organised activities, not only for children but also for adults (coffee mornings to meet other guests, evening bingo, etc). It is well worth spending an afternoon on the terrace of the 'Klein Zwitserland' restaurant which has been built to resemble the bridge of a boat. From here with its great view over the lake, you can sit and watch the sailing boats pass by.

Facilities

Three sanitary buildings offer private cabins, children's toilets, baby bath and facilities for disabled visitors. Children's section in one block. Launderette. Freezer. Shop (daily). Bar/restaurant. Pancake restaurant. Heated indoor pool. Solarium. Play area. Children's farm. Tennis courts. Minigolf. Fishing. Sailing dinghies, motorboats and canoes for hire. Animation programme in high season. Club space with disco. Bicycle hire. Boat launching. Beach. Off site: Riding 5 km. Golf 19 km.

Open: 27 March - 16 October.

Directions

From channel ports, either go north from Amsterdam via A7/E22 through Leeuwarden towards Drachten, or east from Amsterdam via A6, onto the A7 (Groningen), then on N31 (De Haven/ Drachten) and in either case onto N356 towards Bergum following site signs. GPS: N53:11.476 E06:07.457

Charges 2006

Per pitch incl. 2 persons and electricity	€ 17,50 - € 26,00
extra person	€ 4,25

NL5760 Camping de Kuilart

Kuilart 1, NL-8723 CG Koudum (Friesland)
Tel: 0514 52 22 21. Email: info@kuilart.nl

De Kuilart is a well run, modern site by Friesland's largest lake and, with its own marina and private boating facilities, it attracts many watersports enthusiasts. The marina provides windsurfing and sailing lessons and boat hire, and there are special rates at the site for groups and sailing clubs. However, the site also has an excellent indoor pool, as well as an area for lake swimming and on land there are sports facilities and woods for cycling and walking. It may also therefore appeal for a relaxing break in a pleasant area not much visited by British campers. The 450 pitches at De Kuilart are set in groups of 10 to 16 on areas of grass surrounded by well established hedges. There are 175 for touring units, all with electricity (4-16A), water, waste water, WiFi and TV connections, and 20 new pitches with private sanitary facilities. The restaurant provides good views of the lake and woodland. A new children's 'house' is home to the entertainment team and there is an interesting Play Ship on the beach. A member of the Holland Tulip Parcs group.

Facilities

Four modern, heated sanitary blocks well spaced around the site are of above average quality, although showers are on payment and most washbasins (half in private cabins) have only cold water. Launderette. Motorcaravan services. Gas supplies. Restaurant/bar (31/3-29/10). Supermarket (21/4-2/9). Indoor pool (3 sessions daily, 31/3-29/10). Sauna and solarium. Sports field. Play areas. Tennis. Bicycle hire. Fishing. Recreation team (high season). Internet access. Lake swimming area. Marina. Dogs are accepted in certain areas (if booked). Off site: Riding or golf 4 km.

Open: All year.

Directions

Site is southeast of Koudum, on the Fluessen lake. Follow the camping sign off the N359 Bolsward - Lemmer road GPS: N52:54.150 E05:27.972

Charges 2007

Per unit incl. 2 persons and electricity	€ 16,50 - € 21,30
serviced pitch	€ 18,00 - € 22,90
'supercomfort' pitch	€ 23,00 - € 33,30
extra person	€ 3,85

Special weekend rates at B.Hs.
Camping Cheques accepted.

NL6080 Camping de Zeehoeve

Westerzeedijk 45, NL-8862 PK Harlingen (Friesland)

Tel: 0517 41 34 65. Email: info@zeehoeve.nl

Superbly located, directly behind the sea dyke of the Waddensea and just a kilometre from the harbour of Harlingen, De Zeehoeve is an attractive and spacious site. It has 300 pitches (125 for tourers), all with 6A electricity and 20 with water, drainage and electricity. There are 16 pitches with hardstandings for motorcaravans and larger units. Some pitches have views over the Harlingen canal where one can moor small boats. An ideal site for rest and relaxation, for watersports or to visit the attractions of Harlingen and Friesland. After a day of activity, one can wine and dine in the site restaurant or at one of the many pubs in the town. This splendid location allows the opportunity to watch the sun slowly setting from the sea dyke. You can also stroll through Harlingen or take the ferry to Vlieland or Terschelling. It is possible to moor boats at Harlingen, to hire a boat or book an organised sailing or sea fishing trip.

Facilities

Three sanitary blocks include open style washbasins with cold water only, washbasins in cabins with hot and cold water, controllable showers (on payment), family showers and baby bath. Facilities for disabled people. Launderette. Motorcaravan services. Bar/restaurant (1/7-31/8). Internet access. Play area. Bicycle hire. Pedaloes and canoes for hire. Fishing. Extensive entertainment programme in July/Aug. Off site: Beach 200 m. Riding 10 km.

Open: 1 April - 15 October.

Directions

From Leeuwarden take A31 southwest to Harlingen, then follow site signs. GPS: N53:09.742 E05:25.013

Charges 2006

Per unit incl. 2 persons and electricity	€ 14,60 - € 17,10
extra person	€ 3,80
child (4-11 yrs)	€ 3,30
tent (no car) incl. 2 persons	€ 12,10

CAMPING *DE ZEEHOEVE*   Beside the Waddenzee

Part of the famous Eleven-City skating route, "De Zeehoeve" is by the city of Harlingen, the only seaport in the beautiful, historical province of Friesland. You can make a day trip to Vlieland or Terschelling, two of the lovely Wadden Islands and our province has many places of interest, most close to the city itself - the Ald Faers Erf-route, Kazemattenmuseum, Technical Activity Centre Aeolus, the Planetarium in Franeker ans. You can rent bikes, canoe or use pedaloes, cycle, ramble or go sea fishing on the Waddensea - these are just some of the things to see and do in Friesland. The campsite is 1 km. south of Harlingen, with heated modern toilet facilities - launderette - animation in high season - an inland harbour with a trailer slip, and there is accommodation to hire.

Fam. Kleefstra, Westerzeedijk 45, 8862 PK Harlingen
Tel. +31 517-413465, fax +31 517-416971
E-mail: info@zeehoeve.nl www.zeehoeve.nl

NL6030 Recreatieoord Klein Vaarwater

Klein Vaarwaterweg 114, NL-9163 ME Buren (Friesland)

Tel: 0519-542156. Email: info@kleinvaarwater.nl

Recreatieoord Klein Vaarwater is a bustling family holiday park on the interesting island of Ameland. The site is 800 m. from the North-Sea beaches and has its own indoor pool, with bars, restaurants, supermarket and party centre. Klein Vaarwater has 190 touring pitches, of which 130 have electricity, water, waste water and cable. Pitching is off hardcore access lanes, close to nature, on fields taking 6-10 units, on a grass and sand underground. There is some shade from trees and bushes and level pitches are numbered and partly separated by young trees. Touring pitches are on separate fields from mobile homes and holiday bungalows, which take 75% of the site. Those of you who enjoy walking and cycling, can visit the nature reserve of 'Het Oerd' or stroll along the North Sea beaches.

Facilities

Two older style toilet blocks (maintenance variable) with toilets, open style washbasins, pre-set hot showers (coin operated) and facilities for disabled. Laundry. Supermarket. Bar. Restaurants. Snack bar. Café. Boutique. Bicycle hire. Indoor pool with slide and fun paddling pool. Full fitness programme. Playing field. Boules. Bowling alley. Minigolf. Animation programme for young and old. Off site: Beach 800 m. Village of Buren 500 m.

Open: April - October.

Directions

From Leeuwarden, follow N357 all the way north to Holwerd and take the ferry to Ameland (reservations necessary in high season). On the island, follow the signs for Buren and then site signs. GPS: N53:27.215 E05:48.268

Charges 2006

Per person	€ 3,65
child (under 14 yrs)	€ 3,10
pitch with electricity	€ 9,75
Camping Cheques accepted.	

NL6090 Camping Lauwersoog

Strandweg 5, NL-9976 VS Lauwersoog (Groningen)
Tel: 0519 34 91 33. Email: info@lauwersoog.nl

The focus at Camping Lauwersoog is very much on the sea and watersports. One can have sailing lessons or hire canoes and, with a new extension, there is direct access to the beach from the site. Camping Lauwersoog has 450 numbered pitches with 225 for tourers. Electricity (4/6A) is available at 200 pitches and 86 have water, drainage, electricity and cable connections. The pitches are on level, grassy fields (some beside the beach), partly separated by hedges and some with shade from trees. A new building in the marina houses a restaurant, bar, shop and laundry, and also provides beautiful views over the Lauwersmeer. The site's restaurant specialises in seafood and even the entertainment programmes for all ages have a water theme. Youngsters can play on the beach or in the covered play area, whilst adults may join sailing trips organised from the site, or walk and cycle through the Lauwersmeergebied (a national park) or perhaps, if the tide is low, even walk to Schiemonnikoog. The site is close to the harbour where you can take the ferry and let the wind blow away the cobwebs on the large beaches of this beautiful, almost car free island (only residents may take cars).

Facilities

The two toilet blocks for tourers provide washbasins (open style and in cabins), pre-set showers and child size toilets. Facilities for disabled people. Laundry. Campers' kitchen. Motorcaravan service. New restaurant, bar, snack bar and shop. Playground. Sailing school. Canoe hire. Surfing lessons (July/Aug). Bicycle and go-kart hire. Internet access. Extensive entertainment for all ages in high season. Torch useful. Off site: Riding 5 km.

Open: All year.

Directions

Follow N361 from Groningen north to Lauwersoog and then follow site signs.
GPS: N53:24.123 E06:13.039

Charges 2006

Per unit incl. 2 persons, 6A electrcity	€ 24,00
serviced pitch (125 sq.m)	€ 27,00
extra person	€ 4,00
Camping Cheques accepted.	

NL6120 Camping 't Strandheem

Parkweg 2, NL-9865 VP Opende (Groningen)
Tel: 0594 65 95 55. Email: info@strandheem.nl

Camping Strandheem has 330 quite large, numbered pitches (110 sq.m.) some with hardstanding and suitable for motorcaravans. All with electricity, there are 180 used for touring units, partly separated by low hedges but without much shade. Of these, 34 pitches have water points, drainage and cable TV connections. This site provides a base for some interesting excursions. The site itself also has a lot to offer. For youngsters there is an entertainment programme in high season with water games in the lake next to the site, real life theatre, games and craft work, with a new covered play area for bad weather. The De Bruinewoud family will give you a warm welcome.

Facilities

Two modern toilet buildings have washbasins (open style and in cabins), controllable showers, child size toilets and basins, a good baby room and fully equipped bathroom. Facilities for disabled people. Launderette. Motorcaravan service. Shop. Restaurant and bar. Café and snack bar. Covered swimming pool (5 x 5 m). Playgrounds. Covered play area with stage. Minigolf. Fishing. Bicycle hire. Lake with beach (€ 1 p/p per day). Extensive recreation program in July/August. Off site: Lake with beach 100 m. Riding 6 km. Golf 15 km.

Open: 1 April - 1 October.

Directions

Follow A7 west from Groningen towards Heerenveen and take exit 31. Follow campsite signs from there.
GPS: N53:09.167 E06:11.483

Charges 2006

Per unit incl. 2 persons	€ 22,50
extra person	€ 3,75
private sanitary facility	€ 7,50
electricity (4/10A)	€ 2,00
Camping Cheques accepted.	

kawan-villages.com **tel: 00 333 59 59 03 59**

NL5770 Camping Stadspark

Campinglaan 6, NL-9727 KH Groningen (Groningen)

Tel: 0505 25 1624. Email: info@campingstadspark.nl

The Stadspark is a large park to the southwest of the city, well signed and with easy access. The campsite is within the park with many trees and surrounded by water. It has 200 pitches with 150 for touring units, of which 75 have 6A electricity and 30 are fully serviced with electricity, water and drainage. The separate tent area is supervised directly by the manager. Buses for the city leave from right outside and timetables and maps are provided by Mrs Van der Veer, the helpful, English speaking manager. Groningen is a very lively city with lots to do.

Facilities	Directions
Two sanitary blocks, one totally refurbished, provide hot water for showers and dishwashing is now free. Motorcaravan service point. Shop (15/3-15/10). Restaurant, café, bar and takeaway (1/4-15/9). Internet access in reception. Bicycle hire. Some play equipment and small paddling pool. Fishing. Canoeing. Off site: Riding and golf 5 km. Boat launching 6 km.	From Assen on A28 turn left on the A7. Turn on N370 and follow site signs (Stadspark, quite close). GPS: N53:12.054 E06:32.142

Open: 15 March - 15 October.

Charges 2006

Per unit incl. 2 persons	€ 15,00
extra person	€ 2,50
child (2-12 yrs)	€ 1,50
electricity	€ 2,00

No credit cards.

NL5790 Rekreatiepark 't Kuierpadtien

Oranjekanaal NZ 10, NL-7853 TA Wezuperbrug (Drenthe)

Tel: 0591 38 14 15. Email: info@kuierpad.nl

Professionally run, this all year round site is suitable as a night stop, or for longer if you wish to participate in all the activities offered in July and August (on payment). These encompass canoeing, windsurfing, water chutes and the dry-ski slope, which is also open during the winter so that the locals can practise before going en-masse to Austria. The site itself is in a woodland setting on the edge of the village. The 320 flat and grassy pitches for touring units (with 650 in total) are of a fair size. All have 4A electricity and 11 are fully serviced with electricity, TV aerial point, water and drainage. A member of the Holland Tulip Parcs group.

Facilities	Directions
Eight quite acceptable sanitary blocks, including a new one, with hot showers (17.30 - 10.00 in July/Aug). Laundry. Motorcaravan services. Supermarket (1/4-15/9) but bread all year. Restaurant and bar (all year). Takeaway. Indoor pool (all year). Outdoor pool (1/4-1/9). Sauna, solarium and whirlpool. Tennis. Dry ski slope. Play areas. Boules, volleyball, football and basketball. Minigolf. Lake with beach. Boat rental.	From N34 Groningen - Emmen road exit near Emmen onto N31 towards Beilen. Turn right into Schoonord where left to Wezuperbrug. Site is at beginning of village on the right.

Open: All year.

Charges 2006

Per unit incl. 2 persons	€ 20,95 - € 31,60
extra person	€ 5,20

No credit cards.
Camping Cheques accepted.

NL6140 Camping de Valkenhof

Beilerstraat 13a, NL-9431 GA Westerbork (Drenthe)

Tel: 0593 337546. Email: info@camping-de-valkenhof.nl

De Valkenhof is a spacious family site with 180 pitches, partly in the woods and partly on open fields without hedges to separate them. With 160 pitches for touring units, there are 143 with 4A electricity and 11 serviced pitches with electricity, water and drainage. Cars are not permitted on the campsite itself and this, together with the large pitches, provides for a really quiet holiday. Other than a recreation room for youngsters, a pool and sanitary buildings, the site has few amenities but you will find all you need in the village.

Facilities	Directions
Two modern toilet blocks have washbasins (open style and in cabins, only one block with hot water at the basins), pre-set showers, toilets, showers and basins for children and a baby room. Facilities for disabled visitors. Motorcaravan services. Laundry. Basic provisions and some snacks from reception. Swimming pool with slide and paddling pool. Extensive entertainment in high season for children. Boules. Library. Games room. Only gas barbecues are permitted. Off site: Bicycle hire 2 km.	Travelling north from Zwolle on the A28, take exit for Beilen - Westerbork. Follow N31 eastwards and take exit for Westerbork. From there follow site signs.

Open: 1 April - 1 October.

Charges 2006

Per unit incl. 2 persons	€ 7,25
extra person	€ 3,50
serviced pitch	€ 4,00

No credit cards.
Camping Cheques accepted.

NL6160 Camping Ruinen

Oude Benderseweg 11, NL-7963 PX Ruinen (Drenthe)

Tel: **0522 47 17 70**. Email: **info@camping-ruinen.nl**

Camping Ruinen is a large, spacious site with 450 pitches in the woods of Drenthe. All 205 touring pitches have electricity (4/10A) and include 55 serviced pitches with water, drainage, cable TV and electricity connections. The numbered pitches are over 100 sq.m. in size and are on large, grassy fields. They are separated by hedges and in the shade of trees and there are some hardstandings for camper vans. At this comfortable site you can relax by cycling or walking through the woods or over the moors, or join organised trips in groups on a regular basis. There is no need to worry about the children – they will have great fun with Engel and Bengel, who arrange daily adventures, crafts or water games. The site does not have its own pool but the municipal pool is around the corner (passes from reception). Local attractions for children include Speelstad Oranje, a very large play-town, and for adults, activities include a 'whisper tour' by boat through the 'De Weerlibben' national park or a visit to the 'water-town' of Giethoorn.

Facilities

Four well-spaced toilet blocks provide washbasins (open style and in cabins), child-size toilets, bathrooms, child-size baths and a baby room. Facilities for disabled visitors. Laundry. Motorcaravan services. Shop. Restaurant with children's menu. Pancake restaurant. Play areas between the pitches. Giant chess. Boules. Tennis. Minigolf. Bicycle hire. Full entertainment programme in high season. WiFi. Dog are allowed on certain pitches only. Off site: Riding 500 m. Fishing 3 km. Golf 18 km.

Open: 1 April - 1 October.

Directions

From Zwolle follow A28 north and take Ruinen exit. Follow site signs from there.
GPS: N52:46.495 E06:22.196

Charges 2006

Per unit incl. 2 persons	€ 18,40 - € 21,25
extra person	€ 3,70
serviced pitch, plus	€ 3,95

No credit cards.
Camping Cheques accepted.

NL6150 Recreatiepark de Westerbergen

Oshaarseweg 24, NL-7932 PX Echten (Drenthe)

Tel: **0528 251224**. Email: **robin@westerbergen.nl**

Recreatiepark Westerbergen is beautifully situated in the picturesque region of Drenthe. The campsite is divided in two different areas, the campsite itself and the residential park. The campsite provides 600 pitches of which 400 are for touring campers. All pitches have electricity (6-16A) and 132 are equipped with water, drainage and cable television connections. Mostly on a separate field, the marked pitches are of a good size. In the centre of the site there is a pond where children and adults can enjoy themselves when the weather is sunny and warm. During holiday times an animation team organises many activities, for example survival exercises, children's theatre, treasure hunts, discos and many more. The site's swimming pool is covered and there is also an outside water area for little ones. There are many things to do and places to see in the surrounding area and the friendly reception staff are happy to provide information.

Facilities

Three good quality toilet blocks have British style toilets and individual washbasins. One block provides facilities for disabled people and for babies. Washing machines and dryer. Motorcaravan services. Shop. Restaurant. Snack bar. Attractive bar and terrace. Two play areas, indoor and outdoor. Minigolf. Laser game. Archery. Quad track. Tennis. Bicycle hire. Fishing. Off site: Golf and riding 4 km.

Open: 25 March - 28 October.

Directions

Using the A28 in the direction of Hoogeveen and Groningen, take exit for Zuidwolde and Echten (25). At the crossing turm left towards Echten and at T-junction turn right (de Leeuweveenseweg). At the end of this road turn left (de Echtenseweg) towards Echten. At the T-junction turn left and follow signs for site. In the village turn left and site is 1 km.
GPS: N52:42.180 E06:22.584

Charges 2006

Per unit with up to 6 persons and electricity	€ 14,00 - € 44,00

Less 20% in low season for over 50s and families with young children.

NL6130 Camping De Vledders

Zeegersweg, NL-9469 PS Schipborg (Drenthe)

Tel: **050 4091489**. Email: **info@devledders.nl**

Camping De Vledders is set in the centre of one of the most beautiful nature reserves in Holland, between the Drentsche Hondsrug and the Drentsche AA river. This attractive site is landscaped with many varieties of trees and shrubs. About one third of the site is aimed at tourers with pitching is on rectangular, grassy fields, separated by well kept hedges. There is some road noise. The level pitches are around 100 sq.m in size with some shade provided at the back from mature trees and hedges. Static units and seasonal pitches are on separate fields. In one corner of the site there is an attractive lake with sandy beaches. Boating, swimming and even windsurfing are possible on the lake. De Vledders is close to the sub-tropical pool at Zuidlaren and the 'Sprookjeshof', a theme park featuring all the well known fairy tales. Those of you looking for a quiet holiday in beautiful surroundings with many possibilities for walking and cycling will have a relaxing holiday here. The interesting old city of Groningen is only a 10 minute drive and even accessible by bicycle.

Facilities

Two toilet blocks with toilets, washbasins (open style and in cabins) and controllable hot showers. Family shower rooms. Baby room. En-suite facilities for disabled people. Shop for basics. Snack bar. TV in reception. Lake with fishing, boating, windsurfing. Volleyball. Football field. Riding. Nordic walking. Playground. Some animation for children in season. Torch useful. Off site: Sub-tropical pool in Zuidlaren. Sprookjeshof theme park in Zuidlaren. City of Groningen.

Open: April - October.

Directions

From the A28 take exit 35 and continue towards Zuidlaren. Just before Zuidlaren follow signs for Schipborg and then site signs.
GPS: N52:04.756 E06:39.937

Charges 2007

Per unit incl. 2 persons and electricity	€ 20,25
extra person	€ 2,75

NL5810 Recreatiepark de Luttenberg

Heuvelweg 9, NL-8105 SZ Luttenberg (Overijssel)

Tel: 0572 30 14 05. Email: info@luttenberg.nl

This woodland site is near the Sallandse Heuvelrug nature reserve and is well placed for relaxing walking and cycling tours. It is a large park with 90 seasonal pitches around the perimeter and 200 touring pitches (all with 10A electricity) in a central area off tarmac access roads. The large, individual pitches are numbered and separated, in rows divided by hedges and trees, with easy access. The new 25 m. pool, on-site activities and an animal enclosure, provide plenty to keep younger visitors happy. A member of the Holland Tulip Parcs group.

Facilities

New heated sanitary block with controllable showers gives a satisfactory overall provision together with two other blocks. All are heated and each provides hot showers on payment. Outside, under cover dishwashing points. Motorcaravan services. Gas supplies. Small shop for essentials including bread. Bar and restaurant (low season: Tues. and Fri-Sun). Barbecue with seating. Swimming pool (15/5-15/9). Tennis. Boules. Bicycle hire. Minigolf. Off site: Fishing 1.5 km. Riding 6 km.

Open: 31 March - 1 October.

Directions

From N35 Zwolle - Almelo turn on N348 Ommen road east of Raalte, then turn to Luttenberg and follow signs. From A1 (Amsterdam - Hengelo) take exit 23 at Deventer on N348, then as above. GPS: N52:25.698 E06:27.676

Charges 2006

Per unit incl. 2 persons and electricity	€ 24,50
extra person (over 1 yr)	€ 3,50

Less 15% outside 15/7-1/9. No credit cards. Camping Cheques accepted.

NL6480 Camping De Molenhof

Kleijsenweg 7, NL-7667 RS Reutum/Weerselo (Overijssel)

Tel: 0541 661201. Email: info@demolenhof.nl

De Molenhof is a pleasant family site where you can enjoy the real Twent hospitality. It has 450 well laid out pitches of which 430 are for touring units, all with water, drainage, electricity (10A) and cable connections. This is a real family site and children under the age of 12 years will particularly enjoy themselves in the covered, adventure playground, the two swimming pools (one outdoor, one covered) with a large slide on the outside and with the entertainment team that provides a full daily programme in high season. Older guests are not forgotten – the site organises sports tournaments or you can take a tour with a tilt-cart through the woods and visit the windmill at the entrance.

Facilities

Four toilet blocks, three in 'fairy tale' style for children, provide washbasins (open style and in cabins), adult and child size toilets and basins, controllable showers, bathrooms and a baby room. Launderette. Motorcaravan service. Well stocked shop. Bar/restaurant. Pancake restaurant. Swimming pools. Playgrounds (1 covered). Sports court. Tennis court. Volleyball. Fishing. Bicycle and go-kart hire. Boules. Extensive entertainment program in high season. Off site: Beach and riding 6 km. Golf 8 km.

Open: 31 March - 30 October.

Directions

Follow A1 from Amsterdam east to Hengelo and take exit 31, Hengelo Noord. Go through Deurningen to Weerselo and from there the N343 towards Tubbergen and site signs. GPS: N52:21.928 E06:50.591

Charges 2006

Per pitch incl. 2 persons incl. services	€ 32,00
incl. 3 persons	€ 37,00
extra person	€ 5,00

Camping Cheques accepted.

NL6470 Camping De Papillon

Kanaalweg 30, NL-7591 NH Denekamp (Overijssel)

Tel: 0541 351670. Email: info@depapillon.nl

De Papillon is perhaps one of the best campsites in The Netherlands. The campsite is well thought through with an eye for detail and for nature and the environment. For example, at the toilet blocks, waste water from the showers is used to flush the toilets and all buildings are heated by solar energy. In one area of the site the natural environment has been restored to the original heathland. This is a great destination for a holiday amongst nature. The 285 pitches are spacious (an average of 110-120 sq.m. and all have electricity (4-10A).

Facilities

Two large sanitary buildings with showers, toilets, washbasins in cabins, facilities for babies and for disabled visitors. Laundry room. Supermarket, restaurant, bar and takeaway. Heated pool with children's pool and sliding roof. Lake swimming with sandy beach. Adventure play area and smaller play areas. Bicycle hire. Fishing pond.

Open: 1 April - 1 October (bungalows all year).

Directions

From the A1 take exit 32 (Oldenzaal - Denekamp) and continue to Denekamp. Pass Denekamp and turn right at the village of Noord-Deurningen and follow signs to the campsite.

Charges 2006

Per unit incl. 2 persons	€ 24,50
extra person	€ 4,00

NL5985 Kampeercentrum De Beerze Bulten

Kampweg 1, NL-7736 PK Beerze/Ommen (Overijssel)

Tel: 0523 25 13 98. Email: info@beerzebulten.nl

Kampeercentrum De Beerze Bulten is a large holiday park with all amenities one could think of. Beside reception is a large, partly underground 'Rabbit Hole' providing a large indoor playground for children, a theatre for both indoor and outdoor shows and a buffet. De Beerze Bulten has over 500 pitches, all for touring units. In the shade of mature trees in woodland, all the pitches are level and numbered, all with 6/10A electricity, water, waste water and cable. Centrally located on the site is a full 'wellness' spa centre with a heated indoor and outdoor pool, a fun paddling pool, jet stream, several different saunas and a water playground. Here there are also full fitness facilities and a special 'salt cave' treatment for those suffering from asthma or skin troubles. To the back of the site is large lake area with a sandy beach and adventure play equipment. De Beerze Bulten will provide a relaxing and active family holiday and if the site doesn't offer enough, there is always the extensive surrounding woodland for walking and cycling.

Facilities

Several toilet blocks, well placed around the site, with toilets, washbasins in cabins and hot showers (key). Laundry. Shop. Bar and restaurant. Snack bar. Heated indoor and outdoor pool with paddling pool, water playground, sauna, jet stream, salt cave, fitness facilities and sunbeds. Multisports court. Bicycle hire. Indoor playground and theatre. Playgrounds. WIFI Internet. Animation team in season. Dogs allowed on some fields.

Open: All year.

Directions

From the A28, take exit 21 for Ommen and continue east towards Ommen. From Ommen, follow N34 northeast and turn south on N36 at crossing. Site is signed from there.

Charges 2007

Per unit incl. 2 persons and full service pitch	€ 25,50 - € 39,50
extra person	€ 3,50 - € 4,50

NL5780 Vakantiepark De Zanding

Vijverlaan 1, NL-6731 CK Otterlo (Gelderland)

Tel: 0318 596111. Email: info@zanding.nl

De Zanding is a family-run, highly-rated site that offers almost every recreational facility, either on site or nearby, that active families or couples might seek. Immediately after the entrance, a lake is to the left where you can swim, fish, sunbathe or try a two-person canoe. There are 463 touring pitches spread around the site (all with 4/10A electricity), some individual and separated, others in more open spaces shaded by trees. Some serviced pitches are in small groups between long stay units and there is another area for tents. Seasonal units and mobile homes take a further 508 pitches.

Facilities

First class sanitary facilities are housed in five modern blocks that are clean, well maintained and well equipped. Good provision for babies and people with disabilities. Laundry. Kitchen. Motorcaravan services. Gas supplies. Supermarket. Restaurant/bar (30/3-28/10). Lake swimming. Fishing. Tennis. Minigolf. Boules. Five play areas. Bicycle hire. Organised activities.

Open: 30 March - 28 October.

Directions

Leave A12 Utrecht - Arnhem motorway at Oosterbeek at exit 25 and join N310 to Otterlo. Then follow camping signs to site, watching carefully for entrance. GPS: N52:05.586 E05:46.654

Charges 2006

Per unit incl. 2 persons and 4A electricity	€ 18,00 - € 29,00
extra person	€ 3,70

Camping Cheques accepted.

 awan

tel: 00 333 59 59 03 59 *kawan-villages.com*

NL5980 Camping De Roos

Beerzerweg 10, NL-7736 PJ Beerze-Ommen (Overijssel)

Tel: 0523 25 12 34. Email: info@campingderoos.nl

De Roos is a family run site in an area of outstanding natural beauty, truly a nature lover's campsite. It is situated in Overijssel's Vecht Valley, a unique region set in a river dune landscape on the River Vecht. The river and its tributary wend their way around and through this spacious campsite. It is a natural setting that the owners of De Roos have carefully preserved. Conserving the environment is paramount here and the 285 pitches and necessary amenities blend into the landscape. Pitches, many with electricity, are naturally sited, some behind blackthorn thickets, in the shadow of an old oak, or in a clearing scattered with wild flowers. For some there are lovely views over the Vecht river. De Roos is a car-free campsite during peak periods – vehicles must be parked at the car park.

Facilities

Four well maintained sanitary blocks are kept fresh and clean. The two larger blocks are heated and include baby bath/shower and wash cabins. Dishwashing sinks. Launderette. Motorcaravan services. Gas supplies. Health food shop and tea room (1/5-1/9). Bicycle hire. Volleyball. Basketball. Boules. Table tennis. Several small playgrounds and field for kite flying. River swimming. Fishing. Dogs are not accepted (and cats must be kept on a lead!). Torch useful. Off site: Riding 6 km. Golf 10 km.

Open: 6 April - 30 September.

Directions

Leave A28 at Ommen exit 21 and join N340 for 19 km. to Ommen. Turn right at traffic lights over bridge and immediately left on local road towards Beerze. Site on left after 7 km. just after Beerze village sign. GPS: N52:30.647 E06:30.922

Charges 2007

Per person (over 3 yrs)	€ 3,40
pitch	€ 15,75
electricity (6A)	€ 2,40

Discounts in low season and special packages.

NL5990 Camping De Vechtstreek

Grote Beltenweg 17, NL-7794 RA Rheeze-Hardenberg (Overijssel)

Tel: 0523 26 13 69. Email: info@sprookjescamping.nl

It would be difficult for any child (or adult) to pass this site and not be drawn to the oversized open story book which marks its entrance. From here young children enter the exciting world of Hannah and Bumpie, two of the nine characters around which this site's fairy-tale theme has been created. The young owners of De Vechtstreek have given their park a special identity by creating this fairy tale. The colourful characters appear throughout the site. Not only is the story acted out in the restaurant at the Saturday children's buffet, the story continues in the indoor water play park which is dominated by Hannah's Castle. This is also a campsite which offers top class facilities. There are 270 touring pitches mostly laid out in bays which accommodate around 12 units. In the centre of each is a small play area. The site has a mature appearance with many trees and shrubs.

Facilities

Three modern, well equipped and heated toilet blocks include a baby room, separate child sections, family showers and dishwashing areas. Excellent laundry room. Sauna, solarium and jacuzzi. Well stocked supermarket. Restaurant, snack bar and takeaway (all season). Play areas. Fairy-tale water play park (heated). Daily activity club. Internet access. Football field. Theatre.

Open: 1 April - 15 September.

Directions

From Ommen take N34 Hardenberg road for 9 km. Turn right on N36 and proceed south for 3.5 km. Turn left at first crossroads and after 200 m. left again on a local road towards Rheeze. Site clearly is signed in 2 km. GPS: N52:32.764 E06:34.249

Charges 2007

Per unit incl. 2 persons	€ 29,50 - € 39,00
extra person	€ 2,75 - € 3,00

NL6000 Vechtdalcamping Het Tolhuis

Het Lageveld 8, NL-7722 HV Dalfsen (Overijssel)

Tel: 0529 458383. Email: tolhuis@gmx.net

Het Tolhuis is a pleasant, well established site with 145 pitches. Of these, 70 are for tourers, arranged on well kept lawns off paved and gravel access roads. All touring pitches have 4/10A electricity, water, waste water, cable and WiFi internet. Some are shaded by mature trees and bushes, others are more in the open. Het Tolhuis is in beautiful surroundings where you can enjoy numerous walking and cycling routes in the tranquil environment alongside the river Vecht. This is also an ideal environment for those who enjoy fishing. The only disadvantage is a railway that runs along the back of the site.

Facilities

Two heated toilet blocks, one immaculate new one to the front and an older one to the back. Family shower rooms. Baby room. Laundry. Small shop. Café for snacks and drinks. Open air pool. Playing field. Playground. Internet. Off site: Restaurant 2 km. Fishing 5 km.

Open: 1 April - 1 October.

Directions

From the A28 take exit 21 and continue east towards Dalfsen. Site is signed in Dalfsen.

Charges 2007

Per unit incl. 2 persons	€ 16,50 - € 24,70
extra person	€ 1,50 - € 2,75

NL5950 Rekreatiecentrum Heumens Bos

Vosseneindseweg 46, NL-6582 BR Heumen (Gelderland)

Tel: 0243 58 14 81. Email: info@heumensbos.nl

The area around Nijmegen, the oldest city in the Netherlands, has large forests for walking or cycling, nature reserves and old towns to explore, as well as being quite close to Arnhem. Mr Van Velzen and his sons took over this site in 2002 and are planning new buildings and an internet point. The site covers 16 ha. and is open over a long season for touring families (no groups of youngsters allowed) all year for bungalows. It offers 165 level, grass touring pitches for touring units, all with electricity (6A) and cable TV (free) connections. Numbered but not separated, in glades of 10 and one large field, all have easy access with cars parked away from the caravans. One small section for motorcaravans has some hardstandings. The restaurant, which offers a good menu and a new terrace, is close to the comfortable bar and snack bar. An open air swimming pool with a small children's pool is maintained at 28 degrees by a system of heat transfer from the air.

Facilities

The main, high quality sanitary building, plus another new block, are modern and heated, providing showers on payment, rooms for families and disabled people and hot water to private cabins and other washbasins. Another smaller building has acceptable facilities. External, covered dishwashing facilities. Smart launderette. Motorcaravan services. Gas supplies. Shop. Bar, restaurant and snack bar (all season). Heated swimming pool (from 1/5). Bicycle hire. All weather tennis courts. Boules. Table tennis. For children a separate glade area with play equipment on sand and grass, Activity and excursion programme (high season). Large wet weather room. Off site: Riding 300 m. Fishing 2 km. Golf 10 km.

Open: 1 April - 1 November.

Directions

From A73 (Nijmegen - Venlo) take exit 3 (4 km. south of Nijmegen) and follow site signs. GPS: N51:46.149 E05:49.230

Charges 2006

Per pitch incl. 2 persons	€ 16,00 - € 24,50
electricity	€ 2,40

Special low season weekends (incl. restaurant meal) and special deal for over 55 yr olds.

NL5870 Camping de Vergarde

Erichemseweg 84, NL-4117 GL Erichem (Gelderland)

Tel: 0344 57 20 17. Email: info@devergarde.nl

De Vergarde has been developed on a former orchard with a beautiful old farmhouse at its entrance. The site is in two sections on either side of a lake. Static holiday caravans are on the left, with the 207 touring pitches to the right. About a third of these are taken by seasonal units. Arranged in sections, each named after a fruit tree, access is good. The pitches are numbered on flat grass and include 225 with electricity (6A), water, drainage and TV connections. There are trees all around the perimeter (but not much shade on the pitches) and the site has a spacious, open feeling with the lake adding to its attractiveness. A member of the Holland Tulip Parcs group.

Facilities

Good sanitary facilities in three blocks. Most, but not all, hot water is on payment. Washing machines. Motorcaravan services. Heated swimming pool (1/5-1/9). Shop (1/5-1/10). Restaurant (1/5-1/10). Play area and large indoor games room. Pony riding. Pets corner. Minigolf. Bicycle hire. Games room. Two tennis courts. Fishing.

Open: 1 March - 30 October.

Directions

From A15 Dordrecht - Nijmegen road exit at Tiel West (also MacDonald's) and follow signs to campsite. GPS: N51:53.939 E05:21.646

Charges guide

Per unit incl. 2 adults	€ 19,00 - € 24,00
extra person (over 2 yrs)	€ 3,00

Special weekly rates. Low season less 20%.

NL5850 Camping de Hooge Veluwe

Koningsweg 14, NL-6816 TC Arnhem (Gelderland)
Tel: 0264 43 22 72. Email: info@dehoogeveluwe.nl

Its situation at the entrance to the Hoge Veluwe National Park with its moors, forests, sand drifts, walking routes and cycle paths, makes this a highly desirable holiday base. The site itself is well managed and laid out in an orderly fashion, with 260 touring pitches, including 85 fully serviced places of 300 sq.m. All have electricity (4/6A), are numbered and laid out in small fields which are divided by hedging. Some are traffic free which means cars must be left in a nearby car park. Mobile homes are discreetly placed mostly in the centre of the site, but the many trees and shrubbery make them unobtrusive, in fact, many have enviable garden areas.

Facilities	Directions
Five excellent, heated sanitary blocks with all facilities, are easily identified by colourful logos. Launderette. Motorcaravan services. Gas supplies. Supermarket. Restaurant. Takeaway. All facilities open all season. TV room. Heated outdoor and indoor pools. Several small play areas. Playground with football pitch, tennis, cycle track, minigolf, etc. Bicycle hire. Organised activities Off site: Riding 50 m. Golf 6 km. Beach 12 km.	Leave A12 motorway at exit 25 (Oosterbeck) and follow signs for Hooge Veluwe. Site is on right in approx. 6 km. From the A50, take exit 21 to Schaarsbergen and follow signs. GPS: N52:01.861 E05:52.008

Open: 26 March - 30 October.

Charges 2006	
Per unit incl. 2 persons and electricity	€ 27,00 - € 26,00
extra person	€ 2,00 - € 4,00

NL6290 Camping Eiland van Maurik

Rijnbandijk 20, NL-4021 GH Maurik (Gelderland)
Tel: 0344 691502. Email: info@eilandvanmaurik.nl

Camping Eiland van Mourik is beside a lake in the centre of an extensive nature and recreation park in the Nederrijn area. These surroundings are ideal for all sorts of activities – swimming, windsurfing, waterskiing or para-sailing, relaxing on the beach or fishing. The site has 365 numbered, flat pitches, with 155 for touring units, all with 10A electricity and cable TV connections and 64 also with water and drainage. There is an animal farm for the children. In the event of bad weather, the site has a gym and an indoor 'play palace' (Avontura), where in high season activities are organised.

Facilities	Directions
The three toilet blocks for tourers include washbasins (open style and in cabins), controllable showers and a baby room. Launderette. Shop. Bar/restaurant (1/4-1/10). Play areas (one indoors). Play field. Tennis. Minigolf. Bicycle hire. Go karts. Riding (part of the activity programme). Tennis. Water skiing. Para-sailing. Animal farm. Entertainment in high season. Gate key deposit € 50. Off site: Shop, restaurant and bar. Golf 9 km.	From Rhenen take the N320 road towards Mourik and signs for 'Eiland Mourik'. GPS: N51:50.586 E05:15.511

Open: 1 April - 1 October.

Charges 2006	
Per unit incl. 2 persons and electricity	€ 17,00 - € 24,50
extra person (under 2 yrs free)	€ 3,50
hikers and cyclists (2 persons)	€ 14,00
Camping Cheques accepted.	

NL5840 Camping de Pampel

Woeste Hoefweg 35, NL-7351 TN Hoenderloo (Gelderland)
Tel: 0553 78 17 60. Email: info@pampel.nl

A site with no static holiday caravans is rare in the Netherlands and this adds to the congenial atmosphere at De Pampel. This is enhanced by its situation deep in the forest, with 9 ha. of its own woods to explore. This peaceful park offers many opportunities for interesting outings with the two National Parks in the vicinity, the Kröller-Muller museum and the cities of Arnhem and Apeldoorn. There are 185 pitches (20 seasonal). You can choose to site yourself around the edge of a large open field with volleyball, etc. in the middle, or pick one of the individual places which are numbered, divided by trees and generally quite spacious. All have 4/16A electricity. The furthest pitches are some distance from the sanitary facilities.

Facilities	Directions
Toilet facilities are good and modern, with free hot showers. Laundry. Shop (1/4-31/10). Restaurant. Snack bar (July/Aug, otherwise weekends only). Swimming pool and fun paddling pool (heated by solar panels; open Easter-Oct). Play area. Pets corner. Sports area. Barbecues by permission only. Dogs are not accepted in high season.	From the A50 Arnhem - Apeldoorn road exit for Hoenderloo and follow signs.

Open: All year.

Charges guide	
Per unit incl. 2 persons	€ 17,50 - € 22,50
extra person	€ 4,00 - € 5,00
electricity (4/6A)	€ 3,00 - € 3,50
Less 20% (excl. electricity) in low seasons.	

NL5960 Camping De Wielerbaan

Zoomweg 7-9, NL-6705 DM Wageningen-Hoog (Gelderland)

Tel: **0317 41 39 64**. Email: **info@wielerbaan.nl**

This family run park has an interesting history and a natural setting at a point where the Veluwe, the valley of Gelderland and the picturesque area of Betuwe meet. Translated 'Wielerbaan' means 'cycle race track' which still stands in the heart of this site. The present owners have utilised this area to accommodate recreation facilities which include an indoor swimming pool. Touring pitches in a meadow setting are serviced with water, electricity and drainage. Planned cycles routes are available at reception, or maps to choose your own way. It is possible to go by boat to Arnhem and worth visiting is the Burgers Zoo, the Zoo of Ouwehand or seeking out the nearby parks (discounted entrance cards are available from the site).

Facilities

Four toilet blocks of a reasonable standard provide wash cabins, showers and a baby room. Launderette. Gas supplies. Shop. Small restaurant. Snacks and takeaway. Library. Swimming pool. Minigolf. Boules. Ten small play areas and organised entertainment in high season. Off site: Golf 500 m. Fishing 5 km. Boat launching.

Open: All year.

Directions

Leave A12 at exit 24 towards Wageningen and continue for 4.5 km. to second roundabout, where site is clearly signed. Follow signs to site, 1.5 km. from the town. GPS: N51:59.199 E05:47.275

Charges 2006

Per unit incl. 2 persons
and electricity   € 19,50 - € 23,50
Less 10% for over 55s at certain times.

NL6190 Rekreatiepark Hazevreugd

Vormtweg 9, NL-8321 NC Urk (Flevoland)

Tel: **0527 681785**. Email: **info@hazevreugd.nl**

Recreatiepark Hazevreugd, set in the Urkerbos on the former island Urk, is a true family site with lots of sporting facilities. You can hire go-karts and bikes, go surfing from the beaches of the Ijsselmeer or go riding in the woods. The site has 220 pitches, 192 for tourers, all with shade and 6A electricity. There are also 63 serviced pitches with water, electricity and drainage and separate pitches for motorcaravans, which will become hardstandings. In high season a professional entertainment team organises sports competitions, scouting expeditions and entertainment evenings. Besides the sporting activities, this site is an excellent base for a visit to the Batavia shipyard in Lelystad where you can see original 17th century ships that sailed to India.

Facilities

Two modern toilet blocks have washbasins (open style and in cabins), pre-set showers, child size toilets, family showers and a baby room. Facilities for disabled visitors. Laundry. Motorcaravan services. Shop (bread to order). Bar/restaurant and snack bar. Outdoor pool (40 sq.m.) with paddling pool. Playground. Sports court. Boules. Off site: Fishing, boat launching and beach 2 km.

Open: April - September.

Directions

Follow the A6 from Almere to the north and take exit 13 to Urk (N352). Site is next to the Urkerbos and well signed.

Charges 2006

Per unit incl. 2 persons   € 15,00 - € 19,50
extra person   € 2,50
No credit cards.

NL5540 Camping De Katjeskelder

Katjeskelder 1, NL-4904 SG Oosterhout (Noord-Brabant)

Tel: **0162 453 539**. Email: **kkinfo@katjeskelder.nl**

This site, for caravans and tents only, is to be found in a wooded setting in a delightful area of Noord Brabant. It is a well established, family run site offering extensive facilities with an impressive ultra-modern reception area. Around the 25 hectare site are mobile homes and bungalows but there are 200 touring pitches, all with electricity and water (between two pitches), plus 13 fully serviced pitches. Cars are prohibited alongside the pitches, but may be parked nearby.

Facilities

Three modern, heated sanitary blocks include a family shower/wash room, baby room and provision for disabled people. Laundry. Supermarket. Restaurant, bar, snack bar, pizzeria and takeaway (the 'Hapjeskat') Indoor tropical pool. Outdoor swimming pools (15/5-31/8). Play field. Tennis. Bicycle hire. Minigolf. Several play areas for small children. Large adventure playground. Off site: Oosterheide nature park and Dorst forest.

Open: All year.

Directions

From A27 Breda - Gorinchem motorway take Oosterhout Zuid exit 17 and follow signs for 7 km. to site GPS: N51:37.799 E04:49.926

Charges 2007

Per unit incl. up to 5 persons   € 22,00 - € 39,00
extra person   € 4,00

NL5910 Vakantiecentrum de Hertenwei

Wellenseind 7-9, NL-5094 EG Lage Mierde (Noord-Brabant)

Tel: 0135 09 12 95

Set in the southwest corner of the country quite close to the Belgian border, this relaxed site covers a large area. In addition to 100 quite substantial bungalows with their own gardens (30 to let, 32 mobile homes, some residential), the site has some 350 touring pitches. These are in four different areas on oblong meadows surrounded by hedges and trees, with the numbered pitches around the perimeters. There is a choice of pitch size (100 or 150 sq.m.) and all have 6A electrical connections, water and drainage, and even a cable TV connection as well. The most pleasant area is probably the small one near the entrance and main buildings – these are a long walk from some of the furthest pitches. Facilities include indoor and outdoor pools and there is a recreation programme in season with films, dances or disco, sports, bingo, etc.

Facilities

Four toilet blocks are of slightly differing types, all of quite good quality and well spaced around the site. Virtually all washbasins in private cabins and the blocks can be heated in cool weather. Units for disabled people, hair washing cabins and baby baths. Launderette. Gas supplies. Motorcaravan services. Supermarket (Easter - end Oct). Bar by indoor pool (13 x 6 m. open all year, admission charged). Three outdoor pools. (12/5-26/8). Restaurant, cafeteria with snack bar (all year). Disco. Tennis courts. Playgrounds. Sauna, solarium and jacuzzi. Bicycle hire. Off site: Supermarket 2 km. Bus service to Tilburg or Eindhoven with stop at entrance. Fishing and riding 4 km.

Open: All year.

Directions

Site is by N269 Tilburg - Reusel road, 2 km. north of Lage Mierde and 16 km. south of Tilburg
GPS: N51:25.241 E05:08.538

Charges 2007

Per unit incl. 2 persons and electricity	€ 20,00 - € 34,25

Less 25-40% in low seasons.

★★★★★

VAKANTIECENTRUM

de hertenwei

WELLENSEIND 7-9
5094 EG LAGE MIERDE
Tel. +31 13 509 12 95
WWW.HERTENWEI.NL

Situated 2 km north of Lage Mierde on the Tilburg - Reusel road (road Nr. 269) surrounded by beautiful woodland. Modern heated sanitary blocks with hot water in basins and showers. Heated swimming pool and children's pool. Indoor pool with hot whirlpool, sauna, solarium. Bar. Supermarket. Washing machines. Snack bar. Restaurant. Discotheque. Tennis courts. Also bungalows and mobile-homes to let: (4–6–8–16–20 persons)

Please send for our free brochure

NL5970 Camping De Paal

Paaldreef 14, NL-5571 TN Bergeyk (Noord-Brabant)

Tel: 0497 57 19 77. Email: info@depaal.nl

A first class campsite, De Paal is especially suitable for families with young children. Situated in 42 hectares of woodland, there are 530 touring pitches, ranging in size up to 150 sq.m. (plus 70 seasonal pitches). The pitches are numbered and separated by trees, with cars either parked on the pitch or in a dedicated parking area. All have 6A electricity, TV, water, drainage and a bin. There are 40 pitches with private sanitary facilities which are partly underground and attractively covered with grass and flowers. With child safety in mind, there is a play area on each group of pitches.

Facilities

High quality sanitary facilities are ultra modern, including cabins, family rooms and baby baths. Facilities for disabled visitors. Launderette. Motorcaravan services. Underground supermarket. Restaurant (high season), bar and snack bar (all season). Indoor pool (supervised in high season). Outdoor pool (May - Sept). Bicycle hire. Tennis. Play areas. Theatre. WiFi. Bicycle storage. Off site: Tennis complex with indoor courts (Sept-May) with 10 outdoor courts (all equipment for hire) and pleasant bar. Riding 500 m.

Open: Easter/1 April - 31 October.

Directions

From E34 Antwerpen-Eindhoven road take exit 32 (Eersel) and follow signs for Bergeyk and site (2 km. from town). GPS: N51:20.147 E05:27.302

Charges guide

Per pitch incl. 2 persons and services	€ 26,00 - € 38,00
extra person (over 1 yr)	€ 5,00
cyclist	€ 9,00

Discounts outside 5/7-16/8 daily 30%, over 7 days 35%, (over 55s 45% for more than 7 days).

NL5900 Beekse Bergen Safari Camping

Beekse Bergen 1, NL-5081 NJ Hilvarenbeek (Noord-Brabant)
Tel: **013 5491100**. Email: **beeksebergen@libema.nl**

Beekse Bergen is a large impressive leisure park set around a very large, attractive lake near Tilberg. The park offers a range of amusements which should keep the most demanding of families happy! These include not only water based activities such as windsurfing, canoeing, jet ski, rowing and fishing, but also a small amusement park, a cinema, tennis courts, minigolf and many more. The lake is bordered by sandy beaches, children's playgrounds, open air swimming areas and water slides. Transport around and across the lake is provided by a little train or a sightseeing boat (in high season). These and most of the amenities are free to campers. Part of the resort is the Beekse Bergen Safari Park with reduced entry for campers. Here you can see the many wild animals from either your own car, a safari bus or two safari boats, the Stanley and the Livingstone. On the far side of the lake, as well as the bungalows and tents, there are two distinct campsites – one on flat meadows surrounded by hedges and trees near the lake, the other in a more secluded wooded area reached by a tunnel under the nearby main road. The 420 numbered pitches are about 100 sq.m, and all have electricity and cable connections (4/6A). There are 62 fully serviced pitches. The Safari Campsite has a 'typical safari environment' and a viewpoint over the Safari Park (with free, unlimited entry for campers staying here; open 24 April - 2 September). There is an independent central complex with catering, playground and launderette, plus an entertainment team. This is an area with many other recreational activities, including the award winning Efteling amusement park.

Facilities

Sanitary facilities are quite adequate in terms of numbers, cleanliness and facilities including some washbasins in private cabins. Launderettes. Restaurants, cafés and takeaway (weekends only in low seasons). Supermarket. Playgrounds. Indoor pool. Beaches and lake swimming. Watersports including rowing boats (free) and canoe hire. Amusements. Tennis. Minigolf. Fishing. Recreation programme. Bicycle hire. Riding. Twin axle caravans not accepted. Off site: Golf 5 km.

Open: 28 March - 26 October.

Directions

From A58/E312 Tilburg - Eindhoven motorway, take exit to Hilvarenbeek on the N269 road. Park and campsite are signed Beekse Bergen.

Charges guide

Per person (from 2 yrs)	€ 7,50
standard pitch incl. electricity	€ 18,50 - € 25,50
serviced pitch	€ 20,00 - € 29,00

Discounts for weekly stays, camping packages available.

NL5880 Vrijetijdspark Vinkeloord

Vinkeloord 1, NL-5382 JX Vinkeloord (Noord-Brabant)
Tel: **0735 34 35 36**. Email: **vinkeloord@libema.nl**

Run by the same group as Beekse Bergen (NL5900), Vinkeloord is a large site which also provides motel accommodation and a bungalow park, in addition to its 500 camping pitches. These are divided into several grassy areas, many in an attractive wooded setting. There are 381 for touring units, all with electrical connections (4-10A and some with full services (water and TV connection). The site is a popular holiday choice with activities organised in the main seasons. The varied amenities are located in and around a modern, central complex. They include heated outdoor swimming pools, an indoor '.sub-tropical' pool with slide and jetstream, and ten-pin bowling alley. A small, landscaped lake has sandy beaches and is overlooked by a large, modern play area. Some of the touring pitches also overlook the water. Campers are entitled to free entry to the adjacent 'Autotron' attraction.

Facilities

Eight toilet blocks are well situated for all parts of the site with a mixture of clean and simple facilities (some unisex) with some warm water for washing and some individual washbasins. Baby room. Supermarket. Bar. Modern, up-market restaurant. Snack bar/takeaway (high season only). Free outdoor heated swimming pools (1/6-1/9). Indoor pool (on payment). Ten-pin bowling alley. Tennis courts. Minigolf. Boules. Sports field. Bicycle hire. Pedaloes. Fishing. Barbecue area. Play areas on sand. Many organised activities in season. Max. 1 dog per pitch.

Open: 29 March - 3 November.

Directions

Site is signed from the N50/A50 road between 's Hertogenbosch and Nijmegen, about 10 km. east of s'Hertogenbosch at Vinkel.

Charges guide

Per person (from 3 yrs)	€ 7,50
standard pitch incl. electricity	€ 15,00 - € 22,00
incl. water and TV connection	€ 17,00 - € 26,00

NL6790 Camping de Kienehoef

Zwembadweg 35 - 37, NL-5491 TE Sint-Oedenrode (Noord-Brabant)

Tel: 0413 47 28 77. Email: info@kienehoef.nl

Camping de Kienehoef is at Sint Oedenrode in Noord Brabant, which boasts many historical sights, including two castles. The site is well cared for and attractively laid out with reception to the right of the entrance and the site facilities to the left. Behind this area is a heated swimming pool. The generous pitches are mostly laid out in bays and placed between trees and shrubs to the right of a long avenue leading through the site. The touring pitches are on three separate fields amongst pitches used for caravan holiday homes.

Facilities

Two modern, clean and well maintained toilet blocks include pre-set showers and some shower/wash cubicles, also family and baby rooms. Separate dishwashing and laundry area with iron and board. Motorcaravan services. Shop, restaurant/bar and snacks (all 1/5-15/9). Heated outdoor pool (1/5-15/9). Lake fishing. Bicycle hire. Sports field, tennis court. Dogs and other pets are not accepted. Off site: Golf 1 km. Riding 15 km.

Open: 28 March - 28 October.

Directions

Leave A2 s'Hertogenbosh - Eindhoven motorway at exit 27 and follow signs to Sint Oedenrode. Site is well signed from village. GPS: N51:34.653 E05:26.809

Charges 2006

Per unit incl. 2 persons and electricity	€ 24,00 - € 29,00
extra person	€ 4,25

Camping Cheques accepted.

NL6530 Terrassencamping Gulperberg Panorama

Berghem 1, NL-6271 NP Gulpen (Limburg)

Tel: 0434 50 23 30. Email: info@gulperberg.nl

Gulperberg Panorama is just three kilometres from the atttractive village of Gulpen. Pitches are large and flat on terraces overlooking the village on one side and open countryside on the other. Many have full services. English is spoken in the reception, although all written information is in Dutch (ask if you require a translation). Gulperberg Panorama is a haven for children. During the high season there is a weekly entertainment programme to keep them occupied. The site is not suitable for visitors with disabilities. Dogs are restricted to one section of the campsite.

Facilities

Four modern sanitary blocks have excellent facilities. Family shower room and baby room. Laundry. Shop (27/4-31/8). Bar. Takeaway. New restaurant with terrace. Swimming pool (29/4-15/9). Three play areas. TV and games room. Extensive family entertainment. Off site: Golf and bicycle hire 3 km. Fishing 4 km. Riding 5 km. Beach 15 km.

Open: Easter - 31 October.

Directions

Gulpen is east of Maastricht. Take N278 Maastricht - Aachen. Site is signed just as you enter Gulpen at the lights. Turn right and follow signs for 3 km.

Charges 2006

Per unit incl. 2 persons	€ 14,10 - € 18,75
with electricity (6A)	€ 15,90 - € 21,00
with services	€ 19,80 - € 24,90
extra person (over 2 yrs)	€ 2,30 - € 3,35

Camping Cheques accepted.

NL5890 Kampeercentrum Klein Canada

Dorpstraat 1, NL-5851 AG Afferden (Limburg)

Tel: 0485 531223. Email: info@kleincanada.nl

Following the war, the family who own this site wanted to emigrate to Canada – they didn't go, but instead created this attractive site with the maple leaf theme decorating buildings, pool and play equipment. Pleasant, farm style buildings adorned with flowers house the main amenities near the entrance and the site has a sheltered atmosphere with many ornamental trees. There are three touring areas, one on an island surrounded by an attractive, landscaped moat used for fishing, the other on flat ground on the other side of the entrance. They provide 195 large, numbered pitches, all with electricity (6-10A), water, drainage and TV connections.

Facilities

Mixed toilet facilities are partially refurbished and include some with washbasins in cubicles. Family facilities. Some pitches have individual units. Motorcaravan services. Gas supplies. Supermarket, Bar, restaurant, snack bar and takeaway (all 1/4-31/10). Outdoor pool (May - Sept). Indoor pool (all year). Sauna and solarium. Tennis. Fishing. Playground. Animals enclosure. Bicycle hire.

Open: All year.

Directions

Afferden is on the N271 between Nijmegen and Venlo. Site is on the N271 and is signed. GPS: N51:38.309 E06:00.228

Charges guide

Per person	€ 3,60
pitch incl. 6A electricity	€ 11,70 - € 22,85

Camping Cheques accepted.

NL6520 Camping BreeBronne

Lange Heide 9, NL-5993 PB Maasbree (Limburg)
Tel: 077 465 23 60. Email: info@breebronne.nl

One of the top campsites in the Netherlands, BreeBronne is set in a forest region beside a large lake. There are 370 pitches, of which 220 are for touring units. They are at least 80 sq.m. in size and all have electricity (10A), water, waste water and cable TV connections. Touring pitches are separated from the static units. The lake provides a sandy beach with water slide and opportunities for swimming, sailing and windsurfing. Alternatively, you can swim in the heated open air pool (May-Aug) or the 'sub-tropical' heated indoor pool with its special children's area (April-Oct). Member of Leading Campings Group.

Facilities

The sanitary facilities are top class with a special section for children, decorated in fairy tale style, and excellent provision for disabled visitors and seniors. Launderette. Dog shower. Solarium. Private bathrooms for hire. 'De Bron' restaurant with regional specialities. Bar. Takeaway. Shop. Play area. Play room. Internet. Tennis. Animation. Off site: The local area has a rich history, with pretty villages and museums.

Open: All year.

Directions

Breebronne lies between Sevenum and Maasbree. From A67 towards Venlo take exit 38 and fork right. After 3 km. turn for Maasbree, then left (Maasbree). On to roundabout, take third exit. BreeBronne is signed. Go through town and fork right after 2 km. to site on left. GPS: N51:22.488 E06:03.657

Charges 2007

Per unit incl 4 persons	€ 27,50 - € 44,30
extra person	€ 4,70

NL6510 Recreatiecentrum de Schatberg

Midden Peelweg 5, NL-5975 MZ Sevenum (Limburg)
Tel: 0774 67 77 77. Email: info@schatberg.nl

In a woodland setting of 86 hectares, this family run campsite is more reminiscent of a holiday village, with a superb range of activities, making it an ideal venue for families. It is well situated for visits to Germany and Belgium, also easily accessible from the port of Zeebrugge. The 600 touring pitches, with electricity (6/10A), cable, water and drainage, average 100 sq.m. in size and are on rough grass terrain mostly with shade, but not separated. Four pitches have private sanitary facilities and some pitches have been renewed. A feature at De Schatberg is the attractive restaurant/bar area and the reception and indoor pool, manned by friendly staff. Look out for the wallabies and the deer!

Facilities

Five modern, fully equipped toilet blocks, supplemented by three small wooden toilet units to save night time walks. Family shower rooms, baby baths and en-suite units for disabled visitors. Washing machines and dryers. Motorcaravan service point. Supermarket. Restaurant, bar and takeaway. Pizzeria. Pancake restaurant. Indoor and outdoor pools. Tennis. Minigolf. Trampoline. Play areas. Fishing. Watersports. Bicycle hire. Mini-train. Internet access. Entertainment for children and adults in high season. Off site: Golf 4 km.

Open: All year.

Directions

Leave A67 Eindhoven - Venlo motorway at Helden exit 38 and follow signs for 1 km. to site. GPS: N51:22.953 E05:58.575

Charges 2007

Per unit incl. up to 4 persons	€ 18,50 - € 33,95
extra person (over 3 yrs)	€ 4,95
dog	€ 4,95
Camping Cheques accepted.	

NL6560 Camping De Maasvallei

Dorperheideweg 34, NL-5944 NK Arcen (Limburg)

Tel: 077 4731564. Email: info@demaasvallei.nl

Set in the pretty countryside around Noord-Limburg and close to the German border this fairly large site has 463 pitches. There are also static caravans, a number of which are to rent, in separate areas. It is well situated for boating on the Maas, or if preferring to relax on site there is a lake and beach. Being a mature site it is surrounded by trees and some pitches benefit from shade. The main facilities such as the restaurant, bar, takeaway, shop, games room and swimming pool are a short walk from reception, with the lake towards the rear of the site.

Facilities

Three clean and heated sanitary blocks (one new) provide showers, wash cabins, baby baths and a family room, Dishwashing and laundry sinks, washing machines and dryers. Motorcaravan service point. Restaurant and bar. Shop. Swimming pool. Bicycle hire. Organised activities in July/August. Dogs are accepted, but only one per family and in a special area. Off site: Fishing 1 km. Golf 2 km.

Open: All year.

Directions

Leave A77 Boxmeer - Goch motorway at exit 2 to join N271 south in the direction of Venlo. Follow N271 for 27 km. and turn left at traffic lights on dual-carriageway onto local road (signed Lingsfort). Continue on local road for 1.8 km. and turn left. Site is on right after 1.6 km. GPS: N51:29.48 E06:12.378

Charges guide

Per unit incl. 2 persons	€ 18,50 - € 26,50
extra person	€ 3,50

NL6540 Camping Rozenhof

Camerig 12, NL-6294 NB Vijlen-Vaals (Limburg)

Tel: 043 455 16 11. Email: info@campingrozenhof.nl

Camping Rosenhof is a friendly, family run site and its hillside location offers views over a valley that has won awards for its natural beauty. This partially wooded, hilly region is popular with countryside lovers, ramblers and cyclists. Rosenhof has 101 pitches arranged on a series of small terraced, hedged meadows. There are 82 used for touring units, some with hardstanding and all with electricity, water and drainage. Mature trees afford some shade. A rustic restaurant, to the left of the wide entrance has a large terrace and, as the site's name suggests, roses and plants are much in evidence.

Facilities

To the rear of reception, the heated modern sanitary unit houses all the usual facilities including controllable showers, washbasins open and in cabins, facilities for disabled people, a baby changing room and family shower room. Washing machines and dryers. Shop. Restaurant/bar and takeaway. Gas supplies. Playground, playroom and pets corner for children. Riding. Bicycle hire. Off site: Fishing 5 km. Golf 9 km.

Open: All year.

Directions

Leave A76/E314 at Knooppunt Bochtolz and follow N281 towards Vaals for 3 km. to junction with the N278. Turn left and then first right to Vijlen. In Vijlen second road to the left, Vijlen Berg, and straight ahead for 4 km to T-junction. Turn right and continue for 2 km to T-unction then left. After 3 km. the site is to the right. GPS: N50:46.189 E05:55.705

Charges 2006

Per unit incl. 2 persons	€ 16,50
extra person (over 3 yrs)	€ 2,00
electricity (4A)	€ 2,50

NL6580 Recreatieterrein De Gronselenput

Haasstao 3, NL-6321 PK Wijlre (Limburg)

Tel: 043 4591645. Email: gronselenput@paasheuvelgroep.nl

Camping Gronselenput is a small, quiet, countryside site located at the end of a tree lined lane. Family run, it has 60 grassy level pitches 55 of which are for tourists, 40 having 6A electricity. With a peaceful location between a wooded hill and the river Geul (fishing allowed with permit), it is popular with visitors with younger children and those seeking a quiet site. Cars are parked separately from the camping area thus ensuring vehicle free space. The site is set out in a series of small hedged meadows with pitches tending to be located around the edges.

Facilities

In the sanitary block hot water for showers and dishwashing is free. Entry to the toilets is directly from outside. Two baby areas. Washing machines and spin dryer. Gas supplies. Shop (excellent English spoken). Bar selling pizzas with a partly covered terrace facing one of the playgrounds. Large room used for organised children's activities. Off site: Riding and bicycle hire 15 km. Golf 25 km.

Open: 1 April - 31 October.

Directions

Leave A4/E314/A76 at Knooppunt Bocholtz 2 km. (not the exit for the town of Bocholtz). Follow the N281 southwest for 5 km. and turn right (northwest) to Wittem on the N278. In Wittem turn right on N595 to Wijlre. Just after entering Wijlre site is signed to the left. GPS: N50:50.530 E05:52.649

Charges 2006

Per unit incl. 2 persons	€ 9,30 - € 14,00
incl. electricity	€ 16,50

MAP 11

A land full of contrasts, from magnificent snow capped mountains, dramatic fjords, vast plateaux with wild untamed tracts, to huge lakes and rich green countryside. With nearly one quarter of the land above the Arctic Circle it is not surprising that Norway has the lowest population density in Europe.

CAPITAL: OSLO

Tourist Office

Norwegian Tourist Board
Charles House, 5 Lower Regent Street
London SW1Y 4LR
Tel: 0207 839 6255
Email: infouk@ntr.no
Internet: www.visitnorway.com

Norway is made up of five regions. In the heart of the eastern region and the oldest of the Scandinavian capitals, Oslo is situated among green hills and vast forest areas, rich in Viking folklore and traditions. If your main reason for visiting Norway is to see the fjords then head to the west. They are magnificent, with waterfalls and mountains that plunge straight down into the fjords. Trondheim, the third largest city, is in the heart of central Norway, steeped in history with a mixture of old wooden houses and modern architecture. Southern Norway sees the most sun, a popular holiday destination for the Norwegians, with a coastline ideal for swimming, sailing, scuba diving and fishing. The north is the 'Land of the Midnight Sun', where the sun never sets in summer and in winter it fails to rise. The scenery is diverse with forested valleys, stark mountains and lush valleys, and there are also coastal cities to explore, including Tromsø, which boasts the world's most northerly brewery.

Population

4.4 million

Climate

Weather can be unpredictable, although less extreme on the west coast. Some regions have 24 hours of daylight in summer but none in winter.

Language

Norwegian, but English is widely spoken.

Telephone

The country code is 00 47.

Money

Currency: Norwegian Krone
Banks: Mon-Fri 09.00-15.00.

Shops

Mon-Fri 09.00-16.00/17.00, Thu 09.00-18.00/20.00 and Sat 09.00-13.00 /15.00.

Public Holidays

New Year's Day; King's Birthday 21 Feb; Holy Thursday; Good Friday; Easter Monday; May Day; Liberation Day 8 May; Constituition Day 17 May; Ascension; Whit Monday; Queen's Birthday 4 July; Saint's Day 19 July; Christmas 25, 26 Dec.

Motoring

Roads are generally uncrowded around Oslo and Bergen but be prepared for tunnels and hairpin bends. Certain roads are forbidden to caravans or best avoided (advisory leaflet from the Norwegian Tourist Office). Vehicles must have sufficient road grip and in winter it may be necessary to use winter tyres with or without chains. Vehicles entering Bergen on week-days must pay a toll and other tolls are also levied on certain roads.

NO2610 Neset Camping

N-4741 Byglandsfjord (Aust-Agder)

Tel: **37 93 42 55**. Email: **post@neset.no**

On a semi-promontory on the shores of the 40 km. long Byglandsfjord, Neset is a good centre for activities or as a stop en route north from the ferry port of Kristiansand (from England or Denmark). Byglandsfjord offers good fishing (mainly trout) and the area has marked trails for cycling, riding or walking in an area famous for its minerals. Neset is situated on well kept grassy meadows by the lake shore with the water on three sides and the road on the fourth and provides 200 unmarked pitches with electricity and cable TV available. The main building houses reception, a small shop and a restaurant with fine views over the water. This is a well run, friendly site where one could spend an active few days.

Facilities

Three modern sanitary blocks which can be heated, all with comfortable hot showers (some on payment), washing up facilities (metered hot water) and a kitchen. Restaurant and takeaway (15/6-15/8). Shop (1/5-1/10). Campers' kitchen. Playground. Lake swimming, boating and fishing. Excellent new barbecue area and hot tub. Bicycle, canoe and pedalo hire. Climbing, rafting and canoeing courses arranged (including trips to see beavers and elk). Cross-country ski-ing possible in the area in winter. Off site: Rock climbing wall.

Open: All year.

Directions

Site is on route 9, 2.5 km. north of the town of Byglandsfjord on the eastern shores of the lake. GPS: N58:41.309 E07:48.079

Charges guide

Per person	NOK 10
child (5-12 yrs)	NOK 5
pitch	NOK 150
tent and motorcycle	NOK 120
electricity	NOK 30

Camping Cheques accepted.

Neset Camping

4741 Byglnadsford
Aust-Agder
Norway
Tel: +47 37934050
post@neset.no
www.neset.no

Open all year

NO2600 Rysstad Feriesenter

N-4748 Rysstad (Aust-Agder)

Tel: **37 93 61 30**. Email: **post@rysstadferie.no**

Setesdal is on the upper reaches of the Otra river which runs north from the southern port of Kristiansand and right up to the southern slopes of Hardangervidda. It is an area famous for its colourful mining history (silver) and for its vibrant art (especially music) and folklore. The silversmith Trygve Rysstad now runs the Rysstad Feriesenter, founded by his father in the '50s. The site occupies a wide tract of woodland between the road and the river towards which it shelves gently, affording a splendid view of the valley and the towering mountains opposite. The site is in effect divided into two sections; one is divided by trees and hedges into numbered pitches, some occupied by chalets, the other is an adjacent open field and 20 electrical connections are available (6 with satellite TV).

Facilities

Sanitary facilities under the reception block have showers on payment, washbasins in cubicles, dishwashing sinks and a cooker. Laundry facilities. Play area and amusement hut. Sports field. Fishing, swimming and boating (boats for hire). Fitness track. Bicycle hire. Centre includes café, mini shop and restaurant. Handicraft shop. Attractive area on the river's edge for barbecues and entertainment with an arena type setting. Off site: Village within walking distance. Bank, shop, petrol station.

Open: 1 May - 1 October.

Directions

Site is about 1 km. south of junction between route 9 (from Kristiansand) and the extended route 45 (from Stravanger). GPS: N59:05.464 E07:32.434

Charges 2007

Per person	NOK 20
child (4-12 yrs)	NOK 10
caravan or tent	NOK 130
hiker	NOK 60
electricity	NOK 25

NO2660 Preikestolen Camping

Jørssangvegen 265, N-4100 Jørpehand (Rogaland)

Tel: 51 74 97 25. Email: info@preikestolencamping.com

Taking its name from one of Norway's best known attractions, the Preikestolen (Pulpit Rock) cliff formation, Preikestolen Camping is situated in the beautiful region of Rogaland, surrounded by high mountains and deep fjords. The famous and outstanding cliff of Preikestolen was probably formed by the action of frost over 10,000 years ago. From the cliff, 604 m. above fjord level, there are magnificent views over Lysefjorden with its green glacier water. This is a site where you easily could stay a few days to explore the beautiful region. The site is laid out in a relaxed way with a level grass area where trees and bushes create pleasant little 'rooms' for your tent, caravan or motorcaravan. There are 100 pitches, 56 with electricity (10/16A), water tap and waste water drainage.

Facilities

The modern heated sanitary block has showers, washbasins in cubicles and facilities for disabled visitors. Room with sinks but no cookers. All with free hot water. Washing machines and dryers. Motorcaravan services. Freezer. Small shop and craft shop (15/5-15/9). Restaurant and takeaway (15/5-15/9). Fishing. Internet (WiFi). Off site: Preikestolen. Golf 0.5 km. Riding 25 km.

Open: 1 April - 1 October.

Directions

Site is on road 13, 3 km. south of Jörpeland. Follow signs to site. GPS: N58:59.933 E06:05.530

Charges guide

Per person	NOK 25
child	NOK 15
pitch	NOK 110 - 130
electricity	NOK 25

NO2590 Sandviken Camping

N-3650 Tinn Austbygd (Telemark)

Tel: 35 09 81 73. Email: kontakt@sandviken-camping.no

Sandviken is a remote, lakeside site, in scenic location, suitable for exploring Hardangervidda. With its own shingle beach, at the head of Tinnsjo Lake, it provides 150 grassy, mostly level, pitches. In addition to 50 seasonal units and 12 cabins, there are 85 numbered tourist pitches with electricity (10/16A), plus an area for tents, under trees along the waterfront. The office/reception kiosk also sells sweets, soft drinks, ices etc. and a baker calls daily in July. A 1 km. stroll takes you to the tiny village of Tinn Austbygde which has a mini-market, bakery, café, bank, garage and post office.

Facilities

Tidy heated sanitary facilities includes some washbasins in cubicles, showers on payment, sauna, solarium and a dual-purpose disabled/family bathroom with ramped access and baby mat. Kitchen and laundry rooms (hot water on payment). Motorcaravan services. Kiosk (20/6-1/9). Playground. TV and games room. Minigolf. Fishing and watersports. Boat hire. Off site: Riding 15 km.

Open: All year.

Directions

Easiest access is via the Rv 37 from Gransherad along the western side of the lake. GPS: N59:59.352 E08:49.069

Charges guide

Per person	NOK 15
child (4-18 yrs)	NOK 10
caravan or motorcaravan	NOK 110 - 130
tent and car	NOK 95 - 115

NO2315 Ringoy Camping

N-5782 Kinsarvilk (Hordaland)

Tel: 53 66 39 17

Although the village of Ringoy is quiet and peaceful, it occupies a pivotal position, lying not only midway between two principal ferry ports of Upper Hardangerfjord (Kinsarvik and Brimnes), but also near the junction of two key roads (routes 7 and 13). There are several sites at the popular nearby resort town of Kinsarvik, but none compares for situation or atmosphere with the small, simple Ringoy site. This site is basically a steeply sloping field running down from the road to the tree-lined fjord, with flat areas for camping along the top and the bottom of the field. The owners, the Raunsgard family are particularly proud of the site's remarkable shore-side barbecue facilities. On arrival you find a place as there is no reception – someone will call between 8 and 9 pm.

Facilities

The toilet block is small and simple (with metered showers), but well designed, constructed and maintained. It is possibly inadequate during peak holiday weeks in July. Rowing boat (free). A new terraced area with electricity and water is planned. Off site: Village mini-market and garage within a minute's walk.

Open: 15 May - 15 September.

Directions

Site is on route 13, midway between Kinsarvik and Brimnes.

Charges guide

Per person	NOK 10
pitch	NOK 100
electricity (10A)	NOK 20

NO2325 Sundal Camping

P.O. Box 5476, N-5476 Mauranger (Hordaland)

Tel: **53 48 41 86**. Email: **sundalcamping@2i.net**

This is an excellent gateway site for fjordland. Maurangerfjord is a steep-sided arm leading off the eastern shore of the middle reaches of the Hardangerfjord. The village of Mauranger commands magnificent views across the waters. Cutting through the village is a turbulent stream, popular with those in search of trout. Its waters are ice cold, for they descend from the nearby Folgefonn ice-cap and its renowned glacier, an hour's brisk walk from the village. Sundal Camping is divided into two sections: a wooded waterfront site, between the local road and the fjord, which combines camping with a small marina; and an open meadow site uphill of the local road.

Facilities

Two well equipped toilet blocks provide most facilities. Stream and sea fishing. Canoe, rowing boat and bicycle hire. Small shop (24/6-15/9). Restaurant during high season and large barbecue area beside stream. Off site: Small hotel adjacent to site with restaurant and bar. Folgefonna Glacier National Park. Rosenkratz mansion. Trout and salmon fishing.

Open: 1 April - 1 October.

Directions

Either from Route 48 which crosses Hardangerfjord by ferry from Gjermundshavn to Lofallstrand from where road 551 runs northeast for 16 km. along the fjord waterfront to Mauranger/Sundal. Or from Odda on 550 and 551 through an 11 km. long tunnel (toll). GPS: N60:07.113 E06:16.085

Charges guide

Per person	NOK 20
pitch incl. electricity	NOK 90

No credit cards.

NO2330 Eikhamrane Camping

N-5776 Nå (Hordaland)

Tel: **53 66 22 48**

Sørfjord, well known for its fruit growing, has long been on a popular route for travellers across Norway via Utne (where Norway's oldest hotel is a tourist attraction in its own right) and a short ferry crossing across Hardangerfjord. Travellers are also attracted by the Folgefonna ice cap, the most accessible of the great glaciers, which lies at the head of Sørfjord. About halfway along the western shore of Sørfjord is Eikhamrane Camping. There is room for 50 units on unmarked, well kept grass with 20 electrical hook ups (10A). There are attractive trees and good gravel roads, with areas of gravel hardstanding for poor weather. Many pitches overlook the fjord where there are also thoughtfully positioned picnic benches.

Facilities

Two small timber toilet blocks, one for toilets with external access, the other for washbasins (open) and showers (on payment). Both are simple but very well kept. Small kitchen (hot water on payment) and two laundry sinks outside, under cover. Watersports (sailing, canoeing and rowing), and fishing in fjord.

Open: 1 June - 31 August only.

Directions

Site is on road 550 just outside the village of Nå, on the western shore of Sørfjord, 32 km. south of Utne and 16 km. north of Odda.
GPS: N60:10.984 E06:33.104

Charges guide

Per person	NOK 10

No credit cards.

NO2350 Espelandsdalen Camping

N-5736 Granvin (Hordaland)

Tel: **56 52 51 67**. Email: **post@espelandsdalencamping.no**

If one follows Hardangerfjord on the map and considers the mighty glacier which once scooped away the land along its path, it is easy to imagine that it started life in Espelandsdalen. Here is the textbook upper glacial valley. Espelandsdalen runs from Granvin to Ulvik, both of which lie at the heads of their respective arms of Hardangerfjord. A minor road (route 572) links the two small towns with sharp climbs at either end (tricky for caravans). This modest lakeside campsite takes about 30 units on grassy meadow below the road running right down to the lake shore. The whole site occupies just over an acre. There are 10 electrical hook ups (10A).

Facilities

A basic sanitary block consists of a washing trough with hot water, a shower on payment and WCs. Some basic foodstuffs are kept in the office. Swimming, fishing and boating in lake. Boat hire.

Open: 1 May - 31 August.

Directions

The northern loop of the 572 road follows Espelandsdalen. Site is on this road, 6 km. from its junction with route 13 at Granvin (steep gradients).

Charges guide

Per person	NOK 10
pitch incl. electricity	NOK 95

No credit cards.

NO2320 Odda Camping

Borsto, N-5750 Odda (Hordaland)

Tel: **41 32 16 10**. Email: **post@oppleve.no**

Bordered by the Folgefonna glacier to the west and the Hardangervidda plateau to the east and south, Odda is an industrial town with electro-chemical enterprises based on zinc mining and hydro-electric power. At the turn of the century Odda was one of the most popular destinations for the European upper classes – the magnificent and dramatic scenery is still there, together with the added interest of the industrial impact which is well recorded at the industrial museum at Tyssedal. This municipal site has been attractively developed on the town's southern outskirts, just over a kilometre from the centre on the shores of the Sandvin lake (good salmon and trout fishing) and on the minor road leading up the Buar Valley to the Buar glacier, Vidfoss Falls and Folgefonna ice cap. It is possible to walk to the ice face but in the later stages this is quite hard going! The site is spread over 2.5 acres of flat, mature woodland, which is divided into small clearings by massive boulders deposited long ago by the departing glacier. Access is by well tended tarmac roads which wind their way among the trees and boulders. There are 60 tourist pitches including 40 with electricity. The site fills up in the evenings and can be crowded with facilities stretched from the end of June to early August.

Facilities

A single timber building at the entrance houses the reception office (often unattended) and the simple, but clean sanitary facilities which provide, for each sex, 2 WCs, one hot shower (on payment) and 3 open washbasins. Small kitchen with dishwashing facilities. Washing machine and dryer in the ladies washroom. Mini shop. A new sanitary block is planned. Off site: Town facilities close.

Open: 15 May - 31 August (or as required, phone site).

Directions

Site is on the southern outskirts of Odda, signed off road to Buar, with a well marked access.
GPS: N60:03.192 E06:32.628

Charges guide

Per person	NOK 10
tent and car	NOK 90
caravan or motorcaravan	NOK 110
electricity	NOK 30

NO2340 Mo Camping

Steinsdalsvegen 117, N-5601 Norheimsund (Hordaland)

Tel: **56 55 17 27**

This attractive site appears to be alongside a small lake but is actually at the head of an arm of Hardanger fjord one of the 'Big Three' of Norway's spectacular fjords. Only 74km from the ferry at Bergen, Mo makes an ideal first stop on entering Norway or the last night as the ferry can be reached in a comfortable 1.5 hours. It also makes a pleasant base to explore this part of the country. W ithin walking distance of the site, accessed along a footpath at the side of the road, the spectacular Steinsdals Falls draw half a million visitors annually to view the falls from behind! This little site is part of a small working farm run by the Mo family. It has 35 unmarked touring places, with 25 electrical connections possible, on a curve of flat grass with areas of hardstanding for poor weather. The camping is divided from the working part of the farm by a line of charming, traditional, wooden farm buildings which include the family home, owners own personal mini museum, (ask to be shown), the reception and toilet facilities. Although offering only the basics, this site is looked after and well situated with many good walks in the area, free fishing on site and a two-seater canoe for hire. Two rooms and an apartment for rent. Good mobile phone reception.

Facilities

Heated sanitary facilities (in a converted barn) include for each sex a shower (10Nkr - 5 mins) and two washbasins. British style toilets. A little restricted, all sanitary facilities are hard-pressed when the site is full. One room provides a laundry sink, washing machine and dryer plus 2 sinks for dishwashing. Hot water on payment. Motorcaravan services. Off site: Shop and filling station 200 m. Town 1 km. Bicycle hire 5 km. Riding 7 km.

Open: 1 June - 31 August only.

Directions

Site is well signed on road 7 1km west of Norheimsund.

Charges guide

Per unit incl. 2 persons and electricity	NOK 120

No credit cards.

NO2360 Ulvik Fjord Camping

N-5730 Ulvik (Hordaland)

Tel: 091 17 66. Email: camping@ulvik.org

Ulvik was discovered by tourists 150 years ago when the first liners started operating to the head of Hardangerfjord, and to this day, a regular stream of cruise liners work their way into the very heartland of Norway. Access is by winding roads, either along the side of the fjord or up a steep narrow road behind the town – probably not to be recommended for caravans. This pretty little site is 500 m. from the centre of the town. It occupies what must once have been a small orchard running down to the fjord beside a small stream. There is room for about 80 units on undulating ground which slopes towards the fjord, with some flat areas and 24 electrical connections and 6 cabins.

Facilities

New facilities in a small wooden building which houses reception and the well kept sanitary facilities. For each sex there are 2 open washbasins, WCs and 2 modern showers on payment. Kitchen with cooker and dishwashing sink. Washing machine. Bicycle hire. Boat slipway, fishing and swimming in fjord. Jetty with rowing boat (free). Large barbecue area and hot tub.
Off site: Hotel opposite, shops and restaurants in town.

Open: 1 May - 15 September.

Directions

Ulvik is reached by road no. 572; the site is on the southern side of the town, opposite the Ulvikfjord Pension. There is a ferry from road no. 7 at Brimnes. Cars and caravans can now connect with road 7 via a tunnel. GPS: N60:33.908 E06:54.487

Charges guide

Per pitch	NOK 100
electricity	NOK 20

NO2460 Prinsen Strandcamping

Gåseid, N-6015 Ålesund (Møre og Romsdal)

Tel: 70 15 52 04. Email: post@prinsencamping.no

Prinsen is a lively, fjordside site, five kilometres from the attractive small town of Alesund. It is a more attractive option than the more crowded sites closer to town, even so, this is mainly a transit and short-stay site. Divided by trees and shrubs, and sloping gently to a small sandy beach with views down Borgundfjord, the site has 150 grassy pitches, 27 cabins and 7 rooms, 110 electricity hook-ups (16A) and 75 cable TV hook-ups. Reception shares space with the kiosk, fresh baked bread can be ordered daily, and English newspapers are also available.

Facilities

The main heated sanitary unit in the reception building is fully equipped with mostly open washbasins, showers on payment and a sauna for each sex. Kitchen with cooker. Laundry. Extra older facilities mainly serving rooms and cabins, but include multi-purpose bathroom for disabled people, families and baby changing (key from reception). Motorcaravan services. Kiosk (1/6-1/9). TV room. Barbecue areas. Playground. Slipway and boat hire. Fishing.
Off site: Restaurant 800 m. Supermarket 1 km.

Open: All year.

Directions

Turn off E136 at roundabout signed to Hatlane and site. Follow signs to site.
GPS: N62:27.848 E06:15.326

Charges guide

Per pitch	NOK 130
electricity	NOK 30

NO2490 Skjerneset Brygge Camping

Ekkilsoya, N-6530 Averoy (Møre og Romsdal)

Tel: 71 51 18 94. Email: info@skjerneset.com

The tiny island of Ekkilsøya lies off the larger island of Averøy and is reached via a side road and bridge from road 64 just south of Bremsnes from where the ferry crosses to Kristiansund. Although the fishing industry here is not what it used to be it is still the dominant activity and Skjerneset Camping has been developed by the Otterlei family to give visitors an insight into this industry and its history. The old 'Klippfisk' warehouse is now a fascinating 'fisherimuseum' and also houses the sanitary facilities with 5 small apartments, a kitchen, laundry, lounges and reception. There is space for 30 units on gravel hardstandings around a rocky bluff and along the harbour's rocky frontage.

Facilities

Unisex sanitary facilities are heated, but basic, and perhaps a little quirky in their layout but include washbasins in cubicles. Two sanitary blocks, one shaped like fishing boat! Kitchen with two full cookers. Small laundry. Motorcaravan service point. Kiosk for basic packet foods. Satellite TV. Motor boat hire. Organised fishing or sightseeing trips in the owner's sea-going boat.

Open: All year.

Directions

Site is on the little island of Ekkilsøya which is reached via a side road running west from the main Rv 64 road, 1.5 km. south of Bremsnes.
GPS: N63:04.881 E07:35.767

Charges guide

Per person	NOK 20
pitch incl. electricity	NOK 105
No credit cards.	

NO2452 Trollveggen Camping

Horgheimseidet, N-6300 Åndalsnes (Møre og Romsdal)

Tel: **71 22 37 00**. Email: **post@trollveggen.no**

The location of this site provides a unique experience – it is set at the foot of the famous vertical cliff of Trollveggen (the Troll Wall), which is Europe's highest vertical mountain face. The site is surrounded by the Troll Peaks and the Romsdalshorn Mountains with the rapid river of Rauma flowing by. Here in the beautiful valley of Romsdalen you have the ideal starting point for trips to many outstanding attractions such as 'The Troll Road' to Geiranger or to the Mandalsfossen waterfalls. In the mountains there are nature trails of various lengths and difficulties. The campsite owners are happy to help you with information. The site is pleasantly laid out in terraces with level grass pitches. The facility block, the four cabins and the reception are all very attractively built with grass roofs. Beside the river is an attractive barbecue area where barbecue parties are sometimes arranged. The town of Åndalsnes is 10 km. away and has a long tourism tradition as a place to visit. It is situated in the inner part of the beautiful Romsdal fjord and has a range of shops and restaurants. This site is a must for people who love nature.

Facilities

One heated toilet block provides washbasins, some in cubicles, and showers on payment. Family room with baby bath and changing mat, plus facilities for disabled visitors. Communal kitchen with cooking rings, small ovens, fridge and sinks. (free hot water). Washing machine, dryer, and laundry sinks. Motorcaravan service point and chemical disposal point. Barbecue area (covered). Playground. Duck pond. Off site: Climbing, glacier walking and hiking. Fjord fishing. Fjord sightseeing trips. The Troll Road. Mardalsfossen (waterfall). Geiranger and Åndalsnes.

Open: 10 May - 20 September.

Directions

Site is located on the E136 road, 10 km. south of Åndalsnes. It is signed. GPS: N62:29.674 E07:45.500

Charges guide

Per unit incl. 2 persons	NOK 100 - 125
electricity	NOK 30

No credit cards.
Camping Cheques accepted.

Trollveggen Camping

www.trollveggen.no
www.camping-east-west.no
Tlf.: +47 71 22 16 31
Fax: +47 71 22 37 00
Mob.: +47 911 27 325
E-mail: post@trollveggen.no

NO2370 Botnen Camping

N-5950 Brekke (Sogn og Fjordane)

Tel: **57 78 54 71**

For those setting forth north on route 1 from Bergen there are suprisingly few attractive sites until one reaches the southern shore of mighty Sognefjord. At Brekke is a well known tourist landmark, the remarkable Breekstranda Fjord Hotel, a traditional turf-roofed complex which tourist coaches are unable to resist. A mile or two beyond the hotel, also on the shore of the fjord, is the family run Botnen Camping. An isolated, simple (2-star) site which slopes steeply, it is well maintained. It has its own jetty and harbour, with rowing boats and canoes for hire, and commands a splendid view across the fjord to distant mountains.

Facilities

Play area. Swimming, fishing and boating in fjord. Boats and canoes for hire.

Open: May - 1 September.

Directions

Site is 2 km off the coast road running west from Brekke.

Charges guide

Per person	NOK 10
child	NOK 5
pitch incl. electricity	NOK 55

NO2450 Bjolstad Camping

N-6445 Malmefjorden (Møre og Romsdal)

Tel: **71 26 56 56**. Email: **post@bjolstad.no**

This is delightful small, rural site, which slopes down to Malmefjorden, a sheltered arm of Fraenfjorden. Bjølstad has space for just 55 touring units on grassy, fairly level, terraces either side of the tarmac central access road. A delight for children is a large, old masted boat which provides hours of fun playing at pirates or Vikings. At the foot of the site is a waterside barbecue area, a shallow, sandy, paddling area for children and a jetty. Both rowing and motorboats (with lifejackets) can be hired, one can swim or fish in the fjord. This site is an ideal base for visiting Molde International Jazz Festival (annually mid-July), or the famous Varden viewpoint with its magnificent views over this 'Town of Roses', the fjord and mountain peaks, both only 15 minutes drive from the site. Further afield, the small town of Bud is famous for its WW2 German coastal fortress, or one can drive the fantastic and scenic Atlantic Highway as it threads its way across the many islands and bridges to the west of Kristiansund.

Facilities

The very basic, clean, heated sanitary unit includes two showers per sex (on payment), plus washbasins with dividers. Small campers' kitchen with two dishwashing sinks and hot-plate. Laundry service at reception. Playground. Boat hire. Fjord fishing and swimming. Dogs are not accepted in cabins. Off site: Riding 9 km. Golf 12 km.

Open: 1 June - 30 September (may before on request).

Directions

Turn off Rv 64 on northern edge of Malmefjorden village towards village of Lindset (lane is oil bound gravel). Site is 1 km. GPS: N62:48.875 E07:13.518

Charges guide

Per person	NOK 10
child	NOK 5
caravan or tent	NOK 100
motorcaravan	NOK 80
electricity	NOK 30

NO2375 Lærdal Ferie & Fritidspark

P.O. Box 7, N-6886 Lærdal (Sogn og Fjordane)

Tel: **57 66 66 95**. Email: **info@laerdalferiepark.com**

This site is beside the famous Sognefjord, the longest fjord in the world. It is ideally situated if you want to explore the glaciers, fjords and waterfalls of the region. The 100 pitches are level with well trimmed grass and connected by tarmac site roads and are suitable for tents, caravans and motorcaravans. There are 80 electrical hook-ups. You can hire boats on the site for short trips on the fjord. There are plenty of opportunities for other outdoor activities such as fishing, climbing and walking. You can choose a short stroll or a longer hike in the 1,000 m. high mountains. The fully licensed restaurant serves traditional meals as well as snacks and pizzas. The site also provides cabins, flats and rooms to rent, plus a brand new motel, all very modern and extremely tastefully designed. The pretty little village of Laerdal, only 400 m. away, is well worth a visit. A walk among the old, small wooden houses is a pleasant and interesting experience.

Facilities

Two modern and well decorated sanitary blocks with washbasins (some in cubicles), showers on payment, and toilets. Facilities for disabled visitors. Children's room. Washing machine and dryer. Kitchen with cookers and hoods. Dishwashing sinks with free hot water. Motorcaravan services and chemical disposal point. Small shop. Restaurant. TV room. Playground. Motorboats, rowing boats, canoes, bicycles and pedal cars for hire. Tennis court. Bicycle hire. Fishing. Internet (WIFI) at reception. Off site: Cruises on the Sognefjord 400 m. The Norwegian Wild Salmon Centre 400 m. The Flåm railway 40 km. Riding 0.5 km. Golf 12 km.

Open: All year.

Directions

Site is on road 5 (from the Oslo - Bergen road, E16) 400 m. north of Laerdal village centre. GPS: N61:05.793 E07:28.414

Charges guide

Per unit incl. 2 persons	NOK 125,00
electricity	NOK 28,00

Camping Cheques accepted.

Check real time availability and at-the-gate prices...

www.**alanrogers**.com

NO2380 Tveit Camping

N-6894 Vangsnes (Sogn og Fjordane)

Tel: **57 69 66 00**. Email: **tveit@online.no**

Located in the district of Vik on the south shore of Sognefjord, 4 km. from the small port of Vangsnes, Tveit Camping is part of a small working farm and it is a charming neat site. Reception and a kiosk open most of the day in high season, with a phone to summon assistance at any time. Four terraces provide 40 pitches with 30 electricity connections (10A) and there are also site owned cabins. On the campsite you will find a restored Iron Age burial mound dating from 350-550AD, whilst the statue of 'Fritjov the Intrepid' towers over the landscape at Vangsnes. It is also possible for families to do easy hikes on the glacier at Nigardsbreen but not at Fjaerland where it is more challenging.

Facilities

Modern, heated sanitary facilities provide showers on payment, a unit for disabled visitors, kitchens with facilities for dishwashing and cooking, and a laundry with washing machine, dryer and iron (hot water on payment). Motorcaravan services. Kiosk (15/6-15/8). TV rooms. Playground. Harbour for small boats, slipway and boat or canoe hire. Fishing. Bicycle hire. Off site: Shop, café and pub by ferry terminal in Vangsnes 4 km. Riding 15 km.

Open: 10 May - 10 October.

Directions

Site is by Rv 13 between Vik and Vangsnes, 4 km. south of Vangsnes.

Charges guide

Per person (over 5 yrs)	NOK 10
pitch	NOK 90
electricity	NOK 20
No credit cards.	

NO2385 PlusCamp Sandvik

Sandvik Sor, N-6868 Gaupne (Sogn og Fjordane)

Tel: **57 68 11 53**. Email: **sandvik@pluscamp.no**

Sandvik is a compact, small site on the edge of the town of Gaupne close to the Nigardsbreen Glacier. It provides 60 touring pitches, 48 with electrical connections (8/16A), arranged on fairly level grassy terrain either side of a gravel access road. A large supermarket, post office, banks, etc. are all within a level 500 m. stroll. A café in the reception building is open in summer for drinks and meals and the small shop sells groceries, soft drinks, sweets, etc. This is a useful site for those using the spectacular Rv 55 high mountain road from Lom to Sogndal or for visiting the Nigardsbreen Glacier and Jostedalsbreen area of Norway.

Facilities

The single, fully equipped, central sanitary unit includes washbasins with dividers and two hot showers per sex (on payment). Multi-purpose unit for families or disabled people. Small campers' kitchen has hot-plates, oven and fridge (all free of charge) together with tables, chairs and TV. Separate laundry with sinks, washing machine and dryer. Shop and small restaurant (1/6-31/8). Playground. Boat hire. Fishing. Bicycle hire. Off site: Nigardsbreen (glacier). Sognefjellet.

Open: All year.

Directions

Signed just off Rv 55 Lom-Sogndal road on eastern outskirts of Gaupne. GPS: N61:24.032 E07:18.029

Charges 2007

Per pitch incl. up to 4 persons	NOK 140
electricity	NOK 30

NO2390 Kjornes Camping

N-6856 Sogndal (Sogn og Fjordane)

Tel: **57 67 45 80**. Email: **camping@kjornes.no**

A beautiful farm site in a prime fjordside location occupying a long open meadow which is terraced down to the tree lined waterside. This site is ideal for those who enjoy peace and quiet, lovely scenery or a spot of fishing. Access is via a very narrow lane with passing places, which drops down towards the fjord three kilometres from Sogndal. The site takes 100 touring units and has 90 electrical connections (16A). There are also some cabins for accommodation on site.

Facilities

The heated sanitary unit is basic but clean, providing open washbasins, and 2 showers per sex (on payment). Small kitchen with dishwashing sink, double hot-plate and fridge. 'Al fresco' laundry with small roof covering the sink, washing machine and dryer. A new kitchen and laundry facilities are planned. Small shop (20/6-20/8). Off site: Hiking, climbing, rafting.

Open: 1 May - 1 October.

Directions

Site is off the Rv 5, 3 km. east of Sogndal, 8 km. west of Kaupanger. GPS: N61:12.674 E07:07.263

Charges guide

Per person	NOK 25
pitch	NOK 80
electricity	NOK 30

NO2400 PlusCamp Jolstraholmen

Postboks 11, N-6847 Vassenden (Sogn og Fjordane)

Tel: **57728907**. Email: **jolstraholmen@pluscamp.no**

This family run site is situated on the E39 between Sognelfjord and Nordfjord. It is actually located between the road and the fast-flowing Jolstra River (renowned for its trout fishing), 1.5 kilometres from the lakeside village of Vassenden, behind the Statoil filling station, restaurant and supermarket complex which is also owned and run by the site owner and his family. The 50 pitches (some marked) are on grass or gravel hardstanding all with electricity (10A) and some have water and waste points. A river tributary runs through the site and forms an island on which some additional tent pitches are located, and there are also 23 cabins.

Facilities

The main heated sanitary facilities, fully equipped in rooms below the complex, include showers on payment) plus one family bathroom per sex. Small unit located on the island. Two small kitchens provide cooking facilities (free of charge). Laundry. Supermarket and café. Restaurant. Garage. Covered barbecue area. Playground. Volleyball. Water slide (open summer, weather permitting). Rafting. Fishing. Guided walks. Boat hire. Off site: Minigolf. 50 m. Ski-slopes within 1 km.

Open: All year.

Directions

Site is beside the E39 road, 1.5 km. west of Vassenden, 18 km. east of Førde. GPS: N61:29.284 E06:40.941

Charges guide

Per unit incl. 1-4 persons	NOK 120 - 155
small tent incl. 2 persons	NOK 75 - 95
electricity	NOK 30

NO2436 Byrkjelo Camping

N-6826 Byrkjelo (Sogn og Fjordane)

Tel: **91 73 65 97**. Email: **byrkjelocamping@sensewave.com**

This neatly laid out and well equipped small site offers 25 large marked and numbered touring pitches, all with electrical connections (10A) and 15 with gravel hardstandings. It is a good value site in a village location with neatly mown grass, attractive trees and shrubs with a warm welcome from the owners. Fishing is possible in the river adjacent to the site. Reception and a small kiosk selling ices, sweets and soft drinks, are housed in an attractive cabin and there is a bell to summon the owners should they not be on site when you arrive.

Facilities

The good heated sanitary unit includes 5 shower rooms each with washbasin, on payment. A multi-purpose unit serves the needs of families with babies and disabled visitors, incorporating a WC, basin and shower with handrails, etc. Campers' kitchen with hot-plates and dining area (all free). Separate laundry. Motorcaravan services. Kiosk. TV room. Minigolf. Small children's playground. Fishing. Swimming pool (20/6-20/8), both heated (charged). Off site: Riding 4 km. Golf 15 km.

Open: 1 May - 1 October.

Directions

Site is beside the E39 in Byrkjelo village, 19 km. east of Sandane. GPS: N61:43.826 E06:30.507

Charges 2007

Per person	NOK 10
child	NOK 5
pitch	NOK 105
electricity	NOK 30

NO2570 Fossheim Hytte & Camping

N-3550 Gol (Buskerud)

Tel: **32 02 95 80**. Email: **foshytte@online.no**

This small touring site, awarded European camping site of the year 1993, lies just four kilometres west of the town, on the banks of the Hallingdal river bank, shaded by elegant tall birch trees. From reception downstream there are mini rapids. Despite being just below the main road and with a railway in the trees on the opposite side of the river, surprisingly little noise penetrates this idyllic setting. There are 50 grassy touring pitches, with electricity (10/16A) available to 40 and cable TV connections for some. Most overlook the river. Trout fishing with a specially constructed wooden walkway and platform for anglers with disabilities.

Facilities

A modern heated toilet unit includes some washbasins in cubicles, separate unit for disabled people and a sauna for each sex. Small kitchen and laundry rooms. Shop with bread to order (1/6-31/8). Large comfortable TV lounge. Motorcaravan services. Play area. Canoe hire. Fishing licences. Hiking trails. Off site: Riding 18 km. Golf 18 km.

Open: 15 May - 15 September.

Directions

Site is 4 km. west of Gol on route Rv 7 leading to Geilo. GPS: N61:41.012 E08:52.485

Charges 2006

Per unit incl. 2 persons	NOK 130 - 190
electricity	NOK 40

NO2510 Håneset Camping

Osloveien, N-7374 Roros (Sør Trøndelag)

Tel: **72 41 06 00**

At first sight Håneset Camping it is neither promising, lying between the main road and the railway, nor is the gritty sloping ground of the site very imaginatively landscaped – for grass, when it grows up here, is rather coarse and lumpy. However, as we soon discovered, it is the best equipped campsite in the town, and ideal to cope with the often cold, wet weather of this bleak 1,000m. high plateau. The 50 unmarked touring pitches all have access to electricity (10/16A), and most facilities are housed in the main complex building. People flock from all over Europe to visit this well preserved mining town. For over 300 years it was one of Europe's leading copper mines, and during all that time it never suffered serious fire. As a result it occupies a special place on UNESCO's world heritage list.

Facilities	Directions
Heated sanitary facilities provide three separate rooms for each sex, fully equipped with showers on payment. Washing machine and two clothes washing sinks. Kitchen. Huge sitting/TV room and two well equipped kitchens which the owners, the Moen family, share fully with their guests, plus 9 rooms for rent. Off site: Town 20 minutes walk.	Site is on the Rv 30 leading south from Røros to Os, 3 km. from Røros. GPS: N62:34.047 E11:21.118

Charges guide

Per pitch incl. 4 persons	NOK 160,00
electricity	NOK 30,00
No credit cards.	

Open: All year.

NO2515 Gjelten Bru Camping

N-2560 Alvdal (Hedmark)

Tel: **62 48 74 44**

Located a few kilometres west of Alvdal, this peaceful little site, with its traditional turf roof buildings, makes an excellent base from which to explore the area. The 50 touring pitches are on level neatly trimmed grass, served by gravel access roads and with electricity (10A) available to all. Some pitches are in the open and others under tall pine trees spread along the river bank. Across the bridge on the other side of the river and main road, the site owners also operate the well stocked market and post office. The UNESCO World Heritage town of Røros is 75 km. to the northeast of this charming little site, and the Dovrefjell National Park is also within comfortable driving distance.

Facilities	Directions
Heated toilet facilities are housed in two buildings. One unit has been refurbished, the other is of newer construction. There is a mix of conventional washbasins and stainless steel washing troughs, and hot showers on payment. Separate unit for disabled visitors. Two small kitchens, one at each block, provide hot-plates and an oven all free of charge. Washing machine. Fishing. Shop (all year). Off site: Supermarket nearby. Bicycle hire 5 km.	On the road 29 at Gjelten 3.5 km. west of Alvdal. Turn over the river bridge opposite village store and post office, and site is immediately on right. GPS: N62:07.871 E10:34.126

Charges 2006

Per pitch	NOK 130
electricity	NOK 20

Open: All year.

NO2525 Østrea Æra Camping

N-2460 Osen (Hedmark)

Tel: **62 44 49 11**. Email: **info@ostre-aera-camping.com**

This all year site is located on the banks of the Osa river, where you can catch trout and prepare it in the site's barbecue hut for dinner. The small town of Rena is 25 km. away, located in the centre of Norway's largest forest and mountain area. This region is ideal for canoeing, fishing, walking and the only limit is your imagination. The site has 90 pitches (including 60 seasonal), all with 10A electricity and on level grass. There are also 20 cabins for rent. A swimming pool is heated during peak season and has a 50 m. slide. Visit in winter for ice fishing in the Osa lake or good ski facilities in Trysil and Reva, cross country as well as downhill.

Facilities	Directions
Two toilet blocks, one small and unheated. Washbasins with dividers and showers on payment. Dishwashing facilities under cover. Small kitchen. Facilities for disabled visitors. Laundry. No kitchen. Small shop. TV room next to reception. Heated pool with 50 m. slide. Football field. Playground. Barbecue hut. WIFI. Fishing.	Site is on road no. 215, 25 km. northeast of Rena, and is signed. GPS: N61:14.148 E11:39.748

Charges 2006

Per unit incl. electricity	NOK 125 - 185

Open: All year.

NO2545 Plus Camp Rustberg

N-2636 Oyer (Oppland)

Tel: **61 27 58 50**. Email: **rustberg@online.no**

Conveniently located beside the E6, 23 km. from the centre of Lillehammer, this attractive terraced site provides a comfortable base for exploring the area. Like all sites along this route it does suffer from road and train noise at times, but the site's facilities and nearby attractions more than compensate for this. There are 70 pitches with 30 available for touring units, most reasonably level and with some gravel hardstandings available for motorcaravans. There are 70 electrical connections. A small open air, heated swimming pool has a water slide. Lillehammer has a pleasant pedestrian precinct, the '94 Olympic Winter Games and Mailhaugen outdoor museum.

Facilities

Heated, fully equipped sanitary facilities include washbasins in cubicles, showers on payment and free saunas. Two good family bathrooms. Unit for disabled people. Campers' kitchen and dining room with dishwashing, microwave oven and double hob (all free). Separate laundry. Motorcaravan services. Restaurant. Solarium (on payment). Kiosk stocking basic foods. Free swimming pool (1/6-31/8, weather ermitting).Playground. Off site: Forest walks directly from site. Golf 7 km. Children's farm and pony riding.

Open: All year.

Directions

Site is well signed from the E6, 20 km. north of Lillehammer (North) exit.
GPS: N61:16.815 E10:21.657

Charges 2006

Per pitch incl. electricity	NOK 150 - 200

NO2615 Olberg Camping

Sandsveien 2, Olberg, N-1860 Trogstad (Østfold)

Tel: **69 82 86 10**. Email: **froesol@online.no**

Olberg is a newly developed, delightful small farm site, close to lake Oyeren and within 70 km. of Oslo. There are 35 large, level pitches and electricity connections (10-16A) are available for 28 units located on neatly tended grassy meadow with trees and shrubs. In high season fresh bread is available (except Sunday) and coffee, drinks, ices and snacks are provided. A short drive down the adjacent lane takes you to the beach on Lake Oyeren, and there are many woodland walks in the surrounding area. The old church and museum at Trøgstad, and Båstad church are worth visiting. Please bear in mind that this is a working farm. Forest and elk 'safaris' are arranged.

Facilities

Excellent, heated sanitary facilities in a purpose built unit created in the end of a magnificent large, modern barn are fully equipped and include a ramp for wheelchair access and one bathroom for families or disabled visitors. Dishwashing under cover with hot and cold water. Washing machine, tumble dryer and ironing board. Small kitchenette with full size cooker and food preparation area. Kiosk. Snacks. Playground. Off site: Fishing 3 km.

Open: 1 April - 1 October, other times by arrangement.

Directions

Site is signed on Rv 22, 20 km. north of Mysen on southern edge of Båstad village.
GPS: N59:41.296 E11:17.575

Charges 2007

Per unit incl. 2 persons	NOK 175
tent incl. 2 persons	NOK 175

NO2415 Kautokeino Fritidssenter & Camping

Suonpatjavri, N-9520 Kautokeino (Finnmark)

Tel: **78 48 57 33**

This is a friendly, lakeside site, 8 km. south of Kautokeino. The 50 pitches are not marked but are generally on a firm sandy base amongst low growing birch trees, with 20 electric hook-ups (16A) available. There are also cabins and motel rooms for rent. Although the grass is trying to grow, the ground is frozen from September until May so there are mainly hardstandings with some grass areas. During the season when there are enough guests, the owner arranges campfires with 'lectures' about the Sami people. There are walks in the area to some special Sami sites. Shops and are in Kautokeino. The site is 35 km. north of the Finnish Border and is one day's drive from North Cape.

Facilities

The modern sanitary building is heated and well maintained, with 2 British style WCs, 2 open washbasins and 2 showers (on payment) per sex. Small kitchen with full cooker. Laundry. Canoes, boats and pedalos for hire.

Open: 1 June - 30 September.

Directions

Site is 8 km. south of Kautokeino on road Rv 93.
GPS: N68:56.841 E23:05.376

Charges guide

Per pitch	NOK 140
electricity	NOK 20

NO2435 Solvang Camping

Box 1280, N-9505 Alta (Finnmark)

Tel: 78 43 04 77

This is a restful little site with a welcoming atmosphere. It is set well back from the main road, so there is no road noise. The site overlooks the tidal marshes of the Altafjord, which are home to a wide variety of birdlife, providing ornithologists with a grandstand view during the long summer evenings bathed by the Midnight Sun. The 30 pitches are on undulating grass amongst pine trees and shrubs, and are not marked, although there are 16 electric hook-ups (16A). The site is run by a church mission organisation (out of season, the site provides holidays for children and carers).

Facilities

New block with reception and floor-heated sanitary facilities with wash basins in cubicles, showers and a family room. Facilities for disabled visitors. Sauna. New kitchen with cooker, sinks and dining area. Washing machine and dryer. Large TV room. Football field. Playground. Off site: Alta Museum. Rock carvings.

Open: 1 June - 10 August.

Directions

Site is signed off the E6, 10 km. north of Alta. GPS: N69:58.781 E23:28.085

Charges guide

Per pitch incl. 2 persons
and electricity . NOK 150

NO2425 Kirkeporten Camping

Box 22, N-9763 Skarsvag (Finnmark)

Tel: 78 47 52 33. Email: kipo@kirkeporten.no

This is the most northerly mainland campsite in the world (71°06) and considering the climate and the wild unspoilt location it has to be one of the best sites in Scandinavia, and also rivals the best in Europe. An added bonus is that the reindeer often come right into the campsite to graze. The 40 pitches, 22 with electricity (16A), are on grass or gravel hardstanding in natural 'tundra' terrain beside a small lake, together with 16 rental cabins and 5 rooms. Sea fishing and photographic trips by boat can be arranged and buses run 4 times a day to Honningsvåg or the Nordkapp Centre. Note: Although overnighting at Nordkapp Centre is permitted, it is on the very exposed gravel carpark with no electric hook-ups or showers.

Facilities

Excellent modern fully sanitary installations in two buildings (with under-floor heating), linked by a covered timber walkway. They include a sauna, two family bathrooms, baby room, and excellent unit for disabled visitors. Laundry. Kitchen, with hot-plates, sinks and a dining area. All have quality fittings, excellent tiling and beautiful woodwork. Motorcaravan service point. Reception, restaurant and mini shop at the entrance open daily. Off site: North Cape, Kirkeporten.

Open: 20 May - 1 September.

Directions

On the island of Magerøya, from Honningsvåg take the E69 for 20 km. then fork right signed Skarsvåg. Site is on left after 3 km. just as you approach Skarsvåg. GPS: N71:06.456 E25:48.761

Charges guide

Per person	NOK 20
pitch	NOK 150
electricity	NOK 20

NO2428 Andenes Camping

Storgata 53, N-8483 Andenes (Nordland)

Tel: 76 14 12 22. Email: erna.strom@norlandia.no

Many campsites in Norway have simple and basic facilities with little evidence of security. Often, one arrives, finds a pitch and you pay later when reception opens. Andenes Camping is a classic example but included in this guide for very special reasons. This extremely popular exposed site at sea level with picturesque mountain backdrop, is only 3 km. from the base of 'Whalesafari'. This company is deemed the world's largest, most successful Arctic whale watching operation for the general public. The site is also an exceptional location for the midnight sun. Lying on the west coast of Andøy between the quiet main road (82) and white sandy beaches, an area of uneven ground provides space for an unspecified number of touring units and you park where you like. Twenty units only can access 16A electricity and if you want electricity you are highly advised to arrive by mid-afternoon.

Facilities

The reception building houses clean separate sex sanitary facilities providing for each 2 toilets, 2 showers with curtain to keep clothes dry and 3 washbasins. Small kitchen (free). Motorcaravan service point. Off site: Well stocked supermarket 250 m.

Open: 1 June - 30 September.

Directions

Travelling north on road 82, site is on left 3 km. before Andenes.

Charges guide

Per pitch	NOK 120
incl. electricity	NOK 130

NO2455 Ballangen Camping

N-8540 Ballangen (Nordland)

Tel: 76 92 76 90. Email: ballcamp@c2i.net

Ballangen is a pleasant, lively site conveniently located on the edge of a fjord with a small sandy beach, with direct access off the main E6 road. The 150 marked pitches are mostly on sandy grass, with electricity (10/16A) available to all. There are a few hardstandings, also 54 cabins for rent. A TV room has tourist information, a coffee and games machines and there is a heated outdoor pool and waterslide (charged), free fjord fishing, and boat hire. An interesting excursion is to the nearby Martinstollen mine where visitors are guided through the dimly lit Olav Shaft 500 m. into the mountain. Narvik with its wartime connections and museums is 40 km.

Facilities	Directions
Toilet facilities in buildings with modern fittings include some washbasins in cubicles. Facilities for disabled visitors, sauna and solarium. Kitchen with 2 cookers and covered seating area. Laundry. Motorcaravan services. Shop. Café and takeaway (main season). Swimming pool (charged). Tennis. Minigolf. Fishing. Golf. Boat and bicycle hire. Pedal car hire. Mini zoo. Playground. Off site: Riding 2 km. Ballangen 4 km. Narvik 40 km.	Access is off the E6, 4 km. north of Ballangen, 40 km. south of Narvik. GPS: N68:20.333 E16:51.468

Charges 2007	
Per pitch	NOK 170
electricity	NOK 40

Open: 1 March - 31 December.

NO2465 Lyngvær Lofoten Bobilcamping

Postboks 30, N-8310 Kabelvag (Nordland)

Tel: 76 07 87 81. Email: relorent@c2i.net

Some camping sites on Lofoten are very basic with extremely limited facilities but Lyngvaer is in complete contrast. In the centre of Lofoten alongside a tidal fjord with mountains all around, the setting and location is quite idyllic. Large terraces provide fine views for most of the 200 pitches, mainly grass, some with hardstanding, with electricity for 110 Boat hire is available and the site has its own waters for salmon and trout fishing. There are also two cabins and eight rooms for rent, all sleeping up to five people. The owners bake their own bread and rolls to order, with other foodstuffs and the like available at a supermarket in Henningsvaer (10 km.).

Facilities	Directions
Toilet facilities are spotlessly clean and good with showers in small cubicles (NkOK10 for 6 minutes). Extra unisex showers and toilets are beside reception. Communal kitchen with cooking, dishwashing and fish freezer (free). Large sitting area with satellite TV. Play areas. Boat hire. Fishing (fish cleaning area).	On disembarking the ferry (Skutvik - Svolvaer) turn southwest on E10 signed Lofoten. Site is on left in 18 km. (There is a campsite about 6 km. from Skutvik on the left on approach, details unknown).

Charges guide	
Per unit incl. 1 person	NOK 100
extra person	NOK 5
electricity	NOK 20

Open: 1 May - 30 September.

NO2475 Saltstraumen Camping

Bok 85, N-8056 Saltstraumen (Nordland)

Tel: 75 58 75 60. Email: saltstraumen@pluscamp.no

On a coastal route, this extremely popular site, in a very scenic location with a magnificent backdrop, is close to the largest Maelstrom in the world. It is an easy short walk to this outstanding phenomenon where in the course of six hours between 33,800 and 82,700 billion gallons of water are pressed through a narrow strait at a rate of about 20 knots. The effect is greatest at new or full moons. The fjord close by (walking distance) is renowned for the prolific numbers of coalfish and cod caught from the shore. Most on site 'have a go' to catch their evening meal. As well as 20 cabins, the site has 60 plain touring pitches mostly on level, gravel hardstandings in rows, each with electricity. The site is 33 km. from Bodø and 50 km. from Fauske. You are advised to arrive by late afternoon.

Facilities	Directions
Basic but heated sanitary facilities are clean and fully equipped. Separate shower areas for men and women have dividers, shower curtains and communal changing (free). Kitchen with two full cookers (free). Laundry. Motorcaravan service point. Fishing. Off site: Well stocked mini supermarket and snack bar outside site entrance.	Travelling from the south: Before Rognan take Rv 812 signed Saltstraumen. At junction with Rv 17 turn right and site is on left immediately after second bridge.

Charges guide	
Per unit incl. 2 persons	NOK 90 - 120
electricity	NOK 30

Open: All year.

NO2485 Krokstrand Camping

Krokstrand, N-8630 Storforshei (Nordland)

Tel: 75 16 60 02

This site is a popular resting place for all nationalities on the long trek to Nordkapp and it is only 18 km. from the Arctic Circle with its Visitor Centre. There are 45 unmarked pitches set amongst birch trees with electrical connections (16A) for 28 units. In late spring and early summer the river alongside, headed by rapids is impressive with the possibility of mountains close by still being snow-capped. The small reception kiosk is open 16.00 - 22.00 hrs in high season, otherwise campers are invited to find a pitch and pay later. For those interested in WW2 history there is the neatly tended grave of a Russian soldier by the site gate.

Facilities

Well maintained, spotlessly clean, small sanitary unit includes two showers per sex (on payment). Laundry with washing machine and dryer. Small kitchen with double hot-plate and dishwashing sink. Motorcaravan services. Brightly painted playground with trampoline. Minigolf. Fishing. Off site: Hotel with café/restaurant just outside site entrance (same ownership as the site).

Open: 1 June - 20 September.

Directions

Entrance is off E6 at Krokstrand village opposite hotel, 18 km. south of the Arctic Circle.

Charges guide

Per person	NOK 10
child	NOK 5
pitch	NOK 80
electricity	NOK 30

No credit cards.

NO2495 Vegset Camping

N-7760 Snasa (Nord-Trøndelag)

Tel: 74 15 29 50. Email: mveg@online.no

This small, basic but pleasant site is seven kilometres south of Snåsa, directly beside the E6 road on the banks of Lake Snåsavatn. It consists of ten site owned chalets, a number of static units and a small area for about 20 touring units on slightly sloping ground. There are 10A electricity connections available. Snåsa is a centre for the South Lapp people who have their own boarding school, museum and information centre there. The Bergasen Nature Reservation is close to the village and is famous for its rare flora, especially orchids. The Gressamoen National Park is also near. For those travelling to or from Northern Norway, Vegset provides a good resting point or night halt.

Facilities

The satisfactory toilet block provides showers (NOK 10), plus a shower with toilet suitable for disabled people. Kitchen. Kiosk selling emergency groceries doubles as a TV room (end June - mid Aug). Swimming, boat hire and fishing (licence from site).

Open: Easter - 10 October.

Directions

Site is just off the E6 road, 7 km. south of Snåsa.

Charges guide

Per pitch	NOK 110
electricity	NOK 30

NO2500 Tråsåvika Camping

Orkanger, N-7354 Viggja (Sør Trøndelag)

Tel: 72 86 78 22. Email: jowiggen@start.no

On a headland jutting into the Trondheimfjord some 40 km. from Trondheim, Trasavika commands an attractive position. For many this compensates for the extra distance into town. The 65 pitches (some slightly sloping) are on an open grassy field at the top of the site, or on a series of terraces below, which run down to the small sandy beach, easily accessed via a well designed gravel service road. There are 48 electricity connections (10A). To one side, on a wooded bluff at the top of the site, are 14 cabins (open all year), many in traditional style with grass roofs. The reception complex also houses a small shop, licensed café with lounge area and a terrace overlooking the entire panorama.

Facilities

The neat, fully equipped, sanitary unit includes two controllable hot showers per sex (on payment). Hot water on payment in kitchen and laundry which have a hot-plate, dish and clothes washing sinks, washing machine and dryer. Shop. Café (20/6-30/8). TV/sitting room. Play area. Jetty and boat hire. Free fjord fishing with catches of good sized cod from the shore.

Open: 1 May - 10 September.

Directions

Site is to the west of Viggja with direct access from the E39 between Orkanger and Buvik, 21 km. from the E6 and 40 km. west of Trondheim.

Charges guide

Per pitch	NOK 140
electricity	NOK 30 - 110

NO2505 Magalaupe Camping

Engan, N-7340 Oppdal (Sør Trøndelag)

Tel: **72 42 46 84**. Email: **camp@magalaupe.no**

This is a rural, good value, riverside site in a sheltered position with easy access from the E6. Fairly simple facilities are offered but there are a host of unusual activities in the surrounding area, including caving, canyoning, rafting, gold panning, mineral hunting, and musk oxen, reindeer and elk safaris. In winter the more adventurous can also go snow-moiling or skiing in the high Dovrefjell National Park. The 52 unmarked and grassy touring pitches (42 with 16A electricity) are in natural surroundings amongst birch trees and rocks and served by gravel access roads. As the site rarely fills up, the simple facilities should be adequate at most times.

Facilities	Directions
Small, clean, heated sanitary unit fully equipped and the showers are on payment. Extra WC/washbasin units in reception building. Small kitchen with dishwashing facilities, hot-plate, fridge and freezer, plus a combined washing/drying machine. Kiosk for ices, soft drinks, etc. Bar (mid June - Aug). TV lounge. Fishing. Bicycle hire. Off site: Supermarkets and other services in Oppdal (11 km). Riding or golf 12 km. Organised walking, cycling and car tours. **Open:** All year.	Site is signed on E6, 11 km. south of Oppdal. GPS: N62:29.822 E09:35.121

Charges guide

Per pitch	NOK 100
tent	NOK 80
electricity	NOK 20
No credit cards.	

NO2432 Harstad Camping

Nesseveien 55, N-9411 Harstad (Troms)

Tel: **77 07 36 62**. Email: **postmaster@harstad-camping.no**

For those visiting or exiting Lofoten and Vesterålen, this well established, popular site close to Harstad, provides an excellent stopping point on Hinnøya, the largest island in Norway. In a delightful setting with fine views, the campsite has space for 120 units as it slopes down to Vågsfjorden. Pitches are not marked but by the waters edge a flat area provides most of the 33 electricity hook-ups (16A). This part of the site is sought after and we advise a mid-afternoon arrival for the possibility of a level pitch and/or electricity connection. A small island very close to the site plays host to a colony of arctic tern. The clean sanitary block has two coin operated showers for each sex and one may have to wait if the site is busy. Catches of fish from the shore are not prolific, although hiring one of the site's boats (rowing or motor) will soon transport you to nearby areas where you are likely to catch good sized cod. The site also has 16 cabins for rent.

Facilities	Directions
Good facilities include British style WCs, washbasins and showers (Nkr 10 for 4 minutes). Room for disabled visitors. Laundry room with sinks (hot water charged). Kitchen with hot plates (free), tables and chairs. Chemical disposal point. Reception (manned 0800-2300 high season) has a small selection of tinned foods (no bread or milk). Off site: One of northern Norway's largest shopping centres, including a garage and a supermarket at 2 km. **Open:** All year.	Travelling north on road 83, site is on right 3 km. before Harstad. After turning right, turn immediate left and site is 1 km. along firm unmade road (site signed from either direction).

Charges guide

Per pitch	NOK 150
incl. electricity	NOK 175

NO2445 Slettnes Fjordcamp

N-9047 Oteren (Troms)

Tel: **77 71 45 08**

Slettnes is a useful stopover southeast of Tromso beside the E6 road. Beside a narrow fjord and surrounded by snowy capped mountains, this is a large site mainly for permanent caravans but with room for 10 touring units.

Facilities	Directions
Sanitary facilities consist of two toilets each for male and female with washbasins with mirror, etc. There are three showers each, communal but with no charge and good hot water. A kitchen houses a sink unit, full size cooker and microwave. **Open:** Contact site.	Site is beside the E6 road 6 km. north of Oteren. GPS: N69:19.239 E20:00.876

Charges guide

Per unit	NOK 100

MAP 9

Portugal is a relatively small country occupying the southwest part of the Iberian peninsula, bordered by Spain in the north and east, with the Atlantic coast in the south and west. In spite of its size, the country offers a tremendous variety in both its way of life and traditions.

CAPITAL: LISBON

Tourist Office
ICEP Portuguese Trade & Tourism Office
2nd Floor 22/25a Sackville Street
London W1S 3LY
Tel: 0845 3551212
E-mail: info@visitportugal.com
Internet: www.visitportugal.com

Most visitors looking for a beach type holiday head for the busy Algarve, with its long stretches of sheltered sandy beaches, and warm, clear Atlantic waters, great for bathing and watersports. With its monuments and fertile rolling hills, central Portugal adjoins the beautiful Tagus river that winds its way through the capital city of Lisbon, on its way to the Altantic Ocean. Lisbon city itself has deep rooted cultural traditions, coming alive at night with buzzing cafes, restaurants and discos. Moving southeast of Lisbon the land becomes rather impoverished, consisting of stretches of vast undulating plains, dominated by cork plantations. Consequently most people head for the walled town of Evora, an area steeped in two thousand years of history. The Portuguese consider the Minho area in the north to be the most beautiful part of their country, with its wooded mountains and wild coastline, a rural and conservative region with picturesque towns.

Population
10 million

Climate
The country enjoys a maritime climate with hot summers and mild winters with comparatively low rainfall in the south, heavy rain in the north.

Language
Portuguese

Telephone
The country code is 00 351.

Money
Currency: The Euro
Banks: Mon-Fri 08.30-11.45 and 13.00-14.45. Some large city banks operate a currency exchange 18.30-23.00.

Shops
Mon-Fri 09.00-13.00 and 15.00-19.00. Sat 09.00-13.00.

Public Holidays
New Year; Carnival (Shrove Tues); Good Fri; Liberty Day 25 Apr; Labour Day; Corpus Christi; National Day 10 June; Saints Days; Assumption 15 Aug; Republic Day 5 Oct; All Saints 1 Nov; Immaculate Conception 8 Dec; Christmas 24-26 Dec.

Motoring
The standard of roads is very variable, even some of the main roads can be very uneven. Tolls are levied on certain motorways (auto-estradas) out of Lisbon, and upon southbound traffic at the Lisbon end of the giant 25th Abril bridge over the Tagus. Parked vehicles must face the same direction as moving traffic.

Portugal

PO8202 Camping Turiscampo

Estrada Nacional, 125, Espiche, P-8600 Lagos (Faro)
Tel: **282 789 265**. Email: **info@turiscampo.com**

This site is being thoughtfully refurbished and updated to include most of the existing infrastructure since it was purchased by the friendly Coll family, who are known to us from their previous Spanish site. Work was still in progress when we visited but the site does show great promise and will become a quality site. The site provides 250 pitches for tourers mainly in rows of terraces, all with electricity and some with shade. They vary in size (70-120 sq.m). The upper areas of the site are being developed and are mostly destined for bungalows (which are generally separate from the touring areas). A new, elevated Californian style pool plus a children's pool have been constructed and the supporting structure is a clever water cascade and surround. There is a large sun lounger area on astroturf. One side of the pool area is open to the road. The restaurant/bar has been tastefully refurbished and Giovanni and staff are delighted to use their excellent English to provide good fare at most reasonable prices (bargain menu of the day for € 6.50). The restaurant has two patios one of which is used for live entertainment and discos in season and the other for dining out. The sea is 2 km. and the city of Lagos 4 km. with all the attractions of the Algarve within easy reach. When complete this will be a very good site for families and for 'Snowbirds' to 'over-winter'.

Facilities

The two existing toilet blocks have been refurbished and a new block added containing modern facilities for disabled campers. Hot water throughout. Facilities for children. Washing machines. Shop (all year). Gas supplies. Restaurant/bar (all year). Swimming pool (March - Oct). Bicycle hire. Internet. Cable TV. Entertainment in high season on the bar terrace. Playground on sand. Adult art workshops, aqua gymnastics and mini-club (5-12 yrs) in season. Bungalows to rent. Petanque. Sports field with basketball, volleyball etc. Off site: Bus to Lagos and other towns from Praia da Luz village 1.5 km. Fishing and beach 2 km. Golf 4 km. Riding 10 km. Sailing 5 km. Boat launching 5 km.

Open: All year.

Directions

Take the N125 from Lagos to Sagres. The impressive entrance is about 3 km. on the right.
GPS: N37:06 W08:43

Charges 2007

Per person	€ 2,90 - € 5,40
child (3-10 yrs)	€ 1,60 - € 2,80
pitch	€ 4,75 - € 12,00
electricity (6/10A)	€ 2,85 - € 3,60

Camping Cheques accepted.

PO8200 Orbitur Camping Valverde

Estrada da Praia da Luz, Valverde, P-8600-148 Lagos (Faro)
Tel: **282 78 92 11**. Email: **info@orbitur.pt**

A little over a kilometre from the village of Praia da Luz and its beach and about 7 km. from Lagos, this large, well run site is certainly worth considering for your holiday stay in the Algarve. It has 600 numbered pitches, of varying size, which are enclosed by hedges. All are on flat ground or broad terraces with good shade in most parts from established trees and shrubs. The site has a swimming pool with a long curling slide and a paddling pool (under 10s free, adults charged). This is an excellent site with well maintained facilities and good security. It attracts a good number of long-term winter visitors and is one of the better Orbitur sites.

Facilities

Six large, clean, toilet blocks have some washbasins and sinks with cold water only, and hot showers. Units for disabled people. Laundry. Motorcaravan services. Supermarket (all year), shops, restaurant and bar complex with both self-service and waiter service in season (closed November). Takeaway. Coffee shop. Swimming pool (April - Sept) with slide and paddling pool (June - Sept). Playground. Tennis. Satellite TV in bar. Disco. Pub. Excursions. Off site: Bus service from site gate. Beach and fishing 1.5 km. Bicycle hire 3 km. Golf 10 km.

Open: All year.

Directions

From Lagos on N125 road, after 7 km. turn south to Praia da Luz. At the town follow Orbitur camping signs. The beach road is narrow and cobbled and is very challenging in a large unit.
GPS: N37:05 W08:43

Charges 2007

Per person	€ 2,90 - € 5,40
child (5-10 yrs)	€ 1,45 - € 2,70
caravan and car	€ 6,70 - € 13,10
electricity	€ 2,40

Off season discounts (up to 70%).

PO8210 Parque de Campismo Albufeira

EN 125 Ferreiras-Albufeira, P-8200-555 Albufeira (Faro)

Tel: **289 58 76 29**. Email: **campingalbufeira@mail.telepac.pt**

The spacious entrance to this site will accommodate the largest of units (watch for severe speed bumps at the barrier). One of the better sites on the Algarve, it has pitches on fairly flat ground with some terracing, trees and shrubs giving reasonable shade in most parts. There are some marked and numbered pitches of 50-80 sq.m. Winter stays are encouraged with many facilities remaining open including a pool. An attractively designed complex of traditional Portuguese style buildings on the hill, with an unusually shaped pool and two more for children, forms the central area of the site. It has large terraces for sunbathing and pleasant views and is surrounded by a variety of flowers, shrubs and well watered lawns, complete with a fountain. The 'à la carte' restaurant, impressive with its international cuisine, and the very pleasant self-service one both have views across the three pools. A pizzeria, bars and a soundproofed disco are great for younger campers.

Facilities

The toilet blocks include hot showers. Launderette. Very large supermarket. Tabac (English papers). Waiter and self-service restaurants. Pizzeria. Bars. Satellite TV. Soundproof disco. Swimming pools. Tennis. Playground. Internet access. First aid post. Car wash. ATM. Car hire.
Off site: Site bus service from gate to Albufeira every 45 minutes (2 km). Theme parks nearby. Beaches.

Open: All year.

Directions

From N125 coast road or N264 (from Lisbon) at new junctions follow N395 to Albufeira. Site is about 2 km. on the left. GPS: N37:06 W08:15

Charges 2006

Per person	€ 5,20
child (4-10 yrs)	€ 2,60
pitch	€ 5,60 - € 11,95
electricity (10A)	€ 2,85

Check real time availability and at-the-gate prices...

www.**alanrogers**.com

PO8220 Orbitur Camping Quarteira

Estrada da Fonte Santa, Avenida Sá Cameiro, P-8125-618 Quarteira (Faro)

Tel: 289 30 28 26. Email: info@orbitur.pt

This is a large, busy attractive site on undulating ground with some terracing, taking 795 units. On the outskirts of the popular Algarve resort of Quarteira, it is 600 m. from a sandy beach which stretches for a kilometre to the town centre. Many of the unmarked pitches have shade from tall trees and there are a few small individual pitches of 50 sq.m. with electricity and water which can be reserved. There are 680 electrical connections. Like others along this coast, the site encourages long winter stays. There is a large restaurant and supermarket with a separate entrance for local trade.

Facilities

Five toilet blocks provide British and Turkish style toilets, washbasins with cold water, hot showers plus facilities for disabled visitors. Washing machines. Motorcaravan services. Gas supplies. Supermarket. Self-service restaurant (closed Nov). Separate takeaway (from late May). Swimming pools (April - Sept). General room with bar and satellite TV. Tennis. Open air disco (high season). Off site: Bus from gate to Faro. Fishing 1 km. Bicycle hire (summer) 1 km. Golf 4 km.

Open: All year.

Directions

Turn off N125 for village of Almancil. In the village take road south to Quarteira. Site is on the left 1 km. after large, official town welcome sign. GPS: N37:04 W08:05

Charges 2007

Per person	€ 2,90 - € 5,40
child (5-10 yrs)	€ 1,45 - € 2,70
caravan and car	€ 6,70 - € 13,10
electricity	€ 2,40

Off season discounts (up to 70%).

PO8410 Parque de Campismo de Armacão de Pera

P-8365 Armacão de Pera (Faro)

Tel: 282 31 22 96. Email: camping_arm_pera@hotmail.com

A modern site with a wide attractive entrance and a large external parking area, the 1,200 pitches are in zones on level grassy sand. They are marked by trees that provide some shade, and are easily accessed from tarmac and gravel roads. Electricity is available for most pitches. The facilities are good. The self service restaurant, bar and well stocked supermarket should cater for most needs, and you can relax around the swimming pools. The disco near the entrance and café complex is soundproofed which should ensure a peaceful night for non-revellers.

Facilities

Three modern sanitary blocks provide British and Turkish style WCs and showers with hot water on payment. Facilities for disabled campers. A reader reports that maintenance can be variable. Laundry. Supermarket. Self-service restaurant (all year). Three bars (one all year). Swimming and paddling pools (May - Sept; charged per day; no lifeguard). Games and TV rooms. Tennis. Well maintained play area. ATM. Off site: Bus to town from gate. Fishing, bicycle hire and watersports nearby.

Open: All year.

Directions

Site is west of Albufeira. Turn off N125/IC4 road in Alcantarilha, taking the EN269-1 towards the coast. Site is on left before Armação de Pêra. There are sites with similar names in the area, so be sure to find the right one. GPS: N37:06 W08:21

Charges 2006

Per person	€ 2,50 - € 5,50
child (4-10 yrs)	€ 1,60 - € 3,20
pitch incl. electricity (6A)	€ 6,50 - € 11,50

Min. stay 3 nights 1 June - 31 Aug.

PO8430 Orbitur Camping Sagres

Cerro das Moitas, P-8650-998 Sagres (Faro)

Tel: 282 62 43 71. Email: info@orbitur.pt

Camping de Sagres is a pleasant site at the western tip of the Algarve, not very far from the lighthouse in the relatively unspoilt southwest corner of Portugal. With 960 pitches for tents and 120 for tourers, the sandy pitches, some terraced, are located amongst pine trees that give good shade. There are some hardstandings for motorhomes and electricity throughout. The fairly bland restaurant, bar and café/grill provide a range of reasonably priced meals. This is a reasonable site for those seeking winter sun, or as a base for exploring this 'Land's End' region of Portugal.

Facilities

Three spacious toilet blocks are showing some signs of wear but provide hot and cold showers and washbasins with cold water. Washing machines. Motorcaravan services. Supermarket (all year). Restaurant/bar and café/grill (all Easter and June-Oct). Satellite TV. Bicycle hire. Barbecue area. Playground. Fishing. Medical post. Car wash. Off site: Buses from village 1 km. Beach and fishing 2 km. Boat launching 8 km. Golf 12 km.

Open: All year.

Directions

From Sagres, turn off the N268 road west onto the EN268. After about 2 km. the site is signed off to the right. GPS: N37:01 W08:56

Charges 2007

Per person	€ 2,40 - € 4,40
child (5-10 yrs)	€ 1,20 - € 2,20
caravan and car	€ 5,40 - € 10,60
electricity (6A)	€ 2,40

PO8230 Camping Olhão

Pinheiros de Marim, P-8700 Olhão (Faro)

Tel: 289 70 03 00. Email: parque.campismo@sbsi.pt

This site, with around 800 pitches, is open all year. It has many mature trees providing good shade. The pitches are marked, numbered and in rows divided by shrubs, although levelling will be necessary and the trees make access tricky on some. There is electricity for 102 pitches (6A) and a separate area for tents. Permanent and long stay units take 20% of the pitches, the touring pitches filling up quickly in July and August, so arrive early. There is some noise nuisance from an adjacent railway. The site has a relaxed, casual atmosphere. Amenities include very pleasant swimming pools and tennis courts, a reasonable restaurant/bar and a café/bar with TV and games room. All are very popular with the local Portuguese who pay to use the facilities. The large, sandy beaches in this area are on offshore islands reached by ferry and are, as a result, relatively quiet; some are reserved for naturists. This site can get very busy in peak periods and maintenance can be variable. There was a large, low season British contingent when we visited, enjoying the low prices.

Facilities

Eleven sanitary blocks are adequate, clean when seen, and are specifically sited to be a maximum of 50 m. from any pitch. One block has facilities for disabled visitors. Laundry. Excellent supermarket. Kiosk. Restaurant/bar (all year). Café and general room with cable TV. Playgrounds. Swimming pools (April - Sept) and tennis courts (fees for both). Bicycle hire. Internet at reception. Off site: Bus service to the ferry at Olhao 50 m. from site. Indoor pool 2 km. Riding 1 km. Fishing 2 km. Golf 20 km.

Open: All year.

Directions

Just over 1 km. east of Olhão, on EN125, take turn to Pinheiros de Marim. Site is back off the road on the left. Look for very large, white, triangular entry arch as the site name is different on the outside wall. GPS: N37:02 W07:49

Charges 2006

Per person	€ 2,20 - € 4,00
child (5-12 yrs)	€ 1,20 - € 2,20
pitch incl. electricity	€ 4,95 - € 12,30

Less for longer winter stays.

Camping Olhão ★★★ Open All Year
Tennis Football Bar Swimming Pool Restaurant Bungalows Mobile Homes
parque.campismo@sbsi.pt
Algarve - Portugal   www.sbsi.pt/camping   351 289 700 300

PO8170 Parque de Campismo São Miguel

São Miguel, Odeceixe, P-7630-592 Odemira (Beja)

Tel: 282 947145. Email: camping.sao.miguel@mail.telepac.pt

Nestled in green hills near two pretty white villages, 4 km. from the beautiful Praia Odeceixe (beach) is the attractive camping park São Miguel. Unusually the site works on a maximum number of 700 campers, you find your own place (there are no defined pitches) under the tall trees, there are ample electrical points, and the land slopes away gently. Wooden chalet style accommodation to rent is in a separate area, but some mobile homes share the two traditional older style but clean sanitary blocks. The main building with its traditional Portuguese architecture is built around two sides of a large grassy square. It houses reception, restaurant, bars and supermarket.

Facilities

Two older style toilet blocks with British style WCs and free hot showers. Washing machines. Toilets and basins for disabled campers but no shower. Shop (June -Sept). Self-service restaurant (March-Oct). Bar, snacks and pizzeria (June-Sept). Satellite TV. Playground. Tennis (charged). Swimming pool (charged). Dogs are not accepted. Torches useful. Off site: Bus service. Odeceixe 2 km. Beach, fishing and sailing 4 km. Riding 20 km.

Open: All year.

Directions

Between Odemira and Lagos on the N120 just before the village of Odeceixe on the main road well signed. GPS: N37:26 W08:45

Charges 2006

Per person	€ 3,50 - € 5,50
child (5-10 yrs)	€ 2,00 - € 3,00
pitch incl. electricity	€ 9,75 - € 15,25

Plus 7% VAT.

PO8150 Orbitur Camping Costa da Caparica

Avenida Alfonso de Albuquerque, Quinta de St Antonio, P-2825-450 Costa da Caparica (Setubal)

Tel: **212 90 13 66**. Email: **info@orbitur.pt**

This is very much a site for 600 permanent caravans but it has relatively easy access to Lisbon (just under 20 km.) via the motorway, by bus or even by bus and ferry if you wish. It is situated near a small resort, favoured by the Portuguese themselves, which has all the usual amenities plus a good sandy beach (200 m. from the site) and promenade walks. There is a small area for touring units which includes some larger pitches for motorcaravans. We see this very much as a site to visit Lisbon rather than for prolonged stays. Some activities and shows are organised in season.

Facilities	Directions
The three toilet blocks have mostly British style toilets, washbasins with cold water and some hot showers - they come under pressure when the site is full. Facilities for disabled visitors. Washing machine. Motorcaravan services. Supermarket. Large bar/restaurant (not Nov). TV room (satellite). Playground. Gas supplies. Off site: Bus service from site gate. Fishing 1 km. Riding 4 km. Golf 5 km.	Cross the Tagus bridge (toll) on A2 motorway going south from Lisbon, immediately take the turning for Caparica and Trafaria. At 7 km. marker on IC20 turn right (no sign) - the site is at the second roundabout. GPS: N38:39.22 W09:14.33

Open: All year.

Charges 2007

Per person	€ 2,70 - € 4,80
caravan and car	€ 6,70 - € 12,50
electricity	€ 2,40 - € 3,00

PO8130 Orbitur Camping Guincho

E.N. 247, Lugar da Areia - Guincho, P-2750-053 Cascais (Lisbon)

Tel: **214 87 04 50**. Email: **info@orbitur.pt**

Although this is a popular site for permanent Portuguese units with 1,295 pitches, it is nevertheless quite attractively laid out among low pine trees and with the A5 autostrada connection to Lisbon (30 km), it provides a useful alternative to sites nearer the city. This is viewed as an alternative for visiting Lisbon, not a holiday site. There is a choice of pitches (small – mainly about 50 sq.m.) mostly with electricity, although siting amongst the trees may be tricky, particularly when the site is full. Located behind sand dunes and a wide, sandy beach, the site offers a wide range of facilities.

Facilities	Directions
Three sanitary blocks, one refurbished, are in the older style but are clean and tidy. Washbasins with cold water but no hot showers. Facilities for disabled visitors. Washing machines and dryers. Motorcaravan services. Gas. Supermarket. Restaurant, bar and terrace (all year). General room with TV. Tennis. Playground. Entertainment in summer. Chalets to rent. Off site: Bus service. Riding 500 m. Beach 800 m. Fishing 1 km. Golf 3 km. Excursions.	Approach from either direction on N247. Turn inland 6.5 km. west of Cascais at camp sign. Travelling direct from Lisbon, the site is well signed as you leave the A5 autopista. GPS: N38:43.27 W09:28.00

Open: All year.

Charges 2007

Per person	€ 2,70 - € 4,80
child (5-10 yrs)	€ 1,35 - € 2,40
caravan and car	€ 6,70 - € 12,50
electricity	€ 2,40 - € 3,00

PO8450 Parque de Campismo Colina do Sol

Serra Dos Mangues, P-2465 São Martinho do Porto (Leiria)

Tel: **262 98 97 64**. Email: **parque.colima.sol@dix.pt**

Colina do Sol is a well appointed site with its own swimming pool and near the beach. Only 2 km. from the small town of São Martinho do Porto, it has around 350 pitches marked by fruit and ornamental trees on grassy terraces. Electricity (6A) is available. The attractive entrance with its beds of bright flowers, is wide enough for even the largest of outfits, and the surfaced roads are very pleasant for manoeuvring. There is a warm welcome and good English is spoken. The beach is at the rear of the site, with access via a gate which is locked at night. We are told that swimming in the sea requires great care when there are large waves – there is no lifeguard. This is a convenient base for exploring the Costa de Prata.

Facilities	Directions
Two large, clean and modern toilet blocks provide British style WCs (some with bidets), washbasins - some with hot water. Dishwashing and laundry sinks are outside but covered. Motorcaravan services. Supermarket. Bar and restaurant (1/7-31/8). Satellite TV. Swimming pool (1/7-10/9). Off site: Bus to nearby towns. Shop, restaurant and bar within 200 m. Beach (no lifeguard).	Turn from EN 242 (Caldas-Nazaré) road northeast of San Martinho do Porto. Site is clearly signed. GPS: N39:31.37 W09:07.38

Open: All year excl. 25 December.

Charges 2006

Per person	€ 3,65 - € 4,30
child (4-10 yrs)	€ 1,79 - € 2,10
pitch incl. electricity	€ 9,52 - € 12,45

PO8110 Orbitur Camping Valado

Rua dos Combatentes do Ultramar, 2, Valado, P-2450-148 Nazaré (Leiria)

Tel: 262 56 11 11. Email: info@orbitur.pt

This popular site is close to the old, traditional fishing port of Nazaré which has now become something of a holiday resort and popular with coach parties. The large sandy beach in the town (about 2 km. steeply downhill from the site) is sheltered by headlands and provides good swimming. The campsite is on undulating ground under pine trees, has 503 pitches and, although some smallish individual pitches with electricity and water can be reserved, the bulk of the site is not marked out and units are close together during July/August. About 375 electrical connections are available.

Facilities

The three toilet blocks have British and Turkish style WCs, washbasins (some cold water) and 17 hot showers, all very clean when inspected. Laundry. Motorcaravan services. Gas supplies. Supermarket (all season). Bar, snack bar and restaurant with terrace (Easter and June-Oct 18.00-21.00 only). TV/general room. Playground. Tennis. Off site: Bus service 20 m. Fishing and bicycle hire 2 km.

Open: 1 February - 30 November.

Directions

Site is on the Nazaré - Alcobaca N8-5 road, 2 km. east of Nazaré.

Charges 2007

Per person	€ 2,20 - € 4,00
child (5-10 yrs)	€ 1,10 - € 2,00
caravan and car	€ 4,65 - € 9,90
electricity	€ 2,40

Off season discounts (up to 70%).

PO8480 Orbitur Camping Foz do Arelho

Rua Maldonado Freitas, P-2500-516 Foz do Arelho (Leiria)

Tel: 262 97 86 83. Email: info@orbitur.pt

This is a large and roomy ex-municipal site and improvements are still taking place. It is 2 km. from the beach and has a new central complex with a most impressive swimming pool and separated children's pool with lifeguard. Pitches are generally sandy with some hardstandings. They vary in size and are unmarked on two main levels with wide tarmac roads. There is some shade and all touring pitches have electricity (5/15A). The large two storey, brick-faced building contains all the site's leisure facilities but has no ramped access and there are no sanitary facilities anywhere on site for disabled campers. This building is somewhat sterile and the furniture is bland but there are pleasant views over the pool from the restaurant and terrace.

Facilities

Four identical modern sanitary buildings (solar heating) with seatless British and Turkish style WCs and free showers. Washing machine. No facilities for disabled campers. No chemical disposal. Supermarket. Bar/snacks and restaurant (closed November). Games room. Playground – supervision needed. Bus service. Torches useful. Off site: Bus 500 m. Town 2 km. Fishing 2 km.

Open: All year.

Directions

Site is north of Lisbon and west of Caldos la Rainha. From the A8 take N360 to Foz de Arelho. Site is well signed. GPS: N39:25.84 W09:12.05

Charges 2007

Per person	€ 2,60 - € 4,60
child (5-10 yrs)	€ 1,30 - € 2,30
caravan and car	€ 5,80 - € 11,20
electricity	€ 2,40

PO8100 Orbitur Camping São Pedro de Moel

Rua Volta do Sete, P-2430 São Pedro de Moel (Leiria)

Tel: 244 59 91 68. Email: info@orbitur.pt

This quiet and very attractive site is situated under tall pines, on the edge of the rather select small resort of São Pedro de Moel. This is a shady site which can be crowded in July and August. The 525 pitches are in blocks and are unmarked (cars may be parked separately) with 404 electrical connections. A few pitches are used for permanent units. Although there are areas of soft sand, there should be no problem in finding a firm place. The large restaurant and bar are modern as is the superb swimming pool, paddling pool and flume (there is a lifeguard). The attractive, sandy beach is about 500 m. walk downhill from the site (you can take the car, although parking may be difficult in the town) and is sheltered from the wind by low cliffs.

Facilities

Four clean toilet blocks have mainly British style toilets (some with bidets), some washbasins with hot water. Hot showers are mostly in one block. Laundry. Motorcaravan services. Gas supplies. Supermarket. Restaurant and bar with terrace (closed in November). Swimming pools (31/3-30/9). Satellite TV. Games room. Playground. Tennis. Off site: Bus service 100 m. Beach 500 m. Fishing 1 km.

Open: All year.

Directions

Site is 9 km. west of Marinha Grande, on the right as you enter São Pedro de Moel. GPS: N39:45.45 W09:01.60

Charges 2007

Per person	€ 2,70 - € 4,80
child (5-10 yrs)	€ 1,30 - € 2,40
caravan and car	€ 6,70 - € 12,50
electricity	€ 2,40 - € 3,00

PO8460 Camping Caravaning Vale Paraiso

E.N. 242, P-2450-138 Nazaré (Leiria)

Tel: **262 56 18 00**. Email: **info@valeparaiso.com**

A pleasant, well managed site, Vale Paraiso improves every year, with the latest additions being new reception buildings and pool areas. The owners are keen to welcome British visitors and English is spoken. The site is by the main N242 road in eight hectares of undulating pine woods. There are over 600 shady pitches, many on sandy ground only suitable for tents. For other units there are around 250 individual pitches of varying size on harder ground with electricity available. A large range of sporting and leisure activities includes an excellent outdoor pool and paddling pool with sunbathing areas. The adventure playground is very safe with new equipment. There is a pleasant bar, and innovative takeaway selling roasts and a lower level restaurant/bar. Several long beaches of white sand are within 2-15 km. allowing windsurfing, sailing or surfing. Animation for children and evening entertainment is organised in season. Nazaré is an old fishing village with narrow streets, a harbour and marina and many outdoor bars and cafés, with a lift to Sitio. There is much of historical interest in the area although the mild Atlantic climate is also conducive to just relaxing.

Facilities

Spotless sanitary facilities have hot water throughout. Nearly all WCs are British style. Modern facilities for disabled people. Baby baths. Washing machine and dryers. Motorcaravan services. Supermarket (1/5-30/9). Restaurant (March - Sept). Café/bar with satellite TV (all year). Brilliant takeaway. Tabac. Swimming and paddling pools (March - Sept; free for under 11s). Petanque. Leisure games. Amusement hall. Bicycle hire. Safety deposit. Gas supplies. E-mail and fax facilities. Apartments to rent. Off site: Bus service from gate. Fishing 1.5 km. Boat launching 2.5 km. Riding 5 km. Golf 35 km.

Open: All year excl. 10-26 December.

Directions

Site is 2 km. north of Nazaré on the EN242 Marinha Grande road.

Charges 2007

Per person	€ 3,10 - € 4,20
child (3-10 yrs)	€ 1,50 - € 2,00
electricity (4-10A)	€ 2,50

Credit cards accepted for amounts over € 150. Camping Cheques accepted.

PO8400 Campismo O Tamanco

Casas Brancas II, P-3100-231 Louriçal (Leiria)

Tel: **236 95 25 51**. Email: **campismo.o.tamanco@mail.telepac.pt**

O Tamanco is a peaceful countryside site, with a homely, almost farmstead atmosphere. You will have chickens and ducks wandering around and there is a Burro here. The young Dutch owners, Irene and Hans, are sure to give you a warm welcome at this delightful little site. The 100 good sized pitches are separated by cordons of all manner of fruit trees, ornamental trees and flowering shrubs, on level grassy ground. There is electricity (6/16A) to 72 pitches and 5 pitches are suitable for large motorhomes. The site is lit and there is nearly always space available. The swimming pool is very pleasant, as is the small bar and a restaurant (with vegetarian menu options). Courses in printing and sculpture are arranged at certain times of the year. There may also be entertainment for the children during the day. The site is extremely popular with the Dutch, mature couples and winter campers. One can fish or swim in a nearby lake and the resort beaches are a short drive. There is some road noise on pitches at the front of the site.

Facilities

The single toilet block provides very clean and generously sized facilities including washbasins in cabins, with easy access for disabled visitors. As facilities are limited they may be busy in peak periods. Hot water throughout. Washing machine. Bar/restaurant. Roofed patio with fireplace. TV room/lounge (satellite). Internet access. Swimming pool. Off site: Bus service 1 km. Lake 2 km. Beach 11 km. Market in nearby Lourical every Sunday.

Open: 1 February - 31 October.

Directions

From N109/IC1 (Leira - Figuera de Foz) road, 25 km. south of Figuera in Matos de Carriço, turn on to N342 road (signed Louriçal 6 km). Site is 1.5 km. on the left. GPS: N39:59.50 W08:47.31

Charges 2006

Per person	€ 3,30
child (up to 5 yrs)	€ 1,75
pitch	€ 4,90 - € 6,00
electricity (6A)	€ 2,45 - € 3,35

Winter discounts up to 40%. No credit cards.

PO8050 Orbitur Camping São Jacinto

E.N. 327, km 20, São Jacinto, P-3800-909 Aveiro (Aveiro)

Tel: **234 83 82 84**. Email: **info@orbitur.pt**

This small site is in the São Jacinto nature reserve, on a peninsula between the Atlantic and the Barrinha, with views to the mountains beyond. The area is a weekend resort for locals and can be crowded in high season – it may therefore be difficult to find space in July/Aug, particularly for larger units. This is not a large site, taking 169 units on unmarked pitches, but in most places trees provide natural limits and shade. Swimming and fishing are both possible in the adjacent Ria, or the sea, 20 minutes walk from a guarded back gate.

Facilities

Two toilet blocks, very clean when inspected, contain the usual facilities. Dishwashing and laundry sinks. Washing machine and ironing board in a separate part of the toilet block. Motorcaravan services. Shop (all season). Restaurant, bar and snack bar (Easter and June-Oct). Playground. Five bungalows to rent. Off site: Bus service 20 m. Fishing 200 m. Bicycle hire 10 km.

Open: 1 February - 31 October.

Directions

Turn off N109 at Estarreja to N109-5 to cross bridge over Ria da Gosta Nova and on to Torreira and São Jacinto. From Porto go south N1/09, turn for Ovar on the N327 which leads to São Jacinto.

Charges 2007

Per person	€ 2,20 - € 4,00
child (5-10 yrs)	€ 1,10 - € 2,00
pitch incl. electricity	€ 7,05 - € 12,30

Off season discounts (up to 70%).

PO8060 Camping Costa Nova

Quinta dos Patos, Costa Nova do Prado, P-3830 Gafanha da Encarnação (Aveiro)

Tel: **234 393220**. Email: **info@campingcostanova.com**

This campsite has been recommended by our agent and we plan to undertake a full inspection in 2007. Camping Costa Nova is situated between a river and the sea with a large sandy beach. The grass and sand pitches are provided with electricity hook ups, but there is little shade. This site is ideal for those who enjoy watersports and the surroundings offer plenty of sites of interest to explore.

Facilities

Sanitary facilities with free hot water. Laundry room. Restaurant. Takeaway. Snake. Bar. Shop. Games room. Disco. TV. Play area. Off site: Beach 500 m. Fishing.

Open: 16 January - 14 December.

Directions

On the IP5 travelling from Aveiro East towards Barra, cross the bridge. At roundabout take third exit and site is well signed.

Charges 2007

Per unit with electricity	€ 6,30 - € 8,70
person	€ 3,70
child (under 10 yrs)	€ 1,80

Costa Nova - Ilhavo

PO8370 Parque de Campismo de Cerdeira

P-4840 Campo do Gerês (Braga)

Tel: 253 35 1005. Email: **info@parquecerdeira.com**

Located in the National Park of Peneda Gerês, amidst spectacular mountain scenery, this excellent site offers modern facilities in a truly natural area. The National Park is home to all manner of flora, fauna and wildlife, including the roebuck, wolf and wild boar. The well fenced, professional and peaceful site has some 600 good sized, unmarked, mostly level, grassy pitches in a shady woodland setting. Electricity is available for most pitches, though some long leads may be required. A very large timber complex, tastefully designed with the use of noble materials, granite and wood, provides a superb restaurant with a comprehensive menu. A pool with a separated section for toddlers is a welcome, cooling relief in the height of summer. There are unlimited opportunities in the immediate area for fishing, riding, canoeing, mountain biking and climbing, so take advantage of this quality mountain hospitality.

Facilities

Four very clean sanitary blocks provide mixed style WCs, controllable showers and hot water. Dishwashing and laundry sinks under cover. Laundry. Gas supplies. Mini-market. Restaurant/bar (15/4- 30/9, plus weekends and holidays). Playground. Bicycle hire. TV room (satellite). Medical post. Good tennis courts. Minigolf. Car wash. Barbecue area. Torches useful. English spoken. Attractive bungalows to rent. Dogs are not accepted in July/August. Off site: Fishing and riding 800 m. Off site: Fishing and riding 800 m.

Open: All year.

Directions

From north, N103 (Braga-Chaves), turn left at N205 (7.5 km north of Braga). Follow N205 to Caldelas Terras de Bouro and Covide where site is clearly marked to Campo do Geres. An eastern approach from the N103 is for the adventurous but will be rewarded by magnificent views over mountains and lakes. GPS: N41:45.811 W08:11.33

Charges 2007

Per person	€ 3,20 - € 4,50
child (5-11 yrs)	€ 2,00 - € 3,00
pitch	€ 4,30 - € 7,50
electricity (6/10A)	€ 2,50 - € 3,50

PO8030 Orbitur Camping Rio Alto

E.N. 13 - km 13 - Rio Alto-Est, Estela, P-4570-275 Póvoa de Varzim (Porto)

Tel: 252 61 56 99. Email: **info@orbitur.pt**

This site makes an excellent base for visiting Porto which is some 35 km. south of Estela. It has around 700 pitches on sandy terrain and is next to what is virtually a private beach. There are some hardstandings for caravans and motorcaravans and electrical connections to most pitches (long leads may be required). The area for tents is furthest from the beach and windswept, stunted pines give some shade. There are arrangements for car parking away from camping areas in peak season. There is a quality restaurant, snack bar and a large swimming pool plus across the road from reception. An 18 hole golf course is adjacent and huge nets along one side of the site protect campers from any stray balls. The beach is accessed via a novel double tunnel in two lengths of 40 metres under the dunes (open 09.00-19.00). The beach shelves steeply at some tidal stages (lifeguard 15/6-15/9).

Facilities

Four well equipped toilet blocks have hot water. Washing machines and ironing facilities. Facilities for disabled campers. Gas supplies. Restaurant, bar, snack bar and mini-market (all year). Swimming pool (1/6-30/9). Tennis. Playground. Games room. Surfing. TV. Medical post. Car wash. Evening entertainment twice weekly in season. Off site: Fishing 800 m. Golf 1 km. Bicycle hire 13 km. Riding 19 km.

Open: All year.

Directions

From A28 take exit 7 for Estela to EN13 coast road. Turn north for 1 km. and at hotel turn left towards the sea, 12 km. north of Póvoa de Varzim. Travel 2.6 km. along the narrow cobbled road. Look to the right for an Orbitur sign (well back from the road) and take for 0.8 km. to site (speed bumps).

Charges 2007

Per person	€ 2,70 - € 4,80
child (5-10 yrs)	€ 1,35 - € 2,40
caravan and car	€ 6,70 - € 12,50
electricity (5/15A)	€ 2,40 - € 3,00
Off season discounts (up to 70%).	

MAP 7

Slovakia

Slovakia is a small scale country in the heart of Europe, consisting of a narrow strip of land between the spectacular Tatra Mountains and the river Danube. Picturesque, there are historic castles, evergreen forests, rugged mountains, cave formations, and deep lakes and valleys.

CAPITAL: BRATISLAVA

Tourist Office
Czech & Slovak Tourist Centre
16 Frognal Parade
Finchley Road
London NW3 5HG
Tel: 020 7794 3263 Fax: 020 7794 3265
E-mail: info@czechtravel.co.uk
Internet: www.slovakiatourism.sk

Slovakia has much to offer the visitor with an abundance of year round natural beauty. Its terrain varies impressively; the Carpathian Arc Mountains take up nearly half the country and include the Tatra Mountains, with their rugged peaks, deciduous forests and lakes. Southern and eastern Slovakia is mainly a lowland region and home to many thermal springs, with several open to the public for bathing. Many Hungarians have moved to this area and there is a strong Hungarian influence.

Slovakia has over four thousand registered caves, twelve are open to the public and vary from drop stone to glacial; each one claims to have healing benefits for respiratory disorders. The capital, Bratislava is situated on the river Danube and directly below the Carpathian Mountains. Although it may not be as glamorous as Prague, it contains many fascinating buildings from nearly every age and is a lively cheerful city.

Population
5.4 million

Climate
Cold winters and mild summers.
Hot summers and some rain in the eastern lowlands.

Language
Slovak

Telephone
The country code is 00 421.

Money
Currency: The Koruna
Banks: Mon-Fri 08.00-13.00 and 14.00-17.00.

Shops
Mon-Fri 09.00-12.00 and 14.00-18.00.
Some remain open at midday.
Sat 09.00-midday.

Public Holidays
New Year; Easter Mon; May Day; Liberation Day 8 May; Saints Day 5 July; Festival Day 5 July; Constitution Day 1 Sept; All Saints 1 Nov; Christmas 24-26 Dec.

Motoring
A full UK driving licence is acceptable. The major route runs from Bratislava via Trencin, Banska, Bystrica, Zilina and Poprad to Presov. A windscreen sticker which is valid for a year must be purchased at the border crossing for use on certain motorways. Vehicles must be parked on the right.

SK4900 Autocamping Trusalová

SK-03853 Turany (Zilina)

Tel: **043 4292 636**

Autocamping Trusalová is situated right on the southern edge of the Malá Fatra National Park, northeast of the historic town of Martin which has much to offer to tourists. The town is perhaps best known for the engineering works which produced most of the tanks for the Warsaw Pact countries, but is now the home of Volkswagen Slovakia. Paths from the site lead into the Park making it an ideal base for walkers and serious hikers who wish to enjoy this lovely region. The site is in two halves, one on the left of the entrance and the other behind reception on a slight slope. Surrounded by trees with a stream along one side, pitches are grass from a hard road with room for about 150 units and there are some bungalows. We received a most friendly welcome from the German speaking staff. A quiet, orderly and pleasant campsite.

Facilities

Each half has its own old, but clean and acceptable, toilet provision including hot water in basins, sinks and showers. Motorcaravan service point. Each section has a covered barbecue area with raised fire box, chimney, tables and chairs. Volleyball. TV lounge. Playground. Outdoor chess board. Bicycle hire. Off site: Bar just outside site. Restaurants 500 m. or 1 km. Shops 3 km.

Open: 1 June - 15 September.

Directions

Turn north between the Auto Alles car dealer and the Restaurica of the same name on road 18/E50 near the village of Turany to campsite.

Charges guide

Per person	SKK 40
pitch	SKK 80
No credit cards.	

SK4905 ATC Stara Hora

Oravska Priehrada, SK-02901 Namestovo (Zilina)

Tel: **043 55 22 223**. Email: **camp.s.hora@stonline.sk**

Stara Hora has a beautiful location on the Orava artificial lake. It is in the northeast of Slovakia in the Tatra Mountains and attracts visitors from all over Europe which creates a happy and sometimes noisy atmosphere. The site has its own pebble beach with a large grass area behind it for sunbathing. The lake provides opportunities for fishing, boating and sailing and the area is good for hiking and cycling and in winter, it is a popular skiing area. Autocamping Stara Hora is on steeply sloping ground with 160 grassy pitches, all for touring units and with 10A electricity. The lower pitches are level and have good views over the lake, pitches at the top are mainly used by tents.

Facilities

The new modern toilet block has British style toilets, open washbasins and controllable hot showers (free). It could be pressed in high season and hot water to the showers is only available from 7.00-10.00 in the morning and from 19.00-22.00 in the evening. Dishwashing. Shop for basics. Bar and lakeside bar. Restaurant. Playground (a new one is planned). Volleyball. Pedalo, canoe and rowing boat hire. Waterskiing. Fishing (with permit). Torch useful.

Open: May - September.

Directions

From Ruzomberok take E77 road north towards Trstena. Turn left in Tvrdoöin on the 520 road towards Námestovo. Site is on the right. GPS: N49:21.560 E19:33.300

Charges 2006

Per person	SKK 80
child	SKK 40
pitch incl. car	SKK 100
electricity	SKK 80

SK4910 Autocamping Turiec

Kolonia hviezda 92, SK-03608 Martin (Zilina)

Tel: **043 428 4215**. Email: **recepcia@autocampingturiec.sk**

Turiec is situated in northeast Slovakia, 1.5 km. from the small village of Vrutky, 4 km. north of Martin, at the foot of the Lucanska Mala Fatra mountains and with castles nearby. This good site has views towards the mountains and is quiet and well maintained. There is room for about 30 units on grass inside a circular tarmac road with some shade from tall trees. Electrical connections are available for all places. You will receive a friendly welcome from Viktor Matovcik and his wife Lydia who are constantly improving the site.

Facilities

One acceptable sanitary block to the side of the camping area, but in winter the facilities in the bungalow at the entrance are used. Cooking facilities. Restaurant/snack bar in summer. Badminton. Volleyball. Swimming pool 1.5 km. Rest room with TV. Small games room. Covered barbecue. Off site: Shop outside entrance.

Open: All year.

Directions

Site is signed from E18 road (Zilina - Martin) in the village of Vrutky, 3 km. northwest of Martin. Turn south on the bend and follow signs to Martinské Hole.

Charges 2006

Per unit incl. 2 persons, electricity	€ 13,00

SK4935 ATC Bystrina

SK-03101 Demanovska Dolina (Zilina)

Tel: **044 55 48 163**. Email: **hotelbystrina@stonline.sk**

Autocamping Bystrina forms part of the Bystrina Hotel complex which is located in the beautiful Tatra Mountains. There are 150 touring pitches on hilly ground on open, grassy fields which are unmarked. Shade from a few mature trees is available in some areas and there are 60 electricity connections (6/10A). The toilet block is adequate and in front of the site is a new bar/restaurant under the same management. This area is ideal for those who enjoy walking, climbing and mountain biking or people who just wish to relax in this beautiful mountain region.

Facilities	Directions
The basic toilet block has British style toilets, open washbasins and controllable, hot showers (free). Washing machine and ironing board. Dishwashing. Off site: Restaurant 200 m.	From Liptovsk" Mikuláö follow 584 road south towards Demänovská Dolina and then site signs. GPS: N49:07.961 E19:34.458

Open: 1 May - 30 September.

Charges guide

Per person	SKK 90
pitch incl. car	SKK 110 - 150
electricity	SKK 100

SK4920 Autocamping Trencin

Na Ostrove, P.O. Box 10, SK-91101 Trencin (Trencin)

Tel: **032 743 4013**. Email: **autocamping.tn@mail.pvt.sk**

Trencin is an interesting town with a long history and dominated by the partly restored castle which towers high above. The small site with room for 30 touring units (all with electricity) and rooms to let, stands on an island about one kilometre from town centre opposite a large sports complex. Pitches occupy a grass area surrounded by bungalows, although when the site is busy, campers park between and almost on top of the bungalows. There is some rail noise. This is a very neat, tidy friendly site with German spoken during our visit.

Facilities	Directions
Toilet block is old but tiled and clean with hot water in the washbasins (in cabins with curtains) and showers (doors and curtains) under cover but not enclosed. Hot water for washing clothes and dishes. Electric cookers, fridge/freezer, tables and chairs. Little shade. Bar in high season. Boating and fishing in river. Off site: Restaurants 200 m. Shops 300 m. Tennis, indoor and outdoor swimming pools within 400 m.	Initially you need to follow signs for 61 Zilina and having crossed the river, bear left. Turn left at first main traffic lights, under the railway and left again. Then turn right after the stadium. Site is over the canal, on the left. GPS: N48:52.996 E18:02.440

Open: 1 May - 15 September.

Charges 2006

Per person	SKK 170 - 200
child (6-12 yrs)	SKK 100
pitch incl. electricity	SKK 120 - 200

SK4925 Camping Lodenica

Sinava 1, SK-92101 Piestany (Trnava)

Tel: **033 76 26 093**

This site is 1.5 kilometres south of the most important spa in the Slovak Republic and lies in a quiet forest setting on the shores of the Sinava lake, close to the town of Pieötany. The site is only four kilometres from the main motorway between Bratislava and Trenc'n and therefore useful as a night stop when travelling between Poland and Hungary or the Czech Republic. Lodenica is divided into three main camping areas with 250 pitches (150 with electricity), the first right behind the entrance and a large, circular field with pitching close to the electricity boxes. Pitches on the second field to the back are separated by low hedges and the third field is in the 'Arena' and surrounded by a wooden fence, rather like a fortress. Among the pitches are mature trees which provide shade. Very disappointing at this site are the toilet blocks, which are old and need refurbishing.

Facilities	Directions
One traditional toilet block with toilets, open style washbasins (cold water only) and hot showers. Laundry with 5 sinks. Campers' kitchen with gas hob and oven. Good value bar/restaurant. Playing field. Rowing boats, canoes and surfboards for hire at the lake. Water-skiing. Bicycle hire. Off site: Fishing and beach 200 m. Pieötany town with shops, hot food, bars, indoor and outdoor pools 1.5 km. Riding 5 km.	Take motorway form Bratislava towards Trencin and exit at Piestany. At first main junction turn right at traffic lights and go south. Turn left at the hospital towards site. GPS: N48:39.450 E17:49.442

Open: 1 May - 30 September.

Charges guide

Per person	SKK 90
child (5-14 yrs)	SKK 40
pitch	SKK 120
electricity	SKK 70

SK4950 Autocamping Zlaté Piesky

Senecka cesta c 2, SK-82104 Bratislava (Bratislava)

Tel: **0244 45 05 92**. Email: **kempi@netax.sk**

Bratislava undoubtedly has charm, being on the Danube and having a number of interesting buildings and churches in its centre. However, industry around the city, particularly en-route to the camp from the south, presents an ugly picture and gives no hints of the hidden charms. Zlate Piesky (golden sands) is part of a large, lakeside sports complex which is also used during the day in summer by local residents. The site is on the northeast edge of the city with 200 touring pitches, 120 with electrical connections, on level grass under tall trees. Twenty well equipped and many more simple bungalows for hire are spread around the site. An attractive lakeside recreation area also has pedaloes for hire and fitness area in the park, plus water skiing/boarding where you are propelled by something akin to a ski lift. For a night stop or a short stay, this might suit.

Facilities

Four toilet blocks, two for campers and two for day visitors, are good and clean. Two restaurants, one with waiter service, the other self service. Many small snack bars. Shops. Lake for swimming and watersports with large beach area. Table tennis. Minigolf. Play areas. Room with billiards and electronic games. Disco. Off site: Tesco supermarket nearby.

Open: 1 May - 15 October.

Directions

From E75 Bratislava - Trencin motorway exit towards Zlate Piesky just north of the airport. Head towards Bratislava on the 61/E571 and immediately after the footbridge turn left at the traffic lights. The site is a little way ahead on the left.

Charges 2006

Per person	SKK 100
child (4-15 yrs)	SKK 50
pitch	SKK 110 - 160
electricity	SKK 90

No credit cards.

SK4980 Autocamping Levocská Dolina

Kovásvá vila 2, SK-05401 Levoca (Presov)

Tel: **053 451 2701**. Email: **rzlevoca@pobox.sk**

According to the owner, Mr Rusnák, this campsite is one of the top ten sites in Slovakia and he aims to become the best Slovakian site within two years. Autocamping Levocská has been a campsite for over 40 years with Mr Rusnák as its manager. Five years ago, following much negotiation with the State, the city of Levoca and the former Hungarian owners (who owned it before 1920), he was able to purchase it. The site forms part of a restaurant and pension business and the good value restaurant is welcoming. The entrance is attractively landscaped with varieties of shrubs and colourful flowers and the whole site looks well cared for. There are 60 pitches (all for tourers) and 23 electricity connections. On grassy fields with views of the mountains, there is some terracing. The main road runs steeply uphill and then continues on grass roads. This may cause larger units some difficulty in bad weather. This is a good base form which to explore the Tatra Mountains or visit the Ice Caves.

Facilities

Well renovated toilet block with British style toilets, open washbasins and controllable, hot showers (free). Campers' kitchen. Dishwashing. Sauna. Whirlpool. Bar/restaurant. Basic playground. Torch useful. Off site: Lake with pedalo hire 300 m. Doböinska Ice Caves and Slovakian Paradise. Town of Levoca.

Open: All year.

Directions

From Liptovsk˝ Mikuláö, take the E50 road east towards Levoca. In Levoca follow site signs.

Charges guide

Per person	SKK 70
child	SKK 45
pitch	SKK 90 - 125

This is just a sample of the campsites we have inspected and selected in Central Europe. For more campsites and further information, please see the Alan Rogers Central Europe guide.

MAP 1

What Slovenia lacks in size it makes up for in exceptional beauty. Situated between Italy, Austria, Hungary and Croatia, it has a diverse landscape with stunning Alps, rivers, forests and the warm Adriatic coast.

CAPITAL: LJUBLJANA

Tourist Office

Slovenian Tourist Office
South Marlands, Itchingfield,
Horsham RH13 0NN
Tel: 0870 225 5305 Fax: 0208 5842 017
E-mail: slovenia.tourism@virgin.net
Internet: www.slovenia-tourism.info

With its snow capped Julian Alps and the picturesque Triglav National park that include the beautiful lakes of Bled and Bohinj, and the peaceful Soca River, it is no wonder that the northwest region of Slovenia is so popular. Stretching from the Alps down to the Adriatic coast is the picturesque Karst region, with pretty olive groves and thousands of spectacular underground caves, including the Postojna and Skocjan caves. Although small, the Adriatic coast has several bustling beach towns such as the Italianised Koper resort and the historic port of Piran, with many opportunities for watersports and sunbathing. The capital Ljubljana is centrally located, with Renaissance, Baroque and Art Nouveau architecture, you will find most points of interest are along the Ljubljana river. Heading eastwards the landscape becomes gently rolling hills, and is largely given over to vines (home of Lutomer Riesling). Savinja with its spectacular Alps is the main area for producing wine.

Population

1.9 million

Climate

Warm summers, cold winters with snow in the Alps.

Language

Slovene, with German often spoken in the north and Italian in the west.

Telephone

The country code is 386.

Money

Currency: Slovene Tolar
Banks: Mon-Fri 8.30-16.30 with a lunch break 12.30-14.00, plus Saturday mornings 8.30-11.30.

Shops

Shops usually open by 8am sometimes 7am. Closing times vary widely.

Public Holidays

New Year; Culture Day 8 Feb; Easter Monday; Resistance Day 27 Apr; Labour Day 1-2 May; National Day 25 Jun; Peoples' Day 22 July; Assumption; Reformation Day 31 Oct; All Saint's Day; Christmas Day; Independence Day 26 Dec.

Motoring

Small but expanding network of motorways radiating from Ljubljana (there may be tolls). Secondary roads often poorly maintained. Tertiary roads are often gravel (known locally as 'white roads' and shown thus on road maps). Road markings and signs are generally good.

SV4150 Kamp Kamne

Franc Voga, Dovje 9, SLO-4281 Mojstrana (Slovenia)

Tel: 04 589 1105. Email: info@campingkamne.com

For visitors proceeding down the 202 road, from Italy or the Wurzen Pass, towards the prime attractions of the twin lakes of Bled and Bohinj, a delightfully informal little site is to be found just outside the village of Mojstrana. For those arriving via the Karawanker Tunnel the diversion along the 202 is very well worth it. Owner Franc Voga opened the site as recently as 1989, on a small terraced orchard. He has steadily developed the facilities, adding a small pool, a tennis court and improved all other facilities. The little reception doubles as a bar where locals wander up for a beer and a chat while enjoying the view across the valley of the Julian Alps.

Facilities

The small excellent sanitary block is of a high quality and well maintained. Reception/bar. Small swimming pool. Tennis court. Franc's English is good and his daughter Anna is fluent. Twice weekly excursions to the mountains (free)in July and August. Two new apartments now available to rent. Off site: Walking trails.

Open: All year.

Directions

Site is well marked on north side of the 202 4 km. from Jesenice, just to west of exit for Mojstrana. GPS: N46:27.872 E13:57.472

Charges 2007

Per person	€ 5,00 - € 6,00
child (7-17 yrs)	€ 4,00 - € 4,50
electricity	€ 2,00

SV4210 Camping Sobec

Sobceva cesta 25, SLO-4248 Lesce (Slovenia)

Tel: 04 5353 700. Email: sobec@siol.net

Sobec is situated in a valley between the Julian Alps and the Karavanke Mountains, in a pine grove between the Sava Dolinka river and a small lake. It is only 3 km. from Bled and 20 km. from the Karavanke Tunnel. There are 500 unmarked pitches on level, grassy fields off tarmac access roads (450 for touring units), all with 16A electricity. Shade is provided by mature pine trees and younger trees separate some pitches. Some pitches have views over the lake, which has an enclosed area providing safe swimming for children.

Facilities

Three traditional style toilet blocks (two refurbished, one old) with mainly British style toilets, washbasins in cabins and controllable hot showers. Child-size toilets and basins. Well equipped baby room. Facilities for disabled visitors. Laundry facilities. Dishwashing under cover. Motorcaravan service point. Supermarket, bar/restaurant with stage for live performances. Playgrounds. Rafting, canyoning and kayaking organised. Mini-club. Tours to Bled and the Narodni National Park. Off site: Golf and riding 2 km.

Open: 21 April - 30 September.

Directions

Site is off the main road from Lesce to Bled and well signed just outside Lesce. GPS: N46:21.364 E14:08.995

Charges 2007

Per person	€ 9,70 - € 11,50
child (7-14 yrs)	€ 7,30 - € 8,60
electricity (16A)	€ 3,00
dog	€ 3,00

SV4235 Kamp Klin

Lepena 1, SLO-5232 Soca (Slovenia)

Tel: 05 3889 513. Email: kampklin@volja.net

Kamp Klin is next to the confluence of the Soca and Lepenca rivers and is surrounded by mountains. Being next to two rivers, the site is also a suitable base for fishing, kayaking and rafting. Kamp Klin is privately owned and there is a 'pension' next door, all run by the Zorc family, who serve the local dishes with compe (potatoes), cottage cheese, grilled trout and local salami in the restaurant. The campsite has only 50 pitches, all for tourers and with electricity, on one large, grassy field, connected by a circular, gravel access road. The site is attractively landscaped with flowers and young trees, but this also means there is not much shade. Some pitches are right on the bank of the river (unfenced) and there are beautiful views of the river and the mountains.

Facilities

One modern toilet block and a 'portacabin' style unit with toilets and controllable showers. Laundry with sinks. Dishwashing (inside). Bar/restaurant. Play field. Beach volleyball. Fishing (permit required). Torch useful. Off site: Riding 500 m. Bicycle hire 10 km.

Open: All year.

Directions

Site is on the main Kranjska Gora - Bovec road. Well signed in Soca. Access is via a sharp turn from the main road and over a small bridge that may be difficult for larger units. GPS: N46:19.804 E13:38.640

Charges guide

Per person	€ 5,50 - € 7,20
child (7-12 yrs)	€ 2,80 - € 3,60
electricity	€ 2,40

SV4200 Camping Bled

Kidriceva 10c, Sl, SLO-4260 Bled (Slovenia)
Tel: 04 575 2000. Email: info@camping.bled.si

On the western tip of Lake Bled is Camping Bled. The waterfront here is a small public beach immediately behind which gently runs a sloping narrow wooded valley. Pitches at the front, used mainly for over-nighters, are now marked, separated by young trees and enlarged, bringing the total number down to 280. In areas at the back, visitors are free to pitch where they like. Unlike at many other Slovenian sites the number of statics (and semi-statics) here appears to be carefully controlled with touring caravans, motorcaravans and tents predominating. Some visitors might well be disturbed by the noise coming from trains as they hurtle out of a high tunnel overlooking the campsite on the line from Bled to Bohinj. But this is a small price to pay for the pleasure of being in a pleasant site from which the lake, its famous little island, its castle and its town can be explored.

Facilities

Toilet facilities in five blocks are of a high standard (with free hot showers). Two blocks are heated. Solar energy used. Backpackers' kitchen. Washing machines and dryers. Chemical disposal point. Motorcaravan services. Gas supplies. Fridge hire. Supermarket. Restaurant. Play area and children's zoo. Games hall. Beach volleyball. Trampolines. Organised activities in July/Aug. including children's club, excursions and sporting activities. Live entertainment. Mountain bike tours. Fishing. Bicycle hire. Internet access. Off site: Riding 3 km. Golf 5 km. Within walking distance of waterfront and town. Restaurants.

Open: 1 April - 15 October.

Directions

From the town of Bled drive along south shore of lake to its western extremity (some 2 km) to the site. GPS: N46:21.693 E14:04.845

Charges 2007

Per person	€ 8,50 - € 11,50
child (7-13 yrs)	€ 5,95 - € 8,05
electricity	€ 3,00
dog	€ 1,50 - € 2,50

Less 10% for stays over 6 days.
Camping Cheques accepted.

CAMPING BLED
Come and find yourself...

Camping Bled, Kidričeva 10c, 4260 Bled, Slovenija
Tel: +386 (0) 4 575 20 00
Fax: +386 (0) 4 575 20 02
www.camping-bled.com
E-mail: info@camping.bled.si

SV4250 Camping Danica Bohinj

Triglavska 60, SLO-4265 Bohinjska Bistrica (Slovenia)
Tel: 04 574 7820. Email: tdbohinj@bohinj.si

For those wanting to visit the famous Bohinj valley, which stretches like a fjord right into the heart of the Julian Alps, an ideal site is Danica Bohinj site which lies in the valley three kilometres downstream of the lake. The fact that the manager on the site, Marjan Malej, is the director of the local tourist association is an indication of the local community's well deserved pride in their own campsite. Danica occupies a rural site that stretches from the main road leading into Bohinj from Bled (25 kms. away), to the bank of the newly formed Sava river. It is basically flat meadow, broken up by lines of natural woodland. This excellent site has 150 pitches, 135 for touring units, all with 6A electricity and forms an ideal base for the many sporting activities the area has to offer.

Facilities

Two good toilet blocks with toilets, open plan washbasins and hot showers. Facilities for disabled visitors. Laundry with washing machines and dryers. Ironing board. Chemical disposal point. Motorcaravan service point. Volleyball. Football. Tennis. Small shop. Café. Fishing. Bicycle hire. Organised excursions in the Triglavski National Park. Off site: Riding 5 km. Canoeing, kayakingand rafting.

Open: May - September.

Directions

Driving from Bled to Bohinj, the well signed site lies just behind the village of Bohinjska Bistrica on the right-hand (north) side of the road.
GPS: N46:16.401 E13:56.921

Charges 2006

Per person	SIT 1370 - 1920
child (7-14 yrs)	SIT 1050 - 1413
electricity	SIT 500

SV4330 Camping Pivka Jama

Veliki Otok 50, SLO-6230 Postojna (Slovenia)

Tel: **05 720 39 93**. Email: **autokamp.pivka.jama@siol.net**

Postojna is renowned for its extraordinary limestone caves which form one of Slovenia's prime tourist attractions. Among campers it is also renowned for the campsite situated in the forest only four kilometres from the caves. Pivka Jama is a most convenient site for the visitor, being midway between Ljubljana and Piran and only about an hour's pleasant drive from either. This good site is deep in what appears to be primeval forest, cleverly cleared to take advantage of the broken limestone forest bedrock. The 300 pitches are not clustered together but nicely segregated under trees and in small clearings, all connected by a neat network of paths and slip roads. Some level, gravel hardstandings are provided. The facilities are both excellent and extensive and run with obvious pride by enthusiastic staff. It even has its own local caves (the Pivka Jama) which can spare its visitors the commercialisation of Postojna.

Facilities

Two toilet blocks with very good facilities. Washing machines. Motorcaravan service point. Chemical disposal point. Campers' kitchen with hobs. Supermarket. Bar/restaurant. Swimming pool and paddling pool. Volleyball. Basketball. Tennis. Table tennis. Bicycle hire. Daytrips to Postojna Caves and other excursions organised. Off site: Fishing 5 km. Riding or skiing 10 km. Golf 30 km.

Open: March - October.

Directions

Site is 5 km. from Postojna. Take the road leading east from Postojna and then north west towards the Postojna Cave. Site is well signed 4 km. further along this road. GPS: N45:48.320 E14:12.274

Charges 2006

Per person	€ 9,40 - € 10,30
child (7-14 yrs)	€ 7,30 - € 8,10
electricity	€ 3,70

SV4405 Camping Menina

Varpolje 105, SLO-3332 Recica ob Savinji (Slovenia)

Tel: **03 5835 027**. Email: **info@campingmenina.com**

The Menina site is in the heart of the 35 km. long Upper Savinja Valley, surrounded by 2,500 m. high mountains and unspoilt nature. It is being improved every year by the young, enthusiastic owner, Jurij Kolenc and has 200 pitches, all for touring units, on grassy fields under mature trees and with access from gravel roads. All have 4-10A electricity. The Savinja river runs along one side of the site, but if its water is too cold for swimming, the site also has a lake which can be used for swimming as well. This site is a perfect base for walking or mountain biking in the mountains (a wealth of maps and routes is available from reception). Rafting, canyoning and kayaking, or visits to a fitness studio, sauna or massage salon are organised.

Facilities

The traditional style toilet block has modern fittings with toilets, open plan basins and controllable hot showers and the site reports that a new second block is ready. Motorcaravan service point. Bar/restaurant with open air terrace (evenings only) and open air kitchen. Playing field. Fishing. Mountain bike hire. Volleyball. Basketball. Giant chess. Russian bowling. Excursions (52). Live music and gatherings around the camp fire. Off site: Fishing 2 km. Recica and other villages with much culture and folklore are close.

Open: 1 April - 15 November.

Directions

From Ljubljana take A1 towards Celje. Exit at Trnava and turn north towards Mozirje. Follow signs Recica ob Savinj from there. Continue through Recica to Nizka and follow site signs. GPS: N46:18.701 E14:54.548

Charges 2007

Per person	€ 5,00 - € 6,50
child (5-15 yrs)	€ 3,50 - € 4,50
electricity	€ 2,00 - € 2,20
dog	€ 2,00 - € 2,20

This is just a sample of the campsites we have inspected and selected in Central Europe. For more campsites and further information, please see the Alan Rogers Central Europe guide.

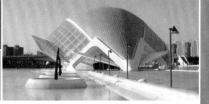

One of the largest countries in Europe with glorious beaches, a fantastic sunshine record, vibrant towns and laid back sleepy villages, plus a diversity of landscape, culture and artistic traditions, Spain has all the ingredients for a great holiday.

Spain

CAPITAL: MADRID

Tourist Office

Spanish National Tourist Office,
22/23 Manchester Square, London W1U 3PX
Tel: 020 7486 8077
Email: info.londres@tourspain.es
Internet: www.spain.info

Spain has a huge choice of beach resorts. With charming villages and attractive resorts, the Costa Brava boasts spectacular scenery with towering cliffs and sheltered coves. There are plenty of lively resorts, including Lloret, Tossa and Calella, plus several quieter ones. Further along the east coast, the Costa del Azahar stretches from Vinaros to Almanzora, with the great port of Valencia in the centre. Orange groves abound. The central section of the coastline, the Costa Blanca, has 170 miles or so of silvery-white beaches. Benidorm is the most popular resort. The Costa del Sol lies in the south, home to more beaches and brilliant sunshine, whilst in the north the Costa Verde is largely unspoiled, with clean water, sandy beaches and rocky coves against a backdrop of mountains.

Beaches and sunshine aside, Spain also has plenty of great cities and towns to explore, including Barcelona, Valencia, Seville, Madrid, Toledo and Bilbao, all offering an array of sights, galleries and museums.

Population

39.5 million

Climate

Spain has a very varied climate. The north is temperate with most of the rainfall; dry and very hot in the centre; subtropical along the Mediterranean.

Language

Castilian Spanish is spoken by most people with Catalan (northeast), Basque (north) and Galician (northwest) used in their respective areas.

Telephone

The country code is 00 34.

Money

Currency: The Euro
Banks: Mon-Fri 09.00-14.00.
Sat 09.00-13.00.

Shops

Mon-Sat 09.00-13.00/14.00 and 15.00/16.00-19.30/20.00. Many close later.

Public Holidays

New Year; Epiphany; Saint's Day 19 Mar; Maundy Thurs; Good Fri; Easter Mon; Labour Day; Saint's Day 25 July; Assumption 15 Aug; National Day 12 Oct; All Saints Day 1 Nov; Constitution Day 6 Dec; Immaculate Conception 8 Dec; Christmas Day.

Motoring

The surface of the main roads is on the whole good, although secondary roads in some rural areas can be rough and winding. Tolls are payable on certain roads and for the Cadi Tunnel, Vallvidrera Tunnel and the Tunnel de Garraf on the A16.

ES8020 Camping Internacional de Amberes

Playa de la Rubina, E-17487 Empúria-brava (Girona)

Tel: 972 450 507. Email: info@inter-amberes.com

Situated in the 'Venice of Spain', Empuria Brava is interlaced with inland waterways and canals, where many residents and holidaymakers moor their boats directly outside their homes on the canal banks. Internacional Amberes is a large friendly site 50 m. from the wide, sandy beach, which is bordered on the east and west by the waterway canals. The site has 950 touring pitches, most enjoying some shade from strategically placed trees. All have electricity and water connections. Amberes is a surprisingly pretty and hospitable site where people seem to make friends easily and get to know other campers and the staff. The restaurant and bar are close to the site entrance and the cuisine is so popular that locals use it too. Unusually the swimming pool is on an elevated terrace, raised out of view of most onlookers with sunbathing areas and a small children's pool adjoining. A shallow river runs through the site and the children can amuse themselves catching the colourful crawfish that abound here. A 'secret garden' style minigolf course is special to this site. The site can arrange temporary moorings for boats at Empuria Brava on request. The sea breeze here appears regularly during the afternoon so watersports are very good and hire facilities are available.

Facilities

Toilet facilities are in five fully equipped blocks. Washing machines. Motorcaravan services. New supermarket, bakery and shop. Restaurant/bar. Disco bar. Takeaway. Pizzeria. Watersports - windsurfing school. Organised sports activities, children's programmes and entertainment. Swimming pool. Playgrounds. Tennis. Internet and WiFi. Apartments. Off site: Beach 200 m. Fishing 300 m. Bicycle hire 500 m. Riding 1 km. Golf 12 km.

Open: 1 April - 15 October.

Directions

Empuria Brava is north of Girona and east of Figueres on the coast. From AP7/E15 take exit 3 south or exit 4 north (note there is no exit 3 north) and then N11 to the C260 towards Roses. At Empuria Brava follow camping signs to site. GPS: N42:15.160 E03:07.902

Charges 2006

Per person over 3 yrs	€ 3,10 - € 3,30
pitch incl. electricity	€ 9,50 - € 28,50

ES8080 Camping El Delfin Verde

Ctra de Torroella de Montgri, E-17257 Torroella de Montgri (Girona)

Tel: 972 758 454. Email: info@eldelfinverde.com

A large, popular and high quality site in a quiet location, El Delfin Verde has its own long beach stretching along its frontage. A prime feature of the site is an attractive large pool in the shape of a dolphin with a total area of 1,800 sq.m. This is a large site with 1420 touring pitches and approximately 6,000 visitors at peak times. It is well managed by friendly staff. Level grass pitches nearer the beach are marked and many are separated by small fences and hedging. All have electrical connections (5/6A) and access to water points. A stream runs through the centre of the site. There is shade in some of the older parts and a particularly pleasant area of pine trees in the centre provides marked but not separated pitches (sandy and not so level).The pool has two island areas, one containing a huge fountain which can be lit at night. In the main season an elevated area with a large bar, full restaurant and a separate takeaway give wonderful views over the huge pool. There is a further restaurant with slightly cheaper, good value food in the main complex with an open air arena for entertainment. El Delfin Verde is a large and cheerful holiday site with many good facilities, sports and a free family entertainment programme in season. It is well worth considering for your Costa Brava holidays. Used by British tour operators (60 pitches).

Facilities

Six excellent large and refurbished toilet blocks plus a seventh smaller block, all with resident cleaners, have showers using desalinated water and some washbasins in cabins. Laundry facilities. Motorcaravan services. Supermarket and shops. Swimming pools (with lifeguard). Two restaurants, grills and pizzerias. Three bars. 'La Vela' barbecue and party area. Large sports area. 2 km. exercise track. Dancing and floor shows weekly in season. Excursions. Bicycle hire. Minigolf. Playground. Trampolines. Fishing. Hairdresser. Car servicing. Gas supplies. Internet access. Dogs are not accepted in high season (11/7-14/8). Off site: Golf 4 km (20% discount). Riding 4 km.

Open: 8 April - 15 October

Directions

Torroella de Montgri is close to the coast east of Girona. From A7/E15 take exit 6 and C66 (Palafrugell). Then the GI 642 east to Parlava and turn north on C31 (L'Escala). Cross river Ter and turn east on C31 (Ulla and Torroella de Montgri). Site signed off the C31 and is at end of long approach road. Watch out for white dolphin marker and flags by road side on left. GPS: N42:00.718 E03:11.284

Charges 2006

Per person	€ 3,50 - € 4,00
child (2-9 yrs)	€ 3,00 - € 3,50
pitch incl. electricity	€ 13,00 - € 38,00
dog (excl 11/7-14/8)	€ 3,50

All plus 7% VAT. Special offers on long stays in low season.

ES8035 Camping L'Amfora

2 Avenida Josep Tarradellas, E-17470 Sant Pere Pescador (Girona)

Tel: **972 520540**. Email: **info@campingamfora.com**

This is a superb spacious and friendly family site with a Greek theme, which is manifested mainly in the restaurant and pool areas. The site is spotlessly clean and well maintained and the owner operates in an environmentally friendly way. There are 830 pitches (730 for touring), all with 10A electrical connections and most with a water tap, on level grass with trees and shrubs. Of these, 64 pitches are large (180 sq.m.), made for two units per pitch and each with an individual sanitary facility (toilet, shower and washbasin). In addition to the individual units, three main sanitary blocks (one heated) offer free hot water, washbasins in cabins, hairdryers and baby rooms. There is extra provision near the pool area. Access is good for disabled visitors. An inviting terraced bar and self-service restaurant overlook four large swimming pools (one for children) with two water slides. Ambitious evening entertainment (pub, disco, shows) and children's animation are organised in season and a choice of watersports activities is available on the beach.

Facilities

Three main toilet blocks, one heated, provide washbasins in cabins and free showers. Baby rooms. Laundry facilities. Motorcaravan services. Supermarket. Terraced bar, self service and waiter service restaurants. Takeaway. Restaurant and bar on the beach with limited menu (high season). Disco-bar. Swimming pools (1/5-30/9). Gymnasium. Petanque. Tennis. Bicycle hire. Minigolf. Playground. Entertainment and activities. Windsurfing. Boat launching and sailing. Fishing. Exchange facilities. Games and TV rooms. Internet room and WiFi. Car wash. Torches required in beach areas. Off site: Riding 2 km. Golf 8 km.

Open: 31 March - 30 September.

Directions

Sant Pere Pescadore is on the coast between Roses and L'Escala. From the AP7/E15 take exit 4 onto the N11 north towards Figueres and then C31 towards Torroella de Fluvia. Take Vilamacolum road east and continue to Sant Pere. Site well signed in town.

Charges 2006

Per person	€ 3,20 - € 4,20
pitch (100 sq.m.)	€ 13,00 - € 32,00
with individual sanitary unit	€ 19,00 - € 50,00

Children free low season. Senior citizens specials. Electricity (10A) included. Plus 7% No credit cards. Camping Cheques accepted.

ES8030 Camping Nautic Almata

Ctra Sant Pere Pescador, km 11.6, E-17486 Castelló d'Empúries (Girona)

Tel: **972 454 477**. Email: **info@almata.com**

In the Bay of Roses, south of Empuria Brava and beside the Parc Natural dels Aiguamolls de l'Empordá, this is a site of particular interest for nature lovers (especially bird watchers). Beautifully laid out, it is arranged around the river and waterways, so will suit those who like to be close to water or who enjoy watersports and boating. It is worth visiting because of its unusual aspects and the feeling of being on the canals, as well as being a high quality beachside site. A large site, there are 1,109 well kept, large, numbered pitches, all with electricity and on flat, sandy ground. There are some pitches right on the beach. As you drive through the natural park to the site watch for the warning signs for frogs on the road and enjoy the wild flamingos alongside the road.. The name no doubt derives from the fact that boats can be tied up at the small marina within the site and a slipway also gives access to a river and thence to the sea. Throughout the season there is a varied entertainment programme for children and adults. The facilities on this site are impressive. Some tour operators use the site.

Facilities

Toilet blocks of a high standard include some en-suite showers with basins. Good facilities for disabled visitors. Washing machines. Gas supplies. Excellent supermarket. Restaurant and bar. Two separate bars by beach where discos held in main season. Water-ski and windsurfing schools. 300 sq.m. swimming pool. Tennis, squash, volleyball and 'fronton' (all free). Minigolf. Games room. Extensive riding tuition with own stables and stud. Children's play park (near river). Fishing (licence required). Car, motorcycle and bicycle hire. Hairdresser. Torches are useful near beach. Off site: Canal trips 18 km. Aquatic Park 20 km.

Open: 14 May - 18 September, including all facilities.

Directions

Site is signed at 26 km. marker on C252 between Castello d'Empuries and Vildemat, then 7 km. to site. Alternatively, on San Pescador - Castello d'Empuries road head north and site is signed,

Charges 2006

Per pitch	€ 18,60 - € 37,25
person (over 3 yrs)	€ 1,75 - € 3,50
dog	€ 4,00 - € 5,10
boat or jetski	€ 7,40 - € 10,00

All plus 7% VAT. No credit cards.

ES8040 Camping Las Dunas

Ctra Santa Marti d'Empuries - Sant Pere, E-17470 Sant Pere Pescador (Girona)

Tel: **972 521 717**. Email: **info@campinglasdunas.com**

Las Dunas is an extremely large, impressive and well organised site with many on site activities and an ongoing programme of improvements. It has direct access to a superb sandy beach that stretches along the site for nearly a kilometre with a windsurfing school and beach bar. There is also a much used swimming pool with large double children's pools. Las Dunas is very large, with 1,700 individual hedged pitches (1,479 for tourers) of around 100 sq.m. laid out on flat ground in long, regular parallel rows. All have electrical connections and 180 also have water and drainage. Shade is available in some parts of the site. Member of Leading Campings Group. Pitches are usually available, even in the main season. Much effort has gone into planting palms and new trees here and the results are very attractive. The large restaurant and bar have spacious terraces overlooking the swimming pools and you can enjoy a very pleasant more secluded cavern styled pub. A magnificent disco club is close by in a soundproof building (although people returning from this during the night can be a problem for pitches in the central area of the site). With free quality entertainment of all types in season and positive security arrangements, this is a great site for families with teenagers. Everything is provided on site so you don't need to leave it during your stay.

Facilities

Five excellent large toilet blocks (with resident cleaners 07.00-21.00) have British style toilets, controllable hot showers and washbasins in cabins. Excellent facilities for youngsters, babies and disabled people. Laundry facilities. Motorcaravan services. Extensive supermarket and other shops. Large bar with terrace. Large restaurant. Takeaway. Ice-cream parlour. Beach bar in main season. Disco club. Swimming pools. Playgrounds. Tennis. Minigolf. Sailing/windsurfing school and other watersports. Programme of sports, games and entertainment, partly in English (15/6-31/8). Exchange facilities. ATM. Safety deposit. Internet café. WiFi. Dogs taken in one section. Torches required in some areas.

Open: 19 May - 2 September.

Directions

L'Escala is northeast of Girona on coast between Palamos and Roses. From A7/E15 autostrada take exit 5 towards L'Escala on GI 623. Turn north 2 km. before reaching L'Escala towards Sant Marti d'Ampurias. Site well signed. GPS: N42:09.659 E03:08.087

Charges 2006

Per person	€ 3,00 - € 4,00
child (2-10 yrs)	€ 2,50 - € 3,00
standard pitch incl. electricity	€ 13,00 - € 39,00
water and drainage	€ 1,00 - € 3,00
dog	€ 3,00 - € 4,00

All plus 7% VAT.

1ª Cat

N 42°.21.248
E 3° 08.645

Camping Nautic Almata
Ctra. Giv-6216
17486 Castelló d'Empuries
Costa Brava-Girona-España
Tel:(34)972 454477
Fax:(34)972 454686
info@almata.com
www.almata.com

ES8008 Camping Joncar Mar

Ctra Figueres s/n, E-17480 Roses (Girona)

Tel: 972 256 702. Email: info@campingjoncarmar.com

Family owned since 1977, Jonca Mar is a mature, all year site with basic facilities. Its strength is its location with the beach promenade just outside the gate, and the many resort leisure facilities and local cultural attractions readily available to customers. The site is divided by a minor road and most leisure facilities are on one side of the site. There are no views and the site has some apartment blocks around the periphery. Pitches are small (60 sq.m) with 6A electricity. Some pitches require long electricity leads and long stay customers have arranged unpleasant systems of hoses draining into road drains. The modest pool has a shallow area at right angles at one end for children, but no barrier separating it from deeper water, so small children will need supervision. The pool is overlooked by a restaurant area offering an uncomplicated 'eat all you can' fixed evening buffet menu, which is open to the street and thus non-camping customers. We met a few regular, low season British customers who stated that this was a two star site in a five star location, but they seemed happy, especially as it was relatively free from biting insects which plague some sites hereabouts. The site offers a very basic, no frills service which will only appeal to a limited number of campers.

Facilities

Two dated, refurbished toilet blocks are well positioned on the main side of the site and the third very tired block on the other side is due for refurbishment. No formal facilities for disabled visitors. Washing machine. Small shop. Small bar and buffet restaurant. Swimming pool. Basic play area. TV in bar. Limited animation programme. Internet. Torches useful. Off site: Nearest beach 50 m. Public transport 600 m. Bicycle hire 100 m. Riding 3 km.

Open: All year.

Directions

Roses is north of Girona and east of Figueres on the coast. From AP7/E15 take exit 3 south or exit 4 north (there is no exit 3 northbound) and then the N11 to the C260 and on to Roses. Site is well signed before you enter the town – follow camping signs initially.

Charges 2006

Per person	€ 5,15 - € 5,30
child (under 10 years)	€ 3,45 - € 3,55
pitch incl. electricity (10A)	€ 13,95 - € 15,20

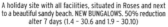

A holiday site with all facilities, situated in Roses and next to a beautiful sandy beach. NEW BUNGALOWS. 50% reduction alter 7 days (1.4 – 30.6 and 1.9 – 30.10)

Camping Caravaning **JONCAR MAR** Str. Figueras, s/n • Postadr. Apartado 483 E-17480 ROSES
Costa Brava • Tel./Fax: 0034 972 25 67 02 • www.campingjoncarmar.com info@campingjoncarmar.com

ES8060 Camping La Ballena Alegre 2

Ctra San Marti d'Empuries s/n, E-17470 San Pere Pescador (Girona)

Tel: 902 510 520. Email: infb2@ballena-alegre.com

La Ballena Alegre 2 is partly in a lightly wooded setting, partly open, and has some 1,800 m. of frontage directly onto an excellent beach of soft golden sand (cleaned daily). They claim that none of the 1,531 touring pitches is more than 100 m. from the beach. The site has won Spanish tourist board awards and is keen on ecological fitness. Electrical connections (5/10A) are available in all parts and there are 91 fully serviced pitches. It is a great site for families.

Facilities

Seven well maintined toilet blocks are of a very high standard. Facilities for children, babies and disabled campers. Launderette. Motorcaravan services. Gas supplies. Supermarket. New restaurant. Self-service restaurant and bar. Takeaway. Pizzeria and beach bar in high season. Swimming pool complex. Jacuzzi. Tennis. Watersports. Fitness centre. Bicycle hire. Playgrounds. Sound proofed disco. Dancing twice weekly and organised activities all season. ATM. Off site: Go-karting nearby with bus service. Fishing 300 m. Riding 2 km.

Open: 12 May - 24 September.

Directions

From A7 Figueres - Girona autopista take exit 5 to L'Escala GI 623 for 18.5 km. At roundabout take sign to Sant Marti d'Empúries and follow camp signs. Access has now been entirely asphalted. GPS: N42:09.194 E03:06.749

Charges 2006

Per person	€ 3,30 - € 3,50
child (3-9 yrs)	€ 2,50 - € 2,75
pitch incl. electricity	€ 14,90 - € 50,50

All plus 7% VAT. Discount of 10% on pitch charge for pensioners all season. No credit cards.

ES8012 Camping Mas Nou

Ctra Figueres - Roses, km. 38, E-17486 Castelló d'Empúries (Girona)

Tel: **972 454 175**. Email: **info@campingmasnou.com**

Some two kilometres from the sea on the Costa Brava, this is a surprisingly tranquil site in two parts on either side of the access road. One part contains the pitches and toilet blocks, the other houses the impressive leisure complex. There are 450 neat, level and marked pitches on grass and sand, a minimum of 70 sq.m. but most 80-100 sq.m, and 300 with electricity (6/10A). The leisure complex is across the road from reception and features a huge L-shaped swimming pool with a paddling area. A formal restaurant has ajoining bar, pleasant terrace crêperie and rotisseria under palms. A barbecue/rotisseria in another part of the site offers takeaway meals (in season). The site owns the large souvenir shop on the entrance road. There are many traditional bargains here and it is worth having a good look around as the prices are extremely good. Lots of time and money goes into the cleanliness of this site and it is good very for families. Ask about the origin of the site coat of arms. The Bay of Roses and the Medes islands have a natural beauty and a visit to Dali's house or the museum (the house is fascinating) will prove he was not just a surrealist painter.

Facilities

Three excellent, fully equipped sanitary blocks include baby baths, good facilities for disabled visitors. Washing machines. Supermarket and other shops. Bar/restaurant. Takeaway. Swimming pool with life guard (from 1/6). Tennis. Minigolf. Mini club (July/Aug). Play area. Electronic games. Off site: Riding 1.5 km. Fishing or bicycle hire 2 km. Beach 2.5 km. Aquatic Park. Romanica tour of famous local churches.

Open: 31 March - 30 September.

Directions

From A7 use exit 3. Mas Nou is 2 km. east of Castelló d'Empúries, on the Roses road, 10 km. from Figueres. Do not turn left across the main road but continue to the roundabout and return. GPS: N42:15.935 E03:06.150

Charges 2007

Per person	€ 2,30 - € 4,40
child (4-11 yrs)	€ 1,60 - € 3,10
pitch	€ 7,50 - € 11,90
electricity	€ 2,90 - € 4,10
dog	free - € 1,90

All plus 7% VAT.

Camping Cheques accepted.

awan
ES CAMPINGS

tel: 00 333 59 59 03 59 *kawan-villages.com*

ES8050 Camping Aquarius

Playa s/n, E-17470 Sant Pere Pescador (Girona)

Tel: **972 520 003**. Email: **camping@aquarius.es**

A smart and efficient family site, Aquarius has direct access to a quiet sandy beach that slopes gently and provides good bathing (the sea is shallow for quite a long way out). One third of the site has good shade with a park-like atmosphere. There are 447 pitches with electricity (6/16A). Markus Rupp and his wife are keen to make their visitors experience a happy one and even issue flags to denote the number of years they have stayed at the site. The site is ideal for those who really like sun and sea, with a quiet situation. Mr Rupp has a background in architecture and a wealth of knowledge on the whole Catalan area and culture. The family is justifiably proud of their most attractive site which they continually upgrade and improve. The fountain at the entrance, the fishponds and the water features in the restaurant are soothing and pleasing. A small stage close to the restaurant is used for live entertainment in season. The spotless beach bar complex with shaded terraces, satellite TV and evening entertainment, has marvellous views over the Bay of Roses. The 'Surf Center' with rentals, school and shop is ideal for enthusiasts and beginners alike.

Facilities

Attractively tiled, fully equipped, large toilet blocks provide some cabins for each sex. Excellent facilities for disabled people, plus baths for children. Superb new block has under-floor heating and features family cabins with showers and basins. Laundry facilities. Gas supplies. Motorcaravan services. Full size refrigerators. Supermarket. Pleasant restaurant and bar with terrace. Takeaway. Children's play centre (with qualified attendant), playground near the beach and games hall. TV room. 'Surf Center'. Minigolf. Bicycle hire. Barbecue and dance once weekly when numbers justify. ATM. Internet access. WiFi. (Note: no pool). Off site: Fishing and boat launching 3 km. Riding 6 km. Golf 15 km.

Open: 15 March - 31 October.

Directions

Sant Pere Pescadore is south of Perpignan on coast between Roses and L'Escala. From the AP7/E15 take exit 4 onto N11 north towards Figueres and then the C31 towards Torroella de Fluvia. Take the Vilamacolum road east and continue to Sant Pere Pescadore. Site well signed in town. GPS: N42:10.614 E03:06.478

Charges 2006

Per person	€ 2,75 - € 3,30
child (2-12 yrs)	free - € 2,40
pitch	€ 7,15 - € 35,00
electricity	€ 2,80

All plus 7% VAT. Discounts for pensioners on longer stays. No credit cards.

E-17470 Sant Pere Pescador
COSTA BRAVA · SPAIN
Tel. +34 972 520 003
Fax +34 972 550 216
www.aquarius.es

A Family Paradise!

Well kept family site situated at a wide and sandy beach, ideal and safe for children.
Excellent amenities and a friendly staff provide a wonderful holiday.

♦ Large serviced pitches
♦ Luxury mobile-homes to rent
♦ Discounts and special offers in low season

Open
15th March
31st October

ES8103 Camping El Maset

Playa de Sa Riera, E-17255 Begur (Girona)

Tel: **972 623 023**. Email: **info@campingelmaset.com**

A delightful little gem of a site in lovely surroundings, El Maset has 116 pitches, of which just 20 are slightly larger for caravans or motorcaravans, the remainder suitable only for tents. The owner of some 40 years, Sr Juan Perez is delightful and his staff are very helpful. The site entrance is steep and access to the caravan pitches can be quite tricky. However, the owner's son will tow your caravan to your pitch. All these pitches have electricity, water and drainage with some shade.

Facilities

Good sanitary facilities in three small blocks are kept very clean. Baby facilities. Washing machines and dryers. Bar/restaurant, takeaway (all season). Shop (from May). Swimming pool (all season). Solarium. Play area. Excellent games room.Dogs are not accepted.

Open: Easter - 24 September.

Directions

From the C31 Figueres - Palamos road south of Pals, north of Palafrugell, take GI653 to Begur. Site is 2 km. north of town. GPS: N41:58.116 E03:12.601

Charges 2007

Per person	€ 4,70 - € 6,70
pitch incl. electricity	€ 8,80 - € 18.70

ES8102 Camping Resort Mas Patoxas Bungalow Park

Ctra C31 Palafrugell-Pals, km. 339, E-17256 Pals (Girona)

Tel: 972 636 928. Email: info@campingmaspatoxas.com

This is a mature and well laid out site for those who prefer to be apart from, but within easy travelling distance of, the beaches (5 km.) and town (1 km.). It has a very easy access and is set on a slight slope with wide avenues on level terraces providing over 400 grassy pitches of a minimum 72 sq.m. All have electricity (5A) and water; many have drainage as well. There are some very pleasant views and shade from a variety of mature trees. Both bar and restaurant terraces give views over the pools and distant hills. The air-conditioned restaurant/bar provides both waiter service meals and takeaway food to order (weekends only mid Sept - April) and entertainment takes place on a stage below the terraces during high season. The restaurant menu is varied and very reasonable. We were impressed with the children's mini-club activity when we visited. There is a large, supervised irregularly shaped swimming pool with triple flume, a separate children's pool and a generous sunbathing area at the poolside and on the surrounding grass.

Facilities

Three modern sanitary blocks provide controllable hot showers, some washbasins with hot water. Baby bath and three cabins for children. No specific facilities for disabled people. Laundry facilities. Well stocked shop (1/4-30/9). Restaurant/bar, pizzeria and takeaway (all 1/4-30/9). Swimming pool (15/6-30/9). Tennis. Entertainment in high season. Fridges for rent. Gas supplies. Torches useful in some areas. Off site: Bus service from site gate. Bicycle hire or riding 2 km. Fishing or golf 4 km.

Open: 12 January - 16 December.

Directions

Site is east of Girona and approx. 1.5 km. south of Pals at km. 339 on the C31 Figueres-Palamos road, just north of Palafugel. GPS: N41:57.311 E03:09.478

Charges 2007

Per unit incl. 2 persons	
and electricity	€ 15,00 - € 41,00
extra person	€ 3,60 - € 5,25
child (1-10 yrs)	€ 3,00 - € 3,75
dog	€ 2,10 - € 3,15

Plus 7% VAT. Special low season offers.

ES8090 Camping Cypsela

Ctra de Pals - Platja de Pals, E-17256 Platja de Pals (Girona)

Tel: 972 667 696. Email: info@cypsela.com

This impressive, de-luxe site with lush vegetation and trees is very efficiently run. The main part of the camping area is pinewood, with 661 clearly marked touring pitches of varying categories on sandy gravel, all with electricity and some with full facilities. The 228 'Elite' pitches of 120 sq.m. are impressive. The site has many striking features, one of which is the sumptuous complex of sport facilities and amenities near the entrance. This provides a fine large swimming pool, a good children's pool and playgrounds, two excellent squash courts, a tennis court, fitness room, and other entertainment rooms.

Facilities

Four sanitary blocks are of excellent quality with comprehensive cleaning schedules and solar heating. Three have washbasins in cabins and three have amazing children's rooms. Superb facilites for disabled people. Serviced launderette. Supermarket and other shops. Restaurant, cafeteria and takeaway. Bar. Hairdresser. Swimming pools. Tennis. Squash. Football. Minigolf. Skating rink. Fitness room. Solarium. Air conditioned social/TV room. Barbecue and party area. Children's club. Comprehensive animation programme in season. Organised sports and games activities. Games room. Business and internet centre. Medical centre. Gas supplies. ATM. Dogs are not accepted. Off site: Bicycle hire 150 m. Golf 1 km. Fishing 2 km.

Open: 12 May - 23 September.

Directions

Platja de Pals is southeast of Girona on the coast. From the AP7/E15 at Girona take exit 6 towards Palamos on the C66. This road changes number to the C31 near La Bisbal. 7.5 km past La Bisbal, exit to Pals on the GI 652. Follow signs for Platja de Pals. At El Masos take the 6502 for 1 km. Main entrance for Cypsela is on the left between the white metal fencing. GPS: N41:59.317 E03:11.083

Charges 2006

Per person	€ 5,40
child (2-10 yrs)	€ 4,25
pitch acc. to season and services	€ 17,30 - € 52,50

ES8072 Camping Les Medes

Paratge Camp de L'Arbre, E-17258 L'Estartit (Girona)

Tel: 972 751 805. Email: campinglesmedes@cambrescat.es

Les Medes is different from some of the 'all singing, all dancing' sites so popular along this coast and the friendly family of Pla-Coll are rightly proud of their award wining site and provide a very warm welcome. With just 172 pitches, the site is small enough for the owners to know their visitors and, being campers themselves, they have been careful in planning their top class facilities and are aware of environmental issues. The level, grassy pitches range in size from 60-80 sq.m. depending on your unit. All have electricity (5,6 or 10A) and the larger ones (around half) also have water and drainage.

Facilities

Two modern spacious sanitary blocks can be heated and are extremely well maintained. Washbasins in cabins, top class facilities for disabled people and baby baths. Washing machines and dryer. Motorcaravan services. Bar with snacks (all year). Good value restaurant (1/4-31/10). Shop. Outdoor swimming and paddling pools (15/6-15/9). Indoor pool with sauna, solarium (15/9-15/6). Masseur. Play area. TV room. Internet access and Wifi. Excursions (July/Aug). Diving activities. Bicycle hire. Dogs only accepted at certain times. Torches are useful. Off site: Riding 400 m. Fishing 800 m. Beach 800 m. Medes Natural Reserve 1.5 km. Estartit 2 km. Golf 8 km.

Open: All year excl. November.

Directions

Site is signed from the main Torroella de Montgri - L'Estartit road GE641. Turn right after Camping Castel Montgri, at Joc's hamburger/pizzeria and follow signs. GPS: N42:02.900 E03:11.273

Charges 2007

Per person	€ 6,70
child (0-10 yrs)	€ 4,75
pitch	€ 15,00
electricity	€ 3,90

All plus 7% VAT. Discounts outside high season and special offers for low season longer stays. No credit cards.

ES8074 Camping Paradis

Avenida de Montgó 260, E-17130 L'Escala (Girona)

Tel: **972 770 200**. Email: **info@campingparadis.com**

If you prefer a quieter site out of the very busy resort of L'Escala then this site is an excellent option. This large, family run site has a dynamic owner Marti, who speaks excellent English. The site is divided by the beach access road and has its own private access to the very safe and unspoilt beach. There are 646 pitches, all with electricity (10A), some on sloping ground although the pitches themselves tend to be flat. Established pine trees provide shade for most places with more coverage on the western side of the site. Non-stop maintenance ensures that all facilities at this site are of a high standard. There are three swimming pools, the largest with an idyllic and most unusual setting on the top of a cliff overlooking the Bay of Roses. A CCTV security system monitors the pools and general security from a purpose built centre.

Facilities

Modern, fully equipped sanitary blocks are kept very clean. Washing machines and dryers. Shop, extensive modern complex of restaurants, bars and takeaways (all open all season). Swimming pools (1/5-20/9). Pool bar. Play areas. Fishing. Kayak hire. Organised activities for children in high season. ATM machine. Private access to beach. Off site: Cala Montgo beach 100 m. with a charming bay of soft sand offering all manner of watersports, pretty restaurants and a disco in season. Road train service to town centre from outside site. Riding 2 km. Golf 10 km.

Open: 17 March - 14 October.

Directions

Leave autopista A7 at exit 5 heading for Viladimat, then L'Escala. Site is well signed from town centre. Follow signs for Montgo and site is south of town beside the coast.

Charges 2007

Per person	€ 2,80 - € 5,00
child (3-10yrs)	€ 2,00 - € 3,50
pitch	€ 10,70 - € 23,60
electricity	€ 3,40

Plus 7% VAT. No credit cards.

ES8101 Camping Playa Brava

Avenida del Grau, 1, E-17256 Platja de Pals (Girona)

Tel: **972 636 894**. Email: **info@playabrava.com**

This is a pleasant site with an open feel which has access to a large sandy beach (200 m.) and a freshwater lagoon. On both you can enjoy watersports and you may launch your own boat. The ground is level and very grassy with shade provided for the 500 pitches by a mixture of conifer and broad-leaf trees. Electricity is provided (5A) and about a third of the pitches (75-85 sq m) have water and drainage. The air of spaciousness continues around the large swimming pool. There are no fences but huge grass sunbathing areas, the whole being overlooked by the restaurant terrace.

Facilities

Five modern, fully equipped toilet blocks include facilities for disabled visitors. Washing machines and dryers. Motorcaravan service point. Bar/restaurant. Takeaway. Supermarket. Swimming pool. Tennis. Volleyball. 5-a-side soccer. Minigolf. Play area on grass. Fishing. Watersports on river and beach, including sheltered lagoon for windsurfing learners. Internet access. Satellite TV. ATM. Gas supplies. Torches required in some areas. Dogs are not accepted. Off site: Two 18 hole golf courses 1 km. Bicycle hire 3 km. Riding 5 km.

Open: 14 May - 18 September.

Directions

Platja de Pals is southeast of Girona on the coast. From the AP7/E15 at Girona take exit 6 towards Palamos on the C66. This road changes number to the C31 near La Bisbal. 7.5 km past La Bisbal, exit to Pals on the GI 652. Follow signs for Platja de Pals. At El Masos take the 6502 east to the coast. Travel through Sa Piera (site signed). Site on left just before road ends at beach car park. GPS: N42:00.106 E03:11.621

Charges 2007

Per person	€ 2,00 - € 3,00
child (2-9 yrs)	free - € 2,00
senior (over 60 yrs)	free - € 3,00
pitch incl. electricity	€ 23,00 - € 38,00

All plus 7% VAT. Discount for longer stays in low season. No credit cards.

ES8170 Camping Valldaro

Apdo 57, Avenida Castell d'Aro 63, E-17250 Platja d'Aro (Girona)

Tel: **972 817 515**. Email: **info@valldaro.com**

Valldaro is 600 m. back from the sea at Platja d'Aro, a small, bright resort with a long, wide beach and plenty of amusements. It is particularly pleasant during out of peak weeks and is popular with British and Dutch visitors. Like a number of other large Spanish sites, Valldaro has been extended and many pitches have been made larger, bringing them up to 80 or 100 sq.m. There are now 1,200 pitches with 660 available for tourers. The site is flat, with pitches in rows divided up by access roads. You will probably find space here even at the height of the season. The newer section has its own vehicle entrance (the nearest point to the beach) and can be reached via a footbridge; it is brought into use at peak times. It has some shade and its own toilet block, as well as a medium-sized swimming pool of irregular shape with a grassy sunbathing area and adjacent bar/snack bar and takeaway. The original pool (36 x 18 m.) is adjacent to the attractive Spanish-style restaurant which also offers takeaway fare. There are 400 permanent Spanish pitches and 150 mobile homes and chalets to rent, but these are in separate areas and do not impinge on the touring pitches.

Facilities

Four sanitary blocks are of a good standard and are well maintained. Child-size toilets. Washbasins (no cabins) and adjustable showers (temperature perhaps a bit variable). Two supermarkets and general shops. Two restaurants. Large bar. Swimming pools. Tennis. Minigolf with snack bar. Playgrounds. Sports ground. Children's club. Organised entertainment in season. Hairdresser. Internet. WiFi. Satellite TV. Gas supplies. Off site: Fishing, bicycle hire and golf 1 km. Riding 4 km.

Open: 23 March - 30 September.

Directions

Platja d'Aro is on the coast southeast of Girona. From Girona on the AP7/E15 take exit 7 to Sant Feliu on C65. On C65 at km. 313 take exit to Platja d'Aro (road number changes here to C31). In 200 m. at roundabout take GI 662 towards Platja d'Aro. Site is at km 4. If approaching from Palomas, access is via Platja d'Aro centre, exit on the GI 662 as the GI 662 cannot be accessed from the C31 southbound. GPS: N41:48.856 E03:02.622

Charges 2006

Per person	€ 3,35 - € 5,50
child (2-10 yrs)	€ 2,25 - € 3,15
pitch incl. electricity	€ 16,50 - € 37,20
dog	€ 2,35

All plus 7% VAT. Discounts in low seasons. Camping Cheques accepted.

Check real time availability and at-the-gate prices...

 www.**alanrogers**.com

ES8100 Camping Inter-Pals

Avenida Mediterrania, E-17256 Platja de Pals (Girona)

Tel: 972 636 179. Email: interpals@interpals.com

Set on sloping ground with tall pine trees providing shade and about 500 metres from the beach, Inter-Pals has 625 terraced pitches (including 280 for touring units and 250 for tents). It is sister site to no. ES8170 Valldaro. Arranged on level terraces, mostly with shade, some of the terraced pitches have views of the sea through the trees. The main entrance and its drive resembles a pretty village street as the bungalows are set on both sides of the street which is lined with traditional lamp-posts. Continuing the village theme is a row of shops where you will find most camper's needs. The formal restaurant with good value menu and choice of takeaway overlooks the pools. The site is close to Platja de Pals which is a long sandy unspoilt stretch of beach, a discreet area, part of which is now an official naturist beach. The pretty town of Pals is close by along with a good golf course. The site will assist with touring plans of the area.

Facilities

Three well maintained toilet blocks include facilities for disabled campers. Laundry facilities. Gas supplies. Fridge/TV rental. Shops. Restaurant/bar. Pizzeria with dancing and entertainment area. Café/bar by entrance. Swimming pool. Tennis. Playground. Organised activities and entertainment in high season. Excursions. Watersports arranged. ATM. Internet access. Some breeds of dog are excluded (check with site). New mini adventure park. Medical centre. Torch useful. Off site: Fishing 200 m. Bicycle hire 500 m. Golf 1 km. Riding 10 km.

Open: 19 March - 2 October

Directions

Site is on the road leading off the Torroella de Montgri-Bagur road north of Pals and going to Playa de Pals (Pals beach). GPS: N41:58.868 E03:11.985

Charges 2007

Per person	€ 3,60 - € 5,50
child (3-10 yrs)	€ 2,60 - € 3,25
pitch	€ 16,60 - € 29,30
small tent and car	€ 14,00 - € 19,00
dog	€ 2,80 - € 2,90

Plus 7% VAT. Discounts for long stays in low season. No credit cards.
Camping Cheques accepted.

ES8104 Camping Begur

Ctra d'Esclanya, km. 2, E-17255 Begur (Girona)

Tel: **972 623 201**. Email: **info@campingbegur.com**

The owners here have made a massive investment in making the site a pleasant place to spend some time. There are some good supporting facilities including a pleasant swimming pool at its centre. The bar and snack bar are part of this new pool complex and it has been well designed with terraces and sunbathing area. The touring areas are protected from the sun by mature trees and the 317 pitches are informally arranged on sloping sandy ground (chocks useful). Most pitches have electricity (10A), water and drainage. A few mobile homes and apartments are scattered around the slopes. Environmental activities are encouraged including visits to the revolutionary water cleansing plant deep in the woods. There are many sporting facilities including a well equipped weight training room (free). A huge supermarket is just outside the gate, used by locals and the new restaurant here is now open. The bays of the Costa Brava are just 1.5 km. away.

Facilities

Two modern toilet blocks are fully equipped and include really large showers. Excellent facilites for disabled campers. Baby bath. Washing machines and dryers. Motorcaravan services. Bar and snacks. Swimming pools (all season). Table tennis. Boules. Weight training room. Play area. Some animation in high season. Children's entertainment in high season. Little farm with ponies, goat and chickens. Internet access. Off site: Restaurant and supermarket just outside gate. Village and beaches 1.5 km. Fishing 3 km. Golf 10 km. Riding 15 km.

Open: 1 April - 30 September.

Directions

From Girona take road east to La Bisbal and Palafrugell then Begur. Turn south towards Fornells, the site is well signed 3 km. south of Begur.

Charges 2007

Per person	€ 3,00 - € 5,70
child (3-10 yrs)	€ 1,40 - € 3,10
pitch with electricity	€ 8,80 - € 18,90
animal	€ 2,60 - € 5,30

No credit cards.

ES8130 Camping Internacional de Calonge

Ctra Sant Feliu/Guixols - Palamos, E-17251 Calonge (Girona)

Tel: 972 651 233. Email: info@intercalonge.com

This spacious, well laid out site has access to the fine beach by a footbridge over the coast road, or you can take the little road train as the site is on very sloping ground. Calonge is a family site with two good sized pools on different levels, a paddling pool plus large sunbathing areas. The site's 800 pitches are on terraces and all have electricity (5A) with 167 available for winter use. A large proportion are suitable for touring units (the remainder for tents) being set on attractively landscaped terraces. Access to some pitches may be a little difficult. There is good shade from the tall pine trees and some views of the sea through the foliage, although the views from the upper levels are taken by the tour operator and mobile home pitches. The pools are overlooked by the restaurant terrace which has great views over the mountains. A nature area within the site is used for walks or picnics. A separate area within the site is set aside for visitors with dogs (including a dog shower!)

Facilities

Generous sanitary provision in new or renovated blocks include some washbasins in cabins. One block is heated in winter. Laundry facilities. Motorcaravan services. Gas supplies. Shop (31/3-31/10). Bar/restaurant (31/3-21/10). Patio bar (pizza and takeaway). Swimming pools (31/3-30/9). Playground. Electronic games. Rather noisy disco two nights a week (but not late). Bicycle hire. Tennis. Hairdresser. ATM. Internet. Torches necessary in some areas. Off site: Fishing 300 m. Golf 3 km. Riding 10 km. Supermarket 500 m.

Open: All year.

Directions

Site is on the inland side of the coast road between Palamos and Platja d'Aro. Take the C31 south to the 661 at Calonge. At Calonge follow signs to the C253 towards Platja d'Aro and on to site which is well signed.

Charges 2007

Per person	€ 3,40 - € 6,80
child (3-10 yrs)	€ 1,75 - € 3,85
pitch incl. electricity	€ 11,30 - € 25,00

All plus 7% VAT. Discounts for longer stays Oct - end May. No credit cards.

ES8392 Camping El Garrofer

Ctra 246 km 39, E-08870 Sitges (Barcelona)

Tel: 938 941 780. Email: info@garroferpark.com

This large, pine covered site, alongside fields of vines, is 800 m. from the beach, close to the pleasant town of Sitges. It has over 500 pitches of which 380 with 6A electricity are for tourers, including 28 with water used for large motorcaravans. Everything is kept clean and the pitches are tidy and shaded, all with electricity (6A). The amenity buildings are along the site perimeter next to the road which absorbs most of the road noise. The permanent pitches are grouped in a completely separate area. A varied menu is offered in the cosy restaurant with a small terrace. Everything is cooked to perfection and complemented with the wines of the Penedes DO made hereabouts (the restaurant has a local reputation and is used by non campers – the menu of the day is great value). A traditional bar is alongside and from here you can see the pretty mosaic clad play area (the 'Gaudi touch' which is also evident elsewhere). An ambitious animation programme is conducted for children in summer. Late evening Salsa classes were offered for adults when we visited. A small swimming pool with sunbathing areas is welcome on hot summer days or you can walk to the very pleasant beach (ten minutes from a gate at the back of the site). The town of Sitges is an attractive resort with seaside entertainments and is well worth exploring. Open most of the year the site offers all manner of adventure activities (extra charge) which may be organized through reception and there are many things to see here – we especially recommend a visit to Monserrat.

Facilities

Two of the three sanitary blocks have been refurbished and provide roomy showers and special bright facilities for children. Separate baby room with bath. Good facilities for disabled campers. Laundry. Bar/restaurant. Shop (reception in low season). Swimming pool. Golf packages. Practice golf. Tennis. Play area for older children and fenced play area for toddlers. Bicycle hire. Boules. Off site: Bus from outside site to Barcelona. Golf, riding and fishing 0.5 km.

Open: All year excl. 18 December - 16 January.

Directions

From A16/C32 autopista take exit 26 towards Vilanova/St Pere Ribes. From Tarragona, go under autopista, around roundabout and back to the other side to pick up site sign (towards Sitges). Follow C-246 to km. 39; site entrance is not too easy to see beside old large tree. GPS: N41:14.033 E01:46.835

Charges 2006

Per person	€ 2,68 - € 4,71
child (1-9 yrs)	€ 1,82 - € 3,64
pitch incl. electricity	€ 14,35 - € 18,53

Plus 7% VAT.

Check real time availability and at-the-gate prices...
www.alanrogers.com

429

ES8210 Camping Tucan

Ctra de Blanes - Lloret, E-17310 Lloret de Mar (Girona)

Tel: **972 369 965**. Email: **info@campingtucan.com**

Situated on the busy Costa Brava near Lloret de Mar, Camping Tucan is well placed to access all the attractions of the area. Views over the mountains are mixed with views of the nearby town. The 250 good size pitches all have electricity, and are laid out in a herring-bone pattern with areas dedicated to singles, families with young children and couples who enjoy the quiet. Pitches are on terraces, flat surfaced with gravel and many are shaded. Tucan is a lively site with a variety of activities including an animation programme for children and modest entertainment at night. Activities on the site centre around the pleasant pool, bar, restaurant and terrace all of which are close to reception. There is a separate, largely independent facility for young people at the rear of the site.

Facilities

Two modern toilet blocks include washbasins with hot water and facilities for disabled visitors, although access is difficult. All very clean when seen. Washing machine. Gas supplies. Shop. Busy bar and good restaurant. Takeaway. Swimming pools and indoor solarium. Playground and fenced play area for toddlers. TV in bar. Bicycle hire. Animation in high season. Mini-club. Off site: Town 500 m. Nearest beach 600 m. Riding 1 km. Golf 4 km.

Open: 1 April - 30 September.

Directions

From A7/E4, A19 or N11 Girona - Barcelona roads take an exit for Lloret de Mar. Site is 1 km. west of the town, well signed and is at the base of the hill off the roundabout. The entrance can get congested in busy periods. GPS: N41:41.832 E02:49.310

Charges 2006

Per person	€ 4,20 - € 6,50
child (1-9 yrs)	€ 3,15 - € 4,40
pitch	€ 4,20 - € 10,30
electricity	€ 3,30 - € 4,30
animal	€ 1,80

ES8200 Camping Cala Llevadó

Ctra GI-682 de Tossa - Lloret, pk. 18,9, E-17320 Tossa de Mar (Girona)

Tel: **972 340 314**. Email: **info@calallevado.com**

For splendour of position Cala Llevadó can compare with almost any in this book. A beautifully situated cliff-side site, it has fine views of the sea and coast below. It is shaped something like half a bowl with steep slopes. High up in the site with a superb aspect, is the attractive restaurant/bar with a large terrace overlooking the pleasant swimming pool. There are terraced, flat areas for caravans and tents (with electricity) on the upper levels of the two slopes, with a great many individual pitches for tents scattered around the site. Some pitches have fantastic settings and views. There is usually car parking close to these pitches, although in some areas cars may be required to park separately. The steepness of the site would make access difficult for disabled people or those with limited mobility. One beach is for all manner of watersports within a buoyed area and there is a sub-aqua diving school. Some other pleasant little coves can also be reached by climbing down on foot (with care!). Cala Llevadó is luxurious and has much character and the atmosphere is informal and very friendly. Many of the 577 touring pitches are available for caravans with 10A electricity. There are a few tour operator pitches (45) and 26 bungalows. The site is peacefully situated but only five minutes away from the busy resort of Tossa – take a look at the town where the castle is beautifully lit by night or if you visit in July enjoy the many lively fiestas. The botanic garden on the site is charming with many of the plants, flowers and trees of the region.

Facilities

Four very well equipped toilet blocks are immaculately maintained and well spaced around the site. Baby baths. Laundry facilities. Motorcaravan services. Gas supplies. Fridge hire. Large supermarket. Restaurant/bar (5/5-28/9). Swimming and paddling pools. Three play areas. Botanic garden. Entertainment for children (4-12 yrs). Sailing, water ski and windsurfing school. Fishing. Excursions. Internet access anf WiFi. Torches definitely needed in some areas. Off site: Bicycle hire 3 km. Large complex adjacent for sports, activities and swimming.

Open: 1 May - 30 September, including all amenities.

Directions

Cala Llevadó is southeast of Girona on the coast. Leave the AP7/E15 at exit 7 to the C65 Sant Feliu road and then take C35 southeast to the GI 681 to Tossa de Mare. Site is signed off the GI 682 Lloret - Tossa road at km 18.9, about 3 km. from Tossa. Route avoids difficult coastal road. GPS: N41:42.769 E02:54.374

Charges 2006

Per person	€ 4,90 - € 7,90
child (4-12 yrs)	€ 3,00 - € 4,30
pitch incl. car	€ 8,25 - € 16,10
electricity	€ 3,95 - € 4,30
Plus 7% VAT.	

sènia

Good campings.
Good people.

CALIDAD TURISTICA

Sant Pere Pescador
Girona
Rupit
Lloret de Mar
Pineda de Mar
arcelona

Online Booking < < <

w w w . s e n i a . b i z

ES8482 Camping La Pineda de Salou

Ctra Costa Tarragona - Salou km 5, E-43481 La Pineda (Tarragona)
Tel: **977 37 30 80**. Email: **info@campinglapineda.com**

La Pineda is just outside Salou towards Tarragona and this site is just 300 m. from the Aquapark and 2.5 km. from Port Aventura, to which there is an hourly bus service from outside the site entrance. There is some noise from this road. The site has a fair-sized swimming pool adjoining a smaller, heated one, open from mid June, behind large hedges close to the entrance. A large terrace has sun loungers, and various entertainment aimed at young people is provided in season. The 366 flat pitches are mostly shaded and of about 70 sq.m. All have 5A electricity. The beach is about 400 m. The simple restaurant/bar is shaded and has a large cactus garden to the rear. This is a plain, friendly and convenient site, with reasonable rates, probably best used for visiting Tarragona and Port Aventura, or exploring the local area, rather than for extended stays. Note: the site is reasonably close to a large industrial centre.

Facilities

Sanitary facilities are mature but clean with baby bath, dishwashing and laundry sinks. Facilities for disabled visitors. Two washing machines in each block. The second building is opened in high season only. Gas supplies. Shop (1/7-31/8). Restaurant and snacks (1/7-31/8). Swimming pools (1/7-31/8). Bar (all season). Small TV room. Bicycle hire. Games room. Playground (3-12 yrs). Entertainment (1/7-30/8). Torches may be required. Off site: Beach and fishing 400 m. Golf 12 km.

Open: All year.

Directions

From A7 just southwest of Tarragona take exit 35 and follow signs to La Pineda and Port Aventura then campsite signs appear. GPS: N41:05.310 E01:10.947

Charges 2006

Per person	€ 4,30 - € 6,00
child (1-10 yrs)	€ 2,90 - € 4,50
pitch incl. car	€ 10,40 - € 20,20
electricity	€ 3,50

All plus 7% VAT.

ES8420 Camping Stel

Ctra N340, km. 1182, E-43883 Roda de Bará (Tarragona)
Tel: **977 802 002**. Email: **rodadebara@stel.es**

Camping Stel is situated between the pre-Littoral mountains and the sea. The rectangular site is between the N340 road and the excellent beach, with the railway running close to the bottom of the site. Beach access is gained through a gate and under the railway – there is rail noise on the lower pitches. The pitches are generally in rows with hedges around the rows but at the lower end of the site the layout is less formal. Many pitches have individual sinks. There is a separate area where no radio or TV is allowed ensuring peace and quiet.

Facilities

Four clean, fully equipped, sanitary blocks. One offers excellent facilities for children and disabled campers and four high standard private cabins. Baby baths. Large launderette. Motorcaravan service area. Supermarket and tourist shop. Bar/restaurant and snack bar. Swimming pools.(4/4-28/9) Outdoor sports area. Gym. Bicycle hire. Miniclub and some adult entertainment in high season. Internet room. Hairdresser. ATM. Dogs are not accepted. Off site: Fishing from beach. Golf and riding 4 km.

Open: 4 April - 30 September.

Directions

Site is at 1182 km. marker on the N340 near Arc de Bara, between Tarragona and Vilanova.
GPS: N41:10 E01:27.84

Charges 2006

Per person	€ 6,70
child (3-10 yrs)	€ 5,20
pitch incl. electricity	€ 20,80 - € 24,35
with water and drainage	€ 25,10 - € 29,35

All plus 7% VAT.
Camping Cheques accepted.

kawan-villages.com **tel: 00 333 59 59 03 59**

kawan VILLAGES CAMPINGS

ES8390 Camping Vilanova Park

Ctra de l'Arboc, km. 2.5, E-08800 Vilanova i la Geltru (Barcelona)

Tel: **93 893 34 02**. Email: **info@vilanovapark.es**

Sitting on the terrace of the bustling but comfortable restaurant at Vilanova Park, it is difficult to believe that in 1908 this was a Catalan farm and then, quite lacking in trees, it was known as 'Rock Farm'. Since then imaginative planting has provided literally thousands of trees and gloriously colourful shrubs making a most attractive, large campsite, with an impressive range of high quality amenities and facilities open all year. There are 248 marked pitches for touring units in separate areas. All have 6A electricity, 133 also have water and some larger pitches (100 sq.m.) also have drainage. The terrain, hard surfaced and mostly on very gently sloping ground, has many trees and considerable shade. At present there are 865 pitches with a significant proportion occupied by bungalows and chalets carefully designed to fit into the environment. The really good amenities include a second pool higher up in the site with marvellous views across the town to the sea and a second, more intimate restaurant for that special romantic dinner overlooking the twinkling evening lights. The original pool has water jets and a coloured floodlit fountain playing at night time, which complement the dancing and entertainment taking place on the stage in the courtyard overlooking the pool. An unusual attraction is a Nature Park and mini-zoo with deer and birdlife, which has pleasant picnic areas and views. An indoor pool, sauna and gym are planned which will be appreciated by winter visitors as will the excursion programmes to Barcelona, Monserrat and Bodegas Torres for wine tasting. There is a transfer service from both Barcelona and Reus airports.

Facilities

All toilet blocks are of excellent quality, can be heated and have washbasins (over half in cabins) with free hot water, and others of standard type with cold water. Serviced laundry. Motorcaravan services. Supermarket. Souvenir shop. Restaurants. Bar with simple meals (all year). Swimming pools (outdoor 1/4 - 15/10, indoor all year). Play areas. Games room. Tennis. Bicycle hire. Tennis. ATM and exchange facilities. Off site: Fishing 4 km. Golf 5 km. Good train service from Vilanova to Barcelona, not so good the other way (to Tarragona). Vilanova town and beach are 4 km (local bus service).

Open: All year.

Directions

Site is 4 km. northwest of Vilanova i la Geltru towards L'Arboc (BV2115). From the A7 Tarragona - Barcelona take exit 29 onto C15 to Vilanova, then C31 El Vendrell road (km. 153) then onto BV2115.

Charges 2007

Per person	€ 4,40 - € 7,75
child (4-12 yrs)	€ 2,65 - € 4,86
pitch incl. electricity	€ 13,05 - € 20,35
with water	€ 15,80 - € 23,13

All plus 7% VAT. Excellent deals for retired people on longer stays.

Camping Cheques accepted.

ES8481 Camping Cambrils Park

Avenida Mas Clariana s/n., E-43850 Cambrils (Tarragona)

Tel: **977 351 031**. Email: **mail@cambrilspark.es**

This is a superb site for a camping holiday providing for all family members, whatever their age. A drive lined with palm trees and flowers leads from a large, very smart round reception building at this impressive modern site. Sister site to no. ES8480, it is set 500 metres back from the excellent beach in a generally quiet setting with outstanding facilities. The 684 slightly sloping, grassy pitches of around 90 sq.m. are numbered and separated by trees. All have 10A electricity, 55 have water and waste water connections, some having more shade than others. The marvellous central lagoon pool complex with three pools and water slides is the main focus of the site with a raised wooden 'poop deck' sunbathing area with palm surrounds that doubles as an entertainment stage at night. There is a huge bar/terrace area for watching the magnificent floodlit spectacles, along with an excellent restaurant in the old farmhouse with an adjacent takeaway. By day there is a small bar at a lower level in the pool where you can enjoy a cool drink from submerged stools, plus a dryer version on the far side of the bar or just relax on the spacious grass sunbathing areas. There are a number of tour operator pitches and attractive thatched chalets. A fabulous jungle theme children's pool is nearer the entrance – they love it, especially the elephants! An extra pool for adults has been added here, along with a snack bar.

Facilities

Four excellent sanitary buildings provide some washbasins in cabins, superb units for disabled visitors and immaculate, decorated baby sections. Dishwashing and laundry sinks. Huge serviced laundry. Motorcaravan services. Car wash. Restaurant. Takeaway. Huge supermarket, souvenir shop and 'panaderia' (fresh-baked bread and croissants). Swimming pools with lifeguards. Minigolf. Tennis Multi-games court. Petanque. Animation and entertainment all season. Mini-club. Internet café. Medical centre. ATM. Gas supplies. Dogs are not accepted. Off site: Beach 500 m. Fishing, bicycle hire 400 m. Riding 3 km. Port Aventura theme park 4 km. Golf 7 km.

Open: 7 April - 8 October.

Directions

Site is about 1.5 km west of Salou. From the A7 take exit 35 and at roundabout take signs for Cambrils. Follow new dual-carriageway around the back of Salou and site is signed at last roundabout towards Cambrils. GPS: N41:04.584 E01:06.527

Charges 2006

Per person	€ 6,00
child (4-12 yrs)	€ 4,00
pitch incl. electricity	€ 12,00 - € 37,00
pitch with water and waste water	€ 14,00 - € 39,00

All plus 7% VAT. Special offers, plus low season discounts for pensioners. Camping Cheques accepted.

ES8470 Camping La Siesta

Calle Ctra Norte 37, E-43840 Salou (Tarragona)

Tel: **977 380 852**. Email: **info@camping-lasiesta.com**

The palm bedecked entrance of La Siesta is only 250 m. from the pleasant sandy beach and close to the life of the resort of Salou. The site is divided into 470 pitches which are large enough and have electricity (10A), with smaller ones for tents. Many pitches are provided with artificial shade and within some there is one box for the tent or caravan and a shared one for the car. There is considerable shade from the trees and shrubs that are part of the site's environment. In high season, the siting of units is carried out by the friendly management. Young campers are located separately to the rear of the site. The town is popular with British and Spanish holidaymakers and has just about all that a highly developed Spanish resort can offer. For those who do not want to share the busy beach, there is a large, free swimming pool which is elevated above pitch level. The restaurant, which overlooks the good-sized pool, has a comprehensive menu and wine list, competing well with the town restaurants. A bar is alongside with TV and a large terrace, part of which is given over to entertainment in high season. A suprisingly large supermarket caters for most needs in season.

Facilities

Three bright and clean sanitary blocks provide very reasonable facilities. Motorcaravan services. Supermarket. Various vending machines. Self-service restaurant and bar with cooked dishes to take away. Dancing some evenings till 11 pm. Swimming pool (300 sq.m. open all season). Playground. Medical service daily in season. ATM point. Torches may be required. Off site: Many shops, restaurants and bars near. Port Aventura is close. Bicycle hire 200 m. Fishing 500 m. Riding amd golf 6 km.

Open: 14 March - 3 November.

Directions

Leave A7 at exit 35 for Salou. Site is signed off the Tarragona/Salou road and from the one way system in the town of Salou. The site is in the town so keep a sharp eye for the small signs. GPS: N41:04.666 E01:08.352

Charges 2006

Per person	€ 3,90 - € 7,55
child (4-9 yrs)	€ 3,10 - € 4,00
pitch	€ 3,10 - € 15,10
electricity	€ 2,70 - € 3,20

All plus 7% VAT. No credit cards.

ES8483 Camping Tamarit Park

N340 km 1172, Tamarit, E-43008 Tarragona (Tarragona)
Tel: **977 650 128**. Email: **tamaritpark@tamarit.com**

This is a marvellous, beach-side site, attractively situated at the foot of Tamarit castle at one end of a superb one kilometre long beach of fine sand. The 734 pitches, 50 of which are virtually on the beach, are marked out on hard sand and grass and some are separated by green vegetation which provides good shade. All pitches have electricity (6A). Long leads and metal awning pegs may be required in places but wide internal roads give good access for even the largest of units (American motorhomes accepted). There is some train noise.

Facilities

Sanitary blocks (one heated) are modern and tiled, providing good facilities. Unfortunately the showers have push-button controlled hot water with tap controlled cold. Private bathrooms to rent. Laundry. Motorcaravan services. Gas supplies. Shop, bar/restaurant and takeaway (all until 15/10). Swimming pool (15/5-15/10). Minigolf. Playground. Animation programme in season. Fishing. Internet access. Barbecues not permtted. Off site: Riding 1 km. Bicycle hire 2 km. Golf 8 km.

Open: All year.

Directions

From A7 take exit 32 towards Tarragona and continue for 4.5 km. At roundabout (km. 1172) turn back towards Atafulla/Tamarit and after just 200 m. turn right to Tamarit. Take care over railway bridge, then turn immediately sharp right. Site entrance is 1 km. GPS: N41:07.943 E01:21.652

Charges 2006

Per person	€ 4,50
child (1-12 yrs)	€ 3,50
pitch acc. to size and season	€ 16,00 - € 44,00

ES8508 Camping Poboleda

Placa de les Casetes s/n, E-43376 Poboleda (Tarragona)
Tel: **977 827197**. Email: **poboleda@campingsonline.com**

Time stands still at this unique site hidden away in a corner of the village, watched over by La Morera de Montsant, a peak of the Serra del Montsant. Situated among olive groves, yet almost in the heart of the lovely old village of Poboleda, it is an idyllic site for tents, small caravans and motorcaravans. Large units may have problems negotiating the narrow village streets. The 151 pitches of 80 sq.m. are set under olive and almond trees. Fairly level and 70 with 4A electricity, they provide a peaceful haven broken only by the peal of church bells or bird song. The young manager is enthusiastic and proud of the facilities offered which are quite unexpected and special. Behind the modern reception is a traditional, comfortablly furnished room with piano and TV, which doubles as a peaceful cool area for relaxing if it is too hot on the terrace. Here you can have breakfast or order a drink. The village is on the doorstep for other needs. The mellow terraced pool area is a lovely surprise and very welcome. There is plenty to do, walking or climbing, visiting the region's vineyards and enjoying the local cuisine. A must to visit is the monastery of Poblet nearby.

Facilities

One small block, open all year, is fully equipped, as is a larger block open for high season. Shower for children. Facilities for disabled people (key). Laundry service. Breakfast can be ordered. Bar. Swimming pool (24/6-11/9). Tennis. Boules. Off site: Beach and Port Aventura 30 km. Fishing 12 km. Bicycle hire 10 km.

Open: All year.

Directions

Bypass Reus (west of Tarragona) on N420. After Borges del Camp pick up C242, signed Alforja. Continue over Coll d'Alforja. Watch for left turn (T702) for Pobodeda. Continue for 6 km. to village. Watch for tent signs and follow carefully through narrow village streets. Not advised for large units.

Charges 2007

Per person	€ 4,50
pitch incl. electricity	€ 12,50 - € 13,00

ES8410 Camping Playa Bara

Ctra N340, km. 1183, E-43883 Roda de Bará (Tarragona)

Tel: **977 802 701**. Email: **info@barapark.es**

This is a most impressive, family owned site near the beach, which has been carefully designed and developed. On entry you find yourself in a beautifully sculptured, tree-lined drive with an accompanying aroma of pine and woodlands and the sound of waterfalls close by. Considering its size, with over 850 pitches, it is still a very green and relaxing site with an immense range of activities. It is well situated with a 50 m. walk to a long sandy beach via a tunnel under the railway (some noise) to a new promenade with palms and a quality beach bar and restaurant. Much care with planning and in the use of natural stone; palms, shrubs and flowering plants gives a most pleasing tropical appearance to all aspects of the site. The owners have excelled themselves in the design of the impressive terraced Roman-style pool complex, which is the central feature of the site. This complex is really amazing. Sunbathe on the pretty terraces or sip a drink whilst seated at the bar stools submerged inside one of the pools or enjoy the panorama over the sea from the rooftop spa or the upper Roman galley bar surrounded by stylish friezes. A separate attractive amphitheatre seats 2,000 and is used to stage very professional entertainment in season. Pitches vary in size and are being progressively enlarged; the older ones terraced and well shaded with pine trees, the newer ones more open, with a variety of trees and bushes forming separators between them. All have electricity (5A) and a sink with water. Arrive early to find space in peak weeks.

Facilities

Excellent, fully equipped toilet blocks include private cabins and excellent facilities for children and disabled visitors. Private facilities to hire. Superb launderette. Triple motorcaravan service points. Supermarket and several other shops. Full restaurant. Large bar with simpler meals and takeaway. Three other bars. Pleasant bar/restaurant on beach. Swimming pools. Jacuzzi/hydro-massage. Fronton and tennis (floodlit). Junior club. Sports area. Windsurfing school. Gym. Massage. Petanque. Minigolf. Fishing. Entertainment centre. ATM. Hairdresser. Internet room. Medical centre. Flights and excursions booked. WiFi. Off site: Bicycle hire 2 km. Riding 3 km. Golf 4 km.

Open: 23 March - 25 September, with all amenities.

Directions

From the A7 take exit 31. Site entrance is at the 1183 km. marker on the main N340 just opposite the Arco de Bara Roman monument from which it takes its name.

Charges 2006

Per person	€ 3,00 - € 9,40
child (1-9 yrs)	€ 2,00 - € 6,60
pitch	€ 3,50 - € 9,40
electricity	€ 3,20

All plus 7% VAT. Low season reductions for pensioners and all sports charges reduced by 90%.

ES8480 Camping & Bungalows Sanguli

Prolongacion Calle, Apdo de Correos 123, E-43840 Salou (Tarragona)

Tel: **977 381 641**. Email: **mail@sanguli.es**

Sanguli is a superb site boasting excellent pools and ambitious entertainment. Owned, developed and managed by a local Spanish family, it provides for all the family with everything open when the site is open. There are 1,220 pitches of varying size (75-90 sq.m) and all have electricity. About 160 are used by tour operators and 140 for bungalows. A wonderful selection of trees, palms and shrubs provides natural shade. The good sandy beach is little more than 100 metres across the coast road and a small railway crossing (a little noise). Although large, Sanguli maintains a quality family atmosphere due to the efforts of the very keen and efficient staff. The owners are striving to achieve the 'Garden of Eden' that is their dream. There are three very attractive pool areas, one (heated) near the entrance with a grassy sunbathing area partly shaded and a second deep one with water slides that forms part of the excellent sports complex (with fitness centre, tennis courts, minigolf and football practice area). The third pool is the central part of the amphitheatre area at the top of the site which includes an impressive Roman style building with huge portals, containing a bar and restaurant with terraces. An amphitheatre seats 2,000 campers and treats them to very professional free nightly entertainment (1/5-30/9). All the pools have adjacent amenity areas and bars. A real effort is made to cater for the young including teenagers with a 'Hop Club' (entertainment for 13-17 year olds), along with an internet room. Located near the centre of Salou, the site can offer the attractions of a busy resort while still being private and it is only 3 km. from Port Aventura. This is a large, professional site providing something for all the family, but still capable of providing peace and quiet for those looking for it.

Facilities

The quality sanitary facilities are constantly improved and are always exceptional, including many individual cabins with en-suite facilities. A new block also has excellent facilities for babies. All are kept very clean. Launderette with service. Motorcaravan services. Bars and restaurant with takeaway. Swimming pools. Jacuzzi. Fitness centre. Sport complex. Fitness room (charged). Playgrounds including adventure play area. Mini-club, teenagers club. Internet room. Upmarket minigolf. First-aid room. Gas supplies. Off site: Fishing and bicycle hire 100 m. Riding 3 km. Golf 6 km. Resort entertainment.

Open: 24 March - 29 October.

Directions

On west side of Salou about 1 km. from the centre, site is well signed from the coast road to Cambrils and from the other town approaches.

Charges 2006

Per person	€ 6,00
child (4-12 yrs)	€ 4,00
pitch incl. electricity	€ 12,00 - € 37,00
incl. water	€ 14,00 - € 39,00

All plus 7% VAT. Less 25-45% outside high season for longer stays. Special long stay offers for senior citizens.

ES8536 Camping Caravanning Ametlla Village Platja

Apdo. Correus 240, Paraje Santes Creus, E-43860 Ametlla de Mar (Tarragona)

Tel: **977 267 784**. Email: **info@campingametlla.com**

This site within a protected area has been well thought out and is startling in the quality of service provided, the finish and the materials used in construction. The 373 pitches are on a terraced hillside above colourful coves with shingle beaches and two small associated lagoons (with a protected fish species). The many bungalows here have been tastefully incorporated. There are great views, particularly from the friendly restaurant. There is some train noise. The site is used by tour operators (30 pitches). It is a very good site for families or for just relaxing. The site is environmentally correct and local planning regulations are extremely tight including the types of trees that may be planted. No transit traffic is allowed within the site in high season. Animation is organised for children in high season and there is a well equipped fitness room (free). There are good quality pools (with lifeguard) and a sub-aqua diving school operates on the site in high season and beginners may try a dive. This most attractive small site is in an idyllic situation near the picturesque fishing village of L'Ametlla de Mar, famous for its fish restaurants, and within the Ebro Delta nature reserve. It is about 20 minutes from Europe's second largest theme park, Port Aventura, but as there is no regular bus service your own transport is required (the owners arrange free buses to the local disco each Wednesday).

Facilities

Three really good toilet blocks. Some private cabins with WC and washbasin. Motorcaravan services. Gas supplies. Supermarket (1/4-30/9; small shop incl. bread at other times). Good restaurant with snack menu and bar with TV (1/4-30/9). Swimming pool. Sub-aqua diving. Kayaking. Fishing. Children's club and play area. Fitness room. Bicycle hire. Entertainment (July/Aug). Barbecue area. Fishing. Off site: Boat launching 3 km. Golf 15 km.

Open: All year.

Directions

From A7/E15 (Barcelona - Valencia) take exit 39 for L'Ametlla de Mar. Follow large white signs and site is 2.5 km. south of the village.

Charges 2006

Per person	€ 2,30 - € 5,30
child (under 10 yrs)	€ 1,85 - € 4,30
pitch incl. electricity	€ 7,70 - € 18,50

All plus 7% VAT. Less for longer stays, especially in low season.

PARC DE VACANCES

Sangulí Salou

CAMPING & BUNGALOW PARK
●●●● 1ª CAT.

✉ Apartat de Correus 123
43840 SALOU • Tarragona • España
📞 Camping   +34 977 38 16 41
📞 Bungalow +34 977 38 90 05
   Fax   +34 977 38 46 16
@ mail@sanguli.es
   www.sanguli.es

Online   Booking: www.sanguli.es

Luxurious holidays at the Costa Daurada

Salou • Costa Daurada • España

ES8530 Playa Montroig Camping Resort

Apdo 3, N340 km. 1136, E-43300 Montroig (Tarragona)

Tel: **977 810 637**. Email: **info@playamontroig.com**

What a superb site! Playa Montroig is about 30 kilometres beyond Tarragona set in its own tropical gardens with direct access to a very long soft sand beach. The main part of the site lies between the sea, road and railway (as at other sites on this coast, there is some train noise) with a huge underpass. The site is divided into spacious, marked pitches with excellent shade provided by a variety of lush vegetation including very impressive palms set in wide avenues. There are 1,950 pitches, all with electricity and 330 with water and drainage. Some 48 pitches are directly alongside the beach. Member of Leading Campings Group. They are somewhat expensive and extremely popular. The site has many outstanding features: there is an excellent pool complex near the entrance with two pools (one heated for children). A quality restaurant serves traditional Catalunian fare (seats 150) and overlooks an entertainment area where you may watch genuine Flamenco dancing and buffet food is served (catering for 1,000). A large terrace bar dispenses drinks or if you yearn for louder music there is a disco and smaller bar. Activities for children are very ambitious – there is even a ceramics kiln (multi-lingual carers). 'La Carpa', a spectacular open air theatre, is an ideal setting for daily keep fit sessions and the professional entertainment provided. If you are 5-11 years old you can explore the 'Tam-Tam Eco Park', a 20,000 sq.m. forest zone where experts will teach about the natural life of the area. Bathing, windsurfing, surfboarding two diving rafts and many beach sports are available on the beach. This is an excellent site and there is insufficient space here to describe all the available activities. We recommend it for families with children of all ages and there is much emphasis on providing activities outside the high season.

Facilities

Fifteen sanitary buildings, some small, but of very good quality with toilets and washbasins, others really excellent, air conditioned larger buildings housing large showers, washbasins (many in private cabins) and separate WCs. Facilities for disabled campers and for babies. Several launderettes. Motorcaravan services. Good shopping centre. Restaurants and bars. Fitness suite. Eco-park. TV lounges (3). Beach bar. Playground. Free kindergarten. Sports area. Tennis. Minigolf. Organised activities. Windsurfing and water skiing courses. Surfboard and pedalo hire. Bicycle hire. Internet café. Gas supplies. Dogs are not accepted. Off site: Riding and golf 3 km.

Open: 1 March - 31 October.

Directions

Site entrance is off main N340 nearly 30 km. southwest from Tarragona. From motorway take Cambrils exit and turn west on N340 at 1136 km marker.

Charges 2006

Per unit incl 2 persons and electricity	€ 13,00 - € 30,00
premium pitch	€ 26,00 - € 95,00
extra person	€ 5,00 - € 6,00
child (1-9 yrs)	free - € 5,00

All plus 7% VAT. Discounts for longer stays and for pensioners.

See advertisement on the back cover

ES8535 Camping-Pension Cala d'Oques

Via Augusta s/n, E-43890 Hospitalet del Infante (Tarragona)

Tel: **977 823 254**. Email: **kroller@tinet.org**

This peaceful and delightful site has been developed with care and dedication by Elisa Roller over 30 years or so and she now runs it with the help of her daughter Kim. Part of its appeal lies in its situation beside the sea with a wide beach of sand and pebbles, its amazing mountain backdrop and the views across the bay to the town and part by the atmosphere created by Elisa, and staff – friendly, relaxed and comfortable. There are 255 pitches, mostly level and laid out beside the beach, with more behind on wide, informal terracing. Odd pine and olive trees are an attractive feature and provide some shade. Electricity is available although long leads may be needed in places. The restaurant with its homely touches has a super menu and a reputation extending well outside the site (the excellent cook has been there for many years) and the family type entertainment is in total contrast to that provided at the larger, brasher sites of the Costa Daurada. Gates provide access to the pleasant beach with useful cold showers to wash the sand away. Torches are needed at night..

Facilities

Toilet facilities are in the front part of the main building. Clean and neat, there is hot water to showers (hot water by token but free to campers - a device to guard against unauthorised visitors from the beach). New heated unit with toilets and washbasins for winter use. Additional small block with toilets and washbasins at the far end of the site. Motorcaravan service point. Restaurant/bar and shop (1/4-30/9). Play area. Kim's kids club. Fishing. Internet point. Gas supplies. Off site: Village facilities, incl. shop and restaurant 1.5 km. Bicycle hire or riding 2 km.

Open: All year.

Directions

Hospitalet del Infante is south of Tarragona, accessed from the A7 (exit 38) or from the N340. From the north take first exit to Hospitalet del Infante at the 1128 km. marker. Follow signs in village, site is 2 km, by the sea. GPS: N40:58.666 E00:54.203

Charges 2006

Per person	€ 4,85 - € 8,25
pitch incl. electricity	€ 8,35 - € 15,90

Discounts for seniors and for longer stays.
No credit cards.

ES8540 Camping Caravaning La Torre del Sol

Ctra N340, km. 1136, E-43300 Montroig (Tarragona)

Tel: 977 810 486. Email: info@latorredelsol.com

A pleasant banana tree-lined approach road gives way to avenues of palms as you arrive at Torre del Sol, sister site to Templo del Sol (ES8537N). Torre del Sol is a very large site occupying a good position with direct access to the clean, soft sand beach, complete with a beach bar. Strong features here are 800 metres of clean beach-front with a special Mediterranean type of pitch, and the entertainment that is provided all season. There is a separate area where the 'Happy Camp' team will take your children to camp overnight in the Indian reservation, plus they can amuse them two days a week with other activities. The cinema doubles as a theatre to stage shows all season. A complex of three pools, thoughtfully laid out with grass sunbathing areas and palms has a lifeguard. There is good shade on a high proportion of the 1,500 individual, numbered pitches. All have electricity and are mostly of about 70-80 sq.m. There is wireless internet access throughout the site. There is usually space for odd nights but for good places between 10/7-16/8 it is best to reserve (only taken for a stay of seven nights or more). Part of the site is between the railway and the sea so there is train noise. We were impressed with the provision of season-long entertainment and to give parents a break whilst children were in the safe hands of the animation team who ensure they enjoy the novel 'Happy Camp' and various workshops.

Facilities

Four very well maintained, fully equipped, toilet blocks include units for disabled people and babies. Washing machines. Shops. Full restaurant. Takeaway. Bar with large terrace where entertainment held daily all season. Beach bar. Pizzeria. Open roof cinema; 3 TV lounges. Well sound-proofed disco. Swimming pools (two heated). Solarium. Sauna. Jacuzzi. Tennis. Squash. Minigolf. Sub-aqua diving. Bicycle hire. Fishing. Windsurfing school; sailboards and pedaloes for hire. Playground, crèche and Happy Camp. Business centre with IT equipment. No animals permitted. No jet skis. Off site: Golf 4 km.

Open: 15 March - 20 October.

Directions

Entrance is off main N340 road by 1136 km. marker, about 30 km. from Tarragona towards Valencia. From motorway take Cambrils exit and turn west on N340. GPS: N41:02 E00:58.49

Charges 2007

Per unit incl. 2 adults	
and electricity	€ 19,70 - € 58,80
extra person	€ 3,25 - € 9,00
child (0-10 yrs)	free - € 7,15

All plus 7% VAT.
Camping Cheques accepted.

awan
ES CAMPINGS

tel: 00 333 59 59 03 59   *kawan-villages.com*

Check real time availability and at-the-gate prices...
www.alanrogers.com

ES8479 Camping Playa Cambrils – Don Camilo

Ctra Cambrils - Salou km. 1.5, E-43850 Cambrils (Tarragona)

Tel: **977 361 490**. Email: **camping@playacambrils.com**

Almost completely canopied by trees which provide welcome shade on hot days, the site is 300 m. from the beach across a busy road. It is mature and has had some recent renovations. The small (60 sq.m.) pitches are on flat ground, divided by hedges. There are many permanent pitches and half the site is given up to chalet style accomodation. Large units are placed in a dedicated area where the trees are higher. The pool complex includes a functional glassed restaurant and bar with a distinct Spanish flavour reflected in the menu and tapas available all day. As this is a popular site with Spanish families it is a good place to practice your language. The pool is long and narrow with separate children's pool and a large paved area for soaking up the sun. Entertainment for children is organised by a good animation team. A big building at one end of the site consists of the supermarket, an attended electronic games room and a large play room.

Facilities

One modern sanitary building, and one large plus one small refurbished block offer reasonable facilities with British style WCs and free showers in separate buildings. Facilities for disabled campers. Laundry facilities. Supermarket (April-Sept). Bar/snacks and separate restaurant (April-Sept). Swimming pool. Playground. Animation in high season. Mini-club. Huge electronic games room. Torches useful. Off site: Resort town has a range of shops, bars and restaurants. Bicycle hire 500 m. Fishing and golf 1 km. Riding 1.5 km.

Open: 15 March - 12 October.

Directions

Leave A7 autopista at exit 37 and head for Cambrils and then to the beach. Turn left along beach road. Site is 1 km. east of Cambrils Playa and is well signed as you leave Cambrils marina.

Charges 2006

Per person	€ 2,15 - € 4,20
child (under 9 yrs)	free - € 3,15
pitch	€ 10,00 - € 24,00

ES8559 Azahar Residencial Camping & Bungalow Park

Ptda. Villarroyos, s/n, E-12598 Peñiscola (Castelló)

Tel: **964 475 480**. Email: **info@campingazahar.com**

Set inland (3 km.) from the busy coastal resort of Peñiscola, Camping Azahar is set amongst the orange groves. The site has 110 level touring pitches, all with access to electricity (6/10A) and accessed by wide, gravel roads. Shade is provided by young trees and three large, barn-type roof structures. The pitches are not separated and those undercover are big enough to suit larger units. Although this is a new site, there are already plans for development. These include an extra toilet block and a spa that will provide saunas, sun beds, jacuzzi, hydrotherapy pool and massage rooms.

Facilities

One modern toilet block in the centre of the site includes open style washbasins. Washing machine. Shop. Bar/restaurant with small terrace (all year). Outdoor swimming pool (Easter - Sept). Play area. Minigolf. Bicycle hire. Internet access. Animals not accepted July/Aug. Off site: Costa Azahar shopping and entertainment complex 1 km. Irta mountains 3 km. Peñiscola 3 km. Fishing and golf 5 km. Beach, and sailing 5 km.

Open: All year.

Directions

From A7 (Barcelona - Valencia) take exit 43 and N340 towards Peñiscola which will direct you onto the Cv141. Approaching outskirts of the town turn left signed Camping Azahar and follow signs.

Charges 2006

Per unit incl. 2 persons, 3A electricity	€ 12,00 - € 15,00
extra person	€ 2,50 - € 4,20
child (3-10 yrs)	€ 1,80 - € 3,00

ES8580 Bonterra Park

Avenida de Barcelona 47, E-12560 Benicasim (Castelló)

Tel: 964 300 007. Email: info@bonterrapark.com

If you are looking for a town site which is not too crowded and has very good facilities, this one may be for you, as there are few quality sites in the local area and this is open all year. It is a 300 metre walk to a good, shady beach – and parking is not too difficult. The site has 331 pitches (70-90 sq.m), all with electricity (6/10A) and a variety of bungalows. Bonterra has a clean and neat appearance with reddish soil, palms, grass and a number of trees which give good shade. There is a little road and rail noise. The site has an attractive pool complex including a covered pool for the winter months. The beach is good for scuba diving or snorkelling – hire facilities are available at Benicasim. This is a well run, Mediterranean style site useful for visiting local attractions such as the Carmelite monastery at Desierto de las Palmas, six kilometres distant or the historic town of Castellon.

Facilities

Four attractive, well maintained sanitary blocks provide some private cabins, washbasins with hot water, others with cold. Baby and dog showers. Facilities for disabled campers. Laundry. Motorcaravan services. Restaurant/bar. Shop (all year). Swimming pool, covered pool and children's pool. Playground (some concrete bases). Tennis. Multi-sport court. Gymnasium. Disco. Bicycle hire. Mini-club. Satellite TV. Internet access (WiFi). Off site: Town facilities. Sandy beach and fishing 500 m. Riding 3 km. Boat launching 5 km. Golf 10 km. Nature Park.

Open: All year.

Directions

Site is about 1 km. east of Benicasim village with access off the old main N340 road running parallel with the coast. The road re-numbering here is very confusing but there are many blue signs to the site with the campsite name so it is not difficult to find. Coming from the north, turn left at sign 'Benicasim por la costa'. On the A7 from the north use exit 45, from the south exit 46. GPS: N40:03 W00:04.46

Charges 2007

Per person	€ 3,40 - € 5,00
child (3-9 yrs)	€ 2,85 - € 4,00
pitch acc. to type and season	€ 14,35 - € 34,75

All plus 7% VAT. Less in low season and special long stay rates excl. July/Aug.

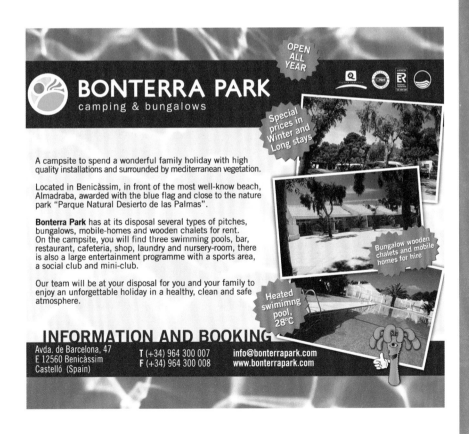

ES8560 Camping Playa Tropicana

Playa Tropicana, E-12579 Alcossebre (Castelló)

Tel: **964 412 463**. Email: **info@playatropicana.com**

Playa Tropicana is a unique site which will strike visitors immediately as being very different. It has been given a tropical theme with scores of 'Romanesque' white statues around the site including in the sanitary blocks. The site has 300 marked pitches separated by lines of flowering bushes under mature trees. The pitches vary in size (50-100 sq.m), most are shaded and there are electricity connections throughout (some need long leads). 50 pitches have water and drainage. It has a delightful position away from the main hub of tourism, alongside a good sandy beach which shelves gently into the clean waters. To gain access to this it is necessary to cross a pretty promenade in front of the site, which also has statues. It is in a quiet position and it is a drive rather than a walk to the centre of the village resort. The theme extends into an excellent restaurant where, in high season, you may dine on the upper terrace with uninterrupted sea views. A variety of entertainment is provided and there is also a children's club and social room with films and soft drinks bar in high season. The site has several large water features by the high quality restaurant (some are very cheeky!). Aviaries are housed in a corner of the site.

Facilities

Three sanitary blocks delightfully decorated, fully equipped and of excellent standard, include washbasins in private cabins. Baby baths and facilities for disabled people. Washing machine. Motorcaravan services. Gas supplies. Large supermarket. Superb restaurant, a little expensive. (Easter - late Sept). Swimming pool (18 x 11 m.) and children's pool. Playground. Bicycle hire. Children's club. Fishing. Torches necessary in some areas. No TVs allowed in July/Aug. Dogs are not accepted. Off site: Fishing and watersports on the beaches. Riding and boat launching 3 km. Golf 25 km.

Open: All year.

Directions

Alcoceber (or Alcossebre) is between Peniscola and Oropesa. Turn off N340 at 1018 km. marker towards Alcossebre on CV142. Just before entering town proceed through the traffic lights to main road. At next junction, turn right and follow coast road to site in 2.5 km. The sliding gate is on the coast road and a bell is on the right side.

Charges 2007

Per unit incl 2 persons and electricity	€ 18,00 - € 60,00
extra person	€ 3,50 - € 7,00
child (1-10 yrs)	€ 2,50 - € 6,00

Electricity and VAT included.
Many discount schemes out of season.
Camping Cheques accepted.

ES8615 Kiko Park Oliva

E-46780 Oliva (Valencia)
Tel: 962 850905. Email: kikopark@kikopark.com

Kiko Park is a smart site nestled behind protective sand dunes alongside a 'blue flag' beach. There are sets of attractively tiled steps over the dunes or a long boardwalk near the beach bar (good for prams and wheelchairs) to take you to the fine white sandy beach and the sea. The 180 large pitches all have electricity and the aim is to progressively upgrade all these to serviced 'super' pitches. There are plenty of flowers, hedging and trees adding shade, privacy and colour. A new outdoor pool complex with a spa, whirl pool, solarium, gym and a pool bar was added in 2006. An award-winning restaurant with architecture that reminds one of a ship is near the tropical style beach-bar, both overlooking the marina, beautiful beach and sea. This is an excellent site for watersport enthusiasts, as it is beside a marina for boat launching. A wide variety of entertainment is provided all year and Spanish lessons are taught along with dance class and aerobics during the winter. The site is run by the second generation of a family involved in camping for 30 years and their experience shows. They are brilliantly supported by a friendly, efficient team who speak many languages. The narrow roads leading to the site can be a little challenging for very large units but it is worth the effort.

Facilities

Four modern sanitary blocks are very clean with large showers, washbasins (a few in cabins), British style WCs and excellent facilities for disabled visitors. Laundry. Motorcaravan services. Supermarket. Restaurant. Bar with TV. Beach-side bar and restaurant (all year). Swimming pools and gym. Playground. Watersports. Diving school in high season (from mid-June). Entertainment for children from mid-June. Petanque. Bicycle hire. Off site: The footpath to the marina leads into the town - 10 minutes walk. Indoor pool 1 km. Golf 5 km. Riding 7 km.

Open: All year.

Directions

From A7 north of Benidorm take exit 61 to the town and then the beach; site is at the northwest end.

Charges 2006

Per person	€ 2,70 - € 5,50
child (under 10 yrs)	€ 2,20 - € 4,80
pitch acc. to services and season	€ 9,30 - € 29,00
dog	€ 0,60 - € 2,20
electricity (per kWh)	€ 0,30

ES8675 Camping Vall de Laguar

C/Sant Antonio 24, La Vall de Laguar, E-03791 Campell (Alacant)
Tel: 96 557 74 90. Email: info@campinglaguar.com

Near the pretty mountain-top village of Campell, this new site is perched high on the side of a mountain with breathtaking views of hilltop villages, the surrounding hills and distant sea. With a wholehearted welcome from the owners, the well maintained site promises a real taste of Spain. The pitches, pool, terrace and restaurant all share the views. The 68 average size gravel pitches are on terraces and all have electricity and water. Trees and hedges now give ample shade.

Facilities

Two new sanitary blocks have excellent clean facilities including some for disabled campers. Washing machines and dryers. Restaurant with pretty terrace. Bar and pool bar. Swimming pool and small pool bar. Small entertainment programme in high season. Barbecue area with sinks. Torches useful. Off site: Attractive town close by. Golf and beach 18 km.

Open: All year.

Directions

Site is 20 km. west of Xabia/Javea. From A7/E15 exit 62 head to Beniarbeig on minor road. From there to Sanet, Benidoleig and finally Vall de Laguar. Site is well signed from the town and sits above it.

Charges 2006

Per person	€ 3,90
pitch incl. electricity	€ 10,85 - € 11,30
Minimum charge Easter and July/August	€ 19.23

445

ES8625 Kiko Park Rural

Ctra Embalse Contreras, km. 3, E-46317 Villargordo del Cabriel (Valencia)

Tel: **962 139 082**. Email: **kikoparkrural@kikopark.com**

Approaching Kiko Park Rural, you will see a small hilltop village appearing in a landscape of mountains, vines and a jewel-like lake. Kiko was a small village and farm and the village now forms the campsite and accommodation. Amenities are contained within the architecturally authentic buildings, some old and some new. The 103 pitches (with 6A electricity and water) all have stunning views, as do the swimming and paddling pools. Generous hedge plantings have been made which already afford some privacy.

Facilities

Three toilet blocks are very well equipped, including excellent facilities for disabled people. Motorcaravan services. Gas. Well stocked shop. Excellent restaurant. Pleasant bar. Swimming and paddling pools. Very good playground. Bicycle hire. Animation in high season. Many activities can be arranged, including white water rafting, gorging, orienteering, trekking and riding. Large families and groups catered for. Off site: Fishing, canoeing and windsurfing on the lake. Village 3 km.

Open: All year.

Directions

From autopista A7/E15 on Valencia ring road (near the airport) take A3 to west. Villagordo del Cabriel is 80 km. towards Motilla. Take the village exit and follow signs through village and over a hill – spot the village on a hill 2 km. away. That is the campsite!

Charges 2007

Per person	€ 4,60 - € 5,75
pitch	€ 6,30 - € 13,00

Camping Cheques accepted.

ES8754 Camping Jávea

Ctra Cabo de la Nao, km. 1, E-03730 Jávea (Alacant)

Tel: **965 791 070**. Email: **info@camping-javea.com**

The 200 metre long access road to this site is a little unkempt as it passes some factories, but all changes on the final approach with palms, orange and pine trees, the latter playing host to a colony of parakeets. English is spoken at reception. The boxed hedges and palms surrounding this area with a backdrop of hills dotted with villas presents an attractive setting. Three hectares provides space for 214 numbered pitches with 179 for touring units. Flat, level and rectangular in shape, the pitches vary in size 60-80 sq.m. (not advised for caravans or motorhomes with an overall length exceeding 7 m). All have a granite chip surface and 8A electricity. Being a typical Spanish site, the pitches are not separated so units may be close to each other. Some pitches have artificial shade, although for most the pruned eucalyptus and pepper trees will suffice. The area has a large number of British residents so a degree of English is spoken by many shopkeepers and many restaurants provide multi language menus. Besides being popular for a summer holiday, Camping Javea is open all year and could be of interest to those that wish to 'winter' in an excellent climate.

Facilities

Two very clean, fully equipped, sanitary blocks include two children's toilets plus a baby bath. Two washing machines. Fridge hire. Small bar and restaurant where in high season you purchase bread and milk. Large swimming pool with lifeguard and sunbathing lawns. Play area. Boules. Electronic barriers (deposit for card). Caravan storage. Off site: Sandy beach 3 km. Old and New Javea within easy walking distance with supermarkets and shops catering for all needs.

Open: All year.

Directions

Exit N332 for Javea on A134, continue in direction of Port (road changes to CV 734). At roundabout (Lidl supermarket) turn right signed Arenal Platges and Cabo de la Nao. Straight on at next roundabout to camping sign and slip road in 100 m. If you miss slip road go back from next roundabout.

Charges 2007

Per person	€ 4,50 - € 5,30
child	€ 4,08 - € 4,80
pitch incl. electricity	€ 14,79 - € 16,80

ES8755 Camping Caravanning Moraira

Camino Paellero 50, E-03724 Moraira-Teulada (Alacant)

Tel: **965 745 249**. Email: **campingmoraira@campingmoraira.com**

This small hillside site with some views over the town and marina is quietly situated in an urban area amongst old pine trees and just 400 metres from a sheltered bay. Terracing provides shaded pitches of varying size, some really quite small (access to some of the upper pitches may be difficult for larger units). Some pitches have water and drainage and a few have sea views. There are electricity connections. An attractive irregularly shaped pool with paved sunbathing terrace is below the small bar/restaurant and terrace. The pool has observation windows where you can watch the swimmers, and is used for sub-aqua instruction. The site runs a professional diving school for all levels (the diving here is good and the water warm, even in winter). A sandy beach is 1.5 km. A large, painted water tower stands at the top of the site. The reception building is being extended to provide a range of new facilities.

Facilities

The high quality toilet block, with polished granite floors and marble fittings, is built to a unique and ultra-modern design with extra large free hot showers. Washing machine and dryer. Motorcaravan services. Bar/restaurant and shop (1/7-30/9). Small swimming pool (all year). Sub-aqua with instruction. Tennis. Torches may be required. Off site: Shops, bars and restaurants within walking distance. Beach 1.5 km. Fishing 400 m. Bicycle hire 1 km. Golf 8 km.

Open: All year.

Directions

Site is best approached from Teulada. From A7 exit 63 take N332 and in 3.5 km. turn right (Teulada and Moraira). In Teulada fork right to Moraira. At junction at town entrance turn right signed Calpe and in 1 km. turn right into road to site on bend immediately after Res. Don Julio.

Charges 2006

Per person	€ 4,70
child (4-9 yrs)	€ 3,60
pitch incl. electricity	€ 13,70 - € 15,80

All plus 7% VAT. Less 15-60% in low season.

ES8681 Camping Villasol

Avenida Bernat de Sarria, E-03503 Benidorm (Alacant)

Tel: **965 850 422**. Email: **camping-villasol@dragonet.es**

Benidorm is increasingly popular for winter stays and Villasol is a genuinely good, purpose built modern site. Many of the 309 well separated pitches are arranged on wide terraces which afford views of the mountains surrounding Benidorm. All pitches (80-85 sq.m.) have electricity and satellite TV connections, with 160 with full services for seasonal use. Shade is mainly artificial. Reservations are only accepted for winter stays of over three months (from 1 Oct). There is a small indoor pool, heated for winter use, and a very attractive, large outdoor pool complex (summer only).

Facilities

Modern toilet blocks provide free, controllable hot water to showers and washbasins and British WCs. Good facilities for disabled campers. Laundry facilities. Good value restaurant. Bar. Shop. Swimming pools, outdoor and indoor. Playground. Evening entertainment programme. Dogs are not accepted. Off site: Fishing and bicycle hire 1.3 km. Golf 8 km.

Open: All year.

Directions

From autopista exit 65 (Benidorm) and turn left at second set of traffic lights. After 1 km. at another set of lights turn right, then right again at next lights. Site is on right in 400 m. From northern end of N332 bypass follow signs for Playa Levante..

Charges 2006

Per person	€ 5,00 - € 6,50
pitch incl. electricity	€ 14,00 - € 21,80

All plus 7% VAT.

ES8743 Complejo Ecoturistico Marjal

Ctra N-332, km 73.4, E-03140 Guardamar del Segura (Alacant)

Tel: 966 725 022. Email: camping@marjal.com

Marjal is located beside the estuary of the Segura river, alongside the pine and eucalyptus forests of the Dunas de Guardamar natural park. The fine sandy beach can be reached through the forest (800 m). This is a new site with a huge lagoon-style pool and a superb sports complex. There are 212 pitches on this award winning site, all with water, electricity, drainage and satellite TV points, the ground covered with crushed marble, making the pitches clean and pleasant. There is some shade and the site has an open feel with lots of room for manoeuvring. Reception is housed within a delicately coloured building complete with a towering Mirador, topped by a weather-vane depicting the 'Garza Real' (heron) bird which frequents the local area and forms part of the site logo. The large leased restaurant overlooks the pools and the river that leads to the sea in the near distance. This situation is shared with the taperia (high season) and bar with large terraces fringed by trees, palms and pomegranates. The impressive pool/lagoon complex (1,100 sq.m) has a water cascade, an island bar plus bridge, one part sectioned as a pool for children and a jacuzzi. The extensive sports area is also impressive with qualified instructors who will customise your fitness programme whilst consulting the doctor. No effort has been spared here, the quality heated indoor pool, light-exercise room, sauna, solarium, beauty salon, fully equipped gym and changing rooms, including facilities for disabled visitors, are of the highest quality. Aerobics and physiotherapy are also on offer. All activities are discounted for campers. A programme of entertainment is provided for adults and children in season by a professional animation team.

Facilities

Three excellent heated toilet blocks have free hot water, elegant separators between sinks, spacious showers and some cabins. Each block has high quality facilities for babies and disabled campers, modern laundry and dishwashing rooms. Car wash. Well stocked supermarket. Restaurants. Bar. Large outdoor pool complex (1/6-31/10). Heated indoor pool (low season). Fitness suite. Jacuzzi. Sauna. Solarium. Aerobics and aquarobics. Play room. Minigolf. Floodlit tennis and soccer pitch. Bicycle hire. Games room. TV room. ATM. Business centre. Internet access. Off site: Beach 800 m. Riding or golf 4 km.

Open: All year.

Directions

On N332 40 km. south of Alicante, site is on the sea side between 73 and 74 km. markers.

Charges 2006

Per person	€ 5,00 - € 7,00
child (4-12 yrs)	€ 2,50 - € 4,00
pitch	€ 18,00 - € 30,00
electricity	€ 2,00 - € 3,00

All plus 7% VAT.

ES8683 Camping Benisol

Avenida de la Comunidad Valenciana s/n, E-03500 Benidorm (Alacant)

Tel: 965 851 673. Email: campingbenisol@yahoo.es

Camping Benisol is a well developed and peaceful site with lush, green vegetation and a mountain background. Mature hedges and trees afford privacy to each pitch and some artficial shade is provided where necessary. There are 298 pitches of which around 115 are for touring units (60-80 sq.m). All have electrical hook-ups (4/6A) and 75 have drainage. All the connecting roads are now surfaced with tarmac. Some day-time road noise should be expected. The site has an excellent restaurant serving traditional Spanish food at great prices, with a pretty, shaded terrace overlooking the pool with its palms and thatched pool bar.

Facilities

Modern sanitary facilities, heated in winter and kept very clean, have free, solar heated hot water to washbasins, showers and sinks. Laundry facilities. Gas supplies. Restaurant with terrace and bar (all year, closed 1 day a week). Shop. Swimming pool (Easter - Nov). Small, old-style play area. Minigolf. Jogging track. Tennis. Golf driving range. ATM. Off site: Riding 1 km. Bicycle hire 3 km. Fishing (sea) 3 km. Golf 14 km. Bus route.

Open: All year.

Directions

Site is northeast of Benidorm. Exit N332 at 152 km. marker and take turn signed Playa Levant. Site is 100 m. on left off the main road, well signed.

Charges 2006

Per person	€ 4,90 - € 5,25
child (1-10 yrs)	€ 4,00 - € 4,40
pitch incl. electricity	€ 16,05 - € 18,80

All plus 7% VAT. Less 15-60% in low seasons.
No credit cards.

ES8689 Camping Playa del Torres

Partida Torres Norte 11, Apdo. Correus 243, E-03570 Villajoyosa (Alacant)

Tel: 966 810 031. Email: into@playadeltonnes.com

Jacinto and Mercedes have a pretty beachside site with the lower part set under eucalyptus trees. Reception is placed in one of the site's tasteful wooden buildings close to the beach (excellent English is spoken). If you prefer a smaller site away from the 'high rise' and bustle of Benidorm offering high quality this could be for you. The 85 lower pitches, some large, are on flat ground with shade. 10 good pitches are right alongside the beach fence (book early). All have electricity (16A), some are fully serviced and there are ample water fountains around the site along with efficient, modern lighting.

Facilities

The sanitary building is of a high specification, as are the fittings within, including excellent showers. Laundry. Bar. Cafeteria. Shop. Swimming pool. Children's play area. Petanque. Fishing. Barbecues. Freezer. Satellite TV. Reception will assist with all tourist activities.
Off site: Riding 100 m. Golf 18 km. Serious or recreational walking and climbing is possible about 20 minutes away from the site. Benidorm is very close.

Open: All year.

Directions

From Villajoyosa on N332, site is 1 km. east of the town. Look for clear site signs towards beach. From Benidorm on N332, site is 3 km. on the left, but a left turn is prohibited. Proceed 400 m. to traffic lights to turn, then proceed as above.

Charges 2006

Per person	€ 4,90
child (4-13 yrs)	€ 3,80
pitch	€ 4,90 - € 35,00
electricity (plus meter)	€ 3,97

Plus 7% VAT. Less 5-50% for low season stays of 7 days or more.

ES8742 Camping Internacional La Marina

Ctra N332 km 76, E-03194 La Marina (Alacant)

Tel: **965 419 200**. Email: **info@campinglamarina.com**

Efficiently run by a friendly Belgian family, La Marina has 370 pitches of seven different types and size ranging from about 50 sq.m. for tents to 100 sq.m. with electricity (10A), TV, water and drainage. Artificial shade is provided and the pitches are extremely well maintained on level, well drained ground with a special area allocated for tents in a small orchard. The lagoon swimming pool complex is absolutely fabulous and has something for everyone (with lifeguards). William Le Metayer, the owner, is passionate about La Marina and it shows in his search for perfection. A magnificent new, modern building houses some superb extra amenities. Member of Leading Campings Group. These include a relaxed business centre with internet access, a tapas bar decorated with amazing ceramics (handmade by the owner's mother) and a quality restaurant with a water fountain feature and great views of the lagoon. There is also a conference centre and an extensive library, with the whole of the lower ground floor dedicated to children with a play area and a 'cyber zone' for teenagers. With a further bar and a soundproofed disco, the building is of an exceptional, eco-friendly standard. A fine fitness centre and covered, heated pool (14 x 7 m) are close by. A pedestrian gate at the rear of the site gives access to the long sandy beach through the coastal pine forest that is a feature of the area. We recommend this site very highly whatever type of holidaying camper you may be.

Facilities

The elegant sanitary blocks offer the very best of modern facilities. Heated in winter, they include private cabins and facilities for disabled visitors. Laundry facilities Motorcaravan services. Gas. Supermarket. Bars. Restaurant (all year). Swimming pools (1/4-15/10). Indoor pool. Fitness centre. Sauna. Play rooms. Extensive activity and entertainment programme. Sports area. Tennis. Huge playground. Hairdresser. Off site: Fishing 800 m. Boat launching 5 km. Golf 7 km. Bicycle hire 8 km. Riding 15 km. Hourly bus service from outside the gate. Theme parks.

Open: All year.

Directions

Site is 2 km. west of La Marina. Leave N332 Guardamara de Segura - Santa Pola road at 75 km. marker if travelling north, or 78 km. marker if travelling south. Site is well signed.

Charges 2006

Per person	€ 5,00 - € 7,20
child (under 10 yrs)	€ 3,50 - € 4,80
pitch incl. electricty, acc. to type and season	€ 19,10 - € 37,20
dog	€ 1,00 - € 2,00

Plus 7% VAT. Seven grades of pitch.
Less in low season, plus good discounts for longer stays 16/9-14/6, excluding Easter.

Check real time availability and at-the-gate prices...

www.**alanrogers**.com

ES8685 Camping Caravaning El Raco

Avenida Doctor Severo Ochoa, s/n, E-03500 Benidorm (Alacant)

Tel: 96 586 8552. Email: campingraco@inicia.es

This purpose built site with good facilities and very competitive prices provides about 1,000 pitches (180 for touring units). There is wide access from the Rincon de Loix road. The site is quietly situated 1.5 km. from the town, Levante beach and promenade. It has wide tarmac roads and pitches of 80 sq.m. or more, separated by low cypress hedging and some trees which provide some shade. Satellite TV connections are provided to each pitch, with 94 with all services including electricity.

Facilities

Four large toilet blocks are well equipped. Facilities for disabled people. Dishwashing sinks. Laundry facilities. Gas supplies. Motorcaravan services. Restaurant. Bar. Well stocked shop. Busy bar with TV also open to public and good value restaurant. Outdoor swimming pool, no slides or diving board (1/4-31/10). Indoor heated pool (1/11-31/3). Playground. ATM. Off site: Beach 1 km. Bicycle hire 2 km. Golf 6 km. Theme parks.

Open: All year.

Directions

From autopista exit 65 (Benidorm, Levante) at second set of traffic lights turn left on N332 (Altea, Valencia). After 1.5 km. turn right (Levante Playa), then straight on at next lights for 300 m. to site on right. From north on N332 follow signs for Playa Levante (or Benidorm Palace). At lights turn left.

Charges 2006

Per person	€ 5,00 - € 5,80
pitch incl. electricity	€ 14,60 - € 18,60

VAT included. No credit cards.

ES8687 Camping Cap Blanch

Playa de Cap Blanch 25, E-03590 Altea (Alacant)

Tel: 965 845 946. Email: capblanch@ctv.es

This well run, small site has plenty of character. It is open all year and is very popular for winter stays. Alongside the beach road, it has direct access to the pebble beach and is within a few hundred yards of all Albir's shops and restaurants. The 250 pitches on flat, hard gravel are of a good size and well maintained with 5A electricity. The site tends to be full in winter and is very popular with several nationalities, especially the Dutch. For winter stays, it would pay to get there before Christmas as January and February are the peak months.

Facilities

The refurbished sanitary block can be heated and provides good facilities including some washbasins in cabins, baby facilities and a room for disabled visitors (both these accessed by key). Motorcaravan services. Gas supplies. Laundry. Bar and restaurant. Takeaway. Playground. Tennis. Boules. Fitness centre. Organised entertainment and courses. ATM. Off site: Restaurants, shops and commercial centre close. Golf 0.5 km. Bicycle hire 1 km.

Open: All year.

Directions

Site is on the Albir - Altea coast road and can be reached from either end. From N332, north or south, watch for sign Playa del Albir and proceed through Albir to the coast road. Site is on north side of Albir.

Charges 2006

Per person	€ 3,50 - € 5,50
pitch incl. car	€ 8,50 - € 24,00
electricity	€ 3,00 - € 4,50

VAT included.

ES8745 Camping La Fuente

Camino de La Bocamina, E-30626 Banos de Fortuna (Murcia)

Tel: 968 685125. Email: info@campingfuente.com

Located in an area known for its thermal waters since Roman and Moorish times and with just 62 pitches, La Fuente is a gem. The main attraction here is the huge pool complex where the water is constant at 36 degrees all year. The site is in two sections, one where pitches are in standard rows and the other where they are in circles around blocks. The flat pitches are on shingle, have 10A electricity, and unusually all have their own mini-sanitary block. There is accommodation on site but it is separate from the camping area. Unusually winter is high season here.

Facilities

All pitches have their own facilities including a unit for disabled campers. Washing machines and dryers. High quality restaurant shared with accommodation guests. Snack bar by pool. Supermarket. Bicycle hire. Communal barbecues. New jacuzzi. Off site: Spa town, massage therapies, hot pools. Golf and riding 20 km.

Open: All year.

Directions

From A7/E15 Alicante - Murcia road take C3223 to Fortuna then follow signs to Banos de Fortuna. The site with its bright yellow walls can be easily seen from the road and is very well signed in the town. GPS: N38:12.409 W01:06.439

Charges 2006

Per person	€ 3,25
pitch (with private sanitary facilities)	€ 8,00 - € 10,00
electricity (plus € 0.22 per kWh)	€ 1,50

ES8753 Caravaning La Manga

Autovia Cartagena - La Manga Salida 11, E-30370 La Manga del Mar Menor (Murcia)

Tel: 902 021 352. Email: lamanga@caravaning.es

This is a very large well equipped, 'holiday style' site with its own beach and both indoor and outdoor pools. With a good number of typical Spanish long stay units, the length of the site is impressive (1 km.) and a bicycle is very helpful for getting about. The 1,000 regularly laid out, gravel touring pitches (84 or 110sq. m.) are generally separated by hedges which also provide a degree of shade. Each has 10A electricity supply, water and the possibility of satellite TV reception. This site's excellent facilities are ideally suited for holidays in the winter when the weather is very pleasantly warm.

Facilities

Seven clean toilet blocks of standard design, well spaced around the site, include washbasins (with hot water in five blocks). Laundry. Gas supplies. Large supermarket. Restaurant. Bar. Snack bar. Swimming pool complex (April - Sept). Indoor pool, gym, sauna, jacuzzi and massage service. Open air cinema (April - Sept). Tennis. Petanque. Minigolf. Play area. Watersports school. Internet café (also WiFi). Off site: Bus to Cartagena from outside site. Golf, bicycle hire and riding 5 km.

Open: All year.

Directions

Use exit (Salida) 15 from MU312 dual-carriageway towards Cabo de Palos, signed Playa Honda (site signed also). Cross road bridge and double back on yourself. Site entrance is clearly visible beside dual-carriageway with many flags flying.

Charges 2007

Per pitch incl. 2 persons	€ 20,00 - € 32,50
extra person	€ 3,75 - € 4,80

Electricity incl. All plus 7% VAT.
Camping Cheques accepted.

ES8752 Camping Naturista El Portus

El Portus, E-30393 Cartagena (Murcia)

Tel: 968 553 052. Email: elportus@elportus.com

Set in a secluded south facing bay fringed by mountains, El Portus is a fairly large naturist site enjoying magnificent views and with direct access to a small sand and pebble beach. This part of Spain enjoys almost all year round sunshine. There are some 400 pitches, 300 for tourers, ranging from 60-100 sq.m, all but a few having electricity (6A). They are mostly on fairly level, if somewhat stony and barren ground. El Portus has a reasonable amount of shade from established trees.

Facilities

Five acceptable toilet blocks, all unisex, are of varying styles and fully equipped. Showers all with hot water. Unit for disabled visitors. Washing machines. Motorcaravan services. Well stocked shop. Bar with TV and libary. Restaurants. Swimming pools. Play area. Tennis. Scuba-diving club (high season).Windsurfing. Spanish lessons. Small boat moorings. Entertainment (high season).

Open: All year.

Directions

Site is on the coast, 10 km. west of Cartagena. Follow signs to Mazarron then E22 to Canteras. Site is well signed for 4 km.

Charges 2006

Per person	€ 6,00
pitch incl. 6A electricity	€ 19,00

Plus 7% VAT.
Camping Cheques accepted.

ES8748 Camping Los Madriles

Ctra de la Azohia, km. 4.5, E-30868 Isla Plana (Murcia)

Tel: 968 152 151. Email: camplosmadriles@terra.es

An exceptional site with super facilities, Los Madriles is run by a hard working team, with constant improvements being made. Twenty kilometres west of Cartegena, the approach to the site and the surrounding area is fairly unremarkable, but the site is not. A fairly steep access road leads to the 311 flat, good to large size terraced pitches, each having electricity, water and a waste point. Most have shade from large trees and a number benefit from panoramic views of the sea or behind to the mountains. The site has huge rectangular and lagoon style pools with water sprays and jacuzzis.

Facilities

Four sanitary blocks and one small toilet block provide excellent facilities, including services in one block for disabled campers. Private wash cabins. Washing machines and dryers. Motorcaravan services. Car wash. Restaurant/snack bar. Bar. Supermarket. Swimming pools with jacuzzi. Boules. Play areas. Bicycle hire. ATM. Dogs and other animals are not accepted. Torches useful. Off site: Town close by. Fishing 800 m. (Licence required, purchase in Puerto Mazarron). Boat launching 3 km. Riding 6 km. Golf 20 km. Beach 800 m.

Open: All year.

Directions

From north: From E15/A7 take exit 627 signed MU602, Cartagena and Fuente Alamo. After 5 km. turn right on MU603 signed Mazarron (do not turn into Mazarron). Continue towards Puerto Mazarron and take N332 (Cartagena). On reaching coast continue with N332. Shortly at roundabout turn right towards Isla Plana and La Azohia. Site is signed and is in 5 km. GPS: N37:34.761 W01:11.71

Charges 2007

Per person	€ 4,20 - € 5,20
pitch incl. electricity	€ 15,80 - € 18,80

(453)

ES8763 Camping Cabo de Gata

Ctra Cabo de Gata s/n, Cortijo Ferrón, E-04150 Cabo de Gata (Almeria)

Tel: **950 160 443**. Email: **info@campingcabodegata.com**

Since this medium sized site opened in 1993, it has strived continually to make improvements and today can be regarded as a very pleasant, all year campsite offering facilities to a good standard. Very popular with British visitors through the winter, it is located within the Cabo de Gata-Nijar natural park and set in open farmland, yet is only a 1 km. walk from a fine sandy beach. The 250 gravel pitches are level and of a reasonable size, with 6/16A electricity and limited shade from maturing trees or canopies. There are specific areas for very large units and 7 chalets for rent. A modern, airy reception is adjacent to internet facilities, whilst the nearby irregularly shaped swimming pool in close proximity to the bar/restaurant are both first class. To the west, Salinas de Acosta and the lighthouse at Faro de Gata (fine views). The salinas are reknowned for their bird life and from one of the hides you will see large flocks of pink flamingo and many other species. Almeria has many quality shops and the Alcazaba (955 A.D.), whilst a short drive inland near Tabernas, Mini Hollywood (Clint Eastwood sphagetti western fame) and the white washed village of Nijar noted for its basketry and rugs.

Facilities

Two, well-maintained, clean toilet blocks provide all the necessary sanitary facilities. including British type WCs, washbasins and free hot showers. Facilities for disabled campers. Restaurant, bar and shop (open all year). Swimming pool. Tennis court. Small playground. Library. Bicycle hire. English spoken. Entertainment programme. Off site: Nearest beach 1 km. Bus 1 km. Fishing 1 km. Golf 10 km. Riding 15 km.

Open: All year.

Directions

From A7-E15 take exit 460 or 467 and follow signs for Retamar via N344 and for Cabo de Gata. The final stretch of road is in a poor state of repair due to restrictions imposed within the natural park.

Charges 2006

Per person	€ 5,00
child (3-10 yrs)	€ 4,50
pitch incl. electricity (6-16A)	€ 12,85 - € 14,90

Camping Cheques accepted.

ES9290 Camping El Balcon de Pitres

E-18414 Pitres (Granada)

Tel: **958 766111**. Email: **info@balcondepitres.com**

A simple country site perched high in the mountains of the Alpujarras, on the south side of the Sierra Nevada, El Balcon de Pitres has its own rustic charm. Many thousands of trees planted around the site provide shade. There are stunning views from some of the 175 level grassy pitches (large units may find pitch access difficult). The garden is kept green by spring waters, which you can hear and sometimes see, tinkling away in places. The Lopez family, have built this site from barren mountain top to cool oasis in the mountains in just fifteen years.

Facilities

Two toilet blocks provide adequate facilities but the steeply sloping site is unsuitable for disabled campers and thus there are no facilities for them. Snack bar. Bar. Shop (closed Tuesdays). Swimming pools (extra charge, € 2.40 adult € 1.50 child). Bicycle hire. Torches useful. Off site: Fishing. Canyoning. Trekking. Parascending. Quad bikes. Sports centre for football.

Open: All year.

Directions

Site is about 30 km. northeast of Motril. Heading south on A44 (E902) exit 164 (Lanjaron) onto E348 towards Orgiva. Fork left at sign (A4132) Pampaneira 8 km. Continue to Pitres (7 km). Site signed. (Steep and winding roads). GPS: N36:55.911 W03:19.961

Charges 2006

Per person	€ 5,00
pitch incl. electricity (2A)	€ 10,00 - € 13,50

ES9285 Camping Las Lomas

Ctra de Sierra Nevada, E-18160 Güejar-Sierra (Granada)

Tel: 958 484 742. Email: laslomas@campings.net

This site is high in the Güéjar Sierra and looks down on the Patano de Canales reservoir. After a wonderful drive to Güéjar-Sierra, you are rewarded with a site boasting excellent facilities. It is set on a slope but the pitches have been levelled and are quite private, with high separating hedges and many mature trees giving good shade (some pitches are fully serviced, with sinks and most have electricity). The large bar/restaurant complex and pools have wonderful views over the lake and a grassed sunbathing area runs down to the fence (safe) looking over the long drop below. A new feature is luxury rooms for rent, including one with a superb spa which is for hire by the hour. Any infirm visitors will need a car to get around as the inclines are extreme.

Facilities

Pretty sanitary blocks (heated in winter) provide clean facilities. First class facilities for disabled campers and well equipped baby room (key at reception). Spa for hire. Motorcaravan services. Good supermarket. Restaurant/bar. Swimming pool. Play area. Table tennis. Minigolf. Basketball. Many other activities including parascending. Barbecue. Internet access. Torches useful. Off site: Buses to village and Granada (15 km). Tours of the Alhambra organised. Useful site for winter skiing.

Open: All year.

Directions

Heading south towards Granada on A44 (E902 Jaén - Motril) take exit 132 onto A395 (Alhamba/Sierra Nevada). After 4 km. marker, exit 5B (Sierra Nevada). At 7 km marker, exit right onto slip road. At junction turn left (Cenes de la Vega/Güéjar-Sierra). In 200 m. turn right on A4026. In 1.6 km. turn left (Güéjar-Sierra). Drive uphill, past dam and site is on right in 2.8 km.

Charges 2006

Per person	€ 4,00 - € 5,00
child (2-10 yrs)	€ 3,00 - € 4,00
pitch	€ 10,00 - € 12,00
VAT included.	

CAMPING CARAVANING
Restaurante

LAS LOMAS

Güejar-Sierra, km 6,5
E-18160 GÜEJAR-SIERRA
Tel. 0034 958 48 47 42
Fax 0034 958 48 47 42
laslomas@campings.net
www.campinglaslomas.com
A first class site with all facilities.
In quiet surroundings in midst of nature.

DISCOVER the SIERRA NEVADA and GRANADA Road...

ES9280 Camping Sierra Nevada

Avenida Madrid 107, E-18014 Granada (Granada)

Tel: 958 150 062. Email: campingmotel@terra.es

This is a good site either for a night stop or for a stay of a few days while visiting Granada and for a city site it is surprisingly pleasant. Quite large, it has an open feeling and, to encourage you to stay a little longer, an irregular shape pool with a smaller children's pool open in high season. There is some traffic noise around the pool as it is on the road boundary. With 148 pitches for touring units, the site is in two connected parts with more mature trees and facilities to the northern end.

Facilities

Two very modern sanitary blocks, with excellent facilities, including cabins, very good facilities for disabled people and babies. Washing machines. Motorcaravan services. Gas supplies. Shop (15/3-15/10). Swimming pools with lifeguards and charge of € 1.50 (15/6-15/9). Bar/restaurant by pool. Tennis. Table tennis. Petanque. Large playground. Doctor lives on site. Off site: Fishing 10 km. Golf 12 km. Bus station 50 m. from site gate.

Open: 1 March - 31 October.

Directions

Site is just outside the city to north, on road to Jaén and Madrid. From autopista, take Granada North - Almanjayar exit 123 (close to central bus station). Follow road back towards Granada and site is on the right, well signed. From other roads join the motorway to access the correct exit. GPS: N37:12.241 W03:37.022

Charges 2006

Per person	€ 5,25
pitch incl. electricity	€ 15,60
VAT included.	

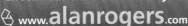

ES9081 Camping Villsom

Ctra Sevilla - Cadiz, km 554.8, E-41700 Sevilla (Sevilla)
Tel: **954 720 828**

This city site was one of the first to open in Spain and it is still owned by the same pleasant family. The administrative building consists of a peaceful and attractive bar with patio and satellite TV (where breakfast is served) and there is a pleasant, small reception area. It is a good site for visiting Seville with a frequent bus service to the centre. Camping Villsom has around 180 pitches which are level and shaded. A huge variety of trees and palms are to be seen around the site and in summer the bright colours of the flowers are very pleasing.

Facilities

Sanitary facilities require modernisation in some areas. Some washbasins have cold water only. Laundry facilities. Small shop selling basic provisions. Bar with satellite TV (open July/Aug). Swimming pool (June-Sept). Putting. Table tennis. Drinks machine. Off site: Bus stop close. Most town facilities including restaurant, supermarket, cinema and theatre.

Open: All year.

Directions

On main Seville - Cadiz NIV road travelling from Seville take exit at km. 553 signed Dos Hermanos - Isla Menor. Go under road bridge and turn immediately right (Isla Mentor) to site 80 m. on right. GPS: N37:16.641 W05:56.210

Charges guide

Per person	€ 3,60
pitch incl. electricity	€ 7,40 - € 10,05

All plus 7% VAT.

ES9082 Camping Sevilla

Ctra N-IV, km. 534, E-41007 Sevilla (Sevilla)
Tel: **954 514 379**

This site is ideal for visiting the fascinating city of Seville. It is just south of the perimeter of Seville airfield, by day with your ear defenders, you can practise your plane-spotting, but thankfully the usual mandatory respite exists at night, although you are fairly close to the main Seville - Madrid road. With a pretty entrance, this is a flat, sandy site with 85 pitches of varying size for motorcaravans and caravans, plus 450 for tents. Electricity (6/10A) is available. Trees provide some pitches with shade, others have artificial shade. There is the constant change-over bustle of all nationalities coming to visit Seville.

Facilities

Buildings housing the sanitary and supporting facilities are round in shape and a happy yellow colour. Half of the showers are cold water only. Blocks are kept very clean. Two excellent motorcaravan service points. Supermarket, bar and restaurant (high season). Small bar/snack area (low season). Swimming pools (June - Sept; charged). Internet access. Off site: Bus service 600 m.

Open: All year.

Directions

From any route follow signs to the airport (very easy) and you will pick up signs for the campsite from any direction. Be sure to follow signs carefully. GPS: N37:24.994 W05:55.048

Charges guide

Per person	€ 3,25
pitch incl. electricity	€ 7,75 - € 8,75

Plus 7% VAT. No credit cards.

ES8800 Camping Marbella Playa

Ctra N-340, km. 192,800, E-29600 Marbella (Málaga)
Tel: **952 833 998**. Email: **recepcion@campingmarbella.com**

This large site is 12 kilometres east of the internationally famous resort of Marbella with public transport available to the town centre and local attractions. A sandy beach is about 150 metres away with direct access. There are 430 individual pitches of up to 70 sq.m. with natural shade (additional artificial shade is provided to some), and electricity (10/20A) available throughout. The site is busy throughout the high season but the high staff/customer ratio and the friendly staff approach ensures a comfortable stay. A large pool complex with a restaurant/bar provides a very attractive feature.

Facilities

Four sanitary blocks of mixed ages, are fully equipped and well maintained. Three modern units for disabled visitors. Large supermarket with butcher and fresh vegetable counter. Bar, restaurant and café (all open all year). Supervised swimming pool (free - April/Sept). Playground (on gritty sand). Torches necessary in beach areas. Off site: Bus service 150 m. Fishing 100 m. Golf and bicycle hire 5 km. Riding 10 km. Beach 200 m.

Open: All year.

Directions

Site is 12 km. east of Marbella with access close to the 193 km. point on the main N340 road. GPS: N36:29.476 W04:45.795

Charges guide

Per person	€ 2,80 - € 4,65
child (1-10 yrs)	€ 3,90
pitch incl. electricity	€ 15,75 - € 25,55

All plus 7% VAT. Reductions (up to 50%) for long stays and senior citizens outside 16/6-31/8.

ES8802 Camping Cabopino

Ctra N340, km 194.7, E-29600 Marbella (Málaga)

Tel: **952 834 373**. Email: **info@campingcabopino.com**

This large mature site is alongside the main N340 Costa del Sol coast road, 12 km. east of Marbella and 15 km. from Fuengirola. The Costa del Sol is also known as the Costa del Golf and fittingly there is a major golf course alongside the site. The site is set amongst tall pine trees which provide shade for the sandy pitches (there are some huge areas for large units). The 400 touring pitches, a mix of level and sloping, all have electricity. There is an area on the western side for groups of youngsters.

Facilities

Four mature but very clean sanitary blocks provide hot water throughout (may be under pressure at peak times). Washing machines. Bar/restaurant and takeaway. Shop. Swimming pools (one open all year). Play area. Some evening entertainment. Excursions can be booked. ATM. Torches necessary in the more remote parts of the site. Off site: Beach 600 m. Fishing, bicycle hire and riding within 1 km. Golf 7 km.

Open: All year.

Directions

Site is 12 km. from Marbella. Approaching Marbella from the east, leave the N340 at the 194 km. marker (signed Cabopino). Site is off the roundabout at the top of the slip road.

Charges 2006

Per unit incl. 2 persons and electricity	€ 17,10 - € 28,70
extra person	€ 3,45 - € 5,75

Plus 7% VAT.

Camping Cheques accepted.

tel: **00 333 59 59 03 59** *kawan-villages.com*

ES8859 Camping Roche

N-340 km 19,5, Carril de Pilahito, E-11140 Conil de la Frontera (Cádiz)

Tel: **956 442 216**. Email: **info@campingroche.com**

This campsite has been recommended by our agent in Spain and we plan to undertake a full inspection in 2007. Camping Roche is situated in a pine forest near white sandy beaches in the lovely region of Andalusia. A family site, it offer a variety of facilities including a sports area and swimming pools. Games for children are organised. There are pleasant paths for mountain biking.

Facilities

Bar and restaurant. Supermarket. Sports area. Swimming pool. Off site: Bus stop 3 km.

Open: All year.

Directions

From the N340 (Cádiz - Algeciras) turn off to site at km. 19,5 point. From Conil, take El Pradillo road.

Charges 2006

Per unit with 2 persons and electricity	€ 16,35 - € 25,00
extra person	€ 3,55 - € 5,50

This is just a sample of the campsites we have inspected and selected in Spain & Portugal. For more campsites and further information, please see the Alan Rogers Spain & Portugal guide.

ES8865 Camping Playa Las Dunas de San Anton

P Maritimo de la Puntilla s/n, E-11500 El Puerto de Santa Maria (Cádiz)

Tel: 956 872 210. Email: info@lasdunascamping.com

This site lies within the Parque Natural Bahia de Les Dunes and is adjacent to the long and gently sloping golden sands of Puntilla beach. This is a pleasant and peaceful site (though very busy in August) with some 400 separate marked pitches, 140 for tourers, with much natural shade and ample electrical connections (5/10A). Motorcaravans park in an area called the Oasis which is very pretty. Tent and caravan pitches, under mature trees, are terraced and separated by low walls. A spacious site with a tranquil setting, it is popular with people who wish to 'winter over' in peace.

Facilities

Immaculate modern sanitary facilities with separate facilities for disabled campers and a baby room. Laundry facilities are excellent. Gas supplies. Bar/restaurant (all year). Supermarket (high season). Very large swimming pool (supervised) and toddlers pool (high season). Play areas. Night security all year. Off site: Fishing 500 m. Riding and golf 2 km. Municipal sports centre. Local buses for town and cities visits and a ferry to Cadiz.

Open: All year.

Directions

Site is 5 km. north of Cadiz off N1V route. Take road to Puerto Santa Maria, site is very well signed throughout the town (small yellow signs high on posts).

Charges 2006

Per person	€ 3,79 - € 4,21
child	€ 3,24 - € 3,60
pitch incl. electricity (5A)	€ 8,59 - € 10,85

ES8860 Camping Fuente del Gallo

Apto. 48, E-11149 Conil de la Frontera (Cádiz)

Tel: 956 440 137. Email: camping@campingfuentedelgallo.com

Fuente del Gallo extends a warm welcome to British visitors, particularly as one half of the ownership is Irish. The attractive pool, restaurant and bar complex with its large, shaded terace, are very welcoming in the height of summer. The site is well maintained with 221 pitches allocated to touring units. Each pitch has 10A electricity and a number of trees create shade to some pitches. Although the actual pitch areas are generally a good size, the majority are long and narrow. This could, in some cases, prevent the erection of an awning and your neighbour may feel close. In low season it is generally accepted to make additional use of an adjoining pitch. Good beaches are relatively near at 300 m. with access gained by steps through new houses with palm-lined roads. Helpful, friendly staff will assist in booking discounted trips to nearby attractions or even further afield to Africa. Cadiz, probably the oldest town in Spain, is worth a visit and in particular the old part with its narrow streets (many pedestrianised) and numerous shops.

Facilities

Two modernised and very clean sanitary blocks include excellent services for babies and disabled visitors and hot water at all facilities. Laundry room with two washing machines. Motorcaravan services. Gas supplies. Well-stocked shop. Attractive bar and restaurant (breakfast served). TV and games rooms. Swimming pool (all season, lifeguard in high season when there is a small charge) with paddling pool. Play area. Safety deposit boxes. Excursions. Torches useful. Off site: Watersports on beach. Fishing 300 m. Riding 1 km. Bicycle and motor scooter hire 2 km. Golf 5 km.

Open: Easter - 3 September.

Directions

From Cadiz-Algeciras road (N340) at km. 23.00, follow signs to Conil de la Frontera town centre, then shortly right to Fuente del Gallo and 'playas', following signs. GPS: N36:17.776 W06:06.611

Charges 2006

Per person	€ 5,40
child (3-10 yrs)	€ 4,40
pitch	€ 8,80 - € 9,50
electricity	€ 4,50
All plus 7% VAT. Less 11-30% for longer stays (except Jul/Aug).	

Check real time availability and at-the-gate prices...

www.alanrogers.com

ES8873 Camping La Aldea

El Rocio, E-21750 Almonte (Huelva)

Tel: **95944 2677**. Email: **info@campinglaaldea.com**

This impressive site lies just on the edge of the Parque Nacional de Donana, southwest of Sevilla on the outskirts of El Rocio. The town hosts a fiesta at the end of May with over one million people attending the local shrine. They travel for days in processions with cow drawn or motorized vehicles to attend. If you want to stay this weekend book well in advance! The well planned, modern site is well set out and the 246 pitches have natural shade from trees or artificial shade and 10A electricity. There are 52 serviced pitches with water and sewerage. There are also pitches for tents and bungalows for rent. The facilities are new, large and very clean. A beautiful waiter service restaurant (where the Spanish eat) provides lovely local food. The staff are welcoming and helpful with plenty of tourist information to hand. Expeditions on horseback or by 4x4 vehicle can be arranged in the national park.

Facilities

Two sanitary blocks provide excellent facilities including provision for disabled visitors. Motorcaravan service point. Swimming pool (May - Oct). Restaurant and bar in separate new complex. Shop. Internet connection. Playground. Off site: Bus stop 5 minutes walk. Huelva and Sevilla are about an hour's drive. Beach 15 km.

Open: All year excl. 25 December - 5 January.

Directions

From main Huelva - Sevilla road E1/A49 take exit 48 and drive south through Almonte to outskirts of El Rocio. Site is on left just past 25 km. marker. Go down to the roundabout and back up to be on the right side of the road to turn in.

Charges 2006

Per person	€ 4,00 - € 5,00
child	€ 3,00 - € 4,00
pitch incl. car	€ 7,00 - € 11,00
electricity	€ 4,00

Less 10-15% for low season stays over 3 days.

Camping La Aldea
Road El Rocio, km 25. Apdo. Correos 1
E-21750 El Rocio-Almonte (Huelva)
Tel./fax: 0034 959 442 677
www.campinglaaldea.com
info@campinglaaldea.com

Situated en El Rocio, at the gate of the natural Park Doñana and only 15 min. from the beach of Matalascañas. Excursions to the famous religious pilgrimage place of Almonte, Lugares Colombinos and Seville. The camp site is open all year. Swimming pool, supermarket and all facilities of a good holiday site.

ES9080 Camping Municipal El Brillante

Avenida del Brillante 50, E-14012 Córdoba (Córdoba)

Tel: **957 403 836**. Email: **elbrillante@campings.net**

For a municipal site this is impressive. Cordoba is one of the hottest places in Europe and the superb pool here is more than welcome. If you really want to stay in the city, then this large site is a good choice. It has 120 neat pitches of gravel and sand, the upper pitches covered by artificial and natural shade but the lower, newer area with little. The site becomes very crowded in high season. The entrance is narrow and may be congested so care must be exercised – there is a lay-by just outside.

Facilities

The toilet blocks have been renovated and an impressive newer block has facilities for babies and disabled people. Motorcaravan services. Gas supplies. Bar and restaurant (1/4-30/9). Shop (all year). Swimming pool (15/6-15/9). Play area. Off site: Bus service to city centre from outside site. Commercial centre 300 m. (left out of site, right at traffic lights).

Open: All year.

Directions

Site is on the north side of the river. From the NIV/E25 road from Madrid, take exit at km. 403 (the middle of three for Cordoba) and follow signs for Mosque/Cathedral into city centre. Pass it (on right) and turn right onto the main avenue. Continue and take right fork following signs for campsite.

Charges 2006

Per unit incl. 2 persons	€ 17,80
extra person (over 10 yrs)	€ 4,50

No credit cards.

ES9089 Camping Despenaperros

Ctra Infanta Elena, E-23213 Santa Elena (Jaén)

Tel: **953 664 192**. Email: **campingdesp@navegalia.com**

This site is on the edge of Santa Elena in a natural park with shade from mature pine trees. This is a good place to stay en-route from Madrid to the Costa del Sol or to just explore the surrounding countryside. The 116 pitches are fully serviced including a satellite TV/internet link. All rubbish must be taken to large bins outside the site gates (a long walk from the other end of the site). The site is run in a very friendly manner where nothing is too much trouble. Reception has a monitor link with tourist information and access to the region's sites of interest.

Facilities

Two traditional, central sanitary blocks have Turkish style WCs and well equipped showers. One washing machine (launderette in town). Shop. Excellent bar (all year) and charming restaurant (12/3-20/10). Swimming pools (15/6-15/9). Tennis. First aid room. Caravan storage. Night security. Off site: Walking, riding and mountain sports nearby. The main road gives good access to Jaen and Valdepenas.

Open: All year.

Directions

Travelling north towards Madrid on A4 (E5) take exit 259 (Santa Elena). Drive through town and site is on right up steep slope (alternative entrance for tall vehicles – ask at reception). Travelling south towards Bailén take exit 257 and as above.

Charges 2006

Per person	€ 3,27 - € 3,50
pitch incl. electricity	€ 8,94 - € 9,35

All plus 7% VAT.

ES9027 Camping Parque Natural de Monfrague

Ctra Plasencia-Trujillo km 10, E-10680 Malpartida de Plasencia (Cáceres)

Tel: **927 459 233**

Situated on the edge of the Monfrague National Park, this well managed site owned by the Barrado family, has fine views to the Sierra de Mirabel and delightful surrounding countryside. Many of the 130 good-sized pitches are grassed on slightly sloping terraced ground. Scattered trees offer a degree of shade, there are numerous water points and electricity is rated at 10A. It would prove difficult to find a more suitable location for those that savour peace, quiet, study of yesteryear, flora and fauna. On rare occasions a goods train travels along the nearby railway line. Used by locals, the air-conditioned restaurant provides good quality food at very acceptable prices. An evening meal on the veranda as the sun sets will provide fond memories of a rewarding holiday. Created as a National Park in 1979, Monfrague is now recognised as one of the best locations in Europe for anyone with any degree of interest in birdwatching. Nearby Plasencia has a medieval aqueduct, fine cathedral (14th C.) and the town's original twin ring of walls containing 68 towers. To the south, the classic historical towns of Merida, Caceres and Trujillo.

Facilities

Large modern toilet blocks, fully equipped, are very clean. Facilities for disabled campers and baby baths. Laundry. Motorcaravan service point. Supermarket/shop. Restaurant, bar and coffee shop. TV room with recreational facilities. Swimming and paddling pools (June - Sept). Play area. Tennis. Bicycle hire. Riding. Animation for children in season. Barbecue areas. Guided safaris into the Park for birdwatching at an acceptable price. Off site: Large supermarket at Plasencia.

Open: All year.

Directions

On the N630, from the north take EX-208 (previously C524) Plasencia - Trujillo; site on left in 6 km. From the south turn right just south of Plasencia on the EX-108 (previously C511) towards of Malpartida de Plasencia. Right at main junction on EX-208 to site.

Charges 2006

Per person	€ 3,70
child (3-12 yrs)	€ 3,20
pitch	€ 6,20

VAT included. Camping Cheques accepted.

ES9086 Cáceres Camping

Ctra N630, km. 549.5, E-10005 Cáceres (Cáceres)

Tel: **927 233 100**. Email: **info@campingcaceres.com**

Recommended by our agent in Spain, we plan to conduct a full inspection of this all-year site in 2007. Cáceres Camping is quite a small site, located to the west of the interesting city of Cáceres, a World Heritage site. There are 130 pitches here, and, unusually, each has a chalet providing a shower, washbasin and toilet. The pitches are of a reasonable size (80 sq.m.) and are well shaded. A range of leisure facilities is provided, including a swimming pool and a separate children's pool. Cáceres is a city with much interest, and a fascinating history – cave paintings on the city outskirts date back 30,000 years! The city is capital of High Extremadura and close by, the Montanchez mountain range offers many opportunities for walking and cycling.

Facilities

Individual wash blocks. Bar, restaurant, cafeteria and takeaway meals. Supermarket. Swimming pool, children's pool. Playground. Entertainment programme in high season. Sports pitch planned for 2007. Chalets and apartments for rent. Off site: City centre 2 km. Golf, walking and cycling opportunities.

Open: All year.

Directions

From the east (E90 motorway) take the N521 to Cáceres. Continue on this road to the west of the city. At the large roundabout, 'Campo de Futbol Principe Felipe', the site is signed to the right.

Charges 2006

Per person	€ 3,70
child	€ 3,20
pitch	€ 10,00
electricity	€ 3,00

Ctra. N-630, km. 549,5
E-10005 CÁCERES
Tel/Fax: 927 233 100

Cáceres camping
www.campingcaceres.com
info@campingcaceres.com

Fantastic site in the town of Caceres, open throughout the year and with installations of the first category. Private individual sanitary install. on each site – equipped wooden bungalows – studio's for 2 p. – Wi-Fi service in install. –social room w. TV – launderette – supermarket – cafeteria and restaurant with terrace – 2 swimming pools and large green areas with children's playground and sports zone.

ES9028 Camping Las Villuercas

Ctra Villanueva, E-10140 Guadalupe (Cáceres)

Tel: **927 367 139**

This rural site nestles in an attractive valley northwest of Guadalupe. The 50 pitches (25 with 10A electricity) are level and of a reasonable size; although large units may experience difficulty in getting into the more central pitches. With an abundance of mature trees most pitches offer some degree of shade. A river runs alongside the site and the ground can be muddy in very wet periods. The site is co-located with hostel accommodation. The restaurant provides excellent food at low prices and leads to a pretty patio with overhead vines and potted plants allowing elevated views of the pools.

Facilities

The single toilet block is older in but very clean, one area for women and one for men, providing British type WCs, washbasins and showers (hot water is from a 40 litre immersion heater which could be overwhelmed in busy periods). Facilities for disabled visitors. Laundry facilities. Restaurant. Bar. Swimming pools. Shop. Tennis. Small playground. Barbecue area. Safe deposit. Medical post. No English spoken. Off site: Riding 2 km. Fishing 3 km.

Open: 1 March - 30 November.

Directions

From NV/E90 Madrid - Mérida exit at Navelmoral de la Mata. Follow south to Guadalupe on the CC713 (83 km). Site is 2 km. from Guadalupe (near Monastery). From further southwest take exit 102 off main E90/NV (northeast of Merida). Follow signs (Guadalupe). Go through a few villages and near the 72 km. marker turn left to site, 100 m. on right.

Charges 2006

Per person	€ 3,00
child (2-12 yrs)	€ 2,50
pitch	€ 5,00 - € 5,50
electricity	€ 2,50

No credit cards.

ES9087 Camping Mérida

Ctra NV Madrid-Port, km. 336.6, E-06800 Mérida (Badajoz)
Tel: 924 303 453. Email: proexcam@jet.es

Camping Mérida is situated alongside the main N-V road to Madrid, the restaurant, café and pool complex separating the camping site area from the road where there is considerable noise. The site has 80 good sized pitches, most with some shade and on sloping ground, with ample electricity connections (long leads may be needed) and hedges with imaginative topiary. No English is spoken, but try out your Spanish. Reception is open until midnight. Camping Mérida is ideal as a base to tour the local area or as an overnight stop en route when travelling either north/south or east/west.

Facilities

The central sanitary facility includes hot and cold showers, British style WCs. Gas supplies. Small shop for essentials. Busy restaurant/cafeteria and bar, also open to the public. Medium sized swimming and paddling pools (May-Sept). Bicycle hire. Play area (unfenced and near road). Caravan storage. Torches useful. Off site: Town 5 km.

Open: All year.

Directions

Site is alongside NV road (Madrid-Lisbon), 5 km. east of Mérida, at km. 336.6. From east take exit 334 and follow camping signs (doubling back). Site is actually on the 630 road that runs alongside the new motorway. GPS: N38:56.143 W06:18.306

Charges 2006

Per person	€ 3,15
pitch incl. electricity	€ 9,30
All plus VAT.	

ES9090 Camping El Greco

Ctra CM-4000 km. 0,7, Puebla de Montalban, E-45004 Toledo (Toledo)
Tel: 925 220 090

Toledo was the home of the Grecian painter and the site that bears his name boasts a beautiful view of the ancient city from the restaurant, bar and superb pool. The friendly, family owners make you welcome and are proud of their site which is the only one in Toledo (it can get crowded). The 150 pitches are of 80 sq.m. with electricity and shade from strategically planted trees. Most have separating hedges that give privacy, with others in herring bone layouts that make for interesting parking in some areas. The river Tagus streches alongside the site which is fenced for safety.

Facilities

Two sanitary blocks, both modernised include facilities for disabled campers and everything is of the highest standard and kept very clean. Laundry. Motorcaravan services. Swimming pool (15/6-15/9; charged). Restaurant/bar (1/4-30/9) with good menu and fair prices. Small shop in reception. Ice machine. Off site: Fishing in river. Golf 10 km. Riding 15 km. An hourly air-conditioned bus service runs from the gates to the city centre, touring the outside of the walls first.

Open: All year.

Directions

Site is on C4000 road on the edge of the town, signed towards Puebla de Montelban; site signs also in city centre. From Madrid on N401, turn off right towards Toledo city centre but turn right again at the roundabout at the gates to the old city. Site is signed from the next right turn.

Charges 2006

Per person	€ 5,56
pitch	€ 5,35 - € 10,48
electricity (6A)	€ 3,75
Plus 7% VAT.	

ES9098 Camping Rio Mundo

Ctra Comarcal 412, km. 205, Mesones, E-02449 Molinicos (Albacete)
Tel: 967 433230. Email: riomundo@campingriomundo.com

This typically Spanish site is situated in the Sierra de Alcaraz (south of Albacete), just off the scenic route 412 between Elche de la Sierra and Valdepeñas. The drive to this site is through beautiful scenery (well worth the drive) and although from the west the main road is winding in some places, it should cause no problems if driven carefully. Shade is provided either by trees or by artificial means for the 100 pitches and electricity is supplied to the centre ones. It is a beautiful setting with majestic mountains and wonderful countryside which begs to be explored.

Facilities

One toilet block provides clean modern facilities. Basic toilet facilities for disabled people. Washing machine. Small shop for basics. Outside bar serving snacks with covered seating area. Another bar by the swimming pool. Playground. Petanque. Barbecue area.

Open: 18 March - 12 October.

Directions

Site is just off the 412 road which runs west to east, between the A30 and 322 roads south of Albacete. Turn at km. 205 on the 412, 5 km. east of village of Riopar and west of Elche de la Sierra. Follow signs to site. The road narrows to one lane for a few hundred yards but keep straight on for 1-2 km. to site.

Charges 2006

per person	€ 3,45 - € 4,45
pitch incl. electricity	€ 10,60 - € 12,85

ES9200 Caravanning El Escorial

Apdo. Correos 8, Ctra M600, km. 3.5, E-28280 El Escorial (Madrid)

Tel: **918 902 412**. Email: **info@campingelescorial.com**

There is a shortage of good sites in the central regions of Spain, but this is one (albeit rather expensive). El Escorial is very large, there are 1,358 individual pitches of which about 600 are for touring, with the remainder used for permanent or seasonal units, but situated to one side of the site. The pitches are shaded (ask for a pitch without a low tree canopy if you have a 3 metre high motorcaravan). There are another 250 pseudo 'wild' spaces for tourists on open fields, with good shade from mature trees (long cables may be necessary for electricity). The general amenities are good and include three swimming pools (unheated), plus a paddling pool in a central area with a bar/restaurant with terrace and plenty of grassy sitting out areas. At weekends in high season the site can be noisy. It is well situated for sightseeing visits especially to the magnificent El Escorial monastery (5 km). Also, the enormous civil war monument of the Valle de los Caidos is very close plus Madrid and Segovia both at 50 km.

Facilities

One large toilet block for the touring pitches, plus two smart, small blocks for the 'wild' camping area, are all fully equipped with some washbasins in cabins. Baby baths. Facilities for disabled campers. The blocks can be heated. Large supermarket (1/3-31/10). Restaurant/bar and snack bar (1/3-31/10). Disco-bar. Swimming pools. Three tennis courts. Two well equipped playgrounds on sand. ATM. Off site: Town 3 km. Riding or golf 7 km.

Open: All year.

Directions

From the south go through town of El Escorial, and follow M600 Guadarrama road. Site is between the 2 and 3 km. markers north of the town on the right. From the north use A6 autopista and exit 47 to M600 towards El Escorial town. Site is on the left.

Charges 2006

Per person	€ 5,35
child (3-10 yrs)	€ 5,20
caravan or tent and car	€ 10,55
motorcaravan	€ 9,20
electricity	€ 3,75

VAT included. No credit cards.

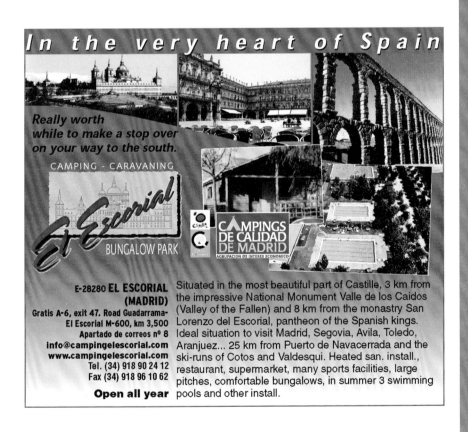

ES9210 Camping Pico de la Miel

Ctra NI Madrid - France, km. 58, E-28751 La Cabrera (Madrid)

Tel: **918 688 082**. Email: **pico-miel@picodelamiel.com**

Pico de la Miel is a very large site 60 kilometres north of Madrid. Mainly a long-stay site for Madrid, there is a huge number of very well established, fairly old statics. There is a small separate area with its own toilet block for touring units. The 60 pitches are on rather poor, sandy grass, some with artificial shade. Others, not so level, are under sparse pine trees and there are yet more pitches for tents (the ground could be hard for pegs). The noise level from the many Spanish customers is high and you will have a chance to practice your Spanish! Electricity connections are available. Tall hedges abound and with the trees, make it resemble a giant maze. No internal signs are provided and the long walk to the pool can be a challenge. The site is well signed and easy to find, two or three kilometres southwest off the main N1 road, with an amazing mountain backdrop.

Facilities

Dated but clean tiled toilet block, with some washbasins in cabins. It can be heated. En-suite unit with ramp for disabled visitors. Motorcaravan services. Gas supplies. Shop. Restaurant/ Bar (all year). Excellent swimming pool complex (15/6-15/9). Tennis. Playground. Off site: Bicycle hire and riding 200 m. Fishing 8 km.

Open: All year.

Directions

Site is well signed from the N1. Going south use exit 60, going north exit 57 or 60, and follow site signs. GPS: N40:51.547 W03:37.034

Charges 2006

Per person	€ 5,40
child (2-9 yrs)	€ 4,70
caravan or tent	€ 5,20 - € 5,40
car	€ 5,20
motorcaravan	€ 8,60

All plus 7% VAT. Less 10-25% for longer stays.

ES9019 Camping La Pesquera

Ctra de Caceres - Arrabal, E-37500 Ciudad Rodrigo (Salamanca)

Tel: **923 481 348**

This modest little site has just 54 pitches and is located near the Rio Agueda looking up to the magnificent fortress ramparts of Ciudad Rodrigo. Entry to the site is through a municipal park with a large play area. Whilst the site is small, it can take even the largest units, the centrally located facilities have all been refurbished to a high standard, the pitches are flat and grassy and the roads are well maintained gravel. The pitches are shaded by trees by day and there is site lighting at night although you may find torches useful due to the tree canopy.

Facilities

Attractive ochre stone sanitary building with British WCs and free hot showers. Facilities for disabled campers. Washing machine. Basics sold from bar in high season. Bar/snacks (April - Sept). Playground outside gates. Barbecue outside gate. Torches useful. Off site: River fishing 1 km. Riding 5 km. Superb walking area.

Open: 25 April - 30 September.

Directions

Site is southwest of Salamancar close to Ciudad Rodrigo. From the E80 N260, any direction, take the 526 to Coria. Site is alongside river directly off the road and well signed.

Charges 2006

Per person	€ 3,20
child (up to 12 yrs)	€ 3,00
tent/caravan and car	€ 3,20
motorcaravan	€ 6,40
electricity	€ 3,00

ES9242 Camping El Acueducto

Avenida D. Juan de Borbón, 49, Ctra CL601, km. 112, E-40004 Segovia (Segovia)

Tel: 921 425 000. Email: campingsg@navegalia.com

Located right on the edge of the interesting city of Segovia with lovely views across the open plain with mountains in the background, this is a family run, typically Spanish site. The grass pitches are mostly of medium size, although a few pitches near the gate would have room for larger motor-caravans. Reception is small but the owner is helpful and speaks good English. El Acueducto is well positioned for discovering Segovia. About three miles away, Segovia is deeply and haughtily Castilian, with plenty of squares and mansions from its days of Golden Age grandeur, when it was a royal resort.

Facilities

Two traditional style toilet blocks provide basic facilities, a laundry room and dishwashing sinks, all of which are clean. Small shop for basics. Bar. Two swimming pools. Table tennis. Large play area. Off site: Large restaurant a few yards along the road providing good food. Bus service into city centre. Madrid is within driving distance.

Open: 1 April - 30 September.

Directions

From the north on N1 (Burgos - Madrid) take exit 99 on N110 towards Segovia. On outskirts of city take third exit on N603 signed Madrid. Pass one exit to Segovia and take second signed Segovia and La Granja. At roundabout turn right towards Segovia. Site is 500 yards on right.

Charges 2006

Per person	€ 4,50 - € 5,00
pitch	€ 14,00 - € 15,50

ES9026 Camping El Burro Blanco

Camino de las Norias s/n, E-37660 Miranda del Castañar (Salamanca)

Tel: 923 161 100. Email: elburroblanco@internet-rural.com

Set on a hill top, within the Sierra Peña de Francia is the romantic walled village of Miranda del Castañar with its charming, crumbling castle. This site has been developed by a Dutch team including husband and wife Jeff and Yvonne and their friend Paul. You are welcomed at the gate and are walked around the facilities. The number of pitches has been reduced to 30 (all now 80 to 120 sq.m.), mostly level with some terracing and 25 with electricity. The pitches are beautifully set in 3.5 hectares of the most attractive woodland.

Facilities

One central modern sanitary facility, fully equipped includes a baby bath. Two washbasins have hot water. Out of season part of the unit is closed and therefore facilities are unisex. Launderette. Gas supplies. Library with book swap and small bar. Off site: Restaurants, bars, shops and ATM in village 600 m. Municipal swimming pool nearby, river swimming and fishing 1.5 km.

Open: 1 April - 1 October.

Directions

From north - south direction take Salamanca - Coria road southwest for about 70 km. through Vecinos, Linares de Rio Frio towards Coria. The road to Miranda is 7 km. northeast of village of Cepeda. Turn off main road and after 1.2 km. turn left on concrete road. Follow for 1.1 km. (a short stretch unmade) to site. GPS: N40:28.488 W05:59.931

Charges 2007

Per person	€ 4,80
pitch incl. electricity	€ 10,50

Plus 7% VAT. No credit cards.

ES9023 Camping Camino de Santiago

Casco Urbano, E-09110 Castrojeriz (Burgos)

Tel: 947 377 255. Email: campingcastro@eresmas.com

This tranquil site lies to the west of Burgos on the outskirts of Castrojeriz, a small unspoilt Spanish rural town. In a superb location, almost in the shadow of the ruined castle high on the hillside, it will appeal to those who like peace and a true touring campsite without all the modern trimmings, and at a reasonable cost. The 50 marked pitches are level, grassy and divided by hedges, with electricity (5A) and drainage available to all. There is also a number of permanent pitches. Mature trees provide shade and there is a pretty orchard in one corner of the site.

Facilities

Adequate sanitary facilities with showers, British and Turkish style WCs, and washbasins with cold water only. These facilities are in older style, but are well maintained and clean. Washing machine. Bar (serving coffee and soft drinks). Games room. Tennis. Play area. Bicycle hire. Barbecue area. Note: the present owner is looking to sell the site so things may change.

Open: 1 March - 30 November.

Directions

From N120/A231 (Leon - Burgos), turn on BU404 (Villasandino, Castrojeriz). Turn left at crossroads on southwest side of town, then left at site sign. GPS: N42:17.484 W04:07.899

Charges 2006

Per person	€ 3,75
pitch incl. electricity	€ 6,50 - € 8,00

All plus 7% VAT.

465

ES9029 Camping El Astral

Camino de Pollos 8, E-47100 Tordesillas (Valladolid)

Tel: 983 770 953. Email: info@campingelastral.es

The site is in a prime position alongside the wide River Duero (safely fenced). It is homely and run by a charming man, Eduardo Gutierrez, who has excellent English and is ably assisted by brother Gustavo and sister Lola. The site is generally flat with 154 pitches separated by thin hedges. They vary in size from 60 - 80 sq.m. with mature trees providing shade. There is an electricity pylon tucked in one corner of the site but this is hardly noticeable. This is a friendly site ideal for exploring the area as you move through Spain.

Facilities

One attractive sanitary block including two cabins with WC, bidet and washbasin. Some facilities for disabled campers, including ramps. Baby room in ladies' area. Washing machines. Motorcaravan services. Supermarket. Bar. Restaurant fequented by locals. Swimming and paddling pools (1/6-15/9). Playground. Tennis (high season). Minigolf. English speaking staff. Local bus service. Animation daily in high season. Torches are useful.

Open: 1 April - 30 September.

Directions

Tordesillas is 28 km. southwest of Valladolid. From all directions, leave the main road towards Tordesillas and follow signs to campsite or 'Parador' (a hotel opposite the site). GPS: N41:29.779 W05:00.312

Charges 2007

Per person	€ 4,20 - € 6,00
child (0-12 yrs)	€ 3,30 - € 5,00
pitch incl. electricity (5A)	€ 11,30 - € 14,50

Plus 7% VAT. Discounts in low season.

kawan-villages.com **tel: 00 333 59 59 03 59**   *kawan* VILLAGES CAMPINGS

ES9024 Camping As Cancelas

Rue do 25 de Xullo 35, E-15704 Santiago de Compostela (A Coruña)

Tel: 981 580 476. Email: info@campingascancelas.com

The beautiful city of Santiago has been the destination for European Christian pilgrims for centuries and they now follow ancient routes to this unique city, the whole of which is a national monument. The As Cancelas campsite is excellent for sharing the experiences of these pilgrims in the city and around the magnificent cathedral. It has 156 marked pitches (30-70 sq.m), arranged in terraces and divided by trees and shrubs. On a hillside overlooking the city, the views are very pleasant, but the site has a steep approach road and access to most of the pitches can be a challenge for large units. Electrical hook-ups (5A) are available, the site is lit at night and a security guard patrols. There are many legendary festivals and processions here, the main one being on July 25th, especially in holy years (when the Saint's birthday falls on a Sunday). Examine for yourself the credibility of the fascinating story of the arrival of the bones of St James at Compostela (Compostela translates as 'field of stars'), and also discover why the pilgrims dutifully carry a scallop shell on their long journey. There are many pilgrims' routes, including one commencing from Fowey in Cornwall.

Facilities

Two very modern toilet blocks are fully equipped, with ramped access for disabled campers. The quality and cleanliness of the fittings and tiling is good. Laundry with service wash for a small fee. Small mini market (open July/Aug.). Restaurant. Bar with TV. (main season). Well kept, unsupervised swimming pool and children's pool. Small playground. Off site: Regular bus service runs into the city from near football ground 200 m. from site. Huge commercial centre (open late and handy for off season use) 20 minutes walk downhill (uphill on the return!).

Open: All year.

Directions

From motorway AP9-E1 take exit 67 and follow signs for 'Casco Historico' and 'Centro Ciudad' then follow site signs.

Charges 2007

Per person	€ 4,00 - € 5,25
child (up to 12 yrs)	€ 2,50 - € 4,00
pitch	€ 8,00 - € 11,00
electricity	€ 3,30

All plus VAT.

Check real time availability and at-the-gate prices...

www.alanrogers.com

ES8942 Camping Los Manzanos

Ctra Santa Cruz - Meiras, km. 0,7, E-15179 Santa Cruz (A Coruña)

Tel: **981 614 825**. Email: **info@camping-losmanzanos.com**

Los Manzanos has a steep access drive to the main buildings and is divided by a stream into two sections linked by a bridge. Pitches for larger units are marked and numbered, 85 with electricity (12A) and, in one section, there is a fairly large, unmarked field for tents. Some aircraft noise should be expected as the site is under the flight path to La Coruña (but no aricraft at night). The site impressed us as being very clean, even when full, which it tends to be in high season. Some huge interesting stone sculptures create focal points and conversation pieces.

Facilities

One good toilet block provides modern facilities including free hot showers. Small shop with fresh produce daily (limited outside July/Aug). High quality restaurant/bar (July/Aug). Swimming pool with lifeguard, free to campers (15/6-15/9). Playground. Barbecue area. Bungalows for rent. Off site: Bus service at end of drive. Beach and fishing 800 m. Bicycle hire 2 km. Golf and riding 8 km.

Open: Easter - 15 September.

Directions

The nearest large city is La Coruna. From A9/E1 going south, take exit 7 for 'O Burgo'. Site is north of Oleiras, in Santa Cruz on the road to Meiras heading out of town, and is well signed from there.

Charges 2006

Per person	€ 5,00
pitch incl. electricity	€ 13,20 - € 13,80

All plus 7% VAT.

ES8940 Camping Los Cantiles

Ctra N634, km. 502,7, E-33700 Luarca (Asturias)

Tel: **985 640 938**. Email: **cantiles@campingloscantiles.com**

Luarca is a picturesque little place with a pretty inner harbour and two sandy beaches, and Los Cantiles is two kilometres to the east of town on a cliff top that juts out into the sea, giving excellent views from some pitches and the sound of the waves to soothe you to sleep. The site is well maintained and is a pleasant place to stop along this under-developed coastline. The 150 pitches, 99 with electricity, are mostly on level grass, divided by huge hedges of hydrangeas and bushes. Some pitches have gravel surfaces. There is a separate area for late arrivals in high season.

Facilities

Two modern, fully equipped sanitary blocks (one in low season which is heated in winter) are kept very clean. Facilities for disabled people and babies. Laundry. Freezer service. Gas supplies. Small shop (July-Sept). Bar with snacks (1/7-15/9). Cooking facilities (own gas). Bicycle hire. Torches helpful after midnight. English is spoken. Off site: Bar/restaurant and shop 300 m. Luarca 2 km. Beach and fishing 700 m. Riding 4 km.

Open: All year.

Directions

Luarca is 85 km. west of Gijon. From N632 Gijon - La Coru–a road turn south at 154 km. marker onto N634 for Luarca. After km. 502 marker east of Luarca, site is well signed to the left through an estate. GPS: N43:32.953 W06:31.459

Charges 2007

Per person	€ 4,00
pitch incl. electricity	€ 8,95 - € 10,95

Plus 7% VAT. No credit cards.

ES8945 Camping Lagos de Somiedo

Valle de Lago, E-33840 Somiedo (Asturias)

Tel: **985 763 776**

This is a most unusual gem of a small site in the Parque Natural de Somieda. Winding narrow roads with challenging rock overhangs, hairpin bends and breathtaking views (for 8 km.) finally bring you to the lake and campsite at an elevation of 1,200 m. This is a site for 4x4s, powerful small camper-vans and cars – not for medium or large motorhomes, and caravans are not accepted. It is not an approach for the faint hearted! The friendly Lana family make you welcome at their unique site, which is for those who wish to explore the natural values of the Park without the 'normal' amenities.

Facilities

There are British style toilets and free hot water to clean hot showers and washbasin. Facilities for babies and children. Washing machine. Combined reception, small restaurant, bar and reference section. Shop for bread, milk and other essentials, plus local produce and crafts. Horses for hire, trekking. Lectures on flora, fauna, history and culture. Fishing (licence required). Barbecue area. Small play area. Gas supplies. Off site: The very small village is 500 m. and it maintains the Spanish customs and traditions of this area.

Open: Easter - 15 October.

Directions

From N634 via Oviedo turn left at 442 km. marker on AS-15 signed Parque Natural de Somiedo. At 9 km. marker past Longoria, turn left on AS-227. At 38 km. marker, turn left into Pol de Somiedo. Follow signs for Valle de Lago and El Valle; 8 km. of hairpin bends from Pola, passing Urria on the left, brings you to the valley. Site is signed on the right.

Charges 2006

Per person	€ 4,50
pitch incl. car	€ 7,00

All plus 7% VAT.

ES8955 Camping Caravaning Arenal de Moris

A8 Salida 337, E-33344 Caravia Alta (Asturias)

Tel: 985 853 097. Email: camoris@teleline.es

This smart, well run site is close to three fine sandy beaches so gets very busy at peak times. It has a backdrop of the mountains in the nature reserve known as the Sueve which is important for a breed of short Asturian horses, the 'Asturcone'. The site has 330 grass pitches (269 for touring units) of 40-70 sq.m. and with 200 electricity connections available (5A). With little shade, some pitches are terraced with others on an open, slightly sloping field with views of the sea.

Facilities

Three sanitary blocks provide comfortable, controllable showers (no dividers) and vanity style washbasins, laundry facilities and external dishwashing (cold water). Supermarket. Bar/restaurant. Swimming pool. Tennis. Play area in lemon orchard. English is spoken. Off site: Fishing 200 m. Golf 5 km. Riding, bicycle hire and sailing 10 km. Bar and restaurants in village 2 km. Beach 200 m.

Open: 1 June - 17 September.

Directions

Caravia Alta is 50 km. east of Gijón, Leave A8 Santander - Oviedo motorway at km. 337 exit, turn left on N632 towards Colunga and site is signed to right in village, near 16 km. marker. GPS: N43:28.349 W05:10.999

Charges 2006

Per person	€ 5,00
pitch incl. electricity	€ 10,80 - € 14,07

ES8961 Camping El Helguero

Ctra Santillana-Comillas, E-39527 Ruiloba (Cantabria)

Tel: 942 722 124. Email: reservas@campingelhelguero.com

This site, in a peaceful location surrounded by tall trees and impressive towering rock formations, caters for 240 units (of which 100 are seasonal) on slightly sloping ground. There are many marked pitches on different levels, all with access to electricity (5A), but with varying amounts of shade. There are also attractive tent and small camper sections set close in to the rocks and some site owned chalets. The site gets very crowded in high season, so it is best to arrive early if you haven't booked. The reasonably sized swimming pool and children's pool have access lifts for disabled campers.

Facilities

Three well placed toilet blocks, although old, are clean and all include controllable showers and hot and cold water to all basins. Facilities for children and disabled visitors. Washing machines and dryers. Motorcaravan services. Small supermarket (July/Aug). Bar/snack bar plus separate more formal restaurant. Swimming pool (caps compulsory). Playground. Activities and entertainment (high season). ATM. Torches useful in some places. Off site: Bus service 500 m. Bar/restaurants in village (walking distance). Beach, fishing, sailing, golf and riding, all 3 km. Santillana del Mar 12 km.

Open: 1 April - 30 September.

Directions

Site is 45 km. west of Santander. From A8 (Santander - Oviedo) take km. 249 exit (Cabezón and Comillas) and turn north on Ca135 towards Comillas, At km. 7 turn right on Ca359 to Ruilobuca and Barrio la Iglesia. After village turn right up hill on Ca358 to site on right (note: signs refer to 'Camping Ruiloba'). GPS: N43:22.973 W04:14.880

Charges 2007

Per person	€ 3,80 - € 4,50
pitch	€ 3,80 - € 9,00
electricity	€ 3,45
Camping Cheques accepted.	

ES8962 Camping La Isla Picos de Europa

Picos de Europa, E-39570 Potes-Turieno (Cantabria)

Tel: 942 730 896. Email: campicoseuropa@terra.es

La Isla is beside the road from Potes to Fuente Dé, with many mature trees giving good shade and glimpses of the mountains above. Established for over 25 years, a warm welcome awaits you from the owners (who speak good English) and a most relaxed and peaceful atmosphere exists in the site. The 121 unmarked pitches are arranged around an oval gravel track under a variety of fruit and ornamental trees. Electricity (6A) is available to all pitches, although some need long leads. A small bar and restaurant are located under dense trees by the small river which runs through the site.

Facilities

Single, clean and smart sanitary block retains the style of the site. It includes washbasins with cold water. Washing machine. Gas supplies. Freezer service. Small shop and restaurant/bar (all season). Small swimming pool (caps compulsory; 1/5-30/9). Play area. Barbecue area. Fishing. Bicycle hire. Riding. Off site: Shops, bars and restaurants plus Monday morning market in Potes 4 km. Fuente Dé and its spectcular cable-car ride 18 km.

Open: 1 April - 30 October.

Directions

Potes is 110 km. southwest of Santander. From A8/N634 (Santander - Oviedo) take km. 272 exit for Unquera. Take N621 south to Panes and travel up spectacular gorge (care needed if towing) to Potes. Site is on right of N621, 4 km. beyond Potes.

Charges guide

Per person	€ 3,30 - € 3,60
pitch incl. electricity	€ 8,90 - € 12,20
All plus VAT. Low season reductions.	

ES9000 Camping Playa Joyel

Playa de Ris, E-39180 Noja (Cantabria)

Tel: 942 630 081. Email: playajoyel@telefonica.net

This very attractive holiday and touring site is some 40 kilometres from Santander and 80 kilometres from Bilbao. It is a busy, high quality, comprehensively equipped site by a superb beach providing 1,000 well shaded, marked and numbered pitches with 3A electricity available. These include 80 large pitches of 100 sq.m. Some 250 pitches are occupied by tour operators or seasonal units. This well managed site has a lot to offer for family holidays with much going on in high season when it gets crowded. The swimming pool complex with lifeguard is free to campers and the superb beaches are cleaned daily 15/6-20/9. One of the beach exits leads to the main beach, or if you turn left out of the other you will find a safe, placid estuary with water at rising tide. An unusual feature is the natural park within the site boundary which has a great selection of animals to see. It overlooks a protected area of marsh where European birds spend the winter. There are security patrols at night.

Facilities

Six excellent, spacious and fully equipped toilet blocks include baby baths. Large laundry. Motorcaravan services. Gas supplies. Freezer service. Supermarket (all season). General shop. Kiosk. Restaurant and takeaway (1/7-31/8). Bar and snacks (all season). Swimming pools, bathing caps compulsory (20/5-15/9). Entertainment organised with a soundproof pub/disco (July-Aug). Gym park. Tennis. Playground. Riding. Fishing. Natural animal park. Hairdresser (July/Aug). Medical centre. Torches necessary in some areas. Dogs and other animals are not accepted. Off site: Bicycle hire and large sports complex with multiple facilities including an indoor pool 1 km. Sailing and boat launching 10 km. Riding and golf 20 km.

Open: Easter - 30 September.

Directions

From A8 (Bilbao - Santander) take km. 185 exit and N634 towards Beranga. Almost immediately turn right on Ca147 to Noja. In 10 km. turn left at multiple campsite signs and go through town. At beach roundabout turn left and continue to site at end of road. GPS: N43:29.369 W03:32.220

Charges 2007

Per person	€ 3,70 - € 5,50
child (3-9 yrs)	€ 2,50 - € 4,00
pitch	€ 12,00 - € 21,00
electricity	€ 3,00 - € 4,00

All plus 7% VAT. No credit cards.

Camping Cheques accepted.

ES9035 Camping Portuondo

Ctra Gernika - Bermeo, E-48360 Mundaka (Bizkaia)

Tel: **946 877 701**. Email: **recepcion@campingportuondo.com**

From some of the 98 pitches on this well kept site there are stunning views over the ocean and estuary. Among the lovely gardens, the pitches are mainly for tents and smaller vans, but there are six large pitches at the lower levels for caravans and motorhomes. However, it must be stressed that access is difficult as the road is very steep and there is no turning space. In high season (July/August) it is best to ring to book your space. English is spoken and the friendly owner is keen to help you.

Facilities

Two fully equipped toilet blocks can be heated and include mostly British WCs and a smart baby room. Washing machines and dryers. Shop . Bar and two restaurants, all open to public (16/1-14/12). Takeaway (15/6-15/9). Swimming pools (15/6-15/9). Barbecue area. Torches may be helpful. Off site: Fishing 100 m. Beaches 500 m bracing walk. Surfing on Mundaka beach 500 m. Boat launching 1 km. Shops, bars and restaurants 2 km. Riding 8 km. Bicycle hire 10 km. Golf 40 km. Buses to Bilbao and Gernika (every 30 mins) 300 m.

Open: All year.

Directions

Mundaka is 35 km. northeast of Bilbao. From A8 (San Sebastián - Bilbao) take exit 18 and follow signs for Gernika on Bi635. Continue on Bi2235 towards Bermeo. Site is on right approaching Mundaka but because of oblique, steep (18%) access, continue nearly 2 km. and use slip road to turn in filling station on left. GPS: N43:23.951 W02:41.766

Charges 2006

Per person	€ 4,75 - € 5,20
pitch incl. electricity	€ 13,40 - € 13,85

All plus 7% VAT. Less 5-10% for longer stays.

ES9043 Camping Caravanning Errota el Molino

E-31150 Mendigorria (Navarra)

Tel: **948 340 604**. Email: **info@campingelmolino.com**

This is an extensive site set by an attractive weir near the town of Mendigorria, alongside the river Arga. It takes its name from an old disused water-mill (molino) close by. The site is split into separate permanent and touring sections. The touring area is a new development with good-sized flat pitches with electricity and water for tourers, and a separate area for tents. Many trees have been planted around the site but there is still only minimal shade. The chirpy owner Anna Beriain will give you a warm welcome. Reception is housed in the lower part of a long building along with the bar/snack bar which has a cool shaded terrace, a separate restaurant and a supermarket. The upper floor of this building is dormitory accommodation for backpackers. The site has a boat launching facility and an ambitious watersport programme in season with a safety boat. There are pedaloes and canoes for hire. The site is busy during the festival of San Fermín (bull running) in July in Pamplona (28 km).

Facilities

The well equipped toilet block is very clean and well maintained, with cold water to washbasins. Facilities for disabled campers. Washing machine. Large restaurant, pleasant bar. Supermarket (Easter - Sept). Superb new swimming pools for adults and children. Bicycle hire. Riverside bar. Weekly animation programme (July/Aug) and many sporting activities. Squash courts. Internet access. Pleasant river walk. Torches useful. Off site: Bus to Pamplona 500 m. Riding 15 km. Golf 35 km.

Open: All year.

Directions

Mendigorria is 30 km. southwest of Pamplona. From A15 San Sebastian - Zaragoza motorway, leave Pamplona bypass on A12 towards Logroño. Leave at km. 23 on NA601 to hill-top town of Mendigorria. At crossroads turn right towards Larraga and down hill to site. GPS: N42:37.497 W01:50.533

Charges 2006

Per person	€ 4,30
pitch incl. car and electricity	€ 11,90

Plus 7% VAT. Discounts outside high season. Camping Cheques accepted.

ES9042 Camping Etxarri

Paraje Dambolintxulo s/n, E-31820 Etxarri-Aranatz (Navarra)

Tel: **948 460 537**. Email: **info@campingetxarri.com**

Situated in the Valle de la Burunda the site is a peaceful oasis with superb views of the 1,300 m. high San-Donato Mountains. The approach to the constantly improving site is via a road lined by huge 300 year old oak trees, which are a feature of the site. There are 100 average sized pitches on flat ground, 50 for tourers, with 6A electricity to all and water to 25. Animation is organised in August for children. The site gets very crowded during the Fiestas de San Fermín (bull-running) in Pamplona early in July. It is essential to make a reservation if you wish to stay.

Facilities

The single toilet block has good facilities including baby bath. Laundry. Gas supplies. Essential supplies kept in high season. Bar (1/4-30/9). Restaurant and takeaway (1/6-15/9). Large swimming pool with children's pool (15/6-15/9) also open to the public and can get crowded. Bicycle hire. Minigolf. Play area. Off site: Bus and trains nearby. Bars, restaurants and shops 2 km. Golf, fishing, riding all 20 km. Pamplona 40 km.

Open: 1 April - 1 October.

Directions

Etxarri-Aranatz is 40 km. northwest of Pamplona. From A8 (San Sebastian - Bilbao) take A15 towards Pamplona, then 20 km. northwest of Pamplona, take A10 west towards Vitoria/Gasteix. At km. 19 take NA120 to and through town following site signs. Turn left after crossing railway to site at end of road.

Charges 2006

Per person	€ 2,90 - € 3,95
pitch incl. electricity	€ 6,70 - € 8,15

ES9060 Camping Peña Montañesa

Ctra Ainsa - Francia, km. 2, E-22360 Labuerda (Huesca)

Tel: **974 500 032**. Email: **info@penamontanesa.com**

A large site situated quite high up in the Pyrenees near the Ordesa National Park, Peña Montanesa is easily accessible from Ainsa or from France via the Bielsa Tunnel (steep sections on the French side). The site is essentially divided into three sections opening progressively throughout the season and all have shade. The 288 pitches on fairly level grass are of about 75 sq.m. and 10A electricity is available on virtually all. Grouped near the entrance are the facilities that make the site so attractive, including a fair sized outdoor pool and a glass-covered indoor pool with jacuzzi and sauna.

Facilities

A newer toilet block, heated when necessary, has free hot showers but cold water to open plan washbasins. Facilities for disabled visitors. Small baby room. Washing machine. Bar. Restaurant. Takeaway. Supermarket. Outdoor pool (1/3-1/10). Indoor pool (all year). Playground. Bicycle hire. Riding. Rafting. Only gas barbecues are permitted.

Open: All year.

Directions

Site is 2 km. from Ainsa, on the road from Ainsa to France. GPS: N42:26.112 E00:08.171

Charges 2006

Per person	€ 4,40 - € 5,75
child (1-9 yrs)	€ 3,44 - € 4,50
pitch incl. electricity	€ 16,75 - € 21,25
All plus 7% VAT.	

ES9062 Camping Boltaña

Ctra N-260, km 442, E-22340 Boltaña (Huesca)

Tel: **974 502 347**. Email: **info@campingboltana.com**

Nestled in the Rio Ara valley, surrounded by the Pyrennees mountains and below a tiny but enchanting, historic, hill top village, is the very pretty, thoughtfully planned Camping Boltana. Generously sized, grassy pitches have good shade from a variety of trees and a stream meanders through the campsite. The landscaping includes ten charming rocky water gardens (though these can dry up in summer months) and a covered pergola doubles as an eating and play area. A stone building houses the site's reception, social room and supermarket.

Facilities

Two modern sanitary blocks include facilities for disabled visitors and laundry facilities. Casual restaurant and bar and a more formal restaurant (April-Oct). Supermarket. Swimming pools (15/5-30/9). Playground. Barbecues. Animation for children (high season). Pentanque. Guided tours, plus hiking, canyoning, rafting, climbing, mountain biking and caving. Torches useful in some parts. Off site: Local bus service.

Open: All year.

Directions

South of the Park Nacional de Ordesa, site is about 50 km. from Jaca near Ainsa. From Ainsa travel northwest on N260 toward Boltaña (near 443 km. marker) and 1 km. from Boltaña turn south toward Margudged. Site is well signed and is 1 km. along this road. GPS: N42:25.811 E00:04.729

Charges 2006

Per person	€ 5,00
pitch incl. car	€ 10,00 - € 10,60
Camping Cheques accepted.	

ES9125 Camping Lago Barasona

Ctra N-123a, km. 25, E-22435 La Puebla de Castro (Huesca)

Tel: **974 545 148**. Email: **info@lagobarasona.com**

This site, alongside its associated ten room hotel, is beautifully positioned on terraces across a road from the shores of the Lago de Barasona (a large reservoir), with views of hills and the distant Pyrenees. The very friendly, English speaking owner is keen to please and has applied very high standards throughout the site. The grassy, fairly level pitches are generally around 100 sq.m. with 35 high quality pitches of 110 sq m for larger units. All have electricity (6/10A), many are well shaded and some have great views of the lake and/or hills. Waterskiing and other watersports are available in July and August. You may swim and fish in the lake which has a shallow area extending for around 20 m. If you prefer, the site has a round outdoor pool plus the pleasant rectangular pool in the hotel (these open from as early as April when the weather is often quite warm). There are two excellent restaurants here one being in the hotel the other with a pretty terrace with wonderful views. The menu and cooking is outstanding, specialising in the regional cuisine. The disco and bar area is well away from the site by the lakeside. This is a most pleasant and peaceful site in a lovely area and will suit families who wish for quality and choice in their camping. The views really are beautiful.

Facilities

Two toilet blocks in modern buildings have high standards and hot water throughout including cabins (3 for ladies, 1 for men). Bar/snack bar and two excellent restaurants (open all season). Shop (15/5-15/9). Swimming pools (15/5-15/9). Tennis. Mountain bike hire. Canoe, windsurfing motor boat and pedalo hire. Mini-club (high season). Lake swimming, fishing, canoeing, etc. Walking (maps provided). Money exchange. Mini-disco. Off site: Riding 4 km.

Open: All year.

Directions

Site is on the west bank of the lake, close to km. 25 on the N123A, 6 km. south of Graus (about 80 km. north of Lleida/Lerida). Travelling from the south, the site is on the left from a newly built roundabout and slip road.
GPS: N42:08.498 E00:18.915

Charges 2007

Per person	€ 3,90 - € 5,50
child (2-10 yrs)	€ 3,20 - € 4,65
pitch incl. electricity	€ 8,60 - € 15,80

Plus 7% VAT. Camping Cheques accepted.

 *kawan-villages.com* tel: **00 333 59 59 03 59** *kawan* VILLAGES CAMPING

ES9105 Camping Lago Park

Ctra Alhama de Aragon-Nuevalos, E-50210 Nuevalos (Zaragoza)

Tel: **976 849 038**

Lago Park is situated in an attractive area which receives many visitors for the Monasterio de Piedra just 3 km. distant and it enjoys pleasant views of the surrounding mountains. This site is suitable for transit stops or if you wish to visit the monasterio as it is the only one hereabouts and appears to make the most of that fact. It is not recommended for extended stays. Set on a steep hillside, the 300 pitches (250 for tourers) are on terraces. Only the lower rows are suitable for large caravans. These pitches are numbered and marked by trees, most having electricity (10A). Facilities on site include a large pool (unheated and chilly with its mountain water), a restaurant/bar and small shop. The restaurant is disappointing with restricted hours, mediocre cooking and is pricey, but there are many restaurants in town. The site is just outside the attractive village, between lake and mountains.

Facilities

The single sanitary block has Turkish and British style WCs. washbasins with hot water and controllable hot showers (no dividers). Restaurant/bar (June-Sept). Shop (all season). Swimming pool (late June-Sept). Play area. Gas supplies. Torches needed in some areas. Off site: Fishing 300 m. Riding 2 km.

Open: 1 April - 30 September.

Directions

From Zaragoza (120 km.) take fast A2/N11/E90 road and turn onto C202 road beyond Calatayud to Nuévalos (25 km.). From Madrid, exit A2 at Alhama de Aragón (13 km.). Follow signs for Monasterio de Piedra from all directions.

Charges 2007

Per person	€ 5,60
child (3-10 yrs)	€ 5,50
pitch incl. electricity	€ 10,50 - € 14,60

MAP 11

With giant lakes and waterways, rich forests, majestic mountains and glaciers, and vast, wide open countryside, Sweden is almost twice the size of the UK but with a fraction of the population.

CAPITAL: STOCKHOLM

Tourist Office

Swedish Travel and Tourism Council
Swedish House, 5 Upper Montagu Street
London W1H 2AG
Tel: 020 7870 5600
Fax: 020 7724 5872
Email: info@swetourism.org.uk
Internet: www.visit-sweden.com

The beautiful southwest region, otherwise known as the 'Swedish Lake and Glass country', is easily accessible by ferry or overland from Norway. The area is dominated by two great lakes, Vänern and Vättern, Europe's second and third largest lakes. There are also many fine beaches with picturesque harbours and historic ports such as Gothenburg, Helsingborg and Malmö, which is now linked by a bridge to Copenhagen. Stockholm, the capital, is a delightful place built on fourteen small islands on the eastern coast. It is an attractive, vibrant city, with magnificent architecture, fine museums and historic squares. Moving northwards into central and northern Sweden, you'll discover beautiful forests and around 96,000 lakes, which are perfect for ice skating (in winter!) and you may even see moose and reindeer. Today Sweden enjoys one of the highest standards of living in the world and a quality of life to go with it.

Population

9 million

Climate

Sweden enjoys a temperate climate thanks to the Gulf Stream. There is generally less rain and more sunshine in the summer than in Britain.

Language

Swedish. English is fairly widely spoken.

Telephone

The country code is 00 46.

Money

Currency: The Krona
Banks: Mon-Fri 09.30-15.00. Some city banks stay open until 17.30/18.00 on Thursdays (regions may vary).

Shops

Mon-Fri 09.00-18.00.
Sat 09.00-13.00/16.00. Some department stores remain open until 20.00/22.00.

Public Holidays

New Year; Epiphany; Easter Mon; Labour Day; Ascension; Whit Sun; Constitution Day June 6; Mid-summer Festival; All Saints; Christmas Dec 24-26.

Motoring

Roads are generally much quieter than in the UK. Dipped headlights are obligatory. Away from large towns, petrol stations rarely open 24 hours but most have self service pumps (with credit card payment). Buy diesel during working hours, it may not be available at self service pumps.

SW2706 Lisebergs Camping Askim Strand

Marholmsvagen, S-436 45 Askim (Hallands Län)

Tel: **031 286 261**. Email: **askim.strand@liseberg.se**

Within easy reach of the city, this is a very pleasantly located site, close to a long gently sloping beach which is very popular for bathing. As a result the area behind the campsite is populated by many holiday homes and cabins. A very open site with very little shade, it has 266 mostly level, grassy pitches all with 10A electricity, plus two areas for tents. Many pitches are fairly compact, although there are some larger ones. The key card entry system operates the entrance barrier and access to the buildings and there is a night security guard (June-Aug). Reception has a range of tourist information, and can provide details of reductions on bus and taxi fares to the city, also selling the Göteborg Card.

Facilities

Two heated sanitary buildings, the larger one fairly new, the smaller recently refitted. Both are maintained to a high standard and provide all the usual facilities, including a good suite for small children, dishwashing sinks, laundry, kitchens with cooking facilities, and a unit for disabled visitors. Hot water is free. Motorcaravan services. Snack bar (July). Playground. TV room. Bicycle hire. Off site: Small shop just outside the site. Göteborg city. Golf 2 km.

Open: 20 April - 2 September.

Directions

About 10 km. south of Göteborg, take exit signed Mölndal S and ports (Hamnar). Take the Rv 159 towards Frolunda, and watch for a slip-road to the right. After 200 m. turn left at the roundabout, signed Askim, and follow signs to campsite. GPS: N57:37.699 E11:55.231

Charges 2006

Per pitch	SEK 140 - 325

Only pitches with electricity available for high season.

SW2640 Krono Camping Båstad-Torekov

S-260 93 Torekov (Skåne Län)

Tel: **0431 364 525**. Email: **torekov@kronocamping.se**

Part of the Kronocamping chain, this campsite is 500 m. from the fishing village of Torekov, 14 km. west of the home of the Swedish tennis WCT Open at Båstad on the stretch of coastline between Malmö and Göteborg. Useful en route from the most southerly ports, it is a very good site and worthy of a longer stay for relaxation. It has 510 large pitches (390 for touring units), all numbered and marked, mainly in attractive natural woodland (mostly pine and birch), with some on more open ground close to the shore. Of these, 300 have electricity (10A) and cable TV, 77 also having water and drainage. WIFI internet access is possible on 50% of the pitches. The modern reception complex is professionally run and is also home for a good shop, a snack bar, restaurant, and pizzeria. The spacious site covers quite a large area and there is a cycle track along the shore to the beach with bathing. Games for children are organised in high season and there is an outdoor stage for musical entertainment and dancing (also in high season). This well run site is a pleasant place to stay.

Facilities

Three very good sanitary blocks with free hot water and facilities in for babies and disabled visitors (in each block). Laundry. Cooking facilities and dishwashing. Motorcaravan service point. Bar. Restaurant, pizzeria and snack bar with takeaway (15/5-30/8). Shop and kiosk. Minigolf. Sports fields. Play areas and adventure park for children. Bicycle hire. TV room. Beach. Fishing. Off site: Tennis close. Golf 1 km. Riding 3 km. Games, music and entertainment in high season.

Open: 15 April - 19 September.

Directions

From E6 Malmö - Göteborg road take Torekov/Båstad exit and follow signs for 20 km. towards Torekov. Site is signed 1 km. before village on right. GPS: N56:25.858 E12:38.433

Charges guide

Per unit incl electricity/TV connection	SEK 185 - 270
tent pitch	SEK 140 - 215

Camping Cheques accepted.

SW2630 Röstånga Camping & Bad

Blinkarpsvägen 3, S-260 24 Röstånga (Skåne Län)

Tel: 04 35 91064. Email: nystrand@msn.com

Beside the Söderåsen National Park, this scenic campsite has its own fishing lake and many activities for the whole family. There are 100 large, level, grassy pitches with electricity (10A) and a quiet area for tents with a view over the fishing lake. The tent area has its own service building and several barbecue places. A large holiday home and 14 pleasant cabins are available to rent all year round. A pool complex adjacent to the site provides a 50 metre swimming pool, three children's pools and a water slide, all heated during peak season. A one day visit is free for campers. Activities are arranged on the site in high season, including a children's club with exciting activities such as treasure hunts and gold panning, and for adults aqua-aerobics, Nordic walking and tennis. The Söderåsen National Park offers hiking and bicycle trails. The friendly staff will be happy to help you to plan interesting excursions in the area.

Facilities

Four good, heated sanitary blocks with free hot water and facilities for babies and disabled visitors. Laundry with washing machines and dryers. Kitchen with cooking rings, oven and microwave. Motorcaravan service point. Small shop at reception. Bar, restaurant and takeaway. Minigolf. Tennis. Fitness trail. Fishing. Canoe hire. Children's club. Off site: Swimming pool complex adjacent to site (one visit free for campers). Many golf courses nearby.

Open: 31 March - 29 October.

Directions

From Malmö: drive towards Lund and follow road no. 108 to Röstånga. From Stockholm: turn off at Östra Ljungby and take road no. 13 to Röstånga. In Röstånga drive through the village on road no. 108 and follow the signs. GPS: N55:59.795 E13:16.803

Charges 2006

Per pitch	SEK 130 - 165
electricity	SEK 35

Camping Cheques accepted.

Röstånga Camping & Bad

We offer you and your family a complete resort with a large heated Poolarea and Fishinglakes by the National Parc of Söderåsen-Sweden.

Blinkarpsvägen 3
26024 RÖSTÅNGA - Sweden
Phone: 0435 - 910 64
Telefax: 0435 - 916 52
E-mail: nystrand@msn.com

www.rostangacamping.se

SW2645 FirstCamp Mölle

S-260 42 Mölle (Skåne Län)

Tel: 042 347384. Email: mollehassle@telia.com

FirstCamp Mölle is a family campsite with a fine location at the foot of the Kullaberg, which marks the point where the Atlantic divides into the Kattegatt and Øresund. This site is open all year and has been recommended to us and we plan to undertake a full inspection during the 2007 season. There are 250 pitches here, generally of a good size and with electrical connections. The nearby Kullaberg Nature Park is dramatic and well worth a visit. The region is also well known for its ceramics and many potters and artists have settled in the area. On-site amenities include a heated paddling pool and water games complex. The nearest beach is 1.5 km. distant and is popular for kayaking and fishing.

Facilities

Bar, cafeteria and takeaway food. Small shop. Sauna. Minigolf. Sports pitch. Heated paddling pool. Bicycle hire. Riding. TV room. Entertainment and children's activity programme (high season). Motorcaravan services. Chalets for rent. Off site: Nearest beach 1.5 km. Golf 4 km. Kayaking 2 km. Kullaberg Nature Park (1 km). Mölle lighthouse (the brightest in Scandinavia!) 6 km.

Open: All year.

Directions

From Helsingborg take the E4 north and then join road 111 towards Höganäs. Pass through this town and follow signs to Mölle and the campsite.

Charges 2006

Per pitch	SEK 150 - 240
electricity	SEK 45
tent pitch	SEK 110 - 240

SW2650 Skånes Djurparks Camping

Jularp, S-243 93 Höör (Skåne Län)

Tel: 0413 553270. Email: info@grottbyn.se

This site is probably one of the most unusual we feature. It is next to the Skånes Djurpark – a zoo park with Scandinavian species – and has on site a reconstructed Stone Age Village. The site is located in a sheltered valley and has 110 large, level grassy pitches for caravans and motorhomes all with 10A electricity and a separate area for tents. The most unusual feature of the site is the sanitary block – it is underground! The fully air-conditioned building houses a superb and ample complement of facilities. The site also has a number of underground, caveman style, 8 bed (dormitory type) holiday units which can be rented by families or private groups (when not in use by schools on educational trips to the Stone Age Village). They open onto a circular courtyard with a barbecue and camp fire area and have access to the kitchens and dining room in the sanitary block. There are good walks through the nature park and around the lakes, where one can see deer, birds and other wildlife. Well placed for the Copenhagen - Malmö bridge or the ferries, this is also a site for discerning campers who want something distinctly different.

Facilities

The underground block includes roomy showers, two fully equipped kitchens, laundry and separate drying room and an enormous dining/TV room. Facilities for disabled people and baby changing. Cooking facilities. Laundry. A small new block and motorcaravan service point are planned. Mini-shop and café (15/6-15/8). Small heated family swimming pool (15/6-15/8). Playground. Stone Age Village. Off site: Restaurant just outside the entrance. Fishing 1.8 km. Bicycle hire 5 km. Riding and golf 8 km.

Open: All year (full services 15/6-10/8).

Directions

Turn off no. 23 road 2 km. north of Höör (at roundabout) and follow signs for Skånes Djurpark. Campsite entrance is off the Djurpark car park. GPS: N55:57.222 E13:32.289

Charges 2006

Per unit	SEK 160
electricity	SEK 30 - 40

Skånes Djurparks Camping

Jularp, S-243 93 Höör
Tel: 0046 413 55 33 270 • e-mail: info@grottbyn.se

SW2655 Tingsryds Camping

Mårdslyckesand, S-362 91 Tingsryd (Kronobergs Län)

Tel: 0477 10554. Email: tingsryd.camping@swipnet.se

A pleasant, well managed site by Lake Tiken, Tingsryds Camping is well placed for Sweden's Glass District. The 200 large pitches are arranged in rows divided by trees and shrubs, with some along the edge of a lakeside path (public have access). All have electricity (10/16A) and there is shade in parts. The facilities are housed in buildings near the site entrance, with the reception building having the restaurant, café, bar and a small shop. Adjacent to the site is a small beach, grassy lying out area, playground and lake swimming area and three tennis courts.

Facilities

Heated sanitary facilities are in two well maintained buildings, one including showers, mostly with curtains (on payment, communal undressing), the other a campers' kitchen. Dishwashing sinks. Facilities for disabled people. Laundry with free ironing. Motorcaravan services. Shop (1/5-15/9). Restaurant and cafe (1/5-15/9). Minigolf. Playground. Boules. Lake swimming. Beach volleyball. Canoe hire. Fishing. Bicycle hire. Off site: Golf 15 km.

Open: 5 April - 20 October (full service 24/5-19/8).

Directions

Site is 1 km. from Tingsryd off road no. 120, well signed around the town. GPS: N56:31.723 E14:57.688

Charges guide

Per unit	SEK 135 - 180

SW2705 Lisebergsbyn Karralund

Olbersgatan 9, S-416 55 Goteborg (Västra Götalands Län)

Tel: 031 840 500. Email: karralund@liseberg.se

Well positioned for visiting the city, this busy, well maintained site has 190 marked pitches, 152 with electricity (10A) and cable TV, 42 hardstandings, and several areas for tents. Pitches do vary in size, some are fairly compact and there are no dividing hedges, consequently units can be rather close together. Additionally there are cabins for rent, a budget hotel and a youth hostel. All this makes for a very busy site in the main season, which in this case means June, July and August. An advance telephone call to check for space is advisable. A breakfast buffet is served in low season and there is a restaurant 300 m. from the site entrance. Reception has a range of tourist information.

Facilities

Two heated sanitary buildings, the larger one fairly new, and a smaller, older one with limited facilities, are well maintained and cleaned. They provide all the usual facilities, with controllable hot showers, a suite for small children, dishwashing sinks and a laundry, kitchens with cooking facilities and a complete unit for disabled visitors. Motorcaravan services. Shop. Playground. TV room. Off site: Göteborg city with Liseberg amusement park.

Open: All year (full services 9/5-28/8.

Directions

Site is about 2.5 km. east of city centre. Follow signs to Lisebergsbyn and campsite symbol from E20, E6 or Rv 40. GPS: N57:42.293 E12:01.790

Charges guide

Per pitch	SEK 150 - 225
electricity	SEK 45
tent and car	SEK 95 - 245

Only pitches with electricity available in high season.

SW2665 Jönköping Swecamp Villa Björkhagen

Friggagatan 31, S-554 54 Jonkoping (Jönköpings Län)

Tel: 036 122863. Email: villabjorkhagen@swipnet.se

Overlooking Lake Vättern, Villa Björkhagen is a good site, useful as a break in the journey across Sweden or visiting the city during a tour of the Lakes. It is on raised ground overlooking the lake, with some shelter in parts. There are 280 pitches on well kept grass which, on one side, slopes away from reception. Some pitches on the other side of reception are flat and there are 200 electrical (10A), 100 cable TV and 40 water connections available. Jönköping is one of Sweden's oldest trading centres with a Charter dating back to 1284 and several outstanding attractions.

Facilities

Heated sanitary facilities include hot showers on payment (some in private cubicles) and a sauna, plus provision for disabled visitors and babies. Laundry. Dishwashing facilities. Motorcaravan services. Gas supplies. Mini-market (all year). Restaurant (1/5-30/9). Playground. TV room. Minigolf. Off site: Swimming pool complex 500 m. Fishing 500 m. Golf 1 km. Riding 7 km.

Open: All year (full services 1/5-30/9).

Directions

Site is well signed from the E4 road on eastern side of Jönköping. Watch carefully for exit on this fast road. GPS: N57:47.221 E14:13.077

Charges guide

Per unit incl. all persons	SEK 170 - 220
incl. electricity/TV connection	SEK 200 - 250

Camping Cheques accepted.

SW2670 Grannastrandens Familjecamping

Box 14, S-563 21 Granna (Jönköpings Län)

Tel: 0390 10706

This large, lakeside site with modern facilities and busy continental feel, is set below the old city of Gränna. Flat fields separate Gränna from the shore, one of which is occupied by the 25 acres of Grännastrandens where there are 450 numbered pitches, including a tent area and some seasonal pitches. The site is flat, spacious and very regularly laid out on open ground with only a row of poplars by the lake to provide shelter, so a windbreak may prove useful against any onshore breeze. About 230 pitches have electricity (10A). Obviously the great attraction here is the lake.

Facilities

The large, sanitary block in the centre of the site has modern, well kept facilities including British style WCs, some with external access, washbasins, and free hot showers, some in private cubicles. Dishwashing and laundry sinks. Laundry facilities. Provision for disabled people. Cooking facilities. Motorcaravan services. Shop (15/6-20/8). TV room. Playground. Lake swimming area. Boating and fishing. Off site: Café outside site (1/5-31/8) or town restaurants close. Bus stop nearby. Golf 6 km.

Open: 1 May - 30 September.

Directions

Take Gränna exit from E4 road (no camping sign) 40 km. north of Jönköping. Site is signed in the centre of the town, towards the harbour and ferry. GPS: N58:01.657 E14:27.482

Charges guide

Per unit	SEK 160
incl. electricity and satellite TV connection	SEK 200

477

SW2675 Västervik Lysingsbadet

Lysingsvägen, S-593 53 Västervik (Kalmar Län)
Tel: **0490 88920**. Email: **lysingsbadet@vastervik.se**

One of the largest sites in Scandinavia, Lysingsbadet has unrivalled views of the 'Pearl of the East Coast' – Västervik and its fjords and islands. There are around 1,000 large, mostly marked and numbered pitches, spread over a vast area of rocky promontory and set on different plateau, terraces, in valleys and woodland, or beside the water. It is a very attractive site, and one which never really looks or feels crowded even when busy. There are 83 full service pitches with TV, water and electrical connections, 163 with TV and electricity and 540 with electricity only, the remainder for tents. Reception is smart, efficient and friendly with good English spoken. An hourly bus service to Västervik runs from the site entrance from June to August. On site facilities include a full golf course, minigolf, heated outdoor pool complex with water slide and poolside café, sauna and solarium, playgrounds, boat hire, tennis, basketball, volleyball and fishing. For children, Astrid Lindgren's World theme park at Vimmerby is an easy day trip away and for adults the delights of the old town of Västervik and its shopping.

Facilities

Ten modern toilet blocks of various ages and designs house a comprehensive mix of showers, basins and WCs. All have good quality fittings and are kept very clean. Several kitchens with dishwashing sinks, cookers and hoods. Four laundry rooms. All facilities and hot water are free. Campers are issued with key cards which operate the barriers and gain access to sanitary blocks, pool complex and other facilities. Motorcaravan services. Supermarket (15/5-31/8). Restaurant and café/takeaway (12/6-138). Swimming pool complex (1/6-31/8). Golf. Minigolf. Tennis. Bicycle and boat hire. Fishing. Entertainment and dances in high season. Playgrounds. Quick Stop service. Bus service. Off site: Riding 10 km.

Open: All year.

Directions

Turn off E22 for Västervik and follow signs for Lysingsbadet. GPS: N57:44.294 E16:40.119

Charges 2006

Per pitch	€ 15,00 - € 27,00
incl. electricity	€ 20,00 - € 32,00
incl. TV connection	€ 21,00 - € 33,00

SW2680 Krono Camping Saxnäs

S-386 95 Färjestaden (Kalmar Län)
Tel: **0485 35700**. Email: **saxnas@kronocamping-oland.se**

Well placed for touring Sweden's Riviera and the fascinating and beautiful island of Öland, this family run site, part of the Krono group, has 420 marked and numbered touring pitches. Arranged in rows on open, well kept grassland dotted with a few trees, all have electricity (10A), 320 have TV connections and 112 also have water. An unmarked area without electricity can accommodate around 60 tents. The site has about 130 long stay units and cabins for rent. Reception is efficient and friendly with good English spoken. In high season children's games are organised and dances are held twice weekly, with other activities on other evenings. The sandy beach slopes very gently and is safe for children. Nearby attractions include the 7 km. long Öland road bridge and the 400 old windmills on the island (in the 19th century there were 2,000). The southern tip of Öland , Ottenby, is a paradise for bird watchers. Kalmar and its castle, museums and old town on the mainland, Eketorp prehistoric fortified village, Öland Djurpark. The Swedish Royal family's summer residence, Solliden, is well worth a visit.

Facilities

Three heated sanitary blocks provide a good supply of roomy shower cubicles, washbasins, some washbasin/WC suites and WCs. Facilities for babies and disabled visitors. Well equipped laundry room. Good kitchen with cookers, microwaves and dishwasher (free), and dishwashing sinks. Hot water is free throughout. Gas supplies. Motorcaravan services. Shop (1/5-30/8). Pizzeria, licensed restaurant and café (all 1/5-30/8). Bar (1/7-31/7). Playgrounds. Bouncing castle. Boules. Beach with volleyball. Fishing. Canoe hire. Bicycle hire. Minigolf. Family entertainment and activities. Football. Off site: Golf 0.5 km. Riding 2 km.

Open: 17 April - 11 September.

Directions

Cross Öland road bridge from Kalmar on road no. 137. Take exit for Öland Djurpark/Saxnäs, then follow campsite signs. Site is just north of the end of the bridge. GPS: N56:41.236 E16:28.909

Charges guide

Per pitch	SEK 100 - 205
incl. electricity	SEK 140 - 255
incl. electricity/TV connection	SEK 150 - 265
Weekend and weekly rates available.	

SW2690 Krono Camping Böda Sand

S-380 75 Byxelkrok (Kalmar Län)

Tel: 0485 22200. Email: bodasand@kronocampingoland.se

KronoCamping Böda Sand is beautifully situated at the northern end of the island of Øland and is one of Sweden's largest and most modern campsites. Most of the 1,300 pitches have electricity (10/16A) and TV connections, 130 have water and waste water drainage. The pitches and 123 cabins for rent are spread out in a pine forest, very close to the fabulous 10 km. long, white sand beach. Here you will also find a restaurant, kiosks, toilets and beach showers, and a relaxation centre with an indoor/outdoor pool. The reception, the toilet blocks and the services at this site are excellent.

Facilities

Seven heated sanitary blocks provide a good supply of roomy shower cubicles, washbasins, some washbasin suites and WCs, plus soothing music! Facilities for babies and disabled visitors. Well equipped laundry rooms. Excellent kitchens. Dishwashers (free) and sinks. Motorcaravan services. Supermarket and bakery. Pizzeria, café, pub and licensed restaurant. Takeaway. Bicycle hire, pedal cars and pedal boat hire. WIFI. Tennis. Badminton. Minigolf. 9-hole golf course. Indoor/outdoor swimming pool (on the beach). Family entertainment and activities.

Open: 1 May - 31 August.

Directions

From Kalmar cross the Øland road bridge on road no. 137. On Øland follow road no. 136 towards Borgholm and Byxelkrok. Turn left at the roundabout north of Böda and follow the campsite signs to Kronocamping Böda Sand.

Charges 2006

Per pitch	SEK 155 - 235
incl. electricity	SEK 195 - 285

SW2710 Lidköping SweCamp Kronocamping

Läckögatan, S-531 54 Lidköping (Västra Götalands Län)

Tel: 0510 26804. Email: info@kronocamping.com

This high quality, attractive site provides 423 pitches on flat, well kept grass. It is surrounded by some mature trees, with the lake shore as one boundary and a number of tall pines have been left to provide shade and shelter. There are 374 pitches with electricity (10A) and TV connections and 91 with water and drainage also, together with 60 cabins for rent. The site takes a fair number of seasonal units. There is a small shop (a shopping centre is very close) and a fully licensed restaurant with conservatory seating area in the reception complex. Very good playgrounds are provided.

Facilities

Excellent, modern sanitary facilities are in two blocks with under-floor heating. Hot water is free. Make up and hairdressing areas, baby room and facilities for disabled people. Private cabins. Dishwashing sinks. Good kitchens with cookers and microwaves. Motorcaravan services. Small shop. Restaurant. Minigolf. Volleyball. Playgrounds. TV room. Games and amusements room. Bicycle hire. Lake swimming, fishing and watersports. Off site: Swimming pool adjacent. Riding 4 km. Golf 6 km. The castle of Läckö, Kinnekulle, Spiken's fishing harbour.

Open: All year (full services 8/6-15/8).

Directions

From Lidköping town junctions follow signs towards Läckö then pick up camping signs and continue to site. GPS: N58:30.889 E13:08.390

Charges guide

Per pitch	SEK 155 - 200
with electricity/TV connection	SEK 175 - 235

SW2715 Gröne Backe Camping & Stugor

Södra Moränvägen, S-66832 Ed (Västra Götalands Län)

Tel: 0534 10144. Email: gronebackecamping@telia.com

In the heart of the beautiful Dalsland region, this pleasant, well shaded (mostly pine) site is open all year. It is well laid out, mostly overlooking the Lilla Le lake, and there is easy access from road no. 164. There are 180 pitches, most with electricity (10A) and special areas for tents. Also on the site are 11 cabins for rent and 40 seasonal pitches. A small shop and café are at the reception building. This pleasant, friendly family site is easy to find and the location makes it ideal for a longer stay.

Facilities

Three heated toilet blocks, two in the centre, one at reception, provide washbasins both vanity type and in cubicles. Showers (on payment). Baby rooms. Facilities for disabled visitors. Laundry. Cooking facilities. Motorcaravan services. Small shop. Café. Internet and WiFi. Playground. Minigolf. Canoes, rowing boats, bicycles and pedal cars for hire. Beach.

Open: All year.

Directions

Site is on road no. 164 at Ed, and is well signed. GPS: N58:53.965 E11:56.092

Charges 2006

Per unit	SEK 135 - 230

SW2720 Tidaholm-Hökensås Semesterby och Camping

Hakangen, S-522 91 Tidaholm (Västra Götalands Län)

Tel: 0502 230 53. Email: info@hokensas-semesterby.com

Hökensås is located just west of Lake Vättern and south of Tidaholm, in a beautiful nature reserve of wild, unspoiled scenery. The park is based on a 100 km. ridge, a glacier area with many impressive boulders and ice age debris but now thickly forested with majestic pines and silver birches, with a small, brilliant lake at every corner. This pleasant campsite is part of a holiday complex that includes wooden cabins for rent. It is relaxed and informal, with over 200 pitches either under trees or on a more open area at the far end, divided into rows by wooden rails. These are numbered and electricity (10A) is available on 135. Tents can go on the large grassy open areas by reception. The forests and lakes provide wonderful opportunities for walking, cycling (gravel tracks and marked walks) angling, swimming and when the snow falls, winter sports. This site is a find for all kinds of people who enjoy outdoor activities.

Facilities

The original sanitary block near reception is supplemented by one in the wooded area, both refurbished. Hot showers in cubicles with communal changing area are free. Separate saunas for each sex and facilities for disabled visitors and babies. Campers' kitchen at each block with cooking, dishwashing and laundry facilities (irons on loan from reception). Small, but well stocked shop. Very good angling shop. Fully licensed restaurant with takeaway. Playground. Tennis. Minigolf. Sauna. Lake swimming. Fishing. Off site: The town of Tidaholm and Lake Hornborga. Fishing 2 km. Riding 10 km. Bicycle hire 15 km.

Open: All year (full services 20/6-11/8).

Directions

Approach site from no. 195 western lake coast road. at Brandstorp, about 40 km. north of Jönköping, turn west at petrol station and camp sign signed Hökensås. Site is about 9 km. up this road. GPS: N58:05.890 E14:04.480

Charges guide

Per unit (more for Midsummer celebrations)	SEK 110
electricity	SEK 35 - 45

SW2725 Hafsten Swecamp Resort

S-451 96 Uddevalla (Västra Götalands Län)

Tel: 0522 644117. Email: info@hafsten.se

This privately owned site on the west coast is situated on a peninsula overlooking the magnificent coastline of Bohuslän. Open all year, it is a lovely terraced site with a beautiful, shallow and child-friendly sandy beach and many nature trails in the vicinity. There are 160 touring pitches, all with electricity (10A), 70 of them with water and drainage. In all, there are 300 pitches including a tent area and 60 cottages of a high standard. Amenities include two clean and well maintained service buildings, a pub, a fully licensed restaurant with wine from their own French vineyard, a takeaway and a well stocked shop. There are plenty of activities available including, canoeing, fishing, horse riding, minigolf, tennis, clay pigeon shooting, water slide and a paddling pool (charged), boat and motor boat hire. Troubadour evenings are arranged during the summer. Almost any activity can be arranged on the site or elsewhere by the friendly owners if they are given advance notice.

Facilities

Two heated sanitary buildings provide the usual facilities. Showers are on payment. Kitchen with good cooking facilities and dishwashing sinks, dining room. Laundry with washing machines, dryers and iron with ironing boards. Units for disabled visitors Motorcaravan services. Shop. Restaurant, takeaway and pub. Troubadour evenings. TV room. Relaxation centre with sauna and jacuzzi (charged). Water slide (charged). Internet access (WIFI). Riding. Minigolf. Tennis. Playground. Off site: Nordens Ark (animal park) 40 km. Havets hus (marine museum) 30 km. Golf 13 km. Shopping centre 13 km.

Open: All year.

Directions

From the E6, north Uddevalla, at Torpmotet exit take the 161 road towards Lysekil. At the Rotviksbro roundabout take the 161 road towards Orust. The exit to the site is located further on road 2 km. on the left. Follow the signs for 4 km. It is a narrow, one way road for motorcaravans and caravans. GPS: N58:18.881 E11:43.40

Charges guide

Per pitch	SEK 150
incl. electricity	SEK 180

SW2730 Ekuddens Camping

Strandbadet, S-542 00 Mariestad (Västra Götalands Län)

Tel: 0501 10637. Email: a.appelgren@mariestad.mail.telia.com

Ekuddens occupies a long stretch of the eastern shore of Lake Vänern to the northwest of the town, in a mixed woodland setting, and next door to the municipal complex of heated outdoor pools and sauna. The lake, of course, is also available for swimming or boating and there are bicycles, tandems and canoes for hire at the tourist information office. The spacious site can take 350 units and there are 230 electrical hook-ups (10A). Most pitches are under the trees but some at the far end are on more open ground with good views over the lake. The site becomes very busy in high season.

Facilities

Sanitary facilities are in three clean low wooden cabins. Free hot showers in cubicles. Facilities for disabled visitors with good access ramps. Baby changing rooms. Kitchens with cooking and dining facilities. Shop. Licensed bar. Takeaway (high season). Playground. Minigolf. TV room. Lake swimming, boating and fishing. Off site: Swimming pools adjacent. Golf 4 km. Bicycle 3 km. Riding 7 km.

Open: 1 May - 15 September (full services 15/6-15/8).

Directions

Site is 2.5 km. northwest of the town and well signed at junctions on the ring road. From the E20 motorway take exit for Mariestad S. and follow signs in the direction of Marieholm.
GPS: N58:42.943 E13:47.723

Charges guide

Per pitch	SEK 120 - 150
electricity	SEK 30

SW2735 Daftö Feriecenter

S-452 97 Stromstad (Västra Götalands Län)

Tel: 0526 260 40. Email: info@dafto.com

This extremely high quality, open all year site, is beautifully situated on the west coast, 5 km. south of the small 'summer town' of Strömstad. A very large site, some parts are terraced, other areas are open, some parts are shady. In total there are 650 pitches with 350 for touring, all with electrical hook-ups (10A, CEE plugs). In addition there are 125 modern, very well equipped chalets of various sizes. The facilities are of very high quality with everything you possibly want in four clean and attractive blocks. Member of Leading Campings Group.

Facilities

Four toilet blocks of excellent quality, with washbasin cubicles, showers, family rooms, a children's bathroom, sun beds, saunas and make up rooms. Units for disabled visitors. Kitchen with cookers, microwaves and sinks. Laundry facilities. Shop. Fully licensed restaurant. Heated pool (peak season). Games and TV rooms. Minigolf. Bicycle hire. Football. Children's club. Boat excursions and seal safaris. Internet access and WiFi for hire.

Open: All year excl. 22 December - 6 January.

Directions

Daftö is 5 km south of Strömstad on road 176. It is signed. GPS: N58:54.256 E11:12.007

Charges guide

Per pitch incl. electricity (max. 5 persons)	SEK 200 - 320
incl. water and drainage	SEK 200 - 330
tent incl. 2 persons	SEK 65 - 195

SW2740 Laxsjons Camping och Friluftsgard

S-660 10 Dals Långed (Västra Götalands Län)

Tel: 0531 30010. Email: office@laxjon.se

In the beautiful Dalsland region, Laxsjöns is an all year round site, catering for winter sports enthusiasts as well as summer tourists and groups. On the shores of the lake, the site is in two main areas – one flat, near the entrance, with hardstandings and the other on attractive, sloping, grassy areas adjoining. In total there are 300 places for caravans or motorcaravans, all with electricity (10/16A), plus more for tents. Leisure facilities on the site include minigolf, trampolines and a playground. A restaurant is at the top of the site with a good range of dishes in high season. In addition, there is a lake for swimming, fishing and canoeing (boats available).

Facilities

The main toilet block has hot showers (on payment), washbasins in cubicles, WCs and a hairdressing cubicle. With a further small block at the top of the site, the provision should be adequate. Facilities for disabled visitors. Laundry with drying rooms for bad weather. Cooking rooms for tenters. Restaurant (high season). Shop. Minigolf. Playground. Lake for swimming, Fishing and boating.

Open: All year (full services 22/6-15/8).

Directions

From Åmål take road no. 164 towards Bengtfors, then the 172 towards Billingsfors and Dals Långed. Site is signed about 5 km. south of Billinsfors, 1 km. down a good road. From the south, (Uddevalla) take road 172. From the west (Strömstad) take the 164 towards Bengtfors and 5 km. south of Billingsfors turn right towards Långed for 1 km.
GPS: N58:57.172 E12:15.14

Charges 2006

Per pitch	SEK 135 - 155

SW2750 FirstCamp Årjäng, Sommarvik

Sommarvik, S-672 91 Årjäng (Värmlands Län)

Tel: 0573 12060. Email: **swecamp@sommarvik.se**

This is a good site in beautiful surroundings with some of the 300 pitches overlooking the clear waters of the Västra Silen lake in peaceful countryside. The numbered pitches are arranged in terraces on a hillside interspersed with pines and birches, with half set aside for static units and 20 for tents. The remaining touring pitches all have 10A electricity hook-ups and 40 also include water and drainage. The site also has 60 chalets for rent. A large restaurant offers a full range of meals, soft drinks, beers, wines and takeaway meals. Close to reception, a heated swimming pool with a paddling pool, terraces and sun loungers has fine views down the lake. The pool and most activities on site attract daily charges. The lake with its sandy beach is popular and safe for children. There are plenty of activities available including canoeing, rowing boats, windsurfing, fishing, football, an attractive water featured minigolf, sauna, quizzes, guided walks and sightseeing trips. It is possible to ride trolleys around the area on disused railway tracks, go gold panning or slip into nearby Norway and visit Oslo. This site makes an ideal base to explore this scenic region in summer or winter when skiing is an additional attraction.

Facilities

Five sanitary units of varying sizes provide shower cubicles (hot showers on payment), washbasins, toilets, family bathrooms, facilities for disabled persons and baby changing. All are clean and acceptable but may be stretched in high season. Campers kitchens with cookers and sinks. Laundry facilities. Motorcaravan services. All activities and amenities are open 1/6-31/8. Small shop 1/5-30/9. Bar, restaurant and takeaway 15/6-20/8. Good play areas. Bicycle hire. Internet access. 'Quick stop' pitches for overnight stays. Youth hostel and conference centre also on site. Off site: Indoor pool complex 3 km. Riding 5 km. Golf 9 km.

Open: All year.

Directions

Site is well signed on road 172.3km south of its junction with the E18 close to Årjäng. GPS: N59:22.059 E12:08.377

Charges 2006

Per pitch	SEK 160
incl. electricity and water	SEK 180 - 260

Camping Cheques accepted.

SW2755 Alevi Camping

Fastnäs 53, S-68051 Stöllet (Värmlands Län)

Tel: 0563 86050. Email: **info@alevi-camping.com**

Alevi Camping is a small, welcoming site with 60 large pitches, 5 cabins and 2 tepees for hire. Open all year, the site is situated on the bank of the river Klarälven, the longest river in Sweden. With its own beach this is a perfect place for swimming, fishing, canoeing and rafting. The site, which had its first season in 2006, offers large level pitches all with electricity (4/10A). The county of Värmland is famous for its lakes, rivers and forests. There, if you are lucky, you can see the 'big four' predators of Scandinavia – wolf, bear, wolverine and lynx. Further up the river, at Sysslebäck, you can build your own log raft for a slow journey down the river. The rafts are fully equipped with a tent and whatever you need for a few days on the water. The site owners are happy to help you to find the perfect activity for a pleasant stay.

Facilities

One new sanitary block with free hot water. Unisex toilets and showers. Washbasins, both vanity style and in cubicles. Facilities for babies and disabled visitors. Family room. Good campers' kitchen. Motorcaravan services. Reception with small shop, restaurant, takeaway. TV room. Canoes and bicycle hire. River beach. Barbecue area. Sauna. Playground. Fishing. Skiing in winter. Off site: Supermarket 10 minutes by car.

Open: All year.

Directions

Site is between Ekshärad and Stöllet on road no. 62. Follow signs. GPS: N60:17.116 E13:24.404

Charges 2007

Per unit incl. 5 persons	SEK 130 - 140
with private sanitary facilities	SEK 210 - 230
electricity	SEK 35 - 65
dog	SEK 10,00

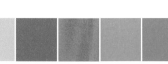

SW2760 Frykenbadens Camping

Frykenbaden, S-665 91 Kil (Värmlands Län)

Tel: **0554 40940**. Email: **frykenbaden@telia.com**

Frykenbaden Camping is in a quiet wooded area on the southern shore of Lake Fryken, taking 200 units on grassy meadows surrounded by trees. One area nearer the lake is gently sloping, the other is flat with numbered pitches arranged in rows, all with electricity (10A). Reception, a good shop, restaurant and takeaway are located in a traditional Swedish house surrounded by lawns sloping down to the shore, with minigolf, a play barn and playground, with pet area also close by. Tables and benches are near the lake, where swimming and canoeing are possible. A good value restaurant is at the adjacent golf club which can be reached by a pleasant walk. Fryken is a long, narrow lake, said to be one of the deepest in Sweden, and it is a centre for angling. Frykenbadens Camping is a quiet, relaxing place to stay, away from the busier and more famous lakes. There are plenty of other activities in the area (golf, riding, ski-ing in winter) and Kil is not too far from the Norwegian border.

Facilities

The main sanitary block is of good quality and heated in cool weather with showers on payment, open washbasins, a laundry room and room for families or disabled people. A further small block has equally good facilities. Well equipped camper's kitchen with ovens, hobs and sinks. Shop. Snack bar, restaurant and takeaway. Minigolf. Children's play barn and playground. Lake swimming. Canoes and bicycles for hire. Off site: Golf 1 km. Go-karts, riding, jogging track 4 km.

Open: All year (full services 19/6-15/8).

Directions

Site is signed from the no. 61 Karlstad - Arvika road, then 4 km. towards lake following signs. GPS: N59:32.775 E13:20.479

Charges guide

Per pitch	SEK 110 - 150
electricity	SEK 40

SW2780 Gustavsvik Camping

Sommarrovägen, S-702 30 Ørebro (Ørebro Län)

Tel: **019 196950**. Email: **camping@gustavsvik.se**

Gustavsvik is one of the most modern and most visited camping and leisure parks in Sweden. It is ideally situated almost half way between Oslo and Stockholm or Gothenburg and Stockholm, at the junction of the E18 and E20 roads. This large campsite provides 720 marked and numbered pitches partly shaded by birch and pine trees, 488 with electrical connections, 440 with cable TV and 56 with water and waste water drainage. There are also three partly shaded areas for tents.The amenities offered by the leisure park include adventure golf, a mini zoo, children's playgrounds, pools and a water slide and a swimming lake, plus a private fishing lake. It is also adjacent one of Europe's largest and most comprehensive swimming complexes. For those looking for shopping and other tourist attractions (for example, the old castle), the town centre of Ørebro is within walking distance. Gustavsvik's golf course is nearby the site and it not far to Marieberg shopping centre with an IKEA branch.

Facilities

Two excellent heated toilet blocks including washbasins with dividers, free hot showers, family rooms, facilities for disabled visitors and children's facilities in each block. Make up rooms. Very well equipped kitchens with free hot water, dishwasher and sinks. Dining area. Washing machine and dryers. Chemical disposal and motorcaravan service points. Shower room for pets. Well stocked shop. Restaurant and pub, fast food and takeaway. TV room and playroom for children. Arcade with games room, internet room. Adventure golf. Tennis. Beach volleyball. Football. Swimming pool with waterslide. Swimming lake. Fishing lake. Mini zoo for children. Bicycle hire. Off site: Adjacent comprehensive pool complex. Golf. Ørebro city centre with its castle. Marieberg shopping centre. Vadköping (old town) and Karlslund manor house and gardens.

Open: 15 April - 6 November (full services 10/6-14/8).

Directions

Site is 1 km. south of Ørebro town centre. Follow signs from E18/E20 or main road 50/51.

Charges guide

Per pitch	SEK 190 - 305

SW2800 Glyttinge Camping

Berggärdsvägen, S-584 37 Linköping (Østergötlands Län)

Tel: 013 174 928

Only five minutes by car from the Ikea Shopping Mall and adjacent to a good swimming pool complex, Glyttinge is a most attractive site with a mix of terrain – some flat, some sloping and some woodland. A top quality site with enthusiastic and friendly management, it is maintained to a very high standard and flowers, trees and shrubs everywhere give it a cosy garden like atmosphere. There are 222 good size, mostly level pitches of which 120 have electricity (10A) and 35 are fully serviced. Children are well catered for – the manager has laid out a wonderful, fenced and very safe children's play area and, in addition, parents can rent (minimal charge) tricycles, pedal cars, scooters and carts.

Facilities

The main, central toilet block is modern and exceptionally well maintained. It has showers in cubicles, washbasin and WC suites and hand dryers. Separate facilities for disabled visitors. Baby rooms. Laundry. Solarium. Kitchen and dining/TV room, fully equipped. Motorcaravan services. Mini-shop (15/6-15/8). Minigolf. Football. Bicycle hire. Playground. Off site: Swimming pool complex adjacent (15/5-25/8). Riding and golf 3 km. Fishing 5 km.

Open: 27 April - 1 October.

Directions

Exit E4 Helsingborg - Stockholm road north of Linköping at signs for Ikea and site. Turn right at traffic lights and camp sign and follow signs to site. GPS: N58:26.282 E15:32.692

Charges guide

Per unit	SEK 140 - 165
electricity	SEK 35

Low season discounts for pensioners.

SW2805 Kolmårdens Camping & Stugby

S-618 34 Kolmården (Østergötlands Län)

Tel: 011 398 250. Email: info@kolmardenscamping.se

This is a family site, open all year, located on Bråviken Bay, south of Stockholm which has been recommended by a reader. We plan to undertake a full inspection during the 2007 season. The site is just 4 km. from Kolmården zoo, one of Sweden's most popular family attractions. There are 320 pitches here, of which 180 have electrical connections (10A). Some pitches have sea views, and there is also a large open area for tents. There are a good range of amenities here including a 120 m. water slide and children's playground. Adjacent to the site is a handicraft village and the Sjöstugans restaurant.

Facilities

Bar and snack bar. Restaurant. Takeaway food. Supermarket. TV room. Sauna. Entertainment and children's activity programme (high season). Direct access to the sea. Waterslide. Play area. Rowing boats. Minigolf. Chalets for rent. Off site: Kolmården zoo 4 km. Stockholm 140 km. Golf 18 km. Riding 2 km.

Open: All year.

Directions

Take the Kolmården exit from the E4 motorway (23 km. north of Norrkoping). The site is well signed from this point.

Charges 2006

Per pitch	SEK 140 - 195
electricity	SEK 35

kawan-villages.com **tel: 00 333 59 59 03 59**

SW2820 Skantzö Bad u. Camping

Box 506, S-737 27 Hallstahammar (Västmanlands Län)

Tel: 0220 24305. Email: skantzo@hallstahammar.se

A very comfortable and pleasant municipal site just off the main E18 motorway from Oslo to Stockholm, this has 200 large marked and numbered pitches, 156 of these with electricity (10A). The terrain is flat and grassy, there is good shade in parts and the site is well fenced. There are 23 alpine style cabins for rent with window boxes of colourful flowers. Reception is very friendly. Direct access to the towpath of the Strömsholms Kanal and nearby is the Kanal Museum.

Facilities

One sanitary block is maintained and equipped to a high standard, including free hot showers (in cubicles with washbasin), facilities for disabled people and baby changing. Another unit has been added at the far end of the site and both are heated. Campers' kitchen. Laundry facilities. Motorcaravan services. Barbecue grill area. Cafeteria and shop (18/5-19/8). Swimming pool and waterslide (19/5 -19/8). Minigolf. Tennis. Playground. Bicycle hire. Fishing. Canoe hire. Off site: Golf 9 km.

Open: 1 May - 30 September.

Directions

Turn off E18 at Hallstahammar and follow road no. 252 to west of town centre and signs to campsite. GPS: N59:36.647 E16:12.925

Charges guide

Per unit	SEK 125 - 155
electricity	SEK 35

SW2825 Camping Herrfallet

S-732 92 Arboga (Västmanlands Län)

Tel: 0589 40110. Email: reception@herrfallet.se

Open all year, Herrfallets Camping is situated on a peninsula, a designated nature reserve, on Lake Hjälmaren, one of Sweden's large lakes. There is a 1 km. long sandy beach on the site and the atmosphere is friendly and 'green'. All the 100 touring pitches have electricity hook-ups (10A) and the area is neatly laid out overlooking the lake where you can hire boats, canoes, pedal boats and go fishing. Fishing is free. You can explore the beautiful and peaceful surroundings by bike which you hire at reception. There are 40 large cottages of an excellent standard and 5 a bit smaller (for 2 people). These are situated close to the beach where you can swim in the clear water.

Facilities

Two sanitary blocks, one basic for the summer season, one new with central heating. Open washbasins, showers (charged). Provision for disabled visitors. Fully equipped kitchen, laundry and ironing facilities. Baby room. Motorcaravan service point. Sauna cottage with shower and relaxing room. Lapland hut (Sami style) for barbecue parties (charged). Shop (peak season). Restaurant and bar. Takeaway. Pedal car, pedal boat, bicycle, canoe and boat hire. Fishing (free). Minigolf. Beach volleyball. Football. Fitness trail. Playground. Internet access. Off site: Arboga 15 km. Julita mansion (old orchard) 30 km. Golf 15 km.

Open: All year (full services 27/5-28/8).

Directions

Follow signs from the E20/E18. Turn off at Sätra exit towards Arboga and cross the river. Follow signs towards Herrfallet/Västermo. 15 km from Arboga. GPS: N59:16.620 E15:54.180

Charges guide

Per pitch	SEK 150 - 220
incl. electricity (10A)	SEK 195 - 265
incl. water and drainage	SEK 195 - 295

SW2842 Bredäng Camping Stockholm

Stora Sällskapets väg, S-127 31 Skärholmen (Stockholms Län)

Tel: 08 977 071. Email: bredangcamping@telia.com

Bredängs is a busy city site, with easy access to Stockhom city centre. Large and fairly level, with very little shade, there are 380 pitches, including 115 with hardstanding and 204 with electricity (10A), and a separate area for tents. Reception is open from 07.00-23.00 in the main season (12/6-20/8), reduced hours in low season, and English is spoken. A Stockholm card is available, or a three-day public transport card. Stockholm has many events and activities, you can take a circular tour on a free sightseeing bus, various boat and bus tours, or view the city from the Kaknäs Tower (155 m). The nearest Metro station is five minute walk, trains run about every ten minutes between 05.00 and 02.00, and the journey takes about twenty minutes. The local shopping centre is five minutes away and a two minute walk through the woods brings you to a very attractive lake and beach.

Facilities

Four heated sanitary units of a high standard provide British style WCs, controllable hot showers, with some washbasins in cubicles. One has a baby room, a unit for disabled people and a first aid room. Cooking and dishwashing facilities are in three units around the site. Laundry facilities. Motorcaravan services and car wash. Shop and fully licensed restaurant (both 1/5-8/9). Sauna. Playground. Bicycle hire. Off site: Fishing 0.5 km.

Open: 15 April - 10 October.

Directions

Site is about 10 km. southwest of city centre. Turn off E4/E20 at Bredängs signpost and follow clearly marked site signs. GPS: N59:17.736 E17:55.389

Charges 2006

Per person	SEK 95 - 100
pitch	SEK 180 - 210
electricity	SEK 40
Discounts for pensioners in low season.	

Attractively located campsite, only 10 km Southwest of Stockholm.
You are very welcome!

Bredäng Camping Stockholm
Stora Sällskapets Väg
12731 Skärholmen, Sweden
Tel. +46 8 97 70 71
Fax +46 8 708 72 62
E-mail: bredangcamping@telia.com
www.camping.se/a04

SW2840 Stockholm Swecamp Flottsbro

Box 1073, S-141 22 Huddinge (Stockholms Län)
Tel: **08 535 327 00**. Email: **info@flottsbro.se**

Flottsbro is a neat, small site with good quality facilities and very good security system (including a night guard), located some 18 km. south of Stockholm. There are 80 large numbered pitches for caravans and motorhomes and a separate unmarked area for tents. Pitches are arranged on level terraces, 52 with electricity (10A), but the site itself is sloping and the restaurant is at the bottom with all the ski facilities and further good sanitary facilities with a sauna. Campers have keys to the barrier and toilet blocks. The site has a small lakeside beach with grass area and a playground. The area is also good for walking, cycling and cross-country skiing.

Facilities	Directions
Two modern sanitary facilities include free showers, a suite for disabled people, baby facilities and a family bathroom. Excellent campers' kitchen with electric cookers and sinks with hot water. Washing machine, dryer (charged for) and sink. Sauna. Shop (high season). Restaurant. Minigolf. Volleyball. Frisbee. Jogging track. Canoe hire. Playground. Off site: Large supermarket and rail station are 10 minutes by car from the site. Golf and riging 15 km. Stockholm 15 km.	Turn off the E4 - E20 at Huddinge onto road no.259. After 2 km. turn right and follow signs to Flottsbro. GPS: N59:13.826 E17:53.291

Charges 2006

Per pitch	SEK 180 - 220
electricity	SEK 40

Open: All year.

SW2836 Mora Parkens Camping

Box 294, S-792 25 Mora (Dalarnas Län)
Tel: **0250 27600**. Email: **moraparken@mora.se**

Mora, at the northern end of Lake Silijan is surrounded by small localities all steeped in history and culture. On the island of Sollerön, south of Mora, is evidence of a large Viking burial ground. Traditional handicrafts are still alive in the region. Travel to Nusnäs, an old village with documents going back to the Middle Ages and see the production of the brightly coloured wooden horse. Every household should have two for luck. Winding country roads lead you through rich farmland to the pretty half timbered houses in Bergkarlås/Vattnås. Mora is lively, friendly and attractive. The campsite which is good for family holidays is only 10 minutes walk from the town. The camping area is large, grassy, open and flat. It is bordered by clumps of trees and a stream. The staff are pleasant and helpful.

Facilities	Directions
Four fully equipped toilet blocks. Campers' kitchen. Laundry. Shop. Restaurant/bar. Sauna. Fishing.Minigolf. Playground. Canoe hire. Internet access. Off site: Swimming pools. Zorn Museum. Orsa Bear Park. Dalhalla (limestone quarry) musical stage. Nusträs.	Follow signs to centre of town. Campsite is clearly signed from the town centre and is next to Zorngården and Zorn museum.

Charges guide

Per pitch with electricity	SEK 185 - 140
tent	SEK 140

Full services mid June - mid August.

Open: All year.

Check real time availability and at-the-gate prices...
www.**alanrogers**.com

SW2845 Svegs Camping

Kyrkogränd 1, S-842 32 Sveg (Jämtlands Län)

Tel: 0680 13025

On the 'Inlandsvägen' route through Sweden, the town centre is only a short walk from this neat, friendly site. Two supermarkets, a café and tourist information office are adjacent. The 80 pitches are in rows, on level grass, divided into bays by tall hedges, and with electricity (10/16A) available to 70. The site has boats, canoes and bicycles for hire, and the river frontage has a barbecue area with covered seating and fishing platforms. Alongside the river with its fountain, and running through the site is a pleasant well lit riverside walk.

Facilities

In the older style, sanitary facilities are functional rather than luxurious, providing stainless steel washing troughs, controllable hot showers with communal changing areas, and a unit for disabled visitors. Although a little short on numbers, facilities will probably suffice at most times as the site is rarely full. Kitchen and dining room with TV. Dishwashing sinks. Washing machine and dryers, and an ironing board (iron on loan from reception). TV room. Minigolf. Canoe, boat and bicycle hire. Fishing.

Open: All year.

Directions

Site is off road 45 behind the tourist information office in Sveg. Site is signed.
GPS: N62:01.964 E14:21.869

Charges guide

Per unit	SEK 130
tent	SEK 90
electricity	SEK 25

SW2850 Østersunds Camping

Krondikesvagen 95, S-831 46 Østersund (Jämtlands Län)

Tel: 063 144 615. Email: ostersundscamping@ostersund.se

Østersund lies on Lake Storsjön, which is Sweden's Loch Ness, with 200 sightings of the monster dating back to 1635, and more recently captured on video in 1996. Also worthy of a visit is the island of Frösön where settlements can be traced back to pre-historic times. This large site has 254 pitches, electricity (10A) and TV socket available on 131, all served by tarmac roads. There are also 41 tarmac hardstandings available, and over 220 cottages, cabins and rooms for rent. Adjacent to the site are the municipal swimming pool complex, a Scandic hotel with restaurant and a Statoil filling station.

Facilities

Toilet facilities are in three units, two including controllable hot showers (on payment) with communal changing areas, suites for disabled people and baby changing. The third has four family bathrooms each containing WC, basin and shower. Two kitchens, each with full cookers, hobs, fridge/freezers and double sinks (all free of charge), and excellent dining rooms. Washing machines, dryers and free drying cabinet. Very good motorhome service point suitable for all types of unit including American RVs. Children's playground. Off site: Østersund, Frösön.

Open: All year.

Directions

Site is south of the town on the road towards Torvalla. Turn by Statoil station and site entrance is immediately on right. It is well signed from around the town. GPS: N63:09.565 E14:40.413

Charges 2006

Per unit incl. electricity	SEK 120 - 185
incl. water and drainage	SEK 230 - 260

SW2853 Snibbens Camping & Stugby och Vandrarhem

Hälledal 527, S-870 16 Ramvik (Västernorrlands Län)

Tel: 061 240 505

Probably you will stop here for one night as you travel the E4 coast road and stay a week. It is a truly beautiful location in the area of 'The High Coast' listed as a World Heritage Site. During high season Snibbens is a busy, popular site but remains quiet and peaceful. Besides 30 bungalows for rent there are 50 touring places, each with a 16A electricity, set amongst delightful scenery on the shores of Lake Mörtsjön. The welcoming owners take you to your adequately sized grass pitch set amongst spacious trees.

Facilities

Excellent, spotlessly clean facilities include controllable showers and partitioned washbasins. Baby changing facilities. Two kitchens with hot plates, microwaves and a mini oven. Laundry room. Small shop (15/6-20/8). Rowing boats and pedaloes for hire. Minigolf. Free fishing for site guests. Youth hostel. Off site: Small supermarket 800 m. Golf 20 km.

Open: 30 April - 15 September.

Directions

Travelling north on the E4 and immediately prior to Höga Kusten bridge (one of the largest in Europe) take road 90 signed Kramfors. Site is directly off road 90 on left in 3 km, well signed.
GPS: N62:47.943 E17:52.188

Charges 2006

Per unit	SEK 140
incl. electricity	SEK 155

sw2855 Flogsta Camping

S-872 80 Kramfors (Västernorrlands Län)

Tel: 0612 10005. Email: flogsta@basterang.se

Kramfors lies just to the west of the E4, and travellers may well pass by over the new Höga Kusten bridge (one of the largest in Europe), and miss this friendly little site. This area of Ådalen and the High Coast, reaches as far as Ørnsköldsvik. The attractive garden-like campsite has 50 pitches, 21 with electrical connections (10A), which are arranged on level grassy terraces, separated by shrubs and trees into bays of 2-4 units. All overlook the heated outdoor public swimming pool complex and attractive minigolf course. The non-electric pitches are on an open terrace nearer reception.

Facilities

Sanitary facilities comprise nine bathrooms, each with British style WC, basin with hand dryer, shower. Laundry facilities. More WCs and showers are in the reception building with a free sauna. A new toilet block has a sauna and outside hot tub. A separate building houses a kitchen, with hot-plates, fridge/freezer and TV/dining room (all free). The reception building has a small shop and snack-bar. Playground. Snowmobile hire. Off site: Fishing 10 km. Golf and riding 15 km.

Open: All year.

Directions

Signed from road 90 in the centre of Kramfors, the site lies to the west in a rural location beyond a housing estate and by the Flogsta Bad, a municipal swimming pool complex.

GPS: N62:55.537 E17:45.385

Charges 2006

Per unit	SEK 125
electricity	SEK 25

sw2857 Strömsund Swecamp

Box 500, S-833 24 Strömsund (Jämtlands Län)

Tel: 0670 16410. Email: stromsund.turism@stromsund.se

A quiet waterside town on the north - south route 45 known as the Inlandsväen, Stromsund is a good place to begin a journey on the Wilderness Way. This is route 342 which heads northwest towards the mountains at Gäddede and the Norwegian border. Being on the confluence of many waterways, there is a wonderful feeling of space and freedom in Stromsund. In the forests there are well marked trails. Walk here alone at midnight on Midsummer's Eve in an intense blue light – nothing moves as the path ahead leads deeper into the dense forest – it is a memorable experience. The campsite is set on a gentle grassy slope backed by forest. Another part of the site, across the road, overlooks the lake. Cabins are set in circular groups of either six or seven. The site is owned by the town council.

Facilities

Excellent facilities include two toilet blocks, one on each side of the road. Both contain showers, toilets, washbasins with dividers and under-floor heating. Facilities for disabled visitors. Laundry. Campers' kitchen with cooking rings, microwave and sinks. Motorcaravan service point. Bicycle, canoe, pedalo and boat hire. Play area. Off site: Municipal pool is next to the site.

Open: All year.

Directions

Site is 700 m. south of Stomsund on route 45.

GPS: N63:50.787 E15:32.023

Charges guide

Per pitch	SEK 120
electricity	SEK 30 - 50
Full services mid June - mid August.	

sw2860 First Camp Umeå

S-906 54 Umeå (Västerbotens Län)

Tel: 090 702 600. Email: umea@firstcamp.se

An ideal stop-over for those travelling the E4 coastal route, or a good base from which to explore the area, this campsite is 6 km. from the centre of this university city. It is almost adjacent to the Nydalsjön lake, which is ideal for fishing, windsurfing and bathing. There are 450 grassy pitches arranged in bays of 10-20 units, 320 with electricity (10A or 16A), and some are fully serviced. Outside the site, adjacent to the lake, are football pitches, an open air swimming pool, minigolf, mini-car driving school, beach volleyball and a mini-farm.

Facilities

The new large, heated, central sanitary unit includes controllable hot showers with communal changing areas. (Facilities stretched in high season). Kitchen. Large dining room. TV. Laundry facilities. Shop (25/5-21/8). Fully licensed restaurant. WiFi. Walk-on chess. Volleyball. Playgrounds. Bicycle hire. Rowing boat hire. Fishing in the lake. Canoes and pedal cars for hire. Adventure golf. Off site: Riding adjacent. Golf 18 km.

Open: All year (full services 25/5-12/8).

Directions

A camping sign on the E4 at a set of traffic lights 5km north of the town directs you to the site. Direction also indicates Holmsund and Vassa.

GPS: N63:50.596 E20:20.432

Charges 2006

Per pitch	SEK 160 - 180
incl. electricity	SEK 200 - 220
Camping Cheques accepted.	

SW2865 Camp Gielas

Järnvägsgatan 111, S-933 34 Arvidsjaur (Norrbottens Län)

Tel: 0960 55600. Email: gielas@arvidsjaur.se

A modern municipal site with excellent sporting facilities on the outskirts of the town, Gielas is well shielded on all sides by trees, providing a very peaceful atmosphere. The 160 pitches, 81 with electricity (10A) and satellite TV connections, are level on sparse grass and accessed by tarmac roadways. The sauna and showers, sporting, gymnasium and Internet facilities at the sports hall are free to campers. Also on site is a snackbar. The lake on the site is suitable for boating, bathing and fishing. There is a swimming pool and a 9-hole golf course nearby, and hunting trips can be arranged.

Facilities

Two modern, heated sanitary units provide controllable hot showers and a unit for disabled visitors. Well equipped kitchens (free). Washing machine and dryer. The unit by the tent area also has facilities for disabled people and baby changing. Snack bar. Tennis courts. Minigolf. Children's playgrounds. Sauna. Sporting facilities. Boat and canoe hire. Pedal Cars. Lake swimming. Fishing. Winter golf course on snow on site. Off site: Golf 200 m. Bowling centre and riding 500 m. Bicycle hire 2 km.

Open: All year.

Directions

Site is on road 95 3 km. south of town centre. GPS: N65:34.955 E19:11.412

Charges 2006

Per unit	SEK 140 - 165

SW2870 Jokkmokks Camping Center

Box 75, S-962 22 Jokkmokk (Norrbottens Län)

Tel: 0971 12370. Email: campingcenter@jokkmokk.com

This attractive site is just 8 km. from the Arctic Circle. Large and well organised, the site is bordered on one side by the river and with woodland on the other, just 3 km. from the town centre. It has 170 level, grassy pitches, with an area for tents, plus 59 cabins for rent. Electricity (10A) is available to all touring pitches. The site has a heated open air pool complex open in summer (no lifeguard). There are opportunities for snow-mobiling, cross-country skiing in spring, or ice fishing in winter. Nearby attractions include the first hydro-electric power station at Porjus, built 1910-15, with free tours between 15/6-15/8, Vuollerim (40 km.) reconstructed 6,000 year old settlement, with excavations of the best preserved Ice Age village, or try visiting for the famous Jokkmokk Winter Market (first Thurs-Sat February) or the less chilly Autumn Market (end of August).

Facilities

Heated sanitary buildings provide mostly open washbasins and controllable showers - some are curtained with a communal changing area, a few are in cubicles with divider and seat. A unit by reception has a baby bathroom, a fully equipped suite for disabled visitors, games room, plus a very well appointed kitchen and launderette. A further unit with WCs, basins, showers plus a steam sauna, is by the pool. Shop, restaurant and bar (in summer). Takeaway (high season). Swimming pools (25 x 10 m. main pool with water slide, two smaller pools and paddling pool). Sauna. Bicycle hire. Children's playground and adventure playground. Minigolf. Football field. Games machines. Free fishing. Off site: Riding 2 km.

Open: All year (for groups on request).

Directions

Site is 3 km. from the centre of Jokkmokk on road 97. GPS: N66:35.698 E19:53.562

Charges guide

Per caravan or motorcaravan	SEK 120 - 150
hiker and small tent	SEK 70
car and small tent	SEK 90
electricity	SEK 30

MAP 1

A small, wealthy country, be known for its outstanding mountainous scenery, fine cheeses, delicious chocolate Swiss bank accounts and enviable lifestyles. Centrally situated in Europe it shares its borde with four countries: France, Austria, Germany and Italy, each one having its own cultural influence on Switzerland.

CAPITAL: BERN

Tourist Office

Switzerland Tourism
Swiss Centre, 10 Wardour Street
London W1D 6QF
Tel: 020 7292 1550 Fax: 020 7292 1599
Email: info.uk@switzerland.com
Internet: www.myswitzerland.com

The landscape of Switzerland boasts mountains, valleys, waterfalls and glaciers. The Bernese Oberland is probably the most visited area, with picturesque villages, lakes and awe inspiring peaks, including the towering Eiger, Mönch and Jungfrau. The highest Alps are those of Valais in the southwest where the small busy resort of Zermatt gives access to the Matterhorn. The southeast of Switzerland has densely forested mountain slopes and the wealthy and glamorous resort of St Moritz. Zurich in the north is a German speaking city with a wealth of sightseeing, particularly in the old town area with its 16th and 17th century houses. Geneva, Montreux and Lausanne on the northern shores of Lake Geneva make up the bulk of French Switzerland, with vineyards that border the lakes and medieval towns. The southernmost canton, Ticino, is home to the Italian speaking Swiss, with the Mediterranean style lakeside resorts of Lugano and Locarno.

Population

7.1 million

Climate

Mild and refreshing in the northern plateau. South of the Alps it is warmer, influenced by the Mediterranean. The Valais is noted for its dryness.

Language

German in central and eastern areas, French in the west and Italian in the south. Raeto-Romansch is spoken in the southeast. English is spoken by many.

Telephone

The country code is 00 41.

Money

Currency: Swiss franc
Banks: Mon-Fri 08.30-16.30. Some close for lunch.

Shops

Mon-Fri 08.00- 12.00 and 14.00- 18.00. Sat 08.00-16.00. Often closed Monday mornings.

Public Holidays

New Year; Good Fri; Easter Mon; Ascension; Whit Mon; National Day 1 Aug; Christmas 25 Dec. Other holidays are observed in individual Cantons.

Motoring

The road network is comprehensive and well planned. An annual road tax is levied on all cars using Swiss motorways and the 'Vignette' windscreen sticker must be purchased at the border (credit cards not accepted), or in advance from the Swiss National Tourist Office, plus a separate one for a towed caravan or trailer.

CH9180 Camping Buchhorn

CH-9320 Arbon (Thurgau)

Tel: 071 446 65 45. Email: info@camping-arbon.ch

This small but clean and pleasant site is directly beside Lake Bodensee in the town's parkland. The site is well shaded but few of the touring pitches are by the water's edge. An overflow field used for tents is next door. There are many static caravans but said to be room for 100 tourists. Pitches are on a mixture of gravel and grass, on flat areas on either side of access roads, most with 6A electricity. Cars may have to parked elsewhere. A railway runs directly along one side but one gets used to the noise from small and infrequent trains. A single set of buildings provide all the site's amenities. There is access for boats from the campsite, but powered craft must be under a certain h.p. (take advice on this from the management). There are splendid views across this large inland sea and interesting boats ply up and down between Constance and Lindau and Bregenz. The town swimming lido in the lake, with a restaurant, is quite close. This is a beautiful area and the site is well placed for touring around Lake Bodensee. The weather can be unsettled in this region. Children under 16 must be accompanied by a parent or guardian.

Facilities

Toilet facilities are clean and modern, and should just about suffice in high season. Washing machine, dryer and drying area. Fridge. Shop (basic supplies, drinks and snacks - all season). General room. Playground. Gates closed 12-14.00 hrs daily. Dogs are not accepted. Off site: Tennis 150 m. Town swimming lido 400 m. Watersports and steamer trips are available on the lake, walks and marked cycle tracks around it. Nature reserve.

Open: April - October.

Directions

On Arbon-Konstanz road 13. From the A1 take the Arbon West exit and head towards the town. Straight on at the lights and turn left just after the town sign. Turn left again and head towards the warehouses. Turn right and the site is straight ahead.

Charges 2006

Per person	CHF 6,50 - 6,75
child (6-16 yrs)	CHF 3,00 - 3,10
pitch incl. car and electricity	CHF 14,50 - 15,00
small tent	CHF 5,50 - 5,70
car	CHF 3,00 - 3,10

CH9420 Camping Manor Farm 1

Manor Farm AG, CH-3800 Interlaken-Thunersee (Bern)

Tel: 033 822 22 64. Email: manorfarm@swisscamps.ch

Manor Farm has been popular with British visitors for many years, as this is one of the traditional touring areas of Switzerland. The flat terrain is divided entirely into 525 individual, numbered pitches which vary considerably both in size (60-100 sq.m.) and price with 10A electricity available and shade in some places. There are 144 equipped with electricity, water, drainage and 55 also have cable TV connections. Reservations are made although you should find space except perhaps in late July/early August, but the best places may then be taken. Around 30% of the pitches are taken by permanent or letting units and there is a tour operator presence. The site lies outside the town on the northern side of the Thuner See, with most of the site between road and lake but with one part on the far side of the road. Interlaken is rather a tourist town but the area is rich in scenery, with innumerable mountain excursions and walks available. The lakes and Jungfrau railway are near at hand. Manor Farm is efficiently and quite formally run, with good English spoken.

Facilities

Six separate toilet blocks are practical, heated and fully equipped. They include free hot water for baths. Twenty private units are for rent. Laundry facilities. Motorcaravan services. Gas supplies. Shop (1/4-15/10). Site-owned restaurant adjoining (1/3-30/11). Snack bar with takeaway (July/Aug). TV room. Playground and paddling pool. Minigolf. Bicycle hire. Sailing and windsurfing school. Lake swimming. Boat hire. Fishing. Daily activity and entertainment programme in high season. Excursions. Off site: Golf 500 m. (handicap card). Riding 3 km. Good area for cycling and walking.

Open: All year.

Directions

Site is 3 km. west of Interlaken along the road running north of the Thuner See towards Thun. Follow signs for 'Camp 1'. From A8 (bypassing Interlaken) take exit 24 marked 'Gunten, Beatenberg', which is a spur road bringing you out close to site. GPS: N46:40.949 E07:49.068

Charges 2006

Per person	CHF 5,00 - 10,00
child (6-15 yrs)	CHF 2,35 - 4,70
pitch	CHF 6,25 - 38,00
electricity (6A)	CHF 3,50 - 4,50

Various discounts for longer stays.

CH9330 TCS Camping Bettlereiche

CH-3770 Gwatt (Bern)

Tel: 033 336 40 67. Email: camping.gwatt@bluewin.ch

Bettlereiche is an ideal site for those who wish to explore this part of the Bernese Oberland and who would enjoy staying on a small site in a quiet area, away from the larger sites and town atmosphere of Interlaken. There are 85 numbered, but unmarked pitches for tourists, most with 4A electricity available, and about the same number of static units. There are hard access roads but cars must be parked away from the pitches. Although there are some trees, there is little shade in the main camping area. Direct access to the lake is available for swimming and boating. The site has a cared for air and the friendly management speak good English. Part of the restaurant is reserved for young people. Some animation in high season.

Facilities

Single, modern, well constructed sanitary block, fully equipped with hot water provided for washbasins in cabins (cold otherwise). Facilities should be adequate in high season. Room for disabled visitors. Washing machine and dryer. Motorcaravan services. Well stocked shop. Restaurant. Lake swimming and boating. Off site: Many cycle tracks.

Open: 1 April - 1st week in October.

Directions

From Berne-Thun-Interlaken autoroute, take exit Thun-Süd for Gwatt and follow signs for Gwatt. Site is signed near town centre to the left. GPS: N46:43.594 E07:37.671

Charges 2006

Per person	CHF 9,10 - 11,10
child (6-16 yrs)	CHF 4,25 - 5,25
caravan or motorcaravan	CHF 16,00 - 21,00
tent	CHF 7,00 - 17,00
electricity	CHF 3,00

CH9360 Camping Grassi

CH-3714 Frutigen (Bern)

Tel: 033 671 11 49. Email: campinggrassi@bluewin.ch

This is a small site with about half the pitches occupied by static caravans, used by their owners for weekends and holidays. The 70 or so places available for tourists are not marked out but it is said that the site is not allowed to become overcrowded. Most places are on level grass with two small terraces at the end of the site. There is little shade but the site is set in a river valley with trees on the hills which enclose the area. Electricity is available for all pitches but long leads may be required in parts. It would make a useful overnight stop en-route for Kandersteg and the railway station where cars can join the train for transportation through the Lotschberg Tunnel to the Rhône Valley and Simplon Pass, or for a longer stay to explore the Bernese Oberland.

Facilities

The well constructed, heated sanitary block is of good quality. Washing machine and dryer. Gas supplies. Motorcaravan services. Rest room with TV. Kiosk (1/6-31/8). Play area and play house. Mountain bike hire and tours. Fishing. Bicycle hire. Off site: Shops and restaurants 10 minutes walk away in village. Riding 2 km. Outdoor and indoor pools, tennis and minigolf in Frutigen. Skiing and walking.

Open: All year.

Directions

Take Kandersteg road from Spiez and leave at Frutigen Dorf exit from where site is signed. GPS: N46:34.925 E07:38.431

Charges 2006

Per person	CHF 6,40
child (1-16 yrs)	CHF 1,50 - 3,20
pitch	CHF 8,00 - 14,00

Camping Grassi Frutigen

Located off the road, alongside the Engstligen Stream, this is the location for the quiet and well equipped site in the summer holiday resort of Frutigen, about 15 km from Spiez, Adelboden and Kandersteg

- Inexhaustible choice of excursions
- Free loan of bicycles, guided mountainbike tours

Winter camping: to skiing resorts of Adelboden, Kandersteg, Elsigenalp, Swiss ski-school, only 10–12 km.

Infos: W. Glausen, CH-3714 Frutigen
Tel. 0041-(0)33 - 671 11 49, Fax 0041-(0)33 - 671 13 80
E-mail: campinggrassi@bluewin.ch
www.camping-grassi.ch

CH9055 TCS Camping Fanel

CH-3236 Gampelen (Bern)

Tel: 032 313 23 33. Email: camping.gampelen@tcs.ch

This Swiss Touring Club site is particularly suited to families with children. From the terrace of a well provisioned self service restaurant there is a view of the small swimming pool and the large grass area that leads to the gently shelving waters of the lake and a small wooden jetty. The site has 900 pitches (150 for tourists) which means that it could become quite busy at weekends and holidays. The level, grass pitches have electricity and some young trees provide shade. This quiet site is located in a protected nature area, a habitat for beavers, wild boar and foxes.

Facilities

Three modern, well maintained toilet blocks with free showers and washbasins in cabins. Facilities for disabled people. Baby room. Laundry room with washing machines and dryers. Motorcaravan service point. Modern, well appointed self service restaurant with takeaway. Shop. Gas supplies. Internet access. Play area. Bicycle hire. Archery.

Open: 1 April - 1 October.

Directions

Site is on the northeastern shore of Lake Neuchatel. From A1 exit 29 (Murten) or exit 30 (Kerzers) travel north towards Neuchatel as far as village of Gampelen where site is well signed. GPS: N47:00.407 E007:02.42

Charges 2006

Per person	CHF 6,60 - 7,60
child	CHF 3,30 - 3,80
pitch	CHF 10,40 - 26,00
electricity	CHF 3,00 - 4,00

CH9460 Camping Jungfrau

CH-3822 Lauterbrunnen (Bern)

Tel: 033 856 20 10. Email: info@camping-jungfrau.ch

This friendly site has a very imposing situation in a steep valley with a fine view of the Jungfrau at the end. It is a popular site and, although you should usually find space, in season do not arrive too late. A fairly extensive area with grass pitches and hard surfaced access roads. All 391 pitches (250 for touring) have shade in parts, electrical connections (13A) and 50 have water and drainage also. About 30% of the pitches are taken by seasonal caravans and it is used by two tour operators. The von Allmen family own and run the site and provide a warm welcome (English is spoken). You can laze here amid real mountain scenery, though it does lose the sun a little early. There are naturally many more active things to do – mountain walks or climbing, trips up the Jungfrau railway or one of the mountain lifts or excursions by car.

Facilities

Three fully equipped modern sanitary blocks can be heated in winter and also provide facilities for disabled visitors. Baby baths. Laundry facilities. Motorcaravan services. Supermarket. Self-service restaurant with takeaway (May-end Oct). General room with tables and chairs, TV, jukebox, drink machines, amusements. Playgrounds and covered play area. Excursions and some entertainment in high season. Mountain bike hire. Internet point. ATM. Drying room. Ski store. Off site: Free bus to ski station (in winter only).

Open: All year.

Directions

Go through Lauterbrunnen and fork right at far end before road bends left, 100 m. before church. The final approach is not very wide.
GPS: N46:35.284 E07:54.646

Charges 2006

Per person	CHF 8,40 - 9,90
child (6-15 yrs)	CHF 4,20 - 4,90
pitch	CHF 18,00
car	CHF 3,50

Discounts for camping carnet and for stays over 3 nights outside high season.

The ideal, family-friendly campsite that's also been family-run for 50 years, at the foot of the giant Eiger, Mönch and Jungfrau mountains in the valley of the waterfalls. At the centre of the world renowned hiking and skiing areas of the "Jungfrau region". Very modern facilities. Restaurant, grocery shop, children's playground – free ski bus in winter. Sports facilities close by. Specially adapted for motor caravans. Bungalows, caravans, bed/breakfast, winter season sites.

Open the whole year round!

CAMPING JUNGFRAU AG, the von Allmen and Fuchs families, CH-3822 LAUTERBRUNNEN
✆ ++41 (0)33 856 20 10, Fax ++41 (0)33 856 20 20
E-Mail: info@camping-jungfrau.ch, Internet: www.camping-jungfrau.ch

495

CH9410 Camping Stuhlegg

Stueleggstr. 7, CH-3704 Krattigen (Bern)

Tel: 033 654 27 23. Email: campstuhlegg@bluewin.ch

On the outskirts of the village of Krattigen, Camping Stuhlegg is a quiet and attractive site, located well above the lake and with beautiful, wide-ranging views over the lake to the mountains beyond. The 65 touring pitches are arranged on grassy terraced areas, some for motorcaravans having hardstanding. A few young trees provide shade. The friendly bar and bistro is also popular as a meeting point for the villagers, which gives a touch of local colour. This is a site where you can enjoy the fresh mountain air the scenery and relax. The site owner, Herr Schweizer, speaks excellent English. He is only too willing to advise on activities and excursions that can be undertaken in the region. In addition, the Krattigen guest information booklet is available in English and is a wealth of diverse information. Here you can discover where in the village good home Swiss cooking can be tried, what boat, train and bus excursions are available, museums to visit or where the William Tell play, in Swiss German, can be seen.

Facilities

Two modern sanitary facilities, the one near the entrance is heated, the other at the top of the site is for summer use and unheated. They contain all the usual facilities, showers operate with either coins or with tokens. Laundry room. Baby bath. Motorcaravan service point. Shop. Bar (all year) and bistro with takeaway (closed Nov). Swimming pool. TV room. Play area. Internet point. Off site: Plenty of footpaths in the immediate area. Bicycle hire 800 m. Riding, golf and fishing 4 km.

Open: All year.

Directions

Site is almost halfway between Spiez and Interlaken on the southern side of the Thunersee. Leave A8 at exit 20 and follow signs for Krattigen. Site is signed at top of village to the right (north). GPS: N46:39.475 E07:43.076

Charges 2006

Per person	CHF 4,50 - 5,00
child	CHF 2,50 - 3,00
pitch	CHF 10,00 - 16,00
electricity	CHF 4,00

CH9440 Camping Jungfraublick

Gsteigstrasse 80, Matten, CH-3800 Interlaken (Bern)

Tel: 033 822 44 14. Email: info@jungfraublick.ch

The Berner Oberland is one of the most scenic and well known areas of Switzerland with Interlaken probably the best known summer resort. Situated in the village of Matten, Jungfraublick is a delightful, medium sized site with splendid views up the Lauterbrunnen valley to the Jungfrau mountain. The 90 touring pitches 60-75 sq.m. with electricity connections (6A) are in regular rows on level, cut grass. A number of fruit trees adorn but do not offer much shade. The 35 static caravans to one side of the tourist area do not intrude. There is some traffic noise from the main road.

Facilities

Fully equipped sanitary facilities and provision for disabled visitors. Showers are on payment, as is hot water for dishwashing. Washing machines and dryers. Motorcaravan services. Shop for basics (from 1/6). Small swimming pool (12 x 8 m.) open mid-June - end-Aug. according to the weather. Heated rest room with TV and electronic games. Barbecues must be off the ground. Off site: Wilderswil train station 10 minutes walk. Bicycle hire 700 m. Town 1 km. Golf, riding and fishing 4 km.

Open: 1 May - 20 September.

Directions

Take the Lauterbrunnen exit 25 from the N8 motorway, turn towards Interlaken. Site is within 500 m. on left. GPS: N46:40.345 E07:52.058

Charges 2006

Per person	CHF 7,60 - 8,60
child (4-16 yrs)	CHF 3,50 - 4,20
pitch acc. to size and season	CHF 8,00 - 30,00
electricity (6A)	CHF 1,10 - 3,20

CH9480 Camping Gletscherdorf

Gletscherdorf 31, CH-3818 Grindelwald (Bern)
Tel: 033 853 14 29. Email: info@gletscherdorf.ch

Set in a flat river valley on the edge of Grindelwald, one of Switzerland's well known winter and summer resorts, Gletscherdorf enjoys wonderful mountain views, particularly of the nearby north face of the Eiger. The site has 120 pitches, 60 for touring units. Most are marked and have electricity connections (10A), with a few others in an overflow field. There is a good community room with tables and chairs. This is, above all, a very quiet, friendly site for those who wish to enjoy the peaceful mountain air, walking, climbing and exploring with a mountain climbing school in Grindelwald.

Facilities

Excellent small, heated, fully equipped, sanitary block. Washing machines and dryer. Motorcaravan services. Gas supplies. Small shop for basic food items. Torches useful. Dogs are not accepted. Off site: Bicycle hire or golf 1 km. Indoor pool 1 km. Town shops and restaurants within walking distance.

Open: 1 May - 20 October.

Directions

To reach site, go into town and turn right at camp signs after town centre; approach road is quite narrow and steep down hill but there is an easier departure road. GPS: N46:37.264 E08:02.718

Charges 2007

Per person	CHF 7,50
child (6-15 yrs)	CHF 3,50
pitch	CHF 6,00 - 17,00
electricity	CHF 3,50 - 4,00

CH9450 TCS Camping Seeblick

Campingstrasse 14, CH-9450 Bonigen (Bern)
Tel: 033 822 1143. Email: camping.boenigen@tcs.ch

This small, quiet site, bordered on two sides by Lake Brienz, is only 1.5 kilometres from the centre of Interlaken and the autoroute exit. It is therefore a useful site, not only to spend time on and enjoy the views, but also as an ideal base to tour this picturesque region, dominated by the Eiger and Jungfrau mountains. Almost all the 107 pitches are available for tourists. On level grassy ground and under tall trees, all have electricity. With magnificent views over the lake, gates give direct access to a footpath and to the lake shores. Interlaken is a tourist centre in the Berner Oberland, a region that has a great deal to offer, from sky diving to leisurely boat or train excursions. It pays to spend some time looking through the many tourist brochures available in reception and talking to the site manager Herr Krahenbiihl to find activities and places to visit that particularly attract you. This is a region that has something for everyone.

Facilities

A well maintained, modern sanitary block has free showers and some washbasins in cabins. Facilities for disabled people. Baby room. Washing machine and dryer. Motorcaravan service point. Small shop sells gas and provides essentials. Informal bar and snack bar with takeaway food. Small solar heated swimming pool, and paddling pool. Play area.

Open: 31 March - 1 October.

Directions

Site is beside the Brienzer See in the eastern suburbs of Interlaken. From A8 take exit 26 (Interlaken Ost) and follow signs for Bönigen and then site signs. GPS: N46:41.480 E007:53.61

Charges 2006

Per person	CHF 5,60 - 7,40
child	CHF 2,80 - 3,70
pitch	CHF 17,00 - 20,00
electricity	CHF 4,00

CH9510 Camping Aaregg

Seestrasse 26, CH-3855 Brienz am See (Bern)

Tel: 033 951 18 43. Email: mail@aaregg.ch

Brienz in the Bernese Oberland is a delightful little town on the lake of the same name and the centre of the Swiss wood carving industry. Camping Aaregg is an excellent site situated on the southern shores of the lake with splendid views across the water to the mountains. There are 60 static caravans occupying their own area and 240 tourist pitches, all with electricity (10A). Of these, 16 are larger with hardstandings, water and drainage also and many of these have good lake views. Pitches fronting the lake have a surcharge. The trees and flowers make an attractive and peaceful environment. An excellent base from which to explore the many attractions of this scenic region, and is a useful night stop when passing from Interlaken to Luzern. Nearby at Ballenberg is the fascinating Freilichtmuseum, a very large open-air park of old Swiss houses which have been brought from all over Switzerland and re-erected in groups. Traditional Swiss crafts are demonstrated in some of these.

Facilities

New very attractive sanitary facilities built and maintained to first class standards. Showers with washbasins. Washbasins (open style and in cubicles). Children's section. Family shower rooms. Baby changing room. Facilities for disabled visitors. Laundry facilities and dishwashing room. Motorcaravan services. Pleasant restaurant with terrace and takeaway in season. Play area. English is spoken.

Open: 1 April - 31 October.

Directions

Site is on road B6 on the east of Brienz. Entrance between BP and Esso filling stations, well signed. From the Interlaken-Luzern motorway, take Brienz exit and turn towards Brienz, site then on the left.

Charges 2006

Per person	CHF 9,00
child (6-16 yrs)	CHF 4,50
pitch incl. electricity	CHF 14,00 - 22,00

Low season less 10%.

CH9500 Camping Hofstatt-Derfli

CH-9500 Hasliberg Goldern (Bern)

Tel: 033 971 37 07. Email: welcome@derfli.ch

This attractive new site has been created by a goldsmith and her husband. Small and family run, with 45 pitches, it is in a quiet location, over 1,000 metres high at the end of a small village in the Berner Oberland. One innovation is the one metre high mushrooms – with their white dotted red tops they are difficult to miss. They provide the electrical supply points for the 35 touring pitches and site lighting. The grass pitches are level, some with gravel hardstanding for motorcaravans and the gently sloping site is partly surrounded by trees with mountain top views across the valley.

Facilities

Well maintained, all the year round, sanitary facilities are housed in the main building. Showers controllable and free, some washbasins in cabins. Facilities for disabled people. Baby areas. Kitchen to rent in community room. Laundry facilities. Motorcaravan service point, Small shop. Play area. Bicycle hire. Ski and snowboard room, ski lifts at 1.5 and 2 km. Off site: Shop and restaurant 300 meters in village. Lots of scenic walking in the region.

Open: 15 May - 31 Oct. and 15 Dec. - 30 April.

Directions

Site is 25 km. east-northeast of Interlaken. From A8 exit 30 (Unterbach) follow signs for Luzern and Brünig Pass. At the top Brünig Pass follow signs for Hasliberg (you may spot a dwarf on a swing). Head towards Hasliberg Goldern. Site signed at end of village on the right. GPS: N46:43.231 E08:11.757

Charges 2006

Per person	CHF 7,00 - 8,00
pitch	CHF 8,00 - 18,00
electricity per kWh	CHF 0,50

CH9570 Camping Eienwäldli

Wasserfallstraße 108, CH-6390 Engelberg (Unterwalden)

Tel: 041 6371949. Email: info@eienwaeldli.ch

This super site has facilities which must make it one of the best in Switzerland. It is situated in a beautiful location 3,500 feet above sea level, surrounded by mountains on the edge of the delightful village of Engelberg. Half of the site is taken up by static caravans which are grouped together at one side. The camping area is in two parts – nearest the entrance there are 57 hardstandings for caravans and motorcaravans, all with electricity (metered) and beyond this is a flat meadow for about 70 tents. The reception building houses the pool complex, shop, a café/bar and rooms and apartments to rent. There is also a restaurant opposite the entrance. The indoor pool has recently been most imaginatively rebuilt as a Felsenbad spa bath with adventure pool, steam and relaxing grottoes, Kneipp's cure, children's pool with water slides, solarium, Finnish sauna and eucalyptus steam bath (charged for). Being about 35 km. from Luzern by road and with a rail link, it makes a quiet, peaceful base from which to explore the Vierwaldstattersee region, walk in the mountains or just enjoy the scenery. The area is famous as a winter sports region and summer tourist resort.

Facilities

The excellent toilet block, heated in cool weather, has free hot water in washbasins (in cabins) and (on payment) showers. Washing machines and dryers. Shop. Café/bar. Small lounge. Indoor pool complex. Ski facilities. Playground. Torches useful. TV. Internet access. Golf. Off site: Golf driving range and 18-hole course near. Fishing and bicycle hire 1 km. Riding 2 km.

Open: All year.

Directions

From N2 Gotthard motorway, leave at exit 33 'Stans-Sud' and follow signs to Engelberg. Turn right at T-junction on edge of town and follow signs to 'Wasserfall' and site. GPS: N46:48.564 E08:25.42

Charges 2006

Per person	CHF 8,00 - 9,00
child (6-15 yrs)	CHF 4,00 - 4,50
pitch	CHF 12,00 - 14,00
electricity (plus meter)	CHF 2,00

Credit cards accepted (surcharge).

CH9495 Camping Balmweid

Balmweidstrasse 22, CH-3860 Meiringen (Bern)

Tel: 033 971 51 15. Email: Info@camping-meiringen.ch

This good, family run site is peaceful, just south of the village of Meiringen on the route to the Grimsel Pass and Susten Passes. With a backdrop of steep cliffs it has good views of the adjacent mountains and forest-covered slopes. It provides 180 pitches of which 120 are for tourers, 64 with 10A electricity. Whilst this is a good site on which to base a longer stay, it is also useful as an overnight stop en-route to the Grimsel Pass or for a rest having faced the challenges that the Pass has to offer.

Facilities

The excellent and well maintained heated sanitary block in the reception building has WCs, showers and washbasins. Facilities for disabled visitors. Dishwashing area. Washing machines and dryer. Motorcaravan service point. Restaurant and shop. TV Room. Playground. Covered communal grill area. Internet access.

Open: All year.

Directions

From Meiringen the site is well signed to the south. At roundabout turn left and then left again in about 200 m. From Bern and Interlaken just go straight on at the roundabout signed 'Grimsel'.

Charges 2006

Per person	CHF 7,00 - 8,00
child (3-16 yrs)	CHF 1,00 - 4,00

CH9110 TCS Camping Seeland

CH-6204 Sempach-Stadt (Luzern)

Tel: 041 460 14 66. Email: camping.sempach@tcs.ch

Lucerne is a very popular city in the centre of Switzerland and Camping Seeland makes a peaceful base from which to visit the town and explore the surrounding countryside or, being a short way from the main N2 Basel - Chiasso motorway, is a convenient night stop if passing through. This neat, tidy site has 200 grass pitches for tourists, all with electricity (6A), a few with gravel hardstanding on either side of hard roads under trees with further places on the perimeter in the open. There are about 235 static caravans. A small river runs through the site with a connecting covered bridge.

Facilities

Three good quality sanitary blocks have the usual facilities including excellent facilities for disabled visitors and a baby room. Washing machine and dryer. Motorcaravan service point. Excellent self-service bar/restaurant with terrace overlooking the play area, lake and surrounding hills. Shop. Children's paddling pool and playground. Fishing. Lakeside beach. Off site: Shops and restaurants in the village. Tennis courts, boat and bicycle hire, minigolf and golf club. Hot air ballooning, river rafting and archery can be arranged. Windsurfing school nearby.

Open: 31 March - 1 October.

Directions

From the N2 take exit 21 for Sempach and follow signs for Sempach and site.
GPS: N47:07.529 E08:11.397

Charges 2006

Per person	CHF 6,20 - 8,00
child (6-15 yrs)	CHF 3,10 - 4,00
caravan or motorcaravan	CHF 16,00 - 30,00
small tent	CHF 8,00 - 10,00
electricity	CHF 4,00
Camping Cheques accepted.	

CH9115 TCS Camping Steinibachried

CH-6048 Horw-Luzern (Luzern)

Tel: 041 340 35 58. Email: camping.horw@tcs.ch

Situated in the southern suburbs of Luzern and with easy autoroute access, this site is a very convenient base for visiting what is quite deservedly a popular tourist area. The level, grassed site provides 100 touring pitches with electricity, separated into rows by trees and hedges. It is dominated by the Pilatus mountains, over 2,000 metres high. The peaks and mountain top restaurants offer fantastic views and can be reached by cable car on the steepest cog railway in the world from Alpnachstad. Access to the lake is over a wooden walkway which passes through a small protected nature area.

Facilities

Single, well maintained toilet block to one end of tourist area. Showers are free, some washbasins in cabins. Facilities for disabled visitors. Baby room. Washing machine and dryer. Motorcaravan service point. Gas supplies. Small shop. Bar with terrace. Convenient self service restaurant with takeaway. New play area.

Open: 31 March - 1 October.

Directions

Site is 4 km. south of Luzern centre and borders the Vierwaldstatter See. Leave motorway 2 at exit 28 Luzern/Horw. Site is signed at roundabout towards Horw-Sud. GPS: N47:00.711 E008:18.66

Charges 2006

Per person	CHF 5,80 - 7,80
child (6-15 yrs)	CHF 2,90 - 3,90
pitch	CHF 15,00 - 20,00
electricity	CHF 3,00 - 4,00

CH9130 Camping Vitznau

CH-6354 Vitznau (Luzern)

Tel: 041 397 12 80. Email: camping-vitznau@bluewin.ch

Camping Vitznau is situated in the small village of the same name, above and overlooking Lake Luzern, with splendid views across the water to the mountains on the other side. It is a small, neat and tidy site very close to the delightful village on the narrow, winding, lakeside road. The 120 pitches for caravans or motorhomes (max length 8 m.) have 15A electricity available to most and all have fine views. They are on level, grassy terraces with hard wheel tracks for motorcaravans and separated by tarmac roads. There are separate places for tents.

Facilities	Directions
The single, well constructed sanitary block provides free hot showers (water heated by solar panels). Laundry and dishwashing facilities. Gas supplies. Motorcaravan services. Shop. General room for wet weather. Games room. Small heated swimming pool and children's splash pool (1/5-30/9). Off site: Restaurants five minutes walk. Fishing or bicycle hire within 1 km. Watersports. Golf 15 km.	Site is signed from the centre of Vitznau. GPS: N47:00.403 E08:29.174

Open: 1 April - 31 October.

Charges 2006

Per person	CHF 8,00 - 10,00
child (4-13 yrs)	CHF 4,00 - 5,00
pitch acc. to size and season	CHF 15,00 - 30,00
dog	CHF 3,00
electricity	CHF 4,00

CH9820 Camping Pradafenz

Girabadaweg 34, CH-7075 Churwalden (Graubünden)

Tel: 081 382 19 21. Email: camping@pradafenz.ch

In the heart of the village of Churwalden on the Chur - St Moritz road, Pradafenz makes a convenient night stop and being amidst the mountains, is also an excellent base for walking and exploring this scenic area. At first sight, this appears to be a site for static holiday caravans but three large rectangular terraces at the front take 50 touring units. This area has a hardstanding of concrete frets with grass growing through and 'super-pitch' facilities of electricity (10A), drainage, gas and TV sockets. A flat meadow is also available for tents or as an over-flow for caravans.

Facilities	Directions
The main sanitary block is half underground, well appointed and heated. It includes some washbasins in cabins. Baby room. Another good, heated small block is in the tourist section. Laundry facilities. Motorcaravan services. Gas supplies. Small restaurant also selling basics. Bicycle hire. Fishing. Torches useful. Off site: Restaurants and shops 300 m. in village. Municipal outdoor pool 500 m. Riding 3.5 km. Golf 5 km.	From Chur take road towards Lenzerheide. It is initially a fairly long, steep climb with one tight hairpin. In centre of Churwalden turn right in front of the tourist office towards the site.

Open: 29 May - 31 October and 15 December - 19 April.

Charges 2006

Per person	CHF 7,00 - 7,50
child (2-16 yrs)	CHF 4,50 - 4,80
pitch incl. electricity	CHF 12,50 - 18,00

CH9830 Camping Sur En

CH-7554 Sur En / Sent (Graubünden)

Tel: 081 866 35 44. Email: wb@bluewin.ch

Sur-En is at the eastern end of the Engadine valley, about 10 km. from the Italian and Austrian borders. The area is, perhaps, better known as a skiing region, but has summer attractions as well. This level site is in an open valley with little shade. They say there is room for 120 touring units on the meadows where pitches are neither marked nor numbered; there are electricity connections for all. As you approach on road 27 and spot the site way below under the shadow of a steeply rising, wooded mountain, the drop may appear daunting. However, as you drive it becomes reasonable.

Facilities	Directions
The modern, heated sanitary block is good with some extra facilities in the main building. Washing machine and dryer. Motorcaravan services. Shop and good restaurant (15/12-15/4 and 1/5-31/10) with covered terrace. Takeaway (high season). Swimming pool (1/6-15/10). Bicycle hire. Fishing. Entertainment in July/Aug. A symposium for sculptors is held during the second week in July. Excursions arranged in high season. Off site: Golf 8 km. Bus service to Scuol for train to St Moritz.	From Zernez on road 27 go straight over at roundabout at Scuol, then down hill. Ignore site at bottom and keep driving east. Note Sent village high above and a small lake in the valley below. After 250 m. turn right (Sur-En). Road is a steady, winding descent. Cross timber bridge (3.8 m.) to site. GPS: N46:49.06 E10:21.57

Open: All year.

Charges 2006

Per person	CHF 5,00 - 5,80
child (6-16 yrs)	CHF 2,50 - 2,90
pitch incl. electricity	CHF 13,90 - 17,80

CH9850 TCS Camping Neue Ganda

CH-7302 Landquart (Graubünden)

Tel: 081 322 39 55. Email: camping.landquart@tcs.ch

Situated close to the Klosters, Davos road and the nearby town of Landquart, this valley campsite provides a comfortable night-stop near the A13 motorway. The 80 tourist pitches are not marked or separated but are all on level grass off a central tarmac road through the long, narrow wooded site. All pitches have 6/10A electricity. The many static caravans are mostly hidden from view situated in small alcoves. A modern, timber cladded building at the entrance houses all the necessary facilities – reception, community room and sanitary facilities. The restaurant/shop adjacent is open all the year.

Facilities

The toilet block is extremely well appointed and can be heated. Facilities for disabled visitors. Baby room. Washing machine and dryer. Drying room. Motorcaravan services. Restaurant. Shop. Internet access. Off site: Tennis, riding and canoeing nearby.

Open: 6 April - 23 October, 19 December - 20 March.

Directions

From A13 motorway take Landquart exit and follow road to Davos. After crossing large bridge, go down slip-road before petrol station where site is signed on right. At the bottom turn left under road and right towards site. GPS: N46:58.14 E09:35.36

Charges guide

Per person	CHF 5,00 - 6,20
child	CHF 2,50 - 3,10
pitch incl. electricity	CHF 19,00 - 21,00
Camping Cheques accepted.	

CH9855 Camping Cavresc

CH-7746 Le Prese (Graubünden)

Tel: 081 844 07 97. Email: camping.cavresc@bleuwin.ch

Le Prese is on the Tirano to St Moritz road, south of the Bernina Pass. Camping Cavresc is on grassy meadows in the Valposchiano valley and, with its southern climate, peaceful ambience and beautiful views, is a very good, newly built site with ultramodern sanitary facilities. There are 30 flat, level pitches, all with 10A electricity and water, plus a large area for tents. There is no shade. If the campsite reception is unmanned, walk back into town, as the Sertori family who own the site also run the small well-stocked supermarket. Le Prese is close to Italy and the Poschiavo Lake.

Facilities

The excellent toilet block is very well maintained. Showers on payment. Facilities for disabled visitors. Washing machine and dryer. Motorcaravan services. Restaurant/bar. Small shop. Swimming pool (high season). Off site: Le Prese 250 m. Windsurfing and sailing and of course skiing.

Open: All year.

Directions

Coming from Italy on road no. 29, the site is towards the end of the town. Turn right towards Pagnoncini and Cantone and site is on right in about 100 m. Go over a humpback bridge at the entrance. GPS: N46:17.33 E10:04.51

Charges 2006

Per person	CHF 10,00 - 12,00
child (6-16 yrs)	CHF 4,00 - 6,00
pitch incl. electricity	CHF 10,00 - 19,00

CH9860 Camping Plauns

Morteratsch, CH-7504 Pontresina (Graubünden)

Tel: 081 842 62 85. Email: plauns@bluewin.ch

This is a mountain site in splendid scenery near St Moritz. Pontrasina is at the mouth of the Bernina Pass road (B29) which runs from Celerina in the Swiss Engadine to Titana in Italy. Camping Plauns, some 4 km. southeast of Pontresina, is situated in the valley between fir-clad mountains at 1,850 m. above sea level. There are about 250 pitches for tourists in summer, all with electricity, some in small clearings amongst trees and some in a larger open space. In winter the number is reduced to 40.

Facilities

Three fully equipped toilet blocks, one old and two new, modern and excellent, and can be heated in cool weather. Some washbasins in private cabins and showers on payment. Facilities for disabled visitors. Washing machines, dryers and drying room. Well stocked shop. Grill-snack bar for drinks or simple meals. TV room. Internet access. Bicycle hire. Playground. Torch useful. Off site: Restaurant 1 km. Entertainment programme offered, winter and summer, at nearby Pontresina.

Open: 1 June - 15 October, 15 December - 15 April.

Directions

Site is on B29, the road to Tirano and Bernina Pass, about 4 km. southeast of Pontresina, well signed. GPS: N46:27.42 E09:56.04

Charges 2006

Per person	CHF 8,50
child (6-15 yrs)	CHF 4,00 - 5,50
pitch	CHF 5,00 - 15,00
electricity	CHF 3,00 - 4,50

CH9865 TCS Camping Fontanivas

CH-7180 Disentis (Graubünden)

Tel: 081 947 44 22. Email: camping.disentis@tcs.ch

Nestled in the Surselva valley with superb views the campsite with its own lake is also appealing. Surrounded by tall pine trees, the site is owned by the Touring Club of Switzerland, the Swiss version of the AA, and provides flat, level pitches, all with 6A electricity. There are plenty of opportunities for walks, nature trails and cycle rides, whilst the more adventurous can enjoy themselves canyoning, rafting, hang-gliding or mountain biking. The Medelser Rhine near Disentis is known to be the richest place in gold in the country.

Facilities

The excellent sanitary block is well maintained with free showers for all and a hairdryer for the ladies. Facilities for disabled visitors. Baby room. Washing machine and dryer. Motorcaravan services. Shop. Restaurant/bar. Caravans and tent bungalows to rent. Off site: Disentis 700 m. Indoor pool. Fishing.

Open: End April - end September.

Directions

From Andermatt take the Oberalppass to Disentis. Go through the town and at T-junction turn left towards Lukmanier. Go down the hill (past drooping power cables) and turn left into site.

Charges 2006

Per person	CHF 5,00 - 6,00
child (6-15 yrs)	CHF 2,50 - 3,00
pitch incl. electricity	CHF 9,60 - 20,80

Camping Cheques accepted.

CH9160 TCS Camping Rheinwiesen

CH-8246 Langwiesen (Schaffhausen)

Tel: 052 659 3300. Email: camping.schaffhausen@tcs.ch

Rheinwiesen is a friendly site in a very pleasant setting on the banks of the Rhine, with some tall trees, amongst which are some attractive willows. It is level and grassy, the first half quite open and the rest of the touring area wooded, with numbered pitches (mostly small – up to 70 sq.m.), many under tall trees. There are many day visitors in summer as the site is ideally placed for swimming, canoeing and diving in the Rhine. Dogs are not accepted at any time. Whilst here, you would not want to miss the impressive waterfalls at Schaffhausen, 150 m. wide and 25 m. high.

Facilities

For tourers, there is an old but clean building which might be under pressure at the busiest times. Washing machine and dryer. Two very deep, large waste collectors. Bar/snack bar with covered terrace for burgers etc. open daily. Bread to order, some essentials kept. Pool room also used as wet weather rest room. Two shallow open air paddling pools, with play area close by. Table tennis, table football. Off site: Shop 500 m.

Open: 27 April - 29 September.

Directions

From Schaffhausen head east towards Kreuzlingen (road no. 14) for approx. 2.5 km. Site is signed just before Langwiesen. If coming from the east, it is a tight turn into the site. GPS: N47:41.240 E08:39.35

Charges guide

Per person	CHF 5,00 - 6,80
child (6-16yrs)	CHF 2,50 - 3,40
pitch	CHF 13,20 - 18,00
small tent	CHF 6,60 - 8,60

Camping Cheques accepted.

CH9175 Camping Giessenpark

CH-7310 Bad Ragaz (St Gallen)

Tel: 081 302 37 10

The luxury spa resort of Bad Ragaz nestles in the Rhine valley and Giessenpark surrounds this site, which is located in a forest. There are 86 flat, level gravel pitches of which 52 are for touring, all with access to electricity (10A). The Rhine and the extensive park are within a minutes walk and add to the peaceful nature of the site. The local authority swimming pool is nearby, which is open from mid May to mid September. There is also a children's pool in a large play area about 200 m. from the site.

Facilities

Good, modern toilet is well maintained with free showers. Facilities for disabled visitors. Baby room. Sinks with hot water for laundry and dishwashing. Washing machine and dryer. Motorcaravan services. Shop (limited). Restaurant. Off site: Bad Ragaz 1 km.

Open: All year.

Directions

From the A13 take Bad Ragaz exit and turn towards the town. At roundabout bear right and go through a golf course. Pass Spa supermarket, over small bridge and turn right immediately, then right again towards the site.

Charges guide

Per person	CHF 7,00
child (3-12 yrs)	CHF 3,00
pitch	CHF 6,00 - 10,00
with electricity	CHF 15,00

CH9185 Camping Fischerhaus

Promenadenstraße 52, CH-8280 Kreuzlingen (Thurgau)

Tel: **071 688 49 03**. Email: **fischerhaus@swisscamps.ch**

Camping Fischerhaus is tucked behind the town's light industrial estate and next to Lake Constance. It provides 250 pitches of which 150 are for tourers, all with 10A electricity supply. The seasonal pitches are grouped together near reception and the lakeside, although from the site it is hardly visible. The touring pitches are grass, level and located towards the back of the site, a short walk from the main sanitary block. The town of Kreuzlingen is a short walk away along the banks of the lake past a marina.

Facilities

The main sanitary block, near reception, has WCs, showers and facilities for disabled visitors. The second block, near the area used by tourers, just has WCs. Good dishwashing area. Washing machines and dryer. Chemical disposal point. Small shop for basics. Restaurant and bar. Playground. Fishing. Dogs are not accepted. Off site: The adjoining swimming pool is no longer free to campers.

Open: 31 March - 28 October.

Directions

Site is at the east side of Kreuzlingen on the banks of Lake Constance. It is well signed from all directions as is the adjoining swimming pool.

Charges 2006

Per person	CHF 9,00
child (3-15 yrs)	CHF 4,50
tent	CHF 6,00 - 12,00
caravan or motorcaravan	CHF 10,00 - 15,00
car	CHF 4,50

Camping Fischerhaus, CH-8280 Kreuzlingen

Kreuzlingen

Information & brochures:
Tel: 0041(0)71 688 49 03

Camping Fischerhaus – an
oasis of relaxation
in a unique location

www.kreuzlingen.ch/camping

CH9180 Camping Buchhorn

CH-9320 Arbon (Thurgau)

Tel: **071 446 65 45**. Email: **info@camping-arbon.ch**

This small but clean and pleasant site is directly beside Lake Bodensee in the town's parkland. The site is well shaded but few of the touring pitches are by the water's edge. An overflow field used for tents is next door. There are many static caravans but said to be room for 100 tourists. Pitches are on a mixture of gravel and grass, on flat areas on either side of access roads, most with 6A electricity. Cars may have to parked elsewhere. A railway runs directly along one side but one gets used to the noise from small and infrequent trains. A single set of buildings provide all the site's amenities.

Facilities

Toilet facilities are clean and modern, and should just about suffice in high season. Washing machine, dryer and drying area. Fridge. Shop (basic supplies, drinks and snacks - all season). General room. Playground. Gates closed 12-14.00 hrs daily. Dogs are not accepted. Off site: Tennis 150 m. Town swimming lido 400 m. Watersports and steamer trips are available on the lake, walks and marked cycle tracks around it. Nature reserve.

Open: April - October.

Directions

On Arbon-Konstanz road 13. From the A1 take the Arbon West exit and head towards the town. Straight on at the lights and turn left just after the town sign. Turn left again and head towards the warehouses. Turn right and the site is straight ahead.

Charges 2006

Per person	CHF 6,50 - 6,75
child (6-16 yrs)	CHF 3,00 - 3,10
pitch incl. car and electricity	CHF 14,50 - 15,00
small tent	CHF 5,50 - 5,70
car	CHF 3,00 - 3,10

CH9010 TCS Camping Zum Muttenhof

Glutzenhopstr. 1, CH-4500 Solothurn (Solothurn)

Tel: 032 621 8935. Email: camping.solothurn@tcs.ch

The Swiss Camping Club site is like many in their ownership with excellent facilities and pleasant location. There are 166 level, grass pitches including 116 for touring units, all with electricity and 12 also have water and drainage. A small marina adjoining the site is under the same ownership. The site is close to the large town of Solothurn, on the banks of the Aare. Although it is behind the town's football stadium and close to some high-rise flats, there are pleasant views of the local hills.

Facilities

Two extremely well maintained sanitary blocks. Dishwashing area. Washing machines and dryer. Chemical disposal point. Motorcaravan service point. Small shop for basics. Restaurant overlooking marina. Playground. Small, unheated children's pool. Internet access. Off site: Large municipal swimming pool 200 m. Solothurn and the River Aare. The stork colony at Altreu.

Open: 1 March - 3 January.

Directions

Site is on the western outskirts of Solothurn. From A5 motorway at Solothurn Sud take exit 32 and follow sign for Solothurn, then Zentrum then Biel. Site on Soloturn-Biel road near football stadium.

Charges 2006

Per person	CHF 6,00 - 7,60
child (6-15 yrs)	CHF 3,00 - 3,80
tent or caravan	CHF 16,00 - 21,00
motorhome	CHF 22,00 - 25,00
electricity	CHF 4,00

Camping Cheques accepted.

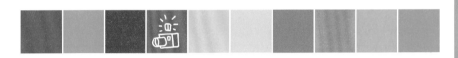

CH9000 Camping Waldhort

Heideweg 16, CH-4153 Reinach bei Basel (Basel-Land)

Tel: 061 711 64 29. Email: camp.waldhort@gmx.ch

This is a satisfactory site for night halts or for visits to Basel. Although there are almost twice as many static caravan pitches as spaces for tourists, this site, on the edge of a residential district, is within easy reach of the city by tram. It is flat, with 210 level pitches on grass with access from the tarmac road which circles round inside the site. Trees are now maturing to give some shade. All pitches have electricity (10A). Owned and run by the Camping and Caravanning Club of Basel, it is neat, tidy and orderly and there is usually space available. An extra, separate camping area has been added behind the tennis club which has pleasant pitches and good sanitary facilities.

Facilities

The good quality, fully equipped, central sanitary block includes facilities for babies and disabled people. Washing machine and dryer. Kitchen with gas rings. Fridge for ice packs. Motorcaravan services. Small shop with terrace for drinks. Children's playground with two small pools. Table tennis. Swimming pool and tennis next to site.

Open: 1 March - 28 October.

Directions

Take Basel - Delémont motorway spur, exit at 'Reinach-Nord' and follow camp signs. GPS: N47:29.954 E07:36.119

Charges 2006

Per person	CHF 8,00
child (6-14 yrs)	CHF 4,50
tent	CHF 11,00
caravan or motorcaravan	CHF 18,00

Electricity included.

CH9880 Camping Lido Mappo

Via Mappo, CH-6598 Tenero (Ticino)
Tel: 091 745 14 37. Email: camping@lidomappo.ch

Lido Mappo lies on the lakeside at the northeast tip of Lake Maggiore, about 5 km. from Locarno, and has views of the surrounding mountains and hills across the lake. The site is attractively laid out in rows of individual, numbered pitches, half for tents and half for caravans and mostly split up by access roads or hedges. The pitches (418 for touring) vary in size, those by the lake costing more and most are well shaded. Electricity (10A) is available on all pitches. With helpful English speaking staff, this is a quiet site with its own narrow, mainly sandy beach. Boats can be brought and left on the shore or at moorings; a jetty has been constructed for these.

Facilities

The five, recently renovated toilet blocks can be heated in cool weather and are well kept. They include individual washbasins, all in cabins for women and some for men. Facilities for disabled people. Baby room. Laundry facilities. Cooking facilities. Refrigerated compartments for hire. Motorcaravan services. Supermarket. Restaurant/bar. Takeaway. TV room. Large playground. Lake swimmming. Fishing. First-aid post. Dogs are not accepted. Off site: Bicycle hire. Riding 3 km. Golf 5 km.

Open: 18 March - 23 October.

Directions

On Bellinzona - Locarno road 13, exit Tereno site is signed at roundabout. GPS: N46:10.625 E08:50.570

Charges 2006

Per unit incl. 2 persons and electricity	CHF 34,00 - 49,00
lakeside pitch incl. 2 persons and electricity	CHF 44,00 - 75,00
Less 5% for stays over 10 days and 10% over 21 days.	

CH9950 TCS Camping Piodella

CH-6933 Muzzano (Ticino)
Tel: 091 994 77 88. Email: camping.muzzano@tcs.ch

This modernised site, on the edge of Lake Lugano facing south down the lake must rank as one of the best in Switzerland. There are 265 numbered pitches (212 for touring units) all with 10A electricity and 26 with water connections. There is shade in the older part nearest the lake and young trees in the new area. Cars must be parked in the car park, not by your pitch. The site is a short way from the airport so there may be some aircraft noise. Well placed for exploring Lugano, southern Switzerland and northern Italy, or simply to enjoy the facilities of the site.

Facilities

The original refurbished toilet block and a splendid new one which includes a baby room and a bathroom for disabled visitors, are heated in cool weather. Washing machines and dryers. Motorcaravan services. Gas supplies. Shop. Bar/restaurant with pleasant terrace. Swimming pools (May - mid Oct). Day and TV rooms. Playground. Two tennis courts. Marina. Off site: Bicycle hire 2 km. Riding 4 km. Golf 5 km.

Open: All year excl. 24 October - 10 December.

Directions

Piodella is on Bellinzona-Ponte Tresa road; take motorway exit 49 Lugano-Nord for Ponte Tresa and turn left at T-junction in Agno. Follow signs for Piodella or TCS at roundabout. Site is at south end of the airport. GPS: N45:59.755 E08:54.503

Charges 2006

Per person	CHF 7,20 - 9,20
pitch	CHF 18,00 - 37,50
electricity	CHF 4,50

CH9890 Camping Campofelice

Via alle Brere 7, CH-6598 Tenero (Ticino)
Tel: 091 745 1417

The largest site in Switzerland, it is bordered on the front by Lake Maggiore and on one side by the Verzasca estuary, where the site has its own harbour. Campofelice is divided into rows, with 1,030 individual pitches of average size on flat grass on either side of hard access roads. Mostly well shaded, all pitches have electricity (10A) and some also have water, drainage and TV connections. Pitches near the lake cost more (not available for motorcaravans). A special area is reserved for small tents. English is spoken at this good, if rather expensive site. Member of Leading Campings Group.

Facilities

The six heated toilet blocks are of excellent quality. Washing machines and dryers. Motorcaravan services. Gas supplies. Supermarket. Restaurant. Tennis. Minigolf. Bicycle hire. Playground. Doctor calls. Dogs are not accepted Off site: Fishing 500 m. Waterskiing and windsurfing 1 km. Boat hire 5 km. Riding 6 km. Golf 8 km.

Open: 31 March - 27 October.

Directions

On the Bellinzona-Locarno road 13, exit Tereno. Site is signed at roundabout. GPS: N46:10.114 E08:51.355

Charges 2006

Per unit incl. 2 persons	CHF 38,00 - 84,00
Some pitches have min. stay regulations.	

CH9970 TCS Camping Parco al Sole

CH-6866 Meride (Ticino)

Tel: **091 646 43 30**. Email: **camping.meride@tcs.ch**

Meride is a small village in the extreme south of Switzerland with the Italian border close on three sides. A little remote, Parco al Sole is on a slight slope 1 km. before the village, with mountain views. There is space for 64 small units, with electricity connections available for 40, and 16 static caravans. The pitches are not numbered or marked out and caravans are placed between tall trees or on an open space. When the site is busy units could be crowded. Cars are parked near the entrance. Parco al Sole is better for a few days stay to explore the area rather than as a single night stop.

Facilities

A good quality sanitary block with the usual facilities, free hot water and a baby room. 'Grotto Cafe' with a log fire during cool weather where drinks and simple meals are offered and limited basic food supplies can be obtained. H.heated swimming pool (1/61-30/8) and paddling pool. Playground. Some animation is organised in high season. TV and videos (in café).

Open: 1 May - 25 September.

Directions

From N2 motorway take exit 52 for Mendrisio towards Stabio, Varese. Head to Rancate then Basazio, Arzo and Meride. Site signed (about 6 km. from motorway exit). Road to site is narrow. Any problems follow signs for camping Serpiano until village of Meride. GPS: N45:53.332 E08:56.93

Charges 2006

Per person	CHF 6,20 - 7,80
caravan or tent	CHF 13,30 - 17,60
motorcaravan	CHF 17,20 - 21,60
electricity	CHF 3,00
Camping Cheques accepted.	

CH9520 Camping du Botza

Route du Camping 1, CH-1963 Vétroz (Valais)

Tel: **027 346 1940**. Email: **info@botza.ch**

Situated in the Rhone Valley at a height of 460 m. and not far from the autoroute, this is a pleasant site with views of the surrounding mountains. It is set in a peaceful wooded location, even though it is close to an industrial zone. There are 128 individual touring pitches, ranging in size (60-130 sq.m.) all with 4A electricity, many with some shade and 25 with water and drainage. Considerable investment has taken place in making the site environmentally friendly with solar power used to heat the pool and sanitary blocks and a large recycling facility. English is spoken. The gates are locked at night.

Facilities

Some private cabins in the heated sanitary block. Washing machines and dryers. Shop. Pizzeria. Swimming pool (15/5-1/9). Playground. Table tennis. Volleyball. Tennis court. Internet access. Off site: Many walks alongside small streams nearby. Good cycle track. Riding 2 km. Golf 8 km. The historic town of Sion is 8 km.

Open: All year.

Directions

From the A9/E62 between Sion and Martigny, take exit 25 Conthey/Vetroz and go south towards 'zone industrial', after 200 m. turn right to 'Camping 9.33 Botza' and follow signs. Site is 2.5 km. from autoroute exit. GPS: N46:12.21 E07:16.44

Charges 2006

Per person	CHF 5,00 - 8,20
pitch incl. electricity	CHF 14,30 - 26,90

CH9600 Camping Rive-Bleue

Bouveret Plage, CH-1897 Bouveret (Valais)

Tel: **024 481 21 61**. Email: **info@camping-rive-bleue.ch**

At the eastern end of Lac Léman with mountain views, the main feature of this site is the very pleasant lakeside lido only a short walk of 300 m. from the site and with free entry for campers. It has an 'Aquaparc' pool with a water toboggan and sunbathing areas, boating facilities with storage for sailboards, canoes, inflatables etc, sailing school, pedaloes for hire. The site has 220 marked pitches on flat grass, half in the centre with 6A electricity, the other half round the perimeter.

Facilities

Two decent toilet blocks have washbasins with cold water in the old block, hot in the new, and pre-set free hot showers. Shop, restaurant by beach (both all season). Bicycle hire. Fishing. Covered area for cooking with electric rings and barbecue. Drying room. Motorcaravan services (Euro-relais; CHF 12).

Open: 1 April - 1 October.

Directions

Leave motorway 5, south of Montreux, at exit 16 (Villeneuve) and follow signs for Evian. Just after passing town sign for Le Bouveret, turn right, north, and follow Aquaparc and site signs. GPS: N46:23.194 E06:51.610

Charges 2006

Per person	CHF 7,90 - 9,70
motorcaravan or caravan	CHF 10,50 - 13,80
tent	CHF 8,60 - 12,50
electricity	CHF 3,50

CH9640 Camping de la Sarvaz

Route de Fully, CH-1913 Saillon (Valais)

Tel: 027 744 13 89. Email: info@sarvaz.ch

The Rhone valley in Valais with its terraced vineyards provides a beautiful setting for this site. Family owned and run, Camping de la Sarvaz provides excellent facilities and would be a good base for relaxing or for the more energetic walking, cycling, climbing or skiing. The site adjoins a restaurant/bar. It has 30 level touring pitches all with electricity, 19 of which have water and drainage. Lovely mountain views surround the site and there are 5 chalets to rent. An inflatable pool is available from May to September. English is spoken.

Facilities

Modern, heated sanitary facilities are of very high standards, very well maintained. Free showers. Additional toilets on the first floor. Facilities for disabled people. Baby room. Washing machine and dryer. Motorcaravan services. Shop (all season). Restaurant/bar (all season, not Mondays and Tuesdays). Volleyball. Good play area. Internet access. Off site: Saillon 2 km. with Thermal centre and spa.

Open: All year excl. 16 November - 15 December.

Directions

From the A9 take exit 23 for Saxon/Saillon. Follow signs to Saillon then turn right towards the site, which is 3 km. from the autoroute exit. GPS: N46:09.593 E07:10.053

Charges 2006

Per person	CHF 8,00
child (6-16 yrs)	CHF 4,00
pitch	CHF 16,00
electricity	CHF 3,30 - 4,40

CH9855 Camping Cavresc

CH-7746 Le Prese (Graubünden)

Tel: 081 844 07 97. Email: camping.cavresc@bleuwin.ch

Le Prese is on the Tirano to St Moritz road, south of the Bernina Pass. Camping Cavresc is on grassy meadows in the Valposchiano valley and, with its southern climate, peaceful ambience and beautiful views, is a very good, newly built site with ultramodern sanitary facilities. There are 30 flat, level pitches, all with 10A electricity and water, plus a large area for tents. There is no shade. If the campsite reception is unmanned, walk back into town, as the Sertori family who own the site also run the small well-stocked supermarket. Le Prese is close to Italy and the Poschiavo Lake.

Facilities

The excellent toilet block is very well maintained. Showers on payment. Facilities for disabled visitors. Washing machine and dryer. Motorcaravan services. Restaurant/bar. Small shop. Swimming pool (high season). Off site: Le Prese 250 m. Windsurfing and sailing and of course skiing.

Open: All year.

Directions

Coming from Italy on road no. 29, the site is towards the end of the town. Turn right towards Pagnoncini and Cantone and site is on right in about 100 m. Go over a humpback bridge at the entrance. GPS: N46:17.33 E10:04.51

Charges 2006

Per person	CHF 10,00 - 12,00
child (6-16 yrs)	CHF 4,00 - 6,00
pitch incl. electricity	CHF 10,00 - 19,00

CH9660 Camping Des Glaciers

CH-1944 La Fouly (Valais)

Tel: 027 783 17 35. Email: camping.glaciers@st-bernard.ch

Camping Des Glaciers at 1,600 m. above sea level is set amidst magnificent mountain scenery in a quiet, peaceful location in the beautiful Ferret Valley. The site offers some pitches in an open, undulating meadow and the rest are level, individual plots of varying size in small clearings, between bushes and shrubs or under tall pines. All of the 170 places have 25A electricity. The charming lady owner, Mme Darbellay, who has run the site for over 35 years, is fluent in six languages and always ready to welcome you to this peaceful haven and to give information on the locality.

Facilities

Three sanitary units of exceptional quality and heated when necessary. Hot water is free in all washbasins (some in cabins), showers and sinks. British style WCs. Washing machines and dryers in each block, one block has a drying room, another a baby room. Gas supplies. Motorcaravan services. Small shop. Recreation room with TV. Playground. Torches may be useful. Off site: Shop and restaurant 500 m. Bicycle hire 500 m. Riding 8 km.

Open: 15 May - 30 September.

Directions

Leave Martigny-Gd St Bernard road (no. 21) at Orsieres and follow signs (Ferret vally or La Fouly). Site is signed on right at end of La Fouly village. GPS: N45:56.008 E07:05.620

Charges 2006

Per person	CHF 6,50
child (2-12 yrs)	CHF 3,50
baby	CHF 2,00
pitch	CHF 10,00 - 16,00
electricity	CHF 3,50

CH9670 Camping de Molignon

CH-1984 Les Haudères (Valais)

Tel: **027 283 12 40**. Email: **info@molignon@ch**

De Molignon, surrounded by mountains, is a quiet, peaceful place 1,450 m above sea level; although there may be some road noise, the rushing stream and the sound of cow bells are likely to be the only disturbing factor in summer. The 100 pitches for tourists (75 with 10A electricity) are on well tended, level terraces leading down to the river. Good English is spoken by the owner's son who is now running the site, who will be pleased to give information on all that is available from the campsite.

Facilities

Two fully equipped sanitary blocks, heated in cool weather, with free hot showers. Baby room. Washing machines and dryer. Kitchen for hikers. Motorcaravan services. Gas supplies. Shop for basic supplies (15/6-15/9). Restaurant. Heated swimming pool with cover for cool weather (6 x 12 m). Sitting room for games and reading. Playground. Guided walks, climbing, geological museum, winter skiing. Fishing. Off site: Tennis and hang-gliding near. Bicycle hire 1 km. Riding 15 km. Langlauf in winter.

Open: All year.

Directions

Follow signs southwards from Sion for the Val d'Herens through Evolène to Les Haudères where site is signed on the right at the beginning of the village. GPS: N46:05.670 E07:29.849

Charges 2006

Per person	CHF 6,20 - 6,30
child (4-16 yrs)	CHF 3,60
pitch	CHF 9,80 - 16,00
electricity	CHF 3,00

Less 10% in low season.

CH9680 TCS Camping Bois de Finges

CH-3960 Sierre (Valais)

Tel: **027 455 02 84**. Email: **camping.sierre@tcs.ch**

This site is situated in the middle of the 'Bois des Finges' pine forest on a rocky wooded hillside. It is attractive and well maintained with much to offer for the naturalist. With 100 pitches cut out of the hillside, some are difficult to access but the manager will help. They can take units of up to 7 metres but mainly smaller units and tents in some parts. All pitches are screened by trees and 62 have 4A electricity (long leads useful). Staff are welcoming and helpful but little English is spoken. Useful for an overnight stop. There is road noise from a quarry opposite.

Facilities

Two very clean and well maintained wooden toilet blocks are fully equipped. Freezer, washing machine and dryer. Motorcaravan service point. Well stocked but limited shop and snack bar. Outdoor heated pool (6 x12 m) and paddling pool. Well appointed play area. Tennis. Table tennis. Bicycle hire. Barbecues are not permitted. Torches are useful. Off site: Sierre 1 km. Walking and hiking area. Fishing (licence required) 900 m. Golf and riding 3 km.

Open: 15 April - 3 October.

Directions

Leave motorway at exit 29, Sierre East. Follow sign for Sierre. Site is signed on the right (TCS) within 200 m. GPS: N46:17.633 E07:33.472

Charges 2006

Per person	CHF 6,00 - 7,00
child	CHF 3,00 - 3,50
pitch	CHF 8,00 - 20,00
electricity	CHF 3,50

Camping Cheques accepted.

CH9720 Camping Bella-Tola

Waldstrasse 57, CH-3952 Susten (Valais)

Tel: **027 473 14 91**. Email: **info@bella-tola.ch**

An attractive site with good standards, Bella-Tola is on the hillside above Susten (east of Sierre) with good views over the Rhône valley. Extensive terracing has been carried out and most of the pitches are now terraced and flat. All of the 180 individually numbered pitches have electricity connections. The fullest season is 10/7-10/8, but they say that there is usually room somewhere. Used by tour operators (20%). Guests are requested to comply with environmental rules by sorting rubbish as directed.

Facilities

Three good quality modern sanitary blocks should be quite sufficient, with some washbasins in cabins. Free hot water in washbasins, showers and sinks for clothes and dishes, plus baby rooms. Facilities for disabled visitors. Washing machines, dryers and irons. Motorcaravan services. Shop. Restaurant/bar. Takeaway (1/7-31/8). Heated swimming pool (25/5-16/9). Torches advised. WiFi (free). Off site: Riding and tennis. Golf 4 km.

Open: 5 May - 30 September.

Directions

Travelling eastwards from Sierre along main road, small site road is to the right(south)just after entering Susten (site signed). GPS: N46:17.937 E07:38.194

Charges 2006

Per person	CHF 10,00
child (2-16 yrs)	CHF 5,00 - 7,00
pitch acc. to type and season	CHF 15,00 - 26,00
electricity	CHF 3,60

Less 25% on person and pitch fees outside July/Aug.

CH9730 Camping Gemmi

Briannenstrasse 4, CH-3952 Susten-Leuk (Valais)

Tel: 027 473 11 54. Email: info@campgemmi.ch

The Rhône Valley is a popular through route to Italy via the Simplon Pass and a holiday region in its own right. Gemmi is a delightful small, friendly site in a scenic location with 65 level pitches, all with 16A electricity, on well tended grass amidst a variety of trees, some of which offer shade. 40 pitches also have water and drainage. The pleasant, friendly owner speaks fluent English, maintains high standards and has established a campsite mainly for tourists with few resident static units. A site more suitable for the mature camper.

Facilities

A modern sanitary block, partly heated, is of excellent quality and kept very clean. It includes some washbasins in cabins. Eight private bathrooms for hire on weekly basis. Washing machines and dryers. Motorcaravan services. Gas supplies. Shop. Small bar/restaurant where snacks and limited range of local specialities served. Terrace bar and snack restaurant. Playground. Tennis. Table tennis. Internet access. Swimming and walking near. Off site: Golf 500 m. Riding 2 km. Fishing 6 km.

Open: 22 April - 14 October.

Directions

From east (Visp), turn left 1 km. after sign for Agarn Feithieren. From west (Sierre), turn right 2 km. after Susten at sign for Camping Torrent and Gemmi. GPS: N46:17.880 E07:39.544

Charges 2006

Per person	CHF 7,00 - 9,00
child (1-6 yrs)	CHF 3,50 - 5,00
child (6-16 yrs)	CHF 5,00 - 6,50
pitch	CHF 11,00 - 15,00
pitch with drainage	CHF 15,00 - 19,00

CH9740 Camping Attermenzen

CH-3928 Randa (Valais)

Tel: 027 967 13 79. Email: rest.camping@rhone.ch

Randa, a picturesque Valais village, at 1,409 m. is a beautiful location for a campsite and ideal for those wishing to visit Zermatt only 10 km. away. Reception is open from mid-June to mid-September, otherwise call at the restaurant (closed on Tuesdays). Unmarked pitches are on an uneven field with some areas that are fairly level and electricity is within easy reach. A paradise for walking, climbing, mountaineering and mountain biking and surrounded by famous 4,000 m. peaks, such as the Dom and Weisshorn, this site also offers good modern facilities with a restaurant and bar next door.

Facilities

The sanitary block is of a good standard and well maintained with free showers. Washing machine. Shop (June-Sept). Gas supplies. Restaurant/bar. Takeaway. Off site: Zermatt 10 km.

Open: 1 May - 31 October.

Directions

From A9 at Visp turn right at roundabout (Zermatt). Go through the 3.3 km. long tunnel and follow road towards Zermatt. Go through Stalden and turn right at roundabout (Zermatt). Site is about 1 km. after Randa village on the left. GPS: N46:05.08 E07:46.54

Charges 2006

Per person	CHF 6,00
child	CHF 3,00
pitch incl. electricity	CHF 11,00 - 13,00

CH9770 Camping Santa Monica

Kantonstrasse/Turtig, CH-3942 Raron (Valais)

Tel: 027 934 24 24. Email: info@santa-monica.ch

We offer several different styles of campsite in the Rhône Valley including this pleasant, well tended site, that is open all year. About half of this site is occupied by static caravans and chalets, but these are to one side leaving two flat, open meadows for touring. The 270 level pitches (120 for touring units) all have electricity (16A) and are roughly defined by saplings. Being right beside the main road 9 (some road noise), makes this a good base either for a night stop or for exploring the area. With mountain views, across the valley, it has an air of peace.

Facilities

Two heated toilet blocks have free hot water in washbasins and sinks and on payment in the showers. Facilities for disabled visitors. Private cabins to rent. Motorcaravan services (Euro-Relais). Gas supplies. Bar, restaurant and shop (1/5-31/10). Small pool and child's pool (1/6-30/9). Playground and play house. Volleyball. Table tennis. Bicycle hire. Ski room. Walking country, cable cars near. Off site: Shops and restaurants near. Tennis courts next door. Riding 10 km.

Open: All year.

Directions

On the south side of road 9 between Visp and Susten, signed. GPS: N46:18.172 E07:48.155

Charges 2006

Per person	CHF 5,00 - 6,00
child (6-16 yrs)	CHF 3,00 - 4,00
motorcaravan	CHF 9,50 - 15,00
tent	CHF 5,00 - 6,00
electricity	CHF 3,00

Special offers in low season.

CH9775 Camping Schwimmbad Mühleye

CH-3930 Visp (Valais)

Tel: 027 946 20 84. Email: info@camping-visp.ch

Camping Mühleye is a popular family site located in the Valais, close to Brig, and has been recommended by our Swiss agent. We we hope to undertake a full inspection here in 2007. The site has 148 grassy pitches, ranging in size from 50-150 sq.m, including a number of super pitches (with electricity, water and drainage). The town of Visp is just 800m away and the site is a useful base for exploring the region. On-site amenities include a large swimming pool with children's games. In high season, an entertainment and activity programme is organised and includes guided walks in the surrounding mountains. The site lies at the heart of the Upper Valais and the resorts of Saas Fee and Zermatt are within easy access. Close at hand, there are countless opportunities for walking and mountain biking.

Facilities

Restaurant, snack bar and takeaway meals. Supermarket. Swimming pool with water slide and children's games. Playground. Entertainment and activity programme in high season. Off site: Visp centre 800 m. Zermatt 36 km. Saas Fee 25 km. Riding. Cycling and walking trails. Golf.

Open: Mid April - end October.

Directions

Take the eastbound A9 motorway from Montreux to Sierre and continue to Visp on road 9. The site is located close to the town centre and is well signed.

Charges 2006

Per person	CHF 5,80 - 6,40
child (6-16 yrs)	CHF 3,20 - 3,90
pitch with electricity	CHF 13,00 - 15,30
larger pitch with water and waste water	CHF 18,70 - 22,20

CH9300 Camping Le Bivouac

Route des Paccots 21, CH-1618 Châtel-St-Denis (Fribourg)

Tel: 021 948 78 49. Email: info@le-bivouac.ch

A pleasant little site in the mountains north of Montreux, Le Bivouac has its own small swimming pool and children's pool. Most of the best places here are taken by seasonal caravans (130) and there are now only about 30 pitches for tourists. Electrical connections (10A) are available and there are five water points. The site is also open for winter sports caravanning and all the sanitary facilities are heated. Entertainment is organised for adults and children in high season. This is a good centre for walking and excursions and there is a friendly welcome from the owner M. Fivaz.

Facilities

The good toilet facilities in the main building include pre-set, free hot water in washbasins, showers and sinks for laundry and dishes. Baby room. Gas supplies. Shop (1/7-31/8). Bar (1/6-30/9). Swimming pool (1/6-15/9). Room for general use adjoining. Fishing. Off site: Bicycle hire 2 km. Riding 4 km. Bus passes the gate.

Open: 1 April - 30 September.

Directions

From motorway 12/E27 Bern-Vevey take Châtel St Denis exit no. 2 and turn towards Les Paccots (about 1 km). Site is is on left up hill. GPS: N46:31.508 E06:55.097

Charges 2006

Per person	CHF 5,00 - 6,00
child (6-16 yrs)	CHF 3,00 - 4,00
pitch	CHF 15,00
electricity	CHF 4,00

No credit cards. Less 10% on showing this guide. Euros are accepted.

CH9790 Camping Augenstern

Postfach 16, CH-3998 Reckingen (Valais)

Tel: 027 973 13 95. Email: info@campingaugenstern.ch

The village of Reckingen is about half way between Brig and the Furka/Grimsel passes. You can still get the train with car and caravan, or motorcaravan from Oberwald to Andermatt to avoid the steep climbs and descents of the Furka Pass, but in doing so you will miss some unforgettable scenery. This family run site, at 1,326 m. provides 100 flat, level pitches for touring units, all with 10A electricity and not much shade. It provides an excellent base for walking, climbing or cycling as well as rafting on the Rhone in the summer or skiing in the winter.

Facilities

The toilet block is good and is well maintained. Showers on payment. Motorcaravan services. Restaurant/bar with satellite TV. Shop in high season. Bicycle hire. Off site: Large swimming pool complex 200 m. Reckingen 500 m. Riding 800 m.

Open: 15 May - 15 October, 15 December - 15 March.

Directions

From the no. 19 road turn south in Reckingen next to church. Go down hill, along one-way street and over railway (carefully!) and bridge. Over next bridge and right to end of lane past swimming pool. GPS: N46:27.900 E08:14.658

Charges 2006

Per person	CHF 7,50
child (0-12 yrs)	CHF 4,00
pitch	CHF 9,50
electricity	CHF 4,00

Camping Augenstern ***

• A wonderful and quiet camp site, most beautifully situated in Obergoms (Wallis) between Gletsch and Brig, just near the passes
• Directly connected with the Rhone • Matterhorn-Gotthard railway and busses for the public traffic • Ideally situated for rafting, biking, climbing, skiing, (Nordic)walking, paragliding, delta gliding, etc.
• The famous Riederalp, Bettmeralp and Matterhorn in the region of the camp site • Park restaurant and breathtaking terrace with an excellent menu and Wallis specials • Public swimming pool situated at the camping area • Reservations possible • Also wintercamping.

Camping-Restaurant Augenstern, **Arne und Annet Kruit, CH-3998 Reckingen**
Phone: +41-(0)27 973 13 95, Fax: +41-(0)27-973 26 77
E-Mail: info@campingaugenstern.ch, www.campingaugenstern.ch

CH9015 Camping Tariche

Tariche, St Ursanne, CH-2883 Montmelon (Jura)

Tel: 032 433 4619. Email: info@tariche.ch

This lovely site is some 6 km. off the main road along a steep wooded valley, through which flows the Doub on its brief excursion through Switzerland from France. If you're looking for peace and tranquillity then this is a distinct possibility for a short or long stay. A very small friendly site, owned and managed by Vincent Gigandet, there are just 15 touring pitches. It is ideal for walking, fishing or for the more active, the possibility of kayaking along the Doub (the river is not suitable for swimming). Medieval St Ursanne, said to be the most beautiful village in the canton, is some 7 km. away. There you will find 16th century town gates and bridge and a 12th century church surrounded by ancient houses. Not too far distant is Delemont, the Jura's capital. A local artist, Michel Marchand, runs introductory lessons in watercolour painting.

Facilities

The modern, heated toilet block is of a high standard with free showers. Washing machine and dryer. Motorcaravan services. Good kitchen facilities include oven, hob and refrigerator. Restaurant with shaded terrace overlooking the play area so that adults can enjoy a drink and keep watch whilst enjoying the river views. Fishing. Off site: St Ursanne 7 km.

Open: 1 March - 31 October.

Directions

From the A16 take exit for St Ursanne (at the end of the tunnel). Turn left towards town. At roundabout turn left and go past first campsite. After 5.6 km. site is on the left next to the restaurant.

Charges 2006

Per person	CHF 8,20
child	CHF 4,00
pitch	CHF 8,00 - 20,00
electricity	CHF 3,00

CH9040 Camping des Pêches

Route du Port, CH-2525 Le Landeron (Neuchâtel)

Tel: 032 751 29 00. Email: info@camping-lelanderon.ch

This recently constructed, touring campsite is on the side of Lake Biel and river Thienne, and close to the old town of Le Landeron. The site is divided into two sections, one side of the road for static caravans, and on the other is the modern campsite for tourists. The 220 pitches are all on level grass, numbered but not separated, a few with shade, all with electricity (10A) and many conveniently placed water points. All the facilities are exceptionally well maintained and in pristine condition during our visit throughout a busy holiday weekend.

Facilities

The spacious, modern sanitary block contains all the usual facilities including a food preparation area with six cooking rings, a large freezer and refrigerator. Payment for showers is by card. Baby room. Laundry facilities. Motorcaravan service point. Community room and small café in reception building. Children's playground. Bicycle hire. TV and general room. Treatment room. Card barrier. Off site: Fishing 300 m. Swimming pool 300 m. (16/5-1/9; charged). Golf and riding 7 km.

Open: 1 April - 15 October.

Directions

Le Landeron is signed from the Neuchâtel - Biel motorway, exit 19 and site is well signed from the town. GPS: N47:03.177 E07:04.184

Charges 2006

Per person	CHF 8,00
child (6-16 yrs)	CHF 4,00
pitch incl. car	CHF 14,50 - 15,00
tent and car	CHF 11,50 - 13,50
electricity	CHF 3,50

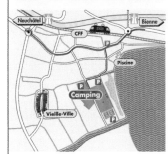

LE LANDERON «Camp des Pêches»★★★★

Quiet and well equipped site for tourists (40'000m2) for a restoring holiday or a short stay in an attractive countryside:

- Idyllic mediaeval town with Gothic town hall, museum, castle, chapels and historic fountains – surrounded by gardens and well-known vineyards
- On the shores of the lake of Bienne with a picturesque harbour, heated olympique swimming pool and restaurant (300m)
- Nice promenades along the river Thielle and walking tours to the Chasseral (1609m)

Camp des Pêches, CH-2525 Le Landeron
Phone 0041-32-751 29 00, Fax 0041-32-751 63 54
www.camping-lelanderon.ch

CH9240 Camping Le Petit Bois

CH-1110 Morges (Vaud)

Tel: 021 801 12 70. Email: camping.morges@tes.ch

This excellent TCS campsite is on the edge of Morges, a wine-growing centre with a 13th century castle, on Lake Geneva about 8 km. west of Lausanne. Flowers, shrubs and trees adorn the site and the neat, tidy lawns make a most pleasant environment. There are 170 grass pitches for tourists, all with 6A electricity and laid out in a regular pattern from wide hard access roads on which cars stand. There are eight larger pitches for motorcaravans with electricity, water and drainage. The friendly managers speak good English, and will advise on local attractions.

Facilities

Two well built, fully equipped, modern toilet blocks include hot water in half the washbasins and sinks and showers. Separate block with excellent baby room and cosmetics room. Facilities for disabled visitors. Washing machines, dryers and irons. Motorcaravan services. Restaurant and takeaway. Shop. Playground. Boules. Bicycle and scooter hire. Small general room. Internet point. Entertainment (high season). Picnic area. Fishing. Bicycle hire. Off site: Swimming pool adjacent. Small harbour. Town centre. Tennis.

Open: 23 March - 21 October.

Directions

Leave Autoroute Lausanne - Geneva A1 at exit 15 (Morges-ouest). Turn towards town and signs for site. GPS: N46:30.274 E06:29.350

Charges 2006

Per person	CHF 6,00 - 7,40
pitch	CHF 18,50 - 23,00
electricity (6/10A)	CHF 4,50 - 5,50
Camping Cheques accepted.	

513

CH9270 Camping De Vidy

Chemin du Camping 3, CH-1007 Lausanne (Vaud)

Tel: 021 622 50 00. Email: info@campinglausannevidy.ch

The ancient city of Lausanne spills down the hillside towards Lake Geneva until it meets the peaceful park in which this site is situated. The present owners have enhanced its neat and tidy appearance by planting many flowers and shrubs. Hard access roads separate the site into sections for tents, caravans and motorcaravans, with 10A electrical connections in all parts, except the tent areas. Pitches are on flat grass, numbered but not marked out, with 260 (of 350) for tourists. 20 are fully serviced and some large pitches near the lake are suitable for American type motorhomes. The lakeside bar/restaurant (also open to the public) provides entertainment in season in the various rooms so that the young and not so young can enjoy themselves without impinging on each other. Although only minutes from the city centre, only a gentle hum of traffic can be heard. A public footpath separates the site from the lakeside, but there is good access. The World HQ of the Olympic movement is adjacent in the pleasant park, which is also available for games and walking.

Facilities

Two excellent sanitary blocks, one heated, have mostly British, some Turkish style WCs, hot water in washbasins, sinks and showers with warm, pre-mixed water. Facilities for disabled people. A third small block has been added. Motorcaravan services (Euro-Relais; CHF 10 for overnight guests, 20 otherwise). Gas supplies. Shop and self-service bar/restaurant (1/5-30/9). Takeaway (high season). Playground. Evening entertainment in high season. Internet point. Lake swimming. Fishing. Off site: Bus service into Lausanne. Boat excursions on the lake.

Open: All year.

Directions

Site is left of road to Geneva, 500 m. west of La Maladière. Take autobahn Lausanne-Süd, exit no.3 La Maladière, and at this roundabout almost turn back on yourself following signs for CIO and camping. At traffic lights turn left, then on for site. Take care at La Maladière roundabout (large trolley buses).

Charges 2006

Per person	CHF 7,00
pitch	CHF 10,00 - 18,00
electricity	CHF 3,00 - 4,00

No credit cards.

CH9900 Camping Delta

Via Respini 7, CH-6600 Locarno (Ticino)

Tel: 091 751 60 81. Email: info@campingdelta.com

Camping Delta is actually within the Locarno town limits, only some 800 m. from the centre, and it has a prime position right by the lake, with bathing direct from the site, and next to the municipal lido and sports field. Boats can be put on the lake and the site also has some moorings on an estuary at one side, with a jetty. It has 300 pitches on flat ground of 80-100 sq.m. of which 255 are available for touring units. They are marked out but are not divided. Delta is a well run and well situated site. Locarno is host to an International Film Festival, classical and jazz concerts and exhibitions.

Facilities

The single toilet block is very clean and should be adequat except perhaps at the busiest times. There are washbasins (some in cabins for women), showers and sinks. Washing machine and dryer. Motorcaravan services. Small supermarket. Restaurant/bar. Fitness centre. Playgrounds. Baby sitting. Volleyball/badminton. Amusements. Entertainment and excursions. Fishing. Bicycle hire. Internet access. Kayaks and electric bikes for hire. Dogs are not accepted. Off site: Golf 200 m. Riding 4 km.

Open: 1 March - 31 October.

Directions

From central Locarno follow signs to Camping Delta, Lido or Stadio along the lake. Beware that approaching from south there are also Delta signs which lead you to Albergo Delta in quite the wrong place. GPS: N46:09.538 E08:48.133

Charges 2006

Per person	CHF 11,00 - 18,00
child (3-15 yrs)	CHF 6,00
pitch (depending on type)	CHF 21,00 - 57,00
electricity	CHF 5,00

Check real time availability and at-the-gate prices...

www.alanrogers.com

Open All Year

The following sites are understood to accept caravanners and campers all year round. Please refer to the site's individual entry for details.

Andorra
AN7145   Valira
AN7143   Xixerella

Austria
AU0035   Alpin Seefeld
AU0055   Arlberg
AU0475   Brunner am See
AU0480   Burgstaller
AU0070   Hofer
AU0502   Im Thermenland
AU0515   Katschtal
AU0170   Kranebitten
AU0220   Krismer
AU0262   Oberwötzlhof
AU0045   Ötztal
AU0155   Prutz
AU0405   Ramsbacher
AU0440   Schluga
AU0065   Seehof
AU0102   Stadlerhof
AU0110   Tirol Camp
AU0100   Toni
AU0180   Woferlgut
AU0160   Zell am See
AU0090   Zillertal-Hell
AU0040   Zugspitze

Belgium
BE0590   De Gavers
BE0560   De Lombarde
BE0740   Eau Rouge
BE0732   Floreal La Roche
BE0555   Klein Strand
BE0670   La Clusure
BE0655   Lilse Bergen
BE0580   Memling
BE0735   Petite Suisse
BE0700   Spa d'Or
BE0675   Spineuse
BE0725   Val de L`Aisne
BE0710   Vallée de Rabais
BE0530   Waux-Hall
BE0780   Wilhelm Tell

Croatia
CR6745   Bi-Village

Czech Republic
CZ4880   Roznov
CZ4850   Sokol Troja

Denmark
DK2015   Ådalens
DK2255   Feddet
DK2044   Hampen Sø
DK2140   Jesperhus
DK2020   Mogeltonder
DK2150   Solyst
DK2046   Trelde Næs

Finland
FI2970   Nallikari
FI2850   Rastila

France
FR37130   Chlorophylle Parc
FR79020   Courte Vallée
FR47150   Guillalmes
FR47150   Guillalmes
FR88040   Lac de Bouzey
FR65080   Lavedan
FR86040   Le Futuriste
FR06080   Les Cigales
FR88130   Vanne de Pierre

Germany
DE3415   Adam
DE3025   Alfsee
DE3685   Allweglehen
DE3452   Alte Sägemühle
DE3632   Altmühltal
DE3065   am Bärenbache
DE3255   Am Königsberg
DE3021   Am Stadtwaldsee
DE3847   Auensee
DE3436   Bankenhof
DE3710   Bayerischer Wald
DE3445   Belchenblick
DE3210   Biggesee
DE3432   Bonath
DE3697   Dreiqueller
DE3627   Ellwangen
DE3836   Erzgebirgsblick
DE3439   Freiburg
DE3650   Gitzenweiler
DE3215   Goldene Meile
DE3202   Grav-Insel
DE3455   Gugel`s
DE3080   Hardausee
DE3254   Harfenmühle
DE3820   Havelberge
DE3490   Hegau
DE3411   Heidehof
DE3437   Hochschwarzwald
DE3256   Hunsrück
DE3440   Kirchzarten
DE3406   Kleinenzhof
DE3008   Klüthseecamp
DE3833   LuxOase
DE3222   Moselbogen
DE3185   Münster

DE3450   Münstertal
DE3720   Naabtal
DE3610   Nürnberg
DE3855   Oberhof
DE3420   Oberrhein
DE3055   Prahljust
DE3010   Röders Park
DE3242   Schinderhannes
DE3002   Schlei-Karschau
DE3427   Schwarzwälder Hof
DE3275   Seepark
DE3180   Sonnenwiese
DE3850   Strandbad Aga
DE3070   Süd-See
DE3030   Tecklenburg
DE3280   Teichmann
DE3212   Wirfttal
DE3003   Wulfener Hals

Greece
GR8525   Chrissa
GR8330   Ionion Beach

Hungary
HU5210   Diófaház
HU5150   Fortuna
HU5300   Kek-Duna

Italy
IT6403   Baciccia
IT6889   Costa Verde
IT6401   Dei Fiori
IT6778   Fabulous
IT6814   Flaminio
IT6053   Fusina
IT6208   Gamp
IT6923   Jonio
IT6667   La Finoria
IT6930   Marinello
IT6200   Olympia
IT6242   Orta
IT6935   Rais Gerbi
IT6780   Roma
IT6919   Scarabeo
IT6661   Toscana Village
IT6412   Valdeiva

Liechtenstein
FL7580   Mittagspitze

Luxembourg
LU7670   Ardennes
LU7850   Fuussekaul
LU7700   Gaalgebierg
LU7880   Trois Frontières
LU7770   Val d'Or

Netherlands

NL5660	Amsterd'se Bos
NL5985	Beerze Bulten
NL6520	BreeBronne
NL5600	Delftse Hout
NL5620	Duinrell
NL5910	Hertenwei
NL5540	Katjeskelder
NL5640	Kijkduinpark
NL5890	Klein Canada
NL5630	Koningshof
NL5790	Kuierpadtien
NL5760	Kuilart
NL6090	Lauwersoog
NL6560	Maasvallei
NL5500	Pannenschuur
NL6540	Rozenhof
NL6930	Schoneveld
NL5735	Tempelhof
NL5960	Wielerbaan
NL5560	Wijde Blick

Norway

NO2515	Gjelten Bru
NO2510	Håneset
NO2432	Harstad
NO2400	Jolstraholmen
NO2375	Lærdal
NO2505	Magalaupe
NO2610	Neset
NO2615	Olberg
NO2525	Østrea Æra
NO2460	Prinsen
NO2545	Rustberg
NO2475	Saltstraumen
NO2385	Sandvik
NO2590	Sandviken
NO2490	Skjerneset

Portugal

PO8210	Albufeira
PO8410	Armacao-Pera
PO8150	Caparica
PO8370	Cerdeira
PO8480	Foz do Arelho
PO8130	Guincho
PO8230	Olhao
PO8220	Quarteira
PO8030	Rio Alto
PO8100	S Pedro-Moel
PO8430	Sagres
PO8170	São Miguel

PO8202	Turiscampo
PO8200	Valverde

Slovakia

SK4980	Levocská Dolina
SK4910	Turiec

Slovenia

SV4150	Kamne
SV4235	Klin

Spain

ES8536	Ametlla
ES9024	As Cancelas
ES8559	Azahar
ES8683	Benisol
ES9062	Boltana
ES8580	Bonterra
ES8763	Cabo de Gata
ES8802	Cabopino
ES9086	Cáceres
ES8535	Cala d`Oques
ES8130	Calonge
ES8687	Cap Blanch
ES9089	Despenaperros
ES9290	El Balcon
ES9080	El Brillante
ES9200	El Escorial
ES9090	El Greco
ES8752	El Portus
ES8685	El Raco
ES9043	Errota el Molino
ES8754	Javea
ES8008	Joncar Mar
ES8615	Kiko
ES8625	Kiko Rural
ES8745	La Fuente
ES8753	La Manga
ES8742	La Marina
ES9125	Lago Barasona
ES9285	Las Lomas
ES8940	Los Cantiles
ES8748	Los Madriles
ES8800	Marbella Playa
ES8743	Marjal
ES9087	Merida
ES9027	Monfrague
ES8755	Moraira
ES9060	Peña Montañesa
ES9210	Pico-Miel
ES8482	Pineda de Salou
ES8689	Playa del Torres
ES8865	Playa Las Dunas

ES8560	Playa Tropicana
ES8508	Poboleda
ES9035	Portuondo
ES8859	Roche
ES9082	Sevilla
ES8483	Tamarit
ES8675	Vall de Laguar
ES8390	Vilanova Park
ES8681	Villasol
ES9081	Villsom

Sweden

SW2755	Alevi
SW2855	Flogsta
SW2840	Flottsbro
SW2760	Frykenbaden
SW2865	Gielas
SW2715	Gröne Backe
SW2725	Hafsten
SW2825	Herrfallet
SW2720	Hökensås
SW2870	Jokkmokks
SW2805	Kolmårdens
SW2740	Laxsjons
SW2710	Lidköping
SW2705	Lisebergsbyn
SW2645	Mölle
SW2836	Mora Parkens
SW2850	Ostersunds
SW2665	Rosenlund
SW2650	Skånes
SW2750	Sommarvik
SW2857	Strömsund
SW2845	Svegs
SW2860	Umeå
SW2675	Västervik Swe

Switzerland

CH9495	Balmweid
CH9855	Cavresc
CH9270	De Vidy
CH9520	Du Botza
CH9570	Eienwäldli
CH9175	Giessenpark
CH9360	Grassi
CH9460	Jungfrau
CH9420	Manor Farm
CH9670	Molignon
CH9770	Santa Monica
CH9410	Stuhlegg
CH9830	Sur En

Dogs

For the benefit of those who want to take their dogs with them or for people who do not like dogs at the sites they visit, we list here those sites that have indicated to us that they do not accept dogs. If you are, however, planning to take your dog we do advise you to check first – there may be limits on numbers, breeds, etc. or times of the year when they are excluded.

Never – these sites do not accept dogs at any time:

Austria
AU0445 Kotschach Mauthen
AU0090 Zillertal-Hell

Croatia
CR6731 Valalta
CR6736 Valdaliso

Czech Republic
CZ4690 Slunce

France
FR84020 Bélézy
FR17010 Bois Soleil
FR01080 Etang du Moulin
FR47150 Guillalmes
FR85210 Les Ecureuils
FR46040 Moulin de Laborde
FR24040 Moulin du Roch

Germany
DE3260 Bad Dürkheim
DE3233 Holländischer Hof
DE3005 Schnelsen Nord

Greece
GR8700 Erodios

Hungary
HU5090 Füred
HU5380 Venus

Italy
IT6820 Baia Domizia
IT6677 Baia Gabbiani
IT6286 Baia Verde
IT6263 Bella Italia

IT6627 Boschetto di Piemma
IT6678 Butteri
IT6036 Ca'Pasquali
IT6032 Cavallino
IT6675 Cieloverde
IT6357 Cisano & San Vito
IT6199 Corones
IT6401 Dei Fiori
IT6256 Del Garda
IT6645 Delle Piscine
IT6358 Delle Rose
IT6804 Eurcamping
IT6040 Garden Paradiso
IT6015 Il Tridente
IT6055 Isamar
IT6021 Italy
IT6013 Lido
IT6033 Malibu Beach
IT6056 Miramare (Chioggia)
IT6046 Miramare
            (Punta Sabbioni)
IT6022 Portofelice
IT6003 Pra' Delle Torri
IT6673 Puntala
IT6419 River
IT6047 Scarpiland
IT6359 Serenella
IT6819 Settebello
IT6629 Tripesce
IT6020 Union Lido
IT6034 Waikiki

Netherlands
NL6470 De Papillon
NL6790 Kienehoef
NL6960 Klepperstee
NL5680 Noordduinen
NL6330 Scheleberg
NL6840 Vogelenzang
NL6925 Weltevreden

Portugal
PO8060 Costa Nova
PO8170 São Miguel

Spain
ES9086 Cáceres
ES8481 Cambrils
ES8090 Cypsela
ES8103 El Maset
ES8748 Los Madriles
ES8101 Playa Brava
ES9000 Playa Joyel
ES8530 Playa Montroig
ES8560 Playa Tropicana
ES8859 Roche
ES8420 Stel (Roda)
ES8540 Torre del Sol
ES8681 Villasol

Switzerland
CH9180 Buchhorn
CH9890 Campofelice
CH9900 Delta
CH9185 Fischerhaus
CH9480 Gletscherdorf
CH9160 Rheinwiesen

Maybe – accepted but with certain restrictions:

Austria
AU0400 Arneitz
AU0227 Camp Grän
AU0060 Natterer See
AU0232 Sonnenberg

Belgium
BE0670 La Clusure
BE0550 Nieuwpoort
BE0595 Oudenaarde
BE0565 Westende

France
FR23010 Château de Poinsouze
FR74060 La Colombière
FR24100 Le Moulinal
FR34130 Le Neptune
FR83200 Les Pêcheurs

Germany
DE3232 Family Club
DE3442 Herbolzheim
DE3440 Kirchzarten
DE3686 Strandcamping

DE3070 Süd-See
DE3465 Wirthshof
DE3003 Wulfener Hals

Italy
IT6889 Costa Verde
IT6606 Europa
IT6000 Mare Pineta
IT6631 Mareblu
IT6660 Maremma
IT6930 Marinello
IT6996 Mariposa
IT6813 Porticciolo
IT6935 Rais Gerbi
IT6620 Riccione
IT6865 Riva di Ugento

Luxembourg
LU7770 Val d'Or

Netherlands
NL6520 BreeBronne
NL5980 De Roos
NL5600 Delftse Hout

NL5790 Kuierpadtien
NL6560 Maasvallei
NL6950 Renesse
NL6140 Valkenhof
NL6000 Vechtdalcamping
NL5580 Veerhoeve
NL5560 Wijde Blick

Portugal
PO8210 Albufeira
PO8370 Cerdeira

Spain
ES8559 Azahar
ES8580 Bonterra
ES8160 Cala Gogo
ES8080 Delfin Verde
ES8072 Les Medes

Switzerland
CH9880 Lido Mappo

We have had very favourable feedback from readers concerning our choice of naturist sites, which we first introduced several years ago. Over the last few years we have gradually added a few more.

There is no need to be a practising naturist before visiting these sites. In fact, as far as British visitors are concerned, many are what might be described as 'holiday naturists' as distinct from the practice of naturism at other times. The emphasis in all the sites featured in this guide at least, is on naturism as 'life in harmony with nature', and respect for oneself and others and for the environment, rather than simply on nudity. In fact nudity is really only obligatory in the area of the swimming pools.

There are a number of rules, which amount to sensible and considerate guidelines designed to ensure that no-one invades someone elses privacy, creates any nuisance, or damages the environment. Whether as a result of these rules, the naturist philosophy generally, or the attitude of site owners and campers alike, we have been very impressed by all the naturist sites we have selected. Without exception they had a friendly and welcoming ambience, were all extremely clean and tidy, and, in most cases, provided much larger than average pitches, with a wide range of activities both sporting and cultural.

The purpose of our including a number of naturist sites in our guide is to provide an introduction to naturist camping in Europe for British holidaymakers; we were actually surprised by the number of British campers we met on naturist sites, many of whom had 'stumbled across naturism almost by accident'.

have you visited

www.alanrogers.com

yet?

INSPECTED CAMPSITES & SELECTED

Alan Rogers

Our website has fast become the first-stop for countless caravanners, motorhome owners and campers all wanting reliable, impartial and detailed information for their next trip.

It features a fully searchable database of the best campsites in the UK & Ireland, and the rest of Europe: over 2,000 campsites in 26 countries. All are Alan Rogers inspected and selected, allowing you to find the site that's perfect for you, with the reassurance of knowing we've been there first.

Travelling

When taking your car (and caravan, tent or trailer tent) or motorcaravan to the continent you do need to plan in advance and to find out as much as possible about driving in the countries you plan to visit. Whilst European harmonisation has eliminated many of the differences between one country and another, it is well worth reading the short notes we provide in the introduction to each country in this guide in addition to this more general summary.

Of course, the main difference from driving in the UK is that in mainland Europe you will need to drive on the right. Without taking extra time and care, especially at busy junctions and conversely when roads are empty, it is easy to forget to drive on the right. Remember that traffic approaching from the right usually has priority unless otherwise indicated by road markings and signs. Harmonisation also means that most (but not all) common road signs are the same in all countries.

Your vehicle

Book your vehicle in for a good service well before your intended departure date. This will lessen the chance of an expensive breakdown. Make sure your brakes are working efficiently and that your tyres have plenty of tread (3 mm. is recommended, particularly if you are undertaking a long journey).

Also make sure that your caravan or trailer is roadworthy and that its tyres are in good order and correctly inflated. Plan your packing and be careful not to overload your vehicle, caravan or trailer – this is unsafe and may well invalidate your insurance cover (it must not be more fully loaded than the kerb weight of the insured vehicle).

Check all the following:

- ☐ GB sticker. If you do not display a sticker, you may risk an on-the-spot fine as this identifier is compulsory in all countries. Euro-plates are an acceptable alternative within the EU (but not outside). Remember to attach another sticker (or Euro-plate) to caravans or trailers. Only GB stickers (not England, Scotland, Wales or N. Ireland) stickers are valid in the EU.

- ☐ Headlights. As you will be driving on the right you must adjust your headlights so that the dipped beam does not dazzle oncoming drivers. Converter kits are readily available for most vehicle, although if your car is fitted with high intensity headlights, you should check with your motor dealer. Check that any planned extra loading does not affect the beam height.

- ☐ Seatbelts. Rules for the fitting and wearing of seatbelts throughout Europe are similar to those in the UK, but it is worth checking before you go. Rules for carrying children in the front of vehicles vary from country to country. It is best to plan not to do this if possible.

- ☐ Door/wing mirrors. To help with driving on the right, if your vehicle is not fitted with a mirror on the left hand side, we recommend you have one fitted.

- ☐ Fuel. Leaded and Lead Replacement petrol is increasingly difficult to find in Northern Europe.

Travelling continued

Compulsory additional equipment

The driving laws of the countries of Europe still vary in what you are required to carry in your vehicle, although the consequences of not carrying a required piece of equipment are almost always an on-the-spot fine.

To meet these requirements we suggest that you carry the following:

- ☐ Fire extinguisher
- ☐ First aid kit
- ☐ Basic tool kit
- ☐ Spare bulbs

- ☐ Two warning triangles – two are required in some countries at all times, and are compulsory in most countries when towing.

- ☐ High visibility vest – now compulsory in Spain, Italy and Austria (and likely to become compulsory throughout the EU) in case you need to walk on a motorway. In Spain we are told that you need a vest for every occupant of the car, and that they must be carried inside the car, not in the boot.

Insurance and Motoring Documents

Vehicle insurance

Contact your insurer well before you depart to check that your car insurance policy covers driving outside the UK. Most do, but many policies only provide minimum cover (so if you have an accident your insurance may only cover the cost of damage to the other person's property, with no cover for fire and theft).

To maintain the same level of cover abroad as you enjoy at home you need to tell your vehicle insurer. Some will automatically cover you abroad with no extra cost and no extra paperwork. Some will say you need a Green Card (which is neither green nor on card) but won't charge for it. Some will charge extra for the Green Card. Ideally you should contact your vehicle insurer 3-4 weeks before you set off, and confirm your conversation with them in writing.

Breakdown insurance

Arrange breakdown cover for your trip in good time so that if your vehicle breaks down or is involved in an accident it (and your caravan or trailer) can be repaired or returned to this country. This cover can usually be arranged as part of your travel insurance policy (see below) and this usually includes a Bail Bond for Spain.

Documents you must take with you

You may be asked to show your documents at any time so make sure that they are in order, up-to-date and easily accessible while you travel. These are what you need to take:

- ☐ Passports (you may also need a visa in some countries if you hold either a UK passport not issued in the UK or a passport that was issued outside the EU)

- ☐ Motor Insurance Certificate, including Green Card (or Continental Cover clause)

- ☐ DVLC Vehicle Registration Document plus, if not your own vehicle, the owner's written authority to drive.

- ☐ A full valid Driving Licence (not provisional). The new photo style licence is now mandatory in most European countries).

insure**4**campers.com

Taking your own caravan, motorhome or tent abroad?

European Camping Holiday Insurance

Our specially tailored travel insurance policies provide exactly the right cover for a self-drive camping holiday in Europe at the lowest possible price. Our policies have been adapted to cover the often-unique risks associated with a camping holiday in Europe. For example, policies include cover for valuables stored in your vehicle overnight on a campsite* (loss from unattended vehicles is often excluded from general travel insurance policies).

Specialist insurance for campers and caravanners can include*:

- **Payment towards additional accommodation costs following loss of own tent**
- **Specific tent and camping equipment cover**
- **Reimbursement of caravan insurance excess.**
- **Theft of valuables from an unattended vehicle whilst parked on a campsite.**
- **Increased car hire limits when towing a caravan or trailer (Plus policies)**

* see policy wording for details

Single Trip Policies

Our **Personal Insurance** provides access to the services of Inter Group Assistance Services (IGAS) and Global Excel, two of the UK's largest assistance companies. Experienced multi-lingual personnel provide a caring, efficient service 24 hours a day. They are backed by a medical team who include in-house doctors and nurses headed by specialist medical consultants.

- **24 hour travel advice line and medical assistance**
- **Authorisation of medical costs and payment guarantees**
- **Air ambulance repatriation/evacuation**
- **Repatriation due to serious illness of relatives at home**
- **Medical escorts and regular liaison with overseas doctors providing treatment**

Our **European Vehicle Assistance** cover is provided by Green Flag who, with over 25 years' experience, provide assistance to over 3 million people each year. With a Europe-wide network of over 7,500 garages and agents, you know you're in very safe hands.

Both IGAS and Green Flag are very used to looking after the needs of campsite-based holidaymakers and are very familiar with the location of most European campsites, with contacts at garages, doctors and hospitals nearby.

Green Flag
motoring assistance

Combined Personal and Vehicle Assistance Insurance

PREMIER COUPLES PACKAGE
£57* 18 days cover for motorhome + 2 adults

PREMIER FAMILY PACKAGE
£89* 18 days cover for car + caravan + 2 adults + dependent children under 16

* Based on vehicles under 5 years old

SAVE WITH ANNUAL POLICIES

If you are likely to take more than one overseas holiday in the next 12 months then our Annual multi-trip policies could save you a great deal of money. European self-drive personal cover for a couple starts at just **£69** and the whole family can be covered for just **£89**.

One call and you're covered **0870 405 4059**

Travelling continued

Personal Holiday insurance

Even though you are just travelling within Europe you must take out travel insurance. Few EU countries pay the full cost of medical treatment even under reciprocal health service arrangements. The first part of a holiday insurance policy covers people. It will include the cost of doctor, ambulance and hospital treatment if needed. If needed the better companies will even pay for English language speaking doctors and nurses and will bring a sick or injured holidaymaker home by air ambulance.

The second part of a good policy covers things. If someone breaks into your motorhome and steals your passports and money, one phone call to the insurance company will have everything sorted out. If you manage to drive over your camera, it should be covered. NB – most policies have a maximum payment limit per item, do check that any valuables are adequately covered.

An important part of the insurance, often ignored, is cancellation (and curtailment) cover. Few things are as heartbreaking as having to cancel a holiday because a member of the family falls ill. Cancellation insurance can't take away the disappointment, but it makes sure you don't suffer financially as well. For this reason you should arrange your holiday insurance at least eight weeks before you set off.

Whichever insurance you choose we would advise reading very carefully the policies sold by the High Street travel trade. Whilst they may be good, they may not cover the specific needs of campers, caravanners and motorcaravanners.

Telephone 0870 405 4059 for a quote for our European Camping Holiday Insurance with cover arranged through Green Flag Motoring Assistance and Inter Group Assistance Services, one of the UK's largest assistance companies. Alternatively visit our website at www.insure4campers.com.

European Health Insurance Card (EHIC)

Important Changes since E111: Since September 2005 new European Health Insurance Cards have replaced the E111 forms .

Make sure you apply for your EHIC before travelling in Europe. Eligible travellers from the UK are entitled to receive free or reduced-cost medical care in many European countries on production of an EHIC. This free card is available by completing a form in the booklet 'Health Advice for Travellers' from local Post Offices. One should be completed for each family member. Alternatively visit www.dh.gov.uk/travellers and apply on-line. Please allow time to send your application off and have the EHIC returned to you.

The EHIC is valid in all European Community countries plus Iceland, Liechtenstein, Switzerland and Norway. If you or any of your dependants are suddenly taken ill or have an accident during a visit to any of these countries, free or reduced-cost emergency treatment is available - in most cases on production of a valid EHIC. Only state-provided emergency treatment is covered, and you will receive treatment on the same terms as nationals of the country you are visiting. Private treatment is generally not covered, and state-provided treatment may not cover all of the things that you would expect to receive free of charge from the NHS.

Remember an EHIC does not cover you for all the medical costs that you can incur or for repatriation - it is not an alternative to travel insurance. You will still need appropriate insurance to ensure you are fully covered for all eventualities.

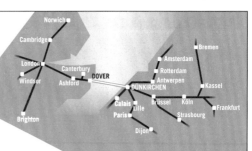
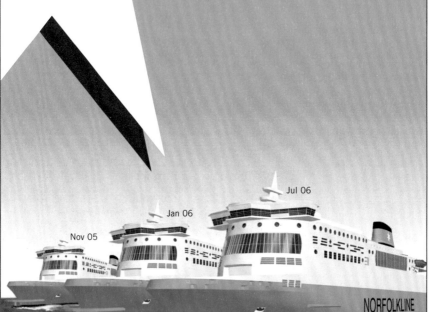

3 ISSUES FOR £1

Our practical titles are packed full of holiday tips, technical advice, reader reviews, superb photography…and much more! So subscribe to Practical Caravan or Practical Motorhome *for just £1.*

- **YOU** get your first 3 issues for £1
- **YOU** save 20% on the shop price after your trial
- **RISK-FREE** offer – you can cancel at any time
- **FREE** delivery, straight to your door!
- **EXCLUSIVE** subscriber offers and discounts

CALL 08456 777 812 NOW!

or visit **www.themagazineshop.com** quote code ALR07

☐ Please start my subscription to Practical Caravan. I will pay £1 for the first 3 issues and £8.16 every 3 issues thereafter, saving 20% on the shop price.

☐ Please start my subscription to Practical Motorhome. I will pay £1 for the first 3 issues and £7.68 every 3 issues thereafter, saving 20% on the shop price.

YOUR DETAILS BLOCK CAPITALS Please (must be completed)

Mr/Mrs/Ms _____ Name _____ Surname _____

Address_____

_____

_____ Postcode_____

Telephone_____

If you are happy to receive offers, news, product and service information from Haymarket Publishing and other carefully selected partners via email and SMS, please tick here ☐.

E-mail_____

Mobile_____

This offer is open to UK residents only and is a Direct Debit only offer. Details of the Direct Debit guarantee are available on request. For international rates please call +44 (0) 1750 724703. Offer ends 31 March 2007. Haymarket Publishing may contact you by post or phone from time to time, with special offers and product information. Please tick this box if you prefer not to receive this information ☐. Occasionally we may pass your details to carefully selected partners whose products we think would be of interest to you. Please tick this box if you prefer not to receive this information ☐.

DIRECT DEBIT DETAILS
Instructions to your Bank or Building Society to pay by Direct Debit

To The Manager: Bank/Building Society

Address

Postcode

Name(s) of Account Holder(s)

Branch Sort Code

Bank/Building Society account number

Reference Number (for office use only)

Signature(s)

DIRE
Originators ID No. 85

Instruction to your Bank or Building Society
Please pay Haymarket Publishing Services Ltd Direct Debits from the account detailed in this instruction subject to the safeguards assured by the Direct Debit Guarantee. I understand that this instruction may stay with Haymarket Publishing Services Ltd an if so, details will be passed electronically to my Bank/Building Society.

ALR0

Please return this form to: Practical Caravan/Motorhome
FREEPOST SEA 14716 Haywards Heath RH16 3BR

Save up to 60% on your holiday

Camping Cheque

- Over 575 sites – all just £10.30 per night
- Maximum flexibility - go as you please
- Fantastic Ferry Deals

Last year 250,000 people used nearly 1.6 million Camping Cheques and enjoyed half-price holidays around Europe. Make sure you don't miss out this year.

Huge off peak savings

Over 575 quality campsites, in 21 European countries, including the UK, all at just £10.30 per night for pitch + 2 adults, including electricity. That's a saving of up to 60% off normal site tariffs.

ferry savings

Ask about our famous special offers

- ☑ Caravans/trailers from **£7***each way
- ☑ Motorhomes Priced As Cars*

*Conditions apply – ask for details

CALL NOW

for your FREE

Holiday Savings

guide

FOR FULL INFORMATION VISIT

www.campingcheque.co.uk

Buy Cheques, check ferry availability, book everything on-line AND SAVE!

0870 405 4057

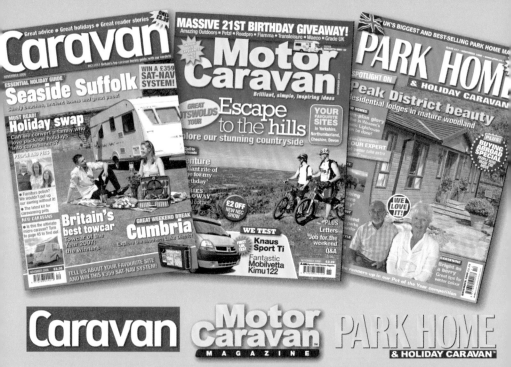

How do I save miles of driving in

France or Spain?

We know a way

Take one of our direct routes from Portsmouth, Poole or Plymouth and save yourself miles of unnecessary driving. You'll find your holiday begins the moment you step on board. And all for less than you'd expect.

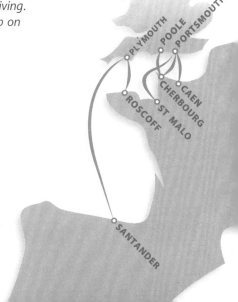

UnityPlus
CARD

NEW

Whether you have a caravan, a motorhome or a tent, the UnityPlus Card
is for you. It's not a club but it offers great benefits and it's free! Quite
simply, it offers unique discounts for campers and caravanners on a
range of products including cheap ferry deals, discounted holidays,
camping accessories, specialist insurance and more.

Full details at www.unity-plus.com
Request your UnityPlus Card today!

The Leading Campsites
in Europe

LeadingCampings – the pleasure of leisure.

We create that high level touring camping that you deserve for the most precious weeks of the year. 32 LeadingCampings throughout Europe guarantee first class vacations: in tent, caravan, motorcaravan or a wide range of rental accommodation. Enjoy also first class wellness spas, restaurants, sports and entertainment facilities. In this camping guide all entries of LeadingCampings are highlighted as 'member of the LeadingCampings'. Visit us on internet, order your personal LeadingCard and profit from all its benefits. You are welcome!

www.leadingcampings.com

LeadingCampings

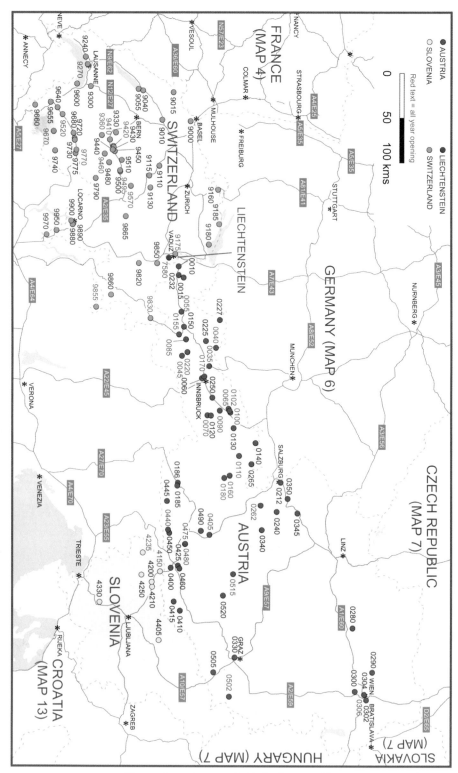

Please refer to the numerical index (page 551) for campsite page references

BELGIUM   NETHERLANDS
LUXEMBOURG

Red text = all year opening

0   50 kms   100 kms

6030   6090   EMDEN

GRONINGEN
6040   5770
6120

6080

5710   A28/E232
6820   5760   6140   5790

5735   6160
A7/E22   6150

5700   6190   5990
5980   5985
6000
NETHERLANDS   5810   6470
5720   6480
AMSTERDAM   A1/E30
6870   5670   ENSCHEDE
6840
5660   6830   6130
5680   5630
5620   6330   5780
5640   DEN HAAG   5850   6310
5600   5960   ARNHEM
ROTTERDAM   5870   GERMANY
6290   (MAP 6)
6960   6970   5950

5560   6950   5880
5540   5890
5570   5580   6790   ESSEN
5620   6560
6925   6920   6915   EINDHOVEN
5510   6930   5900   6520   A61/E31
5500   5910   DUSSELDORF
0660   5970
0655
ANTWERPEN   KOLN
0578   BRUGGE
OOSTENDE   0580   0780
0560   0565   0555   AKEN
0520   0550   GENT   A4/E40
0610   6580
0600   6530
A10/E17   0630   6540
BRUSSEL   LUIK
0570   0595   0590   0640
BELGIUM   0705   0700
LILLE   0740
0530   CHARLEROI   0730
0725   A60/E42
ARRAS   A2/E19   0735   7880
0770   0732   7780
0670   7770   7680
0720   7670   7650
7890   7870
7850   7640
7620   7610
AMIENS   0675   0680
N43/E44   0712   0715   LUXEMBOURG   7660
FRANCE   0710
(MAP 4)   7700

A1/E19

Please refer to the numerical index (page 551) for campsite page references

535

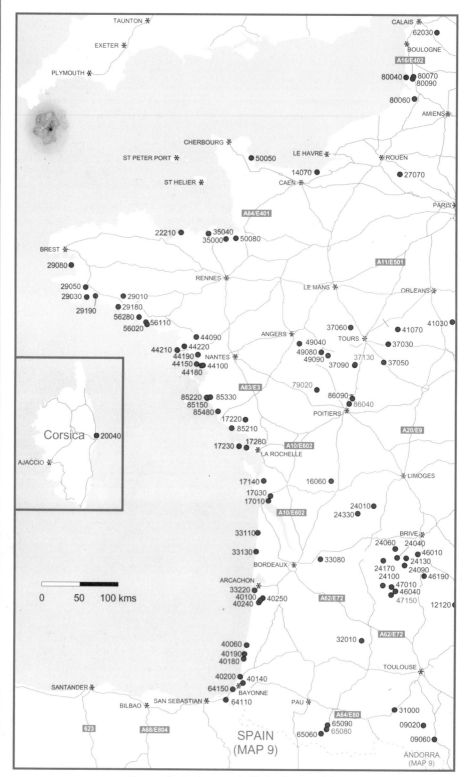

TAUNTON ✱

EXETER ✱

PLYMOUTH ✱

CALAIS ✱
62030 ●
BOULOGNE ✱
A16/E402
80040 ●● 80070
80090
80060 ●
AMIENS ✱

CHERBOURG ✱
ST PETER PORT ✱
LE HAVRE ✱
✱ ROUEN
50050 ●
14070 ●
27070 ●
ST HELIER ✱
CAEN ✱
PARIS ✱

A84/E401

22210 ●
35040 ●
35000 ●● 50080

BREST ✱
29080 ●

RENNES ✱
LE MANS ✱
ORLEANS ✱

A11/E501

29050 ●
29030 ●●
29010 ●
29190
29180 ●
56280 ●
56020 ●● 56110

37060 ●
41070 ●
41030 ●
37030 ●

ANGERS ✱
49040 ●
TOURS ✱
44090 ●
44220 ●
44210 ●●
44190 ●● NANTES ✱
44150 ●● 44100
44180 ●
49080 ●
49090 ●
37130
37090 ●
37050 ●

85220 ● 85330
85150 ●
85480 ●
A83/E3
79020
86090 ●
86040 ●
POITIERS ✱

17220 ●
85210 ●

Corsica ● 20040
17230 ●
17280 ●
17230 ●
A10/E602
LA ROCHELLE

AJACCIO ✱

17140 ●
16060 ●
✱ LIMOGES
17030 ●
17010 ●
24010 ●
A10/E602
24330 ●

A20/E9

33110 ●
BRIVE ✱
24060 ● 24040
33130 ●
46010 ●
24130
24170 ● 24090
24100 ● 46190
47010 ●
46040
47150

33080 ●
BORDEAUX ✱
ARCACHON ✱
33220 ●✱
40100 ● 40250
40240 ●
A62/E72
12120 ●

0   50   100 kms

40060 ●
40190 ●
40180 ●

32010 ●

A62/E72

TOULOUSE ✱

40200 ●
40140 ●
SANTANDER ✱
64150 ●✱
BAYONNE
64110 ●
BILBAO ✱
SAN SEBASTIAN ✱
PAU ✱
31000 ●
A64/E80
65090 ●
09020 ●
623
A68/E804
65060 ●
65080
09060 ●

SPAIN
(MAP 9)
ANDORRA
(MAP 9)

Please refer to the numerical index (page 551) for campsite page references

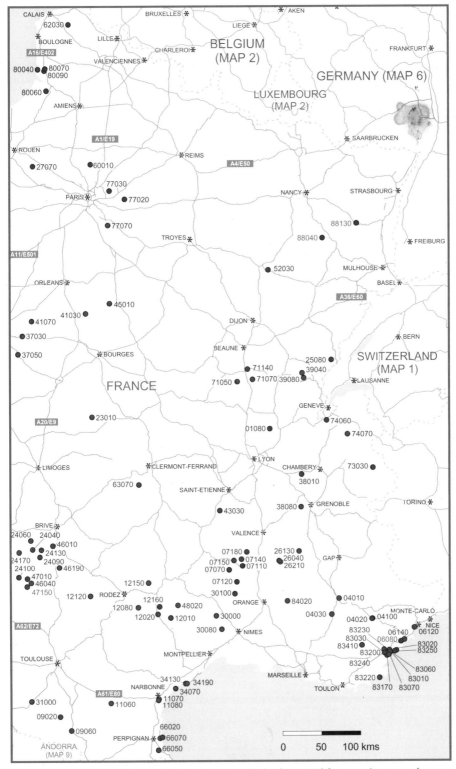

CALAIS ✳
62030 ●
BRUXELLES ✳
LIEGE ✳
AKEN ✳
BOULOGNE ✳
LILLE ✳
A16/E402
CHARLEROI ✳
BELGIUM
(MAP 2)
FRANKFURT ✳
VALENCIENNES ✳
GERMANY (MAP 6)
80040 ● ● 80070
80090
80060 ●
LUXEMBOURG
(MAP 2)
AMIENS ✳
SAARBRUCKEN ✳
✳ ROUEN
A1/E19
REIMS ✳
A4/E50
27070 ●
60010 ●
77030 ●
PARIS ✳
77020 ●
NANCY ✳
STRASBOURG ✳
88130 ●
FREIBURG ✳
77070 ●
TROYES ✳
88040 ●
A11/E501
52030 ●
MULHOUSE ✳
BASEL ✳
ORLEANS ✳
A36/E60
45010 ●
41030 ●
DIJON ✳
BERN ✳
41070 ●
37030 ●
BEAUNE ✳
SWITZERLAND
(MAP 1)
37050 ●
BOURGES ✳
25080 ●
39040 ●
71140 ●
FRANCE
71050 ●
71070 ● 39080 ●
LAUSANNE ✳
23010 ●
GENEVE ✳
A20/E9
74060 ●
01080 ●
74070 ●
LIMOGES ✳
CLERMONT-FERRAND ✳
LYON ✳
CHAMBERY ✳
73030 ●
63070 ●
SAINT-ETIENNE ✳
38010
38080 ●
GRENOBLE ✳
TORINO ✳
43030 ●
A62/E72
BRIVE ✳
VALENCE ✳
24060 ● 24040
46010 ●
26130 ●
GAP ✳
24130
07180 ●
26040 ●
24170 ● 24090
07150 ● 07140
26210 ●
24100
46190 ●
07070 ● 07110
47010 ●
12150 ●
07120 ●
46040 ●
12120 ●
RODEZ ✳
30100 ●
04010 ●
47150
MONTE-CARLO ✳
12160 ●
84020 ●
04100 ●
NICE ✳
12080 ●
48020 ●
ORANGE ✳
04020 ●
06140
06120
12020 ● 12010 ●
30000 ●
04030 ●
83230
06080 ●
83030
83020
30080 ●
NIMES ✳
83410
83250
TOULOUSE ✳
83200 ●
83060
MONTPELLIER ✳
83240
83010
31000 ●
MARSEILLE ✳
83220 ●
83170 83070
A61/E80
34130 ●
34190 ●
09020 ●
11060 ●
34070
TOULON ✳
11070
09060 ●
NARBONNE ✳
11080
ANDORRA
(MAP 9)
PERPIGNAN ✳
66020 ●
66070
66050 ●

0   50   100 kms

Please refer to the numerical index (page 551) for campsite page references

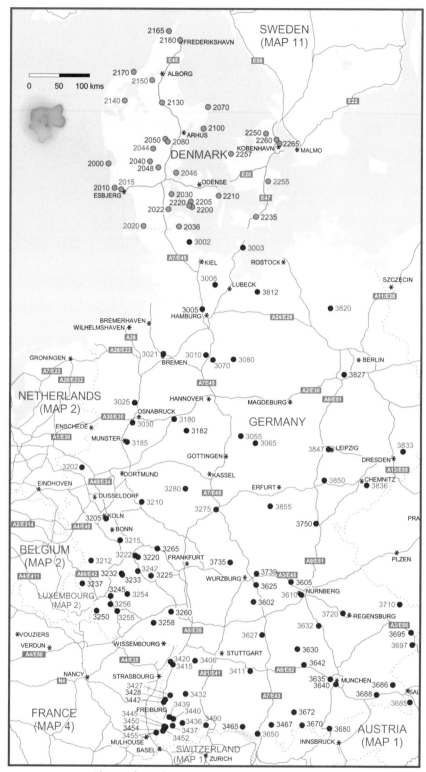

Please refer to the numerical index (page 551) for campsite page references

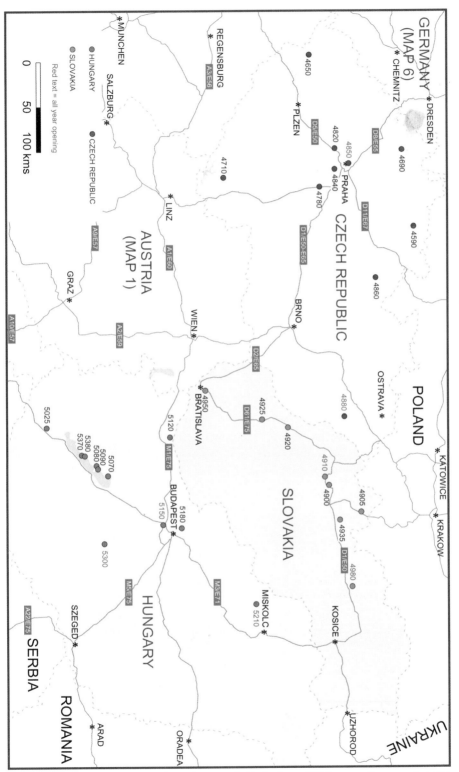

GERMANY
(MAP 6)
* CHEMNITZ
* DRESDEN

* REGENSBURG
*

A3/E6

* MUNCHEN

SALZBURG
*

GRAZ
*

SLOVAKIA
HUNGARY
CZECH REPUBLIC

Red text = all year opening

0   50   100 kms

4650

D8/E55

4690

4590

4860

D5/E50
4820
4850
4840
PRAHA
4780
* PLZEN
D11/E67

D1/E50-E55

4710

LINZ
*
A1/E60

AUSTRIA
(MAP 1)

A9/E57

WIEN
*

A2/E59

BRNO
*

CZECH REPUBLIC

OSTRAVA *

POLAND

4880

D2/E65

4950
BRATISLAVA
*

4925
D61/E75
4920

4910
4900

4905

4935
D1/E50
4980

SLOVAKIA

KATOWICE
*

KRAKOW
*

A10/E57

5025

5380
5370
5080
5090
5070

5120

M1/E75

BUDAPEST
*
5180

5150

5300

M5/E75

SZEGED
*

A22/E75

SERBIA

HUNGARY

M3/E71

MISKOLC
*
5210

KOSICE
*

UZHOROD
*

UKRAINE

ARAD
*

ORADEA
*

ROMANIA

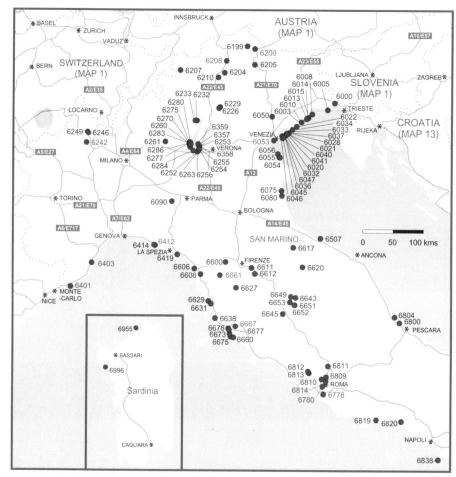

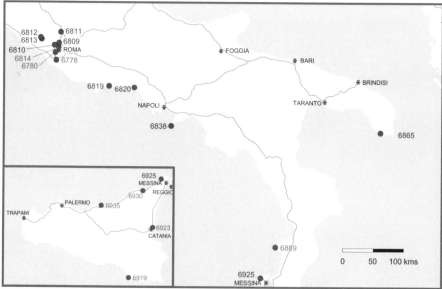

Please refer to the numerical index (page 551) for campsite page references

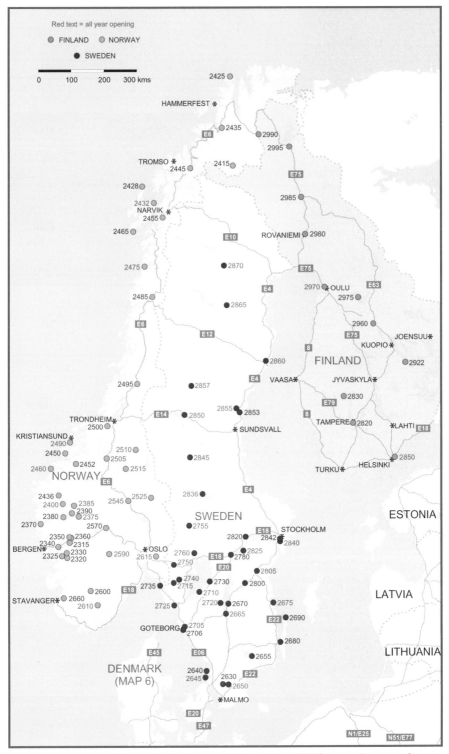

Red text = all year opening

○ FINLAND   ○ NORWAY
● SWEDEN

0   100   200   300 kms

2425

HAMMERFEST✳

2435
2990
2995

TROMSO✳
2445   2415

E6

E75

2428

2432
NARVIK✳
2455

2985

2465

E10

ROVANIEMI 2980

2475

2870

E75

2485

E6

2865

2970 OULU
2975

E4

E12

2960

E63

E75
KUOPIO✳

JOENSUU✳

2922

8

2860

FINLAND

2495

2857

E14   2850

2855 2853

E4   VAASA✳

JYVASKYLA✳

TRONDHEIM✳
2500

SUNDSVALL✳

8   2830

E79

KRISTIANSUND✳
2490
2450
2460   2452
NORWAY   E6

2510
2505
2515

2845

TAMPERE✳ 2820

LAHTI✳ E18

TURKU✳   HELSINKI 2850

2436
2400   2385
2390
2380   2375
2370   2570
2350 2360
2340   2315
BERGEN✳   2330
2325   2320

2545   2525

2836

E4

ESTONIA

SWEDEN
2755

2820
2842

STOCKHOLM
2840

E18

2590

✳OSLO
2615

2760
2750

2825
2780

E18
E20

2805

2735

2740
2715

2730

2800

LATVIA

STAVANGER✳   2660
2610

2600   E18

2725

2710
2720

2670
2665

2675

E22 2690

GOTEBORG
2705
2706

2680

E45   E06

2655

LITHUANIA

DENMARK
(MAP 6)

2640
2645

2630   E22
2650

E20

✳MALMO

E47

N1/E25   N51/E77

Please refer to the numerical index (page 551) for campsite page references

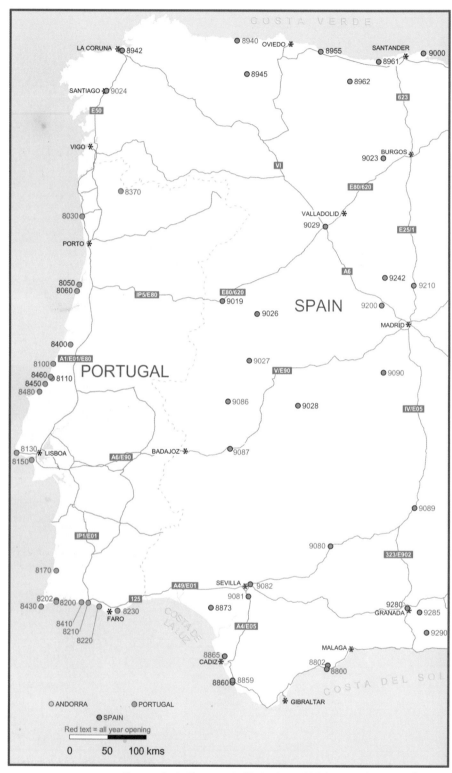

COSTA VERDE

LA CORUNA ✳ 8942
8940
OVIEDO ✳
8955
SANTANDER ✳
8961
9000

8945
8962

SANTIAGO ✳ 9024

E50

VIGO ✳

BURGOS ✳
9023

VI

E80/620

8370

E25/1

VALLADOLID ✳
9029

8030

PORTO ✳

A6
9242
9210

8050
8060

IP5/E80
E80/620
9019
9026
SPAIN
9200
MADRID ✳

8400

8100
A1/E01/E80
9027
PORTUGAL
9090

8460
8450
8110
V/E90

8480
9086
9028
IV/E05

8130
LISBOA ✳
BADAJOZ ✳
8150
A6/E90
9087

9089

IP1/E01

9080

8170
323/E902

8202
8200
A49/E01
SEVILLA ✳ 9082
9280
8430
125
9081
GRANADA ✳ 9285
8410
✳ 8230
8873
9290
8210
FARO
A4/E05
8220

8865
MALAGA ✳
8802
CADIZ ✳
8800
8860
8859
COSTA DEL SOL

○ ANDORRA   ● PORTUGAL
● SPIN ✳ GIBRALTAR

○ SPAIN

Red text = all year opening

0   50   100 kms

Please refer to the numerical index (page 551) for campsite page references

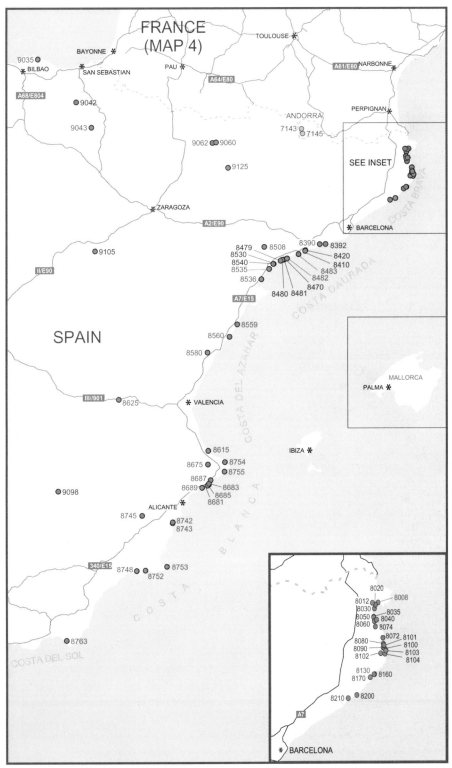

Please refer to the numerical index (page 551) for campsite page references

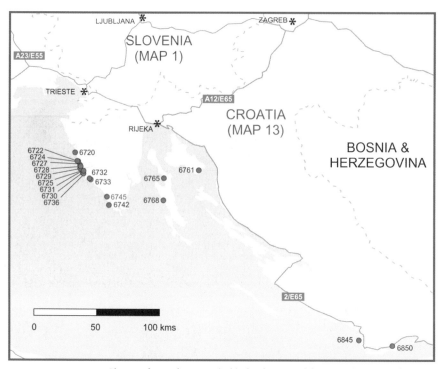

Please refer to the numerical index (page 551) for campsite page references

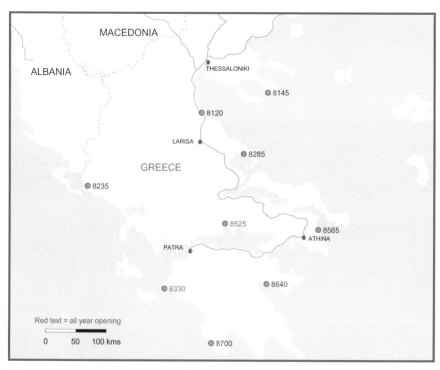

NOTE: For technical reasons, maps 5 and 12 have been omitted from this year's guide.
Campsites in the countries of the Baltic States, Poland and Romania are not included this year,
but are available in our guide to Central Europe.

Town and Village Index

Andorra
Andorra la Vella   16
La Massana   16
Xixerella   16

Austria
Abtenau   34
Aschau im Zillertal   27
Bairisch Kölldorf   38
Bruck   33
Döbriach   41, 45
Ehrwald   20
Faak am See   40
Fieberbrunn   26
Fügen   24
Grän   30
Graz   38
Hermagor-Presseggersee 42, 43
Innsbruck   27
Itter ba Hopfgarten   28
Jerzens   24
Kössen   28
Kötschach Mauthen   44
Kramsach   23, 25, 26
Landeck   29
Längenfeld   22
Leibnitz   39
Lienz   29
Maholmhof   31
Maltatal   42
Mondsee   34
Mühlen   39
Nassereith   30
Natters   20
Nenzing   18
Nußdorf am Attersee   34
Nüziders bei Bludenz   19
Obertraun   35
Ossiach   45
Peterdorf   39
Pettneu am Arlberg   23
Prutz   29
Raggal   18
Rauchenbichl   32
Rennweg   44
Salzburg   32
Schönbühel   36
Seefeld   22
St Margareten im Rosental   40
St Martin bei Lofer   32
St Primus   40
St Wolfgang   36
Tulln   36
Umhausen   30
Villach Landskron   44
Volders   25
Weer bei Schwaz   31
Wien   37, 38
Zell-am-See   31
Zell-am-Ziller   24

Belgium
Amberloup   58
Attert   57
Bachte-Maria-Leerne   53
Brugge   49
Bure-Tellin   52
De Haan   50
Deinze   53
Dochamps   51

Erezee   59
Gent   53
Geraardsbergen   52
Gierle   54
Grimbergen   53
Ieper   50
Jabbeke   48
Koksijde aan Zee   47
La Roche-en-Ardenne 55, 60
Lille   54
Lombardsijde Middelkerke   49
Manhay   59
Mons   48
Neufchâteau   56
Nieuwpoort   47
Opglabbeek   60
Oteppe   57
Oudenaarde   52
Overijse   54
Poupehan-sur-Semois   58
Sart-lez-Spa   55
Stavelot   51
Tintigny   58
Turnhout   56
Virton   57
Westende   49

Croatia
Baska   72
Bijela Uvala   63
Cervar   62
Cesta Valalta-Lim bb. 66
Cres Island   70
Fazana   69
Huljerat b.b.   73
Koversada   66
Martinscica   70
Monsena bb,   67, 72
Polari bb   68
Porec   62, 63
Porto Sole   65
Primosten   73
Pula   68
Rovinj   66-69, 72
Seget Donji   73
Valkanela   64
Vrsar   64-66
Zelena Laguna   63

Czech Republic
Benesov u Prahy   76
Chrustenice   76
Chvalsiny   78
Dolni Branna   77
Dolni Brezany   75
Horní Paseky   78
Kostelec n Orlicí   77
Lodenice   76
Plzenska   78
Praha   75
Roznov pod Radhostem   78
Velká Hledsebe   78
Vrchlabi   77
Zandov   76
Zlatniky - Liben   75

Denmark
Årgab   80
Blavand   81
Bojden   89

Broager   83
Charlottenlund   92
Diernæs   82
Ebberup   90
Ebeltoft   86
Esbjerg V-Sædding   80
Fåborg   89
Fakse   91
Fjerritslev   88
Føllenslev   90
Fredericia   84
Frederikshaven   88
Give   83
Grenå   86
Haderslev   82
Hampen   83
Hårby   89
Harderslev   82
Helnæs   90
Hesselager   89
Hillerod   91
Hobro   86
Hvide Sande   80
Jelling   84
Laven   85
Mogeltonder   80
Nærum   92
Nibe   87
Nykobing Mors   81
Ry   85
Sakskobing   90
Silkeborg   85
Skiveren/Aalbæk   87
Tonder   80
Trelde   84

Finland
Helsinki   94
Iisalmi   96
Ivalo   98
Karigasniemi   98
Manamansalo   96
Oulun Kaupunki   96
Rovaniemi   97
Sodankylä   97
Tampere   94
Varkaus   95
Virrat   95

France
Agde   186, 188
Agos Vidalos   182
Airvault   135
Alèria   203
Allés-sur-Dordogne   164
Andelys   114
Anduze   182
Argelès-Gazost   182
Aubenas   172
Autrans   142
Baguer-Pican   106
Barjac   184
Bédoin   179
Bénodet   100
Bidart   152
Bignac   160
Biron   163
Biscarosse   148, 151
Boisset-et-Gaujac   182
Bouillancourt-sous-Miannay 116

Bourdeaux	175	Millau	157	Telgruc-sur-Mer	104
Boussac-Bourg	168	Moliets-Plage	150	Trogues	129, 130
Brem sur Mer	126	Montcabrier	164	Ucel	172
Brissac	134	Montclar	183	Urrugne	155
Cagnes-sur-Mer	189	Montignac	162	Vallon-Pont-d'Arc	173
Candé-sur-Beuvron	133	Montsoreau	135	Vaubarlet	169
Canet-en-Roussillon	188, 190	Moyenneville	116	Vielle-St Girons	148
Carnac	112	Murol	169	Vieux-Mareuil	164
Castellane	176	Nampont-St Martin	117	Villecroze - Les Grottes	202
Caudon par Montfort	162	Nant-d'Aveyron	156	Villefranche-de-Rouergue	160
Cavalaire-sur-Mer	199	Narbonne	183, 184	Villeneuve-de-Berg	170
Chalon sur Saône	138	Neydens	141	Villers-sur-Authie	118
Chatillon	141	Niozelles	179	Vitrac	162
Clohars-Carnoët	105	Orouet	125	Volonne	178
Concarneau Cedex	103	Palau del Vidre	188		
Condat	166	Peigney	120	**Germany**	
Crespian	183	Peisey-Nancroix	143	Aitrang	225
Darbres	172	Pierrefitte-sur-Sauldre	132	Amtsberg	216
Dol-de-Bretagne	106	Poilly	132	Asbacherhütte	246
Eperlecques	115	Pommeuse	118	Bad Dürkheim	248
Erdeven	111	Pontchâteau	107	Bad Griesbach	227
Erquy	100	Pontorson	114	Bad Wildbad	229
Estaing	181	Pornic	105, 108	Badenweiler	230
Forcalquier	179	Privas	172	Barntrup	210
Fort-Mahon-Plage	115	Pyla-sur-Mer	147	Berchtesgaden	226
Francueil-Chenonceaux	130	Quimper	101	Braunlage	208
Fréjus	192, 196	Ravenoville-Plage	113	Bremen	206
Fresne-sur-Authie	117	Rivière-sur-Tarn	159	Bühl	229
Fumel	166	Roquebrune-sur-Argens		Clausthal-Zellerfeld	207
Gien	132		194, 198, 200	Creglingen-Münster	239
Gigny-sur-Saône	138	Route de la Châtre	168	Donautat	227
Guérande	112	Saint Cyr	135	Dresden	216
Houlgate	113	Saint Malo	104	Eggelstetten	221
Hourtin-Plage	144	Saint Marcel	138	Ellwangen	239
Ile d'Offard	134	Sainte-Mère-Eglise	113	Erlangen-Dechsendorf	218
Ile de Ré	124	Sainte-Sigolène	169	Ettenheim	234
Jablines	119	Salles-Curan	158	Flessenow	214
Jard-sur-Mer	127	Sanchey	119	Frankenhain	217
La Bastide-de-Sérou	180	Sanguinet	152	Freiburg	234
La Couarde sur Mer	124	Sarlat-la-Canéda	160, 162, 163	Frickenhausen	218
La Flotte en Ré	124	Saumur	134	Füssen im Allgäu	224
La Plaine-sur-Mer	106	Sauveterre-la-Lemance	167	Gemünden-Hofstetten	220
La Rochette	119	Séniergues	166	Gera-Aga	217
La Romieu	180	Sérignan	186	Groß Quassow	215
La Trinité-sur-Mer	112	Sonzay	128	Güls	242
Labenne Océan	151	Souillac-sur-Dordogne	165	Hamburg	206
Lac Chambon	169	St Aygulf	200	Hausbay-Pfalzfeld	245
Lac de Pareloup	158	St Boil	140	Herbolzheim	231
Lacanau-Océan	146	St Brévin-les-Pins	110	Hohegeiss	208
Langres	120	St Dié-des-Vosges	120	Irring b. Passau	227
Largentière	170	St Emilion	144	Isny	238
Lau-Balagnas	182	St Geniez-d'Olt	158	Issigau	221
Le Cannet	191	St Georges-de-Didonne	122	Kipfenberg	219
Le Château-d'Oléron	121	St Georges-les-Baillargeaux	136	Kirchheim	241
Le Croisic	108	St Hilaire-de-Riez	120	Kirchzarten	231
Le Grand-Bornand	142	St Jean-de-Monts	125, 126	Klein Rönnau	212
Le Poët Célard	174	St Jouan des Guerets	104	Kleinröhrsdorf	216
Le Pouldu	105	St Julien-en-Genevois	141	Koblenz	242
Les Abrets	142	St Just-Luzac	122	Köln-Poll	211
Loches en Touraine	129	St Léon-sur-Vézère	162	Krün / Obb	225
Locunolé	102	St Leu-d'Esserent	115	Lahnstein	242
Malbuisson	140	St Martin de Seignanx	143	Laichingen	239
Mandelieu-la-Napoule	191	St Pardoux	161	Leipzig	217
Marigny	141	St Paul de Varax	171	Leiwen	246
Martres-Tolosane	181	St Privat de Champclos	184	Limburg an der Lahn	240
Medis	121	St Raphaël	202	Lindau-Oberreitnau	223
Melun	119	St Raphaël – Agay	192	Lorch am Rhine	241
Menglon	174	Ste Nathalène	163	Markdorf	237
Messanges	154	Ste Reine de Bretagne	107	Mesenich bei Cochem	246
Meyrueis	170	Tarascon-sur-Ariege	181	Mühlhausen bei Augsburg	224

München	222	**Italy**		S. Anna di Chioggia	307
Münster	210	Aglientu	340	S. Arcangelo Magione	325
Münstertal	235	Alghero	340	S. Arcangelo sul Trasimeno	324
Neuenburg (am Rhein)	232	Ameglia	266	S. Baronto di	
Neuerburg	244	Baia Domizia	334	Lamporecchio	314
Nürnberg	218	Bardolino	282	S. Croce Camerina	338
Oberhof	217	Bibione	296	S. Felice del Benaco	267, 272,
Olpe-Sondern	211	Bibione-Pineda	292, 294		277, 280
Pielenhofen	228	Bracciano	330, 331	S. Gimignano	314
Potsdam	214	Calceranica al Lago	286	S. Maria di Leuca	336
Prien am Chiemsee	226	Caorle	291	S. Nicolo di Ricadi	334
Rabenkirchen-Faulück	212	Capo Vaticano di Ricadi	334	S. Remo	264
Reinsfeld	248	Castiglione del Lago	325	S. Vincenzo	317
Remagen	243	Castiglione della Pescaia	318	Salto di Fondi	331
Rheinmunster	228	Catania	337	Sarteano	318
Rieste	207	Cavallino-Treporti	294-301	Scarlino	322
Saarburg	247	Cecina Mare	316	Silvi	332
Seelbach	232	Ceriale	264	Sottomarina	307
Senheim	244	Chioggia	308	Tabiano di	
Soltau	206	Chiusa	286	Salsomaggiore Terme	309
Sommerach am Main	219	Cisano di Bardolino	276	Toblach	288
Stadtkyll	243	Cortina d'Ampezzo	290	Torre del Lago Puccini	312
Staufen	237	Deiva Marina	262, 263	Treporti	306
Suderburg/Hosseringen	209	Eraclea Mare	295	Trieste	280
Sulzburg	236	Fiano Romano	326	Troghi - Firenze	313
Tecklenburg-Leeden	209	Figline Valdarno	315	Tuoro sul Trasimeno	323
Tengen	238	Finale di Pollina	339	Ugento	336
Titisee	236	Fiorenzuola di Focara	311	Vada	316
Todtnau-Muggenbrunn	230	Fondotoce di Verbania	261	Verbania Fondotoce	260
Trippstadt	247	Fusina	304	Völs am Schlern	285
Vlotho	209	Gavorrano	320		
Vöhl-Herzhausen	240	Grado	283	**Liechtenstein**	
Waging am See	227	Iseo	266	Triesen	341
Wesel	210	Isolaverde	307		
Wietzendorf	208	Laives (Bolzano)	287	**Luxembourg**	
Wolfach-Halbmeil	230	Lazise	270, 272	Boulaide	349
Wolfstein	248	Lévico Terme	289	Diekirch	349
Wulfen auf Fehmarn	213	Lido degli Scacchi	310	Enscherange	346
Zwiesel	219	Lido di Jésolo	302, 308	Esch-sur-Alzette	348
		Lido Estensi	309	Heiderscheid	348
Greece		Lignano Sabbiadoro	283	Hosingen	345
Assini	252	Manerba del Garda	276-279	Kockelscheuer	345
Chrisso	251	Marina del Cantone	333	Larochette	343
Delphi	251	Marina di Grosseto	321	Larochette/Medernach	344
Gialova	252	Massa Lubrense	333	Lieler	349
Glifa	251	Messina	338	Maulusmühle	346
Igoumenitsa	250	Molina di Ledro	288	Nommern	343
Kato Gatzea	251	Moniga del Garda	274	Obereisenbach	347
Koroni	252	Montopoli	319	Reisdorf	344
Nafplio	252	Novafeltria	311		
Neos Marmaras	250	Ognina	337	**Netherlands**	
Neos Panteleimonas	250	Oliveri	337	Afferden	378
Platamon-Pieria	250	Oriago	302	Amstelveen	360
Plataria	250	Orta San Giulio	262	Amsterdam	359
Pylos	252	Pacengo	268	Arcen	380
Rafina	252	Passignano sul Trasimeno	323	Arnhem	374
Vartholomino Ilias	251	Perticara	311	Beerze-Ommen	371
		Peschiera del Garda	269, 274	Bergeyk	376
Hungary		Pieve di Ledro	290	Berkhout	363
Aszófô	254	Pineta di Vignola Mare	340	Bloemendaal aan Zee	361
Balatonalmádi	254	Pisa	312	Breskens	352
Balatonfüred	256	Prad am Stilfserjoch	284	Buren	365
Balatonszepezd	254	Punta Ala	320	Callantsoog	362
Dunafoldvar	258	Punta Sabbioni	300, 301	Dalfsen	372
Györszentivan-Kertváros	257	Rasun	283	Delft	357
Szilvásvárad	258	Riccione	310	Den Haag	357
Törökbálint	256	Rivoltella	268	Denekamp	370
Üröm	257	Rodia	338	Echten	368
Zalakaros	258	Roma	326-330	Erichem	373
		Roseto Degli Abruzzi	332	Groede	352

Groningen	367	Malmefjorden	388	Turany		408
Gulpen	378	Mauranger	384			
Harlingen	365	Nå	384	**Slovenia**		
Hellevoetsluis	357	Norheimsund	385	Bled		413
Heumen	373	Odda	385	Bohinjska Bistrica		413
Hilvarenbeek	377	Olberg	392	Lesce		412
Kamperland	353	Oppdal	396	Mojstrana		412
Katwijk	358	Orkanger	395	Postojna		414
Koudum	364	Osen	391	Recica ob Savinji		414
Lage Mierde	376	Osloveien	391	Soca		412
Lauwersoog	366	Oteren	396			
Loosdrecht	362	Oyer	392	**Spain**		
Luttenberg	370	Roros	391	Alcossebre		444
Maasbree	379	Rysstad	382	Almonte		459
Maurik	374	Saltstraumen	394	Altea		452
Nieuwvliet	351	Sandvik Sor	389	Ametlla de Mar		438
Noord-Scharwoude	360	Skarsvag	393	Banos de Fortuna		452
Oosterhout	375	Snasa	395	Begur	422,	428
Opende	366	Sogndal	389	Benicasim		443
Otterlo	372	Storforshei	305	Benidorm	447, 448,	452
Ouddorp	358	Suonpatjavri	392	Boltaña		471
Renesse	355	Tinn Austbygd	383	Cabo de Gata		454
Reutum/Weerselo	370	Trogstad	392	Cáceres		461
Rheeze-Hardenberg	372	Ulvik	386	Calonge	428,	429
Rijnsburg	356	Vangsnes	389	Cambrils	434,	442
Ruinen	368	Vassenden	390	Campell		445
Schipborg	369	Viggja	395	Caravia Alta		468
Sevenum	379			Carril de Pilahito		457
Sint-Oedenrode	378	**Portugal**		Cartagena		453
Sumar	364	Albufeira	399	Castelló d`Empúries	418,	419
Uitdam	361	Armacao de Pera	400	Castrojeriz		465
Urk	375	Aveiro	405	Ciudad Rodrigo		464
Vijlen-Vaals	380	Campo do Gerês	406	Conil de la Frontera	457,	458
Vinkeloord	377	Cascais	402	Córdoba		459
Vogelenzang	363	Cerro das Moitas	400	El Escorial		463
Wageningen-Hoog	375	Costa da Caparica	402	El Puerto de Santa Maria		458
Wassenaar	359	Costa Nova do Prado	405	El Rocio		459
Wemeldinge	354	Espiche	398	Empúria-brava		416
Westerbork	367	Estela	406	Etxarri-Aranatz		471
Wezuperbrug	367	Foz do Arelho	403	Granada		455
Wijlre	380	Gafanha da Encarnação	405	Guadalupe		461
Wolphaartsdijk	353, 354	Lagos	398	Guardamar del Segura		448
Workum	363	Louriçal	404	Güejar-Sierra		455
Zouteland	352	Nazaré	403, 404	Hospitalet del Infante		440
		Odeceixe	401	Isla Plana		453
Norway		Odemira	401	Jávea		446
Ålesund	386	Olhao	401	L`Estartit		424
Alta	393	Pinheiros de Marim	401	L'Escala		425
Alvdal	391	Póvoa de Varzim	406	La Cabrera		464
Åndalsnes	387	Quarteira	400	La Manga del Mar Menor		453
Andenes	393	Quinta de Ste Antonio	402	La Marina		450
Averoy	386	Quinta dos Patos	405	La Pineda		432
Ballangen	394	Sagres	400	La Puebla de Castro		472
Borsto	385	Sao Jacinto	405	La Vall de Laguar		445
Brekke	387	Sao Martinho do Porto	402	Labuerda		471
Byglandsfjord	382	São Miguel	401	Lloret de Mar		430
Byrkjelo	390	Sao Pedro de Moel	403	Luarca		467
Ekkilsoya	386	Valado	403	Malpartida de Plasencia		460
Engan	396	Valverde	398	Marbella	456,	457
Gåseid	386			Mendigorria		470
Gaupne	389	**Slovakia**		Mérida		462
Gol	390	Bratislava	410	Mesones		462
Granvin	384	Demanovska Dolina	409	Miranda del Castañar		465
Harstad	396	Levoca	410	Molinicos		462
Horgheimseidet	387	Martin	408	Montroig	440,	441
Jørpehand	383	Na Ostrove	409	Moraira-Teulada		447
Kabelvag	394	Namestovo	408	Mundaka		470
Kautokeino	392	Oravska Priehrada	408	Noja		469
Kinsarvilk	383	Piestany	409	Nuevalos		472
Lærdal	388	Trencin	409	Oliva		445

Pals	423	Hakangen	480	Engelberg		499
Peñiscola	442	Hallstahammar	484	Frutigen		494
Pitres	454	Höör	476	Gampelen		494
Platja d'Aro	426, 428	Huddinge	486	Grindelwald		497
Platja de Pals	424, 427, 426	Jokkmokk	489	Gwatt		492
Playa de la Rubina	416	Jonkoping	477	Hasliberg Goldern		498
Playa de Ris	469	Jularp	476	Horw-Luzern		500
Playa de Sa Riera	422	Kil	483	Interlaken	491, 496
Poboleda	436	Kolmården	484	Interlaken-Thunersee		492
Potes-Turieno	468	Kramfors	488	Krattigen		496
Puebla de Montalban	462	Läckögatan	479	Kreuzlingen		504
Roda de Bará	432, 437	Lidköping	479	La Fouly		508
Roses	420	Linköping	484	Landquart		502
Ruiloba	468	Lysingsvägen	478	Langwiesen		503
Salou	434, 438	Mårdslyckesand	476	Lausanne		515
Sant Pere Pescador	417-422	Marholmsvagen	474	Lauterbrunnen		495
Santa Cruz	467	Mariestad	481	Le Landeron		513
Santa Elena	460	Mölle	475	Le Prese		502
Santiago de Compostela	466	Mora	486	Les Haudères		509
Segovia	465	Örebro	483	Locarno		515
Sevilla	456	Ostersund	487	Martigny		508
Sitges	429	Ramvik	487	Matten		496
Somiedo	467	Röstånga	475	Meiringen		500
Tamarit	436	Skärholmen	485	Meride		507
Tarragona	436	Södra Moränvägen	479	Montmelon		512
Toledo	462	Sommarrovägen	483	Morges		513
Tordesillas	466	Sommarvik	482	Morteratsch		502
Torroella de Montgrí	416	Stöllet	482	Muzzano		506
Tossa de Mar	430	Stromstad	481	Pontresina		502
Valle de Lago	467	Strömsund	488	Randa		510
Vilanova i la Geltru	433	Sveg	487	Raron		510
Villajoyosa	450	Tidaholm	480	Reckingen		512
Villargordo del Cabriel	446	Tingsryd	476	Reinach bei Basel		505
		Torekov	474	Saillon		508
Sweden		Uddevalla	480	Sempach-Stadt		500
Arboga	485	Umeå	488	Sierre		509
Årjäng	482	Västervik	478	Solothurn		505
Arvidsjaur	489			St Ursanne		512
Askim	474	**Switzerland**		Sur En / Sent		501
Berggärdsvägen	484	Arbon	504	Susten		509
Byxelkrok	479	Bad Ragaz	503	Susten-Leuk		510
Dals Långed	481	Bonigen	497	Tariche		512
Ed	479	Bouveret	507	Tenero		506
Färjestaden	478	Brienz am See	498	Vétroz		507
Frykenbaden	483	Châtel-St-Denis	511	Visp		511
Goteborg	477	Churwalden	501	Vitznau		501
Granna	477	Disentis	503			

Widely regarded as the 'Bible' by site owners and readers alike, there is no better guide when it comes to forming an independent view of a campsite's quality. When you need to be confident in your choice of campsite, you need the Alan Rogers Guide.

☑ Sites only included on merit

☑ Sites cannot pay to be included

☑ Independently inspected, rigorously assessed

☑ Impartial reviews

☑ 40 years of expertise

Andorra
AN7143 Xixerella 16
AN7145 Valira 16

Austria
AU0010 Nenzing 18
AU0015 Grosswalsertal 18
AU0035 Alpin Seefeld 22
AU0040 Zugspitze 20
AU0045 Ötztal 22
AU0055 Arlberg 23
AU0060 Natterer See 20
AU0065 Seehof 23
AU0070 Hofer 24
AU0080 Schloß-Camping 25
AU0085 Mountain Camp
Pitztal 24
AU0090 Zillertal-Hell 24
AU0100 Toni 25
AU0102 Stadlerhof 26
AU0110 Tirol Camp 26
AU0120 Aufenfeld 27
AU0130 Schloßberg Itter 28
AU0140 Wilder Kaiser 28
AU0150 Riffler 29
AU0155 Prutz 29
AU0160 Zell am See 31
AU0170 Kranebitten 27
AU0180 Woferlgut 33
AU0185 Seewiese 29
AU0212 Stadtblick 32
AU0220 Krismer 30
AU0225 Schloß
Fernsteinsee 30
AU0227 Camp Grän 30
AU0232 Sonnenberg 19
AU0240 Appesbach 36
AU0250 Alpencamping 31
AU0262 Oberwötzlhof 34
AU0265 Grubhof 32
AU0280 Stumpfer 36
AU0290 Tulln 36
AU0300 Rodaun 37
AU0302 Neue Donau 37
AU0304 Wien-Sud 37
AU0306 Wien West 38
AU0330 Central 38
AU0340 Am See 35
AU0345 Gruber 34
AU0350 Mond See Land 34
AU0400 Arneitz 40
AU0405 Ramsbacher 44
AU0410 Turnersee 40
AU0415 Rosental Roz 40
AU0425 Berghof 44
AU0440 Schluga 43
AU0445 Kotschach
Mauthen 44
AU0450 Schluga See 42
AU0460 Ossiachersee 45
AU0475 Brunner am See 45
AU0480 Burgstaller 41
AU0490 Maltatal 42
AU0502 Im Thermenland 38
AU0505 Leibnitz 39

AU0515 Katschtal 39
AU0520 Badesee 39

Belgium
BE0520 De Blekker 47
BE0530 Waux-Hall 48
BE0550 Nieuwpoort 47
BE0555 Klein Strand 48
BE0560 De Lombarde 49
BE0565 Westende 49
BE0570 Jeugdstadion 50
BE0578 Ter Duinen 50
BE0580 Memling 49
BE0590 De Gavers 52
BE0595 Oudenaarde 52
BE0600 Groeneveld 53
BE0610 Blaarmeersen 53
BE0630 Grimbergen 53
BE0640 Druivenland 54
BE0655 Lilse Bergen 54
BE0660 Baalse Hei 56
BE0670 La Clusure 52
BE0675 Spineuse 56
BE0680 Sud 57
BE0700 Spa d'Or 55
BE0705 Hirondelle 57
BE0710 Vallée de Rabais 57
BE0712 Ile De Faigneul 58
BE0715 Chênefleur 58
BE0720 Tonny 58
BE0725 Val de L'Aisne 59
BE0730 Moulin-Malempre 59
BE0732 Floreal La Roche 60
BE0735 Petite Suisse 51
BE0740 Eau Rouge 51
BE0770 Vieux Moulin 55
BE0780 Wilhelm Tell 60

Croatia
CR6720 Ulika 62
CR6722 Zelena Laguna 62
CR6724 Bijela Uvala 63
CR6725 Porto Sole 65
CR6727 Valkanela 64
CR6728 Orsera 64
CR6729 Koversada 66
CR6730 Amarin 67
CR6731 Valalta 66
CR6732 Polari 68
CR6733 Vestar 69
CR6736 Valdaliso 72
CR6742 Stoja 68
CR6745 Bi-Village 69
CR6761 Zablace 72
CR6765 Kovacine 70
CR6768 Slatina 70
CR6845 Adriatic 73
CR6850 Camp Seget 73

Czech Republic
CZ4590 Lisci Farma 77
CZ4650 Luxor 78
CZ4690 Slunce 76
CZ4710 Chvalsiny 78
CZ4780 Konopiste 76

CZ4820 Valek 76
CZ4840 Oase 75
CZ4850 Sokol Troja 75
CZ4860 Orlice 77
CZ4880 Roznov 78

Denmark
DK2000 Nordsø 80
DK2010 Hvidbjerg Strand 81
DK2015 Ådalens 80
DK2020 Mogeltonder 80
DK2022 Vikær Diernæs 82
DK2030 Sandersvig 82
DK2036 Gammelmark 83
DK2040 Riis 83
DK2044 Hampen Sø 83
DK2046 Trelde Næs 84
DK2048 Faarup Sø 84
DK2050 Terrassen 85
DK2070 Fornæs 86
DK2080 Holmens 85
DK2100 Blushoj 86
DK2130 Hobro Gattenborg 86
DK2140 Jesperhus 81
DK2150 Solyst 87
DK2165 Skiveren 87
DK2170 Klim Strand 88
DK2180 Nordstrand 88
DK2200 Bojden 89
DK2205 Logismosestrand 89
DK2210 Bøsøre 89
DK2220 Helnæs 90
DK2235 Sakskobing Gron 90
DK2250 Hillerød 91
DK2255 Feddet 91
DK2257 Vesterlyng 90
DK2260 Nærum 92
DK2265 Charlottenlund 92

Finland
FI2820 Tampere Härmälä 94
FI2830 Lakari 95
FI2850 Rastila 94
FI2922 Taipale 95
FI2960 Koljonvirta 96
FI2970 Nallikari 96
FI2975 Manamansalo 96
FI2980 Ounaskoski 97
FI2985 Sodankylä Nilimella 97
FI2990 Tenorinne 98
FI2995 Ukonjarvi 98

France
FR01080 Etang du Moulin 171
FR04010 Hippocampe 178
FR04020 Le Camp
du Verdon 176
FR04030 Moulin de Ventre 179
FR04100 International 176
FR06080 Les Cigales 191
FR06120 Green Park 189
FR06140 Ranch 191
FR07070 Les Ranchisses 170
FR07110 Le Pommier 170
FR07120 L'Ardéchois 173

FR07140	Les Lavandes	172
FR07150	Domaine de Gil	172
FR07180	Ardèche	172
FR09020	L'Arize	180
FR09060	Le Pré Lombard	181
FR11060	Arnauteille	183
FR11070	Les Mimosas	183
FR11080	La Nautique	184
FR12010	Val de Cantobre	156
FR12020	Les Rivages	157
FR12080	Les Genêts	158
FR12120	Rouergue	160
FR12150	Marmotel	158
FR12160	Les Peupliers	159
FR14070	La Vallée	113
FR16060	Marco de Bignac	160
FR17010	Bois Soleil	122
FR17030	Le Bois Roland	121
FR17140	Sequoia Parc	122
FR17220	La Brande	121
FR17230	L'Océan	124
FR17280	La Grainetière	124
FR20040	Riva Bella	203
FR22210	Bellevue	100
FR23010	Château de	
	Poinsouze	168
FR24010	Le Verdoyer	161
FR24040	Moulin du Roch	160
FR24060	Le Paradis	162
FR24090	Soleil Plage	162
FR24100	Le Moulinal	163
FR24130	Grottes de Roffy	163
FR24170	Port de Limeuil	164
FR24330	Etang Bleu	164
FR25080	Les Fuvettes	140
FR26040	Le Couspeau	174
FR26130	Hirondelle	174
FR26210	Bois du Chatelas	175
FR27070	l'Isle des Trois Rois	114
FR29010	Ty-Nadan	102
FR29030	Du Letty	100
FR29050	Orangerie de	
	Lanniron	101
FR29080	Le Panoramic	104
FR29180	Les Embruns	105
FR29190	Les Prés Verts	103
FR30000	Gaujac	182
FR30080	Mas de Reilhe	183
FR30100	La Sablière	184
FR31000	Le Moulin	181
FR32010	Florence	180
FR33080	Barbanne	144
FR33110	Côte d'Argent	144
FR33130	Les Grands Pins	146
FR33220	Petit Nice	147
FR34070	Sérignan Plage	186
FR34130	Le Neptune	186
FR34190	Champs Blancs	188
FR35000	Vieux Chêne	106
FR35040	P'tit Bois	104
FR37030	Moulin Fort	130
FR37050	La Citadelle	129
FR37060	Arada Parc	128
FR37090	La Rolandière	130
FR37130	Parc des Allais	129
FR38010	Coin Tranquille	142
FR38080	Au Joyeux Réveil	142
FR39040	La Pergola	141
FR39080	Domaine de	
	l'Epinette	141
FR40060	Eurosol	148
FR40100	La Rive	148
FR40140	Lou P'tit Poun	143
FR40180	Le Vieux Port	154
FR40190	Saint Martin	150
FR40200	Sylvamar	151
FR40240	Mayotte Vacances	151
FR40250	Les Grands Pins	152
FR41030	Alicourts	132
FR41070	Grande Tortue	133
FR43030	Vaubarlet	169
FR44090	Deffay	107
FR44100	Le Patisseau	105
FR44150	La Tabardière	106
FR44180	Boutinardière	108
FR44190	Le Fief	110
FR44210	de l'Ocean	108
FR44220	Parc de Léveno	112
FR45010	Bois du Bardelet	132
FR46010	Paille Basse	165
FR46040	Moulin de	
	Laborde	164
FR46190	Domaine de la	
	Faurie	166
FR47010	Moulin du Périé	167
FR47150	Guillalmes	166
FR48020	Capelan	170
FR49040	Etang	134
FR49080	Ile d'Offard	134
FR49090	Isle Verte	135
FR50050	Le Cormoran	113
FR50080	Haliotis	114
FR52030	Lac de la Liez	120
FR56020	La Plage	112
FR56110	Moustoir	112
FR56280	Les Sept Saints	111
FR60010	Campix	115
FR62030	Château de	
	Gandspette	115
FR63070	Le Pré Bas	169
FR64110	Col d'Ibardin	155
FR64150	Residence des Pins	152
FR65060	Pyrenees Natura	181
FR65080	Lavedan	182
FR65090	Soleil du Pibeste	182
FR66020	Ma Prairie	188
FR66050	Le Haras	188
FR66070	Le Brasilia	190
FR71050	Moulin de	
	Collonge	140
FR71070	Epervière	138
FR71140	Pont de	
	Bourgogne	138
FR73030	Les Lanchettes	143
FR74060	La Colombière	141
FR74070	Escale	142
FR77020	Le Chêne Gris	118
FR77030	Jablines	119
FR77070	Belle Etoile	119
FR79020	Courte Vallée	135
FR80040	Le Royon	115
FR80060	Val de Trie	116
FR80070	Ferme des Aulnes	117
FR80090	Val d'Authie	118
FR83010	Pins Parasol	192
FR83020	Esterel	192
FR83030	Leï Suves	194
FR83060	La Baume	196
FR83070	Etoile d'Argens	200
FR83170	La Bergerie	194
FR83200	Les Pêcheurs	198
FR83220	Cros de Mouton	199
FR83230	Colombier	196
FR83240	Moulin des Iscles	200
FR83250	Douce Quiétude	202
FR83410	Le Ruou	202
FR84020	Bélézy	179
FR85150	La Yole	125
FR85210	Les Ecureuils	127
FR85220	Acapulco	126
FR85330	Cap Natur'	128
FR85480	Le Chaponnet	126
FR86040	Le Futuriste	136
FR86090	Saint Cyr	135
FR88040	Lac de Bouzey	119
FR88130	Vanne de Pierre	120

Germany
DE3002	Schlei-Karschau	212
DE3003	Wulfener Hals	213
DE3005	Schnelsen Nord	206
DE3008	Klüthseecamp	212
DE3010	Röders Park	206
DE3021	Am Stadtwaldsee	206
DE3025	Alfsee	207
DE3030	Tecklenburg	209
DE3055	Prahljust	207
DE3065	am Bärenbache	208
DE3070	Süd-See	208
DE3080	Hardausee	209
DE3180	Sonnenwiese	209
DE3182	Teutoburger Wald	210
DE3185	Münster	210
DE3202	Grav-Insel	210
DE3205	Stadt Köln	211
DE3210	Biggesee	211
DE3212	Wirfttal	243
DE3215	Goldene Meile	243
DE3220	Burg Lahneck	242
DE3222	Moselbogen	242
DE3225	Suleika	241
DE3232	Family Club	246
DE3233	Holländischer Hof	244
DE3237	In der Enz	244
DE3242	Schinderhannes	245
DE3245	Sonnenberg	246
DE3250	Warsberg	247
DE3254	Harfenmühle	246
DE3255	Am Königsberg	248
DE3256	Hunsrück	248
DE3258	Sägmühle	247
DE3260	Bad Dürkheim	248
DE3265	Lahn	240
DE3275	Seepark	241
DE3280	Teichmann	240

DE3406	Kleinenzhof	229
DE3411	Heidehof	239
DE3415	Adam	229
DE3420	Oberrhein	228
DE3427	Schwarzwälder	
	Hof	232
DE3428	Oase	234
DE3432	Bonath	230
DE3436	Bankenhof	236
DE3437	Hochschwarzwald	230
DE3439	Freiburg	234
DE3440	Kirchzarten	231
DE3442	Herbolzheim	231
DE3445	Belchenblick	237
DE3450	Münstertal	235
DE3452	Alte Sägemühle	236
DE3454	Badenweiler	230
DE3455	Gugel's	232
DE3465	Wirthshof	237
DE3467	Isnycamping	238
DE3490	Hegau	238
DE3602	Romantische Str.	239
DE3605	Rangau	218
DE3610	Nürnberg	218
DE3625	Frickenhausen	218
DE3627	Ellwangen	239
DE3630	Donau-Lech	221
DE3632	Altmühltal	219
DE3635	Obermenzing	222
DE3640	Thalkirchen	222
DE3642	Lech	224
DE3650	Gitzenweiler	223
DE3670	Hopfensee	224
DE3672	Elbsee	225
DE3680	Tennsee	225
DE3685	Allweglehen	226
DE3686	Strandcamping	227
DE3688	Panorama Harras	226
DE3695	Dreiflüsse	227
DE3697	Dreiqueller	227
DE3710	Bayerischer Wald	219
DE3720	Naabtal	228
DE3735	Schönrain	220
DE3739	Katzenkopf	219
DE3750	Issigau	221
DE3812	Flessenow	214
DE3820	Havelberge	215
DE3827	S'souci-Gaisberg	214
DE3833	LuxOase	216
DE3836	Erzgebirgsblick	216
DE3847	Auensee	217
DE3850	Strandbad Aga	217
DE3855	Oberhof	217
Greece		
GR8120	Poseidon Beach	250
GR8145	Areti	250
GR8235	Kalami Beach	250
GR8285	Hellas	
	International	251
GR8330	Ionion Beach	251
GR8525	Chrissa	251
GR8565	Kokkino Limanaki	252
GR8640	Kastraki	252
GR8700	Erodios	252

Hungary		
HU5025	Zalatour	258
HU5070	Kristof	254
HU5080	Diana	254
HU5090	Füred	256
HU5120	Pihenö	257
HU5150	Fortuna	256
HU5180	Jumbo	257
HU5210	Diófaház	258
HU5300	Kek-Duna	258
HU5380	Venus	254
Italy		
IT6000	Mare Pineta	280
IT6003	Pra' Delle Torri	291
IT6005	Europa	283
IT6008	Sabbiadoro	283
IT6010	Capalonga	292
IT6013	Lido	292
IT6014	Internazionale	296
IT6015	Il Tridente	294
IT6020	Union Lido	298
IT6021	Italy	295
IT6022	Portofelice	295
IT6028	Vela Blu	296
IT6032	Cavallino	300
IT6033	Malibu Beach	308
IT6034	Waikiki	308
IT6036	Ca'Pasquali	294
IT6037	Jésolo	302
IT6040	Garden Paradiso	295
IT6041	Europa (Cavallino)	301
IT6045	Marina Venezia	301
IT6046	Miramare	
	(Punta Sabbioni)	300
IT6047	Scarpiland	306
IT6050	Serenissima	302
IT6053	Fusina	304
IT6054	Oasi	307
IT6055	Isamar	307
IT6056	Miramare	
	(Chioggia)	308
IT6075	Florenz	310
IT6080	Mare Pineta	309
IT6090	Arizona	309
IT6199	Corones	283
IT6200	Olympia	288
IT6204	Seiser Alm	285
IT6205	Dolomiti	290
IT6207	Sägemühle	284
IT6208	Gamp	286
IT6210	Steiner	287
IT6226	Punta Lago	286
IT6229	Lévico	289
IT6232	Al Sole	288
IT6233	Al Lago	290
IT6242	Orta	262
IT6246	Isolino	260
IT6249	Continental	261
IT6252	San Francesco	268
IT6253	Piani di Clodia	270
IT6254	Lido	268
IT6255	La Quercia	272
IT6256	Del Garda	269
IT6260	Europa Silvella	267

IT6261	Del Sole	266
IT6263	Bella Italia	274
IT6270	La Gardiola	280
IT6275	Fornella	272
IT6277	Fontanelle	274
IT6280	Week-End	277
IT6283	La Rocca	276
IT6284	Belvedere	279
IT6286	Baia Verde	278
IT6357	Cisano & San Vito	276
IT6358	Delle Rose	270
IT6359	Serenella	282
IT6401	Dei Fiori	264
IT6403	Baciccia	264
IT6412	Valdeiva	262
IT6414	Arenella	263
IT6419	River	266
IT6507	Panorama	311
IT6600	Barco Reale	314
IT6606	Europa	312
IT6608	Torre Pendente	312
IT6611	Il Poggetto	313
IT6612	Norcenni	315
IT6617	Perticara	311
IT6620	Riccione	310
IT6627	Boschetto	
	di Piemma	314
IT6629	Tripesce	316
IT6631	Mareblu	316
IT6638	Park Albatros	317
IT6643	Village Europa	323
IT6645	Delle Piscine	318
IT6649	Punta Navaccia	323
IT6651	Polvese	324
IT6652	Italgest	325
IT6653	Listro	325
IT6660	Maremma	318
IT6661	Toscana Village	319
IT6667	La Finoria	320
IT6673	Puntala	320
IT6675	Cieloverde	321
IT6677	Baia Gabbiani	322
IT6678	Butteri	322
IT6778	Fabulous	326
IT6780	Roma	328
IT6800	Europe Garden	332
IT6804	Eurcamping	332
IT6809	Tiber	327
IT6810	Seven Hills	326
IT6811	I Pini	326
IT6812	Roma Flash	330
IT6813	Porticciolo	331
IT6814	Flaminio	330
IT6819	Settebello	331
IT6820	Baia Domizia	334
IT6838	Nettuno	333
IT6865	Riva di Ugento	336
IT6889	Costa Verde	334
IT6919	Scarabeo	338
IT6923	Jonio	337
IT6925	Il Peloritano	338
IT6930	Marinello	337
IT6935	Rais Gerbi	339
IT6955	La Tortuga	340
IT6996	Mariposa	340

Liechtenstein
FL7580 Mittagspitze 341

Luxembourg
LU7610 Birkelt 343
LU7620 Nommerlayen 343
LU7640 Auf Kengert 344
LU7650 De la Sûre 344
LU7660 Kockelscheuer 345
LU7670 Ardennes 345
LU7680 Kohnenhof 347
LU7700 Gaalgebierg 348
LU7770 Val d'Or 346
LU7780 Woltzdal 346
LU7850 Fuussekaul 348
LU7870 De la Sûre 349
LU7880 Trois Frontières 349
LU7890 Haute Sûre 349

Netherlands
NL5500 Pannenschuur 351
NL5510 Groede 352
NL5540 Katjeskelder 375
NL5560 Wijde Blick 355
NL5570 Molenhoek 353
NL5580 Veerhoeve 353
NL5600 Delftse Hout 357
NL5620 Duinrell 359
NL5630 Koningshof 356
NL5640 Kijkduinpark 357
NL5660 Amsterd'se Bos 360
NL5670 Gaasper 359
NL5680 Noordduinen 358
NL5700 Molengroet 360
NL5710 It Soal 363
NL5720 Uitdam 361
NL5735 Tempelhof 362
NL5760 Kuilart 364
NL5770 Stadspark 367
NL5780 Zanding 372
NL5790 Kuierpadtien 367
NL5810 Luttenberg 370
NL5850 Hooge Veluwe 374
NL5870 Vergarde 373
NL5880 Vinkeloord 377
NL5890 Klein Canada 378
NL5900 Beekse Bergen 377
NL5910 Hertenwei 376
NL5950 Heumens Bos 373
NL5960 Wielerbaan 375
NL5970 De Paal 376
NL5980 De Roos 371
NL5985 Beerze Bulten 371
NL5990 Vechtstreek 372
NL6000 Vechtdalcamping 372
NL6030 Klein Vaarwater 365
NL6040 Bergumermeer 364
NL6080 Zeehoeve 365
NL6090 Lauwersoog 366
NL6120 Strandheem 366
NL6130 De Vledders 369
NL6140 Valkenhof 367
NL6150 de Westerbergen 368
NL6160 Engeland 368
NL6190 Hazevreugd 375

NL6290 Eiland-Maurik 374
NL6310 Arnhem 374
NL6470 De Papillon 370
NL6480 Molenhof 370
NL6510 Schatberg 379
NL6520 BreeBronne 379
NL6530 Panorama 378
NL6540 Rozenhof 380
NL6560 Maasvallei 380
NL6580 De Gronselenput- 380
NL6790 Kienehoef 378
NL6820 Westerkogge 363
NL6830 Mijnden 362
NL6840 Vogelenzang 363
NL6870 De Lakens 361
NL6915 Linda 354
NL6920 Veerse Meer 354
NL6925 Weltevreden 352
NL6930 Schoneveld 352
NL6950 Renesse 355
NL6960 Klepperstee 358
NL6970 Weergors 357

Norway
NO2315 Ringoy 383
NO2320 Odda 385
NO2325 Sundal 384
NO2330 Eikhamrane 384
NO2340 Mo 385
NO2350 Espelandsdalen 384
NO2360 Ulvik Fjord 386
NO2370 Botnen 387
NO2375 Lærdal 388
NO2380 Tveit 389
NO2385 Sandvik 389
NO2390 Kjornes 389
NO2400 Jolstraholmen 390
NO2415 Kautokeino 392
NO2425 Kirkeporten 393
NO2428 Andenes 393
NO2432 Harstad 396
NO2435 Solvang 393
NO2436 Byrkjelo 390
NO2445 Slettnes 396
NO2450 Bjolstad 388
NO2452 Trollveggen 387
NO2455 Ballangen 394
NO2460 Prinsen 386
NO2465 Lyngvær 394
NO2475 Saltstraumen 394
NO2485 Krokstrand 305
NO2490 Skjerneset 386
NO2495 Vegset 395
NO2500 Tråsåvika 395
NO2505 Magalaupe 396
NO2510 Håneset 391
NO2515 Gjelten Bru 391
NO2525 Østrea Æra 391
NO2545 Rustberg 392
NO2570 Fossheim 390
NO2590 Sandviken 383
NO2600 Rysstad 382
NO2610 Neset 382
NO2615 Olberg 392
NO2660 Preikestolen 383

Portugal
PO8030 Rio Alto 406
PO8050 Sao Jacinto 405
PO8060 Costa Nova 405
PO8100 S Pedro-Moel 403
PO8110 Valado 403
PO8130 Guincho 402
PO8150 Caparica 402
PO8170 São Miguel 401
PO8200 Valverde 398
PO8202 Turiscampo 398
PO8210 Albufeira 399
PO8220 Quarteira 400
PO8230 Olhao 401
PO8370 Cerdeira 406
PO8400 O Tamanco 404
PO8410 Armacao-Pera 400
PO8430 Sagres 400
PO8450 Colina-Sol 402
PO8460 Vale Paraiso 404
PO8480 Foz do Arelho 403

Slovakia
SK4900 Trusalová 408
SK4905 Stara Hora 408
SK4910 Turiec 408
SK4920 Trencin 409
SK4925 Lodenica 409
SK4935 Bystrina 409
SK4950 Zlaté Piesky 410
SK4980 Levocská Dolina 410

Slovenia
SV4150 Kamne 412
SV4200 Bled 413
SV4210 Sobec 412
SV4235 Klin 412
SV4250 Danica Bohinj 413
SV4330 Pivka Jama 414
SV4405 Menina 414

Spain
ES8008 Joncar Mar 420
ES8012 Mas Nou 419
ES8020 Amberes 416
ES8030 Nautic Almata 418
ES8035 Amfora 417
ES8040 Las Dunas 418
ES8050 Aquarius 422
ES8060 Ballena Alegre 2 420
ES8072 Les Medes 424
ES8074 Paradis 425
ES8080 Delfin Verde 416
ES8090 Cypsela 424
ES8100 Inter-Pals 427
ES8101 Playa Brava 426
ES8102 Mas Patoxas 423
ES8103 El Maset 422
ES8104 Begur 428
ES8130 Calonge 429
ES8160 Cala Gogo 428
ES8170 Valldaro 426
ES8200 Cala Llevadó 430
ES8210 Tucan 430
ES8390 Vilanova Park 433

ES8392	El Garrofer	429
ES8410	Playa Bara	437
ES8420	Stel (Roda)	432
ES8470	La Siesta	434
ES8479	Playa Cambrils	
	(Don Camilo)	442
ES8480	Sanguli	438
ES8481	Cambrils	434
ES8482	Pineda de Salou	432
ES8483	Tamarit	436
ES8508	Poboleda	436
ES8530	Playa Montroig	440
ES8535	Cala d'Oques	440
ES8536	Ametlla	438
ES8540	Torre del Sol	441
ES8559	Azahar	442
ES8560	Playa Tropicana	444
ES8580	Bonterra	443
ES8615	Kiko	445
ES8625	Kiko Rural	446
ES8675	Vall de Laguar	445
ES8681	Villasol	447
ES8683	Benisol	448
ES8685	El Raco	452
ES8687	Cap Blanch	452
ES8689	Playa del Torres	450
ES8742	La Marina	450
ES8743	Marjal	448
ES8745	La Fuente	452
ES8748	Los Madriles	453
ES8752	El Portus	453
ES8753	La Manga	453
ES8754	Javea	446
ES8755	Moraira	447
ES8763	Cabo de Gata	454
ES8800	Marbella Playa	456
ES8802	Cabopino	457
ES8859	Roche	457
ES8860	Fuente del Gallo	458
ES8865	Playa Las Dunas	458
ES8873	La Aldea	459
ES8940	Los Cantiles	467
ES8942	Los Manzanos	467
ES8945	Lagos-Somiedo	467
ES8955	Arenal-Moris	468
ES8961	El Helguero	468
ES8962	La Isla	468
ES9000	Playa Joyel	469
ES9019	La Pesquera	464
ES9023	Santiago	465
ES9024	As Cancelas	466
ES9026	Burro Blanco	465
ES9027	Monfrague	460
ES9028	Villuercas	461
ES9029	El Astral	466
ES9035	Portuondo	470
ES9042	Etxarri	471
ES9043	Errota el Molino	470
ES9060	Peña Montañesa	471
ES9062	Boltana	471
ES9080	El Brillante	459
ES9081	Villsom	456
ES9082	Sevilla	456
ES9086	Cáceres	461
ES9087	Merida	462
ES9089	Despenaperros	460
ES9090	El Greco	462
ES9098	Rio Mundo	462
ES9105	Lago Park	472
ES9125	Lago Barasona	472
ES9200	El Escorial	463
ES9210	Pico-Miel	464
ES9242	El Acueducto	465
ES9280	Sierra Nevada	455
ES9285	Las Lomas	455
ES9290	El Balcon	454
Sweden		
SW2630	Röstånga	475
SW2640	Båstad-Torekov	474
SW2645	Mölle	475
SW2650	Skånes	476
SW2655	Tingsryds	476
SW2665	Rosenlund	477
SW2670	Grannastrandens	477
SW2675	Västervik Swe	478
SW2680	Saxnäs	478
SW2690	Böda Sand	479
SW2705	Lisebergsbyn	477
SW2706	Askim Strand	474
SW2710	Lidköping	479
SW2715	Gröne Backe	479
SW2720	Hökensås	480
SW2725	Hafsten	480
SW2730	Ekuddens	481
SW2735	Daftö	481
SW2740	Laxsjons	481
SW2750	Sommarvik	482
SW2755	Alevi	482
SW2760	Frykenbaden	483
SW2780	Gustavsvik	483
SW2800	Glyttinge	484
SW2805	Kolmårdens	484
SW2820	Skantzö Bad	484
SW2825	Herrfallet	485
SW2836	Mora Parkens	486
SW2840	Flottsbro	486
SW2842	Bredängs	485
SW2845	Svegs	487
SW2850	Ostersunds	487
SW2853	Snibbens	487
SW2855	Flogsta	488
SW2857	Strömsund	488
SW2860	Umeå	488
SW2865	Gielas	489
SW2870	Jokkmokks	489
Switzerland		
CH9000	Waldhort	505
CH9010	Zum Muttenhof	505
CH9015	Tariche	512
CH9040	Des Pêches	513
CH9055	Fanel	494
CH9110	Seeland	500
CH9115	Steinibachried	500
CH9130	Vitznau	501
CH9160	Rheinwiesen	503
CH9175	Giessenpark	503
CH9180	Buchhorn	504
CH9185	Fischerhaus	504
CH9240	Petit Bois	513
CH9270	De Vidy	515
CH9300	Le Bivouac	511
CH9330	Bettlereiche	492
CH9360	Grassi	494
CH9410	Stuhlegg	496
CH9420	Manor Farm	492
CH9430	Lazy Rancho 4	491
CH9440	Jungfraublick	496
CH9450	Seeblick	497
CH9460	Jungfrau	495
CH9480	Gletscherdorf	497
CH9495	Balmweid	500
CH9500	Hofstatt-Derfli	498
CH9510	Aaregg	498
CH9520	Du Botza	507
CH9570	Eienwäldli	499
CH9600	Rive-Bleue	507
CH9640	de la Sarvaz	508
CH9655	Les Neuvilles	508
CH9660	Des Glaciers	508
CH9670	Molignon	509
CH9680	Bois de Finges	509
CH9720	Bella-Tola	509
CH9730	Gemmi	510
CH9740	Attermenzen	510
CH9770	Santa Monica	510
CH9775	Mühleye	511
CH9790	Augenstern	512
CH9820	Pradafenz	501
CH9830	Sur En	501
CH9850	Neue Ganda	502
CH9855	Cavresc	502
CH9860	Plauns	502
CH9865	Fontanivas	503
CH9880	Lido Mappo	506
CH9890	Campofelice	506
CH9900	Delta	515
CH9950	Piodella	506
CH9970	Parco al Sole	507

Andorra
AN7145	Valira	16
AN7143	Xixerella	16

Austria
AU0250	Alpencamping	31
AU0035	Alpin Seefeld	22
AU0340	Am See	35
AU0240	Appesbach	36
AU0055	Arlberg	23
AU0400	Arneitz	40
AU0120	Aufenfeld	27
AU0520	Badesee	39
AU0425	Berghof	44
AU0475	Brunner am See	45
AU0480	Burgstaller	41
AU0227	Camp Grän	30
AU0330	Central	38
AU0015	Grosswalsertal	18
AU0345	Gruber	34
AU0265	Grubhof	32
AU0070	Hofer	24
AU0502	Im Thermenland	38
AU0515	Katschtal	39
AU0445	Kotschach	
	Mauthen	44
AU0170	Kranebitten	27
AU0220	Krismer	30
AU0505	Leibnitz	39
AU0490	Maltatal	42
AU0350	Mond See Land	34
AU0085	Mountain Camp	
	Pitztal	24
AU0060	Natterer See	20
AU0010	Nenzing	18
AU0302	Neue Donau	37
AU0262	Oberwötzlhof	34
AU0460	Ossiachersee	45
AU0045	Ötztal	22
AU0155	Prutz	29
AU0405	Ramsbacher	44
AU0150	Riffler	29
AU0300	Rodaun	37
AU0415	Rosental Roz	40
AU0225	Schloß	
	Fernsteinsee	30
AU0130	Schloßberg Itter	28
AU0080	Schloß-Camping	25
AU0440	Schluga	43
AU0450	Schluga See	42
AU0065	Seehof	23
AU0185	Seewiese	29
AU0232	Sonnenberg	19
AU0102	Stadlerhof	26
AU0212	Stadtblick	32
AU0280	Stumpfer	36
AU0110	Tirol Camp	26
AU0100	Toni	25
AU0290	Tulln	36
AU0410	Turnersee	40
AU0306	Wien West	38
AU0304	Wien-Sud	37
AU0140	Wilder Kaiser	28
AU0180	Woferlgut	33
AU0160	Zell am See	31
AU0090	Zillertal-Hell	24
AU0040	Zugspitze	20

Belgium
BE0660	Baalse Hei	56
BE0610	Blaarmeersen	53
BE0715	Chênefleur	58
BE0520	De Blekker	47
BE0590	De Gavers	52
BE0560	De Lombarde	49
BE0640	Druivenland	54
BE0740	Eau Rouge	51
BE0732	Floreal La Roche	60
BE0630	Grimbergen	53
BE0600	Groeneveld	53
BE0705	Hirondelle	57
BE0712	Ile De Faigneul	58
BE0570	Jeugdstadion	50
BE0555	Klein Strand	48
BE0670	La Clusure	52
BE0655	Lilse Bergen	54
BE0580	Memling	49
BE0730	Moulin-Malempre	59
BE0550	Nieuwpoort	47
BE0595	Oudenaarde	52
BE0735	Petite Suisse	51
BE0700	Spa d'Or	55
BE0675	Spineuse	56
BE0680	Sud	57
BE0578	Ter Duinen	50
BE0720	Tonny	58
BE0725	Val de L`Aisne	59
BE0710	Vallée de Rabais	57
BE0770	Vieux Moulin	55
BE0530	Waux-Hall	48
BE0565	Westende	49
BE0780	Wilhelm Tell	60

Croatia
CR6845	Adriatic	73
CR6730	Amarin	67
CR6724	Bijela Uvala	63
CR6745	Bi-Village	69
CR6850	Camp Seget	73
CR6765	Kovacine	70
CR6729	Koversada	66
CR6728	Orsera	64
CR6732	Polari	68
CR6725	Porto Sole	65
CR6768	Slatina	70
CR6742	Stoja	68
CR6720	Ulika	62
CR6731	Valalta	66
CR6736	Valdaliso	72
CR6727	Valkanela	64
CR6733	Vestar	69
CR6761	Zablace	72
CR6722	Zelena Laguna	62

Czech Republic
CZ4710	Chvalsiny	78
CZ4780	Konopiste	76
CZ4590	Lisci Farma	77
CZ4650	Luxor	78
CZ4840	Oase	75
CZ4860	Orlice	77
CZ4880	Roznov	78
CZ4690	Slunce	76
CZ4850	Sokol Troja	75
CZ4820	Valek	76

Denmark
DK2015	Ådalens	80
DK2100	Blushoj	86
DK2200	Bojden	89
DK2210	Bøsøre	89
DK2265	Charlottenlund	92
DK2048	Faarup Sø	84
DK2255	Feddet	91
DK2070	Fornæs	86
DK2036	Gammelmark	83
DK2044	Hampen Sø	83
DK2220	Helnæs	90
DK2250	Hillerød	91
DK2130	Hobro Gattenborg	86
DK2080	Holmens	85
DK2010	Hvidbjerg Strand	81
DK2140	Jesperhus	81
DK2170	Klim Strand	88
DK2205	Logismosestrand	89
DK2020	Mogeltonder	80
DK2260	Nærum	92
DK2000	Nordsø	80
DK2180	Nordstrand	88
DK2040	Riis	83
DK2235	Sakskobing Gron	90
DK2030	Sandersvig	82
DK2165	Skiveren	87
DK2150	Solyst	87
DK2050	Terrassen	85
DK2046	Trelde Næs	84
DK2257	Vesterlyng	90
DK2022	Vikær Diernæs	82

Finland
FI2960	Koljonvirta	96
FI2830	Lakari	95
FI2975	Manamansalo	96
FI2970	Nallikari	96
FI2980	Ounaskoski	97
FI2850	Rastila	94
FI2985	Sodankylä Nilimella	97
FI2922	Taipale	95
FI2820	Tampere Härmälä	94
FI2990	Tenorinne	98
FI2995	Ukonjarvi	98

France
FR85220	Acapulco	126
FR41030	Alicourts	132
FR37060	Arada Parc	128
FR07180	Ardèche	172
FR11060	Arnauteille	183
FR38080	Au Joyeux Réveil	142
FR33080	Barbanne	144
FR84020	Bélézy	179
FR77070	Belle Etoile	119
FR22210	Bellevue	100
FR45010	Bois du Bardelet	132
FR26210	Bois du Chatelas	175
FR17010	Bois Soleil	122
FR44180	Boutinardière	108
FR60010	Campix	115
FR85330	Cap Natur`	128
FR48020	Capelan	170
FR34190	Champs Blancs	188
FR62030	Château de	
	Gandspette	115
FR23010	Château de	
	Poinsouze	168
FR37130	Parc des Allais	129
FR38010	Coin Tranquille	142
FR64110	Col d`Ibardin	155
FR83230	Colombier	196
FR33110	Côte d`Argent	144
FR79020	Courte Vallée	135
FR83220	Cros de Mouton	199
FR44210	de l`Ocean	108

FR44090 Deffay 107	FR09060 Le Pré Lombard 181	DE3685 Allweglehen 226
FR07150 Domaine de Gil 172	FR80040 Le Royon 115	DE3452 Alte Sägemühle 236
FR39080 Domaine de l'Epinette 141	FR83410 Le Ruou 202	DE3632 Altmühltal 219
	FR24010 Le Verdoyer 161	DE3065 am Bärenbache 208
FR46190 Domaine de la Faurie 166	FR40180 Le Vieux Port 154	DE3255 Am Königsberg 248
	FR83030 Leï Suves 194	DE3021 Am Stadtwaldsee 206
FR83250 Douce Quiétude 202	FR06080 Les Cigales 191	DE3847 Auensee 217
FR29030 Du Letty 100	FR85210 Les Ecureuils 127	DE3260 Bad Dürkheim 248
FR71070 Epervière 138	FR29180 Les Embruns 105	DE3454 Badenweiler 230
FR74070 Escale 142	FR25080 Les Fuvettes 140	DE3436 Bankenhof 236
FR83020 Esterel 192	FR12080 Les Genêts 158	DE3710 Bayerischer Wald 219
FR49040 Etang 134	FR33130 Les Grands Pins 146	DE3445 Belchenblick 237
FR24330 Etang Bleu 164	FR40250 Les Grands Pins 152	DE3210 Biggesee 211
FR01080 Etang du Moulin 171	FR73030 Les Lanchettes 143	DE3432 Bonath 230
FR83070 Etoile d'Argens 200	FR07140 Les Lavandes 172	DE3220 Burg Lahneck 242
FR40060 Eurosol 148	FR11070 Les Mimosas 183	DE3630 Donau-Lech 221
FR80070 Ferme des Aulnes 117	FR83200 Les Pêcheurs 198	DE3695 Dreiflüsse 227
FR32010 Florence 180	FR12160 Les Peupliers 159	DE3697 Dreiqueller 227
FR30000 Gaujac 182	FR29190 Les Prés Verts 103	DE3672 Elbsee 225
FR41070 Grande Tortue 133	FR07070 Les Ranchisses 170	DE3627 Ellwangen 239
FR06120 Green Park 189	FR12020 Les Rivages 157	DE3836 Erzgebirgsblick 216
FR24130 Grottes de Roffy 163	FR56280 Les Sept Saints 111	DE3232 Family Club 246
FR47150 Guillalmes 166	FR40140 Lou P'tit Poun 143	DE3812 Flessenow 214
FR50080 Haliotis 114	FR66020 Ma Prairie 188	DE3439 Freiburg 234
FR04010 Hippocampe 178	FR16060 Marco de Bignac 160	DE3625 Frickenhausen 218
FR26130 Hirondelle 174	FR12150 Marmotel 158	DE3650 Gitzenweiler 223
FR27070 l'Isle des Trois Rois 114	FR30080 Mas de Reilhe 183	DE3215 Goldene Meile 243
FR49080 Ile d'Offard 134	FR40240 Mayotte Vacances 151	DE3202 Grav-Insel 210
FR04100 International 176	FR71050 Moulin de Collonge 140	DE3455 Gugel's 232
FR49090 Isle Verte 135		DE3080 Hardausee 209
FR77030 Jablines 119	FR46040 Moulin de Laborde 164	DE3254 Harfenmühle 246
FR17230 L'Océan 124		DE3820 Havelberge 215
FR07120 L'Ardéchois 173	FR04030 Moulin de Ventre 179	DE3490 Hegau 238
FR09020 L'Arize 180	FR83240 Moulin des Iscles 200	DE3411 Heidehof 239
FR83060 La Baume 196	FR47010 Moulin du Périé 167	DE3442 Herbolzheim 231
FR83170 La Bergerie 194	FR24040 Moulin du Roch 160	DE3437 Hochschwarzwald 230
FR17220 La Brande 121	FR37030 Moulin Fort 130	DE3233 Holländischer Hof 244
FR37050 La Citadelle 129	FR56110 Moustoir 112	DE3670 Hopfensee 224
FR74060 La Colombière 141	FR29050 Orangerie de Lanniron 101	DE3256 Hunsrück 248
FR17280 La Grainetière 124		DE3237 In der Enz 244
FR11080 La Nautique 184	FR35040 P'tit Bois 104	DE3467 Isnycamping 238
FR39040 La Pergola 141	FR46010 Paille Basse 165	DE3750 Issigau 221
FR56020 La Plage 112	FR44220 Parc de Léveno 112	DE3739 Katzenkopf 219
FR40100 La Rive 148	FR33220 Petit Nice 147	DE3440 Kirchzarten 231
FR37090 La Rolandière 130	FR83010 Pins Parasol 192	DE3406 Kleinenzhof 229
FR30100 La Sablière 184	FR71140 Pont de Bourgogne 138	DE3008 Klüthseecamp 212
FR44150 La Tabardière 106		DE3265 Lahn 240
FR14070 La Vallée 113	FR24170 Port de Limeuil 164	DE3642 Lech 224
FR85150 La Yole 125	FR65060 Pyrenees Natura 181	DE3833 LuxOase 216
FR88040 Lac de Bouzey 119	FR06140 Ranch 191	DE3222 Moselbogen 242
FR52030 Lac de la Liez 120	FR64150 Residence des Pins 152	DE3185 Münster 210
FR65080 Lavedan 182	FR20040 Riva Bella 203	DE3450 Münstertal 235
FR17030 Le Bois Roland 121	FR12120 Rouergue 160	DE3720 Naabtal 228
FR66070 Le Brasilia 190	FR86090 Saint Cyr 135	DE3610 Nürnberg 218
FR04020 Le Camp du Verdon 176	FR40190 Saint Martin 150	DE3428 Oase 234
	FR17140 Sequoia Parc 122	DE3855 Oberhof 217
FR85480 Le Chaponnet 126	FR34070 Sérignan Plage 186	DE3635 Obermenzing 222
FR77020 Le Chêne Gris 118	FR65090 Soleil du Pibeste 182	DE3420 Oberrhein 228
FR50050 Le Cormoran 113	FR24090 Soleil Plage 162	DE3688 Panorama Harras 226
FR26040 Le Couspeau 174	FR40200 Sylvamar 151	DE3055 Prahljust 207
FR44190 Le Fief 110	FR29010 Ty-Nadan 102	DE3605 Rangau 218
FR86040 Le Futuriste 136	FR80090 Val d'Authie 118	DE3010 Röders Park 206
FR66050 Le Haras 188	FR12010 Val de Cantobre 156	DE3602 Romantische Str. 239
FR31000 Le Moulin 181	FR80060 Val de Trie 116	DE3827 S'souci-Gaisberg 214
FR24100 Le Moulinal 163	FR88130 Vanne de Pierre 120	DE3258 Sägmühle 247
FR34130 Le Neptune 186	FR43030 Vaubarlet 169	DE3242 Schindelhannes 245
FR29080 Le Panoramic 104	FR35000 Vieux Chêne 106	DE3002 Schlei-Karschau 212
FR24060 Le Paradis 162		DE3005 Schnelsen Nord 206
FR44100 Le Patisseau 105	**Germany**	DE3735 Schönrain 220
FR07110 Le Pommier 170	DE3415 Adam 229	DE3427 Schwarzwälder Hof 232
FR63070 Le Pré Bas 169	DE3025 Alfsee 207	

DE3275	Seepark	241	IT6205	Dolomiti	290	IT6252	San Francesco	268
DE3245	Sonnenberg	246	IT6804	Eurcamping	332	IT6919	Scarabeo	338
DE3180	Sonnenwiese	209	IT6005	Europa	283	IT6047	Scarpiland	306
DE3205	Stadt Köln	211	IT6606	Europa	312	IT6204	Seiser Alm	285
DE3850	Strandbad Aga	217	IT6041	Europa (Cavallino)	301	IT6359	Serenella	282
DE3686	Strandcamping		IT6260	Europa Silvella	267	IT6050	Serenissima	302
	Waging	227	IT6800	Europe Garden	332	IT6819	Settebello	331
DE3070	Süd-See	208	IT6778	Fabulous	326	IT6810	Seven Hills	326
DE3225	Suleika	241	IT6814	Flaminio	330	IT6210	Steiner	287
DE3030	Tecklenburg	209	IT6075	Florenz	310	IT6809	Tiber	327
DE3280	Teichmann	240	IT6277	Fontanelle	274	IT6608	Torre Pendente	312
DE3680	Tennsee	225	IT6275	Fornella	272	IT6661	Toscana Village	319
DE3182	Teutoburger Wald	210	IT6053	Fusina	304	IT6629	Tripesce	316
DE3640	Thalkirchen	222	IT6208	Gamp	286	IT6020	Union Lido	298
DE3250	Warsberg	247	IT6040	Garden Paradiso	295	IT6412	Valdeiva	262
DE3212	Wirfttal	243	IT6811	I Pini	326	IT6028	Vela Blu	296
DE3465	Wirthshof	237	IT6925	Il Peloritano	338	IT6643	Village Europa	323
DE3003	Wulfener Hals	213	IT6611	Il Poggetto	313	IT6034	Waikiki	308
			IT6015	Il Tridente	294	IT6280	Week-End	277
Greece			IT6014	Internazionale	296			
GR8145	Areti	250	IT6055	Isamar	307	**Liechtenstein**		
GR8525	Chrissa	251	IT6246	Isolino	260	FL7580	Mittagspitze	341
GR8700	Erodios	252	IT6652	Italgest	325			
GR8285	Hellas		IT6021	Italy	295	**Luxembourg**		
	International	251	IT6037	Jésolo	302	LU7670	Ardennes	345
GR8330	Ionion Beach	251	IT6923	Jonio	337	LU7640	Auf Kengert	344
GR8235	Kalami Beach	250	IT6667	La Finoria	320	LU7610	Birkelt	343
GR8640	Kastraki	252	IT6270	La Gardiola	280	LU7650	De la Sûre	344
GR8565	Kokkino Limanaki	252	IT6255	La Quercia	272	LU7870	De la Sûre	349
GR8120	Poseidon Beach	250	IT6283	La Rocca	276	LU7850	Fuussekaul	348
			IT6955	La Tortuga	340	LU7700	Gaalgebierg	348
Hungary			IT6229	Lévico	289	LU7890	Haute Sûre	349
HU5080	Diana	254	IT6013	Lido	292	LU7660	Kockelscheuer	345
HU5210	Diófaház	258	IT6254	Lido	268	LU7680	Kohnenhof	347
HU5150	Fortuna	256	IT6653	Listro	325	LU7620	Nommerlayen	343
HU5090	Füred	256	IT6033	Malibu Beach	308	LU7880	Trois Frontières	349
HU5180	Jumbo	257	IT6000	Mare Pineta	280	LU7770	Val d'Or	346
HU5300	Kek-Duna	258	IT6080	Mare Pineta	309	LU7780	Woltzdal	346
HU5070	Kristof	254	IT6631	Mareblu	316			
HU5120	Pihenö	257	IT6660	Maremma	318	**Netherlands**		
HU5380	Venus	254	IT6045	Marina Venezia	301	NL5660	Amsterd'se Bos	360
HU5025	Zalatour	258	IT6930	Marinello	337	NL6310	Arnhem	374
			IT6996	Mariposa	340	NL5900	Beekse Bergen	377
Italy			IT6056	Miramare		NL5985	Beerze Bulten	371
IT6233	Al Lago	290		(Chioggia)	308	NL6040	Bergumermeer	364
IT6232	Al Sole	288	IT6046	Miramare		NL6520	BreeBronne	379
IT6414	Arenella	263		(Punta Sabbioni)	300	NL6580	De Gronselenput-	
IT6090	Arizona	309	IT6838	Nettuno	333		Wijlre	380
IT6403	Baciccia	264	IT6612	Norcenni	315	NL6870	De Lakens	361
IT6820	Baia Domizia	334	IT6054	Oasi	307	NL5970	De Paal	376
IT6677	Baia Gabbiani	322	IT6200	Olympia	288	NL6470	De Papillon	370
IT6286	Baia Verde	278	IT6242	Orta	262	NL5980	De Roos	371
IT6600	Barco Reale	314	IT6507	Panorama	311	NL6130	De Vledders	369
IT6263	Bella Italia	274	IT6638	Park Albatros	317	NL6150	de Westerbergen	368
IT6284	Belvedere	279	IT6617	Perticara	311	NL5600	Delftse Hout	357
IT6627	Boschetto di		IT6253	Piani di Clodia	270	NL5620	Duinrell	359
	Piemma	314	IT6651	Polvese	324	NL6290	Eiland-Maurik	374
IT6678	Butteri	322	IT6813	Porticciolo	331	NL6160	Engeland	368
IT6036	Ca'Pasquali	294	IT6022	Portofelice	295	NL5670	Gaasper	359
IT6010	Capalonga	292	IT6003	Pra' Delle Torri	291	NL5510	Groede	352
IT6032	Cavallino	300	IT6226	Punta Lago	286	NL6190	Hazevreugd	375
IT6675	Cieloverde	321	IT6649	Punta Navaccia	323	NL5910	Hertenwei	376
IT6357	Cisano & San Vito	276	IT6673	Puntala	320	NL5950	Heumens Bos	373
IT6249	Continental	261	IT6935	Rais Gerbi	339	NL5850	Hooge Veluwe	374
IT6199	Corones	283	IT6620	Riccione	310	NL5710	It Soal	363
IT6889	Costa Verde	334	IT6865	Riva di Ugento	336	NL5540	Katjeskelder	375
IT6401	Dei Fiori	264	IT6419	River	266	NL6790	Kienehoef	378
IT6256	Del Garda	269	IT6780	Roma	328	NL5640	Kijkduinpark	357
IT6261	Del Sole	266	IT6812	Roma Flash	330	NL5890	Klein Canada	378
IT6645	Delle Piscine	318	IT6008	Sabbiadoro	283	NL6030	Klein Vaarwater	365
IT6358	Delle Rose	270	IT6207	Sägemühle	284	NL6960	Klepperstee	358

NL5630	Koningshof	356
NL5790	Kuierpadtien	367
NL5760	Kuilart	364
NL6090	Lauwersoog	366
NL6915	Linda	354
NL5810	Luttenberg	370
NL6560	Maasvallei	380
NL6830	Mijnden	362
NL5700	Molengroet	360
NL5570	Molenhoek	353
NL6480	Molenhof	370
NL5680	Noordduinen	358
NL5500	Pannenschuur	351
NL6530	Panorama	378
NL6950	Renesse	355
NL6540	Rozenhof	380
NL6510	Schatberg	379
NL6930	Schoneveld	352
NL5770	Stadspark	367
NL6120	Strandheem	366
NL5735	Tempelhof	362
NL5720	Uitdam	361
NL6140	Valkenhof	367
NL6000	Vechtdalcamping	372
NL5990	Vechtstreek	372
NL5580	Veerhoeve	353
NL6920	Veerse Meer	354
NL5870	Vergarde	373
NL5880	Vinkeloord	377
NL6840	Vogelenzang	363
NL6970	Weergors	357
NL6925	Weltevreden	352
NL6820	Westerkogge	363
NL5960	Wielerbaan	375
NL5560	Wijde Blick	355
NL5780	Zanding	372
NL6080	Zeehoeve	365

Norway

NO2428	Andenes	393
NO2455	Ballangen	394
NO2450	Bjolstad	388
NO2370	Botnen	387
NO2436	Byrkjelo	390
NO2330	Eikhamrane	384
NO2350	Espelandsdalen	384
NO2570	Fossheim	390
NO2515	Gjelten Bru	391
NO2510	Håneset	391
NO2432	Harstad	396
NO2400	Jolstraholmen	390
NO2415	Kautokeino	392
NO2425	Kirkeporten	393
NO2390	Kjornes	389
NO2485	Krokstrand	305
NO2375	Lærdal	388
NO2465	Lyngvær	394
NO2505	Magalaupe	396
NO2340	Mo	385
NO2610	Neset	382
NO2320	Odda	385
NO2615	Olberg	392
NO2525	Østrea Æra	391
NO2660	Preikestolen	383
NO2460	Prinsen	386
NO2315	Ringoy	383
NO2545	Rustberg	392
NO2600	Rysstad	382
NO2475	Saltstraumen	394
NO2385	Sandvik	389
NO2590	Sandviken	383

NO2490	Skjerneset	386
NO2445	Slettnes	396
NO2435	Solvang	393
NO2325	Sundal	384
NO2500	Tråsåvika	395
NO2452	Trollveggen	387
NO2380	Tveit	389
NO2360	Ulvik Fjord	386
NO2495	Vegset	395

Portugal

PO8210	Albufeira	399
PO8410	Armacao-Pera	400
PO8150	Caparica	402
PO8370	Cerdeira	406
PO8450	Colina-Sol	402
PO8060	Costa Nova	405
PO8480	Foz do Arelho	403
PO8130	Guincho	402
PO8040	O Tamanco	404
PO8230	Olhao	401
PO8220	Quarteira	400
PO8030	Rio Alto	406
PO8100	S Pedro-Moel	403
PO8430	Sagres	400
PO8050	Sao Jacinto	405
PO8170	São Miguel	401
PO8202	Turiscampo	398
PO8110	Valado	403
PO8460	Vale Paraiso	404
PO8200	Valverde	398

Slovakia

SK4935	Bystrina	409
SK4980	Levocská Dolina	410
SK4925	Lodenica	409
SK4905	Stara Hora	408
SK4920	Trencin	409
SK4900	Trusalová	408
SK4910	Turiec	408
SK4950	Zlaté Piesky	410

Slovenia

SV4200	Bled	413
SV4250	Danica Bohinj	413
SV4150	Kamne	412
SV4235	Klin	412
SV4405	Menina	414
SV4330	Pivka Jama	414
SV4210	Sobec	412

Spain

ES8020	Amberes	416
ES8536	Ametlla	438
ES8035	Amfora	417
ES8050	Aquarius	422
ES8955	Arenal-Moris	468
ES9024	As Cancelas	466
ES8559	Azahar	442
ES8060	Ballena Alegre 2	420
ES8104	Begur	428
ES8683	Benisol	448
ES9062	Boltana	471
ES8580	Bonterra	443
ES9026	Burro Blanco	465
ES8763	Cabo de Gata	454
ES8802	Cabopino	457
ES9086	Cáceres	461
ES8535	Cala d'Oques	440
ES8160	Cala Gogo	428
ES8200	Cala Llevadó	430

ES8130	Calonge	429
ES8481	Cambrils	434
ES8687	Cap Blanch	452
ES8090	Cypsela	424
ES8080	Delfin Verde	416
ES9089	Despenaperros	460
ES9242	El Acueducto	465
ES9029	El Astral	466
ES9290	El Balcon	454
ES9080	El Brillante	459
ES9200	El Escorial	463
ES8392	El Garrofer	429
ES9090	El Greco	462
ES8961	El Helguero	468
ES8103	El Maset	422
ES8752	El Portus	453
ES8685	El Raco	452
ES9043	Errota el Molino	470
ES9042	Etxarri	471
ES8860	Fuente del Gallo	458
ES8100	Inter-Pals	427
ES8754	Javea	446
ES8008	Joncar Mar	420
ES8615	Kiko	445
ES8625	Kiko Rural	446
ES8873	La Aldea	459
ES8745	La Fuente	452
ES8962	La Isla	468
ES8753	La Manga	453
ES8742	La Marina	450
ES9019	La Pesquera	464
ES8470	La Siesta	434
ES9125	Lago Barasona	472
ES9105	Lago Park	472
ES8945	Lagos-Somiedo	467
ES8040	Las Dunas	418
ES9285	Las Lomas	455
ES8072	Les Medes	424
ES8940	Los Cantiles	467
ES8748	Los Madriles	453
ES8942	Los Manzanos	467
ES8800	Marbella Playa	456
ES8743	Marjal	448
ES8012	Mas Nou	419
ES8102	Mas Patoxas	423
ES9087	Merida	462
ES9027	Monfrague	460
ES8755	Moraira	447
ES8030	Nautic Almata	418
ES8074	Paradis	425
ES9060	Peña Montañesa	471
ES9210	Pico-Miel	464
ES8482	Pineda de Salou	432
ES8410	Playa Bara	437
ES8101	Playa Brava	426
ES8479	Playa Cambrils (Don Camilo)	442
ES8689	Playa del Torres	450
ES9000	Playa Joyel	469
ES8865	Playa Las Dunas	458
ES8530	Playa Montroig	440
ES8560	Playa Tropicana	444
ES8508	Poboleda	436
ES9035	Portuondo	470
ES9098	Rio Mundo	462
ES8859	Roche	457
ES8480	Sanguli	438
ES9023	Santiago	465
ES9082	Sevilla	456
ES9280	Sierra Nevada	455
ES8420	Stel (Roda)	432

ES8483	Tamarit	436	SW2836	Mora Parkens	486	CH9865	Fontanivas	503
ES8540	Torre del Sol	441	SW2850	Ostersunds	487	CH9730	Gemmi	510
ES8210	Tucan	430	SW2665	Rosenlund	477	CH9175	Giessenpark	503
ES8675	Vall de Laguar	445	SW2630	Röstånga	475	CH9480	Gletscherdorf	497
ES8170	Valldaro	426	SW2680	Saxnäs	478	CH9360	Grassi	494
ES8390	Vilanova Park	433	SW2650	Skånes	476	CH9500	Hofstatt-Derfli	498
ES8681	Villasol	447	SW2820	Skantzö Bad	484	CH9460	Jungfrau	495
ES9081	Villsom	456	SW2853	Snibbens	487	CH9440	Jungfraublick	496
ES9028	Villuercas	461	SW2750	Sommarvik	482	CH9430	Lazy Rancho 4	491
			SW2857	Strömsund	488	CH9300	Le Bivouac	511
Sweden			SW2845	Svegs	487	CH9655	Les Neuvilles	508
SW2755	Alevi	482	SW2655	Tingsryds	476	CH9880	Lido Mappo	506
SW2706	Askim Strand	474	SW2860	Umeå	488	CH9420	Manor Farm	492
SW2640	Båstad-Torekov	474	SW2675	Västervik Swe	478	CH9670	Molignon	509
SW2690	Böda Sand	479				CH9775	Mühleye	511
SW2842	Bredängs	485	**Switzerland**			CH9850	Neue Ganda	502
SW2735	Daftö	481	CH9510	Aaregg	498	CH9970	Parco al Sole	507
SW2730	Ekuddens	481	CH9740	Attermenzen	510	CH9240	Petit Bois	513
SW2855	Flogsta	488	CH9790	Augenstern	512	CH9950	Piodella	506
SW2840	Flottsbro	486	CH9495	Balmweid	500	CH9860	Plauns	502
SW2760	Frykenbaden	483	CH9720	Bella-Tola	509	CH9820	Pradafenz	501
SW2865	Gielas	489	CH9330	Bettlereiche	492	CH9160	Rheinwiesen	503
SW2800	Glyttinge	484	CH9680	Bois de Finges	509	CH9600	Rive-Bleue	507
SW2670	Grannastrandens	477	CH9180	Buchhorn	504	CH9770	Santa Monica	510
SW2715	Gröne Backe	479	CH9890	Campofelice	506	CH9450	Seeblick	497
SW2780	Gustavsvik	483	CH9855	Cavresc	502	CH9110	Seeland	500
SW2725	Hafsten	480	CH9640	de la Sarvaz	508	CH9115	Steinibachried	500
SW2825	Herrfallet	485	CH9270	De Vidy	515	CH9410	Stuhlegg	496
SW2720	Hökensås	480	CH9900	Delta	515	CH9830	Sur En	501
SW2870	Jokkmokks	489	CH9660	Des Glaciers	508	CH9015	Tariche	512
SW2805	Kolmårdens	484	CH9040	Des Pêches	513	CH9130	Vitznau	501
SW2740	Laxsjons	481	CH9520	Du Botza	507	CH9000	Waldhort	505
SW2710	Lidköping	479	CH9570	Eienwäldli	499	CH9010	Zum Muttenhof	505
SW2705	Lisebergsbyn	477	CH9055	Fanel	494			
SW2645	Mölle	475	CH9185	Fischerhaus	504			

Acknowledgements

We would like to thank the following national and regional Tourist Boards for supplying photographs for use in this guide:

Andorra Tourist Office

Toerisme Vlaanderen

Croatian National Tourist Board

Danish Tourism Board

Bayern Tourismus

Hungarian Tourist Board

Italian Tourist Board

Liechtenstein Tourist Board

Luxembourg Tourist Office
Bourscheid Castle © Konrad Scheel
Vianden Castle overlooking the Old Town
© Marc Theis
Market town of Esch-sur-Sure © Marc Theis

Netherlands Tourist Board

Norwegian Tourist Board
North Cape Midnight Sun © Trym Ivar Bergsmo
Geirangerfjord © Per Eide
Sorlandet Lyngor © Niels Jorgensen

Portuguese National Tourism Office

Slovakia Travel

Turespana
L'Atmella de Mar © F. Ontanon
Broto © Oscar Masats

Costa Brava Girona Tourist Board

Sweden Travel & Travel Tourism Council

Switzerland Tourism